Readings in Medieval History

Readings in Medieval History

fourth edition
edited by Patrick J. Geary

University of Toronto Press

Library and Archives Canada Cataloguing in Publication

Readings in medieval history / edited by Patrick J. Geary.—4th ed.

Includes bibliographical references.
ISBN 978-1-4426-0120-8

1. Middle Ages—Sources. I. Geary, Patrick J., 1948–

D113.R42 2010   940.1   C2010-903469-4

We welcome comments and suggestions regarding any aspect of our publications—please feel free to contact us at news@utphighereducation.com or visit our Internet site at www.utphighereducation.com.

North America
5201 Dufferin Street
North York, Ontario, Canada, M3H 5T8

2250 Military Road
Tonawanda, New York, USA, 14150

ORDERS PHONE: 1-800-565-9523
ORDERS FAX: 1-800-221-9985
ORDERS E-MAIL: utpbooks@utpress.utoronto.ca

UK, Ireland, and continental Europe
NBN International
Estover Road, Plymouth, PL6 7PY, UK
ORDERS PHONE: 44 (0) 1752 202301
ORDERS FAX: 44 (0) 1752 202333
ORDERS E-MAIL: enquiries@nbninternational.com

The University of Toronto Press acknowledges the financial support for its publishing activities of the Government of Canada through the Book Publishing Industry Development Program (BPIDP).

Printed in Canada

For my students and especially in memory of

BRIDGET BERNADETTE PHILLIPS

1966–1989

whose tragic death cut short a career of great promise

CONTENTS

PREFACE

ANY HISTORIAN WILL TELL you that the real fun in history comes from reading and analyzing primary sources: those documents, monuments, tools, and buildings actually created by the people we study. Regardless of how well researched or written, no secondary history book can provide the same thrill as reading the actual words of a twelfth-century abbot or listening to the testimony of a woman hauled before a court of inquisition. History, after all, is the active and creative process of interpreting the distant echoes of the past; it is not the passive memorization of facts, dates, and other people's theories. Canned history is no more appealing than canned food: fresh is always better, and growing your own is the best. Even the best textbook or scholarly synthesis is only the opinion of some historian about the significance of the material that he or she has read. In a sense, the author has already had all the fun: reading, interpreting, synthesizing, and making sense of these voices of the past. Unless we know the sources that the author has used, we can have only a distant sense of whether to accept, reject, or modify his or her conclusions. Only by reading these primary sources for ourselves can we develop our own critical, independent evaluation of the people who produced them and thus become historians, ready to participate in a dialogue with others who have read these texts before and offered their interpretations.

Because this active involvement with primary sources is at the heart of studying history, this volume places at the disposal of students beginning their exploration of medieval Europe some of these documents so that they can actually participate in the historical enterprise. Obviously this book cannot reproduce the feeling of anticipation as one sits in a great European library and opens a massive parchment manuscript, or the excitement of untying a bundle of charters written by monastic scribes over a thousand years ago. Nor can translations convey the complexities and problems of the original languages: every translation, it has been said, is a "polite lie." Still, I hope that these documents will bring students more than merely a deeper knowledge of the received tradition of medieval history. The recognition of the fragmentary and ambiguous nature of the documentation with which historians have reconstructed the past should inspire in students a healthy skepticism toward these syntheses. Moreover, it should engender in them an impatience to acquire the necessary linguistic and technical skills to do their own medieval history and to do it better than their predecessors and teachers.

Accordingly this book is designed to provide primary material with which students can participate in the historical process, not to argue for any particular interpretations or to serve merely as an illustration of currently fashionable historical theses. Four principles have guided the selection of the documents it contains.

First, entire documents or long excerpts have been included whenever possible. Truncated and severely abridged "snippets" do not allow students to understand enough of the form and context of these sources to attempt their own analyses. The result is a volume containing fewer texts than might be desired, but because of their length students and instructors should be able to do more with those that are included. I particularly regret that, with the exception of the Old High German Song of Hildebrand, I was forced to exclude literary sources. However, excellent and inexpensive translations of the classics of medieval literature are generally available for students and can supplement the harder-to-find historical sources in this volume. Likewise, I regret that except to a very limited extent, the Orthodox and Islamic worlds of the Middle Ages are not represented in this reader. To do these complex civilizations justice would have fundamentally changed the nature of this volume: they deserve primary-source readers of their own.

Second, rather than selecting widely different texts to illustrate particular issues, I have grouped some texts to form a dossier in which the individual documents relate to each other. This is of course what the practicing historian attempts to compile and examine. Examples such as the series of documents concerning land holding from Cluny, two accounts of the meeting between Otto III and the Polish prince Bolesław Chrobry in 1000, a group of Florentine catasto filings from a single family, or two Spanish law codes dealing with Jews, Muslims, and heretics, provide students with the opportunity to pose historical questions from a variety of differing perspectives. Likewise, it should be possible for students to make valid connections among documents across units. Thus, for example, the selection from the *Theodosian Code* can be related to texts from the Salic law, Anglo-Saxon law, twelfth-century Italian legal contracts, the *Saxon Mirror*, and Spanish urban law. Guibert of Nogent's autobiography can be compared with that of Emperor Charles IV and *The Book of Margery Kempe*. Anselm of Canterbury's argument for the existence of God can be compared with that of Thomas Aquinas. The selection from the eleventh-century *Domesday Book* concerning Huntingdonshire lends itself to comparison with the Huntingdonshire Eyre of 1286.

Third, whenever possible the documents presented here have been selected because they have been the objects of significant scholarship available in English. Nothing is more frustrating for a student beginning to develop an interest in medieval history than to find the issues he or she raises in relationship to a particular text have been discussed only in continental languages. Thus, for example, one reason for the selection of the book of the *Miracles of St. Foy* rather than other hagiographic texts is that it has been the subject of a number of recent studies in English from a variety of perspectives. The example of an inquisitorial dossier comes from Montaillou, brilliantly if controversially studied by Emmanuel Le Roy Ladurie. Similarly, the growing interest in the multi-ethnic and multi-cultural world of the Iberian peninsula explains the inclusion of Spanish material.

Finally, although I have my own prejudices and preferences in terms of how one does history, I have made a sincere effort to provide the raw material for many types of historical investigations. There is no one exercise that can be done with each document, no single way that an instructor can make use of them. Nor is there one point of view toward which the selection of documents tacitly point.

Of course, the perspective and competence of the investigator limit every historical enterprise, and this volume is no exception. One could easily compile an equally valuable alternative list of readings to this one, and one could validly object to the geographical limitations from which the sources are taken. I have tried to take into account the range of documents my colleagues are currently using by surveying and examining medievalist syllabuses and other source books. I have selected accurate translations or made new ones, attempting whenever possible to select translations whose publishers charge reasonable fees to reproduce in order to keep the price of the book as low as possible. Finally, I have included a number of hitherto untranslated texts in order to provide the sorts of documents representative of the types of sources to which medievalists are turning in contemporary research.

Don LePan, who first suggested that a new medieval reader was needed and encouraged me to undertake it, deserves much of the credit for this book. I would also like to thank Barbara Rosenwein, Susanna Foster Baxandall, George Beech, and Jonathan M. Elukin for their contributions. I owe a lasting debt of gratitude to John William Rooney, Jr., who first introduced me to the joy of reading the sources of medieval history. Wolter Braamhorst and Anne Picard spent many hours assisting me in finding appropriate translations and editions. Edward Schoolman worked with me on the glossary. J. Patout Burns, Richard Kay, and Ronald Finucane provided many useful corrections and suggestions for revisions. Also critical to the success of this *Reader* has been the feedback I have received from the users of the first three editions. Clearly the book has proven useful to many teachers and students, and many have shared with Don LePan and me their suggestions for how to make the book still better.

In this new, fourth edition, the first prepared for the University of Toronto Press, we have taken advantage of the many written comments that we have received through the years. First, we include a glossary of technical vocabulary, particularly words that appear in more than one source. We add recommended readings that can provide students with more information on the text. Finally, we have responded to requests for more women's voices, more legal material, and more coverage outside of western Europe. In particular, this edition contains a long selection from the ninth-century aristocratic woman Dhuoda's advice to her son; a selection from the *Saxon Mirror*, the first German language summary of customary law, and a passage from the twelfth-century *Deeds of the Princes of the Poles*. We hope that this new edition, like the three that preceded it, will continue to open a world of excitement and wonder to students of the Middle Ages by allowing them to participate in the joys of the historian's craft.

Patrick J. Geary

LATE ANTIQUITY

1. *THEODOSIAN CODE*

THE THEODOSIAN CODE WAS the first official collection of imperial general constitutions (composed between 313 and 438) dealing with a large number of public, private, and church issues. Its compilation was ordered by Emperor Theodosius II (401–450) as part of his concern with legal education. It was completed in 438 and adopted in both the eastern and western portions of the Roman Empire.

The work is arranged in sixteen books, each composed of a number of titles. In the east it was superseded by the codification of Justinian but continued to be the authoritative collection of Roman law in the barbarian kingdoms of western Europe. As such, it had an enormous influence on the formation of western barbarian and medieval law.

The following selection is Book III, which treats contracts, betrothal, marriage, dowries, divorce, and care of minors.

Source: *The Theodosian Code and Novels and the Sirmondian Constitutions*, trans. Clyde Pharr in collaboration with Theresa Sherrer Davidson and Mary Brown Pharr (Princeton: Princeton University Press, 1952), 63–81.

Further Reading: John F. Matthews, *Laying Down the Law: A Study of the Theodosian Code* (New Haven: Yale University Press, 2000).

Title 1: Contracts of Purchase
(*De Contrahenda Emptione*)

1. Emperor Constantine Augustus to Profuturus, Prefect of the Annona.
It is not at all fitting that the good faith of sale and purchase should be broken, when no duress was exerted through fraud. For a contract that has been executed without any flaw must not be disturbed by a litigious controversy because of the sole complaint that the price was too cheap.

Posted on the ides of August in the fifth consulship of Constantine Augustus and the consulship of Licinius Caesar.—August 13, 319.

INTERPRETATION: When a thing has been purchased for a definite price that is agreed upon between the buyer and seller, although it is worth more than it is sold for at the present, this only must be investigated, whether the person who is proved to have purchased it has committed no fraud or violence. If the seller should wish to revoke the sale, by no means shall he be permitted to do so.

2. The same Augustus to Gregorius.
The purchaser shall assume the tax assessment[1] of property that is purchased, and no person shall be permitted either to buy or sell property without its tax assessment.

1. Moreover, in accordance with this law, there must henceforth be a public or fiscal inspection, so that if any property should be sold without its tax assessment and this fact should be reported by another, the seller, indeed, shall lose the landholding, and the purchaser for his part shall lose

---

1   That is, payments of the taxes assessed on the property.

the price that he has paid, since the fisc shall vindicate both.

1a. It is also Our pleasure that no person shall engage in the sale of anything whatsoever unless at the time when the contract between the seller and the buyer is formally executed, a certain and true ownership is proved by the neighbors. To such an extent shall the precaution prescribed by this law be observed that even if "benches," or strips of land, as they are commonly called, are sold, the proof of showing ownership shall be fulfilled.

2. Nor shall the formalities between the buyer and the seller be solemnized in hidden corners, but fraudulent sales shall be completely buried and shall perish.

Given on the day before the nones of February at Constantinople in the year of the consulship of Felicianus and Titianus.—February 4, 337.

INTERPRETATION: If any person should purchase a villa, he shall know that he has purchased the obligation of the tribute of the thing itself as well as the right to the landholding, because no person is permitted either to buy or sell a farm without the tribute or fiscal payment. But if any person should dare to sell or presume to purchase anything when the fiscal payment had been concealed, those between whom such a contract has been made by a secret transaction should know that both the purchaser shall lose the price and the seller shall lose the landholding, because it is ordered that the neighbors of the property which is sold must be witnesses and present, to the extent that even in the case of things of slight value, if anything is sold for use, it is Our pleasure that it shall be shown to the neighbors and thus purchased, in order that the property of others may not be sold.

3. *Emperor Julian Augustus to Julianus, Count of the Orient.*
We order that the constitution of My paternal uncle, Constantine, shall be repealed, in which he commanded that minor women who were united with husbands in marriage should be able to negotiate sales without the interposition of a decree, if their husbands should suppose that they ought to give their consent as well as provide their subscription to the documents. For it is absurd that husbands who are at times needy men should be obligated for their wives, because when the right itself of the sale is not valid, these women are able to recover their own property from those persons who have participated in the illicit contracts. 1. Therefore We revive the old law, that on no account shall any sale whatsoever be valid when it has been contracted by a minor, whether a man or a woman, without the interposition of a decree.

Given on the eighth day before the ides of December at Antioch in the year of the consulship of the Most Noble Mamertinus and Nevitta.— December 6, 362.

INTERPRETATION: It had been ordained by a law of the Emperor Constantine that minor women who had husbands could sell anything from their own resources with the consent of their husbands. But this ordinance is abrogated by the present law, and the following rule must be observed, namely, that if under the compulsion of necessity men or women who are minors should wish to sell anything, whoever should wish to buy it shall be protected by the authorization of the judge or by the consent of the municipal council; for otherwise a sale made by minors will not be valid.

4. *Emperors Gratian, Valentinian, and Theodosius Augustuses to Hypatius, Praetorian Prefect.*
If a person in his majority and approved as capable of administering his own patrimony should sell a landed estate, even though it is situated at a distance and even though, perchance, in some cases the entire estate has not been sold, he shall not thereafter obtain the right of recovery on the ground that the price was too cheap.

1. He shall not be allowed to contrive delays by means of unfounded objections, namely, that he should allege that the value of the property was unknown to him, since he ought to know the value, that is, the worth and income of his own family property.

Given on the sixth day before the nones of May at Milan in the year of the second consulship of Merobaudes and the consulship of Saturninus.— May 2, 383.

INTERPRETATION: If any person, already of full legal age and able to manage his own household, should sell his villa, house, or anything else at a definite price and if, perchance, later he should wish to claim in opposition that he received a smaller price than the property was worth, because he says, perhaps, that he was ignorant of the value of the land which he sold, since it was located at a distance, the sale cannot be revoked for that reason. For a person of full age could have known what sort of thing he sold or at what price the thing to be sold could be valued.

5. The same Augustuses to Cynegius, Praetorian Prefect.

No Jew whatever shall purchase a Christian slave or contaminate an ex-Christian with Jewish religious rites. But if a public investigation should disclose that this has been done, the slave shall be forcibly taken away, and such masters shall undergo a punishment suitable and appropriate for the crime. It is further added that if there should be found among the Jews any slaves who are either still Christians or ex-Christian Jews, they shall be redeemed from this unworthy servitude by the Christians upon payment of a suitable price.

Received on the tenth day before the kalends of October at Rhegium in the year of the consulship of Richomer and Clearchus.—September 22, 384.

INTERPRETATION: It must be observed above all things else that no Jew shall be permitted to have a Christian slave; indeed, if a Jew should have a Christian slave, he shall under no circumstances dare to presume to transfer him to his own religious faith. If he should do this, he shall know that his slaves will be forcibly taken from him, and he shall undergo a punishment suited to so great a crime. For before this law was issued, it had been decreed that if a Christian slave had been contaminated by Jewish pollution, his master should know that the price which he had paid for the slave would be refunded to him by the Christians in order that the slave might remain in the Christian faith.

6. The same Augustuses to Flavianus, Praetorian Prefect of Illyricum and Italy.

Formerly the right had been granted to near kinsmen and to co-owners to exclude extraneous persons from a purchase,[2] and men could not, in accordance with their own decision, sell any property which they had for sale. But because this appears to be a grave injustice, which is veiled by the empty pretext of honor, that men should be compelled to do anything about their own property against their will, this former law is hereby annulled, and each person shall be able to seek and approve a purchaser according to his own decision.

Given on the sixth day before the kalends of June at Vincentia in the year of the consulship of Titianus and Symmachus.—May 27, 391.

INTERPRETATION: A former ordinance of the law had provided that if one co-owner, because of some necessity, should wish to sell a thing, an extraneous person should not have the opportunity to buy it. But this imperial indulgence is approved as better, namely, that any person shall have the right to use his unconstrained decision concerning his own property. He may pass over his co-owners and near kinsmen and have the unrestricted privilege of selling to whomever he wishes.

7. The same Augustuses to Remigius, Augustal Prefect.

If persons of full legal capacity should once enter into a contract of purchase and sale, it cannot be invalidated on the ground that too small a price has been paid.

Given on the third day before the kalends of April at Constantinople in the year of the fourth consulship of Arcadius Augustus and the third consulship of Honorius Augustus.—March 30, 396.

INTERPRETATION: When an agreement has been made between any two persons concerning the price of anything, although the thing has been bought for a less price than it was worth, the sale shall by no means be revoked.

---

2   Of property held in common.

8. The same Augustuses to Messala, Praetorian Prefect.

(After other matters.) If any persons by flight should desert the compulsory public services, either municipal or provincial, that have been enjoined upon them and should suppose that they may enter into clandestine contracts, they shall understand that these artifices will profit them nothing, and the purchaser shall be fined the price that he has paid. (Etc.)

Given on the twelfth day before the kalends of September in the year of the consulship of the Most Noble Theodorus.—August 21, 399.

INTERPRETATION: If any persons should attempt to escape the compulsory public services which are due to the municipal council or their own municipality and should wish to sell their property secretly, they shall know that what they have done cannot be valid, and that they themselves will be recalled to the services due. Those persons also who bought the property shall lose the price.

9. Emperors Honorius and Theodosius Augustuses to the People.

We command that the sales, gifts, and compromises which have been extorted through the exercise of power[3] shall be invalidated.

Given on the thirteenth day before the kalends of March at Constantinople in the year of the tenth consulship of Honorius Augustus and the sixth consulship of Theodosius Augustus.—February 17, 415.

INTERPRETATION: All men shall know that whatever they have given or sold under the compulsion of very powerful persons can be recovered.

10. Honorius and Theodosius Augustuses to Palladius, Praetorian Prefect.

There is said to exist a superfluous belief of some persons that the right to purchase has been denied to persons placed in administrative offices and in the imperial service, although a law of the sainted Honorius, issued to Palladius, Praetorian Prefect, and included in the Theodosian corpus, is read as having given this right to such persons.

Title 2: The Annulment of Provisions for Forfeiture (*De Commissoria Rescindenda*)

1. Emperor[4] Constantine Augustus to the People.

Since among other captious practices, the harshness of the provision for forfeiture is especially increasing, it is Our pleasure that such provision shall be invalidated and that hereafter all memory of it shall be abolished. If any person, therefore, is suffering under such a contract, he shall be relieved by this sanction which cancels all such past and present arguments and prohibits them for the future. For We order that creditors shall surrender the property[5] and recover that which they have given.[6]

Given on the day before the kalends of February at Sofia (Serdica) in the year of the seventh consulship of Constantine Augustus and the consulship of Constantius Caesar.—January 31, 326; [320].

INTERPRETATION: Those written acknowledgements of debt are called agreements for forfeiture in which a debtor through necessity promises in a written acknowledgement of debt to sell to his own creditor a thing which he had pledged for a time to the creditor. This law cancels any such agreement for forfeiture which has been made and absolutely prohibits one to be made. Thus if any creditor should appear to have bought property of his debtor under such a pretext, he shall not delude himself with written documents, but as soon as the debtor wishes, who sold when oppressed by debt, the creditor shall recover his money, and the debtor shall receive back his property.

---

3   The merciless exploitation of the poor and weak by the rich and powerful was extremely common. It was often forbidden by the emperors, but the various laws against it were apparently ineffectual.

4   Some of the dates provided in the text are incorrect; suggested corrections appear after these.

5   Which they have accepted as a pledge.

6   As a loan.

Title 3: Fathers Who Have Sold Their Children
(*De Patribus Qui Filios Distraxerunt*)

1. Emperors Valentinian, Theodosius, and Arcadius Augustuses to Tatianus, Praetorian Prefect.
All those persons whom the piteous fortune of their parents has consigned to slavery while their parents thereby were seeking sustenance shall be restored to their original status of free birth. Certainly no person shall demand repayment of the purchase price, if he has been compensated by the slavery of a free-born person for a space of time that is not too short.

Given on the fifth day before the ides of March at Milan in the year of the consulship of Tatianus and Symmachus.—March 11, 391.

INTERPRETATION: If a father, forced by need, should sell any free-born child whatsoever, the child cannot remain in perpetual slavery, but if he has made compensation by his slavery, he shall be restored to his free-born status without even the repayment of the purchase price.

Title 4: Aedilician Actions (*De Aedilicis Actionibus*)

1. Emperors Valentinian, Theodosius, and Arcadius Augustuses to Nebridius, Prefect of the City.
Once a contract of good faith has been completed and a slave has been received and the price paid, the right to recover the purchase price shall be granted to the purchaser of the slave only if he can produce the slave who he claims is a fugitive. This rule, indeed, is prescribed by law not only in the case of barbarian slaves, but also in the case of provincial slaves.

Given on the third day before the kalends of July at Constantinople in the year of the consulship of Emperor Designate Honorious and the Most Noble Evodius.—June 29, 386.

INTERPRETATION: When the price of a slave has been agreed upon between the buyer and seller and a deed of sale has been written, such sale can by no means be revoked, unless by chance the buyer should prove that the slave is a fugitive, and then he shall have permission to recover the price if he should restore the slave to the seller.

Title 5: Betrothal and Prenuptial Gifts
(*De Sponsalibus Et Ante Nuptias Donationibus*)

1. Emperor Constantine Augustus to Rufinus, Praetorian Prefect.
It was the will of Our father that no act of generosity should be valid unless it was entered in the public records. We decree also that, after the time of promulgation of this law, gifts between betrothed persons, as well as those between all other persons, shall be valid only if they are accompanied by the attestation of the public records.

Given on the fourth day before the ides of May at Sirmium in the year of the fifth consulship of Constantine Augustus and the consulship of Licinius Caesar.—May 12, 319; 352.

INTERPRETATION: Before the time of the above law, gifts were valid even without the attestation of the public records. But now, after the above law, no nuptial or any other gift of anything whatsoever, between any persons whatsoever, can be valid if it has not been formally registered in the public records.

2. The same Augustus to Maximus, Prefect of the City.
Since We are displeased with the opinion of the ancients which decreed that gifts to a betrothed woman were valid even though the marriage did not follow, We order that those negotiations between betrothed persons which are conducted with due legal formality with the intention of making gifts shall be made subject to the following conditions: whether it appears that persons live under paternal power or that they are in any manner legally independent, if, either of their own volition or with the mutual consent of their parents, they should make presents to each other as though with a view to future matrimony, and if indeed the man of his own accord should be unwilling to take the woman as his wife, he shall not recover that which has been given and delivered by him; if any part of the promised gift remains in the possession of the donor, it shall be transferred to the betrothed woman without any evasion. 1. But if the responsibility for failure to contract the marriage is revealed to have been that of the betrothed woman or of the person under

whose power she lives, then all gifts shall be returned to the betrothed man or his heirs without any diminution.

2. These provisions shall similarly be observed also if a gift has been made to a betrothed man on the part of the woman betrothed to him. There shall be no further inquiry into reasons for failure to contract the marriage. Thus, for example, the morals or the low birth, perhaps, of either party may not be alleged, and no other obstacle may be adduced which anyone might consider unsuitable, since long before the betrothal was contracted, all these things should have been foreseen. Therefore, only the intention shall be investigated, and a change of intention shall suffice for either restitution or recovery of the gifts that have been made, since, after the elimination of all pretexts, it shall be necessary for nothing further to be established, except the evidence as to which party said that the marriage which was to be contracted was not acceptable.

3. Since it is possible that before the marriage is contracted, one of the two may die while his intention to marry is still unchanged, We consider it suitable that when the one to whom a gift has been made completes his days before the marriage, whatever has been given under the title of a betrothal gift or donated in any other way shall be restored to the person who made the gift. Also, if the person who presented a gift should die before the wedding, the gift shall be immediately invalidated and that property which was presented shall be restored to the heirs of the donor without any hindrance.

4. We decree that this benefit shall extend even to the person of the father and mother and of children also, if there were any from a former marriage; if in any manner any of these persons should succeed to the inheritance of the deceased. But if none of these persons should be an heir of the deceased, but some one from the remaining[7] degrees should succeed to the inheritance, the gifts shall become valid even though because of death the marriage was not confirmed, since We believe that suitable provisions should be made only for those persons.[8]

Given on the seventeenth day before the kalends of November: October 16. Posted on the sixth day before the aforesaid kalends at Rome in the year of the fifth consulship of Constantine Augustus and the consulship of Licinius Caesar.—October 27, 319.

INTERPRETATION: Whenever betrothed persons have made a specific agreement concerning their future marriage, and the man, either with the consent of his parents or of his own free will if he is legally independent, has written a deed of gift of his betrothal bounty to his betrothed and has confirmed this deed of gift with all the formality of written documents, provided also that it shall be proved that public records were made in conformity with the law and that formal induction into the land and delivery of movables followed, then if anything should pass into the right and ownership of the betrothed woman by such a formal gift and if later, after the aforesaid formal documents have been executed, the man should voluntarily refuse to accept as his wife the woman whom he betrothed, he shall not demand back anything that has been delivered. If he is proved to have in his possession any of the property thus formally specified and delivered, it shall be transferred without any delay to the ownership of the betrothed woman whom he was unwilling to accept.

It is unnecessary to explain the remainder of the above law because it is annulled by the subsequent laws.

3. The same Augustus to Valerianus, Acting Vicar of the Prefect.
Although in matters of gain it is not customary to assist women who are ignorant of the law, the statutes of former emperors declare that this rule does not apply as against one who is still under age. 1. Lest, therefore, when marital affection has vanished, some cruel decision should be made, We decree that if property has been given and delivered to a prospective wife who is under age at the time of marriage, this property cannot be recovered on the grounds that the former husband refused to register the gift in the public records.

---

7   The more remote degrees of kinship than those mentioned above.
8   The ones specified above.

Given on the fourth day before the kalends of May in the year of the consulship of Gallicanus and Symmachus.—April 28, 330.

INTERPRETATION: Although even in the case of women, who can at times be excused because of their frailty, the law is unwilling to assist them in some cases if they have been negligent, nevertheless, in the above law it was the emperor's will that especial provision should be made for them, so that if any girl should be united to a husband in her pupillary years and her husband should through negligence fail to register his betrothal bounty in the public records, she shall know that by the benefit of this law, even if public records are lacking, the gift will remain in her ownership with indefeasible title.

4. *The same Augustus to Pacatianus, Praetorian Prefect.*

If any man should contract for the marriage of a girl to himself and should fail to effect such marriage within two years, and if after this time has elapsed the girl should proceed to marry another, no fraud shall be imputed to her for hastening her marriage and not allowing her marriage vows to be mocked any longer.

Given on the day before the ides of April at Marcianopolis in the year of the consulship of Pacatianus and Hilarianus.—April 12, 332.

5. *The same Augustus to Pacatianus, Praetorian Prefect.*

The father of a girl or her tutor, curator, or any kinsman, shall not be permitted to give her in marriage to another after having previously betrothed her to a soldier. If the girl should be given in marriage to another within two years, the person guilty of such perfidy shall be exiled by relegation to an island. But if after an interval of two years has elapsed since the marriage was agreed upon, the person who betrothed the girl[9] should marry her to another, it shall be attributed to the fault of the betrothed man[10] rather than to that of the girl, and the person who gave the girl in marriage to another husband after two years shall suffer no injury.

Given on the day before the ides of April at Marcianopolis in the year of the consulship of Pacatianus and Hilarianus.—April 12, 332.

INTERPRETATION: If any person, either a private citizen or a soldier, after his betrothal to a girl, should make a definite agreement concerning the marriage with her father, tutor, curator, or near kinsman, he must effect the marriage within two years after this definite agreement. But if on account of the procrastination or negligence of the betrothed man, a period of two years should elapse and the girl should marry another man, both she herself and the kinsman who delivered her in marriage shall be free from calumny. For the fault is that of the man who, by delaying his own marriage, gave to another man the opportunity to marry the girl. If she should be given in marriage to another man within two years, the rules to be observed will be understood more clearly from the subsequent law.

6. *The same Augustus to Tiberianus, Vicar of Spain.*

If a man should make gifts to his betrothed when a kiss has been exchanged as a pledge and if it should happen that either the man or the woman should die before the marriage, We order that one half of the things given shall belong to the survivor; the other half shall belong to the heirs of the deceased man or woman, of whatever degree such heirs may be and by whatever right they may succeed to the inheritance, so that it appears that one half the gift shall remain valid and one half shall be annulled. But when no kiss has been exchanged as a pledge, if either of the betrothed persons should die, the whole gift shall be invalidated and shall be restored to the betrothed donor or to his heirs.

1. If a woman should give anything to her betrothed under the title of betrothal gifts, a thing which rarely occurs, and if it happens that either the man or the woman dies before the marriage, whether or not a kiss has been exchanged as a pledge, the whole gift shall be invalidated, and the ownership of the things shall be transferred to the betrothed woman who gave it or to her heirs.

---

9   To a soldier.
10   The soldier who had thus delayed the marriage of the girl to himself.

Given on the ides of July at Constantinople: July 15, 335. Received on the fourteenth day before the kalends of May at Hispalis in the year of the consulship of Nepotianus and Facundus.—April 18, 336.

INTERPRETATION: If when a betrothal has been solemnized and a kiss has been exchanged as a pledge, the betrothed man should make some gift to the betrothed woman, and if perchance he should die before the marriage, then the girl, in case she survives, shall be able to vindicate one half of the things which had been formally given to her, and the heirs of the deceased shall acquire one half, in whatsoever order, according to the degree of succession, they may come. But if a kiss should not be exchanged as a pledge, and the betrothed man should die, the girl shall not be able to vindicate any of the things given or delivered to her. But if anything should be given by the girl to the betrothed man and she should die, whether or not a kiss has been exchanged as a pledge, the parents or near kinsmen of the girl shall recover all that which the girl gave.

7. …[11]

… provided that … has been preserved, the gift shall have complete validity, although he did not arrange for the certification of public records in testimony thereof. Certainly, a group of people assembled as witnesses of these vows is sufficiently competent. But in the case of all other gifts, the execution of public records shall be required in accordance with the constitutions of Our sainted father.[12]

Given on the fifth day before the ides of Ju …[13] at Köln in the year of the consulship of Amantius and Albinus.—June 9 (July 11), 345.

8. *Emperor Julian Augustus to Hypatius, Vicar of the City of Rome.*[14]
Whenever any gifts consisting of landed estates that are subject to either Italian, stipendiary, or tributary rights are given and pledged by a stipulation to a betrothed woman in her minority, with a view to future marriage, such bounty shall be supported by perpetual validity, even though it should appear that the formality of delivery was lacking; provided, however, that even in the case of those gifts which are bestowed upon minors, the execution of public records shall be demanded in all cases.

Given on the ninth day before the kalends of M(arch) at Antioch in the year of the fourth consulship of Julian Augustus and the consulship of Sallustius.—February 21, 363.

9. *Emperors Valentinian, Valens, and Gratian Augustuses to Probus, Praetorian Prefect.*
Before marriage many things are delivered with all due formality under the title of betrothal gifts, and these gifts must not by any means contribute to loss on the part of the donor. But if the girl should die during the marriage, they shall revert to the advantage of the said donor in disregard, of course, of the old law. Therefore, the claim of the father and other near kinsmen shall be annulled, and such gifts shall be returned without delay to those persons who appear to have presented them before the marriage was contracted.

Given on the third day before the ides of July at Trier in the year of the consulship of Valentinian and Valens Augustuses.—July 13, 368; 367; 373.

10. *Emperors Gratian, Valentinian, and Theodosius Augustuses to Eutropius, Praetorian Prefect.*
If, after anything has been given as earnest under the title of betrothal gifts, either of the betrothed persons should die, We order that whatever has been given shall be restored, unless the deceased person had previously given cause for the non-performance of the marriage rites.

11　The first part of the constitution has been lost.
12　Constantine the Great.
13　Since the ms. is defective, the month is uncertain.
14　Estates subject to Italian rights had certain privileges that were not held by stipendiary or tributary estates, since Italian estates were originally those of the Roman conquerors, while stipendiary and tributary estates were originally those of conquered peoples. These distinctions were gradually abolished in the time of the Empire.

Given on the fifteenth day before the kalends of July at Thessalonica in the year of the fifth consulship of Gratian Augustus and the first consulship of Theodosius Augustus.—June 17, 380.

11. The same Augustuses to Eutropius, Praetorian Prefect.

When betrothal gifts have been made to a girl before her tenth year, We remit the fourfold penalty for the father, mother, tutor, or any person, even though the marriage should not follow; and if the girl should die in the meantime, We order that the betrothal gifts shall be restored to her betrothed. 1. But if the father or any other person who has charge of the girl's affairs should suppose that he should retain the pledges which he has received in the girl's tenth year or later, and before her twelfth year, that is, until the end of her eleventh year, then if, when the time for the marriage arrives, he should be false to his trust, he shall become obligated to the fourfold penalty.

2. But for a widow, since she is not assisted by the privilege of age, there is a different rule, namely, that if she does not effect her marriage, she shall be liable to the fourfold penalty according to the ancient constitution.

3. Moreover, when any person makes an agreement concerning the marriage of a girl after the completion of her twelfth year, if indeed the person making the agreement is the girl's father, he shall obligate himself, but if her mother or a curator or other near kinsman, the girl shall become obligated.

4. But there shall be reserved to the girl against her mother, tutor, curator, or such near kinsman, an unimpaired action, on the basis of what is fair and just with regard to those pledges which she restored from her own resources according to the penalty of the law, provided that she can prove that she had been compelled by the aforesaid persons to consent to receive what was given as earnest.

Given on the fifteenth day before the kalends of July at Thessalonica in the year of the fifth consulship of Gratian Augustus and the first consulship of Theodosius Augustus.—June 17, 380.

INTERPRETATION: If, before a girl has reached her tenth year, her father or mother or, if the father should be lacking, her tutor, curator, or any near kinsman, should make an agreement concerning her marriage and should accept betrothal gifts, and if afterwards he should change his mind and wish to reject the person whom he had formerly accepted, he shall not be condemned to the fourfold penalty, but shall restore only what he had received. Certainly, also if the girl should die, only that shall be returned which had been received. But if, when the girl is in her tenth year and until the completion of her eleventh year, she herself, or her parents, tutors and curators should retain the earnest which had been received, the following rule must be observed, namely, that if the person who made the agreement concerning the marriage of the girl should wish to prove false to the agreement and should reject the man whose betrothal gifts had been received, he shall be liable to the fourfold penalty, without doubt. But if he should return the pledges received before the girl's eleventh year is completed, he shall fear no malicious charges concerning the earnest which had been accepted. On the other hand, if the girl should be a widow, she shall not be able to defend herself on the ground of her age,[15] if she should turn her affections elsewhere and should wish to reject her former betrothed. Then whatever she has accepted under the title of betrothal gifts she shall return fourfold. But if after the girl's twelfth year, her father should wish to do otherwise than he promised concerning her marriage, her father himself shall be held liable to the fourfold penalty. If the father is dead and the mother, tutor, curator or any near kinsman should make a definite agreement concerning the marriage of the girl and the girl should prefer to wed another, she herself out of her own resources shall make reparation to her former betrothed in the amount of four times the value of what she received. This condition, however, shall be observed, that she can bring suit afterwards against the aforesaid persons, if under their compulsion she unwillingly accepted the pledges of the man whom she later refused.

---

15 That is, she may not claim the privileges granted to women who were minors.

12. Emperors Honorius and Theodosius Augustuses to Marinianus, Praetorian Prefect.

(After other matters.) If a father should enter into a pact concerning the marriage of his daughter and he should not be able to reach the time of the marriage because he perished by human lot, the decision which is proved to have been made by the father shall remain valid and binding between the betrothed, and a compromise shall not be permitted to have any weight if it is proved to have been made by the guardian to whose administration the interests of the minor pertain. 1. For it is thoroughly unjust that the decision of a tutor or curator, who has perhaps been bribed, should be admitted as against the father's wish, since frequently even the determination of a woman herself is found to work against her own interests. (Etc.)

Given on the third day before the nones of November at Ravenna in the year of the thirteenth consulship of Our Lord Honorius Augustus and the tenth consulship of Our Lord Theodosius Augustus.—November 3, 422.

INTERPRETATION: When a definite agreement concerning the marriage of a girl has been made by the decision of her father, if by human lot the father should die before the girl is married, the agreement cannot be changed in any way, and the girl shall not have the liberty to do anything else even if her mother or tutor or curator or near kinsmen should perhaps wish that she accept another rather than the man her father chose. But the promise of her father with reference to the man whom he himself accepted as her betrothed shall remain valid, and in no way shall the girl be permitted in accordance with her own plan to desire anything contrary to the wishes of her father.

13. Emperors Theodosius and Valentinian Augustuses to Hierius, Praetorian Prefect.

(After other matters.) If a deed or gift has been validated before marriage by the formality of registration in the public records, there shall be no inquiry as to whether delivery of the gift either preceded or followed the marriage or was altogether omitted. In the case of a gift which is less than two hundred solidi in its total value, the execution of public records shall not be required. 1. We do not permit these advantages to be denied to a wife or to those persons who succeed to her rights, who may be deceived through the fraud of her husband or the dishonesty of his heirs or through legal technicalities, even though either through ignorance or cunning the deed of gift should make mention of things to be given as dowry, but such gifts shall be extracted from the husband or his heirs and shall be restored. That law also shall remain in force which makes just provision for women of minor age, even when the attestation of the public records has been omitted, if they have been deprived of their father's aid. (Etc.)

Given on the tenth day before the kalends of March at Constantinople in the year of the consulship of Taurus and Felix.—February 21, 428.

INTERPRETATION: If a betrothal gift should be entered in the public records before marriage, it cannot be invalidated even though the thing given is not delivered. But in the case of a gift, the total value of which is found to be less than two hundred solidi, even when a public record of it is lacking, no chicanery can be employed against women under cover of any cunning device or objection, but any writing whatever which indicates the day and the time shall suffice. Therefore, whether a gift is one which is made by entry in the public records without delivery, or whether it is one which is less than two hundred solidi in value, it shall not be invalidated by any arguments resting upon chicanery in any respect, but the things shall be exacted from the husband or his heirs who shall be ordered to restore them to the woman. Nevertheless, the benefit of the law shall remain valid concerning those women who are married during their minority after their father's death, so that a deed of gift of any amount whatever, when made in writing, shall stand with complete validity, even though it has not been registered in the public records.

14. …

… the betrothed man or the betrothed woman may violate this regulation without any hazard. But the fifteenth constitution of the fifteenth title of the third book of the Theodosian Code confirms the threatened penalty to the extent of double indemnity in cases of agreements for marriage.

Title 6: If the Governor of a Province or Persons Connected with Him Should Give Betrothal Gifts (*Si Provinciae Rector Vel Ad Eum Pertinentes Sponsalia Dederint*)

1. Emperors Gratian, Valentinian, and Theodosius Augustuses to Eutropius, Praetorian Prefect.
(After other matters.) If betrothal gifts should be given by persons who hold positions of public power and honor in the administration of provinces and who, therefore, can intimidate parents, tutors, curators, or the women themselves who are about to contract the marriage, We order that if either the parents or the women themselves should change their minds thereafter, they shall not only be released from the toils of the law and free from the fourfold penalty which it has established, but in addition they shall keep as gain the things given as pledges if they should suppose that they ought not to be returned. 1. So widely do We intend this provision to extend that We decree that it shall apply not only to such administrators, but also to sons, grandsons, near kinsmen, associates and confidential advisers of administrations, provided, however, that the administrators had given them assistance. 2. However, We do not forbid that marriage to be effected thereafter which was obligated by means of an earnest at the time of such administration, on account of those persons about whom We have spoken, if the consent of the betrothed woman should accede thereto.

Given on the fifteenth day before the kalends of July at Thessalonica in the year of the fifth consulship of Our Lord Gratian Augustus and the first consulship of Our Lord Theodosius Augustus.—June 17, 380.

INTERPRETATION: If any judges[16] of provinces or any persons in administrative offices, while holding the aforesaid positions of honor, should have with them their adult sons or near kinsmen or any persons who appear to be associated with them in their administration, if they should use their power to threaten the parents or perchance to intimidate tutors or curators or the girls themselves, if they should give anything in the name of betrothal gifts or as earnest for the purpose of obligating the household of any person, and if the parents or the girls themselves should wish to resist this desire,[17] they shall have the unrestricted right to refuse that which they appear to have thus accepted. They shall know that the fourfold penalty shall not be exacted of them, but also those gifts which it appears that they accepted through terror they shall retain to their own profit, if they so wish, and they cannot be constrained to return them unless perchance they should wish to do so of their own free will. For if, after the end of such administration, the desire of the parents or the girls should remain unchanged with regard to marriage with those persons who had given betrothal gifts, the marriage thus chosen may follow.

Title 7: Marriage (*De Nuptiis*)

1. Emperors Valentinian, Valens, and Gratian Augustuses to the Senate.
A widow less than twenty-five years of age, even though she enjoys the freedom derived from emancipation, shall not enter into a subsequent marriage without the consent of her father or in opposition to his will. Therefore, the intermediaries and marriage brokers, the corrupt bearers of secret messages back and forth, shall cease. No person shall purchase a noble marriage,[18] no person shall solicit one; but the kinsmen shall be consulted publicly, and a number of nobles shall be admitted. 1. But if in the choice of a marriage the woman's desire should conflict with the decision of her near kinsmen, it is Our pleasure that, as has been sanctioned in the case of marriages of girls who are pupils, the authority of a judicial trial shall be added to the investigation that must be held, so that if the suitors are equal in birth and character, the person whom the woman herself approves, consulting her own interests, shall be adjudged preferable. 2. But lest perchance even honorable marriages should be impeded by those persons who, as kinsmen in the nearest degree, would be called to the inheritances of such widows, if a suspicion of this kind should arise, it is Our will that the authority and judgment of those

---

16   Governors, the judges ordinary.
17   Of the administrators. Or: if the parents or the girls themselves should wish to oppose their previous agreement.
18   Marriage with a person of noble rank.

persons shall prevail who, even though death should intervene, could not receive the benefit of the inheritance.

Given on the seventeenth day before the kalends of August in the year of the second consulship of Gratian Augustus and the consulship of Probus.— July 16, 371.

INTERPRETATION: If a widow who has not yet arrived at her twenty-fifth year during her father's lifetime should wish to enter into a subsequent marriage, she shall know that, even though she has acquired her freedom by emancipation, her marriage is subject to the control of her father and does not rest upon her own desire, and her consent must conform to the choice of her father and not that of any friends or comrades whatever. But if indeed the father of such a widow is dead, even so she shall not have the right to marry according to her own individual choice, but in the interests of an honorable condition of marriage, the judgment of the near kinsmen must be followed. But if there should be two suitors, the near kinsmen must certainly be consulted, and the judge[19] also must not be ignored, who shall take into consideration the desire of the woman only in the interest of the more honorable man. He shall not give assent to the wishes of those near kinsmen only who labour under the suspicion of desiring the inheritance and who, perhaps, while they delay the wedding, appear to be awaiting the death of the woman with a view to their succession to the inheritance. But if such a condition should arise, the choice of those persons rather must be followed who can acquire nothing from the inheritance of the aforesaid woman.

2. Emperors Valentinian, Theodosius, and Arcadius Augustuses to Cynegius, Praetorian Prefect.
No Jew shall receive a Christian woman in marriage, nor shall a Christian man contract a marriage with a Jewish woman. For if any person should commit an act of this kind, the crime of this misdeed shall be considered as the equivalent of adultery, and freedom to bring accusation shall be granted also to the voices of the public.

Given on the day before the ides of March at Thessalonica in the year of the second consulship of Theodosius Augustus and the consulship of the Most Noble Cynegius.—March 14, 388.

INTERPRETATION: By the severity of this law it is prohibited that a Jew should enjoy marriage with a Christian woman or that a Christian man should receive a Jewish woman as his wife. But if any persons should involve themselves in such a union, contrary to Our prohibition, they shall know that they will be prosecuted and subjected to the same punishment as that which is inflicted upon adulterers, and that the right to bring accusation of this crime and the prosecution of it shall be allowed not only to near kinsmen but also to everyone.

3. Emperors Theodosius and Valentinian Augustuses to Hierius, Praetorian Prefect.
If instruments[20] of prenuptial gifts or dowries should be lacking and if the solemn procession and other wedding ceremonies should be omitted, no person shall suppose that on this account a marriage otherwise legally entered into shall lack validity or that the rights of legitimacy can be taken from children born of such a marriage, when the marriage is contracted of persons of equally honorable status, when it is preceded by no law, and when it is confirmed by the consent of the parties and the reliable testimony of friends. (Etc.)

Given on the tenth day before the kalends of March at Constantinople in the year of the consulship of Felix and Taurus.—February 21, 428.

INTERPRETATION: If any such exigency should arise that a marriage should lack the due formalities, or even that betrothal gifts cannot be made or the bestowal of a dowry executed, yet if the parties should unite in marriage by mutual consent, when they are persons of equal status, a suitable choice and the agreement of the parties shall suffice, provided, however, that the knowledge of friends shall act as surety of the marriage; then if such a situation should occur, the marriage shall be approved as valid and the children as legitimate.

---

19 The governor of the province, the judge ordinary.
20 Documentary evidence, such as deeds of gift and dowry agreements.

Title 8: Subsequent Marriages
(*De Secundis Nuptiis*)

1. Emperors Gratian, Valentinian, and Theodosius Augustuses to Eutropius, Praetorian Prefect.
If any woman who has lost her husband should hasten to marry another man within the period of a year (for We add a small amount of time to be observed after the ten months period, although We consider even that to be very little) she shall be branded with the marks of disgrace and deprived of both the dignity and rights of a person of honorable and noble status. She shall also forfeit all the property which she has obtained from the estate of her former husband, either by the right of betrothal gifts or by the will of her deceased husband. She shall know also that she shall expect no help from Us through either a special grant of imperial favor or an annotation.

Given on the third day before the kalends of June at Constantinople in the year of the consulship of Eucherius and Syagrius.—May 30, 381.

INTERPRETATION: If within a year after the death of her husband a woman should marry another man, she shall know that she will subject herself to infamy and be rendered infamous to such a degree that she shall forfeit any betrothal gifts that she has received by the bounty of her former husband or anything that he has given to her by his testament, and all this property shall go to his children. If there should be no children, the said property shall profit those persons who are akin to the former husband in the nearest degree, and they shall be able to vindicate this property for themselves through the right of inheritance.

2. The same Augustuses to Florus, Praetorian Prefect.
When a woman passes to a subsequent marriage, if she has children born from a prior marriage, anything that she has received from the property of her former husband by right of betrothal gifts, or anything that she has also received upon celebration of the marriage, or anything that she has acquired from the property of her former husband by gifts made in expectation of death or by testament, either by direct right or under the title of a trust or legacy or as a reward through any other form of munificent liberality, all this she shall have the right to transmit undiminished, just as she received it, to the children which she has from her prior marriage, or to any one of these children upon whom the mother believes she ought to bestow the judgment of her liberality in view of the merits of such child, provided that this child should be one of those whom We consider most worthy of such a succession. Such a woman shall not presume or have the power to alienate any part of such property to any extraneous person whatsoever or to successors born from the union of the second marriage. She shall have the right of possession only to the last day of her life, and she shall not be allowed the power of alienation also. For if any of the aforesaid property, through a fraud of evil intent, should be transferred by the mother who possesses it to any other person whatsoever, it must be restored by compensation out of her own resources, whereby the property shall go undiminished and unimpaired to those persons whom We have designated as heirs.

1. We also add to the law the following provision, namely, that if any son from the aforesaid children who are proved to have been born from the former marriage should perhaps die, leaving one or more sisters but no brother, and thus, by benefit of the decree of the Senate, he should appear to provide for the mother a place as heir along with the sisters; or if a daughter should die leaving no brother alive, but only her mother and sisters as survivors and should thus preserve for the mother an opportunity to enter upon the inheritance for a half portion, whatever the mother shall appear to have obtained by the benefit of succession,[21] she shall be granted only the possession thereof to the last day of her life in accordance with her due portion. She shall leave everything to the surviving children who were born of her prior marriage, and she shall not have the power to will such property to any extraneous person or to alienate any of it.

2. But if she should have no children as her successors from the prior marriage, or if such child or children should have died, she shall hold

---

21 As an heir.

in fully legal ownership all property which she has received in any manner, and she shall have the unlimited power to acquire ownership from these children and to give it by testament to whomever she wishes.

3. It is Our will that husbands also shall be admonished by a similar example of both piety and law. Although We do not constrain them by the bond, so to speak, of a sanction very severely imposed upon them, nevertheless We restrain them by the law of religion, that they may know that which is enjoined upon mothers by the necessity of the law, as here set forth, is more readily expected of them in consideration of justice, in order that, if necessity should so persuade, in the case of men, too, there should not have to be exacted from them by the aid of a sanction that which meanwhile may properly be desired and expected.

Given on the sixteenth day before the kalends of January at Constantinople in the year of the consulship of Antonius and Syagrius.—December 17, 382.

INTERPRETATION: If a woman should lose her husband and afterward should enter into another marriage at the statutory time, that is, when a year has elapsed, and if she should have children by her former husband, she shall preserve for such children all the property which she has received through any betrothal bounty or gift made at the time of the wedding, and she shall know that this property must not be transferred to other or extraneous persons. But whatever the former husband has given to his wife by a testament or trust fund or under the title of legacy or in expectation of death, this property that the wife has received by such a gift, she shall have the unlimited power to bestow, either upon all the children or upon one for the merit of such child's service, if she should so wish; but she shall not be permitted to alienate any of the property of her former husband away from his children. But if she should presume to do this, she must know that compensation must be made out of her own resources.

The emperor supposed that the following provision especially should be included in this law, namely, that if a woman should proceed to another marriage, and if, of the children which she had

born from her prior marriage, a son should die, in case that he leaves surviving a mother and sisters, or at least a sister and does not leave a brother, who would be able to exclude the mother, then by the benefit of the law the mother and the daughters or daughter shall succeed to equal shares. But if a daughter should die and should leave only a mother and sisters, the mother shall acquire half the inheritance of the deceased daughter, and half shall accrue to the sisters, whether there be one or many, under the condition, however, that while the mother lives, she shall possess only in usufruct the half which she has acquired from such inheritance of a son or daughter. After her death she shall leave this property to the remaining children, if any have survived from her former marriage, and she shall not have the liberty to transfer it to other persons either by testament or by gift. But if no children by her former husband should survive, then any property whatever that she has received on this account she shall vindicate for herself as though it were her own property, and she shall lawfully transmit it to whomever she may wish. In this law also it was the emperor's will that a similar condition should be observed if a father whose wife had died should proceed to a subsequent marriage, so that, if there should be sons or daughters by his former wife, of whom some should die and make a place for the father in the succession to their own portion, after the father's death, this portion which was left to him should accrue to the brothers and sisters who survive from his prior marriage, and it could not pass to other persons through paternal power.

3. Emperors Honorius and Theodosius Augustuses to Johannes, Praetorian Prefect.
No person shall have any doubt that a woman shall have a usufruct to the last day of her life in the property which she received at the time of her marriage, even though she should perchance proceed to a subsequent marriage after the statutory time has elapsed and even though there should be children of the prior marriage. The ownership of such property shall be preserved for those persons to whom the most sacred imperial laws have reserved the entire right after the death of the woman, which right it is manifestly established is transmitted to the children of the prior marriage.

Given on the tenth day before the kalends of July at Ravenna in the year of the ninth consulship of Our Lord Honorius Augustus and the fifth consulship of Our Lord Theodosius Augustus.—June 22, 412.

INTERPRETATION: It is very well known that a woman vindicates to her ownership such property as she receives from her husband at the time of her wedding. If her husband should chance to die, leaving children, however, and the woman should lawfully proceed to another marriage after the period of mourning has elapsed, to the last day of her life she shall hold a usufruct of the property thus given to her. But after the death of the woman, all such property shall revert to the children of the former husband, and the mother is not permitted to transfer any of it to the ownership of others while the children are living.

Title 9: If a Woman to Whom Her Husband Left a Usufruct Should Subsequently Marry
(*Si Secundo Nupserit Mulier Cui Maritus Usumfructum Reliquerit*)

1. Emperors Arcadius and Honorius Augustuses to Asterius, Count of the Orient.
By a clear decision We indicate that the regulations which have been established by Our Clemency concerning prenuptial gifts are far different from those which have been established concerning property from a man's own patrimony, the usufruct of which he has left to his wife by his own will. For in the case of such usufruct of a portion of his own property which a man by executing his last will leaves to his wife, it is Our will that the woman shall be threatened with the loss of this usufruct immediately after her subsequent marriage, in accordance with that law which has indubitably been issued concerning this special point. But as to the usufruct of property given before marriage, those rules shall be observed which an earlier, most salutary law has decreed with a full regulation.
Given on the sixteenth day before the kalends of March at Constantinople in the year of the fourth consulship of Honorius Augustus and the

consulship of Eutychianus.—February 14, 398.

INTERPRETATION: With a clear interpretation the emperor has explained these two legal provisions, namely, that if the husband at his death should leave to his wife, in addition to the betrothal gift, a usufruct on property of his own patrimony, she shall possess that which has been left to her according to his will, on condition that if afterwards the woman should marry another man, she shall immediately restore the usufruct acquired under the will to the children of the man from whom she had obtained the usufruct. But she shall rightfully retain the usufruct of the betrothal gift until her death, just as another law previously indicated. Whence the ownership of this property shall revert after the mother's death to the children of the husband who gave it.

Title 10: If Marriage Should be Petitioned for in Accordance With a Rescript
(*Si Nuptiae Ex Rescripto Petantur*)

1. Emperors Honorius and Theodosius Augustuses to Theodorus, Praetorian Prefect.
Some men, in disregard of the provision of the ancient law, suppose that they may request from Us by surreptitious supplication permission for a marriage to which they know they are not entitled, and they pretend that they have the girl's consent. Therefore We prohibit betrothals of such a kind by the ordinance of the present law. 1. If any person, therefore, in violation of this ordinance, should obtain such permission to marry by a surreptitious supplication, he shall not doubt that he will suffer the forfeiture of his goods and the punishment of deportation. He shall also know that he forfeits the right of marriage which he obtained by such a forbidden usurpation; that he cannot have legally born children in this manner; and that he has never obtained an effective permission by the grant of the requested indulgence or the imperial annotation. Excepted herefrom are those persons whom the law of Our father of triumphal memory[22] did not forbid to supplicate, after the pattern of the imperial indulgences, for the marriage of cousins, that is, of persons related

---

22 Theodosius I. The law is not extant.

in the fourth degree. Those persons also shall be excepted who desire that the solemn engagement of parents as to the marriage of their daughters shall be fulfilled or who request the return of betrothal gifts, that is, of gifts given in the name of earnest, together with the fourfold penalty, under the provisions of the laws. 2. For We forbid that We be requested by supplication to grant permission for a marriage which should properly be impetrated[23] in accordance with the wish of the parents or of the adult girls or the women themselves. But if a marriage is refused which has previously been promised and some lawsuit arises under the provision of these statutes, We do not forbid that We be consulted about the law.

Given on the tenth day before the kalends of February at Ravenna in the year of the eighth consulship of Our Lord Honorius Augustus and the third consulship of Our Lord Theodosius Augustus.—January 23, 409.

INTERPRETATION: Occasionally it happens that some man, forgetful of the severity of the law, dares to employ surreptitious methods in dealing with the imperial majesty, that he seeks for himself permission granted by an imperial order for a marriage which he is not entitled to obtain, and that he lies about the consent of the parents or of the girl; wherefore, the emperor prohibits such audacity. If any man, therefore, should suppose that he should obtain the right to marry through such surreptitious methods, he shall know that he will be punished by the forfeiture of his property and exile by relegation; that he shall not have the marriage which he sought in such a manner; that the children born of a union contracted through such an arrangement and by such corrupt solicitation shall not be called legitimate, and that not even through a supplication to the emperor shall he obtain pardon for such presumption. But in the case of persons connected by kinship in the fourth degree who have entered into a presumptuous union, although such a union is infamous, nevertheless, if the parties should supplicate the emperor, he will grant a pardon. Those persons shall not be prohibited from seeking an ordinance of His Majesty, since they are united in marriage

pursuant to an agreement of the parents. But if any man to whom a girl was betrothed while her parents were living is scorned by the girl after the death of her parents, according to the tenor of the law he shall recover fourfold those things which he has given or presented in the name of earnest. But if arrangements have not previously been made, the emperor, with all severity, prohibits the request by supplication of permission to marry. But if any man should make a marriage agreement with the parents of a girl or with the girl herself, and one of the contracting parties should wish to abandon the agreement, We do not forbid the person who is scorned to consult Us. (The remainder of this law has already been expounded elsewhere.)

Title 11: If a Person Endowed With Any Administrative Power Should Seek to Marry a Woman Against Her Will (*Si Quacumque Praeditus Potestate Nuptias Petat Invitae*)

1. Emperors Gratian, Valentinian, and Theodosius Augustuses to Neoterius, Praetorian Prefect.
If a person endowed with ordinary authority[24] or with any administrative authority whatever, should use the advantage of his power in connection with contracting a marriage to which the woman herself or her parents are averse, whether the girl is a pupil, a maiden or widow living with her father, a widow of independent status, or in short, a woman of any condition whatever, and if such administrator should be found to show or to have shown his menacing favor toward unwilling persons whose interests are here considered, We decree that he shall be liable to a fine of ten pounds of gold, and We forbid him, when he has retired from his high office, to usurp the high rank thus acquired. If he should refuse to obey the sanction of Our statute with respect to the vindication of the honor which he has wrongfully used, the following penalty is provided, namely, that in every case for a continuous period of two years he shall not be allowed to live in the province in which he committed such usurpation.
1. Because, however, We realize that certain households and certain parents must be further

---

23 Obtained by request or entreaty.
24 Administrative authority, as of the governors, the judges ordinary.

protected against hidden malice, We order that if any parent or any woman whatsoever should be assailed by hidden promises or threats through the judge[25] with regard to that marriage to which the woman has disdained to give her consent, such persons may immediately file an attestation. Whereupon they, together with their household and that of their family, shall cease to belong to his jurisdiction; the defenders of each municipality and the apparitors of the aforesaid judge shall attend to this matter. 2. If such depravity should be that of the judge ordinary, all jurisdiction over the aforesaid household in all matters, civil and criminal, shall belong to the vicar as long as the aforesaid judge ordinary is in authority. However, if the vicar or a person of similar authority should undertake to exercise coercion in contracting such a marriage, the judge ordinary in turn shall become the intercessor. But if the judge and vicar should both be suspected, the protection of such households particularly shall devolve upon the illustrious prefect as long as the aforesaid judge or vicar is in office.

Given on the fifteenth day before the kalends of July at Thessalonica in the year of the fifth consulship of Gratian Augustus and the first consulship of Theodosius Augustus.—June 17, 380.

INTERPRETATION: If any judge who administers a province, or even if any person to whom is entrusted the administration of municipalities or districts, through his authority should assign to himself for marriage a maiden, against the will of her parents, or even a widow who is either of independent status or a pupil, and if, contrary to the interests of this woman, by means of terror and collusion of any persons whatever, such woman should be assigned against her will to be married to those persons concerning whom the emperor speaks—if anyone should presume to do this, he shall know that he will be condemned to the payment of ten pounds of gold, stripped of his high rank, and prohibited for a period of two years from entering the province in which he had been judge. But this law provides a special grant of imperial favor, as a protection against such men, to parents and to women themselves when they are of independent status, and to those persons who exercise guardianship over minors, namely, that they shall have the right to file their attestations before other judges or in the nearest municipalities and to be defended by their protection. Thus if there should be another high official in the same province, as, for example, if there should be two judges, one administering private rights and the other imperial rights, and if, in this situation, any person is oppressed by one of these judges, he shall be defended by the protection of the other, or at least he shall have recourse to the magnificent authority,[26] who can bring this information to the ears of the emperor.

Title 12: Incestuous Marriages
(*De Incestis Nuptiis*)

1. Emperors Constantius and Constans Augustuses to the Provincials of Phoenicia.
If any man should be so abominable as to presume that a daughter of a brother or of a sister should be made his wife, and if he should fly to her embrace, not as her paternal or maternal uncle, he shall be held subject to a sentence of capital punishment.

Given on the day before the kalends of April at Antioch in the year of the third consulship of Constantius Augustus and the second consulship of Constans Augustus.—March 31, 342.

INTERPRETATION: If any man should presume to enter into an incestuous union with the daughter of his brother or of his sister, he shall know that he will undergo the peril of capital punishment.

2. Emperors Constantius and Constans Augustuses and Julian Caesar to Volusianus, Praetorian Prefect.
Although the ancients believed it lawful for a man to marry his brother's wife after the marriage of his brother had been dissolved, and lawful also for a man, after the death or divorce of his wife, to contract a marriage with a sister of the said wife, all men shall abstain from such marriages, and they shall not suppose that legitimate children may be begotten from such a union. For it is established that children so born are spurious.

---

25 The governor of the province.
26 The praetorian prefect.

Given on the day before the kalends of May at Rome in the year of the consulship of Arbitio and Lollianus.—April 30, 355.

INTERPRETATION: Licence is absolutely denied a man to marry a woman who has been his brother's wife or for the same man to have two sisters to wife, for the children born of such a union are not considered legitimate.

3. Emperors Arcadius and Honorius Augustuses to Eutychianus, Praetorian Prefect.

The decrees shall remain undisturbed with regard to those persons who have been either absolved or punished in any manner under the law formerly issued. But hereafter, if any person should defile himself by an incestuous marriage with his own first cousin, the daughter of his sister or brother, or finally with any man's wife whose marriage to him has been forbidden and condemned, he shall indeed be exempt from the punishment designated by the law, that is, the punishment of fire and proscription, and he shall have the right to hold his own property as long as he lives. But he shall not be considered as having a wife or as having children born from her. 1. Absolutely nothing shall be given by him during his lifetime or left by him at his death to the aforesaid wife, even through an interposed person. 2. If perchance any dowry has been formally given, specified, or promised, it shall accrue to the resources of Our fisc in accordance with the ancient law. 3. He shall leave nothing by his testament to extraneous persons, but whether he dies testate or intestate, he shall be succeeded, according to the statutes and the law, by those persons, if there be any, who are born of statutory and legal marriage; that is, in the case of descendants, by a son, daughter, grandson, granddaughter, great grandson, great granddaughter; in the case of ascendants, by a father, mother, grandfather, grandmother; in the case of collaterals, by a brother, sister, paternal uncle, or paternal aunt.

4. Indeed, he shall have the power to make a testament only to the extent that he may leave what he wishes, subject to the provisions of the law and statutes, to those persons alone whom We order to succeed by the terms of the imperial statute; provided, however, that if any of those persons whom We have mentioned should be proved to have participated in contracting the incestuous marriage and to have entered into the plan, he shall be absolutely barred from the inheritance of the deceased, and into his place shall succeed that person who is found to rank next after him in the order of kinship. 5. Certainly these provisions which We have made concerning men shall be observed also by women who pollute themselves by marriage with the aforesaid persons. 6. But if none of the aforementioned persons should survive, a place shall be open to the fisc.[27] 7. We order to be subject to the restraints and conditions of this law any person who perchance previously, that is, before the promulgation of this law, has been contaminated by the illicit crimes of the aforesaid marriages and has been able in any manner to avoid detection.

Given on the seventh day before the ides of December at Constantinople in the year of the fourth consulship of Arcadius Augustus, and the third consulship of Honorius Augustus.—December 7 (6), 396.[28]

INTERPRETATION: After the provisions of the former law which was issued about such persons, the emperor commands that the following rules shall be observed, namely, that if any person should unite to himself in a criminal marriage a sister's or a brother's daughter, a cousin of the third degree,[29] or even a cousin of more remote degree, or the wife[30] of his brother, such person shall be exempt from the penalty of the law, that is, severe punishment and proscription, but he shall be subjected to the punishment that he shall be separated from such a union and that if there are any children, they shall not be considered his heirs. But both parties[31] shall be branded with infamy, with the provision that, by special grant of imperial favor, they shall appear only to have possession

---

27   That is, the right to receive the inheritance shall be available to the fisc, if the properly qualified heirs are lacking.

28   The date is doubtful, since Caesarius was prefect until July 13, 397, and was succeeded by Eutychianus on September 4, 397.

29   A first cousin.

30   The former wife.

31   Both parties to the union.

of their own property; but they shall presume to enter into no contract. They shall be deprived of the right to make gifts and to execute testaments. But such a husband shall bestow nothing upon the woman herself whom he has thus married, and if the husband and wife have exchanged gifts at the time of the marriage, such gifts shall be confiscated to the fisc. Even if they should have children, none of their property shall pass to such children through a supposititious[32] person or any other person or by fictitious gift, but at their death their property shall pass by intestate succession to those lawful heirs who are admitted to the inheritance according to their rank in the line of succession, up to a certain degree of kinship. They are permitted the right to make a testament for the benefit of those persons only for whom they are allowed by law to make testaments, so that from these persons they may designate as heirs those persons whom they choose; provided, however, that if any of these persons are shown to have given their approval to such a union, they shall be excluded from the inheritance, and they shall make place for others who come in the next degree. Indeed, if there should be a lack of such near kinsmen that the law calls to the succession, then the fisc shall take possession of their property.

4. Emperors Honorius and Theodosius Augustuses to Aurelianus, Praetorian Prefect for the second time.
A man shall be considered as though he had committed incest, if after the death of a former wife he should presume to select her sister for marriage. A woman, also, shall be held to an equal and similar accountability if after the death of her husband she should presume to aspire to a marriage with his own brother. It will undoubtedly follow that the children of such a cohabitation will not be considered legitimate, they shall not be in the power of their father, and they shall not receive the paternal inheritance as family heirs.
Given on the seventeenth day before the kalends of January at Constantinople in the year of the tenth consulship of Our Lord Honorius Augustus and the sixth consulship of Our Lord Theodosius Augustus.—December (May) 16, 415.

INTERPRETATION: If any woman should marry the husband[33] of her sister after the death of the latter, or if any man should be united by a subsequent marriage to his deceased wife's sister, such persons shall know that they are infamous as a result of such a union. The children born of this union are excluded from the succession and shall not be reckoned as children.

Title 13: Dowries (*De Dotibus*)

1. Emperors Constantius and Constans Augustuses to Philippus, Praetorian Prefect.
An action on morals cannot be extended beyond the person accused, and it shall not be granted against an heir nor assigned to an heir.
Given on the twelfth day before the kalends of October in the year of the consulship of Limenius and Catullinus.—September 20, 349.

INTERPRETATION: If a husband should accuse his wife with respect to her morals, that is, of sorcery, adultery or other similar crimes, and if his wife should then die, her heirs cannot be accused because a crime dies with its author. Also if a husband who has accused his wife should die, the wife cannot be accused by the heir of the husband.

2. Emperor Julian Augustus to Mamertinus, Praetorian Prefect.
In the restoration of dowries, it is Our pleasure that rights of retention created by law and by pacts shown to be consistent with the law shall also be preserved unbroken and inviolate by the authority of this sanction.
Given on the fourth day before the kalends of March in the year of the fourth consulship of Julian Augustus and the consulship of Sallustius.—February 26, 363.

INTERPRETATION: This law prescribes that pacts made between a husband and wife, which were made relative to a dowry and which are consistent with the law, shall be valid, just as all other pacts. But since this statute evidently does not set forth the provisions concerning retentions from a dowry, such provisions must be sought in

---

32 Fraudulently substituted or pretended.
33 The former husband.

the body of the law, that is, in the Sentences of Paulus under the title, Dowries, or at any rate in the Responses of Paulus under the title, *A Wife's Property.*

3. Emperors Honorius and Theodosius Augustuses to Marinianus, Praetorian Prefect.
(After other matters.) If while a marriage subsists it should chance that the husband should be destroyed by the lot of fate, the dowry which is said to have been given or promised out of his wife's property shall revert to the woman, and the heir of the deceased shall not dare to vindicate for himself any of the property which has reverted to the woman as the result of her husband's death.

1. If perchance, while the marriage subsists, the dowry has been returned to a wife by her husband, a transaction which cannot stand according to the laws, because it is understood to be analogous to a gift,[34] and if the wife should die, the dowry, together with the fruits thereof from the day that the dowry was returned to her, shall be restored to the husband by her heirs; but the ownership of the same cannot be alienated by the husband away from the children born of the aforesaid woman. (Etc.)

Given on the third day before the nones of November at Ravenna in the year of the thirteenth consulship of Honorius Augustus and the tenth consulship of Theodosius Augustus.—November 3, 422.

INTERPRETATION: If perchance a husband should die and his wife should survive him, the woman shall recover for her own ownership any property which had been given to her husband as a dowry, and the heirs of the deceased husband shall not presume to vindicate it. Indeed, if the husband, while he was living, had perhaps returned that property which he had received from his wife as dowry, since such a return is like a gift, this act shall have no validity. If the woman should die, such property cannot be vindicated by her heirs, but it is ordered that, together with its fruits, it shall be restored to her husband; provided, however, that if there should be children, they shall not vindicate this property for themselves as though a part of their mother's estate during the lifetime of their father, and the father shall have nothing therefrom except the usufruct, nor shall he have the unrestricted right to transfer such property to another person; but after his death all of it shall revert to their common children.

4. Emperors Theodosius and Valentinian Augustuses to Hierius, Praetorian Prefect.
(After other matters.) We decree that any sort of words whatever shall suffice for the exaction of a dowry, if its delivery has once been agreed upon, even though a formal statement or stipulation with reference to the promise of the property of the dowry did not follow. (Etc.)

Given on the tenth day before the kalends of March at Constantinople in the year of the consulship of Felix and Taurus.—February 21, 428.

INTERPRETATION: A dowry, that is, whatever is given by[35] a woman to her husband at the time of marriage, is ordered to be valid with respect to its fulfillment or its exaction, even though a stipulation of the promiser and the legally prescribed words should be lacking.

Title 14: Marriages With Foreigners
(*De Nuptiis Gentilium*)

1. Emperors Valentinian and Valens Augustuses to Theodosius, Master of the Horse.
No provincial, of whatever rank or class he may be, shall marry a barbarian wife, nor shall a provincial woman be united with any foreigner. But if there should be any alliances between provincials and foreigners through such marriages and if anything should be disclosed as suspect or criminal among them, it shall be expiated by capital punishment.

Given on the fifth day before the kalends of January in the year of the consulship of Valentinian and Valens Augustuses.—December 28, 370 or 373; May 28, 368.

---

34   Gifts between husbands and wives were forbidden.
35   On behalf of.

INTERPRETATION: No Roman shall presume to have a barbarian wife of any nation whatever, nor shall any Roman woman be united in marriage with a barbarian. But if they should do this, they shall know that they are subject to capital punishment.

Title 15: Sureties of Dowries
(*De Fidejussoribus Dotium*)

1. Emperors Valentinian, Theodosius, and Arcadius Augustuses to Martinianus, Count of the Orient.
Henceforth We absolve all sponsors or sureties from their promises in guaranteeing any solemn agreement for a dowry.

Given on the third day before the ides of November at Constantinople in the year of the second consulship of Arcadius Augustus, and the consulship of Rufinus.—November 11 [10], 392.

INTERPRETATION: If any person should become surety of a woman for the payment of a dowry, he shall not be held liable for such guaranty.

Title 16: Notices of Divorce (*De Repudiis*)

1. Emperor Constantine Augustus to Ablavius, Praetorian Prefect.
It is Our pleasure that no woman, on account of her own depraved desires, shall be permitted to send a notice of divorce to her husband on trumped up grounds, as, for instance, that he is a drunkard or a gambler or a philanderer, nor indeed shall a husband be permitted to divorce his wife on every sort of pretext. But when a woman sends a notice of divorce, the following criminal charges only shall be investigated, that is, if she should prove that her husband is a homicide, a sorcerer, or a destroyer of tombs, so that the wife may thus earn commendation and at length recover her entire dowry. For if she should send a notice of divorce to her husband on grounds other than these three criminal charges, she must leave everything, even her last hairpin, in her husband's home, and as punishment for her supreme self-confidence, she shall be deported to an island. In the case of a man also, if he should send a notice of divorce, inquiry shall be made as to the following three criminal charges, namely, if he wishes to divorce her as an adulteress, a sorceress, or a procuress. For if he should cast off a wife who is innocent of these crimes, he must restore her entire dowry, and he shall not marry another woman. But if he should do this, his former wife shall be given the right to enter and seize his home by force and to transfer to herself the entire dowry of his later wife in recompense for the outrage inflicted upon her.

Given ... in the year of the consulship of Bassus and Ablavius.—331

INTERPRETATION: The right to send a notice of divorce is extended to a wife or husband for certain approved reasons and causes; for they are forbidden to dissolve a marriage for a trivial charge. If perchance a woman should say that her husband is either a drunkard or given to licentiousness, she shall not send him notice of divorce on that account. But if perchance she should prove that he is either a homicide, a sorcerer, or a violator of tombs, the husband who is convicted of these crimes appears to be justly divorced, without any fault of the woman; and she may recover her dowry and depart. If the woman should not be able to prove such crimes, she shall be subjected to the following punishment: namely, that she shall forfeit both the dowry which she had given or which had been given on her behalf and the gift[36] which she received, and she shall also be liable to exile by relegation. But if a man should cast off his wife, he also is not permitted to divorce her for a trivial quarrel, as often happens, unless perhaps he should be able to prove that she is an adulteress, a sorceress, or a procuress. But if he cannot prove this, he shall restore her dowry to the woman, and he shall not presume to take another wife. But if perchance he should attempt to do so, the woman who was cast off, though innocent, shall have the right to vindicate for herself her husband's home and all his substance. It is recognized that this is ordained in order that if a woman should be unjustly divorced, she is ordered to acquire the dowry of the second wife also.

36　The betrothal and prenuptial gifts.

2. Emperors Honorius, Theodosius, and Constantius Augustuses to Palladius, Praetorian Prefect.

If a woman should serve notice of divorce upon her husband and separate from him and if she should prove no grounds for divorce, the gifts shall be annulled which she had received when betrothed. She shall also be deprived of her dowry, and she shall be sentenced to the punishment of deportation. We deny her not only the right to a union with a subsequent husband, but even the right of postliminium. But if a woman who has revolted against her marriage should prove merely flaws of character and ordinary faults, she shall lose her dowry and restore to her husband all gifts, and never at all shall she be associated in marriage with any man. In order that she may not defile her widowhood with wanton debauchery, we grant to the repudiated husband the right to bring an accusation.

1. It remains to say that if a woman who withdraws should prove serious grounds and a conscience involved in great crimes, she shall obtain possession of her dowry and shall also retain the betrothal bounty, and she shall regain the right to marry after a period of five years from the day of the divorce. For then it will appear that she has done this from loathing of her own husband rather than from a desire for another husband.

2 (1). Certainly if the husband should be the first to give notice of divorce and if he should charge his wife with a grave crime, he shall prosecute the accused woman in accordance with the law, and when he has obtained his revenge, he shall both get possession of her dowry and recover his bounty to her, and he shall acquire the unrestricted right to marry another woman immediately. 3. If it is a fault of character and not of criminality, the husband shall recover his gifts but relinquish the dowry, and he shall have the right to marry another woman after a period of two years. 4. But if the husband should wish to dissolve the marriage because of a mere disagreement and should charge the repudiated woman with no vices or sins, he shall lose both his gifts and the dowry and be compelled to live in perpetual celibacy; he shall suffer punishment for his insolent divorce in the sadness of solitude; and the woman shall be granted the right to marry after

the termination of a year. Moreover, We order to be preserved the guarantees of the ancient law in regard to the retentions of dowries, on account of children.

Given on the sixth day before the ides of March at Ravenna in the year of the consulship of Eustathius and Agricola.—March 10, 421.

INTERPRETATION: If a woman should be the first to serve a notice of divorce upon her husband and should not prove the statutory grounds for divorce, she shall forfeit the betrothal bounty, and she shall not recover that which she gave her husband as dowry. In addition, she shall also be sent into exile by relegation, and she shall not have the right to marry another man. If, however, after divorcing her husband, she should become involved in adultery, her husband shall have the right to prosecute her even after the divorce. But if a woman who has separated from her husband should prove that he is guilty of grave and definite crimes, she shall both recover her dowry and vindicate that which her husband bestowed upon her as a betrothal bounty, and she shall have the unrestricted right of marriage after five years.

Indeed, if the husband should be the first to serve notice of divorce, he shall secure his revenge on grounds approved by law, he shall vindicate his dowry of his repudiated wife, shall recover his betrothal gifts, and shall have the right to marry another woman immediately if he wishes. If indeed there were no definite crimes, but, as often happens, the husband is displeased with the frivolity of his wife's character, he shall recover his gifts and shall restore to her immediately anything which he has received from her, after a period of two years he shall have the right to marry another wife. But if no defect of character should be proved but merely mental discord, the innocent woman who is rejected by her husband shall both vindicate the gifts made to her by the man and shall recover her dowry. But he shall remain alone forever and shall not presume to associate himself in marriage with another woman. The woman, however, is permitted to proceed to another marriage after a year if she should so wish. But for the sake of their common children, if there should be any, the emperor orders those rules to be observed which have been established in the law concerning retentions according to the number of children, which law Paulus sets forth in his Book of Responses under the title *A Wife's Property*.

Title 17: The Creation of Tutors and Curators
(*De Tutoribus Et Curatoribus Creandis*)

1. Emperor Constantine Augustus and the Caesar to Bassus, Prefect of the City.
It is Our pleasure that in all litigation, no person who has attained the age of puberty[37] shall have legal capacity unless by the interposition of a decree a curator has been appointed for him,[38] either for the purpose of administering his patrimony or for the purpose of the lawsuit, so that, in accordance with the preceding statutes of Our Providence, when a suit has been legally instituted, the controversy may be tried in the courts and settled.

Given on the fourth day before the ides of October at Aquileia in the year of the fifth consulship of Constantine Augustus and the consulship of Licinius Caesar.—October 12, 319; 318.

INTERPRETATION: If an action is brought as though against a pupil,[39] although he should appear to be an adult,[40] such person cannot take part in the lawsuit unless perchance his age should be confirmed by attestation of the municipal council, or at any rate a curator should be provided who may defend the patrimony or lawsuit of the ward.

2. The same Augustus and Caesar to the People.
A consanguineous paternal uncle shall not refuse the statutory guardianship over a woman.

Given on the day before the kalends of January in the year of the seventh consulship of the Augustus Himself and the consulship of the Caesar.—December 31, 326.

3. Emperors Valentinian, Theodosius, and Arcadius Augustuses to Proculus, Prefect of the City.
The Illustrious prefect of the City, with the assistance of ten men selected from the membership of the Most August Senate, together with the Most Noble praetor who presides over suits involving guardianship, shall provide that suitable persons, of any rank whatever, shall be obligated to act as tutors and curators.

1. Certainly, those who judge this matter shall decide with free judgment and without liability. If one nominee should not be adequate for administering the pupil's property, it shall be proper, according to the ancient law, that several shall be called to this duty and that the person whom the aforesaid group adjudges the most competent for administering the pupil's affairs shall obtain such administration by the decision of the prefect alone.

2. Hence in this manner, those present at the council shall remain free of fear, and from this deliberation of prudent men, legalized protection shall be provided for both young children and adults.

3 (1). However, it is evident that We have decreed the preceding regulation concerning those persons for whom there are available neither testamentary nor statutory guardians of a suitable mode of life, age and property. For when, perchance, such men are offered, We rightly prescribe that they can be held obligated if they should acquire no grounds of defense through their privileges. 4 (2). Moreover, We decree that all other provisions that have been prescribed by the ancient laws concerning the case of minors shall remain inviolate.

Given on the sixth day before the kalends of January at Milan in the year of the consulship of Timasius and Promotus.—December 27, 389.

INTERPRETATION: As often as the problem arises concerning the guardianship of pupils, the chief decurions of the municipality, along with the judge, must select either a tutor or a curator, according to the age of the minor, so that a person who undertakes a tutelage as the result of such a selection can be secure. However, this manner of selection shall be observed in connection with those persons whose appointment has

---

37 *puber*, an adult, a male over fourteen or a female over twelve and under twenty-five years of age.
38 The guardianship of minors was a compulsory public service, without remuneration. It could not be evaded except by some legally recognized excuse.
39 Under the age of puberty.
40 Under twenty-five years of age, but over the age of puberty.

not been directed by testament and who have not been assigned to this office through close kinship. Concerning the other interests of minors, indeed, the emperor commands that the provisions of former laws shall be observed.

4. The same Augustuses to Tatianus, Praetorian Prefect.
If mothers who have lost their husbands should demand tutelage over their children to administer their affairs, before confirmation of such an office can legally come to them, they shall state in the public records that they will not proceed to another marriage.

1. Certainly, no woman is forced to make such a choice, but she shall comply of her own free will with the conditions which We have prescribed. For if she prefers to choose another marriage, she must not administer the guardianship of her children.

2. In order that such a woman may not easily be taken by storm after she has lawfully undertaken the guardianship, We order that, first of all, the property of any man who eagerly seeks the marriage of a woman who is administering the guardianship shall be obligated and held liable for the accounts of the children, so that nothing may be lost to them through negligence or through fraud. 3. To the aforesaid provisions We add the following: that a woman who has attained her majority shall have the right to petition for a guardianship when a statutory tutor is lacking or when such a person is excused from serving as tutor by reason of his privilege, or when he is excluded as being of the class of suspect, or when he is found to be incapable of managing even his own property because of mental or physical infirmity. 4. But if women should avoid the guardianship and should prefer marriage, and no statutory tutor can be called to such cases, then only the Illustrious prefect of the City, with the assistance of the praetor who presides over the appointment of tutors or the judges who administer the law in the provinces, shall, after investigation, order guardians of another order to be appointed for minors.

Given on the twelfth day before the kalends of February at Milan in the year of the fourth consulship of Valentinian Augustus and the consulship of Neoterius.—January 21, 390.

INTERPRETATION: If women whose husbands are dead should themselves wish to undertake the guardianship of their children, before they may assume this responsibility, they shall formally declare in the public records that they will not marry. However, this declaration must not be extorted from them, but if they prefer, they shall so state of their own free will. For if they desire to proceed to subsequent marriages, they cannot administer the guardianship of their children. When men request the mothers of young children to marry them, they too shall know that if a woman has begun to administer the tutelage of her children, and later marries, the man whom she takes as her consort in marriage shall know that his property will be obligated, and he himself will be responsible for rendering an account to the minors.

There is the further provision that a woman is forbidden to undertake a guardianship unless she has attained her majority. As to those persons, indeed, who come to a guardianship by statute, if any one of them should appear either to be mistaken as to his resources or to be worthless in character, he cannot be admitted to the guardianship, lest the property of the minors should be lost. But those persons shall undertake the guardianship who are characterized by integrity of mind and who are definitely connected by a near degree of kinship. For if the aforesaid persons should be lacking and the mother should be unwilling to undertake the guardianship, then, as has been previously provided, tutors shall be assigned to minors by the selection of the judges or the provincials.[41]

Title 18: Those Persons Who Shall Petition (*Qui Petant*)

1. Emperors Constantius Augustus and Julian Caesar to Our Very Dear Orfitus, Greetings.
Grandfathers also and grandmothers shall be held obligated to the necessity of requesting the appointment of tutors if both testamentary and statutory guardianship should be lacking for their

---

41 The municipal councils.

grandchildren of pupillary age. For if perchance a tutor should not be requested, in accordance with the provisions of the ancient laws, those persons to whom the inheritance could have come shall forfeit the benefit of the succession.

Given on the ides of July in the year of the ninth consulship of Constantius Augustus and the second consulship of Julian Caesar.—July 15, 357.

INTERPRETATION: If there should be no paternal grandfather, the emperor orders that even the maternal grandfather and the paternal and maternal grandmothers shall be bound by the command of the law to request tutors for young children, provided that testamentary or statutory tutors are proved to be lacking. But if they should scorn to provide tutors for their young grandchildren, the emperor orders that they shall be subjected to the following penalty, namely, that if perchance the "mournful" inheritance should accrue from the estates of minors for whom they have either not sought or not wished to provide tutors, they shall be considered as extraneous persons.

2. ... [42]

Title 30: The Administration and Liability of Tutors and Curators (De Administratione Et Periculo Tutorum Et Curatorum)

1. Emperor Constantine Augustus.
Minors shall not be prohibited from vindicating for themselves the property of their tutors or curators, as though it were obligated under title of a pledge, if such tutors or curators should become indebted to them on account of the duties of their administration.

Given on the seventh day before the kalends of April in the year of the consulship of Volusianus and Annianus.—March 26, 314.

INTERPRETATION: If any tutor or curator should be proved to be a debtor to minors through negligence of his administration, he shall know that his own property is so obligated that

if he should not render satisfaction, after his account has been deducted,[43] his goods shall be held as a pledge by the minors.

2. The same Augustus to Maximus, Prefect of the City.
(After other measures.) The guardians of minors shall make good the value of the property lost,[44] if through them the conditions attached to the gifts should be neglected. (Etc.)

Given on the third day before the nones of February at Rome in the year of the consulship of Sabinus and Rufinus Augustus.—(January 30) February 3, 316; 323; 320.

INTERPRETATION: If in the case of gifts which can be made to minors, the formality or condition of a gift should not be fulfilled through the tutor's negligence or collusion, he shall be compelled to pay out of his own property that which the minor has lost.

3. The same Augustus to the People.
... or curator shall be solicitous to make repeated inspections in order to see that the aforesaid articles are unharmed. As to superfluous animals of minors also, We do not forbid that they be sold.

Given on the ides of March at Sirmium in the year of the seventh consulship of Constantine Augustus and the consulship of Constantius Caesar.—March 15, 326; 329.

4. The same Augustus to all Provincials.
(After other matters.) If guardians of minors, that is, tutors or curators, as co-owners of property that is being sued for in litigation should decline to declare, as the law requires, but contrary to the prohibition, they should name the aforesaid minors, the guardians shall pay to the fisc out of their own resources as much money as is computed to be a third of the estimated value of the property involved in the litigation, since minors, whether pupils or adults, must lose nothing, no matter what the outcome of the suit. However, if the guardians should be paupers, they shall suffer diminution of status and shall cease to be

---

42 A constitution has been lost.

43 An account of his own expenses incurred for the benefit of the minor during the course of his guardianship.

44 To the minors by reason of the negligence of the guardians.

Roman citizens, but in such a way that the rights of the minors themselves shall be preserved unimpaired. (Etc.)

Given on the kalends of August 12 in the year of the consulship of Bassus and Ablavius.—August 1, 331.

5. The same Augustus to Felix.
Since landholdings held by emphyteutic tenure[45] are being torn from the possessions of minors as a result of default involving forfeiture which occurred through neglect or betrayal by tutors or curators, it is Our pleasure that if during the administration of a tutor or curator, the landed estates of a minor should lose the prerogative of emphyteutic tenure through an offense involving forfeiture, they shall restore to the minor from their own resources, under the threat of a severe sentence, as much as it shall be determined that the property forfeited was worth.

Given on the fourteenth day before the kalends of May at Constantinople in the year of the consulship of Dalmatius and Zenophilus.—April 18, 333.

INTERPRETATION: If perchance it should occur that, subject to any kind of payment whatever, minors should hold by emphyteutic tenure a landed estate, that is, property of the fisc which their parents had obtained the right to hold, and if this estate should be diminished or certainly if it should be taken away from them through the negligence or betrayal of the tutor, whatever may be lost shall be restored by the tutor or curator.

6. Emperors Arcadius and Honorius Augustuses to Eutychianus, Praetorian Prefect.
The very moment that they are instituted, tutors shall immediately appear before the judges, so that, in the presence of the chief decurions, the defender, and public office staffs,[46] an inventory shall be made with due formality, and all the gold and silver found in the pupil's substance, as well as anything else that does not suffer change with the lapse of time, shall be marked with the seals of the judges, senators and public office staffs, and placed in safest custody by the authorization of a

public order. There shall be no expectation of interest, nor shall any change be made in any event whatever, until the ward, having become an adult, attains legal age, when he does not so much begin to have time for lawsuits as to rejoice that he has been restored so soon to his whole patrimony.

1. Since a moderate fortune, too, must be considered, if perchance movables alone, and no immovables, are left to a person as an inheritance, and no income from landed estates can be reckoned upon, out of which the pupil's household or the pupil himself can be supported, either suitable estates shall be purchased with the aforesaid movables, or if perchance, as usually happens, suitable estates cannot be found, in accordance with the general rule of the ancient law, an income shall accrue from interest. Thus in this case also, in which there is no hope for income from landed estates, the needs of the minor shall be provided from the income of his movable property; and in the former case[47] interest shall by no means be sought without the risk of the tutor.

Given on the sixth day before the kalends of March at Constantinople in the year of the fourth consulship of Arcadius Augustus, and the third consulship of Honorius Augustus.—February 25, 396(?).

INTERPRETATION: As soon as any person enters upon a guardianship, he shall immediately summon the chief decurions of the municipality and the defender, together with his office staff, while he takes an inventory and makes a written record of the property of the pupil which he has received. If there should be any money or silver or things which cannot perish with age, he shall deposit them after they have been marked with the seals of the aforesaid officials, and in no event shall such property be diminished. The aforesaid persons shall know that while the pupil is in his minority, this property shall not be entrusted to him for the purpose of lawsuits or for any other reasons, but it shall be preserved in all its entirety until his mature age. In all other matters there shall be profitable diligence. If the resources of a minor are of less value, so that he has no

---

45 A form of lease requiring the lessee to make improvements to the property during the term of the lease.
46 The office staffs of the public officials of the district.
47 If suitable estates can be purchased for the minor.

patrimony, and his substance is found to consist of movables only, the tutors shall know that they will be permitted to undertake to sell the movables and to purchase fields, so that they may provide for the minors in this respect. But if there is no substance of such value that a land estate can be purchased with it, the tutors are ordered to use diligence in collecting the money and to acquire profit for the pupil from the earnings of interest or from any other sources. If perchance the substance of the minor should be very small, then the property shall be kept intact, and means of subsistence shall be furnished to the pupil. If this is done, the pupil shall not seek interest from the tutor.

Title 31: Exemption from Tutelage
(*De excusatione tutelae*)

1. Emperors Arcadius and Honorius Augustuses to Flavianus, Prefect of the City.
(After other matters.) We grant to the shipmasters themselves exemption from tutelage or curatorship to this extent, namely, that they shall be obligated to perform such duties for minors of their own guild only.
    Given on the third day before the nones of March at Milan in the year of the consulship of Stilicho and Aurelianus.—March 5, 400.

Title 32: The Landed Estates of Minors Shall Not Be Alienated Without a Decree
(*De praendiis minorum sine decreto non alienandis*)

1. Emperor Constantine Augustus to Severus.
A minor who is less than twenty-five years of age shall be able to vindicate a landed estate or a rustic slave which was alienated without the issuance of a decree, even though he has not applied

for restoration to his original condition; provided that if, following upon the publication of this law, so little time before the end of the twenty-fifth year should remain that a lawsuit already begun cannot be terminated within the limits of the aforesaid year, the lawsuit that is begun can be continued. 1. Those persons also whom this same law has found past their twenty-fifth and within their twenty-sixth year shall not delay to commence their petitions, since the time limits for a lawsuit thus begun shall be concluded at the twenty-sixth year.

2. But if any persons should attempt to sue after this time, they shall be rejected, so that the possessor shall now be certain and secure.[48]
    Given on the fifteenth day before the kalends of January at Sofia (Serdica) in the year of the consulship of Probianus and Julianus.—December 18, 322; 325.

2. Emperors …
Even if any minor should be found obligated, either in the name of his father or in his own name, on account of urgent fiscal debts only or as a consequence of private contracts, the interposition of a decree shall be granted by the Constantinian Praetor after the reasons have been exactly proved, so that after the reliability of the facts has been revealed, a sale may remain valid.[48] Since these things are so, tutors also who are suspect must be sued in the court of the said praetor; an action also must be granted, provided, of course, that the laws shall be observed and that recourse may be had finally to Your Experience, if, while the trial is being conducted before either of the two praetors, the aid of an appeal should be interposed by one of the parties, so that you as the sublime judge may weigh the merits of the appeal.
    Given …—December 31, 326(?).

---

48 In his possession.
49 Minors were not permitted to sell property without a decree, which could be granted for various reasons, such as urgent debts.

2. AUGUSTINE OF HIPPO

AUGUSTINE OF HIPPO (354–430) had the most profound influence in medieval culture of any ancient writer. Born in North Africa to Roman non-Christian parents, his transformation to being the most important Christian thinker of his time was a long process, which included a pagan education followed by work as a teacher of rhetoric, as well as periods when he followed Manichaeism (as outlined in his autobiographical *Confessions*). After Augustine's conversion in 386, his writings demonstrate his strong opposition to both Manichaeism and Christian heresies; however, his most influential works were his treatise *On Christian Doctrine* and his great *City of God*.

In the first, finished in 426, Augustine outlined what became the universal means of interpreting sacred Scripture and other texts through to the twelfth century. The particular passages below discuss his fundamental distinction between the use and enjoyment of creation, and his theory of signs.

Augustine wrote the *City of God* over a long period, completing it only in 426. The work began as a defense against the charge that Christianity had led to the misfortunes of the Roman Empire culminating in the sacking of Rome by the Visigoths in 410. It became a broad-ranging meditation on the nature of good and evil, human society, and government and formed the foundation of all medieval political theory.

Source: Philip Schaff (ed.), *A Select Library of the Nicene and Post-Nicene Fathers of the Christian Church*, vol. II, trans. Marcus Dods (Buffalo: Christian Literature Co., 1987).

Further Reading: G. O'Daly, *Augustine's* City of God: *A Reader's Guide* (Oxford: Clarendon Press, 1999).

On Christian Doctrine

Preface: Showing that to teach rules for the interpretation of scripture is not a superfluous task.

1. There are certain rules for the interpretation of Scripture which I think might with great advantage be taught to earnest students of the word, that they might profit not only from reading the works of others who have laid open the secrets of sacred writings, but also from themselves opening such secrets to others. These rules I propose to teach to those who are able and willing to learn, if God our Lord do not withhold from me, while I write, the thoughts He is wont to vouchsafe to me in my meditations on this subject. But before I enter upon this undertaking, I think it well to meet the objections of those who are likely to take exception to the work, or who would do so, did I not conciliate them beforehand. And if, after all, men should still be found to make objections, yet at least they will not prevail with others over

whom they might have influence, did they not find them forearmed against their assaults, to turn them back from a useful study to the dull sloth of ignorance.

2. There are some, then, likely to object to this work of mine, because they have failed to understand the rules here laid down. Others, again, will think that I have spent my labour to no purpose, because, though they understand the rules, yet in their attempts to apply them and to interpret Scripture by them, they have failed to clear up the point they wish cleared up; and these, because they have received no assistance from this work themselves, they will give it as their opinion that it can be of no use to anybody. There is a third class of objectors who either really do understand Scripture well, or think they do, and who, because they know (or imagine) that they have attained a certain power of interpreting the sacred books without reading any directions of the kind that I

propose to lay down here, will cry out that such rules are not necessary for any one, but that everything rightly done towards clearing up the obscurities of Scripture could be better done by the unassisted grace of God.

3. To reply briefly to all these: To those who do not understand what is here set down, my answer is, that I am not to be blamed for their want of understanding. It is just as if they were anxious to see the new or the old moon, or some very obscure star, and I should point it out with my finger; if they had not sight enough to see even my finger, they would surely have no right to fly into a passion with me on that account. As for those who, even though they know and understand my directions, fail to penetrate the meaning of obscure passages in Scripture, they may stand for those who, in the case I have imagined, are just able to see my finger, but cannot see the stars at which it is pointed. And so both these classes had better give up blaming me, and pray instead that God would grant them the sight of their eyes. For though I can move my finger to point out an object, it is out of my power to open men's eyes that they may see either the fact that I am pointing, or the object at which I point.

4. But now as to those who talk vauntingly of Divine Grace, and boast that they understand and can explain Scripture without the aid of such directions as those I now propose to lay down, and who think, therefore, that what I have undertaken to write is entirely superfluous. I would such persons could calm themselves so far as to remember that, however justly they may rejoice in God's great gift, yet it was from human teachers that they themselves learned to read. Now, they would hardly think it right that they should be held in contempt by the Egyptian monk Antony, a just and holy man, who, not being able to read himself, is said to have committed the Scriptures to memory through hearing them read by others, and by dint of wise meditations to have arrived at a thorough understanding of them; or by that barbarian slave Christianus, of whom I have lately heard from very respectable and trustworthy witnesses, who, without any teaching from man, attained a full knowledge of the art of reading

simply through prayer that it might be revealed to him; after three days' supplication obtaining his request that he might read through a book presented to him on the spot by the astonished bystanders.

5. But if any one thinks that these stories are false, I do not strongly insist on them. For, as I am dealing with Christians who profess to understand the Scriptures without any directions from man (and if the fact be so, they boast of a real advantage, and one of no ordinary kind), they must surely grant that every one of us learnt his own language by hearing it constantly from childhood, and that any other language we have learnt,—Greek, or Hebrew, or any of the rest,—we have learnt either in the same way, by hearing it spoken, or from a human teacher. Now, then, suppose we advise all our brethren not to teach their children any of these things, because on the outpouring of the Holy Spirit the apostles immediately began to speak the language of every race; and warn every one who has not had a like experience that he need not consider himself a Christian, or may at least doubt whether he has yet received the Holy Spirit? No, no; rather let us put away false pride and learn whatever can be learnt from man; and let him who teaches another communicate what he has himself received without arrogance and without jealousy. And do not let us tempt Him in whom we have believed, lest, being ensnared by such wiles of the enemy and by our own perversity, we may even refuse to go to the churches to hear the Gospel itself, or to read a book, or to listen to another reading or preaching, in the hope that we shall be carried up to the third heaven, "whether in the body or out of the body," as the apostle says, and there hear unspeakable words, such as it is not lawful for man to utter, or see the Lord Jesus Christ and hear the Gospel from his own lips rather than from those of men.

6. Let us beware of such dangerous temptations of pride, and let us rather consider the facts that the Apostle Paul himself, although stricken down and admonished by the voice of God from heaven, yet was sent to a man to receive the sacraments and be admitted into the Church; and that Cornelius the centurion, although an angel announced to

him that his prayers were heard and his alms had in remembrance, yet was handed over to Peter for instruction, and not only received the sacraments from the apostle's hands, but was also instructed by him as to the proper objects of faith, hope, and love. And without doubt it was *possible* to have done everything through the instrumentality of angels, but the condition of our race would have been more degraded if God had not chosen to make use of men as the ministers of His word to their fellow-men. For how could that be true which is written, "The temple of God is holy, which temple ye are," if God gave forth no oracles from His human temple, but communicated everything that He wished to be taught to men by voices from heaven, or through the ministration of angels? Moreover, love itself, which binds men together in the bond of unity, would have no means of pouring soul into soul, and, as it were, mingling them one with another, if men never learnt anything from their fellow-men.

7. And we know that the eunuch who was reading Isaiah the prophet, and did not understand what he read, was not sent by the apostle to an angel, nor was it an angel who explained to him what he did not understand, nor was he inwardly illuminated by the grace of God without the interposition of man; on the contrary, at the suggestion of God, Philip, who *did* understand the prophet, came to him, and sat with him, and in human words, and with a human tongue, opened to him the Scriptures. Did not God talk with Moses, and yet he, with great wisdom and entire absence of jealous pride, accepted the plan of his father-in-law, a man of an alien race, for ruling and administering the affairs of the great nation entrusted to him? For Moses knew that a wise plan, in whatever mind it might originate, was to be ascribed not to the man who devised it, but to Him who is the Truth, the unchangeable God.

8. In the last place, every one who boasts that he, through divine illumination, understands the obscurities of Scripture, though not instructed in any rules of interpretation, at the same time believes, and rightly believes, that this power is not his own, in the sense of originating with himself, but is the gift of God. For so he seeks God's glory, not his own. But reading and understanding, as he does, without the aid of any human interpreter, why does he himself undertake to interpret for others? Why does he not rather send them direct to God, that they too may learn by the inward teaching of the Spirit without the help of man? The truth is, he fears to incur the reproach: "Thou wicked and slothful servant, thou oughtest to have put my money to the exchangers." Seeing, then, that these men teach others, either through speech or writing, what they understand, surely they cannot blame me if I likewise teach not only what they understand, but also the rules of interpretation they follow. For no one ought to consider anything as his own, except perhaps what is false. All truth is of Him who says, "I am the truth." For what have we that we did not receive? and if we have received it, why do we glory, as if we had not received it?

9. He who reads to an audience pronounces aloud the words he sees before him: he who teaches reading, does it that others may be able to read for themselves. Each, however, communicates to others what he has learnt himself. Just so, the man who explains to an audience the passages of Scripture he understands is like one who reads aloud the words before him. On the other hand, the man who lays down rules for interpretation is like one who teaches reading, that is, shows others how to read for themselves. So that, just as he who knows how to read is not dependent on some one else, when he finds a book, to tell him what is written in it, so the man who is in possession of the rules which I here attempt to lay down, if he meet with an obscure passage in the books which he reads, will not need an interpreter to lay open the secret to him, but, holding fast by certain rules, and following up certain indications, will arrive at the hidden sense without any error, or at least without falling into any gross absurdity. And so although it will sufficiently appear in the course of the work itself that no one can justly object to this undertaking of mine, which has no other object than to be of service, yet as it seemed convenient to reply at the outset to any who might make preliminary objections, such is

the start I have thought good to make on the road I am about to traverse in this book.

BOOK I. Containing a general view of the subjects treated in Holy Scripture.

Chapter 1.—The interpretation of Scripture depends on the discovery and enunciation of the meaning, and is to be undertaken in dependence on God's aid.

1. There are two things on which all interpretation of Scripture depends: the mode of ascertaining the proper meaning, and the mode of making known the meaning when it is ascertained. We shall treat first of the mode of ascertaining, next of the mode of making known, the meaning;—a great and arduous undertaking, and one that, if difficult to carry out, it is, I fear, presumptuous to enter upon. And presumptuous it would undoubtedly be, if I were counting on my own strength; but since my hope of accomplishing the work rests on Him who has already supplied me with many thoughts on this subject, I do not fear but that He will go on to supply what is yet wanting when once I have begun to use what He has already given. For a possession which is not diminished by being shared with others, if it is possessed and not shared, is not yet possessed as it ought to be possessed. The Lord saith, "Whosoever hath, to him shall be given," He will give, then, to those who have; that is to say, if they use freely and cheerfully what they have received, He will add to and perfect His gifts. The loaves in the miracle were only five and seven in number before the disciples began to divide them among the hungry people. But when once they began to distribute them, though the wants of so many thousands were satisfied, they filled baskets with the fragments that were left. Now, just as that bread increased in the very act of breaking it, so those thoughts which the Lord has already vouchsafed to me with a view to undertaking this work will, as soon as I begin to impart them to others, be multiplied by His grace, so that, in this very work of distribution in which I have engaged, so far from incurring loss and poverty, I shall be made to rejoice in a marvellous increase of wealth.

Chapter 2.—What a thing is, and what a sign.

2. All instruction is either about things or about signs; but things are learnt by means of signs. I now use the word "thing" in a strict sense, to signify that which is never employed as a sign of anything else: for example, wood, stone, cattle, and other things of that kind. Not, however, the wood which we read Moses cast into the bitter waters to make them sweet, nor the stone which Jacob used as a pillow, nor the ram which Abraham offered up instead of his son; for these, though they are things, are also signs of other things. They are signs of another kind, those which are never employed except as signs: for example, words. No one uses words except as signs of something else; and hence may be understood what I call signs: these things, to wit, which are used to indicate something else. Accordingly, every sign is also a thing; for what is not a thing is nothing at all. Every thing, however, is not also a sign. And so, in regard to this distinction between things and signs, I shall, when I speak of things, speak in such a way that even if some of them may be used as signs also, that will not interfere with the division of the subject according to which I am to discuss things first and signs afterwards. But we must carefully remember that what we have now to consider about things is what they are in themselves, not what other things they are signs of.

Chapter 3.—Some things are for use, some for enjoyment.

3. There are some things, then, which are to be enjoyed, others which are to be used, others still which enjoy and use. Those things which are objects of enjoyment make us happy. Those things which are objects of use assist, and (so to speak) support us in our efforts after happiness, so that we can attain the things that make us happy and rest in them. We ourselves, again, who enjoy and use these things, being placed among both kinds of objects, if we set ourselves to enjoy those which we ought to use, are hindered in our course, and sometimes even led away from it; so that, getting entangled in the love of lower gratifications, we lag behind in, or even altogether turn back

from, the pursuit of the real and proper objects of enjoyment.

Chapter 4.—Difference of use and enjoyment.

4. For to enjoy a thing is to rest with satisfaction in it for its own sake. To use, on the other hand, is to employ whatever means are at one's disposal to obtain what one desires, if it is a proper object of desire; for an unlawful use ought rather to be called an abuse. Suppose, then, we were wanderers in a strange country, and could not live happily away from our fatherland, and that we felt wretched in our wandering, and wishing to put an end to our misery, determined to return home. We find, however, that we must make use of some mode of conveyance, either by land or water, in order to reach that fatherland where our enjoyment is to commence. But the beauty of the country through which we pass, and the very pleasure of the motion, charm our hearts, and turning these things which we ought to use into objects of enjoyment, we become unwilling to hasten the end of our journey; and becoming engrossed in a factitious delight, our thoughts are diverted from that home whose delights would make us truly happy. Such is a picture of our condition in this life of mortality. We have wandered far from God; and if we wish to return to our Father's home, this world must be used, not enjoyed, that so the invisible things of God may be clearly seen, being understood by the things that are made,—that is, that by means of what is material and temporary we may lay hold upon that which is spiritual and eternal.

BOOK II.

Chapter 1.—Signs, their nature and variety.

1. As when I was writing about things, I introduced the subject with a warning against attending to anything but what they are in themselves, even though they are signs of something else, so now, when I come in its turn to discuss the subject of signs, I lay down this direction, not to attend to what they are in themselves, but to the fact that they are signs, that is, to what they signify. For a sign is a thing which, over and above the

impression it makes on the senses, causes something else to come into the mind as a consequence of itself: as when we see a footprint, we conclude that an animal whose footprint this is has passed by; and when we see smoke, we know that there is fire beneath; and when we hear the voice of a living man, we think of the feeling in his mind; and when the trumpet sounds, soldiers know that they are to advance or retreat, or do whatever else the state of battle requires.

2. Now some signs are natural, others conventional. Natural signs are those which, apart from any intention or desire of using them as signs, do yet lead to the knowledge of something else, as, for example, smoke when it indicates fire. For it is not from any intention of making it a sign that it is so, but through attention to experience we come to know that fire is beneath, even when nothing but smoke can be seen. And the footprint of an animal passing by belongs to this class of signs. And the countenance of an angry or sorrowful man indicates the feeling in his mind, independently of his will: and in the same way every other emotion of the mind is betrayed by the tell-tale countenance, even though we do nothing with the intention of making it known. This class of signs, however, it is no part of my design to discuss at present. But as it comes under this division of the subject, I could not altogether pass it over. It will be enough to have noticed it thus far.

Chapter 2.—Of the kind of signs we are now concerned with.

3. Conventional signs, on the other hand, are those which living beings mutually exchange for the purpose of showing, as well as they can, the feelings of their minds, or their perceptions, or their thoughts. Nor is there any reason for giving a sign except the desire of drawing forth and conveying into another's mind what the giver of the sign has in his own mind. We wish, then, to consider and discuss this class of signs so far as men are concerned with it, because even the signs which have been given us of God, and which are contained in the Holy Scriptures, were made known to us through men—those, namely, who wrote the Scriptures. The beasts, too, have certain

signs among themselves by which they make known the desires in their mind. For when the poultry-cock has discovered food, he signals with his voice for the hen to run to him, and the dove by cooing calls his mate, or is called by her in turn; and many signs of the same kind are matters of common observation. Now whether these signs, like the expression or the cry of a man in grief, follow the movement of the mind instinctively and apart from any purpose, or whether they are really used with the purpose of signification, is another question, and does not pertain to the matter in hand. And this part of the subject I exclude from the scope of this work as not necessary to my present object.

Chapter 3.—Among signs, words hold the chief place.

4. Of the signs, then, by which men communicate their thoughts to one another, some relate to the sense of sight, some to that of hearing, a very few to the other senses. For, when we nod, we give no sign except to the eyes of the man to whom we wish by this sign to impart our desire. And some convey a great deal by the motion of the hands: and actors by movements of all their limbs give certain signs to the initiated, and, so to speak, address their conversation to the eyes: and the military standards and flags convey through the eyes the will of the commanders. And all these signs are as it were a kind of visible words. The signs that address themselves to the ear are, as I have said, more numerous, and for the most part consist of words. For though the bugle and the flute and the lyre frequently give not only a sweet but a significant sound, yet all these signs are very few in number compared with words. For among men words have obtained far and away the chief place as a means of indicating the thoughts of the mind. Our Lord, it is true, gave a sign through the odour of the ointment which was poured out upon his feet; and in the sacrament of His body and blood He signified His will through the sense of taste; and when by touching the hem of His garment the woman was made whole, the act was not wanting in significance. But the countless multitude of the signs through which men express their thoughts consist of words. For I have been able to put into

words all those signs, the various classes of which I have briefly touched upon, but I could by no effort express words in terms of those signs….

Chapter 17.—Origin of the legend of the nine Muses.

27. For we must not listen to the falsities of heathen superstition, which represent the nine muses as daughters of Jupiter and Mercury. Varro refutes these, and I doubt whether any one can be found among them more curious or more learned in such matters. He says that a certain state (I don't recollect the name) ordered from each of three artists a set of statues of the Muses, to be placed as an offering in the temple of Apollo, intending that whichever of the artists produced the most beautiful statues, they should select and purchase from him. It so happened that these artists executed their works with equal beauty, that all nine pleased the state, and that all were bought to be dedicated in the temple of Apollo; and he says that afterwards Hesiod the poet gave names to them all. It was not Jupiter, therefore, that begat the nine Muses, but three artists created three each. And the state had originally given the order for three, not because it had seen them in visions, nor because they had presented themselves in that number to the eyes of any of the citizens, but because it was obvious to remark that all sound, which is the material of song, is by nature of three kinds. For it is either produced by the voice, as in the case of those who sing with the mouth without an instrument; or by blowing, as in the case of trumpets and flutes; or by striking, as in the case of harps and drums, and all other instruments that give their sound when struck.

Chapter 18.—No help is to be despised, even though it come from a profane source.

28. But whether the fact is as Varro has related, or is not so, still we ought not to give up music because of the superstition of the heathen, if we can derive anything from it that is not of use for the understanding of Holy Scripture; nor does it follow that we must busy ourselves with their theatrical trumpery because we enter upon an investigation about harps and other instruments, that

may help us to lay hold upon spiritual things. For we ought not to refuse to learn letters because they say that Mercury discovered them; nor because they have dedicated temples to Justice and Virtue, and prefer to worship in the form of stones things that ought to have their place in the heart, ought we on that account to forsake justice and virtue. Nay, but let every good and true Christian understand that wherever truth may be found, it belongs to his Master; and while he recognizes and acknowledges the truth, even in their religious literature, let him reject the figments of superstition, and let him grieve over and avoid men who, "when they knew God, glorified him not as God, neither were thankful; but became vain in their imaginations, and their foolish heart was darkened. Professing themselves to be wise, they became fools, and changed the glory of the uncorruptible God into an image made like to corruptible man, and to birds, and four-footed beasts, and creeping things."[1]

Chapter 19.—Two kinds of heathen knowledge.

29. But to explain more fully this whole topic (for it is one that cannot be omitted), there are two kinds of knowledge which are in vogue among the heathen. One is the knowledge of things instituted by men, the other of things which they have noted, either as transacted in the past or as instituted by God. The former kind, that which deals with human institutions, is partly superstitious, partly not.

Chapter 20.—The superstitious nature of human institutions.

30. All the arrangements made by men for the making and worshipping of idols are superstitious, pertaining as they do either to the worship of what is created or of some part of it as God, or to consultations and arrangements about signs and leagues with devils, such, for example, as are employed in the magical arts, and which the poets are accustomed not so much to teach as to celebrate. And to this class belong, but with a bolder reach of deception, the books of the haruspices and augurs. In this class we must place also all

amulets and cures which the medical art condemns, whether these consist in incantations, or in marks which they call *characters*, or in hanging or tying on or even dancing in a fashion certain articles, not with reference to the condition of the body, but to certain signs hidden or manifest; and these remedies they call by the less offensive name of *physica*, so as to appear not to be engaged in superstitious observances, but to be taking advantage of the forces of nature. Examples of these are the ear-rings on the top of each ear, or the rings of ostrich bone on the fingers, or telling you when you hiccup to hold your left thumb in your right hand.

31. To these we may add thousands of the most frivolous practices, that are to be observed if any part of the body should jump, or if, when friends are walking arm-in-arm, a stone, or a dog, or a boy, should come between them. And the kicking of a stone, as if it were a divider of friends, does less harm than to cuff an innocent boy if he happens to run between men who are walking side by side. But it is delightful that the boys are sometimes avenged by the dogs; for frequently men are so superstitious as to venture upon striking a dog who has run between them,—not with impunity however, for instead of a superstitious remedy, the dog sometimes makes his assailant run in hot haste for a real surgeon. To this class, too, belong the following rules: To tread upon the threshold when you go back to bed if any one should sneeze when you are putting on your slippers; to return home if you stumble when going to a place; when your clothes are eaten by mice, or to be more frightened at the prospect of coming misfortune than grieved by your present loss. Whence that witty saying of Cato, who, when consulted by a man who told him that mice had eaten his boots, replied, "That is not strange, but it would have been very strange indeed if the boots had eaten the mice."

Chapter 21.—Superstition of astrologers.

32. Nor can we exclude from this kind of superstition those who were called *genethliaci*, on account of their attention to birthdays, but are now

---

1   Rom. 1:20.

commonly called *mathematici*. For these, too, although they may seek with pains for the true position of the stars at the time of our birth, and may sometimes even find it out, yet in so far as they attempt thence to predict our actions, grievously err, and sell inexperienced men into a miserable bondage. For when any freeman goes to an astrologer of this kind, he gives money that he may come away the slave either of Mars or of Venus, or rather, perhaps, of all the stars to which those who first fell into this error, and handed it on to posterity, have given the names either of beasts, or of men with a view to confer honor on those men. And this is not to be wondered at, when we consider that even in times more recent and nearer our own, the Romans made an attempt to dedicate the star which we call Lucifer to the name and honor of Caesar. And this would, perhaps, have been done, and the name handed down to distant ages, only that his ancestress Venus had given her name to this star before him, and could not by any law transfer to her heirs what she had never possessed, nor sought to possess, in life. For where a place was vacant, or not held in honor of any of the dead of former times, the usual proceeding in such cases was carried out. For example, we have changed the names of the months Quintilis and Sextilis to July and August, naming them in honor of the men Julius Cæsar and Augustus Cæsar; and from this instance any one who cares can easily see that the stars spoken of above formerly wandered in the heavens without the names they now bear. But as the men were dead whose memory people were either compelled by royal power or impelled by human folly to honor, they seemed to think that in putting their names upon the stars they were raising the dead men themselves to heaven. But whatever they may be called by men, still there are stars which God has made and set in order after His own pleasure, and they have a fixed movement, by which the seasons are distinguished and varied. And when any one is born, it is easy to observe the point at which this movement has arrived, by use of the rules discovered and laid down by those who are rebuked by Holy Writ in these terms: "For if they were able to know so much that they could weigh the world, how did they not more easily find out the Lord thereof?"

Chapter 22.—The folly of observing the stars in order to predict the events of a life.

33. But to desire to predict the characters, the acts, and the face of those who are born from such an observation, is a great delusion and great madness. And among those at least who have any sort of acquaintance with matters of this kind (which, indeed, are only fit to be unlearnt again), this superstition is refuted beyond the reach of doubt. For the observation is of the position of the stars, which they call constellations, at the time when the person was born about whom these wretched men are consulted by their still more wretched dupes. Now it may happen that, in the case of twins, one follows the other out of the womb so closely that there is no interval of time between them that can be apprehended and marked in the position of the constellations. Whence it necessarily follows that twins are in many cases born under the same stars, while they do not meet with equal fortune either in what they do or what they suffer, but often meet with fates so different that one of them has a most fortunate life, the other a most unfortunate. As, for example, we are told that Esau and Jacob were born twins, and in such close succession, that Jacob, who was born last, was found to have laid hold with his hand upon the heel of his brother, who preceded him. Now, assuredly, the day and the hour of the birth of these two could not be marked in any way that would not give both the same constellation. But what a difference there was between the characters, the actions, the labors, and the fortunes of these two, the Scriptures bear witness, which are now so widely spread as to be in the mouth of all nations.

34. Nor is it to the point to say that the very smallest and briefest moment that separates the birth of twins, produces great effects in nature, and in the extremely rapid motion of the heavenly bodies. For, although I may grant that it does produce the greatest effects, yet the astrologer cannot discover this in the constellations, and it is by looking into these that he professes to read the fates. If, then, he does not discover the difference when he examines the constellations, which must, of course, be the same whether he is consulted about Jacob

or his brother, what does it profit him that there is a difference in the heavens, which he rashly and carelessly brings into disrepute, when there is no difference in his chart, which he looks into anxiously but in vain? And so these notions also, which have their origin in certain signs of things being arbitrarily fixed upon by the presumption of men, are to be referred to the same class as if they were leagues and covenants with devils.

Chapter 23.—Why we repudiate arts of divination.

35. For in this way it comes to pass that men who lust after evil things are, by a secret judgment of God, delivered over to be mocked and deceived, as the just reward of their evil desires. For they are deluded and imposed on by the false angels, to whom the lowest part of the world has been put in subjection by the law of God's providence, and in accordance with His most admirable arrangement of things. And the result of these delusions and deceptions is, that through these superstitions and baneful modes of divination, many things in the past and future are made known, and turn out just as they are foretold; and in the case of those who practice superstitious observances, many things turn out agreeably to their observances, and ensnared by these successes, they become more eagerly inquisitive, and involve themselves further and further in a labyrinth of most pernicious error. And to our advantage, the Word of God is not silent about this species of fornication of the soul; and it does not warn the soul against following such practices on the ground that those who profess them speak lies, but it says, "Even if what they tell you should come to pass, hearken not unto them." For though the ghost of the dead Samuel foretold the truth to King Saul, that does not make such sacrilegious observances as those by which his ghost was brought up the less detestable; and though the ventriloquist woman in the Acts of the Apostles bore true testimony to the apostles of the Lord, the Apostle Paul did not spare the evil spirit on that account, but rebuked and cast it out, and so made the woman clean.

36. All arts of this sort, therefore, are either nullities, or are part of a guilty superstition, springing out of a baleful fellowship between men and devils, and are to be utterly repudiated and avoided by the Christian as the covenants of a false and treacherous friendship. "Not as if the idol were anything," says the apostle; "but because the things which they sacrifice they sacrifice to devils and not to God; and I would not that ye should have fellowship with devils."[2] Now, what the apostle has said about idols and the sacrifices offered in their honor, that we ought to feel in regard to all fancied signs which lead either to the worship of idols, or to worshipping creation or its parts instead of God, or which are connected with attention to medicinal charms and other observances; for these are not appointed by God as the public means of promoting love towards God and our neighbor, but they waste the hearts of wretched men in private and selfish striving after temporal things. Accordingly, in regard to all these branches of knowledge, we must fear and shun the Devil their prince, strive only to shut and bar the door against our return. As, then, from the stars which God created and ordained, men have drawn lying omens of their own fancy, so also from things that are born, or in any other way come into existence under the government of God's providence, if there chance only to be something unusual in the occurrence,—as when a mule brings forth young, or an object is struck by lightning,—men have frequently drawn omens by conjectures of their own, and have committed them to writing, as if they had drawn them by rule.

Chapter 24.—The intercourse and agreement with demons which superstitious observances maintain.

37. And all these omens are of force just so far as has been arranged with the devils by that previous understanding in the mind which is, as it were, the common language, but they are all full of hurtful curiosity, torturing anxiety, and deadly slavery. For it was not because they had meaning that they were attended to, but it was by attending to and marking them that they came to have

---

2　1 Corinthians 10:20.

meaning. And so they are made different for different people, according to their several notions and prejudices. For those spirits which are bent upon deceiving, take care to provide for each person the same sort of omens as they see his own conjectures and preconceptions have already been entangled in. For, to take an illustration, the same figure of the letter X, which is made in the shape of a cross, means one thing among the Greeks and another among the Latins, not by nature, but by agreement and pre-arrangement as to its signification; and so, any one who knows both languages uses this letter in a different sense when writing to a Greek from that in which he uses it when writing to a Latin. And the same sound, *beta*, which is the name of a letter among the Greeks, is the name of a vegetable among the Latins; and when I say, *lege*, these two syllables mean one thing to a Greek and another to a Latin. Now, just as all these signs affect the mind according to the arrangements of the community in which each man lives, and affect different men's minds differently, because these arrangements are different; and as, further, men did not agree upon them as signs because they were already significant, but on the contrary they are now significant because they have agreed upon them; in the same way also, those signs by which the ruinous intercourse with devils is maintained have meaning just in proportion to each man's observations. And this appears quite plainly in the rites of the augurs; for they, both before they observe the omens and after they have completed their observations, take pains not to see the flight or hear the cry of the birds, because these signs are of no significance apart from the previous arrangement in the mind of the observer.

Chapter 25.—In human institutions which are not superstitious, there are some things superfluous and some convenient and necessary.

38. But when all these have been cut away and rooted out of the mind of the Christian, we must then look at human institutions which are not superstitious, that is, such as are not set up in association with devils, but by men in association with one another. For all arrangements that are in force among men, because they have agreed among themselves that they should be in force, are human institutions; and of these, some are matters of superfluity and luxury, some of convenience and necessity. For if those signs which the actors make in dancing were of force by nature, and not by the arrangement and agreement of men, the public crier would not in former times have announced to the people of Carthage, while the pantomime was dancing, what it meant to express,—a thing still remembered by many old men from whom we have frequently heard it. And we may well believe this, because even now, if any one who is unaccustomed to such follies goes into the theatre, unless some one tells him what these movements mean, he will give his whole attention to them in vain. Yet all men aim at a certain degree of likeness in their choice of signs, that the signs may as far as possible be like the things they signify. But because one thing may resemble another in many ways, such signs are not always of the same significance among men, except when they have mutually agreed upon them.

39. But in regard to pictures and statues, and other works of this kind, which are intended as representations of things, nobody makes a mistake, especially if they are executed by skilled artists, but every one, as soon as he sees the likenesses, recognizes the things they are likenesses of. And this whole class are to be reckoned among the superfluous devices of men, unless when it is a matter of importance to inquire in regard to any of them, for what reason, where, when, and by whose authority it was made. Finally, the thousands of fables and fictions, in whose lies men take delight, are human devices, and nothing is to be considered more peculiarly man's own and derived from himself than anything that is false and lying. Among the convenient and necessary arrangements of men with men are to be reckoned whatever differences they choose to make in bodily dress and ornament for the purpose of distinguishing sex or rank; and the countless varieties of signs without which human intercourse either could not be carried on at all, or would be carried on at great inconvenience; and the arrangements as to weights and measures, and the stamping and weighing of coins, which are peculiar to each state and people, and other things of the same kind.

Now these, if they were not devices of men, would not be different in different nations, and could not be changed among particular nations at the discretion of their respective sovereigns.

40. This whole class of human arrangements, which are of convenience for the necessary intercourse of life, the Christian is not by any means to neglect, but on the contrary should pay a sufficient degree of attention to them, and keep them in memory.

Chapter 26.—What human contrivances we are to adopt, and what we are to avoid.

For certain institutions of men are in a sort of way representations and likenesses of natural objects. And of these, such as have relation to fellowship with devils must, as has been said, be utterly rejected and held in detestation; those, on the other hand, which relate to the mutual intercourse of men, are, so far as they are not matters of luxury and superfluity, to be adopted, especially the forms of letters which are necessary for reading, and the various languages as far as is required—a matter I have spoken of above. To this class also belong shorthand characters, those who are acquainted with which are called shorthand writers. All these are useful, and there is nothing unlawful in learning them, nor do they involve us in superstition, or enervate us by luxury, if they only occupy our minds so far as not to stand in the way of more important objects to which they ought to be subservient.

Chapter 27.—Some departments of knowledge, not of mere human invention, aid us in interpreting Scripture.

41. But, coming to the next point, we are not to reckon among human institutions those things which men have handed down to us, not as arrangements of their own, but as the result of investigation into the occurrences of the past, and into the arrangements of God's providence. And of course, some pertain to the bodily senses, some to the intellect. Those which are reached by the bodily senses we either believe on testimony, or perceive when they are pointed out to us, or infer from experience.

Chapter 28.—To what extent history is an aid.

42. Anything, then, that we learn from history about the chronology of past times assists us very much in understanding the Scriptures, even if it be learnt without the pale of the Church as a matter of childish instruction. For we frequently seek information about a variety of matters by use of the Olympiads, and the names of the consuls; and ignorance of the consulship in which our Lord was born, and that in which He suffered, has led some into the error of supposing that He was forty-six years of age when He suffered, that being the number of years He was told by the Jews the temple (which He took as a symbol of His body) was in building. Now we know on the authority of the evangelist that He was baptized; but the number of years He lived afterwards, although by putting His actions together we can make it out, yet that no shadow of doubt might arise from another source, can be ascertained more clearly and more certainly from a comparison of profane history with the Gospel. It will still be evident, however, that it was not without a purpose it was said that the temple was forty and six years in building; so that, as this cannot be referred to our Lord's age, it may be referred to the more secret formation of the body which, for our sakes, the only-begotten Son of God, by whom all things were made, condescended to put on.

43. As to the utility of history, moreover, passing over the Greeks, what a great question our own Ambrose has set at rest! For, when the readers and admirers of Plato dared calumniously to assert that our Lord Jesus Christ learnt all those sayings of His, which they are compelled to admire and praise, from the books of Plato—because (they urged) it cannot be denied that Plato lived long before the coming of our Lord!—did not the illustrious bishop, when by his investigations into profane history he had discovered that Plato was through Jeremiah's means initiated into our literature, so as to be able to teach and write those views of his which are so justly praised? For not even Pythagoras himself, from whose successors these men assert Plato learnt theology, lived at a date prior to the books of that Hebrew race, among whom the worship of one God sprang up, and of whom as concerning the flesh our Lord

came. And thus, when we reflect upon the dates, it becomes much more probable that those philosophers learnt whatever they said that was good and true from our literature, than that the Lord Jesus Christ learnt from the writings of Plato,—a thing which it is the height of folly to believe.

44. And even when in the course of an historical narrative former institutions of men are described, the history itself is not to be reckoned among human institutions; because things that are past and gone and cannot be undone are to be reckoned as belonging to the course of time, of which God is the author and governor. For it is one thing to tell what has been done, another to show what ought to be done. History narrates what has been done, faithfully and with advantage; but the books of the haruspices, and all writings of the same kind, aim at teaching what ought to be done or observed, using the boldness of an adviser, not the fidelity of a narrator.

Chapter 29.—To what extent natural science is an exegetical aid.

45. There is also a species of narrative resembling description, in which not a past but an existing state of things is made known to those who are ignorant of it. To this species belongs all that has been written about the situation of places, and the nature of animals, trees, herbs, stones, and other bodies. And of this species I have treated above, and have shown that this kind of knowledge is serviceable in solving the difficulties of Scripture, not that these objects are to be used conformably to certain signs as nostrums or the instruments of superstition; for that kind of knowledge I have already set aside as distinct from the lawful and free kind now spoken of. For it is one thing to say: If you bruise down this herb and drink it, it will remove the pain from your stomach; and another to say: If you hang this herb round your neck, it will remove the pain from your stomach. In the former case the wholesome mixture is approved of, in the latter the superstitious charm is condemned; although indeed, where incantations and invocations and marks are not used, it is frequently doubtful whether the thing that is tied or fixed in any way to the body to cure it, acts by a natural virtue, in which case it may be freely used; or acts by a sort of charm, in which case it becomes the Christian to avoid it the more carefully, the more efficacious it may seem to be. But when the reason why a thing is of virtue does not appear, the intention with which it is used is of great importance, at least in healing or in tempering bodies, whether in medicine or in agriculture.

46. The knowledge of the stars, again, is not a matter of narration, but of description. Very few of these, however, are mentioned in Scripture. And as the course of the moon, which is regularly employed in reference to celebrating the anniversary of our Lord's passion, is known to most people; so the rising and setting and other movements of the rest of the heavenly bodies are thoroughly known to very few. And this knowledge, although in itself it involves no superstition, renders very little, indeed almost no assistance, in the interpretation of Holy Scripture, and by engaging the attention unprofitably is a hindrance rather; and as it is closely related to the very pernicious error of the diviners of the fates, it is more convenient and becoming to neglect it. It involves, moreover, in addition to a description of the present state of things, something like a narrative of the past also; because one may go back from the present position and motion of the stars, and trace by rule their past movements. It involves also regular anticipations of the future, not in the way of forebodings and omens, but by way of sure calculation; not with the design of drawing any information from them as to our own acts and fates, in the absurd fashion of the *genethliaci*, but only as to the motions of the heavenly bodies themselves. For, as the man who computes the moon's age can tell, when he has found out her age to-day, what her age was any number of years ago, or what will be her age any number of years hence, in just the same way men who are skilled in such computations are accustomed to answer like questions about every one of the heavenly bodies. And I have stated what my views are about all this knowledge, so far as regards its utility.

Chapter 30.—What the mechanical arts contribute to exegetics.

47. Further, as to the remaining arts, whether those by which something is made which, when

the effort of the workman is over, remains as a result of his work, as, for example, a house, a bench, a dish, and other things of that kind; or those which, so to speak, assist God in His operations, as medicine, and agriculture, and navigation; or those whose sole result is an action, as dancing, and racing, and wrestling;—in all these arts experience teaches us to infer the future from the past. For no man who is skilled in any of these arts moves his limbs in any operation without connecting the memory of the past with the expectation of the future. Now of these arts a very superficial and cursory knowledge is to be acquired, not with a view to practicing them (unless some duty compel us, a matter on which I do not touch at present), but with a view to forming a judgment about them, that we may not be wholly ignorant of what Scripture means to convey when it employs figures of speech derived from these arts.

Chapter 31.—Use of dialectics. Of fallacies.

48. There remain those branches of knowledge which pertain not to the bodily senses, but to the intellect, among which the science of reasoning and that of number are the chief. The science of reasoning is of very great service in searching into and unraveling all sorts of questions that come up in Scripture, only in the use of it we must guard against the love of wrangling, and the childish vanity of entrapping an adversary. For there are many of what are called *sophisms*, inferences in reasoning that are false, and yet so close an imitation of the true, as to deceive not only dull people, but clever men too, when they are not on their guard. For example, one man lays before another with whom he is talking, the proposition, "What I am, you are not." The other assents, for the proposition is in part true, the one man being cunning and the other simple. Then the first speaker adds: "I am a man;" and when the other has given his assent to this also, the first draws his conclusion: "Then you are not a man." Now of this sort of ensnaring arguments, Scripture, as I judge, expresses detestation in that place where it is said, "There is one that showeth wisdom in words, and is hated;" although indeed, a style of speech which

is not intended to entrap, but only aims at verbal ornamentation more than is consistent with seriousness of purpose, is also called sophistical.

49. There are also valid processes of reasoning which lead to false conclusions, by following out to its logical consequences the error of the man with whom one is arguing; and these conclusions are sometimes drawn by a good and learned man, with the object of making the person from whose error these consequences result, feel ashamed of them, and of thus leading him to give up his error, when he finds that if he wishes to retain his old opinion, he must of necessity also hold other opinions which he condemns. For example, the apostle did not draw true conclusions when he said, "Then is Christ not risen," and again, "Then is our preaching vain, and your faith is also vain";[3] and further on drew other inferences which are all utterly false; for Christ has risen, the preaching of those who declared this fact was not in vain, nor was their faith in vain who had believed it. But all these false inferences followed legitimately from the opinion of those who said that there is no resurrection of the dead. These inferences, then, being repudiated as false, it follows that since they would be true if the dead rise not, there will be a resurrection of the dead. As, then, valid conclusions may be drawn not only from true but from false propositions, the laws of valid reasoning may easily be learnt in the schools, outside the pale of the Church. But the truth of propositions must be inquired into in the sacred books of the Church.

Chapter 32.—Valid logical sequence is not devised but only observed by man.

50. And yet the validity of logical sequences is not a thing devised by men, but is observed and noted by them that they may be able to learn and teach it; for it exists eternally in the reason of things, and has its origin with God. For as the man who narrates the order of events does not himself create that order; and as he who describes the situations of places, or the natures of animals, or roots, or minerals, does not describe arrangements of man; and as he who points out the stars and their

3   1 Corinthians 15:14.

movements does not point out anything that he himself or any other man has ordained;—in the same way, he who says, "When the consequent is false, the antecedent must also be false," says what is most true; but he does not himself make it so, he only points out that it is so. And it is upon this rule that the reasoning I have quoted from the Apostle Paul proceeds. For the antecedent is, "There is no resurrection of the dead,"—the position taken up by those whose error the apostle wished to overthrow. Next, from this antecedent, the assertion, viz., that there is no resurrection of the dead, the necessary consequence is, "Then Christ is not risen." But this consequence is false, for Christ has risen; therefore the antecedent is also false. But the antecedent is, that there is no resurrection of the dead. Now all this is briefly expressed thus: If there is no resurrection of the dead, then is Christ not risen; but Christ is risen, therefore there is a resurrection of the dead. This rule, then, that when the consequent is removed, the antecedent must also be removed, is not made by man, but only pointed out by him. And this rule has reference to the validity of the reasoning, not to the truth of the statements.

Chapter 33.—False inferences may be drawn from valid reasonings, and vice versa.

51. In this passage, however, where the argument is about the resurrection, both the law of the inference is valid, and the conclusion arrived at is true. But in the case of false conclusions, too, there is a validity of inference in some such way as the following. Let us suppose some man to have admitted: If a snail is an animal, it has a voice. This being admitted, then, when it has been proved that the snail has no voice, it follows (since when the consequent is proved false, the antecedent is also false) that the snail is not an animal. Now this conclusion is false, but it is a true and valid inference from the false admission. Thus, the truth of a statement stands on its own merits; the validity of an inference depends on the statement or the admission of the man with whom one is arguing. And thus, as I said above, a false inference may be drawn by a valid process of reasoning, in order that he whose error we wish to correct may be sorry that he has admitted the antecedent, when

he sees that its logical consequences are utterly untenable. And hence it is easy to understand that as the inferences may be unsound where the opinions are false, so the inferences may be unsound where the opinions are true. For example, suppose that a man propounds the statement, "If this man is just, he is good," and we admit its truth. Then he adds, "But he is not just;" and when we admit this too, he draws the conclusion, "Therefore he is not good." Now although every one of these statements may be true, still the principle of the inference is unsound. For it is not true that, as when the consequent is proved false the antecedent is also false, so when the antecedent is proved false the consequent is false. For the statement is true, "If he is an orator, he is a man." But if we add, "He is not an orator," the consequence does not follow, "He is not a man."

Chapter 34.—It is one thing to know the laws of inference, another to know the truth of opinions.

52. Therefore it is one thing to know the laws of inference, and another to know the truth of opinions. In the former case we learn what is consequent, what is inconsequent, and what is incompatible. An example of a consequent is, "If he is an orator, he is a man;" of an inconsequent, "If he is a man, he is an orator;" of an incompatible, "If he is a man, he is a quadruped." In these instances we judge of the connection. In regard to the truth of opinions, however, we must consider propositions as they stand by themselves, and not in their connection with one another; but when propositions that we are sure about are joined by a valid inference to propositions that are true and certain, they themselves, too, necessarily become certain. Now some, when they have ascertained the validity of the inference, plume themselves as if this involved also the truth of the propositions. Many, again, who hold the true opinions have an unfounded contempt for themselves, because they are ignorant of the laws of inference; whereas the man who knows that there is a resurrection of the dead is assuredly better than the man who only knows that it follows that if there is no resurrection of the dead, then is Christ not risen.

Chapter 35.—The science of definition is not false, though it may be applied to falsities.

53. Again, the science of definition, of division, and of partition, although it is frequently applied to falsities, is not itself false, nor framed by man's device, but is evolved from the reason of things. For although poets have applied it to their fictions, and false philosophers, or even heretics—that is, false Christians—to their erroneous doctrines, that is no reason why it should be false, for example, that neither in definition, nor in division, nor in partition, is anything to be included that does not pertain to the matter in hand, nor anything to be omitted that does. This is true, even though the things to be defined or divided are not true. For even falsehood itself is defined when we say that falsehood is the declaration of a state of things which is not as we declare it to be; and this definition is true, although falsehood itself cannot be true. We can also divide it, saying that there are two kinds of falsehood, one in regard to things that cannot be true at all, the other in regard to things that are not, though it is possible that they might be, true. For example, the man who says that seven and three are eleven, says what cannot be true under any circumstances; but he who says that it rained on the kalends of January, although perhaps the fact is not so, says what possibly might have been. The definition and division, therefore, of what is false may be perfectly true, although what is false cannot, of course, itself be true.

Chapter 36.—The rules of eloquence are true, though sometimes used to persuade men of what is false.

54. There are also certain rules for a more copious kind of argument, which is called eloquence, and these rules are not the less true that they can be used for persuading men of what is false; but as they can be used to enforce the truth as well, it is not the faculty itself that is to be blamed, but the perversity of those who put it to a bad use. Nor is it owing to an arrangement among men that the expression of affection conciliates the hearer, or that a narrative, when it is short and clear, is effective, and that variety arrests men's attention without wearying them. And it is the same with

other directions of the same kind, which, whether the cause in which they are used be true or false, are themselves true just in so far as they are effective in producing knowledge or belief, or in moving men's minds to desire and aversion. And men rather found out that these things are so, than arranged that they should be so.

Chapter 37.—Use of rhetoric and dialectic.

55. This art, however, when it is learnt, is not to be used so much for ascertaining the meaning as for setting forth the meaning when it is ascertained. But the art previously spoken of, which deals with inferences, and definitions, and divisions, is of the greatest assistance in the discovery of the meaning, provided only that men do not fall into the error of supposing that when they have learnt these things they have learnt the true secret of a happy life. Still, it sometimes happens that men find less difficulty in attaining the object for the sake of which these sciences are learnt, than in going through the very intricate and thorny discipline of such rules. It is just as if a man wishing to give rules for walking should warn you not to lift the hinder foot before you set down the front one, and then should describe minutely the way you ought to move the hinges of the joints and knees. For what he says is true, and one cannot walk in any other way; but men find it easier to walk by executing these movements than to attend to them while they are going through them, or to understand when they are told about them. Those, on the other hand, who cannot walk, care still less about such directions, as they cannot prove them by making trial of them. And in the same way a clever man often sees that an inference is unsound more quickly than he apprehends the rules for it. A dull man, on the other hand, does not see the unsoundness, but much less does he grasp the rules. And in regard to all these laws, we derive more pleasure from them as exhibitions of truth, than assistance in arguing or forming opinions, except perhaps that they put the intellect in better training. We must take care, however, that they do not at the same time make it more inclined to mischief or vanity,—that is to say, that they do not give those who have learnt them an inclination to lead people astray by plausible speech and catching questions, or make them think that they have

attained some great thing that gives them an advantage over the good and innocent.

Chapter 38.—The science of numbers not created, but only discovered, by man.

56. Coming now to the science of numbers, it is clear to the dullest apprehension that this was not created by man, but was discovered by investigation. For, though Virgil could at his own pleasure make the first syllable of *Italia* long, while the ancients pronounced it short, it is not in any man's power to determine at his pleasure that three times three are not nine, or not make a square, or are not the triple of three, nor one and a half times the number six, or that it is not true that they are not the double of any number because odd numbers have no half. Whether, then, numbers are considered in themselves, or as applied to the laws of figures, or of sounds, or of other motions, they have fixed laws which were not made by man, but which the acuteness of ingenious men brought to light.

57. The man, however, who puts so high a value on these things as to be inclined to boast himself one of the learned, and who does not rather inquire after the source from which those things which he perceives to be true derive their truth, and from which those others which he perceives to be unchangeable also derive their truth and unchangeableness, and who, mounting up from bodily appearances to the mind of man, and finding that it too is changeable (for it is sometimes instructed, at other times uninstructed), although it holds a middle place between the unchangeable truth above it and the changeable things beneath it, does not strive to make all things redound to the praise and love of the one God from whom he knows that all things have their being;—the man, I say, who acts in this way may seem to be learned, but wise he cannot in any sense be deemed.

Chapter 39.—To which of the above-mentioned studies attention should be given, and in what spirit.

58. Accordingly, I think that it is well to warn serious and able young men, who fear God and are seeking for happiness of life, not to venture heedlessly upon the pursuit of the branches of learning that are in vogue beyond the pale of the Church of Christ, as if these could secure for them the happiness they seek; but soberly and carefully to discriminate among them. And if they find any of those which have been instituted by men varying by reason of the varying pleasure of their founders, and unknown by reason of erroneous conjectures, especially if they involve entering into fellowship with devils by means of leagues and covenants about signs, let these be utterly rejected and held in detestation. Let the young men also withdraw their attention from such institutions of men as are unnecessary and luxurious. But for the sake of the necessities of this life we must not neglect the arrangements of men that enable us to carry on intercourse with those around us. I think, however, there is nothing useful in the other branches of learning that are found among the heathen, except information about objects, either past or present, that relate to the bodily senses, in which are included also the experiments and conclusions of the useful mechanical arts, except also the sciences of reasoning and of number. And in regard to all these we must hold by the maxim, "Not too much of anything;" especially in the case of those which, pertaining as they do to the senses, are subject to the relations of space and time.

59. What, then, some men have done in regard to all words and names found in Scripture, in the Hebrew, and Syriac, and Egyptian, and other tongues, taking up and interpreting separately such as were left in Scripture without interpretation; and what Eusebius has done in regard to the history of the past with a view to the questions arising in Scripture that require a knowledge of history for their solution;—what, I say, these men have done in regard to matters of this kind, making it unnecessary for the Christian to spend his strength on many subjects for the sake of a few items of knowledge, the same, I think, might be done in regard to other matters, if any competent man were willing in a spirit of benevolence to undertake the labour for the advantage of his brethren. In this way he might arrange in their several classes, and give an account of the unknown places, and animals, and plants, and trees, and stones, and metals, and other species of things that are

mentioned in Scripture, taking up these only, and committing his account to writing. This might also be done in relation to numbers, so that the theory of those numbers, and those only, which are mentioned in Holy Scripture, might be explained and written down. And it may happen that some or all of these things have been done already (as I have found that many things I had no notion of have been worked out and committed to writing by good and learned Christians), but are either lost amid the crowds of the careless, or are kept out of sight by the envious. And I am not sure whether the same thing can be done in regard to the theory of reasoning; but it seems to me it cannot, because this runs like a system of nerves through the whole structure of Scripture, and on that account is of more service to the reader in disentangling and explaining ambiguous passages, of which I shall speak hereafter, than in ascertaining the meaning of unknown signs, the topic I am now discussing.

Chapter 40.—Whatever has been rightly said by the heathen, we must appropriate to our use.

60. Moreover, if those who are called philosophers, and especially the Platonists, have said aught that is true and in harmony with our faith, we are not only not to shrink from it, but to claim it for our own use from those who have unlawful possession of it. For, as the Egyptians had not only the idols and heavy burdens which the people of Israel hated and fled from, but also the vessels and ornaments of gold and silver, which the same people when going out of Egypt appropriated to themselves, designing them for a better use, not doing this on their own authority, but by the command of God, the Egyptians themselves, in their ignorance, providing them with things which they themselves were not making a good use of; in the same way all branches of heathen learning have not only false and superstitious fancies and heavy burdens of unnecessary toil, which every one of us, when going out under the leadership of Christ from the fellowship of the heathen, ought to abhor and avoid; but they contain also liberal instruction which is better adapted to the use of the truth, and some most excellent precepts of morality; and some truths in regard even to the worship of the One God are found among them.

Now these are, so to speak, their gold and silver, which they did not create themselves, but dug out of the mines of God's providence which are everywhere scattered abroad, and are perversely and unlawfully prostituting to the worship of devils. These, therefore, the Christian, when he separates himself in spirit from the miserable fellowship of these men, ought to take away from them, and to devote to their proper use in preaching the Gospel. Their garments, also,—that is, human institutions such as are adapted to that intercourse with men which is indispensable in this life,—we must take and turn to a Christian use.

61. And what else have many good and faithful men among our brethren done? Do we not see with what a quantity of gold and silver and garments Cyprian, that most persuasive teacher and most blessed martyr, was loaded when he came out of Egypt? How much Lactantius brought with him? And Victorinus, and Optatus, and Hilary, not to speak of living men! How much Greeks out of number have borrowed! And prior to all these, that most faithful servant of God, Moses, had done the same thing; for of him it is written that he was learned in all the wisdom of the Egyptians. And to none of all these would heathen superstition (especially in those times when, kicking against the yoke of Christ, it was persecuting the Christians) have ever furnished branches of knowledge it held useful, if it had suspected they were about to turn them to the use of worshipping the One God, and thereby overturning the vain worship of idols. But they gave their gold and their silver and their garments to the people of God as they were going out of Egypt, not knowing how the things they gave would be turned to the service of Christ. For what was done at the time of the exodus was no doubt a type prefiguring what happens now. And this I say without prejudice to any other interpretation that may be as good, or better.

Chapter 41.—What kind of spirit is required for the study of Holy Scripture.

62. But when the student of the Holy Scriptures, prepared in the way I have indicated, shall enter upon his investigations, let him constantly meditate upon that saying of the apostle's, "Knowledge puffeth up, but charity edifieth." For so he will feel

that, whatever may be the riches he brings with him out of Egypt, yet unless he has kept the passover, he cannot be safe. Now Christ is our passover sacrificed for us, and there is nothing the sacrifice of Christ more clearly teaches us than the call which He himself addresses to those whom He sees toiling in Egypt under Pharoah: "Come unto me, all ye that labor and are heavy laden, and I will give you rest. Take my yoke upon you, and learn of me; for I am meek and lowly in heart; and ye shall find rest unto your souls. For my yoke is easy, and my burden is light." To whom is it light but to the meek and lowly in heart, whom knowledge doth not puff up, but charity edifieth? Let them remember, then, that those who celebrated the passover at that time in type and shadow, when they were ordered to mark their door-posts with the blood of the lamb, used hyssop to mark them with. Now this is a meek and lowly herb, and yet nothing is stronger and more penetrating than its roots; that being rooted and grounded in love, we may be able to comprehend with all saints what is the breadth, and length, and depth, and height,—that is, to comprehend the cross of our Lord, the breadth of which is indicated by the transverse wood on which the hands are stretched, its length by the part from the ground up to the cross-bar on which the whole body from the head downwards is fixed, its height by the part which is hidden, being fixed in the earth. And by this sign of the cross all Christian action is symbolized, viz., to do good works in Christ, to cling with constancy to Him, to hope for heaven, and not to desecrate the sacraments. And purified by this Christian action, we shall be able to know even "the love of Christ which passeth knowledge," who is equal to the Father, by whom all things, were made, "that we may be filled with all the fullness of God." There is besides in hyssop a purgative virtue, that the breast may not be swollen with that knowledge which puffeth up, nor boast vainly of the riches brought out from Egypt. "Purge me with hyssop," the psalmist says, "and I shall be clean; wash me, and I shall be whiter than snow. Make me to hear joy and gladness." Then he immediately adds, to show that it is purifying from pride that is indicated by hyssop, "that the bones which Thou hast broken may rejoice."

Chapter 42.—Sacred Scripture compared with profane authors.

63. But just as poor as the store of gold and silver and garments which the people of Israel brought with them out of Egypt was in comparison with the riches which they afterwards attained at Jerusalem, and which reached their height in the reign of King Solomon, so poor is all the useful knowledge which is gathered from the books of the heathen when compared with the knowledge of Holy Scripture. For whatever man may have learnt from other sources, if it is hurtful, it is there condemned; if it is useful, it is therein contained. And while every man may find there all that he has learnt of useful elsewhere, he will find there in much greater abundance things that are to be found nowhere else, but can be learnt in the wonderful sublimity and wonderful simplicity of the Scriptures.

When, then, the reader is possessed of the instruction here pointed out, so that unknown signs have ceased to be a hindrance to him; when he is meek and lowly of heart, subject to the easy yoke of Christ, and loaded with His light burden, rooted and grounded and built up in faith, so that knowledge cannot puff him up, let him then approach the consideration and discussion of ambiguous signs in Scripture. And about these I shall now, in a third book, endeavor to say what the Lord shall be pleased to vouchsafe.

City of God

BOOK I.

Preface, explaining his design in undertaking this work.

The glorious city of God is my theme in this work, which you, my dearest son Marcellinus,[4] suggested, and which is due to you by my promise. I have undertaken its defense against those who prefer their own gods to the Founder of this city,— a city surpassingly glorious, whether we view it as it still lives by faith in this fleeting course of time, and sojourns as a stranger in the midst of the ungodly, or as it shall dwell in the fixed stability of its eternal seat, which it now with patience waits for, expecting until "righteousness shall return unto judgment,"[5] and it obtain, by virtue of its excellence, final victory and perfect peace. A great work this, and an arduous; but God is my helper. For I am aware what ability is requisite to persuade the proud how great is the virtue of humility, which raises us, not by a quite human arrogance, but by a divine grace, above all earthly dignities that totter on this shifting scene. For the King and Founder of this city of which we speak, has in Scripture uttered to His people a dictum of the divine law in these words: "God resisteth the proud, but giveth grace unto the humble."[6] But this, which is God's prerogative, the inflated ambition of a proud spirit also affects, and dearly loves that this be numbered among its attributes, to

> "Show pity to the humbled soul,
> And crush the sons of pride."[7]

And therefore, as the plan of this work we have undertaken requires, and as occasion offers, we must speak also of this earthly city, which, though it be mistress of the nations, is itself ruled by its lust of rule.

Chapter 1.—Of the adversaries of the name of Christ, whom the barbarians for Christ's sake spared when they stormed the city.

For to this earthly city belong the enemies against whom I have to defend the city of God. Many of them, indeed, being reclaimed from their ungodly error, have become sufficiently creditable citizens of this city; but many are so inflamed with hatred against it, and are so ungrateful to its Redeemer for His signal benefits, as to forget that they would now be unable to utter a single word to its prejudice, had they not found in its sacred places, as they fled from the enemy's steel, that life in which they now boast themselves.[8] Are not those very Romans, who were spared by the barbarians through their respect for Christ, become enemies to the name of Christ? The reliquaries of the martyrs and the churches of the apostles bear witness to this; for in the sack of the city they were open sanctuary for all who fled to them, whether Christian or pagan. To their very threshold the bloodthirsty enemy raged; there his murderous fury owned a limit. Thither did such of the enemy as had any pity convey those to whom they had given quarter, lest any less mercifully disposed might fall upon them. And, indeed, when even those murderers who everywhere else showed themselves pitiless came to those spots where that was forbidden which the license of war permitted in every other place, their furious rage for slaughter was bridled, and their eagerness to take prisoners was quenched. Thus escaped multitudes who now reproach the Christian religion, and impute to Christ the ills that have befallen their city; but the preservation of their own life— a boon which they owe to the respect entertained for Christ by the barbarians—they attribute not to our Christ, but to their own good luck. They

---

4   Marcellinus was a friend of Augustine who urged him to write this work. He was commissioned by the Emperor Honorius to convene a conference of Catholic and schismatic Donatist bishops in the summer of 411, and conceded the victory to the Catholics; but on account of his rigor in executing the laws against the Donatists, he fell victim to their revenge and was honored by a place among the martyrs.

5   Psalm 94:15.

6   James 4:6.

7   *Aeneid* VI, 853.

8   Augustine refers to the sacking of the city of Rome by the West-Gothic King Alaric in 410. He was the most humane of the barbaric invaders and conquerors of Rome and had embraced Arian Christianity (probably from the teaching of Ulphilas, the Arian bishop and translator of the Bible). He spared the Catholic Christians.

ought rather, had they any right perceptions, to attribute the severities and hardships inflicted by their enemies, to that divine providence which is wont to reform the depraved manners of men by chastisement, and which exercises with similar afflictions the righteous and praiseworthy,—either translating them, when they have passed through the trial, to a better world, or detaining them still on earth for ulterior purposes. And they ought to attribute it to the spirit of these Christian times, that, contrary to the custom of war, these bloodthirsty barbarians spared them, and spared them for Christ's sake, whether this mercy was actually shown in promiscuous places, or in those places specially dedicated to Christ's name, and of which the very largest were selected as sanctuaries, that full scope might thus be given to the expansive compassion which desired that a large multitude might find shelter there. Therefore ought they to give God thanks, and with sincere confession flee for refuge to His name, that so they may escape the punishment of eternal fire—they who with lying lips took upon them this name, that they might escape the punishment of present destruction. For of those whom you see insolently and shamelessly insulting the servants of Christ, there are numbers who would not have escaped that destruction and slaughter had they not pretended that they themselves were Christ's servants. Yet now, in ungrateful pride and most impious madness, and at the risk of being punished in everlasting darkness, they perversely oppose that name under which they fraudulently protected themselves for the sake of enjoying the fruits of this brief life....

Chapter 8.—Of the advantages and disadvantages which often indiscriminately accrue to good and wicked men.

Will someone say, Why, then, was this divine compassion extended even to the ungodly and ungrateful? Why, but because it was the mercy of Him who daily "maketh His sun to rise on the evil and on the good, and sendeth rain on the just and on the unjust."[9] For though some of these men, taking thought of this, repent of their wickedness

and reform, some, as the apostle says, "despising the riches of His goodness and long-suffering, after their hardness and impenitent heart, treasure up unto themselves wrath against the day of wrath and revelation of the righteous judgment of God, who will render to every man according to his deeds":[10] nevertheless does the patience of God still invite the wicked to repentance, even as the scourge of God educates the good to patience. And so, too, does the mercy of God embrace the good that it may cherish them, as the severity of God arrests the wicked to punish them. To the divine providence it has seemed good to prepare in the world to come for the righteous good things, which the unrighteous shall not enjoy; and for the wicked evil things, by which the good shall not be tormented. But as for the good things of this life, and its ills, God has willed that these should be common to both; that we might not too eagerly covet the things which wicked men are seen equally to enjoy, nor shrink with an unseemly fear from the ills which even good men must suffer.

There is, too, a very great difference in the purpose served both by those events which we call adverse and those called prosperous. For the good man is neither uplifted with the good things of time, nor broken by its ills; but the wicked man, because he is corrupted by this world's happiness, feels himself punished by its unhappiness. Yet often, even in the present distribution of temporal things, does God plainly evince His own interference. For if every sin were now visited with manifest punishment, nothing would seem to be reserved for the final judgment; on the other hand, if no sin received now a plainly divine punishment, it would be concluded that there is no divine providence at all. And so of the good things of this life: if God did not by a very visible liberality confer these on some of those persons who ask for them, we should say that these good things were not at His disposal; and if He gave them to all who sought them, we should suppose that such were the only rewards of His service; and such a service would make us not godly, but greedy rather, and covetous. Wherefore, though good and bad men suffer alike, we must not suppose that there is no difference between the men

---

9   Matthew 5:45.
10   Romans 2:6.

themselves, because there is no difference in what they both suffer. For even in the likeness of the sufferings, there remains an unlikeness in the sufferers; and though exposed to the same anguish, virtue and vice are not the same thing. For as the same fire causes gold to glow brightly, and chaff to smoke; and under the same flail the straw is beaten small, while the grain is cleansed; and as the lees are not mixed with the oil, though squeezed out of the vat by the same pressure, so the same violence of affliction proves, purges, clarifies the good, but damns, ruins, exterminates the wicked. And thus it is that in the same affliction the wicked detest God and blaspheme, while the good pray and praise. So material a difference does it make, not what ills are suffered, but what kind of man suffers them. For, stirred up with the same movement, mud exhales a horrible stench, and ointment emits a fragrant odor.

Chapter 9.—Of the reasons for administering correction to bad and good together.

What, then, have the Christians suffered in that calamitous period, which would not profit every one who duly and faithfully considered the following circumstances? First of all, they must humbly consider those very sins which have provoked God to fill the world with such terrible disasters; for although they be far from the excesses of wicked, immoral, and ungodly men, yet they do not judge themselves so clean removed from all faults as to be too good to suffer for these even temporal ills. For every man, however laudably he lives, yet yields in some points to the lust of the flesh. Though he do not fall into gross enormity of wickedness, and abandoned viciousness, and abominable profanity, yet he slips into some sins, either rarely or so much the more frequently as the sins seem of less account. But not to mention this, where can we readily find a man who holds in fit and just estimation those persons on account of whose revolting pride, luxury, and avarice, and cursed iniquities and impiety, God now smites the earth as His predictions threatened? Where is the man who lives with them in the style in which it becomes us to live with them? For often we wickedly blind ourselves to the occasions of teaching and admonishing them, sometimes even of reprimanding and chiding them, either

because we shrink from the labor or are ashamed to offend them, or because we fear to lose good friendships, lest this should stand in the way of our advancement, or injure us in some worldly matter, which either our covetous disposition desires to obtain, or our weakness shrinks from losing. So that, although the conduct of wicked men is distasteful to the good, and therefore they do not fall with them into that damnation which in the next life awaits such persons, yet, because they spare their damnable sins through fear, therefore, even though their own sins be slight and venial, they are justly scourged with the wicked in this world, though in eternity they quite escape punishment. Justly, when God afflicts them in common with the wicked, do they find this life bitter, through love of whose sweetness they declined to be bitter to these sinners.

If anyone forbears to reprove and find fault with those who are doing wrong, because he seeks a more seasonable opportunity, or because he fears they may be made worse by his rebuke, or that other weak persons may be disheartened from endeavoring to lead a good and pious life, and may be driven from the faith; this man's omission seems to be occasioned not by covetousness, but by a charitable consideration. But what is blameworthy is, that they who themselves revolt from the conduct of the wicked, and live in quite another fashion, yet spare those faults in other men which they ought to reprehend and wean them from; and spare them because they fear to give offense, lest they should injure their interests in those things which good men may innocently and legitimately use,—though they use them more greedily than becomes persons who are strangers in this world, and profess the hope of a heavenly country. For not only the weaker brethren who enjoy married life, and have children (or desire to have them), and own houses and establishments, whom the apostle addresses in the churches, warning and instructing them how they should live, both the wives with their husbands, and the husbands with their wives, the children with their parents, and parents with their children, and servants with their masters, and masters with their servants,—not only do these weaker brethren gladly obtain and grudgingly lose many earthly and temporal things on account of which they dare not offend men whose polluted and wicked life greatly displeases them; but those also who live at a higher level, who are not entangled in the meshes of married life, but use meager food and raiment, do not often take thought of their own safety and good name, and abstain from finding fault with the wicked, because they fear their wiles and violence. And although they do not fear them to such an extent as to be drawn to the commission of like iniquities, nay, not by any threats or violence soever; yet those very deeds which they refuse to share in the commission of, they often decline to find fault with, when possibly they might by finding fault prevent their commission. They abstain from interference, because they fear that, if it fail of good effect, their own safety or reputation may be damaged or destroyed; not because they see that their preservation and good name are needful, that they may be able to influence those who need their instruction, but rather because they weakly relish the flattery and respect of men, and fear the judgments of the people, and the pain or death of the body; that is to say, their non-intervention is the result of selfishness, and not of love.

Accordingly this seems to me to be one principal reason why the good are chastised along with the wicked, when God is pleased to visit with temporal punishments the profligate manners of a community. They are punished together, not because they have spent an equally corrupt life, but because the good as well as the wicked, though not equally with them, love this present life; while they ought to hold it cheap, that the wicked, being admonished and reformed by their example, might lay hold of life eternal. And if they will not be the companions of the good in seeking life everlasting, they should be loved as enemies, and be dealt with patiently. For so long as they live, it remains uncertain whether they may not come to a better mind. These selfish persons have more cause to fear than those to whom it was said through the prophet, "He is taken away in his iniquity, but his blood I will require at the watchman's hand." For watchmen or overseers of the people are appointed in churches, that they may unsparingly rebuke sin. Nor is that man guiltless of the sin we speak of, who, though he be not a watchman,

yet sees in the conduct of those with whom the relationships of this life bring him into contact, many things that should be blamed, and yet overlooks them, fearing to give offense, and lose such worldly blessings as may legitimately be desired, but which he too eagerly grasps. Then, lastly, there is another reason why the good are afflicted with temporal calamities—the reason which Job's case exemplifies: that the human spirit may be proved, and that it may be manifested with what fortitude of pious trust, and with how unmercenary a love, it cleaves to God....

(BOOK XIX)

Chapter 4.—What the Christians believe regarding the supreme good and evil, in opposition to the philosophers, who have maintained that the supreme good is in themselves.

If, then, we be asked what the city of God has to say upon these points, and, in the first place, what its opinion regarding the supreme good and evil is, it will reply that life eternal is the supreme good, death eternal the supreme evil, and that to obtain the one and to escape the other we must live rightly. And thus it is written, "The just lives by faith,"[11] for we do not as yet see our good, and must therefore live by faith; neither have we in ourselves power to live rightly, but can do so only if He who has given us faith to believe in His help do help us when we believe and pray. As for those who have supposed that the sovereign good and evil are to be found in this life, and have placed it either in the soul or the body, or, to speak more explicitly, either in pleasure or in virtue, or in both; in repose or in virtue, or in both; in pleasure and repose, or in virtue, or in all combined; in the primary objects of nature, or in virtue, or in both,—all these have, with a marvelous shallowness, sought to find their blessedness in this life and in themselves. Contempt has been poured upon such ideas by the Truth, saying by the prophet, "The Lord knoweth the thoughts of men" (or, as the Apostle Paul cites the passage, "The Lord knoweth the thoughts of the *wise*") "that they are vain."[12]

---

11   Habakkuk 2:4; Romans 1:17.
12   1 Corinthians 3:20.

For what flood of eloquence can suffice to detail the miseries of this life? Cicero, in the *Consolation* on the death of his daughter, has spent all his ability in lamentation; but how inadequate was even his ability here? For when, where, how, in this life can these primary objects of nature be possessed so that they may not be assailed by unforeseen accidents? Is the body of the wise man exempt from any pain which may dispel pleasure, from any disquietude which may banish repose? The amputation or decay of the members of the body puts an end to its integrity, deformity blights its beauty, weakness its health, lassitude its vigor, sleepiness or sluggishness its activity,—and which of these is it that may not assail the flesh of the wise man? Comely and fitting attitudes and movements of the body are numbered among the prime natural blessings; but what if some sickness makes the members tremble? what if a man suffers from curvature of the spine to such an extent that his hands reach the ground, and he goes upon all-fours like a quadruped? Does not this destroy all beauty and grace in the body, whether at rest or in motion? What shall I say of the fundamental blessings of the soul, sense and intellect, of which the one is given for the perception, and the other for the comprehension of truth? But what kind of sense is it that remains when a man becomes deaf and blind? where are reason and intellect when disease makes a man delirious? We can scarcely, or not at all, refrain from tears, when we think of or see the actions and words of such frantic persons, and consider how different from and even opposed to their own sober judgment and ordinary conduct their present demeanor is. And what shall I say of those who suffer from demoniacal possession? Where is their own intelligence hidden and buried while the malignant spirit is using their body and soul according to his own will? And who is quite sure that no such thing can happen to the wise man in this life? Then, as to the perception of truth, what can we hope for even in this way while in the body, as we read in the true book of Wisdom, "The corruptible body weigheth down the soul, and the earthly tabernacle presseth down the mind that museth upon many things?"[13] And eagerness, or desire of action, if this is the right meaning to put on the Greek ρμη, is also reckoned among the primary advantages of nature; and yet is it not this which produces those pitiable movements of the insane, and those actions which we shudder to see, when sense is deceived and reason deranged?

In fine, virtue itself, which is not among the primary objects of nature, but succeeds to them as the result of learning, though it holds the highest place among human good things, what is its occupation save to wage perpetual war with vices,—not those that are outside of us, but within; not other men's, but our own,—a war which is waged especially by that virtue which the Greeks call σωφροσυνη, and we temperance, and which bridles carnal lusts, and prevents them from winning the consent of the spirit to wicked deeds? For we must not fancy that there is no vice in us, when, as the apostle says, "The flesh lusteth against the spirit;" for to this vice there is a contrary virtue, when, as the same writer says, "The spirit lusteth against the flesh."[14] "For those two," he says, "are contrary one to the other, so that you cannot do the things which you would." But what is it we wish to do when we seek to attain the supreme good, unless that the flesh should cease to lust against the spirit, and that there be no vice in us against which the spirit may lust? And as we cannot attain to this in the present life, however ardently we desire it, let us by God's help accomplish at least this, to preserve the soul from succumbing and yielding to the flesh that lusts against it, and to refuse our consent to the perpetration of sin. Far be it from us, then, to fancy that while we are still engaged in this intestine war, we have already found the happiness which we seek to reach by victory. And who is there so wise that he has no conflict at all to maintain against his vices?

What shall I say of that virtue which is called prudence? Is not all its vigilance spent in the discernment of good from evil things, so that no mistake may be admitted about what we should desire and what avoid? And thus it is itself a proof that we are in the midst of evils, or that evils are in us; for it teaches us that it is an evil to consent to sin, and a good to refuse this consent. And yet

---

13   Wisd. ix. 15.
14   Galatians 5:17.

this evil, to which prudence teaches and temperance enables us not to consent, is removed from this life neither by prudence nor by temperance. And justice, whose office it is to render to every man his due, whereby there is in man himself a certain just order of nature, so that the soul is subjected to God, and the flesh to the soul, and consequently both soul and flesh to God,—does not this virtue demonstrate that it is as yet rather laboring towards its end than resting in its finished work? For the soul is so much the less subjected to God as it is less occupied with the thought of God; and the flesh is so much the less subjected to the spirit as it lusts more vehemently against the spirit. So long, therefore, as we are beset by this weakness, this plague, this disease, how shall we dare to say that we are safe? and if not safe, then how can we be already enjoying our final beatitude? Then that virtue which goes by the name of fortitude is the plainest proof of the ills of life, for it is these ills which it is compelled to bear patiently. And this holds good, no matter though the ripest wisdom co-exists with it. And I am at a loss to understand how the Stoic philosophers can presume to say that these are no ills, though at the same time they allow the wise man to commit suicide and pass out of this life if they become so grievous that he cannot or ought not to endure them. But such is the stupid pride of these men who fancy that the supreme good can be found in this life, and that they can become happy by their own resources, that their wise man, or at least the man whom they fancifully depict as such, is always happy, even though he become blind, deaf, dumb, mutilated, racked with pains, or suffer any conceivable calamity such as may compel him to make away with himself; and they are not ashamed to call the life that is beset with these evils happy. O happy life, which seeks the aid of death to end it? If it is happy, let the wise man remain in it; but if these ills drive him out of it, in what sense is it happy? Or how can they say that these are not evils which conquer the virtue of fortitude, and force it not only to yield, but so to rave that it in one breath calls life happy and recommends it to be given up? For who is so blind as not to see that if it were happy it would not be fled from? And if they say we should flee from it on account of the infirmities that beset it, why then do

they not lower their pride and acknowledge that it is miserable? Was it, I would ask, fortitude or weakness which prompted Cato to kill himself? for he would not have done so had he not been too weak to endure Cæsar's victory. Where, then, is his fortitude? It has yielded, it has succumbed, it has been so thoroughly overcome as to abandon, forsake, flee this happy life. Or was it no longer happy? Then it was miserable. How, then, were these not evils which made life miserable, and a thing to be escaped from?

And therefore, those who admit that these are evils, as the Peripatetics do, and the Old Academy, the sect which Varro advocates, express a more intelligible doctrine; but theirs also is a surprising mistake, for they contend that this is a happy life which is beset by these evils, even though they be so great that he who endures them should commit suicide to escape them. "Pains and anguish of body," says Varro, "are evils, and so much the worse in proportion to their severity; and to escape them you must quit this life." What life, I pray? This life, he says, which is oppressed by such evils. Then it is happy in the midst of these very evils on account of which you say we must quit it? Or do you call it happy because you are at liberty to escape these evils by death? What, then, if by some secret judgment of God you were held fast and not permitted to die, nor suffered to live without these evils? In that case, at least, you would say that such a life was miserable. It is soon relinquished, no doubt, but this does not make it not miserable; for were it eternal, you yourself would pronounce it miserable. Its brevity, therefore, does not clear it of misery; neither ought it to be called happiness because it is a brief misery. Certainly there is a mighty force in these evils which compel a man—according to them, even a wise man—to cease to be a man that he may escape them, though they say, and say truly, that it is as it were the first and strongest demand of nature that a man cherish himself, and naturally therefore avoid death, and should so stand his own friend as to wish and vehemently aim at continuing to exist as a living creature, and subsisting in this union of soul and body. There is a mighty force in these evils to overcome this natural instinct by which death is by every means and with all a man's efforts avoided, and to overcome it is desired, sought after, and if it cannot in any other way be obtained, is inflicted by the man on himself. There is a mighty force in these evils which make fortitude a homicide,—if, indeed, that is to be called fortitude which is so thoroughly overcome by these evils, that it not only cannot preserve by patience the man whom it undertook to govern and defend, but is itself obliged to kill him. The wise man, I admit, ought to bear death with patience, but when it is inflicted by another. If, then, as these men maintain, he is obliged to inflict it on himself, certainly it must be owned that the ills which compel him to this are not only evils, but intolerable evils. The life, then, which is either subject to accidents, or environed with evils so considerable and grievous, could never have been called happy, if the men who give it this name had condescended to yield to the truth, and to be conquered by valid arguments, when they inquired after the happy life, as they yield to unhappiness, and are overcome by overwhelming evils, when they put themselves to death, and if they had not fancied that the supreme good was to be found in this mortal life; for the very virtues of this life, which are certainly the best and most useful possessions, are all the more telling proofs of its miseries in proportion as they are helpful against the violence of its dangers, toils, and woes. For if these are true virtues,—and such cannot exist save in those who have true piety,—they do not profess to be able to deliver the men who possess them from all miseries; for true virtues tell no such lies, but they profess that by the hope of the future world this life, which is miserably involved in the many and great evils of this world, is happy as it is also safe. For if not yet safe, how could it be happy? And therefore the Apostle Paul, speaking not of men without prudence, temperance, fortitude, and justice, but of those whose lives were regulated by true piety, and whose virtues were therefore true, says, "For we are saved by hope: now hope which is not seen is not hope; for what a man seeth, why doth he yet hope for? But if we hope for that we see not, then do we with patience wait for it."[15] As, therefore, we are saved, so we are made happy by hope. And as we do not as yet possess a present, but look for a future salvation, so is it with our happiness, and this "with patience;"

for we are encompassed with evils, which we ought patiently to endure, until we come to the ineffable enjoyment of unmixed good; for there shall be no longer anything to endure. Salvation, such as it shall be in the world to come, shall itself be our final happiness. And this happiness these philosophers refuse to believe in, because they do not see it, and attempt to fabricate for themselves a happiness in this life, based upon a virtue which is as deceitful as it is proud.

Chapter 5.—Of the social life, which, though most desirable, is frequently disturbed by many distresses.

We give a much more unlimited approval to their idea that the life of the wise man must be social. For how could the city of God (concerning which we are already writing no less than the nineteenth book of this work) either take a beginning or be developed, or attain its proper destiny, if the life of the saints were not a social life? But who can enumerate all the great grievances with which human society abounds in the misery of this mortal state? Who can weigh them? Hear how one of their comic writers makes one of his characters express the common feelings of all men in this matter: "I am married; this is one misery. Children are born to me; they are additional cares." What shall I say of the miseries of love which Terence also recounts—"slights, suspicions, quarrels, war to-day, peace tomorrow?" Is not human life full of such things? Do they not often occur even in honorable friendships? On all hands we experience these slights, suspicions, quarrels, war, all of which are undoubted evils; while, on the other hand, peace is a doubtful good, because we do not know the heart of our friend, and though we did know it to-day, we should be as ignorant of what it might be tomorrow. Who ought to be, or who are more friendly than those who live in the same family? And yet who can rely even upon this friendship, seeing that secret treachery has often broken it up, and produced enmity as bitter as the amity was sweet, or seemed sweet by the most perfect dissimulation? It is on this account that the words of Cicero so move the heart of every one, and provoke a sigh: "There are no snares more

---

15   Romans 8:25.

dangerous than those which lurk under the guise of duty or the name of the relationship. For the man who is your declared foe you can easily baffle by precaution; but this hidden, intestine, and domestic danger not merely exists, but overwhelms you before you can foresee and examine it."[16] It is also to this that allusion is made by the divine saying, "A man's foes are those of his own household,"[17]—words which one cannot hear without pain; for though a man have sufficient fortitude to endure it with equanimity, and sufficient sagacity to baffle the malice of a pretended friend, yet if he himself is a good man, he cannot but be greatly pained at the discovery of the perfidy of wicked men whether they have always been wicked and merely feigned goodness, or have fallen from a better to a malicious disposition. If, then, home, the natural refuge from the ills of life, is itself not safe, what shall we say of the city, which, as it is larger, is so much the more filled with lawsuits civil and criminal, and is never free from the fear, if sometimes from the actual outbreak, of disturbing and bloody insurrections and civil wars?…

Chapter 9.—Of the friendship of the holy angels, which men cannot be sure of in this life, owing to the deceit of the demons who hold in bondage the worshippers of a plurality of gods.

The philosophers who wished us to have the gods for our friends rank the friendship of the holy angels in the fourth circle of society, advancing now from the three circles of society on earth to the universe, and embracing heaven itself. And in this friendship we have indeed no fear that the angels will grieve us by their death or deterioration. But as we cannot mingle with them as familiarly as with men (which itself is one of the grievances of this life), and as Satan, as we read, sometimes transforms himself into an angel of light, to tempt those whom it is necessary to discipline, or just to deceive, there is great need of God's mercy to preserve us from making friends of demons in disguise, while we fancy we have good angels for our friends; for the astuteness and deceitfulness of these wicked spirits is equaled by their hurtfulness. And is this not a great misery of human life, that we are involved in such ignorance as, but for God's mercy, makes us a prey to these demons? And it is very certain that the philosophers of the godless city, who have maintained that the gods were their friends, had fallen a prey to the malignant demons who rule that city, and whose eternal punishment is to be shared by it. For the nature of these beings is sufficiently evinced by the sacred or rather sacrilegious observances which form their worship, and by the filthy games in which their crimes are celebrated, and which they themselves originated and exacted from their worshippers as a fit propitiation.

Chapter 10.—The reward prepared for the saints after they have departed the trial of this life.

But not even the saints and faithful worshippers of the one true and most high God are safe from the manifold temptations and deceits of the demons. For in this abode of weakness, and in these wicked days, this state of anxiety has also its use, stimulating us to seek with keener longing for that security where peace is complete and unassailable. There we shall enjoy the gifts of nature, that is to say, all that God the Creator of all natures has bestowed upon ours,—gifts not only good, but eternal,—not only of the spirit, healed now by wisdom, but also of the body renewed by the resurrection. There the virtues shall no longer be struggling against any vice or evil, but shall enjoy the reward of victory, the eternal peace which no adversary shall disturb. This is the final blessedness, this the ultimate consummation, the unending end. Here, indeed, we are said to be blessed when we have such peace as can be enjoyed in a good life; but such blessedness is mere misery compared to that final felicity. When we mortals possess such peace as this mortal life can afford, virtue, if we are living rightly, makes a right use of the advantages of this peaceful condition; and when we have it not, virtue makes a good use even of the evils a man suffers. But this is true virtue, when it refers all the advantages it makes a good use of, and all that it does in making good use of good and evil things, and itself also, to that end in which we shall enjoy the best and greatest peace possible.

---

16   *In Verrem*, ii. 1. 15.

17   Matthew 10:36.

Chapter 11.—Of the happiness of the eternal peace, which constitutes the end or true perfection of the saints.

And thus we may say of peace, as we have said of eternal life, that it is the end of our good; and the rather because the Psalmist says of the city of God, the subject of this laborious work, "Praise the Lord, O Jerusalem; praise thy God, O Zion: for He hath strengthened the bars of thy gates; He hath blessed thy children within thee; who hath made thy borders peace."[18] For when the bars of her gates shall be strengthened, none shall go in or come out from her; consequently we ought to understand the peace of her borders as that final peace we are wishing to declare. For even the mystical name of the city itself, that is, *Jerusalem*, means, as I have already said, "Vision of Peace." But as the word peace is employed in connection with things in this world in which certainly life eternal has no place, we have preferred to call the end or supreme good of this city life eternal rather than peace. Of this end the apostle says, "But now, being freed from sin, and become servants to God, ye have your fruit unto holiness, and the end life eternal."[19] But, on the other hand, as those who are not familiar with Scripture may suppose that the life of the wicked is eternal life, either because of the endless punishment of the wicked, which forms a part of our faith, and which seems impossible unless the wicked live for ever, it may therefore be advisable, in order that every one may readily understand what we mean, to say that the end or supreme good of this city is either peace in eternal life, or eternal life in peace. For peace is a good so great, that even in this earthly and mortal life there is no word we hear with such pleasure, nothing we desire with such zest, or find to be more thoroughly gratifying. So that if we dwell for a little longer on this subject, we shall not, in my opinion, be wearisome to our readers, who will attend both for the sake of understanding what is the end of this city of which we speak, and for the sake of the sweetness of peace which is dear to us all....

Chapter 21.—Whether there ever was a Roman Republic answering to the definitions of Scipio in Cicero's dialogue.

This, then, is the place where I should fulfill the promise I gave in the second book of this work, and explain, as briefly and clearly as possible, that if we are to accept the definitions laid down by Scipio in Cicero's *De Republica*, there never was a Roman republic; for he briefly defines a republic as the weal of the people. And if this definition be true, there never was a Roman republic, for the people's weal was never attained among the Romans. For the people, according to his definition, is an assemblage associated by a common acknowledgement of right and by a community of interests. And what he means by a common acknowledgement of right he explains at large, showing that a republic cannot be administered without justice. Where, therefore, there is no true justice, there can be no right. For that which is done right is justly done, and what is unjustly done cannot be done by right. For the unjust inventions of men are neither to be considered nor spoken of as rights; for even they themselves say that right is that which flows from the fountain of justice, and deny the definition which is commonly given by those who misconceive the matter, that right is that which is useful to the stronger party. Thus, where there is not true justice there can be no assemblage of men associated by a common acknowledgment of right, and therefore there can be no people, as defined by Scipio or Cicero; and if no people, then no weal of the people, but only of some promiscuous multitude unworthy of the name of people. Consequently, if the republic is the weal of the people, and there is no people if it be not associated by a common acknowledgement of right, and if there is no right where there is no justice, then most certainly it follows that there is no republic where there is no justice. Further, justice is that virtue which gives every one his due. Where, then, is the justice of man, when he deserts the true God and yields himself to impure demons? Is this to give every one his due? Or is he who keeps back a piece of ground from the purchaser, and gives it to a man

---

18 Psalm 147:13.
19 Romans 6:22.

who has no right to it, unjust, while he who keeps back himself from the God who made him, and serves wicked spirits, is just?

This same book, *De Republica*, advocates the cause of justice against injustice with great force and keenness. The pleading for injustice against justice was first heard, and it was asserted that without injustice a republic could neither increase nor even subsist, for it was laid down as an absolutely unassailable position that it is unjust for some men to rule and some to serve; and yet the imperial city to which the republic belongs cannot rule her provinces without having recourse to this injustice. It was replied in behalf of justice, that this ruling of the provinces is just, because servitude may be advantageous to the provincials, and is so when rightly administered,—that is to say, when lawless men are prevented from doing harm. And further, as they became worse and worse so long as they were free, they will improve by subjection. To confirm this reasoning, there is added an eminent example drawn from nature: for "why," it is asked, "does God rule man, the soul the body, the reason the passions and other vicious parts of the soul?" This example leaves no doubt that, to some, servitude is useful; and, indeed, to serve God is useful to all. And it is when the soul serves God that it exercises a right control over the body; and in the soul itself the reason must be subject to God if it is to govern as it ought the passions and other vices. Hence, when a man does not serve God, what justice can we ascribe to him, since in this case his soul cannot exercise a just control over the body, nor his reason over his vices? And if there is no justice in such an individual, certainly there can be none in a community composed of such persons. Here, therefore, there is not that common acknowledgement of right which makes an assemblage of men a people whose affairs we call a republic. And why need I speak of the advantageousness, the common participation in which, according to the definition, makes a people? For although, if you choose to regard the matter attentively, you will see that there is nothing advantageous to those who live godlessly, as every one lives who does not serve God

but demons, whose wickedness you may measure by their desire to receive the worship of men though they are most impure spirits, yet what I have said of the common acknowledgement of right is enough to demonstrate that, according to the above definition, there can be no people, and therefore no republic, where there is no justice. For if they assert that in their republic the Romans did not serve unclean spirits, but good and holy gods, must we therefore again reply to this evasion, though already we have said enough, and more than enough, to expose it? He must be an uncommonly stupid, or a shamelessly contentious person, who has read through the foregoing books to this point, and can yet question whether the Romans served wicked and impure demons. But, not to speak of their character, it is written in the law of the true God, "He that sacrificeth unto any god save unto the Lord only, he shall be utterly destroyed."[20] He, therefore, who uttered so menacing a commandment decreed that no worship should be given either to good or bad gods....

Chapter 24.—The definition which must be given of a people and a republic, in order to vindicate the assumption of these titles by the Romans and by other kingdoms.

But if we discard this definition of a people, and, assuming another, say that a people is an assemblage of reasonable beings bound together by a common agreement as to the objects of their love, then, in order to discover the character of any people, we have only to observe what they love. Yet whatever it loves, if only it is an assemblage of reasonable beings and not of beasts, and is bound together by an agreement as to the objects of love, it is reasonably called a people; and it will be a superior people in proportion as it is bound together by higher interests, inferior in proportion as it is bound together by lower. According to this definition of ours, the Roman people is a people, and its weal is without doubt a commonwealth or republic. But what its tastes were in its early and subsequent days, and how it declined into sanguinary seditions and then to social and civil wars, and so burst asunder or rotted off the bond of

---

20 Exodus 22:20.

concord in which the health of a people consists, history shows, and in the preceding books I have related at large. And yet I would not on this account say either that it was not a people, or that its administration was not a republic, so long as there remains an assemblage of reasonable beings bound together by a common agreement as to the objects of love. But what I say of this people and of this republic I must be understood to think and say of the Athenians or any Greek state, of the Egyptians, of the early Assyrian Babylon, and of every other nation, great or small, which had a public government. For, in general, the city of the ungodly, which did not obey the command of God that it should offer no sacrifice save to Him alone, and which, therefore, could not give to the soul its proper command over the body, nor to the reason its just authority over the vices, is void of true justice.

Chapter 25.—That where there is no true religion there are no true virtues.

For though the soul may seem to rule the body admirably, and the reason the vices, if the soul and reason do not themselves obey God, as God has commanded them to serve Him, they have no proper authority over the body and the vices. For what kind of mistress of the body and the vices can that mind be which is ignorant of the true God, and which, instead of being subject to His authority, is prostituted to the corrupting influences of the most vicious demons? It is for this reason that the virtues which it seems to itself to possess, and by which it restrains the body and the vices that it may obtain and keep what it desires, are rather vices than virtues so long as there is no reference to God in the matter. For although some suppose that virtues which have a reference only to themselves, and are desired only on their own account, are yet true and genuine virtues, the fact is that even then they are inflated with pride, and therefore to be reckoned vices rather than virtues. For as that which gives life to the flesh is not derived from the flesh, but is above it, so that which gives blessed life to man is not derived from man, but is something above him; and what

I say of man is true of every celestial power and virtue whatsoever.

Chapter 26.—Of the peace which is enjoyed by the people that are alienated from God, and the use made of it by the people of God in the time of its pilgrimage.

Wherefore, as the life of the flesh is the soul, so the blessed life of man is God, of whom the sacred writings of the Hebrews say, "Blessed is the people whose God is the Lord." Miserable, therefore, is the people which is alienated from God. Yet even this people has a peace of its own which is not to be lightly esteemed, though, indeed, it shall not in the end enjoy it, because it makes no good use of it before the end. But it is our interest that it enjoy this peace meanwhile in this life; for as long as the two cities are commingled, we also enjoy the peace of Babylon. For from Babylon the people of God is so freed that it meanwhile sojourns in its company. And therefore the apostle also admonished the Church to pray for kings and those in authority, assigning as the reason, "that we may live a quiet and tranquil life in all godliness and love."[21] And the prophet Jeremiah, when predicting the captivity that was to befall the ancient people of God, and giving them the divine command to go obediently to Babylonia, and thus serve their God, counselled them also to pray for Babylonia, saying, "In the peace thereof shall ye have peace,"—the temporal peace which the good and the wicked together enjoy.

Chapter 27.—That the peace of those who serve God cannot in this mortal life be apprehended in its perfection.

But the peace which is peculiar to ourselves we enjoy now with God by faith, and shall hereafter enjoy eternally with Him by sight. But the peace which we enjoy in this life, whether common to all or peculiar to ourselves, is rather the solace of our misery than the positive enjoyment of felicity. Our very righteousness, too, though true in so far as it has respect to the true good, is yet in this life of such a kind that it consists rather in the

---

21   1 Timothy 2:2.

2. AUGUSTINE OF HIPPO

remission of sins than in the perfecting of virtues. Witness the prayer of the whole city of God in its pilgrim state, for it cries to God by the mouth of all its members, "Forgive us our debts as we forgive our debtors." And this prayer is efficacious not for those whose faith is "without works and dead," but for those whose faith "worketh by love." For as reason, though subjected to God, is yet "pressed down by the corruptible body," so long as it is in this mortal condition, it has not perfect authority over vice, and therefore this prayer is needed by the righteous. For though it exercises authority, the vices do not submit without a struggle. For however well one maintains the conflict, and however thoroughly he has subdued these enemies, there steals in some evil thing, which, if it do not find ready expression in act, slips out by the lips, or insinuates itself into the thought; and therefore his peace is not full so long as he is at war with his vices. For it is a doubtful conflict he wages with those that resist, and his victory over those that are defeated is not secure, but full of anxiety and effort. Amidst these temptations, therefore, of all which it has been summarily said in the divine oracles, "Is not human life upon earth a temptation?" who but a proud man can presume that he so lives that he has no need to say to God, "Forgive us our debts?" And such a man is not great, but swollen and puffed up with vanity, and is justly resisted by Him who abundantly gives grace to the humble. In this, then, consists the righteousness of a man, that he submit himself to God, his body to his soul, and his vices, even when they rebel, to his reason, which either defeats or at least resists them; and also that he beg from God grace to do his duty, and the pardon of his sins, and that he render to God thanks for all the blessings he receives. But, in that final peace to which all our righteousness has reference, and for the sake of which it is maintained, as our nature shall enjoy a sound immortality and incorruption, and shall have no more vices, and as we shall experience no resistance either from ourselves or from others, it will not be necessary that reason should rule vices which no longer exist, but God shall rule the man, and the soul shall rule the body, with a sweetness and facility suitable to the felicity of a life which is done with bondage. And this condition shall there be eternal, and we shall be assured of its eternity; and thus the peace of this blessedness and the blessedness of this peace shall be the supreme good.

Chapter 28.—The end of the wicked.

But, on the other hand, they who do not belong to this city of God shall inherit eternal misery, which is also called the second death, because the soul shall then be separated from God its life, and therefore cannot be said to live, and the body shall be subjected to eternal pains. And consequently this second death shall be the more severe, because no death shall terminate it. But war being contrary to peace, as misery to happiness, and life to death, it is not without reason asked what kind of war can be found in the end of the wicked answering to the peace which is declared to be the end of the righteous? The person who puts this question has only to observe what it is in war that is hurtful and destructive, and he shall see that it is nothing else than the mutual opposition and conflict of things. And can he conceive a more grievous and bitter war than that in which the will is so opposed to passion, and passion to the will, that their hostility can never be terminated by the victory of either, and in which the violence of pain so conflicts with the nature of the body, that neither yields to the other? For in this life, when this conflict has arisen, either pain conquers and death expels the feeling of it, or nature conquers and health expels the pain. But in the world to come the pain continues that it may torment, and the nature endures that it may be sensible of it; and neither ceases to exist, lest punishment also should cease. Now, as it is through the last judgment that men pass to these ends, the good to the supreme good, the evil to the supreme evil, I will treat of this judgment in the following book.

3. ST. PERPETUA

The Passion of Saints Perpetua and Felicitas

VIBIA PERPETUA, A MEMBER of a high-ranking Roman family, was arrested along with four other Christians under a decree of Emperor Septimus Severus in 202 during a period of intense persecution. She was executed in the arena in Carthage on March 7, 203. Her *Passion*, or account of her martyrdom, was apparently written in large part by Perpetua herself, making it one of the few texts by a woman from this period. An unknown contemporary author wrote the beginning and end of the text, placing it in the tradition of Monatism, a Christian movement that emphasized female prophesy and strict asceticism, and encouraged Christians to seek martyrdom. The *Passion*, with its prophetic visions linked to scriptural imagery and its prominent female voice, had a great influence in later martyrologies not only in North Africa, but in the eastern Mediterranean as well.

Source: *Acts of the Christian Martyrs*, trans. H.R. Musurillo (Oxford: Clarendon Press, 1972), 106–31

Further Reading: Brent D. Shaw, "The Passion of Perpetua," *Past & Present* 139 (1993): 3–45.

---

1. The deeds recounted about the faith in ancient times were a proof of God's favor and achieved the spiritual strengthening of men as well; and they were set forth in writing precisely that honor might be rendered to God and comfort to men by the recollection of the past through the written word. Should not then more recent examples be set down that contribute equally to both ends? For indeed these too will one day become ancient and needful for the ages to come, even though in our own day they may enjoy less prestige because of the prior claim of antiquity.

Let those then who would restrict the power of the one Spirit to times and seasons look to this: the more recent events should be considered the greater, being later than those of old, and this is a consequence of the extraordinary graces promised for the last stage of time. For *in the last days, God declares, I will pour out my Spirit upon all flesh and their sons and daughters shall prophesy and on my manservants and my maidservants I will pour my Spirit, and the young men shall see visions and the old men shall dream dreams.* So too we hold in honor and acknowledge not only new prophecies but new visions as well, according to the promise. And we consider all the other functions of the Holy Spirit as intended for the good of the Church; for the same Spirit has been sent to distribute all his gifts to all, as the Lord apportions to everyone. For this reason we deem it imperative to set them forth and to make them known through the word for the glory of God. Thus no one of weak or despairing faith may think that supernatural grace was present only among men of ancient times, either in the grace of martyrdom or of visions, for God always achieves what he promises, as a witness to the non-believer and a blessing to the faithful.

And so, my brethren and little children, *that which we have heard and have touched with our hands we proclaim also to you, so that* those of you that were witnesses may recall the glory of the Lord and those that now learn of it through hearing *may have fellowship* with the holy martyrs and, through them, *with* the Lord *Christ Jesus,* to whom belong splendor and honor for all ages. Amen.

2. A number of young catechumens were arrested, Revocatus and his fellow slave Felicitas, Saturninus and Secundulus, and with them Vibia Perpetua, a newly married woman of good family and upbringing. Her mother and father were still alive and one of her two brothers was a catechumen like herself. She was about twenty-two years old and had an infant son at the breast. (Now

from this point on the entire account of her ordeal is her own, according to her own ideas and in the way that she herself wrote it down.)

3. While we were still under arrest (she said) my father out of love for me was trying to persuade me and shake my resolution. "Father," said I, "do you see this vase here, for example, or water pot or whatever?"

"Yes, I do," said he.

And I told him: "Could it be called by any other name than what it is?"

And he said: "No."

"Well, so too I cannot be called anything other than what I am, a Christian."

At this my father was so angered by the word "Christian" that he moved towards me as though he would pluck my eyes out. But he left it at that and departed, vanquished along with his diabolical arguments. For a few days afterwards I gave thanks to the Lord that I was separated from my father, and I was comforted by his absence. During these few days I was baptized, and I was inspired by the Spirit not to ask for any other favor after the water but simply the perseverance of the flesh. A few days later we were lodged in the prison; and I was terrified, as I had never before been in such a dark hole. What a difficult time it was! With the crowd the heat was stifling; then there was the extortion of the soldiers; and to crown all, I was tortured with worry for my baby there. Then Tertius and Pomponius, those blessed deacons who tried to take care of us, bribed the soldiers to allow us to go to a better part of the prison to refresh ourselves for a few hours. Everyone then left that dungeon and shifted for himself. I nursed my baby, who was faint from hunger. In my anxiety I spoke to my mother about the child, I tried to comfort my brother, and I gave the child in their charge. I was in pain because I saw them suffering out of pity for me. These were the trials I had to endure for many days. Then I got permission for my baby to stay with me in prison. At once I recovered my health, relieved as I was of my worry and anxiety over the child. My prison had suddenly become a palace, so that I wanted to be there rather than anywhere else.

4. Then my brother said to me: "Dear sister, you are greatly privileged; surely you might ask for a vision to discover whether you are to be condemned or freed." Faithfully I promised that I would, for I knew that I could speak with the Lord, whose great blessings I had come to experience. And so I said: "I shall tell you tomorrow." Then I made my request and this was the vision I had.

I saw a ladder of tremendous height made of bronze, reaching all the way to the heavens, but it was so narrow that only one person could climb up at a time. To the sides of the ladder were attached all sorts of metal weapons: there were swords, spears, hooks, daggers, and spikes; so that if anyone tried to climb up carelessly or without paying attention, he would be mangled and his flesh would adhere to the weapons.

At the foot of the ladder lay a dragon of enormous size, and it would attack those who tried to climb up and try to terrify them from doing so. And Saturus was the first to go up, he who was later to give himself up of his own accord. He had been the builder of our strength, although he was not present when we were arrested. And he arrived at the top of the staircase and he looked back and said to me:

"Perpetua, I am waiting for you. But take care; do not let the dragon bite you."

"He will not harm me," I said, "in the name of Christ Jesus."

Slowly, as though he were afraid of me, the dragon stuck his head out from underneath the ladder. Then, using it as my first step, I trod on his head and went up.

Then I saw an immense garden, and in it a grey-haired man sat in shepherd's garb; tall he was, and milking sheep. And standing around him were many thousands of people clad in white garments. He raised his head, looked at me, and said:

"I am glad you have come, my child."

He called me over to him and gave me, as it were, a mouthful of the milk he was drawing; and I took it into my cupped hands and consumed it. And all those who stood around said: "Amen!" At the sound of this word I came to, with the taste of something sweet still in my mouth. I at once told this to my brother, and we realized that we would have to suffer, and that from now on we would no longer have any hope in this life.

5. A few days later there was a rumor that we were going to be given a hearing. My father also arrived from the city, worn with worry, and he came to see me with the idea of persuading me.

"Daughter," he said, "have pity on my grey head—have pity on me your father, if I deserve to be called your father, if I have favored you above all your brothers, if I have raised you to reach this prime of your life. Do not abandon me to be the reproach of men. Think of your brothers, think of your mother and your aunt, think of your child, who will not be able to live once you are gone. Give up your pride! You will destroy all of us! None of us will ever be able to speak freely again if anything happens to you."

This was the way my father spoke out of love for me, kissing my hands and throwing himself down before me. With tears in his eyes he no longer addressed me as his daughter but as a woman. I was sorry for my father's sake, because he alone of all my kin would be unhappy to see me suffer.

I tried to comfort him saying: "It will all happen in the prisoner's dock as God wills; for you may be sure that we are not left to ourselves but are all in his power."

And he left me in great sorrow.

6. One day while we were eating breakfast we were suddenly hurried off for a hearing. We arrived at the forum, and straight away the story went about the neighborhood near the forum and a huge crowd gathered. We walked up to the prisoner's dock. All the others when questioned admitted their guilt. Then, when it came my turn, my father appeared with my son, dragged me from the step, and said "Perform the sacrifice—have pity on your baby!"

Hilarianus the governor, who had received his judicial powers as the successor of the late proconsul Minucius Timinianus, said to me: "Have pity on your father's grey head; have pity on your infant son. Offer the sacrifice for the welfare of the emperors."

"I will not," I retorted.

"Are you a Christian?" said Hilarianus.

And I said: "Yes, I am."

When my father persisted in trying to dissuade me, Hilarianus ordered him to be thrown to the ground and beaten with a rod. I felt sorry for father, just as if I myself had been beaten. I felt

sorry for his pathetic old age.

Then Hilarianus passed sentence on all of us: we were condemned to the beasts, and we returned to prison in high spirits. But my baby had got used to being nursed at the breast and to staying with me in prison. So I sent the deacon Pomponius straight away to my father to ask for the baby. But father refused to give him over. But as God willed, the baby had no further desire for the breast, nor did I suffer any inflammation; and so I was relieved of any anxiety for my child and of any discomfort in my breasts.

7. Some days later when we were all at prayer, suddenly while praying I spoke out and uttered the name Dinocrates. I was surprised; for the name had never entered my mind until that moment. And I was pained when I recalled what had happened to him. At once I realized that I was privileged to pray for him. I began to pray for him and to sigh deeply for him before the Lord. That very night I had the following vision. I saw Dinocrates coming out of a dark hole, where there were many others with him, very hot and thirsty, pale and dirty. On his face was the wound he had when he died.

Now Dinocrates had been my brother according to the flesh; but he had died horribly of cancer of the face when he was seven years old, and his death was a source of loathing to everyone. Thus it was for him that I made my prayer. There was a great abyss between us: neither could approach the other. Where Dinocrates stood there was a pool full of water; and its rim was higher than the child's height, so that Dinocrates had to stretch himself up to drink. I was sorry that, though the pool had water in it, Dinocrates could not drink because of the height of the rim. Then I woke up, realizing that my brother was suffering. But I was confident that I could help him in his trouble; and I prayed for him every day until we were transferred to the military prison. For we were supposed to fight with the beasts at the military games to be held on the occasion of the Emperor Geta's birthday. And I prayed for my brother day and night with tears and sighs that this favor might be granted me.

8. On the day we were kept in chains, I had this vision shown to me. I saw the same spot that I had

seen before, but there was Dinocrates all clean, well dressed, and refreshed. I saw a scar where the wound had been; and the pool that I had seen before now had its rim lowered to the level of the child's waist. And Dinocrates kept drinking water from it, and there above the rim was a golden bowl full of water. And Dinocrates drew close and began to drink from it, and yet the bowl remained full. And when he had drunk enough of the water, he began to play as children do. Then I awoke, and I realized that he had been delivered from his suffering.

9. Some days later, an adjutant named Pudens, who was in charge of the prison, began to show us great honor, realizing that we possessed some great power within us. And he began to allow many visitors to see us for our mutual comfort.

Now the day of the contest was approaching, and my father came to see me overwhelmed with sorrow. He started tearing the hairs from his beard and threw them on the ground; he then threw himself on the ground and began to curse his old age and to say such words as would move all creation. I felt sorry for his unhappy old age.

10. The day before we were to fight with the beasts I saw the following vision. Pomponius the deacon came to the prison gates and began to knock violently. I went out and opened the gate for him. He was dressed in an unbelted white tunic, wearing elaborate sandals. And he said to me: "Perpetua, come; we are waiting for you."

Then he took my hand and we began to walk through rough and broken country. At last we came to the amphitheater out of breath, and he led me into the center of the arena.

Then he told me: "Do not be afraid. I am here, struggling with you." Then he left.

I looked at the enormous crowd who watched in astonishment. I was surprised that no beasts were let loose on me; for I knew that I was condemned to die by the beasts. Then out came an Egyptian against me, of vicious appearance, together with his seconds, to fight with me. There also came up to me some handsome young men to be my seconds and assistants. My clothes were stripped off, and suddenly I was a man. My seconds began to rub me down with oil (as they are wont to do before a contest). Then I saw the Egyptian on the other side rolling in the dust. Next there came forth a man of marvelous stature, such that he rose above the top of the amphitheater. He was clad in a beltless purple tunic with two stripes (one on either side) running down the middle of his chest. He wore sandals that were wondrously made of gold and silver, and he carried a wand like an athletic trainer and a green branch on which there were golden apples.

And he asked for silence and said: "If this Egyptian defeats her he will slay her with the sword. But if she defeats him, she will receive this branch." Then he withdrew.

We drew close to one another and began to let our fists fly. My opponent tried to get hold of my feet, but I kept striking him in the face with the heels of my feet. Then I was raised up into the air and I began to pummel him without as it were touching the ground. Then when I noticed there was a lull, I put my two hands together linking the fingers of one hand with those of the other and thus I got hold of his head. He fell flat on his face and I stepped on his head.

The crowd began to shout and my assistants started to sing psalms. Then I walked up to the trainer and took the branch. He kissed me and said to me: "Peace be with you, my daughter!" I began to walk in triumph towards the Gate of Life [the *Porta Sanavivaria* by which victorious gladiators or those spared by the people could leave]. Then I awoke. I realized that it was not with wild animals that I would fight but with the Devil, but I knew that I would win the victory. So much for what I did up until the eve of the contest. About what happened at the contest itself, let him write of it who will.

11. But the blessed Saturus has also made known his own vision and he has written it out with his own hand. We had died, he said, and had put off the flesh, and we began to be carried towards the east by four angels who did not touch us with their hands. But we moved along not on our backs facing upwards but as though we were climbing up a gentle hill. And when we were free of the world, we first saw an intense light. And I said to Perpetua (for she was at my side): "This is what the Lord promised us. We have received his promise."

While we were being carried by these four angels, a great open space appeared, which seemed to be a garden, with rose bushes and all manner of flowers. The trees were as tall as cypresses, and their leaves were constantly falling. In the garden there were four other angels more splendid than the others. When they saw us they paid us homage and said to the other angels in admiration: "Why, they are here! They are here!"

Then the four angels that were carrying us grew fearful and set us down. Then we walked across to an open area by way of a broad road, and there we met Jucundus, Saturninus, and Artaxius, who were burnt alive in the same persecution, together with Quintus who had actually died as a martyr in prison. We asked them where they had been. And the other angels said to us: "First come and enter and greet the Lord."

12. Then we came to a place whose walls seemed to be constructed of light. And in front of the gate stood four angels, who entered in and put on white robes. We also entered and we heard the sound of voices in unison chanting endlessly: "*Holy, holy, holy!*" In the same place we seemed to see an aged man with white hair and a youthful face, though we did not see his feet. On his right and left were four elders, and behind them stood other aged men. Surprised, we entered and stood before a throne: four angels lifted us up and we kissed the aged man and he touched our faces with his hand. And the elders said to us: "Let us rise." And we rose and gave the kiss of peace. Then the elders said to us: "Go and play."

To Perpetua I said: "Your wish is granted."

She said to me: "Thanks be to God that I am happier here now than I was in the flesh."

13. Then we went out and before the gates we saw the bishop Optatus on the right and Aspasius the presbyter and teacher on the left, each of them far apart and in sorrow. They threw themselves at our feet and said: "Make peace between us. For you have gone away and left us thus."

And we said to them: "Are you not our bishop, and are you not our presbyter? How can you fall at our feet?"

We were very moved and embraced them. Perpetua then began to speak with them in Greek, and we drew them apart into the garden under a rose arbor.

While we were talking with them, the angels said to them: "Allow them to rest. Settle whatever quarrels you have among yourselves." And they were put to confusion. Then they said to Optatus: "You must scold your flock. They approach you as though they had come from the games, quarreling about the different teams."

And it seemed as though they wanted to close the gates. And there we began to recognize many of our brethren, martyrs among them. All of us were sustained by a most delicious odor that seemed to satisfy us. And then I woke up happy.

14. Such were the remarkable visions of these martyrs, Saturus and Perpetua, written by themselves. As for Secundulus, God called him from this world earlier than the others while he was still in prison, by a special grace that he might not have to face the animals. Yet his flesh, if not his spirit, knew the sword.

15. As for Felicitas, she too enjoyed the Lord's favor in this wise. She had been pregnant when she was arrested, and was now in her eighth month. As the day of the spectacle drew near she was very distressed that her martyrdom would be postponed because of her pregnancy; for it is against the law for women with child to be executed. Thus she might have to shed her holy, innocent blood afterwards along with others who were common criminals. Her comrades in martyrdom were also saddened; for they were afraid that they would have to leave behind so fine a companion to travel alone on the same road to hope. And so, two days before the contest, they poured forth a prayer to the Lord in one torrent of common grief. And immediately after their prayer the birth pains came upon her. She suffered a good deal in her labor because of the natural difficulty of an eight months' delivery.

Hence one of the assistants of the prison guards said to her: "You suffer so much now—what will you do when you are tossed to the beasts? Little did you think of them when you refused to sacrifice."

"What I am suffering now," she replied, "I suffer by myself. But then another will be inside me who will suffer for me, just as I shall be suffering for him."

And she gave birth to a girl; and one of the sisters brought her up as her own daughter.

16. Therefore, since the Holy Spirit has permitted the story of this contest to be written down and by so permitting has willed it, we shall carry out the command or, indeed, the commission of the most saintly Perpetua, however unworthy I might be to add any thing to this glorious story. At the same time I shall add one example of her perseverance and nobility of soul.

The military tribune had treated them with extraordinary severity because on the information of certain very foolish people he became afraid that they would be spirited out of the prison by magical spells.

Perpetua spoke to him directly. "Why can you not even allow us to refresh ourselves properly? For we are the most distinguished of the condemned prisoners, seeing that we belong to the emperor; we are to fight on his very birthday. Would it not be to your credit if we were brought forth on the day in a healthier condition?"

The officer became disturbed and grew red. So it was that he gave the order that they were to be more humanely treated; and he allowed her brothers and other persons to visit, so that the prisoners could dine in their company. By this time the adjutant who was head of the jail was himself a Christian.

17. On the day before, when they had their last meal, which is called the free banquet [the public feast given to the condemned], they celebrated not a banquet but rather a love feast. They spoke to the mob with the same steadfastness, warned them of God's judgment, stressing the joy they would have in their suffering, and ridiculing the curiosity of those that came to see them. Saturus said: "Will not tomorrow be enough for you? Why are you so eager to see something that you dislike? Our friends today will be our enemies on the morrow. But take careful note of what we look like so that you will recognize us on the day." Thus everyone would depart from the prison in amazement, and many of them began to believe.

18. The day of their victory dawned, and they marched from the prison to the amphitheater joyfully as though they were going to heaven, with calm faces, trembling, if at all, with joy rather than fear. Perpetua went along with shining countenance and calm step, as the beloved of God, as a wife of Christ, putting down everyone's stare by her own intense gaze. With them also was Felicitas, glad that she had safely given birth so that now she could fight the beasts, going from one blood bath to another, from the midwife to the gladiator, ready to wash after childbirth in a second baptism. They were then led up to the gates and the men were forced to put on the robes of priests of Saturn, the women the dress of the priestesses of Ceres. But the noble Perpetua strenuously resisted this to the end. "We came to this of our own free will that our freedom should not be violated. We agreed to pledge our lives provided that we would do no such thing. You agreed with us to do this." Even injustice recognized justice. The military tribune agreed. They were to be brought into the arena just as they were. Perpetua then began to sing a psalm: she was already treading on the head of the Egyptian. Revocatus, Saturninus, and Saturus began to warn the onlooking mob. Then when they came within sight of Hilarianus, they suggested by their motions and gestures: "You have condemned us, but God will condemn you" was what they were saying.

At this the crowds became enraged and demanded that they be scourged before a line of gladiators. And they rejoiced at this that they had obtained a share in the Lord's sufferings.

19. But he who said, "Ask and you shall receive," answered their prayer by giving each one the death he had asked for. For when ever they would discuss among themselves their desire for martyrdom, Saturninus indeed insisted that he wanted to be exposed to all the different beasts, that his crown might be all the more glorious. And so at the outset of the contest he and Revocatus were matched with a leopard, and then while in the stocks they were attacked by a bear. As for Saturus, he dreaded nothing more than a bear, and he counted on being killed by one bite of a leopard. Then he was matched with a wild boar; but the gladiator who had tied him to the animal was gored by the boar and died a few days after the contest, whereas Saturus was only dragged

along. Then when he was bound in the stocks awaiting the bear, the animal refused to come out of the cages, so that Saturus was called back once more unhurt.

20. For the young women, however, the Devil had prepared a mad heifer. This was an unusual animal, but it was chosen that their sex might be matched with that of the beast. So they were stripped naked, placed in nets and thus brought out into the arena. Even the crowd was horrified when they saw that one was a delicate young girl and the other was a woman fresh from child birth with the milk still dripping from her breasts. And so they were brought back again and dressed in unbelted tunics.

First the heifer tossed Perpetua and she fell on her back. Then sitting up she pulled down the tunic that was ripped along the side so that it covered her thighs, thinking more of her modesty than of her pain. Next she asked for a pin to fasten her untidy hair: for it was not right that a martyr should die with her hair in disorder, lest she might seem to be mourning in her hour of triumph.

Then she got up. And seeing that Felicitas had been crushed to the ground, she went over to her, gave her hand, and lifted her up. Then the two stood side by side. But the cruelty of the mob was by now appeased, and so they were called back through the Gate of Life.

There Perpetua was held up by a man named Rusticus who was at the time a catechumen and kept close to her. She awoke from a kind of sleep (so absorbed had she been in ecstasy in the Spirit) and she began to look about her. Then to the amazement of all she said: "When are we going to be thrown to that heifer or whatever it is?"

When told that this had already happened, she refused to believe it until she noticed the marks of her rough experience on her person and her dress. Then she called for her brother and spoke to him together with the catechumens and said: "You must all *stand fast in the faith* and love one another, and do not be weakened by what we have gone through."

21. At another gate Saturus was earnestly addressing the soldier Pudens. "It is exactly," he said, "as I foretold and predicted. So far not one animal has touched me. So now you may believe me with all your heart: I am going in there and I shall be finished off with one bite of the leopard." And immediately as the contest was coming to a close a leopard was let loose, and after one bite Saturus was so drenched with blood that as he came away the mob roared in witness to his second baptism: "Well washed! Well washed [an ironic use of the greeting to bathers in the public baths]!" For well washed indeed was one who had been bathed in this manner.

Then he said to the soldier Pudens: "Goodbye. Remember me, and remember the faith. These things should not disturb you but rather strengthen you."

And with this he asked Pudens for a ring from his finger, and dipping it into his wound he gave it back to him again as a pledge and as a record of his bloodshed.

Shortly after he was thrown unconscious with the rest in the usual spot to have his throat cut. But the mob asked that their bodies be brought out into the open that their eyes might be the guilty witnesses of the sword that pierced their flesh. And so the martyrs got up and went to the spot of their own accord as the people wanted them to, and kissing one another they sealed their martyrdom with the ritual kiss of peace. The others took the sword in silence and without moving, especially Saturus, who being the first to climb the stairway was the first to die. For once again he was waiting for Perpetua. Perpetua, however, had yet to taste more pain. She screamed as she was struck on the bone; then she took the trembling hand of the young gladiator and guided it to her throat. It was as though so great a woman, feared as she was by the unclean spirit, could not be dispatched unless she herself were willing.

Ah, most valiant and blessed martyrs! Truly are you called and chosen for the glory of Christ Jesus our Lord! And any man who exalts, honors, and worships his glory should read for the consolation of the Church these new deeds of heroism which are no less significant than the tales of old. For these new manifestations of virtue will bear witness to one and the same Spirit who still operates, and to God the Father almighty, to his Son Jesus Christ our Lord, to whom is splendor and immeasurable power for all the ages. Amen.

4. TACITUS

Germania

IN 98 THE ROMAN historian Cornelius Tacitus (ca. 56–ca. 120) wrote a brief description of the Germanic peoples living beyond the Rhine. The *Germania* was his second work, written after the *Life of Agricola* (a biography and tribute to his father-in-law and the elaboration of his life as a model for Roman senatorial behavior) but in the years before his two major historical works, the *Historiae* and *Annales*. His account is based on the writings of previous geographers and historians, especially Pliny the Elder's lost *German Wars*, as well as on interviews with people who had first-hand experience with the Germanic peoples. Although largely accurate in its details, the treatise organizes and filters Tacitus' data through the classical ethnological categories. Its purpose was less to inform Romans about the Germans than to criticize Roman customs and morals by contrasting them with those of the barbarians.

Source: *Tacitus. Dialogus, Agricola, Germania* (London: Heineman, 1914). *Germania* translated by Maurice Hutton, revised by D. LePan, 1989.

Further Reading: Ronald H. Martin, *Tacitus* (Berkeley: University of California Press, 1981).

1 Undivided Germany is separated from the Gauls, Rhaetians, and Pannonians by the rivers Rhine and Danube: from the Sarmatians and Dacians by mutual fear or mountains: the rest of it is surrounded by the ocean, which enfolds wide peninsulas and islands of vast expanse, some of whose people and kings have but recently become known to us: war has lifted the curtain.

The Rhine, rising from the inaccessible and precipitous crest of the Rhaetian Alps, after turning west for a reach of some length is lost in the North Sea. The Danube pours from the sloping and not very lofty ridge of Mount Abnoba, and visits several peoples on its course, until at length it emerges by six of its channels into the Pontic Sea: the seventh mouth is swallowed in marshes.

2 As for the Germans themselves, I should suppose them to be native to the area and only very slightly blended with new arrivals from other races or regions; for in ancient times people who sought to migrate reached their destination by sea and not by land; while, in the second place, the great ocean on the further side of Germany—at the opposite end of the world, so to speak, from us—is rarely visited by ships from our world. Besides, even apart from the perils of an awful and unknown sea, who would have left Asia or Africa or Italy to look for Germany? With its wild scenery and harsh climate it is pleasant neither to live in nor look upon unless it be one's home.

Their ancient hymns—the only record of history which they possess—celebrate a god Tuisto, a scion of the soil, and his son Mannus as the founders of their race. To Mannus they ascribe three sons, from whose names the tribes of the seashore came to be known as Ingaevones, the central tribes as Herminones, and the rest as Istaevones. Some authorities, using the license which pertains to antiquity, claim more sons for the god and a larger number of race names: Marsi, Gambrivii, Suebi, Vandilii. These are, they say, real and ancient names, while the name of "Germany" is new. The first tribes in fact to cross the Rhine and expel the Gauls, though now called Tungri, were then styled Germans: so little by little the name—a tribal, not a national, name—prevailed, until the whole people were called by the artificial name of "Germans," first only by the victorious tribe in order to intimidate the Gauls, but afterwards among themselves also.

3 The authorities also record how Hercules appeared among the Germans, and on the eve of battle the natives chant "Hercules, the first of brave men." They use as well another chant—"barritus" is the name they use for it—to inspire courage; and they forecast the results of the coming battle from the sound of the cry. Intimidation or timidity depends on the concert of the warriors; the chant seems to them to mean not so much unison of voices as union of hearts; the object they specially seek is a certain volume of hoarseness, a crashing roar, their shields being brought up to their lips, that the voice may swell to a fuller and deeper note by means of the echo.

To return. Ulysses also—in the opinion of some authorities—was carried during his long and legendary wanderings into this ocean, and reached the lands of Germany. Asciburgium, which stands on the banks of the Rhine and has inhabitants today, was founded, they say, and named by him; further, they say that an altar dedicated by Ulysses, who added to his own inscription that of his father Laertes, was once found at the same place, and that certain monuments and barrows, marked with Greek letters, are still extant on the borderland between Germany and Rhaetia. I have no intention of furnishing evidence to establish or refute these assertions: every one according to his temperament may minimize or magnify their credibility.

4 Personally, I agree with those who hold that in the peoples of Germany there has been given to the world a nation untainted by intermarriage with other peoples, a peculiar people and pure, like no one but themselves; whence it comes that their physique, in spite of their vast numbers, is identical: fierce blue eyes, red hair, tall frames. They are powerful too, but only spasmodically; they have no fondness for feats of endurance or for hard work. Nor are they well able to bear thirst and heat; to cold and hunger, thanks to the climate and the soil, they are accustomed.

5 There are some varieties in the appearance of the country, but in general it is a land of bristling forests and unhealthy marshes; the rainfall is heavier on the side of Gaul; the winds are higher on the side of Noricum and Pannonia.

It is fertile in cereals, but unkind to fruit-bearing trees; it is rich in flocks and herds, but for the most part they are undersized. Even the cattle lack natural beauty and majestic brows. The pride of the people is rather in the number of their beasts, which constitute the only form of wealth they value.

The gods have denied them gold and silver, whether in mercy or in wrath I find it hard to say. Not that I would assert that Germany has no veins bearing gold or silver, for who has explored there? At any rate, they are not affected, like their neighbors, by the use and possession of such things. One may see among them silver vases, given as gifts to their commanders and chieftains, but treated as of no more value than earthenware. Although the border tribes for purposes of trade treat gold and silver as precious metals, and recognize and collect certain coins of our money, the tribes of the interior practice barter in the simpler and older fashion. The coinage which appeals to them is the old and long-familiar: the denarii with milled edges, showing the two-horsed chariot. They prefer silver to gold: not that they have any feeling in the matter, but because a number of silver pieces is easier to use for people whose purchases consist of cheap objects of general utility.

6 Even iron is not plentiful among them, as may be gathered from the style of their weapons. Few have swords or the longer kind of lance: they carry short spears, in their language "*frameae*," with a narrow and small iron head, so sharp and so handy in use that they fight with the same weapon, as circumstances demand, both at close quarters and at a distance. The mounted man is content with a shield and *framea*: the infantry launch showers of

spears as well, each man a volley, and are able to hurl these great distances, for they wear no outer clothing, or at most a light cloak.

Their garb is for the most part quite plain; only shields are decorated, each a few colours. Few have breast-plates: scarcely one or two at most have metal or hide helmets. The horses are conspicuous for neither beauty nor speed; but then neither are they trained like our horses to run in shifting circles: the Germans ride them forwards only or to the right, with but one turn from the straight, dressing the line so closely as they wheel that no one is left behind. In general there is more strength in their infantry, and accordingly cavalry and infantry fight in one body; the swift-footed infantryman, whom they pick out of the whole body of warriors and place in front of the line, are well-adapted to cavalry battles. The number of these men is fixed—one hundred from each canton, and among themselves "the Hundred" is the precise name they use. What was once a number only has become a title and a distinction. The battle-line itself is arranged in wedges. To retire, provided you press on again, they treat as a question of tactics, not of cowardice; they carry off their dead and wounded even in drawn battles. To have abandoned one's shield is the height of disgrace. The man so dishonored cannot be present at religious rites, nor attend a council; many survivors of war have ended their infamy with a noose.

7 They choose their kings on the grounds of birth, their generals on the basis of courage. The authority of their kings is not unlimited or arbitrary; their generals control them by example rather than command, the troops admiring their energy and the conspicuous place they take in front of the line. But anything beyond this—capital punishment, imprisonment, even a blow—is permitted only to the priests, and then not as a penalty or under the general's orders, but in obedience to the god whom they believe accompanies them on campaign. Certain totems, in fact, and emblems are fetched from groves and carried into battle. The strongest incentive to courage lies in this, that neither chance nor casual grouping makes the squadron or the wedge, but family and kinship. Close at hand, too, are their dearest, so that they hear the wailing voices of women and cries of children. Here are the witnesses who are in each man's eyes most precious; here the praise he covets most. The warriors take their wounds to mother and wife, who do not shrink from counting the hurts and demanding a sight of them: they give to the combatants food and encouragement.

8 Tradition relates that some battles that seemed lost have been restored by the women, by their incessant prayers and by the baring of their breasts; for so it is brought home to the men that slavery, which they dread much more keenly on their women's account, is close at hand. It follows that the loyalty of those tribes is more effectively guaranteed if you hold, among other hostages, girls of noble birth.

Further, they conceive that in women is a certain uncanny and prophetic sense: they neither scorn to consult them nor slight their answers. In the reign of Vespasian of happy memory we saw Velaeda treated as a deity by many during a long period; but in ancient times they also reverenced Albruna and many other women—in no spirit of flattery, nor for the manufacture of goddesses.

9 Of the gods they most worship Mercury, to whom on certain days they count even the sacrifice of human life lawful. Hercules and Mars they appease with such animal life as is permissible. A section of the Suebi sacrifices also to Isis[1]: the cause and origin of this foreign worship I have not succeeded in discovering, except that the emblem itself, which takes the shape of a Liburnian galley, shows that the ritual is imported.

Apart from this they deem it incompatible with the majesty of the heavenly host to confine the gods within walls, or to mold them into any likeness of the human face. They consecrate groves and thickets, and they give divine names to that mysterious presence which is visible only to the eyes of faith.

10 To divination and casting lots they pay as much attention as any one. The method of drawing lots is uniform. A bough is cut from a nut-bearing tree

---

1   Egyptian mother goddess widely worshiped in the Roman Empire.

and divided into slips. These are distinguished by certain runes and spread casually and at random over white cloth. Afterwards, should the inquiry be official the priest of the state, if private the father of the family in person, after prayers to the gods and with eyes turned to heaven takes up one slip at a time till he has done this on three separate occasions. After taking the three he interprets them according to the runes which have already been stamped on them. If the message is a prohibition, no inquiry on the same matter is made during the same day; if the message gives permission, further confirmation is required by means of divination. Among the Germans divination by consultation of the cries and flight of birds is well known. Another form of divination peculiar to them is to seek the omens and warnings furnished by horses.

In the same groves and thickets are fed certain white horses, never soiled by mortal use. These are yoked to a sacred chariot and accompanied by the priest and king, or other chief of the state, who then observe their neighing and snorting. On no other form of divination is more reliance placed, not merely by the people but also by their leaders. The priests they regard as the servants of the gods, but the horses are their confidants.

They have another method of taking divinations, by means of which they probe the issue of serious wars. A member of the tribe at war with them is somehow or other captured and pitted against a selected champion of their own countrymen, each in his tribal armor. The victory of one or the other is taken as a presage.

11 On small matters the chiefs consult, on larger questions the community; but with this limitation: even when the decision rests with the people, the matter is considered first by the chiefs. They meet, unless there is some unforeseen and sudden emergency, on days set apart—when the moon is either new or full. They regard these times as the most auspicious for the transaction of business. They count not days as we do, but by nights and their decisions and proclamations are subject to this principle; the night, that is, seems to take precedence over the day.

It is a foible of their freedom that they do not meet at once and when commanded, but waste two or three days by dilatoriness in assembling. When they are finally ready to begin, they take their seats carrying arms. Silence is called for by the priests, who then have the power to force obedience. Then a king or a chief is listened to, in order of age, birth, glory in war, or eloquence. Such figures command attention through the prestige which belongs to their counsel rather than any prescriptive right to command. If the advice tendered is displeasing, the people reject it with groans; if it pleases them, they clash their spears. The most complimentary expression of assent is this martial approbation.

12 At this assembly it is also permissible to lay accusations and to bring capital charges. The nature of the death penalty differs according to the offense: traitors and deserters are hung from trees; cowards, poor fighters and notorious evil-livers are plunged in the mud of marshes with a hurdle on their heads. These differences of punishment follow the principle that crime should be blazoned abroad by its retribution, but shameful actions hidden. Lighter offenses have also a measured punishment. Those convicted are fined a certain number of horses or cattle. Part of the fine goes to the king or the state; part is paid to the person who has brought the charge or to his relatives. At the same gatherings are selected chiefs, who administer law through the cantons and villages: each of them has one hundred assessors from the people to act as his responsible advisors.

13 They do no business, public or private, without arms in their hands; yet the custom is that no one takes arms until the state has endorsed this competence. Then in the assembly itself one of the chiefs or his father or his relatives equip the young man with shield and spear. This corresponds with them to the toga, and is youth's first public distinction; before that he was merely a member of the household, now he becomes a member of the state. Conspicuously high birth, or great services on the part of their ancestors may win the chieftain's approval even for the very young men. They mingle with the others, men of maturer strength and tested by long years and have no shame to be seen among the chief's retinue. In the retinue itself degrees are observed at the chief's discretion;

there is great rivalry among the retainers to decide who shall have the first place with chief, and among the chieftains as to who shall have the largest and most enthusiastic retinue. It is considered desirable to be surrounded always with a large band of chosen youths—glory in peace, in war protection. Nor is this only so with a chief's own people; with neighboring states also it means name and fame for a man that his retinue be conspicuous for number and character. Such men are in demand for embassies, and are honored with gifts; often, by the mere terror of their name, they are able to break the back of opposition in war.

14 When the battlefield is reached it is a reproach for a chief to be surpassed in prowess and a reproach for his retinue not to equal the prowess of its chief. Much worse, though, is to have left the field and survived one's chief; this means lifelong infamy and shame. To protect and defend the chief and to devote one's own feats to his glorification is the gist of their allegiance. The chief fights for victory, but the retainers for the chief.

Should it happen that the community where they are born has been drugged with long years of peace and quiet, many of the high-born youth voluntarily seek those tribes which are at the time engaged in some war; for rest is unwelcome to the race, and they distinguish themselves more readily in the midst of uncertainties: besides, you cannot keep up a great retinue except by war and violence. It is the generous chief that the warriors expect to give them a particular war-horse or murderous and masterful spear. Banquetings and a certain rude but lavish outfit take the place of salary. The material for this generosity comes through war and foray. You will not so readily persuade a German to plow the land and wait for the year's returns as to challenge the enemy and earn wounds. Besides, it seems limp and slack to get with the sweating of your brow what you can gain with the shedding of your blood.

15 When they are not warring, they spend much time hunting, but more in idleness—creatures who eat and sleep, the best and bravest warriors doing nothing, having handed over the charge of their home, hearth and estate to the women and the old men and the weakest members of the family. For themselves they vegetate by that curious incongruity of temperament which makes of the same men such lovers of slumber and such haters of quiet.

It is the custom in their states for each man to bestow upon the chief unasked some portion of his cattle or crops. It is accepted as a compliment, but also serves the chief's needs. The chiefs appreciate still more the gifts of neighboring tribes, which are sent not merely by individuals but by the community—selected horses, heavy armor, bosses and bracelets; by this time we have taught them to accept money also.

16 It is well known that none of the German tribes live in cities, that individually they do not permit houses to touch each other. They live separated and scattered, according as spring-water, meadow, or grove appeals to each man. They lay out their villages not, after our fashion, with buildings contiguous and connected; everyone keeps a clear space round his house, whether it be a precaution against the chances of fire or just ignorance of building. They have not even learned to use quarry-stone or tiles: the timber they use for all purposes is unshaped, and stops short of all ornament or attraction. Certain buildings are smeared with a stucco bright and glittering enough to be a substitute for paint and frescoes. They are in the habit also of opening pits in the earth and piling dung in quantities on the roof, as a refuge from the winter or a root-house, because such places lessen the harshness of frost. If an enemy comes, he lays waste the open, but the hidden and buried houses are either missed outright or escape detection just because they require a search.

17 For clothing all wear a cloak, fastened with a clasp, or, in its absence a thorn. They spend whole days on the hearth round the fire with no other covering. The richest men are distinguished by the wearing of underclothes—not loose, like those of Parthians and Sarmatians, but drawn tight, throwing each limb into relief.

They wear also the skins of wild beasts: the tribes adjoining the river-bank in casual fashion, the inland tribes with more attention, since they cannot depend on traders for clothing. The beasts for this purpose are selected, and the hides so taken are checkered with the pied skins of the creatures native to the outer ocean and its unknown waters.

The women have the same dress as the men, except that very often long linen garments, striped with purple, are in use for the women. The upper part of this costume does not widen into sleeves; their arms and shoulders are therefore bare, as is the adjoining portion of the breast.

18 None the less the marriage tie with them is strict; you will find nothing in their character to praise more highly. They are almost the only barbarians who are content with a wife apiece. The very few exceptions have nothing to do with passion, but consist of those with whom polygamous marriage is eagerly sought for the sake of their high birth.

As for the dowry, it is not the wife who brings it to the husband, but the husband to the wife. The parents and relations are present to approve these gifts—gifts not devised for ministering to female fads, nor for the adornment of the person of the bride, but oxen, a horse and bridle, a shield and spear or sword. It is to share these things that the wife is taken by the husband, and she in turn brings some piece of armor to her husband. Here is the gist of the bond between them, here in their eyes its mysterious sacrament, the divinity which hedges it. Thus the wife may not imagine herself released from the practice of heroism, released from the chances of war; she is warned by the very rites with which her marriage begins that she comes to share with her husband hard work and peril. Her fate will be the same as his in peace and in panic, her risks the same. This is the moral of the yoked oxen, of the bridled horse, of the exchange of arms; so she must live and so she must die. The things she takes she is to hand over inviolate to her children, fit to be taken by her daughters-in-law and passed on again to her grandchildren.

19 So their life is one of fenced-in chastity. There is no arena with its seductions, no dinner-tables with their provocations to corrupt them. Of the exchange of secret letters men and women alike are innocent. Adultery is very rare among these people. Punishment is prompt and is the husband's prerogative: the wife's hair is close-cropped, she is stripped of her clothes, her husband drives her from his house in the presence of his relatives and pursues her with blows through the length of the village. For lost chastity there is no pardon; neither beauty nor youth nor wealth will find the sinner a husband. No one laughs at vice there; no one calls seduction the spirit of the age. Better still are those tribes where only maids marry and where a woman makes an end, once and for all, with the hopes and vows of a wife. So they take one husband only, just as one body and one life, in order that there may be no second thoughts, no belated fancies, and in order that their excessive desire may be not for the man, but for marriage. To limit the number of their children or to put to death any of the later children is considered abominable. Good habits have more force with them than good laws elsewhere.

20 The children in every house grow up amid nakedness and squalor into that girth of limb and frame which is to our people a marvel. Its own mother suckles each at her breast; children are not passed on to nursemaids and wet-nurses.

Nor can master be recognized from servant by having been spoiled in his upbringing. Master and servant live in the company of the same cattle and on the same mud floor till years separate the free-born and character claims her own.

The virginity of young men is long preserved, and their powers are therefore inexhaustible. Nor for the girls is there any hothouse forcing; they pass their youth in the same way as the boys. Their stature is as tall; when they reach the same strength they are mated, and the children reproduce the vigor of the parents. Sisters' children mean as much to their uncle as to their father: some tribes regard this blood-tie as even closer and more sacred than that between son and father, and in taking hostages make it the basis of their demand, as though they thus secure loyalty more surely and have a wider hold on the family.

However, so far as succession is concerned, each man's children are his heirs, and there is no will. If there are no children, the nearest degrees of relationship for the holding of property are brothers, paternal uncles, and maternal uncles. The more relations a man has and the larger the number of his connections by marriage, the more influence has he in his age; it does not pay to have no ties.

21 It is incumbent to take up the feuds of one's father or kinsman no less than his friendships. But such feuds do not continue unappeasable; even homicide may be atoned for by a fixed number of cattle and sheep. The whole family thereby receives satisfaction to the public advantage, for feuds are more dangerous among a free people.

No race indulges more lavishly in hospitality and entertainment. To close the door against any human being is a crime. Everyone according to his means welcomes guests generously. Should there not be enough, he who is your host goes with you next door, without an invitation, but it makes no difference; you are received with the same courtesy. Stranger or acquaintance, no one distinguishes them where the right of hospitality is concerned. It is customary to speed the parting guest with anything he fancies. There is the same readiness in turn to ask of him: gifts are the Germans' delight, but they neither count upon what they have given, nor are bound by what they have received.

22 On waking from sleep, which they generally prolong in the day, they wash, usually in warm water, since winter bulks so large in their lives. After washing they take a meal, seated apart, each at his own table. Then, arms in hand, they proceed to business, or, just as often, to revelry. To drink heavily day and night is a reproach to no man. Brawls are frequent, as you would expect among heavy drinkers: these seldom terminate with abuse, more often in wounds and bloodshed. Nevertheless the mutual reconciliation of enemies, the forming of family alliances, the appointment of chiefs, the question even of war or peace, are usually debated at these banquets; as though at no other time were the mind more open to obvious, or better warmed to larger, thoughts. The people are without craft or cunning, and expose in the freedom of revelry the heart's secrets; so every mind is bared to nakedness. On the next day the matter is handled afresh. So the principle of each debating season is justified: deliberation comes when people are incapable of pretense, but

decision when they are secure from illusion.

23 For drink they use a liquid distilled from barley or wheat, after fermentation has given it a certain resemblance to wine. The tribes nearest the river also buy wine. Their diet is simple: wild fruit, fresh venison, curdled milk. They banish hunger without sauce or ceremony, but there is not the same temperance in facing thirst: if you humor their drunkenness by supplying as much as they crave, they will be vanquished through their vices as easily as on the battlefield.

24 Their shows are all of one kind, and the same whatever the gathering may be: naked youths, for whom this is a form of professional acting, jump and bound between swords and upturned spears. Practice has made them dexterous and graceful. Yet they do not perform for hire or gain: however daring be the sport, the spectator's pleasure is the only price they ask.

Gambling, one may be surprised to find, they practise in all seriousness in their sober hours, with such recklessness in winning or losing that, when all else has failed, they stake personal liberty on the last and final throw.

The loser faces voluntary slavery; though he may be the younger and the stronger man, he will still allow himself to be bound and sold. Such is the Germans' persistence in wrongdoing, or their good faith, as they themselves style it. Slaves so acquired they trade, in order to deliver themselves as well as the slave from the humiliation involved in such victory.

25 Their other slaves are not organized in our fashion: that is, by a division of the services of life among them. Each of them remains master of his own house and home: the master requires from the slave as serf a certain quantity of grain or cattle or clothing. The slave so far is subservient; but the other services of the household are discharged by the master's wife and children. To beat a slave or coerce him with hard labor and imprisonment is rare. If slaves are killed, it is not usually to preserve strict discipline, but in a fit of fury like an enemy, except that there is no penalty to be paid.

Freedmen are not much above slaves. Rarely are they of any weight in the household, never in politics, except in those states which have kings. Then they climb above the free-born and above the nobles; in other states the disabilities of the freedman are the evidence of freedom.

26 To charge interest, let alone interest at high rates, is unknown and the principle of avoiding usury is accordingly better observed than if there had been actual prohibition.

Land is taken up by a village as a whole, in quantity according to the number of cultivators. They then distribute it among themselves on the basis of rank, such distribution being made easy by the amount of land available. They change the arable land yearly, and there is still land to spare, for they do not strain the fertility and resources of the soil by tasking them, through the planting of vineyards, the setting apart of water-meadows, or the irrigation of vegetable gardens. Grain is the only harvest required of the land. Accordingly the year itself is not divided into as many parts as with us: winter, spring, summer have a meaning and a name; the gifts of autumn and its name are alike unknown.

27 In burial there is no ostentation. The only ceremony is to burn the bodies of their notables with special kinds of wood. They build a pyre, but do not load it with palls or spices. The man's armor and some of his horse also is added to the fire. The tomb is a mound of turf: the difficult and tedious tribute of a monument they reject as too heavy on the dead. Weeping and wailing they put away quickly; sorrow and sadness linger. Lamentation becomes women: men must restrain their emotion.

So much in general we have ascertained concerning the origin of the undivided Germans and their customs. I shall now set forth the habits and customs of the several nations, and the extent to which they differ from each other; and explain what tribes have migrated from Germany to the Gallic provinces.

28 That the fortunes of Gaul were once higher than those of Germany is recorded on the supreme authority of Julius of happy memory. Therefore it is easy to believe that the Gauls at one time crossed over into Germany; small chance there was of the river preventing each tribe, as it became powerful, from seizing new land, which had not yet been divided into powerful kingdoms. Accordingly the country between the Hercynian forest and the rivers Rhine and Moenus was occupied by the Helvetii, and the country beyond by the Boii, both Gallic races. The name Boihaemum still testifies to the old traditions of the place, though here has been a change of occupants.

Whether, however, the Aravisci migrated into Pannonia from the Osi, or the Osi into Germany from the Aravisci, must remain uncertain, since their speech, habits, and type of character are still the same. Originally, in fact, there was the same misery and the same freedom on either bank of the river, the same advantages and the same drawbacks.

The Treveri and Nervi conversely go out of their way in their ambition to claim a German origin, as though this illustrious ancestry delivers them from any affinity with the indolent Gaul.

On the river bank itself are planted certain peoples who are unquestionably German: Vangiones, Triboci, Nemetes. Not even the Ubii, though they have earned the right to be a Roman colony and prefer to be called "Agrippinenses" after the name of their founder, blush to own their German origin. They originally came from beyond the river. After they had given proof of their loyalty, they were placed in charge of the bank itself, in order to block the way to others, not in order to be under supervision.

Of all these races the most manly are the Batavi, who occupy only a short stretch of the river bank, but with it the island in the stream. They were once a tribe of the Chatti, and on account of a rising at home they crossed the river onto lands which later became part of the Roman Empire. Their distinction persists and the emblem of their ancient alliance with us; they are not insulted, that is, by the exaction of tribute, and there is no tax-farmer to oppress them. Immune from burdens and contributions, and set apart for fighting purposes only, they are reserved for war to be, as it were, our arms and weapons. Equally loyal are the tribe of the Mattiaci; for the greatness of the Roman nation has projected the awe felt for our empire beyond the Rhine, and beyond the long-established frontier. So by site and territory they belong to their own bank, but by sentiment and thought they act with us, and are similar in all respects to the Batavi, except that hitherto both the soil and the climate of their land make them more lively.

I should not count among the people of Germany, though they have established themselves beyond the Rhine and Danube, the tribes who cultivate "the tithe-lands." All the wastrels of Gaul, plucking courage from misery, took possession of that disputed land. Later, since the frontier line has been drawn and the garrisons pushed forward, these lands have been counted as an outlying corner of the empire and a part of the Roman province.

30 Beyond these people are the Chatti. The front of their settlements begins with the Hercynian forest. The land is not so low and marshy as the other states of the level German plain; yet even where the hills cover a considerable territory they gradually fade away, and so the Hercynian forest, after escorting its Chatti to the full length of their settlement, drops them in the plain. This tribe has hardier bodies than the others, close-knit limbs, a forbidding expression, and more strength of the intellect. There is much method in what they do, for Germans at least, and much shrewdness. They elect magistrates and listen to the man elected; know their place in the ranks and recognize opportunities; reserve their attack; have a time for everything; entrench at night; distrust luck, but rely on courage; and—the rarest thing of all, and usually attained only through Roman discipline—depend on the initiative of the general rather than on that of the soldier. Their whole strength lies in their infantry, whom they load with iron tools and baggage, in addition to their arms. Other Germans may be seen going to battle, but the Chatti go to war. Forays and casual fighting are rare with them. The latter method no doubt is part of the strength of cavalry—to win suddenly, that is, and as suddenly to retire. For the speed of cavalry is near allied to panic, but the deliberate action of infantry is more likely to be resolute.

31 One ceremony that is practised by other German peoples only occasionally, depending on preference, has with the Chatti become a convention: to let the hair and beard grow when a youth has attained manhood, and to remove this manly facial garb only after an enemy has been slain. Standing above the bloody spoil, they dismantle their faces again, and advertise that then and not before have they paid the price of their birthpangs, and are worthy of their kin and country. Cowards and weaklings remain unkempt. The bravest also wear a ring of iron—the badge of shame on other occasions among this people— as a symbolic band from which each man frees himself by the slaughter of an enemy. This symbolism is very popular, and men already growing grey still wear this uniform for the pointing finger of friend and foe. Every battle begins with these men: the front rank is made up of them and is a curious sight. But, even in peace they do not allow a tamer life to enervate them. None of them has a house or land or any business. Wherever they go they are entertained; they waste the possessions of others and are indifferent to their own, until age and loss of blood make them unequal to such demanding heroism.

32 Next to the Chatti come the Usipi and Tencteri, on the Rhine banks where the river has ceased to shift its bed and has become fit to serve as a boundary. The Tencteri, in addition to the general reputation as the race of warriors, excel in the accomplishments of trained horsemen. Even the fame of the Chattan infantry is not greater than that of their cavalry. Their ancestors established the precedent, and succeeding generations vie with them. Horsemanship is the diversion of children, the center of competition for youth, and the abiding interest of age. Horses descend with servants, house, and regular inheritance. The heir to the horse, however, is not as in other things the eldest son but the confident soldier and the better man.

33 Next to the Tencteri one originally came across the Bructeri. The Chamavi and Angrivarii are said to have trekked there recently, after the Bructeri had been expelled or cut to pieces by the joint action of neighboring peoples. Whether this was from disgust at their arrogance or from the attractions of plunder, or because Heaven leans to

the side of Rome cannot be said. But Heaven did not grudge us a dramatic battle; over sixty thousand men fell, not before the arms and spears of Rome, but—what was even a greater triumph for us—merely to delight our eyes. Long may such behavior last, I pray, and persist among the German nations—if they feel no love for us, at least may they feel hatred for each other. Now that the destinies of the empire have passed their zenith, Fortune can guarantee us nothing better than discord among our foes.

34 The Angrivarii and Chamavi are surrounded to the south by the Dulgubnii and the Chasuarii and other tribes not so well known to history. To the north follow the Frisii: they are called the Greater or Lesser Frisii according to the measure of their strength. These two tribes border the Rhine down to the ocean, and also fringe the great lakes which the fleets of Rome navigate. In that quarter we have even reached the ocean itself, and beyond our range are rumored to stand the pillars of Hercules. Did Hercules really visit those shores, or is it only that we have agreed to credit all marvels everywhere to him? Nor did Drusus Germanicus lack audacity as an explorer but Ocean vetoed inquiry into either itself or Hercules. Soon the attempt was abandoned, and it came to be judged more reverent to believe in the works of deities than to comprehend them.

35 Thus far we have been enquiring into Western Germany. At this point the country falls away with a great bend towards the north. First in this area come the Chauci. Though they start next to the Frisii and occupy part of the seaboard, they also border on all of the tribes just mentioned, and finally edge away south as far as the Chatti. This vast block of territory is not merely held by the Chauci but filled by them. They are the noblest of the German tribes, and prefer to protect their vast domain by justice alone. They are neither grasping nor lawless; in peaceful seclusion they provoke no wars and despatch no raiders on marauding forays. The special proof of their great strength is, indeed, just this, that they do not depend for their superior position on injustice. Yet they are ready with arms, and, if circumstances should require, with armies, men and horse in abundance. So, even though they keep the peace, their reputation does not suffer.

36 Bordering the Chauci and the Chatti are the Cherusci. For long years they have been unassailed and have encouraged an abnormal and languid peacefulness. It has been a pleasant rather than a sound policy. With lawlessness and strength on either side of you, you will find no true peace; where might is right, self-control and righteousness are titles reserved for the stronger. Accordingly, the Cherusci, who were once styled just and generous, are now described as indolent and shortsighted, while the good luck of the victorious Chatti has been credited to them as wisdom. The fall of the Cherusci dragged down the Fosi also, a neighboring tribe. They share the adversity of the Cherusci on even terms, though they have only been dependents in their prosperity.

37 This same "sleeve" or peninsula of Germany is the home of the Cimbri, who dwell nearest the ocean. They are a small state today, but rich in memories. Broad traces of their ancient fame are still extant—a spacious camp on each bank (of the Rhine), by the circuit of which you can even today measure the size and skill of the nation and get some sense of that mighty trek.

Our city was in its six hundred and fortieth year when the Cimbrian armies were first heard of, in the consulship of Caecilius Metellus and Papirius Carbo. If we count from that date to the second consulship of the Emperor Trajan, the total amounts to about two hundred and ten years. For that length of time the conquest of Germany has been in process. Between the beginning and end of that long period there have been many mutual losses. Neither Samnite nor Carthaginian, neither Spain nor Gaul, nor even the Parthians have taught us more lessons. The German fighting for liberty has been a keener enemy than the absolutism of Arsaces. What has the East to taunt us with, apart from the overthrow of Crassur—the East which itself fell at the feet of a Ventidius and lost Pacorus?

But the Germans routed or captured Carbo and Cassius and Aurelius Scaurus and Servilius Caepio and Gnaeus Mallius, and wrested five consular armies in one campaign from the people of Rome, and even from a Caesar wrested Varus and three legions with him. Nor was it without paying the price that Marius smote them in Italy, and Julius of happy memory in Gaul, and Drusus, Nero, and Germanicus in their own homes. Soon after that the great tragedy threatened by Gaius Caesar turned into a farce. Then came peace until, on the opportunity offered by our own dissensions and by civil war, the Germans carried the legions' winter quarters by storm and even aspired to the Gallic provinces. Finally they were repulsed, and they have in recent years gratified us with more triumphs than victories.

38 Now I must speak of the Suebi, who do not comprise only one tribe, as with the Chatti and the Tencteri. Rather they occupy the greater part of Germany, and are still distinguished by special national names, though styled in general Suebi. One mark of the race is to comb the hair back over the side of the face and tie it low in a knot behind. This distinguishes the Suebi from other Germans, and the free-born of the Suebi from the slave. In other tribes, whether from some relationship to the Suebi or, as often happens, from imitation, the same thing may be found, but it is rare and confined to the period of youth. Among the Suebi, even till the hair is grey they twist the rough locks backward, and often knot them on the very crown. The chieftains wear theirs somewhat more ornamentally, and are to this extent interested in appearances, but innocently so. It is not for making love or being made love to, but rather that men who are to face battle are—in the eyes of their foes—more terrifying with these adornments heightening their stature.

39 The Semnones are described as the most ancient and best-born tribe of the Suebi; this is confirmed by religious rite. At fixed seasons all the tribes of the same blood gather with their delegations at a certain forest that is hallowed by visions beheld by their ancestors and by the awe of the ages. After publicly offering up a human life, they celebrate the grim "initiation" of their barbarous worship. There is a further tribute which they pay to the grove; no one enters it until he has been bound with a chain. He puts off his freedom, and advertises in his person the might of the deity. If he

chances to fall, he must not be lifted up or rise—he must writhe along the ground until he is out again. The whole superstition comes to this, that it was here where the race arose, here where dwells the god who is lord of all things; everything else is subject to him. The prosperity of the Semnones enforces the idea; they occupy one hundred cantons, and their magnitude leads them to consider themselves the head of the Suebi.

40 The Langobardi, conversely, are distinguished by lack of number. Set in the midst of numberless and powerful tribes, they find safety not in submissiveness, but in peril and pitched battle. Then come the Reudigni and the Aviones, and the Anglii and the Varini, the Eudoses and Suardones and Nuithones. These tribes are protected by forests and rivers. There is nothing noteworthy about them individually, except that they worship in common Nerthus, or Mother Earth, and conceive her as intervening in human affairs, and riding in procession through the cities of men. In an island of the ocean is a holy grove, and in it a consecrated chariot, covered with robes. A single priest is permitted to touch it; he interprets the presence of the goddess in her shrine, and follows with deep reverence as she rides away, drawn by cows. Then come days of rejoicing, and all places keep holiday, as many as she thinks worthy to receive and entertain her. They make no war, take no arms. Every weapon is put away; peace and quiet rules until the same priest returns the goddess to her temple, when she has had her fill of the society of mortals. After this the chariot and the robes, and, if you are willing to credit it, the deity in person, are washed in a sequestered lake. Slaves perform this duty and are then straightaway swallowed by the same lake. Hence a mysterious terror and ignorance full of piety as to what it may be which men only behold to die.

41 These sections on the Suebi extend into the more secluded parts of Germany. Nearer to us—to follow the course of the Danube, as before I followed the Rhine—comes the state of the Hermunduri. They are loyal to Rome, and with them alone among Germans business is transacted not on the river bank, but far within the frontier in the most thriving colony of the province of

Rhaetia. They cross the river everywhere without supervision, and while we let other peoples see only our fortified camps, to them we have thrown open our houses and homes because they do not covet them. Among the Hermunduri rises the River Albis—a river once famous, now a name only.

42 Next to the Hermunduri are the Naristi and then the Marcomani and the Quadi. The fame and strength of the Marcomani are outstanding; their very home was won by their bravery, through the expulsion in ancient times of the Boii. Nor are the Naristi and Quadi inferior to them. These tribes are, so to speak, the brow of Germany, so far as Germany is wreathed by the Danube. The Marcomani and the Quadi retained kings of their own race down to our time—the noble houses of Maroboduus and Tudrus. Now they submit to foreign kings also, but the force and power of their kings rest on the influence of Rome. Occasionally they are assisted by our armed intervention: more often by subsidies, out of which they get as much help.

43 Behind them are the Marsigni, Cotini, Osi, and Buri, enclosing the Marcomani and Quadi from the rear. Among these the Marsigni and Buri in language and culture recall the Suebi. As for the Cotini and Osi, the Gallic tongue of the first and the Pannonian of the second prove not to be Germans; so does their submission to tribute. This tribute is imposed upon them as foreigners in part by the Sarmatae, in part by the Quadi. The Cotini, to their shame, even have iron-mines to work. All these peoples have little level land, but occupy the summits and ridges of mountains. In fact, a continuous range parts and cuts Suebia in two.

Beyond the range are many races. The most widely diffused name is that of the Lugii, which extends over several states. It will be sufficient to have named the strongest: Harii, Helvecones, Manimi, Elisii, Nahanarvali. Among the Nahanarvali one is shown a grove, the seat of a prehistoric ritual. A priest presides in female dress; but according to the Roman interpretation the gods recorded in this fashion are Castor and Pollux. That at least is the spirit of the godhead here recognized, whose name is the Alci. No images are in use; there is no sign of foreign superstition. Nevertheless they worship these deities as brothers and as youths.

But to return. The Harii, apart from the strength in which they surpass the peoples just enumerated, are fierce in nature, and augment this natural ferocity by the help of art and season. They blacken their shields and dye their bodies; they choose pitchy nights for their battles; by sheer panic and darkness they strike terror like an army of ghosts. No enemy can face this novel and, as it were, phantasmagorical vision. In every battle, after all, the eye is conquered first.

Beyond the Lugii is the monarchy of the Gotones. The hand upon the reins closes somewhat tighter here than among the other tribes of Germans, but not so tight yet as to destroy freedom. Then immediately following them and on the ocean are the Rugii and the Lemovii. The distinguishing features of all these tribes are round shields, short swords, and a submissive bearing before their kings.

44 Beyond these tribes the states of the Suiones, on the ocean, possess not merely arms and men but powerful fleets. The style of their ships differs in this respect: there is a prow at each end, with a beak ready to be driven forwards. They neither work a ship with sails, nor add oars in banks to the side; the gearing of the oars is detached as on certain rivers, and reversible as occasion demands for movement in either direction.

Among these peoples respect is paid to wealth, and one man is accordingly supreme, with no restrictions and with an unchallenged right to obedience. Nor is there any general carrying of arms here, as among the other Germans. Rather they are locked up in charge of a custodian, who is a slave. The ocean forbids sudden inroads from enemies; and, besides, bands of armed men, with nothing to do, easily become riotous: it is not in the king's interest to put a noble or a freemen or even a freedman in charge of the arms.

45 Beyond the Suiones is another sea, sluggish and almost motionless, with which the earth is girdled and bounded. Evidence for this is furnished by the brilliance of the last rays of the sun, which remain so bright from his setting to his rising

again as to dim the stars. Faith adds further that the sound of the sun's emergence is audible and the forms of his horses visible, with the spikes of his crown.

So far (and here rumor speaks the truth), and so far only, does Nature reach.

We must now turn to the right-hand shore of the Suebic Sea. Here it washes the tribes of the Aestii; there customs and dress are Suebic, but their language is nearer British.

They worship the mother of the gods. As an emblem of that superstition they wear the figures of wild boars; this boar takes the place of arms or of any other protection, and guarantees to the votary of the goddess a mind at rest even in the midst of foes. They use swords rarely, clubs frequently. Grain and other products of the earth they cultivate with a patience out of keeping with the lethargy customary to Germans. They ransack the sea also, and are the only people who gather in the shallows and on the shore itself amber, which they call in their tongue "glaesum."

Nor have they, being barbarians, inquired or learned what substance or process produces it. It lay there long among the rest of the flotsam and jetsam of the sea, until Roman luxury gave it a name. To the natives it is useless. It is gathered crude and is forwarded to Rome unshaped; the barbarians are astonished to be paid for it. Yet you may infer that it is the gum of trees; certain creeping and even winged creatures are continually found embedded in it. They have been entangled in its liquid form, and, as the material hardens, are imprisoned. I should suppose therefore that just as in the secluded places in the East, where frankincense and balsam are exuded, so in the islands and lands of the West there are groves and glades more than ordinarily luxuriant. These are tapped and liquefied by the rays of the sun as it approached, and ooze into the nearest sea, whence by the force of tempests they are stranded on the shores opposite. If you try the qualities of amber by setting fire to it, it kindles like a torch, feeds an oily and odorous flame, and soon dissolves into something like pitch and resin.

Adjacent to the Suiones come the tribes of the Sitones, resembling them in all other respects, and differing only in this, that among them the woman rules. To this extent they have fallen lower not merely than freemen but even than slaves.

46 Here Suebia ends. As for the tribes of the Peucini, Venedi, and Fenni, I am in doubt whether to count them as Germans or Sarmatians. Though the Peucini, whom some men call Bastarnae, in language, culture, fixity of habitation, and house-building, conduct themselves as Germans, all are dirty and lethargic. The faces of the chiefs, too, owing to intermarriage, wear to some extent the degraded aspect of Sarmatians while the Venedi have contracted many Sarmatian habits; they are caterans [robbers], infesting all the hills and forests which lie between the Peucini and the Fenni.

And yet these peoples are preferably entered as Germans, since they have fixed abodes, and carry shields, and delight to use their feet and to run fast, all of which are traits opposite to those of the Sarmatians, who live in wagons and on horseback.

The Fenni live in astonishing barbarism and disgusting misery: no arms, no horses, no fixed homes; herbs for their food, skins for their clothing, earth for their bed. Arrows are all their wealth and for want of iron they tip them with bone. This same hunting is the support of the women as well as of the men, for they accompany the men freely and claim a share of the spoil. Nor have their infants any shelter against wild beasts and rain, except the covering afforded by a few intertwined branches. To these the hunters return: these are the refuge of age; and yet the people think it happier so than to groan over field labor, be encumbered with house-service, and be for ever exchanging their own and their neighbors' goods with alternate hopes and fears. Unconcerned towards men, unconcerned towards Heaven, they have achieved a consummation very difficult: they have nothing even to ask for.

Beyond this all else that is reported is legendary: that the Hellusii and Oxiones have human faces and features, the limbs and bodies of beasts. It has not been so ascertained, and I shall leave it an open question.

5. JORDANES

History of the Goths

JORDANES WAS A SIXTH-CENTURY Goth or Alan who had been notary to Gunthigis-Baza, a Gothic chieftain, but who spent part of his later life in Constantinople, where in 551 he composed his *History of the Goths*, largely a summary of Cassidorus' now lost work of the same name. It combines genuine Gothic oral traditions into the traditional framework of classical ethnography to present the Goths within the broader perspective of Roman and Christian history.

Source: *The Gothic History of Jordanes*, trans. Charles C. Mierow (Princeton: Princeton University Press, 1915).

Further Reading: James J. O'Donnell, "The Aims of Jordanes," *Historia: Zeitschrift für Alte Geschichte* 31 (1982): 223–40.

The United Goths

IV Now from this island of Scandza, as from a hive of races or a womb of nations, the Goths are said to have come forth long ago under their king, Berig by name. As soon as they disembarked from their ships and set foot on the land, they straightway gave their name to the place. And even to-day it is said to be called Gothiscandza. Soon they moved from here to the abodes of the Ulmerugi, who then dwelt on the shores of Ocean, where they pitched camp, joined battle with them and drove them from their homes. Then they subdued their neighbors, the Vandals, and thus added to their victories. But when the number of the people increased greatly and Filimer, son of Gadaric, reigned as king—about the fifth since Berig—he decided that the army of the Goths with their families should move from that region. In search of suitable homes and pleasant places they came to the land of Scythia, called *Oium* in that tongue. Here they were delighted with the great richness of the country, and it is said that when half the army had been brought over, the bridge whereby they had crossed the river fell in utter ruin, nor could anyone thereafter pass to or fro. For the place is said to be surrounded by quaking bogs and an encircling abyss, so that by this double obstacle nature has made it inaccessible. And even to-day one may hear in that neighborhood the lowing of cattle and may find traces of men, if we are to believe the stories of travelers, although we must grant that they hear these things from afar.

This part of the Goths, which is said to have crossed the river and entered with Filimer into the country of Oium, came into possession of the desired land, and there they soon came upon the race of the Spali, joined battle with them and won the victory. Thence the victors hastened to the farthest part of Scythia, which is near the sea of Pontus; for so the story is generally told in their early songs, in almost historic fashion. Ablabius also, a famous chronicler of the Gothic race, confirms this in his most trustworthy account. Some of the ancient writers also agree with the tale. Among these we may mention Josephus, a most reliable relator of annals, who everywhere follows the truth and unravels from the beginning the origin of things;—but why he has omitted the beginnings of the race of the Goths, of which I have spoken, I do not know. He barely mentions Magog of that stock, and says they were Scythians by race and were called so by name.

Before we enter on our history, we must describe the boundaries of this land, as it lies.

V Now Scythia borders on the land of Germany as far as the source of the river Ister and the expanse of the Morsian Swamp. It reaches even to the rivers Tyra, Danaster and Vagosola, and the great Danaper, extending to the Taurus range—not the mountains in Asia but our own, that is, the

Scythian Taurus—all the way to Lake Maeotis. Beyond Lake Maeotis it spreads on the other side of the straits of Bosphorus to the Caucasus Mountains and the river Araxes. Then it bends back to the left behind the Caspian Sea, which comes from the northeastern ocean in the most distant parts of Asia, and so is formed like a mushroom, at first narrow and then broad and round in shape. It extends as far as the Huns, Albani and Seres. This land, I say—namely, Scythia, stretching far and spreading wide—has on the east the Seres, a race that dwelt at the very beginning of their history on the shore of the Caspian Sea. On the west are the Germans and the river Vistula; on the arctic side, namely the north, it is surrounded by Ocean; on the south by Persis, Albania, Hiberia, Pontus and the farthest channel of the Ister, which is called the Danube all the way from the mouth to the source. But in that region where Scythia touches the Pontic coast it is dotted with towns of no mean fame:—Borysthenis, Olbia, Callipolis, Cherson, Theodosia, Careon, Myrmicion and Trapezus. These towns the wild Scythian tribes allowed the Greeks to build to afford them the means of trade. In the midst of Scythia is the place that separates Asia and Europe, I mean the Rhipaeian mountains, from which the mighty Tanais flows. This river enters Maeotis, a marsh having circuit of one hundred and four miles and never subsiding to a depth of less than eight cubits.

In the land of Scythia to the westward dwells, first of all, the race of the Gepidae, surrounded by great and famous rivers. For the Tisia flows through it on the north and northwest, and on the southwest is the great Danube. On the east it is cut by the Flutausis, a swiftly eddying stream that sweeps whirling into the Ister's waters. Within these rivers lies Dacia, encircled by the lofty Alps as by a crown. Near their left ridge, which inclines toward the north, and beginning at the source of the Vistula, the populous race of the Venethi dwell, occupying a great expanse of land. Though their names are now dispersed amid various clans and places, yet they are chiefly called Sclaveni and Antes. The abode of the Sclaveni extends from the city of Noviodunum and the lake called Mursianus to the Danaster, and northward as far as the Vistula. They have swamps and forests

for their cities. The Antes, who are the bravest of these peoples dwelling in the curve of the sea of Pontus, spread from the Danaster to the Danaper, rivers that are many days' journey apart. But on the shore of Ocean, where the floods of the river Vistula empty from three mouths, the Vidivarii dwell, a people gathered out of various tribes. Beyond them the Aesti, a subject race, likewise hold the shore of Ocean. To the south dwell the Acatziri, a very brave tribe ignorant of agriculture, who subsist on their flocks and by hunting. Farther away and above the Sea of Pontus are the abodes of the Bulgares, well known from the disasters our neglect has brought upon us. From this region the Huns, like a fruitful root of bravest races, sprouted into two hordes of people. Some of these are called Altziagiri, others Sabiri; and they have different dwelling places. The Altziagiri are near Cherson, where the avaricious traders bring in the goods of Asia. In summer they range the plains, their broad domains, wherever the pasturage for their cattle invites them, and betake themselves in winter beyond the sea of Pontus. Now the Hunuguri are known to us from the fact that they trade in marten skins. But they have been cowed by their bolder neighbors.

We read that in their first abode the Goths dwelt in the land of Scythia near Lake Maeotis; in their second in Moesia, Thrace and Dacia, and in their third they dwelt again in Scythia, above the sea of Pontus. Nor do we find anywhere in their written records legends which tell of their subjection to slavery in Britain or in some other island, or of their redemption by a certain man at the cost of a single horse. Of course if anyone in our city says that the Goths had an origin different from that I have related, let him object. For myself, I prefer to believe what I have read, rather than put trust in old wives' tales.

To return, then, to my subject. The aforesaid race of which I speak is known to have had Filimer as king while they remained in their first home in Scythia near Maeotis. In their second home, that is, in the countries of Dacia, Thrace and Moesia, Zalmoxes reigned, whom many annals mention as a man of remarkable learning in philosophy. Yet even before this they had a learned man Zeuta, and after him Dicineus; and the third was Zalmoxes of whom I have made mention above.

Nor did they lack teachers of wisdom. Wherefore the Goths have ever been wiser than other barbarians and were nearly like the Greeks, as Dio relates, who wrote their history and annals with a Greek pen. He says that those of noble birth among them, from whom their kings and priests were appointed, were called first Tarabostesei and then Pilleati. Moreover so highly were the Getae praised that Mars, whom the fables of poets call the god of war, was reputed to have been born among them. Hence Vergil says:

"Father Gradivus rules the Getic fields."

Now Mars has always been worshipped by the Goths with cruel rites, and captives were slain as his victims. They thought that he who is lord of war ought to be appeased by the shedding of human blood. To him they devoted the first share of the spoil, and in his honor arms stripped from the foe were suspended from trees. And they had more than all other races a deep spirit of religion, since the worship of this god seemed to be really bestowed upon their ancestor.

In their third dwelling place, which was above the Sea of Pontus, they had now become more civilized and, as I have said before, were more learned. Then the people were divided under ruling families. The Visigoths served the family of the Balthi and the Ostrogoths served the renowned Amali. They were the first race of men to string the bow with cords, as Lucan, who is more of a historian than a poet, affirms:

"They string Armenian bows with Getic
    cords."

In earliest times they sang of the deeds of their ancestors in strains of song accompanied by the cithara; chanting of Eterpamara, Hanala, Fritigern, Vidigoia and others whose fame among them is great; such heroes as admiring antiquity scarce proclaims its own to be. Then, as the story goes, Vesosis waged a war disastrous to himself against the Scythians, whom ancient tradition asserts to have been the husbands of the Amazons. Concerning these female warriors Orosius speaks in convincing language. Thus we can clearly prove that Vesosis then fought with the Goths, since we know surely that he waged war with the husbands of the Amazons. They dwelt at that time along a bend of Lake Maeotis, from the river Borysthenes, which the natives call the Danaper, to the stream of the Tanais. By the Tanais I mean the river which flows down from the Rhipaeian mountains and rushes with so swift a current that when the neighboring streams or Lake Maeotis and the Bosphorus are frozen fast, it is the only river that is kept warm by the rugged mountains and is never solidified by the Scythian cold. It is also famous as the boundary of Asia and Europe. For the other Tanais is the one which rises in the mountains of the Chrinni and flows into the Caspian Sea. The Danaper begins in a great marsh and issues from it as from its mother. It is sweet and fit to drink as far as half-way down its course. It also produces fish of a fine flavour and without bones, having only cartilage as the frame-work of their bodies. But as it approaches the Pontus it receives a little stream called Exampaeus, so very bitter that although the river is navigable for the length of a forty days' voyage, it is so altered by the water of this scanty stream as to become tainted and unlike itself, and flows thus tainted into the sea between Greek towns of Callipidae and Hypanis. At its mouth there is an island named Achilles. Between these two rivers is a vast land filled with forests and treacherous swamps.

VI This was the region where the Goths dwelt when Vesosis, king of the Egyptians, made war upon them. Their king at that time was Tanausis. In a battle at the river Phasis (whence come the birds called pheasants, which are found in abundance at the banquets of the great all over the world), Tanausis, king of the Goths, met Vesosis, king of the Egyptians, and there inflicted a severe defeat upon him, pursuing him even to Egypt. Had he not been restrained by the waters of the impassable Nile and the fortifications which Vesosis had long ago ordered to be made against the raids of the Ethiopians, he would have slain him in his own land. But finding he had no power to injure him there, he returned and conquered almost all Asia and made it subject and tributary to Sornus, king of the Medes, who was then his dear friend. At that time some of his victorious army, seeing that the subdued provinces were rich and fruitful, deserted their companies and of their own accord remained in various parts of Asia. From their name or race Pompeius Trogus says the stock of the Parthians had its origin. Hence even to-day in the Scythian tongue they are called Parthi, that is, Deserters. And in consequence of their descent they are archers—almost alone among the nations of Asia—and are very valiant warriors. Now in regard to the name, though I have said they were called Parthi because they were deserters, some have traced the derivation of the word otherwise, saying that they were called Parthi because they fled from their kinsmen. Now when this Tanausis, king of the Goths, was dead, his people worshipped him as one of their gods.

VII After his death, while the army under his successors was engaged in an expedition in other parts, a neighboring tribe attempted to carry off women of the Goths as booty. But they made a brave resistance, as they had been taught to do by their husbands, and routed in disgrace the enemy who had come upon them. When they had won this victory, they were inspired with greater daring. Mutually encouraging each other, they took up arms and chose two of the bolder, Lampeto and Marpesia, to act as their leaders. While they were in command, they cast lots both for the defense of their own country and the devastation of other lands. So Lampeto remained to guard their native land and Marpesia took a company of women and led this novel army into Asia. After conquering various tribes in war and making others their allies by treaties, she came to the Caucasus. There she remained for some time and gave the place the name Rock of Marpesia, of which also Vergil makes mention:

"Like to hard flint or the Marpesian Cliff."

It was here Alexander the Great afterwards built gates and named them the Caspian Gates, which now the tribe of the Lazi guard as a Roman outpost. Here, then the Amazons remained for some time and were much strengthened. Then they departed and crossed the river Halys, which flows near the city of Gangra, and with equal success subdued Armenia, Syria, Cilicia, Galatia, Pisidia and all the places of Asia. Then they turned to Ionia and Aeolia, and made provinces of them after their surrender. Here they ruled for some time and even founded cities and camps bearing their name. At Ephesus also they built a very

costly and beautiful temple for Diana, because of her delight in archery and the chase—arts to which they were themselves devoted. Then these Scythian-born women, who had by such a chance gained control over the kingdoms of Asia, held them for almost a hundred years, and at last came back to their own kinsfolk in the Marpesian rocks I have mentioned above, namely in the Caucasus mountains....

VIII Fearing their race would fail, they sought marriage with neighboring tribes. They appointed a day for meeting once in every year, so that when they should return to the same place on that day in the following year each mother might give over to the father whatever male child she had borne, but should herself keep and train for warfare whatever children of the female sex were born. Or else, as some maintain, they exposed the males, destroying the life of the ill-fated child with a hate like that of a stepmother. Among them childbearing was detested, though everywhere else it is desired. The terror of their cruelty was increased by common rumor; for what hope, pray, would there be for a captive, when it was considered wrong to spare even a son? Hercules, they say fought against them and overcame Menalippe, yet more by guile than by valor. Theseus, moreover, took Hippolyte captive, and of her he begat Hippolytus. And in later times the Amazons had a queen named Penthesilea, famed in the tales of the Trojan war. These women are said to have kept their power even to the time of Alexander the Great.

IX But say not "Why does a story which deals with the men of the Goths have so much to say of their women?" Hear, then, the tale of the famous and glorious valor of the men. Now Dio,[1] the historian and diligent investigator of ancient times, who gave to his work the title "Getica" (and the Getae we have proved in a previous passage to be Goths, on the testimony of Orosius Paulus)—this Dio, I say, makes mention of a later king of theirs named Telefus. Let no one say that this name is quite foreign to the Gothic tongue, and let no one who is ignorant cavil at the fact that the tribes of men make use of many names, even as

---

1   Cassius Dio, (ca. 155–ca. 229), Roman historian whose history of Rome in 80 books, written in Greek, only partially survives.

the Romans borrow from the Macedonians, the Greeks from the Romans, the Sarmatians from the Germans, and the Goths frequently from the Huns. This Telefus, then, a son of Hercules by Auge, and the husband of a sister of Priam, was of towering stature and terrible strength. He matched his father's valor by virtues of his own and also recalled the traits of Hercules by his likeness in appearance. Our ancestors called his kingdom Moesia. This province has on the east the mouths of the Danube, on the south Macedonia, on the west Histria and on the north the Danube. Now this king we have mentioned carried on wars with the Greeks, and in their course he slew in battle Thesander, the leader of Greece. But while he was making a hostile attack upon Ajax and was pursuing Ulysses, his horse became entangled in some vines and fell. He himself was thrown and wounded in the thigh by a javelin of Achilles, so that for a long time he could not be healed. Yet, despite his wound, he drove the Greeks from his land. Now when Telefus died, his son Eurypylus succeeded to the throne, being a son of the sister of Priam, king of the Phrygians. For love of Cassandra he sought to take part in the Trojan war, that he might come to the help of her parents and his own father-in-law; but soon after his arrival he was killed....

XI Then when Buruista was king of the Goths, Dicineus came to Gothia at the time when Sulla ruled the Romans. Buruista received Dicineus and gave him almost royal power. It was by his advice that the Goths ravaged the lands of the Germans, which the Franks now possess. Then came Caesar, the first of all the Romans to assume imperial power and to subdue almost the whole world, who conquered all kingdoms and even seized islands lying beyond our world, reposing in the bosom of Ocean. He made tributary to the Romans those that knew not the Roman name even by hearsay, and yet was unable to prevail against the Goths, despite his frequent attempts. Soon Gaius Tiberius reigned as third emperor of the Romans, and yet the Goths continued in their kingdom unharmed. Their safety, their advantage, their one hope lay in this, that whatever their counselor Dicineus advised should by all means be done; and they judged it expedient that they should labor for its accomplishment. And when he saw that their

minds were obedient to him in all things and that they had natural ability, he taught them almost the whole of philosophy, for he was a skilled master of this subject. Thus by teaching them ethics he restrained their barbarous customs; by imparting a knowledge of physics he made them live naturally under laws of their own, which they possess in written form to this day and call *belagines*. He taught them logic and made them skilled in reasoning beyond all other races; he showed them practical knowledge and so persuaded them to abound in good works. By demonstrating theoretical knowledge he urged them to contemplate the courses of the twelve signs and the planets passing through them, and the whole of astronomy. He told them how the disc of the moon gains increase or suffers loss, and showed them how much the fiery globe of the sun exceeds in size our earthly planet. He explained the names of the three hundred and forty-six stars and told through what signs in the arching vault of the heavens they glide swiftly from their rising to their setting. Think, I pray you, what pleasure it was for these brave men, when for a little space they had leisure from warfare, to be instructed in the teachings of philosophy! You might have seen one scanning the position of the heavens and another investigating the nature of plants and bushes. Here stood one who studied the waxing and waning of the moon, while still another regarded the labors of the sun and observed how these bodies which were hastening to go toward the east are whirled around and borne back to the west by the rotation of the heavens. When they had learned the reason, they were at rest. These and various other matters Dicineus taught the Goths in his wisdom and gained marvelous repute among them, so that he ruled not only the common men but their kings. He chose from among them those that were at that time of noblest birth and superior wisdom and taught them theology, bidding them worship certain divinities and holy places. He gave the name of Pilleati to the priests he ordained, I suppose because they offered sacrifice having their heads covered with tiaras, which we otherwise call *pillei*. But he bade them call the rest of their race Capillati. This name the Goths accepted and prized highly, and they retain it to this day in their songs.

After the death of Dicineus, they held Comosicus in almost equal honor, because he was not inferior in knowledge. By reason of his wisdom he was accounted their priest and king, and he judged the people with the greatest uprightness.

XII When he too had departed from human affairs, Coryllus ascended the throne as king of the Goths and for forty years ruled his people in Dacia. I mean ancient Dacia, which the race of the Gepidae now possesses. This country lies across the Danube within sight of Moesia, and is surrounded by a crown of mountains. It has only two ways of access, one by way of Boutae and the other by Tapae. This Gothia, which our ancestors called Dacia and now, as I have said, is called Gepidia, was then bounded on the east by the Roxolani, on the west by the Iazygres, on the north by the Sarmatians and Basternae and on the south by the river Danube. The Iazyges are separated from the Roxolani by the Aluta river only.

And since mention has been made of the Danube, I think it not out of place to make brief notice of so excellent a stream. Rising in the fields of the Alamanni, it receives sixty streams which flow into it here and there in the twelve hundred miles from its source to its mouths in the Pontus, resembling a spine interwoven with ribs like a basket. It is indeed a most vast river. In the language of the Bessi it is called the Hister, and it has profound waters in its channel to a depth of quite two hundred feet. This stream surpasses in size all other rivers, except the Nile. Let this much suffice for the Danube. But let us now with the Lord's help return to the subject from which we have digressed.

XIII Now after a long time, in the reign of the Emperor Domitian, the Goths, through fear of his avarice, broke the truce they had long observed under other emperors. They laid waste the bank of the Danube, so long held by the Roman Empire, and slew the soldiers and their generals. Oppius Sabinus was then governor of that province, after Agrippa, while Dorpaneus held command over the Goths. Thereupon the Goths made war and conquered the Romans, cut off the head of Oppius Sabinus and invaded and boldly plundered many castles and cities belonging to the emperor. In this plight of his countrymen Domitian hastened with all his might to Illyricum, bringing with him the troops of almost the entire empire. He sent Fuscus before him as his general with picked soldiers. Then joining boats together like a bridge, he made his soldiers cross the river Danube above the army of Dorpaneus. But the Goths were on the alert. They took up arms and presently overwhelmed the Romans in the first encounter. They slew Fuscus, the commander, and plundered the soldiers' camp of its treasure. And because of the great victory they had won in this region, they thereafter called their leaders, by whose good fortune they seemed to have conquered, not mere men, but demigods, that is *Ansis*. Their genealogy I shall run through briefly, telling the lineage of each and the beginning and the end of this line. And do thou, O reader, hear me without repining; for I speak truly.

XIV Now the first of these heroes, as they themselves relate in their legends, was Gapt, who begat Hulmul. And Hulmul begat Augis; and Augis begat him who was called Amal, from whom the name of Amali comes. This Amal begat Hisarnis. Hisarnis moreover begat Ostrogotha, and Ostrogotha begat Hunuil, and Hunuil likewise begat Athal. Athal begat Achiulf and Oduulf. Now Achiulf begat Ansila and Ediulf, Vultuulf and Hermanaric. And Vultuulf begat Valaravans and Valaravans begat Vandalarius; Vandalarius begat Thiudimer and Valamir and Vidimer; and Thiudimer begat Theodoric. Theodoric begat Amalasuentha; Amalasuentha bore Athalaric and Mathesuentha to her husband Eutharic, whose race was thus joined to hers in kinship. For the aforesaid Hermanaric, the son of Achiulf, begat Hunimund, and Hunimund begat Thorismud. Now Thorismud begat Beremud, Beremud begat Veteric, and Veteric likewise begat Eutharic, who married Amalasuentha and begat Athalaric and Mathesuentha. Athalaric died in the years of his childhood, and Mathesuentha married Vitiges, to whom she bore no child. Both of them were taken together by Belisarius to Constantinople. When Vitiges passed from human affairs, Germanus the patrician, a nephew of the Emperor Justinian, took Mathesuentha in marriage and made her a Patrician Ordinary.[2] And of her he begat a son, also called Germanus. But upon the death of

---

2 A high Roman dignity.

Germanus, she determined to remain a widow. Now how and in what wise the kingdom of the Amali was overthrown we shall keep to tell in its proper place, if the Lord help us....

XVII From this city [Marcianople], as we were saying, the Getae returned after a long siege to their own land, enriched by the ransom they had received. Now the race of the Gepidae was moved with envy when they saw them laden with booty and so suddenly victorious everywhere, and made war on their kinsmen. Should you ask how the Getae and Gepidae are kinsmen, I can tell you in a few words. You surely remember that in the beginning I said the Goths went forth from the bosom of the island of Scandza with Berig, their king, sailing in only three ships toward the hither shore of Ocean, namely to Gothiscandza. One of these three ships proved to be slower than the others, as is usually the case, and thus is said to have given the tribe their name, for in their language *gepanta* means slow. Hence it came to pass that gradually and by corruption the name Gepidae was coined for them by way of reproach. For undoubtedly they too trace their origin from the stock of the Goths, but because, as I have said, *gepanta* means something slow and stolid, the word Gepidae arose as a gratuitous name of reproach. I do not believe this is very far wrong, for they are slow of thought and too sluggish for quick movement of their bodies.

These Gepidae were then smitten by envy while they dwelt in the province of Spesis on an island surrounded by the shallow waters of the Vistula. This island they called, in the speech of their fathers, Gepedoios; but it is now inhabited by the race of the Vividarii, since the Gepidae themselves have moved to better lands. The Vividarii are gathered from various races into this one asylum, if I may call it so, and thus they form a nation. So then, as we were saying, Fastida, king of the Gepidae, stirred up his quiet people to enlarge their boundaries by war. He overwhelmed the Burgundians, almost annihilating them, and conquered a number of other races also. He unjustly provoked the Goths, being the first to break the bonds of kinship by unseemly strife. He was greatly puffed up with vain glory, but in seeking to acquire new lands for his growing nation, he

only reduced the numbers of his own countrymen. For he sent ambassadors to Ostrogotha, to whose rule Ostrogoths and Visigoths alike, that is, the two peoples of the same tribe, were still subject. Complaining that he was hemmed in by rugged mountains and dense forests, he demanded one of two things, that Ostrogotha should either prepare for war or give up part of his lands to them. Then Ostrogotha, king of the Goths, who was a man of firm mind, answered the ambassadors that he did indeed dread such a war and that it would be a grievous and infamous thing to join battle with their kin—but he would not give up his lands. And why say more? The Gepidae hastened to take arms and Ostrogotha likewise moved his forces against them, lest he should seem a coward. They met at the town of Galtis, near which the river Auha flows, and there both sides fought with great valor; indeed the similarity of their arms and of their manner of fighting turned them against their own men. But the better cause and their natural alertness aided the Goths. Finally night put an end to the battle as a part of the Gepidae were giving way. Then Fastida, king of the Gepidae, left the field of slaughter and hastened to his own land, as much humiliated with shame and disgrace as formerly he had been elated with pride. The Goths returned victorious, content with the retreat of the Gepidae, and dwelt in peace and happiness in their own land as long as Ostrogotha was their leader.

XVIII After his death, Cniva divided the army into two parts and sent some to waste Moesia, knowing that it was undefended through the neglect of the emperors. He himself with seventy thousand men hastened to Euscia, that is, Novae. When driven from this place by the general Gallus, he approached Nicopolis, a very famous town situated near the Iatrus river. This city Trajan built when he conquered the Sarmatians and named it the City of Victory. When the Emperor Decius drew near, Cniva at last withdrew to the regions of Haemus, which were not far distant. Thence he hastened to Philippopolis, with his forces in good array. When the Emperor Decius learned of his departure, he was eager to bring relief to his own city and, crossing Mount Haemus, came to Beroa. While he was resting his horses and his weary army in that place, all at once Cniva and his Goths fell upon him like a thunderbolt. He cut the Roman army to pieces and drove the emperor, with a few who had succeeded in escaping, across the Alps again to Euscia in Moesia, where Gallus was then stationed with a large force of soldiers as guardian of the frontier. Collecting an army from this region as well as from Oescus, he prepared for the conflict of the coming war. But Cniva took Philippopolis after a long siege and then, laden with spoil, allied himself to Priscus, the commander in the city, to fight against Decius. In the battle that followed they quickly pierced the son of Decius with an arrow and cruelly slew him. His father saw it, and although he is said to have exclaimed, to cheer the hearts of his soldiers: "Let no one mourn; the death of one soldier is not a great loss to the republic," he was yet unable to endure it, because of his love for his son. So he rode against the foe, demanding either death or vengeance, and when he came back to Abrittus, a city of Moesia, he was himself cut off by the Goths and slain, thus making an end of his dominion and of his life. This place is to-day called the Altar of Decius, because he there offered strange sacrifices to idols before the battle.

XIX Then upon the death of Decius, Gallus and Volusianus succeeded to the Roman Empire. At this time a destructive plague, almost like death itself, such as we suffered nine years ago, blighted the face of the whole earth and especially devastated Alexandria and all the land of Egypt. The historian Dionysius[3] gives a mournful account of it and Cyprian,[4] our own bishop and venerable martyr in Christ, also describes it in his own book entitled "On Mortality." At this time the Goths frequently ravaged Moesia, through the neglect of the emperors. When a certain Aemilianus saw that they were free to do this, and that they could not be dislodged by anyone without great cost to the republic, he thought that he too might be able to achieve fame and fortune. So he seized the rule in Moesia and, taking all the soldiers he could gather, began to plunder cities and people. In the next few months, while an armed host was

being gathered against him, he wrought no small harm to the state. Yet he died almost at the beginning of his evil attempt, thus losing at once his life and the power he coveted. Now though Gallus and Volusianus, the emperors we have mentioned, departed this life after remaining in power for barely two years, yet during this space of two years which they spent on earth they reigned amid universal peace and favor. Only one thing was laid to their charge, namely the great plague. But this was an accusation made by ignorant slanderers, whose custom it is to wound the lives of others with their malicious bite. Soon after they came to power they made a treaty with the race of the Goths. When both rulers were dead, it was no long time before Gallienus usurped the throne.

XX While he was given over to luxurious living of every sort, Respa, Veduc and Thuruar, leaders of the Goths, took ship and sailed across the strait of the Hellespont to Asia. There they laid waste many populous cities and set fire to the renowned temple of Diana at Ephesus, which, as we have said before, the Amazons built. Being driven from the neighborhood of Bithynia, they destroyed Chalcedon, which Cornelius Avitus afterwards restored to some extent. Yet even to-day, though it is happily situated near the royal city, it still shows some traces of its ruin as a witness to posterity. After their success, the Goths recrossed the strait of the Hellespont, laden with booty and spoil, and returned along the same route by which they had entered Asia, sacking Troy and Ilium on the way. These cities, which had scarce recovered a little from the famous war with Agamemnon, were thus destroyed anew by the hostile sword. After the Goths had thus devastated Asia, Thrace next felt their ferocity. For they went thither and presently attacked Anchiali, a city at the foot of Haemus and not far from the sea. Sardanapalus, king of the Parthians, had built this city long ago between an inlet of the sea and the base of Haemus. There they are said to have stayed for many days, enjoying the baths of the hot springs which are situated about twelve miles from the city of Anchiali. There they gush from the depths

---

3   Dionysius of Alexandria, third-century Egyptian bishop.
4   Cyprian, Bishop of Carthage (d. 258).

of their fiery source, and among the innumerable hot springs of the world they are particularly famous and efficacious to heal the sick.

XXI After these events, the Goths had already returned home when they were summoned at the request of the Emperor Maximian to aid the Romans against the Parthians. They fought for him faithfully, serving as auxiliaries. But after Caesar Maximian by their aid had routed Narseus, king of the Persians, the grandson of Sapor the Great, taking as spoil all his possessions, together with his wives and his sons, and when Diocletian had conquered Achilles in Alexandria and Maximianus Herculius had broken the Quinquegentiani in Africa, thus winning peace for the empire, they began rather to neglect the Goths.

Now it had been a hard matter for the Roman army to fight against any nations whatsoever without them. This is evident from the way in which the Goths were so frequently called upon. Thus they were summoned by Constantine to bear arms against his kinsman Licinius. Later, when he was vanquished and shut up in Thessalonica and deprived of his power, they slew him with the sword of Constantine the victor. In like manner it was the aid of the Goths that enabled him to build the famous city that is named after him, the rival of Rome, inasmuch as they entered into a truce with the emperor and furnished him forty thousand men to aid him against various peoples. This body of men, namely, the Allies, and the service they rendered in war are still spoken of in the land to this day. Now at that time they prospered under the rule of their kings Ariaric and Aoric. Upon their death Geberich appeared as successor to the throne, a man renowned for his valor and noble birth.

XXII For he was the son of Hilderith, who was the son of Ovida, who was the son of Nidada; and by his illustrious deeds he equaled the glory of his race. Soon he sought to enlarge his country's narrow bounds at the expense of the race of the Vandals and Visimar, their king. This Visimar was of the stock of the Asdingi, which is eminent among them and indicates a most warlike descent, as Dexippus the historian relates. He states furthermore that by reason of the great extent of their country they could scarcely come from Ocean to our frontier in a year's time. At that time they dwelt in the land where the Gepidae now live, near the rivers Marisia, Miliare, Gilpil and the Grisia, which exceeds in size all previously mentioned. They then had on the east the Goths, on the west the Marcomanni, on the north the Hermunduli and on the south the Hister, which is also called the Danube. At the time when the Vandals were dwelling in this region, war was begun against them by Geberich, king of the Goths, on the shore of the river Marisia which I have mentioned. Here the battle raged for a little while on equal terms. But soon Visimar himself, the king of the Vandals, was overthrown, together with the greater part of his people. When Geberich, the famous leader of the Goths, had conquered and spoiled the Vandals, he returned to his own place whence he had come. Then the remnant of the Vandals who had escaped, collecting a band of their unwarlike folk, left their ill-fated country and asked Emperor Constantine for Pannonia. Here they made their home for about sixty years and obeyed the commands of the emperors like subjects. A long time afterward they were summoned thence by Stilicho, Master of the Soldiery, Ex-Consul and Patrician, and took possession of Gaul. Here they plundered their neighbors and had no settled place of abode.

XXIII Soon Geberich, king of the Goths, departed from human affairs and Hermanaric, noblest of the Amali, succeeded to the throne. He subdued many warlike peoples of the north and made them obey his laws, and some of our ancestors have justly compared him to Alexander the Great. Among the tribes he conquered were the Golthescytha, Thiudos, Inaunxis, Vasinabroncae, Merens, Mordens, Imniscaris, Rogas, Tadzans, Athaul, Navego, Bubegenae and Coldae. But though famous for his conquest of so many races, he gave himself no rest until he had slain some in battle and then reduced to his sway the remainder of the tribe of the Heruli, whose chief was Alaric. Now the aforesaid race, as the historian Ablabius tells us, dwelt near Lake Maeotis in swampy places which the Greeks call *hele*; hence they were named Heluri. They were a people swift of foot, and on that account were the more swollen with pride, for there was at that time no race that did not choose from them its light-armed troops for battle. But though their quickness often saved them from others who made war upon them, yet they were overthrown by the slowness and steadiness of the Goths; and the lot of fortune brought it to pass that they, as well as the other tribes, had to serve Hermanaric, king of the Getae. After the slaughter of the Heruli, Hermanaric also took arms against the Venethi. This people, though despised in war, was strong in numbers and tried to resist him. But a multitude of cowards is of no avail, particularly when God permits an armed multitude to attack them. These people, as we started to say at the beginning of our account or catalogue of nations, though off-shoots from one stock, have now three names, that is, Venethi, Antes and Sclaveni. Though they now rage in war far and wide, in consequence of our neglect, yet at that time they were all obedient to Hermanaric's commands. This ruler also subdued by his wisdom and might the race of the Aesti, who dwell on the farthest shore of the German Ocean, and ruled all the nations of Scythia and Germany by his own prowess alone.

XXIV But after a short space of time, as Orosius relates, the race of the Huns, fiercer than ferocity itself, flamed forth against the Goths. We learn from old traditions that their origin was as follows: Filimer, king of the Goths, son of Gadaric the Great, who was the fifth in succession to hold the rule of the Getae after their departure from the island of Scandza—and who, as we have said, entered the land of Scythia with his tribe—found among his people certain witches, whom he called in his native tongue *Haliurunnae*. Suspecting these women, he expelled them from the midst of his race and compelled them to wander in solitary exile afar from his army. There the unclean spirits, who beheld them as they wandered through the wilderness, bestowed their embraces upon them and begat this savage race, which dwelt at first in the swamps, a stunted, foul and puny tribe, scarcely human and having no language save one which bore but slight resemblance to human speech. Such was the descent of the Huns who came to the country of the Goths.

This cruel tribe, as Priscus the historian relates, settled on the farther bank of the Maeotic swamp. They were fond of hunting and had no skill in any other art. After they had grown to a nation, they disturbed the peace of neighboring races by theft and rapine. At one time, while hunters of their tribe were as usual seeking for game on the farthest edge of Maeotis, they saw a doe unexpectedly appear to their sight and enter the swamp, acting as guide of the way; now advancing and again standing still. The hunters followed and crossed on foot the Maeotic swamp, which they had supposed was impassable as the sea. Presently the unknown land of Scythia disclosed itself and the doe disappeared. Now in my opinion the evil spirits, from whom the Huns are descended, did this from envy of the Scythians. And the Huns, who had been wholly ignorant that there was another world beyond Maeotis, were now filled with admiration for the Scythian land. As they were quick of mind, they believed that this path, utterly unknown to any age of the past, had been divinely revealed to them. They returned to their tribe, told them what had happened, praised Scythia and persuaded the people to hasten thither along the way they had found by the guidance of the doe. As many as they captured, when they thus entered Scythia for the first time, they sacrificed to Victory. The remainder they conquered and made subject to themselves. Like a whirlwind of nations they swept across the great swamp and at once fell upon the Alpidzuri, Alcildzuri, Itimari, Tuncarsi and Boisci, who bordered on that part of Scythia. The Alani also, who were their equals in battle, but unlike them in civilization, manners and appearance, they exhausted by their incessant attacks and subdued. For by the terror of their features they inspired great fear in those whom perhaps they did not really surpass in war. They made their foes flee in horror because their swarthy aspect was fearful, and they had, if I may call it so, a sort of shapeless lump, not a head, with pin-holes rather than eyes. Their hardihood is evident in their wild appearance, and they are beings who are cruel to their children on the very day they are born. For they cut the cheeks of the males with a sword, so that before they receive the nourishment of milk they must learn to endure wounds. Hence they grow old beardless and their young men are without comeliness, because a face furrowed by the sword spoils by its scars the natural beauty of a beard. They are short in stature, quick in bodily movement, alert horsemen, broad shouldered, ready in the use of bow and arrow, and have firm-set necks which are ever erect in pride. Though they live in the form of men, they have the cruelty of wild beasts.

When the Getae beheld this active race that had invaded many nations, they took fright and consulted with their king how they might escape from such a foe. Now although Hermanaric, king of the Goths, was the conqueror of many tribes, as we have said above, yet while he was deliberating on this invasion of the Huns, the treacherous tribe of the Rosomoni, who at that time were among those who owed him their homage, took this chance to catch him unawares. For when the king had given orders that a certain woman of the tribe I have mentioned, Sunilda by name, should be bound to wild horses and torn apart by driving them at full speed in opposite directions (for he was roused to fury by her husband's treachery to him), her brothers Sarus and Ammius came to avenge their sister's death and plunged a sword into Hermanaric's side. Enfeebled by this blow, he dragged out a miserable existence in bodily weakness. Balamber, king of the Huns, took advantage of his ill health to move an army into the country of the Ostrogoths, from whom the Visigoths had already separated because of some dispute. Meanwhile Hermanaric, who was unable to endure either the pain of his wound or the inroads of the Huns, died full of days at the great age of one hundred and ten years. The fact of his death enabled the Huns to prevail over those Goths who, as we have said, dwelt in the east and were called Ostrogoths.

The Divided Goths: Visigoths

XXV The Visigoths, who were their other allies and inhabitants of the western country, were terrified as their kinsmen had been, and knew not how to plan for their safety against the race of the Huns. After long deliberation by common consent they finally sent ambassadors into Romania to the Emperor Valens, brother of Valentinian, the elder emperor, to say that if he would give them part of Thrace or Moesia to keep, they would submit themselves to his laws and commands. That he might have greater confidence in them, they promised to become Christians, if he would give them teachers who spoke their language. When Valens learned this, he gladly and promptly granted what he had himself intended to ask. He received the Getae into the region of Moesia and placed them there as a wall of defense for his kingdom against other tribes. And since at that time the Emperor Valens, who was infected with the Arian perfidy, had closed all the churches of our party, he sent as preachers to them those who favored his sect. They came and straightway filled a rude and ignorant people with the poison of their heresy. Thus the Emperor Valens made the Visigoths Arians rather than Christians. Moreover, from the love they bore them, they preached the Gospel both to the Ostrogoths and to their kinsmen the Gepidae, teaching them to reverence the heresy, and they invited all people of their speech everywhere to attach themselves to this sect. They themselves, as we have said, crossed the Danube and settled Dacia Ripensis, Moesia and Thrace by permission of the emperor.

XXVI Soon famine and want came upon them, as often happens with a people not yet well settled in a country. Their princes and the leaders who ruled them in place of kings, that is Fritigern, Alatheus and Safrac, began to lament the plight of their army and begged Lupicinus and Maximus, the Roman commanders, to open a market. But to what will not the "cursed lust for gold" compel men to assent? The generals, swayed by avarice, sold them at a high price not only the flesh of sheep and oxen, but even the carcasses of dogs and unclean animals, so that a slave would be bartered for a loaf of bread or ten pounds of meat. When their goods and chattels failed, the greedy trader demanded their sons in return for the necessities of life. And the parents consented even to this, in order to provide for the safety of their children, arguing that it was better to lose liberty than life; and indeed it is better that one be sold, if he will be mercifully fed, than that he should be kept free only to die.

Now it came to pass in that troublous time that Lupicinus, the Roman general, invited Fritigern, a chieftain of the Goths, to a feast and, as the event revealed, devised a plot against him. But Fritigern, thinking no evil, came to the feast with a few followers. While he was dining in the praetorium he heard the dying cries of his ill-fated men, for, by order of the general, his soldiers were slaying his companions who were shut up in another part of the house. The loud cries of the dying fell upon ears already suspicious, and Fritigern at once perceived the treacherous trick. He drew his sword and with great courage dashed quickly from the banqueting-hall, rescued his men from their threatening doom and incited them to slay the Romans. Thus these valiant men gained the chance they had longed for—to be free to die in battle rather than to perish of hunger—and immediately took arms to kill the generals Lupicinus and Maximus. Thus that day put an end to the famine of the Goths and the safety of the Romans, for the Goths no longer as strangers and pilgrims, but as citizens and lords, began to rule the inhabitants and to hold in their own right all the northern country as far as the Danube.

When the Emperor Valens heard of this at Antioch, he made ready an army at once and set out for the country of Thrace. Here a grievous battle took place and the Goths prevailed. The emperor himself was wounded and fled to a farm near Hadrianople. The Goths, not knowing that an emperor lay hidden in so poor a hut, set fire to it (as is customary in dealing with a cruel foe), and thus he was cremated in royal splendor. Plainly it was a direct judgment of God that he should be burned with fire by the very men whom he had perfidiously led astray when they sought the true faith, turning them aside from the flame of love into the fire of hell. From this time the Visigoths, in consequence of their glorious victory, possessed Thrace and Dacia Ripensis as if it were their native land.

XXVII Now in the place of Valens, his uncle, the Emperor Gratian established Theodosius the Spaniard in the eastern empire. Military discipline was soon restored to a high level, and the Goths, perceiving that the cowardice and sloth of former princes had ended, became afraid. For the emperor was famed alike for his acuteness and discretion. By stern commands and by generosity and kindness he encouraged a demoralized army to deeds of daring. But when the soldiers, who had obtained a better leader by the change, gained new confidence, they sought to attack the Goths and drive them from the borders of Thrace. But as Emperor Theodosius fell so sick at this time that his life was almost despaired of, the Goths were again inspired with courage. Dividing the Gothic army, Fritigern set out to plunder Thessaly, Epirus and Achaia, while Alatheus and Safrac with the rest of the troops made for Pannonia. Now the Emperor Gratian had at this time retreated from Rome to Gaul because of the invasions of the Vandals. When he learned that the Goths were acting with greater boldness because Theodosius was in despair of his life, he quickly gathered an army and came against them. Yet he put no trust in arms, but sought to conquer them by kindness and gifts. So he entered on a truce with them and made peace, giving them provisions.

XXVIII When the Emperor Theodosius afterwards recovered and learned that the Emperor Gratian had made a compact between the Goths and the Romans, as he had himself desired, he was very well pleased and gave his assent. He gave gifts to King Athanaric, who had succeeded Fritigern, made an alliance with him and in the most gracious manner invited him to visit him in Constantinople. Athanaric very gladly consented and as he entered the royal city exclaimed in wonder, "Lo, now I see what I have often heard of with unbelieving ears," meaning the great and famous city. Turning his eyes hither and thither, he marveled as he beheld the situation of the city, the coming and going of the ships, the splendid walls, and the people of divers nations gathered like a flood of waters streaming from different regions into one basin. So too, when he saw the army in array, he said, "Truly the emperor is a god on earth, and whoso raises a hand against him is guilty of his own blood." In the midst of his admiration and the enjoyment of even greater honors at the hand of the emperor, he departed this life after the space of a few months. The emperor had such affection for him that he honored Athanaric even more when he was dead than during his lifetime, for he not only gave him a worthy burial, but himself walked before the bier at the funeral. Now when Athanaric was dead, his whole army continued in the service of the Emperor Theodosius and submitted to the Roman rule, forming as it were one body with the imperial soldiery. The former service of the Allies under the Emperor Constantine was now renewed and they were again called Allies. And since the emperor knew that they were faithful to him and his friends, he took from their number more than twenty thousand warriors to serve against the tyrant Eugenius who had slain Gratian and seized Gaul. After winning the victory over this usurper, he wreaked his vengeance upon him.

XXIX But after Theodosius, the lover of peace and of the Gothic race, had passed from human cares, his sons began to ruin both empires by their luxurious living and to deprive their Allies, that is to say the Goths, of the customary gifts. The contempt of the Goths for the Romans soon increased, and for fear their valor would be destroyed by long peace, they appointed Alaric king over them. He was of famous stock, and his nobility was second only to that of the Amali, for he came from the family of the Balthi, who because of their daring valor had long ago received among their race the name *Baltha*, that is, The Bold. Now when this Alaric was made king, he took counsel with his men and persuaded them to seek a kingdom by their own exertions rather than serve others in idleness. In the consulship of Stilicho and Aurelian he raised an army and entered Italy, which seemed to be bare of defenders, and came through Pannonia and Sirmium along the right side. Without meeting any resistance, he reached the bridge of the river Candidianus at the third milestone from the royal city of Ravenna.

This city lies amid the streams of the Po between swamps and the sea, and is accessible only on one side. Its ancient inhabitants, as our ancestors relate, were called *a vero*, that is "Laudable." Situated in a corner of the Roman Empire above the Ionian Sea, it is hemmed in like an island by a flood of rushing waters. On the east it has no sea, and one who sails straight to it from the region of Corcyra and those parts of Hellas sweeps with his oars along the right hand coast, first touching Epirus, then Dalmatia, Liburnia and Histria and at last the Venetian Isles. But on the west it has swamps through which a sort of door has been left by a very narrow entrance. To the north is an arm of the Po, called the Fossa Asconis. On the south likewise is the Po itself, which they call the King of the rivers of Italy; and it has also the name Eridanus. This river was turned aside by the Emperor Augustus into a very broad canal which flows through the midst of the city with a seventh part of its stream, affording a pleasant harbor at its mouth. Men believed in ancient times, as Dio relates, that it would hold a fleet of two hundred and fifty vessels in its safe anchorage. Fabius[5] says that this, which was once a harbor, now displays itself like a spacious garden full of trees; but from them hang not sails but apples. The city boasts of three names and is happily placed in its threefold location. I mean to say the first is called Ravenna and the most distant part Classis; while midway between the city and the sea is Caesarea, full of luxury. The sand of the beach is fine and suited for riding.

XXX But as I was saying, when the army of the Visigoths had come into the neighborhood of the city, they sent an embassy to the Emperor Honorius, who dwelt within. They said that if he would permit the Goths to settle peaceably in Italy, they would so live with the Roman people that men might believe them both to be of one race; but if not, whoever prevailed in war should drive out the other, and the victor should henceforth rule unmolested. But the Emperor Honorius feared to make either promise. So he took counsel with his senate and considered how he might drive them from the Italian borders. He finally decided that Alaric and his race, if they were able to do so, should be allowed to seize for their own home the provinces farthest away, namely Gaul and Spain. For at this time he had almost lost them, and moreover they had been devastated by the invasion of Gaiseric, king of the Vandals. The grant was confirmed by an imperial rescript, and the Goths, consenting to the arrangement, set out for the country given them.

When they had gone away without doing any harm in Italy, Stilicho, the Patrician and father-in-law of the Emperor Honorius—for the

---

5   Possibly a reference to Fabius Rusticus, a first-century Roman historian?

emperor had married both his daughters, Maria and Thermantia, in succession, but God called both from this world in their virgin purity—this Stilicho, I say, treacherously hurried to Pollentia, a city in the Cottian Alps. There he fell upon the unsuspecting Goths in battle, to the ruin of all Italy and his own disgrace. When the Goths suddenly beheld him, at first they were terrified. Soon regaining their courage and arousing each other by brave shouting, as is their custom, they turned to flight the entire army of Stilicho and almost exterminated it. Then forsaking the journey they had undertaken, the Goths with hearts full of rage returned again to Liguria whence they had set out. When they had plundered and spoiled it, they also laid waste Aemilia, and then hastened toward the city of Rome along the Flaminian Way, which runs between Picenum and Tuscia, taking as booty whatever they found on either hand. When they finally entered Rome, by Alaric's express command they merely sacked it and did not set the city on fire, as wild peoples usually do, nor did they permit serious damage to be done to the holy places. Thence they departed to bring like ruin upon Campania and Lucania, and then came to Bruttii. Here they remained a long time and planned to go to Sicily and thence to the countries of Africa.

Now the land of the Bruttii is at the extreme southern bound of Italy, and a corner of it marks the beginning of the Apennine mountains. It stretches out like a tongue into the Adriatic Sea and separates it from the Tyrrhenian waters. It chanced to receive its name in ancient times from a Queen Bruttia. To this place came Alaric, king of the Visigoths, with the wealth of all Italy which he had taken as spoil, and from there, as we have said, he intended to cross over by way of Sicily to the quiet land of Africa. But since man is not free to do anything he wishes without the will of God, that dread strait sunk several of his ships and threw all into confusion. Alaric was cast down by his reverse and, while deliberating what he should do, was suddenly overtaken by an untimely death and departed from human cares. His people mourned for him with the utmost affection. Then turning from its course the river Busentus near the city of Consentia—for this stream flows with its wholesome waters from the foot of a mountain

near that city—they led a band of captives into the midst of its bed to dig out a place for his grave. In the depths of the pit they buried Alaric, together with many treasures, and then turned the waters back into their channel. And that none might ever know the place, they put to death all the diggers. They bestowed the kingdom of the Visigoths on Athavulf his kinsman, a man of imposing beauty and great spirit; for though not tall of stature, he was distinguished for beauty of face and form.

XXXI When Athavulf became king, he returned again to Rome, and whatever had escaped the first sack his Goths stripped bare like locusts, not merely despoiling Italy of its private wealth, but even of its public resources. The Emperor Honorius was powerless to resist even when his sister Placidia, the daughter of the Emperor Theodosius by his second wife, was led away captive from the city. But Athavulf was attracted to her nobility, beauty and chaste purity, and so he took her to wife in lawful marriage at Forum Julii, a city of Aemilia. When the barbarians learned of this alliance, they were the more effectually terrified, since the empire and the Goths now seemed to be made one. Then Athavulf set out for Gaul, leaving Honorius Augustus stripped of his wealth, to be sure, yet pleased at heart because he was now a sort of kinsman of his. Upon his arrival the neighboring tribes who had long made cruel raids into Gaul—Franks and Burgundians alike—were terrified and began to keep within their own borders. Now the Vandals and the Alani, as we have said before, had been dwelling in both Pannonias by permission of the Roman emperors. Yet fearing they would not be safe even here if the Goths should return, they crossed over into Gaul. But no long time after they had taken possession of Gaul they fled thence and shut themselves up in Spain, for they still remembered from the tales of their forefathers what ruin Geberich, king of the Goths, had long ago brought on their race, and how by his valor he had driven them from their native land. And thus it happened that Gaul lay open to Athavulf when he came. Now when the Goth had established his kingdom in Gaul, he began to grieve for the plight of the Spaniards and planned to save them from the attacks of the Vandals. So Athavulf left with a few faithful men at Barcelona his treasures and those who were unfit for war, and entered the interior of Spain. Here he fought frequently with the Vandals and, in the third year after he had subdued Gaul and Spain, fell pierced through the groin by the sword of Euervulf, a man whose short stature he had been wont to mock. After his death Segeric was appointed king, but he too was slain by the treachery of his own men and lost both his kingdom and his life even more quickly than Athavulf.

XXXII Then Valia, the fourth from Alaric, was made king, and he was an exceeding stern and prudent man. The Emperor Honorius sent an army against him under Constantius, who was famed for his achievements in war and distinguished in many battles, for he feared that Valia would break the treaty long ago made with Athavulf and that, after driving out the neighboring tribes, he would again plot evil against the empire. Moreover Honorius was eager to free his sister Placidia from the disgrace of servitude, and made an agreement with Constantius that if by peace or war or any means soever he could bring her back to the kingdom, he should have her in marriage. Pleased with this promise, Constantius set out for Spain with an armed force and in almost royal splendor. Valia, king of the Goths, met him at a pass in the Pyrenees with as great a force. Hereupon embassies were sent by both sides and it was decided to make peace on the following terms, namely that Valia should give up Placidia, the emperor's sister, and should not refuse to aid the Roman Empire when occasion demanded.

Now at that time a certain Constantine usurped imperial power in Gaul and appointed as Caesar his son Constans, who was formerly a monk. But when he had held for a short time the empire he had seized, he was himself slain at Arelate and his son at Vienne. Jovinus and Sebastian succeeded them with equal presumption and thought they might seize the imperial power; but they perished by a like fate.

Now in the twelfth year of Valia's reign the Huns were driven out of Pannonia by the Romans and Goths, almost fifty years after they had taken possession of it. Then Valia found that the Vandals had come forth with bold audacity from the interior of Galicia, whither Athavulf had long ago driven them, and were devastating and plundering everywhere in his own territories, namely in the land of Spain. So he made no delay but moved his army against them at once, at about the time when Hierius and Ardabures had become consuls.

XXXIII But Gaiseric, king of the Vandals, had already been invited into Africa by Boniface, who had fallen into a dispute with the Emperor Valentinian and was able to obtain revenge only by injuring the empire. So he invited them urgently and brought them across the narrow strait known as the Strait of Gades, scarcely seven miles wide, which divides Africa from Spain and unites the mouth of the Tyrrhenian Sea with the waters of Ocean. Gaiseric, still famous in the City for the disaster of the Romans, was a man of moderate height and lame in consequence of a fall from his horse. He was a man of deep thought and few words, holding luxury in disdain, furious in his anger, greedy for gain, shrewd in winning over the barbarians and skilled in sowing the seeds of dissension to arouse enmity. Such was he who, as we have said, came at the solicitous invitation of Boniface to the country of Africa. There he reigned for a long time, receiving authority, as they say, from God Himself. Before his death he summoned the band of his sons and ordained that there should be no strife among them because of desire for the kingdom, but that each should reign in his own rank and order as he survived the others; that is, the next younger should succeed his elder brother, and he in turn should be followed by his junior. By giving heed to this command they ruled their kingdom in happiness for the space of many years and were not disgraced by civil war, as is usual among other nations; one after another receiving the kingdom and ruling the people in peace.

Now this is their order of succession: first, Gaeseric who was the father and lord, next Huneric, the third Gunthamund, the fourth Thrasamund, and the fifth Ilderich. He was driven from his throne and slain by Gelimer, who destroyed his race by disregarding his ancestor's advice and setting up a tyranny. But what he had done did not remain unpunished, for soon the vengeance of the Emperor Justinian was manifested against him. With his whole family and that wealth over which he gloated like a robber, he was taken to Constantinople by that most renowned warrior Belisarius, Master of the Soldiery of the East, Ex-Consul Ordinary and Patrician. Here he afforded a great spectacle to the people in the Circus.[6] His repentance, when he cast himself down from his royal state, came too late. He died as a mere subject and in retirement, though he had formerly been unwilling to private life. Thus after a century Africa, which in the division of the earth's surface is regarded as the third part of the world, was delivered from the yoke of the Vandals and brought back to the liberty of the Roman Empire. The country which the hand of the heathen had long ago cut off from the body of the Roman Empire, by reason of the cowardice of emperors and the treachery of generals, was now restored by a wise prince and a faithful leader and to-day is happily flourishing. And though, even after this, it had to deplore the misery of civil war and the treachery of the Moors, yet the triumph of the Emperor Justinian, vouchsafed him by God, brought to a peaceful conclusion what he had begun. But why need we speak of what the subject does not require? Let us return to our theme.

Now Valia, king of the Goths, and his army fought so fiercely against the Vandals that he would have pursued them even into Africa, had not such a misfortune recalled him as befell Alaric when he was setting out for Africa. So when he had won great fame in Spain, he returned after a bloodless victory to Tolosa, turning over to the Roman Empire, as he had promised, a number of provinces which he had rid of his foes. A long time after this he was seized with sickness and departed this life. Just at that time Beremud, the son of Thorismud, whom we have mentioned above in the genealogy of the family of the Amali, departed with his son Veteric from the Ostrogoths, who still submitted to the oppression of the Huns in the land of Scythia, and came to the kingdom of the Visigoths. Well aware of his valor and noble birth, he believed that the kingdom would be more readily bestowed upon him by his kinsmen, inasmuch as he was known to be the heir of many kings. And who would hesitate to choose one of the Amali, if there were an empty throne? But he was not himself eager to make known who he

was, and so upon the death of Valia the Visigoths made Theodorid his successor. Beremud came to him and, with the strength of mind for which he was noted, concealed his noble birth by prudent silence, for he knew that those of royal lineage are always distrusted by kings. So he suffered himself to remain unknown, that he might not bring the established order into confusion. King Theodorid received him and his son with special honor and made him partner in his counsels and a companion at his board; not for his noble birth, which he knew not, but for his brave spirit and strong mind, which Beremud could not conceal.

XXXIV And what more? Valia (to repeat what we have said) had but little success against the Gauls, but when he died the more fortunate and prosperous Theodorid succeeded to the throne. He was a man of the greatest moderation and notable for vigor of mind and body. In the consulship of Theodosius and Festus the Romans broke the truce and took up arms against him in Gaul, with the Huns as their auxiliaries. For a band of the Gallic Allies, led by Count Gaina, had aroused the Romans by throwing Constantinople into a panic. Now at that time the Patrician Aëtius was in command of the army. He was of the bravest Moesian stock, the son of Gaudentius and born in the city of Durostorum. He was a man fitted to endure the toils of war, born expressly to serve the Roman state; and by inflicting crushing defeats he had compelled the proud Suavi and barbarous Franks to submit to Roman sway. So then, with the Huns as allies under their leader Litorius, the Roman army moved in array against the Goths. When the battle lines of both sides had been standing for a long time opposite each other, both being brave and neither side the weaker, they struck a truce and returned to their ancient alliance. And after the treaty had been confirmed by both and an honest peace was established, they both withdrew.

During this peace Attila was lord over all the Huns and almost the sole earthly ruler of all the tribes of Scythia; a man marvelous for his glorious fame among all nations. The historian Priscus,[7] who was sent to him on an embassy by the younger Theodosius, says this among other things:

---

6   The hippodrome of Constantinople.

7   Fifth-century Roman historian whose work, surviving only in fragments, probably covered the period of ca. 433–474.

"Crossing mighty rivers—namely, the Tisia and Tibisia and Dricca—we came to the place where long ago Vidigoia, bravest of the Goths, perished by the guile of the Sarmatians. At no great distance from that place we arrived at the village where King Attila was dwelling, a village, I say, like a great city, in which we found wooden walls made of smooth-shining boards, whose joints so counterfeited solidity that the union of the boards could scarcely be distinguished by close scrutiny. There you might see dining halls of large extent and porticoes planned with great beauty, while the courtyard was bounded by so vast a circuit that its very size showed it was the royal palace." This was the abode of Attila, the king of all the barbarian world; and he preferred this as a dwelling to the cities he captured.

XXXV Now this Attila was the son of Mundiuch, and his brothers were Octar and Ruas who are said to have ruled before Attila, though not over quite so many tribes as he. After their death he succeeded to the throne of the Huns, together with his brother Bleda. In order that he might first be equal to the expedition he was preparing, he sought to increase his strength by murder. Thus he proceeded from the destruction of his own kindred to the menace of all others. But though he increased his power by this shameful means, yet by the balance of justice he received the hideous consequences of his own cruelty. Now when his brother Bleda, who ruled over a great part of the Huns, had been slain by his treachery, Attila united all the people under his own rule....

XXXVI Now when Gaiseric, king of the Vandals, whom we mentioned shortly before, learned that his mind was bent on the devastation of the world, he incited Attila by many gifts to make war on the Visigoths, for he was afraid that Theodorid, king of the Visigoths, would avenge the injury done to his daughter. She had been joined in wedlock with Huneric, the son of Gaiseric, and at first was happy in this union. But afterwards he was cruel even to his own children, and because of the mere suspicion that she was attempting to poison him, he cut off her nose and mutilated her ears. He sent her back to her father in Gaul thus despoiled of her natural charms. So the wretched girl presented a pitiable aspect ever after, and the cruelty which would stir even strangers still more surely incited her father to vengeance. Attila, therefore, in his efforts to bring about the wars long ago instigated by the bribe of Gaiseric, sent ambassadors into Italy to the Emperor Valentinian to sow strife between the Goths and the Romans, thinking to shatter by civil discord those whom he could not crush in battle. He declared that he was in no way violating his friendly relations with the empire, but that he had a quarrel with Theodorid, king of the Visigoths. As he wished to be kindly received, he filled the rest of the letter with the usual flattering salutations, striving to win credence for his falsehood. In like manner he despatched a message to Theodorid, king of the Visigoths, urging him to break his alliance with the Romans and reminding him of the battles to which they had recently provoked him. Beneath his great ferocity he was a subtle man, and fought with craft before he made war.

Then the Emperor Valentinian sent an embassy to the Visigoths and their king Theodorid, with this message: "Bravest of nations, it is the part of prudence for us to unite against the lord of the earth who wishes to enslave the whole world; who requires no just cause for battle, but supposes whatever he does is right. He measures his ambition by his might. License satisfies his pride. Despising law and right, he shows himself an enemy to Nature herself. And thus he, who clearly is the common foe of each, deserves the hatred of all. Pray remember—what you surely cannot forget—that the Huns do not overthrow nations by means of war, where there is an equal chance, but assail them by treachery, which is a greater cause for anxiety. To say nothing about ourselves, can you suffer such insolence to go unpunished? Since you are mighty in arms, give heed to your own danger and join hands with us in common. Bear aid also to the empire, of which you hold a part. If you would learn how such an alliance should be sought and welcomed by us, look into the plans of the foe."

By these and like arguments the ambassadors of Valentinian prevailed upon King Theodorid. He answered them, saying: "Romans, you have attained your desire; you have made Attila our foe also. We will pursue him wherever he summons us, and though he is puffed up by his victories over divers races, yet the Goths know how to fight this haughty foe. I call no war dangerous save one whose cause is weak; for he fears no ill on whom Majesty has smiled." The nobles shouted assent to the reply and the multitude gladly followed. All were fierce for battle and longed to meet the Huns, their foe. And so a countless host was led forth by Theodorid, king of the Visigoths, who sent home four of his sons, namely Friderich and Eurich, Retemer and Himnerith, taking with him only the two elder sons, Thorismud and Theodorid, as partners of his toil. O brave array, sure defense and sweet comradeship, having the aid of those who delight to share in the same dangers!

On the side of the Romans stood the Patrician Aëtius, on whom at that time the whole empire of the west depended; a man of such wisdom that he had assembled warriors from everywhere to meet them on equal terms. Now these were his auxiliaries: Franks, Sarmatians, Armoricians, Liticians, Burgundians, Saxons, Riparians, Olibriones (once Roman soldiers and now the flower of the allied forces), and some other Celtic or German tribes. And so they met in the Catalaunian Plains, which are also called Mauriacian, extending in length one hundred *leuva*, as the Gauls express it, and seventy in width. Now a Gallic *leuva* measures a distance of fifteen hundred paces. That portion of the earth accordingly became the threshing-floor of countless races. The two hosts bravely joined battle. Nothing was done under cover, but they contended in open fight. What just cause can be found for the encounter of so many nations, or what hatred inspired them all to take arms against each other? It is proof that the human race lives for its kings, for it is at the mad impulse of one mind a slaughter of nations takes place, and at the whim of a haughty ruler that which nature has taken ages to produce perishes in a moment.

XXXVII But before we set forth the order of the battle itself, it seems needful to relate what had already happened in the course of the campaign, for it was not only a famous struggle but one that was complicated and confused. Well then, Sangiban, king of the Alani, smitten with fear of what might come to pass, had promised to surrender to Attila, and to give into his keeping Aureliani, a city of Gaul wherein he dwelt. When Theodorid and Aëtius learned of this, they cast up great earthworks around that city before Attila's arrival and kept watch over the suspected Sangiban, placing him with his tribe in the midst of their auxiliaries. Then Attila, king of the Huns, was taken aback by this event and lost confidence in his own troops, so that he feared to begin the conflict. While he was meditating on flight—a greater calamity than death itself—he decided to inquire into the future through soothsayers. So, as was their custom, they examined the entrails of cattle and certain streaks in bones that had been scraped, and foretold disaster to the Huns. Yet as a slight consolation they prophesied that the chief commander of the foe they were to meet should fall and mar by his death the rest of the victory and the triumph. Now Attila deemed the death of Aëtius a thing to be desired even at the cost of his own life, for Aëtius stood in the way of his plans. So although he was disturbed by this prophecy, yet inasmuch as he was a man who sought counsel of omens in all warfare, he began the battle with anxious heart at about the ninth hour of the day, in order that the impending darkness might come to his aid if the outcome should be disastrous.

XXXVIII The armies met, as we have said, in the Catalaunian Plains. The battle field was a plain rising by a sharp slope to a ridge, which both armies sought to gain; for advantage of position is a great help. The Huns with their forces seized the right side, the Romans, the Visigoths and their allies the left, and then began a struggle for the yet untaken crest. Now Theodorid with the Visigoths held the right wing and Aëtius with the Romans the left. They placed in the center Sangiban (who, as said before, was in command of the Alani), thus contriving with military caution to surround by a host of faithful troops the man in whose loyalty they had little confidence. For one who has difficulties placed in the way of his flight readily submits to the necessity of fighting. On the other side, however, the battle line of the Huns was arranged so that Attila and his bravest followers were stationed in the center. In arranging them thus the king had chiefly his own safety in view, since by his position in the very midst of his race he would be kept out of the way of threatening danger. The innumerable peoples of the divers tribes, which he had subjected to his sway, formed the wings. Amid them was conspicuous the army of the Ostrogoths under the leadership of the brothers Valamir, Thiudimer and Vidimer, nobler even than the king they served, for the might of the family of the Amali rendered them glorious. The renowned king of the Gepidae, Ardaric, was there also with a countless host, and because of his great loyalty to Attila, he shared his plans. For Attila, comparing them in his wisdom, prized him and Valamir, king of the Ostrogoths, above all the other chieftains. Valamir was a good keeper of secrets, bland of speech and skilled in wiles, and Ardaric, as we have said, was famed for his loyalty and wisdom. Attila might well feel sure that they would fight against the Visigoths, their kinsmen. Now the rest of the crowd of kings (if we may call them so) and the leaders of various nations hung upon Attila's nod like slaves, and when he gave a sign even by a glance, without a murmur each stood forth in fear and trembling, or at all events did as he was bid. Attila alone was king of all kings over all and concerned for all.

So then the struggle began for the advantage of position we have mentioned. Attila sent his men to take the summit of the mountain, but was outstripped by Thorismud and Aëtius, who in their effort to gain the top of the hill reached higher ground and through this advantage of position easily routed the Huns as they came up.

XXXIX Now when Attila saw his army was thrown into confusion by this event, he thought it best to encourage them by an extemporaneous address on this wise: "Here you stand, after conquering mighty nations and subduing the world. I therefore think it foolish for me to goad you with words, as though you were men who had not been proved in action. Let a new leader or an untried army resort to that. It is not right for me to say anything common, nor ought you to listen. For what is war but your usual custom? Or what is sweeter for a brave man than to seek revenge with his own hand? It is a right of nature to glut the soul with vengeance. Let us then attack the foe eagerly; for they are ever the bolder who make the attack. Despise this union of discordant races! To defend oneself by alliance is proof of cowardice.

See, even before our attack they are smitten with terror. They seek the heights, they seize the hills and, repenting too late, clamor for protection against battle in the open fields. You know how slight a matter the Roman attack is. While they are still gathering in order and forming in one line with locked shields, they are checked, I will not say by the first wound, but even by the dust of battle. Then on to the fray with stout hearts, as is your wont. Despise their battle line. Attack the Alani, smite the Visigoths! Seek swift victory in that spot where the battle rages. For when the sinews are cut the limbs soon relax, nor can a body stand when you have taken away the bones. Let your courage rise and your own fury burst forth! Now show your cunning, Huns, now your deeds of arms! Let the wounded exact in return the death of his foe; let the unwounded revel in the slaughter of the enemy. No spear shall harm those who are sure to live; and those who are sure to die Fate overtakes even in peace. And finally, why should Fortune have made the Huns victorious over so many nations, unless it were to prepare them for the joy of this conflict. Who was it revealed to our sires the path through the Maeotian swamp, for so many ages a closed secret? Who, moreover, made armed men yield to you, when you were as yet unarmed? Even a mass of federated nations could not endure the sight of the Huns. I am not deceived in the issue; here is the field so many victories have promised us. I shall hurl the first spear at the foe. If any can stand at rest while Attila fights, he is a dead man." Inflamed by these words, they all dashed into battle.

XL And although the situation was itself fearful, yet the presence of their king dispelled anxiety and hesitation. Hand to hand they clashed in battle, and the fight grew fierce, confused, monstrous, unrelenting—a fight whose like no ancient time has ever recorded. There such deeds were done that a brave man who missed this marvelous spectacle could not hope to see anything so wonderful all his life long. For, if we may believe our elders, a brook flowing between low banks through the plain was greatly increased by blood from the wounds of the slain. It was not flooded by showers, as brooks usually rise, but was swollen by a strange stream and turned into a torrent by the increase of blood. Those whose wounds drove them to slake their parching thirst drank water mingled with gore. In their wretched plight they were forced to drink what they thought was the blood they had poured from their own wounds.

Here King Theodorid, while riding by to encourage his army, was thrown from his horse and trampled under foot by his own men, thus ending his days at a ripe old age. But others say he was slain by the spear of Andag of the host of the Ostrogoths, who were then under the sway of Attila. This was what the soothsayers had told to Attila in prophecy, though he understood it of Aëtius. Then the Visigoths, separating from the Alani, fell upon the horde of the Huns and nearly slew Attila. But he prudently took flight and straightway shut himself and his companions within the barriers of the camp, which he had fortified with wagons. A frail defense indeed; yet there they sought refuge for their lives, whom but a little while before no walls of earth could withstand. But Thorismud, the son of King Theodorid, who with Aëtius had seized the hill and repulsed the enemy from the higher ground, came unwittingly to the wagons of the enemy at night, thinking he had reached his own lines. As he was fighting bravely, someone wounded him in the head and dragged him from his horse. Then he was rescued by the watchful care of his followers and withdrew from the fierce conflict. Aëtius also became separated from his men in the confusion of night and wandered about in the midst of the enemy. Fearing disaster had happened, he went about in search of the Goths. At last he reached the camp of his allies and passed the remainder of the night in the protection of their shields.

At dawn on the following day, when the Romans saw the fields were piled high with bodies and that the Huns did not venture forth, they thought the victory was theirs, but knew that Attila would not flee from the battle unless overwhelmed by a great disaster. Yet he did nothing cowardly, like one that is overcome, but with clash of arms sounded the trumpets and threatened an attack. He was like a lion pierced by hunting spears, who paces to and fro before the mouth of his den and dares not spring, but ceases not to terrify the neighborhood by his roaring. Even so this warlike king at bay terrified his conquerors.

Therefore the Goths and Romans assembled and considered what to do with the vanquished Attila. They determined to wear him out by a siege, because he had no supply of provisions and was hindered from approaching by a shower of arrows from the bowmen placed within the confines of the Roman camp. But it was said that the king remained supremely brave even in this extremity and had heaped up a funeral pyre of horse saddles, so that if the enemy should attack him, he was determined to cast himself into the flames, that none might have the joy of wounding him and that the lord of so many races might not fall into the hands of his foes.

XLI Now during these delays in the siege, the Visigoths sought their king and the king's sons their father, wondering at his absence when success had been attained. When, after a long search, they found him where the dead lay thickest, as happens with brave men, they honored him with songs and bore him away in the sight of the enemy. You might have seen bands of Goths shouting with dissonant cries and paying honor to the dead while the battle still raged. Tears were shed, but such as they were accustomed to devote to brave men. It was death indeed, but the Huns are witness that it was a glorious one. It was a death whereby one might well suppose the pride of the enemy would be lowered, when they beheld the body of so great a king borne forth with fitting honors. And so the Goths, still continuing the rites due to Theodorid, bore forth the royal majesty with sounding arms, and valiant Thorismud, as befitted a son, honored the glorious spirit of his dear father by following his remains.

When this was done, Thorismud was eager to take vengeance for his father's death on the remaining Huns, being moved to this both by the pain of bereavement and the impulse of that valor for which he was noted. Yet he consulted with the Patrician Aëtius (for he was an older man and of more mature wisdom) with regard to what he ought to do next. But Aëtius feared that if the Huns were totally destroyed by the Goths, the Roman Empire would be overwhelmed, and urgently advised him to return to his own dominions to take up the rule which his father had left. Otherwise his brothers might seize their father's possessions and obtain the power over the Visigoths. In this case Thorismud would have to fight fiercely and, what is worse, disastrously with his own countrymen. Thorismud accepted the advice without perceiving its double meaning, but followed it with an eye toward his own advantage. So he left the Huns and returned to Gaul. Thus while human frailty rushes into suspicion, it often loses an opportunity of doing great things.

In this most famous war of the bravest tribes, one hundred and sixty-five thousand are said to have been slain on both sides, leaving out of account fifteen thousand of the Gepidae and Franks, who met each other the night before the general engagement and fell by wounds mutually received, the Franks fighting for the Romans and the Gepidae for the Huns.

Now when Attila learned of the retreat of the Goths, he thought it a ruse of the enemy—for so men are wont to believe when the unexpected happens—and remained for some time in his camp. But when a long silence followed the absence of the foe, the spirit of the mighty king was aroused to the thought of victory and the anticipation of pleasure, and his mind turned to the old oracles of his destiny.

Thorismud, however, after the death of his father on the Catalaunian Plains where he had fought, advanced in royal state and entered Tolosa. Here although the throng of his brothers and brave companions were still rejoicing over the victory he yet began to rule so mildly that no one strove with him for the succession to the kingdom.

XLII But Attila took occasion from the withdrawal of the Visigoths, observing what he had often desired—that his enemies were divided. At length feeling secure, he moved forward his array to attack the Romans. As his first move he besieged the city of Aquileia, the metropolis of Venetia, which is situated on a point or tongue of land by the Adriatic Sea. On the eastern side its walls are washed by the river Natissa, flowing from Mount Piccis. The siege was long and fierce, but of no avail, since the bravest soldiers of the Romans withstood him from within. At last his army was discontented and eager to withdraw. Attila chanced to be walking around the

walls, considering whether to break camp or delay longer, and noticed that the white birds, namely, the storks, who build their nests in the gables of houses, were bearing their young from the city and, contrary to their custom, were carrying them out into the country. Being a shrewd observer of events, he understood this and said to his soldiers: "You see the birds foresee the future. They are leaving the city sure to perish and are forsaking strongholds doomed to fall by reason of imminent peril. Do not think this a meaningless or uncertain sign; fear, arising from the things they foresee, has changed their custom." Why say more? He inflamed the hearts of his soldiers to attack Aquileia again. Constructing battering rams and bringing to bear all manner of engines of war, they quickly forced their way into the city, laid it waste, divided the spoil and so cruelly devastated it as scarcely to leave a trace to be seen. Then growing bolder and still thirsting for Roman blood, the Huns raged madly through the remaining cities of the Veneti. They also laid waste Mediolanum, the metropolis of Liguria, once an imperial city, and gave over Ticinum to a like fate. Then they destroyed the neighboring country in their frenzy and demolished almost the whole of Italy.

Attila's mind had been bent on going back to Rome. But his followers, as the historian Priscus relates, took him away, not out of regard for the city to which they were hostile, but because they remembered the case of Alaric, the former king of the Visigoths. They distrusted the good fortune of their own king, inasmuch as Alaric did not live long after the sack of Rome, but straightway departed this life. Therefore while Attila's spirit was wavering in doubt between going and not going, and he still lingered to ponder the matter, an embassy came to him from Rome to seek peace. Pope Leo himself came to meet him in the Ambuleian district of the Veneti at the well-traveled ford of the river Mincius. Then Attila quickly put aside his usual fury, turned back on the way he had advanced from beyond the Danube and departed with the promise of peace. But above all he declared and avowed with threats that he would bring worse things upon Italy, unless they sent him Honoria, the sister of the Emperor Valentinian and daughter of Augusta Placidia, with her due share of the royal wealth. For it was said that Honoria, although bound to chastity for the honor of the imperial court and kept in constraint by command of her brother, had secretly despatched a eunuch to summon Attila that she might have his protection against her brother's power; a shameful thing, indeed, to get license for her passion at the cost of the public weal.

XLIII So Attila returned to his own country, seeming to regret the peace and to be vexed at the cessation of war. For he sent ambassadors to Marcian, emperor of the east, threatening to devastate the provinces, because that which had been promised him by Theodosius, a former emperor, was in no wise performed, and saying that he would show himself more cruel to his foes than ever. But as he was shrewd and crafty, he threatened in one direction and moved his army in another; for in the midst of these preparations he turned his face towards the Visigoths who had yet to feel his vengeance. But here he had not the same success as against the Romans. Hastening back by a different way than before, he decided to reduce to his sway that part of the Alani which was settled across the river Loire, in order that by attacking them, and thus changing the aspect of the war, he might become a more terrible menace to the Visigoths. Accordingly he started from the provinces of Dacia and Pannonia, where the Huns were then dwelling with various subject peoples, and moved his array against the Alani. But Thorismud, king of the Visigoths, with like quickness of thought perceived Attila's trick. By forced marches he came to the Alani before him, and was well prepared to check the advance of Attila when he came after him. They joined battle in almost the same way as before at the Catalaunian Plains, and Thorismud dashed his hopes of victory, for he routed him and drove him from the land without a triumph, compelling him to flee to his own country. Thus while Attila, the famous leader and lord of many victories, sought to blot out the fame of his destroyer and in this way to annul what he had suffered at the hands of the Visigoths, he met a second defeat and retreated ingloriously. Now after the bands of the Huns had been repulsed by the Alani, without any hurt to his own men, Thorismud departed for Tolosa. There he established a settled peace for his people and in the

third year of his reign he fell sick. While letting blood from a vein, he was betrayed to his death by Ascalc, a client, who told his foes that his weapons were out of reach. Yet grasping a foot-stool in the one hand he had free, he became the avenger of his own blood by slaying several of those that were lying in wait for him.

XLIV After his death, his brother Theodorid succeeded to the kingdom of the Visigoths and soon found that Riciarius his kinsman, the king of the Suavi, was hostile to him. For Riciarius, presuming on his relationship to Theodorid, believed that he might seize almost the whole of Spain, thinking the disturbed beginning of Theodorid's reign made the time opportune for this trick. The Suavi formerly occupied as their country Galicia and Lusitania, which extend on the right side of Spain along the shore of Ocean. To the east is Austrogonia, to the west, on a promontory, is the sacred monument of the Roman general Scipio, to the north Ocean, and to the south Lusitania and the Tagus river, which mingles golden grains in its sands and thus carries wealth in its worthless mud. So then Riciarius, king of the Suavi, set forth and strove to seize the whole of Spain. Theodorid, his kinsman, a man of moderation, sent ambassadors to him and told him quietly that he must not only withdraw from the territories that were not his own, but furthermore that he should not presume to make such an attempt, as he was becoming hated for his ambition. But with arrogant spirit he replied: "If you murmur here and find fault with my coming, I shall come to Tolosa where you dwell. Resist me there, if you can." When he heard this, Theodorid was angry and, making a compact with all the other tribes, moved his array against the Suavi. He had as his close allies Gundiuch and Hilperic, kings of the Burgundians. They came to battle near the river Ulbius, which flows between Asturica and Hiberia, and in the engagement Theodorid with the Visigoths, who fought for the right, came off victorious, overthrowing the entire tribe of the Suavi and almost exterminating them. Their king Riciarius fled from the dread foe and embarked upon a ship. But he was beaten back by another foe, the adverse wind of the Tyrrhenian Sea, and so fell into the hands of the Visigoths. Thus though he changed from sea to land, the wretched man did not avert his death.

When Theodorid had become the victor, he spared the conquered and did not suffer the rage of conflict to continue, but placed over the Suavi whom he had conquered one of his own retainers, named Agrivulf. But Agrivulf soon treacherously changed his mind, through the persuasion of the Suavi, and failed to fulfil his duty. For he was quite puffed up with tyrannical pride, believing he had obtained the province as a reward for the valor by which he and his lord had recently subjugated it. Now he was a man born of the stock of the Varni, far below the nobility of Gothic blood, and so was neither zealous for liberty nor faithful toward his patron. As soon as Theodorid heard of this, he despatched a force to cast him out from the kingdom he had usurped. They came quickly and conquered him in the first battle, inflicting a punishment befitting his deeds. For he was captured, taken from his friends and beheaded. Thus at last he was made aware of the wrath of the master he thought might be despised because he was kind. Now when the Suavi beheld the death of their leader, they sent priests of their country to Theodorid as suppliants. He received them with the reverence due their office and not only granted the Suavi exemption from punishment, but was moved by compassion and allowed them to choose a ruler of their own race for themselves. The Suavi did so, taking Rimismund as their prince. When this was done and peace was everywhere assured, Theodorid died in the thirteenth year of his reign.

XLV His brother Eurich succeeded him with such eager haste that he fell under dark suspicion. Now while these and various other matters were happening among the people of the Visigoths, the Emperor Valentinian was slain by the treachery of Maximus, and Maximus himself, like a tyrant, usurped the rule. Gaiseric, king of the Vandals, heard of this and came from Africa to Italy with ships of war, entered Rome and laid it waste. Maximus fled and was slain by a certain Ursus, a Roman soldier. After him Majorian undertook the government of the western empire at the bidding of Marcian, emperor of the east. But he too ruled but a short time. For when he had moved his forces against the Alani who were

harassing Gaul, he was killed at Dertona near the river named Ira. Severus succeeded him and died at Rome in the third year of his reign. When the Emperor Leo, who had succeeded Marcian in the eastern empire, learned of this, he chose as emperor his Patrician Anthemius and sent him to Rome. Upon his arrival he sent against the Alani his son-in-law Ricimer, who was an excellent man and almost the only one in Italy at that time fit to command the army. In the very first engagement he conquered and destroyed the host of the Alani, together with their king, Beorg.

Now Eurich, king of the Visigoths, perceived the frequent change of Roman emperors and strove to hold Gaul by his own right. The Emperor Anthemius heard of it and asked the Brittones for aid. Their King Riotimus came with twelve thousand men into the state of the Bituriges by the way of Ocean, and was received as he disembarked from his ships. Eurich, king of the Visigoths, came against them with an innumerable army, and after a long fight he routed Riotimus, king of the Brittones, before the Romans could join him. So when he had lost a great part of his army, he fled with all the men he could gather together, and came to the Burgundians, a neighboring tribe then allied to the Romans. But Eurich, king of the Visigoths, seized the Gallic city of Arverna; for the Emperor Anthemius was now dead. Engaged in fierce war with his son-in-law Ricimer, he had worn out Rome and was himself finally slain by his son-in-law and yielded the rule to Olybrius.

At that time Aspar, first of the Patricians and a famous man of the Gothic race was wounded by the swords of the eunuchs in his palace at Constantinople and died. With him were slain his sons Ardabures and Patriciolus, the one long a Patrician, and the other styled a Caesar and son-in-law of the Emperor Leo. Now Olybrius died barely eight months after he had entered upon his reign, and Glycerius was made Caesar at Ravenna, rather by usurpation than by election. Hardly had a year been ended when Nepos, the son of the sister of Marcellinus, once a Patrician, deposed him from his office and ordained him bishop at the Port of Rome.

When Eurich, as we have already said, beheld these great and various changes, he seized the city of Arverna, where the Roman general Ecdicius was at that time in command. He was a senator of most renowned family and the son of Avitus, a recent emperor who had usurped the reign for a few days—for Avitus held the rule for a few days before Olybrius, and then withdrew of his own accord to Placentia, where he was ordained bishop. His son Ecdicius strove for a long time with the Visigoths, but had not the power to prevail. So he left the country and (what was more important) the city of Arverna to the enemy and betook himself to safer regions. When the Emperor Nepos heard of this, he ordered Ecdicius to leave Gaul and come to him, appointing Orestes in his stead as Master of the Soldiery. This Orestes thereupon received the army, set out from Rome against the enemy and came to Ravenna. Here he tarried while he made his son Romulus Augustulus emperor. When Nepos learned of this, he fled to Dalmatia and died there, deprived of his throne, in the very place where Glycerius, who was formerly emperor, held at that time the bishopric of Salona.

XLVI Now when Augustulus had been appointed emperor by his father Orestes in Ravenna, it was not long before Odoacer, king of the Torcilingi, invaded Italy, as leader of the Sciri, the Heruli and allies of various races. He put Orestes to death, drove his son Augustulus from the throne and condemned him to the punishment of exile in the Castle of Lucullus in Campania. Thus the western empire of the Roman race, which Octavianus Augustus, the first of the Augusti, began to govern in the seven hundred and ninth year from the founding of the city, perished with this Augustulus in the five hundred and twenty-second year from the beginning of the rule of his predecessors and those before them, and from this time onward kings of the Goths held Rome and Italy. Meanwhile Odoacer, king of nations, subdued all Italy and then at the very outset of his reign slew Count Bracila at Ravenna that he might inspire a fear of himself among the Romans. He strengthened his kingdom and held it for almost thirteen years, even until the appearance of Theodoric, of whom we shall speak hereafter.

XLVII But first let us return to that order from which we have digressed and tell how Eurich, king of the Visigoths, beheld the tottering of the Roman Empire and reduced Arelate and Massilia to his own sway. Gaiseric, king of the Vandals, enticed him by gifts to do these things, to the end that he himself might forestall the plots which Leo and Zeno had contrived against him. Therefore he stirred the Ostrogoths to lay waste the eastern empire and the Visigoths the western, so that while his foes were battling in both empires, he might himself reign peacefully in Africa. Eurich perceived this with gladness and, as he already held all of Spain and Gaul by his own right, proceeded to subdue the Burgundians also. In the nineteenth year of his reign he was deprived of his life at Arelate, where he then dwelt. He was succeeded by his own son Alaric, the ninth in succession from the famous Alaric the Great to receive the kingdom of the Visigoths. For even as it happened to the line of the Augusti, as we have stated above, so too it appears in the line of the Alarici, that kingdoms often come to an end in kings who bear the same name as those at the beginning. Meanwhile let us leave this subject, and weave together the whole story of the origin of the Goths, as we promised.

The Divided Goths: Ostrogoths

XLVIII Since I have followed the stories of my ancestors and retold to the best of my ability the tale of the period when both tribes, Ostrogoths and Visigoths, were united, and then clearly treated of the Visigoths apart from the Ostrogoths, I must now return to those ancient Scythian abodes and set forth in like manner the ancestry and deeds of the Ostrogoths. It appears that at the death of their king, Hermanaric, they were made a separate people by the departure of the Visigoths, and remained in their country subject to the sway of the Huns; yet Vinitharius of the Amali retained the insignia of his rule. He rivalled the valor of his grandfather Vultuulf, although he had not the good fortune of Hermanaric. But disliking to remain under the rule of the Huns, he withdrew a little from them and strove to show his courage by moving his forces against the country of the Antes. When he attacked them, he was beaten in the first encounter. Thereafter he did valiantly and, as a terrible example, crucified their king, named Boz, together with his sons and seventy nobles, and left their bodies hanging there to double the fear of those who had surrendered. When he had ruled with such license for barely a year, Balamber, king of the Huns, would no longer endure it, but sent for Gesimund, son of Hunimund the Great. Now Gesimund, together with a great part of the Goths, remained under the rule of the Huns, being mindful of his oath of fidelity. Balamber renewed his alliance with him and led his army up against Vinitharius. After a long contest, Vinitharius prevailed in the first and in the second conflict, nor can any say how great slaughter he made of the army of the Huns. But in the third battle, when they met each other unexpectedly at the river named Erac, Balamber shot an arrow and wounded Vinitharius in the head, so that he died. Then Balamber took to himself in marriage Vadamerca, the grand-daughter of Vinitharius, and finally ruled all the people of the Goths as his peaceful subjects, but in such a way that one ruler of their own number always held the power over the Gothic race, though subject to the Huns.

And later, after the death of Vinitharius, Hunimund ruled them, the son of Hermanaric, a mighty king of yore; a man fierce in war and of famous personal beauty, who afterwards fought successfully against the race of the Suavi. And when he died, his son Thorismud succeeded him, in the very bloom of youth. In the second year of his rule he moved an army against the Gepidae and won a great victory over them, but is said to have been killed by falling from his horse. When he was dead, the Ostrogoths mourned for him so deeply that for forty years no other king succeeded in his place, and during all this time they had ever on their lips the tale of his memory. Now as time went on, Valamir grew to man's estate. He was the son of Thorismud's cousin Vandalarius. For his son Beremud, as we have said before, at last grew to despise the race of the Ostrogoths because of the overlordship of the Huns, and so had followed the tribe of the Visigoths to the western country, and it was from him Veteric was descended. Veteric also had a son Eutharic, who married Amalasuentha, the daughter of Theodoric, thus uniting again the stock of the Amali which had divided long ago. Eutharic begat Athalaric and

Mathesuentha. But since Athalaric died in the years of his boyhood, Mathesuentha was taken to Constantinople by her second husband, namely Germanus, a nephew of the Emperor Justinian, and bore a posthumous son, whom she named Germanus.

But that the order we have taken for our history may run its due course, we must return to the stock of Vandalarius, which put forth three branches. This Vandalarius, the great grand-nephew of Hermanaric and cousin of the aforesaid Thorismud, vaunted himself among the race of the Amali because he had begotten three sons, Valamir, Thiudimer and Vidimer. Of these Valamir ascended the throne after his parents, though the Huns as yet held the power over the Goths in general as among other nations. It was pleasant to behold the concord of these three brothers; for the admirable Thiudimer served as a soldier for the empire of his brother Valamir, and Valamir bade honors be given him, while Vidimer was eager to serve them both. Thus regarding one another with common affection, not one was wholly deprived of the kingdom which two of them held in mutual peace. Yet, as has often been said, they ruled in such a way that they respected the dominion of Attila, king of the Huns. Indeed they could not have refused to fight against their kinsmen the Visigoths, and they must even have committed parricide at their lord's command. There was no way whereby any Scythian tribe could have been wrested from the power of the Huns, save by the death of Attila—an event the Romans and all other nations desired. Now his death was as base as his life was marvelous....

We shall not omit to say a few words about the many ways in which his shade was honored by his race. His body was placed in the midst of a plain and lay in state in a silken tent as a sight for men's admiration. The best horsemen of the entire tribe of the Huns rode around in circles, after the manner of circus games, in the place to which he had been brought and told of his deeds in a funeral dirge in the following manner: "The chief of the Huns, King Attila, born of his sire Mundiuch, lord of bravest tribes, sole possessor of the Scythian and German realms—powers unknown before—captured cities and terrified both empires of the Roman world and, appeased by their prayers, took annual tribute to save the rest from plunder. And when he had accomplished all this by the favor of fortune, he fell not by wound of the foe, nor by treachery of friends, but in the midst of his nation at peace, happy in his joy and without sense of pain. Who can rate this as death, when none believes it calls for vengeance?" When they had mourned him with such lamentations, a *strava*, as they call it, was celebrated over his tomb with great reveling. They gave way in turn to the extremes of feeling and displayed funereal grief alternating with joy. Then in the secrecy of night they buried his body in the earth. They bound his coffins, the first with gold, the second with silver and the third with the strength of iron, showing by such means that these three things suited the mightiest of kings; iron because he subdued the nations, gold and silver because he received the honors of both empires. They also added the arms of foemen won in the fight, trappings of rare worth, sparkling with various gems, and ornaments of all sorts whereby princely state is maintained. And that so great riches might be kept from human curiosity, they slew those appointed to the work—a dreadful pay for their labor; and thus sudden death was the lot of those who buried him as well as of him who was buried.

L … When Ardaric, king of the Gepidae, learned this, he became enraged because so many nations were being treated like slaves of the basest condition, and was the first to rise against the sons of Attila. Good fortune attended him, and he effaced the disgrace of servitude that rested upon him. For by his revolt he freed not only his own tribe, but all the others who were equally oppressed; since all readily strive for that which is sought for the general advantage. They took up arms against the destruction that menaced all and joined battle with the Huns in Pannonia, near a river called Nedao. There an encounter took place between the various nations Attila had held under his sway. Kingdoms with their peoples were divided, and out of one body were made many members not responding to a single impulse. Being deprived of their head, they madly strove against each other. They never found their equals ranged against them without harming each other by wounds mutually given. And so the bravest nations tore

themselves to pieces. For then, I think, must have occurred a most remarkable spectacle, where one might see the Goths fighting with pikes, the Gepidae raging with the sword, the Rugi breaking off the spears in their own wounds, the Suavi fighting on foot, the Huns with bows, the Alani drawing up a battle-line of heavy-armed and the Heruli of light-armed warriors.

Finally, after many bitter conflicts, victory fell unexpectedly to the Gepidae. For the sword and conspiracy of Ardaric destroyed almost thirty thousand men, Huns as well as those of the other nations who brought them aid. In this battle fell Ellac, the elder son of Attila, whom his father is said to have loved so much more than all the rest that he preferred him to any child or even to all the children in his kingdom. But fortune was not in accord with his father's wish. For after slaying many of the foe, it appears that he met his death so bravely that if his father had lived, he would have rejoiced at his glorious end. When Ellac was slain, his remaining brothers were put to flight near the shore of the Sea of Pontus, where we have said the Goths first settled. Thus did the Huns give way, a race to which men thought the whole world must yield. So baneful a thing is division, that they who used to inspire terror when their strength was united, were overthrown separately. The cause of Ardaric, king of the Gepidae, was fortunate for the various nations who were unwillingly subject to the rule of the Huns, for it raised their long downcast spirits to the glad hope of freedom. Many sent ambassadors to the Roman territory, where they were most graciously received by Marcian, who was then emperor, and took the abodes allotted them to dwell in. But the Gepidae by their own might won for themselves the territory of the Huns and ruled as victors over the extent of Dacia, demanding of the Roman Empire nothing more than peace and an annual gift as a pledge of their friendly alliance. This the emperor freely granted at the time, and to this day that race receives its customary gifts from the Roman emperor.

Now when the Goths saw the Gepidae defending for themselves the territory of the Huns, and the people of the Huns dwelling again in their ancient abodes, they preferred to ask for lands from the Roman Empire, rather than invade the lands of others with danger to themselves. So they received Pannonia, which stretches in a long plain, being bounded on the east by Upper Moesia, on the south by Dalmatia, on the west by Noricum and on the north by the Danube. This land is adorned with many cities, the first of which is Sirmium and the last Vindobona. But the Sauromatae, whom we call Sarmatians, and the Cemandri and certain of the Huns dwelt in Castra Martis, a city given them in the region of Illyricum. Of this race was Blivila, Duke of Pentapolis, and his brother Froila and also Bessa, a Patrician in our time. The Sciri, moreover, and the Sadagarii and certain of the Alani with their leader, Candac by name, received Scythia Minor and Lower Moesia. Paria, the father of my father Alanoviiamuth (that is to say, my grandfather), was secretary to this Candac as long as he lived. To his sister's son Gunthigis, also called Baza, the Master of the Soldiery, who was descended from the stock of the Amali, I also, Jordanes, although an unlearned man before my conversion, was secretary. The Rugi, however, and some other races asked that they might inhabit Bizye and Arcadiopolis. Hernac, the younger son of Attila, with his followers, chose a home in the most distant part of Lesser Scythia. Emnetzur and Ultzindur, kinsmen of his, won Oescus and Utus and Almus in Dacia on the banks of the Danube, and many of the Huns, then swarming everywhere, betook themselves into Romania, and from them the Sacromontisi and the Fossatisii of this day are said to be descended.

LI There were other Goths also, called the Lesser, a great people whose priest and primate was Vulfila, who is said to have taught them to write. And to-day they are in Moesia, inhabiting the Nicopolitan region as far as the base of Mount Haemus. They are a numerous people, but poor and unwarlike, rich in nothing save flocks of various kinds and pasture-lands for cattle and forests for wood. Their country is not fruitful in wheat and other sorts of grain. Some of them do not know that vineyards exist elsewhere, and they buy their wine from neighboring countries. But most of them drink milk.

LII Let us now return to the tribe with which we started, namely the Ostrogoths, who were dwelling in Pannonia under their king Valamir and his brothers Thiudimer and Vidimer. Although their territories were separate, yet their plans were one. For Valamir dwelt between the rivers Scarniunga and Aqua Nigra, Thiudimer near Lake Pelso and Vidimer between them both. Now it happened that the sons of Attila, regarding the Goths as deserters from their rule, came against them as though they were seeking fugitive slaves, and attacked Valamir alone, when his brothers knew nothing of it. He sustained their attack, though he had but few supporters, and after harassing them a long time, so utterly overwhelmed them that scarcely any portion of the enemy remained. The remnant turned in flight and sought the parts of Scythia which border on the stream of the river Danaper, which the Huns call in their own tongue the Var. Thereupon he sent a messenger of good tidings to his brother Thiudimer, and on the very day the messenger arrived he found even greater joy in the house of Thiudimer. For on that day his son Theodoric was born, of a concubine Erelieva indeed, and yet a child of good hope.

Now after no great time King Valamir and his brothers Thiudimer and Vidimer sent an embassy to the Emperor Marcian, because the usual gifts which they received like a New Year's present from the emperor, to preserve the compact of peace, were slow in arriving. And they found that Theodoric, son of Triarius, a man of Gothic blood also, but born of another stock, not of the Amali, was in great favor, together with his followers. He was allied in friendship with the Romans and obtained an annual bounty, while they themselves were merely held in disdain. Thereat they were aroused to frenzy and took up arms. They roved through almost the whole of Illyricum and laid it waste in their search for spoil. Then the emperor quickly changed his mind and returned to his former state of friendship. He sent an embassy to give them the past gifts, as well as those now due, and furthermore promised to give these gifts in future without any dispute. From the Goths the Romans received as a hostage of peace Theodoric, the young child of Thiudimer, whom we have mentioned above. He had now attained the age of seven years and was entering upon his eighth. While his father hesitated about giving him up, his uncle Valamir besought him to do it, hoping that peace between the Romans and the Goths might thus be assured. Therefore Theodoric was given as a hostage by the Goths and brought to the city of Constantinople to the Emperor Leo and, being a goodly child, deservedly gained the imperial favor.

LIII Now after firm peace was established between Goths and Romans, the Goths found that the possessions they had received from the emperor were not sufficient for them. Furthermore, they were eager to display their wonted valor, and so began to plunder the neighboring races around them, first attacking the Sadagis who held the interior of Pannonia. When Dintzic, king of the Huns, a son of Attila, learned this, he gathered to him the few who still seemed to have remained under his sway, namely, the Ultzinzures, the Angisciri, the Bittugures and the Bardores. Coming to Bassiana, a city of Pannonia, he beleaguered it and began to plunder its territory. Then the Goths at once abandoned the expedition they had planned against the Sadagis, turned upon the Huns and drove them so ingloriously from their own land that those who remained have been in dread of the arms of the Goths from that time even down to the present day.

When the tribe of the Huns was at last subdued by the Goths, Hunimund, chief of the Suavi, who was crossing over to plunder Dalmatia, carried off some cattle of the Goths which were straying over the plains; for Dalmatia was near Suavia and not far distant from the territory of Pannonia, especially that part where the Goths were then staying. So then, as Hunimund was returning with the Suavi to his own country, after he had devastated Dalmatia, Thiudimer the brother of Valamir, king of the Goths, kept watch on their line of march. Not that he grieved so much over the loss of his cattle, but he feared that if the Suavi obtained this plunder with impunity, they would proceed to greater license. So in the dead of night, while they were asleep, he made an unexpected attack on them, near Lake Pelso. Here he so completely crushed them that he took captive and sent into slavery under the Goths even Hunimund, their king, and all of his army who had escaped the sword. Yet as he was a great lover of mercy, he granted pardon after taking vengeance and became reconciled to the Suavi. He adopted as his son the same man whom he had taken captive, and sent him back with his followers into Suavia. But Hunimund was unmindful of his adopted father's kindness. After some time he brought forth a plot he had contrived and aroused the tribe of the Sciri, who then dwelt above the Danube and abode peaceably with the Goths. So the Sciri broke off their alliance with them, took up arms, joined themselves to Hunimund and went out to attack the race of the Goths. Thus war came upon the Goths who were expecting no evil, because they relied upon both of their neighbors as friends. Constrained by necessity they took up arms and avenged themselves and their injuries by recourse to battle. In this battle, as King Valamir rode on his horse before the line to encourage his men, the horse was wounded and fell, overthrowing its rider. Valamir was quickly pierced by his enemies' spears and slain. Thereupon the Goths proceeded to exact vengeance for the death of their king, as well as for the injury done them by the rebels. They fought in such wise that there remained of all the race of the Sciri only a few who bore the name, and they with disgrace. Thus were all destroyed.

LIV The kings [of the Suavi], Hunimund and Alaric, fearing the destruction that had come upon the Sciri, next made war upon the Goths, relying upon the aid of the Sarmatians, who had come to them as auxiliaries with their kings Beuca and Babai. They summoned the last remnants of the Sciri, with Edica and Hunuulf, their chieftains, thinking they would fight the more desperately to avenge themselves. They had on their side the Gepidae also, as well as no small reinforcements from the race of the Rugi and from others gathered here and there. Thus they brought together a great host at the river Bolia in Pannonia and encamped there. Now when Valamir was dead, the Goths fled to Thiudimer, his brother. Although he had long ruled along with his brothers, yet he took the insignia of increased authority and summoned his younger brother Vidimer and shared with him the cares of war, resorting to arms under compulsion. A battle was fought and the party of the Goths was found to be so much the stronger that the plain was drenched in the blood of their fallen foes and looked like a crimson sea. Weapons and corpses, piled up like hills, covered the plain for more than ten miles. When the Goths saw this, they rejoiced with joy unspeakable, because by this great slaughter of their foes they had avenged the blood of Valamir their king and the injury done themselves. But those of the innumerable and motley throng of the foe who were unable to escape, though they got away, nevertheless came to their own land with difficulty and without glory.

LV After a certain time, when the wintry cold was at hand, the river Danube was frozen over as usual. For a river like this freezes so hard that it will support like a solid rock an army of footsoldiers and wagons and sledges and whatsoever vehicles there may be—nor is there need of skiffs and boats. So when Thiudimer, king of the Goths, saw that it was frozen, he led his army across the Danube and appeared unexpectedly to the Suavi from the rear. Now this country of the Suavi has on the east the Baiovari, on the west the Franks, on the south the Burgundians and on the north the Thuringians. With the Suavi there were present the Alamanni, then their confederates, who also ruled the Alpine heights, whence several streams flow into the Danube, pouring in with a great rushing sound. Into a place thus fortified King Thiudimer led his army in the winter-time and conquered, plundered and almost subdued the race of the Suavi as well as the Alamanni, who were mutually banded together. Thence he returned as victor to his own home in Pannonia and joyfully received his own son Theodoric, once given as hostage to Constantinople and now sent back by the Emperor Leo with great gifts. Now Theodoric had reached man's estate, for he was eighteen years of age and his boyhood was ended. So he summoned certain of his father's adherents and took to himself from the people his friends and retainers—almost six thousand men. With these he crossed the Danube, without his father's knowledge, and marched against Babai, king of the Sarmatians, who had just won a victory over Camundus, a general of the Romans, and was ruling with insolent pride. Theodoric came upon him and slew him, and taking as booty his slaves and treasure, returned victorious to his father.

Next he invaded the city of Singidunum, which the Sarmatians themselves had seized, and did not return to the Romans, but reduced it to his own sway.

LVI Then as the spoil taken from one and another of the neighboring tribes diminished, the Goths began to lack food and clothing, and peace became distasteful to men for whom war had long furnished the necessaries of life. So all the Goths approached their king Thiudimer and, with great outcry, begged him to lead forth his army in whatsoever direction he might wish. He summoned his brother and, after casting lots, bade him go into the country of Italy, where at this time Glycerius ruled as emperor, saying that he himself as the mightier would go to the east against a mightier empire. And so it happened. Thereupon Vidimer entered the land of Italy, but soon paid the last debt of fate and departed from earthly affairs, leaving his son and namesake Vidimer to succeed him. The Emperor Glycerius bestowed gifts upon Vidimer and persuaded him to go from Italy to Gaul, which was then harassed on all sides by various races, saying that their own kinsmen, the Visigoths, there ruled a neighboring kingdom. And what more? Vidimer accepted the gifts and, obeying the command of the Emperor Glycerius, pressed on to Gaul. Joining with his kinsmen the Visigoths, they again formed one body, as they had been long ago. Thus they held Gaul and Spain by their own right and so defended them that no other race won the mastery there.

But Thiudimer, the elder brother, crossed the river Savus with his men, threatening the Sarmatians and their soldiers with war if any should resist him. From fear of this they kept quiet; moreover they were powerless in the face of so great a host. Thiudimer, seeing prosperity everywhere awaiting him, invaded Naissus, the first city of Illyricum. He was joined by his son Theodoric and the Counts Astat and Invilia, and sent them to Ulpiana by way of Castrum Herculis. Upon their arrival the town surrendered, as did Stobi later; and several places of Illyricum, inaccessible to them at first, were thus made easy of approach. For they first plundered and then ruled by right of war Heraclea and Larissa, cities of Thessaly. But Thiudimer the king, perceiving his own good fortune and that of his son, was not content with this alone, but set forth from the city of Naissus, leaving only a few men behind as a guard. He himself advanced to Thessalonica, where Hilarianus the Patrician, appointed by the emperor, was stationed with his army. When Hilarianus beheld Thessalonica surrounded by an entrenchment and saw that he could not resist attack, he sent an embassy to Thiudimer the king and by the offer of gifts turned him aside from destroying the city. Then the Roman general entered upon a truce with the Goths and of his own accord handed over to them those places they inhabited, namely Cyrrhus, Pella, Europus, Methone, Pydna, Beroea, and another which is called Dium. So the Goths and their king laid aside their arms, consented to peace and became quiet. Soon after these events, King Thiudimer was seized with a mortal illness in the city of Cyrrhus. He called the Goths to himself, appointed Theodoric his son as heir of the kingdom and presently departed this life.

LVII When the Emperor Zeno heard that Theodoric had been appointed king over his own people, he received the news with pleasure and invited him to come and visit him in the city, sending an escort of honor. Receiving Theodoric with all due respect, he placed him among the princes of his palace. After some time Zeno increased his dignity by adopting him as his son-in-arms and gave him a triumph in the city at his expense. Theodoric was made Consul Ordinary also, which is well known to be the supreme good and highest honor in the world. Nor was this all, for Zeno set up before the royal palace an equestrian statue to the glory of this great man.

Now while Theodoric was in alliance by treaty with the empire of Zeno and was himself enjoying every comfort in the city, he heard that his tribe, dwelling as we have said in Illyricum, was not altogether satisfied or content. So he chose rather to seek a living by his own exertions, after the manner customary to his race, rather than to enjoy the advantages of the Roman Empire in luxurious ease while his tribe lived apart. After pondering these matters, he said to the emperor: "Though I lack nothing in serving your empire, yet if Your Piety deem it worthy, be pleased to hear the desire of my heart." And when as usual he had been granted permission to speak freely, he said: "The western country, long ago governed by the rule of your ancestors and predecessors, and that city which was the head and mistress of the world—wherefore is it now shaken by the tyranny of the Torcilingi and the Rugi? Send me there with my race. Thus if you but say the word, you may be freed from the burden of expense here, and, if by the Lord's help I shall conquer, the fame of Your Piety shall be glorious there. For it is better that I, your servant and your son, should rule that kingdom, receiving it as a gift from you if I conquer, than that one whom you do not recognize should oppress your Senate with his tyrannical yoke and a part of the republic with slavery. For if I prevail, I shall retain it as your grant and gift; if I am conquered, Your Piety will lose nothing—nay, as I have said, it will save the expense I now entail." Although the emperor was grieved that he should go, yet when he heard this he granted what Theodoric asked, for he was unwilling to cause him sorrow. He sent him forth enriched by great gifts and commended to his charge the Senate and the Roman people.

Therefore Theodoric departed from the royal city and returned to his own people. In company with the whole tribe of the Goths, who gave him their unanimous consent, he set out for Hesperia. He went in straight march through Sirmium to the places bordering on Pannonia and, advancing into the territory of Venetia as far as the bridge of the Sontius, encamped there. When he had halted there for some time to rest the bodies of his men and pack-animals, Odoacer sent an armed force against him, which he met on the plains of Verona and destroyed with great slaughter. Then he broke camp and advanced through Italy with greater boldness. Crossing the river Po, he pitched camp near the royal city of Ravenna, about the third milestone from the city in the place called Pineta. When Odoacer saw this, he fortified himself within the city. He frequently harassed the army of the Goths at night, sallying forth stealthily with his men, and this not once or twice, but often; and thus he struggled for almost three whole years. But he labored in vain, for all Italy at last called Theodoric its lord and the empire obeyed his nod. But Odoacer, with his few adherents and the Romans who were present, suffered daily from war and famine in Ravenna. Since he accomplished nothing, he sent an embassy and begged for mercy. Theodoric first granted it and afterwards deprived him of his life.

It was in the third year after his entrance into Italy, as we have said, that Theodoric, by advice of the Emperor Zeno, laid aside the garb of a private citizen and the dress of his race and assumed a costume with a royal mantle, as he had now become the ruler over both the Goths and Romans. He sent an embassy to Lodoin, king of the Franks, and asked for his daughter Audefleda in marriage. Lodoin freely and gladly gave her, and also his sons Celdebert and Heldebert and Thiudebert, believing that by this alliance a league would be formed and that they would be associated with the race of the Goths. But that union was of no avail for peace and harmony, for they fought fiercely with each other again and again for the lands of the Goths; but never did the Goths yield to the Franks while Theodoric lived.

LVIII Now before he had a child from Audefleda, Theodoric had children of a concubine, daughters begotten in Moesia, one named Thiudigoto and another Ostrogotho. Soon after he came to Italy, he gave them in marriage to neighboring kings, one to Alaric, king of the Visigoths, and the other to Sigsimund, king of the Burgundians. Now Alaric begat Amalaric. While his grandfather Theodoric cared for and protected him—for he had lost both parents in the years of childhood—he found that Eutharic, the son of Veteric, grandchild of Beremud and of Thorismud, and a descendant of the race of the Amali, was living in Spain, a young man strong in wisdom and valor and health of body. Theodoric sent for him and gave him his daughter Amalasuentha in marriage. And that he might extend his family as much as possible, he sent his sister Amalafrida (the mother of Theodahad, who was afterwards king) to Africa as wife of Thrasamund, king of the Vandals, and her daughter Amalaberga, who was his own niece, he united with Herminefred, king of the Thuringians.

Now he sent his Count Pitza, chosen from among the chief men of his kingdom, to hold the city of Sirmium. He got possession of it by driving out its king Thrasaric, son of Thraustila, and keeping his mother captive. Thence he came with two thousand infantry and five hundred horsemen to aid Mundo against Sabinian, Master of the Soldiery of Illyricum, who at that time had made ready to fight with Mundo near the city named Margoplanum, which lies between the Danube and Margus rivers, and destroyed the Army of Illyricum. For this Mundo, who traced his descent from the Attilani of old, had fled from the tribe of the Gepidae and was roaming around beyond the Danube in waste places where no man tilled the soil. He had gathered around him many outlaws and ruffians and robbers from all sides and had seized a tower called Herta, situated on the bank of the Danube. There he plundered his neighbors in wild license and made himself king over his vagabonds. Now Pitza came upon him when he was nearly reduced to desperation and was already thinking of surrender. So he rescued him from the hands of the Sabinian and made him a grateful subject of his king Theodoric.

Theodoric won an equally great victory over the Franks through his Count Ibba in Gaul, when more than thirty thousand Franks were slain in battle. Moreover, after the death of his son-in-law Alaric, Theodoric appointed Thiudis, his armor-bearer, guardian of his grandson Amalaric in Spain. But Amalaric was ensnared by the plots of the Franks in early youth and lost at once his kingdom and his life. Then his guardian Thiusis, advancing from the same kingdom, assailed the Franks and delivered the Spaniards from their disgraceful treachery. So long as he lived he kept the Visigoths united. After him Thiudigisclus obtained the kingdom and, ruling but a short time, met his death at the hands of his own followers. He was succeeded by Agil, who holds the kingdom to the present day. Athanagild has rebelled against him and is even now provoking the might of the Roman Empire. So Liberius the Patrician is on the way with an army to oppose him. Now there was not a tribe in the west that did not serve Theodoric while he lived, either in friendship or by conquest.

LIX When he had reached old age and knew that he should soon depart this life, he called together the Gothic counts and chieftains of his race and appointed Athalaric as king. He was a boy scarce ten years old, the son of his daughter Amalasuentha, and he had lost his father Eutharic. As though uttering his last will and testament, Theodoric adjured and commanded them to honor their king, to love the Senate and Roman people and to make sure of the peace and good will of the emperor of the east, as next after God.

They kept this command fully so long as Athalaric their king and his mother lived, and ruled in peace for almost eight years. But as the Franks put no confidence in the rule of a child and furthermore held him in contempt, and were also plotting war, he gave back to them those parts of Gaul which his father and grandfather had seized. He possessed all the rest in peace and quiet. Therefore when Athalaric was approaching the age of manhood, he entrusted to the emperor of the east both his own youth and his mother's widowhood. But in a short time the ill-fated boy was carried off by an untimely death and departed from earthly affairs. His mother feared she might be despised by the Goths on account of the weakness of her sex. So after much thought she decided, for the sake of relationship, to summon her cousin Theodahad from Tuscany, where he led a retired life at home, and thus she established him on the throne. But he was unmindful of their kinship and, after a little time, had her taken from the palace at Ravenna to an island of the Bulsinian lake where he kept her in exile. After spending a very few days there in sorrow, she was strangled in the bath by his hirelings.

LX When Justinian, the emperor of the east, heard this, he was aroused as if he had suffered personal injury in the death of his wards. Now at that time he had won a triumph over the Vandals in Africa, through his most faithful Patrician Belisarius. Without delay he sent his army under this leader against the Goths at the very time when his arms were yet dripping with the blood of the Vandals. This sagacious general believed he could not overcome the Gothic nation, unless he should first seize Sicily, their nursing-mother. Accordingly he did so. As soon as he entered Trinacria, the Goths, who were besieging the town of Syracuse, found that they were not succeeding and surrendered of their own accord to Belisarius, with their leader Sinderith. When the Roman general reached Sicily, Theodahad sought out Evermud, his son-in-law, and sent him with an army to guard the strait which lies between Campania and Sicily and sweeps from a bend of the Tyrrhenian Sea into the vast tide of the Adriatic. When Evermud arrived, he pitched his camp by the town of Rhegium. He soon saw that his side was the weaker. Coming over with a few close and faithful followers to the side of the victor and willingly casting himself at the feet of Belisarius, he decided to serve the rulers of the Roman Empire. When the army of the Goths perceived this, they distrusted Theodahad and clamored for his expulsion from the kingdom and for the appointment as king of their leader Vitiges, who had been his armor-bearer. This was done; and presently Vitiges was raised to the office of king on the Barbarian Plains. He entered Rome and sent on to Ravenna the men most faithful to him to demand the death of Theodahad. They came and executed his command. After King Theodahad was slain, a messenger came from the king—for he was already king in the Barbarian Plains—to proclaim Vitiges to the people.

Meanwhile the Roman army crossed the strait and marched toward Campania. They took Naples and pressed on to Rome. Now a few days before they arrived, King Vitiges had set forth from Rome, arrived at Ravenna and married Mathesuentha, the daughter of Amalasuentha and grand-daughter of Theodoric, the former king. While he was celebrating his new marriage and holding court at Ravenna, the imperial army advanced from Rome and attacked the strongholds in both parts of Tuscany. When Vitiges learned of this through messengers, he sent a force under Hunila, a leader of the Goths, to Perusia which was beleaguered by them. While they were endeavoring by a long siege to dislodge Count Magnus, who was holding the place with a small force, the Roman army came upon them, and they themselves were driven away and utterly exterminated. When Vitiges heard the news, he raged like a lion and assembled all the host of the Goths. He advanced from Ravenna and harassed the walls of Rome with a long siege. But after fourteen months his courage was broken and he raised the siege of the city of Rome and prepared to overwhelm Ariminum. Here he was baffled in like manner and put to flight; and so he retreated to Ravenna. When besieged there, he quickly and willingly surrendered himself to the victorious side, together with his wife Mathesuentha and the royal treasure.

And thus a famous kingdom and most valiant race, which had long held sway, was at last overcome in almost its two thousand and thirtieth year by that conqueror of many nations, the Emperor Justinian, through his most faithful consul Belisarius. He gave Vitiges the title of Patrician and took him to Constantinople, where he dwelt for more than two years, bound by ties of affection to the emperor, and then departed this life. But his consort Mathesuentha was bestowed by the emperor upon the Patrician Germanus, his nephew. And of them was born a son (also called Germanus) after the death of his father Germanus. This union of the race of the Anicii with the stock of the Amali gives hopeful promise, under the Lord's favor, to both peoples.

Conclusion

And now we have recited the origin of the Goths, the noble line of the Amali and the deeds of brave men. This glorious race yielded to a more glorious prince and surrendered to a more valiant leader, whose fame shall be silenced by no ages or cycles of years; for the victorious and triumphant Emperor Justinian and his consul Belisarius shall be named and known as Vandalicus, Africanus and Geticus.

Thou who readest this, know that I have followed the writings of my ancestors, and have culled a few flowers from their broad meadows to weave a chaplet for him who cares to know these things. Let no one believe that to the advantage of the race of which I have spoken—though indeed I trace my own descent from it—I have added aught besides what I have read or learned by inquiry. Even thus I have not included all that is written or told about them, nor spoken so much to their praise as to the glory of him who conquered them.

6. HILDEBRANDSLIED

THE FRAGMENTARY SONG OF *Hildebrand and Hadubrand*, the oldest extant continental Germanic heroic poem, was copied into a manuscript in the monastery of Fulda around 800. The current scholarly opinion is that the poem was composed in the eighth century in Lombardy, drawing on a much older Gothic tradition of the fifth and sixth centuries concerning the family of the Brandings: Heribrand, Hildebrand, and Hadubrand. Versions of the legend spread throughout the Germanic and Celtic worlds from Germany to Scandinavia to Ireland. The poem presents the complex world of late antiquity from the perspective of the Barbarians as well as the tragic conflict between honor and kindred.

Source: *Von Hildebrand und Hadubrand: Lied—Sage—Mythos*, trans. Sigfried Gutenbrunner (Heidelberg: Winter, 1976).

Further Reading: Cyril Edwards, *The Beginnings of German Literature: Comparative and Interdisciplinary Approaches to Old High German* (Rochester: Camden House, 2002).

The Song of Hildebrand and Hadubrand

That I heard it said …[1]
that two warriors encountered each other
Hildebrand and Hadubrand, between their
    two armies.
Son and father looked to their armor,
They prepared their battle-dress, their swords
    the heroes belted fast
Over their ring-armor, and then they rode to
    the battle.
Hildebrand spoke, Heribrand's son; he was
    the older man,
Experienced in the world. He began to ask
With few words, who his father was
From among the heroes of the people …
… "or of what ancestry are you?
Name but one, the others I will know,
Youth, in the kingdoms all the kindreds are
    known to me."
Hadubrand spoke, Hildebrand's son:
"Long ago our people told me,
The elders and sages who had lived long,
That my father was called Hildebrand, I am
    called Hadubrand.
Long ago he went east, fled the anger of
    Odoacer,
With Dietrich [Theoderic] and his many
    swordsmen.

He established misery in the land
The woman in the home, the small child,
He robbed of their inheritance, and then rode
    east.
Therefore my father was and remained for
    Dietrich
Indispensable, he was such a reliable man.
He was a great enemy of Odoacer But he was
    the best of the swords with Dietrich;
He was always at the head of the army;
    swordplay was always dear to him.
He was known to many brave men.
I do not imagine that he still wanders the
    earth."
Hildebrand spoke, Heribrand's son:
"The Father of All above in heaven knows
That never before have you exchanged speech
    with so close a kinsman."
Then he took from his arm a twisted ring,
Made from Emperor's gold, as the king had
    given it to him,
The lord of the Huns: "This I give to you as a
    gift!"
Hadubrand spoke, Hildebrand's son:
"With the spear should one receive gifts,
Point against point.
You old Hun, outrageous trickster,

---

1   Ellipses indicate lost portions of the poem.

You entice me with your words, you want to
    cast me down with the spear,
You have become so old that you intend only
    treachery.
This men have told me who have traveled to
    the sea
And westward over the earth-encircling sea:
    War took him away,
Hildebrand is dead, Heribrand's son."
Hildebrand spoke, Heribrand's son:
"In truth I hear it and see it in your war-gear,
That you have at home a lord so good
That under this prince you would never be
    exiled." …
"Now sorrow, ruling god, the destiny of woe
    fulfills itself!
I have traveled through sixty summers and
    winters,
Always I was counted among the most
    forward
But before none of the cities did I come to die;
Now my child must kill me with the sword,

Must lay me low with the death-ax, or else I
    must become his killer!
Now you lightly wish, if you have the power,
To win the armor of so old a hero,
To capture the spoils if you have the right to
    them!"
He would be the most repulsive of all the East
    people (said Hildebrand)
Who would refuse you battle, now he gladly
    desires
Hand to hand battle with you! May the
    encounter decide
Which of us must today lose his armor
Or possess both coats of mail.
Then first they sprang at each other with
    spears
In hard attacks; the shields protect them.
Then they rush together to bitter swordplay,
The bright shields strike sorrowfully
Until the linden wood became light to them
Ground away by the weapons …

7. THE TOMB OF CHILDERIC, FATHER OF CLOVIS

IN 1653 THE TOMB of the Frankish chieftain Childeric (d. 481 or 482) was discovered at Tournai, Belgium. Most of the extremely precious objects from the tomb were stolen and destroyed in the nineteenth century. However, descriptions and sketches of them, as well as objects recently discovered in the area surrounding the tomb, have made it possible to reconstruct the multi-ethnic and multi-cultural world of such Germanic chieftains.

These objects include a lance and an ax typical of northern Gaul and particularly of "Frankish" warriors. Childeric's cruciform broach or fibula is of Roman origin, and similar pieces have been found in Hungary and the former Czechoslovakia. His signet ring with its inscription "Childerici regis" is also typically Roman, although the inscription itself, indicating that he is a king, is a barbarian title granted perhaps but not carried by Romans. Another fibula found recently near the tomb appears to be Anglo-Saxon. Childeric's long sword and shorter sword with a single blade resemble others found in Pannonia, and the cloisonné enamels of bees and other zoomorphic motifs indicate a strong oriental influence although they were probably produced in northern Gaul. Finally, the form of burial itself, although difficult to interpret, apparently was a tumulus or mound in which the chieftain and at least one horse were buried, while a herd of at least thirty horses were killed and buried around his tomb. Such a burial is much more typical of Alans and Sarmats from Iran than of western Germanic peoples.

Source: Patrick Périn and Laure-Charlotte Feffer, *Les Francs*, vol. I: *À la conquête de la Gaule*, trans. Joelle Favreau (Paris: Colin, 1987), 119–33.

Further Reading: Bonnie Effros, *Merovingian Mortuary Archaeology and the Making of the Early Middle Ages* (Berkeley: University of California Press, 2003).

Childeric's tomb was discovered on May 27, 1653, at 3 p.m. by a deaf-mute mason, Adrien Quinquin, during the Saint-Brice hospice reconstructions in Tournai. At 2.50 m deep, Quinquin brought to light the remnants of a leather bag full of gold coins, then a gold bracelet, fragments of iron and, most importantly, a large quantity of jewelry cloisonné with garnet. Among these objects was a gold signet ring with the inscription CHILDERICI REGIS. In fact it was the tomb of Childeric, Clovis's father.

Exceptional in its value, the funeral artifacts found in Childeric's tomb are also remarkable for their precise dating. It was in 481 or 482 that Clovis succeeded his father. The date of his father's death is corroborated by the signet ring. Indeed, this date constitutes an exact *terminus ante quem* for the dating of the objects gathered in Tournai in 1653, corroborated by the period of issue of the most recent coins found in the royal grave (bearing the effigy of the Emperor Zeno).

Dated to the third quarter of the fifth century, these funeral artifacts still raise two problems: first, the identification of some of their components because of the almost total ignorance of their original sites in the tomb; second, the appreciation of the circumstances that led to the accumulation of all these objects, modest or precious.

While it is possible to allocate precisely the cloisonné ornaments which belonged to the long sword and to the scramasax [single-edged short sword], and to attribute to the royal costume some accessories (belt and shoe buckles, cruciform buckle, purse clasp) and jewels (bracelets, signet ring, ring), archeologists still remain divided as to the identification of other objects, considered by some as clothing accessories and by others as ornaments for the harness of the royal horse. It is the same for the possibility of an adjacent woman's burial place, granted to Basina[1](second skullcap, sphere of rock crystal characteristic of a woman's costume). The apparent presence of the tomb of a horse (whose head was found) also divides the archeologists: was the entire horse buried, or the head only, or merely the harness? The three possibilities are all plausible, taking into account other similar discoveries.

As controversial is the question of influences reflected by the components of Childeric's funeral artifacts. In a schematic manner, one can try to isolate several lines of influence. The spear and the ax, classic during that era in northern Gaul, must be attributed to the "Frankish" warlike style. The gold cruciform buckle of Roman origin (similar to those found in the tombs of Barbarian princes of Apahida, in Hungary, and of Blucina, in the former Czechoslovakia), as well as the signet ring (also present in Apahida), illustrate in an eloquent way that the "Roman" style was adopted by Barbarian princes in contact with the Empire. Childeric's tomb also reveals the style then common to the Germans as a whole and even to other Barbarians such as the Alani-Sarmatians (Iranians): the actual funeral pomp (possibly completed by the presence of an adjacent tomb for a horse, with the collective sacrifice of a herd of domestic horses); the presence on the right wrist of a permanently fixed solid gold bracelet which, as in the Apahida, Blucina, and Pouan (Aube) tombs, showed the princely status of these wealthy warriors.

Of other influences, perhaps the most spectacular can be termed "Danubian." Parallels between the tombs of Tournai and Pouan and those of wealthy warriors from the oriental Germanic world (more precisely of the Danubian regions such as the Gepide burial places of Apahida and the Lombard or Skire tombs of Blucina), were identified long ago. In all these cases the tomb has held a long sword and a straight sword with a narrow blade and only one cutting edge; clothing accessories such as massive belt buckles equipped with tongues with large shields; and the ornaments of cloisonné jewelry. These parallels suggest that Childeric's tomb must be directly related to the Germanic tombs which were part of the contemporary Germanic culture that survived the fall of the Hunnic Empire in 455. The parallels should not be assumed to result from Attila and the Huns' raid in Gaul in 451. Indeed, at the end of the fourth century and during the first half of the fifth century, some rare discoveries in occidental Europe (men's tombs at Wolfsheim, Altussheim, and Mundolsheim, in the Middle Rhine or vicinity; Béja in Portugal; women's tombs of Hochfelden in Alsace and of Airan in Calvados) testify that there were already contacts with the Danubian regions. These contacts were broadened during the second half of the fifth century and facilitated the adoption and imitation by the occidental Barbarian courts of some styles popular in the oriental Germanic world.

While the cloisonné enamel objects of Childeric's tomb, and in particular the sword and scramasax sword, testify to the remarkable work of several workshops or of several goldsmiths, it does not seem possible today to try to separate those that could have been imported from the Danubian regions or fabricated at the Frankish court by goldsmiths who were native to these regions from those that were produced by local craftsmen imitating the oriental productions. The most plausible hypothesis, supported by the presence of decorated designs that were totally foreign to the oriental world, is that all of Childeric's funeral artifacts were made in northern Gaul by goldsmiths who were either of oriental origin or were working largely according to the traditions of oriental goldsmiths (among which some probably were not "Barbarians," but, for example, Greeks).

Recent excavations in Tournai around the Saint-Brice church have shed some new light on the archeological environment of Childeric's tomb. For example, until 1983 it was thought that this royal burial, established on the site of an old

---

1   Daughter of Chilperic.

Roman necropolis of the first and second centuries, was isolated. While the recent research had not been able to date this graveyard to the late Empire, it nonetheless has revealed the presence of a series of Merovingian burial places dating from the second half of the fifth century to the seventh century. However, it has not been possible to determine whether the oldest ones among them were prior or contemporary to Childeric's tomb. Therefore it is now established that the royal grave was part of an original core of a Merovingian necropolis and may have marked its beginning.

Several Merovingian burial places have been found to contain rich funeral artifacts: proof that Tournai remained an important town at the beginning of the early Middle Ages, even though it was no longer a Merovingian capital. Also

significant has been the discovery of three collective burial places of horses, each containing a dozen animals, most of them stallions. These burial places, which lacked artifacts, have been dated to the second half of the fifth century or to the beginning of the sixth century (C14 dating, between 430 and 560 and more probably 440 and 540). Taking into consideration that their location was around 20 m from Childeric's tomb, it is likely that they bear some direct relation to the royal burial. Thus a new detail may be added to our picture of the funeral splendor of Clovis's father: the collective sacrifice of a whole herd of domestic horses. There are no precise parallels for this exceptional ritual in the occidental Germanic world; indeed, in Westphalia as well as in Thuringia, such burials involved only two or three horses.

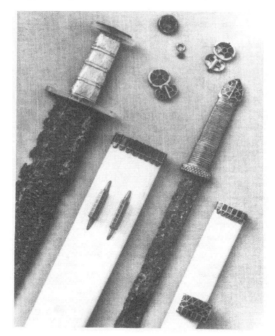

"Treasure of Pouan." The sword and the scramasax.

Childeric's tomb. Zoomorphic purse clasps.

Two gold bees cloisonné with garnet from the "Childeric's treasure."

The signet ring of Childeric I.

Gilded silver bracelet with zoomorphic ends.

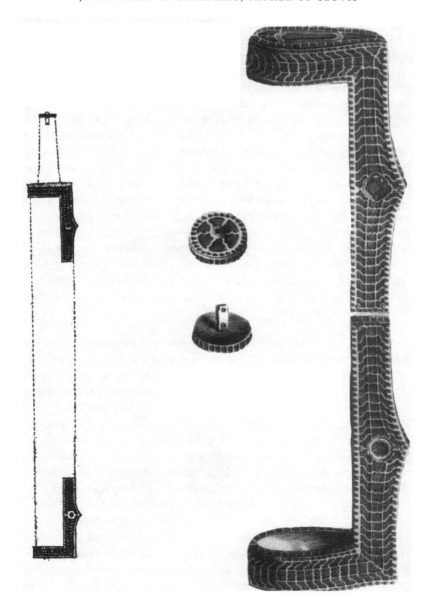

Childeric's tomb. Reconstruction of the scramasax sheath. Knob of button and scramasax appliqués of cloisonné goldsmith work.

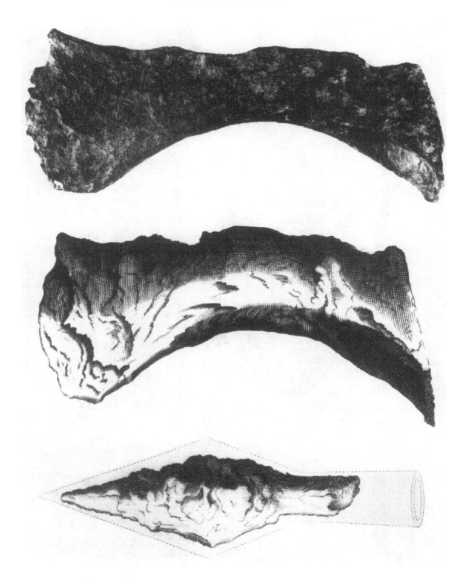

Childeric's tomb. Frankish battle-ax. Spear.

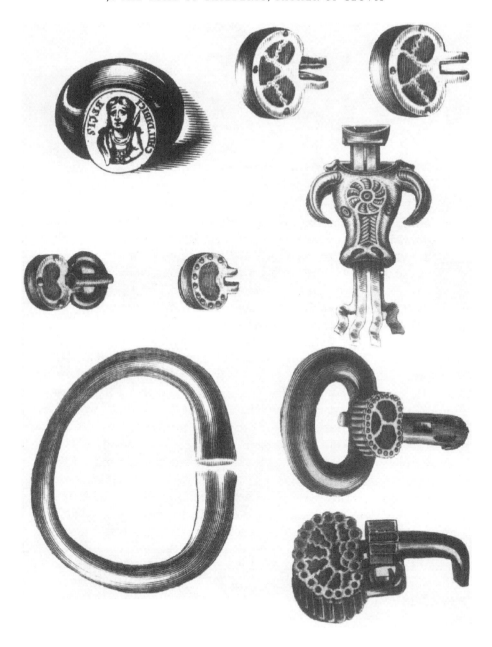

Childeric's tomb. Signet ring and gold bracelet. Belt and shoe buckles and appliqués.

Collective tomb of horses near Childeric's tomb.

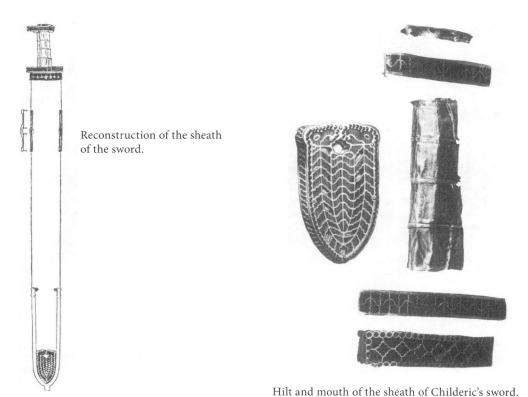

Reconstruction of the sheath
of the sword.

Hilt and mouth of the sheath of Childeric's sword.

Anglo-Saxon–type buckle with zoomorphic and anthropomorphic design, sixth century.

8. SALIC LAW

THE FIRST CODIFICATION OF Salic law took place under King Clovis (481–511) and represents the shift from oral tradition to a literary one for the Franks. The laws were drawn up with the assistance of Gallo-Romans trained in the Roman legal tradition. However they also contain much that may date from Frankish customs from as early as the fourth century. The Salic Franks, from which these laws derive their name, were originally members of a single tribe, the *Salii*, who eventually became the most dominant group within the Frankish confederation. These laws would have been applicable throughout Clovis's kingdom, except for the Gallo-Romans still following Roman legal precedents.

Source: E.F. Henderson (ed.), *Select Historical Documents of the Middle Ages* (London: George Bell, 1892), 176–89.

Further Reading: Patrick Wormald, "Lex Scripta and Verbum Regis: Legislation and Germanic Kinship, from Euric to Cnut," in P.H. Sawyer and I.N. Wood (eds.), *Early Medieval Kingship* (Leeds: The School of History, University of Leeds, 1977), 105–38.

Title I. Concerning Summonses.

1. If any one be summoned before the "Thing" by the king's law, and do not come, he shall be sentenced to 600 denars, which make 15 shillings (solidi).

2. But he who summons another, and does not come himself, shall, if a lawful impediment have not delayed him, be sentenced to 15 shillings, to be paid to him whom he summoned.

3. And he who summons another shall walk with witnesses to the home of that man, and, if he be not at home, shall bid the wife or any one of the family to make known to him that he has been summoned to court.

4. But if he be occupied in the king's service he can not summon him.

5. But if he shall be inside the hundred[1] seeing about his own affairs, he can summon him in the manner explained above.

Title II. Concerning Thefts of Pigs, etc.

1. If any one steal a suckling pig, and it be proved against him, he shall be sentenced to 120 denars, which make three shillings.

2. If any one steal a pig that can live without its mother, and it be proved on him, he shall be sentenced to 40 denars—that is, 1 shilling.

3. If any one steal 25 sheep where there were no more in that flock, and it be proved on him, he shall be sentenced to 2500 denars—that is, 62 shillings.

Title III. Concerning Thefts of Cattle.

4. If any one steal that bull which rules the herd and never has been yoked, he shall be sentenced to 1800 denars, which make 45 shillings.

5. But if that bull is used for the cows of three villages in common, he who stole him shall be sentenced to three times 45 shillings.

6. If any one steal a bull belonging to the king he shall be sentenced to 3600 denars, which make 90 shillings.

---

1   A small territorial subdivision that may have corresponded to the land sufficient to sustain one hundred families.

Title IV. Concerning Damage done among Crops or in any Enclosure.

1. If any one finds cattle or a horse, or flocks of any kind in his crops, he shall not at all mutilate them.

2. If he do this and confess it, he shall restore the worth of the animal in place of it, and shall himself keep the mutilated one.

3. But if he have not confessed it, and it have been proved on him, he shall be sentenced, besides the value of the animal and the fines for delay, to 600 denars, which make 15 shillings. …

Title XI. Concerning Thefts or Housebreakings of Freemen.

1. If any freeman steal, outside of the house, something worth 2 denars, he shall be sentenced to 600 denars, which make 15 shillings.

2. But if he steal, outside of the house, something worth 40 denars, and it be proved on him, he shall be sentenced, besides the amount and the fines for delay, to 1400 denars, which make 35 shillings.

3. If a freeman break into a house and steal something worth 2 denars, and it be proved on him, he shall be sentenced to 15 shillings.

4. But if he shall have stolen something worth more than 5 denars, and it have been proved on him, he shall be sentenced, besides the worth of the object and the fines for delay, to 1400 denars, which make 35 shillings.

5. But if he have broken, or tampered with, the lock, and thus have entered the house and stolen anything from it, he shall be sentenced, besides the worth of the object and the fines for delay, to 1800 denars, which make 45 shillings.

6. And if he have taken nothing, or have escaped by flight, he shall, for the housebreaking alone, be sentenced to 1200 denars, which make 30 shillings.

Title XII. Concerning Thefts or Housebreakings on the Part of Slaves.

1. If a slave steal, outside of the house, something worth two denars, he shall, besides paying the worth of the object and the fines for delay, be stretched out and receive 120 blows.

2. But if he steal something worth 40 denars, he shall either be castrated or pay 6 shillings. But the lord of the slave who committed the theft shall restore to the plaintiff the worth of the object and the fines for delay.

Title XIII. Concerning Rape committed by Freemen.

1. If three men carry off a free-born girl, they shall be compelled to pay 30 shillings.

2. If there are more than three, each one shall pay 8 shillings.

3. Those who shall have been present with boats shall be sentenced to three shillings.

4. But those who commit rape shall be compelled to pay 2500 denars, which make 63 shillings.

5. But if they have carried off that girl from behind lock and key, or from the spinning room, they shall be sentenced to the above price and penalty.

6. But if the girl who is carried off be under the king's protection, then the "frith" [peace money] shall be 2500 denars, which make 63 shillings.

7. But if a bondsman of the king, or a leet, should carry off a free woman, he shall be sentenced to death.

8. But if a free woman have followed a slave of her own will, she shall lose her freedom.

9. If a free-born man shall have taken an alien bondswoman, he shall suffer similarly.

10. If any body take an alien spouse and join her to himself in matrimony, he shall be sentenced to 2500 denars, which make 63 shillings.

Title XIV. Concerning Assault and Robbery.

1. If any one have assaulted and plundered a free man, and it be proved on him, he shall be sentenced to 2500 denars, which make 63 shillings.

2. If a Roman have plundered a Salian Frank, the above law shall be observed.

3. But if a Frank have plundered a Roman, he shall be sentenced to 35 shillings.

4. If any man should wish to migrate, and has permission from the king, and shall have shown this in the public "Thing": whoever, contrary to the decree of the king, shall presume to oppose him, shall be sentenced to 8000 denars, which make 200 shillings.

Title XV. Concerning Arson.

1. If any one shall set fire to a house in which men were sleeping, as many freemen as were in it can make complaint before the "Thing"; and if any one shall have been burned in it, the incendiary shall be sentenced to 2500 denars, which make 63 shillings. …

Title XVII. Concerning Wounds.

1. If any one have wished to kill another person, and the blow have missed, he on whom it was proved shall be sentenced to 2500 denars, which make 63 shillings.

2. If any person have wished to strike another with a poisoned arrow, and the arrow have glanced aside, and it shall be proved on him, he shall be sentenced to 2500 denars, which make 63 shillings.

3. If any person strike another on the head so that the brain appears, and the three bones which lie above the brain shall project, he shall be sentenced to 1200 denars, which make 30 shillings.

4. But if it shall have been between the ribs or in the stomach, so that the wound appears and reaches to the entrails, he shall be sentenced to 1200 denars—which make 30 shillings—besides five shillings for the physician's pay.

5. If any one shall have struck a man so that blood falls to the floor, and it be proved on him, he shall be sentenced to 600 denars, which make 15 shillings.

6. But if a freeman strike a freeman with his fist so that blood does not flow, he shall be sentenced for each blow—up to 3 blows—to 120 denars, which make 3 shillings.

Title XVIII. Concerning him who, before the King, accuses an Innocent Man.

If any one, before the king, accuse an innocent man who is absent, he shall be sentenced to 2500 denars, which make 63 shillings.

Title XIX. Concerning Magicians.

1. If any one have given herbs to another so that he die, he shall be sentenced to 200 shillings (or shall surely be given over to fire).

2. If any person have bewitched another, and he who was thus treated shall escape, the author of the crime, who is proved to have committed it, shall be sentenced to 2500 denars, which make 63 shillings. …

Title XXIV Concerning the Killing of Little Children and Women.

1. If any one have slain a boy under 10 years—up to the end of the tenth—and it shall have been proved on him, he shall be sentenced to 24000 denars, which make 600 shillings. …

3. If any one have hit a free woman who is pregnant, and she dies, he shall be sentenced to 28000 denars, which make 700 shillings. …

6. If any one have killed a free woman after she has begun bearing children, he shall be sentenced to 24000 denars, which make 600 shillings.

7. After she can have no more children, he who kills her shall be sentenced to 8000 denars, which make 200 shillings. ...

Title XXX. Concerning Insults.

... 3. If any one, man or woman, shall have called a woman harlot, and shall not have been able to prove it, he shall be sentenced to 1800 denars, which make 45 shillings.

4. If any person shall have called another "fox," he shall be sentenced to 3 shillings.

5. If any man shall have called another "hare," he shall be sentenced to 3 shillings.

6. If any man shall have brought it up against another that he have thrown away his shield, and shall not have been able to prove it, he shall be sentenced to 120 denars, which make 3 shillings.

7. If any man shall have called another "spy" or "perjurer," and shall not have been able to prove it, he shall be sentenced to 600 denars, which make 15 shillings. ...

Title XXXIII. Concerning the Theft of Hunting Animals.

... 2. If any one have stolen a tame marked stag[-hound?] trained to hunting, and it shall have been proved through witnesses that his master had him for hunting, or had killed him with two or three beasts, he shall be sentenced to 1800 denars, which make 45 shillings.

Title XXXIV. Concerning the Stealing of Fences.

1. If any man shall have cut 3 staves by which a fence is bound or held together, or have stolen or cut the heads of 3 stakes, he shall be sentenced to 600 denars, which make 15 shillings.

2. If any one shall have drawn a harrow through another's harvest after it has sprouted, or shall have gone through it with a wagon where there was no road, he shall be sentenced to 120 denars, which make 3 shillings.

3. If any one shall have gone, where there is no way or path, through another's harvest which has already become thick, he shall be sentenced to 600 denars, which make 15 shillings. ...

Title XLI. Concerning the Murder of Free Men.

1. If any one shall have killed a free Frank, or a barbarian living under the Salic law, and it have been proved on him, he shall be sentenced to 8000 denars.

2. But if he shall have thrown him into a well or into the water, or shall have covered him with branches or anything else, to conceal him, he shall be sentenced to 24000 denars, which make 600 shillings.

3. But if any one has slain a man who is in the service of the king, he shall be sentenced to 24000 denars, which make 600 shillings.

4. But if he have put him in the water or a well, and covered him with anything to conceal him, he shall be sentenced to 72000 denars, which make 1800 shillings.

5. If any one have slain a Roman who eats in the king's palace, and it have been proved on him, he shall be sentenced to 12000 denars, which make 300 shillings.

6. But if the Roman shall not have been a landed proprietor and table companion of the king, he who killed him shall be sentenced to 4000 denars, which make 100 shillings.

7. But if he shall have killed a Roman who was obliged to pay tribute, he shall be sentenced to 63 shillings. ...

9. If any one have thrown a free man into a well, and he have escaped alive, he (the criminal) shall be sentenced to 4000 denars, which make 100 shillings. ...

Title XLV. Concerning Migrators.

1. If any one wish to migrate to another village and if one or more who live in that village do not wish to receive him,—if there be only one who objects, he shall not have leave to move there.

2. But if he shall have presumed to settle in that village in spite of his rejection by one or two men, then some one shall give him warning. And if he be unwilling to go away, he who gives him warning shall give him warning, with witnesses, as follows: I warn thee that thou may'st remain here this next night as the Salic law demands, and I warn thee that within 10 nights thou shalt go forth from this village. After another 10 nights he shall again come to him and warn him again within 10 nights to go away. If he still refuse to go, again 10 nights shall be added to the command, that the number of 30 nights may be full. If he will not go away even then, then he shall summon him to the "Thing," and present his witnesses as to the separate commands to leave. If he who has been warned will not then move away, and no valid reason detains him, and all the above warnings which we have mentioned have been given according to law: then he who gave him warning shall take the matter into his own hands and request the "comes"[2] to go to that place and expel him. And because he would not listen to the law, that man shall relinquish all that he has earned there, and, besides, shall be sentenced to 1200 denars, which make 30 shillings.

3. But if anyone have moved there, and within 12 months no one have given him warning, he shall remain as secure as the other neighbors.

Title XLVI. Concerning Transfers of Property.

1. The observance shall be that the Thunginus or Centenarius shall call together a "Thing," and shall have his shield in the "Thing," and shall demand three men as witnesses for each of the three transactions. He (the owner of the land to be transferred) shall seek a man who has no connection with himself, and shall throw a stalk into his lap. And to him into whose lap he has thrown the stalk he shall tell, concerning his property, how much of it—or whether the whole or a half—he wishes to give. He in whose lap he threw the stalk shall remain in his (the owner's) house, and shall collect three or more guests, and shall have the property—as much as is given him—in his power. And, afterwards, he to whom that property is entrusted shall discuss all these things with the witnesses collected afterwards, either before the king or in the regular "Thing," he shall give the property up to him for whom it was intended. He shall take the stalk in the "Thing," and, before 12 months are over, shall throw it into the lap of him whom the owner has named heir; and he shall restore not more nor less, but exactly as much as was entrusted to him.

2. And if any one shall wish to say anything against this, three sworn witnesses shall say that they were in the "Thing" which the Thunginus or Centenarius[3] called together, and that they saw that man who wished to give his property throw a stalk into the lap of him whom he had selected. They shall name by name him who threw his property into the lap of the other, and, likewise, shall name him whom he named his heir. And three other sworn witnesses shall say that he in whose lap the stalk was thrown had remained in the house of him who gave his property, and had there collected three or more guests, and that they had eaten porridge at table, and that he had collected those who were bearing witness, and that those guests had thanked him for their entertainment. All this those other sworn witnesses shall say, and that he who received that property in his lap in the "Thing" held before the king, or in the regular public "Thing," did publicly, before the people, either in the presence of the king or in the public "Thing"—namely on the Mallberg, before the "Thunginus"—throw the stalk into the lap of him whom the owner had named as heir. And thus 9 witnesses shall confirm all this. ...

Title L. Concerning Promises to Pay.

1. If any freeman or leet have made to another a promise to pay, then he to whom the promise was made shall, within 40 days or within such term

---

2   A royal official responsible for an administrative area later known as a county.
3   Royal officials with judicial powers subordinate to the count.

as was agreed when he made the promise, go to the house of that man with witnesses, or with appraisers. And if he (the debtor) be unwilling to make the promised payment, he shall be sentenced to 15 shillings above the debt which he had promised.

2. If he then be unwilling to pay, he (the creditor) shall summon him before the "Thing" and thus accuse him: "I ask thee, 'Thunginus,' to bann my opponent who made me a promise to pay and owes me a debt." And he shall state how much he owes and promised to pay. Then the "Thunginus" shall say: "I bann thy opponent to what the Salic law decrees." Then he to whom the promise was made shall warn him (the debtor) to make no payment or pledge of payment to any body else until he have fulfilled his promise to him (the creditor). And straightway on that same day, before the sun sets, he shall go to the house of that man with witnesses, and shall ask if he will pay that debt. If he will not, he (the creditor) shall wait until after sunset; then, if he shall have waited until after sunset, 120 denars, which make 3 shillings shall be added on to the debt. And this shall be done up to 3 times in 3 weeks. And if at the third time he will not pay all this, it (the sum) shall increase to 360 denars, or 9 shillings: so, namely, that, after each admonition or waiting until after sunset, 3 shillings shall be added to the debt.

3. If any one be unwilling to fulfil his promise in the regular assembly,—then he to whom the promise was made shall go to the count of that place, in whose district he lives, and shall take the stalk and shall say: oh count, that man made me a promise to pay, and I have lawfully summoned him before the court according to the Salic law on this matter; I pledge thee myself and my fortune that thou may'st safely seize his property. And he shall state the case to him, and shall tell how much he (the debtor) had agreed to pay. Then the count shall collect 7 suitable bailiffs, and shall go with them to the house of him who made the promise and shall say: thou who art here present pay voluntarily to that man what thou didst promise, and choose any two of these bailiffs who shall appraise that from which thou shalt pay; and make good what thou dost owe, according to a just appraisal. But if he will not hear, or be absent,

then the bailiffs shall take from his property the value of the debt which he owes. And, according to the law, the accuser shall take two thirds of that which the debtor owes, and the count shall collect for himself the other third as peace money; unless the peace money shall have been paid to him before in this same matter.

4. If the count have been appealed to, and no sufficient reason, and no duty of the king, have detained him—and if he have put off going, and have sent no substitute to demand law and justice: he shall answer for it with his life, or shall redeem himself with his "wergeld." …

Title LIV. Concerning the Slaying of a Count.

1. If any one slay a count, he shall be sentenced to 24000 denars, which make 600 shillings.

Title LV. Concerning the Plundering of Corpses.

… 2. If any one shall have dug up and plundered a corpse already buried, and it shall have been proved on him, he shall be outlawed until the day when he comes to an agreement with the relatives of the dead man, and they ask for him that he be allowed to come among men. And whoever, before he come to an arrangement with the relative, shall give him bread or shelter—even if they are his relations or his own wife—shall be sentenced to 600 denars, which make 15 shillings.

3. But he who is proved to have committed the crime shall be sentenced to 8000 denars, which make 200 shillings.

Title LVI. Concerning him who shall have scorned to come to Court.

1. If any man shall have scorned to come to court, and shall have put off fulfilling the injunction of the bailiffs, and shall have not been willing to consent to undergo the fine, or the kettle ordeal, or anything prescribed by law: then he (the plaintiff) shall summon him to the presence of the king. And there shall be 12 witnesses who—3 at a time being sworn—shall testify that they were present when the bailiff enjoined him (the accused) either to go to the kettle ordeal, or to agree concerning

the fine; and that he had scorned the injunction. Then 3 others shall swear that they were there on the day when the bailiffs enjoined that he should free himself by the kettle ordeal or by composition; and that 40 days after that, in the "mallberg," he (the accuser) had again waited until after sunset, and that he (the accused) would not obey the law. Then he (the accuser) shall summon him before the king for a fortnight thence; and three witnesses shall swear that they were there when he summoned him and when he waited for sunset. If he does not then come, those 9, being sworn, shall give testimony as we have above explained. On that day likewise, if he do not come, he (the accuser) shall let the sun go down on him, and shall have 3 witnesses who shall be there when he waits till sunset. But if the accuser shall have fulfilled all this, and the accused shall not have been willing to come to any court, then the king, before whom he has been summoned, shall withdraw his protection from him. Then he shall be guilty, and all his goods shall belong to the fisc, or to him to whom the fisc may wish to give them. And whoever shall have fed or housed him—even if it were his own wife—shall be sentenced to 600 denars, which make 15 shillings; until he (the debtor) shall have made good all that has been laid to his charge.

Title LVII. Concerning the "Chrenecruda."

1. If any one have killed a man, and, having given up all his property, has not enough to comply with the full terms of the law, he shall present 12 sworn witnesses to the effect that, neither above the earth nor under it, has he any more property than he has already given. And he shall afterwards go into his house, and shall collect in his hand dust from the four corners of it, and shall afterwards stand upon the threshold, looking inwards into the house. And then, with his left hand, he shall throw over his shoulder some of that dust on the nearest relative that he has. But if his father and (his father's) brothers have already paid, he shall then throw that dust on their (the brothers') children—that is, over three (relatives) who are nearest on the father's and three on the mother's side. And after that, in his shirt, without girdle and without shoes, a staff in his hand, he shall spring over the hedge. And then those three shall pay half of what is lacking of the compounding money or the legal fine; that is, those others who are descended in the paternal line shall do this.

2. But if there be one of those relatives who has not enough to pay his whole indebtedness, he, the poorer one, shall in turn throw the "chrenecruda" on him of them who has the most, so that he shall pay the whole fine.

3. But if he also have not enough to pay the whole, then he who has charge of the murderer shall bring him before the "Thing," and afterwards to 4 Things, in order that they (his friends) may take him under their protection. And if no one have taken him under his protection—that is, so as to redeem him for what he can not pay—then he shall have to atone with his life. ...

Title LIX. Concerning Private Property.

1. If any man die and leave no sons, if the father and mother survive, they shall inherit.

2. If the father and mother do not survive, and he leave brothers or sisters, they shall inherit.

3. But if there are none, the sisters of the father shall inherit.

4. But if there are no sisters of the father, the sisters of the mother shall claim that inheritance.

5. If there are none of these, the nearest relatives on the father's side shall succeed to that inheritance.

6. But of Salic land no portion of the inheritance shall come to a woman; but the whole inheritance of the land shall come to the male sex. ...

Title LXII. Concerning Wergeld.

1. If any one's father have been killed, the sons shall have half the compounding money (wergeld); and the other half the nearest relatives, as well on the mother's as on the father's side, shall divide among themselves.

2. But if there are no relatives, paternal or maternal, that portion shall go to the fisc.

9. BISHOPS REMIGIUS OF REIMS AND AVITUS OF VIENNE

Letters to Clovis

THE FOLLOWING TWO LETTERS are the only contemporary records directly addressed to Clovis. Remigius of Reims (ca. 437–533) wrote to Clovis shortly after he succeeded his father Childeric in 481/82 and well before his victory over Syagrius at Soissons in 486 or his conversion. The letter of Avitus was written after Clovis's conversion to Orthodox Christianity. From the letter it is unclear whether Clovis was converted from paganism, as Gregory of Tours asserts, or from Arianism.

Source: *Christianity and Paganism, 350–750*, trans. J.N. Hillgarth (Philadelphia: University of Pennsylvania Press, 1986).

Further Reading: Ian Wood, *The Merovingian Kingdoms: 450–751* (London: Longman, 1994).

Bishop Remigius of Reims to Clovis (ca. 481).

To the celebrated and rightly magnificent Lord, King Clovis, Bishop Remigius.
A strong report has come to us that you have taken over the administration of the Second Belgic Province. There is nothing new in that you now begin to be what your parents always were. First of all, you should act so that God's Judgment may not abandon you and that your merits should maintain you at the height where you have arrived by your humility. For, as the proverb says, man's acts are judged. You ought to associate with yourself counselors who are able to do honor to your reputation. Your deeds should be chaste and honest. You should defer to your bishops and always have recourse to their advice. If you are on good terms with them your province will be better able to stand firm. Encourage your people, relieve the afflicted, protect widows, nourish orphans, so shine forth that all may love and fear you. May justice proceed from your mouth. Ask nothing of the poor or of strangers, do not allow yourself to receive gifts from them. Let your tribunal be open to all men, so that no man may leave it with the sorrow [of not having been heard]. You possess the riches your father left you. Use them to ransom captives and free them from servitude. If someone is admitted to your presence let him not feel he is a stranger. Amuse yourself with young men, deliberate with the old. If you wish to reign, show yourself worthy to do so.

Bishop Avitus to King Clovis.

The followers of [Arian] error have in vain, by a cloud of contradictory and untrue opinions, sought to conceal from your extreme subtlety the glory of the Christian name. While we committed these questions to eternity and trusted that the truth of each man's belief would appear at the Future Judgment, the ray of truth has shone forth even among present shadows. Divine Providence has found the arbiter of our age. Your choice is a general sentence. Your Faith is our victory. Many others, in this matter, when their bishops or friends exhort them to adhere to the True Faith, are accustomed to oppose the traditions of their race and respect for their ancestral cult; thus they culpably prefer a false shame to their salvation. While they observe a futile reverence for their parents [by continuing to share their] unbelief, they confess that they do not know what they should choose to do. After this marvelous deed guilty shame can no longer shelter behind this excuse. Of all your ancient genealogy you have chosen to keep only your own nobility, and you have willed that your race should derive from you all the glories which adorn high birth. Your ancestors have prepared a great destiny for you; you willed to prepare better things [for those who will follow you]. You follow your ancestors in reigning in this world; you have opened the way to your descendants to a heavenly reign. Let Greece indeed rejoice it has elected an emperor who shares our Faith; it is no longer alone in deserving such a favor. Your sphere also burns with its own brilliance, and, in the person of a king, the light of a rising sun shines over the western lands. It is right that this light began at the Nativity of Our Redeemer, so that the waters of rebirth have brought you forth to salvation the very day that the world received the birth of its Redemption, the Lord of Heaven. The day celebrated as the Lord's Nativity is also yours, in which you have consecrated your soul to God, your life to your contemporaries, your glory to posterity.

What should be said of the glorious solemnity of your regeneration? If I could not assist in person among the ministers [of the rite] I shared in its joy. Thanks to God, our land took part in the thanksgiving, for, before your Baptism, a messenger of Your Most Subtle Humility informed us that you were a "competens" [that is, to be baptized within forty days]. Therefore the sacred night [of Christmas] found us sure of what you would do. We saw (with the eyes of the spirit) that great sight, when a crowd of bishops around you, in the ardor of their holy ministry, poured over your royal limbs the waters of life; when that head feared by the peoples bowed down before the servants of God; when your royal locks, hidden under a helmet, were steeped in holy oil; when your breast, relieved of its cuirass, shone with the same whiteness as your baptismal robes. Do not doubt, most flourishing of kings, that this soft clothing will give more force to your arms: whatever Fortune has given up to now, this Sanctity will bestow.

I would wish to add some exhortations to your praises if anything escaped either your knowledge or your attention. Should we preach the Faith to the convert who perceived it without a preacher; or humility, which you have long shown toward us [bishops], although you only owe it to us now, after your profession of Faith; or mercy, attested, in tears and joy to God and men, by a people once captive, now freed by you? One wish remains for me to express. Since God, thanks to you, will make of your people His own possession, offer a part of the treasure of Faith which fills your heart to the peoples living beyond you, who, still living in natural ignorance, have not been corrupted by the seeds of perverse doctrines [that is, Arianism]. Do not fear to send them envoys and to plead with them the cause of God, who has done so much for your cause. So that the other pagan peoples, at first being subject to your empire for the sake of religion, while they still seem to have another ruler, may be distinguished rather by their race than by their prince. [End of letter missing.]

10. GREGORY OF TOURS

History of the Franks

GREGORY OF TOURS (CA. 540–594) was a member of an illustrious Gallo-Roman family that for centuries had dominated the episcopal see of Tours, where he himself was bishop beginning in 573. His *History of the Franks* is the most important source for early Frankish history. Gregory was primarily concerned in his history with Orthodox Christianity, with his community of Tours, and with his Gallo-Roman aristocratic colleagues. He worked closely with the Frankish kings, whom he saw as instruments of divine providence. These concerns are evident in the following passages. The first is his account of Clovis. Written almost a century after the events it describes, it is largely unreliable as a detailed account of Clovis but essential for understanding the meaning of Clovis to later Frankish history. The other selections show Gregory's activities as peacemaker in Tours and his involvement with his contemporary kings of the Franks.

Source: Gregory of Tours, *The History of the Franks*, trans. Lewis Thorpe (Harmondsworth: Penguin, 1974).

Further Reading: Kathleen Mitchell and Ian Wood (eds.), *The World of Gregory of Tours* (Leiden: Brill, 2002).

Excerpts from Book II

12. Childeric, King of the Franks, whose private life was one long debauch, began to seduce the daughters of his subjects. They were so incensed about this that they forced him to give up his throne. He discovered that they intended to assassinate him and he fled to Thuringia. He left behind a close friend of his who was able to soothe the minds of his angry subjects with his honeyed words. Childeric entrusted to him a token which should indicate when he might return to his homeland. They broke a gold coin into two equal halves. Childeric took one half with him and the friend kept the other half. "When I send my half to you," said his friend, "and the two halves placed together make a complete coin, you will know that you may return home safe and sound." Childeric then set out for Thuringia and took refuge with King Bisinus and his wife Basina. As soon as Childeric had gone, the Franks unanimously chose as their king that same Aegidius who, as I have already said, had been sent out of Rome as commander of the armies. When Aegidius had reigned over the Franks for eight years, Childeric's faithful friend succeeded in pacifying them secretly and he sent messengers to the exile with the half of the broken coin which he had in his possession. By this token Childeric knew for sure that the Franks wanted him back, indeed that they were clamoring for him to return, and he left Thuringia and was restored to his throne. Now that Bisinus and Childeric were both kings, Queen Basina, about whom I have told you, deserted her husband and joined Childeric. He questioned her closely as to why she had come from far away to be with him, and she is said to have answered: "I know that you are a strong man and I recognize ability when I see it. I have therefore come to live with you. You can be sure that if I knew anyone else, even far across the sea, who was more capable than you, I should have sought him out and gone to live with him instead." This pleased Childeric very much and he married her. She became pregnant and bore a son whom she named Clovis. He was a great man and became a famous soldier.

13. After the death of Saint Arthemius, Venerandus, a man of senatorial rank, was consecrated as Bishop of Clermont-Ferrand. Paulinus gives us information as to what sort of man this bishop was:

> Today when you see bishops as worthy of the Lord as Emperius of Toulouse, Simplicius of

Vienne, Armandus of Bordeaux, Diogenianus of Albi, Venerandus of Clermont, Alithius of Cahors and now Pegasus of Périgueux, you will see that we have excellent guardians of all our faith and religion, however great may be the evils of our age.

Venerandus is said to have died on Christmas Eve. The next morning the Christmas procession was also his funeral cortège. After his death the most shameful argument arose among the local inhabitants concerning the election of a bishop to replace him. Different factions were formed some of which wanted this man and others that, and there was great dissension among the people. One Sunday when the electing bishops were sitting in conclave, a woman wearing a veil over her head to mark the fact that she was a true servant of God came boldly in and said: "Listen to me, priests of the Lord! You must realize that it is true that not one of those whom they have put forward for the bishopric finds favor in the sight of God. This very day the Lord in person will choose Himself a bishop. Do not inflame the people or allow any more argument among them, but be patient for a little while, for the Lord will now send to us the man who is to rule over our church." As they sat wondering at her words, there came in a man called Rusticus, who was himself a priest of the diocese of this city of Clermont-Ferrand. He was the very man who had been pointed out to the woman in a vision. As soon as she set eyes on him she cried: "That is the man whom the Lord elects! That is the man whom He has chosen to be your bishop! That is the man whom you must consecrate!" As she spoke the entire population forgot all its previous disagreement and shouted that this was the correct and proper choice. To the great joy of the populace Rusticus was set on the episcopal throne and inducted as bishop. He was the seventh to be made bishop in Clermont-Ferrand.

14. In the city of Tours Bishop Eustochius died in the seventeenth year of his episcopate. Perpetuus was consecrated in his place, being the fifth bishop after Saint Martin. When Perpetuus saw how frequently miracles were being performed at Saint Martin's tomb and when he observed how small was the chapel erected over the saint's body, he decided that it was unworthy of these wonders. He had the chapel removed and he built in its place the great church which is still there some five hundred and fifty yards outside the city. It is one hundred and sixty feet long by sixty feet broad; and its height up to the beginning of the vaulting is forty-five feet. It has thirty-two windows in the sanctuary and twenty in the nave, with forty-one columns. In the whole building there are fifty-two windows, one hundred and twenty columns and eight doorways, three in the sanctuary and five in the nave. The great festival of the church has a threefold significance: it marks the dedication of the building, the translation of the saint's body and his ordination as a bishop. You should observe this feast-day on July 4; and you should remember that Saint Martin died on November 11. If you celebrate this faithfully you will gain the protection of the saintly bishop in this world and the next. The vault of the tiny chapel which stood there before was most elegantly designed, and so Bishop Perpetuus thought it wrong to destroy it. He built another church in honor of the blessed apostles Peter and Paul, and he fitted this vault over it. He built many other churches which still stand firm today in the name of Christ.

15. At this time the church of the blessed martyr Symphorian of Autun was built by the priest Eufronius, and later on Eufronius was elected as bishop of that city. It was he who, in great devotion, sent the marble lid which covers the tomb of Saint Martin.

16. After the death of Bishop Rusticus, Saint Namatius became the eighth Bishop of Clermont-Ferrand. It was he who built by his effort the church which still stands and which is considered to be the oldest within the city walls. It is one hundred and fifty feet long, sixty feet wide inside the nave and fifty feet high as far as the vaulting. It has a rounded apse at the end, and two wings of elegant design on either side. The whole building is constructed in the shape of a cross. It has forty-two windows, seventy columns and eight doorways. In it one is conscious of the fear of God and of a great brightness, and those at prayer are often aware of a most sweet and aromatic odor which is being wafted towards them. Round the

sanctuary it has walls which are decorated with mosaic work made of many varieties of marble. When the building had been finished for a dozen years, the saintly bishop sent priests to Bologna, the city in Italy, to procure for him the relics of Saint Agricola and Saint Vitalis, who, as I have shown, were assuredly crucified in the name of Christ our Lord.

17. The wife of Namatius built the church of Saint Stephen in the suburb outside the walls of Clermont-Ferrand. She wanted it to be decorated with colored frescoes. She used to hold in her lap a book from which she would read stories of events which happened long ago, and tell the workmen what she wanted painted on the walls. One day as she was sitting in the church and reading these stories, there came a poor man to pray. He saw her in her black dress, a woman already far advanced in age. He thought that she was one of the needy, so he produced a piece of bread, put it in her lap and went on his way. She did not scorn the gift of this poor man, who had not understood who she was. She took it, and thanked him, and put it on one side. She ate it instead of her other food and each day she received a blessing from it until it was all eaten up.

18. Childeric fought a battle at Orleans. Odovacar with his Saxons penetrated as far as Angers. A great pestilence caused the death of many people. Aegidius died and left a son called Syagrius. After the death of Aegidius, Odovacar took hostages from Angers and other places. The Bretons were expelled from Bourges by the Goths and many were killed at Bourg-de-Déois. Count Paul, who had Roman and Frankish troops under his command, attacked the Goths and seized booty from them. Odovacar reached Angers, but King Childeric arrived there on the following day: Count Paul was killed and Childeric occupied the city. On that day the church-house was burnt down in a great fire.

19. While these things were happening a great war was waged between the Saxons and the Romans. The Saxons fled and many of their men were cut down by the Romans who pursued them. Their islands[1] were captured and laid waste by the Franks, and many people were killed. In the ninth month of that year there was an earthquake. Odovacar made a treaty with Childeric and together they subdued the Alamanni, who had invaded a part of Italy.

20. During the fourteenth year of his reign, Euric, King of the Goths, put Duke Victorius in charge of the seven cities. Victorius went straight to Clermont-Ferrand and made certain additions to the city. The underground chapels which he constructed are still there today. It was he who had erected in the church of Saint Julian the columns which are still part of the building. He also built the church of Saint Lawrence and the church of Saint Germanus in Saint-Germain-Lanbron. Victorius was nine years in Clermont. He spread a number of scandalous rumors about the Senator Eucherius. Eucherius was thrown into prison. In the middle of the night Victorius had him brought out, he was attached to an old wall and then Victorius had the wall knocked down on top of him. Victorius was far too much given to irregular affairs with women. He was afraid of being assassinated by the men of Clermont and he fled to Rome. There he began to live the same loose life and he was stoned to death. Euric reigned for another four years after the death of Victorius. He died in the twenty-seventh year of his reign. There again occurred a big earthquake.

21. When Bishop Namatius died in Clermont-Ferrand, Eparchius succeeded him. He was a most saintly and devout man. At that time the church had very little property inside the city walls. The bishop had his lodging in what is now called the sacristy. He was in the habit of getting up in the middle of the night to give thanks to God before the high altar in his cathedral. One night it happened that as he went into the church he found it full of devils and Satan himself sitting on his own episcopal throne made up to look like a painted woman. "You hideous prostitute," said the bishop, "is it not enough that you infect other places with every imaginable sort of foulness, without your defiling the throne consecrated to the Lord

---

1   These were islands in the River Loire between Saumur and Angers which had been occupied by piratical bands of Saxons.

by sitting your revolting body down on it? Leave the house of God this instant and stop polluting it with your presence!" "Since you give me the title of prostitute," said Satan, "I will see that you yourself are constantly harassed with sexual desire." As he said this he disappeared into thin air. It is true that the bishop was tempted by lusts of the flesh, but he was protected by the sign of the Cross and the Devil was unable to harm him.

According to all accounts it was Eparchius who built the monastery on top of Mont Chantoin, where the oratory now is, and there he would go into retreat during the holy days of Lent. On the day of the Lord's Supper he would process down to his cathedral, escorted by his clergy and the townsfolk, and accompanied by a great singing of psalms.

When Eparchius died he was succeeded by Sidonius Apollinaris, one-time Prefect of the City, a man of most noble birth as honors are counted in this world, and one of the leading senators of Gaul, so noble indeed that he married the daughter of the Emperor Avitus. In his time, while Victorius, about whom I have already told you, was still in Clermont, there lived in the monastery of Saint-Cyr in the same city an abbot called Abraham, who, thanks to his predecessor and namesake, was greatly distinguished by his faith and good works, as I have told you in my other book where his life is recorded.

22. The saintly Sidonius was so eloquent that he would often speak extempore in public without hesitating in the slightest and express whatever he had to say with the greatest clarity. One day it happened that he went to the monastery church of which I have told you, for he had been invited there for a festival. Some malicious person removed the book with which it was his habit to conduct the church service. Sidonius was so well versed in the ritual that he took them through the whole service of the festival without pausing for a moment. This was a source of wonder to everyone present and they had the impression that it must be an angel speaking rather than a man. I have described this in more detail in the preface of the book which I wrote about the Masses composed by Sidonius. He was a very saintly man and, as I have said, a member of one of the foremost

senatorial families. Without saying anything to his wife he would remove silver vessels from his home and give them away to the poor. When she found out what he had done, she used to grumble at him; then he would buy the silver vessels back from the poor folk and bring them home again.

23. At the time when Sidonius was living a saintly life here on earth and was completely devoted to the service of the Lord, two priests rebelled against him. They removed from him all control over the property of his church, reduced him to a very straitened way of life and submitted him to every kind of contumely. God in His clemency did not permit this insult to go long unpunished. One of these two insidious men, who was unworthy to be called by the name of priest, had threatened the night before to drag Sidonius out of his own church. When he got up the next morning on hearing the bell which called to matins, this man was full of spite against the holy man of God, and was busy turning over in his mind how he could best carry out a plan which he had formed the previous evening. He went off to the lavatory and while he was occupied in emptying his bowels he lost his soul instead. A boy was waiting outside with a candle, expecting his master to emerge at any moment. Day dawned. His accomplice, the other priest, sent someone to see what had happened. "Come quickly," said the messenger, "don't hang about in there any longer, we must do together what we planned yesterday." The dead man gave no answer. The boy lifted up the curtain of the lavatory and found his master dead on the seat. From this we may deduce that this man was guilty of a crime no less serious than that of Arius, who in the same way emptied out his entrails through his back passage in the lavatory. This, too, smacks of heresy, that one of God's bishops should not be obeyed in his own church, the man to whom had been entrusted the task of feeding God's flock, and that someone else to whom nothing at all had been entrusted, either by God or by man, should have dared to usurp his authority.

After that the saintly bishop, to whom, mark you, there still remained one of his two enemies, was restored to his authority. Some time later Sidonius fell ill with a very high temperature. He ordered his attendants to carry him into the church. He was borne inside and a great crowd of men and women, and of little children, too, gathered round him, weeping and saying: "Good shepherd, why are you deserting us? To whom will you abandon us, your orphan children? If you die, what sort of life can we expect? Will there be anyone left to season our lives with the salt of wisdom and to inspire in us the fear of the Lord's name with the same insight which you have shown?" The citizens of Clermont wept as they said these things and others like them. Finally Bishop Sidonius answered them, for the Holy Spirit moved him to do so. "Do not be afraid, my people," said he. "My brother Aprunculus is still alive and he will be your bishop." Those who were present did not understand him, and they thought that he was wandering in his mind.

After the death of Sidonius, the evil priest, the second of the two, the one who was still alive, blinded with greed, immediately laid hands on the property of the church, as if he were already bishop. "God has at last taken notice of me," said he, "for He knows that I am more just than Sidonius and He has granted me this power." He rode proudly through the whole city. On the Sunday following the death of the holy bishop, this priest prepared a feast in the church-house and ordered all the townspeople to be invited. He showed no respect for the senior among them, but took his place at the table first. The cup-bearer passed him a goblet of wine and said: "My lord, I have just seen a vision and this I will describe to you, if you permit. I saw it this very Sunday evening. I perceived a great hall, and in this hall there was placed a throne, and on this throne there sat a man, a sort of judge who seemed to have authority over everyone else present. A great throng of priests in white garments stood round him, and there were immense crowds of people of all sorts, so many that I could not count them. While I watched, and trembled as I watched, I saw the blessed Sidonius standing far off as if on a dais, and he was rebuking that dear friend of yours, the priest who died some years ago. The priest was worsted in this argument, and the King had him shut up in the deepest and smallest dungeon. When he had been put away, Sidonius turned on you, saying that you had been implicated in the crime for which the other had just been condemned. Then the judge

began to make urgent inquiries to find someone whom he could send to you. I hid myself in the crowd and stood well back, holding my own counsel, for fear that I myself should be sent, for after all I know you very well. While I stood silent and lost in thought everyone else disappeared and I was left all alone in this public place. The judge called me forward and I went up to him. At the sight of him in all his dignity and splendor I lost control of myself and began to sway on my feet from sheer panic. 'Do not be afraid, my boy,' said he. 'Go and tell that priest: "Be present to answer the charge, for Sidonius has stipulated that you be summoned." You must go quickly, for the King commanded me to say what I have said, and he made this dire threat to me: "If you do not speak you will die a frightful death." As his servant said this the priest fell down dead on the spot and the goblet slid out of his hand. He was picked up dead from the couch on which he was reclining, and they buried him and so despatched him to join his accomplice in hell. The Lord passed this earthly judgement on those two unruly priests: one suffered the fate of Arius, and the other was dashed headlong from the very summit of his pride, like Simon Magus at the behest of the holy apostle. No one can doubt that these two who plotted together against their holy bishop now have their place side by side in nethermost hell.

Meanwhile rumors of the approach of the Franks were being repeated on all sides in these regions and everyone looked forward with great excitement to the moment when they would take over the government. Saint Aprunculus, the bishop of the city of Langres, had fallen into ill-favor with the Burgundes. The hatred which they bore him became daily more bitter and an order went out that he should be executed in secret. This came to his ears and one night he was lowered down from the walls of Dijon. He escaped to Clermont-Ferrand and in accordance with the word of God, placed in the mouth of Sidonius, he became the eleventh bishop of that city.

24. In the days of Bishop Sidonius there was a great famine in Burgundy. The inhabitants were widely scattered over the countryside and there was nobody to distribute food to the poor. Then Ecdicius, one of the senators and a close relative of Sidonius,

with the help of God found a wonderful solution. He sent his servants and horses and carts through the neighboring cities and brought in those who were suffering from starvation. They went out and collected all the poor and needy they could find and brought them in to where Ecdicius lived. Throughout the long period of famine he provided them with food and so saved them from dying of hunger. There were, so they say, more than four thousand of them, both men and women. When the time of plenty returned, he arranged transport home again for them and took each man and woman back to where he or she lived. After they had gone a voice was heard from Heaven, saying to him: "Ecdicius, Ecdicius, because you have done this thing you and your descendants will never lack food; for you have obeyed my word and by feeding the poor you have stayed my hunger, too." Many witnesses have reported how swift this Ecdicius was to take action. There is a story that he once repelled a strong force of Goths with only ten men to help him. Saint Patiens, Bishop of Lyons, is said to have succored his people in just the same way during the famine. There is still in existence a letter written by Saint Sidonius in which he praises Patiens very highly for this.

25. At the same time Euric, king of the Goths, crossed the Spanish frontier and began a terrible persecution of the Christians in Gaul. Without ado he cut off the heads of all who would not subscribe to his heretical opinions, he imprisoned the priests, and the bishops he either drove into exile or had executed. He ordered the doorways of the churches to be blocked with briers so that the very difficulty of finding one's way in might encourage men to forget their Christian faith. It was mainly the district between the River Garonne and the Pyrenees and the towns of the two Aquitaines which suffered from this violent attack.[2] We still possess a letter by the noble Sidonius written to Bishop Basilus about this, in which he gives full details. Soon afterwards the persecutor died, struck down by the vengeance of God.

26. Not long afterwards Saint Perpetuus, bishop of the city of Tours, reached the end of his life,

having been bishop for thirty years. Volusianus, a man of senatorial rank, was appointed in his place. He was regarded with suspicion by the Goths. In the seventh year of his episcopate he was dragged off as a captive to Spain and there he soon died. Verus succeeded him and was ordained as the seventh bishop after Saint Martin.

27. The next thing which happened was that Childeric died. His son Clovis replaced him on the throne. In the fifth year of his reign, Syagrius, the king of the Romans and the son of Aegidius, was living in the city of Soissons, where Aegidius himself used to have his residence. Clovis marched against him with his blood-relation Ragnachar, who also had high authority, and challenged him to come out to fight. Syagrius did not hesitate to so do, for he was not afraid of Clovis. They fought each other and the army of Syagrius was annihilated. He fled and made his way as quickly as he could to King Alaric II in Toulouse. Clovis summoned Alaric to surrender the fugitive, informing him that he would attack him in his turn for having given Syagrius refuge. Alaric was afraid to incur the wrath of the Franks for the sake of Syagrius and handed him over bound to the envoys, for the Goths are a timorous race. When Clovis had Syagrius in his power he ordered him to be imprisoned. As soon as he had seized the kingdom of Syagrius he had him killed in secret. … Clovis waged many wars and won many victories. In the tenth year of his reign he invaded the Thuringians and subjected them to his rule.

28. The king of the Burgundes was called Gundioc; he was of the family of that King Athanaric who persecuted the Christians and about whom I have told you. He had four sons: Gundobad, Godigisel, Chilperic and Gundomar. Gundobad killed his brother Chilperic and drowned Chilperic's wife after tying a stone round her neck. He drove Chilperic's two daughters into exile: the elder, whose name was Chroma, became a religious, and the younger was called Clotild. Clovis often sent envoys to Burgundy and they saw the girl Clotild. They observed that she was an elegant young woman and clever for her years, and they

---

2   The district between the Garonne and the Pyrenees, then known as Novempopulana, is now Gascony. The "two Aquitaines," Aquitania Prima and Aquitania Secunda, are the district between the River Garonne and the River Loire.

discovered that she was of the blood royal. They reported all this to Clovis and he immediately sent more messengers to Gundobad to ask for her hand in marriage. Gundobad was afraid to refuse and he handed Clotild over to them. They took her back with them, and presented her to their king. Clovis already had a son called Theuderic by one of his mistresses, but he was delighted when he saw Clotild and made her his wife.

29. The first child which Clotild bore for Clovis was a son. She wanted to have her baby baptized, and she kept on urging her husband to agree to this. "The gods whom you worship are no good," she would say. "They haven't even been able to help themselves, let alone others. They are carved out of stone or wood or some old piece of metal. The very names which you have given them were the names of men, not of gods. Take your Saturn, for example, who ran away from his own son to avoid being exiled from his kingdom, or so they say; and Jupiter, that obscene perpetrator of all sorts of mucky deeds, who couldn't keep his hands off other men, who had his fun with all his female relatives and couldn't even refrain from intercourse with his own sister,

'... Jovisque
Et soror et coniunx,'[3]

to quote her own words. What have Mars and Mercury ever done for anyone? They may have been endowed with magic arts, but they were certainly not worthy of being called divine. You ought instead to worship Him who created at a word and out of nothing heaven, and earth, the sea and all that therein is, who made the sun to shine, who lit the sky with stars, who peopled the water with fish, the earth with beasts, the sky with flying creatures, at whose nod the fields became fair with fruits, the trees with apples, the vines with grapes, by whose hand the race of man was made, by whose gift all creation is constrained to serve in deference and devotion the man He made." However often the queen said this, the king came no nearer to belief. "All these things have been created and produced at the command of *our* gods," he would answer. "It is obvious that *your* God can do nothing, and there is no proof that he is a God at all."

The queen, who was true to her faith, brought her son to be baptized. She ordered the church to be decorated with hangings and curtains, in the hope that the king, who remained stubborn in the face of argument, might be brought to the faith by ceremony. The child was baptized; he was given the name Ingomer; but no sooner had he received baptism than he died in his white robes. Clovis was extremely angry. He began immediately to reproach his queen. "If he had been dedicated in the name of my gods," he said, "he would have lived without question; but now that he has been baptized in the name of your God he has not been able to live a single day!" "I give thanks to Almighty God," replied Clotild, "the Creator of all things, who has not found me completely unworthy, for He has deigned to welcome into His kingdom a child conceived in my womb. I am not at all cast down in my mind because of what has happened, for I know that my child, who was called away from this world in his white baptismal robes, will be nurtured in the sight of God."

Some time later Clotild bore a second son. He was baptized Chlodomer. He began to ail and Clovis said: "What else do you expect? It will happen to him as it happened to his brother: no sooner is he baptized in the name of your Christ than he will die!" Clotild prayed to the Lord and at His command the baby recovered.

30. Queen Clotild continued to pray that her husband might recognize the true God and give up his idol-worship. Nothing could persuade him to accept Christianity. Finally war broke out against the Alamanni and in this conflict he was forced by necessity to accept what he had refused of his own free will. It so turned out that when the two armies met on the battlefield there was a great slaughter and the troops of Clovis were rapidly being annihilated. He raised his eyes to heaven when he saw this, felt compunction in his heart and was moved to tears. "Jesus Christ," he said, "you who Clotild maintains to be the Son of the living God, you who design to give help to those in travail and victory to those who trust in you, in faith I beg the glory of your help. If you will give me victory over my enemies, and if I may have evidence of that miraculous power which the

---

3   And both the sister and lover of Jove [Jupiter]. Virgil, *Aeneid*, 1.46–47.

people dedicated to your name say that they have experienced, then I will believe in you and I will be baptized in your name. I have called upon my own gods, but, as I see only too clearly, they have no intention of helping me. I therefore cannot believe that they possess any power, for they do not come to the assistance of those who trust them. I now call upon you. I want to believe in you, but I must first be saved from my enemies." Even as he said this the Alamanni turned their backs and began to run away. As soon as they saw that their king was killed, they submitted to Clovis. "We beg you," they said, "to put an end to this slaughter. We are prepared to obey you." Clovis stopped the war. He made a speech in which he called for peace. Then he went home. He told the queen how he had won a victory by calling on the name of Christ. This happened in the fifteenth year of his reign.

31. The queen then ordered Saint Remigius, bishop of the town of Rheims, to be summoned in secret. She begged him to impart the word of salvation to the king. The bishop asked Clovis to meet him in private and began to urge him to believe in the true God, Maker of heaven and earth, and to forsake his idols, which were powerless to help him or anyone else. The king replied: "I have listened to you willingly, holy father. There remains one obstacle. The people under my command will not agree to forsake their gods. I will go and put to them what you have just said to me." He arranged a meeting with his people, but God in his power had preceded him, and before he could say a word all those present shouted in unison: "We will give up worshipping our mortal gods, pious king, and we are prepared to follow the immortal God about whom Remigius preaches." This news was reported to the bishop. He was greatly pleased and he ordered the baptismal pool to be made ready. The public squares were draped with colored cloths, the churches were adorned with white hangings, the baptistry was prepared, sticks of incense gave off clouds of perfume, sweet-smelling candles gleamed bright and the holy place of baptism was filled with divine fragrance. God filled the hearts of all present with such grace that they imagined

themselves to have been transported to some perfumed paradise. King Clovis asked that he might be baptized first by the bishop. Like some new Constantine he stepped forward to the baptismal pool, ready to wash away the sores of his old leprosy and to be cleansed in flowing water from the sordid stains which he had borne so long. As he advanced for his baptism, the holy man of God addressed him in these pregnant words: "Bow your head in meekness, Sicamber.[4] Worship what you have burnt, burn what you have been wont to worship."

Saint Remigius was a bishop of immense learning and a great scholar more than anything else, but he was also famous for his holiness and he was the equal of Saint Silvester for the miracles which he performed. We still have an account of his life, which tells how he raised a man from the dead. King Clovis confessed his belief in God Almighty, three in one. He was baptized in the name of the Father, the Son and the Holy Ghost, and marked in holy chrism with the sign of the Cross of Christ. More than three thousand of his army were baptized at the same time. His sister Albofled was baptized, but she soon after died and was gathered to the Lord. The king grieved over her death, but Saint Remigius sent him a consoling letter which began with these words:

I am greatly distressed and I share your grief at the loss of your sister of pious memory. We can take consolation in this, that she has met her death in such a way that we can look up to her instead of mourning for her.

Another sister of Clovis, called Lanthechild, was converted at the same time. She had accepted the Arian heresy, but she confessed the triune majesty of the Father, the Son and the Holy Ghost, and received the holy chrism.

32. At this time the two brothers Gundobad and Godigisel ruled over the territory round the Rhône and the Saône and the province of Marseilles. Like their subjects they belonged to the Arian sect. They were enemies, and when Godigisel heard of the victories won by King Clovis he sent envoys

---

4   The Merovingians claimed to be descended from the Sicambri.

to him in secret. "If you help me to attack my brother," he said, "so that I can kill him in battle or drive him out of his territory, I will pay you any annual tribute which you may care to exact." Clovis gladly accepted the offer and in his turn promised to help Godigisel wherever occasion should arise. They chose a suitable moment and Clovis marched his army against Gundobad. As soon as he heard of this, Gundobad, who knew nothing of his brother's treachery, sent a message to Godigisel. "Come to my assistance," he said, "for the Franks are marching against us and are invading our territory which they plan to capture. Let us make a common front against this people which hates us, for if we are not united we shall suffer the same fate which others have met before us." Godigisel answered: "I am coming with my army and I will support you." The three kings each put his army in the field, Clovis marching against Gundobad and Godigisel. They arrived with all their military equipment at a fortified place called Dijon. When battle was joined on the River Ouche, Godigisel went over to Clovis and their united forces crushed the army of Gundobad. Gundobad turned his back and fled when he saw the treachery of his brother, about whom he had no suspicion. He made his way along the banks of the Rhône and took refuge in the city of Avignon. As for Godigisel, once the victory was won, he promised to hand over part of his kingdom to Clovis and then went home in peace and entered Vienne in triumph, as if he were still master of his own territory. Clovis called up more troops and set out in pursuit of Gundobad, planning to extract him from Avignon and kill him. When Gundobad learned this he was panic-stricken, for he was afraid of being killed at any moment. He had with him a man of some distinction called Aridius. Aridius was astute and full of energy. Gundobad summoned this man to him and said: "I am surrounded by pitfalls and what to do I cannot tell. These barbarians have launched this attack against me. If they kill us two they will ravage the whole neighborhood." "You must do all you can to propitiate this savage creature," answered Aridius, "or else you are done for. If you agree, I will run away from you and pretend to go over to his side. When I have joined him I will see to it that no harm is done to you or to this region. If

you will only carry out my plan in all its details, the Lord God in his compassion will assure you a happy outcome." "I will do whatever you say," replied Gundobad. Having received his answer, Aridius bade him goodbye and left him. He made his way to Clovis. "I am your humble slave, most pious king," said he. "I have deserted the wretched Gundobad and come to join your forces. If you are prepared to accept me kindly, then you and your descendants will find in me a faithful and trustworthy retainer." Clovis accepted this offer without hesitating for a moment and kept Aridius by his side. He was a wonderful raconteur, full of good advice, sound in judgement and apparently trustworthy. Clovis remained encamped with his entire army round the city walls. "If you who are a king with absolute power would deign to accept a little advice from me who am no one," said Aridius to him, "this is the loyal proposition which I should like to put to you. What I am going to say will be to your advantage and at the same time to the advantage of the cities through which you propose to pass. What is the point of keeping all these troops under arms when your enemy is safe in a stronghold which is too well fortified for you to capture? You are destroying the fields, spoiling the meadows, cutting up the vineyards, ruining the olive-groves and ravaging the whole countryside, which is a very fruitful one. In doing this you are causing no harm whatsoever to Gundobad. Why don't you send an ultimatum to him to say that he must pay whatever annual tribute you care to exact? In that way the region will be saved and he will have to submit to you and pay tribute to you for ever. If he doesn't accept this, you can do whatever you wish." Clovis accepted the advice of Aridius and sent his army home. Then he dispatched envoys to Gundobad and ordered him to pay yearly tribute. Gundobad paid up for the year in question and promised that he would do the same from then onwards.

33. Later on Gundobad recovered his strength and scorned to pay King Clovis the tribute which he had been promised. He marched his army against his brother Godigisel and besieged him inside his city of Vienne. Once provisions began to run short among the common people, Godigisel was afraid that the lack of food might extend to him also,

and he ordered them to be driven out of the town. This was done, but along with them was expelled the engineer who was in charge of the aqueduct. He was very indignant at having been ejected with the others. He went in a rage to Gundobad and revealed to him how he might break into the city and take vengeance on his brother. With this engineer to show them the way, Gundobad's army was led along the aqueduct. At their head marched a number of sappers with iron crowbars. There was a water-gate blocked by a great stone. Under the direction of the engineer they heaved this stone on one side with their crowbars, made their way into the city and attacked from the rear the defenders, who were still busy shooting their arrows from the wall. A trumpet-call was sounded from the center of the city, the besiegers attacked the gateways, burst them open and rushed in. The townsfolk were caught between two fires and cut to pieces by two forces. Godigisel took refuge in one of the heretic churches, but he was killed there and his Arian bishop with him. The Franks who had been with Godigisel banded together in one of the towers. Gundobad gave orders that none of them should be maltreated. When he had disarmed them he sent them in exile to King Alaric in Toulouse. All the Gallo-Roman senators and the Burgundes who had sided with Godigisel were killed out of hand. This whole region, which is now called Burgundy, Gundobad took under his own rule. He instituted milder laws among the Burgundes, to stop them treating the Romans unjustly.

34. Gundobad came to realize that the religious tenets of the heretics were of no avail. He accepted that Christ, the Son of God, and the Holy Ghost are equal with the Father, and he asked the saintly Bishop of Vienne to arrange for him to be anointed with the chrism in secret. "If you really believe what the Lord has Himself taught us," said the bishop, "then you should carry it out. Christ said: 'Whosoever therefore shall confess me before men, him I will confess also before my Father which is in heaven. But whosoever shall deny me before men, him will I also deny before my Father which is in heaven.' In the same way He gave advice to the holy and blessed apostles, whom He loved so much, saying: 'But beware of men: for they will deliver you up to the councils, and they will scourge you in their synagogues; and ye shall be brought before governors and kings for my sake, for a testimony against them and the Gentiles.' You are a king and you need not fear to be taken in charge by anyone: yet you are afraid of your subjects and you do not dare to confess in public your belief in the Creator of all things. Stop being so foolish and confess in front of them all what you say you believe in your heart. The blessed apostle said: 'For with the heart man believeth unto righteousness; and with the mouth confession is made unto salvation.' Similarly the prophet said: 'I will give thee thanks in the great congregation: I will praise thee among much people.' And again: 'I will praise thee, O Lord, among the people: I will sing unto thee among the nations.' You are afraid of your people. Do you not realize that it is better that the people should accept your belief, rather than that you, a king, should pander to their every whim? You are the leader of your people; your people is not there to lord it over you. When you go to war, you yourself march at the head of the squadrons of your army and they follow where you lead. It is therefore preferable that they should learn the truth under your direction, rather than that at your death they should continue in their errors. For 'God is not mocked,' nor can He love the man who for an earthly kingdom refuses to confess Him before all the world." Gundobad was worsted in this argument, but to his life's end he persisted in his obstinacy, refusing to confess in public that the three persons of the Trinity are equal.

At this time Saint Avitus was at the height of his eloquence. Certain heresies began to be current in the town of Constantinople, first that of Eutyches and then that of Sabellius, who maintained that our Lord Jesus Christ had nothing about Him which was divine. At the request of King Gundobad Avitus wrote polemics against these heresies. We still possess these admirable letters, which at once denounced the heresy and supported the Church of God. He wrote a book of *Homilies*, six books in verse on the creation of the world and other cognate subjects, and nine books of *Letters*, among which are included the ones already mentioned. In the homily which he composed on the Rogations he says that these ceremonies, which we celebrate before the triumph of our Lord's Ascension, were instituted by Mamertus, bishop of that same town of Vienne of which Avitus held the episcopate when he was writing, at a time when the townsfolk were terrified by a series of portents. Vienne was shaken by frequent earthquakes, and savage packs of wolves and stags came in through the gates and ranged through the entire city, fearing nothing and nobody, or so he writes. These portents continued throughout the whole year. As the season of the feast of Easter approached, the common people in their devotion expected God's compassion on them, hoping that this day of great solemnity might see an end of their terror. However, on the very vigil of the holy night, when the rite of Mass was being celebrated, the king's palace inside the city walls was set ablaze by fire sent by God. The congregation was panic-stricken. They rushed out of the church, for they thought that the whole town would be destroyed by this fire, or else that the earth would open and swallow it up. The holy bishop was prostrate before the altar, imploring God's mercy with tears and lamentations. What more should I say? The prayers of this famous bishop rose to heaven above and, so to speak, his floods of tears put out the fire in the palace. While this was going on, the feast of the Ascension of our Lord was coming nearer, as I have told you. Mamertus told the people to fast, he instituted a special form of prayer, a religious service and a grant of alms to the poor in thanksgiving. All the horrors came to an end. The story of what had happened spread through all the provinces and led all the bishops to copy what this particular prelate had done in faith. Down to our own times these rites are celebrated with a contrite spirit and a grateful heart in all our churches to the glory of God.

35. When Alaric II, the King of the Goths, observed that King Clovis was beating one race of people after another, he sent envoys to him. "If you agree," said he, "it seems to me that it would be a good thing, my dear brother, if, with God's approval, we two were to meet." Clovis did agree. He traveled to meet Alaric and the two of them came together near the village of Amboise, on an island in the Loire, in territory belonging to Tours. They conferred with each other, sat side by side at the meal table, swore eternal friendship and went home again in peace. At that time a great many people in Gaul were very keen on having the Franks as their rulers.

36. It was as a direct result of this that Quintianus, the Bishop of Rodez, fell into disfavor and was driven out of his city. The townsfolk started saying to him: "If you had your way, the Franks would take over our territory." Not long after this an open quarrel started between him and his flock. The Goths who were resident in Rodez suspected him, and the Rhuténois themselves went so far as to accuse him of wishing to accept the rule of the Franks. They plotted together and planned to assassinate him. When Quintianus came to hear of this, he fled one night and left the city with the more trustworthy among his attendants. He reached Clermont-Ferrand and there he was kindly received by Saint Eufrasius, who had succeeded to Aprunculus, himself a native of Dijon. Eufrasius gave him accommodation, with fields around and vineyards, for, as he said: "The resources of this diocese are sufficient to support us both: that charity which the blessed apostle preached must continue between God's ministers." The Bishop of Lyons also made over to Quintianus certain church property which he administered in Clermont. Other details concerning Saint Quintianus, the wrongs which were done to him and the miracles which the Lord deigned to perform through his agency, are described in my *Vitae Patruum* [*Lives of the Fathers*], in the chapter devoted to him.

37. "I find it hard to go on seeing these Arians occupy a part of Gaul," said Clovis to his ministers. "With God's help let us invade them. When we have beaten them, we will take over their territory." They all agreed to this proposal. An army was assembled and Clovis marched on Poitiers. Some of his troops passed through land belonging to Tours. In respect for Saint Martin, Clovis ordered that they should requisition nothing in this neighborhood except fodder and water. One of the soldiers found some hay belonging to a poor man. "The King commanded that nothing should be requisitioned except fodder, didn't he?" said this

man. "Well, this is fodder. We shan't be disobeying his orders if we take it." He laid hands on the poor man and took his hay by main force. This was reported to Clovis. He drew his sword and killed the soldier on the spot. "It is no good expecting to win this fight if we offend Saint Martin," said he. This was enough to ensure that the army took nothing else from this region. The King sent messengers to the church of Saint Martin. "Off with you," he said, "and see if you can bring me some good tidings from God's house." He loaded them with gifts which they were to offer to the church. "Lord God," said he, "if You are on my side and if You have decreed that this people of unbelievers, who have always been hostile to You, are to be delivered into my hands, deign to show me a propitious sign as these men enter Saint Martin's church, so that I may know that You will support your servant Clovis." The messengers set out on their journey and came to Tours as Clovis had commanded. As they entered the church, it happened that the precentor was just beginning to intone this antiphon: "For thou hast girded me with strength unto the battle: thou hast subdued under me those that rose up against me. Thou hast also given me the necks of mine enemies: that I might destroy them that hate me." When the messengers heard this psalm, they gave thanks to God. They made their vows to the saint and went happily back to report to the king. When Clovis reached the Vienne with his army, he was at a loss to know where to cross, for the river was swollen with heavy rains. That night he prayed that God might deign to indicate a ford by which he might make the crossing. As day dawned an enormous doe entered the water, as if to lead them at God's command. The soldiers knew that where the doe had crossed they could follow. The King marched towards Poitiers, and while he and his army were encamped there a pillar of fire rose from the church of Saint Hilary. It seemed to move towards Clovis as a sign that with the support of the blessed saint he might the more easily overcome the heretic host, against which Hilary himself had so often done battle for the faith. Clovis forbade his troops to take any booty as they marched in, or to rob any man of his possessions.

At that time on the outskirts of Poitiers there dwelt a saintly abbot called Maxentius, who lived as a God-fearing recluse in his monastery. There is no point in my giving the name of the monastery, as it is now called the Cell of Saint Maxentius. When the monks saw a squadron of troops coming nearer and nearer to their monastery they begged their abbot to come out of his cell to give his blessing to the soldiers. He was a long time coming, and they were so frightened that they burst the door open and pushed him out of his cell. He showed no fear. He walked towards the troops, as if to ask them not to molest him. One of the soldiers drew his sword to strike Maxentius over the head. His arm went stiff on a level with the saint's feet and asked his forgiveness. When his companions saw what had happened, they rushed back to the army in great consternation, for they were afraid that they might all pay for it with their lives. The blessed saint rubbed the man's arm with holy oil, made the sign of the Cross over him, and he immediately recovered. As a result of what Maxentius had done the monastery remained unharmed. He performed many other miracles, as the diligent reader will discover if he peruses the abbot's *Vita*. This happened in the fifteenth year of the reign of Clovis.

Meanwhile King Clovis met Alaric II, king of the Goths, on the battlefield of Vouillé, near the tenth milestone outside Poitiers. Some of the soldiers engaged hurled their javelins from a distance, others fought hand to hand. The Goths fled, as they were prone to do, and Clovis was the victor, for God was on his side. As one of his allies he had the son of Sigibert the Lame,[5] called Chloderic. Sigibert had been lame since he was wounded in the knee when fighting against the Alamanni at the fortress of Zülpich. Clovis killed Alaric, but, as the Goths fled, two of them suddenly rushed up in the scrum, one on this side and one on that, and struck at the Frankish king with their spears. It was his leather corselet which saved him and the sheer speed of his horse, but he was very near to death. A large force of Auvergnats took part in the battle, for they had come under the command of Apollinaris; their leaders, who were of senatorial rank, were killed. Amalaric, the

---

5   Sigibert the Lame, King of the Ripuarian Franks.

son of Alaric, escaped from the conflict and fled to Spain, where he later ruled his father's kingdom wisely. Clovis sent his own son Theuderic through Albi and the town of Rodez to Clermont-Ferrand. As he moved forward Theuderic subjected to his father's rule all the towns which lay between the two frontiers of the Goths and the Burgundes. Alaric II had reigned for twelve years. Clovis wintered in the town of Bordeaux. He removed all Alaric's treasure from Toulouse and went to Angoulême. There the Lord showed him such favor that the city walls collapsed of their own weight as he looked at them. Clovis drove the Goths out of Angoulême and took command of the city. With his victory consolidated he then returned to Tours. There he gave many gifts to the church of Saint Martin.

38. Letters reached Clovis from the Emperor Anastasius to confer the consulate on him. In Saint Martin's church he stood clad in a purple tunic and the military mantle, and he crowned himself with a diadem. He then rode out on his horse and with his own hand showered gold and silver coins among the people present all the way from the doorway of Saint Martin's church to Tours cathedral. From that day on he was called Consul or Augustus. He left Tours and travelled to Paris, where he established the seat of his government. Theuderic came to join him in Paris.

39. When Eustochius, Bishop of Tours, died, Licinius was ordained bishop in his place. He was the eighth after Saint Martin. The war which I have just described was waged during the episcopate of Licinius, and it was in his time that King Clovis came to Tours. Licinius is said to have been in the East and to have visited the holy places. They even say that he went to Jerusalem and saw on a number of occasions the site of our Lord's Passion and Resurrection, about which we read in the Gospels.

40. While Clovis was resident in Paris he sent secretly to the son of Sigibert, saying: "Your father is old and he is lame in one leg. If he were to die, his kingdom would come to you of right, and my alliance would come with it." Chloderic was led astray by his lust for power and began

to plot his father's death. One day Sigibert went out of the city of Cologne and crossed the Rhine, for he wanted to walk in the forest of Buchau. At midday he took a siesta in his tent, and his son set assassins on him and had him murdered, so that he might gain possession of his kingdom. By the judgement of God Chloderic fell into the pit which he had dug for his own father. He sent messengers to King Clovis to announce his father's death. "My father is dead," said he, "and I have taken over his kingdom and his treasure. Send me your envoys and I will gladly hand over to you anything which you may care to select from this treasure." "I thank you for your good will," answered Clovis. "I ask you to show all your treasure to my messengers, but you may keep it." The envoys came and Chloderic showed his father's treasure to them. They inspected everything. "It was in this coffer that my father used to keep all his gold coins," said Chloderic. "Plunge your hand right to the bottom," they answered, "to see how much is there." As he leant forward to do this, one of the Franks raised his hand and split Chloderic's skull with his double-headed axe. This unworthy son thus shared the fate of his father. When Clovis heard that both Sigibert and his son were dead, he came to Cologne himself and ordered the inhabitants to assemble. "While I was out sailing on the River Scheldt," said he, "Chloderic, the son of your king, my brother, was busy plotting against his father and putting it out that I wanted him killed. As Sigibert fled through the forest of Buchau, Chloderic set assassins on him and had him murdered. While Chloderic was showing his father's treasure, he in his turn was killed by somebody or other. I take no responsibility for what has happened. It is not for me to shed the blood of one of my fellow kings, for that is a crime; but since things have turned out in this way, I will give you my advice and you must make of it what you will. It is that you should turn to me and put yourself under my protection." When they heard what he had to say, they clashed their shields and shouted their approval. Then they raised Clovis up on a shield and made him their ruler. In this way he took over both the kingship and the treasure of Sigibert and submitted Sigibert's people to his own rule. Day in day out God submitted the enemies of Clovis to his dominion and increased his power, for he walked before Him with an upright heart and did what was pleasing in His sight.

41. Clovis next marched against Chararic.[6] When Clovis was fighting against Syagrius, this Chararic, who had been summoned to his aid, remained neutral, giving help to neither side and awaiting the issue of the conflict, so that he might offer the hand of friendship to whichever leader was victorious. This was the reason why Clovis now attacked him in his wrath. He hemmed Chararic in by some stratagem and made him prisoner. Chararic and his son were both bound and then Clovis had their hair cut short. He ordered Chararic to be ordained as a priest and he made his son a deacon. Chararic objected to this humiliation and burst into tears. His son is said to have exclaimed: "These leaves have been cut from wood which is still green and not lacking in sap. They will soon grow again and be larger than ever; and may the man who has done this deed perish equally quickly." The statement came to the ears of Clovis. As they were threatening to let their hair grow again and then to kill him, he had their heads cut off. When they were dead he took possession of their kingdom, their treasure and their people.

42. There lived in Cambrai at this time a king called Ragnachar who was so sunk in debauchery that he could not even keep his hands off the women of his own family. He had an adviser named Farro who was given to the same filthy habits. It was said of Farro that when food, or a present, or indeed any gift was brought to the king, Ragnachar would say that it was good enough for him and his dear Farro. This situation roused their Frankish subjects to the utmost fury. Clovis gave a bribe, of golden arm-bands and sword-belts to the *leudes* of Ragnachar, to encourage them to call him in against their King. These ornaments looked like gold, but they were really of bronze very cleverly gilded. Clovis marched his army against Ragnachar. Ragnachar sent spies to discover the strength of the invaders. When the spies returned, he asked them just how strong the enemy was. "Strong enough for you and your dear Farro," they

replied. Clovis arrived in person and drew up his line of battle. Ragnachar witnessed the defeat of his army and prepared to slip away in flight. He was arrested by his own troops and with his arms tied behind his back he was brought before Clovis. His brother Ricchar was dragged in with him. "Why have you disgraced our Frankish people by allowing yourself to be bound?" asked Clovis. "It would have been better for you had you died in battle." He raised his axe and split Ragnachar's skull. Then he turned to Ricchar and said: "If you had stood by your brother, he would not have been bound in this way." He killed Ricchar with a second blow of his axe. When these two were dead, those who had betrayed them discovered that the gold which they had received from Clovis was counterfeit. When they complained to Clovis, he is said to have answered: "This is the sort of gold which a man can expect when he deliberately lures his lord to death." He added that they were lucky to have escaped with their lives, instead of paying for the betrayal of their rulers by being tortured to death. When they heard this, they chose to beg forgiveness, saying that it was enough for them if they were allowed to live. The two kings of whom I have told you, Ragnachar and Ricchar, were relatives of Clovis. At his command their brother Rignomer was also put to death in Le Mans. As soon as all three were slain, Clovis took over their kingdom and their treasure. In the same way he encompassed the death of many other kings and blood-relations of his whom he suspected of conspiring against his kingdom. By doing this he spread his dominion over the whole of Gaul. One day when he had called a general assembly of his subjects, he is said to have made the following remark about the relatives whom he had destroyed: "How sad a thing it is that I live among strangers like some solitary pilgrim, and that I have none of my own relations left to help me when disaster threatens!" He said this not because he grieved for their deaths, but because in his cunning way he hoped to find some relative still in the land of the living whom he could kill.

43. At long last Clovis died in Paris. He was buried in the Church of the Holy Apostles, which he and

---

6   Chararic, a king of the Salian Franks.

his queen Clotild had built. He expired five years after the battle of Vouillé. He had reigned for thirty years and he was forty-five years old. From the passing of Saint Martin until the death of King Clovis, which happened in the eleventh year of the episcopate of Licinius, Bishop of Tours, there are counted one hundred and twelve years. After the death of her husband Queen Clotild came to live in Tours. She served as a religious in the church of Saint Martin. She lived all the rest of her days in this place, apart from an occasional visit to Paris. She was remarkable for her great modesty and her loving kindness.

Excerpt from Book VII

47. A most serious civil discord now arose between the citizens of Tours. When Sichar, the son of John, was enjoying himself in the village of Manthelan, as part of the Christmas festivities, with Austregesil and a number of other local folk, the village priest sent one of his servants to invite some of the men to come and have a drink in his house. When the servant arrived, one of the men who were invited drew his sword and hit him. He fell down dead. Sichar was a personal friend of the priest. As soon as he heard that the priest's servant had been killed, he seized his weapons and went to the church to wait for Austregesil. When Austregesil was informed of this, he snatched up his own weapons and went to look for Sichar. A pitched battle ensued. In the end a number of people slipped away on both sides, and Sichar was brought safely out by some of the clerics. He sought refuge in the country estate where he lived. In the priest's house he left behind four of his servants who had been wounded, together with some money and some of his effects. Once Sichar had fled, Austregesil launched a second attack, killed the four servants, and stole the gold and silver with the other things. The two parties were called up before a tribunal of citizens. Their verdict was that Austregesil, who had committed murder, killed Sichar's servants and removed his goods without having any right to them, was guilty in the eyes of the law. A few days after the case had been tried, Sichar heard that the goods which Austregesil had stolen were now in the hands of a man called Auno, Auno's son, and his

brother Eberulf. Sichar thereupon dismissed the tribunal from his mind as if it had never been, sought the help of a certain Audinus and started an affray by attacking those three in the middle of the night with a gang of armed men. He broke into the house where they were sleeping, murdered Auno, his son and his brother, killed their servants and stole not only all their portable property but also their herds. When I came to hear of this I was greatly disturbed. In conjunction with the judge I sent a message to them, summoning them to appear before me to see if the matter could be settled rationally, so that they might part in peace without the feud going any further. They duly arrived and a number of townsfolk with them. "Men," said I, "You must stop this riotous behavior and not let the wrong which has been done spread any wider. I have already lost several sons of the Church, and I have reason to fear that I may well lose others in this feud. I ask you to keep the peace. Whichever of you has done wrong, let him pay for it in brotherly love, and then all of you make peace, so that, if God grants, you may be worthy to receive the kingdom of heaven. He Himself has said: 'Blessed are the peacemakers: for they shall be called the children of God.' [Matthew 5, 9]. If he who is ordered to pay a fine lacks the wherewithal, the Church will provide it, rather than see any man lose his soul." When I had finished speaking, I offered money belonging to the Church. The supporters of Chramnesind, who was there to demand justice for the killing of his father, brother and uncle, refused to accept it. When they had all gone off, Sichar made ready to go to see the King. With this in mind he set off first for Poitiers to visit his wife. There he was exhorting one of his slaves to get on with his work, and had just taken hold of a stick and was belaboring him with it, when the slave dragged Sichar's sword from his belt and had the effrontery to wound his master with it. Sichar fell to the ground. His friends ran up. The slave was seized, he was cruelly beaten, his hands and feet were cut off, and he was hanged from the gallows. Meanwhile the news reached Tours that Sichar was dead. When Chramnesind heard of this, he sent word to his friends and relations, and hurried off to Sichar's house. He stole everything that he could lay his hands on, killed a few slaves, burned down not only Sichar's house but also those of his neighbors who lived in the same estate, and carried off with him all the cattle and every other movable object. The parties concerned were summoned to appear before the judge in the city to plead their cases. The judgement of the court was that Chramnesind, who had refused to accept the compensation offered and had then proceeded to burn down the houses, should forfeit half of the sum previously awarded to him. This decision was made against the letter of the law, in an attempt to persuade them to make peace. It was further decreed that Sichar should pay the remaining half of the compensation. In effect the money was provided by the Church. Thus the compensation which the judges had demanded was duly paid over, and securities were lodged in court. Both parties swore an oath that they would never make further trouble against each other. So the feud came to an end.

Excerpts from Book IX

19. The civil discord between the townsfolk of Tours, which I described above as having spent its force, broke out once more with renewed fury. After having murdered Chramnesind's relatives, Sichar formed a great friendship with him, and they became so devoted to each other that they often had meals together and even slept in the same bed. One day as twilight was falling Chramnesind ordered his supper to be prepared and then invited Sichar round to eat with him. He came, and they both sat down to table. Sichar drank far more wine than he could carry and began to boast at Chramnesind's expense. He is reported to have said: "Dear brother, you ought to be grateful to me for having killed off your relations. There is plenty of gold and silver in your house now that I have recompensed you for what I did to them. If it weren't for the fact that the fine which I've paid has restored your finances, you would still today be poor and destitute." When he heard Sichar's remarks, Chramnesind was sick at heart. "If I don't avenge my relatives," he said to himself, "they will say that I am as weak as a woman, for I no longer have the right to be called a man!" Thereupon he blew the lights out and hacked Sichar's skull in two. Sichar uttered a low moan as life left his body, then he fell dead to the floor. The servants who had come with him lost no time in making off. Chramnesind stripped Sichar's corpse of its clothes and hung it from a post in his garden-fence. He then climbed on a horse and went off to find the king. He entered a church and threw himself at Childebert's feet. "Mighty king!" he said, "I come to plead for my life. I have killed the man who in secret destroyed my relations and then stole all their possessions." He explained what had happened, point by point. Queen Brunhild took it very ill that Sichar, who was under her protection, should have been killed in this way, and she began to rage at Chramnesind. When he saw that she was against him, he fled to the village of Bouges in the Bourges area, where his people came from, this being under the jurisdiction of King Guntram. Tranquilla, Sichar's wife, abandoned her children and her husband's property in Tours and Poitiers, and went off to join her own relations in the village of Pont-sur-Seine. There she married again.

Sichar was only about twenty when he died. He was a loose-living young man, drunken and murderous, causing trouble to all sorts of people when he was in liquor. Chramnesind went to the king a second time. The judgement was that he must prove that he had taken life in order to avenge an affront, and this he did. In view of the fact that she had taken Sichar under her protection, Queen Brunhild ordered Chramnesind's property to be sequestered. Eventually his goods were handed back by Flavinius, one of the queen's retainers. Chramnesind rushed off to Count Aginus and obtained a letter of restitution from him. It was to Flavinius that the queen had made over his possessions.

20. In the thirteenth year of Childebert's reign, just as I had hurried off to Metz to meet the king, I received a command to go to King Guntram on an embassy. I found him in the town of Chalon-sur-Saône. "Noble king," said I, "your illustrious nephew Childebert sends to you his sincerest greetings. He thanks you warmly for your loving kindness and the constant encouragement which you give him to do that which is pleasing in God's sight, which is acceptable to you and in the best interests of his own people. He promises to carry

out everything that was agreed between you, and he pledges himself not to contravene any article of the treaty he signed by you both." "As far as I am concerned," replied the king, "I have little reason to feel grateful to Childebert. Why, he has already broken the promises which he made to me! He has not made over to me my part of the town of Senlis. He has not returned to me those men who, for my own well-being, I wished to summon back from his kingdom, seeing that they were hostile to my interests. How then can you stand there and say that this precious nephew of mine is determined in no way to contravene any article of the treaty signed by us both?"

To this I made the following reply: "Childebert has no intention of contravening any of the provisions. On the contrary, he really is determined to see that they are all carried out. As for the one to which you refer, if you wish to proceed to a partition of Senlis, it can be made immediately and you can take over your third of the town without delay. As far as the men to whom you have referred are concerned, give me their names in writing and you will see that all the promises made in the treaty will be honored."

When I had finished my speech, the king ordered the treaty to be read aloud once more in the hearing of all who were present.

Text of the Treaty. When, in the name of Christ, the most noble Lords King Guntram and King Childebert, and the most renowned Lady Queen Brunhild, met at Andelot to reaffirm their friendship and, after full debate, to put to an end any circumstance whatsoever which might prove to be a cause of dispute between them, it was settled, approved and mutually agreed, by the grace of God, and with the approval of their bishops and their military leaders that, for as long as Almighty God should preserve them in their lives here below, they should maintain good faith one with another, in pure loving kindness and singleness of heart.

§. Insofar as King Guntram, according to the terms of the alliance into which he had entered with King Sigibert of blessed memory, has claimed as his own the entire domain which King Sigibert had inherited from the lands owned by Charibert, and in so far as King Childebert has wished to recover from all this that portion which his own father had possessed, it is agreed between them and after full debate decided that the third part of the city of Paris, with its territory and its inhabitants, which came to King Sigibert by signed treaty from the lands ruled over by Charibert, together with the castles of Châteaudun and Vendôme, and all that the aforesaid King possessed with right of free passage in the region of Etampes and Chartres, with the lands concerned and the people who lived there, shall remain in perpetuity under the jurisdiction and dominion of King Guntram, this in addition to what he, Guntram, had already inherited from the lands ruled over by Charibert during the lifetime of King Sigibert.

§. It is further agreed that from this day forward King Childebert shall hold under his dominion the city of Meaux, two thirds of Senlis, and the cities of Tours, Poitiers, Avranches, Aire, Couserans, Labourd and Albi, with their territories.

§. The following condition shall be observed, that whichever of the aforesaid kings may by God's decree survive the other, given that other has passed away from the light of this world without male issue, shall inherit the kingdom of that other, in its entirety and in perpetuity, and, by God's grace, hand it down to his own descendants.

§. It is further most specifically agreed, and it shall be observed come what may, that whatsoever King Guntram has donated to his daughter Clotild, or may, by God's grace, in the future donate, in property of all kinds, in men, cities, lands or revenues, shall remain in her power and under her control. It is agreed that if she shall decide of her own free will to dispose of any part of the lands or revenues or monies, or to donate them to any person, by God's grace they shall not be taken from him at any time or by any other person. Moreover, she herself shall, under the protection and guardianship of King Childebert, hold secure, in all honor and dignity, everything of which she shall stand possessed at the death of her father.

§. In addition to this and under the same terms, King Guntram promises that if, in the light of human frailty, it should come to pass, and may God in His compassion not permit this, for Guntram himself would certainly not wish to live to see the day, that King Childebert should pass away from the light of this world leaving Guntram still alive, he, Guntram, will take under his own guardianship and protection, with all loving-kindness, her Majesty the Queen Brunhild, mother of King Childebert, Brunhild's daughter Chlodosind, the sister of King Childebert, as long as she remain in the land of the Franks, and Childebert's queen, Faileuba, as if she were his own dear sister, and her daughters, too; and he will ensure that they may hold in all security and peace, and in all honor and dignity, such men and such goods, such cities, lands, revenues, rights of all sorts and wealth of all kinds, as at this present time they are seen to hold, or as, in the future, with Christ to guide them, they are able lawfully to acquire. If of their own free will they wish to dispose of or to grant to any person any part of their lands, revenues or monies, this shall be secured in safe possession in perpetuity, and their wish shall not be annulled at any time by any other person.

§. As to the cities of Bordeaux, Limoges, Cahors, Lescar and Cieutat, which, as is unquestioned, Galswinth, sister of the Lady Brunhild, acquired as dowry, or as *morgengabe*, that is as a morning-gift, on her first coming to the land of the Franks, and which the Lady Brunhild is recognized to have inherited, by the decree of King Guntram and with the agreement of the Franks, during the lifetime of Chilperic and King Sigibert, it is agreed that the Lady Brunhild shall forthwith receive into her possession the city of Cahors, with its lands and all its inhabitants, but that King Guntram shall hold the other cities named above as long as he lives, on this condition, that

after his death they shall pass, God willing, in all security, into the possession of the Lady Brunhild, it being understood that, as long as King Guntram lives, they shall not under any pretext or at any time be claimed by the Lady Brunhild, or by her son King Childebert, or by his sons.

§. It is further agreed that King Childebert shall hold in its entirety the town of Senlis, but that, by the transfer to his lands of that third part of Ressons which is in King Childebert's possession, compensation shall be given to King Guntram for that third part of Senlis which is rightly claimed by him.

§. It is furthermore agreed that in accordance with the treaty made between King Guntram and King Sigibert of blessed memory, those *leudes* who, on the death of King Lothar, first took oaths of loyalty to King Guntram, but who can be shown since then to have transferred their allegiance elsewhere; shall be brought back from the places in which they are known to have taken up residence. In the same way those *leudes* who, after the death of King Lothar, are known first to have taken oaths of loyalty to King Sigibert, and then to have transferred their allegiance elsewhere, shall be brought back.

§. Furthermore, whatsoever the aforementioned kings have conferred upon the churches or upon their own faithful subjects, or may in future, by God's grace, and in lawful fashion, wish to confer upon them, shall be held by them in all security.

§. Whatsoever any faithful subject, in either of the two kingdoms, may justly and legally hold in his possession, shall in no way be open to question, for he shall be permitted to retain the things which are his. If, during interregna, anything is taken away from anyone through no fault of his own, an inquiry shall be held and restoration shall be made. Whatsoever, through the munificence of earlier kings, down to the death of King Lothar of blessed memory, any man has possessed, let him continue to possess it in security. Whatsoever has been taken away from our faithful subjects since then must be restored immediately.

§. Insofar as one single unequivocal treaty has now been accepted in God's name by the aforesaid kings, it is agreed that, in both kingdoms and for the faithful subjects of both kingdoms, the right of free passage shall at no time be refused to any person who may wish to travel on public affairs or on private business. It is furthermore agreed that neither king shall invite the *leudes* of the other king to join him, and that, if they should come, he shall not receive them. If, as the result of some misdemeanor, the *leudes* of one king seek refuge in the territory of the other king, they shall be handed back and punished in accordance with their crime.

§. It is further resolved to add to the treaty that, if at any time, on any pretext, any one of the parties concerned should fail to observe its provisions, he must forfeit all benefits conferred in the present or promised for the future, to the advantage of him who shall have carried out all the provisions in full detail, this latter then being absolved in all respects from being bound by his oath.

§. Now that agreement has been come to on all these points, the parties concerned swear in the name of God Almighty, and by the inseparable Trinity, by all things divine and by the awful Day of Judgement, that they will observe, in full detail, without fraud or treachery or wish to deceive, each and every provision as it is written above.

§. This treaty was made on November 28, in the twenty-sixth year of the reign of King Guntram and in the twelfth year of the reign of King Childebert.

When this treaty had been read aloud, the king said: "May I be struck by the judgement of God, if I break any of the provisions contained in that!" Then he turned to Felix, who had come with me. "Tell me, Felix," he said, "is it really true that you have established friendly relations between my sister Brunhild and that enemy of God and man, Fredegund?" Felix said that it was not. I spoke up and said: "The king need not question the fact that the 'friendly relations' which have bound them together for so many years are still being fostered by them both. That is to say, you may be quite sure that the hatred which they have borne each other for many a long year, far from withering away, is still as strong as ever. Noble king, it is a great pity that you cannot bring yourself to be less kindly disposed towards Queen Fredegund. We have so often remarked that you receive her envoys with more consideration than you give to ours." "You may be quite sure in your turn, bishop," answered King Guntram, "that I receive Fredegund's envoys in this way simply in order to maintain friendly relations with my nephew Childebert. I can hardly be offering ties of genuine friendship to a woman who on more than one occasion has sent her men to murder me!"

As soon as the king stopped speaking, Felix said: "I believe that it has come to your august ears that Recared has sent envoys to your nephew to ask for the hand in marriage of Chlodosind, your own niece and your brother's daughter. Childebert has, however, refused to give any promise without your express approval." "It cannot be a good thing," answered the king, "that my niece should set out for a land in which her sister met her end. I cannot accept it as right that my niece Ingund's death should go unavenged." "They are very keen to prove themselves guiltless of this," said Felix, "either by swearing oaths, or by any other means which you may propose. Only give your consent that Chlodosind may be betrothed to Recared as he asks!" "If my nephew carries out all that has been written into the treaty, and that with his full approval," answered Guntram, "I, for my part, will agree to what he wishes in this other matter." We promised that Childebert would fulfil all the conditions.

"Childebert further asks of you, in your loyalty to your own kith and kin," went on Felix, "that you send him help against the Longobards, so that he may drive them out of Italy and win back the territory which his father claimed during his lifetime. Then, with your assistance, the rest of Italy can be restored to Imperial rule." "I will never send my troops to Italy," answered the king, "for in doing so I should encompass their certain death. A terrible epidemic is raging in that country at this moment."

"You have put the request to your nephew," said I in my turn, "that all the bishops of his realm should meet together, since there are so many other matters which need to be settled. Your nephew has always been of the opinion, and in this he follows the canonical use, that each metropolitan should hold a meeting of the bishops of his own province, and then anything which is wrong in his own diocese can be put right as they may decide. What reason can there be for calling such a huge council together in one place? No threat is being made to the doctrine of the Church. No new heresy is being spawned. What need can there be for so many bishops to meet together in a single council?" "There are many matters which need to be settled," answered Guntram. "Many evil deeds are being committed, there is a decline in personal morality, for instance, and there are many other things which we need to discuss together. Above all, and more important than all the rest, for the issue concerns God Himself, you need to discover how Bishop Praetextatus came to be struck down in his own cathedral. Then there should be an inquiry into the case of those who are accused of the crime of *luxuria*.[7] If they are proved guilty, they should be punished as their fellow-bishops decide, but if they are found to be innocent, the injustice of the accusation should be made public." He then ordered the council to be deferred until the first day of June.

As soon as our interview was over, we processed to the cathedral. It was the feast-day of our Lord's Resurrection. When Mass was over, Guntram asked us to eat with him. The abundance of dishes on the table was only rivalled by the full contentment which we felt in our hearts. The king talked of God, of building new churches, of succoring the poor. From time to time he laughed out loud, as he coined some witty phrase, thereby ensuring that we shared his happiness. Among the other things which he said, he kept returning to this: "If only my nephew keeps his promises! All that I have is his! If he takes offense because I grant

an audience to my nephew Lothar's envoys, am I such a fool that I cannot mediate between them and so stop their quarrel from spreading? I am quite sure that it is better to end that quarrel, instead of letting it drag on. If I do recognize Lothar as my nephew, I will give him two or three cities in some part or other of my dominions, so that he may not feel that he is disinherited from my kingdom. Childebert has no reason to take offense if I make these gifts to Lothar." He also said a number of things. He was extremely friendly towards us and loaded us with gifts. He then bade us farewell, exhorting us always to give Childebert such counsel as would make his life easier.

21. As I have often told you, King Guntram was well known for his charity and much given to vigils and fasting.

At this time it was reported that Marseilles was suffering from a severe epidemic of swelling in the groin and that this disease had quickly spread to Saint Symphorien-d'Ozon, a village near Lyons. Like some good bishop providing the remedies by which the wounds of a common sinner might be healed, King Guntram ordered the entire people to assemble in church and Rogations to be celebrated there with great devotion. He then commanded that they should eat and drink nothing else but barley bread and pure water, and that all should be regular in keeping the vigils. His orders were obeyed. For three days his own alms were greater than usual, and he seemed so anxious about all his people that he might well have been taken for one of our Lord's bishops, rather than for a king. He put his hope in the compassion of our Lord, directing all his prayers towards Him, for through His agency he believed with perfect faith that his wishes would be realized.

The faithful had a story which they used to tell about Guntram. There was a woman whose son was seriously ill of quartan ague [malaria]. As the boy lay tossing on his bed, his mother pushed her way through the vast crowds and came up behind the King. Without his noticing she cut a few threads from his cloak. She steeped these threads in water and then gave the infusion to her son to drink. The fever left him immediately and he

---

7   Illicit sexual desire.

became well again. I accept this as true, for I have often heard men possessed of a devil call upon Guntram's name when the evil spirit was in them, and through his miraculous powers confess their crimes.

22. As I have just said, the city of Marseilles was suffering from a most serious epidemic. I want to tell you exactly how this came about. At the time Bishop Theodore had gone to see King Childebert, for he had some complaint or other to make against the patrician Nicetius. The king paid little attention to what Theodore had to say, so the bishop prepared to return home. In the meantime a ship from Spain put into port with the usual kind of cargo, unfortunately also bringing with it the source of this infection. Quite a few of the townsfolk purchased objects from the cargo and in less than no time a house in which eight people lived was left completely deserted, all the inhabitants having caught the disease. The infection did not spread through the residential quarter immediately. Some time passed and then, like a cornfield set alight, the entire town was suddenly ablaze with the pestilence. For all that Bishop Theodore came back and took up residence in Saint Victor's Church, together with the seven poor folk who remained at his side. There he stayed throughout the whole of the catastrophe which assailed his city, giving up all his time to prayers and vigils, and imploring God in his mercy to put an end to the slaughter and to allow the people some peace and quiet. At the end of two months the plague burned itself out. The population returned to Marseilles, thinking themselves safe. Then the disease started again and all who had come back died. On several occasions later on Marseilles suffered from an epidemic of this sort.

23. Ageric, Bishop of Verdun, fell seriously ill. Day after day he tortured himself with the thought that it was his fault that Guntram Boso had been killed, in that he had stood surety for him. The fact that Berthefried had been slain in the oratory of his church-house was another cause of chagrin to him. Then there was this last straw, that he faced the daily reminder of having Guntram's sons living with him. "It is my fault that you are left orphans," he kept saying to them. As I have

told you, these things weighed heavily upon him. He suffered from black depression, virtually giving up eating, and so died and was buried. Abbot Buccovald put in for the bishopric, but he had no success. By royal decree the Referendary Charimer was appointed, this also being the wish of the people. Abbot Buccovald was passed over, but they used to say that he was a proud man, hence his nickname, Buccus Validus.

Licerius, Bishop of Arles, died. With the backing of Bishop Syagrius, Virgil, Abbot of Autun, replaced him in his cathedral....

30. At the request of Bishop Maroveus King Childebert sent tax inspectors to Poitiers: Florentianus, Mayor of the Queen's Household, and Romulf, Count of his own Palace. Their orders were to prepare new tax-lists and to instruct the people to pay the taxes which had been levied from them in the time of Childebert's father. Many of those who were on the lists had died, and, as a result, widows, orphans and infirm folk had to meet a heavy assessment. The inspectors looked into each case in turn: they granted relief to the poor and infirm, and assessed for taxation all who were justly liable.

After this they came to Tours. When they announced that they were about to tax the townsfolk, and that they had in their possession tax-lists showing how the people had been assessed in the time of earlier kings, I gave them this answer: "It is undeniable that the town of Tours was assessed in the days of King Lothar. The books were taken off to be submitted to the king. Lothar had them thrown into the fire, for he was greatly overawed by our bishop, Saint Martin. When Lothar died, my people swore an oath of loyalty to King Charibert, and he swore in his turn that he would not make any new laws or customs, but would secure to them the conditions under which they had lived in his father's reign. He promised that he would not inflict upon them any new tax-laws which would be to their disadvantage. Gaiso, who was count at that time, took the tax-lists, which, as I have said, had been drawn up by earlier tax inspectors, and began to exact payment. He was opposed by Bishop Eufronius, but he went off to the king with the money which he had collected illegally and showed to him the tax-lists in which the assessment was set down. King Charibert sighed, for he feared the miraculous power of Saint Martin, and he threw the lists into the fire. The money which had been collected he sent back to Saint Martin's church, swearing that no public taxation should ever again be forced upon the people of Tours. King Sigibert held this city after Charibert's death, but he did not burden it with taxation. In the same way Childebert has made no demands in the fourteen years during which he has reigned since his father's death. The city has not had to face any tax-assessment at all. It lies in your power to decide whether or not tax should be collected; but beware of the harm which you will do if you act contrary to the king's sworn agreement." When I had finished speaking, they made the following reply: "You see that we hold in our hands the book which lists the tax-assessment for your people." "That book was not issued by the king's treasury," I answered. "For all these long years it has been in abeyance. I would not be at all surprised if it had been kept carefully in someone's house out of hatred for these townsfolk of mine. God will surely punish the individuals who have produced it after such a long passage of time, just to despoil my citizens." That very day the son of Audinus, the man who had produced the inventory, caught a fever. He died three days later. We then sent representatives to the king, to ask that he send instructions and make clear just what his orders were. An official letter came back almost immediately, confirming the immunity from taxation of the people of Tours, out of respect for Saint Martin. As soon as they had read it, the men who had been sent on the mission returned home.

11. *LIFE OF SAINT BALTHILD*

BALTHILD, WIFE OF KING Clovis II (639–657) rose from Anglo-Saxon slave to Frankish queen and regent for her son Clothar III. Her *Life* was written shortly her death, probably by a nun of Chelles (near modern-day Paris), the monastery she was forced to enter after a palace coup overthrew her regency. The account presents, although in veiled manner, both the possibilities and dangers facing a Frankish queen who, lacking the support of powerful family members, looked to ecclesiastical institutions to protect her position and that of her son.

Source: *Sainted Women of the Dark Ages*, ed. and trans. Jo Ann McNamara and John E. Halborg, with E. Gordon Whatley (Durham and London: Duke University Press, 1992).

Further Reading: Janet L. Nelson, "Queens as Jezebels: the Careers of Brunhild and Balthild in Merovingian History," in D. Baker (ed.), *Medieval Women* (Oxford: Blackwell, 1978), 31–77.

Here Begins the Prologue to the Life of Lady Balthild the Queen

1. Most beloved brothers, I have been commanded by the prelate Christ, to accomplish a simple and pious work. My lack of skill and experience prevents me from setting forth an exquisite narrative in learned language. But the power of heartfelt love more strongly commands us not to be puffed up with vain glory and simply bring the truth to light. For we know that the lord Jesus Christ asked for fruit from the fig tree, not leaves. And likewise we have determined that the fruit of truth shall not be hidden but shine forth upon a candlestick for the advancement and edification of many. Though less skilled in scholarship, we are all the more eager to cultivate a plain and open style so as to edify the many people who, like prudent bees seeking sweet nectar from the flowers, seek from simple words the burgeoning truth that edifies but does not flatter and puff up the one who hears it. Thus may the compendium of piety be thrown open to those who desire to imitate her. Therefore in what follows we have shown forth the truth as best we can, not for detractors but rather for the faithful.

Here Begins the Life of the Blessed Queen Balthild

2. The blessed Lord, "who will have all men to be saved, and to come unto the knowledge of the truth,"[1] works "all in all"[2] both "to will and to do."[3] By the same token, among the merits and virtues of the saints, praise should first be sung of Him Who made the humble great and raised the pauper from the dunghill and seated him among the princes of his people. Such a one is the woman present to our minds, the venerable and great lady Balthild the queen. Divine Providence called her from across the seas. She, who came here as God's most precious and lofty pearl, was sold at a cheap price. Erchinoald,[4] a Frankish magnate and most illustrious man, acquired her and in his service the girl behaved most honorably. And her pious and admirable manners pleased this prince and all his servants. For she was kindhearted and sober and prudent in all her ways, careful and plotting evil for none. Her speech was not frivolous nor her words presumptuous but in every way she behaved with utmost propriety. And since she was of the Saxon race, she was graceful in form with refined features, a most seemly woman with a smiling face and serious gait. And she so showed herself just as she ought in all things, that she

---

1   1 Timothy 2:4.
2   1 Corinthians 15:28.
3   Philippians 2:3–4.
4   Neustrian mayor of the palace.

pleased her master and found favor in his eyes. So he determined that she should set out the drinking cup for him in his chamber and, honored above all others as his housekeeper, stand at his side always ready to serve him. She did not allow this dignity to make her proud but rather kept her humility. She was all obedience to her companions and amiable, ministering with fitting honor to her elders, ready to draw the shoes from their feet and wash and dry them. She brought them water to wash themselves and prepared their clothing expeditiously. And she performed all these services with good spirits and no grumbling.

3. And from this noble conduct, the praise and love of her comrades for her increased greatly. She gained such happy fame that, when the said lord Erchinoald's wife died, he hoped to unite himself to Balthild, that faultless virgin, in a matronal bed. But when she heard of this, she fled and most swiftly took herself out of his sight. When she was called to the master's chamber she hid herself secretly in a corner and threw some vile rags over herself so that no one could guess that anyone might be concealed there. Thus for the love of humility, the prudent and astute virgin attempted to flee as best she could from vain honors. She hoped that she might avoid a human marriage bed and thus merit a spiritual and heavenly spouse. But doubtless, Divine Providence brought it about that the prince, unable to find the woman he sought, married another wife. Thereafter it happened, with God's approval, that Balthild, the maid who escaped marriage with a lord, came to be espoused to Clovis, son of the former king Dagobert. Thus by virtue of her humility she was raised to a higher rank. Divine dispensation determined to honor her in this station so that, having scorned the king's servant, she came to be coupled with the king himself and bring forth royal children. And these events are known to all for now her royal progeny rule the realm.

4. She upon whom God conferred the grace of prudence obeyed the King with vigilant care as her lord, acted as a mother to the princes, as a daughter to priests, and as a most pious nurse to children and adolescents. And she was amiable to all, loving priests as fathers, monks as brothers, a pious nurse to the poor. And she distributed generous alms to every one. She guarded the princes' honor by keeping their intimate counsels secret. She always exhorted the young to strive for religious achievement and humbly and assiduously suggested things to the king for the benefit of the church and the poor. For, desiring to serve Christ in the secular habit at that time, she frequented daily prayers commending herself with tears to Christ, the King of heaven. The pious king, impressed by her faith and devotion, delegated his faithful servant the abbot Genesius as her helper. Through his hands, she ministered to priests and poor alike, feeding the needy and clothing the naked and taking care to order the burial of the dead, funneling large amounts of gold and silver through him to convents of men and virgins. Afterwards that servant of Christ, Genesius, by Christ's order, was ordained bishop of Lyon in Gaul. But at that time, he was busy about the palace of the Franks. And as we have said, by King Clovis's order, Lady Balthild followed the servant of God's advice in providing alms through him to every poor person in many places.

5. What more? In accordance with God's will, her husband King Clovis migrated from the body and left his sons with their mother. Immediately after him her son Clothar took up the kingdom of the Franks, maintaining peace in the realm, with the most excellent princes, Chrodebert, Bishop of Paris, Lord Ouen and Ebroin, Mayor of the Palace with the rest of the elders and many others. Then to promote peace, by command of Lady Balthild with the advice of the other elders, the people of Austrasia accepted her son Childeric as their king and the Burgundians were united with the Franks. And we believe, under God's ordinance, that these three realms then held peace and concord among themselves because of Lady Balthild's great faith.

6. Then following the exhortations of good priests, by God's will working through her, Lady Balthild prohibited the impious evil of the simoniac heresy, a depraved custom which stained the church of God, whereby episcopal orders were obtained for a price. She proclaimed that no payment could be exacted for receipt of a sacred rank. Moreover,

she, or God acting through her, ordained that yet another evil custom should cease, namely, that many people determined to kill their children rather than nurture them, for they feared to incur the public exactions which were heaped upon them by custom, which caused great damage to their affairs. In her mercy, that lady forbade anyone to do these things. And for all these deeds, a great reward must surely have awaited her.

7. Who can count how many and how great her services were to religious communities? She showered great estates and whole forests upon them for the construction of their cells and monasteries. And at Chelles, in the region of Paris, she built a great community of virgins as her own special house of God. There she established the maiden Bertilla, God's serving girl, as the first to hold the place of their mother. And there in turn the venerable Lady Balthild had determined she would finally go to live under the rule of religion and to rest in peace and in truth she fulfilled her desire with willing devotion. Whatever wonders God works through His saints and His chosen ones should not be passed over, for they contribute to His praise. For, as Scripture says, "God does wonders in his saints."[5] For His Holy Spirit, the Paraclete, dwells within and cooperates with the benevolent heart as it is written: "All things work together for good to them that love God."[6] And thus it was spoken truly of this great woman. As we said, neither our tongue nor any others, however learned as I believe, can give voice to all the good she did. How much consolation and help did she lavish on the houses of God and on the poor for the love of Christ and how many advantages and comforts did she confer on them? And what of the monastery called Corbie in the parish of Amiens that she built at her own expense? There the venerable man, Lord Theofredus, now a bishop but then the abbot, ruled a great flock of brothers whom Lady Balthild had requested from the most saintly Lord Waldebert, then abbot of the monastery of Luxeuil, who wondrously had them sent to that same convent which all agree in praising to this very day.

8. What more? At Jumièges, the religious man Lord Philibert was given a great wood from the fisc where his community has settled and other gifts and pastures were also conceded from the fisc for the building of this same monastery. And how many great farms and talents of gold and silver did she give to Lord Lagobert at Curbio? She took off a girdle from her regalia, which had encircled her own holy loins, and gave it to the brothers to devote to alms. And she dispensed all this with a benign and joyous soul, for as the scripture says: "The Lord loveth a cheerful giver."[7] And likewise to Fontanelle and Logium, she conceded many things. As to Luxeuil and the monasteries in Burgundy, who can tell how many whole farms and innumerable gifts of money she gave? And what did she do for Jouarre, whence she gathered the Lady Bertilla abbess of Chelles and other sacred virgins? How many gifts of wealth and land? And similarly she often directed gifts to holy Fara's monastery. And she granted many great estates to the basilicas of the saints and monasteries of the city of Paris, and enriched them with many gifts. What more? As we have said, we cannot recount these things one by one, not even half of them, and to give an account of all the blessings she conferred is utterly beyond our powers.

9. We should not pass over, however, what she did in her zealous love of God for the older basilicas of the saints, Lord Denis and Lord Germanus and Lord Médard and Saint Peter or the Lord Anianus, and Saint Martin, or wherever something came to her notice. She would send orders and letters warning bishops and abbots that the monks dwelling in those places ought to live according to their holy rule and order. And that they might agree more freely, she ordered their privileges confirmed and granted immunities that it might please them all the more to beseech Christ the highest King to show mercy to the king and give peace. And let it be remembered, since it increases the magnitude of her own reward, that she prohibited the sale of captive Christian folk to outsiders and gave orders through all the lands

---

5   Psalm 67:36.

6   Romans 8:28.

7   2 Corinthians 9:7.

that no one was to sell captive Christians within the borders of the Frankish realm. What is more, she ordered that many captives should be ransomed, paying the price herself. And she installed some of the captives she released and other people in monasteries, particularly as many men and women of her own people as possible and cared for them. For as many of them as she could persuade thereto, she commended to holy communities and bade that they might pray for her. And even to Rome, to the basilicas of Peter and Paul, and the Roman poor, she directed many and large gifts.

10. And as we have said before, it was her own holy intention to convert to this monastery of religious women which she had built at Chelles. But the Franks delayed much for love of her and would not have permitted this to happen except that there was a commotion made by the wretched Bishop Sigobrand whose pride among the Franks earned him his mortal ruin. Indeed, they formed a plan to kill him against her will. Fearing that the lady would act heavily against them, and wish to avenge him, they suddenly relented and permitted her to enter the monastery. There can be no doubt that the princes' motives were far from pure. But the lady, considering the will of God rather than their counsel, thought it a dispensation from God so that, whatever the circumstances, she might have the chance to fulfill her holy plan under Christ's rule. And conducted by several elders, she came to her aforesaid monastery of Chelles and there she was received into the holy congregation by the holy maidens, as was fitting, honorably and with sufficient love. But at first she had no small complaint against those whom she had so sweetly nurtured. For they suspected her of false motives or else simply attempted to return evil for good. Hastily conferring with the priests about this, she mercifully indulged them in the delay and begged that they would forgive the commotion in her heart. And afterwards by the largesse of God, peace was fully restored between them.

11. And indeed, she loved her sisters with the most pious affection as her own daughters and she obeyed their most holy abbess as a mother. She showed herself as a servant and lowliest bondwoman to them from holy devotion, even while she still ruled the public palace, and had often visited the community. One example of her great humility was the way she would valiantly take care of the dirtiest cleaning jobs for the sisters in the kitchen, personally cleaning up the dung from the latrine. And she did all this gladly and in perfect joy of spirit, doing such humble service for Christ's sake. For who would believe that one so sublime in power would take care of things so vile? Only if she were driven by the fullest love of Christ could it be expected. And she prayed constantly, persistently, devoutly, tearfully. She frequently attended divine reading and gave constant comfort to the sick through holy exhortation and frequent visits. Through the achievement of charity, she grieved with the sorrowful, rejoiced with the joyful and, that all might be comforted, she often made suggestions for their improvement humbly to the lady abbess. And that lady amiably gave heed to her petitions for truly in them as in the apostles, there was but one heart and one soul, and they loved each other tenderly in Christ.

12. Then the Lady Balthild became physically ill of body and suffered wearily from pain in the bowels caused by a serious infection, and but for the doctors' efforts she would have died. But she always had more confidence in celestial medicine for her health. So, with a holy and pious conscience, she never ceased to thank God for chastising. She gave her astute advice at all times and—example of great humility—she provided a pattern of piety in her service to her sisters. She often consulted with the mother of the monastery as to how they might always call on the king and queen and their honored nobles with gifts, as was customary, that the house of God might continue to enjoy the good fame with which it began. Thus it would not lose but always remain in loving affection with all its friends and grow stronger in the name of God, as it is written: "It is fitting to have good report of them which are without."[8] Particularly, she urged them always to care for the poor and for guests with the utmost zeal, out of love and mercy

---

8   1 Timothy 3:7.

and the mother of the monastery heard her salutary admonitions willingly for love of Christ and did all with gladness of heart. Nor did she ever cease to carry out all this and to increase the rewards of her community.

13. And as her glorious death approached, a clear vision was shown to her. Before holy Mary's altar, a ladder stood upright whose height reached the heavens. Angels of God were going up and down and there the Lady Balthild made her ascent. Through this revelation, she was clearly given to understand that her sublime merit, patience and humility, would take her to the heights of the eternal King who would swiftly reward her with an exalted crown. The lady knew, from this clear vision, that it would not be long before she would migrate from her body and come where she had already laid up her best treasures. And she ordered that this be concealed from her sisters so that until her passing the vision was not revealed lest it cause painful grief to the sisters or the mother of the monastery. But she on her part devoted herself with ever greater piety and good spirits to holy prayer, commending herself ever more zealously, humbly, and in contrition of heart to the celestial king, the Lord Jesus Christ. As much as she could, she concealed the weight of her pain and consoled Lady Bertilla and the rest of the sisters saying that her illness was not serious, that she was convalescent, dissimulating what was to come so that afterwards they took comfort in believing that the blow fell suddenly and she went unexpectedly from life.

14. And when the lady felt her end to be truly near, she raised her holy mind to Heaven. And having made certain that she would be awarded the great prize that the blessed receive, she vehemently forbade her attendants to say how sick she was to the other sisters or to the abbess who was ill herself lest she be distracted by a multitude of even heavier sorrows. At the time there was an infant, her goddaughter whom she wished to take with her. And she was suddenly snatched from her body and preceded her to the tomb. Then full of faith, she crossed herself. Raising pious eyes and holy hands to heaven, the saint's soul was released from the chains of her flesh in peace. And immediately her chamber glittered brightly with the light of divine splendor. And no doubt with that light, a chorus of angels and her faithful old friend Bishop Genesius came to receive that most holy soul as her great merits deserved.

15. For a little while, the sisters attending her, stifled their sorrowful groans. They said nothing of her death and, as she had ordered, remained silent and told only those priests who commended her most blessed soul to the Lord. But when the abbess and all the congregation learned what had happened they asked tearfully how this universally desired jewel could have been snatched away so suddenly without warning, without knowing the hour of her departure. And stupefied, they all prostrated themselves on the ground in grief and with profuse tears and fearful groans, gave thanks to the pious Lord and praised Him together. Then they commended her holy soul to Christ, the pious King, that He might escort her to holy Mary in the chorus and company of the saints. Then they buried her with great honor and much reverence as was proper. And Lady Bertilla the abbess, with solicitous striving for piety, earnestly commended her to the holy priests in several churches that her holy name be carefully commemorated in the sacred oblations. And they still celebrate her merits in many places.

16. To her followers, she left a holy example of humility and patience, mildness and overflowing zest for loving; nay more, infinite mercy, astute and prudent vigilance, pure confessions. She showed that everything should be done as a result of consultation and that nothing should be done without consent but that all actions should be temperate and rational. She left this rule of piety as a model to her companions and now for her holy virtues and many other merits she has received the prize of the crown that the Lord set aside for her long ago. So she is happy among the angels in the Lord's sight and as His spouse rejoices forever among the white-garbed flock of virgins enjoying the immense and everlasting joy she had always desired. And in order to make known her sublime merits to the faithful, God in his goodness has effected many miracles at her holy tomb. For whoever came there seized by fever, or vexed with

demons, or worn with toothache, if they had faith, was immediately cured through divine virtue and her holy intercession from whatever plague or illness. Safe and sound, they went out in the Lord's name as was manifested not long ago in the case of a certain boy.

17. A certain venerable man, Bishop Leudegund, came from Provence, a faithful friend to the monastery of Chelles. His son was possessed by a demon so violent that his companions could only control him if his hands and feet were bound, for with great cruelty he tore apart all he could reach. But when they brought him into the place of her holy sepulcher and laid him half-alive on the pavement, the ferocious demon grew stiff and terrified with fear of God and fell silent. Divine power made him flee from the boy forthwith. And the boy rose up confidently, crossed himself and, giving thanks to God, returned to his own unharmed and in his right mind.

18. Now let us recall that there have been other noble queens in the realm of the Franks who worshipped God: Clothild, King Clovis's queen of old, niece of King Gundobad. Her husband was a mighty pagan but she drew him, with many other Frankish leaders, to Christianity and the Catholic faith by holy exhortations. She led them to construct a church in honor of Saint Peter at Paris, and she built the original community of virgins for Saint George at Chelles and in honor of the saints and to store up her future reward she founded many others which she endowed with much wealth. And likewise we are told of Queen Ultragotha of the most Christian king Childebert, that she was a comforter of the poor and helper of the monks who served God. And also, there was the most faithful handmaid Radegund, King Clothar's queen of elder time, whom the grace of the Holy Spirit enkindled so that she relinquished her husband during his life and consecrated herself to the Lord Christ under the holy veil. And we may read in her acts of all the good she did for Christ her spouse.

19. But it is only right that we meditate instead on her who is our subject here, Lady Balthild whose many good deeds have been done in our time and whose acts are best known to us. We have commemorated a few of these many acts and cannot think her merits inferior to those who came before her for we know she surpassed them in zealous striving for what is holy. For after performing many good deeds to the point of evangelical perfection, she at last surrendered herself freely to holy obedience and happily ended her life as a religious, a true *monacha*.[9] Her sacred obit and holy feast are celebrated on the third calends of February. She lies entombed in Chelles, her monastery, while truly she reigns gloriously with Christ in Heaven in perpetual joy never, we trust, to forget her faithful friends. And as well as we could, if not as much as we ought, in fervent charity we have striven to follow your orders. Forgive our lack of skill and for our sins of negligence we pray for charity's sake that you ask the good Lord to exonerate us. May the peace of the Lord be with you to Whom be glory from everlasting to everlasting. Amen.

---

9   Female monk.

EARLY ITALY

12. SAINT BENEDICT

Rule for Monasteries

BENEDICT OF NURSIA (CA. 480–547) began his religious life as a hermit near Subiaco, a small town near Rome. He went on to found twelve monasteries, the most important being Monte Cassino. His *Rule*, derived largely from an earlier anonymous *Rule of the Master*, first became widely known in the middle of the seventh century. By the ninth century it had become the dominant monastic rule in the West, a position that it holds to the present day.

Source: *St. Benedict's Rule for Monasteries*, trans. Leonard J. Doyle (Collegeville, MN: The Liturgical Press, 1948).

Further Reading: Adalbert de Vogüé, *Saint Benedict: the Man and his Work* (Petersham, MA: St. Bebe's Publications, 2006).

Prologue

Jan. 1—May 2—Sept. 1[1]

Listen, my son, to your master's precepts, and incline the ear of your heart. Receive willingly and carry out effectively your loving father's advice, that by the labor of obedience you may return to Him from whom you had departed by the sloth of disobedience.

To you, therefore, my words are now addressed, whoever you may be, who are renouncing your own will to do battle under the Lord Christ, the true King, and are taking up the strong, bright weapons of obedience.

And first of all, whatever good work you begin to do, beg of Him with most earnest prayer to perfect it, that He who has now deigned to count us among His sons may not at any time be grieved by our evil deeds. For we must always so serve Him with the good things he has given us, that He will never as an angry Father disinherit His children, nor ever as a dread Lord, provoked by our evil actions, deliver us to everlasting punishment as wicked servants who would not follow Him to glory.

Jan. 2—May 3—Sept. 2

Let us arise, then, at last, for the Scripture stirs us up, saying, "Now is the hour for us to rise from sleep." Let us open our eyes to the deifying light, let us hear with attentive ears the warning which the divine voice cries daily to us, "Today if you hear His voice, harden not your hearts." And again, "He who has ears to hear, let him hear what the Spirit says to the churches." And what does He say? "Come, My children, listen to Me; I will teach you the fear of the Lord. Run while you have the light of life, lest the darkness of death overtake you."

Jan. 3—May 4—Sept. 3

And the Lord, seeking His laborer in the multitude to whom He thus cries out, says again, "Who is the man who will have life, and desires to see

---

1 In Benedictine monasteries, sections of the Rule are read each day. The date references indicate those days of the year on which each section is read in the communal assembly or chapter.

good days?" And if, hearing Him, you answer, "I am he," God says to you, "If you will have true and everlasting life, keep your tongue from evil and your lips that they speak no guile. Turn away from evil and do good; seek after peace and pursue it. And when you have done these things, My eyes shall be upon you and My ears open to your prayers; and before you call upon Me, I will say to you, 'Behold, here I am.'"

What can be sweeter to us, dear brethren, than this voice of the Lord inviting us? Behold, in His loving kindness the Lord shows us the way of life.

Jan. 4—May 5—Sept. 4

Having our loins girded, therefore, with faith and the performance of good works, let us walk in His paths by the guidance of the Gospel, that we may deserve to see Him who has called us to His kingdom.

For if we wish to dwell in the tent of that kingdom, we must run to it by good deeds or we shall never reach it.

But let us ask the Lord, with the Prophet, "Lord, who shall dwell in Your tent, or who shall rest upon Your holy mountain?"

After this question, brethren, let us listen to the Lord as He answers and shows us the way to that tent, saying, "He who walks without stain and practices justice; he who speaks truth from his heart; he who has not used his tongue for deceit; he who has done no evil to his neighbor; he who has given no place to slander against his neighbor."

It is he who, under any temptation from the malicious devil, has brought him to naught by casting him and his temptation from the sight of his heart; and who has laid hold of his thoughts while they were still young and dashed them against Christ.

It is they who, fearing the Lord, do not pride themselves on their good observance; but, convinced that the good which is in them cannot come from themselves and must be from the Lord, glorify the Lord's work in them, using the words of the Prophet, "Not to us, O Lord, not to us, but to Your name give the glory." Thus also the Apostle Paul attributed nothing of the success of his preaching to himself, but said, "By the grace of God I am what I am." And again he says, "He who glories, let him glory in the Lord."

Jan. 5—May 6—Sept. 5

Hence the Lord says in the Gospel, "Whoever listens to these words of Mine and acts upon them, I will liken him to a wise man who built his house on rock. The floods came, the winds blew and beat against that house, and it did not fall, because it was founded on rock."

Having given us these assurances, the Lord is waiting every day for us to respond by our deeds to His holy admonitions. And the days of this life are lengthened and a truce granted us for this very reason, that we may amend our evil ways. As the apostle says, "Do you not know that God's patience is inviting you to repent?" For the merciful Lord tells us, "I desire not the death of the sinner, but that he should be converted and live."

Jan. 6—May 7—Sept. 6

So, brethren, we have asked the Lord who is to dwell in His tent, and we have heard His commands to anyone who would dwell there; it remains for us to fulfil those duties.

Therefore we must prepare our hearts and our bodies to do battle under the holy obedience of His commands; and let us ask God that He be pleased to give us the help of His grace for anything which our nature finds hardly possible. And if we want to escape the pains of hell and attain life everlasting, then, while there is still time, while we are still in the body and are able to fulfil all these things by the light of this life, we must hasten to do now what will profit us for eternity.

Jan. 7—May 8—Sept. 7

And so we are going to establish a school for the service of the Lord. In founding it we hope to introduce nothing harsh or burdensome. But if a certain strictness results from the dictates of equity for the amendment of vices or the preservation of charity, do not be at once dismayed and fly from the way of salvation, whose entrance cannot but be narrow. For as we advance in the religious life and in faith, our hearts expand and we run the way of God's commandments and with unspeakable sweetness of love. Thus, never departing from His school, but persevering in the monastery according to His teaching until death, we may by patience share in the sufferings of Christ and deserve to have a share also in His kingdom.

Chapter 1—On the Kinds of Monks

Jan. 8—May 9—Sept. 8

It is well known that there are four kinds of monks. The first kind are the Cenobites: those who live in monasteries and serve under a rule and an Abbot.

The second kind are the Anchorites or Hermits: those who, no longer in the first fervor of their reformation, but after long probation in a monastery, having learned by the help of many brethren how to fight against the Devil, go out well armed from the ranks of the community to the solitary combat of the desert. They are able now, with no help save from God, to fight single-handed against the vices of the flesh and their own evil thoughts.

The third kind of monks, a detestable kind, are the Sarabaites. These, not having been tested, as gold in the furnace, by any rule or by the lessons of experience, are as soft as lead. In their works they still keep faith with the world, so that their tonsure marks them as liars before God. They live in twos or threes, or even singly, without a shepherd, in their own sheepfolds and not in the Lord's. Their law is the desire for self-gratification: whatever enters their mind or appeals to them, that they call holy; what they dislike, they regard as unlawful.

The fourth kind of monks are those called Gyrovagues. These spend their whole lives tramping from province to province, staying as guests in different monasteries for three or four days at a time. Always on the move, with no stability, they indulge their own wills and succumb to the allurements of gluttony, and are in every way worse than the Sarabaites. Of the miserable conduct of such men it is better to be silent than to speak.

Passing these over, therefore, let us proceed, with God's help, to lay down a rule for the strongest kind of monks, the Cenobites.

Chapter 2—What Kind of Man the Abbot Ought to Be

Jan. 9—May 10—Sept. 9

An Abbot who is worthy to be over a monastery should always remember what he is called, and live up to the name of Superior. For he is believed to hold the place of Christ in the monastery, being called by a name of His, which is taken from the words of the apostle: "You have received a Spirit of adoption as sons, by virtue of which we cry, 'Abba—Father!'"

Therefore the Abbot ought not to teach or ordain or command anything which is against the Lord's precepts; on the contrary, his commands and his teaching should be a leaven of divine justice kneaded into the minds of his disciples.

Jan. 10—May 11—Sept. 10

Let the Abbot always bear in mind that at the dread Judgment of God there will be an examination of these two matters: his teaching and the obedience of his disciples. And let the Abbot be sure that any lack of profit the master of the house may find in the sheep will be laid to the blame of the shepherd. On the other hand, if the shepherd has bestowed all his pastoral diligence on a restless, unruly flock and tried every remedy for their unhealthy behavior, then he will be acquitted at the Lord's Judgment and may say to the Lord with the Prophet: "I have not concealed Your justice within my heart; Your truth and Your salvation I have declared. But they have despised and rejected me." And then finally let death itself, irresistible, punish those disobedient sheep under his charge.

Jan. 11—May 12—Sept. 11

Therefore, when anyone receives the name of Abbot, he ought to govern his disciples with a twofold teaching. That is to say, he should show them all that is good and holy by his deeds even more than by his words, expounding the Lord's commandments in words to the intelligent among his disciples, but demonstrating the divine precepts by his actions for those of harder hearts and ruder minds. And whatever he has taught his disciples to be contrary to God's law, let him indicate by his example that it is not to be done, lest, while preaching to others, he himself be found reprobate, and lest God one day say to him in his sin, "Why do you declare My statutes and profess My covenant with your lips, whereas you hate discipline and have cast My words behind you?" And again, "You were looking at the speck in your brother's eye, and did not see the beam in your own."

Jan. 12—May 13—Sept. 12

Let him make no distinction of persons in the monastery. Let him not love one more than another, unless it be one whom he finds better in good works or in obedience. Let him not advance one of noble birth ahead of one who was formerly a slave, unless there be some other reasonable ground for it. But if the Abbot for just reason think fit to do so, let him advance one of any rank whatever. Otherwise let them keep their due places; because, whether slaves or freemen, we are all one in Christ and bear an equal burden of service in the army of the same Lord. For with God there is no respect of persons. Only for one reason are we preferred in His sight: if we be found better than others in good works and humility. Therefore let the Abbot show equal love to all and impose the same discipline on all according to their deserts.

Jan. 13—May 14—Sept. 13

In his teaching the Abbot should always follow the apostle's formula: "Reprove, entreat, rebuke"; threatening at one time and coaxing at another as the occasion may require, showing now the stern countenance of a master, now the loving affection of a father. That is to say, it is the undisciplined and restless whom he must reprove rather sharply; it is the obedient, meek and patient whom he must entreat to advance in virtue; while as for the negligent and disdainful, these we charge him to rebuke and correct.

And let him not shut his eyes to the faults of offenders; but, since he has the authority, let him cut out those faults by the roots as soon as they begin to appear, remembering the fate of Heli, the priest of Silo. The well-disposed and those of good understanding let him correct with verbal admonition the first and second time. But bold, hard, proud and disobedient characters he should curb at the very beginning of their ill-doing by stripes and other bodily punishments, knowing that it is written, "The fool is not corrected with words," and again, "Beat your son with the rod and you will deliver his soul from death."

Jan. 14—May 15—Sept. 14

The Abbot should always remember what he is and what he is called, and should know that to whom more is committed, from him more is required. Let him understand also what a difficult and arduous task he has undertaken: ruling souls and adapting himself to a variety of characters. One he must coax, another scold, another persuade, according to each one's character and understanding. Thus he must adjust and adapt himself to all in such a way that he may not only suffer no loss in the flock committed to his care, but may even rejoice in the increase of a good flock.

Jan. 15—May 16—Sept. 15

Above all let him not neglect or undervalue the welfare of the souls committed to him, in a greater concern for fleeting, earthly, perishable things; but let him always bear in mind that he has undertaken the government of souls and that he will have to give an account of them.

And if he be tempted to allege a lack of earthly means, let him remember what is written: "First seek the kingdom of God and His justice, and all these things shall be given you besides." And again: "Nothing is wanting to those who fear Him."

Let him know, then, that he who has undertaken the government of souls must prepare himself to render an account of them. Whatever number of brethren he knows he has under his care, he may be sure beyond doubt on Judgment Day he will have to give the Lord an account of all these souls, as well as of his own soul.

Thus the constant apprehension about his coming examination as shepherd concerning the sheep entrusted to him, and his anxiety over the account that must be given for others, make him careful of his own record. And while by his admonitions he is helping others to amend, he himself is cleansed of his faults.

Chapter 3—On Calling the Brethren for Counsel

Jan. 16—May 17—Sept. 16

Whenever any important business has to be done in the monastery, let the Abbot call together the whole community and state the matter to be acted upon. Then, having heard the brethren's advice, let him turn the matter over in his own mind and do what he shall judge to be most expedient. The reason we have said that all should be called for counsel is that the Lord often reveals to the younger what is best.

Let the brethren give their advice with all the deference required by humility, and not presume stubbornly to defend their opinions; but let the decision rather depend on the Abbot's judgment, and all submit to whatever he shall decide for their welfare.

However, just as it is proper for the disciples to obey their master, so also it is his function to dispose all things with prudence and justice.

Jan. 17—May 18—Sept. 17

In all things, therefore, let us all follow the Rule as guide, and let no one be so rash as to deviate from it. Let no one in the monastery follow his own heart's fancy; and let no one presume to contend with his Abbot in an insolent way or even outside of the monastery. But if anyone should presume to do so, let him undergo the discipline of the Rule. At the same time, the Abbot himself should do all things in the fear of God and in observance of the Rule, knowing that beyond a doubt he will have to render an account of all his decisions to God, the most just Judge.

But if the business to be done in the interests of the monastery be of lesser importance, let him take counsel with the seniors only. It is written, "Do everything with counsel, and you will not repent when you have done it."

Chapter 4—What Are the Instruments of Good Works

Jan. 18—May 19—Sept. 18

1. In the first place, to love the Lord God with the whole heart, the whole soul, the whole strength.
2. Then, one's neighbor as oneself.
3. Then not to murder.
4. Not to commit adultery.
5. Not to steal.
6. Not to covet.
7. Not to bear false witness.
8. To respect all men.
9. And not to do to another what one would not have done to oneself.
10. To deny oneself in order to follow Christ.
11. To chastise the body.
12. Not to become attached to pleasures.
13. To love fasting.
14. To relieve the poor.
15. To clothe the naked.
16. To visit the sick.
17. To bury the dead.
18. To help in trouble.
19. To console the sorrowing.
20. To become a stranger to the world's ways.
21. To prefer nothing to the love of Christ.

Jan. 19—May 20—Sept. 19

22. Not to give way to anger.
23. Not to nurse a grudge.
24. Not to entertain deceit in one's heart.
25. Not to give a false peace.
26. Not to forsake charity.
27. Not to swear, for fear of perjuring oneself.
28. To utter truth from heart and mouth.
29. Not to return evil for evil.
30. To do no wrong to anyone, and to bear patiently wrongs done to oneself.
31. To love one's enemies.
32. Not to curse them who curse us, but rather to bless them.
33. To bear persecution for justice's sake.
34. Not to be proud.
35. Not addicted to wine.
36. Not a great eater.
37. Not drowsy.
38. Not lazy.
39. Not a grumbler.
40. Not a detractor.
41. To put one's hope in God.
42. To attribute to God, and not to self, whatever good one sees in oneself.
43. But to recognize always that the evil is one's own doing, and to impute it to oneself.

Jan. 20—May 21—Sept. 20

44. To fear the Day of Judgment.
45. To be in dread of hell.
46. To desire eternal life with all the passion of the spirit.
47. To keep death daily before one's eyes.
48. To keep constant guard over the actions of one's life.
49. To know for certain that God sees one everywhere.

50. When evil thoughts come into one's heart, to dash them against Christ immediately.
51. And to manifest them to one's spiritual father.
52. To guard one's tongue against evil and depraved speech.
53. Not to love much talking.
54. Not to speak useless words or words that move to laughter.
55. Not to love much or boisterous laughter.
56. To listen willingly to holy reading.
57. To devote oneself frequently to prayer.
58. Daily in one's prayers, with tears and sighs, to confess one's past sins to God, and to amend them for the future.
59. Not to fulfil the desires of the flesh; to hate one's own will.
60. To obey in all things the commands of the Abbot, even though he himself (which God forbid) should act otherwise, mindful of the Lord's precept, "Do what they say, but not what they do."
61. Not to wish to be called holy before one is holy; but first to be holy, that one may be truly so called.

Jan. 21—May 22—Sept. 21
62. To fulfil God's commandments daily in one's deeds.
63. To love chastity.
64. To hate no one.
65. Not to be jealous, not to harbor envy.
66. Not to love contention.
67. To beware of haughtiness.
68. And to respect the seniors.
69. To love the juniors.
70. To pray for one's enemies in the love of Christ.
71. To make peace with one's adversary before the sun sets.
72. And never to despair of God's mercy.

These, then, are the tools of the spiritual craft. If we employ them unceasingly day and night, and return them on the Day of Judgment, our compensation from the Lord will be that wage He has promised: "Eye has not seen, nor ear heard, what God has prepared for those who love Him."

Now the workshop in which we shall diligently execute all these tasks is the enclosure of the monastery and stability in the community.

Chapter 5—On Obedience

Jan. 22—May 23—Sept. 22
The first degree of humility is obedience without delay. This is the virtue of those who hold nothing dearer to them than Christ; who, because of the holy service they have professed, and the fear of hell, and the glory of life everlasting, as soon as anything has been ordered by the Superior, receive it as a divine command and cannot suffer any delay in executing it. Of these the Lord says, "As soon as he heard, he obeyed Me." And again to teachers He says, "He who hears you, hears Me."

Such as these, therefore, immediately leaving their own affairs and forsaking their own will, dropping the work they were engaged in and leaving it unfinished, with the ready step of obedience follow up with their deeds the voice of him who commands. And so as it were at the same moment the master's command is given and the disciple's work is completed, the two things being speedily accomplished together in the swiftness of the fear of God by those who are moved with the desire of attaining life everlasting. That desire is their motive for choosing the narrow way, of which the Lord says, "Narrow is the way that leads to life," so that, not living according to their own choice nor obeying their own desires and pleasures but walking by another's judgment and command, they dwell in monasteries and desire to have an Abbot over them. Assuredly such as these are living up to that maxim of the Lord in which he says, "I have come not to do My own will, but the will of Him who sent Me."

Jan. 23—May 24—Sept. 23
But this very obedience will be acceptable to God and pleasing to men only if what is commanded is done without hesitation, delay, lukewarmness, grumbling, or objection. For the obedience given to Superiors is given to God, since He Himself has said, "He who hears you, hears Me." And the disciples should offer their obedience with a good will, for "God loves a cheerful giver." For if the disciple obeys with an ill will and murmurs, not necessarily with his lips but in his heart, then

even though he fulfil the command yet his work will not be acceptable to God, who sees that his heart is murmuring. And, far from gaining a reward for such work as this, he will incur the punishment due to murmurers, unless he amend and make satisfaction.

Chapter 6—On the Spirit of Silence

Jan. 24—May 25—Sept. 24

Let us do what the Prophet says: "I said, 'I will guard my ways, that I may not sin with my tongue. I have set a guard to my mouth.' I was mute and was humbled, and kept silence even from good things." Here the Prophet shows that if the spirit of silence ought to lead us at times to refrain even from good speech, so much the more ought the punishment for sin make us avoid evil words.

Therefore, since the spirit of silence is so important, permission to speak should rarely be granted even to perfect disciples, even though it be for good, holy, edifying conversation; for it is written, "In much speaking you will not escape sin," and in another place, "Death and life are in the power of the tongue."

For speaking and teaching belong to the master; the disciple's part is to be silent and to listen. And for that reason if anything has to be asked of the Superior, it should be asked with all the humility and submission inspired by reverence.

But as for coarse jests and idle words or words that move to laughter, these we condemn everywhere with a perpetual ban, and for such conversation we do not permit a disciple to open his mouth.

Chapter 7—On Humility

Jan. 25—May 26—Sept. 25

Holy Scripture, brethren, cries out to us, saying, "Everyone who exalts himself shall be humbled, and he who humbles himself shall be exalted." In saying this it shows us that all exaltation is a kind of pride, against which the Prophet proves himself to be on guard when he says, "Lord, my heart is not exalted, nor are mine eyes lifted up; neither have I walked in great matters, nor in wonders above me." But how has he acted? "Rather have I been of humble mind than exalting myself; as a weaned child on its mother's breast, so You solace my soul."

Hence, brethren, if we wish to reach the very highest point of humility and to arrive speedily at that heavenly exaltation to which ascent is made through the humility of this present life, we must by our ascending actions erect the ladder Jacob saw in his dream, on which Angels appeared to him descending and ascending. By that descent and ascent we must surely understand nothing else than this, that we descend by self-exaltation and ascend by humility. And the ladder thus set up is our life in the world, which the Lord raises up to heaven if our heart is humbled. For we call our body and soul the sides of the ladder, and into these sides our divine vocation has inserted the different steps of humility and discipline we must climb.

Jan. 26—May 27—Sept. 26

The first degree of humility, then, is that a person keep the fear of God before his eyes and beware of ever forgetting it. Let him be ever mindful of all that God has commanded; let his thoughts constantly recur to the hell-fire which will burn for their sins those who despise God, and to the life everlasting which is prepared for those who fear Him. Let him keep himself at every moment from sins and vices, whether of the mind, the tongue, the hands, the feet, or the self-will, and check also the desires of the flesh.

Jan. 27—May 28—Sept. 27

Let a man consider that God is always looking at him from heaven, that his actions are everywhere visible to the divine eyes and are constantly being reported to God by the Angels. This is what the Prophet shows us when he represents God as ever present within our thoughts, in the words "Searcher of minds and hearts is God" and again in the words "The Lord knows the thoughts of men." Again he says, "You have read my thoughts from afar" and "The thoughts of men will confess to You."

In order that he may be careful about his wrongful thoughts, therefore, let the faithful brother say constantly in his heart, "Then shall I be spotless before Him if I have kept myself from my iniquity."

Jan. 28—May 29—Sept. 28

As for self-will, we are forbidden to do our own will by the Scripture, which says to us, "Turn away from your own will," and likewise by the prayer in which we ask God that His will be done in us. And rightly we are taught not to do our own will when we take heed to the warning of Scripture: "There are ways which to men may seem right, but the ends of them plunge into the depths of hell"; and also when we tremble at what is said of the careless: "They are corrupt and have become abominable in their wills."

And as for the desires of the flesh, let us believe with the Prophet that God is ever present to us, when he says to the Lord, "Every desire of mine is before You."

Jan. 29—May 30—Sept. 29

We must be on our guard, therefore, against evil desires, for death lies close by the gate of pleasure. Hence the Scripture gives this command: "Go not after your concupiscences."

So therefore, since the eyes of the Lord observe the good and the evil and the Lord is always looking down from heaven on the children of men "to see if there be anyone who understands and seeks God," and since our deeds daily, day and night, are reported to the Lord by the Angels assigned to us, we must constantly beware, brethren, as the Prophet says in the Psalm, lest at any time God see us falling into evil ways and becoming unprofitable; and lest, having spared us for the present because in His kindness He awaits our reformation, He say to us in the future, "These things you did, and I held My peace."

Jan. 30—May 31—Sept. 30

The second degree of humility is that a person love not his own will nor take pleasure in satisfying his desires, but model his actions on the saying of the Lord, "I have come not to do My own will, but the will of Him who sent Me." It is written also, "Self-will has its punishment, but constraint wins a crown."

Jan. 31—June 1—Oct. 1

The third degree of humility is that a person for love of God submit himself to his Superior in all obedience, imitating the Lord, of whom the apostle says, "He became obedient even unto death."

Feb. 1—June 2—Oct. 2

The fourth degree of humility is that he hold fast to patience with a silent mind when in this obedience he meets with difficulties and contradictions and even any kind of injustice, enduring all without growing weary or running away. For the Scripture says, "He who perseveres to the end, he it is who shall be saved"; and again, "Let your heart take courage, and wait for the Lord!"

And to show how those who are faithful ought to endure all things, however contrary, for the Lord, the Scripture says in the person of the suffering, "For Your sake we are put to death all the day long; we are considered as sheep marked for slaughter." Then, secure in their hope of a divine recompense, they go on with joy to declare, "But in all these trials we conquer, through Him who has granted us His love." Again, in another place the Scripture says, "You have tested us, O God; You have tried us as silver is tried, by fire; You have brought us into a snare; You have laid afflictions on our back." And to show that we ought to be under a Superior, it goes on to say, "You have set men over our heads."

Moreover, by their patience those faithful ones fulfil the Lord's command in adversities and injuries: when struck on one cheek, they offer the other; when deprived of their tunic, they surrender also their cloak; when forced to go a mile, they go two; with the Apostle Paul they bear with the false brethren and bless those who curse them.

Feb. 2—June 3—Oct. 3

The fifth degree of humility is that he hide from his Abbot none of the evil thoughts that enter his heart or the sins committed in secret, but that he humbly confess them. The Scripture urges us to this when it says, "Reveal your way to the Lord and hope in Him," and again, "Confess to the Lord, for He is good, for His mercy endures forever." And the Prophet likewise says, "My offense I have made known to You, and my iniquities I have not covered up. I said: 'I will declare against myself my iniquities to the Lord'; and 'You forgave the wickedness of my heart.'"

Feb. 3—June 4—Oct. 4
The sixth degree of humility is that a monk be content with the poorest and worst of everything, and that in every occupation assigned him he consider himself a bad and worthless workman, saying with the Prophet, "I am brought to nothing and I am without understanding; I have become as a beast of burden before You, and I am always with You."

Feb. 4—June 5—Oct. 5
The seventh degree of humility is that he consider himself lower and of less account than anyone else, and this not only in verbal protestation but also with the most heartfelt inner conviction, humbling himself and saying with the Prophet, "But I am a worm and no man, the scorn of men and the outcast of the people. After being exalted, I have been humbled and covered with confusion." And again, "It is good for me that You have humbled me, that I may learn Your commandments."

Feb. 5—June 6—Oct. 6
The eighth degree of humility is that a monk do nothing except what is commended by the common Rule of the monastery and the example of the elders.

Feb. 6—June 7—Oct. 7
The ninth degree of humility is that a monk restrain his tongue and keep silence, not speaking until he is questioned. For the Scripture shows that "in much speaking there is no escape from sin" and that "the talkative man is not stable on the earth."

Feb. 7—June 8—Oct. 8
The tenth degree of humility is that he be not ready and quick to laugh, for it is written, "The fool lifts up his voice in laughter."

Feb. 8—June 9—Oct. 9
The eleventh degree of humility is that when a monk speaks he do so gently and without laughter, humbly and seriously, in few and sensible words, and that he be not noisy in his speech. It is written, "A wise man is known by the fewness of his words."

Feb. 9—June 10—Oct. 10
The twelfth degree of humility is that a monk not only have humility in his heart but also by his very appearance make it always manifest to those who see him. That is to say that whether he is at the Work of God, in the oratory, in the monastery, in the garden, on the road, in the fields or anywhere else, and whether sitting, walking or standing, he should always have his head bowed and his eyes towards the ground. Feeling the guilt of his sins at every moment, he should consider himself already present at the dread Judgment and constantly say in his heart what the publican in the Gospel said with his eyes fixed on the earth: "Lord, I am a sinner and not worthy to lift up my eyes to heaven"; and again with the Prophet: "I am bowed down and humbled everywhere."

Having climbed all these steps of humility, therefore, the monk will presently come to that perfect love of God, which casts out fear. And all those precepts which formerly he had not observed without fear, he will now begin to keep by reason of that love, without any effort, as though naturally and by habit. No longer will his motive be the fear of hell, but rather the love of Christ, good habit and delight in the virtues which the Lord will deign to show forth by the Holy Spirit in His servant now cleansed from vice and sin.

Chapter 8—On the Divine Office during the Night

Feb. 10—June 11—Oct. 11
In winter time, that is, from the Calends of November until Easter, the brethren shall rise at what is calculated to be the eighth hour of the night, so that they may sleep somewhat longer than half the night and rise with their rest completed. And the time that remains after the Night Office should be spent in study by those brethren who need a better knowledge of the Psalter or the lessons.

From Easter to the aforesaid Calends of November, the hour of rising should be so arranged that the Morning Office, which is to be said at daybreak, will follow the Night Office after a very short interval, during which the brethren may go out for the necessities of nature.

Chapter 9—How Many Psalms Are to Be Said at the Night Office

Feb. 11—June 12—Oct. 12

In winter time as defined above, there is first this verse to be said three times: "O Lord, open my lips, and my mouth shall declare Your praise." To it is added Psalm 3 and the "Glory be to the Father," and after that Psalm 94 to be chanted with an antiphon or even chanted simply. Let the Ambrosian hymn follow next, and then six Psalms with antiphons. When these are finished and the verse said, let the Abbot give a blessing; then, all being seated on the benches, let three lessons be read from the book on the lectern by the brethren in their turns, and after each lesson let a responsory be chanted. Two of the responsories are to be said without a "Glory be to the Father"; but after the third lesson let the chanter say the "Glory to the Father," and as soon as he begins it let all rise from their seats out of honor and reverence to the Holy Trinity.

The books to be read at the Night Office shall be those of divine authorship, of both the Old and New Testament, and also the explanations of them which have been made by well known and orthodox Catholic Fathers.

After these three lessons with their responsories let the remaining six Psalms follow, to be chanted with "Alleluia." After these shall follow the lesson from the apostle, to be recited by heart, the verse and the petition of the litany, that is "Lord have mercy on us." And so let the Night Office come to an end.

Chapter 10—How the Night Office Is to Be Said in Summer Time

Feb. 12—June 13—Oct. 13

From Easter until the Calends of November let the same number of Psalms be kept as prescribed above; but no lessons are to be read from the book, on account of the shortness of the nights. Instead of those three lessons let one lesson from the Old Testament be said by heart and followed by a short responsory. But all the rest should be done as has been said, that is to say that never fewer than twelve Psalms should be said at the Night Office, not counting Psalm 3 and Psalm 94.

Chapter 11—How the Night Office Is to Be Said on Sundays

Feb. 13—June 14—Oct. 14

On Sunday the hour of rising for the Night Office should be earlier. In that Office let the measure already prescribed be kept, namely the singing of six Psalms and a verse. Then let all be seated on the benches in their proper order while the lessons and their responsories are read from the book, as we said above. These shall be four in number, with the chanter saying the "Glory be to the Father" in the fourth responsory only, and all rising reverently as soon as he begins it.

After these lessons let six more Psalms with antiphons follow in order, as before, and a verse; and then let four more lessons be read with their responsories in the same way as the former.

After these let there be three canticles from the book of the Prophets, as the Abbot shall appoint, and let these canticles be chanted with "Alleluia." Then when the verse has been said and the Abbot has given the blessing, let four more lessons be read, from the New Testament, in the manner prescribed above.

After the fourth responsory let the Abbot begin the hymn "We praise You, O God." When this is finished the Abbot shall read the lesson from the book of the Gospels, while all stand in reverence and awe. At the end let all answer "Amen," and let the Abbot proceed at once to the hymn "To You be praise." After the blessing has been given, let them begin the Morning Office.

This order for the Night Office on Sunday shall be observed the year around, both summer and winter; unless it should happen (which God forbid) that the brethren be late in rising, in which case the lessons or the responsories will have to be shortened somewhat. Let every precaution be taken, however, against such an occurrence; but if it does happen, then the one through whose neglect it has come about should make due satisfaction to God in the oratory.

Chapter 12—How the Morning Office Is to Be Said

Feb. 14—June 15—Oct. 15
The Morning Office on Sunday shall begin with Psalm 66 recited straight through without an antiphon. After that let Psalm 50 be said with "Alleluia," then Psalms 117 and 62, the Canticle of Blessing and the Psalms of praise; then a lesson from the Apocalypse to be recited by heart, the responsory, the Ambrosian hymn, the verse, the canticle from the Gospel book, the litany, and so the end.

Chapter 13—How the Morning Office Is to be Said on Weekdays

Feb. 15—June 16—Oct. 16
On weekdays the Morning Office shall be celebrated as follows. Let Psalm 66 be said without an antiphon and somewhat slowly, as on Sunday, in order that all may be in time for Psalm 50, which is to be said with an antiphon. After that let two other Psalms be said according to custom, namely: on Monday Psalms 5 and 35, on Tuesday Psalms 42 and 56, on Wednesday Psalms 63 and 64, on Thursday Psalms 87 and 89, on Friday Psalms 75 and 91, and on Saturday Psalm 142 and the canticle from Deuteronomy, which is to be divided into two sections each terminated by a "Glory to the Father." But on the other days let there be a canticle from the Prophets, each on its own day as chanted by the Roman Church. Next follow the Psalms of praise, then a lesson of the apostle to be recited from memory, the responsory, the Ambrosian hymn, the verse, the canticle from the Gospel book, the litany, and so the end.

Feb. 16—June 17—Oct. 17
The Morning and Evening Offices should never be allowed to pass without the Superior saying the Lord's Prayer in its place at the end so that all may hear it, on account of the thorns of scandal which are apt to spring up. Thus those who hear it, being warned by the covenant which they make in that prayer when they say, "Forgive us as we forgive," may cleanse themselves of faults against that covenant.

But at the other Offices let the last part only of that prayer be said aloud, so that all may answer, "But deliver us from evil."

Chapter 14—How the Night Office Is to Be Said on the Feasts of the Saints

Feb. 17—June 18—Oct. 18
On the feasts of Saints and on all festivals let the Office be performed as we have prescribed for Sundays, except that the Psalms, the antiphons and the lessons belonging to that particular day are to be said. Their number, however, shall remain as we have specified above.

Chapter 15—At What Times "Alleluia" Is to Be Said

Feb. 18—June 19—Oct. 19
From holy Easter until Pentecost without interruption let "Alleluia" be said both in the Psalms and in the responsories. From Pentecost to the beginning of Lent let it be said every night with the last six Psalms of the Night Office only. On every Sunday, however, outside of Lent, the canticles, the Morning Office, Prime, Terce, Sext and None[2] shall be said with "Alleluia," but Vespers with antiphons.

The responsories are never to be said with "Alleluia" except from Easter to Pentecost.

Chapter 16—How the Work of God Is to Be Performed during the Day

Feb. 19—June 20—Oct. 20
"Seven times in the day," says the Prophet, "I have rendered praise to You." Now that sacred number of seven will be fulfilled by us if we perform the Offices of our service at the time of the Morning Office, of Prime, of Terce, of Sext, of None, of Vespers and of Compline, since it was of these day Hours that he said, "Seven times in the day I have rendered praise to You." For as to the Night Office the same Prophet says, "In the middle of the night I arose to glorify You."

Let us therefore bring our tribute of praise to our Creator "for the judgments of His justice" at these times: the Morning Office, Prime, Terce,

---

2   The "little hours" of monastic prayer are at ca. 6, 8, and 11 a.m. and 2 p.m.

Sext, None, Vespers, and Compline; and in the night let us arise to glorify Him.

Chapter 17—How Many Psalms Are to Be Said at These Hours

Feb. 20—June 21—Oct. 21

We have already arranged the order of the psalmody for the Night and Morning Offices; let us now provide for the remaining Hours. At Prime let three Psalms be said, separately and not under one "Glory to the Father." The hymn of that Hour is to follow the verse "Incline unto my aid, O God," before the Psalms begin. Upon completion of the three Psalms let one lesson be recited, then a verse, the "Lord, have mercy on us" and the concluding prayers.

The Offices of Terce, Sext and None are to be celebrated in the same order, that is: "Incline unto my aid, O God," the hymn proper to each Hour, three Psalms, lesson and verse, "Lord, have mercy on us" and concluding prayers.

If the community is a large one, let the Psalms be sung with antiphons; but if small, let them be sung straight through.

Let the Psalms of the Vesper Office be limited to four, with antiphons. After these Psalms the lesson is to be recited, then the responsory, the Ambrosian hymn, the verse, the canticle from the Gospel book, the litany, the Lord's Prayer and the concluding prayers.

Let Compline be limited to the saying of three Psalms, which are to be said straight through without antiphon, and after them the hymn of that Hour, one lesson, a verse, the "Lord, have mercy on us," the blessing and the concluding prayers.

Chapter 18—In What Order the Psalms Are to Be Said

Feb. 21—June 22—Oct. 22

Let this verse be said: "Incline unto my aid, O God: O Lord, make haste to help me," and the "Glory be to the Father"; then the hymn proper to each Hour.

Then at Prime on Sunday four sections of Psalm 118 are to be said; and at each of the remaining Hours, that is Terce, Sext and None, three sections of the same Psalm 118.

At Prime on Monday let three Psalms be said, namely Psalms 1, 2 and 6. And so each day at Prime until Sunday let three Psalms be said in numerical order, to Psalm 19, but with Psalms 9 and 17 each divided into two parts. Thus it comes about that the Night Office on Sunday always begins with Psalm 20.

Feb. 22—June 23—Oct. 23

At Terce, Sext and None on Monday let the nine remaining sections of Psalm 118 be said, three at each of these Hours.

Psalm 118 having been completed, therefore, on two days, Sunday and Monday, let the nine Psalms from Psalm 119 to Psalm 127 be said at Terce, Sext and None, three at each Hour, beginning with Tuesday. And let these same Psalms be repeated every day until Sunday at the same Hours, while the arrangement of hymns, lessons and verse is kept the same on all days; and thus Prime on Sunday will always begin with Psalm 118.

Feb. 23—June 24—Oct. 24

Vespers are to be sung with four Psalms every day. These shall begin with Psalm 109 and go on to Psalm 147, omitting those which are set apart for other Hours; that is to say that with the exception of Psalms 117 to 127 and Psalms 133 and 142, all the rest of these are to be said at Vespers. And since there are three Psalms too few, let the longer ones of the above number be divided, namely Psalms 138, 143 and 144. But let Psalm 116 because of its brevity be joined to Psalm 115.

The order of the Vesper Psalms being thus settled, let the rest of the Hour—lesson, responsory, hymn, verse and canticle—be carried out as we prescribed above.

At Compline the same Psalms are to be repeated every day, namely Psalms 4, 90 and 133.

(Feb. 24 in leap year; otherwise added to the preceding)—June 25—Oct. 25

The order of psalmody for the day Hours being thus arranged, let all the remaining Psalms be equally distributed among the seven Night Offices by dividing the longer Psalms among them and assigning twelve Psalms to each night.

We strongly recommend, however, that if this distribution of the Psalms is displeasing to anyone, he should arrange them otherwise, in whatever way he considers better, but taking care that the Psalter with its full number of 150 Psalms be chanted every week and begun again every Sunday at the Night Office. For those monks show themselves too lazy in the service to which they are vowed, who chant less than the Psalter with the customary canticles in the course of a week, whereas we read that our holy Fathers strenuously fulfilled that task in a single day. May we, lukewarm that we are, perform it at least in a whole week!

Chapter 19—On the Manner of Saying the Divine Office

Feb. 24 (25)—June 26—Oct. 26
We believe that the divine presence is everywhere and that "the eyes of the Lord are looking on the good and the evil in every place." But we should believe this especially without any doubt when we are assisting at the Work of God. To that end let us be mindful always of the Prophet's words, "Serve the Lord in fear" and again "Sing praises wisely" and "In the sight of the Angels I will sing praise to You." Let us therefore consider how we ought to conduct ourselves in the sight of the Godhead and of His Angels, and let us take part in the psalmody in such a way that our mind may be in harmony with our voice.

Chapter 20—On Reverence in Prayer

Feb. 25 (26)—June 27—Oct. 27
When we wish to suggest our wants to men of high station, we do not presume to do so except with humility and reverence. How much the more, then, are complete humility and pure devotion necessary in supplication of the Lord who is God of the universe! And let us be assured that it is not in saying a great deal that we shall be heard, but in purity of heart and in tears of compunction. Our prayer, therefore, ought to be short and pure, unless it happens to be prolonged by an inspiration of divine grace. In community, however,

let prayer be very short, and when the Superior gives the signal let all rise together.

Chapter 21—On the Deans of the Monastery

Feb. 26 (27)—June 28—Oct. 28
If the community is a large one, let there be chosen out of it brethren of good repute and holy life, and let them be appointed deans. These shall take charge of their deaneries in all things, observing the commandments of God and the instructions of their Abbot.

Let men of such character be chosen deans that the Abbot may with confidence share his burdens among them. Let them be chosen not by rank but according to their worthiness of life and the wisdom of their doctrine.

If any of these deans should become inflated with pride and found deserving of censure, let him be corrected once, and again, and a third time. If he will not amend, then let him be despised and another put in his place who is worthy of it.

And we order the same to be done in the case of the Prior.

Chapter 22—How the Monks Are to Sleep

Feb. 27 (28)—June 29—Oct. 29
Let each one sleep in a separate bed. Let them receive bedding suitable to their manner of life, according to the Abbot's directions. If possible let all sleep in one place; but if the number does not allow this, let them take their rest by tens and twenties with the seniors who have charge of them.

A candle shall be kept burning in the room until morning.

Let the monks sleep clothed and girded with belts and cords—but not with their knives at their sides, lest they cut themselves in their sleep—and thus be always ready to rise without delay when the signal is given and hasten to be before one another at the Work of God, yet with all gravity and decorum.

The younger brethren shall not have beds next to one another, but among those of the older ones.

When they rise for the Work of God let them gently encourage one another, that the drowsy may have no excuse.

Chapter 23—On Excommunication for Faults

Feb. 28 (29)—June 30—Oct. 30
If a brother is found to be obstinate, or disobedient, or proud, or murmuring, or habitually transgressing the Holy Rule in any point and contemptuous of the orders of his seniors, the latter shall admonish him secretly a first and a second time, as Our Lord commands. If he fails to amend, let him be given a public rebuke in front of the whole community. But if even then he does not reform, let him be placed under excommunication, provided that he understands the seriousness of that penalty; if he is perverse, however, let him undergo corporal punishment.

Chapter 24—What the Measure of Excommunication Should Be

Mar. 1—July 1—Oct. 31
The measure of excommunication or of chastisement should correspond to the degree of fault, which degree is estimated by the Abbot's judgment.

If a brother is found guilty of lighter faults, let him be excluded from the common table. Now the program for one deprived of the fellowship of the table shall be as follows: In the oratory he shall intone neither Psalm nor antiphon nor shall he recite a lesson until he has made satisfaction; in the refectory he shall take his food alone after the community meal, so that if the brethren eat at the sixth hour, for instance, that brother shall eat at the ninth, while if they eat at the ninth hour he shall eat at the evening, until by a suitable satisfaction he obtains pardon.

Chapter 25—On Weightier Faults

Mar. 2—July 2—Nov. 1
Let the brother who is guilty of a weightier fault be excluded both from the table and from the oratory. Let none of the brethren join him either for company or for conversation. Let him be alone at the work assigned him, abiding in penitential sorrow and pondering that terrible sentence of the apostle where he says that a man of that kind is handed over for the destruction of the flesh, that the spirit may be saved in the day of the Lord. Let him take his meals alone in the measure and at

the hour which the Abbot shall consider suitable for him. He shall not be blessed by those who pass by, nor shall the food that is given him be blessed.

Chapter 26—On Those Who without an Order Associate with the Excommunicated

Mar. 3—July 3—Nov. 2
If any brother presumes without an order from the Abbot to associate in any way with an excommunicated brother, or to speak with him, or to send him a message, let him incur a similar punishment of excommunication.

Chapter 27—How Solicitous the Abbot Should Be for the Excommunicated

Mar. 4—July 4—Nov. 3
Let the Abbot be most solicitous in his concern for delinquent brethren, for "it is not the healthy but the sick who need a physician." And therefore he ought to use every means that a wise physician would use. Let him send "senpectae," that is, brethren of mature years and wisdom, who may as it were secretly console the wavering brother and induce him to make humble satisfaction; comforting him that he may not "be overwhelmed by excessive grief," but that, as the apostle says, charity may be strengthened in him. And let everyone pray for him.

For the Abbot must have the utmost solicitude and exercise all prudence and diligence lest he lose any of the sheep entrusted to him. Let him know that what he has undertaken is the care of weak souls and not a tyranny over strong ones; and let him fear the Prophet's warning through which God says, "What you saw to be fat you took to yourselves, and what was feeble you cast away." Let him rather imitate the loving example of the Good Shepherd who left the ninety-nine sheep in the mountains and went to look for the one sheep that had gone astray, on whose weakness He had such compassion that He deigned to place it on His own sacred shoulders and thus carry it back to the flock.

Chapter 28—On Those Who Will Not Amend after Repeated Corrections

Mar. 5—July 5—Nov. 4
If a brother who has been frequently corrected for some fault, and even excommunicated, does not amend, let a harsher correction be applied, that is, let the punishment of the rod be administered to him.

But if he still does not reform or perhaps (which God forbid) even rises up in pride and wants to defend his conduct, then let the Abbot do what a wise physician would do. Having used applications, the ointments of exhortation, the medicines of the Holy Scriptures, finally the cautery of excommunication and of the strokes of the rod, if he sees that his efforts are of no avail, let him apply a still greater remedy, his own prayers and those of his own brethren, that the Lord, who can do all things, may restore health to the sick brother.

But if he is not healed even in this way, then let the Abbot use the knife of amputation, according to the apostle's words, "Expel the evil one from your midst," and again, "If the faithless one departs, let him depart," lest one diseased sheep contaminate the whole flock.

Chapter 29—Whether Brethren Who Leave the Monastery Should Be Received Again

Mar. 6—July 6—Nov. 5
If a brother who through his own fault leaves the monastery should wish to return, let him first promise full reparation for his having gone away; and then let him be received in the lowest place, as a test of his humility. And if he should leave again, let him be taken back again, and so a third time; but he should understand that after this all way of return is denied him.

Chapter 30—How Boys Are to Be Corrected

Mar. 7—July 7—Nov. 6
Every age and degree of understanding should have its proper measure of discipline. With regard to boys and adolescents, therefore, or those who cannot understand the seriousness of the penalty of excommunication, whenever such as these are delinquent let them be subjected to terms by harsh beatings, that they may be cured.

Chapter 31—What Kind of Man the Cellarer of the Monastery Should Be

Mar. 8—July 8—Nov. 7
As cellarer of the monastery let there be chosen from the community one who is wise, of mature character, sober, not a great eater, not haughty, not excitable, not offensive, not slow, not wasteful, but a God-fearing man who may be like a father to the whole community.

Let him have charge of everything. He shall do nothing without the Abbot's orders, but keep to his instructions. Let him not vex the brethren. If any brother happens to make some unreasonable demand of him, instead of vexing the brother with a contemptuous refusal he should humbly give the reason for denying the improper request.

Let him keep guard over his own soul, mindful always of the apostle's saying that "he who has ministered well acquires for himself a good standing."

Let him take the greatest care of the sick, of children, of guests and of the poor, knowing without doubt that he will have to render an account for all these on the Day of Judgment.

Let him regard all the utensils of the monastery and its whole property as if they were the sacred vessels of the altar. Let him not think that he may neglect anything. He should be neither a miser nor a prodigal and squanderer of the monastery's substance, but should do all things with a measure and in accordance with the Abbot's instructions.

Mar. 9—July 9—Nov. 8
Above all things let him have humility; and if he has nothing else to give let him give a good word in answer, for it is written: "A good word is above the best gift."

Let him have under his care all that the Abbot has assigned to him, but not presume to deal with what he has forbidden him.

Let him give the brethren their appointed allowance of food without any arrogance or delay, that they may not be scandalized, mindful of the Word of God as to what he deserves "who shall scandalize one of the little ones."

If the community is a large one, let helpers be given him, that by their assistance he may fulfil with a quiet mind the office committed to him.

The proper times should be observed in giving the things that have to be given and asking for the things that have to be asked for, that no one may be troubled or vexed in the house of God.

Chapter 32—On the Tools and Property of the Monastery

Mar. 10—July 10—Nov. 9

For the care of the monastery's property in tools, clothing and other articles let the Abbot appoint brethren on whose manner of life and character he can rely; and let him, as he shall judge to be expedient, consign the various articles to them, to be looked after and to be collected again. The Abbot shall keep a list of these articles, so that as the brethren succeed one another in their assignments he may know what he gives and what he receives back.

If anyone treats the monastery's property in a slovenly or careless way, let him be corrected. If he fails to amend, let him undergo the discipline of the Rule.

Chapter 33—Whether Monks Ought to Have Anything of Their Own

Mar. 11—July 11—Nov. 10

This vice especially is to be cut out of the monastery by the roots. Let no one presume to give or receive anything without the Abbot's leave, or to have anything as his own—anything whatever, whether book or tablets or pen or whatever it may be—since they are not permitted to have even their bodies or wills at their own disposal; but for all their necessities let them look to the Father of the monastery. And let it be unlawful to have anything which the Abbot has not given or allowed. Let all things be common to all, as it is written, and let no one say or assume that anything is his own. But if anyone is caught indulging in this most wicked vice, let him be admonished once and a second time. If he fails to amend, let him undergo punishment.

Chapter 34—Whether All Should Receive in Equal Measure What Is Necessary

Mar. 12—July 12—Nov. 11

Let us follow the Scripture, "Distribution was made to each according as anyone had need." By this we do not mean that there should be respecting of persons (which God forbid), but consideration for infirmities. He who needs less should thank God and not be discontented; but he who needs more should be humbled by the thought of his infirmity rather than feeling important on account of the kindness shown him. Thus all the members will be at peace.

Above all, let not the evil of murmuring appear for any reason whatsoever in the least word or sign. If anyone is caught at it, let him be placed under very severe discipline.

Chapter 35—On the Weekly Servers in the Kitchen

Mar. 13—July 13—Nov. 12

Let the brethren serve one another, and let no one be excused from the kitchen service except by reason of sickness or occupation in some important work. For this service brings increase of reward and of charity. But let helpers be provided for the weak ones, that they may not be distressed by this work; and indeed let everyone have help, as required by the size of the community or the circumstances of the locality. If the community is a large one, the cellarer shall be excused from the kitchen service; and so also those whose occupations are of greater utility, as we said above. Let the rest serve one another in charity.

The one who is ending his week of service shall do the cleaning on Saturday. He shall wash the towels with which the brethren wipe their hands and feet; and this server who is ending his week, aided by the one who is about to begin, shall wash the feet of all the brethren. He shall return the utensils of his office to the cellarer clean and in good condition, and the cellarer in turn shall consign them to the incoming server, in order that he may know what he gives out and what he receives back.

Mar. 14—July 14—Nov. 13

An hour before the meal let the weekly servers each receive a drink and some bread, over and above the appointed allowance, in order that at the meal time they may serve their brethren without murmuring and without excessive fatigue. On solemn days, however, let them wait until after Mass.

Immediately after the Morning Office on Sunday, the incoming and outgoing servers shall prostrate themselves before all the brethren in the oratory and ask their prayers. Let the server who is ending his week say this verse: "Blessed are You, O Lord God, who have helped me and consoled me." When this has been said three times and the outgoing server has received his blessing, then let the incoming server follow and say, "Incline unto my aid, O God; O Lord, make haste to help me." Let this also be repeated three times by all, and having received his blessing let him enter his service.

Chapter 36—On the Sick Brethren

Mar. 15—July 15—Nov. 14

Before all things and above all things, care must be taken of the sick, so that they will be served as if they were Christ in person; for He Himself said, "I was sick, and you visited Me," and, "What you did for one of these least ones, you did for Me." But let the sick on their part consider that they are being served for the honor of God, and let them not annoy their brethren who are serving them by their unnecessary demands. Yet they should be patiently borne with, because from such as these is gained a more abundant reward. Therefore the Abbot shall take the greatest care that they suffer no neglect.

For these sick brethren let there be assigned a special room and an attendant who is God-fearing, diligent and solicitous. Let the use of baths be afforded the sick as often as may be expedient; but to the healthy, and especially to the young, let them be granted more rarely. Moreover, let the use of meat be granted to the sick who are very weak, for the restoration of their strength; but when they are convalescent, let all abstain from meat as usual.

The Abbot shall take the greatest care that the sick be not neglected by the cellarers or the attendants; for he also is responsible for what is done wrongly by his disciples.

Chapter 37—On Old Men and Children

Mar. 16—July 16—Nov. 15

Although human nature itself is drawn to special kindness towards these times of life, that is towards old men and children, still the authority of the Rule should also provide for them. Let their weakness be always taken into account, and let them by no means be held to the rigor of the Rule with regard to food. On the contrary, let a kind consideration be shown to them, and let them eat before the regular hours.

Chapter 38—On the Weekly Reader

Mar. 17—July 17—Nov. 16

The meals of the brethren should not be without reading. Nor should the reader be anyone who happens to take up the book; but there should be a reader for the whole week, entering that office on Sunday. Let this incoming reader, after Mass and Communion, ask all to pray for him that God may keep him from the spirit of pride. And let him intone the following verse, which shall be said three times by all in the oratory: "O Lord, open my lips, and my mouth shall declare thy praise." Then, having received a blessing, let him enter on the reading.

And let absolute silence be kept at table, so that no whispering may be heard nor any voice except the reader's. As to the things they need while they eat and drink, let the brethren pass them to one another so that no one need ask for anything. If anything is needed, however, let it be asked for by means of some audible sign rather than by speech. Nor shall anyone at table presume to ask questions about the reading or anything else, lest that give occasion for talking; except that the Superior may perhaps wish to say something briefly for the purpose of edification.

The brother who is reader for the week shall take a little refreshment before he begins to read, on account of the Holy Communion and lest perhaps the fast be hard for him to bear. He shall take his meal afterwards with the kitchen and table servers of the week.

The brethren are not to read or chant in order, but only those who edify their hearers.

Chapter 39—On the Measure of Food

Mar. 18—July 18—Nov. 17

We think it sufficient for the daily dinner, whether at the sixth or the ninth hour, that every table have two cooked dishes, on account of individual infirmities, so that he who for some reason cannot eat of the one may make his meal of the other. Therefore let two cooked dishes suffice for all the brethren; and if any fruit or fresh vegetables are available, let a third dish be added.

Let a good pound weight of bread suffice for the day, whether there by only one meal or both dinner and supper. If they are to have supper, the cellarer shall reserve a third of that pound, to be given them at supper.

But if it happens that the work was heavier, it shall lie within the Abbot's discretion and power, should it be expedient, to add something to the fare. Above all things, however, over-indulgence must be avoided and a monk must never be overtaken by indigestion; for there is nothing so opposed to the Christian character as over-indulgence, according to Our Lord's words, "See to it that your hearts be not burdened with over-indulgence."

Young boys shall not receive the same amount of food as their elders, but less; and frugality shall be observed in all circumstances.

Except the sick who are very weak, let all abstain entirely from eating the flesh of four-footed animals.

Chapter 40—On the Measure of Drink

Mar. 19—July 19—Nov. 18

"Everyone has his own gift from God, one in this way and another in that." It is therefore with some misgiving that we regulate the measure of other men's sustenance. Nevertheless, keeping in view the needs of weaker brethren, we believe that a hemina[3] of wine a day is sufficient for each. But those to whom God gives the strength to abstain should know that they will receive a special reward.

If the circumstances of the place, or the work, or the heat of summer require a greater measure, the Superior shall use his judgment in the matter, taking care always that there be no occasion for surfeit or drunkenness. We read, it is true, that wine is by no means a drink for monks; but since the monks of our day cannot be persuaded of this, let us at least agree to drink sparingly and not to satiety, because "wine makes even the wise fall away."

But where the circumstances of the place are such that not even the measure prescribed above can be supplied, but much less or none at all, let those who live there bless God and not murmur. Above all things do we give this admonition, that they abstain from murmuring.

Chapter 41—At What Hours the Meals Should Be Taken

Mar. 20—July 20—Nov. 19

From holy Easter until Pentecost let the brethren take dinner at the sixth hour and supper in the evening.

From Pentecost throughout the summer, unless the monks have work in the fields or the excessive heat of summer oppresses them, let them fast on Wednesdays and Fridays until the ninth hour; on the other days let them dine at the sixth hour. This dinner at the sixth hour shall be the daily schedule if they have work in the fields or the heat of summer is extreme; the Abbot's foresight shall decide on this. Thus it is said that he should adapt and arrange everything in such a way that souls may be saved and that the brethren may do their work without just cause for murmuring.

From the Ides of September until the beginning of Lent let them always take their dinner at the ninth hour.

In Lent let them dine in the evening. But this evening hour shall be so determined that they will not need the light of a lamp while eating, but everything will be accomplished while it is still daylight. Indeed at all seasons let the hour, whether for supper or for dinner, be so arranged that everything will be done by daylight.

---

3   A measure of disputed size.

Chapter 42—That No One Speak After Compline

Mar. 21—July 21—Nov. 20

Monks ought to be zealous for silence at all times, but especially during the hours of the night. For every season, therefore, whether there be fasting or two meals, let the program be as follows:

If it be a season when there are two meals, then as soon as they have risen from supper they shall all sit together, and one of them shall read the Conferences or the Lives of the Fathers or something else that may edify the hearers; not the Heptateuch or the Book of Kings, however, because it will not be expedient for weak minds to hear those parts of Scripture at that hour; but they shall be read at other times.

If it be a day of fast, then having allowed a short interval after Vespers they shall proceed at once to the reading of the Conferences, as prescribed above; four or five pages being read, or as much as time permits, so that during the delay provided by this reading all may come together, including those who may have been occupied in some work assigned them.

When all, therefore, are gathered together, let them say Compline; and when they come out from Compline, no one shall be allowed to say anything from that time on. And if anyone should be found evading this rule of silence, let him undergo severe punishment. An exception shall be made if the need of speaking to guests should arise or if the Abbot should give someone an order. But even this should be done with the utmost gravity and the most becoming restraint.

Chapter 43—On Those Who Come Late to the Work of God or to Table

Mar. 22—July 22—Nov. 21

At the hour for the Divine Office, as soon as the signal is heard, let them abandon whatever they have in hand and hasten with the greatest speed, yet with seriousness, so that there is no excuse for levity. Let nothing, therefore, be put before the Work of God.

If at the Night Office anyone arrives after the "Glory be to the Father" of Psalm 94—which Psalm for this reason we wish to be said very slowly and protractedly—let him not stand in his usual place in the choir; but let him stand last of all, or in a place set aside by the Abbot for such negligent ones in order that they may be seen by him and by all. He shall remain there until the Work of God has been completed, and then do penance by a public satisfaction. The reason why we have judged it fitting for them to stand in the last place or in a place apart is that, being seen by all, they may amend for very shame. For if they remain outside of the oratory, there will perhaps be someone who will go back to bed and sleep or at least seat himself outside and indulge in idle talk, and thus an occasion will be provided for the evil one. But let them go inside, that they may not lose the whole Office, and may amend for the future.

At the day Hours anyone who does not arrive at the Work of God until after the verse and the "Glory be to the Father" of the first Psalm following it shall stand in the last place, according to our ruling above. Nor shall he presume to join the choir in their chanting until he has made satisfaction, unless the Abbot should pardon him and give him permission; but even then the offender must make satisfaction for his fault.

Mar. 23—July 23—Nov. 22

Anyone who does not come to table before the verse, so that all together may say the verse and the oration and all sit down to table at the same time—anyone who through his own carelessness or bad habit does not come on time shall be corrected for this up to the second time. If then he does not amend, he shall not be allowed to share in the common table, but shall be separated from the company of all and made to eat alone, and his portion of wine shall be taken away from him, until he has made satisfaction and has amended. And let him suffer a like penalty who is not present at the verse said after the meal.

And let no one presume to take any food or drink before or after the appointed time. But if anyone is offered something by the Superior and refuses to take it, then when the time comes that he desires what he formerly refused or something else, let him receive nothing whatever until he has made proper satisfaction.

Chapter 44—How the Excommunicated Are to Make Satisfaction

Mar. 24—July 24—Nov. 23
One who for serious faults is excommunicated from oratory and table shall make satisfaction as follows. At the hour when the celebration of the Work of God is concluded in the oratory, let him lie prostrate before the door of the oratory, saying nothing, but only lying prone with his face to the ground at the feet of all as they come out of the oratory. And let him continue to do this until the Abbot judges that satisfaction has been made. Then, when he has come at the Abbot's bidding, let him cast himself first at the Abbot's feet and then at the feet of all, that they may pray for him.

And next, if the Abbot so orders, let him be received into the choir, to the place which the Abbot appoints, but with the provision that he shall not presume to intone Psalm or lesson or anything else in the oratory without a further order from the Abbot. Moreover, at every Hour, when the Work of God is ended, let him cast himself on the ground in the place where he stands. And let him continue to satisfy in this way until the Abbot again orders him finally to cease from this satisfaction.

But those who for slight faults are excommunicated only from table shall make satisfaction in the oratory, and continue in it till an order from the Abbot, until he blesses them and says, "It is enough."

Chapter 45—On Those Who Make Mistakes in the Oratory

Mar. 25—July 25—Nov. 24
When anyone has made a mistake while reciting a Psalm, a responsory, an antiphon or a lesson, if he does not humble himself there before all by making a satisfaction, let him undergo a greater punishment because he would not correct by humility what he did wrong through carelessness.

But boys for such faults shall be whipped.

Chapter 46—On Those Who Fail in Any Other Matters

Mar. 26—July 26—Nov. 25
When anyone is engaged in any sort of work, whether in the kitchen, in the cellar, in a shop, in the bakery, in the garden, while working at some craft, or in any other place, and he commits some fault, or breaks something, or loses something, or transgresses in any other way whatsoever, if he does not come immediately before the Abbot and the community of his own accord to make satisfaction and confess his fault, then when it becomes known through another, let him be subjected to a more severe correction.

But if the sin-sickness of the soul is a hidden one, let him reveal it only to the Abbot or to a spiritual father, who knows how to cure his own and others' wounds without exposing them and making them public.

Chapter 47—On Giving the Signal for the Time of the Work of God

Mar. 27—July 27—Nov. 26
The indicating of the hour of the Work of God by day and by night shall devolve upon the Abbot, either to give the signal himself or to assign this duty to such a careful brother that everything will take place at the proper hours.

Let the Psalms and the antiphons be intoned by those who are appointed for it, in their order after the Abbot. And no one shall presume to sing or read unless he can fulfil that office in such a way as to edify the hearers. Let this function be performed with humility, gravity and reverence, and by him whom the Abbot has appointed.

Chapter 48—On the Daily Manual Labor

Mar. 28—July 28—Nov. 27
Idleness is the enemy of the soul. Therefore the brethren should be occupied at certain times in manual labor, and again at fixed hours in sacred reading. To that end we think that the times for each may be prescribed as follows.

From Easter until the Calends of October, when they come out from Prime in the morning let them labor at whatever is necessary until about the fourth hour, and from the fourth hour until about the sixth let them apply themselves to reading. After the sixth hour, having left the table, let them rest on their beds in perfect silence; or if anyone may perhaps want to read, let him read to himself in such a way as not to disturb anyone else. Let None be said rather early, at the middle of the eighth hour, and let them again do what work has to be done until Vespers.

And if the circumstances of the place or their poverty should require that they themselves do the work of gathering the harvest, let them not be discontented; for then are they truly monks when they live by the labor of their hands, as did our Fathers and the apostles. Let all things be done with moderation, however, for the sake of the faint-hearted.

Mar. 29—July 29—Nov. 28
From the Calends of October until the beginning of Lent, let them apply themselves to reading up to the end of the second hour. At the second hour let Terce be said, and then let all labor at the work assigned them until None. At the first signal for the Hour of None let everyone break off from his work, and hold himself ready for the sounding of the second signal. After the meal let them apply themselves to their reading or to the Psalms.

On the days of Lent, from morning until the end of the third hour let them apply themselves to their reading, and from then until the end of the tenth hour let them do the work assigned them. And in these days of Lent they shall each receive a book from the library, which they shall read straight through from the beginning. These books are to be given out at the beginning of Lent.

But certainly one or two of the seniors should be deputed to go about the monastery at the hours when the brethren are occupied in reading and see that there be no lazy brother who spends his time in idleness or gossip and does not apply himself to the reading, so that he is not only unprofitable to himself but also distracts others. If such a one be found (which God forbid), let him be corrected once and a second time; if he does not amend, let him undergo the punishment of the Rule in such a way that the rest may take warning.

Moreover, one brother shall not associate with another at unseasonable hours.

Mar. 30—July 30—Nov. 29
On Sundays, let all occupy themselves in reading, except those who have been appointed to various duties. But if anyone should be so negligent and shiftless that he will not or cannot study or read, let him be given some work to do so that he will not be idle.

Weak or sickly brethren should be assigned a task or craft of such a nature as to keep them from idleness and at the same time not to overburden them or drive them away with excessive toil. Their weakness must be taken into consideration by the Abbot.

Chapter 49—On the Observance of Lent

Mar. 31—July 31—Nov. 30
Although the life of a monk ought to have about it at all times the character of a Lenten observance, yet since few have the virtue for that, we therefore urge that during the actual days of Lent the brethren keep their lives most pure and at the same time wash away during these holy days all the negligences of other times. And this will be worthily done if we restrain ourselves from all vices and give ourselves up to prayer with tears, to reading, to compunction of heart and to abstinence.

During these days, therefore, let us increase somewhat the usual burden of our service, as by private prayers and by abstinence in food and drink. Thus everyone of his own will may offer God "with joy of the Holy Spirit" something above the measure required of him. From his body, that is, he may withhold some food, drink, sleep, talking and jesting; and with the joy of spiritual desire he may look forward to holy Easter.

Let each one, however, suggest to his Abbot what it is that he wants to offer, and let it be done with his blessing and approval. For anything done without the permission of the spiritual father will be imputed to presumption and vainglory and will merit no reward. Therefore let everything be done with the Abbot's approval.

Chapter 50—On Brethren Who Are Working Far from the Oratory or Are on a Journey

Apr. 1—Aug. 1—Dec. 1

Those brethren who are working at a great distance and cannot get to the oratory at the proper time—the Abbot judging that such is the case—shall perform the Work of God in the place where they are working, bending their knees in reverence before God.

Likewise those who have been sent on a journey shall not let the appointed Hours pass by, but shall say the Office by themselves as well as they can, and not neglect to render the task of their service.

Chapter 51—On Brethren Who Go Not Very Far Away

Apr. 2—Aug. 2—Dec. 2

A brother who is sent out on some business and is expected to return to the monastery that same day shall not presume to eat while he is out, even if he is urgently requested to do so by any person whomsoever, unless he has permission from his Abbot. And if he acts otherwise, let him be excommunicated.

Chapter 52—On the Oratory of the Monastery

Apr. 3—Aug. 3—Dec. 3

Let the oratory be what it is called, a place of prayer; and let nothing else be done there or kept there. When the Work of God is ended, let all go out in perfect silence, and let reverence for God be observed, so that any brother who may wish to pray privately will not be hindered by another's misconduct. And at other times also, if anyone should want to pray by himself, let him go in simply and pray, not in a loud voice but with tears and fervor of heart. He who does not say his prayers in this way, therefore, shall not be permitted to remain in the oratory when the Work of God is ended, lest another be hindered, as we have said.

Chapter 53—On the Reception of Guests

Apr. 4—Aug. 4—Dec. 4

Let all guests who arrive be received like Christ, for He is going to say, "I came as a guest, and you received Me." And to all let due honor be shown, especially to the domestics of the faith and to pilgrims.

As soon as a guest is announced, therefore, let the Superior or the brethren meet him with all charitable service. And first of all let them pray together, and then exchange the kiss of peace. For the kiss of peace should not be offered until after the prayers have been said, on account of the Devil's deceptions.

In the salutation of all guests, whether arriving or departing, let all humility be shown. Let the head be bowed or the whole body prostrated on the ground in adoration of Christ, who indeed is received in their persons.

After the guests have been received and taken to prayer, let the Superior or someone appointed by him sit with them. Let the divine law be read before the guest for his edification, and then let all kindness be shown him. The Superior shall break his fast for the sake of a guest, unless it happens to be a principal fast day which may not be violated. The brethren, however, shall observe the customary fasts. Let the Abbot give the guests water for their hands; and let both Abbot and community wash the feet of all guests. After the washing of the feet let them say this verse: "We have received Your mercy, O God, in the midst of Your temple."

In the reception of the poor and of pilgrims the greatest care and solicitude should be shown, because it is especially in them that Christ is received; for as far as the rich are concerned, the very fear which they inspire wins respect for them.

Apr. 5—Aug. 5—Dec. 5

Let there be a separate kitchen for the Abbot and guests, that the brethren may not be disturbed when guests, who are never lacking in a monastery, arrive at irregular hours. Let two brethren capable of filling the office well be appointed for a year to have charge of this kitchen. Let them be given such help as they need, that they may serve without murmuring. And on the other hand, when they have less to occupy them, let them go out to whatever work is assigned them.

And not only in their case but in all the offices of the monastery let this arrangement be observed, that when help is needed it be supplied, and again when the workers are unoccupied they do whatever they are bidden.

The guest house also shall be assigned to a brother whose soul is possessed by the fear of God. Let there be a sufficient number of beds made up in it; and let the house of God be managed by prudent men and in a prudent manner.

On no account shall anyone who is not so ordered associate or converse with guests. But if he should meet them or see them, let him greet them humbly, as we have said, ask their blessing and pass on, saying that he is not allowed to converse with a guest.

Chapter 54—Whether a Monk Should Receive Letters or Anything Else

Apr. 6—Aug. 6—Dec. 6
On no account shall a monk be allowed to receive letters, tokens or any little gift whatsoever from his parents or anyone else, or from his brethren, or to give the same, without the Abbot's permission. But if anything is sent him even by his parents, let him not presume to take it before it has been shown to the Abbot. And it shall be in the Abbot's power to decide to whom it shall be given, if he allows it to be received; and the brother to whom it was sent should not be grieved, lest occasion be given to the Devil.

Should anyone presume to act otherwise, let him undergo the discipline of the Rule.

Chapter 55—On the Clothes and Shoes of the Brethren

Apr. 7—Aug. 7—Dec. 7
Let clothing be given to the brethren according to the nature of the place in which they dwell and its climate; for in cold regions more will be needed, and in warm regions less. This is to be taken into consideration, therefore, by the Abbot.

We believe, however, that in ordinary places the following dress is sufficient for each monk: a tunic, a cowl (thick and woolly for winter, thin or worn for summer), a scapular for work, stockings and shoes to cover the feet.

The monks should not complain about the color or the coarseness of any of these things, but be content with what can be found in the district where they live and can be purchased cheaply.

The Abbot shall see to the size of the garments, that they be not too short for those who wear them, but of the proper fit.

Let those who receive new clothes always give back the old ones at once, to be put away in the wardrobe for the poor. For it is sufficient if a monk has two tunics and two cowls, to allow for night wear and for the washing of these garments; more than that is superfluity and should be taken away. Let them return their stockings also and anything else that is old when they receive new ones.

Those who are sent on a journey shall receive drawers from the wardrobe, which they shall wash and restore on their return. And let their cowls and tunics be somewhat better than what they usually wear. These they shall receive from the wardrobe when they set out on a journey, and restore when they return.

Apr. 8—Aug. 8—Dec. 8
For bedding let this suffice: a mattress, a blanket, a coverlet and a pillow.

The beds, moreover, are to be examined frequently by the Abbot, to see if any private property be found in them. If anyone should be found to have something that he did not receive from the Abbot, let him undergo the most severe discipline.

And in order that this vice of private ownership may be cut out by the roots, the Abbot should provide all the necessary articles: cowl, tunic, stockings, shoes, girdle, knife, pen, needle, handkerchief, tablets; that all pretext of need may be taken away. Yet the Abbot should always keep in mind the sentence from the Acts of the Apostles that "distribution was made to each according as anyone had need." In this manner, therefore, let the Abbot consider the weaknesses of the needy and not the ill-will of the envious. But in all his decisions let him think about the retribution of God.

Chapter 56—On the Abbot's Table

Apr. 9—Aug. 9—Dec. 9

Let the Abbot's table always be with the guests and the pilgrims. But when there are no guests, let it be in his power to invite whom he will of the brethren. Yet one or two seniors must always be left with the brethren for the sake of discipline.

Chapter 57—On the Craftsmen of the Monastery

Apr. 10—Aug. 10—Dec. 10

If there are craftsmen in the monastery, let them practice their crafts with all humility, provided the Abbot has given permission. But if any one of them becomes conceited over his skill in his craft, because he seems to be conferring a benefit on the monastery, let him be taken from his craft and no longer exercise it unless, after he has humbled himself, the Abbot again gives him permission.

If any of the work of the craftsmen is to be sold, let those through whose hands the transactions pass see to it that they do not presume to practice any fraud. Let them always remember Ananias and Saphira, lest perhaps the death which these incurred in the body, they themselves and any others who would deal dishonestly with the monastery's property should suffer in the soul. And in the prices let not the sin of avarice creep in, but let the goods always be sold a little cheaper than they can be sold by people in the world, "that in all things God may be glorified."

Chapter 58—On the Manner of Receiving Brethren

Apr. 11—Aug. 11—Dec. 11

When anyone is newly come for the reformation of his life, let him not be granted an easy entrance; but, as the apostle says, "Test the spirits to see whether they are from God." If the newcomer, therefore, perseveres in his knocking, and if it is seen after four or five days that he bears patiently the harsh treatment offered him and the difficulty of admission, and that he persists in his petition, then let entrance be granted him, and let him stay in the guest house for a few days.

After that let him live in the novitiate, where the novices study, eat and sleep. A senior shall be assigned to them who is skilled in winning souls, to watch over them with the utmost care. Let him examine whether the novice is truly seeking God, and whether he is zealous for the Work of God, for obedience and for humiliations. Let the novice be told all the hard and rugged ways by which the journey to God is made.

If he promises stability and perseverance, then at the end of two months let this Rule be read through to him, and let him be addressed thus: "Here is the law under which you wish to fight. If you can observe it, enter; if you cannot, you are free to depart." If he still stands firm, let him be taken to the above-mentioned novitiate and again tested in all patience. And after the lapse of six months let the Rule be read to him, that he may know on what he is entering. And if he still remains firm, after four months let the same Rule be read to him again.

Then, having deliberated with himself, if he promises to keep it in its entirety and to observe everything that is commanded him, let him be received into the community. But let him understand that, according to the law of the Rule, from that day forward he may not leave the monastery nor withdraw his neck from under the yoke of the Rule which he was free to refuse or to accept during that prolonged deliberation.

Apr. 12—Aug. 12—Dec. 12

He who is to be received shall make a promise before all in the oratory of his stability and of the reformation of his life and of obedience. This promise he shall make before God and His Saints, so that if he should ever act otherwise, he may know that he will be condemned by Him whom he mocks. Of this promise of his let him draw up a petition in the name of the Saints whose relics are there and of the Abbot who is present. Let him write this petition with his own hand; or if he is illiterate, let another write it at his request, and let the novice put his mark to it. Then let him place it with his own hand upon the altar; and when he has placed it there, let the novice at once intone this verse: "Receive me, O Lord, according to Your word, and I shall live: and let me not be confounded in my hope." Let the whole community answer this verse three times and add the "Glory be to the Father." Then let the novice brother prostrate himself at each one's feet, that they may pray for him. And from that day forward let him be counted as one of the community.

If he has any property, let him either give it beforehand to the poor or by solemn donation bestow it on the monastery, reserving nothing at all for himself, as indeed he knows that from that day forward he will no longer have power even over his own body. At once, therefore, in the oratory, let him be divested of his own clothes which he is wearing and dressed in the clothes of the monastery. But let the clothes of which he was divested be put aside in the wardrobe and kept there. Then if he should ever listen to the persuasions of the Devil and decide to leave the monastery (which God forbid), he may be divested of the monastic clothes and cast out. His petition, however, which the Abbot has taken from the altar, shall not be returned to him, but shall be kept in the monastery.

Chapter 59—On the Sons of Nobles and of the Poor Who Are Offered

Apr. 13—Aug. 13—Dec. 13
If anyone of the nobility offers his son to God in the monastery and the boy is very young, let his parents draw up the petition which we mentioned above; and at the oblation let them wrap the petition and the boy's hand in the altar cloth and so offer him.

As regards their property, they shall promise in the same petition under oath that they will never of themselves, or through an intermediary, or in any way whatever, give him anything or provide him with the opportunity of owning anything. Or else, if they are unwilling to do this, and if they want to offer something as an alms to the monastery for their advantage, let them make a donation of the property they wish to give to the monastery, reserving the income to themselves if they wish. And in this way let everything be barred, so that the boy may have no expectations whereby (which God forbid) he might be deceived and ruined, as we have learned by experience.

Let those who are less well-to-do make a similar offering. But those who have nothing at all shall simply draw up the petition and offer their son before witnesses at the oblation.

Chapter 60—On Priests Who May Wish to Live in the Monastery

Apr. 14—Aug. 14—Dec. 14
If anyone of the priestly order should ask to be received into the monastery, permission shall not be granted him too readily. But if he is quite persistent in his request, let him know that he will have to observe the whole discipline of the Rule and that nothing will be relaxed in his favor, that it may be as it is written: "Friend, for what have you come?"

It shall be granted him, however, to stand next after the Abbot and to give blessings and celebrate Mass, but only by order of the Abbot. Without such order let him not presume to do anything, knowing that he is subject to the discipline of the Rule; but rather let him give an example of humility to all.

If there happens to be question of an appointment or of some business in the monastery, let him expect the rank due him according to the date of his entrance into the monastery, and not the place granted him out of reverence for the priesthood.

If any clerics, moved by the same desire, should wish to join the monastery, let them be placed in a middle rank. But they too are to be admitted only if they promise observance of the Rule and their own stability.

Chapter 61—How Pilgrim Monks Are to Be Received

Apr. 15—Aug. 15—Dec. 15
If a pilgrim monk coming from a distant region wants to live as a guest of the monastery, let him be received for as long a time as he desires, provided he is content with the customs of the place as he finds them and does not disturb the monastery by superfluous demands, but is simply content with what he finds. If, however, he censures or points out anything reasonably and with the humility of charity, let the Abbot consider prudently whether perhaps it was for that very purpose that the Lord sent him.

If afterwards he should want to bind himself to stability, his wish should not be denied him, especially since there has been opportunity during his stay as a guest to discover his character.

Apr. 16—Aug. 16—Dec. 16

But if as a guest he was found exacting or prone to vice, not only should he be denied membership in the community, but he should even be politely requested to leave, lest others be corrupted by his evil life.

If, however, he has not proved to be the kind who deserves to be put out, he should not only on his own application be received as a member of the community, but he should even be persuaded to stay, that the others may be instructed by his example, and because in every place it is the same Lord who is served, the same King for whom the battle is fought.

Moreover, if the Abbot perceives that he is a worthy man, he may put him in a somewhat higher rank. And not only with regard to a monk but also with regard to those in priestly or clerical orders previously mentioned, the Abbot may establish them in a higher rank than would be theirs by date of entrance if he perceives that their life is deserving.

Let the Abbot take care, however, never to receive a monk from another known monastery as a member of his community without the consent of his Abbot or a letter of recommendation; for it is written, "Do not to another what you would not want done to yourself."

Chapter 62—On the Priests of the Monastery

Apr. 17—Aug. 17—Dec. 17

If an Abbot desire to have a priest or a deacon ordained for his monastery, let him choose one of his monks who is worthy to exercise the priestly office.

But let the one who is ordained beware of self-exaltation or pride; and let him not presume to do anything except what is commanded him by the Abbot, knowing that he is so much the more subject to the discipline of the Rule. Nor should he by reason of his priesthood forget the obedience and the discipline required by the Rule, but make ever more and more progress towards God.

Let him always keep the place which he received on entering the monastery, except in his duties at the altar or in case the choice of the community and the will of the Abbot should promote him for the worthiness of his life. Yet he must understand that he is to observe the rules laid down by deans and Priors.

Should he presume to act otherwise, let him be judged not as a priest but as a rebel. And if he does not reform after repeated admonitions, let even the Bishop be brought in as a witness. If then he still fails to amend, and his offenses are notorious, let him be put out of the monastery, but only if his contumacy is such that he refuses to submit or to obey the Rule.

Chapter 63—On the Order of the Community

Apr. 18—Aug. 18—Dec. 18

Let all keep their places in the monastery established by the time of their entrance, the merit of their lives and the decision of the Abbot. Yet the Abbot must not disturb the flock committed to him, nor by an arbitrary use of his power ordain anything unjustly; but let him always think of the account he will have to render to God for all his decisions and his deeds.

Therefore in that order which he has established or which they already had, let the brethren approach to receive the kiss of peace and Communion, intone the Psalms and stand in choir. And in no place whatever should age decide the order or be prejudicial to it; for Samuel and Daniel as mere boys judged priests.

Except for those already mentioned, therefore, whom the Abbot has promoted by a special decision or demoted for definite reasons, all the rest shall take their order according to the time of their entrance. Thus, for example, he who came to the monastery at the second hour of the day, whatever be his age or his dignity, must know that he is junior to one who came at the first hour of the day. Boys, however, are to be kept under discipline in all matters and by everyone.

Apr. 19—Aug. 19—Dec. 19

The juniors, therefore, should honor their seniors, and the seniors love their juniors.

In the very manner of address, let no one call another by the mere name; but let the seniors call their juniors Brothers, and the juniors call their seniors Fathers, by which is conveyed the reverence due to a father. But the Abbot, since he is believed to represent Christ, shall be called

Lord and Abbot, not for any pretensions of his own but out of honor and love for Christ. Let the Abbot himself reflect on this, and show himself worthy of such an honor.

And wherever the brethren meet one another the junior shall ask the senior for his blessing. When a senior passes by, a junior shall rise and give him a place to sit, nor shall the junior presume to sit with him unless his senior bid him, that it may be as was written, "In honor anticipating one another."

Boys, both small and adolescent, shall keep strictly to their rank in oratory and at table. But outside of that, wherever they may be, let them be under supervision and discipline, until they come to the age of discretion.

Chapter 64—On Constituting an Abbot

Apr. 20—Aug. 20—Dec. 20
In the constituting of an Abbot let this plan always be followed, that the office be conferred on the one who is chosen either by the whole community unanimously in the fear of God or else by a part of the community, however small, if its counsel is more wholesome.

Merit of life and wisdom of doctrine should determine the choice of the one to be constituted, even if he be the last in the order of the community.

But if (which God forbid) the whole community should agree to choose a person who will acquiesce in their vices, and if those vices somehow become known to the Bishop to whose diocese the place belongs, or to the Abbots or the faithful of the vicinity, let them prevent the success of this conspiracy of the wicked, and set a worthy steward over the house of God. They may be sure that they will receive a good reward for this action if they do it with a pure intention and out of zeal for God; as, on the contrary, they will sin if they fail to do it.

Apr. 21—Aug. 21—Dec. 21
Once he has been constituted, let the Abbot always bear in mind what a burden he has undertaken and to whom he will have to give an account of his stewardship, and let him know that his duty is rather to profit his brethren than to

preside over them. He must therefore be learned in the divine law, that he may have a treasure of knowledge from which to bring forth new things and old. He must be chaste, sober and merciful. Let him exalt mercy above judgment, that he himself may obtain mercy. He should hate vices; he should love the brethren.

In administering correction he should act prudently and not go to excess, lest in seeking too eagerly to scrape off the rust he break the vessel. Let him keep his own frailty ever before his eyes and remember that the bruised reed must not be broken. By this we do not mean that he should allow vices to grow; on the contrary, as we have already said, he should eradicate them prudently and with charity, in the way which may seem best in each case. Let him study rather to be loved than to be feared.

Let him not be excitable and worried, nor exacting and headstrong, nor jealous and over-suspicious; for then he is never at rest.

In his commands let him be prudent and considerate; and whether the work which he enjoins concerns God or the world, let him be discreet and moderate, bearing in mind the discretion of holy Jacob, who said, "If I cause my flocks to be overdriven, they will all die in one day." Taking this, then, and other examples of discretion, the mother of virtues, let him so temper all things that the strong may have something to strive after, and the weak may not fall back in dismay.

And especially let him keep this Rule in all its details, so that after a good ministry he may hear from the Lord what the good servant heard who gave his fellow-servants wheat in due season: "Indeed, I tell you, he will set him over all his goods."

Chapter 65—On the Prior of the Monastery

Apr. 22—Aug. 22—Dec. 22
It happens all too often that the constituting of a Prior gives rise to grave scandals in monasteries. For there are some who become inflated with the evil spirit of pride and consider themselves second Abbots. By usurping power they foster scandals and cause dissensions in the community. Especially does this happen in those places where the Prior is constituted by the same Bishop or the

same Abbots who constitute the Abbot himself. What an absurd procedure this is can easily be seen; for it gives the Prior an occasion for becoming proud from the very time of his constitution, by putting the thought into his mind that he is freed from the authority of his Abbot: "For," he will say to himself, "you were constituted by the same persons who constituted the Abbot." From this source are stirred up envy, quarrels, detraction, rivalry, dissensions and disorders. For while the Abbot and the Prior are at variance, their souls cannot but be endangered by this dissension; and those who are under them, currying favor with one side or the other, go to ruin. The guilt for this dangerous state of affairs rests on the heads of those whose action brought about such disorder.

Apr. 23—Aug. 23—Dec. 23
To us, therefore, it seems expedient for the preservation of peace and charity that the Abbot have in his hands the full administration of his monastery. And if possible let all the affairs of the monastery, as we have already arranged, be administered by deans according to the Abbot's directions. Thus, with the duties being shared by several, no one person will become proud.

But if the circumstances of the place require it, or if the community asks for it with reason and with humility, and the Abbot judges it to be expedient, let the Abbot himself constitute as his Prior whomsoever he shall choose with the counsel of God-fearing brethren.

That Prior, however, shall perform respectfully the duties enjoined on him by his Abbot and do nothing against the Abbot's will or direction; for the more he is raised above the rest, the more carefully should he observe the precepts of the Rule.

If it should be found that the Prior has serious faults, or that he is deceived by his exaltation and yields to pride, or if he should be proved to be a despiser of the Holy Rule, let him be admonished verbally up to four times. If he fails to amend, let the correction of regular discipline be applied to him. But if even then he does not reform, let him be deposed from the office of Prior and another be appointed in his place who is worthy of it. And if afterwards he is not quiet and obedient in the community, let him even be expelled from

the monastery. But the Abbot, for his part, should bear in mind that he will have to render an account to God for all his judgments, lest the flame of envy or jealousy be kindled in his soul.

Chapter 66—On the Porters of the Monastery

Apr. 24—Aug. 24—Dec. 24
At the gate of the monastery let there be placed a wise old man, who knows how to receive and to give a message, and whose maturity will prevent him from straying about. This porter should have a room near the gate, so that those who come may always find someone at hand to attend to their business. And as soon as anyone knocks or a poor man hails him, let him answer "Thanks be to God" or "A blessing!" Then let him attend to them promptly, with all the meekness inspired by the fear of God and with the warmth of charity.

Should the porter need help, let him have one of the younger brethren.

If it can be done, the monastery should be so established that all the necessary things, such as water, mill, garden and various workshops, may be within the enclosure, so that there is no necessity for the monks to go about outside of it, since that is not at all profitable for their souls.

We desire that this Rule be read often in the community, so that none of the brethren may excuse himself on the ground of ignorance.

Chapter 67—On Brethren Who Are Sent on a Journey

Apr. 25—Aug. 25—Dec. 25
Let the brethren who are sent on a journey commend themselves to the prayers of all the brethren and of the Abbot; and always at the last prayer of the Work of God let a commemoration be made of all absent brethren.

When brethren return from a journey, at the end of each canonical Hour of the Work of God on the day they return, let them lie prostrate on the floor of the oratory and beg the prayers of all on account of any faults that may have surprised them on the road, through the seeing or hearing of something evil, or through idle talk. And let no one presume to tell another whatever he may have seen or heard outside of the monastery, because this causes very great harm. But if anyone presumes to do so, let him undergo the punishment of the Rule. And let him be punished likewise who would presume to leave the enclosure of the monastery and go anywhere or do anything, however small, without an order from the Abbot.

Chapter 68—If a Brother Is Commanded to Do Impossible Things

Apr. 26—Aug. 26—Dec. 26

If it happens that difficult or impossible tasks are laid on a brother, let him nevertheless receive the order of the one in authority with all meekness and obedience. But if he sees that the weight of the burden altogether exceeds the limit of his strength, let him submit the reasons for his inability to the one who is over him and in a quiet way and at an opportune time, without pride, resistance, or contradiction. And if after these representations the Superior still persists in his decision and command, let the subject know that this is for his good, and let him obey out of love, trusting in the help of God.

Chapter 69—That the Monks Presume Not to Defend One Another

Apr. 27—Aug. 27—Dec. 27

Care must be taken that no monk presume on any ground to defend another monk in the monastery, or as it were to take him under his protection, even though they be united by some tie of blood-relationship. Let not the monks dare to do this in any way whatsoever, because it may give rise to most serious scandals. But if anyone breaks this rule, let him be severely punished.

Chapter 70—That No One Venture to Punish at Random

Apr. 28—Aug. 28—Dec. 28

Every occasion of presumption shall be avoided in the monastery, and we decree that no one be allowed to excommunicate or to strike any of his brethren unless the Abbot has given him the authority. Those who offend in this matter shall be rebuked in the presence of all, that the rest may have fear.

But boys up to 15 years of age shall be carefully controlled and watched by all, yet this too with all moderation and discretion. Anyone, therefore, who presumes without the Abbot's instructions to punish those above that age or who loses his temper with the boys, shall undergo the discipline of the Rule; for it is written, "Do not to another what you would not want done to yourself."

Chapter 71—That the Brethren Be Obedient to One Another

Apr. 29—Aug. 29—Dec. 29

Not only is the boon of obedience to be shown by all to the Abbot, but the brethren are also to obey one another, knowing that by this road of obedience they are going to God. Giving priority, therefore, to the commands of the Abbot and of the Superiors appointed by him (to which we allow no private orders to be preferred), for the rest let all the juniors obey their seniors with all charity and solicitude. But if anyone is found contentious, let him be corrected.

And if any brother, for however small a cause, is corrected in any way by the Abbot or by any of his Superiors, or if he faintly perceives that the mind of any Superior is angered or moved against him, however little, let him at once, without delay, prostrate himself on the ground at his feet and lie there making satisfaction until that emotion is quieted with a blessing. But if anyone should disdain to do this, let him undergo corporal punishment or, if he is stubborn, let him be expelled from the monastery.

Chapter 72—On the Good Zeal Which Monks Ought to Have

Apr. 30—Aug. 30—Dec. 30

Just as there is an evil zeal of bitterness which separates from God and leads to hell, so there is a good zeal which separates from vices and leads to God and to life everlasting. This zeal, therefore, the monks should practice with the most fervent love. Thus they should anticipate one another in honor; most patiently endure one another's infirmities, whether of body or of character; vie in paying obedience one to another—no one following what he considers useful for himself, but rather what benefits another—; tender the charity of brotherhood chastely; fear God in love; love their Abbot with a sincere and humble charity; prefer nothing whatever to Christ. And may He bring us all together to life everlasting!

Chapter 73—On the Fact That the Full Observance of Justice Is Not Established in This Rule

May 1—Aug. 31—Dec. 31
Now we have written this Rule in order that by its observance in monasteries we may show that we have attained some degree of virtue and the rudiments of the religious life.

But for him who would hasten to the perfection of that life there are the teachings of the holy Fathers, the observance of which leads a man to the height of perfection. For what page or what utterance of the divinely inspired books of the Old and New Testaments is not a most unerring role for human life? Or what book of the holy Catholic Fathers does not loudly proclaim how we may come by a straight course to our Creator? Then the Conferences and the Institutes and the Lives of the Fathers, as also the Rule of our holy Father Basil—what else are they but tools of virtue for right-living and obedient monks? But for us who are lazy and ill-living and negligent they are a source of shame and confusion.

Whoever you are, therefore, who are hastening to the heavenly homeland, fulfil with the help of Christ this minimum Rule which we have written for beginners; and then at length under God's protection you will attain to the loftier heights of doctrine and virtue which we have mentioned above.

13. GREGORY THE GREAT

Dialogues

THE BOOK OF *DIALOGUES* traditionally attributed to Pope Gregory the Great (589–604) spread the fame of Benedict across Europe and was one of the most important hagiographical texts (relating the life and miracles of a saint) of the Middle Ages. The second book, *A Life of Benedict of Nursia*, became a model for lives of monastic saints. In this text, the discussion between a master and his student describes Benedict's life and presents him as a model for ascetic devotional practices.

Source: Odo John Zimmerman (ed. and trans.), *Saint Gregory the Great, Dialogues* (New York: The Fathers of the Church, 1959), 55–110.

Further Reading: R. Markus, *Gregory the Great and His World* (Cambridge: Cambridge University Press, 1997).

Book II

Life and Miracles of St. Benedict Founder and Abbot of the Monastery Which Is Known as the Citadel of Campania.

There was a man of saintly life; blessed Benedict was his name, and he was blessed also with God's grace. Even in boyhood he showed mature understanding, for he kept his heart detached from every pleasure with a strength of character far beyond his years. While still living in the world, free to enjoy its earthly advantages, he saw how barren it was with its attractions and turned from it without regret.

He was born in the district of Norcia[1] of distinguished parents, who sent him back to Rome for a liberal education. But when he saw many of his fellow students falling headlong into vice, he stepped back from the threshold of the world in which he had just set foot. For he was afraid that if he acquired any of its learning, he, too, would later plunge, body and soul, into the dread abyss. In his desire to please God alone, he turned his back on further studies, gave up home and inheritance and resolved to embrace the religious life. He took this step, well aware of his ignorance, yet wise, uneducated though he was.

I was unable to learn about all his miraculous deeds. But the few that I am going to relate I know from the lips of four of his own disciples: Constantine, the holy man who succeeded him as abbot; Valentinian, for many years superior of the monastery at the Lateran; Simplicius, Benedict's second successor; and Honoratus, who is still abbot of the monastery where the man of God first lived.

(1) When Benedict abandoned his studies to go into solitude, he was accompanied only by his nurse, who loved him dearly. As they were passing through Affile, a number of devout men invited them to stay there and provided them with lodging near the Church of St. Peter. One day, after asking her neighbors to lend her a tray for cleaning wheat, the nurse happened to leave it on the edge of the table and when she came back found it had slipped off and broken in two. The poor woman burst into tears; she had only borrowed this tray and now it was ruined. Benedict, who had always been a devout and thoughtful boy, felt sorry for his nurse when he saw her weeping. Quietly picking up both the pieces, he knelt down by himself and prayed earnestly to God, even to the point of tears. No sooner had he finished his prayer than he noticed that the two pieces were joined together again, without even a mark to show where the

---

1   A little town about seventy miles northeast of Rome. The saint was born around 480.

tray had been broken. Hurrying back at once, he cheerfully reassured his nurse and handed her the tray in perfect condition.

News of the miracle spread to all the country around Affile and stirred up so much admiration among the people that they hung the tray at the entrance to their church. Ever since then it has been a reminder to all of the great holiness Benedict had acquired at the very outset of his monastic life. The tray remained there many years for everyone to see, and it is still hanging over the doorway of the church in these days of Lombard rule.[2] Benedict, however, preferred to suffer ill-treatment from the world rather than enjoy its praises. He wanted to spend himself laboring for God, not to be honored by the applause of men. So he stole away secretly from his nurse and fled to a lonely wilderness about thirty-five miles from Rome called Subiaco. A stream of cold, clear water running through the region broadens out at this point to form a lake, then flows off and continues on its course.[3] On his way there Benedict met a monk named Romanus, who asked him where he was going. After discovering the young man's purpose, Romanus kept it secret and even helped him carry it out by clothing him with the monastic habit and supplying his needs as well as he could.

At Subiaco, Benedict made his home in a narrow cave and for three years remained concealed there, unknown to anyone except the monk Romanus, who lived in a monastery close by under the rule of Abbot Deodatus. With fatherly concern this monk regularly set aside as much bread as he could from his own portion; then from time to time, unnoticed by his abbot, he left the monastery long enough to take the bread to Benedict. There was no path leading from the monastery down to his cave because of a cliff that rose directly over it. To reach him Romanus had to tie the bread to the end of a long rope and lower it over the cliff. A little bell attached to the rope let Benedict know when the bread was there, and he would come out to get it. The ancient Enemy of mankind grew envious of the kindness shown by

the older monk in supplying Benedict with food, and one day, as the bread was being lowered, he threw a stone at the bell and broke it. In spite of this, Romanus kept on with his faithful service.

At length the time came when almighty God wished to grant him rest from his toil and reveal Benedict's virtuous life to others. Like a shining lamp his example was to be set on a lampstand to give light to everyone in God's house. The Lord therefore appeared in a vision to a priest some distance away, who had just prepared his Easter dinner. "How can you prepare these delicacies for yourself," He asked, "while my servant is out there in the wilds suffering from hunger?"

Rising at once, the priest wrapped up the food and set out to find the man of God that very day. He searched for him along the rough mountain-sides, in the valleys, and through the caverns, until he found him hidden in the cave. They said a prayer of thanksgiving together and then sat down to talk about the spiritual life. After a while the priest suggested that they take their meal. "Today is the great feast of Easter," he added.

"It must be a great feast to have brought me this kind visit," the man of God replied, not realizing after his long separation from men that it was Easter Sunday.

"Today is really Easter," the priest insisted, "the feast of our Lord's Resurrection. On such a solemn occasion you should not be fasting. Besides, I was sent here by almighty God so that both of us could share in His gifts."

After that they said grace and began their meal. When it was over they conversed some more and then the priest went back to his church.

At about the same time some shepherds also discovered Benedict's hiding place. When they first looked through the thickets and caught sight of him clothed in rough skins, they mistook him for some wild animal. Soon, however, they recognized in him a servant of God, and many of them gave up their sinful ways for a life of holiness. As a result, his name became known to all the people in that locality and great numbers visited his cave, supplying him with the food he needed and

---

2   The Lombards, a Germanic people, left their homes along the upper Danube and invaded Italy in 568, establishing a kingdom there which lasted until 774.

3   Subiaco lies along the Anio River about five miles north of Affile. The lake St. Gregory speaks of gave the site its Latin name of *Sublacum*. It was formed by a dam which Emperor Claudius had built across the river, and lasted until 1305 when the dam was destroyed by floods.

receiving from his lips in return spiritual food for their souls.

(2) One day, while the saint was alone, the Tempter came in the form of a little blackbird, which began to flutter in front of his face. It kept so close that he could easily have caught it in his hand. Instead, he made the sign of the cross and the bird flew away. The moment it left, he was seized with an unusually violent temptation. The evil spirit recalled to his mind a woman he had once seen, and before he realized it his emotions were carrying him away. Almost overcome in the struggle, he was on the point of abandoning the lonely wilderness, when suddenly with the help of God's grace he came to himself.

He then noticed a thick patch of nettles and briers next to him. Throwing his garment aside he flung himself into the sharp thorns and stinging nettles. There he rolled and tossed until his whole body was in pain and covered with blood. Yet, once he had conquered pleasure through suffering, his torn and bleeding skin served to drain the poison of temptation from his body. Before long, the pain that was burning his whole body had put out the fires of evil in his heart. It was by exchanging these two fires that he gained the victory over sin. So complete was his triumph that from then on, as he later told his disciples, he never experienced another temptation of this kind.

Soon after, many forsook the world to place themselves under his guidance, for now that he was free from these temptations he was ready to instruct others in the practice of virtue. That is why Moses commanded the Levites to begin their service when they were twenty-five years old or more and to become guardians of the sacred vessels only at the age of fifty.

Peter: The meaning of the passage you quote is becoming a little clearer to me now. Still, I wish you would explain it more fully.

Gregory: It is a well-known fact, Peter, that temptations of the flesh are violent during youth, whereas after the age of fifty concupiscence dies down. Now, the sacred vessels are the souls of the faithful. God's chosen servants must therefore obey and serve and tire themselves out with strenuous work as long as they are still subject to temptations. Only when full maturity has left them undisturbed by evil thoughts are they put in charge of the sacred vessels, for then they become teachers of souls.

Peter: I like the way you interpreted that passage. Now that you have explained what it means, I hope you will continue with your account of the holy man's life.

Gregory: (3) With the passing of this temptation, Benedict's soul, like a field cleared of briers, soon yielded a rich harvest of virtues. As word spread of his saintly life, the renown of his name increased. One day the entire community from a nearby monastery[4] came to see him. Their abbot had recently died, and they wanted the man of God to be their new superior. For some time he tried to discourage them by refusing their request, warning them that his way of life would never harmonize with theirs. But they kept insisting, until in the end he gave his consent.

At the monastery he watched carefully over the religious spirit of the monks and would not tolerate any of their previous disobedience. No one was allowed to turn from the straight path of monastic discipline either to the right or to the left. Their waywardness, however, clashed with the standards he upheld, and in their resentment they started to reproach themselves for choosing him as abbot. It only made them the more sullen to find him curbing every fault and every evil habit. They could not see why they should have to force their settled minds into new ways of thinking.

At length, proving once again that the very life of the just is a burden to the wicked, they tried to find a means of doing away with him and decided to poison his wine. A glass pitcher containing this poisoned drink was presented to the man of God during his meal for the customary blessing. As he made the sign of the cross over it with his hand, the pitcher was shattered, even though it was well beyond his reach at the time. It broke at his blessing as if he had struck it with stone.

Then he realized it had contained a deadly drink which could not bear the sign of life. Still calm and undisturbed, he rose at once and, after

---

4   Usually identified as Vicovaro, about twenty miles farther down the Anio.

gathering the community together, addressed them. "May almighty God have mercy on you," he said. "Why did you conspire to do this? Did I not tell you at the outset that my way of life would never harmonize with yours? Go and find yourselves an abbot to your liking. It is impossible for me to stay here any longer." Then he went back to the wilderness he loved, to live alone with himself in the presence of his heavenly Father.

Peter: I am not quite sure I understand what you mean by saying "to live with himself."

Gregory: These monks had an outlook on religious life entirely unlike his own and were all conspiring against him. Now, if he had tried to force them to remain under his rule, he might have forfeited his own fervor and peace of soul and even turned his eyes from the light of contemplation. Their persistent daily faults would have left him almost too weary to look to his own needs, and he would perhaps have forsaken himself without finding them. For, whenever anxieties carry us out of ourselves unduly, we are no longer with ourselves even though we still remain what we are. We are too distracted with other matters to give any attention whatever to ourselves.

Surely we cannot describe as "with himself" the young man who traveled to a distant country where he wasted his inheritance and then, after hiring himself out to one of its citizens to feed swine, had to watch them eat their fill of pods while he went hungry. Do we not read in Scripture that, as he was considering all he had lost, "he came to himself and said, 'how many hired servants there are in my father's house that have more bread than they can eat'"? If he was already "with himself," how could he have come "to himself"?

Blessed Benedict, on the contrary, can be said to have lived "with himself" because at all times he kept such close watch over his life and actions. By searching continually into his own soul he always beheld himself in the presence of his Creator. And this kept his mind from straying off to the world outside.

Peter: But what of Peter the Apostle when he was led out of prison by an angel? According to the

Scriptures, he, too, "came to himself." "Now I can tell for certain," he said, "that the Lord has sent his angel, to deliver me out of Herod's hands, and from all that the people of the Jews hoped to see."

Gregory: There are two ways in which we can be carried out of ourselves, Peter. Either we fall below ourselves through sins of thought or we are lifted above ourselves by the grace of contemplation. The young man who fed the swine sank below himself as a result of his shiftless ways and his unclean life. The Apostle Peter was also out of himself when the angel set him free and raised him to a state of ecstasy, but he was above himself. In coming to themselves again, the former had to break with his sinful past before he could find his true and better self, whereas the latter merely returned from the heights of contemplation to his ordinary state of mind.

Now, the saintly Benedict really lived "with himself" out in that lonely wilderness by always keeping his thoughts recollected. Yet he must have left his own self far below each time he was drawn heavenward in fervent contemplation.

Peter: I am very grateful to you for that explanation. Do you think it was right, though, for him to forsake this community, once he had taken it under his care?

Gregory: In my opinion, Peter, a superior ought to bear patiently with a community of evil men as long as it has some devout members who can benefit from his presence. When none of the members is devout enough to give any promise of good results, his efforts to help such a community will prove to be a serious mistake, especially if there are opportunities nearby to work more fruitfully for God. Was there anyone the holy man could have hoped to protect by staying where he was, after he saw that they were all united against him?

In this matter we cannot afford to overlook the attitude of the saints. When they find their work producing no results in one place, they move on to another where it can do some good. This explains the action of the blessed Apostle Paul. In order to escape from Damascus, where he was being persecuted, he secured a basket and a rope and had himself secretly lowered over the wall. Yet this outstanding preacher of the Gospel longed to depart and be with Christ, since for him life meant Christ, and death was a prize to be won. Besides being eager for the trials of persecution himself, he even inspired others to endure them. Can we say that Paul feared death, when he expressly declared that he longed to die for the love of Christ? Surely not. But, when he saw how little he was accomplishing at Damascus in spite of all his toil, he saved himself for more fruitful labors elsewhere. God's fearless warrior refused to be held back inside the walls and sought the open field of battle.

Peter: I am sure your conclusion is correct, after the simple proof you gave and that striking example from sacred Scripture. Would you be good enough to return now to the story of this great abbot's life?

Gregory: As Benedict's influence spread over the surrounding countryside because of his signs and wonders, a great number of men gathered round him to devote themselves to God's service. Christ blessed his work and before long he had established twelve monasteries there, with an abbot and twelve monks in each of them. There were a few monks whom he kept with him, since he felt that they still needed his personal guidance.

It was about this time that pious noblemen from Rome first came to visit the saint and left their sons with him to be schooled in the service of God. Thus, Euthicius brought his son Maurus; and Senator Tertullus, Placid—both very promising boys. Maurus, in fact, who was a little older, had already acquired solid virtue and was soon very helpful to his saintly master. But Placid was still only a child.

(4) In one of the monasteries Benedict had founded in that locality, there was a monk who would never remain with the rest of the community for silent prayer. Instead, he left the chapel as soon as they knelt down to pray, and passed the time aimlessly at whatever happened to interest him. His abbot corrected him repeatedly and at length sent him to the man of God. This time the monk received a stern rebuke for his folly and after his return took the correction to heart for a day or two, only to fall back the third day into his old habit of wandering off during the time of

prayer. On learning of this from the abbot, the man of God sent word that he was coming over himself to see that the monk mended his ways.

Upon his arrival at the monastery, Benedict joined the community in the chapel at the regular hour. After they had finished chanting the psalms and had begun their silent prayer, he noticed that the restless monk was drawn outside by a little black boy who was pulling at the edge of his habit.

"Do you see who is leading that monk out of the chapel?" he whispered to Abbot Pompeianus and Maurus.

"No," they replied.

"Let us pray, then," he said, "that you may see what is happening to him."

They prayed for two days, and after that Maurus also saw what was taking place, but Abbot Pompeianus still could not. The next day, when prayers were over, Benedict found the offender loitering outside and struck him with his staff for being so obstinate of heart. From then on the monk remained quietly at prayer like the rest, without being bothered again by the Tempter. It was as if that ancient Enemy had been struck by the blow himself and was afraid to domineer over the monk's thoughts any longer.

(5) Three of the monasteries the saint had built close by stood on the bare rocky heights. It was a real hardship for these monks always to go down to the lake to get water for their daily needs. Besides, the slope was steep and they found the descent very dangerous. The members of the three communities therefore came in a body to see the servant of God. After explaining how difficult it was for them to climb down the mountainside every day for their water supply, they assured him that the only solution was to have the monasteries moved somewhere else.

Benedict answered them with fatherly words of encouragement and sent them back. That same night, in company with the little boy Placid, he climbed to the rocky heights and prayed there for a long time. On finishing his prayer, he placed three stones together to indicate the spot where he had knelt and then went back to his monastery, unnoticed by anyone.

The following day, when the monks came again with their request, he told them to go to the summit of the mountain. "You will find three stones there," he said, "one on top of the other. If you dig down a little, you will see that almighty God has the power to bring forth water even from that rocky summit and in His goodness relieve you of the hardship of such a long climb."

Going back to the place he had described, they noticed that the surface was already moist. As soon as they had dug the ground away, water filled the hollow and welled up in such abundance that today a full stream is still flowing from the top of the mountain into the ravine below.

(6) At another time a simple, sincere Goth came to Subiaco to become a monk, and blessed Benedict was very happy to admit him. One day he had him take a brush hook and clear away the briers from a place at the edge of the lake where a garden was to be planted. While the Goth was hard at work cutting down the thick brush, the iron blade slipped off the handle and flew into a very deep part of the lake, where there was no hope of recovering it.

At this the poor man ran trembling to Maurus and, after describing the accident, told him how sorry he was for his carelessness. Maurus in turn informed the servant of God, who on hearing what had happened went down to the lake, took the handle from the Goth and thrust it in the water. Immediately the iron blade rose from the bottom of the lake and slipped back onto the handle. Then he handed the tool back to the Goth and told him, "Continue with your work now. There is no need to be upset."

(7) Once while blessed Benedict was in his room, one of his monks, the boy Placid, went down to the lake to draw water. In letting the bucket fill too rapidly, he lost his balance and was pulled into the lake, where the current quickly seized him and carried him about a stone's throw from the shore. Though inside the monastery at the time, the man of God was instantly aware of what had happened and called out to Maurus: "Hurry, Brother Maurus! The boy who just went down for water has fallen into the lake, and the current is carrying him away."

What followed was remarkable indeed, and unheard of since the time of Peter the Apostle! Maurus asked for the blessing and on receiving it hurried out to fulfill his abbot's command. He kept on running even over the water till he reached the place where Placid was drifting along helplessly. Pulling him up by the hair, Maurus rushed back to shore, still under the impression that he was on dry land. It was only when he set foot on the ground that he came to himself and looking back realized that he had been running on the surface of the water. Overcome with fear and amazement at a deed he would never have thought possible, he returned to his abbot and told him what had taken place.

The holy man would not take any personal credit for the deed, but attributed it to the obedience of his disciple. Maurus, on the contrary, claimed that it was due entirely to his abbot's command. He could not have been responsible for the miracle himself, he said, since he had not even known he was performing it. While they were carrying on this friendly contest of humility, the question was settled by the boy who had been rescued. "When I was being drawn out of the water," he told them, "I saw the abbot's cloak over my head; he is the one I thought was bringing me to shore."

Peter: What marvelous deeds these are! They are sure to prove inspiring to all who hear of them. Indeed, the more you tell me about this great man, the more eager I am to keep on listening.

Gregory: (8) By this time the people of that whole region for miles around had grown fervent in their love for Christ, and many of them had forsaken the world in order to bring their hearts under the light yoke of the Savior. Now, in a neighboring church there was a priest named Florentius, the grandfather of our subdeacon Florentius. Urged on by the bitter Enemy of mankind, this priest set out to undermine the saint's work. And envious as the wicked always are of the holiness in others which they are not striving to acquire themselves, he denounced Benedict's way of life and kept everyone he could from visiting him.

The progress of the saint's work, however, could not be stopped. His reputation for holiness kept on growing, and with it the number of vocations to a more perfect state of life. This infuriated Florentius all the more. He still longed to enjoy the praise the saint was receiving, yet he was unwilling to lead a praiseworthy life himself.

At length, his soul became so blind with jealousy that he decided to poison a loaf of bread and send it to the servant of God as though it was a sign of Christian fellowship.

Though aware at once of the deadly poison it contained, Benedict thanked him for the gift.

At mealtime a raven used to come out of the nearby woods to receive food from the saint's hands. On this occasion he set the poisoned loaf in front of it and said, "In the name of our Lord Jesus Christ, take this bread and carry it to a place where no one will be able to find it." The raven started to caw and circled round the loaf of bread with open beak and flapping wings as if to indicate that it was willing to obey, but found it impossible to do so. Several times the saint repeated the command. "Take the bread," he said, "and do not be afraid! Take it away from here and leave it where no one will find it." After hesitating a long while, the raven finally took the loaf in its beak and flew away. About three hours later, when it had disposed of the bread, it returned and received its usual meal from the hands of the man of God.

The saintly abbot now realized how deep the resentment of his enemy was, and he felt grieved not so much for his own sake as for the priest's. But Florentius, after his failure to do away with the master, determined instead to destroy the souls of the disciples and for this purpose sent seven depraved women into the garden of Benedict's monastery. There they joined hands and danced together for some time within sight of his followers, in an attempt to lead them into sin.

When the saint noticed this from his window, he began to fear that some of his younger monks might go astray. Convinced that the priest's hatred for him was the real cause of this attack, he let envy have its way, and, taking only a few monks with him, set out to find a new home. Before he left, he reorganized all the monasteries he had founded, appointing priors to assist in governing them, and adding some new members to the communities.

Hardly had the man of God made his humble escape from all this bitterness when almighty God struck the priest down with terrible vengeance. As he was standing on the balcony of his house congratulating himself on Benedict's departure, the structure suddenly collapsed, crushing him to death, though the rest of the building remained undamaged. This accident occurred before the saint was even ten miles away. His disciple Maurus immediately decided to send a messenger with the news and ask him to return, now that the priest who had caused him so much trouble was dead. Benedict was overcome with sorrow and regret on hearing this, for not only had his enemy been killed, but one of his own disciples had rejoiced over his death. And for showing pleasure in such a message he gave Maurus a penance to perform.

Peter: This whole account is really amazing. The water streaming from the rock reminds me of Moses, and the iron blade that rose from the bottom of the lake, of Eliseus. The walking on the water recalls St. Peter, the obedience of the raven, Elias, and the grief at the death of an enemy, David. This man must have been filled with the spirit of all the just.

Gregory: Actually, Peter, blessed Benedict possessed the Spirit of only one Person, the Savior who fills the hearts of all the faithful by granting them the fruits of His Redemption. For St. John says of Him, "There is one who enlightens every soul born into the world; he was the true light." And again, "we have all received something out of his abundance." Holy men never were able to hand on to others the miraculous powers which they received from God. Our Savior was the only one to give His followers the power to work signs and wonders, just as He alone could assure His enemies that He would give them the sign of the prophet Jonas. Seeing this sign fulfilled in His death, the proud looked on with scorn. The humble, who saw its complete fulfillment in His rising from the dead, turned to Him with reverence and love. In this mystery, then, the proud beheld Him dying in disgrace, whereas the humble witnessed His triumph over death.

Peter: Now that you have finished explaining this, please tell me where the holy man settled after his departure. Do you know whether he performed any more miracles?

Gregory: Although he moved to a different place, Peter, his enemy remained the same. In fact, the assaults he had to endure after this were all the more violent, because the very Master of evil was fighting against him in open battle.

The fortified town of Cassino lies at the foot of a towering mountain that shelters it within its slope and stretches upward over a distance of nearly three miles.[5] On its summit stood a very old temple, in which the ignorant country people still worshipped Apollo as their pagan ancestors had done, and went on offering superstitious and idolatrous sacrifices in groves dedicated to various demons.

When the man of God arrived at this spot, he destroyed the idol, overturned the altar and cut down the trees in the sacred groves.[6] Then he turned the temple of Apollo into a chapel dedicated to St. Martin,[7] and where Apollo's altar had stood, he built a chapel in honor of St. John the Baptist. Gradually, the people of the countryside were won over to the true faith by his zealous preaching.

Such losses the ancient Enemy could not bear in silence. This time he did not appear to the saint in a dream or under a disguise, but met him face to face and objected fiercely to the outrages he had to endure. His shouts were so loud that the brethren heard him, too, although they were unable to see him. According to the saint's own description, the Devil had an appearance utterly revolting to human eyes. He was enveloped in fire and, when he raged against the man of God, flames darted from his eyes and mouth. Everyone could hear what he was saying. First he called Benedict by name. Then, finding that the saint would not answer, he broke out in abusive language. "Benedict, Benedict, blessed Benedict!" he would begin, and then add, "You cursed Benedict! Cursed, not blessed! What do you want with me? Why are you tormenting me like this?"

From now on, Peter, as you can well imagine, the Devil fought against the man of God with renewed violence. But, contrary to his plans, all

these attacks only supplied the saint with further opportunities for victory.

(9) One day while the monks were constructing a section of the abbey, they noticed a rock lying close at hand and decided to use it in the building. When two or three did not succeed in lifting it, others joined in to help. Yet it remained fixed in its place as though it was rooted to the ground. Then they were sure that the Devil himself was sitting on this stone and preventing them from moving it in spite of all their efforts.

Faced with this difficulty, they asked Abbot Benedict to come and use his prayers to drive away the Devil who was holding down the rock. The saint began to pray as soon as he got there, and after he had finished and made the sign of the cross, the monks picked up the rock with such care that it seemed to have lost all its previous weight.

(10) The abbot then directed them to spade up the earth where the stone had been. When they had dug a little way into the ground they came upon a bronze idol, which they threw into the kitchen for the time being. Suddenly the kitchen appeared to be on fire and everyone felt that the entire building was going up in flames. The noise and commotion they made in their attempt to put out the blaze by pouring on buckets of water brought Benedict to the scene. Unable to see the fire which appeared so real to his monks, he quietly bowed his head in prayer and soon had opened their eyes to the foolish mistake they were making. Now, instead of the flames the evil spirit had devised, they once more saw the kitchen standing intact.

(11) On another occasion they were working on one of the walls that had to be built a little higher. The man of God was in his room at the time, praying, when the Devil appeared to him and remarked sarcastically that he was on his way to visit the brethren at their work. Benedict quickly sent them word to be on their guard against the evil spirit who would soon be with them. Just as they received his warning, the Devil overturned the

---

5   St. Gregory is referring to the winding path that led up the mountain. The altitude of Monte Cassino is 1,500 feet.

6   Monte Cassino is about seventy-five miles southeast of Rome. St. Benedict arrived there in 529. In addition to the pagan shrines mentioned by St. Gregory, there was also a very ancient fortress on the summit for the defense of the townspeople below and the surrounding plains. The Abbey of Monte Cassino was built entirely within the walls of the fortress and was for that reason known at first as the Citadel of Campania, as we learn from the full title of this book.

7   St. Martin of Tours.

wall, crushing under its ruins the body of a very young monk who was the son of a tax collector.

Unconcerned about the damaged wall in their grief and dismay over the loss of their brother, the monks hurried to Abbot Benedict to let him know of the dreadful accident. He told them to bring the mangled body to his room. It had to be carried in on a blanket, for the wall had not only broken the boy's arms and legs but had crushed all the bones in his body. The saint had the remains placed on the reed matting where he used to pray and after that told them all to leave. Then he closed the door and knelt down to offer his most earnest prayers to God. That very hour, to the astonishment of all, he sent the boy back to his work as sound and healthy as he had been before. Thus, in spite of the Devil's attempt to mock the man of God by causing this tragic death, the young monk was able to rejoin his brethren and help them finish the wall.

Meanwhile, Benedict began to manifest the spirit of prophecy by foretelling future events and by describing to those who were with him what they had done in his absence.

(12) It was a custom of the house, strictly observed as a matter of regular discipline, that monks away on business did not take food or drink outside the monastery. One day, a few of them went out on assignment which kept them occupied till rather late. They stopped for a meal at the house of a devout woman they knew in the neighborhood. On their return, when they presented themselves to the abbot for the usual blessing, he asked them where they had taken their meal.

"Nowhere," they answered.

"Why are you lying to me?" he said. "Did you not enter the house of this particular woman and eat these various foods and have so many cups to drink?"

On hearing him mention the woman's hospitality and exactly what she had given them to eat and drink, they clearly recalled the wrong they had done, fell trembling at his feet, and confessed their guilt. The man of God did not hesitate to pardon them, confident that they would do no further wrong in his absence, since they now realized he was always present with them in spirit.

(13) The monk Valentinian, mentioned earlier in our narrative, had a brother who was a very devout layman. Every year he visited the abbey in order to get Benedict's blessing and see his brother. On the way he always used to fast. Now, one time as he was making this journey he was joined by another traveler who had brought some food along.

"Come," said the stranger after some time had passed, "let us have something to eat before we become too fatigued."

"I am sorry," the devout layman replied. "I always fast on my way to visit Abbot Benedict."

After that the traveler was quiet for a while. But when they had walked along some distance together, he repeated his suggestion. Still mindful of his good resolve, Valentinian's brother again refused. His companion did not insist and once more agreed to accompany him a little further without eating.

Then, after they had covered a great distance together and were very tired from the long hours of walking, they came upon a meadow and a spring. The whole setting seemed ideal for a much needed rest. "Look," said the stranger, "water and a meadow! What a delightful spot for us to have some refreshments! A little rest will give us strength to finish our journey without any discomfort."

It was such an attractive sight and this third invitation sounded so appealing that the devout layman was completely won over and stopped there to eat with his companion. Toward evening he arrived at the monastery and was presented to the abbot. As soon as he asked for the blessing, however, the holy man reproved him for his conduct on the journey. "How is it," he said, "that the evil spirit who spoke with you in the person of your traveling companion could not persuade you to do his will the first and second time he tried, but succeeded on his third attempt?" At this Valentinian's brother fell at Benedict's feet and admitted the weakness of his will. The thought that even from such a distance the saint had witnessed the wrong he had done filled him with shame and remorse.

Peter: This proves that the servant of God possessed the spirit of Eliseus. He, too, was present with one of his followers who was far away.

Gregory: If you will listen a little longer, Peter, I have an incident to tell you that is even more astonishing. (14) Once while the Goths were still in power, Totila their king happened to be marching in the direction of Benedict's monastery.[8] When still some distance away, he halted with his troops and sent a messenger ahead to announce his coming, for he had heard that the man of God possessed the gift of prophecy. As soon as he received word that he would be welcomed, the crafty king decided to put the saint's prophetic powers to a test. He had Riggo, his sword-bearer, fitted out with royal robes and riding boots and directed him to go in this disguise to the man of God. Vul, Ruderic and Blidin, three men from his own bodyguard, were to march at his side as if he really were king of the Goths. To supplement these marks of kingship, Totila also provided him with a sword-bearer and other attendants.

As Riggo entered the monastery grounds in his kingly robes and with all his attendants, Benedict caught sight of him and as soon as the company came within hearing called out from where he sat, "Son, lay aside the robes you are wearing," he said. "Lay them aside. They do not belong to you." Aghast at seeing what a great man he had tried to mock, Riggo sank to the ground, and with him all the members of his company. Even after they had risen to their feet they did not dare approach the saint, but hurried back in alarm to tell their king how quickly they had been detected.

(15) King Totila then went to the monastery in person. The moment he noticed the man of God sitting at a distance, he was afraid to come any closer and fell down prostrate where he was. Two or three times Benedict asked him to rise. When Totila still hesitated to do so in his presence, the servant of Christ walked over to him and with his own hands helped him from the ground. Then he rebuked the king for his crimes and briefly foretold everything that was going to happen to him. "You are the cause of many evils," he said. "You have caused many in the past. Put an end now to your wickedness. You will enter Rome and cross the sea. You will have nine more years to rule, and in the tenth year you will die."

Terrified at these words, the king asked for a blessing and went away. From that time on he was less cruel. Not long after, he went to Rome and then crossed over to Sicily. In the tenth year of his reign he lost his kingdom and his life as almighty God had decreed.

There is also a story about the bishop of Canosa,[9] who made regular visits to the abbey and stood high in Benedict's esteem because of his saintly life. Once while they were discussing Totila's invasion and the downfall of Rome, the bishop said, "The city will be destroyed by this king and left without a single inhabitant."

"No," Benedict assured him, "Rome will not be destroyed by the barbarians. It will be shaken by tempests and lightnings, hurricanes and earthquakes, until finally it lies buried in its own ruins."

The meaning of this prophecy is perfectly clear to us now. We have watched the walls of Rome crumble and have seen its homes in ruins, its churches destroyed by violent storms, and its dilapidated buildings surrounded by their own debris.

Benedict's disciple Honoratus, who told me about the prophecy, admits he did not hear it personally, but he assures me that some of his brethren gave him this account of it.

(16) At about the same time there was a cleric from the church at Aquino[10] who was being tormented by an evil spirit. Constantius, his saintly bishop, had already sent him to the shrines of various martyrs in the hope that he would be cured. But the holy martyrs did not grant him this favor, preferring instead to reveal the wonderful gifts of the servant of God.

As soon as the cleric was brought to him, Benedict drove out the evil spirit with fervent prayers to Christ. Before sending him back to Aquino, however, he told him to abstain from meat thereafter and never to advance to sacred orders "If you ignore this warning," he added, "and present yourself for ordination, you will find yourself once more in the power of Satan."

---

8   The Ostrogoths were a Germanic people from Eastern Europe who had established their kingdom in Italy under Theodoric in
     493. King Totila (541–52) was fighting to re-establish Gothic power there after it had virtually been broken by Emperor Justinian's
     armies during the previous decade. The following events probably took place when Totila was marching on Naples, which he captured in 543. See doc. 5, above, for more on the Ostrogoths.
9   In southeastern Italy, about 120 miles from Monte Cassino.
10   About five miles from Monte Cassino.

The cleric left completely cured, and as long as his previous torments were still fresh in his mind he did exactly as the man of God had ordered. Then with the passing of years, all his seniors in the clerical state died, and he had to watch newly ordained young men moving ahead of him in rank. Finally, he pretended to have forgotten about the saint's warning and, disregarding it, presented himself for ordination. Instantly he was seized by the Devil and tormented mercilessly until he died.

Peter: The servant of God must even have been aware of the hidden designs of Providence, to have realized that this cleric had been handed over to Satan to keep him from aspiring to holy orders.

Gregory: Is there any reason why a person who has observed the commandments of God should not also know God's secret designs? "The man who unites himself to the Lord becomes one spirit with him," we read in sacred Scripture.

Peter: If everyone who unites himself to the Lord becomes one spirit with him, what does the renowned apostle mean when he asks, "Who has ever understood the Lord's thoughts, or been his counselor?" It hardly seems possible to be one spirit with a person without knowing his thoughts.

Gregory: Holy men do know the Lord's thoughts, Peter, in so far as they are one with Him. This is clear from the apostle's words, "Who else can know a man's thoughts, except the man's own spirit that is within him? So no one else can know God's thoughts but the Spirit of God." To show that he actually knew God's thoughts, St. Paul added: "And what we have received is no spirit of worldly wisdom; it is the Spirit that comes from God." And again: "No eye has seen, no ear has heard, no human heart conceived, the welcome God has prepared for those who love him. To us, then, God has made a revelation of it through his Spirit."

Peter: If it is true that God's thoughts are revealed to the apostle by the Holy Spirit, how could he introduce his statement with the words, "How deep is the mine of God's wisdom, of his knowledge; how inscrutable are his judgments, how undiscoverable his ways!" Another difficulty just occurred to me now as I was speaking. In addressing the Lord, David the Prophet declares, "With my lips I have pronounced all the judgments of thy mouth." Surely it is a greater achievement to express one's knowledge than merely to possess it. How is it, then, that St. Paul calls the judgments of God inscrutable, whereas David says he knows them all and has even pronounced them with his lips?

Gregory: I already gave a brief reply to both of these objections when I told you that holy men know God's thoughts in so far as they are one with Him. For all who follow the Lord wholeheartedly are living in spiritual union with Him. As long as they are still weighed down with a perishable body, however, they are not actually united to Him. It is only to the extent that they are one with God that they know His hidden judgments. In so far as they are not yet one with Him, they do not know them. Since even holy men cannot fully grasp the secret designs of God during this present life, they call His judgments inscrutable. At the same time, they understand His judgments and can even pronounce them with their lips; for they keep their hearts united to God by dwelling continually on the words of holy Scripture and on such private revelations as they may receive, until they grasp His meaning. In other words, they do not know the judgments which God conceals but only those which He reveals. That is why, after declaring, "With my lips I have pronounced all the judgments," the Prophet immediately adds the phrase, "of thy mouth," as if to say, "I can know and pronounce only the judgments You have spoken to me. Those You leave unspoken must remain hidden from our minds." So the Prophet and the apostle are in full agreement. God's decisions are truly unfathomable. But, once His mouth has made them known, they can also be proclaimed by human lips. What God has spoken man can know. Of the thoughts He has kept secret man can know nothing.

Peter: That is certainly a reasonable solution to the difficulties that I raised. If you know any other miraculous events in this man's life, would you continue with them now?

Gregory: (17) Under the direction of Abbot Benedict a nobleman named Theoprobus had embraced monastic life. Because of his exemplary life he enjoyed the saint's personal friendship and confidence. One day, on entering Benedict's room, he found him weeping bitterly. After he had waited for some time and there was still no end to the abbot's tears, he asked what was causing him such sorrow, for he was not weeping as he usually did at prayer, but with deep sighs and lamentation.

"Almighty God has decreed that this entire monastery and everything I have provided for the community shall fall into the hands of the barbarians," the saint replied. "It was only with the greatest difficulty that I could prevail upon Him to spare the lives of its members."

This was the prophecy he made to Theoprobus, and we have seen its fulfillment in the recent destruction of his abbey by the Lombards.[11] They came at night while the community was asleep and plundered the entire monastery, without capturing a single monk. In this way God fulfilled His promise to Benedict, His faithful servant. He allowed the barbarians to destroy the monastery, but safeguarded the lives of the religious. Here you can see how the man of God resembled St. Paul, who had the consolation of seeing everyone with him escape alive from the storm, while the ship and all its cargo were lost.

(18) Exhilaratus, a fellow Roman who, as you know, later became a monk was once sent by his master to Abbot Benedict with two wooden flasks of wine. He delivered only one of them, however; the other he hid along the way. Benedict, who could observe even what was done in his absence, thanked him for the flask, but warned him as he turned to go: "Son, be sure not to drink from the flask you have hidden away. Tilt it carefully and you will see what is inside."

Exhilaratus left in shame and confusion and went back to the spot, still wishing to verify the saint's words. As he tilted the flask a serpent crawled out, and at the sight of it he was filled with horror for his misdeed.

(19) Not far from the monastery was a village largely inhabited by people the saintly Benedict had converted from the worship of idols and instructed in the true faith. There were seven nuns living there too, and he used to send one of his monks down to give them spiritual conferences.

After one of these instructions they presented the monk with a few handkerchiefs, which he accepted and hid away in his habit. As soon as he got back to the abbey he received a stern reproof. "How is it," the abbot asked him, "that evil has found its way into your heart?" Taken completely by surprise, the monk did not understand why he was being rebuked, for he had completely forgotten about the handkerchiefs. "Was I not present," the saint continued, "when you accepted those handkerchiefs from the handmaids of God and hid them away in your habit?" The offender instantly fell at Benedict's feet, confessed his fault, and gave up the present he had received.

(20) Once when the saintly abbot was taking his evening meal, a young monk whose father was a high-ranking official happened to be holding the lamp for him. As he stood at the abbot's table the spirit of pride began to stir in his heart. "Who is this," he thought to himself, "that I should have to stand here holding the lamp for him while he is eating? Who am I to be serving him?"

Turning to him at once, Benedict gave the monk a sharp reprimand. "Brother," he said, "sign your heart with the sign of the cross. What are you saying? Sign your heart!" Then, calling the others together, he had one of them take the lamp instead, and told the murmurer to sit down by himself and be quiet. Later, when asked what he had done wrong, the monk explained how he had given in to the spirit of pride and silently murmured against the man of God. At this the brethren all realized that nothing could be kept secret from their holy abbot, since he could hear even the unspoken sentiments of the heart.

(21) During a time of famine the severe shortage of food was causing a great deal of suffering in Campania. At Benedict's monastery the entire grain supply had been used up and nearly all the bread was gone as well. In fact, when mealtime came, only five loaves could be found to set before the community. Noticing how downcast they

---

11   Monte Cassino was destroyed by Duke Zotto in 589 and was not rebuilt until 720, under Abbot Petronax.

were, the saint gently reproved them for their lack of trust in God and at the same time tried to raise their dejected spirits with a comforting assurance. "Why are you so depressed at the lack of bread!" he asked. "What if today there is only a little? Tomorrow you will have more than you need."

The next day 200 measures of flour were found in sacks at the gate of the monastery, but no one ever discovered whose services almighty God had employed in bringing them there. When they saw what had happened, the monks were filled with gratitude and learned from this miracle that even in their hour of need they must not lose faith in the bountiful goodness of God.

Peter: Are we to believe that the spirit of prophecy remained with the servant of God at all times, or did he receive it only on special occasion?

Gregory: The spirit of prophecy does not enlighten the minds of the prophets constantly, Peter. We read in sacred Scripture that the Holy Spirit breathes where He pleases, and we should also realize that He breathes when He pleases. For example, when King David asked whether he could build a temple, the Prophet Nathan gave his consent, but later had to withdraw it. And Eliseus once found a woman in tears without knowing the reason for her grief. This is why he told his servant who was trying to interfere, "Let her alone, for her soul is in anguish and the Lord has hidden it from me and has not told me."

All this reflects God's boundless wisdom and love. By granting these men the spirit of prophecy He raises their minds above the world, and by withdrawing it again He safeguards their humility. When the spirit of prophecy is with them they learn what they are by God's mercy. When the spirit leaves them they discover what they are of themselves.

Peter: This convincing argument leaves no room for doubt about the truth of what you say. Please resume your narrative now, if you recall any other incidents in the life of the blessed Benedict.

Gregory: (22) A Catholic layman once asked him to found a monastery on his estate at Terracina. The servant of God readily consented and, after selecting several of his monks for this undertaking, appointed one of them abbot and another his assistant. Before they left he specified a day on which he would come to show them where to build the chapel, the refectory, a house for guests, and the other buildings they would need. Then he gave them his blessing.

After their arrival at Terracina they looked forward eagerly to the day he had set for his visit and prepared to receive the monks who would accompany him. Before dawn of the appointed day, Benedict appeared in a dream to the new abbot as well as to his prior and showed them exactly where each section of the monastery was to stand. In the morning they told each other what they had seen, but, instead of putting their entire trust in the vision, they kept waiting for the promised visit. When the day passed without any word from Benedict, they returned to him disappointed. "Father," they said, "we were waiting for you to show us where to build, as you assured us you would, but you did not come."

"What do you mean?" he replied. "Did I not come as I promised?"

"When?" they asked.

"Did I not appear to both of you in a dream as you slept and indicate where each building was to stand? Go back and build as you were directed in the vision."

They returned to Terracina, filled with wonder, and constructed the monastery according to the plans he had revealed to them.

Peter: I wish you would explain how Benedict could possibly travel that distance and then in a vision give these monks directions which they could hear and understand while they were asleep.

Gregory: What is there in this incident that should raise a doubt in your mind, Peter? Everyone knows that the soul is far more agile than the body. Yet we have it on the authority of holy Scripture that the Prophet Habacuc was lifted from Judea to Chaldea in an instant, so that he might share his dinner with the Prophet Daniel, and presently found himself back in Judea again. If Habacuc could cover such a distance in a brief moment to take a meal to his fellow Prophet, is it not understandable that Abbot Benedict could go in spirit to his sleeping brethren with the information they required? As the Prophet came in body with food for the body, Benedict came in spirit to promote the life of the soul.

Peter: Your words seem to smooth away all my doubts. Could you tell me now what this saint was like in his everyday speech?

Gregory: (23) There was a trace of the marvelous in nearly every thing he said, Peter, and his words never failed to take effect because his heart was fixed in God. Even when he uttered a simple threat that was indefinite and conditional, it was just as decisive as a final verdict.

Some distance from the abbey two women of noble birth were leading the religious life in their own home. A God-fearing layman was kind enough to bring them what they needed from the outside world. Unfortunately, as is sometimes the case, their character stood in sharp contrast to the nobility of their birth, and they were too conscious of their former importance to practice true humility toward others. Even under the restraining influence of religious life they still had not learned to control their tongues, and the good layman who served them so faithfully was often provoked at their harsh criticisms. After putting up with their insults for a long time, he went to blessed Benedict and told him how inconsiderate they were. The man of God immediately warned them to curb their sharp tongues and added that he would have to excommunicate them if they did not. This sentence of excommunication was not actually pronounced, therefore, but only threatened.

A short time afterward the two nuns died without any sign of amendment and were buried in their parish church. Whenever Mass was celebrated, their old nurse, who regularly made an offering for them, noticed that each time the deacon announced, "The non-communicants must now leave," the nuns rose from their tombs and went outside.[12] This happened repeatedly, until one day she recalled the warning Benedict had given them while they were still alive, when he threatened to deprive them of communion with the Church if they kept on speaking so uncharitably.

The grief-stricken nurse had Abbot Benedict informed of what was happening. He sent her messengers back with an oblation and said, "Have this offered up for their souls during the Holy Sacrifice, and they will be freed from the sentence of excommunication." The offering was made and after that the nuns were not seen leaving the church any more at the deacon's dismissal of the non-communicants. Evidently, they had been admitted to communion with our blessed Lord in answer to the prayers of His servant Benedict.

Peter: Is it not extraordinary that souls already judged at God's invisible tribunal could be pardoned by a man who was still living in the mortal flesh, however holy and revered he may have been?

Gregory: What of Peter the Apostle? Was he not still living in the flesh when he heard the words, "Whatever thou shalt bind on earth shall be bound in heaven, and whatever thou shalt loose on earth shall be loosed in heaven"? All those who govern the Church in matters of faith and morals exercise the same power of binding and loosing that he received. In fact, the Creator's very purpose in coming down from heaven to earth was to impart to earthly man this heavenly power. It was when God was made flesh for man's sake that flesh received its undeserved prerogative of sitting in judgment even over spirits. What raised our weakness to these heights was the descent of an almighty God to the depths of our own helplessness.

Peter: Your lofty words are certainly in harmony with these mighty deeds.

Gregory: (24) One time, a young monk who was too attached to his parents left the monastery without asking for the abbot's blessing and went home. No sooner had he arrived there he died. The day after his burial his body was discovered lying outside the grave. His parents had him buried again, but on the following day found the body unburied as before. In their dismay they hurried to the saintly abbot and pleaded with him to forgive the boy for what he had done. Moved

---

12   The deacon's words applied to the unbaptized and the excommunicated, who were not allowed to remain for the Mass of the Faithful. Their dismissal took place after the Gospel and sermon.

by their tears, Benedict gave them a consecrated Host with his own hands. "When you get back," he said, "place this sacred Host upon his breast and bury him once more."[13] They did so, and thereafter his body remained in the earth without being disturbed again.

Now, Peter, you can appreciate how pleasing this holy man was in God's sight. Not even the earth would retain the young monk's body until he had been reconciled with blessed Benedict.

Peter: I assure you I do. It is really amazing.

Gregory: (25) One of Benedict's monks had set his fickle heart on leaving the monastery. Time and again the man of God pointed out how wrong this was and tried to reason with him but without any success. The monk persisted obstinately in his request to be released. Finally, Benedict lost patience with him and told him to go.

Hardly had he left the monastery grounds when he noticed to his horror that a dragon with gaping jaws was blocking his way. "Help! Help!" he cried out, trembling, "or the dragon will devour me." His brethren ran to the rescue, but could see nothing of the dragon. Still breathless with fright, the monk was only too glad to accompany them back to the abbey. Once safe within its walls, he promised never to leave again. And this time he kept his word, for Benedict's prayers had enabled him to see with his own eyes the invisible dragon that had been leading him astray.

(26) I must tell you now of an event I heard from the distinguished Anthony. One of his father's servants had been seized with a severe case of leprosy. His hair was already falling out and his skin growing thick and swollen. The fatal progress of the disease was unmistakable. In this condition he was sent to the man of God, who instantly restored him to his previous state of health.

(27) Benedict's disciple Peregrinus tells of a Catholic layman who was heavily burdened with debt and felt that his only hope was to disclose the full extent of his misfortune to the man of God. So he went to him and explained that he was being constantly tormented by a creditor to whom he owed twelve gold pieces.

"I am very sorry," the saintly abbot replied. "I do not have that much money in my possession." Then, to comfort the poor man in his need, he added, "I cannot give you anything today, but come back again the day after tomorrow."

In the meantime the saint devoted himself to prayer with his accustomed fervor. When the debtor returned, the monks, to their surprise, found thirteen gold pieces lying on top of a chest that was filled with grain. Benedict had the money brought down at once. "Here, take these," he told him. "Use twelve to pay your creditor and keep the thirteenth for yourself."

I should like to return now to some other events I learned from the saint's four disciples who were mentioned at the beginning of this book.

There was a man who had become so embittered with envy that he tried to kill his rival by secretly poisoning his drink. Though the poison did not prove fatal, it produced horrible blemishes resembling leprosy, which spread over the entire body of the unfortunate victim. In this condition he was brought to the servant of God, who cured the disease with a touch of his hand and sent him home in perfect health.

(28) While Campania was suffering from famine, the holy abbot distributed the food supplies of his monastery to the needy until there was nothing left in the storeroom but a little oil in a glass vessel. One day, when Agapitus, a subdeacon, came to beg for some oil, the man of God ordered the little that remained to be given to him, for he wanted to distribute everything he had to the poor and thus store up riches in heaven.

The cellarer listened to the abbot's command, but did not carry it out. After a while, Benedict asked him whether he had given Agapitus the oil. "No," he replied, "I did not. If I had, there would be none left for the community." This angered the man of God, who wanted nothing to remain in the monastery through disobedience, and he told another monk to take the glass with the oil in it and throw it out the window. This time he was obeyed.

Even though it struck against the jagged rocks of the cliff just below the window, the glass remained intact as if it had not been thrown at all. It

---

13   During the first centuries laypeople were permitted to handle the Blessed Sacrament and even keep it in their homes. The practice of placing a consecrated Host on the bodies of those who died in union with the Church was quite common in St. Benedict's time.

was still unbroken and none of the oil had spilled. Abbot Benedict had the glass brought back and given to the subdeacon. Then he sent for the rest of the community and in their presence rebuked the disobedient monk for his pride and lack of faith.

(29) After that the saint knelt down to pray with his brethren. In the room where they were kneeling there happened to be an empty oil-cask that was covered with a lid. In the course of his prayer the cask gradually filled with oil and the lid started to float on top of it. The next moment the oil was running down the sides of the cask and covering the floor. As soon as he was aware of this, Benedict ended his prayer and the oil stopped flowing. Then, turning to the monk who had shown himself disobedient and wanting in confidence, he urged him again to strive to grow in faith and humility.

This wholesome reprimand filled the cellarer with shame. Besides inviting him to trust in God, the saintly abbot had clearly shown by his miracle what marvelous power such trust possesses. In the future who could doubt any of his promises? Had he not in a moment's time replaced the little oil still left in the glass with a cask that was full to overflowing?

(30) One day, on his way to the Chapel of St. John at the highest point of the mountain, Benedict met the ancient Enemy of mankind, disguised as a veterinarian with medicine horn and triple shackle.

"Where are you going?" the saint asked him.

"To your brethren," he replied with scorn. "I am bringing them some medicine."

Benedict continued on his way and after his prayer hurried back. Meanwhile, the evil spirit entered one of the older monks whom he found drawing water and had thrown him to the ground in a violent convulsion. When the man of God caught sight of this old brother in such torment, he merely struck him on the cheek, and the evil spirit was promptly driven out, never to return.

Peter: I should like to know whether he always obtained these great miracles through fervent prayer. Did he ever perform them at will?

Gregory: It is quite common for those who devoutly cling to God to work miracles in both of these ways, Peter, either through their prayers or by their own power, as circumstances may dictate. Since we read in St. John that "all those who did welcome him he empowered to become the children of God," why should we be surprised if those who are the children of God use this power to work signs and wonders? Holy men can undoubtedly perform miracles in either of the ways you mentioned, as is clear from the fact that St. Peter raised Tabitha to life by praying over her, and by a simple rebuke brought death to Ananias and Sapphira for their lies. Scripture does not say that he prayed for their death, but only that he reprimanded them for the crime they had committed. Now, if St. Peter could restore to life by a prayer and deprive of life by a rebuke, is there any reason to doubt that the saints can perform miracles by their own power as well as through their prayers?

I am now going to consider two instances in the life of God's faithful servant Benedict. One of them shows the efficacy of his prayer; the other, the marvelous powers that were his by God's gift.

(31) In the days of King Totila one of the Goths, the Arian heretic Zalla, had been persecuting devout Catholics everywhere with the utmost cruelty. No monk or cleric who fell into his hands ever escaped alive. In his merciless brutality and greed he was one day lashing and torturing a farmer whose money he was after. Unable to bear it any longer, the poor man tried to save his life by telling Zalla that all his money was in Abbot Benedict's keeping. He only hoped his tormentor would believe him and put a stop to his brutality. When Zalla heard this, he did stop beating him, but immediately bound his hands together with a heavy cord. Then, mounting his horse, he forced the farmer to walk ahead of him and lead the way to this Benedict who was keeping his money.

The helpless prisoner had no choice but to conduct him to the abbey. When they arrived, they found the man of God sitting alone in front of the entrance reading. "This is the Abbot Benedict I meant," he told the infuriated Goth behind him.

Imagining that this holy man could be frightened as readily as anyone else, Zalla glared at him with eyes full of hate and shouted harshly, "Get up! Do you hear? Get up and give back the money this man left with you!" At the sound of this angry voice the man of God looked up from his reading and, as he glanced toward Zalla, noticed the farmer with his hands bound together. The moment he caught sight of the cord that held them, it fell miraculously to the ground. Human hands could never have unfastened it so quickly.

Stunned at the hidden power that had set his prisoner free, Zalla fell trembling to his knees and, bending his stubborn, cruel neck at the saint's feet, begged for his prayers. Without rising from his place, Benedict called for his monks and had them take Zalla inside for some food and drink. After that he urged him to give up his heartless cruelty. Zalla went away thoroughly humbled and made no more demands on this farmer who had been freed from his bonds by a mere glance from the man of God.

So you see, Peter, what I said is true. Those who devote themselves wholeheartedly to the service of God can sometimes work miracles by their own power. Blessed Benedict checked the fury of a dreaded Goth without even rising to his feet, and with a mere glance unfastened the heavy cord that bound the hands of an innocent man. The very speed with which he performed this marvel is proof enough that he did it by his own power.

And now, here is a remarkable miracle that was the result of his prayer. (32) One day, when he was out working in the fields with his monks, a farmer came to the monastery carrying in his arms the lifeless body of his son. Broken-hearted at his loss, he begged to see the saintly abbot and, on learning that he was at work in the fields, left the dead body at the entrance of the monastery and hurried off to find him. By then the abbot was already returning from his work. The moment the farmer caught sight of him he cried out, "Give me back my son! Give me back my son!"

Benedict stopped when he heard this. "But I have not taken your son from you, have I?" he asked.

The boy's father only replied, "He is dead. Come! Bring him back to life."

Deeply grieved by his words, the man of God turned to his disciples. "Stand back, brethren!" he said. "Stand back! Such a miracle is beyond our power. The holy apostles are the only ones who can raise the dead. Why are you so eager to accept what is impossible for us?"

But overwhelming sorrow compelled the man to keep on pleading. He even declared with an oath that he would not leave until Benedict restored his son to life. The saint then asked him where the body was. "At the entrance to the monastery," he answered.

When Benedict arrived there with his monks, he knelt down beside the child's body and bent over it. Then, rising, he lifted his hands to heaven in prayer. "O Lord," he said, "do not consider my sins but the faith of this man who is asking to see his son alive again, and restore to this body the soul You have taken from it."

His prayer was hardly over when the child's whole body began once more to throb with life. No one present there could doubt that this sudden stirring was due to a heavenly intervention. Benedict then took the little boy by the hand and gave him back to his father alive and well.

Obviously, Peter, he did not have the power to work this miracle himself. Otherwise he would not have begged for it prostrate in prayer.

Peter: The way facts bear out your words convinces me that everything you have said is true. Will you please tell me now whether holy men can always carry out their wishes, or at least obtain through prayer whatever they desire?

Gregory: (33) Peter, will there ever be a holier man in this world than St. Paul? Yet he prayed three times to the Lord about the sting in his flesh and could not obtain his wish. In this connection I must tell you how the saintly Benedict once had a wish he was unable to fulfill.

His sister Scholastica, who had been consecrated to God in early childhood, used to visit with him once a year. On these occasions he would go down to meet her in a house belonging to the monastery, a short distance from the entrance.

For this particular visit he joined her there with a few of his disciples and they spent the whole day singing God's praises and conversing about the spiritual life. When darkness was setting in, they took their meal together and continued their conversation at table until it was quite late. Then the holy nun said to him, "Please do not leave me tonight, brother. Let us keep on talking about the joys of heaven till morning."

"What are you saying, sister?" he replied. "You know I cannot stay away from the monastery."

The sky was so clear at the time that there was not a cloud in sight. At her brother's refusal

Scholastica folded her hands on the table and rested her head upon them in earnest prayer. When she looked up again, there was a sudden burst of lightning and thunder, accompanied by such a downpour that Benedict and his companions were unable to set a foot outside the door.

By shedding a flood of tears while she prayed, this holy nun had darkened the cloudless sky with a heavy rain. The storm began as soon as her prayer was over. In fact, the two coincided so closely that the thunder was already resounding as she raised her head from the table. The very instant she ended her prayer the rain poured down.

Realizing that he could not return to the monastery in this terrible storm, Benedict complained bitterly, "God forgive you, sister!" he said. "What have you done?"

Scholastica simply answered, "When I appealed to you, you would not listen to me. So I turned to my God and He heard my prayer. Leave now if you can. Leave me here and go back to your monastery."

This, of course, he could not do. He had no choice now but to stay, in spite of his unwillingness. They spent the entire night together and both of them derived great profit from the holy thoughts they exchanged about the interior life.

Here you have my reason for saying that this holy man was once unable to obtain what he desired. If we consider his point of view, we can readily see that he wanted the sky to remain as clear as it was when he came down from the monastery. But this wish of his was thwarted by a miracle almighty God performed in answer to a woman's prayer. We need not be surprised that in this instance she proved mightier than her brother; she had been looking forward so long to this visit. Do we not read in St. John that God is love? Surely it is no more than right that her influence was greater than his, since hers was the greater love.

Peter: I find this discussion very enjoyable.

Gregory: (34) The next morning Scholastica returned to her convent and Benedict to his monastery. Three days later as he stood in his room looking up toward the sky, he beheld his sister's soul leaving her body and entering the court of heaven in the form of a dove.

Overjoyed at her eternal glory, he gave thanks to God in hymns of praise. Then, after informing his brethren of her death, he sent some of them to bring her body to the monastery and bury it in the tomb he had prepared for himself. The bodies of these two were now to share a common resting place, just as in life their souls had always been one in God.

(35) At another time, the deacon Servandus came to see the servant of God on one of his regular visits. He was abbot of the monastery in Campania that had been built by the late Senator Liberius, and always welcomed an opportunity to discuss with Benedict the truths of eternity, for he, too, was a man of deep spiritual understanding. In speaking of their hopes and longings they were able to taste in advance the heavenly food that was not yet fully theirs to enjoy. When it was time to retire for the night, Benedict went to his room on the second floor of the tower, leaving Servandus in the one below, which was connected with his own by a stairway. Their disciples slept in the large building facing the tower.

Long before the night office began, the man of God was standing at his window, where he watched and prayed while the rest were asleep. In the dead of night he suddenly beheld a flood of light shining down from above more brilliant than the sun, and with it every trace of darkness cleared away. Another remarkable sight followed. According to his own description, the whole world was gathered up before his eyes in what appeared to be a single ray of light. As he gazed at all this dazzling display, he saw the soul of Germanus, the Bishop of Capua, being carried by angels up to heaven in a ball of fire.

Wishing to have someone else witness this great marvel, he called out for Servandus, repeating his name two or three times in a loud voice. As soon as he heard the saint's call, Servandus rushed to the upper room and was just in time to catch a final glimpse of the miraculous light. He remained speechless with wonder as Benedict described everything that had taken place. Then without any delay the man of God instructed the devout Theoprobus to go to Cassino and have a messenger sent to Capua that same night to find out what had happened to Germanus. In carrying out these instructions the messenger discovered that the revered bishop was already dead. When he asked for further details, he learned that his death had occurred at the very time blessed Benedict saw him carried into heaven.

Peter: What an astounding miracle! I hardly know what to think when I hear you say that he saw the whole world gathered up before his eyes in what appeared to be a single ray of light. I have never had such an experience. How is it possible for anyone to see the whole universe at a glance?

Gregory: Keep this well in mind, Peter. All creation is bound to appear small to a soul that sees the Creator. Once it beholds a little of His light, it finds all creatures small indeed. The light of holy contemplation enlarges and expands the mind in God until it stands above the world. In fact, the soul that sees Him rises even above itself, and as it is drawn upward in His light all its inner powers unfold. Then, when it looks down from above, it sees how small everything is that was beyond its grasp before.

Now, Peter, how else was it possible for this man to behold the ball of fire and watch the angels on their return to heaven except with light from God? Why should it surprise us, then, that he could see the whole world gathered up before him after this inner light had lifted him so far above the world? Of course, in saying that the world was gathered up before his eyes I do not mean that heaven and earth grew small, but that his spirit was enlarged. Absorbed as he was in God, it was now easy for him to see all that lay beneath God. In the light outside that was shining before his eyes, there was a brightness which reached into his mind and lifted his spirit heavenward, showing him the insignificance of all that lies below.

Peter: My difficulty in understanding you has proved of real benefit, the explanation it led to was so thorough. Now that you have cleared up this problem for me, would you return once more to your account of blessed Benedict's life?

Gregory: (36) I should like to tell you much more about this saintly abbot, but I am purposely passing over some of his miraculous deeds in my eagerness to take up those of others. There is one

more point, however, I want to call to your attention. With all the renown he gained by his numerous miracles, the holy man was no less outstanding for the wisdom of his teaching. He wrote a Rule for Monks that is remarkable for its discretion and its clarity of language. Anyone who wishes to know more about his life and character can discover in his Rule exactly what he was like as an abbot, for his life could not have differed from his teaching.

(37) In the year that was to be his last, the man of God foretold the day of his holy death to a number of his disciples. In mentioning it to some who were with him in the monastery, he bound them to strict secrecy. Some others, however, who were stationed elsewhere he only informed of the special sign they would receive at the time of his death.

Six days before he died he gave orders for his tomb to be opened. Almost immediately he was seized with a violent fever that rapidly wasted his remaining strength. Each day his condition grew worse until finally, on the sixth day, he had his disciples carry him into the chapel, where he received the Body and Blood of our Lord to gain strength for his approaching end. Then, supporting his weakened body on the arms of his brethren, he stood with his hands raised to heaven and as he prayed he breathed his last.

That day two monks, one of them at the monastery, the other some distance away, received the very same revelation. They both saw a magnificent road covered with rich carpeting and glittering with thousands of lights. From his monastery it stretched eastward in a straight line until it reached up into heaven. And there in the brightness stood a man of majestic appearance, who asked them, "Do you know who passed this way?"

"No," they replied.

"This," he told them, "is the road taken by blessed Benedict, the Lord's beloved, when he went to heaven."

Thus, while the brethren who were with Benedict witnessed his death, those who were absent knew about it through the sign he had promised them. His body was laid to rest in the Chapel of St. John the Baptist, which he had built to replace the altar of Apollo.

(38) Even in the cave at Subiaco, where he had

lived before, this holy man still works numerous miracles for people who turn to him with faith and confidence. The incident I am going to relate happened only recently.

A woman who had completely lost her mind was roaming day and night over hills and valleys, through forests and fields, resting only when she was utterly exhausted. One day, in the course of her aimless wanderings, she strayed into the saint's cave and rested there without the least idea of where she was. The next morning she woke up entirely cured and left the cave without even a trace of her former affliction. After that she remained free from it for the rest of her life.

Peter: How is it that, as a rule, even the martyrs in their care for us do not grant the same great favors through their bodily remains as they do through their other relics? We find them so often performing more outstanding miracles away from their burial places.

Gregory: There is no doubt, Peter, that the holy martyrs can perform countless miracles where their bodies rest. And they do so in behalf of all who pray there with a pure intention. In places where their bodies do not actually lie buried, however, there is danger that those whose faith is weak may doubt their presence and their power to answer prayers. Consequently, it is in these places that they must perform still greater miracles. But one whose faith in God is strong earns all the more merit by his faith, for he realizes that the martyrs are present to hear his prayers even though their bodies happen to be buried elsewhere.

It was precisely to increase the faith of His disciples that the eternal Truth told them, "If I do not go, the Advocate will not come to you." Now certainly the Holy Spirit, the Advocate, is ever proceeding from the Father and the Son. Why, then, should the Son say He will go in order that the Spirit may come, when, actually, the Spirit never leaves Him? The point is that as long as the disciples could see our Lord in His human flesh they would want to keep on seeing Him with their bodily eyes. With good reason, therefore, did He tell them, "If I do not go, the Advocate will not come." What He really meant was, "I cannot teach you spiritual love unless I remove my body from your sight; as long as you continue to see me with your bodily eyes you will never learn to love me spiritually."

Peter: That is a very satisfying explanation.

Gregory: Let us interrupt our discussion for a while. If we are going to take up the miracles of other holy men, we shall need a short period of silence to rest our voices.

14. *LAWS OF ETHELBERT*

ETHELBERT OF KENT (560–616) was the Anglo-Saxon ruler whose hegemony extended over all Britain south of the Humber. He received Augustine of Canterbury and allowed him to begin his mission of the conversion of the Anglo-Saxons. His law code, written in Old English, was probably compiled around 602 and is the earliest Anglo-Saxon legal compilation. Furthermore, it set a precedent in England, and many later Anglo-Saxon kings promulgated their own codes.

Source: Dorothy Whitelock (ed.), *English Historical Documents 500–1042*, vol. 1 (London: Eyre & Spottiswoode, 1955), 391–94.

Further Reading: A.W.B. Simpson, "The Laws of Ethelbert," in M.S. Arnold (ed.), *On the Laws and Customs of England: Essays in Honor of Samuel E. Thorne* (Chapel Hill: University of North Carolina Press, 1981).

1. The property of God and the Church [is to be paid for] with a twelve-fold compensation; a bishop's property with an eleven-fold compensation; a priest's property with a nine-fold compensation; a deacon's property with a six-fold compensation; a cleric's property with a three-fold compensation; the peace of the Church with a two-fold compensation; the peace of a meeting with a two-fold compensation.
2. If the king calls his people to him, and anyone does them injury there, [he is to pay] a two-fold compensation and 50 shillings to the king.
3. If the king is drinking at a man's home, and anyone commits any evil deed there, he is to pay two-fold compensation.
4. If a freeman steal from the king, he is to repay nine-fold.
5. If anyone kills a man in the king's estate, he is to pay 50 shillings compensation.
6. If anyone kills a freeman, [he is to pay] 50 shillings to the king as "lord-ring."[1]
7. If [anyone] kills the king's own smith or his messenger, he is to pay the ordinary wergild.
8. The [breach of the] king's protection,[2] 50 shillings.
9. If a freeman steals from a freeman, he is to pay three-fold, and the king is to have the fine or all the goods.
10. If anyone lies with a maiden belonging to the king, he is to pay 50 shillings compensation.
11. If it is a grinding slave, he is to pay 25 shillings compensation; [if a slave of] the third [class], 12 shillings.
12. The king's *fedesl*[3] is to be paid for with 20 shillings.
13. If anyone kills a man in a nobleman's estate, he is to pay 12 shillings compensation.

---

1 Presumably what is called elsewhere a *manbot*. The term used here is obviously ancient, belonging to a time when payments were more often in rings than in currency. Several of the words in this code are either unique, or used only in poetry, which was conservative in its vocabulary.
2 Offenses against anyone or any place under the king's protection, but also including various acts showing lack of respect. Other persons than the king had their *mund(byrd)*, or "(right of giving) protection."
3 Boarder.

14. If anyone lies with a nobleman's serving-woman, he is to pay 20 shillings compensation.

15. The [breach of a] *ceorl*'s[4] protection: six shillings.

16. If anyone lie with a *ceorl*'s serving-woman, he is to pay six shillings compensation; [if] with a slave-woman of the second [class], 50 *sceattas*;[5] [if with one of] the third [class], 30 *sceattas*.

17. If a man is the first to force his way into a man's homestead, he is to pay six shillings compensation; he who enters next, three shillings; afterwards each [is to pay] a shilling.

18. If anyone provides a man with weapons, when a quarrel has arisen, and [yet] no injury results, he is to pay six shillings compensation.

19. If highway-robbery is committed, he[6] is to pay six shillings compensation.

20. If, however, a man is killed, he is to pay 20 shillings compensation.

21. If anyone kills a man, he is to pay as an ordinary wergild 100 shillings.

22. If anyone kills a man, he is to pay 20 shillings at the open grave, and within 40 days the whole wergild.

23. If the slayer departs from the land, his kinsmen are to pay half the wergild.

24. If anyone binds a free man, he is to pay 20 shillings compensation.

25. If anyone kills a *ceorl*'s dependant, he is to pay six shillings compensation.

26. If [anyone] kills a *l[æ]t*,[7] he is to pay for one of the highest class 80 shillings; if he kills one of the second class, he is to pay 60 shillings; if one of the third class, he is to pay 40 shillings.

27. If a freeman breaks an enclosure, he is to pay six shillings compensation.

28. If anyone seizes property inside, the man is to pay three-fold compensation.

29. If a freeman enters the enclosure, he is to pay four shillings compensation.

30. If anyone kill a man, he is to pay with his own money and unblemished goods, whatever their kind.

31. If a freeman lies with the wife of another freeman, he is to atone with his wergild, and to obtain another wife with his own money, and bring her to the other's home.

32. If anyone thrusts through a true *hamseyld*,[8] he is to pay for it with its value.

33. If hair-pulling occur, 50 *sceattas* [are to be paid] as compensation....

73. If a freewoman, with long hair,[9] commits any misconduct, she is to pay 30 shillings compensation.

74. The compensation for [injury to] a maiden is to be as for a freeman.

75. [Breach of] guardianship over a noble-born widow of the highest class is to be compensated for with 50 shillings.

75.1. that over one of the second class, with 20 shillings; over one of the third class, with 12 shillings; over one of the fourth, with six shillings.

76. If a man takes a widow who does not belong to him, the [penalty for breach of the] guardianship is to be doubled.

77. If anyone buys a maiden, she is to be bought with a [bride] payment, if there is no fraud.

77.1. If, however, there is any fraud, she is to be taken back home, and he is to be given back his money.

78. If she bears a living child, she is to have half the goods, if the husband dies first.

79. If she wishes to go away with the children, she is to have half the goods.

80. If the husband wishes to keep [the children], [she is to have the same share] as a child.

---

4   Though modern English "churl" is the direct descendant of this word, the sense has changed so much that to use it would be misleading. Its normal Old English meaning is a peasant proprietor.

5   A type of silver coin.

6   The man who provided the weapon.

7   Only in Kent is there reference to this class, lower than the *ceorl*, but above the slave.

8   Possibly a fence around a dwelling.

9   This is generally taken to be a distinguishing feature of a free, as opposed to a bond, woman.

81. If she does not bear a child, [her] paternal kinsmen are to have [her] goods and the "morning-gift."[10]

82. If anyone carries off a maiden by force, [he is to pay] to the owner 50 shillings, and afterwards buy from the owner his consent [to the marriage].

83. If she is betrothed to another man at a [bride] price, he[11] is to pay 20 shillings compensation.

84. If a return [of the woman] takes place, [he is to pay] 35 shillings and 15 shillings to the king.

85. If anyone lies with the woman of a servant while her husband is alive, he is to pay a two-fold compensation.

86. If one servant kills another without cause, he is to pay the full value.

87. If a servant's eye or foot is destroyed, the full value is to be paid for him.

88. If anyone binds a man's servant, he is to pay six shillings compensation.

89. Highway robbery of [or by?] a slave is to be three shillings.

90. If a slave steals, he is to pay two-fold compensation.

10 The gift made by the husband to the bride on the morning after the consummation of the marriage.
11 The man who ran off with her.

15. BEDE

History of the English Church and People

BEDE (CA. 672–735) SPENT almost all of his life as a monk in the Northumbrian monastery of St. Paul at Jarrow. His writing included exegetical works, chronology, rhetoric, metrics, natural history, and hagiography, as well as history. His *History of the English Church and People* is the most important narrative source for English history up to 731. Bede was extremely careful in his selection and use of sources, although he carefully molded his work in order to present his own vision of the growth of English Christianity. The following selections present Augustine's mission to England, the life of Bishop Aidan, and the Synod of Whitby.

Source: Leo Sherley-Price (ed. and trans.), *Bede: A History of the English Church and People* (Harmondsworth: Penguin Books, 1955).

Further Reading: James Campbell, *Essays in Anglo-Saxon History: 400–1200* (London: Hambledon Press, 1986).

Book One

Chapter 23: *The holy Pope Gregory sends Augustine and other monks to preach to the English nation, and encourages them in a letter to persevere in their mission* [596 CE]

In the year of our Lord 582, Maurice, fifty-fourth in succession from Augustus, became emperor, and ruled for twenty-one years. In the tenth year of his reign, Gregory, an eminent scholar and administrator, was elected pontiff of the apostolic Roman see, and ruled it for thirteen years, six months, and ten days. In the fourteenth year of the emperor, and about the one hundred and fiftieth year after the coming of the English to Britain, Gregory was inspired by God to send his servant Augustine with several other God-fearing monks to preach the word of God to the English nation. Having undertaken this task in obedience to the Pope's command and progressed a short distance on their journey, they became afraid, and began to consider returning home. For they were appalled at the idea of going to a barbarous, fierce, and pagan nation, of whose very language they were ignorant. They unanimously agreed that this was the safest course, and sent back Augustine—who was to be consecrated bishop in the event of their being received by the English—so that he might humbly request the holy Gregory to recall them from so dangerous, arduous, and uncertain a journey. In reply, the Pope wrote them a letter of encouragement, urging them to proceed on their mission to preach God's word, and to trust themselves to his aid. This letter ran as follows:

"GREGORY, Servant of the servants of God, to the servants of our Lord. My very dear sons, it is better never to undertake any high enterprise than to abandon it when once begun. So with the help of God you must carry out this holy task which you have begun. Do not be deterred by the troubles of the journey or by what men say. Be constant and zealous in carrying out this enterprise which, under God's guidance, you have undertaken: and be assured that the greater the labor, the greater will be the glory of your eternal reward. When Augustine your leader returns, whom We have appointed your abbot, obey him humbly in all things, remembering that whatever he directs you to do will always be to the good of your souls. May Almighty God protect you with His grace, and grant me to see the result of your labors in our heavenly home. And although my office prevents me from working at your side, yet because I long to do so, I hope to share in your joyful reward. God keep you safe, my dearest sons.

"Dated the twenty-third of July, in the fourteenth year of the reign of the most pious

Emperor Maurice Tiberius Augustus, and the thirteenth year after his Consulship: the fourteenth interdiction."

Chapter 24: *Pope Gregory writes commending them to the Bishop of Arles*

The venerable Pontiff also wrote to Etherius, Archbishop of Arles, asking him to offer a kindly welcome to Augustine on his journey to Britain. This letter reads:

"To his most reverend and holy brother and fellow-bishop Etherius: Gregory, servant of the servants of God.

"Religious men should require no commendation to priests who exhibit the love that is pleasing to God; but since a suitable opportunity to write has arisen, We have written this letter to you, our brother, to certify that its bearer, God's servant Augustine, with his companions, of whose zeal we are assured, has been directed by us to proceed to save souls with the help of God. We therefore request Your Holiness to assist them with pastoral care, and to make speedy provision for their needs. And in order that you may assist them the more readily, we have particularly directed Augustine to give you full information about his mission, being sure that when you are acquainted with this, you will supply all their needs for the love of God. We also commend to your love the priest Candidus, our common son in Christ, whom we have transferred to a small patrimony in our church. God keep you safely, most reverend brother.

"Dated the twenty-third day of July, in the fourteenth year of the reign of the most pious Emperor Maurice Tiberius Augustus, and the thirteenth year after his Consulship: the fourteenth interdiction."

Chapter 25: *Augustine reaches Britain, and first preaches in the Isle of Thanet before King Ethelbert, who grants permission to preach in Kent* [*597 CE*]

Reassured by the encouragement of the blessed father Gregory, Augustine and his fellow-servants of Christ resumed their work in the word of God, and arrived in Britain. At this time the most powerful king there was Ethelbert, who reigned in Kent and whose domains extended northwards to the river Humber, which forms the boundary between the north and south Angles. To the east of Kent lies the large island of Thanet, which by English reckoning is six hundred hides in extent; it is separated from the mainland by a waterway about three furlongs broad called the Wantsum, which joins the sea at either end and is fordable only in two places. It was here that God's servant Augustine landed with companions, who are said to have been forty in number. At the direction of blessed Pope Gregory, they had brought interpreters from among the Franks, and they sent these to Ethelbert, saying that they came from Rome bearing very glad news, which infallibly assured all who would receive it of eternal joy in heaven and an everlasting kingdom with the living and true God. On receiving this message, the king ordered them to remain in the island where they had landed, and gave directions that they were to be provided with all necessaries until he should decide what action to take. For he had already heard of the Christian religion, having a Christian wife of the Frankish royal house named Bertha, whom he had received from her parents on condition that she should have freedom to hold and practice her faith unhindered with Bishop Liudhard, whom they had sent as her helper in the faith.

After some days, the king came to the island, and, sitting down in the open air, summoned Augustine and his companions to an audience. But he took precautions that they should not approach him in a house; for he held an ancient superstition that, if they were practicers of magical arts, they might have opportunity to deceive and master him. But the monks were endowed with power from God, not from the Devil, and approached the king carrying a silver cross as their standard and the likeness of our Lord and Savior painted on a board. First of all they offered prayer to God, singing a litany for the eternal salvation both of themselves and of those to whom and for whose sake they had come. And when, at the king's command, they had sat down and preached the word of life to the king and his court, the king said: "Your words and promises are fair indeed; but they are new and uncertain, and I cannot accept them and abandon the age-old beliefs that I have held together with the whole English nation.

But since you have traveled far, and I can see that you are sincere in your desire to impart to us what you believe to be true and excellent, we will not harm you. We will receive you hospitably and take care to supply you with all that you need; nor will we forbid you to preach and win any people you can to your religion." The king then granted them a dwelling in the city of Canterbury, which was the chief city of all his realm, and in accordance with his promise he allowed them provisions and did not withdraw their freedom to preach. Tradition says that as they approached the city, bearing the holy cross and the likeness of our great King and Lord Jesus Christ as was their custom, they sang in unison this litany: "We pray Thee, O Lord, in all Thy mercy, that Thy wrath and anger may be turned away from this city and from Thy holy house, for we are sinners. Alleluia."

Chapter 26: *The life and doctrine of the primitive Church are followed in Kent: Augustine establishes his episcopal see in the king's city*

As soon as they had occupied the house given to them they began to emulate the life of the apostles and the primitive Church. They were constantly at prayer; they fasted and kept vigils; they preached the word of life to whomsoever they could. They regarded worldly things as of little importance, and accepted only the necessities of life from those they taught. They practiced what they preached, and were willing to endure any hardship, and even to die for the truth which they proclaimed. Before long a number of heathen, admiring the simplicity of their holy lives and the comfort of their heavenly message, believed and were baptized. On the east side of the city stood an old church, built in honor of Saint Martin during the Roman occupation of Britain, where the Christian queen of whom I have spoken went to pray. Here they first assembled to sing the psalms, to pray, to say Mass, to preach, and to baptize, until the king's own conversion to the Faith gave them greater freedom to preach and to build and restore churches everywhere.

At length the king himself, among others, edified by the pure lives of these holy men and their gladdening promises, the truth of which they confirmed by many miracles, believed and was baptized. Thenceforward great numbers gathered each day to hear the word of God, forsaking their heathen rites and entering the unity of Christ's holy Church as believers. While the king was pleased at their faith and conversion, it is said that he would not compel anyone to accept Christianity; for he had learned from his instructors and guides to salvation that the service of Christ must be accepted freely and not under compulsion. Nevertheless, he showed greater favor to believers, because they were fellow-citizens of the kingdom of heaven. And it was not long before he granted his teachers in his capital of Canterbury a place of residence appropriate to their station, and gave them possessions of various kinds to supply their wants....

Chapter 29: *Gregory sends Augustine the* pallium, *a letter, and several clergy* [*601 CE*]

Hearing from Bishop Augustine that he had a rich harvest but few to help him gather it, Pope Gregory sent with his envoys several colleagues and clergy, of whom the principal and most outstanding were Mellitus, Justus, Paulinus, and Rufinianus. They brought with them everything necessary for the worship and service of the Church, including sacred vessels, altar coverings, church ornaments, vestments for priests and clergy, relics of the holy apostles and martyrs, and many books. Gregory also sent a letter to Augustine, telling him that he had dispatched the *pallium* to him, and giving him directions on the appointment of bishops in Britain. This letter runs as follows:

"To our most reverend and holy brother and fellow-bishop Augustine: Gregory, servant of the servants of God.

"While Almighty God alone can grant His servants the ineffable joys of the kingdom of heaven, it is proper that we should reward them with earthly honors, and encourage them by such recognition to devote themselves to their spiritual labors with redoubled zeal. And since the new Church of the English has now, through the goodness of God and your own efforts, been brought to the grace of God, we grant you the privilege of wearing the *pallium* in that Church whenever you perform the solemnities of the Mass. You are to consecrate twelve bishops in different places, who will be subject to your jurisdiction: the bishop of the city of London will thenceforward be consecrated by his own synod, and will receive the honor of the *pallium* from this apostolic see which, by divine decree, we at present occupy. We wish you also to send a bishop of your own choice to the city of York, and if that city with the adjoining territory accepts the word of God, this bishop is to consecrate twelve other bishops, and hold the dignity of Metropolitan. If we live to see this, we intend to grant him the *pallium* also, but he is to remain subject to your authority. After your death, however, he is to preside over the bishops whom he has consecrated and to be wholly independent of the Bishop of London. Thenceforward, seniority of consecration is to determine whether the Bishop of London or York takes precedence; but they are to consult one another and take united action in all matters concerning the Faith of Christ, and take and execute all decisions without mutual disharmony.

"You, my brother, are to exercise authority in the Name of our Lord and God Jesus Christ both over those bishops whom you shall consecrate, and any who shall be consecrated by the Bishop of York, and also over all the British bishops. Let Your Grace's words and example show them a pattern of right belief and holy life, so that they may execute their office in right belief and practice and, when God wills, attain the kingdom of heaven. God keep you safe, most reverend brother.

"Dated the twenty-second of June, in the nineteenth year of our most pious Lord and Emperor Maurice Tiberius Augustus ... and the nineteenth after his Consulship: the fourth interdiction."

Chapter 32: *Pope Gregory sends letters and gifts to King Ethelbert*

Pope Gregory also sent a letter to King Ethelbert with many gifts of different kinds, wishing to bestow earthly honors on this king who by his exertions and zeal, and to his great joy, had been brought to knowledge of heavenly glory. A copy of this letter follows.

"To our excellent son, the most glorious King Ethelbert, King of the English: the Bishop Gregory.

"The reason why Almighty God raises good men to govern nations is that through them He may bestow the gifts of His mercy on all whom they rule. We know that this is so in the case of the English nation, over whom you reign so gloriously, so that by means of the good gifts that God grants to you He may bless your people as well. Therefore, my illustrious son, zealously foster the grace that God has given you, and press on with the task of extending the Christian faith among the people committed to your charge. Make their conversion your first concern; suppress the worship of idols, and destroy their shrines; raise the moral standards of your subjects by your own innocence of life, encouraging, warning, persuading, correcting, and showing them an example by your good deeds. God will most surely grant you His rewards in heaven if you faithfully proclaim His Name and truth upon earth; and He whose honor you seek and uphold among your peoples will make your own name glorious to posterity.

"So it was that the devout Emperor Constantine in his day turned the Roman State from its ignorant worship of idols by his own submission to our mighty Lord and God Jesus Christ, and with his subjects accepted Him with all his heart. The result is that his glorious reputation has excelled that of all his predecessors, and he has outshone them in reputation as greatly as he surpassed them in good works. Now, therefore, let Your Majesty make all speed to bring to your subject princes and peoples the knowledge of the One God, Father, Son and Holy Spirit, so that your own merit and repute may excel that of all the former kings of your nation. And when you have thus cleansed your subjects from their sins, you will bear the load of your own sins with greater confidence before the judgment seat of God.

"Our most reverend brother Bishop Augustine has been trained under monastic Rule, has a complete knowledge of holy scripture, and, by the grace of God, is a man of holy life. Therefore I beg you to listen to his advice ungrudgingly, follow it exactly and store it carefully in your memory; for if you listen to him when he speaks in God's name, God himself will listen more readily to the prayers he utters on your behalf. But if you ignore his advice—which God forbid—and disregard him when he speaks for God, how should God pay attention when he speaks for you? Work sincerely and wholeheartedly with him in fervent faith, and support his efforts with all the strength God has given you, so that you may receive a place in the kingdom of Christ, Whose Faith you profess and uphold in your own realm.

"We would also have Your Majesty know what we have learned from the words of Almighty God in holy Scripture, that the end of this present world is at hand and the everlasting kingdom of the Saints is approaching. When the end of the world is near, unprecedented things occur—portents in the sky, terrors from heaven, unseasonable tempests, wars, famines, pestilences, and widespread earthquakes. Not all these things will happen during our own lifetimes, but will all ensue in due course. Therefore, if any such things occur in your own country, do not be anxious, for these portents of the end are sent to warn us to consider the welfare of our souls and remember our last end, so that, when our Judge comes, He may find us prepared by good lives. I have mentioned these matters in this short letter, my illustrious son, in the hope that as the Christian faith grows more strong in your kingdom, our correspondence with you may become more frequent. So my pleasure in addressing you will keep pace with the joy in my heart at the glad news of the complete conversion of your people.

"I have sent some small presents, which will not appear small to you, since you receive them with the blessing of the blessed Apostle Peter. May Almighty God continue to perfect you in His grace, prolong your life for many years, and after this life receive you among the citizens of our heavenly home. May the grace of heaven preserve Your Majesty in safety.

"Dated the twenty-second day of June, in the nineteenth year of our most pious lord and Emperor Maurice Tiberius Augustus, and the eighteenth after his Consulship: the fourth interdiction."

Book Two

Chapter 2: *Augustine urges the British bishops to cement Catholic unity, and performs a miracle in their presence. Retribution follows their refusal [603 CE]*

Meanwhile, with the aid of King Ethelbert, Augustine summoned the bishops and teachers of the nearest British province to a conference at a place still known to the English as Augustine's Oak, which lies on the border between the Hwiccas and the West Saxons. He began by urging them to establish brotherly relations with him in Catholic unity, and to join with him in God's work of preaching the Gospel to the heathen.

Now the Britons did not keep Easter at the correct time, but between the fourteenth and the twentieth days of the moon—a calculation depending on a cycle of eighty-four years. Furthermore, certain other of their customs were at variance with the universal practice of the Church. But despite protracted discussions, neither the prayers nor the advice nor the censures of Augustine and his companions could obtain the compliance of the Britons, who stubbornly preferred their own customs to those in universal use among Christian Churches. Augustine then brought this lengthy and fruitless conference to a close, saying, "Let us ask our Lord, *who makes men to be of one mind* in his Father's house, to grant us a sign from heaven and show us which tradition is to be followed, and by what roads we are to hasten our steps towards His kingdom. Bring in some sick person, and let the beliefs and practice of those who can heal him be accepted as pleasing to God and to be followed by all." On the reluctant agreement of his opponents, a blind Englishman was led in and presented to the British priests, from whose ministry he obtained no healing or benefit. Then Augustine, as the occasion demanded, knelt in prayer to the Father of our Lord Jesus Christ, imploring that the man's lost sight might be restored and prove the means of bringing the light of spiritual grace to the minds of countless believers. Immediately the blind man's sight was restored, and all acknowledged Augustine as the true herald of the light of Christ. The Britons declared that, while they had learnt that what Augustine taught was the true way of righteousness, they could not abandon their ancient customs without the consent and approval of their own people, and therefore asked that a second and fuller conference might be held.

This was arranged, and seven British bishops and many very learned men are said to have attended, who came mainly from their most famous monastery which the English call Bancornaburg [Bangor-is-Coed, co. Flint], then ruled by Abbot

Dinoot. Those summoned to this council first visited a wise and prudent hermit, and enquired of him whether they should abandon their own traditions at Augustine's demand. He answered: "If he is a man of God, follow him." "But how can we be sure of this?" they asked. "Our Lord says, *Take my yoke upon you and learn of Me, for I am meek and lowly in heart*," he replied. "Therefore if Augustine is meek and lowly in heart, it shows that he bears the yoke of Christ himself, and offers it to you. But if he is haughty and unbending, then he is not of God, and we should not listen to him." Then they asked, "But how can we know even this?" Whereupon Augustine, that man of God, is said to have answered them with a threat that was also a prophecy: if they refused to accept peace with their fellow-Christians, they would be forced to accept war at the hands of enemies; and if they refused to preach to the English the way of life, they would eventually suffer at their hands the penalty of death. And, by divine judgment, all these things happened as Augustine foretold.

Some while after this, the powerful king Ethelfrid, whom I have already mentioned, raised a great army at the City of Legions—which the English call Legacestir [Chester], but which the Britons more correctly call Carlegion—and made a great slaughter of the faithless Britons. Before battle was joined, he noticed that their priests were assembled apart in a safer place to pray for their soldiers, and he enquired who they were and what they had come there to do. Most of these priests came from the monastery of Bangor, where there are said to have been so many monks that although it was divided into seven sections, each under its own head, none of these sections contained less than three hundred monks, all of whom supported themselves by manual work. Most of these monks, who had kept a three-day fast, had gathered to pray at the battle, guarded by a certain Brocmail, who was there to protect them from the swords of the barbarians while they were intent on prayer. As soon as King Ethelfrid was informed of their purpose, he said: "If they are crying to their God against us, they are fighting against us even if they do not bear arms." He therefore directed his first attack against them, and then destroyed the rest of the accursed army, not without heavy loss to his own forces. It is said

that of the monks who came to pray about twelve hundred perished in this battle, and only fifty escaped by flight. Brocmail and his men took to their heels at the first assault, leaving those whom they should have protected unarmed and exposed to the swordstrokes of the enemy. Thus, long after his death, was fulfilled Bishop Augustine's prophecy that the faithless Britons, who had rejected the offer of eternal salvation, would incur the punishment of temporal destruction.

Chapter 3: *Augustine consecrates Mellitus and Justus as bishops: his own death* [604 CE]

In the year of our Lord 604, Augustine, Archbishop of Britain, consecrated two bishops, Mellitus and Justus. Mellitus was appointed to preach in the province of the East Saxons, which is separated from Kent by the river Thames, and bounded on the east by the sea. Its capital is the city of London, which stands on the banks of the Thames, and is a trading center for many nations who visit it by land and sea. At this time Sabert, Ethelbert's nephew through his sister Ricula, ruled the province under the suzerainty of Ethelbert, who, as already stated, governed all the English peoples as far north as the Humber. When this province too had received the faith through the preaching of Mellitus, King Ethelbert built a church dedicated to the Holy Apostle Paul in the city of London, which he appointed as the episcopal see of Mellitus and his successors. Augustine also consecrated Justus as bishop of a Kentish city which the English call Hrofescaestir [Rochester] after an early chieftain named Hrof. This lies nearly twenty-four miles west of Canterbury, and a church in honor of Saint Andrew the Apostle was built here by King Ethelbert, who made many gifts to the bishops of both these churches as well as to Canterbury; he later added lands and property for the maintenance of the bishop's household.

When our father Augustine, the beloved of God, died, his body was laid to rest just outside the church of the holy apostles Peter and Paul, since the church was not yet completed or consecrated. But as soon as it was dedicated, his body was brought inside and buried in the north porch with great honor. This is also the last resting-place of all succeeding archbishops except Theodore and Bertwald, whose bodies lie inside the church, no space remaining in the porch. Almost in the center of the church stands an altar dedicated in honor of blessed Pope Gregory, at which a priest of the place says solemn mass in their memory each Saturday. On the tomb of Augustine is inscribed this epitaph:

"Here rests the Lord Augustine, first Archbishop of Canterbury, who, having been sent here by blessed Gregory, Pontiff of the City of Rome, and supported by God with miracles, guided King Ethelbert and his people from the worship of idols to the Faith of Christ. He ended the days of his duty in peace, and died on the twenty-sixth day of May in the above King's reign."

Book Three

Chapter 7: *The West Saxons accept the faith through the teaching of Birinus and his successors Agilbert and Leutherius* [635 CE]

During the reign of Cynegils,[1] the West Saxons, anciently known as the Gewissae, accepted the faith of Christ through the preaching of Bishop Birinus. He had come to Britain at the direction of Pope Honorius [I], having promised the Pope that he would sow the seeds of our holy faith in the distant lands beyond the English dominions where no other teacher had been before him. He was consecrated bishop by Asterius, Bishop of Genoa, at the Pope's command; but when he had reached Britain and entered the territory of the Gewissae, he found them completely heathen, and decided that it would be better to begin to preach the word of God among them rather than seek more distant converts. He therefore evangelized that province, and when he had instructed its king, he baptized him and his people. It happened at the time that the most holy and victorious Oswald was present, who greeted King Cynegils as he came from the font, and offered him an alliance most acceptable to God, taking him as his godson, and his daughter as wife. The two kings gave Bishop Birinus the city of Dorcic [Dorchester, Oxfordshire] for his episcopal see, and there he built and dedicated several churches, and brought many people

to God by his holy labors. He also died and was buried there; and many years later, when Haeddi was bishop, his body was translated to Venta [Winchester] and laid in the church of the blessed apostles Peter and Paul.

On the death of Cynegils, his son Cenwalh succeeded to the throne, but refused to accept the faith and sacraments of Christ. Not long afterwards he lost his kingdom, for he put away his wife, who was sister of Penda, king of Mercia, and took another woman. This led to war, and Cenwalh was driven out of his kingdom and took refuge with Anna, king of the East Angles. There he lived in exile for three years, during which he learned the Christian faith and received baptism. For Anna his host was a good man, and blessed with good and holy children, as I shall mention later.

When Cenwalh had been restored to his kingdom, there arrived in the province a bishop from Gaul named Agilbert, who had been studying the scriptures in Ireland for many years. This bishop came to the king, and voluntarily undertook to evangelize the country. Appreciating his learning and enthusiasm, the king asked him to accept an episcopal see and remain in the province as his chief bishop. Agilbert acceded to the king's request, and presided as bishop for many years. Later, however, the king, who understood only Saxon, grew tired of the bishop's foreign speech, and invited to the province a bishop of his own race called Wini, who had been consecrated in Gaul; and dividing his kingdom into two dioceses, he gave Wini the city of Venta—known by the Saxons as Wintancestir—as his see. This action gravely offended Agilbert, whom the king had not consulted in the matter, and he returned to Gaul, where he became Bishop of Paris and ended his days there at an advanced age. Not many years after Agilbert's departure from Britain, Wini was also driven from his bishopric by the king, and took refuge with Wulfhere, King of Mercia, to whom he offered money for the Bishopric of London, and held it till his death. So for a considerable time the province of the West Saxons remained without any bishop.

During this interval King Cenwalh, who had

---

1   West Saxon king ca. 611 to ca. 643.

often lost large areas of his kingdom to his enemies, eventually remembered that as he had formerly been driven from his throne because of his infidelity and had been restored to it after his acceptance of the Christian faith, so he was now justly deprived of God's protection because his kingdom has no bishop. He therefore sent messengers to Agilbert in Gaul, offering him satisfaction and requesting him to return to his bishopric. But Agilbert sent his regrets, and said that it was impossible for him to return, since he was now responsible for his own bishopric and city of Paris. But not wishing to appear unwilling to help, he sent in his place his nephew, the priest Leutherius[2] who could be made bishop if the king were agreeable, recommending him as worthy of a bishopric. Both king and people welcomed Leutherius with honor, and asked Theodore, then Archbishop of Canterbury, to consecrate him their bishop. He was accordingly consecrated at Canterbury, and for many years wisely ruled the West Saxon see with the full support of the synod.

Chapter 25: *Controversy arises with the Scots over the date of Easter* [*664 CE*]

When Bishop Aidan departed this life, he was succeeded in the Bishopric by Finan, who had been consecrated and sent by the Scots. He built a church in the Isle of Lindisfarne suitable for an episcopal see, constructing it, however, not of stone, but of hewn oak thatched with reeds after the Scots manner. It was later dedicated by the most reverend Archbishop Theodore in honor of the blessed Apostle Peter. But Eadbert, a later Bishop of Lindisfarne, removed the thatch, and covered both roof and walls with sheets of lead.

About this time there arose a great and recurrent controversy on the observance of Easter, those trained in Kent and Gaul maintaining that the Scottish observance was contrary to that of the universal Church. The most zealous champion of the true Easter was a Scot named Ronan, who had been instructed in Gaul and Italy in the authentic practice of the Church. He disputed against Finan and convinced many, or at least persuaded them to make a more careful enquiry into the truth. But

he entirely failed to move Finan, a hot-tempered man whom reproof made more obstinate and openly hostile to the truth. James, formerly the deacon of the venerable Archbishop Paulinus, of whom I have spoken, kept the true and Catholic Easter with all whom he could persuade to adopt the right observance. Also Queen Eanfled and her court, having a Kentish priest named Romanus who followed the Catholic practice, observed the customs she had seen in Kent. It is said that the confusion in those days was such that Easter was sometimes kept twice in one year, so that when the king had ended Lent and was keeping Easter, the queen and her attendants were still fasting and keeping Palm Sunday. During Aidan's lifetime these differences of Easter observance were patiently tolerated by everyone; for it was realized that, although he was in loyalty bound to retain the customs of those who sent him, he nevertheless labored diligently to cultivate the faith, piety, and love that marks out God's saints. He was therefore rightly loved by all, even by those who differed from his opinion on Easter, and was held in high respect not only by ordinary folk, but by Honorius of Canterbury and Felix of the East Angles.

When Finan, who followed Aidan as bishop, died, he was succeeded by another Irishman, Colman, under whom an even more serious controversy arose about Easter and also about other rules of Church discipline. This dispute rightly began to trouble the minds and consciences of many people, who feared that they might have received the name of Christian in vain. Eventually the matter came to the notice of King Oswy and his son Alchfrid. Oswy thought nothing could be better than the Scots teaching, having been instructed and baptized by the Scots and having a complete grasp of their language. But Alchfrid, who had been instructed in the faith by Wilfrid—a very learned man who had gone to Rome to study the doctrine of the Church, and spent a long time at Lyons under Dalfin, Archbishop of Gaul, from whom he had received the tonsure—knew that Wilfrid's doctrine was in fact preferable to all the traditions of the Scots. He had therefore given him a monastery with forty

---

2   Latinized form of the name "'Hlothere."

hides of land at In-Hrypum [Ripon]. Actually, he had given this not long previously to the adherents of the Scottish customs; but since, when offered the alternative, these preferred to give up the place rather than alter their customs, he then offered it to Wilfrid, whose life and teaching made him a worthy recipient. About this time, Agilbert, Bishop of the West Saxons, whom I have mentioned, had come to visit the province of the Northumbrians. He was a friend both of King Alchfrid and of Abbot Wilfrid and stayed with them for some time, and at the king's request he made Wilfrid a priest in his monastery. He also had with him a priest named Agatho. So when discussion arose there on the questions of Easter, the tonsure, and various other church matters, it was decided to hold a synod to put an end to this dispute at the monastery of Streanaeshalch, which means The Bay of the Beacon, then ruled by the Abbess Hilda, a woman devoted to God. Both kings, father and son, came to this synod, and so did Bishop Colman with his Scots clergy, and Bishop Agilbert with the priests Agatho and Wilfrid. James and Romanus supported the latter, while Abbess Hilda and her community, together with the venerable bishop Cedd, supported the Scots. Cedd, who as already mentioned had long ago been ordained by the Scots, acted as a most careful interpreter for both parties at the council.

King Oswy opened by observing that all who served the One God should observe one rule of life, and since they all hoped for one kingdom of heaven, they should not differ in celebrating the sacraments of heaven. The synod now had the task of determining which was the truer tradition, and this should be loyally accepted by all. He then directed his own bishop Colman to speak first, and to explain his own rite and its origin. Then Colman said: "The Easter customs which I observe were taught me by my superiors, who sent me here as a bishop; and all our forefathers, men beloved of God, are known to have observed these customs. And lest anyone condemn or reject them as wrong, it is recorded that they owe their origin to the blessed evangelist Saint John, the disciple especially loved by our Lord, and all the churches over which he presided." When he had concluded these and similar arguments, the king directed Agilbert to explain the origin and authority of his own customs. Agilbert replied: "May I request that my disciple the priest Wilfrid be allowed to speak in my place? For we are both in full agreement with all those here present who support the traditions of our Church, and he can explain our view in the English language more competently and clearly than I can do through an interpreter." When Wilfrid had received the king's command to speak, he said: "Our Easter customs are those that we have seen universally observed in Rome, where the blessed apostles Peter and Paul lived, taught, suffered, and are buried. We have also seen the same customs generally observed throughout Italy and Gaul when we traveled through these countries for study and prayer. Furthermore, we have learnt that Easter is observed by men of different nations and languages at one and the same time, in Africa, Asia, Egypt, Greece, and throughout the world wherever the Church of Christ has spread. The only people who stupidly contend against the whole world are these Scots and their partners in obstinacy the Picts and Britons, who inhabit only a portion of these two uttermost islands of the ocean." In reply to this statement, Colman answered: "It is strange that you call us stupid when we uphold customs that rest on the authority of so great an apostle, who was considered worthy to lean on our Lord's breast, and whose great wisdom is acknowledged throughout the world." Wilfrid replied: "Far be it from us to charge John with stupidity, because he literally observed the Law of Moses at a time when the Church followed many Jewish practices, and the apostles were not able immediately to abrogate the observances of the Law once given by God, lest they gave offence to believers who were Jews (whereas idols, on the other hand, being inventions of the Devil, must be renounced by all converts). For this reason Paul circumcised Timothy, offered sacrifice in the Temple, and shaved his head at Corinth with Aquila and Priscilla, for no other reason than that of avoiding offense to the Jews. For James said to Paul: '*Thou seest, brother, how many thousands of Jews there are which believe; and they are all zealous of the law.*' But today, as the Gospel spreads throughout the world, it is unnecessary and indeed unlawful for the faithful to be circumcised or to offer animals to God in sacrifice. John, following the custom of the Law, used to begin the feast of Easter on the evening of the fourteenth day of the first month, not caring whether it fell on the Sabbath or on any other day. But Peter, when he preached in Rome, remembering that it was on the day after the Sabbath that our Lord rose from the dead and gave the world the hope of resurrection, realized that Easter should be kept as follows: like John, in accordance with the law, he waited for moonrise on the evening of the fourteenth day of the first month. And if the Lord's Day, then called the morrow of the Sabbath, fell on the following day, he began to observe Easter the same evening, as we all do today. But, if the Lord's Day did not fall on the day following the fourteenth day of the moon, but on the sixteenth, seventeenth, or any day up to the twenty-first, he waited until that day, and on the Sabbath evening preceding it he began the observance of the Easter Festival. This evangelical and apostolical tradition does not abrogate but fulfil the Law, which ordained that the Passover be kept between the eve of the fourteenth and twenty-first days of the moon of that month. And this is the custom of all the successors of blessed John in Asia since his death, and is also that of the worldwide Church. This is the true and only Easter to be observed by the faithful. It was not newly decreed by the Council of Nicaea, but reaffirmed by it, as Church history records. It is quite apparent, Colman, that you follow neither the example of John, as you imagine, nor that of Peter, whose tradition you deliberately contradict. Your keeping of Easter agrees neither with the Law nor with the Gospel. For John, who kept Easter in accordance with the decrees of Moses, did not keep to the first day after the Sabbath; but this is not your practice, for you keep Easter only on the first day after the Sabbath. Peter kept Easter between the fifteenth and twenty-first days of the moon; you do not, for you keep it between the fourteenth and twentieth days of the month. As a result, you often begin Easter on the evening of the thirteenth day, which is not mentioned in the Law. Nor did our Lord, the Author and Giver of the Gospel, eat the old Passover or institute the Sacrament of the New Testament to be celebrated by the Church in memory of His Passion on that day, but on the fourteenth. Furthermore, when you keep Easter, you totally exclude the twenty-first day, which the

Law of Moses particularly ordered to be observed. Therefore, I repeat, you follow neither John nor Peter, the Law nor the Gospel, in your keeping of our greatest Festival."

Colman in reply said: "Do you maintain that Anatolius, a holy man highly spoken of in Church history, taught contrary to the Law and the Gospel, when he wrote that Easter should be kept between the fourteenth and twentieth days of the moon? Are we to believe that our most revered Father Columba and his successors, men so dear to God, thought or acted contrary to Holy Scripture when they followed this custom? The holiness of many of them is confirmed by heavenly signs, and their virtues by miracles; and having no doubt that they are Saints, I shall never cease to emulate their lives, customs, and discipline."

"It is well established that Anatolius was a most holy, learned, and praiseworthy man," answered Wilfrid; "but how can you claim his authority when you do not follow his directions? For he followed the correct rule about Easter, and observed a cycle of nineteen years; but either you do not know of this general custom of the Christian Church, or else you ignore it. He calculated the fourteenth day of the moon at Easter according to the Egyptian method, counting it in the evening as the fifteenth day; similarly, he assigned the twentieth to Easter Sunday, regarding it after sunset as the twenty-first day. But it appears that you do not realize this distinction, since you sometimes keep Easter before full moon, that is, on the thirteenth day. And with regard to your Father Columba and his followers, whose holiness you claim to imitate and whose rules and customs you claim to have been supported by heavenly signs, I can only say that when many shall say to our Lord at the day of judgment: *'Have we not prophesied in Thy name, and cast out devils, and done many wonderful works?'* the Lord will reply, *'I never knew you.'* Far be it from me to apply these words to your fathers; for it is more than just to believe good rather than evil of those whom one does not know. So I do not deny that they were true servants of God and dear to Him, and that they loved Him in primitive simplicity but in devout sincerity. Nor do I think that their ways of keeping Easter were seriously harmful, so long as no one came to show them a more perfect way to follow. Indeed, I feel that, if any Catholic reckoner had come to them, they would readily have accepted his guidance, as we know that they readily observed such of God's ordinances as they already knew. But you and your colleagues are most certainly guilty of sin if you reject the decrees of the apostolic see, indeed of the universal Church, which are confirmed by Holy Writ. For, although your Fathers were holy men, do you imagine that they, a few men in a corner of a remote island, are to be preferred before the universal Church of Christ throughout the world? And even if your Columba—or, may I say, ours also if he was the servant of Christ—was a saint potent in miracles, can he take precedence before the most blessed Prince of the Apostles, to whom our Lord said: '*Thou art Peter, and upon this rock I will build my Church, and the gates of hell shall not prevail against it, and I will give unto thee the keys of the kingdom of heaven*'?"

When Wilfrid had ended, the king asked: "Is it true, Colman, that these words were spoken to that Peter by our Lord?" He answered: "It is true, Your Majesty." Then the king said: "Can you show that a similar authority was given to your Columba?" "No," replied Colman. "Do you both agree," the king continued, "that these words were indisputably addressed to Peter in the first place, and that our Lord gave him the keys of the kingdom of heaven?" Both answered: "We do." At this, the king concluded: "Then, I tell you, Peter is guardian of the gates of heaven, and I shall not contradict him. I shall obey his commands in everything to the best of my knowledge and ability; otherwise, when I come to the gates of heaven, there may be no one to open them, because he who holds the keys has turned away."

When the king said this, all present, both high and low, signified their agreement and, abandoning their imperfect customs, hastened to adopt those which they had learned to be better.

16. KING ALFRED

THE FOLLOWING TEXTS RELATE to King Alfred of Wessex (849–899). Alfred led the Anglo-Saxon resistance to Danish invasions, united all of England not under Danish rule, and fostered a reform of English political and cultural life.

Alfred's laws (*Dooms*) were prepared between 871 and 899. Asser, who originally had been a monk and bishop, lived and worked with Alfred and assisted him with his translation of Gregory the Great's *Pastoral Care*; Asser used the Anglo-Saxon Chronicle as a source and Einhard's *Life of Charlemagne* as a model for his *Life of King Alfred*, which survived in only one copy but provides more information about Alfred than any other source and makes him the Anglo-Saxon king for whose reign we have the most information. The letter to Edward the Elder shows the importance of Alfred's legal program.

Source: Dorothy Whitelock (ed.), *English Historical Documents 500–1042*, vol. 1 (London: Eyre & Spottiswoode, 1955), 408–17, 264–76, 176–91.

Further Reading: Richard P. Abels, *Alfred the Great: War, Kingship, and Culture in Anglo-Saxon England* (London: Longman, 1998).

Dooms

Introduction

I, then, King Alfred, have collected these [dooms] and ordered them to be written down, many of those which our predecessors observed and which were also pleasing to me. And those which were not pleasing to me, by the advice of my *Witan*, I have rejected, ordering them to be observed only as amended. I have not ventured to put in writing much of my own, being uncertain what might please those who shall come after us. So I have here collected the dooms that seemed to me the most just, whether they were from the time of Ine, my kinsman, from that of Offa, king of the Mercians, or from that of Aethelbert, the first of the English to receive baptism; the rest I have discarded. I then, Alfred, king of the West Saxons, have shown these to all my *Witan* who have declared it is the will of all that they be observed …

1. First we direct, what is most necessary, that each man keep carefully his oath and pledge.
1.1. If anyone is wrongfully compelled to either of these, [to promise] treachery against his lord or any illegal aid, then it is better to leave it unfulfilled than to perform it.
1.2. [If, however, he pledges what it is right for him to perform,] and leaves it unfulfilled, let him with humility give his weapons and his possessions into his friends' keeping and be 40 days in prison at a king's estate; let him endure there what penance the bishop prescribes for him, and his kinsmen are to feed him if he has no food himself.
1.3. If he has no kinsmen and has not the food, the king's reeve is to feed him.
1.4. If he has to be forced thither, and will not go otherwise, and he is bound, he is to forfeit his weapons and his possessions.
1.5. If he is killed, he is to lie unpaid for.
1.6. If he escapes before the end of the period, and he is caught, he is to be 40 days in prison, as he should have been before.
1.7. If he gets clear, he is to be outlawed, and to be excommunicated from all the churches of Christ.
1.8 If, however, there is secular surety for him, he is to pay for the breach of surety as the law directs him, and for the breach of pledge as his confessor prescribes for him.

2. If anyone for any guilt flees to any one of the monastic houses to which the king's food-rent belongs, or to some other privileged community which is worthy of honor, he is to have a respite of three days to protect himself, unless he wishes to be reconciled.
2.1. If during that respite he is molested with slaying or binding or wounding, each of those [who did it] is to make amends according to the legal

custom, both with wergild and with fine, and to pay to the community 120 shillings as compensation for the breach of sanctuary, and is to have forfeited his own [claim against the culprit].

3. If anyone violates the king's surety, he is to pay compensation for the charge as the law directs him, and for the breach of the surety with five pounds of pure pennies. The breach of the archbishop's surety or of his protection is to be compensated with three pounds; the breach of the surety or protection of another bishop or an ealdorman is to be compensated with two pounds.

4. If anyone plots against the king's life, directly or by harboring his exiles or his men, he is liable to forfeit his life and all that he owes.
4.1. If he wishes to clear himself, he is to do it by [an oath equivalent to] the king's wergild.
4.2 Thus also we determine concerning all ranks, both *ceorl* and noble: he who plots against his lord's life is to be liable to forfeit his life and all that he owns, or to clear himself by his lord's wergild.

5. Also we determine this sanctuary for every church which a bishop has consecrated: if a man exposed to a vendetta reaches it running or riding, no one is to drag him out for seven days, if he can live in spite of hunger, unless he himself fights [his way] out. If however anyone does so, he is liable to [pay for breach of] the king's protection and of the church's sanctuary—more, if he seizes more from there.
5.1. If the community have more need of their church, he is to be kept in another building, and it is to have no more doors than the church.
5.2. The head of that church is to take care that no one give him food during that period.
5.3. If he himself will hand out his weapons to his foes, they are to keep him for 30 days, and send notice about him to his kinsmen.
5.4. Further sanctuary of the church: if any man has recourse to the church on account of any crime which has not been discovered, and there confesses himself in God's name, it is to be half remitted.
5.5 Whoever steals on Sunday or at Christmas or Easter or on the Holy Thursday in Rogation days; each of those we wish to be compensated doubly, as in the Lenten fast.

6. If anyone steals anything in church, he is to pay the simple compensation and the fine normally belonging to that simple compensation, and the hand with which he did it is to be struck off.
6.1 And if he wishes to redeem the hand, and that is allowed to him, he is to pay in proportion to his wergild.

7. If anyone fights or draws his weapon in the king's hall, and he is captured, it is to be at the king's judgment, whether he will grant him death or life.
7.1 If he escapes, and is afterwards captured, he shall always pay for himself with his wergild, and compensate for the crime, with wergild as with fine, according to what he has done.

8. If anyone brings a nun out of a nunnery without the permission of the king or the bishop, he is to pay 120 shillings, half to the king and half to the bishop and the lord of the church which has the nun.
8.1. If she outlives him who brought her out, she is to have nothing of his inheritance.
8.2. If she bears a child, it is not to have any of that inheritance, any more than the mother.
8.3 If her child is killed, the share of the maternal kindred is to be paid to the king; the paternal kindred are to be given their share.

9. If a woman with child is slain when she is bearing the child, the woman is to be paid for with full payment, and the child at half payment according to the wergild of the father's kin.
9.1. The fine is always to be 60 shillings until the simple compensation rises to 30 shillings; when the simple compensation has risen to that, the fine is afterwards to be 120 shillings.
9.2. Formerly, [the fine] for the stealer of gold, the stealer of stud-horses, the stealer of bees, and many fines, were greater than others; now all are alike, except for the stealer of a man: 120 shillings.

10. If anyone lies with the wife of a man of a twelve-hundred wergild, he is to pay to the husband 120 shillings; to a man of a six-hundred wergild 100 shillings is to be paid; to a man of the *ceorl* class 40 shilling one ands is to be paid....

12. If a man burns or fells the wood of another, without permission, he is to pay for each large tree with five shillings, and afterwards for each, no matter how many there are, with fivepence; and 30 shillings as a fine.

13. If at a common task a man unintentionally kills another [by letting a tree fall on him] the tree is to be given to the kinsmen, and they are to have it from that estate within 30 days, or else he who owns the wood is to have the right to it.

14. If anyone is born dumb, or deaf, so that he cannot deny sins or confess them, the father is to pay compensation for his misdeeds.

15. If anyone fights or draws a weapon in the presence of the archbishop, he is to pay 150 shillings as compensation; if this happens in the presence of another bishop or of an ealdorman, he is to pay 100 shillings compensation.

16. If anyone steals a cow or a brood-mare and drives off a foal or a calf, he is to pay a shilling compensation [for the latter], and for the mothers according to their value.

17. If anyone entrusts to another one of his helpless dependants, and he dies during that time of fostering, he who reared him is to clear himself of guilt, if anyone accuses him of any.

18. If anyone in lewd fashion seizes a nun either by her clothes or her breast without her leave, the compensation is to be double that we have established for a lay person.
18.1. If a betrothed maiden commits fornication, if she is of *ceorl* birth, 60 shillings compensation is to be paid to the surety; and it is to be paid in livestock, cattle [only], and one is not to include in it any slave.
18.2. If she is a woman of a six-hundred wergild, 100 shillings are to be given to the surety.
18.3. If she is a woman of a twelve-hundred wergild, 120 shillings are to be paid to the surety.

19. If anyone lends his weapon to another that he may kill a man with it, they may, if they wish, join him to pay the wergild.
19.1. If they do not join, he who lent the weapon is to pay a third part of the wergild and a third part of the fine.
19.2. If he wishes to clear himself, that in making the loan he was aware of no evil intent, he may do so.
19.3. If a sword-polisher receives another man's weapon to polish it, or a smith a man's tool, they both are to give it back unstained,[1] just as either of them had received it; unless either of them had stipulated that he need not be liable to compensation for it.

20. If anyone entrusts property to another man's monk, without the permission of the monk's lord, and it is lost to him, he who owned it before is to bear the loss.

21. If a priest slays another man, he is to be handed over, and all of the [minster] property which he bought for himself, and the bishop is to unfrock him, when he is to be delivered up out of the minster, unless the lord is willing to settle the wergild on his behalf.

22. If anyone brings up a charge in a public meeting before the king's reeve, and afterwards wishes to withdraw it, he is to make the accusation against a more likely person, if he can; if he cannot, he is to forfeit his compensation.

23. If a dog rends or bites a man to death, [the owner] is to pay six shillings at the first offense; if he gives it food, he is to pay on a second occasion 12 shillings, on a third 30 shillings.
23.1. If in any of these misdeeds the dog is destroyed, nevertheless this compensation is still to be paid.
23.2. If the dog commits more offenses, and the owner retains it, he is to pay compensation for such wounds as the dog inflicts, according to the full wergild.

24. If a neat[2] wounds a man, [the owner] is to hand over the neat, or make terms.

---

1 Without it having been used to commit a crime.
2 Domestic cow or ox.

25. If anyone rapes a *ceorl*'s slave-woman, he is to pay five shillings compensation to the *ceorl*, and 60 shillings fine.

25.1. If a slave rape a slave-woman, he is to pay by suffering castration.

26 (29). If anyone with a band of men kills an innocent man of a two-hundred wergild, he who admits the slaying is to pay the wergild and the fine, and each man who was in that expedition is to pay 30 shillings as compensation for being in that band.

27 (30). If it is a man of a six-hundred wergild, each man [is to pay] 60 shillings as compensation for being in that band, and the slayer the wergild and full fine.

28 (31). If he is a man of a twelve-hundred wergild, each of them [is to pay] 120 shillings, and the slayer the wergild and the fine.

28.1 (31.1). If a band of men does this and afterwards wishes to deny it[3] on oath, they are all to be accused; and then they are all collectively to pay the wergild, and all one fine, as is accordant to the wergild.

29 (26). If anyone rapes a girl not of age, that is to be the same compensation as for an adult.

30 (27). If a man without paternal kinsmen fights and kills a man, and if then he has maternal kinsmen, those are to pay a third share of the wergild, [and the associates a third; for the third part] he is to flee.[4]

30.1 (27.1). If he has no maternal kinsmen, the associates are to pay half, and for half he is to flee.

31 (28). If anyone kills a man so placed, if he has no kinsmen, he is to pay half to the king, half to the associates.

32. If anyone is guilty of public slander, and it is proved against him, it is to be compensated for with no lighter penalty than the cutting off of his tongue, with the proviso that it be redeemed at no

cheaper rate than it is valued in proportion to the wergild.

33. If anyone charges another about a pledge sworn by God, and wishes to accuse him that he did not carry out any of those [promises] which he gave him, he [the plaintiff] is to pronounce the preliminary oath in four churches, and the other, if he wishes to clear himself, is to do it in twelve churches.

34. Moreover, it is prescribed for traders; they are to bring before the king's reeve in a public meeting the men whom they take up into the country with them, and it is to be established how many of them there are to be; and they are to take with them men whom they can afterwards bring to justice at a public meeting; and whenever it may be necessary for them to have more men out with them on their journey, it is always to be announced, as often as it is necessary for them, to the king's reeve in the witness of the meeting.

35. If anyone binds an innocent *ceorl*, he is to pay him ten shillings compensation.

35.1. If anyone scourges him, he is to pay him 20 shillings compensation.

35.2. If he places him in the stocks, he is to pay him 30 shillings compensation.

35.3. If in insult he disfigures him by cutting his hair, he is to pay him 10 shillings compensation.

35.4. If, without binding him, he cuts his hair like a priest's, he is to pay him 30 shillings compensation.

36. Moreover, it is established; if anyone has a spear over his shoulder, and a man is transfixed on it, the wergild is to be paid without the fine.

36.1. If he transfixed before his eyes, he is to pay the wergild; if anyone accuses him of intention in this act, he is to clear himself in proportion to the fine, and by that [oath] do away with the fine,

36.2. If the point is higher than the butt end of the shaft. If they are both level, the point and the butt end, that is to be [considered] without risk.

---

3   *I.e.*, each wishes to deny being the actual slayer.
4   This shows that the payment of their proper share frees the kinsmen from the dangers of a vendetta, even if the whole wergild is not paid. The slayer himself remains exposed if his own third is unpaid.

37. If anyone from one district wishes to seek a lord in another district, he is to do so with the witness of the ealdorman, in whose shire he previously served.

37.1. If he do it without his witness, he who accepts him as his man is to pay 120 shillings compensation; he is, however, to divide it, half to the king in the shire in which the man served previously, half in that into which he has come.

37.2. If he has committed any wrong where he was before, he who now receives him as his man is to pay compensation for it, and 120 shillings to the king as fine.

38. If anyone fights in a meeting in the presence of the king's ealdorman, he is to pay wergild and fine, as it is the law, and before that, 120 shillings to the ealdorman as a fine.

38.1. If he disturbs a public meeting by drawing a weapon, [he is to pay] 120 shillings to the ealdorman as a fine.

38.2. If any of this takes place in the presence of the deputy of the king's ealdorman, or of the king's priest, 30 shillings [is to be paid] as a fine.

39. If anyone fights in the house of a *ceorl*, he is to pay six shillings compensation to the *ceorl*.

39.1. If he draws a weapon and does not fight, it is to be half as much.

39.2. If either of these things happens to a man of a six-hundred wergild, it is to amount to threefold the compensation to a *ceorl*; [if] to a man of a twelve-hundred wergild, to double that of the man of the six-hundred wergild.

40. Forcible entry into the king's residence shall be 120 shillings; into the archbishop's, 90 shillings; into another bishop's or an ealdorman's, 60 shillings; into that of a man of a twelve-hundred wergild, 30 shillings; into that of a man of a six-hundred wergild, 15 shillings; forcible entry into a *ceorl*'s enclosure, five shillings.

40.1. If any of this happens when the army has been called out, or in the Lenten fast, the compensations are to be doubled.

40.2. If anyone openly neglects the rules of the Church in Lent without permission, he is to pay 120 shillings compensation.

41. The man who holds bookland, which his kinsmen left to him—then we establish that he may not alienate it from his kindred if there is a document or witness [to show] that he was prohibited from doing so by those men who acquired it in the beginning and by those who gave it to him; and that is then to be declared[5] in the witness of the king and of the bishop, in the presence of his kinsmen.

42. Moreover we command: that the man who knows his opponent[6] to be dwelling at home is not to fight before he asks justice for himself.

42.1. If he has sufficient power to surround his opponent and besiege him there in his house, he is to keep him seven days inside and not fight against him, if he will remain inside; and then after seven days, if he will surrender and give up his weapons, he is to keep him unharmed for 30 days, and send notice about him to his kinsmen and his friends.

42.2. If he, however, reaches a church, it is then to be [dealt with] according to the privilege of the church, as we have said before.

42.3. If he [the attacker] has not sufficient power to besiege him in his house, he is to ride to the ealdorman and ask him for support; if he will not give him support, he is to ride to the king, before having recourse to fighting.

42.4. Likewise, if a man run across his opponent, and did not previously know him to be at home, if he will give up his weapons, he is to be kept for 30 days and his friends informed; if he will not give up his weapons, then he may fight against him. If he is willing to surrender, and to give up his weapons, and after that anyone fights against him, he [who does] is to pay wergild or compensation for wounds according to what he has done, and a fine, and is to have forfeited [the right to avenge] his kinsman.

42.5. Moreover we declare that a man may fight on behalf of his lord, if the lord is being attacked, without incurring a vendetta. Similarly the lord may fight on behalf of his man.

42.6. In the same way, a man may fight on behalf of his born kinsman, if he is being wrongfully attacked, except against his lord; that we do not allow.

42.7. And a man may fight without incurring a

---

5   By whoever is contesting the alienation of the land.
6   A man against whom he has a legitimate blood-feud.

vendetta if he finds another man with his wedded wife, within closed doors or under the same blanket, or with his legitimate daughter or his legitimate sister, or with his mother who was given as a lawful wife to his father.

43. These days are to be given to all free men, but not to slaves or unfree laborers: 12 days at Christmas, and the day on which Christ overcame the Devil, and the anniversary of St. Gregory, and seven days at Easter and seven days after, and one day at the feast of St. Peter and St. Paul, and in harvest-time the whole week before the feast of St. Mary, and one day at the feast of All Saints. And the four Wednesdays in the four Ember weeks[7] are to be given to all slaves, to sell to whomsoever they choose anything of what anyone has given them in God's name, or of what they can earn in any of their leisure moments.[8]

The Treaty between Alfred and Guthrum (886–890)

PROLOGUE. This is the peace which King Alfred and King Guthrum and the councillors of all the English race and all the people which is in East Anglia have all agreed on and confirmed with oaths, for themselves and for their subjects, both for the living and those yet unborn, who care to have God's grace or ours.

1. First concerning our boundaries: up the Thames, and then up the Lea, and along the Lea to its source, then in a straight line to Bedford, then up the Ouse to the Watling Street.[9]

2. This is next, if a man is slain, all of us estimate Englishmen and Dane at the same amount, at eight half-marks[10] of refined gold, except the *ceorl* who occupies rented land, and their [the Danes'] freedmen; these also are estimated at the same amount, both at 200 shillings.

3. And if anyone accuses a king's thegn[11] of manslaughter, if he dares to clear himself by oath, he is to do it with 12 king's thegns; if anyone accuses a man who is less powerful than a king's thegn, he is to clear himself with 12 of his equals and with one king's thegn—and so in every suit which involves more than four mancuses—and if he dare not [clear himself], he is to pay three-fold compensation, according as it is valued.

4. And that each man is to know his warrantor at [the purchase of] men or horses or oxen.

5. And we all agreed on the day when the oaths were sworn, that no slaves nor freemen might go without permission into the army of the Danes, any more than any of theirs to us. But if it happens that from necessity any one of them wishes to have traffic with us, or we with them, for cattle or goods, it is to be permitted on condition that hostages shall be given as a pledge of peace and as evidence so that one may know no fraud is intended.

Letter to King Edward the Elder explaining the history of an estate at Fonthill, Wiltshire (899–924, probably early in the reign)

Sire, I will inform you what happened about the land at Fonthill, the five hides which Æthelhelm Higa is claiming. When Helmstan committed the crime of stealing Æthelred's belt, Higa at once began to bring a charge against him, along with other claimants, and wished to win the land from him by litigation. Then he came to me and begged me to intercede for him, because I had stood sponsor to him at his confirmation before he committed that crime. Then—may God repay his soul—he allowed him to be entitled to prove his right against Æthelhelm as regards the land, because of my advocacy and true account. Then he ordered that they should be brought to agreement, and I was one of the men appointed to do

---

7   The weeks in which occur four sets of three days of fasting, spaced through the year.
8   The rest of the code consists of a tariff of the compensations to be paid for wounds of various kinds and for other injuries.
9   An ancient roadway from Canterbury and St Albans.
10 A mark was a Scandinavian weight, by the end of the next century, and perhaps already, about 3440-3520 grains. The amount here stated may represent a recognized Scandinavian wergild, but, if the ratio of gold to silver was approximately 10:1 at this time, it would not be very far from the wergild of the highest English class.
11 An aristocratic retainer of a king.

it, and Wihtbord and Ælfric, who was then keeper of the wardrobe, and Brihthelm and Wulfhun the Black of Somerton, and Strica and Ubba and more men than I can now name. Then each of them gave his account, and it then seemed to us all that Helmstan should be allowed to come forward with the title-deeds and prove his right to the land, that he had it as Æthelthryth had sold it into Oswulf's possession at a suitable price; and she had told Oswulf that she was entitled to sell it to him because it was her "morning-gift" when she married Æthelwulf. And Helmstan included all this in the oath. And King Alfred had given his signature to Oswulf, when he bought the land from Æthelthryth, that it might thus remain valid, and Edward gave his and Æthelnoth his and Deormod his, and so did each of the men whom one then wished to have. And when we were reconciling them at Wardour, the deed was produced and read, and the signatures were all written on it. Then it seemed to all of us who were at that arbitration that Helmstan was the nearer to the oath on that account.

Then Æthelhelm would not fully assent until we went in to the king and told exactly how we had decided it and why we had decided it; and Æthelhelm stood himself in there with us. And the king stood in the chamber at Wardour—he was washing his hands. When he had finished, he asked Æthelhelm why what we had decided for him did not seem just to him; he said that he could think of nothing more just then than that Helmstan should be allowed to give the oath if he could. I then said that he wished to attempt it, and asked the king to appoint a day for it, and he then did so. And on that appointed day he performed the oath fully. He asked me to help him, and said that he would rather give [the land to me] than that the oath should fail or it ever …. Then I said that I would help him to obtain justice, but never to any wrong, on condition that he granted it to me; and he gave me a pledge to that.

And then we rode on that appointed day, I— and Wihtbord rode with me, and Brihthelm rode there with Æthelhelm; and we all heard that he gave the oath in full. Then we all said that it was a closed suit when the sentence had been fulfilled. And, Sire, when will any suit be ended if one can end it neither with money nor with an oath? And if one wishes to change every judgment which King Alfred gave, when shall we have finished disputing? And he then gave me the title-deed just as he had pledged to do, as soon as the oath was given; and I promised him that he might use the land as long as he lived, if he would keep himself out of disgrace.

Then on top of that—I do not know whether it was a year and a half or two years later—he stole the untended oxen at Fonthill, by which he was completely ruined, and drove them to Chicklade, and there he was discovered, and the man who tracked him rescued the traced cattle [?]. Then he fled, and a bramble scratched him in the face; and when he wished to deny it, that was brought in evidence against him. Then Eanwulf, Peneard's son, who was the reeve, intervened, and took from him all the property that he owned at Tisbury. I then asked him why he did so, and he said that he was a thief, and the property was adjudged to the king, because he was the king's man. And Ordlaf succeeded to his land; because what he was occupying was held on lease from him, he could not forfeit it. And you then pronounced him an outlaw. Then he sought your father's body, and brought a seal[12] to me, and I was with you at Chippenham. Then I gave the seal to you, and you removed his outlawry and gave him the estate to which he still has withdrawn [?]. And I succeeded to my land, and then in your witness and that of your councillors I gave it to the bishop, five hides in exchange for the land of five hides at Lyddiard. And the bishop and all the community granted me the four hides, and the fifth was subject to tithe. Now, Sire, it is very necessary for me that it may remain as it is now arranged and was before. If it shall be otherwise, then I must and will be satisfied with what seems right to you as a charitable gift.

Endorsement
And Æthelhelm Higa retired from the dispute when the king was at Warminster, in the witness of Ordlaf and Osferth and Odda and Wihtbord and Ælfstan the Bald and Æthelnoth.

---

12 Probably a document authenticated by a seal, to show that he had taken an oath at the king's tomb.

Asser's Life of King Alfred

To my venerable and most pious lord, ruler of all the Christians of the island of Britain, Alfred, king of the Anglo-Saxons, Asser, lowest of all the servants of God, wishes thousandfold prosperity in both the present and future life, according to his prayers and desires.

Chap. 1. In the year of our Lord's incarnation 849, Alfred, king of the Anglo-Saxons, was born in the royal residence called Wantage, in the shire which is named Berkshire; which shire is thus called from the wood *Berroc*, where box grows very abundantly ....[13]

Chap. 2. His mother was called Osburh, a very religious woman, noble in character, noble also by birth; for she was the daughter of Oslac, the renowned cupbearer of King Æthelwulf. This Oslac was by race a Goth, for he was sprung from the Goths and Jutes, namely from the stock of Stuf and Wihtgar, two brothers, and also ealdormen, who received the rule over the Isle of Wight from their uncle King Cerdic and his son Cynric, their cousin. They killed the few British inhabitants of the island whom they could find on it at the place called *Wihtgarabyrig*; for the rest of the inhabitants of the island had either already been killed or had fled as exiles ....

Chap. 12. But meanwhile,[14] King Æthelwulf was lingering beyond the sea for some little time, a certain disgraceful thing, contrary to the practice of all Christians, arose to the west of Selwood. For King Æthelbald, son of King Æthelwulf, and Ealhstan, bishop of the church of Somerset, are said to have plotted that King Æthelwulf should not be received again into the kingship when he returned from Rome. This unhappy business, unheard of in all previous ages, very many persons ascribe to the bishop and the ealdorman alone, by whose counsel it is said this deed was done. But there are also many who impute it solely to the royal pride, because that king was stubborn in this affair and in many other wrong acts, as we

have heard from certain men's accounts; and this was proved by the outcome of the affair. For as King Æthelwulf was returning from Rome, his son aforesaid, with all his counselors, or rather conspirators, tried to commit so great a crime as to keep the king out of his own kingdom; but God did not allow it to happen, neither did the nobles of all the Saxon land consent. For, in order that the irremediable danger to the Saxon land from civil war, with father and son at war, or rather with the whole people fighting against one or the other of them, might not grow more fierce and cruel from day to day, the kingdom previously united was by the indescribable forbearance of the father and the assent of all the nobles divided between father and son; and the eastern districts were assigned to the father, the western, on the other hand, to the son. Thus, where the father ought to have reigned by rights, the wicked and stubborn son reigned; for the western part of the Saxon land has always been more important than the eastern.

Chap. 13. When therefore King Æthelwulf arrived from Rome, all the people, as was fitting, rejoiced so greatly at the coming of their lord, that, if he had allowed it, they wished to deprive his stubborn son Æthelbald, with all his counselors, of any share in the kingdom. But he, as we have said, exercising great forbearance and prudent counsel, lest danger should befall the kingdom, would not have it done thus. And without any opposition or illfeeling on his nobles' part, he ordered that Judith, daughter of King Charles, whom he had received from her father, was to sit beside him on the royal throne as long as he lived, contrary to the wrongful custom of that nation. For the people of the West Saxons did not allow the queen to sit next the king, or even to be called queen, but "wife of the king" ....[15]

Chap. 16. Thus King Æthelwulf lived two years after he came back from Rome. During these years, among many other good endeavors in this present life, meditating on his departure on the way of all flesh, he ordered to be written a testamentary, or rather an advisory, letter, so that his sons should

---

13   Here follows his genealogy.
14   *I.e.,* while Æthelwulf was away on his visit to Rome in 855.
15   Here follows a story that this custom arose from the evil behavior of Offa's daughter, Eadburh, wife of Brihtric of Wessex, part of which Asser tells on Alfred's authority.

not dispute unduly among themselves after their father's death; in this he took care to command in writing in due form, a division of the kingdom between his sons, that is to say the two eldest, of his own inheritance between his sons and daughter and his relations also, and of the money, which he should leave, between the needs of the soul and his sons and also his nobles. Concerning this prudent policy we have decided to record a few examples out of many, for posterity to imitate, namely such as are understood to belong particularly to the necessities of the soul. It is unnecessary to insert the rest, which belong to human dispensation, in this little book, lest by its length it should arouse disgust in the readers and also in those desiring to hear it. For the benefit of his soul then, which he had been zealous to promote in all things from the first flower of his youth, he enjoined that his successors after him until the Day of Judgment were always to supply with food, drink and clothing, one poor man, whether a native or foreigner, from every ten hides throughout all his hereditary land, provided that that land was occupied by men and herds, and had not become waste land. He gave orders also that a great sum of money was every year to be taken to Rome for his soul, namely 300 mancuses, which were to be divided there thus: 100 mancuses in honor of St. Peter, especially for the purchase of oil to fill all the lamps of that apostolic church on Easter eve and likewise at cockcrow, and 100 mancuses in honor of St. Paul on the same terms, for the purchase of oil to fill the lamps on Easter eve and at cockcrow, and 100 mancuses also for the universal apostolic pope.

Chap. 17. But when King Æthelwulf was dead, his son Æthelbald, contrary to God's prohibition and Christian dignity, and also against the usage of all pagans, ascending the bed of his father, married Judith, daughter of Charles, king of the Franks, earning much infamy from all who heard of it; and ruled the government of the kingdom of the West Saxons for two and a half years after his father's death. ...

Chap. 21. ... I think that we should return to what specially incited me to this work; that is to say, that I consider that I should insert briefly in this place the little that has come to my knowledge concerning the character of my revered lord, Alfred, king of the Anglo-Saxons, during his childhood and boyhood.

Chap. 22. Now, he was loved by his father and mother, and indeed by everybody, with a united and immense love, more than all his brothers, and was always brought up in the royal court, and as he passed through his childhood and boyhood he appeared fairer in form than all his brothers, and more pleasing in his looks, his words and his ways. And from his cradle a longing for wisdom before all things and among all the pursuits of this present life, combined with his noble birth, filled the noble temper of his mind; but alas, by the unworthy carelessness of his parents and tutors, he remained ignorant of letters until his twelfth year, or even longer. But he listened attentively to Saxon poems day and night, and hearing them often recited by others committed them to his retentive memory. A keen huntsman, he toiled unceasingly in every branch of hunting, and not in vain; for he was without equal in his skill and good fortune in that art, as also in all other gifts of God, as we have ourselves often seen.

Chap. 23. When, therefore, his mother one day was showing him and his brothers a certain book of Saxon poetry which she held in her hand, she said: "I will give this book to whichever of you can learn it most quickly." And moved by these words, or rather by divine inspiration, and attracted by the beauty of the initial letter of the book, Alfred said in reply to his mother, forestalling his brothers, his elders in years though not in grace: "Will you really give this book to one of us, to the one who can soonest understand and repeat it to you?" And, smiling and rejoicing, she confirmed it, saying: "To him will I give it." Then taking the book from her hand he immediately went to his master, who read it. And when it was read, he went back to his mother and repeated it.

Chap. 24. After this he learnt the daily course, that is, the services of the hours, and then certain psalms and many prayers. He collected these into one book and carried it about with him everywhere in his bosom (as I have myself seen) day and night, for the sake of prayer, through all the changes of this present life, and was never parted from it. But alas, what he principally desired, the liberal arts, he did not obtain according to his wish, because, as he was wont to say, there were at that time no good scholars in all the kingdom of the West Saxons.

Chap. 25. He often affirmed with frequent laments and sighs from the bottom of his heart, that among all his difficulties and hindrances in this present life this was the greatest; that, during the time when he had youth and leisure and aptitude for learning, he had no teachers; but when he was more advanced in years, he did have teachers and writers to some extent, when he was not able to study, because he was harassed, nay, rather disturbed, day and night both with illnesses unknown to all the physicians of this island, and with the cares of the royal office at home and abroad, and also with the invasions of pagans by land and sea. Yet, among all the difficulties of this present life, from infancy unto the present day, he has never abandoned that same insatiable longing, and even now still yearns for it....

Chap. 75. Sons and daughters were born to him by the aforesaid wife, namely Æthelflæd, the firstborn, and after her Edward, then Æthelgifu, next Ælfthryth, then Æthelweard, besides those who were snatched away in infancy by an early death.... Æthelflæd, when she reached marriageable age, was joined in matrimony to Æthelred, ealdorman of the Mercians. Æthelgifu, devoted to God as a virgin, subjected and consecrated to the rules of the monastic life, entered the service of God. Æthelweard, the youngest, was given over by the divine counsel and the admirable prudence of the king to the pleasures of literary studies, along with almost all the children of noble birth of the whole country, and also many of humble birth, under the diligent care of masters. In that school, books of both languages, Latin, that is, and English, were assiduously read, and they had leisure for writing; so that before they had the strength for manly pursuits, namely hunting and other pursuits which are fitting for noblemen, they were zealous and skilled in the liberal arts. Edward and Ælfthryth were always brought up in the royal court, with

great care from their tutors and nurses, and indeed, with great affection from all; and until this day they continue there, showing humility, affability and gentleness to all, whether their countrymen or foreigners, and great obedience to their father. Nor, indeed, are they allowed to live idly and carelessly without a liberal education among the other occupations of this present life which are fitting for nobles; for they have learnt carefully psalms and Saxon books, and especially Saxon poems, and they frequently make use of books.

Chap. 76. Meanwhile the king, in the midst of wars and frequent hindrances of this present life, and also of the raids of the pagans and his daily infirmities of body did not cease, single-handed, assiduously and eagerly with all his might, to govern the kingdom, to practice every branch of hunting, to instruct his goldsmiths and aid his craftsmen, and his falconers, hawkers and dog-keepers, to erect buildings to his own new design more stately and magnificent than had been the custom of his ancestors, to recite Saxon books, and especially to learn by heart Saxon poems, and command others to do so. He also was in the habit of hearing daily the divine office, the Mass, and certain prayers and psalms, and of observing both the day and the night hours, and of visiting churches at night-time, as we have said, in order to pray without his followers knowing. Moreover, he showed zeal for almsgiving, and generosity both to his countrymen and to strangers from all nations, and very great and matchless kindness and pleasantness towards all men, and skill in searching into things unknown. And many Franks, Frisians, men of Gaul, pagans, Welsh, Scots and Bretons willingly submitted to his lordship, both noblemen and men of humble rank; and he ruled them all in accordance with his own honorable nature just like his own people, and loved and honored them, and enriched them with money and rights. Also he was accustomed to listen to the Holy Scripture recited by native clergy, but also, if by chance someone had come from elsewhere, to listen with equal earnestness and attention to prayers along with foreigners. He also loved his bishops and all the ecclesiastical order, his ealdormen and his nobles, his officials and all members of his household, with a wonderful affection.

And he himself never ceased among other occupations, day and night, to train their sons, who were being brought up in the royal household, in all good behavior, and to educate them in letters, loving them no less than his own sons. Yet, as if he had no comfort in all these things and as if he suffered no disquiet from within or without, he complained in anxious sadness by day and night to God and to all who were bound to him in close affection, and lamented with repeated sighs, that Almighty God had not made him skilled in divine wisdom and the liberal arts; emulating in this the pious and most illustrious and rich Solomon, king of the Hebrews, who, despising all present glory and riches, sought first wisdom from God, and also found both, wisdom and present glory, as it is written: "Seek therefore first the kingdom of God and his justice, and all these things shall be granted unto you." But God, who always sees into the inmost thoughts, and prompts our designs and all good desires, and also most amply ordains that good desires may be obtained, and who never prompts anyone to desire well without also ordaining what each man well and justly desires to have, stirred up the king's mind from within, not without; as it is written: "I will hear what the Lord God will speak in me." Whenever he could, he would acquire assistants in his good design, who could help him to the desired wisdom, that he might obtain what he longed for. Forthwith, like the prudent bee, which arises in the summer-time at dawn from its beloved cells and, directing its course in swift flight through the unknown ways of the air, alights upon many and various blossoms of herbs, plants and fruits, and finds and carries home what pleases it most, he turned afar the gaze of his mind, seeking abroad what he had not at home, that is, in his own kingdom.

Chap. 77. And then God, suffering no longer his so good and just complaint, sent for the king's goodwill some consolations, certain lights, as it were, namely Wærferth, bishop of the church of Worcester, a man well versed in the divine Scriptures, who at the king's command first translated clearly and beautifully from Latin into the Saxon language the books of the "Dialogues" of Pope Gregory and his disciple Peter, sometimes giving a paraphrase; and then Plegmund,

a Mercian by race, archbishop of the church of Canterbury, a venerable man, endowed with wisdom; also Æthelstan and Wærwulf, priests and chaplains, learned men, of Mercian race. King Alfred summoned these four to him from Mercia, and advanced them with great honors and authority in the kingdom of the West Saxons, in addition to those which Archbishop Plegmund and Bishop Wærferth possessed in Mercia. By the teaching and wisdom of all these men, the king's desire was ceaselessly increased and fulfilled. For by day and night, whenever he had any free time, he ordered books to be read before him by such men, nor indeed did he allow himself to be without any of them. Therefore he obtained a knowledge of almost all books, although he could not as yet by himself understand anything from books, for he had not yet begun to read anything.

Chap. 78. But, since in this matter the royal avarice, praiseworthy as it was, was still unsatisfied, he sent messengers across the sea to Gaul to acquire teachers. From there he summoned Grimbald, priest and monk, a venerable man, an excellent singer, most learned in every way in ecclesiastical studies and the divine Scriptures and adorned with all good qualities; and also John, likewise a priest and monk, a man of very keen intelligence and most learned in all branches of the art of literature, enriched and skilled in many other arts. By their teaching the king's mind was much enriched; he endowed and honored them with great authority.

Chap. 79. At that time I also was summoned by the king, and came to the Saxon land from the western and farthest parts of Wales, and when I had decided to come to him through great tracts of country. I reached the province of the South Saxons, which is called Sussex in the Saxon language, led by guides of that race. There I first saw the king in the royal residence which is called Dean. And when I had been kindly received by him, among other topics of conversation, he asked me pressingly to devote myself to his service and to be a member of his court, and to give up for his sake all that I possessed to the north and west of the Severn; and he promised also to give me a greater recompense. And this he did. I replied that I could not make such a promise carelessly and rashly. For it seemed wrong to me to desert for the sake of any worldly honor and power those so holy places in which I had been reared and educated, tonsured, and finally ordained, unless by force and compulsion. To which he said: "If you cannot accede to this, at least grant to me half of your service, so that you may be six months with me and as many in Wales." To which I replied thus: "I cannot promise this easily and rashly without the counsel of my friends." But indeed, since I realized that he desired my services, though I knew not why, I promised that I would return to him six months later, if my life were spared, with such a reply as might be advantageous for me and mine, and acceptable to him. And when this reply seemed good to him, and I had given a pledge to return at the appointed time, on the fourth day we rode away from him and returned to our own land. But when we had left him, a violent fever laid hold of me in the city of Caer and I was grievously afflicted with it day and night for 12 months and a week without any hope of life. And when I did not come to him at the appointed time, as I had promised, he sent letters to me, which urged me to ride to him and inquired the cause of the delay. But as I could not ride to him, I sent another letter to him, which explained to him the reason for my delay and declared that I would perform what I had promised if I could recover from that sickness. Therefore, when the sickness left me, I devoted myself, as I had promised the king, to his service, by the advice and permission of all our people, for the benefit of that holy place and all dwelling in it, on this condition, that I should spend six months of every year with him, either, if I could, six months at a time, or otherwise by turns spend three months in Wales and three in the Saxon land, and that land should be benefited by the teaching of St. David, yet in every case in proportion to our strength. For our brethren hoped that they would suffer fewer tribulations and injuries from King Hyfaidd—who often plundered that monastery and the diocese of St. David's, sometimes by driving out the bishops who were in charge of it, as he at one time among these drove out Archbishop Nobis, my kinsman, and me myself—if I were to come to the notice and friendship of that king by any kind of agreement.

Chap. 80. For at that time, and for a long time before, all the districts of the southern part of Wales belonged to King Alfred, and still belong to him; for Hyfaidd with all the inhabitants of the region of Dyfed, compelled by the power of the six sons of Rhodri, had submitted to the royal overlordship; also Hywel, son of Rhys, king of Glywyssing, and Brochwel and Ffernfael, the sons of Merwig, kings of Gwent, compelled by the might and tyranny of Ealdorman Æthelred and the Mercians, of their own accord besought the same king that he would be their lord and protector against their enemies. Also Elise, son of Tewdwr, king of Brecknock, forced by the power of the same sons of Rhodri, with his brothers, finally deserted the friendship of the Northumbrians, from which they had no good, but only injury, and came to the king's presence earnestly beseeching his friendship. And when he had been honorably received by the king, and been accepted by him as his son from the hands of the bishop at confirmation, and been enriched by great gifts, he submitted with all his followers to the king's overlordship, on such terms that he would be obedient to the king in all things, just like Æthelred with the Mercians.

Chap. 81. Nor did they all obtain the king's friendship in vain. For those who desired to increase their earthly power, obtained this; those who desired money, obtained money; those who desired friendship, gained friendship; those who desired both, received both. And all had love and guardianship and protection from every side, in as far as the king with his people could defend himself. When, therefore, I came to him at the royal residence which is called *Leonaford*, I was honorably received by him, and remained with him in his court on that occasion for eight months, during which I read to him whatever books he wished and which we had at hand. For it is his most usual habit either himself to read books aloud or to listen to others who read them, day and night, in the midst of all other occupations of mind and body. And when I had frequently asked his permission to return, and could by no means obtain it, at length when I had made up my mind absolutely to demand his permission, I was summoned to him in the early morning of the eve of our Lord's Nativity, and he delivered to me two letters, in which there was a detailed list of all the things belonging to two monasteries, which in Saxon are called Congresbury and Banwell, and on that same day he delivered to me those two monasteries with everything that was in them, and a very costly silk robe, and a strong man's load of incense, adding these words, that he did not give me these small things because he was unwilling to give greater later on. Indeed at a later time he unexpectedly gave me Exeter, with all the diocese belonging to it, in Saxon territory and in Cornwall, besides innumerable daily gifts of all kinds of earthly riches, which it would be tedious to enumerate here lest it should cause weariness to the readers. But do not let anyone think that I have mentioned such gifts in this place out of any vain glory or in flattery, or for the sake of gaining greater honor; for I call God to witness that I have not done so, but only to make clear to those who do not know, how profuse is his generosity. Then at once he gave me leave to ride to those two monasteries, which were filled with all good things, and thence to return to my own country.

Chap. 87. Also in that same year (887) the oft-mentioned Alfred, king of the Anglo-Saxons, first began by the divine inspiration both to read (Latin) and translate on one and the same day. But, that this may be made clear to those ignorant of it, I will take care to explain the reason for this late start.

Chap. 88. For when we were both sitting one day in the royal chamber talking as was our wont, on all sorts of subjects, it happened that I read to him a passage from a certain book. And when he had listened to it intently with both his ears, and pondered it carefully in the depths of this mind, he suddenly showed me a little book, which he constantly carried in the depths of his bosom, in which were contained the daily course and certain psalms and prayers which he had read in his youth, and he ordered me to write that passage in the same little book. And I, hearing this and perceiving in part his eagerness of mind and also his devout wish to study the divine wisdom, gave great thanks to Almighty God, although silently, with hands outstretched to heaven, who had planted so great devotion for the study of wisdom in the king's heart. But when I found no vacant space in that little book, in which I could write

the passage—for it was completely filled with various matters—I hesitated for a little while, principally that I might provoke the king's fine understanding to a greater knowledge of the divine testimonies. And when he urged me to write it as quickly as possible I said to him: "Are you willing that I should write this passage on a separate leaf? For we do not know whether we may not at some time find one or more such passages which may please you; and if this happens unexpectedly, we shall be glad to have kept it apart." And hearing this, he said that it was a good plan. When I heard this I was glad, and hastened to prepare a quire, at the beginning of which I wrote the passage he had commended; and on the same day I wrote by his command no fewer than three other passages which pleased him, in the same quire, as I had foretold. And henceforth as we daily talked together, and searching to this end found other equally pleasing passages, that quire became full; and rightly, as it is written: "The just man builds upon a small foundation and by degrees passes to greater things." Like a most productive bee, traveling far and wide over the marshes in its quest, he eagerly and unceasingly collected many various flowers of Holy Scripture, with which he densely stored the cells of his mind.

Chap. 89. Now, once that passage had been written, he straightway was eager to read and to translate into the Saxon language, and hence to instruct many others. And just as we should learn from that happy thief, who knew the Lord Jesus Christ, his Lord, and indeed the Lord of all, hanging beside him on the venerable gallows of the Holy Cross; for with humble prayers, bending on him his bodily eyes, because he could do nothing else, being all fixed with nails, he called with a lowly voice: "Christ, remember me when thou shalt come into thy kingdom," and on the gallows first began to learn the rudiments of the Christian faith; the king likewise, though in a different way, for he was set with royal power, presumed by the instigation of God to begin his first lessons in holy writings on the festival of St. Martin and he [began] to learn those flowers, which had been gathered from various masters, and to bring them all into the compass of one book although in no order, as they came to hand, until it grew almost to the size of a psalter. This book he used to call his "enchiridion," that is, "hand-book," because he was most careful to have it at hand by day and night. And he found, as he then said, no little comfort in it....

Chap. 91. The king was pierced by many nails of tribulation, although placed in royal power. For, from his twentieth till his forty-fifth year, in which he now is, he has been constantly afflicted with a most severe attack of an unknown malady, so that he has not a single hour's peace, in which he is not either suffering that infirmity or driven almost to despair by apprehension of it. Moreover he was troubled, and with good reason, by the constant inroads of foreign peoples, which he constantly sustained by land and sea without any peaceful interval. What shall I say of his frequent expeditions and battles against the pagans and the incessant cares of government? What of his daily [solicitude] for the nations, which dwell from the Tyrrhenian Sea to the farthest end of Ireland? Indeed, we have even seen and read letters sent to him along with gifts by the patriarch Elias. What of the cities and towns he restored, and the others, which he built where none had been before? Of the buildings made by his instructions with gold and silver, beyond compare? Of the royal halls and chambers constructed admirably in stone and timber at his command? Of the royal residences in stone, moved at the royal command from their ancient sites and beautifully erected in more suitable places? And what of the great trouble and vexation (besides his illness) he had with his own people, who would voluntarily submit to little or no labor for the common needs of the kingdom? Yet, just as a skillful pilot strives to bring his ship, laden with great riches, to the longed-for safe harbor of his native land, though nearly all his sailors are worn out; he, upheld by divine aid, would not allow the helm of the kingdom he had once received to totter or waver, though set alone in the midst of the raging and manifold whirlpools of this present life. For he most wisely brought over and bound to his own will and to the common profit of the whole kingdom his bishops and ealdormen and nobles, and the thegns who were dearest to him, and also his reeves, to whom, after God and the king, the control of the kingdom seems rightly to belong, by gently instructing, flattering, urging,

commanding them, and, after long patience, by punishing sharply the disobedient, and by showing in every way hatred of vulgar folly and obstinacy. But if among these exhortations of the king, his orders were not carried out because of the slackness of the people, or things begun late in time of need were unfinished and of no profit to those who undertook them—for I may tell of fortresses ordered by him and still not begun, or begun too late to be brought to completion—and enemy forces broke in by land or sea, or, as often happened, on every side, the opponents of the royal ordinances then were ashamed with a vain repentance when on the brink of ruin. For by the witness of Scripture I call that repentance vain, by which numberless men sorrow when afflicted with grievous loss for the many ill-deeds they have committed. But though—alas, the pity of it—they are sadly afflicted through this, and moved to tears by the loss of their fathers, wives, children, servants, slaves, handmaids, their labors and all their goods, what help is hateful repentance, when it cannot succor their slain kinsmen, nor redeem captives from odious captivity, nor even can it help themselves, who have escaped, seeing that they have nought with which to sustain their own lives? Grievously afflicted, they then repent with too late repentance, and regret that they have carelessly neglected the king's orders, and with one voice praise the king's wisdom, and promise to fulfill with all their strength what they have before refused, that is, with regard to the building of fortresses and the other things for the common profit of the whole kingdom.

Chap. 92. I do not consider it profitable to pass over in this place his vow and most well thought-out scheme, which he was never able to put aside by any means either in prosperity or adversity. For when in his usual manner he was meditating on the needs of his soul, among other good acts in which he was actively engaged by day and night, he ordered the foundation of two monasteries; one for monks in the place which is called Athelney, which is surrounded on all sides by very great swampy and impassable marshes, so that no one can approach it by any means except in punts or by a bridge which has been made with laborious skill between two fortresses. At the western end of this bridge a very strong fort has been placed of most beautiful workmanship by the king's command. In this monastery he collected monks of various races from every quarter, and set them therein.

Chap. 93. For at first he had no noble or freeman of his nation who would of his own accord enter the monastic life—apart from children, who by reason of their tender age could not yet choose good or refuse evil—for indeed for many years past the desire for the monastic life had been utterly lacking in all that people, and also in many other nations, although there still remains many monasteries founded in that land, but none properly observing the rule of this way of life, I know not why; whether on account of the onslaughts of foreigners, who very often have invaded by land or sea, or on account of the nation's too great abundance of riches of every kind, which I am much more inclined to think the reason for that contempt of the monastic life. For this reason he sought to gather together monks of different race in that monastery.

Chap. 94. First, he appointed John, priest and monk, by race an Old Saxon, as abbot, and then some priests and deacons from across the sea. But when he still had not with these the number he wanted, he also procured many of that same Gallic race, some of whom, being children, he ordered to be educated in that same monastery, and to be raised to the monastic order at a later time. In that monastery I also saw one of pagan race, brought up there and wearing the monastic habit, quite a young man, and not the lowest among them....

Chap. 98. The aforesaid king also ordered to be built another monastery by the east gate of Shaftesbury, as a habitation for nuns, over which he appointed as abbess his own daughter, Æthelgifu, a virgin dedicated to God. And along with her dwell many other noble nuns serving God in the monastic life in the same monastery. He richly endowed these two monasteries with estates and wealth of all kinds.

Chap. 99. When all this was thus settled, he meditated according to his usual practice what he could still add that would further his pious intentions. Things wisely begun and profitably conceived were profitably continued. For long ago he had heard that it was written in the law that the Lord had promised to repay His tithe many times over, and had faithfully kept his promise. Inspired by this example and wishing to excel the practice of his predecessors, the pious thinker promised that he would faithfully and devoutly with all his heart give to God a half part of his service, both by day and night, and also the half part of all the riches which reached him every year by moderate and just acquisition; and this resolve he strove to carry out skillfully and wisely in as far as human discernment can observe and keep it. But, as was his habit, in order that he might carefully avoid what we are warned against in another place in Holy Scripture: "If thou offer aright, but dost not divide aright, thou sinnest," he considered how he might rightly divide what he willingly devoted to God, and, as Solomon says: "The heart of the king"—that is his counsel—"is in the hand of the Lord." Taking counsel from on high, he ordered his officers first to divide into two equal parts all his annual revenue.

Chap. 100. When this was done, he adjudged that the first part should be devoted to secular uses, and ordered that this should be further divided into three parts. The first of these shares he bestowed annually on his fighting men, and also on his noble thegns who dwelt by turns in his court, serving him in many offices. Now the royal household was always managed in three relays; for the followers of the aforesaid king were prudently divided into three companies, so that the first company resided one month in the royal court on duty day and night, and when the month was over and another company arrived, the first went home and remained there for two months, each seeing to his own affairs. So also the second company, when its month was over and the third company arrived, returned home and stayed there for two months. And also the third, having finished one month of service, went home when the first company arrived, to remain there for two months. And by this arrangement the administration of the royal court is taken in turn at all times of this present life.

Chap. 101. Thus, then, did he grant the first of the

three aforesaid shares to such men, to each, however, according to his rank and also to his office; and the second to the craftsmen, whom he had with him in almost countless number, collected and procured from many races, who were men skilled in every kind of earthly craft; and the third share to strangers from every race, who flocked to him from places far and near asking him for money, and even to those who did not ask, to each according to his rank. He gave in a praiseworthy manner with a wonderful liberality, and cheerfully, since it is written: "The Lord loveth a cheerful giver."

Chap. 102. But the second part of all his wealth, which came to him every year from revenue of every kind, and was paid into his treasury, he devoted, as we said a little while back, with all his will, to God, and ordered his officials to divide it most carefully into four equal parts, in such a way, that the first part of this division was to be prudently dispended on the poor of every race who came to him. He used to say in this connexion, that as far as human discretion could ensure it, the saying of the holy Pope Gregory ought to be observed, in which he made a wise observation about the division of alms, saying thus: "Do not give little to whom you should give much, nor much to whom you should give little, nor nothing to whom you should give something, nor anything to whom you should give nothing." And the second part he gave to the two monasteries which he himself had built, and to those serving in them, about which we spoke more fully a little way back; and the third to a school which he had collected very zealously from many nobles of his own race and also boys not of noble birth; and the fourth part to the neighboring monasteries throughout the Saxon kingdom and Mercia. And in some years he also either made gifts, according to his means, to the churches in Wales and Cornwall, Old Brittany, Northumbria, and sometimes even in Ireland, in turn, and to the servants of God dwelling in them, or else he proposed to give them later on, provided his life and prosperity continued....

Chap. 105. When these things had been completely set in order, since he desired as he had vowed to God, to preserve half his service, and to increase it further, in as far as his capacity and his means,

and indeed his infirmity, permitted, he showed himself a minute inquirer into the truth of judgments, and this especially because of his care for the poor, on whose behalf he exerted himself wonderfully by day and by night in the midst of his other duties in this present life. For except for him alone, the poor had no helpers throughout that kingdom, or indeed very few; since almost all the magnates and nobles of that land had turned their minds more to the things of this world than to the things of God; indeed, in the things of this world each regarded more his own private advantage than the common good.

Chap. 106. Also he gave attention to judgments for the benefit of his nobles and common people, for in the assemblies of the ealdormen and the reeves they disagreed among themselves, so that hardly one of them would allow to be valid whatever had been judged by the ealdormen or reeves. And compelled by this perverse and obstinate dissension, all desired to submit to the king's judgment, and both parties quickly hastened to do so. But yet anyone who knew that on his side some injustice had been committed in that suit, was unwilling to approach the judgment of such a judge of his own accord, but only against his will, though compelled to come by force of law and covenant. For he knew that there he could not quickly conceal any part of his ill-doing, and no wonder, since the king was in truth a most skilled investigator into the exercise of justice, as in all other matters. For he shrewdly looked into almost all the judgments of his whole country which were made in his absence, to see whether they were just or unjust, and if truly he could discover any wrong in those judgments, he would on his own authority mildly inquire of those judges, either in person or by some of his faithful followers, why they had given so wrong a judgment, whether from ignorance or out of any kind of ill-will, that is, for love or fear of one party, or hatred of the other, or even for greed of anyone's money. And then, if those judges admitted that they had given such judgments because they knew no better in those cases, he wisely and moderately reproved their inexperience and folly, saying thus: "I am amazed at your presumption, that you have by God's favor and mine assumed the office and status of wise men, but have neglected the study and practice of wisdom. I command you therefore either to resign on the spot the exercise of the worldly authority you hold, or to apply yourselves much more zealously to the study of wisdom." When they had heard these words, the ealdormen and reeves hastened to turn themselves with all their might to the task of learning justice, for they were terrified and as if they had been severely punished; so that in a marvelous fashion almost all the ealdormen, reeves and thegns, who had been untaught from their childhood, gave themselves to the study of letters, preferring thus toilsomely to pursue this unaccustomed study rather than resign the exercise of their authority. But if anyone were unable to make progress in learning to read, either by reason of his age or the too great slowness of an unpractised mind, he ordered his son, if he had one, or some other kinsman, or even, if he had no one else, his own man, free man or slave, whom he had long before made to learn to read, to read Saxon books to him day and night whenever he had any leisure. And, greatly sighing from the bottom of their hearts that they had not applied themselves to such studies in their youth, they considered the youth of this age happy, who could have the good fortune to be trained in the liberal arts, accounting themselves unhappy indeed, since they had neither learnt in their youth, nor were able to learn in their old age, though they ardently desired it. But we have dealt on this quickness of old and young to learn to read to add to knowledge of the aforesaid king.

Anglo-Saxon Chronicle

865 In this year the heathen army encamped on Thanet and made peace with the people of Kent. And the people of Kent promised them money for that peace. And under cover of that peace and promise of money the army stole away inland by night and ravaged all east Kent.

866 In this year Ethelbert's brother Æthelred succeeded to the kingdom of the West Saxons. And the same year a great heathen army came into England and took up winter quarters in East Anglia; and there they were supplied with horses, and the East Angles made peace with them.

867 In this year the army went from East Anglia to Northumbria, across the Humber estuary to the city of York. And there was great civil strife going on in that people, and they had deposed their king Osbert and taken a king with no hereditary right, Æella. And not until late in the year did they unite sufficiently to proceed to fight the raiding army; and nevertheless they collected a large army and attacked the enemy in York, and broke into the city; and some of them got inside, and an immense slaughter was made of the Northumbrians, some inside and some outside, and both kings were killed, and the survivors made peace with the enemy. And the same year Bishop Ealhstan died, and he had held the bishopric of Sherborne for 50 years, and his body is buried in the cemetery there.

868 In this year the same army went into Mercia to Nottingham and took up winter quarters there. And Burgred, king of the Mercians, and his councillors asked Æthelred, king of the West Saxons, and his brother Alfred to help him to fight against the army. They then went with the army of the West Saxons into Mercia to Nottingham, and came upon the enemy in that fortress and besieged them there. There occurred no serious battle there, and the Mercians made peace with the enemy.

869 In this year the raiding army returned to the city of York, and stayed there one year.

870 In this year the raiding army rode across Mercia into East Anglia, and took up winter quarters at Thetford. And that winter King Edmund fought against them, and the Danes had the victory, and killed the king, and conquered all the land. And the same year Archbishop Ceolnoth died.

871 In this year the army came into Wessex to Reading, and three days later two Danish earls rode farther inland. Then Ealdorman Æthelwulf encountered them at Englefield, and fought against them there and had the victory, and one of them, whose name was Sidroc, was killed there. Then four days later King Æthelred and his brother Alfred led a great army to Reading and fought against the army; and a great slaughter was made on both sides and Ealdorman Æthelwulf was killed, and the Danes had possession of the battle-field.

And four days later King Æthelred and his brother Alfred fought against the whole army at Ashdown; and the Danes were in two divisions: in the one were the heathen kings Bagsecg and Healfdene, and in the other were the earls. And then King Æthelred fought against the kings' troop, and King Bagsecg was slain there; and Æthelred's brother Alfred fought against the earls' troop, and there were slain Earl Sidroc the Old, and Earl Sidroc the Younger and Earl Osbearn, Earl Fræna and Earl Harold; and both enemy armies were put to flight and many thousands were killed, and they continued fighting until night.

And a fortnight later King Æthelred and his brother Alfred fought against the army at Basing, and there the Danes had the victory. And two months later, King Æthelred and his brother Alfred fought against the army at *Meretun*, and they were in two divisions; and they put both to flight and were victorious far on into the day; and there was a great slaughter on both sides; and the Danes had possession of the battle-field. And Bishop Heahmind was killed there and many important men. And after this battle a great summer army came to Reading. And afterwards, after Easter, King Æthelred died, and he had reigned five years, and his body is buried at Wimborne minster.

Then his brother Alfred, the son of Æthelwulf, succeeded to the kingdom of the West Saxons. And a month later King Alfred fought with a small force against the whole army at Wilton and put it to flight far on into the day; and the Danes had possession of the battle-field. And during that year nine general engagements were fought against the Danish army in the kingdom south of the Thames, besides the expeditions which the king's brother Alfred and [single] ealdormen and king's thegns often rode on, which were not counted. And that year nine [Danish] earls were killed and one king. And the West Saxons made peace with the enemy that year.

872 In this year the army went from Reading to London, and took up winter quarters there; and then the Mercians made peace with the army.

873 In this year the army went into Northumbria, and it took up winter quarters at Torksey in Lindsey; and then the Mercians made peace with the army.

In this year the army took up winter quarters at Torksey.

874 In this year the army went from Lindsey to Repton and took up winter quarters there, and drove King Burgred across the sea, after he had held the kingdom 22 years. And they conquered all that land. And he went to Rome and settled there; and his body is buried in the church of St. Mary in the English quarter. And the same year they gave the kingdom of the Mercians to be held by Ceolwulf, a foolish king's thegn; and he swore oaths to them and gave hostages, that it should be ready for them on whatever day they wished to have it, and he would be ready, himself and all who would follow him, at the enemy's service.

875 In this year the army left Repton: Healfdene went with part of the army into Northumbria and took up winter quarters by the River Tyne. And the army conquered the land and often ravaged among the Picts and the Strathclyde Britons; and the three kings, Guthrum, Oscetel and Anwend, went from Repton to Cambridge with a great force, and stayed there a year. And that summer King Alfred went out to sea with a naval force, and fought against the crews of seven ships, and captured one ship and put the rest to flight.

876 In this year the enemy army slipped past the army of the West Saxons into Wareham; and then the king made peace with the enemy and they gave him hostages, who were the most important men next to their king in the army, and swore oaths to him on the holy ring[16]—a thing which they would not do before for any nation—that they would speedily leave his kingdom. And then under cover of that, they—the mounted army—stole by night away from the English army to Exeter. And that year Healfdene shared out the

---

16   A sacred ring, normally kept in the inner sanctuary of the heathen temples, and worn by the chief at assemblies, is mentioned in the saga literature of Iceland.

land of the Northumbrians, and they proceeded to plow and to support themselves.

877 In this year the enemy army from Wareham came to Exeter; [and the naval force sailed west along the coast] and encountered a great storm at sea, and 120 ships were lost at Swanage. And King Alfred rode after the mounted army with the English army as far as Exeter, but could not overtake them [before they were in the fortress where they could not be reached]. And they gave him hostages there, as many as he wished to have, and swore great oaths and then kept a firm peace. Then in the harvest season the army went away into Mercia and shared out some of it, and gave some to Ceolwulf.

878 In this year in midwinter after twelfth night the enemy army came stealthily to Chippenham, and occupied the land of the West Saxons and settled there, and drove a great part of the people across the sea, and conquered most of the others; and the people submitted to them, except King Alfred. He journeyed in difficulties through the woods and fen-fastnesses[17] with a small force.

And the same winter the brother of Ivar and Healfdene was in the kingdom of the West Saxons [in Devon], with 23 ships. And he was killed there and 840 men of his army with him. And there was captured the banner which they called "Raven."

And afterwards at Easter, King Alfred with a small force made a stronghold at Athelney, and he and the section of the people of Somerset which was nearest to it proceeded to fight from that stronghold against the enemy. Then in the seventh week after Easter he rode to "Egbert's stone" east of Selwood, and there came to meet him all the people of Somerset and of Wiltshire and of that part of Hampshire which was on this side of the sea, and they rejoiced to see him. And then after one night he went from that encampment to Iley, and after another night to Edington, and there fought against the whole army and put it to flight, and pursued it as far as the fortress, and stayed there a fortnight. And then the enemy gave him preliminary hostages and great oaths that they would leave

his kingdom, and promised also that their king should receive baptism, and they kept their promise. Three weeks later King Guthrum with 30 of the men who were the most important in the army came [to him] at Aller, which is near Athelney, and the king stood sponsor to him at his baptism there; and the unbinding of the chrism[18] took place at Wedmore. And he was twelve days with the king, and he honored him and his companions greatly with gifts.

879 In this year the army went from Chippenham to Cirencester, and stayed there for one year. And the same year a band of vikings assembled and encamped at Fulham by the Thames. And the same year there was an eclipse of the sun for one hour of the day.

880 In this year the army went from Cirencester into East Anglia, and settled there and shared out the land. And the same year the army which had encamped at Fulham went overseas into the Frankish empire to Ghent and stayed there for a year.

881 In this year the army went farther inland into the Frankish empire, and the Franks fought against them; and the Danish army provided itself with horses after that battle.

882 In this year the army went farther into the Frankish empire along the Meuse, and stayed there a year. And the same year King Alfred went out with ships to sea and fought against four crews of Danish men, and captured two of the ships—and the men were killed who were on them—and two crews surrendered to him. And they had great losses in killed or wounded before they surrendered.

883 In this year the army went up the Scheldt to Condé, and stayed there for a year. And Pope Marinus sent some wood of the Cross to King Alfred. And that same year Sigelm and Athelstan took to Rome the alms [which King Alfred had promised thither], and also to India to St. Thomas

---

17 Alkaline wetlands usually fed by underground water sources.

18 For eight days after baptism, white robes were worn and a white cloth was bound round the head after the anointment with the chrism. The ceremony of its removal is what is meant here.

and St. Bartholomew, when the English were en-camped against the enemy army at London; and there, by the grace of God, their prayers were well answered after that promise.

884 In this year the army went up the Somme to Amiens, and stayed there a year.

885 In this year the aforesaid army divided into two [one part going east], the other part to Rochester, where they besieged the city and made other fortifications round themselves. And never-theless the English defended the city until King Alfred came up with his army. Then the enemy went to their ships and abandoned their fortifica-tion, and they were deprived of their horses there, and immediately that same summer they went back across the sea. That same year King Alfred sent a naval force from Kent into East Anglia. Immediately they came into the mouth of the Stour and they encountered 16 ships of vikings and fought against them, and seized all the ships and killed the men. When they turned homeward with the booty, they met a large naval force of vi-kings and fought against them on the same day, and the Danes had the victory.

That same year before Christmas, Charles, king of the Franks, died. He was killed by a boar, and a year previously his brother, who had also held the western kingdom, had died. They were both sons of Louis, who died in the year of the eclipse of the sun. He was the son of that Charles[19] whose daughter Æthelwulf, king of the west Saxons, had married. That same year a large naval force assembled among the Old Saxons and twice in the year there occurred a great battle, and the Saxons had the victory, and with them there were the Frisians.

That same year Charles[20] succeeded to the western kingdom and to all the kingdom on this side of the Mediterranean and beyond this sea, as his great-grandfather[21] had held it, except for Brittany. This Charles was the son of Louis,[22] the brother of the Charles who was the father of Judith whom King Æthelwulf married; and they were sons of Louis.[23] This Louis was the son of the old Charles.[24] This Charles was Pippin's son.

That same year there died the good pope, Marinus, who had freed from taxation the English quarter at the request of Alfred, king [of the West Saxons]. And he had sent him great gifts, includ-ing part of the Cross on which Christ suffered.

And that same year the Danish army in East Anglia violated their peace with King Alfred.

886 In this year the Danish army which had gone east went west again, and then up the Seine, and made their winter quarters there at the town of Paris.

That same year King Alfred occupied London; and all the English people that were not under subjection to the Danes submitted to him. And he then entrusted the borough to the control of Ealdorman Æthelred.[25]

887 In this year the Danish army went up past the bridge at Paris, then up along the Seine to the Marne, and then up the Marne as far as Chézy, and stayed there and in the Yonne area, spending two winters in those two places.

And the same year Charles,[26] king of the Franks, died; and six weeks before he died his brother's son Arnulf had deprived him of the kingdom. The kingdom was then divided into five, and five kings were consecrated to it. It was done, however, with Arnulf's consent and they said that they would hold it under him, for not one of them was born to it in the male line but him alone. Arnulf then lived in the land east of the Rhine, and Rudolf[27] succeeded to the middle

---

19   Charles the Bald (823–877).
20   Charles the Fat (839–888, deposed in 887).
21   Charles the Great (742–814).
22   Louis the German (806–876).
23   Louis the Pious (778–840).
24   Charles the Great.
25   The lord of the Mercians, who married Alfred's daughter, Æthelflæd. Under their rule, Mercia preserved its autonomy.
26   Charles the Fat, who died in January 888.
27   Count of Upper Burgundy.

kingdom and Odo[28] to the western portion; and Berengar[29] and Guido[30] to Lombardy and the lands on that side of the Alps; and they held it with much discord and fought two general engagements, and ravaged the land again and again, and each repeatedly drove out the other.

And the same year in which the army went up beyond the bridge at Paris, Ealdorman Æthelhelm took to Rome the alms of King Alfred and the West Saxons.

888 In this year Ealdorman Beocca took to Rome the alms of the West Saxons and of King Alfred. And Queen Æthelswith, who was King Alfred's sister, died, and her body is buried in Pavia. And the same year Archbishop Æthelred and Ealdorman Æthelwold died in the same month.

889 There was no expedition to Rome in this year, but King Alfred sent two couriers with letters.

890 In this year Abbot Beornhelm took to Rome the alms of the West Saxons and of King Alfred. And the northern king, Guthrum, whose baptismal name was Athelstan, died. He was King Alfred's godson, and he lived in East Anglia and was the first[31] to settle that land.

And the same year the Danish army went from the Seine to St. Lô, which lies between Brittany and France; and the Bretons fought against them and had the victory, and drove them into a river and drowned many of them.

891 In this year the Danish army went east, and King Arnulf with the East Franks, the Saxons and Bavarians fought against the mounted force before the ships arrived, and put it to flight.

And three Scots came to King Alfred in a boat without any oars from Ireland, which they had left secretly, because they wished for the love of God to be in foreign lands, they cared not where. The boat in which they traveled was made of two and a half hides, and they took with them enough food for seven days. And after seven days they came to land in Cornwall, and went immediately to King Alfred. Their names were as follows: Dubslane, Machbethu and Maelinnum. And Swifneh, the best scholar among the Scots, died.

And the same year after Easter, at the Rogation days or before, there appeared the star which is called in Latin *cometa*. Some men say that it is in English the long-haired star, for there shines a long ray from it, sometimes on one side, sometimes on every side.

892 In this year the great Danish army, which we have spoken about before, went back from the eastern kingdom westward to Boulogne, and they were provided with ships there, so that they crossed in one journey, horses and all, and then came up into the estuary of the Lympne with 200 [and 50] ships. That estuary is in East Kent, at the east end of that great wood which we called *Andred*. The wood is from east to west 120 miles long, or longer, and 30 miles broad. The river, of which we spoke before, comes out of the Weald. They rowed their ships up the river as far as the Weald, four miles from the mouth of the estuary, and there they stormed a fortress. Inside that fortification there were a few peasants, and it was only half made.

Then immediately afterwards Hæsten[32] came with 80 ships up the Thames estuary and made himself a fortress at Milton, and the other army made one at Appledore.

893 In this year, that was twelve months after the Danes had built the fortress in the eastern kingdom, the Northumbrians and East Angles had given King Alfred oaths, and the East Angles had given six preliminary hostages; and yet, contrary to those pledges, as often as the other Danish armies went out in full force, they went either with them or on their behalf. And then King Alfred collected his army, and advanced to take up a position between the two enemy forces,

---

28 Count of Paris.
29 Margrave of Friuli.
30 Duke of Spoleto.
31 *I.e.*, of the Danes.
32 Old Norse Hæsteinn (*Hastingus*), a viking leader first heard of on the Loire in 866, who afterwards had an active career on the Continent.

where he had the nearest convenient site with re-gard both to the fort in the wood and the fort by the water, so that he could reach either army, if they chose to come into the open country. Then they went afterwards along the Weald in small bands and mounted companies, by whatever side it was then undefended by the English army. And also they were sought by other bands, almost every day, either by day or by night, both from the English army and from the boroughs. The king had divided his army into two, so that always half its men were at home, half on service, apart from the men who guarded the boroughs. The enemy did not all come out of those encampments more than twice: once when they first landed, before the English force was assembled, and once when they wished to leave those encampments. Then they captured much booty, and wished to carry it north across the Thames into Essex, to meet the ships. Then the English army intercepted them and fought against them at Farnham, and put the enemy to flight and recovered the booty. And the Danes fled across the Thames where there was no ford, and up along the Colne on to an islet. Then the English forced besieged them there for as long as their provisions lasted; but they had completed their term of service and used up their provisions, and the king was then on the way there with the division which was serving with him. When he was on his way there and the other English army was on its way home, and the Danes were remaining behind there because their king had been wounded in the battle, so that they could not move him, those Danes who lived in Northumbria and East Anglia collected some hundred ships, and went south around the coast [And some 40 ships went north around the coast] and besieged a fortress on the north coast of Devon, and those who had gone south besieged Exeter.

When the king heard that, he turned west towards Exeter with the whole army, except for a very inconsiderable portion of the people [who continued] eastwards. They went on until they came to London, and then with the citizens and with the reinforcements which came to them from the west, they went east to Benfleet. Hæsten had then come there with his army which had been at Milton, and the large army which had been at Appledore on the estuary of the Lympne had then also come there. Hæsten had previously

built that fortress at Benfleet; and he was then out on a raid, and the large army was at home. Then the English went there and put the enemy to flight, and stormed the fortress and captured all that was within, both goods, and women and also children, and brought all to London; and they either broke up or burnt all the ships, or brought them to London or to Rochester. And Hæsten's wife and two sons were brought to the king; and he gave them back to him, because one of them was his godson, and the other the godson of Ealdorman Æthelred. They had stood sponsor to them before Hæsten came to Benfleet, and he had given the king oaths and hostages, and the king had also made him generous gifts of money, and so he did also when he gave back the boy and the woman. But immediately they came to Benfleet and had made that fortress, Hæsten ravaged his kingdom, that very province which Æthelred, his son's godfather, was in charge of; and again, a second time, he had gone on a raid in that same kingdom when his fortress was stormed.

When the king had turned west with the army towards Exeter, as I have said before, and the Danish army had laid siege to the borough, they went to their ships when he arrived there. When he was occupied against the army there in the west, and the [other] two Danish armies were assembled at Shoebury in Essex, and had made a fortress there, they went both together up along the Thames, and a great reinforcement came to them both from the East Angles, and the Northumbrians. [They then went up along the Thames until they reached the Severn, then up along the Severn.] Then Ealdorman Æthelred and Ealdorman Æthelhelm and Ealdorman Æthelnoth and the king's thegns who then were at home at the fortresses assembled from every borough east of the Parret, and both west and east of Selwood, and also north of the Thames and west of the Severn, and also some portion of the Welsh people. When they were all assembled, they overtook the Danish army at Buttington on the bank of the Severn, and besieged it on every side in a fortress. Then when they had encamped for many weeks on the two sides of the river, and the king was occupied in the west in Devon against the naval force, the besieged were oppressed by famine, and had eaten the greater part of their horses and the rest had died of starvation. They then came out against the men who were encamped on the east side of the river, and fought against them, and the Christians had the victory. And the king's thegn Ordheah and also many other king's thegns were killed, and a very great [slaughter] of the Danes was made, and the part that escaped were saved by flight.

When they came to Essex to their fortress and their ships, the survivors collected again before winter a large army from the East Angles and Northumbrians, placed their women and ships and property in safety in East Anglia, and went continuously by day and night till they reached a deserted city in Wirral, which is called Chester. Then the English army could not overtake them before they were inside that fortress. However, they besieged the fortress for some two days, and seized all the cattle that was outside, and killed the men whom they could cut off outside the fortress, and burnt all the corn, or consumed it by means of their horses, in all the surrounding districts. And that was twelve months after they had come hither across the sea.

894 And then in this year, immediately after that, the Danish went into Wales from Wirral, because they could not stay there. That was because they were deprived both of cattle and the corn which had been ravaged. When they turned back from Wales with the booty they had captured there, they went, so that the English army could not reach them, across Northumbria and into East Anglia, until they came into east Essex on to an island called Mersea, which is out in the sea.

And when the Danish army which had besieged Exeter turned homewards, they ravaged up in Sussex near Chichester, and the citizens put them to flight and killed many hundreds of them, and captured some of their ships.

Then that same year in early winter the Danes who were encamped on Mersea rowed their ships up the Thames and up the Lea. That was two years after they came hither across the sea.

895 And in the same year the aforesaid army made a fortress by the Lea, 20 miles above London. Then afterwards in the summer a great part of the citizens and also of other people marched till they arrived at the fortress of the Danes, and there they were put to flight and four king's thegns were slain.

Then later, in the autumn, the king encamped in the vicinity of the borough while they were reaping their corn, so that the Danes could not deny them that harvest. Then one day the king rode up along the river, and examined where the river could be obstructed, so that they could not bring the ships out. And when this was carried out, two fortresses were made on the two sides of the river. When they had just begun that work [and had encamped for that purpose], the enemy perceived that they could not bring the ships out. Then they abandoned the ships and went overland till they reached Bridgnorth on the Severn and built that fortress. Then the English army rode after the enemy, and the men from London fetched the ships, and broke up all which they could not bring away, and brought to London those which were serviceable. And the Danes had placed their women in safety in East Anglia before they left that fortress. Then they stayed the winter at Bridgnorth. That was three years after they had come hither across the sea into the estuary of the Lympne.

896 And afterwards in the summer of this year the Danish army divided, one force going into East Anglia and one into Northumbria; and those that were moneyless got themselves ships and went south across the sea to the Seine.

By the grace of God, the army had not on the whole afflicted the English people very greatly; but they were much more seriously afflicted in those three years by the mortality of cattle and men, and most of all in that many of the best king's thegns who were in the land died in those three years. Of those, one was Swithwulf, bishop of Rochester, and Ceolmund, ealdorman of Kent, and Brihtwulf, ealdorman of Essex [and Wulfred, ealdorman of Hampshire], and Ealhheard, bishop of Dorchester, and Eadwulf, a king's thegn in Sussex, and Beornwulf, the town-reeve of Winchester, and Ecgwulf, the king's marshal, and many besides them, though I have named the most distinguished.

In the same year the armies in East Anglia and Northumbria greatly harassed Wessex along the south coast with marauding bands, most of all with the warships which they had built many years before. Then King Alfred had "long ships" built to oppose the Danish warships. They were almost twice as long as the others. Some had 60 oars, some more. They were both swifter and steadier and also higher than the others. They were built neither on the Frisian nor the swifter and steadier Danish pattern, but as it seemed to him himself that they could be most useful. Then on a certain occasion of the same year, six ships came to the Isle of Wight and did great harm there, both in Devon and everywhere along the coast. Then the king ordered [a force] to go thither with nine of the new ships, and they blocked the estuary from the seaward end. Then the Danes went out against them with three ships, and three were on dry land farther up the estuary; the men from them had gone up on land. Then the English captured two of those three ships at the entrance to the estuary, and killed the men, and the one ship escaped. On it also the men were killed except five. These got away because the ships of their opponents ran aground. Moreover, they had run aground very awkwardly; three were aground on that side of the channel on which the Danish ships were aground, and all [the others] on the other side, so that none of them could get to the others. But when the water had ebbed many furlongs from the ships, the Danes from the remaining three ships went to the other three which were stranded on their side, and they then fought there. And there were killed the king's reeve Lucuman, Wulfheard the Frisian, Æbba the Frisian, Æthelhere the Frisian, Æthelfrith the king's *geneat*,[33] and in all 62 Frisians and English and 120 of the Danes. Then, however, the tide reached the Danish ships before the Christians could launch theirs, and therefore they rowed away out. They were then so wounded that they could not row past Sussex, but the sea cast two of them on to the land, and the men were brought to Winchester to the king, and he ordered them to be hanged. And the men who were on the one ship reached East Anglia greatly wounded. That same summer no fewer than 20 ships, men

and all, perished along the south coast. That same year died Wulfric, the king's marshal, who was [also] the Welsh-reeve.

897 In this year, nine days before midsummer, Æthelhelm, ealdorman of Wiltshire, died; and in this year died Heahstan, who was bishop of London.

900 In this year Alfred the son of Æthelwulf died, six days before All Saints' Day. He was king over the whole English people except for that part which was under Danish rule, and he had held the kingdom for one and a half years less than thirty; and then his son Edward succeeded to the kingdom.

In this year King Alfred died on 26 October; and he had held the kingdom 28 years and half a year; then his son Edward succeeded to the kingdom.

Then the atheling Æthelwold, his father's brother's son,[34] rode and seized the residence at Wimborne and at *Twinham*, against the will of the king and his councillors. Then the king rode with the army till he encamped at Badbury near Wimborne, and Æthelwold stayed inside the residence with the men who had given allegiance to him; and he had barricaded all the gates against him, and said that he would either live there or die there. Then meanwhile the atheling rode away by night, and went to the Danish army in Northumbria, and they accepted him as king and gave allegiance to him. Then the woman was seized whom he had taken without the king's permission and contrary to the bishops' orders—for she had been consecrated a nun.

And in this same year Æthelred, who was ealdorman of Devon, died four weeks before King Alfred....

---

33 Companion.

34 He was son of King Ethelred, Alfred's elder brother and predecessor. An atheling was a male member of a royal house and presumed heir to the throne.

17. THEODORE

Penitential

HANDBOOKS OF PENANCE WERE important texts in insular spirituality, designed to direct sinners toward the proper course of penance and prayer. In the course of the seventh and eighth centuries, they spread to the continent and had deep and lasting influence on the development of medieval ethics and spirituality. The penitential attributed to Theodore of Tarsus, Archbishop of Canterbury (ca. 668–690) was one of the most widely disseminated of these handbooks both in England and on the Continent.

Source: John McNeill and Helena M. Gamer, *Medieval Handbooks of Penance: A Translation of the Principal Libri Poenitentiales and selections from related documents* (New York: Columbia University Press, 1938).

Further Reading: Allen J. Frantzen, *The Literature of Penance in Anglo-Saxon England* (New Brunswick, NJ: Rutgers University Press, 1983).

Preface

In the name of Christ. Here begins the preface of the booklet which Father Theodore, having been inquired of by different persons, prepared for the remedy of penance. A pupil of the [North]umbrians, to all Catholics of the English, especially to the physicians of souls, as a suppliant [sends] blessing and greeting in the Lord Christ.

First, then, beloved, from love of your blessedness, I thought it fitting, to set forth whence I have collected the penitential remedies which follow, in order that the law may not, on account of the age or negligence of copyists, be perpetuated in a confused and corrupted state, as is usual—that law which of old time God gave figuratively by its first promulgator and then later committed to the Fathers, that they should make it known to their sons that another generation should be acquainted with it; to wit, the [law of] penance, which the Lord Jesus, when he was baptized before us all, proclaimed as the instrument of his teaching for those who had no means of healing; saying: "Do penance," etc. For the increase of your felicity, He deigned to send from the blessed see of him to whom it is said, "Whatsoever thou shalt loose on earth shall be loosed also in heaven," one by whom this most wholesome treatment of wounds is to be controlled; "for I," says the apostle, "have received of the Lord," and I, beloved, have received

of you, by God's favor, that which, in turn, I have handed over to you. For the greater part of these [decisions] the presbyter Eoda, of blessed memory, whose surname was "Christian," is said, by true report, to have received in answer to his questions from the venerable prelate Theodore. Supplementing these also is that element which the divine grace has in like manner provided to our unworthy hands, the things which that man is likewise reported to have searched out, from a booklet of the Irish. Concerning this book, the aged [Theodore] is said to have expressed the opinion that the author was an ecclesiastic.

Further, not only many men but also women, enkindled by him through these [decisions] with inextinguishable fervor, burning with desire to quench the thirst, made haste in crowds to visit a man undoubtedly of extraordinary knowledge for our age. Hence there has been found in divers quarters that conflicting and confused digest of those rules of the second book compiled with the cases adjudged. For which reason I implore, brethren, the most kind indulgence of your favor, through Him who was crucified and [who] by the shedding of His blood in life mightily confirmed what He had preached, that, if for the interests of the practical service I have committed any sin of rashness or ignorance, you will defend me before Him with the support of your intercession. For I call to witness the Maker of all things, that so far as I know my own heart, I have done these things for the sake of that kingdom of which He has preached; and if, as I fear, I undertake something beyond my talents, then, you thus assisting me, let your good will toward a work so necessary implore the pardon of my sin before Him. For in all these things equally and without invidious discrimination, according as I am able, I carefully select out of the whole the more useful things I have been able to find, and I have collected them, prefixing headings to them one by one. For I believe that men of good spirit give attention to these things, of whom it is said: "On earth peace to men of good will."

Book One

I. Of Excess and Drunkenness

1. If any bishop or deacon or any ordained person has had by custom the vice of drunkenness, he shall either desist or be deposed.

2. If a monk vomits on account of drunkenness, he shall do penance for thirty days.

3. If a presbyter or a deacon [does this] on account of drunkenness, he shall do penance for forty days.

4. If [the offense is] due to weakness or because he has been a long time abstinent and is not accustomed to drink or eat much; or if it is for gladness at Christmas or Easter or for any festival of a saint, and he then has imbibed no more than is commanded by his seniors, no offence is committed. If a bishop commands it no offense is committed, unless he himself does likewise.

5. If a lay Christian vomits because of drunkenness, he shall do penance for fifteen days.

6. Whoever is drunk against the Lord's command, if he has taken a vow of sanctity, shall do penance for seven days on bread and water, or twenty days without fat; or laymen, without beer.

7. Whoever in wickedness makes another drunk, shall do penance for forty days.

8. Whoever vomits from excess shall do penance for three days.

9. If with the sacrifice of communion, he shall do penance for seven days; if on account of weakness, he is without guilt.

II. Of Fornication

1. If anyone commits fornication with a virgin he shall do penance for one year. If with a married woman, for four years, two of these entire, and in the other two during the three forty-day periods[1] and three days a week.

2. He judged that he who often commits fornication with a man or with a beast should do penance for ten years.

3. Another judgment is that he who is joined to beasts shall do penance for fifteen years.

4. He who after his twentieth year defiles himself with a male shall do penance for fifteen years.

5. A male who commits fornication with a male shall do penance for ten years.

6. Sodomites shall do penance for seven years, and the effeminate man as an adultress.

7. Likewise he who commits this sexual offense once shall do penance for four years. If he has been in the habit of it, as Basil says, fifteen years; but if not, one year less[?] as a woman. If he is a boy, two years for the first offense; if he repeats it, four years.

8. If he does this between the thighs, one year, or the three forty-day periods.

9. If he defiles himself, forty days.

10. He who desires to commit fornication, but is

---

1   Probably by the "three forty-day periods" frequently assigned in this penitential, those mentioned in Book II, xiv, 1, below, are to be understood. Some modern writers habitually call these "the three lents."

not able, shall do penance for forty or twenty days.

11. As for boys who mutually engage in vice, he judged that they should be whipped.

12. If a woman practices vice with a woman, she shall do penance for three years.

13. If she practices solitary vice, she shall do penance for the same period.

14. The penance of a widow and of a girl is the same. She who has a husband deserves a greater penalty if she commits fornication.

15. He who ejaculates into the mouth of another shall do penance for seven years; this is the worst of evils. Elsewhere it was his judgment that both [participants in the offense] shall do penance to the end of life; or twelve years, or as above seven.

16. If one commits fornication with his mother, he shall do penance for fifteen years and never change except on Sundays. But this so impious incest is likewise spoken of by him in another way— that he shall do penance for seven years, with perpetual pilgrimage.

17. He who commits fornication with his sister shall do penance for fifteen years in the way which it is stated above of his mother. But this [penalty] he also elsewhere established in a canon as twelve years. Whence it is not unreasonable that the fifteen years that are written apply to the mother.

18. The first canon determined that he who often commits fornication should do penance for ten years; a second canon, seven; but on account of the weakness of man, on deliberation they said he should do penance for three years.

19. If a brother commits fornication with a natural brother, he shall abstain from all kinds of flesh for fifteen years.

20. If a mother imitates acts of fornication with her little son, she shall abstain from flesh for three years and fast one day in the week, that is until vespers.

21. He who amuses himself with libidinous imagination shall do penance until the imagination is overcome.

22. He who loves a woman in his mind shall seek pardon from God; but if he has spoken [to her], that is, of love and friendship, but is not received by her, he shall do penance for seven days.

III. Of Thieving Avarice

1. If any layman carries off a monk from the monastery by stealth, he shall either enter a monastery to serve God or subject himself to human servitude.

2. Money stolen or robbed from churches is to be restored fourfold; from secular persons, twofold.

3. Whoever has often committed theft, seven years is his penance, or such a sentence as his priest shall determine, that is, according to what can be arranged with those whom he has wronged. And he who used to steal, when he becomes penitent, ought always to be reconciled to him against whom he has offended and to make restitution according to the wrong he has done to him; and [in such case] he shall greatly shorten his penance. But if he refuses, or is unable, let him do penance scrupulously for the prescribed time.

4. And he who gives notice of stolen goods shall give a third part to the poor; and whoever treasures up goods in excess through ignorance, shall give a third part to the poor.

5. Whoever has stolen consecrated things shall do penance for three years without fat and then [be allowed to] communicate.

IV. Of Manslaughter

1. If one slays a man in revenge for a relative, he shall do penance as a murderer for seven or ten years. However, if he will render to the relatives the legal price, the penance shall be lighter, that is, [it shall be shortened] by half the time.

2. If one slays a man in revenge for a brother, he

shall do penance for three years. In another place it is said that he should do penance for ten years.

3. But a murderer, ten or seven years.

4. If a layman slays another with malice aforethought, if he will not lay aside his arms, he shall do penance for seven years; without flesh and wine, three years.

5. If one slays a monk or a cleric, he shall lay aside his arms and serve God, or he shall do penance for seven years. He is in the judgment of his bishop. But as for one who slays a bishop or presbyter, it is for the king to give judgment in this case.

6. One who slays a man by command of his lord shall keep away from the church for forty days; and one who slays a man in public war shall do penance for forty days.

7. If through anger, he shall do penance for three years; if by accident, for one year; if by a potion or any trick, seven years or more; if as a result of a quarrel, ten years.

V. Of Those Who Are Deceived by Heresy

1. If one has been ordained by heretics, if he was without blame [in the matter] he ought to be reordained; but if not, he ought to be deposed.

2. If one goes over from the Catholic Church to heresy and afterward returns, he cannot be ordained except after a long probation and in great necessity. Pope Innocent claimed that such a person is not permitted by the authority of the canons to become a cleric [even] after penance. Therefore if Theodore says this: "only in great necessity," as has been said, he permitted the procedure, who often used to say that he wished that the decrees of the Romans should never be changed by him.

3. If one flouts the Council of Nicea and keeps Easter with the Jews on the fourteenth of the moon, he shall be driven out of every church unless he does penance before his death.

4. If one prays with such a person as if he were a Catholic cleric, he shall do penance for a week; if indeed he neglects this, he shall the first time do penance for forty days.

5. If one seeks to encourage the heresy of these people and does not do penance, he shall be likewise driven out; as the Lord saith: "He that is not with me is against me."

6. If one is baptized by a heretic who does not rightly believe in the Trinity, he shall be rebaptized. This we do not believe Theodore to have said [since it is] in opposition to the Nicene council and the decrees of the synod; as is confirmed in connection with the Arian converts who did not rightly believe in the Trinity.[2]

7. If one gives the communion to a heretic or receives it from his hand, and does not know that the Catholic Church disapproves it, when he afterward becomes aware [of this] he shall do penance for an entire year. But if he knows and [yet] neglects [the rule] and afterwards does penance, he shall do penance for ten years. Others judge that he should do penance for seven years and, more leniently, for five.

8. If one, without knowing it, permits a heretic to celebrate the Mass in a Catholic church, he shall do penance for forty days. If [he does this] out of veneration for him [i.e., for the heretic], he shall do penance for an entire year.

9. If [he does this] in condemnation of the Catholic Church and the customs of the Romans, he shall be cast out of the Church as a heretic, unless he is penitent; if he is, he shall do penance for ten years.

10. If he departs from the Catholic Church to the congregation of the heretics and persuades others and afterward performs penance, he shall do penance for twelve years; four years outside the church, and six among the "hearers," and two more out of communion. Of these it is said in a synod: They shall receive the communion or oblation in the tenth year.

---

2   The writer has mistaken the canons of Constantinople (381) for those of Nicaea. The council of Constantinople admitted Arians without rebaptism.

11. If a bishop or an abbot commands a monk to sing a mass for dead heretics, it is not proper or expedient to obey him.

12. If a presbyter is present where he has sung a mass, and another recites the names of dead persons and names heretics together with Catholics, and after the mass he is aware of it, he shall do penance for a week. If he has done it frequently, he shall do penance for an entire year.

13. But if anyone orders a mass for a dead heretic and preserves his relics on account of his piety, because he fasted much, and he does not know the difference between the Catholic faith and that of the Quatrodecimans, and [if he] afterward understands and performs penance, he ought to burn the relics with fire, and he shall do penance for a year. If one knows, however, and is indifferent, when he is moved to penance he shall do penance for ten years.

14. If anyone departs from God's faith without any necessity and afterwards receives penance with his whole heart, he shall do penance among the "hearers"; according to the Nicene council, three years without the church among the penitents, and two years in addition out of communion.

VI. Of Perjury

1. He who commits perjury in a church shall do penance for eleven years.

2. He who [commits perjury] however [because] forced by necessity, for the three forty-day periods.

3. But he who swears on the hand of a man[3]—this is nothing among the Greeks.

4. If, however, he swears on the hand of a bishop or of a presbyter or of a deacon or on an altar or on a consecrated cross and lies, he shall do penance for three years. But if on a cross that is not consecrated, he shall do penance for one year.

5. The penance for perjury is three years.

VII. Of Many and Diverse Evils, and What Necessary Things Are Harmless

1. He who has committed many evil deeds, that is, murder, adultery with a woman and with a beast, and theft, shall go into a monastery and do penance until his death.

2. Of money which has been seized in a foreign province from a conquered enemy, that is, from an alien king who has been conquered, the third part shall be given to the church or to the poor, and penance shall be done for forty days because it was the king's command.[4]

3. He who drinks blood or semen shall do penance for three years.

4. There is pardon for evil imaginations if they are not carried out in action, nor yet by intention.

5. Further, Theodore approved reckoning the twelve three-day periods as the equivalent of a year. Also in the case of sick persons, the value of a man or of a female slave for a year, or to give the half of all his possessions, and if he have defrauded anyone, to restore fourfold, as Christ judged. These are the proofs of what we said in the preface about the booklet of the Irish; in which, as in other matters, sometimes he [the author of the Irish booklet] determined these things therein more leniently, as seemed best to him; it set the measure [of penance] for the week.

6. He who eats unclean flesh or a carcass that has been torn by beasts shall do penance for forty days. But if the necessity of hunger requires it, there is no offense, since a permissible act is one thing and what necessity requires is another.

7. If anyone accidentally touches food with unwashed hands, or [if] a dog, a cat, a mouse, or an unclean animal that has eaten blood [touches it] there is no offense; and if one from necessity eats an animal that seems unclean, whether a bird or a beast, there is no offense.

---

3   Meaning a layman, as indicated by the next canon.

4   The last clause gives the reason for the lightness of the penalty.

8. If a mouse falls into a liquid it shall be removed and sprinkled with holy water, and if it is alive it may be taken [for food]; but if it is dead, all the liquid shall be poured out and not given to man, and the vessel shall be cleansed.

9. Again, if that liquid in which a mouse or a weasel is submerged and dies and contains much food, it shall be purged and sprinkled with holy water and taken if there is need.

10. If birds drop dung into any liquid, the dung shall be removed from it, and it shall be sanctified with [holy] water, and it shall be clean food.

11. Unwittingly to absorb blood with the saliva is not a sin.

12. If without knowing it, one eats what is polluted by blood or any unclean thing, it is nothing; but if he knows, he shall do penance according to the degree of the pollution.

VIII. Of Various Failings of the Servants of God

1. If a priest is polluted in touching or in kissing a woman he shall do penance for forty days.

2. If a presbyter kisses a woman from desire, he shall do penance for forty days.

3. Likewise if a presbyter is polluted through imagination, he shall fast for a week.

4. For masturbation, he shall fast for three weeks.

5. If any presbyter denies penance to the dying, he is answerable for their souls, since the Lord saith, "On whatever day the sinner is converted, he shall live and die." For true conversion is possible in the last hour, since the Lord sees not only the time but the heart; for the thief in his last hour, by a confession of one moment, merited to be in paradise.

6. A monk or a holy virgin who commits fornication shall do penance for seven years.

7. He who often pollutes himself through the violence of his imagination shall do penance for twenty days.

8. He who when asleep in a church pollutes himself shall do penance for three days.

9. For masturbation, the first time he shall do penance for twenty days, on repetition, forty days; for further offenses fasts shall be added.

10. If between the thighs, one year or the three forty-day periods.

11. He who defiles himself shall do penance for forty days; if he is a boy, for twenty days or be flogged. If he is in orders, for the three forty-day periods or a year if he has done it frequently.

12. If anyone renounces the world and afterward resumes a secular habit, if he was a monk and after these things performs penance, he shall do penance for ten years and after the first three years, if he has been approved in all his penance in tears and prayers, the bishop can deal more leniently with him.

13. If he was not a monk when he departed from the Church, he shall do penance for seven years.

14. Basil gave judgment that a boy should be permitted to marry before the age of sixteen if he could not abstain; but that if he is already a monk, [and marries], he is both [classed] among bigamists and shall do penance for one year.

IX. Of Those Who Are Degraded or Cannot Be Ordained

1. A bishop, presbyter, or deacon guilty of fornication ought to be degraded and to do penance at the decision of a bishop; yet they shall take communion. With loss of rank, penance dies, the soul lives.

2. If anyone after he has vowed himself to God takes a secular habit, he assuredly ought not to proceed a second time to any rank.

3. Nor ought a woman [in such case] to take the veil; it is far better that she should not come to prominence in the Church.

4. If any presbyter or deacon marries a strange woman, he shall be deposed before the people.

5. If he commits adultery with her and it comes to the knowledge of the people, he shall be cast out of the Church and shall do penance among the laymen as long as he lives.

6. If anyone has a concubine, he ought not to be ordained.

7. If any presbyter in his own province or in another or wherever he may be found refuses to baptize a sick person who has been committed to him or on account of the exertion of the journey [declines the duty] so that he dies without baptism, he shall be deposed.

8. Likewise he who slays a man or commits fornication, shall be deposed.

9. It is not permitted to ordain a boy brought up in a monastery before the age of twenty-five.

10. If anyone, before or after baptism, marries a twice married woman, as in the case of twice married men, he cannot be ordained.

11. If anyone who is not ordained performs baptism through temerity, he is cut off from the Church and shall never be ordained.

12. If through ignorance anyone has been ordained before he is baptized, those who have been baptized by that pagan ought to be [re]baptized, and he himself shall not be ordained [again].

This, again, is said to have been differently determined by the Roman pontiff of the apostolic see, to the effect that not he who baptizes, even if he is a pagan, but the Spirit of God, ministers the grace of baptism; but also this matter was differently decided in the case of a "pagan" presbyter—he who thinks himself baptized, holding the Catholic faith in his works—these cases are differently decided—that is, that he should have been baptized and ordained.

X. Of Those Who Have Been Baptized Twice; How They Shall Do Penance

1. Those who in ignorance have been twice baptized are not required to do penance for this, except that according to the canons they cannot be ordained unless some great necessity compels it.

2. However, those who have been baptized a second time, not ignorantly, [which is] as if they crucified Christ a second time, shall do penance for seven years on Wednesdays and Fridays and during the forty-day periods, if it was on account of some fault. But if they determined [to be baptized] for the sake of cleanness, they shall do penance in this way for three years.

XI. Of Those Who Despise the Lord's Day, and Neglect the Appointed Fasts of the Church of God

1. Those who labor on the Lord's day, the Greeks reprove the first time; the second, they take something from them; the third time, [they take] the third part of their possessions, or flog them; or they shall do penance for seven days.

2. But if on account of negligence anyone fasts on the Lord's day, he ought to abstain for a whole week. If [he does this] a second time, he shall fast for twenty days; if afterwards forty days.

3. If he fasts out of contempt for the day, he shall be abhorred as a Jew by all the Catholic churches.

4. But if he despises a fast appointed in the Church and acts contrary to the decrees of the elders, not in Lent, he shall do penance for forty days. But if it is in Lent, he shall do penance for a year.

5. If he does it frequently and it has become habitual to him, he shall be cast out of the Church, as saith the Lord: "He that shall scandalize one of these little ones," etc.

XII. Of the Communion of the Eucharist, or the Sacrifice

1. The Greeks, clergy, and laymen, communicate every Lord's day, and those who do not communicate for three Lord's days are to be excommunicated, as the canons state.

2. Likewise the Romans who so wish, communicate; however those who do not so wish are not excommunicated.

3. The Greeks and Romans abstain from women for three days before the [feast of] loaves of proposition, as it is written in the law.

4. Penitents according to the canons ought not to communicate before the conclusion of the penance; we, however, out of pity give permission after a year or six months.

5. He who receives the sacrament after food shall do penance for seven days. (It is in the judgment of his bishop. This point, that it is in the judgment of the bishop, is not added in some texts.)

6. If the host has become corrupted with dirt accumulated by time it is always to be burned with fire.

7. Moreover, it shall be permitted if necessary that confession be made to God alone. And this [word] "necessary" is not in some codices.

8. He who mislays the host, [leaving it] for beasts and birds to devour, if by accident, he shall fast for three weeks; if through neglect, for the three forty-day periods.

XIII. Of Reconciliation

1. The Romans reconcile a man within the apse; but the Greeks will not do this.

2. The reconciliation of the penitents in the Lord's Supper is by the bishops only—and the penance is ended.

3. If it is difficult for the bishop, he can, for the sake of necessity, confer authority on a presbyter, to perform this.

4. Reconciliation is not publicly established in this province, for the reason that there is no public penance either.

XIV. Of the Penance for Special Irregularities in Marriage

1. In a first marriage the presbyter ought to perform Mass and bless them both, and afterwards they shall absent themselves from church for thirty days. Having done this, they shall do penance for forty days, and absent themselves from the prayer; and afterwards they shall communicate with the oblation.

2. One who is twice married shall do penance for a year; on Wednesdays and Fridays and during the three forty-day periods he shall abstain from flesh; however, he shall not put away his wife.

3. He that is married three times, or more, that is a fourth or fifth marriage, or beyond that number, for seven years on Wednesdays and Fridays and during the three forty-day periods they shall abstain from flesh; yet they shall not be separated. Basil so determined, but in the canon four years [are indicated].

4. If anyone finds his wife to be an adultress and does not wish to put her away but has had her in the matrimonial relation to that time, he shall do penance for two years on two days in the week and [shall perform] the fasts of religion; or as long as she herself does penance he shall avoid the matrimonial relation with her, because she has committed adultery.

5. If any man or woman who has taken the vow of virginity is joined in marriage, he shall not set aside the marriage but shall do penance for three years.

6. Foolish vows and those incapable of being performed are to be set aside.

7. A woman may not take a vow without the consent of her husband; but if she does take a vow she can be released, and she shall do penance according to the decision of a priest.

8. He who puts away his wife and marries another shall do penance with tribulation for seven years or a lighter penance for fifteen years.

9. He who defiles his neighbor's wife, deprived of his own wife, shall fast for three years two days a week and in the three forty-day periods.

10. If [the woman] is a virgin, he shall do penance for one year without meat and wine and mead.

11. If he defiles a vowed virgin, he shall do penance for three years, as we said above, whether a child is born of her or not.

12. If she is his slave, he shall set her free and fast for six months.

13. If the wife of anyone deserts him and returns to him undishonored, she shall do penance for one year; otherwise for three years. If he takes another wife he shall do penance for one year.

14. An adulterous woman shall do penance for seven years. And this matter is stated in the same way in the canon.

15. A woman who commits adultery shall do penance for three years as a fornicator. So also shall she do penance who makes an unclean mixture of food for the increase of love.

16. A wife who tastes her husband's blood as a remedy shall fast for forty days, more or less.

17. Moreover, women shall not in the time of impurity enter into a church, or communicate—neither nuns nor laywomen; if they presume [to do this] they shall fast for three weeks.

18. In the same way shall they do penance who enter a church before purification after childbirth, that is, forty days.

19. But he who has intercourse at these seasons shall do penance for twenty days.

20. He who has intercourse on the Lord's day shall seek pardon from God and do penance for one or two or three days.

21. In case of unnatural intercourse with his wife, he shall do penance for forty days the first time.

22. For a graver offense of this kind he ought to do penance as one who offends with animals.

23. For intercourse at the improper season he shall fast for forty days.

24. Women who commit abortion before [the foetus] has life, shall do penance for one year or for the three forty-day periods or for forty days, according to the nature of the offense; and if later, that is, more than forty days after conception, they shall do penance for three years as murderesses, that is for three years on Wednesdays and Fridays and in the three forty-day periods. This according to the canons is judged [punishable by] ten years.

25. If a mother slays her child, if she commits homicide, she shall do penance for fifteen years, and never change except on Sunday.

26. If a poor woman slays her child, she shall do penance for seven years. In the canon it is said that if it is a case of homicide, she shall do penance for ten years.

27. A woman who conceives and slays her child in the womb within forty days shall do penance for one year; but if later than forty days, she shall do penance as a murderess.

28. If an infant that is weak and is a pagan has been recommended to a presbyter [for baptism] and dies [unbaptized], the presbyter shall be deposed.

29. If the neglect is on the part of the parents, they shall do penance for one year; and if a child of

three years dies without baptism, the father and the mother shall do penance for three years. He gave this decision at a certain time because it happened to be referred to him.

30. In the canon, he who slays his child without baptism [is required to do penance for] ten years, but under advisement he shall do penance for seven years.

XV. Of the Worship of Idols

1. He who sacrifices to demons in trivial matters shall do penance for one year; but he who [does so] in serious matters shall do penance for ten years.

2. If any woman puts her daughter upon a roof or into an oven for the cure of a fever, she shall do penance for seven years.

3. He who causes grains to be burned where a man has died, for the health of the living and of the house, shall do penance for five years.

4. If a woman performs diabolical incantations or divinations, she shall do penance for one year or the three forty-day periods, or forty days, according to the nature of the offense. Of this matter it is said in the canon: He who celebrates auguries, omens from birds, or dreams, or any divinations according to the custom of the heathen, or introduces such people into his houses, in seeking out any trick of the magicians—when these become penitents, if they belong to the clergy they shall be cast out; but if they are secular persons they shall do penance for five years.

5. In the case of one who eats food that has been sacrificed and later confesses, the priest ought to consider the person, of what age he was and in what way he had been brought up or how it came about. So also the sacerdotal authority shall be modified in the case of a sick person. And this matter is to be observed with all diligence in all penance always and rigorously in confession, in so far as God condescends to aid.

Book Two

I. Of the Ministry of a Church, or of Its Rebuilding

1. A church may be placed in another place if it is necessary, and it ought not to be sanctified, except that the priest ought to sprinkle it with [holy] water, and in the place of the altar[5] a cross ought to be set.

2. It is acknowledged that two masses may be celebrated in one day on every altar; and he who does not communicate shall not approach the bread nor the kiss [of peace] in the Mass; and he who eats beforehand is not admitted to this kiss.

3. The lumber of a church ought not to be applied to any other work except for another church or for burning with fire or for the benefit of the brethren in a monastery or to bake bread for them; and such things ought not to pass into lay operations.

4. In a church in which the bodies of dead believers are buried, an altar may not be sanctified; but if it seems unsuitable for consecration, when the bodies have been removed and the woodwork of it has been scraped or washed, it[6] shall be re-erected.

5. But if it was previously consecrated, masses may be celebrated in it if religious men are buried there; but if there is a pagan [buried there], it is better to cleanse it and cast [the corpse] out.

6. We ought not to make steps in front of the altar.

7. The relics of saints are to be venerated.

8. If it can be done, a candle should burn near them every night; but if the poverty of the place prevents this, it does them no harm.

9. The incense of the Lord is to be burned on the natal days of saints out of reverence for the day, since they, as lilies, shed an odor of sweetness and asperge the Church of God as a church is asperged with incense, beginning at the altar.

---

5   Meaning, "in the place where the altar formerly stood."
6   Apparently, the altar.

10. A layman ought not to read a lection in a church nor sing the Alleluia, but only the psalms and responses without the Alleluia.

11. As often as they wish, those who dwell in houses may sprinkle them with holy water; and when thou dost consecrate water thou shalt first offer a prayer.

II. Of the Three Principal Orders of the Church

1. A bishop may confirm in a field if it is necessary.

2. Likewise a presbyter may celebrate masses in a field if a deacon or the presbyter himself holds in his hands the chalice and the oblation.

3. A bishop ought not to compel an abbot to go to a synod unless there is also some sound reason.

4. A bishop determines cases of poor men up to fifty solidi; but the king, if [the amount in litigation] is above that sum.

5. A bishop or an abbot may keep a criminal as a slave if he [the criminal] has not the means of redeeming himself.

6. A bishop may absolve from a vow if he will.

7. Only a presbyter may celebrate masses and bless the people on Good Friday and sanctify a cross.

8. A presbyter is not obliged to give tithes.

9. A presbyter must not reveal the sin of a bishop, since he is set over him.

10. The host is not to be received from the hand of a priest who cannot recite the prayers or the lections according to the ritual.

11. If a presbyter sings the responses in the Mass, or anything [else], he shall not remove his cope[7]; moreover, he lays it on his shoulders even when he is reading the Gospel.

12. In the case of a presbyter who is a fornicator, if before he was found out he baptized, those whom he baptized shall be baptized a second time.

13. If any ordained presbyter perceives that he was not baptized, he shall be baptized and ordained again, and all whom he baptized previously shall be baptized.

14. Among the Greeks, deacons do not break the holy bread; neither do they say the collect or the "Dominus vobiscum" or the compline.

15. A deacon may not give penance to a layman, but a bishop or a presbyter ought to give it.

16. Deacons can baptize, and they can bless food and drink; they cannot give the bread.

III. Of the Ordination of Various Persons

1. In the ordination of a bishop the mass ought to be sung by the ordaining bishop himself.

2. In the ordination of a presbyter or of a deacon, the bishop ought to celebrate masses as the Greeks are accustomed to do at the election of an abbot or an abbess.

3. In the ordination of a monk, indeed, the abbot ought to perform the mass and complete three prayers over his head; and for seven days he shall veil his head with his cowl, and on the seventh day the abbot shall remove the veil as in baptism the presbyter is accustomed to take away the veil of the infants; so also ought the abbot to do to the monk, since according to the judgment of the fathers it is a second baptism in which, as in baptism, all sins are taken away.

4. A presbyter may consecrate an abbess with the celebration of the mass.

5. In the ordination of an abbot, indeed, the bishop ought to perform the mass and bless him as he bows his head, with two or three witnesses from among his brethren, and give him the staff and shoes.

---

7   A liturgical vestment in the form of a long cloak.

6. Nuns, moreover, and churches ought always to be consecrated with a mass.

7. The Greeks bless a widow and a virgin together and choose either as an abbess. The Romans, however, do not veil a widow with a virgin.

8. According to the Greeks a presbyter may consecrate a virgin with the sacred veil, reconcile a penitent, and make the oil for exorcism and the chrism of the sick if it is necessary. But according to the Romans these functions appertain to bishops alone.

IV. Of Baptism and Confirmation

1. In baptism sins are remitted; [but] not loose behavior with women, since the children who were born before the baptism of the parents are in such cases in the same status as those born after their baptism.

2. If indeed she who was married before [her] baptism is not regarded as a wife, it follows that the children who were previously begotten can neither be held to be [true] children nor be called brothers among themselves or sharers of the inheritance.

3. If any pagan gives alms and keeps abstinence and [does] other good works which we cannot enumerate, does he not lose these in baptism? No, for he shall not lose any good, but he shall wash away the evil. This Pope Innocent asserted, taking for example what was done concerning the catechumen Cornelius.

4. Gregory Nazianzen declares that the second baptism is that of tears.

5. We believe no one is complete in baptism without the confirmation of a bishop; yet we do not despair.

6. Chrism was established in the Nicene synod.

7. It is not a breach of order if the chrismal napkin is laid again upon another who is baptized.

8. One person may, if it is necessary, be [god]father to a catechumen both in baptism and in confirmation; however, it is not customary, but [usually] separate persons act as godparents in each [office].

9. No one may act as a godparent who is not baptized or confirmed.

10. However, a man may act as a godparent for a woman in baptism, likewise also a woman may act as a godparent for a man.

11. Baptized persons may not eat with catechumens, nor give them the kiss;[8] how much more [must this regulation be observed] in the case of pagans.

V. The Mass of the Dead

1. According to the Roman Church the custom is to carry dead monks or religious men to the church, to anoint their breasts with the chrism, there to celebrate masses for them and then with chanting to carry them to their graves. When they have been placed in the tomb a prayer is offered for them; then they are covered with earth or stone.

2. On the first, the third, the ninth, and also on the thirtieth day a mass is celebrated for them, and, if they wished it, [a mass] is observed a year later.

3. A mass is celebrated for a dead monk on the day of his burial and on the third day; afterward as often as the abbot decides.

4. It is the custom also for masses to be celebrated for monks each week, and for their names to be recited.

5. Three masses in a year [are sung] for dead seculars, on the third, the ninth, and the thirtieth day, since the Lord rose from the dead on the third day and in the ninth hour "he yielded up the ghost, and the children of Israel bewailed Moses for thirty days."

---

8   That is, "the kiss of peace."

6. For a good layman there is to be a mass on the third day; for a penitent on the thirtieth day, or on the seventh, after the fast; since his neighbors ought to fast seven days and to make an offering at the altar, as in Jesus Ben Sirach we read: "And the children of Israel fasted for Saul";[9] afterward, as often as the priest decides.

7. Many say that it is not permissible to celebrate masses for infants of less than seven years; but it is permitted, nevertheless.

8. Dionysius the Areopagite [10] says that he who offers masses for a bad man commits blasphemy against God.

9. Augustine says that masses are to be performed for all Christians, since it either profits them or consoles those who offer or those who seek [to have it done].

10. A presbyter or a deacon who is not permitted to, or who will not, take communion, may not celebrate masses.

VI. Of Abbots and Monks, or of the Monastery

1. Out of humility and with the permission of the bishop an abbot may relinquish his office. But the brethren shall elect an abbot for themselves from among their own number, if they have [a suitable man]; if not, from among outsiders.

2. And the bishop shall not keep an abbot in his office by violence.

3. The congregation ought to elect an abbot after the abbot's death, or while he is alive if he has gone away or sinned.

4. He himself cannot appoint anyone from among his own monks, nor from those without, nor can he give [the office] to another abbot without the decision of the brethren.

5. If, indeed, the abbot has sinned, the bishop cannot take away the property of the monastery, albeit the abbot has sinned; but he shall send him to another monastery, into the power of another abbot.

6. Neither an abbot nor a bishop may transfer the land of a church to another [church] although both are under his authority. If he wishes to change the land of a church, he shall do it with the consent of both [parties].

7. If anyone wishes to set his monastery in another place, he shall do it on the advice of the bishop and of his brethren, and he shall release a presbyter for the ministry of the church in the former place.

8. It is not permissible for men to have monastic women, nor women, men; nevertheless, we shall not overthrow that which is the custom in this region.

9. A monk may not take a vow without the consent of his abbot; if he lacks this, the vow is to be annulled.

10. If an abbot has a monk worthy of the episcopate, he ought to grant this, if it is necessary.

11. A boy may not marry when he has already set before him the vow of a monk.

12. Any monk whom a congregation has chosen to be ordained to the rank of presbyter for them, ought not to give up his former habit of life.

13. But if he is afterwards found to be either proud or disobedient or vicious, and [if] in a better rank [he] seeks a worse life, he shall be deposed and put in the lowest place, or [he shall] make amends with satisfaction.

14. The reception of infirm persons into a monastery is within the authority and liberty of the monastery.

15. Washing the feet of laymen[11] is also within the liberty of a monastery. Except on the Lord's day, it is not obligatory.

---

9   Sirach 46:20.

10   Anonymous theologian philosopher of the late fifth or early sixth century; known as Pseudo-Dionysius.

11   The "pedilavium," or ceremonial foot washing, usually accompanied baptism in the Celtic Church.

16. It is also a liberty of the monastery to adjudge penance to laymen for this is properly a function of the clergy.

VII. The Rite of the Women, or Their Ministry in the Church

1. It is permissible for the women, that is, the handmaidens of Christ, to read the lections and to perform the ministries which appertain to the confession of the sacred altar, except those which are the special functions of priests and deacons.

[In a minority of manuscripts this canon reads]:

Women shall not cover the altar with the corporal nor place on the altar the offerings, nor the cup, nor stand among ordained men in the church, nor sit at a feast among priests.

2. According to the canons it is the function of the bishops and priests to prescribe penance.

[For this canon a number of manuscripts have the following:]

No woman may adjudge penance for anyone, since in the canon no one may [do this] except the priests alone.

3. Women may receive the host under a black veil, as Basil decided.

4. According to the Greeks a woman can make offerings, but not according to the Romans.

VIII. Of the Customs of the Greeks and of the Romans

1. On the Lord's Day the Greeks and the Romans sail and ride; they do not make bread, nor proceed in a carriage, except only to church, nor bathe themselves.

2. The Greeks do not write publicly on the Lord's Day; in the case of special necessity, however, they write at home.

3. The Greeks and the Romans give clothing to their slaves, and they work, except on the Lord's Day.

4. Greek monks do not have slaves; Roman monks have them.

5. On the day before the Lord's nativity, at the ninth hour, when mass is ended, that is, the vigil of the Lord, the Romans eat; but the Greeks take supper [only] when vespers and mass have been said.

6. In the case of plague, both the Greeks and the Romans say that the sick ought to be visited, as [are] other persons, as the Lord commands.

7. The Greeks do not give carrion flesh to swine but allow the skins and leather [of carrion] to be taken for shoes, and the wool and horns may be taken [but] not for any sacred [use].

8. The washing of the head is permitted on the Lord's Day, and it is permitted to wash the feet in a solution of lye; but this washing of the feet is not a custom of the Romans.

IX. Of the Communion of the Irish and Britons Who Are Not Catholic in Respect to Easter and the Tonsure

1. Those who have been ordained by Irish or British bishops who are not Catholic with respect to Easter and the tonsure are not united to the Church, but [they] shall be confirmed again by a Catholic bishop with imposition of hands.

2. Likewise also the churches that have been consecrated by these bishops are to be sprinkled with holy water and confirmed by some collect.

3. Further, we have not the liberty to give them, when they request it, the chrism or the eucharist, unless they have previously confessed their willingness to be with us in the unity of the Church. And likewise a person from among these nations, or anyone who doubts his own baptism, shall be baptized.

X. Of Those Who Are Vexed by the Devil

1. If a man is vexed by the Devil and can do nothing but run about everywhere, and [if he] slays

himself, there may be some reason to pray for him if he was formerly religious.

2. If it was on account of despair, or of some fear, or for some unknown reasons, we ought to leave to God the decision of this matter, and we dare not pray for him.

3. In the case of one who of his own will slays himself, masses may not be said for him; but we may only pray and dispense alms.

4. If any Christian goes insane through a sudden seizure, or as a result of insanity slays himself—there are some who celebrate masses for such a one.

5. One who is possessed of a demon may have stones and herbs, without [the use of] incantation.

XI. Of the Use or Rejection of Animals

1. Animals which are torn by wolves or dogs are not to be eaten, nor a stag nor a goat if found dead, unless perchance they were previously killed by a man, but they are to be given to swine and dogs.

2. Birds and other animals that are strangled in nets are not to be eaten by men; nor if they are found dead after being attacked by a hawk, since it is commanded in the fourth chapter[12] of the Acts of the Apostles to abstain from fornication, from blood, from that which is strangled, and from idolatry.

3. Fish, however, may be eaten, since they are of another nature.

4. They do not forbid horse [flesh], nevertheless it is not the custom to eat it.

5. The hare may be eaten, and it is good for dysentery; and its gall is to be mixed with pepper for [the relief of] pain.

6. If bees kill a man, they ought also to be killed quickly, but the honey may be eaten.

7. If by chance swine eat carrion flesh or the blood of a man, we hold that they are not to be thrown away; nor are hens; hence swine that [only] taste the blood of a man are to be eaten.

8. But as for those which tear and eat the corpses of the dead, their flesh may not be eaten until they become feeble and until a year has elapsed.

9. Animals that are polluted by intercourse with men shall be killed, and their flesh thrown to dogs, but their offspring shall be for use, and their hides shall be taken. However, when there is uncertainty, they shall not be killed.

XII. Of Matters Relating to Marriage

1. Those who are married shall abstain from intercourse for three nights before they communicate.

2. A man shall abstain from his wife for forty days before Easter, until the week of Easter. On this account the apostle says: "That ye may give yourselves to prayer."

3. When she has conceived a woman ought to abstain from her husband for three months before the birth, and afterward in the time of purgation, that is, for forty days and nights, whether she has borne a male or a female child.

4. It is also fully permitted to a woman to communicate before she is to bear a child.

5. If the wife of anyone commits fornication, he may put her away and take another; that is, if a man puts away his wife on account of fornication, if she was his first, he is permitted to take another; but if she wishes to do penance for her sins, she may take another husband after five years.

6. A woman may not put away her husband, even if he is a fornicator, unless, perchance, for [the purpose of his entering] a monastery. Basil so decided.

---

12 Acts 15:20.

7. A legal marriage may not be broken without the consent of both parties.

8. But either, according to the Greeks, may give the other permission to join a monastery for the service of God, and [as it were] marry it, if he [or she] was in a first marriage; yet this is not canonical. But if such is not the case, [but they are] in a second marriage, this is not permitted while the husband or wife is alive.

9. If a husband makes himself a slave through theft or fornication or any sin, the wife, if she has not been married before, has the right to take another husband after a year. This is not permitted to one who has been twice married.

10. When his wife is dead, a man may take another wife after a month. If her husband is dead, the woman may take another husband after a year.

11. If a woman is an adultress and her husband does not wish to live with her, if she decides to enter a monastery she shall retain the fourth part of her inheritance. If she decides otherwise, she shall have nothing.

12. Any woman who commits adultery is in the power of her husband if he wishes to be reconciled to an adulterous woman. If he makes a reconciliation, her punishment does not concern the clergy, it belongs to her own husband.

13. In the case of a man and a woman who are married, if he wishes to serve God[13] and she does not, or if she wishes to do so and he does not, or if either of them is broken in health, they may still be completely separated with the consent of both.

14. A woman who vows not to take another husband after her husband's death and when he is dead, false to her word, takes another and is married a second time, when she is moved by penitence and wishes to fulfill her vow, it is in the power of her husband [to determine] whether she shall fulfill it or not.

15. Therefore, to one woman who after eleven years confessed [such] a vow, Theodore gave permission to cohabit with the man.

16. And if anyone in a secular habit takes a vow without the consent of the bishop, the bishop himself has power to change the decision if he wishes.

17. A legal marriage may take place equally in the day and in the night, as it is written, "Thine is the day and thine is the night."

18. If a pagan puts away his pagan wife, after baptism it shall be in his power to have her or not to have her.

19. In the same way, if one of them is baptized, the other a pagan, as saith the apostle, "If the unbeliever depart, let him depart"; therefore, if the wife of any man is an unbeliever and a pagan and cannot be converted, she shall be put away.

20. If a woman leaves her husband, despising him, and is unwilling to return and be reconciled to her husband, after five years, with the bishop's consent, he shall be permitted to take another wife.

21. If she has been taken into captivity by force and cannot be redeemed, [he may] take another after a year.

22. Again, if she has been taken into captivity her husband shall wait five years; so also shall the woman do if such things have happened to the man.

23. If, therefore, a man has taken another wife, he shall receive the former wife when she returns from captivity, and put away the later one; so also shall she do, as we have said above, if such things have happened to her husband.

24. If an enemy carries away any man's wife, and he cannot get her again, he may take another. To do this is better than acts of fornication.

---

13   That is, to enter a monastery.

25. If after this the former wife comes again to him, she ought not to be received by him, if he has another, but she may take to herself another husband, if she has had [only] one before. The same ruling stands in the case of slaves from over sea.

26. According to the Greeks it is permitted to marry in the third degree of consanguinity, as it is written in the Law; according to the Romans, in the fifth degree; however, in the fourth degree they do not dissolve [a marriage] after it has taken place. Hence they are to be united in the fifth degree; in the fourth, if they are found [already married] they are not to be separated; in the third, they are to be separated.

27. Nevertheless, it is not permitted to take the wife of another after his death [if he was related] in the third degree.

28. On the same conditions a man is joined in matrimony to those who are related to him, and to his wife's relatives after her death.

29. Two brothers may also have two sisters in marriage, and a father and a son [respectively] a mother and her daughter.

30. A husband who sleeps with his wife shall wash himself before he goes into a church.

31. A husband ought not to see his wife nude.

32. If anyone has illicit connection or illicit marriage, it is nevertheless permissible to eat the food which they have, for the prophet has said: "The earth is the Lord's and the fullness thereof."

33. If a man and a woman have united in marriage, and afterward the woman says of the man that he is impotent, if anyone can prove that this is true, she may take another [husband].

34. Parents may not give a betrothed girl to another man unless she flatly refuses [to marry the original suitor]; but she may go to a monastery if she wishes.

35. But if she who is betrothed refuses to live with the man to whom she is betrothed, the money which he gave for her shall be paid back to him, and a third part shall be added; if, however, it is he that refuses, he shall lose the money which he gave for her.

36. But a girl of seventeen years has power over her own body.

37. Until he is fifteen years old a boy shall be in the power of his father, then he can make himself a monk; but a girl of sixteen or seventeen years who was before in the power of her parents [can become a nun]. After that age a father may not bestow his daughter in marriage against her will.

XIII. Of Male and Female Slaves

1. If he is compelled by necessity, a father has the power to sell his son of seven years of age into slavery; after that, he has not the right to sell him without his consent.

2. A person of fourteen [years] can make himself a slave.

3. A man may not take away from his slave money which he has acquired by his labor.

4. If the master of a male and female slave joins them in marriage and the male slave or the female slave is afterward set free, and if the one who is in slavery cannot be redeemed, the one who has been set free may marry a free-born person.

5. If any freeman takes a female slave in marriage, he has not the right to put her away if they were formerly united with the consent of both.

6. If anyone acquires [as a slave] a free woman who is pregnant, the child that is born of her is free.

7. If anyone sets free a pregnant slave woman, the child which she brings forth shall be [in a state] of slavery.

XIV. Of Various Matters

1. There are three legitimate fasts in a year for the people; the forty [days] before Easter, when we pay the tithes of the year, and the forty [days] before the Lord's nativity and the forty days and nights after Pentecost.[14]

2. He who fasts for a dead person aids himself. But to God alone belongs knowledge of the dead person.

3. Laymen ought not to be dilatory with respect to their promises, since death does not delay.

4. On no account may the servant of God fight. Let [the matter] be for consultation by many servants of God.

5. One infant may be given to God at a monastery instead of another, even if [the father] has vowed the other; nevertheless it is better to fulfill the vow.

6. Similarly, cattle of equal value may be substituted if it is necessary.

7. If a king holds the territory of another king, he may give it for [the good of] his soul.

8. If anyone converted from the world to the service of God has any royal specie[15] received from a king, that [specie] is in the power of that king; but if it is from a former king, [now] dead, that which he received shall be as his other goods; it is permissible to give it to God with himself.

9. That which is found on a road may be taken away. If the owner is found, it shall be restored to him.

10. Let the tribute of the church be according to the custom of the province; that is, so that the poor may not so greatly(?) suffer violence on this account in tithes or in any matters.

11. It is not lawful to give tithes except to the poor and to pilgrims, or for laymen [to give] to their own churches.

12. Out of reverence for the new birth, prayer is to be made in the fifty days.[16]

13. Prayer may be [made] under a veil if necessity requires it.

14. The sick may take food and drink at all hours when they desire it or when they are able [to take it] if they cannot [do so] at the proper times.

Epilogue[17]

Our [authors], as we said, have written these [canons] in consultation with the venerable Theodore, archbishop of the English. If some suppose they have in their possession in more satisfactory or better form these two rules,[18] we hope they will well use their own [versions] and not neglect ours, in which the parts which seem corrupted are attributed by all to the fault of both scribes and interpreters—pretty barbarous men—so that by some, even [by] those instructed by him, the defective and incorrect passages are rightly said not to be his decisions. Of these, although they are retained by many here and there and in a confused state, in succeeding books we have been able with the aid of Christ the Lord to set in order impartially according to our ability not a few of the chief things out of them. But being still in doubt about this work, we connect with it passages in certain minor works that are necessary to it, especially in the booklet on penance, which I think can be easily perceived by a discerning person.

It therefore remains further in vindication of our father Theodore to make satisfaction as best we can to you, beloved,[19] who, not finding a full

---

14   These are the "three forty-day periods" ("quadragesimae") frequently referred to in this and some other penitentials.
15   Money in coin.
16   The period between Easter and Pentecost.
17   The epilogue has come down in only two manuscripts, and neither one includes both the beginning and the end. The text is unusually obscure.
18   Probably the two books of the penitential.
19   Literally, "to your love."

exposition in the utterances of other Catholics, have therefore had recourse to him. In all these matters, I, not undeservedly, entreat you, beloved, who have been judging the difficulties of these [inquiries] that on this account you defend me by your merits on the right hand and on the left, while I strive on your behalf in the welter of these [difficulties], Christ being the judge of the contest, against the threatening blows of calumniators. It is easier for these [calumniators] to defame the laborers than to sweat in the zeal of labor; for some of our people have given themselves to abuse the wisest men of the Church of God by the volubility of their tongues. I refer to St. Jerome whom they call an evil speaker to men, to Augustine whom they call loquacious, and to Isidore whom they call an arranger of glosses. I say nothing of the others, when they say that Gregory, our apostle, easily uttered what others had earlier expounded, a follower in the beaten paths of other men. From this source I have recently heard (what I shudder to tell) that a certain gross follower of heathen fables is abusing the promulgator of the Law of God and chronicler of the whole history of creation, saying, "What could Moses himself, the magician, either know or say to him?"

What, then, can my defense be, since I, in comparison to those whom I have mentioned, am nothing. Yet, "by the grace of God, I am what I am"; may it not have been void in me through him who is able to create all things of nothing and to bring to pass great things from little. On this account, if any Catholic author finds anything anywhere in these canons that he is able to amend, he shall have permission from us to do this reasonably, in view of the fact that unless the parts that are not to be followed are suppressed, when they are held of equal validity they occasion contention to those to whom it is said: "not in contention and envy; But put ye on the Lord Jesus Christ."

18. EINHARD

Life of Charles the Great

EINHARD (CA. 770–840), ORIGINALLY from the region of Mainz, was raised in the monastery of Fulda and later educated at the court of Charlemagne. He later served Charlemagne and his son Louis the Pious (778–840) in various capacities at court and on diplomatic missions. Displeased with the direction of Louis's reign, he retired from court in the early 820s and wrote his *Life of Charlemagne* ca. 825/26. The text, which is a classic of medieval biography, demonstrates the author's thorough familiarity with his model Suetonius, the Roman historian who wrote biographies of the emperors, but is also an extremely subtle critique of Charlemagne's successor. Like royal biographers after him such as Joinville, the biographer of St. Louis IX (see below), Einhard attacks the faults of the reigning monarch simply by praising the virtues of his predecessor.

Source: Translated for this anthology by Samuel Epes Turner.

Further Reading: Rosamond McKitterick, *Charlemagne: The Formation of a European Identity* (Cambridge: Cambridge University Press, 2008).

Einhard's Preface

Since I have taken upon myself to narrate the public and private life, and no small part of the deeds, of my lord and foster-father, the most excellent and most justly renowned King Charles, I have condensed the matter into as brief a form as possible. I have been careful not to omit any fact that could come to my knowledge, but at the same time not to offend by a prolix style those minds that despise everything modern, if one can possibly avoid offending by a new work men who seem to despise also the masterpieces of antiquity, the works of most learned and luminous writers. Very many of them, I have no doubt, are men devoted to a life of literary leisure, who feel that the affairs of the present generation ought not to be passed by, and who do not consider everything done today as unworthy of mention and deserving to be given over to silence and oblivion, but are nevertheless seduced by lust of immortality to celebrate the glorious deeds of other times by some sort of composition rather than to deprive posterity of the mention of their own names by not writing at all.

Be this as it may, I see no reason why I should refrain from entering upon a task of this kind, since no man can write with more accuracy than I of events that took place about me, and of facts concerning which I had personal knowledge, ocular demonstration, as the saying goes, and I have no means of ascertaining whether or not any one else has the subject in hand.

In any event, I would rather commit my story to writing, and hand it down to posterity in partnership with others, so to speak, than to suffer the most glorious life of this most excellent king, the greatest of all the princes of his day, and his illustrious deeds, hard for men of later times to imitate, to be wrapped in the darkness of oblivion.

But there are still other reasons, neither unwarrantable nor insufficient, in my opinion, that urge me to write on this subject, namely, the care that King Charles bestowed upon me in my childhood, and my constant friendship with himself and his children after I took up my abode at court. In this way he strongly endeared me to himself, and made me greatly his debtor as well in death as in life, so that were I, unmindful of the benefits conferred upon me, to keep silence concerning the most glorious and illustrious deeds of a man who claims so much at my hands, and suffer his life to lack due eulogy and written memorial, as if he had never lived, I should deservedly appear ungrateful, and be so considered, albeit my powers are feeble, scanty, next to nothing indeed, and not at all adapted to write and set forth a life that would tax the eloquence of a Tully.[1]

I submit the book. It contains the history of a very great and distinguished man; but there is nothing in it to wonder at besides his deeds, except the fact that I, who am a barbarian, and very little versed in the Roman language, seem to suppose myself capable of writing gracefully and respectably in Latin, and to carry my presumption so far as to disdain the sentiment that Cicero is said in the first book of the "Tusculan Disputations" to have expressed when speaking of the Latin authors. His words are: "It is an outrageous abuse both of time and literature for a man to commit his thoughts to writing without having the ability either to arrange them or elucidate them, or attract readers by some charm of style." This dictum of the famous orator might have deterred me from writing if I had not made up my mind that it was better to risk the opinions of the world, and put my little talents for composition to the test, than to slight the memory of so great a man for the sake of sparing myself.

The Life of the Emperor Charles

1. The Merovingian family, from which the Franks used to choose their kings, is commonly said to have lasted until the time of Childeric, who was deposed, shaved and thrust into the cloister by command of the Roman Pontiff Stephen. But although, to all outward appearances, it ended with him, it had long since been devoid of vital strength, and conspicuous only from bearing the empty epithet royal; the real power and authority in the kingdom lay in the hands of the chief officer of the court, the so-called mayor of the palace, and he was at the head of affairs. There was nothing left the king to do but to be content with his name of king, his flowing hair, and long beard, to sit on his throne and play the ruler, to give ear to the ambassadors that came from all quarters, and to dismiss them, as if on his own responsibility, in words that were, in fact, suggested to him, or even imposed upon him. He had nothing that he could call his own beyond this vain title of king and the precarious support allowed by the mayor of the palace in his discretion, except a single country seat, that brought him but a very small income. There was a dwelling house upon this, and a small number of servants attached to it, sufficient to perform the necessary offices. When he had to go abroad, he used to ride in a cart, drawn by a yoke of oxen, driven, peasant-fashion, by a plowman; he rode in this way to the palace and to the general assembly of the people, that met once a year for the welfare of the kingdom, and he returned him in like manner. The mayor of the palace took charge of the government and everything that had to be planned or executed at home and abroad.

2. At the time of Childeric's disposition, Pepin, the father of King Charles, held this office of mayor of the palace, one might almost say, by hereditary right; for Pepin's father, Charles, had received it at the hands of his father, Pepin, and filled it with distinction. It was this Charles that crushed the tyrants who claimed to rule the whole Frank land as their own, and that utterly routed the Saracens, when they attempted the conquest of Gaul, in two great battles—one in Aquitania, near the town of Poitiers, and the other on the River Berre, near Narbonne—and compelled them to return to Spain. This honor was usually conferred by the people only upon men eminent from their illustrious birth and ample wealth. For some years, ostensibly under King Childeric, Pepin, the father of King Charles, shared the duties inherited from

---

1 Marcus Tullius Cicero (106–43 BCE), Roman rhetorician and statesman.

his father and grandfather most amicably with his brother, Carloman. The latter, then, for reasons unknown, renounced the heavy cares of an earthly crown and retired to Rome. Here he exchanged his worldly garb for a cowl, and built a monastery on Mt. Oreste, near the Church of St. Sylvester, where he enjoyed for several years the seclusion that he desired, in company with certain others who had the same object in view. But so many distinguished Franks made the pilgrimage to Rome to fulfill their vows, and insisted upon paying their respects to him, as their former lord, on the way, that the repose which he so much loved was broken by these frequent visits, and he was driven to change his abode. Accordingly, when he found that his plans were frustrated by his many visitors, he abandoned the mountain, and withdrew to the Monastery of St. Benedict, on Monte Cassino, in the province of Samnium, and passed the rest of his days there in the exercises of religion.

3. Pepin, however, was raised, by decree of the Roman Pontiff, from the rank of mayor of the palace to that of king, and ruled alone over the Franks for fifteen years or more. He died of dropsy, in Paris, at the close of the Aquitanian war, which he waged with William, Duke of Aquitania, for nine successive years, and left two sons, Charles and Carloman, upon whom, by the grace of God, the succession devolved.

The Franks, in a general assembly of the people, made them both kings, on condition that they should divide the whole kingdom equally between them, Charles to take and rule the part that had belonged to their father, Pepin, and Carloman the part which their uncle, Carloman, had governed. The conditions were accepted, and each entered into possession of the share of the kingdom that fell to him by this arrangement; but peace was only maintained between them with the greatest difficulty, because many of Carloman's party kept trying to disturb their good understanding, and there were some even who plotted to involve them in a war with each other. The event, however, showed the danger to have been rather imaginary than real, for at Carloman's death his widow fled to Italy with her sons and her principal adherents, and without reason, despite her husband's brother, put herself and her children under the

protection of Desiderius, king of the Lombards. Carloman had succumbed to disease after ruling two years in common with his brother, and at his death Charles was unanimously elected king of the Franks.

4. It would be folly, I think, to write a word concerning Charles's birth and infancy, or even his boyhood, for nothing has ever been written on the subject, and there is no one alive now who can give information of it. Accordingly, I have determined to pass that by as unknown, and to proceed at once to treat of his character, his deeds, and such other facts of his life as are worth telling and setting forth, and shall first give an account of his deeds at home and abroad, then of his character and pursuits, and lastly of his administration and death, omitting nothing worth knowing or necessary to know.

5. His first undertaking in a military way was the Aquitanian war, begun by his father, but not brought to a close; and because he thought that it could be readily carried through, he took it up while his brother was yet alive, calling upon him to render aid. The campaign once opened, he conducted it with the greatest vigor, notwithstanding his brother withheld the assistance that he had promised, and did not desist or shrink from his self-imposed task until, by his patience and firmness, he had completely gained his ends. He compelled Hunold, who had attempted to seize Aquitania after Waifar's death, and renew the war then almost concluded, to abandon Aquitania and flee to Gascony. Even here he gave him no rest, but crossed the River Garonne, built the castle of Fronsac, and sent ambassadors to Lupus, Duke of Gascony, to demand the surrender of the fugitive, threatening to take him by force unless he were promptly given up to him. Thereupon Lupus chose the wiser course, and not only gave Hunold up, but submitted himself, with the province which he ruled, to the king.

6. After bringing this war to an end and settling matters in Aquitania (his associate in authority had meanwhile departed this life), he was induced, by the prayers and entreaties of Hadrian, bishop of the city of Rome, to wage war on the

Lombards. His father before him had undertaken this task at the request of Pope Stephen, but under great difficulties, for certain leading Franks, of whom he usually took counsel, had so vehemently opposed his design as to declare openly that they would leave the king and go home. Nevertheless, the war against the Lombard King Astolf had been taken up and very quickly concluded. Now, although Charles seems to have had similar, or rather just the same grounds for declaring war that his father had, the war itself differed from the preceding one alike in its difficulties and its issue. Pepin, to be sure, after besieging King Astolf a few days in Pavia, had compelled him to give hostages, to restore to the Romans the cities and castles that he had taken, and to make oath that he would not attempt to seize them again: but Charles did not cease, after declaring war, until he had exhausted King Desiderius by a long siege, and forced him to surrender at discretion; driven his son Adalgis, the last hope of the Lombards, not only from his kingdom, but from all Italy; restored to the Romans all that they had lost; subdued Hruodgaus, Duke of Friuli, who was plotting revolution; reduced all Italy to his power, and set his son Pepin as king over it.

At this point I should describe Charles's difficult passage over the Alps into Italy, and the hardships that the Franks endured in climbing the trackless mountain ridges, the heaven-aspiring cliffs and ragged peaks, if it were not my purpose in this work to record the manner of his life rather than the incidents of the wars that he waged. Suffice it to say that this war ended with the subjection of Italy, the banishment of King Desiderius for life, the expulsion of his son Adalgis from Italy, and the restoration of the conquests of the Lombard kings to Hadrian, the head of the Roman Church.

7. At the conclusion of this struggle, the Saxon war, that seems to have been only laid aside for the time, was taken up again. No war ever undertaken by the Frank nation was carried on with such persistence and bitterness, or cost so much labor, because the Saxons, like almost all the tribes of Germany, were a fierce people, given to the worship of devils, and hostile to our religion, and did not consider it dishonorable to transgress and violate all law, human and divine. Then there were peculiar circumstances that tended to cause a breach of peace every day. Except in a few places, where large forests or mountain ridges intervened and made the bounds certain, the line between ourselves and the Saxons passed almost in its whole extent through an open country, so that there was no end to the murders, thefts and arsons on both sides. In this way the Franks became so embittered that they at last resolved to make reprisals no longer, but to come to open war with the Saxons. Accordingly war was begun against them, and was waged for thirty-three successive years with great fury; more, however, to the disadvantage of the Saxons than of the Franks. It could doubtless have been brought to an end sooner, had it not been for the faithlessness of the Saxons. It is hard to say how often they were conquered, and, humbly submitting to the king, promised to do what was enjoined upon them, gave without hesitation the required hostages, and received the officers sent them from the king. They were sometimes so much weakened and reduced that they promised to renounce the worship of devils, and to adopt Christianity, but they were no less ready to violate these terms than prompt to accept them, so that it is impossible to tell which came more easily to them to do; scarcely a year passed from the beginning of the war without such changes on their part. But the king did not suffer his high purpose and steadfastness—firm alike in good and evil fortune—to be turned from the task that he had undertaken; on the contrary, he never allowed their faithless behavior to go unpunished, but either took the field against them in person, or sent his counts with an army to wreak vengeance and exact righteous satisfaction. At last, after conquering and subduing all who had offered resistance, he took ten thousand of those that lived on the banks of the Elbe, and settled them, with their wives and children, in many different bodies here and there in Gaul and Germany. The war that had lasted so many years was at length ended by their acceding to the terms offered by the king; which were renunciation of their national religious customs and the worship of devils, acceptance of the sacraments of the Christian faith and religion, and union with the Franks to form one people.

8. Charles himself fought but two pitched battles in this war, although it was long protracted—one on Mount Osning, at the place called Detmold, and again on the bank of the river Hase, both in the space of little more than a month. The enemy were so routed and overthrown in these two battles that they never afterwards ventured to take the offensive or to resist the attacks of the king, unless they were protected by a strong position. A great many of the Frank as well as of the Saxon nobility, men occupying the highest posts of honor, perished in this war, which only came to an end after the lapse of thirty-two years. So many and grievous were the wars that were declared against the Franks in the meantime, and skillfully conducted by the king, that one may reasonably question whether his fortitude or his good fortune is to be more admired. The Saxon war began two years before the Italian war; but although it went on without interruption, business elsewhere was not neglected, nor was there any shrinking from other equally arduous contests. The king, who excelled all the princes of his time in wisdom and greatness of soul, did not suffer difficulty to deter him or danger to daunt him from anything that had to be taken up or carried through, for he had trained himself to bear and endure whatever came, without yielding in adversity, or trusting to the deceitful favors of fortune in prosperity.

9. In the midst of this vigorous and almost uninterrupted struggle with the Saxons, he covered the frontier by garrisons at the proper points, and marched over the Pyrenees into Spain at the head of all the forces that he could muster. All the towns and castles that he attacked surrendered, and up to the time of his homeward march he sustained no loss whatsoever; but on his return through the Pyrenees he had cause to rue the treachery of the Gascons. That region is well adapted for ambuscades by reason of the thick forests that cover it; and as the army was advancing in the long line of march necessitated by the narrowness of the road, the Gascons, who lay in ambush on the top of a very high mountain, attacked the rear of the baggage train and the rear guard in charge of it, and hurled them down to the very bottom of the valley. In the struggle that ensued, they cut them off to a man; they then plundered the baggage, and

dispersed with all speed in every direction under cover of approaching night. The lightness of their armor and the nature of the battle ground stood the Gascons in good stead on this occasion, whereas the Franks fought at a disadvantage in every respect, because of the weight of their armor and the unevenness of the ground. Eggihard, the king's steward; Anselm, Count Palatine; and Roland, governor of the March of Brittany, with very many others, fell in this engagement. This ill turn could not be avenged for the nonce, because the enemy scattered so widely after carrying out their plan that not the least clue could be had to their whereabouts.

10. Charles also subdued the Bretons, who live on the sea coast, in the extreme western part of Gaul. When they refused to obey him, he sent an army against them, and compelled them to give hostages, and to promise to do his bidding. He afterwards entered Italy in person with his army, and passed through Rome to Capua, a city in Campania, where he pitched his camp and threatened the Beneventans with hostilities unless they should submit themselves to him. Their duke, Aragis, escaped the danger by sending his two sons, Rumold and Grimold, with a great sum of money to greet the king, begging him to accept them as hostages, and promising for himself and his people compliance with all the king's commands, on the single condition that his personal attendance should not be required. The king took the welfare of the people into account rather than the stubborn disposition of the duke, accepted the proffered hostages, and released him from the obligation to appear before him in consideration of his handsome gift. He retained the younger son only as hostage, and sent the elder back to his father, and returned to Rome, leaving commissioners with Aragis to exact the oath of allegiance, and administer it to the Beneventans. He stayed in Rome several days in order to pay his devotions at the holy places, and then came back to Gaul.

11. At this time, on a sudden, the Bavarian war broke out, but came to a speedy end. It was due to the arrogance and folly of Duke Tassilo. His wife, a daughter of King Desiderius, was desirous of avenging her father's banishment through

the agency of her husband, and accordingly induced him to make a treaty with the Huns, the neighbors of the Bavarians on the east, and not only to leave the king's commands unfulfilled, but to challenge him to war. Charles's high spirit could not brook Tassilo's insubordination, for it seemed to him to pass all bounds; accordingly he straightway summoned his troops from all sides for a campaign against Bavaria, and appeared in person with a great army on the river Lech, which forms the boundary between the Bavarians and the Alemanni. After pitching his camp upon its banks, he determined to put the Duke's disposition to the test by an embassy before entering the province. Tassilo did not think that it was for his own or his people's good to persist, so he surrendered himself to the king, gave the hostages demanded, among them his own son Theodo, and promised by oath not to give ear to anyone who should attempt to turn him from his allegiance; so this war, which bade fair to be very grievous, came very quickly to an end. Tassilo, however, was afterward summoned to the king's presence, and not suffered to depart, and the government of the province that he had had in charge was no longer intrusted to a duke, but to counts.

12. After these uprisings had been thus quelled, war was declared against the Slavs who are commonly known among us as Wilzi, but properly, that is to say in their own tongue, are called Welatabians. The Saxons served in this campaign as auxiliaries among the tribes that followed the king's standard at his summons, but their obedience lacked sincerity and devotion. War was declared because the Slavs kept harassing the Abodriti, old allies of the Franks, by continual raids, in spite of all commands to the contrary. A gulf of unknown length, but nowhere more than a hundred miles wide, and in many parts narrower, stretches off towards the east from the Western Ocean. Many tribes have settlements on its shores; the Danes and Swedes, whom we call Northmen, on the northern shore and all the adjacent islands; but the southern shore is inhabited by the Slavs and Aïsti, and various other tribes. The Welatabians, against whom the king now made war, were the chief of these; but in a single campaign, which he conducted in person, he

so crushed and subdued them that they did not think it advisable thereafter to refuse obedience to his commands.

13. The war against the Avars, or Huns, followed, and, except for the Saxon war, was the greatest that was waged; he took it up with more spirit than any of his other wars, and made far greater preparations for it. He conducted one campaign in person in Pannonia, of which the Huns then had possession. He intrusted all subsequent operations to his son, Pepin, and the governors of the provinces, to counts even, and lieutenants. Although they most vigorously prosecuted the war, it only came to a conclusion after a seven years' struggle. The utter depopulation of Pannonia, and the site of the Khan's palace, now a desert, where not a trace of human habitation is visible, bear witness how many battles were fought in those years, and how much blood was shed. The entire body of the Hun nobility perished in this contest, and all its glory with it. All the money and treasure that had been years amassing was seized, and no war in which the Franks have ever engaged within the memory of man brought them such riches and such booty. Up to that time the Huns had passed for a poor people, but so much gold and silver was found in the Khan's palace, and so much valuable spoil taken in battle, that one may well think that the Franks took justly from the Huns what the Huns had formerly taken unjustly from other nations. Only two of the chief men of the Franks fell in this war—Eric, Duke of Friuli, who was killed in Tarsatch, a town on the coast of Liburnia, by the treachery of the inhabitants; and Gerold, governor of Bavaria, who met his death at Pannonia, slain, with two men that were accompanying him, by an unknown hand while he was marshaling his forces for battle against the Huns, and riding up and down the line encouraging his men. This war was otherwise almost a bloodless one so far as the Franks were concerned, and ended most satisfactorily, although by reason of its magnitude it was long protracted.

14. The Saxon war next came to an end as successful as the struggle had been long. The Bohemian and Linonian wars that next broke out could not last long; both were quickly carried through

under the leadership of the younger Charles. The last of these wars was the one declared against the Northmen called Danes. They began their careers as pirates, but afterward took to laying waste the coasts of Gaul and Germany with their large fleet. Their king Godfred was so puffed with vain aspirations that he counted on gaining empire over all Germany, and looked upon Saxony and Frisia as his provinces. He had already subdued his neighbors the Abodriti, and made them tributary, and boasted that he would shortly appear with a great army before Aix-la-Chapelle, where the king held his court. Some faith was put in his words, empty as they sound, and it is supposed that he would have attempted something of the sort if he had not been prevented by a premature death. He was murdered by one of his own bodyguards, and so ended at once his life and the war that he had begun.

15. Such are the wars, most skillfully planned and successfully fought, which this most powerful king waged during the forty-seven years of his reign. He so largely increased the Frank kingdom, which was already great and strong when he received it at his father's hands, that more than double its former territory was added to it. The authority of the Franks was formerly confined to that part of Gaul included between the Rhine and the Loire, the Ocean and the Balearic Sea; to that part of Germany which is inhabited by the so-called Eastern Franks, and is bounded by Saxony and the Danube, the Rhine and the Saale— this stream separates the Thuringians from the Sorabians; and to the country of the Alemanni and Bavarians. By the wars above mentioned he first made tributary Aquitania, Gascony, and the whole of the region of the Pyrenees as far as the River Ebro, which rises in the land of the Navarrese, flows through the most fertile districts of Spain, and empties into the Balearic Sea, beneath the walls of the city of Tortosa. He next reduced and made tributary all Italy from Aosta to Lower Calabria, where the boundary line runs between the Beneventans and the Greeks, a territory more than a thousand miles long; then Saxony, which constitutes no small part of Germany, and is reckoned to be twice as wide as the country inhabited by the Franks, while about equal to it in length; in addition, both Pannonias, Dacia beyond the Danube, and Istria, Liburnia, and Dalmatia, except the cities on the coast, which he left to the Greek emperor for friendship's sake, and because of the treaty that he had made with him. In fine, he vanquished and made tributary all the wild and barbarous tribes dwelling in Germany between the Danube, all of which speak very much the same language, but differ widely from one another chiefly in customs and dress. The chief among them are the Welatabians, the Sorabians, the Abodriti, and the Bohemians, and he had to make war upon these; but the rest, by far the larger number, submitted to him of their own accord.

16. He added to the glory of his reign by gaining the goodwill of several kings and nations; so close, indeed, was the alliance that he contracted with Alfonso, king of Galicia and Asturias, that the latter, when sending letters or ambassadors to Charles, invariably styled himself his man. His munificence won the kings of the Scots also to pay such deference to his wishes that they never gave him any other title than lord, or themselves than subjects or slaves: there are letters from them extant in which these feelings in his regard are expressed. His relations with Aaron, king of the Persians, who ruled over almost the whole of the East, India excepted, were so friendly that this prince preferred his favor to that of all the kings and potentates of the earth, and considered that to him alone marks of honor and munificence were due. Accordingly, when the ambassadors sent by Charles to visit the most holy sepulcher and place of resurrection of our Lord and Savior presented themselves before him with gifts, and made known their master's wishes, he not only granted what was asked, but gave possession of that holy and blessed spot. When they returned, he dispatched his ambassadors with them, and sent magnificent gifts, besides stuffs, perfumes, and other rich products of the Eastern lands. A few years before this, Charles had asked him for an elephant, and he sent the only one that he had. The emperors of Constantinople, Nicephorus, Michael, and Leo, made advances to Charles, and sought friendship and alliance with him by several embassies; and even when the Greeks suspected

him of designing to wrest the empire from them, because of his assumption of the title emperor, they made a close alliance with him, that he might have no cause of offense. In fact, the power of the Franks was always viewed by the Greeks and Romans with a jealous eye, whence the Greek proverb "Have the Frank for your friend, but not for your neighbor."

17. This king, who showed himself so great in extending his empire and subduing foreign nations, and was constantly occupied with plans to that end, undertook also very many works calculated to adorn and benefit his kingdom, and brought several of them to completion. Among these, the most deserving of mention are the basilica of the Holy Mother of God at Aix-la-Chapelle, built in the most admirable manner, and a bridge over the Rhine at Mayence, half a mile long, the breadth of the river at this point. This bridge was destroyed by fire the year before Charles died, but, owing to his death so soon after, could not be repaired, although he had intended to rebuild it in stone. He began two palaces of beautiful workmanship—one near his manor called Ingelheim, not far from Mayence; the other at Nimeguen, on the Waal, the stream that washes the south side of the island of the Batavians. But, above all, sacred edifices were the object of his care throughout his whole kingdom; and whenever he found them falling to ruin from age, he commanded the priests and fathers who had charge of them to repair them, and made sure by commissioners that his instructions were obeyed. He also fitted out a fleet for the war with the Northmen; the vessels required for this purpose were built on the rivers that flow from Gaul and Germany into the Northern Ocean. Moreover, since the Northmen continually overran and laid waste the Gallic and German coasts, he caused watch and ward to be kept in all the harbors, and at the mouths of rivers in all the harbors, and at the mouths of rivers large enough to admit the entrance of vessels, to prevent the enemy from disembarking; and in the South, in Narbonensis and Septimania, and along the whole coast of Italy as far as Rome, he took the same precautions against the Moors, who had recently begun their piratical practices. Hence, Italy suffered no great harm in his time at the hands of the Moors, nor Gaul and Germany from the Northmen, save that the Moors got possession of the Etruscan town of Civita Vecchia by treachery, and sacked it, and the Northmen harried some of the islands in Frisia off the German coast.

18. Thus did Charles defend and increase as well as beautify his kingdom, as is well known; and here let me express my admiration of his great qualities and his extraordinary constancy alike in good and evil fortune. I will now forthwith proceed to give the details of his private and family life.

After his father's death, while sharing the kingdom with his brother, he bore his unfriendliness and jealousy most patiently, and, to the wonder of all, could not be provoked to be angry with him. Later he married a daughter of Desiderius, king of the Lombards, at the instance of his mother; but he repudiated her at the end of a year for some reason unknown, and married Hildegard, a woman of high birth, of Suabian origin. He had three sons by her—Charles, Pepin, and Louis—and as many daughters—Hruodrud, Bertha, and Gisela. He had three other daughters besides these—Theoderada, Hiltrud, and Ruodhaid—two by his third wife, Fastrada, a woman of East Frankish (that is to say, German) origin, and the third by a concubine, whose name for the moment escapes me. At the death of Fastrada, he married Liutgard, an Alemannic woman, who bore him no children. After her death he had three concubines—Gersuinda, a Saxon, by whom he had Adaltrud; Regina, who was the mother of Drogo and Hugh; and Ethelind, by whom he had Theodoric. Charles's mother, Berthrada, passed her old age with him in great honor; he entertained the greatest veneration for her; and there was never any disagreement between them except when he divorced the daughter of King Desiderius, whom he had married to please her. She died soon after Hildegard, after living to see three grandsons and as many granddaughters in her son's house, and he buried her with great pomp in the Basilica of St. Denis, where his father lay. He had an only sister, Gisela, who had consecrated herself to a religious life from girlhood, and he cherished as much affection for her as for his mother. She also died a few years before him in the nunnery where she had passed her life.

19. The plan that he adopted for his children's education was, first of all, to have both boys and girls instructed in the liberal arts, to which he also turned his own attention. As soon as their years admitted, in accordance with the customs of the Franks, the boys had to learn horsemanship, and to practice war and the chase, and the girls to familiarize themselves with cloth-making, and to handle distaff and spindle, that they might not grow indolent through idleness, and he fostered in them every virtuous sentiment. He lost only three of all his children before his death, two sons and one daughter, Charles who was the eldest, Pepin, whom he had made king of Italy, and Hruodrud, his oldest daughter, whom he had betrothed to Constantine, emperor of the Greeks. Pepin left one son, named Bernard, and five daughters, Adelaide, Atula, Guntrada, Berthaid, and Theoderada. The king gave a striking proof of his fatherly affection at the time of Pepin's death: he appointed the grandson to succeed Pepin, and had the granddaughters brought up with his own daughters. When his sons and his daughter died, he was not so calm as might have been expected from his remarkably strong mind, for his affections were no less strong, and moved him to tears. Again, when he was told of the death of Hadrian, the Roman Pontiff, whom he had loved most of all his friends, he wept as much as if he had lost a brother, or a very dear son. He was by nature most ready to contract friendships, and not only made friends easily, but clung to them persistently, and cherished most fondly those with whom he had formed such ties. He was so careful of the training of his sons and daughters that he never took his meals without them when he was at home, and never made a journey without them; his sons would ride at his side, and his daughters follow him, while a number of his bodyguard, detailed for their protection, brought up the rear. Strange to say, although they were very handsome women, and he loved them very dearly, he was never willing to marry any of them to a man of their own nation or to a foreigner, but kept them all at home until his death, saying that he could not dispense with their society. Hence, though otherwise happy, he experienced the malignity of fortune as far as they were concerned; yet he concealed his knowledge of the rumors current in regard to them, and of the suspicions entertained of their honor.

20. By one of his concubines he had a son, handsome in face, but hunchbacked, named Pepin, whom I omitted to mention in the list of his children. When Charles was at war with the Huns, and was wintering in Bavaria, this Pepin shammed sickness, and plotted against his father in company with some of the leading Franks, who seduced him with vain promises of the royal authority. When his deceit was discovered, and the conspirators punished, his head was shaved, and he was suffered, in accordance with his wishes, to devote himself to a religious life in the monastery of Prüm. A formidable conspiracy against Charles had previously been set on foot in Germany, but all the traitors were banished, some of them without mutilations, others after their eyes had been put out. Three of them only lost their lives; they drew their swords and resisted arrest, and, after killing several men, were cut down, because they could not otherwise be overpowered. It is supposed that the cruelty of Queen Fastrada was the primary cause of these plots, and they were both due to Charles's apparent acquiescence in his wife's cruel conduct, and deviation from the usual kindness and gentleness of his disposition. All the rest of his life he was regarded by everyone with the utmost love and affection, so much so that not the least accusation of unjust rigor was ever made against him.

21. He liked foreigners, and was at great pains to take them under his protection. There were often so many of them, both in the palace and the kingdom, that they might reasonably have been considered a nuisance; but he, with his broad humanity, was very little disturbed by such annoyances, because he felt himself compensated for these great inconveniences by the praises of his generosity and the reward of high renown.

22. Charles was large and strong, and of lofty stature, though not disproportionately tall (his height is well known to have been seven times the length of his foot); the upper part of his head was round, his eyes very large and animated, nose a little long, hair fair, and face laughing and merry.

Thus his appearance was always stately and dignified, whether he was standing or sitting; although his neck was thick and somewhat short, and his belly rather prominent; but the symmetry of the rest of his body concealed these defects. His gait was firm, his whole carriage manly, and his voice clear, but not so strong as his size led one to expect. His health was excellent, except during the four years preceding his death, when he was subject to frequent fevers; at the last he even limped a little with one foot. Even in those years he consulted rather his own inclinations than the advice of physicians, who were almost hateful to him, because they wanted him to give up roasts, to which he was accustomed, and to eat boiled meat instead. In accordance with the national custom, he took frequent exercise on horseback and in the chase, accomplishments in which scarcely any peoples in the world can equal the Franks. He enjoyed the exhalations from natural warm springs, and often practiced swimming, in which he was such an adept that none could surpass him; and hence it was that he built his palace at Aix-la-Chapelle, and lived there constantly during his latter years until his death. He used not only to invite his sons to his bath, but his nobles and friends, and now and then a troop of his retinue or bodyguard, so that a hundred or more persons sometimes bathed with him.

23. He used to wear the national, that is to say, the Frank, dress—next to his skin a linen shirt and linen breeches, and above these a tunic fringed with silk; while hose fastened by bands covered his lower limbs, and shoes his feet, and he protected his shoulders and chest in winter by a close-fitting coat of otter or marten skins. Over all he flung a blue cloak, and he always had a sword girt about him, usually one with a gold or silver hilt and belt; he sometimes carried a jeweled sword, but only on great feast-days or at the reception of ambassadors from foreign nations. He despised foreign costumes, however handsome, and never allowed himself to be robed in them, except twice in Rome, when he donned the Roman tunic, chlamys, and shoes; the first time at the request of Pope Hadrian, the second to gratify Leo, Hadrian's successor. On great feast-days he made use of embroidered clothes and shoes bedecked by a golden buckle, and he appeared crowned with a diadem of gold and gems, but on other days his dress varied little from the common dress of the people.

24. Charles was temperate in eating, and particularly so in drinking, for he abominated drunkenness in anybody, much more in himself and those of his household; but he could not easily abstain from food, and often complained that fasts injured his health. He very rarely gave entertainments, only on great feast-days, and then to large numbers of people. His meals ordinarily consisted of four courses, not counting the roast, which his huntsmen used to bring in on the spit; he was more fond of this than any other dish. While at table, he listened to reading or music. The subjects of the readings were the stories and deeds of olden time: he was fond, too, of St. Augustine's books, and especially of the one entitled "The City of God." He was so moderate in the use of wine and all sorts of drink that he rarely allowed himself more than three cups in the course of a meal. In summer, after the midday meal, he would eat some fruit, drain a single cup, put off his clothes and shoes, just as he did for the night, and rest for two or three hours. He was in the habit of awaking and rising from bed four or five times during the night. While he was dressing and putting on his shoes, he not only gave audience to his friends, but if the count of the palace told him of any suit in which his judgment was necessary, he had the parties brought before him forthwith, took cognizance of the case, and gave his decision, just as if he were sitting on the judgment seat. This was not the only business that he transacted at this time, but he performed any duty of the day whatever, whether he had to attend to the matter himself, or to give commands concerning it to his officers.

25. Charles had the gift of ready and fluent speech, and could express whatever he had to say with the utmost clearness. He was not satisfied with command of his native language merely, but gave attention to the study of foreign ones, and in particular was such a master of Latin that he could speak it as well as his native tongue; but he could understand Greek better than he could speak it. He was so eloquent, indeed, that he might have

passed for a teacher of eloquence. He most zealously cultivated the liberal arts, held those who taught them in great esteem, and conferred great honors upon them. He took lessons in grammar of the deacon Peter of Pisa, at that time an aged man. Another deacon, Albin of Britain, surnamed Alcuin, a man of Saxon extraction, who was the greatest scholar of the day, was his teacher in other branches of learning. The king spent much time and labor with him studying rhetoric, dialectics, and especially astronomy; he learned to reckon, and used to investigate the motions of the heavenly bodies most curiously, with an intelligent scrutiny. He also tried to write, and used to keep tablets and blanks in bed under his pillow, that at leisure hours he might accustom his hand to form the letters; however, as he did not begin his efforts in due season, but late in life, they met with ill success.

26. He cherished with the greatest fervor and devotion the principles of the Christian religion, which had been instilled into him from infancy. Hence it was that he built the beautiful basilica at Aix-la-Chapelle, which he adorned with gold and silver and lamps, and with rails and doors of solid brass. He had the columns and marbles for this structure brought from Rome and Ravenna, for he could not find such as were suitable elsewhere. He was a constant worshipper at this church as long as his health permitted, going morning and evening, even after nightfall, besides attending mass; and he took care that all the services there conducted should be administered with the utmost possible propriety, very often warning the sextons not to let any improper or unclean thing be brought into the building or remain in it. He provided it with a great number of sacred vessels of gold and silver and with such a quantity of clerical robes that not even the doorkeepers who fill the humblest office in the church were obliged to wear their everyday clothes when in the exercise of their duties. He was at great pains to improve the church reading and psalmody, for he was well skilled in both, although he neither read in public nor sang, except in a low tone and with others.

27. He was very forward in succoring the poor, and in that gratuitous generosity which the Greeks call alms, so much so that he not only made a point of giving in his own country and his own kingdom, but when he discovered that there were Christians living in poverty in Syria, Egypt, and Africa, at Jerusalem, Alexandria, and Carthage, he had compassion on their wants, and used to send money over the seas to them. The reason that he zealously strove to make friends with the kings beyond the seas was that he might get help and relief to the Christians living under their rule. He cherished the Church of St. Peter the Apostle at Rome above all other holy and sacred places, and heaped its treasury with a vast wealth of gold, silver, and precious stones. He sent great and countless gifts to the popes, and throughout his whole reign the wish that he had nearest at heart was to reestablish the ancient authority of the city of Rome under his care and by his influence, and to defend and protect the Church of St. Peter, and to beautify and enrich it out of his own store above all other churches. Although he held it in such veneration, he only repaired to Rome to pay his vows and make his supplications four times during the whole forty-seven years that he reigned.

28. When he made his last journey thither, he had also other ends in view. The Romans had inflicted many injuries upon the Pontiff Leo, tearing out his eyes and cutting out his tongue, so that he had been compelled to call upon the king for help. Charles accordingly went to Rome, to set in order the affairs of the Church, which were in great confusion, and passed the whole winter there. It was then that he received the titles of Emperor and Augustus, to which he at first had such an aversion that he declared that he would not have set foot in the Church the day that they conferred, although it was a great feast-day, if he could have foreseen the design of the Pope. He bore very patiently with the jealousy which the Roman emperors showed upon his assuming these titles, for they took this step very ill; and by dint of frequent embassies and letters, in which he addressed them as brothers, he made their haughtiness yield to his magnanimity, a quality in which he was unquestionably much their superior.

29. It was after he received the imperial name that, finding the laws of his people very defective

(the Franks have two sets of laws, very different in many particulars), he determined to add what was wanting, to reconcile the discrepancies, and to correct what was vicious and wrongly cited in them. However, he went no further in this matter than to supplement the laws with a few capitularies, and those imperfect ones; but he caused the unwritten laws of all the tribes that came under his rule to be compiled and reduced to writing. He also had the old rude songs that celebrate the deeds and wars of the ancient kings written out for transmission to posterity. He began a grammar of his native language. He gave the months names in his own tongue, in place of the Latin and barbarous names by which they were formerly known among the Franks. He likewise designated the winds by twelve appropriate names; there were hardly more than four distinctive ones in use before. He called January, Wintarmanoth; February, Hornung; March, Lentzinmanoth; April, Ostarmanoth; May, Winnemanoth; June, Brachmanoth; July, Heuvimanoth; August, Aranmanoth; September, Witumanoth; October, Windumemanoth; November, Herbistmanoth; December, Heilagmanoth. He styled the winds as follows; Subsolanus, Ostroniwint; Eurus, Ostsundroni; Euroauster, Sundostroni; Auster, Sundroni; Austro-Africus, Sundwestroni; Africus, Westsundroni; Zephyrus, Westroni; Caurus, Westnordroni; Circius, Nordwestroni; Septentrio, Nordroni; Aquilo, Nordostroni; Vulturnus, Ostnordroni.

30. Toward the close of his life, when he was broken by ill-health and old age, he summoned Louis, king of Aquitania, his only surviving son by Hildegard, and gathered together all the chief men of the whole kingdom of the Franks in a solemn assembly. He appointed Louis, with their unanimous consent, to rule with himself over the whole kingdom, and constituted him heir to the imperial name, placing the diadem upon his son's head, he bade him be proclaimed Emperor and Augustus. This step was hailed by all present with great favor, for it really seemed as if God had prompted him to it for the kingdom's good; it increased the King's dignity, and struck no little terror into foreign nations. After sending his son back to Aquitania, although weak from age he set out to hunt, as usual, near his palace

at Aix-la-Chapelle, and passed the rest of the autumn in the chase, returning thither about the first of November. While wintering there, he was seized, in the month of January, with a high fever, and took to his bed. As soon as he was taken sick, he prescribed for himself abstinence from food, as he always used to do in case of fever, thinking that the disease could be driven off, or at least mitigated, by fasting. Besides the fever, he suffered from a pain in the side, which the Greeks called pleurisy; but he still persisted in fasting, and in keeping up his strength only by draughts taken at very long intervals. He died January twenty-eighth, the seventh day from the time he took to his bed, at nine o'clock in the morning, after partaking of the holy communion, the seventy-second year of his age and the forty-seventh of his reign.

31. His body was washed and cared for in the usual manner, and was then carried to the church, and interred amid the greatest lamentations of all the people. There was some question at first where to lay him, because in his lifetime he had given no directions as to his burial; but at length all agreed that he could nowhere be more honorably entombed than in the very basilica that he had built in the town at his own expense, for the love of God and our Lord Jesus Christ, and in honor of the Holy and Eternal Virgin, His Mother. He was buried there the same day that he died, and a gilded arch was erected above his tomb with his image and an inscription. The words of the inscription were as follows: "In this tomb lies the body of Charles, the Great and Orthodox Emperor, who gloriously extended the kingdom of the Franks, and reigned prosperously for forty-seven years. He died at the age of seventy, in the year of our Lord 814, the 7th Indiction, on the 28th day of January."

32. Very many omens had portended his approaching end, a fact that he had recognized as well as others. Eclipses both of the sun and moon were very frequent during the last three years of his life, and a black spot was visible on the sun for the space of seven days. The gallery between the basilica and the palace, which he had built at great pains and labor, fell in sudden ruin to the ground on the day of the Ascension of our Lord. The

wooden bridge over the Rhine at Mayence, which he had caused to be constructed with admirable skill, at the cost of ten years' hard work, so that it seemed as if it might last forever, was so completely consumed in three hours by an accidental fire that not a single splinter of it was left, except what was under water. Moreover, one day in his last campaign into Saxony against Godfred, king of the Danes, Charles himself saw a ball of fire fall suddenly from the heavens with a great light, just as he was leaving camp before sunrise to set out on the march. It rushed across the clear sky from right to left, and everybody was wondering what was the meaning of the sign, when the horse which he was riding gave a sudden plunge, head foremost, and fell, and threw him to the ground so heavily that his cloak buckle was broken and his sword belt shattered; and after his servants had hastened to him and relieved him of his arms, he could not rise without their assistance. He happened to have a javelin in his hand when he was thrown, and this was struck from his grasp with such force that it was found lying at a distance of twenty feet or more from the spot. Again, the palace at Aix-la-Chapelle frequently trembled, the roofs of whatever buildings he tarried in kept up a continual crackling noise, the basilica in which he was afterwards buried was struck by lightning, and the gilded ball that adorned the pinnacle of the roof was shattered by the thunderbolt and hurled upon the bishop's house adjoining. In this same basilica, on the margin of the cornice that ran around the interior, between the upper and lower tiers or arches, a legend was inscribed in red letters, stating who was the builder of the temple, the last words of which were *Karolus Princeps.* The year that he died it was remarked by some, a few months before his decease, that the letters of the word *Princeps* were so effaced as to be no longer decipherable. But Charles despised, or affected to despise, all these omens, as having no reference whatever to him.

33. It had been his intention to make a will, that he might give some share in the inheritance to his daughters and the children of his concubines; but it was begun too late and could not be finished. Three years before his death, however, he made a division of his treasures, money, clothes, and other movable goods in the presence of his friends and servants, and called them to witness it, that their voices might insure the ratification of the disposition thus made. He had a summary drawn up of his wishes regarding this distribution of his property, the terms and text of which are as follows:

"In the name of the Lord God, the Almighty Father, Son, and Holy Ghost. This is the inventory and division dictated by the most glorious and most pious Lord Charles, Emperor Augustus, in the 811th year of the Incarnation of our Lord Jesus Christ, in the 43rd year of his reign in France and 37th in Italy, the 11th of his empire, and the 4th Indiction, which considerations of piety and prudence have determined him, and the favor of God enabled him, to make of his treasures and money ascertained this day to be in his treasure chamber. In this division he is especially desirous to provide not only that the largess of alms which Christians usually make of their possessions shall be made for himself in due course and order out of his wealth, but also that his heirs shall be free from all doubt, and know clearly what belongs to them, and be able to share their property by suitable partition without litigation or strife. With this intention and to this end he first divided all his substance and movable goods ascertained to be in his treasure chamber on the day aforesaid in gold, silver, precious stones, and royal ornaments into three lots, and has subdivided and set off two of the said lots into twenty-one parts, keeping the third entire. The first two lots have been thus subdivided into twenty-one parts because there are in his kingdom twenty-one recognized metropolitan cities, and in order that each archbishopric may receive by way of alms, at the hands of his heirs and friends, one of the said parts, and that the archbishop who shall then administer its affairs shall take the part given to it, and share the same with his suffragans in such manner that one third shall go to the Church, and the remaining two-thirds be divided among the suffragans. The twenty-one parts into which the first two lots are to be distributed, according to the number of recognized metropolitan cities, have been set apart from one another, and each has been put aside by itself in a box labeled with the name of the city for which it was destined. The names of the cities to which this alms or largess is to be sent are as follows: Rome, Ravenna, Milan, Friuli, Grado, Cologne, Mayence, Salzburg, Treves, Sens, Besançon, Lyons, Rouen, Rheims, Arles, Vienne, Moutiers-en-Tarantaise, Embrun, Bordeaux, Tours, and Bourges. The third lot, which he wishes to be kept entire, is to be bestowed as follows: While the first two lots are to be divided into the parts aforesaid, and set aside under seal, the third lot shall be employed for the owner's daily needs, as property which he shall be under no obligation to part with in order to fulfil any vow, and this as long as he shall be in the flesh, or consider it necessary for his use. But upon his death, or voluntary renunciation of the affairs of this world, this said lot shall be added to the aforesaid twenty-one parts; the second shall be assigned to his sons and daughters, and to the sons and daughters of his sons, to be distributed among them in just and equal partition; the third, in accordance with the custom common among Christians, shall be devoted to the poor; and the fourth shall go to the support of the men servants and maid servants on duty in the palace. It is his wish that to this said third lot of the whole amount, which consists, as well as the rest, of gold and silver, shall be added all the vessels and utensils of brass, iron, and other metals, together with the arms, clothing, and other movable goods, costly and cheap, adapted to divers uses, as hangings, coverlets, carpets, woolen stuffs, leathern articles, pack-saddles, and whatsoever shall be found in his treasure chamber and wardrobe at that time, in order that thus the parts of the said lots may be augmented, and the alms distributed reach more persons. He ordains that his chapel—that is to say, its church property, as well that which he has provided and collected as that which came to him by inheritance from

his father—shall remain entire, and not be disserviced by any partition whatever. If, however, any vessel, books, or other articles be found therein which are certainly known not to have been given by him to the said chapel, whoever wants them shall have them on paying their value at a fair estimation. He likewise commands that the books which he has collected in his library in great numbers shall be sold for fair prices to such as want them, and the money received therefrom given to the poor. It is well known that among his other property and treasures there are three silver tables, and one very large and massive golden one. He directs and commands that the square silver table, upon which there is a representation of the city of Constantinople, shall be sent to the Basilica of St. Peter the Apostle at Rome, with the other gifts destined therefor; that the round one, adorned with a delineation of the city of Rome, shall be given to the Episcopal Church at Ravenna; that the third, which far surpasses the other two in weight and in beauty of workmanship, and is made in three circles, showing the plan of the whole universe, drawn with skill and delicacy, shall go, together with the golden table, fourthly above mentioned, to increase that lot which is to be devoted to his heirs and to alms.

This deed, and the dispositions thereof, he has made and appointed in the presence of the bishops, abbots, and counts able to be present, whose names are hereto subscribed: Bishops—Hildebald, Ricolf, Arno, Wolfar, Bernoin, Laidrad, John, Theodulf, Jesse, Heito, Waltgaud. Abbots—Fredugis, Adalung, Angilbert, Irmino. Counts—Walacho, Meginher, Otulf, Stephen, Unruoch, Burchard, Meginhard, Hatto, Rihwin, Edo, Ercangar, Gerold, Bero, Hildiger, Rocculf."

Charles's son Louis, who by the grace of God succeeded him, after examining this summary, took pains to fulfill all its conditions most religiously as soon as possible after his father's death.

19. SELECTED CAPITULARIES

THE MOST IMPORTANT SOURCE for understanding Carolingian cultural, administrative, and social-reform programs are the capitularies, directives used by the central administration to communicate with local authorities, although some had kingdom-wide distribution. The following examples show the range of these instruments and the various problems of Frankish society they attempt to address.

Source: H.R. Loyn and John Percival, *The Reign of Charlemagne: Documents on Carolingian Government and Administration* (New York: St. Martin's Press, 1975).

Further Reading: Janet L. Nelson, "Literacy in Carolingian Government," in R. McKitterick (ed.), *The Uses of Literacy in the Early Middle Ages* (Cambridge: Cambridge University Press, 1989).

Herstal, 779

In the eleventh auspicious year of the reign of our lord and most glorious king, Charles, in the month of March, there was made a capitulary whereby, there being gathered together in one synod and council the bishops and abbots and illustrious counts, together with our most pious lord, decisions were agreed to concerning certain appropriate matters in accordance with God's will.

1 Concerning the metropolitans, that suffragan bishops should be placed under them in accordance with the canons, and that such things as they see needing correction in their ministry they should correct and improve with willing hearts.

2 Concerning bishops: where at present they are not consecrated they are to be consecrated without delay.

3 Concerning the monasteries that have been based on a rule, that they should live in accordance with that rule; and that convents should preserve their holy order, and each abbess reside in her convent without intermission.

4 That bishops should have authority over the priests and clerks within their dioceses, in accordance with the canons.

5 That bishops should have authority to impose correction on incestuous people, and should have the power of reproving widows within their dioceses.

6 That no one should be allowed to receive another's clerk, or to ordain him to any rank.

7 Concerning tithes, that each man should give his tithe, and that these should be disposed of according to the bishop's orders.

8 Concerning murderers and other guilty men who ought in law to die, if they take refuge in a church they are not to be let off, and no food is to be given to them there.

9 That robbers who are caught within an immunity area should be presented by the justices of that area at the count's court; and anyone who fails to comply with this is to lose his benefice and his office. Likewise a vassal of ours, if he does not carry this out, shall lose his benefice and his office; anyone who has no benefice must pay the fine.

10 Concerning a man who commits perjury, that he cannot redeem if except by losing his hand. But if an accuser wishes to press the charge of perjury they are both to go to the ordeal of the cross; and if the swearer wins, the accuser is to pay the equivalent of his wergeld. This procedure is to be observed in minor cases; in major cases, or in cases involving free status, they are to act in accordance with the law.

11 Concerning the judgement of, and punishment inflicted upon robbers, the synod have ruled that the testimony given by the bishops is probably equivalent to that of the count, provided there is no malice or ill will, and there is no intervention

in the case except in the interests of seeing justice done. And if he [the judge] should maim a man through hatred or ill intent and not for the sake of justice, he is to lose his office and is to be subject to the laws under which he acted unjustly and to the penalty which he sought to inflict.

12 The heads of procedure which our father of happy memory decided upon for his hearings and for his synods; these we wish to preserve.

13 Concerning the properties of the churches from which the *census* now comes, the tithes and ninths should be paid along with that *census*; likewise tithes and ninths are to be given for those properties from which they have not so far come— from fifty *casati* one shilling, from thirty *casati* half a shilling, and from twenty a *tremissis* [*i.e.*, fourpence]. And concerning precarial holdings, where they are now they are to be renewed, and where they are not they are to be recorded. And a distinction should be made between the precarial holdings established by our authority and those which they establish of their own volition from the property of the church itself.

14 Concerning the raising of an armed following, let no one dare to do it.

15 Concerning those who give tribute in candles, and those who are free by deed or charter, the long-standing arrangements are to be observed.

16 Concerning oaths entered into by swearing together in a fraternity, that no one should dare to perform them. Moreover, concerning alms-giving, and fire and shipwreck, even though men enter into fraternities they are not to dare to swear to them.

17 Concerning travelers who are going to the palace or anywhere else, that no one should dare to assault them with an armed band. And let no one presume to take away another's crop when the fields are enclosed, unless he is going to the host or is acting as one of our *missi*; anyone who dares to do otherwise shall make amends for it.

18 Concerning the tolls that have before now been forbidden, let no one exact them except where they have existed from of old.

19 Concerning the sale of slaves, that it should take place in the presence of a bishop or count, or in the presence of an archdeacon or *centenarius*, or in that of a *vicedominus* or a count's justice, or before well-known witnesses; and let no one sell a slave beyond the march. Anyone who does so must pay the fine as many times over as the slaves he sold; and if he does not have the means to pay he must hand himself over in service to the count as a pledge, until such time as he can pay off the fine.

20 Concerning coats of mail, that no one should dare to sell them outside our kingdom.

21 If a count does not administer justice in his district he is to arrange for our *missus* to be provided for from his household until justice has been administered there; and if a vassal of ours does not administer justice, then the count and our *missus* are to stay at his house and live at his expense until he does so.

22 If anyone is unwilling to accept a payment instead of vengeance he is to be sent to us, and we will send him where is likely to do least harm. Likewise, if anyone is unwilling to pay a sum instead of vengeance or to give legal satisfaction for it, it is our wish that he be sent to a place where he can do no further harm.

23 Concerning robbers, our instructions are that the following rules should be observed; for the first offense they are not to die but to lose an eye; for the second offense the robber's nose is to be cut off; for the third offense, if he does not mend his ways, he must die.

Mantua, 781

Concerning the various provisions which we have made known to all men at the general assembly held at Mantua.

1 Concerning the administration of justice in God's Church, in the matter of widows and orphans, and others who need protection, it is our wish and our special instruction that all bishops,

abbots and counts shall both give and accept full justice according to the law.

2 This we have decided, that everyone who has a claim shall make it three times to his count, and shall find suitable men to give truthful witness that he made the claim and was unable to secure justice as a result of it; and if anyone does otherwise, and brings his claim prematurely to the palace, he shall pay the legal penalty.

3 Further, the count shall declare before witnesses on their behalf that he was willing to give them justice, and he shall have his notary write everything down, namely, what claim they made and what justice they received; so that when the people have made their claim the counts can have no excuse unless it is abundantly clear that they were willing to give them justice; also, that the count himself or his advocate can testify by an oath that there was no negligence in giving them justice, and we can know through their report whether they made the claim to them or not.

4 Let this be known to all men, that if anyone makes a claim after the case has been legally closed, he must either receive 15 strokes of the rod or be made to pay 15 shillings.

5 Let no one receive another's priest and allow him to celebrate mass before he has been interviewed and examined by the local bishop.

6 When a bishop goes the round of his parishes, let the count or his agent [sculdhais] give him assistance, so that he can perform his ministry in full, according to the canons.

7 Let no one sell Christian or pagan slaves or arms of any kind or stallions outside our kingdom; anyone who does so must be made to pay our fine, and if he is unable to bring the slaves back he must pay their worth.

8 With regard to tolls; let no one presume to levy a toll except in accordance with ancient custom, and let it be levied only in places recognized by law from of old; anyone who levies it unlawfully must make payment according to the law, and in addition must pay our fine to our *missi*.

9 Concerning the coinage: after the first day of August let no one dare to give or receive the pennies now current; anyone who does so is to pay our fine.

10 Concerning brigands who rarely come before our missi: let the counts seek them out, and keep them on bail or in custody until the missi return to them….

Paderborn, 785 (Capitulary concerning the parts of Saxony)

1 Decisions were taken first on the more important items. All were agreed that the churches of Christ which are now being built in Saxony and are consecrated to God should have no less honor than the temples of idols had, but rather a greater and more surpassing honor.

2 If anyone takes refuge in a church, let no one presume to drive him out of that church by force; rather let him be in peace until he is brought to plead his case, and in honor of God and in reverence for the saints of the church let his life and all his members be respected. But let him pay for his offense according to his means and according to what is decided; and after this let him be brought to the presence of our lord the king, who shall send him wherever in his mercy he shall decide.

3 If anyone makes forcible entry to a church, and steals anything from it by violence or stealth, or if he sets fire to the church, let him die.

4 If anyone in contempt of the Christian faith should spurn the holy Lenten fast and eat meat, let him die; but let the priest enquire into the matter, lest it should happen that someone is compelled by necessity to eat meat.

5 If anyone kills a bishop or a priest or a deacon, he shall likewise pay with his life.

6 If anyone is deceived by the Devil, and believes after the manner of pagans that some man or some woman is a witch and eats people, and if because of this he burns her or gives her flesh to someone to eat or eats it himself, let him pay the penalty of death.

7 If anyone follows pagan rites and causes the body of a dead man to be consumed by fire, and reduces his bones to ashes, let him pay with his life.

8 If there is anyone of the Saxon people lurking among them unbaptized, and if he scorns to come to baptism and wishes to absent himself and stay a pagan, let him die.

9 If anyone sacrifices a man to the Devil, and after the manner of pagans offers him as a victim to demons, let him die.

10 If anyone takes counsel with pagans against Christians, or wishes to persist with them in hostility to Christians, let him die; and anyone who treacherously approves of this against the king or against Christian people, let him die.

11 If anyone is shown to be unfaithful to our lord the king, let him suffer the penalty of death.

12 If anyone rapes the daughter of his lord, he shall die.

13 If anyone kills his lord or his lady, he shall be punished in the same way.

14 However, if anyone has committed these capital crimes and has gone undetected, and goes of his own accord to a priest and is willing to make his confession and undergo a penance, he shall be excused the death penalty on the priest's testimony.

15 On the lesser items all were agreed. For each and every church the people in the area who attend it are to provide a farmstead and two manses of land; and for every 120 men among them, be they noble or free or *lidi*, they are to give a male and a female slave to the church.

16 This too was decided, with Christ's blessing, that any revenue which comes to the royal fisc, whether it be from infringement of the peace or a ban of any kind [*sive in frido sive in qualecumque banno*], or from any other payment due to the king, a tithe is to be given to the churches and the clergy.

17 Likewise, in accordance with God's command, we instruct all men to give a tithe of their substance and labor to their churches and clergy; and let nobles, free men and *lidi* alike make partial return to God for what he has given to each and every Christian.

18 On Sundays there are to be no assemblies or public gatherings, except in cases of great need or when an enemy is pressing; rather let all attend church to hear the word of God, and give their time to prayers and lawful occupations. Likewise on the greater feast-days they should gather to serve God and his Church, and put off secular business.

19 Likewise it was decided to include in these enactments that all infants should be baptized within the year; we have decided further, that if anyone scorns to offer an infant for baptism before a year has gone by, and does not consult a priest or obtain his permission, he shall, if he is of noble birth, pay 120 shillings to the fisc, if he is a free man, 60 shillings, and if he is a *lidus* 30.

20 If anyone contracts a forbidden or unlawful marriage, he shall pay 60 shillings if he is a noble, 30 if he is a free man, and 15 if he is a *lidus*.

21 If anyone offers prayers to springs or trees or groves, or makes an offering after the manner of the gentiles and consumes it in honor of demons, he shall pay 60 shillings if he is a noble, 30 if he is a free man, and 15 is he is a *lidus*. But if they do not have the means to pay at once, they are to be placed in the service of the church until such time as the shillings are paid.

22 It is our order that the bodies of Christian Saxons shall be taken to the church's cemeteries and not to the pagan burial grounds.

23 We have decided to hand over the diviners and sooth-sayers to the churches and the clergy.

24 With regard to robbers and other criminals who flee from one country to another, if anyone receives them into his power, and keeps them with him for seven nights for any purpose other than to bring them to justice, let him pay our fine. Likewise, if the count lets such a man abscond,

and refuses to bring him to justice, and can give no reason for so doing, let him lose his office.

25 With regard to sureties, let no one, under any circumstances, dare to use another man as a surety; anyone who does this shall pay our fine.

26 Let no one take it upon himself to bar the way to any man coming to us to appeal for justice; if anyone tries to do this he shall pay our fine.

27 If any man is unable to find a surety, his property is to be placed in distraint until he finds one. But if he dares to enter his house in defiance of the ban, let him forfeit ten shillings or one ox in payment for the ban, and in addition pay in full his original debt. And if the surety does not keep him to the appointed day, let him lose whatever he stood to lose in his capacity as surety; but let him who was debtor to the surety pay back double the loss that he caused his surety to suffer.

28 With regard to payments and rewards: let no one take reward against an innocent person; if anyone dares to do this, he must pay our fine. And if, which God forbid, it should happen that a count does it, let him lose his office.

29 Let all the counts endeavor to be at peace and concord with one another: and if it should happen that some disagreement or quarrel should arise among them, they must not scorn our help in settling it.

30 If anyone kills a count or conspires to kill him, his inheritance shall be made over to the king and he shall be subject to his jurisdiction.

31 We have given authority to the counts, within the areas assigned to them, to impose a fine of up to 60 shillings for feuds or other major crimes; but for minor offenses we have fixed the limits of the count's fine at 15 shillings.

32 If anyone has to give an oath to a man, let him swear that oath in church on the appointed day; and if he scorns to swear, let him give a pledge; and anyone who shows himself negligent must pay 15 shillings and afterwards give full satisfaction in the case.

33 With regard to perjury, the law of the Saxons is to apply.

34 We forbid the Saxons to come together as a body in public gatherings, except on those occasions when our *missus* assembles them on our instructions; rather, let each and every count hold court and administer justice in his own area. And the clergy are to see to it that this order is obeyed.

Concerning the Saxons, 797

1 In the seven hundred and ninety-seventh year of the incarnation of Our Lord Jesus Christ, and in the thirtieth and twenty-fifth years respectively of the reign of our lord and most mighty king, Charles, there being assembled together at the palace at Aix at his bidding on the twenty-eighth day of October the reverend bishops and abbots and the illustrious counts, and there being also gathered together the Saxons from the several regions—from Westphalia, from Angaria and from Eastphalia—they did all with one mind agree and ordain that for those matters for which the Franks pay 60 shillings if they have offended against the king's ban, the Saxon shall likewise pay, if they have done something contrary to the ban. The matters in question are these: first that the Church, and then that widows, orphans and humble folk generally, should be left in rightful peace and quiet; that no one should dare to commit rape or violence or arson within the neighborhood; and that no one should presume to hold back from military service in defiance of the king's ban.

2 Those who offend in any of the eight matters mentioned are to pay, Saxons and Franks alike, 60 shillings.

3 It was agreed by all the Saxons that, in all cases where Franks are bound by law to pay 15 shillings, the noble Saxons shall pay 12 shillings, free men 5, and *lidi* 3.

4 This also they decided, that when any case is settled within a district by the local authorities, the people of the district are to receive 12 shillings as a fine [*pro districtione*] in the usual way, and they are to have this concession also in payment of the wergeld which it was their custom to have. But if

cases are settled in the presence of the royal *missi*, the people are to have these 12 shillings as wergeld and the royal *missus* is to receive another 12 on the king's behalf, on the grounds that he has been troubled with the matter. If, however, the case is carried through to the palace for a settlement in the king's presence, then both of the 12 shilling payments, that for wergeld and that owed to the local people, making 24 shillings in all, are to be paid to the king's account, on the grounds that the settlement was not arrived at in the district concerned. And if there is anyone who is unwilling to abide by what his neighbors have decided in his district, and who comes to the palace for this reason, and if it is there decided that the original decision was just, he must on the first occasion, as explained above, pay 24 shillings to the king's account; and if he then goes away and refuses to abide by it or to make a just settlement, and is again brought to the palace for this reason and judged, let him pay the 24 shillings twice over; and if, in spite of this, he is detained and brought to the palace for the same reason a third time, let him pay for it three times over to the king.

5 If any noble is summoned to court and refuses to come, let him pay four shillings; free men are to pay two shillings and *lidi* one.

6 In the matter of priests, it was decided that if anyone should presume to do harm to them or to their men, or should take anything from them unlawfully, he should pay back everything to them and make amends twice over.

7 Concerning the king's *missi*, it was decided that if a *missus* should happen to be killed by them [the Saxons], he who dared to do it should pay for him three times over. Likewise, for anything done to their men, they should see that threefold restoration is made and payment given according to their law.

8 Concerning fine-raising, it was decided that no one should dare to do so in his district out of anger or enmity or for any other spiteful motive: there should, however, be an exception if a man is so rebellious that he refuses to accept a court's decision and cannot be otherwise restrained; and if he refuses to come to us and be judged in our presence; in such a case a common hearing should be declared and all the people in the district must come, and if they are unanimous in this court the fine can be raised in order to restrain him. When at this hearing a common course of action is agreed upon, let it be carried out in accordance with their own law, and not through any anger or spiteful intent, but only in order to restrain a man for us. If anyone dares to raise a fine in any other circumstances, let him, as is said above, pay 60 shillings.

9 Likewise, seeing that our lord the king, for the sake of peace and for [preventing] feuds and for other important reasons, wishes to impose a stronger fine [*bannum*], it was decided, with the consent of the Franks and of his faithful Saxons, according to his decision, as the case demands and as opportunity allows, to double the 60 shilling payment; and if anyone goes against this order, let him pay 100 shillings, or even up to a thousand.

10 Concerning the criminals who should (according to the Saxon law code) incur the death penalty, it was decided by all that whoever of them seeks refuge in the royal prerogative it shall be part of that prerogative either to hand the criminal back for punishment, or with their consent to remove him and his wife and family and all his goods from the district, and settle them inside his kingdom or in the march or wherever he wishes, and to have possession of him as though dead.

11 Note should be taken of the proper equivalents of the Saxon shillings; a yearling calf of either sex, in autumn when it is put to byre, is to count for one shilling; likewise in spring, when it comes out of the byre; but afterwards, as it grows older, it should increase in value proportionately. Of oats, the Bortrini must give 40 bushels for a shilling, and of rye 20 bushels; those to the south, however, must give 30 bushels of oats for a shilling and 15 bushels of rye. Of honey, the Bortrini must give one and a half *siccli* for a shilling, while those of the south are to give two *siccli*. Likewise of winnowed barley they are to give the same amount as of rye for one shilling. In silver, 12 pennies make a shilling. And in other media of exchange the values shall be the equivalents in each case.

The Synod of Frankfurt, 794

1 A gathering, under God's blessing, in accordance with the apostolic authority and the order of our most pious lord king, Charles, in the twenty-sixth year of his reign, of all the bishops and priests of the kingdom of the Franks, of Italy, of Aquitaine and Provence in synod and council, among whom, in the holy assembly, was the most gentle king himself. Whereat, under the first and foremost head, there arose the matter of the impious and wicked heresy of Elipandus, bishop of the see of Toledo, and Felix, bishop of Urgel, and their followers, who in their erroneous belief concerning the Son of God assert adoption: this heresy did all the most holy fathers above mentioned repudiate and with one voice denounce, and it was their decision that it should be utterly eradicated from the Holy Church.

2 There was presented for discussion the matter of the new synod of the Greeks, organized at Constantinople on the subject of the adoration of images, in which it was stated that they regarded as anathema those images of the saints which did not have a bearing on the service or adoration of the Holy Trinity; our most holy fathers aforementioned repudiated it and despised all such adoration and service, and argued in condemning it.

3 After this had been dealt with a decision was reached concerning Tassilo, the cousin of our lord king, Charles, who had formerly been duke of Bavaria. He took his stand in the midst of the most holy council, asking pardon for the sins that he had committed, both for those which he had perpetrated in the time of our lord king, Pippin, against him and against the kingdom of the Franks, and for those later ones committed under our lord and most pious king, Charles, in which he had shown himself to be a breaker of his word. He begged to be thought worthy of indulgence from the king, and appeared to do so in all humility, since he wholeheartedly repudiated all anger and scandalous behavior on his part and all things committed against the king to which he had been party. Moreover, all his rights and properties, everything that should lawfully belong to himself or his sons or daughters in the duchy of Bavaria, he disowned and renounced, and forswearing all claims to it for the future irrevocably surrendered it, and along with his sons and daughters commended it to the mercy of the king. Wherefore our lord [the king], moved with pity, both forgave the said Tassilo graciously for the sins he had committed, restored full favor to him, and with compassion received him in love and affection, so that from henceforth he might be secure in the mercy of God. And so he ordered three copies of this decision to be written to the one effect; one he ordered to be kept in the palace, another to be given to the said Tassilo for him to keep by him in the monastery, and the third to be deposited in the chapel of the sacred palace.

4 Our most pious lord the king, with the consent of the holy synod, gave instructions that no man, whether he be cleric or layman, should ever sell corn in time of abundance or in time of scarcity at a greater price than the public level recently decided upon, that is a *modius* of oats one penny, a *modius* of barley two pennies, a *modius* of rye three pennies, a *modius* of wheat four pennies. If he should wish to sell it in the form of bread, he should give 12 loaves of wheat bread, each weighing two pounds, for one penny, and for the same price 15 of equal weight of rye bread, 20 of barley bread of the same weight, and 25 of oat bread of the same weight. For the public corn of our lord the king, if it should be sold, the price is to be two *modii* of oats for a penny, one *modius* of barley for a penny, two pence for a *modius* of rye, and three for a *modius* of wheat. Anyone who holds a benefice of us should take the greatest possible care that, if God but provide, none of the slaves of the benefice should die of hunger; and anything that remains above what is necessary for the household he may freely sell in the manner laid down.

5 Concerning the pennies, you should be fully aware of our edict, that in every place, in every city and in every market these new pennies must be current and must be accepted by everyone. Provided they bear the imprint of our name and are of pure silver and of full weight, if anyone should refuse to allow them in any place, in any transaction of buying and selling, he shall, if he is a free man, pay 15 shillings to the king, and, if he is of servile status and the transaction is his own, shall lose the transaction or be flogged naked at

the stake in the presence of the people; but if he has done it on his lord's orders, the lord, if it is proved against him, shall pay the 15 shillings.

6 It was ordained by our lord the king and by the holy synod that bishops should administer justice in their parishes. And if any person from among the abbots, priests, deacons, subdeacons, monks, and other clerics, or anyone else in the parish should refuse to obey his bishop, let them come to their metropolitan, and let him decide the case along with his suffragans. Our counts also are to come to the bishops' courts. And if there is anything which the metropolitan bishop cannot put right or settle, then let the accusers finally come to us, with the accused and with letters from the metropolitan, that we may know the truth of the matter.

7 It was ruled by our lord the king and by the holy synod that a bishop should not move from one city to another, but should stay and take care of his church; likewise a priest or a deacon should stay in his church according to the canons.

8 With regard to the dispute between Ursio, bishop of Vienne and the advocate of Elifantus, bishop of Arles, there were read letters of St. Gregory, Zosimus, Leo and Symmachus, which made it clear that the church of Vienne should have four suffragan sees, with itself as the fifth over them, and that the church at Arles should have nine suffragan sees under its authority. As to the question of Tarantaise and Embrun and Aix, an embassy was arranged to the apostolic see; and whatever may be decided by the pontiff of the Church of Rome shall be adhered to.

9 It was ruled also by the same our lord the king and by the holy synod that Peter the bishop [of Verdun] should assert before God and his angels and, in the presence of two or three others, as though he were receiving consecration, or indeed in the presence of his archbishop, should swear that he had not conspired for the death of the king or against his kingdom nor been unfaithful to him. The said bishop, since he could find no one with whom he could swear, decided for himself that he would, as God's man, go before the judgement of God, and testify without relics and

without the holy Gospels and solely in the presence of God that he was innocent of these matters, and that in accordance with his innocence God should help this his man, who was bound to submit to his judgement and did so. Yet it was not by order of the king or by the decision of the holy synod but by his own free will that he submitted to God's judgement, and was acquitted by Our Lord and found innocent. Nevertheless, our king in his mercy bestowed his favor on the said bishop and endowed him with his former honors, and would not allow a man whom he perceived to merit nothing harmful to be without honor as a result of the charge alleged against him.

10 It was ruled by our lord the king and decided by the holy synod that Gaerbodus, who said he was a bishop but had no witnesses of his consecration, and yet had sought episcopal insignia from Magnardus the metropolitan bishop (who declared moreover that he was not ordained deacon or priest according to canonical prescription), should be deposed by the said metropolitan or by the other bishops of the province from that rank of bishop which he claimed to have.

11 That monks should not go out for secular business nor to engage in lawsuits, unless they do so in accordance with the precepts of the rule itself.

12 That men should not become recluses unless the bishop of the province and the abbot have previously approved of them, and they are to enter upon their place of retreat according to their arrangements.

13 That an abbot should sleep alongside his monks according to the rule of St. Benedict.

14 That greedy men should not be chosen as cellarers in the monasteries, but that such men should be chosen as the rule of St. Benedict instructs.

15 Concerning a monastery where there are bodies of saints; that it should have an oratory within its cloister where the peculiar and daily office may be done.

16 We have heard that certain abbots, led on by greed, require a payment on behalf of those

entering their monastery. Therefore we and the holy synod have decided that under no circumstances shall money be required for receiving brothers into a holy order, but that they should be received in accordance with the rule of St. Benedict.

17 That an abbot should not be chosen, when the king so orders, in the congregation, except by the consent of the local bishop.

18 That whatever sin is committed by the monks, we do not allow the abbots under any circumstances to blind them or inflict the mutilation of members upon them, unless the discipline of the rule provides for it.

19 That priests, deacons, monks and clerks should not go into taverns to drink.

20 That a bishop should not be permitted to be ignorant of the canons and the rule.

21 That the Lord's day should be observed from evening to evening.

22 That it should not be proper to consecrate bishops in small towns and villages.

23 Concerning other men's slaves, that they should not be taken in by anyone, and should not be ordained by bishops without their lords' permission.

24 Concerning clerks and monks, that they should remain steadfast in their chosen way of life.

25 That in general, tithes and ninths (or the *census*) should be paid by all who owe them, in respect of benefices and Church property, according to the earlier enactments of our lord the king; and every man should give the lawful tithe in respect of his property to the Church. For we have been informed that in that year when the severe famine broke out there was an abundance of empty corn eaten by demons, and voices of reproach were heard.

26 That the church buildings and their roofs should be repaired and restored by those who hold benefices dependent on them. And where, on the testimony of trustworthy men, it is found that they have in their own houses any wood or stone or tiles that were previously on the church buildings, they must restore to the church everything that has been taken from it.

27 Concerning clerks, that they should under no circumstances move from one church to another, nor be taken in without the knowledge of the bishop and letters of commendation from the diocese to which they belonged, lest it should happen that discord arise in the Church as a result. And wherever such men are found, they must all return to their own church; and let no one dare to keep such a man by him once his bishop or abbot has indicated his wish to have him back. And if it should happen that the lord does not know where he should look for his clerk, let the man with whom he is staying keep him in custody and not allow him to wander elsewhere, until such time as he is restored to his lord.

28 That men should not be ordained without restriction [*absolute*].

29 That each and every bishop should give good teaching and instruction to those placed in his charge, so that there will always in God's house be found men who are worthy to be chosen according to the canons.

30 Concerning clerks who quarrel among themselves or who act in opposition to their bishop, they are to take all the measures that the canons prescribe. And if it should happen that a quarrel arises between a clerk and a layman, the bishop and the count should meet together and should with one mind decide the case between them according to what is right.

31 Concerning plots and conspiracies, that they should not occur; and where they are discovered they are to be crushed.

32 That monasteries should be guarded according to the provisions of the canons.

33 That the Catholic faith of the Holy Trinity, the Lord's Prayer and the Creed should be preached and handed on to all men.

34 Concerning the stamping out of greed and covetousness.

35 Concerning the practice of hospitality.

36 Concerning criminals, that they should not be allowed to accuse their superiors or their bishops.

37 Concerning absolution in time of emergency.

38 Concerning priests who have been disobedient towards their bishops; they must under no circumstances communicate with the clerks who live in the king's chapel, unless they have made their peace with their bishop, lest it should happen that excommunication according to the canons should come upon them as a result.

39 If a priest is caught in a criminal act, he should be brought before his bishop and be dealt with according to the ruling of the canons. And if it should happen that he wishes to deny the offense, and his accuser is unable to offer proof of it, and the matter cannot be settled before his bishop, then the decision should be referred to their whole council.

40 Concerning girls who have been deprived of their parents; they should, under the supervision of bishops and priests, be entrusted to suitably sober women, in accordance with the teachings of canonical authority.

41 That no bishop should abandon his proper see by spending his time elsewhere, nor dare to stay on his own property for more than three weeks. And the relatives or heirs of a bishop should in no circumstance inherit after his death any property which was acquired by him after he was consecrated bishop, either by purchase or by gift; rather, it should go in full to the church. Such property as he had before then shall, unless he make a gift from it to the Church, pass to his heirs and relatives.

42 That no new saints should be revered or invoked in prayers, nor memorials of them erected by the wayside; only those are to be venerated in church which have been deservedly chosen on the basis of their passions or their lives.

43 Concerning the destruction of trees and groves, let the authority of the canons be observed.

44 That the chosen judges should not be rejected by either side in a dispute.

45 Concerning their witnesses, let the canons be observed. And small children should not be compelled to swear an oath, as the Guntbadingi do.

46 Concerning young girls, at what time they are to take the veil and what are to be their occupations before the age of 25, the writings of the canons should, if necessary, be consulted.

47 Concerning abbesses who do not live according to the canons or the monastic rule: the bishops are to make inquiries and give notice to the king, so that they may be deprived of their office.

48 Concerning offerings which are made to the Church or for the use of the poor, the provisions of the canons are to be observed; such funds are not to be dispensed except by those appointed by the bishop.

49 Concerning priests, and not ordaining them before their thirtieth year.

50 That when the sacred mysteries are accomplished all men should be peaceable towards one another during the rites of mass.

51 Concerning not reciting names until an oblation is offered.

52 That no one should believe that God cannot be prayed to except in three languages only; since God can be prayed to, and man listened to if his prayers are just, in any language.

53 That no bishop or priest should be allowed to be ignorant of the sacred canons.

54 Concerning churches which are built by free men; it is allowed to bestow them as gifts, or to sell them, provided that no church is destroyed and the daily offices are observed.

55 Our lord the king informed the holy synod that

he had permission of the holy see, that is of Pope Hadrian, to keep Angilramnus the archbishop permanently in his palace to deal with ecclesiastical matters. He asked the synod that he might be allowed to have bishop Hildebald there on the same terms as he had Angilramnus, he had the apostolic permission. The whole synod agreed, and decided that he should be in the palace to deal with ecclesiastical matters.

56 He suggested that the holy synod should think it right to accept Alcuin into its fellowship and prayers, since he was a man of learning in the doctrines of the Church. All the synod agreed to the suggestion of our lord the king, and accepted him into their fellowship and their prayers.

Charles the Great on the study of literature [*De litteris colendis*], end of the eighth century

We, Charles, by the grace of God king of the Franks and Lombards and patrician of the Romans, to Abbot Baugulf and all your congregation and our faithful teachers [*oratoribus*] entrusted to your charge, send affectionate greeting in the name of Almighty God.

Be it known to your devotion, most pleasing in the sight of God, that we, along with our faithful advisers, have deemed it useful that the bishoprics and monasteries which through the favor of Christ have been entrusted to us to govern should, in addition to the way of life prescribed by their rule and practice of holy religion, devote their efforts to the study of literature and to the teaching of it, each according to his ability, to those on whom God has bestowed the capacity to learn; that, just as the observance of a rule gives soundness to their conduct, so also an attention to teaching and learning may give order and adornment to their words, and those who seek to please God by living aright may not fail to please him also by rightness in their speaking. For it is written, "Either by your words shall you be justified, or by your words shall you be condemned" [Matthew 12.27]. For although it is better to do what is right than to know it, yet knowledge comes before action. Thus each man must first learn what he wishes to carry out, so that he will know in his heart all the more fully what he needs to do, in order that his tongue

may run on without stumbling into falsehood in the praise of Almighty God. For since falsehood is to be shunned by all men, how much more should it be avoided, as far as they are able, by those who have been chosen for this one purpose, that they should give special service to truth. Letters have often been sent to us in these last years from certain monasteries, in which was set out what the brothers there living were striving to do for us in their holy and pious prayers; and we found that in most of these writings their sentiments were sound but their speech uncouth. Inwardly their pious devotions gave them a message of truth, but because of their neglect of learning their unskilled tongues could not express it without fault. And so it came about that we began to fear that their lack of knowledge of writing might be matched by a more serious lack of wisdom in the understanding of holy scripture. We all know well that, dangerous as are the errors of words, yet much more dangerous are the errors of doctrine. Wherefore we urge you, not merely to avoid the neglect of the study of literature, but with a devotion that is humble and pleasing to God to strive to learn it, so that you may be able more easily and more rightly to penetrate the mysteries of the holy scriptures. For since there are figures of speech, metaphors and the like to be found on the sacred pages, there can be no doubt that each man who reads them will understand their spiritual meaning more quickly if he is first of all given full instruction in the study of literature. Let men be chosen for this work who have the will and ability to learn and also the desire to instruct others; and let it be pursued with an eagerness equal to my devotion in prescribing it. For we want you, as befits the soldiers of the Church, to be inwardly devout and outwardly learned, pure in good living and scholarly in speech; so that whoever comes to see you in the name of God and for the inspiration of your holy converse, just as he is strengthened by the sight of you, so he may be instructed also by your wisdom, both in reading and chanting, and return rejoicing, giving thanks to Almighty God. Therefore, if you wish to keep our favor, do not neglect to send copies of this letter to all your suffragans and fellow bishops, and to all the monasteries.

De Villis, end of the eighth century

1 It is our wish that those of our estates which we have established to minister to our needs shall serve our purposes and not those of other men.

2 That all our people shall be well looked after, and shall not be reduced to penury by anyone.

3 That the stewards shall not presume to put our people to their own service, and shall not compel them to give their labor or to cut wood or to do any other work for them; and they shall accept no gifts from them, neither a horse nor an ox, nor a cow, nor a pig, nor a sheep, nor a piglet, nor a lamb, nor anything other than bottles of wine, vegetables, fruit, chickens and eggs.

4 If anyone of our people does harm to our interests through theft or any other neglect of duty, let him make good the damage in full, and in addition let him be punished by whipping according to the law, except in the case of murder or arson, for which a fine may be exacted. As far as concerns other men, let the stewards be careful to give them the justice to which they have a right, as the law directs. Our people, as we have said, are to be whipped in preference to being fined. Free men, however, who live on our crown lands [*fiscis*] and estates shall be careful to pay for any wrong they may have done, according to their law; and whatever they may give as their fine, whether it be cattle or any other form of payment, shall be assigned to our use.

5 Wherever it falls to our stewards to see that our work is done, whether it be sowing or plowing, harvesting, haymaking or gathering of grapes, let each one of them, at the appropriate time and place, supervise the work and give instructions as to how it should be done, so that everything may be successfully carried out. If a steward is not in his district, or cannot get to a particular place, let him send a good messenger from among our people, or some other man who can be trusted, to look after our affairs and settle them satisfactorily; and the steward shall be especially careful to send a reliable man to deal with this matter.

6 It is our wish that our stewards shall pay a full tithe of all produce to the churches that are on our estates, and that no tithe of ours shall be paid to the church of another lord except in places where this is an ancient custom. And no clerics shall hold these churches except our own or those from our people or from our chapel.

7 That each steward shall perform his service in full, according to his instructions. And if the necessity should arise for his service to be increased, let him decide whether he should add to the manpower or to the days spent in performing it [*si servitium debeat multiplicare vel noctes*].

8 That our stewards shall take charge of our vineyards in their districts, and see that they are properly worked; and let them put the wine into good vessels, and take particular care that no loss is incurred in shipping it. They are to have purchased other, more special, wine to supply the royal estates. And if they should buy more of this wine than is necessary for supplying our estates they should inform us of this, so that we can tell them what we wish to be done with it. They shall also have slips from our vineyards sent for our use. Such rents from our estates as are paid in wine they shall send to our cellars.

9 It is our wish that each steward shall keep in his district measures for *modii* and *sextaria*, and vessels containing eight *sextaria*, and also baskets of the same capacity as we have in our palace.

10 That our mayors and foresters, our stablemen, cellarers, deans, toll-collectors and other officials shall perform regular services, and shall give pigs in return for their holdings: in place of manual labor, let them perform their official duties well. And any mayor who has a benefice, let him arrange to send a substitute, whose task it will be to carry out the manual labor and other services on his behalf.

11 That no steward, under any circumstances, shall take lodgings for his own use or for his dogs, either among our men or among those living outside our estates.

12 That no steward shall commend a hostage of ours on our estates.

13 That they shall take good care of the stallions, and under no circumstances allow them to stay for long in the same pasture, lest it should be spoiled. And if any of them is unhealthy, or too old, or is likely to die, the stewards are to see that we are informed at the proper time, before the season comes for sending them in among the mares.

14 That they shall look after our mares well, and segregate the colts at the proper time. And if the fillies increase in number, let them be separated so that they can form a new herd by themselves.

15 That they shall take care to have our foals sent to the winter palace at the feast of St. Martin.

16 It is our wish that whatever we or the queen may order any steward, or whatever our officials, the seneschal or the butler, may order them in our name or in the name of the queen, they shall carry out in full as they are instructed. And whoever falls short in this through negligence, let him abstain from drinking from the moment he is told to do so until he comes into our presence or the presence of the queen and seeks forgiveness from us. And if a steward is in the army, or on guard duty, or on a mission, or is away elsewhere, and gives an order to his subordinates and they do not carry it out, let them come on foot to the palace, and let them abstain from food and drink until they have given reasons for failing in their duty in this way; and then let them receive their punishment, either in the form of a beating or in any other way that we or the queen shall decide.

17 A steward shall appoint as many men as he has estates in his district, whose task it will be to keep bees for our use.

18 At our mills they are to keep chickens and geese, according to the mill's importance—or as many as possible.

19 In the barns on our chief estates they are to keep not less than 100 chickens and not less than 30 geese. At the smaller farms they are to keep not less than 50 chickens and not less than 12 geese.

20 Every steward is to see that the produce is brought to the court in plentiful supply throughout the year; also, let them make their visitations for this purpose at least three or four times.

21 Every steward is to keep fishponds on our estates where they have existed in the past, and if possible he is to enlarge them. They are also to be established in places where they have not so far existed but where they are now practicable.

22 Those who have vines shall keep not less than three or four crowns of grapes.

23 On each of our estates the stewards are to have as many byres, pigsties, sheepfolds and goat-pens as possible, and under no circumstances are they to be without them. They are also to have cows provided by our serfs for the performance of their service, so that the byres and plow-teams are in no way weakened by service on our demesne. And when they have to provide meat, let them have lame but healthy oxen, cows or horses which are not mangy, and other healthy animals; and, as we have said, our byres and plow-teams must not suffer as a result of this.

24 Every steward is to take pains over anything he is to provide for our table, so that everything he gives is good and of the best quality, and as carefully and cleanly prepared as possible. And each of them, when he comes to serve at our table, is to have corn for two meals a day for his service; and any other provisions, whether in flour or in meat, are similarly to be of good quality.

25 They are to report on the first of September whether or not there will be food for the pigs.

26 The mayors are not to have more land in their districts than they can ride through and inspect in a single day.

27 Our houses are to have continuous watch-fires and guards to keep them safe. And when our *missi* and their retinues are on their way to or from the palace, they shall under no circumstances take lodging in the royal manor houses, except on our express orders or those of the queen. And the count in his district, or the men whose traditional

custom it has been to look after our *missi* and their retinues, shall continue, as they have done in the past, to provide them with pack-horses and other necessities, so that they may travel to and from the palace with ease and dignity.

28 It is our wish that each year in Lent on Palm Sunday, which is also called Hosanna Sunday, the stewards shall take care to pay in the money part of our revenue according to our instructions, after we have determined the amount of our revenue for the year in question.

29 With regard to these of our men who have cases to plead, every steward is to see to it that they are not compelled to come into our presence to make their plea; and he shall not allow a man to lose, through negligence, the days on which he owes service. And if a serf of ours is involved in a lawsuit outside our estates, his master is to do all he can to see that he obtains justice. And if in a given place the serf has difficulty obtaining it, his master shall not allow him to suffer as a result, but shall make it his business to inform us of the matter, either in person or through his messenger.

30 It is our wish that from all the revenue they shall set aside what is needed for our purposes; and in the same way they are to set aside the produce with which they load the carts that are needed for the army, both those of the householders and those of the shepherds, and they shall keep a record of how much they are sending for this purpose.

31 That in the same way each year they shall set aside what is necessary for the household workers and for the women's workshops; and at the appropriate time they are to supply it in full measure, and must be in a position to tell us how they have disposed of it, and where it came from.

32 That every steward shall make it his business always to have good seed of the best quality, whether bought or otherwise acquired.

33 After all these parts of our revenue have been set aside or sown or otherwise dealt with, anything that is left over is to be kept to await our instructions, so that it can be sold or held in reserve as we shall decide.

34 They are to take particular care that anything which they do or make with their hands—that is, lard, smoked meat, sausage, newly-salted meat, wine, vinegar, mulberry wine, boiled wine, garum, mustard, cheese, butter, malt, beer, mead, honey, wax and flour—that all these are made or prepared with the greatest attention to cleanliness.

35 It is our wish that tallow shall be made from fat sheep and also from pigs; in addition, they are to keep on each estate not less than two fatted oxen, which can be used for making tallow there or can be sent to us.

36 That our woods and forests shall be well protected; if there is an area to be cleared, the stewards are to have it cleared, and shall not allow fields to become overgrown with woodland. Where woods are supposed to exist they shall not allow them to be excessively cut or damaged. Inside the forests they are to take good care of our game; likewise, they shall keep our hawks and falcons in readiness for our use, and shall diligently collect our dues there. And the stewards, or our mayors or their men, if they send their pigs into our woods to be fattened, shall be the first to pay the tithe for this, so as to set a good example and encourage other men to pay their tithe in full in the future.

37 That they shall keep their fields and arable land in good order, and shall guard our meadows at the appropriate time.

38 That they shall always keep fattened geese and chickens sufficient for our use if needed, or for sending to us.

39 It is our wish that the stewards shall be responsible for collecting the chickens and eggs which the serfs and manse-holders contribute each year; and when they are not able to use them they are to sell them.

40 That every steward, on each of our estates, shall always have swans, peacocks, pheasants, ducks, pigeons, partridges and turtle doves, for the sake of ornament.

41 That the buildings inside our demesnes, together with the fences around them, shall be well

looked-after, and that the stables and kitchens, bakeries and wine-presses, shall be carefully constructed, so that our servants who work in them can carry out their tasks properly and cleanly.

42 That each estate shall have in its storeroom beds, mattresses, pillows, bed-linen, table-cloths, seat-covers, vessels of bronze, lead, iron and wood, fire-dogs, chains, pot-hangers, adzes, axes, augers, knives and all sorts of tools, so that there is no need to seek them elsewhere or to borrow them. As to the iron tools which they provide for the army, the stewards are to make it their business to see that these are good, and that when they are returned they are put back into the storeroom.

43 They are to supply the women's workshops with materials at the appropriate times, according to their instructions—that is, linen, wood, woad, vermilion, madder, wool-combs, teazles, soap, oil, vessels and the other small things that are needed there.

44 Two thirds of the Lenten food shall be sent each year for our use—that is, of the vegetables, fish, cheese, butter, honey, mustard, vinegar, millet, panic, dry or green herbs, radishes, turnips, and wax or soap and other small items; and as we have said earlier, they are to inform us by letter of what is left over, and shall under no circumstances omit to do this, as they have done in the past, because it is through those two thirds that we wish to know about the one third that remains.

45 That every steward shall have in his district good workmen—that is, blacksmiths, gold- and silver-smiths, shoemakers, turners, carpenters, shield-makers, fishermen, falconers, soap-makers, brewers (that is, people who know how to make beer, cider, perry or any other suitable beverage), bakers to make bread for our use, net-makers who can make good nets for hunting or fishing or fowling, and all the other workmen too numerous to mention.

46 That the stewards shall take good care of our walled parks, which the people call *brogili*, and always repair them in good time, and not delay so long that it becomes necessary to rebuild them completely. This should apply to all buildings.

47 That our hunters and falconers, and the other servants who are in permanent attendance on us at the palace, shall throughout our estates be given such assistance as we or the queen may command in our letters, on occasions when we send them out on an errand or when the seneschal or butler gives them some task to do in our name.

48 That the wine-presses on our estates shall be kept in good order. And the stewards are to see to it that no one dares to crush the grapes with his feet, but that everything is clean and decent.

49 That our women's quarters shall be properly arranged—that is, with houses, heated rooms and living rooms; and let them have good fences all round, and strong doors, so that they can do our work well.

50 That each steward shall determine how many horses there should be in a single stable, and how many grooms with them. Those grooms who are free men, and have benefices in the district, shall live off those benefices. Similarly the men of the fisc, who hold manses, shall live off them. And those who have no holding shall receive their food from the demesne.

51 Every steward is to take care that dishonest men do not conceal our seed from us, either under the ground or elsewhere, thus making the harvest less plentiful. Similarly, with the other kinds of mischief, let them see to it that they never happen.

52 It is our wish that the men of the fisc, our serfs, and the free men who live on our crown lands and estates shall be required to give all men the full and complete justice to which they are entitled.

53 That every steward shall take pains to prevent our people in his district from becoming robbers and criminals.

54 That every steward shall see to it that our people work well at their tasks, and do not go wasting time at markets.

55 It is our wish that the stewards should record, in one document, any goods or services they have provided, or anything they have appropriated for

our use, and, in another document, what payments they have made; and they shall notify us by letter of anything that is left over.

56 That every steward in his district shall hold frequent hearings and dispense justice, and see to it that our people live a law-abiding life.

57 If any of our serfs should wish to say something to us about his master in connection with our affairs, he is not to be prevented from coming to us. And if a steward should learn that his subordinates wish to come to the palace to lodge a complaint against him, then that steward shall present his arguments against them at the palace, and give reason why we should not be displeased at hearing their complaint. In this way we wish to find out whether they come from necessity or merely on some pretext.

58 When our puppies are entrusted to the stewards they are to feed them at their own expense, or else entrust them to their subordinates, that is, the mayors and deans, or cellarers, so that they in their turn can feed them from their own resources—unless there should be an order from ourselves or the queen that they are to be fed at their own expense. In this case the steward is to send a man to them, to see to their feeding, and is to set aside food for them; and there will be no need for the man to go to the kennels every day.

59 Every steward shall, when he is on service, give three pounds of wax and eight *sextaria* of soap each day; in addition, he shall be sure to give six pounds of wax on St. Andrew's Day, wherever we may be with our people, and a similar amount in mid-Lent.

60 Mayors are never to be chosen from among powerful men, but from men of more modest station who are likely to be loyal.

61 That each steward, when he is on service, shall have his malt brought to the palace; and with him shall come master-brewers who can make good beer there.

62 That each steward shall make an annual statement of all our income, from the oxen which our plowmen keep, from the holdings which owe plowing services, from the pigs, from rents, judgement-fees and fines, from the fines for taking game in our forests without our permission and from the various other payments; from the mills, forests, fields, bridges and ships; from the free men and the hundreds which are attached to our fisc; from the markets; from the vineyards, and those who pay their dues in wine; from hay, firewood and torches, from planks and other timber; from waste land; from vegetables, millet and panic; from wool, linen and hemp; from the fruits of trees; from larger and smaller nuts; from the graftings of various trees; from gardens, turnips, fishponds; from hides, skins and horns; from honey and wax; from oil, tallow and soap; from mulberry wine, boiled wine, mead and vinegar; from beer and from new and old wine; from new and old grain; from chickens and eggs and geese; from the fishermen, smiths, shield-makers and cobblers; from kneading troughs, bins or boxes; from the turners and saddlers; from forges and from mines, that is, from iron- or lead-workings and from workings of any other kind; from people paying tribute; and from colts and fillies. All these things they shall set out in order under separate headings, and shall send the information to us at Christmas time, so that we may know the character and amount of our income from the various sources.

63 With regard to all the things mentioned so far, our stewards should not think it hard of us to make these demands, since it is our wish that they likewise should be able to make demands of their subordinates without giving offense. And all the things that a man ought to have in his house or on his estates, our stewards shall have on our estates.

64 That our carts which go to the army as war-carts shall be well constructed; their coverings shall be well-made of skins, and sewn together in such a way that, should the necessity arise to cross water, they can get across rivers with the provisions inside and without any water being able to get in—and, as we have said, our belongings can get across safely. It is also our wish that flour—12 *modii* of it—should be placed in each cart for our use; and in those carts which carry wine they are to place 12 *modii* according to our measurement,

and they are also to provide for each cart a shield, a lance, a quiver and a bow.

65 That the fish from our fishponds shall be sold, and others put in their place, so that there is always a supply of fish; however, when we do not visit the estates they are to be sold, and our stewards are to get a profit from them for our benefit.

66 They are to give an account to us of the male and female goats, and of their horns and skins; and each year they are to bring to us the newly-salted meat of the fattened goats.

67 With regard to vacant manses and newly acquired slaves, if they have any surplus which they cannot dispose of, they are to let us know.

68 It is our wish that the various stewards should always have by them good barrels bound with iron, which they can send to the army and to the palace, and that they should not make bottles of leather.

69 They shall at all times keep us informed about wolves, how many each of them has caught, and shall have the skins delivered to us. And in the month of May they are to seek out the wolf cubs and catch them, with poison and hooks as well as with pits and dogs.

70 It is our wish that they shall have in their gardens all kinds of plants: lily, roses, fenugreek, costmary, sage, rue, southernwood, cucumbers, pumpkins, gourds, kidney-beans, cumin, rosemary, caraway, chick-pea, squill, gladiolus, tarragon, anise, colocynth, chicory, ammi, sesili, lettuces, spider's foot, rocket salad, garden cress, burdock, penny-royal, hemlock, parsley, celery, lovage, juniper, dill, sweet fennel, endive, dittany, white mustard, summer savory, water mint, garden mint, wild mint, tansy, catnip, centaury, garden poppy, beets, hazelwort, marshmallows, mallows, carrots, parsnip, orach, spinach, kohlrabi, cabbages, onions, chives, leeks, radishes, shallots, cibols, garlic, madder, teazles, broad beans, peas, coriander, chervil, capers, clary. And the gardener shall have house-leeks growing on his house. As for trees, it is our wish that they shall have various kinds of apple, pear, plum, sorb, medlar,

chestnut and peach; quince, hazel, almond, mulberry, laurel, pine, fig, nut and cherry trees of various kinds. The names of apples are: *gozmaringa, geroldinga, crevedella, spirauca*; there are sweet ones, bitter ones, those that keep well, those that are to be eaten straightaway, and early ones. Of pears they are to have three or four kinds, those that keep well, sweet ones, cooking pears and the late-ripening ones.

General capitulary for the *missi*, spring 802

1 Concerning the commission despatched by our lord the emperor. Our most serene and most Christian lord and emperor, Charles, has selected the most prudent and wise from among his leading men, archbishops and bishops, together with venerable abbots and devout laymen, and has sent them out into all his kingdom, and bestowed through them on all his subjects the right to live in accordance with a right rule of law. Wherever there is any provision in the law that is other than right or just he has ordered them to inquire most diligently into it and bring it to his notice, it being his desire, with God's help, to rectify it. And let no one dare or be allowed to use his wit and cunning, as many do, to subvert the law as it is laid down or the emperor's justice, whether it concerns God's churches, or poor people and widows and orphans, or any Christian person. Rather should all men live a good and just life in accordance with God's commands, and should with one mind remain and abide each in his appointed place or profession: the clergy should live a life in full accord with the canons without regard for base gain, the monastic orders should keep their life under diligent control, the laity and secular people should make proper use of their laws, refraining from ill-will and deceit, and all should live together in perfect love and peace. And the *missi* themselves, as they wish to have the favor of Almighty God and to preserve it through the loyalty they have promised, are to make diligent inquiry wherever a man claims that someone has done him an injustice; so everywhere, and amongst all men, in God's holy churches, among poor people, orphans and widows, and throughout the whole people they may administer law and justice in full accordance with the will and the fear of God. And if there be anything which they themselves, together with the

counts of the provinces, cannot correct or bring to a just settlement, they should refer it without any hesitation to the emperor's judgement along with their reports. And in no way, whether by some man's flattery or bribery, or by the excuse of blood relationship with someone, or through fear of someone more powerful, should anyone hinder the right and proper course of justice.

2 Concerning the promise of fealty to our lord the emperor. He has given instructions that in all his kingdom all men, both clergy and laity, and each according to his vows and way of life, who before have promised fealty to him as king, should now make the same promise to him as Caesar; and those who until now have not made the promise are all to do so from 12 years old and upwards. And that all should be publicly informed, so that each man may understand how many important matters are contained in that oath—not only, as many have thought until now, the profession of loyalty to our lord the emperor throughout his life, and the undertaking not to bring any enemy into his kingdom for hostile reasons, nor to consent to or be silent about anyone's infidelity towards him, but also that all men may know that the oath has in addition the following meaning within it.

3 First, that everyone on his own behalf should strive to maintain himself in God's holy service, in accordance with God's command and his own pledge, to the best of his ability and intelligence, since our lord the emperor himself is unable to provide the necessary care and discipline to all men individually.

4 Second, that no man, through perjury or any other craft or deceit, or through anyone's flattery or bribery, should in any way withhold or take away or conceal our lord the emperor's serf, or his landmark, or his land, or anything that is his by right of possession; and that no one should conceal the men of his fisc who run away and unlawfully and deceitfully claim to be free men, nor take them away by perjury or any other craft.

5 That no one should presume to commit fraud or theft or any other criminal act against God's holy churches or against widows or orphans or pilgrims; for the lord emperor himself, after God

and his saints, has been appointed their protector and defender.

6 That no one should dare neglect a benefice held of our lord the emperor, and build up his own property from it.

7 That no one should presume to ignore a summons to the host from our lord the emperor, and that no count should be so presumptuous as to dare to excuse any of those who ought to go with the host, either on the pretext of kinship or through the enticement of any gift.

8 That no one should presume to subvert in any way any edict or any order of our lord the emperor, nor trifle with his affairs nor hinder nor weaken them, nor act in any other way contrary to his will and his instructions. And that no one should dare to be obstructive about any debt or payment that he owes.

9 That no one in court should make a practice of defending another man in an unlawful manner, by arguing the case weakly through a desire for gain, by hampering a lawful judgement by showing off his skill in pleading, or by presenting a weak case in an attempt to do his client harm. Rather should each man plead for himself, be it a question of tax or debt or some other case, unless he is infirm or unacquainted with pleading; for such men the *missi* or the chief men who are in the court or a judge who knows the case can plead it before the court, or if necessary a man can be provided to plead, who is approved by all parties and has a good knowledge of the case at issue; this, however, should only be done at the convenience of the chief men or *missi* who are present. At all events, it must be done in accordance with justice and the law; and no one should be allowed to impede the course of justice by offering a reward or a fee, by skilful and ill-intentioned flattery, or by the excuse of kinship. And let no one make an unlawful agreement with anyone, but let all men be seriously and willingly prepared to see that justice is done.

10–24 [These sections are all on ecclesiastical matters, dealing with the duties and conduct of clergy, monks, etc.]

25 That the counts and *centenarii* should strive to see that justice is done, and should have as assistants in their duties men in whom they can have full confidence, who will faithfully observe justice and the law, will in no wise oppress the poor, and will not dare, for flattery or a bribe, to conceal in any manner of concealment any thieves, robbers or murderers, adulterers, evil-doers and performers of incantations and auguries, and all other sacrilegious people, but rather will bring them to light, that they may receive correction and punishment according to the law, and that with God's indulgence all these evils may be removed from among our Christian people.

26 That the justices should give right judgement according to the written law, and not according to their private opinions.

27 We ordain that no one in all our kingdom, whether rich or poor, should dare to deny hospitality to pilgrims; that is, no one should refuse a roof, a hearth and water to any pilgrims who are traveling the country in the service of God, or to anyone who is journeying for love of God or for the salvation of his soul. And if a man should be willing to offer any further benefit to such people, let him know that God will send him the best reward, as he himself said: "Whoso shall receive one such little child in my name receiveth me"; and in another place, "I was a stranger, and ye took me in" [Matthew 18.5; 25.35].

28 Concerning the commissions coming from our lord the emperor. The counts and the *centenarii* should, as they are desirous of the favor of our lord the emperor, provide for the *missi* who are sent upon them with all possible attention, that they may go about their duties without any delay; and he has given instructions to all men that it is their duty to make such provision, that they suffer no delay to occur anywhere, and that they help them to go upon their way with all haste, and make such provision for this as our *missi* may require.

29 Concerning those poor men who owe payment of the royal fine and to whom the lord emperor in his mercy has given remission; the counts or *missi* are not to have the right for their part to bring constraint upon people so excused.

30 Concerning those whom the lord emperor wishes, with Christ's blessing, to have peace and protection in his kingdom, that is, those who have thrown themselves upon his mercy, those who, whether Christians or pagans, have desired to offer any information, or who from poverty or hunger have sought his intervention; let no one dare to bind them in servitude or take possession of them or dispose of them or sell them, but rather let them stay where they themselves choose, and live there under the lord emperor's protection and in his mercy. If anyone should presume to transgress this instruction, let him know that a man so presumptuous as to despise the lord emperor's orders must pay for it with the loss of his life.

31 For those who administer the justice of our lord the emperor let no one dare to devise harm or injury, nor bring any hostility to bear upon them. Anyone who presumes to do so must pay the royal fine; and if he is guilty of a greater offense, the orders are that he be brought to the king's presence.

32 Murder, by which a great multitude of our Christian people perish, we ordain should be shunned and avoided by every possible means; Our Lord himself forbade hatred and enmity among his faithful, and murder even more. How can a man feel confident that he will be at peace with God, when he has killed the son most close to himself? Or who can believe that Christ Our Lord is on his side, when he has murdered his brother? It is, moreover, a great and unacceptable risk with God the Father and Christ the ruler of heaven and earth to arouse the hostility of men. With men, we can escape for a time by hiding, but even so by some chance of fortune we fall into our enemy's hands; but where can a man escape from God, from whom no secrets are hid? What rashness to think to escape His anger! For this reason we have sought, by every kind of precept, to prevent the people entrusted to us for ruling from perishing as a result of this evil; for he who feels no dread at the anger of God should not receive mild and benevolent treatment from us; rather would we wish a man who had dared to commit the evil act of murder to receive the severest of punishments. Nevertheless, in order that the crime should not increase further, and in order that serious enmity should not arise among Christians when

they resort to murders at the persuasion of the Devil, the guilty person should immediately set about making amends, and should with all possible speed pay the appropriate recompense to the relatives of the dead man for the evil he has done to them. And this we firmly forbid, that the parents of the dead man should dare in any way to increase the enmity arising from the crime committed, or refuse to allow peace when the request is made; rather, they should accept the word given to them and the compensation offered, and allow perpetual peace, so long as the guilty man does not delay payment of the compensation. And when a man sinks to such a depth of crime as to kill his brother or a relative, he must betake himself immediately to the penance devised for him, and to do as his bishop instructs him and without any compromising. He should strive with God's help to make full amends, and should pay compensation for the dead man according to the law and make his peace in full with his kinsmen; and once the parties have given their word let no one dare to arouse further enmity on the matter. And anyone who scorns to pay the appropriate compensation is to be deprived of his inheritance pending our judgement.

33 We forbid absolutely the crime of incest. If anyone is stained by wicked fornication he must in no circumstances be let off without severe penalty, but rather should be punished for it in such a way that others will be deterred from committing the same offense, that filthiness may be utterly removed from our Christian people, and that the guilty person himself may be fully freed from it through the penance that is prescribed for him by his bishop. The woman concerned should be kept under her parents' supervision subject to our judgement. And if such people are unwilling to agree to the bishop's judgement concerning their improvement they are to be brought to our presence, mindful of that exemplary punishment for incest imposed by Fricco upon a certain nun.

34 That all should be fully and well prepared for whenever our order or announcement may come. And if anyone then maintains that he is not ready and disregards our instructions he is to be brought to the palace—and not he alone, but all those who presume to go against our edict or our orders.

35 That all bishops and their priests should be accorded all honor and respect in their service of God's will. They should not dare to stain themselves or others with incestuous unions. They should not presume to solemnize marriages until the bishops and priests, together with the elders of the people, have carefully inquired to see if there be any blood relationship between the parties, and should only then give their blessing to the marriage. They should avoid drunkenness, shun greediness, and not commit theft; disputes and quarrels and blasphemies, whether in normal company or in a legal sense, should be entirely avoided; rather, they should live in love and unity.

36 That all men should contribute to the full administration of justice by giving their agreement to our *missi*. They should not in any way give their approval to the practice of perjury, which is a most evil crime and must be removed from among our Christian people. And if anyone after this is convicted of perjury he should know that he will lose his right hand; but he is also to be deprived of his inheritance subject to our judgement.

37 That those who commit patricide or fratricide, or who kill an uncle or a father-in-law or any of their kinsmen, and who refuse to obey and consent to the judgement of our bishops, priests, and other justices, are for the salvation of their souls and for the carrying out of the lawful judgement to be confined by our *missi* and counts in such custody that they will be safe, and will not pollute the rest of the people, until such time as they are brought to our presence. And in the meantime they are not to have any of their property.

38 The same is to be done with those who are arraigned and punished for unlawful and incestuous unions, and who refuse to mend their ways or submit to their bishops and priests, and who presume to disregard our edict.

39 That no one should dare to steal our beasts in our forests; this we have forbidden already on many occasions, and we now firmly ban it again, that no one should do it any more and should take care to keep the faith which everyone has promised to us and desires to keep. And if any count or *centenarius* or vassal of ours or any of our officials

should steal our game he must at all costs be brought to our presence to account for it. As for the rest of the people, anyone who steals the game in this way should in every case pay the appropriate penalty, and under no circumstances should anyone be let off in this matter. And if anyone knows that it has been done by someone else, in accordance with the faith he has promised to us to keep and has now to promise again he should not dare to conceal this.

40 Finally, therefore, from all our decrees we desire it to be known in all our kingdom through our *missi* now sent out: among the clergy, the bishops, abbots, priests, deacons, clerks, and all monks and nuns, that each one in his ministry or profession should keep our edict or decree, and when it is right should of his good will offer thanks to the people, give them help, or if need be correct them in some way. Similarly for the laity, in all places everywhere, if a plea is entered concerning the protection of the holy churches, or of widows or orphans or less powerful people, or concerning the host, and is argued on these cases, we wish them to know that they should be obedient to our order and our will, that they maintain observance of our edict, and that in all these matters each man strive to keep himself in God's holy service. This in order that everything should be good and well-ordered for the praise of Almighty God, and that we should give thanks where it is due; that where we believe anything to have gone unpunished we should so strive with all earnestness and willingness to correct it that with God's help we may bring it to correction, to the eternal reward both of ourselves and of all our faithful people. Similarly concerning the counts and *centenarii*, our officers [*ministerialibus*], we wish all the things above mentioned in our deliberations to be known. So be it.

Special capitularies for the *missi*, 802.

Capitulary for the missi for Paris and Rouen
In Paris, Meaux, Melun, Provins, Estampes, Chartres and Poissy: Fardulfus and Stephanus. In Le Mans, Exmes, Lisieux, Bayeux, Coutances, Avranches, Evreux and Merey, and for that part of the Seine and Rouen: Bishop Magenardus and Madelgaudus.

Capitulary for the missi for Orleans
First, for the city of Orleans on the Seine, by the direct route, then to Troyes, with the whole of its region, then to Langres, from Langres to the town of Besançon in Burgundy, from there to Autun, and afterwards to the Loire as far as Orleans: those sent are Archbishop Magnus and Count Godefredus.

1 Concerning the oath of fealty, that all should reaffirm it.

2 Concerning bishops and the clergy, whether they are living according to the canons, and whether they are well acquainted with them and are carrying them out.

3 Concerning abbots, whether they are living according to a rule or according to the canons, and whether they are well acquainted with that rule or those canons.

4 Concerning the monasteries where there are monks, whether they live according to the rule in cases where it is part of their vows.

5 Concerning convents, whether the nuns live according to a rule or to the canons, and concerning their cloisters.

6 Concerning secular laws.

7 Concerning perjury.

8 Concerning murder.

9 Concerning adultery and other unlawful acts, whether committed in bishoprics and monasteries and convents or among laymen.

10 Concerning those men who have plundered our benefices and made up their private holdings. Likewise concerning the property of the churches.

11 Concerning those Saxons who have our benefices in Frankia, in what way they cultivate them, and with what degree of care.

12 Concerning the oppressions of poor free men, who owe military service and are oppressed by the justices.

13 That all men be well prepared for whatever order may come from us.

13a Concerning the preparation of ships around the coast.

13b Concerning the free men who live around the coastal regions; if a message should come to them instructing them to come and give assistance, and they refuse to obey it, each of them must pay twenty shillings, a half to his lord and a half to the people. If one of them is a *lidus* he must pay fifteen shillings to the people and give his back to be flogged. If he is a serf he must pay ten shillings to the people and receive the flogging.

14 Concerning the commissions coming to us and the *missi* sent out by us.

15 Concerning those whom we wish to have peace and protection throughout the kingdoms which by the favor of Christ belong to us.

16 Concerning those men who have been killed in administering our justice.

17 Concerning tithes and ninths and the dues to God's churches, that they should be at pains to pay them and to make good what is wanting.

18 Concerning the ban of our lord the emperor and king, and those things for which it has been our wont to exact a fine, that is, violence offered to churches, to widows or orphans or those unable to defend themselves, and rape, and failure to observe a decree concerning the host, that those who offend against the king in these respects should make full reparation.

18a That they make careful enquiries among the bishops, abbots, counts, abbesses and all our vassals, to see what degree of mutual harmony and friendship they have in their various districts, or whether there appears to be any discord among them; and that they be careful to report to us the whole truth of these matters, confirmed by their oath. That all of them should have good administrators [*vicedomos*] and advocates.

19 In addition, they are to enquire into and settle any matter that may be necessary, whether in our jurisdiction or in that of the churches, concerning widows, orphans, minors, and all other persons. And whatever they find that needs correcting, let them take pains to correct it to the best of their ability; what they cannot correct they must have referred to our presence.

The oath whereby I reaffirm that from this day forth, being of sound mind and with no evil intent from my part to his, I am a faithful subject of our lord and most pious emperor, Charles, son of King Pippin and Queen Berthana, for the honor of his kingdom, as a man ought lawfully to be towards his lord; so help me God, and these relics of the saints here situated, for all the days of my life with all my will and with what intelligence God has given me, I will so attend and consent.

Again: the oath whereby I affirm. I am a faithful servant of our lord and most pious emperor, Charles, son of King Pippin and Queen Berthana, as a man lawfully ought to be towards his lord, for his kingdom and for his right. And this oath which I have sworn I shall willingly keep to the best of my knowledge and ability, from this day forth, so help me God, who created heaven and earth, and these relics of saints.

20. DHUODA'S HANDBOOK FOR HER SON
(*LIBER MANUALIS*)

IN 841, NOT LONG after the disastrous battle of Fontenoy in which the sons of Louis the Pious (d. 840) fought each other to a bloody stalemate, Dhuoda wrote a treatise of advice for her fifteen-year-old son William, who was serving King Charles the Bald. This unique text by a Frankish noblewoman shows her education, piety, and deep concern for her family in the tumultuous period of the dissolution of the Carolingian world. Her husband, Bernard of Septimania, had been the closest supporter of Louis the Pious and was firmly in Charles's camp, but Dhuoda feared for her son amid the dangers of the court. Most of the treatise is devoted to William's religious devotion, but Book Three, presented here, focuses on William's reverence to his father, his fealty to his king, and his comportment with other nobles at court. Dhuoda's fears for her son were well founded—seven years later he revolted against Charles and was eventually killed.

Source: *Handbook for William: A Carolingian Woman's Counsel for her Son by Dhuoda*, ed. and trans. with an introduction by Carol Neel (Lincoln & London: University of Nebraska Press, 1991), 21–42.

Further Reading: See the translator's introduction, pp. ix–xxviii, as well as Marcelle Thiebaux (ed. and trans.), *Dhuoda Handbook for her Warrior Son: Liber Manualis*, Cambridge Medieval Classics 8 (Cambridge: Cambridge University Press, 1998), 1–39; and Marie Anne Mayeski, *Dhuoda: Ninth Century Mother and Theologian* (Scranton, PA: University of Scranton Press, 1996).

---

1. On the reverence you should show your father throughout your life.

Now I must do my best to guide you in how you should fear, love, and be faithful to your lord and father, Bernard, in all things, both when you are with him and when you are apart from him. In this Solomon is your teacher and your wisest authority. He chastises you, my son, and says to you in warning, *For God hath made the father* who flourishes in his children *honorable (Ecclus. 3:3).* And likewise: *He that honoreth his father shall have joy in his own children (Ecclus. 2:6)* and *shall enjoy a long life. He that obeyeth the father shall be a comfort to his mother (Ecclus. 3:7). As one that layeth up* good things *(Ecclus. 3:5),* so is he who honors his father. *He that feareth the Lord, honoreth his parents (Ecclus. 3:8). So* honor thy father, my son, and pray for him devotedly, *that thou mayest be longlived upon the land (Ecclus. 20:12),* with a full term of earthly existence. *Remember that thou hadst not been born* but through him *(Ecclus. 7:30).* In every matter be obedient to your father's interest and heed his judgment (compare *Ecclus. 3:2).* If by God's help you come to this, *support the old age of thy father and grieve him not in his life (Ecclus. 3:14). Despise him not when thou art in thy strength (Ecclus. 3:15).*

May you never do this last, and may the earth cover my body before such a thing might happen. But I do not believe that it will. I mention it not because I fear it but rather so that you may avoid it so completely that such a crime never comes to your mind, as I have heard that it indeed has done among many who are not like you. Do not forget the dangers that befell Elias's sons, who disobediently scorned the commands of their father and for this met with a bitter death *(1 Kings 4:11).* Nor should I fail to mention the tree of Absalom, who rebelled against his father and whom a base death brought to a sudden fall. Hung from an oak and pierced by lances, he ended his earthly life in the flower of his youth, with a groan of anguish. Lacking as he did an earthly kingdom, he never reached that highest of kingdoms promised to him *(compare 2 Kings 18:15).*

What of the many more who behave as he did? Their path is perilous. May those who perpetrate such evil suffer accordingly. It is not I who condemn them, but Scripture that promises their condemnation, threatening them terribly and saying, *Cursed is he that honoreth not his father* (Deut. 27:16). And again, *He who curseth his father, dying let him die* (Lev. 20:9) basely and uselessly. If such is the punishment for harsh, evil words alone, what do you think will happen to those who inflict real injury upon their parents and insult the dignity of their fathers? We hear of many in our times who, thinking their present circumstances unjust, consider such crimes without taking into account the past. On them and on those like them fall hatred, jealousy, disaster, and calamity, and *nourishment to their envy* (Gen. 37:8). They lose rather than keep those goods of others that they seek, and they are scarcely able even to keep their own property. I say these things not because I have seen them happen, but because I have read about such matters in books. I have heard of them in the past, you hear about them yourself, and I am hearing them even now. Consider what will happen in the future to those who treat others in this fashion. But God has the power to bring even these people—if there are such—to lament their evil ways and, in their conversion, to do penance and be worthy of salvation. May anyone who behaves so stay away from you, and may God give him understanding.

Everyone, whoever he may be, should consider this, my son: if the time comes that God finds him worthy to give him children of his own, he will not wish them to be rebellious or proud or full of greed, but humble and quiet and full of obedience, so that he rejoices to see them. He who was a son before, small and obedient to his father, may then be fortunate in his own fatherhood. May he who thinks on these things in the hope that they will happen consider too what I have said above. Then "all his limbs" will work "in concert, peacefully" *(Benedict, Rule 34)*.

Hear me as I direct you, my son William, and "listen carefully," follow the "instructions … of a father." Heed the words of the holy Fathers, and *bind them in thy heart* (Prov. 16:20) by frequent reading so that years *of life may be multiplied to thee* (Prov. 4:10) as you grow continually in goodness. For *they that wait upon* (Ps. 36:9)

God, blessing him, obeying the Fathers and complying freely with their precepts—such men *shall inherit the land* (Ps. 36:9). If you listen to what I say above and if you put it into worthy practice, not only will you have success here on this earth, but also you will be found worthy to possess with the saints what the Psalmist describes: *I believe to see the good things of the Lord in the land of the living* (Ps. 26:13). So that this other land may be your inheritance, my son, I pray that he who lives eternally may deign to prepare you to dwell there.

2. On the same topic, on reverence for your father.

In the human understanding of things, royal and imperial appearance and power seem pre-eminent in the world, and the custom of men is to account those men's actions and their names ahead of all others, as though these things were worthy of veneration and as though worldly power were the highest honor. This attitude is testified in the words of him who said, *whether it be to the king as excelling, or to the governors* (1 Pet. 2:13–14). But despite all this, my wish is as follows, my son. In the smallness of my understanding—but also according to God's will—I caution you to render first to him whose son you are special, faithful, steadfast loyalty as long as you shall live. For it is a fixed and unchangeable truth that no one, unless his rank comes to him from his father, can have access to another person at the height of power.

So I urge you again, most beloved son William, that first of all you love God as I have written above. Then love, fear, and cherish your father. Keep in mind that your worldly estate proceeds from his. Recognize that from the most ancient times, men who have loved their fathers and have been truthfully obedient to them have been found worthy to receive God's benediction from those fathers' hands.

3. On the examples of the early Fathers.

We read that Sem, the son of Noah, reached heaven because he loved his father, and so did his brother Japheth. Their father said over their heads as he blessed them: may God bless Sem and Japheth, and may he dwell in their tents *(compare*

Gen. 9:26–27); may they prosper, may they flourish, and may they be enriched in all good things. What shall I say about Cham and others like him? (*compare Gen. 9:22.*)

Is it not necessary for you to know? For it is very useful to discern the meaning of these examples. Let us think upon them always, turning toward those who have been good.

In obeying his father, Isaac was found worthy to share with his wife and descendants many goods in this world, for he received that father's benediction. Isaac is also called *laughter (Gen. 21:16)* in holy Scripture, or "rejoicing," and "rejoicing" is a fitting name for one such as he, just as "mourning" is rightly applied to an idle, confused, and profligate man. So too Jacob, because he loved and obeyed his father, was found worthy to be snatched away from many tribulations and pressing difficulties. He received double and triple benediction from God and from his earthly father, and also from his mother and an angel. It was said to him, *I will bless thee, and I will multiply* your name as *the stars of heaven (Gen. 22:17). You will be blessed and you will be called Israel (Gen. 35:10), for if thou hast been strong against God, how much more shalt thou prevail against* men? *(Gen. 32:28).*

Consider, my son, how strong those are in the secular world who are worthy of God's blessing because of their parents' merits and because of their own filial obedience. If such was the case for Jacob, then you too should fight, seek, struggle, and strive manfully in all situations that you too may be worthy to receive at least that blessing from him who is called God and to receive your inheritance along with Jacob. For it is according to Jacob's model that faults are washed away and vices overcome; all his enemies submitted to the weight of his gentleness as if they wore yokes in his service (*compare Jer. 27:12*). The creator of the world gave Jacob a wife, children, and much material wealth. We read of him that he was always satisfied and rich in this world and that he pleased God in every way.

And what shall I say of Joseph, Jacob's son, who was so loving and obedient to his father that he would have been willing to die for him if God and that father's merits had not protected him? Joseph was betrayed and accused because of his obedience to his father; he was sent to his brothers, and

they sold him. But he feared and avoided fornication with women, maintaining chastity of the mind for God's sake and of the body for his earthly lord's sake. Thus he was worthy to be loved more than all the other servants of his lord. He was imprisoned, he was beaten, and he suffered greatly—all these things for his father's sake, and throughout he gave thanks to God. Finally he was set free of this swarm of troubles and hardships. He became the greatest of counselors and interpreters of dreams; he was raised to great authority and crowned with the highest power. In the royal hall, when he shone forth as the second in command on account of his merits, he was higher in rank than all the rest.

He was called *Joseph … a growing son, a growing son (Gen. 49:22)* and the Egyptians changed his name to ruler of the world and savior (*compare Gen. 49:22*) because of the goodness of his great love. Beautiful in demeanor, beautiful in spirit, beautiful in appearance, he was still more beautiful in understanding, chaste in body and humble in heart. And what else shall I say? Eminent and rich in this world, he was pleasing in everything to God and man alike. Ruling his father and his brothers, governing all of Egypt, he ended his earthly life in peace. Walking *from virtue to virtue (Ps. 83:8)*, he was found worthy in his humility, chastity, and obedience to be joined to God, shining forth in heaven and ruling with the saints in glory. And all this because of his devotion to his father.

Many others who have been obedient to God and mindful of the commands of a devoted father have been honored and respected in the secular world and have safely reached that heavenly reward for which they struggled. May what happened to them happen also for you if the good Lord grants you children. But what else shall I write for you about that humble respect I have described above? I beseech and I caution you that you act worthily toward deserving individuals. Always do good works. And always grow and increase in him who is called God, the maker of heaven and earth, about whom it is written: and he was subject to his parents (*compare Luke 2:51*). May the redeemer of the human race cause you to grow, to progress, and to be enlarged in age and wisdom before God and men (*compare Luke 2:52*). May Jesus Christ, our Lord in whom all good things are possible and who reigns eternally, deign to grant these things to you. Amen.

4. Direction on your comportment toward your lord.

You have Charles[1] as your lord; you have him as lord because, as I believe, God and your father, Bernard, have chosen him for you to serve at the beginning of your career, in the flower of your youth. Remember that he comes from a great and noble lineage on both sides of his family. Serve him not only so that you please him in obvious ways, but also as one clearheaded in matters of both body and soul. Be steadfastly and completely loyal to him in all things.

Think on that excellent servant of the patriarch Abraham. He traveled a great distance to bring back a wife for his master's son (*Gen. 24*). Because of the confidence of him who gave the command and the wise trustworthiness of him who followed it, the task was fulfilled. The wife found great blessing and great riches in her many descendants. What shall I say of the attitude of Joab, of Abner, and of many others toward the king David? (*compare 3 Kings 2.*) Facing dangers on their king's behalf in many places, they desired with all their might to please their lord more than themselves. And what of those many others in holy Scripture who faithfully obeyed their lords' commands? Because of their watchful strength they were found worthy to flourish in this world. For we know that, as Scripture tells, all honor and authority are given by God. Therefore we should serve our lords faithfully, without ill will, without reluctance, and without sluggishness. As we read, *there is no power but from God: and he … that resisteth the power, resisteth the ordinance of God (Rom. 13:1–2).*

That is why, my son, I urge you to keep this loyalty as long as you live, in your body and in your mind. For the advancement that it brings you will be of great value both to you and to those who in turn serve you. May the madness of treachery never, not once, make you offer an angry insult. May it never give rise in your heart to the idea of being disloyal to your lord. There is harsh and shameful talk about men who act in this fashion. I do not think that such will befall you or those who fight alongside you because such an attitude has never shown itself among your ancestors. It has not been seen among them, it is not seen now, and it will not be seen in the future.

Be truthful to your lord, my son William, child of their lineage. Be vigilant, energetic, and offer him ready assistance as I have said here. In every matter of importance to royal power take care to show yourself a man of good judgment—in your own thoughts and in public—to the extent that God gives you strength. Read the sayings and the lives of the holy Fathers who have gone before us. You will there discover how you may serve your lord and be faithful to him in all things. When you understand this, devote yourself to the faithful execution of your lord's commands. Look around as well and observe those who fight for him loyally and constantly. Learn from them how *you may* serve him. Then, informed by their example, with the help and support of God, you will easily reach the celestial goal I have mentioned above. And may your heavenly Lord God be generous and benevolent toward you. May he keep you safe, be your kind leader and your protector. May he deign to assist you in all your actions and be your constant defender. *As it shall be the will* of God *in heaven so be it done (1 Macc. 3:60).* Amen.

5. On taking counsel

If God should someday bring you to such a point that you are found worthy to be called to the council of the magnates, consider carefully on what, when, to whom, and how you should offer worthy and appropriate comment. Act with the advice of those who encourage you to behave loyally in body and in soul. It is written: do everything with counsel, *and thou shalt not repent when thou hast done (Ecclus. 32:34).* Here "everything" refers not to evil deeds offensive to good judgment, but to lofty and generous actions such as enhance the health of soul and body and are beyond reproach;

---

1   Charles the Bald (823–877).

such deeds are useful and steady, of long-enduring effect. As someone said, *what I have said is determined (2 Kings 19:29)*.

Those who do metalwork, when they begin to pound out gold to make it into leaf, wait for the best and most suitable day, weather, and temperature. Then the gold that they work for decoration, brilliant and sparkling even among the finest metals, may shine still more brightly. In the same way, the thought of those in council should in all matters follow the well-reasoned pattern known to the wise. For the speech of one who has good understanding is whiter than snow, sweeter than honey, purer than gold or silver. Why? Because, as Scripture says, from the mouth of a wise man comes honey *(compare Ps. 118:103)*. The eloquence of a great man is therefore a favor greater than silver and gold *(compare Prov. 22:1)* because his lips draw from the honeycomb *(compare Cant. 4:11)* and his words are *pure words ... tried by the fire, purged (Ps. 117)*.

There are no riches where stupidity reigns, and nothing is wanting, nothing an obstacle, in matters where gentle speech prevails *(compare Ecclus. 6:5)*. Whoever tries to be numbered among the wise can be welcome to both God and man and pleasing in every way to his earthly lord. For he will be known as true as gold, seen as whiter than snow. It is written: the mouths of the wise will be bleached whiter than snow *(compare Ps. 50:9)*, and their lips will be the lips of exaltation *(compare Ps. 62:6)*. Such are the lips of those who, with thoughtful counsel, offer speech useful to both God and men and enduring in Christ after its good effect is accomplished.

As for you, my son, believe in God, fear him, and love him. Do not hesitate to cling to him in the flower of your youth. Seek his wisdom and he will grant it to you. For the Apostle James says, *But if any of you want wisdom, let him ask of God, who giveth to all men abundantly, and upbraideth not*, but let him ask *nothing wavering*, and *it shall be given him (James 1:5–6)*, for God wishes to be petitioned. For the Lord says, encouraging us, *Ask, and it shall be given you: seek, and you shall find: knock, and it shall be opened to you (Matt. 7:7)*. I believe confidently in that Lord's generous mercy, freely given. For he who beseeches the Lord with the worthy, pure love of the heart may ask to be given wisdom, counsel, and those other things necessary for the body. Such a man may then believe that God will open to him and that the Lord will give to him *(compare Mark 11:24)*.

Therefore, my son, pray and seek of the Lord, just as a certain man used to pray to him in song. Say with that poet: to you be praise, honor, and power. You who are rich in all things, *give me wisdom*. And again, *Give me wisdom, that sitteth by thy throne, and cast me not off from among thy children (Wisd. 9:4)*. Send *wisdom out from the throne of thy majesty, that she may be with me, and may labor with me (Wisd. 9:10)*, so that I may *discern between good and evil* and be able to judge which is better *(compare Ps. 70:17–189)*. Love this wisdom, even from your youth, and seek it often as you invoke God. And if the good Lord should give it to you, cherish it, and it will embrace you in return. If you have wisdom, you will be the more blessed.

I urge you to make every effort to associate not only with older men who love God and seek wisdom but also with youths who do so, for maturity is rooted in the flower of youth. As someone says, *The things that thou hast not gathered in thy youth, how shalt thou find them in old age? (Ecclus. 25:5)*. *So* seek this in the Lord and say: God, teach me therefore from my youth, and unto old age and gray hairs *(compare 3 Kings 3:9)* my good father will not desert me *(compare 3 Kings 3:9)*. You will be blessed, my son, if you are made learned by him and if you are worthy to be instructed in his law. Indeed, Samuel and David were judges even as boys in the flower of youth according to the custom of the Fathers, and they were again as old men *(compare Benedict, Rule 63)*. They were great counselors to kings in the secular world, and they faithfully gave advice to the leaders of the Gentiles and foreign people. They deserved the victor's palm because of their worthy merits.

Think on the Fathers who went before us; think about Joseph before Pharaoh *(Gen. 41:13ff)*, Daniel before Nabuchodonosor, Baltassar, and Darius and the leaders of the Medes and the Persians *(Dan. 2:27ff, 5:17, 6:3)*. Without abandoning their own ways, these Fathers were always helpful in council. Do not forget Jethro, Moses' kinsman, and how he gave important counsel *(Exod. 18:14–23)*, or how Achior advised Holofernes, prince of the Gentiles *(Jth. 5:5ff)*, or how many more of the ancients faithfully gave excellent counsel to their friends and those around them. In freeing themselves, they were found worthy both of spiritual salvation and of the bounty of those they counseled. Indeed, these Fathers shine forth in the sacred Scriptures, praised much more than others. Why? *Because God hath tried them, and found them worthy (Wisd. 3:5)*, humble and pure in mind and body, informed in their understanding, so that the Lord is known to have joined them, pure as gold, to himself. There is no doubt that they, like the sacrifice of the holocaust *(Wisd. 3:6)*, are brought together with him in his kingdom in spirit and in body along with all the saints.

What shall I, the unworthy, unlucky, and insignificant Dhuoda, say then of you, *my* son? I pray that he who strengthened those men and others like them, he who is called God, may also increase the strength of your manhood now and always. *Nevertheless as it shall be the will of God in heaven so be it done (1 Macc. 3:60)* always in respect to you.

6. More on the same topic. On counselors.

There are some who consider themselves counselors and are not, for they think themselves wise even when this is untrue. I *speak as one less wise: I am more (2 Cor. 11:23)*. But this is not the fault of him in whom all good flourishes. For there are those who give good counsel and do not do it in a good way but in a way neither useful to themselves nor uplifting to another. Why? Because the counsel of such men does not lead to the highest, perfect good of heaven. And there are many who give bad counsel, but without effect. This happens in many, various ways. There were in former times many worthy, good, and truthful men, but today most people are unlike those ancients in many ways. What does this mean for us? Many things are clear in this secular world. For Scripture says, *and because iniquity hath abounded, the charity of many shall grow cold (Matt. 24:12)*. As things are now, one does not know whom to choose as a counselor or whom one ought first to believe, and

for many the hope of finding help from anyone remains uncertain. Read the *Synonyms*.[2]

But you must not despair in this, my son. There are many descended from these ancients who still, with God's help, are willing and able to give counsel that is good, welcome, and appropriate in respect to both themselves and their lords. And all these things happen through him who is called the Most High. For Scripture says, Is *there no physician* in Egypt *or balm in Galaad (Jer. 8:22)*, clear water in Canaan or counselor in Israel? There is indeed, and clear understanding reveals itself in *many* men. God, who gives light to the world and is the angel of good counsel, knows his own. He shows them the words that bring the soul's salvation. May he who was then among the ancients and is now among the living, who is in you, goes out from you, and returns to you, who directs you to fight alongside a worthy, high king to carry out that earthly lord's command—may that God cause you to arrive at that high, right counsel. Amen.

7. Special direction on the same topic.

For you to be such a man depends entirely on the judgment and the power of omnipotent God. If, with the aid of the highest creator, you come to the time that I have mentioned above,[3] fear immoral men and seek out worthy ones. Flee evil men and find good ones *(compare Isidore, Synonyma 2.43, PL 83:355)*. Do not take counsel with a man of ill will or a weak-spirited man or a wrathful man. For he will corrupt you like tin *(compare Isidore, Synonyma 2.43, PL 83:355)*, and under his command you will never rest secure. For the wrath and the envy that come easily to him draw him at once, headlong, to the depths.

Let not your fate be like Achitofel's *(2 Kings 16:15ff)* or like Aman's *(Esther 6:4ff)*, bad and arrogant men whose counsels were worthless and who, when they gave bad advice to their lord, fell headlong in both spirit and body to their deaths. For I wish, my son, that you take pleasure in fighting on your lord's behalf, as did such men as Doeg the Edomite *(1 Kings 21:7, 22:9)* and the

---

2   *Isidore of Seville, Synonyma 2:44.*
3   That is, if William should become one of the king's counselors.

humble Mardochai *(Esther 8:2ff)*. Achitophel offered Absalom the bad counsel that he should rebel against his father, David—and Achitophel did so in order to win the son's favor. But by the will of God *(compare 2 Kings 17:14)*, Achitophel's evil counsels were brought to nothing *(compare 2 Kings 17:14)*. But Chusai *(2 Kings 15:32ff)* and Doeg, a strong man who firmly held his ground against another determined man, remained unshakable in their counsel. On the other hand Aman, on account of the pride in his envious spirit, gave evil counsel to Assuerus so that sons of Israel were killed *(Esther 6:6ff)*. But Mardochai, praying for God's help to liberate himself and his people, gave the same king good counsel, the evidence of loyalty, in order to free and to vindicate himself *(compare Esther 2:22)*. Mardochai began, "Consider, O king."

By God's providence, one man merits salvation with his people. Another, a proud man, goes away empty along with all his house. He is hung on the gallows that in his envy he has prepared for the humble man, so that this evil is turned upon its designer. All by himself he has brought his life, even his body, to a worse end. There is fulfilled in him and in those like him what is said: *He hath conceived sorrow, and brought forth iniquity. He hath opened a pit … and fallen into it (Ps. 7:15–16)*. For he who had prepared evil for his innocent brother has now rushed headlong and straightaway into death. God, who is good and who in his goodness spares the wicked, rightly desires to bring all men to himself through penance. *For he knoweth both the deceiver, and him that is deceived by the deceiver (Ps. 7:15–16)*.

Therefore, my son William, fear immoral men and seek out worthy ones. Flee evil men like those mentioned here, but attach yourself to good men seeking after worthy goals. They offer counsel in the most useful of ways, in their true subjection to the wishes of their lords, and they are found worthy to receive fitting reward both from God and in the secular world. I pray that such counsel as has been in those great men may grow in you now, every day, always, my best of sons.

8. Regarding your lord's family.

As for the great and famous relations and associates of your royal lord—those who are descended from his illustrious father's side as well as those related to him by marriage—fear, love, honor, and cherish them if you and those who fight alongside you are found worthy to serve them in the royal and imperial court or anywhere else you may act on their behalf. In all undertakings in their interest maintain a pure, fitting, and steadfast obedience to them, as well as good faith in the execution of your duties.

Remember how David comported himself toward Jonathan, the son of the king Saul. In every way, throughout his life, he was a pure, faithful, and true supporter of both the father and the son, and also their children, not only during their lives but also after their deaths. Even after their destruction the sweetness of his great love caused him to mourn them with sorrowful tears, greatly lamenting and saying, *How are the valiant fallen in battle (2 Kings 1:25)* and *the weapons of war perished (2 Kings 1:27)*. And also, *I grieve for thee, my brother Jonathan: exceedingly beautiful, and amiable to me above the love of women (2 Kings 1:26)*, *swifter than eagles, stronger than lions (2 Kings 1:23)*. And again, my best of children, *the arrow of Jonathan never turned back (2 Kings 1:22)*. In these and other instances David was filled with grief for the king's son, and with his retainers he mourned deeply over Jonathan's ruin. May you and those who fight alongside you avoid such a fate.

I am having this copied out as an example for you. For when David recovered, as if consoled by the great loyalty of his love for them, he praised his dead friends in another voice, with sighing, *Saul and Jonathan, lovely, and comely in their life, even in death they were not divided (2 Kings 1:23)*. Many who faithfully obeyed the commandments of their lords and their lords' relations are abundantly and honorably praised in sacred Scriptures. Read the book of Kings and the books of the other Fathers, and you will find many.

So, my son William, bear patiently the yoke that governs a servant and be faithful to your lord Charles—whatever sort of lord he may be—and to his worthy relations of both sexes and to all those of royal origins. It is fitting for you and for all those who fight under their royal power to do so, and I wish that you serve them to good ends, faithfully, with all your might. For as we believe, God chose them and established them in royal power, granting them glory almost as great in its likeness to the ancients' as that promised to Abraham, Isaac, and Jacob (*compare Gen. 15:4ff*), and to their worthy children and descendants.

May the omnipotent Father—our strong King, the glorious Highest—make them peaceful and harmonious, seeking concord after the manner of their fathers in this earthly realm. Then they may shine in prosperity and rule, protect, and govern the world and its people with strength in the service of God and his saints. And they may hold and defend our people from the blows of enemies pressing all around, uniting the holy church of God the more firmly in Christ and his true religion. May they see the children of their sons pleasing God in worthy fashion, growing and flourishing, and aiming for heaven through many cycles of the years, persevering in this course until they come happily to the end of their lives. As for you, after you have reached the end of this present life, may he who gives all recompense and all bounty bring you to rest in the kingdom of heaven with those Fathers whom I have mentioned. May he bring you to his kingdom and his glory—you who struggle here to render faithful service both to your several earthly lords and to that singular Lord who gives fitting reward for your merits from his own riches. And may he unite you happily to Christ.

9. Regarding the magnates.

As for the magnates and their counselors—and all those like them who serve faithfully—show them your love, affection, and service often. Do so to them together and individually, to whomever is important at court. Learn attentively from the model of their distinction and adhere to it firmly. For in a house as great as the king's there are, there have been, and there will be, if the good Lord so commands, many conversations. There, one who wishes can learn from others humility, charity, chastity, patience, gentleness, modesty, sobriety, discretion, and other virtues, as well as the desire to do good.

So, my son, while you are a young boy still growing (*compare Gen. 49:22*), learn from those elders whose understanding is rich whatever good you can with the Father's help so you may be pleasing to God before all else and then be useful to man. I urge you to strive to act among your associates, peers, and faithful friends so that your life may hold to a good course, marked with no shame of disloyalty to your lords but with eagerness for good action, in a laudable fashion, worthy and proper. May that God who makes the tongues of infants speak in his praise—as it is written, *out of the mouths of infants (Ps. 8:3)*—himself cause you, filled with the eloquence of worthy, noble men who fear the Lord, to climb to the ranks of heaven.

10. That you accommodate yourself to great and to lesser men.

I need not point out to you that great men as well as lesser should follow the examples of their lords and of the highest magnates. Far from me as you are, you realize that constantly yourself. Still, never doubt that even lesser folk improve themselves after the model of their betters. I urge you not to hesitate to attach yourself to them—and them to you—by large and small favors.

God is the maker of all good things in heaven and earth, but he deigned to show his presence even here below for the sake of the least of his creatures. For as the learned say, even though he is the Most High and the creator of all things, he deigned to take on the form of a servant (*compare Phil. 2:7*). He raises up the powerful so that they may be cast down to the depths, and he exalts the humble "in order then to raise them up to a higher state. It is he, as the prophet says, who is the littlest one multiplying to a thousand, the weak one who becomes the strongest nation." He is great among the least of men, the feeble; he is powerful and manly. We believe in one God, creator, shepherd, and governor of our bodies and our souls, namely that one about whom I have written above. We receive all things from him, whatever seems to be within our power. Every higher creature with the faculty of reason should undoubtedly, whether he is greater or lesser than another, serve and praise his maker; such is fitting. And according to the authority of Scripture, the earth with all that is born of her, *the old with the younger (Ps. 148:12)*, should bless God and give him praise.

There is a short saying: *Let every spirit praise the Lord (Ps. 150:5)*. For it is he who loves the human race, and he does not fail to enrich through his gifts both the great and the small, according to his measure and on the scale of their merits. For he is *not a respecter of persons*, but in all things, when he is besought, he is present to those who fear him *(Acts 10:34–35)* and who do his will.

And if he who is so great acts thus even toward the least of men, what should we who are ourselves of small importance do for those who are even lesser? Those who can give aid should do so and—according to the words and injunctions of the apostle—carry burdens for each other (*compare Gal. 6:2*), the strong for the weak, the capable for those who are not. Then the weak may climb along with the strong, participating in their strength, to that heavenly height promised our forefathers. For the same apostle says: Now you *that are stronger* and more powerful *ought to bear the infirmities of the weak (Rom 15:1)*, so that your *abundance may supply their want (2 Cor. 8:14)* and their poverty.

My son, although you may be the least in stature among those who fight alongside you, you are nevertheless steadfast in your mind. Do not hesitate, I therefore urge you, to examine closely and to imitate the exemplary strength and model of those great men of whom you have read above. Consider great men as high above you, your equals as your betters, and those like you as ahead of you, so that in your attachment to them you may advance the dignity of your ancestors. Rejoice in deep humility, I beseech you, that they all have been set before you as your examples.

For instance, consider the image, metaphorically expressed, of the man about whom it is written, *his hand will be against all men, and all men's hands against him (Gen. 16:12)*. If we understand this short description in a good sense, then I urge that you be such a man in all respects. Then your hand will be ready for worthy action, and you will do your best now and always to give service and honor—not only in words but in deeds, and

with gentle speech—to great men, to lesser men, to those who are your equals, and likewise to the least of men. For it is written about our obligation to give, *God loveth a cheerful giver (2 Cor. 8:14)*. And it is said about words that a good speech is better than the *best gift (James 1:17)*. So you must do both things. If you strive to apply yourself with good will toward all, there will be accomplished in you what is written above. And may your hand, giving free service, be against all in order to give, and may all hands be against you to help you or to reward you according to the merit of your actions.

Love all so that you may be loved by all, and cherish them that you may be cherished. If you love all, all will love you. If you—who are singular—love them, then they—who are plural—will love you. It is written in Donatus' *Art of Poetry*, "I love you and I am loved by you, I kiss you and am kissed by you, I cherish you and am cherished by you, I respect and am respected by you." And again, "I, of me or by me, of me or from me, and O, by me" and more of the same, "them, of them or by them, O, by them," and many other relevant things.[4]

Therefore, my son William, cherish and show respect to whatever one or many persons you wish to respect you. Love, revere, stand by, and honor all, so that you may be found worthy to receive appropriately honorable recompense in all the changeable situations of the world. Toward our edification in this regard a certain learned author offers a brief comparison—an important one, extraordinarily clear in its meaning—with dumb animals. He says in the forty-first Psalm, *As the hart panteth*. For this is what harts do when groups of them begin to cross seas or wide streams with churning waves—they lower their necks one after the other, each putting his head and horns on the back of the previous one, so that as they each rest a little they all may the more easily cross the swift current. The harts have such intelligence and such commensurate discretion that, when they perceive that the one in front is weakening, the leader becomes a follower and eventually the last in line so that the others may assist and support him; then they choose another to go first. Thus, as one individual takes the place

---

4   An obscure reference to a versified version of Donatus' grammar.

of another, each feels the brotherly fellowship of love run through them all. Always careful that the head and antlers of any one of their kind not be plunged into the flood, the harts manage to hold up his head and to keep his antlers visible.

The point of this is not obscure to the learned, for everything is immediately clear in their sight. In the harts' mutual support—in their changing places in line—they show that human beings too must have the brotherly fellowship of love for greater and lesser men alike, in all ways and in all circumstances. We read that this was fulfilled in the past by many men, especially among the holy apostles and those like them. It is written, *For neither was there any one needy among them (Acts 4:34), but all things were common unto them (Acts 4:32).* They had *one heart and one soul (Acts 4: 32)* in God, always feeling brotherly compassion for each other in Jesus Christ.

Just as the harts support and sustain each other's heads and antlers, so those who have faith in Christ hold up their hearts and keep their minds always on him. He who was born king of David's seed for the salvation of the human race and descended to the depth of this sea of battering waves has raised his horn to liberate his people (*compare Luke 1:69*). Acting of his grace, he has found those who were lying in darkness, and rising from that depth he has visited them (*compare Luke 1:78*) and raised them to the heights. He offers his example lest we be lost in the turmoil of the deep sea or in the blinding mud of desire and cupidity, so that we may hold up our hearts in perseverance and say with the apostle, *But our conversation is in heaven (Phil. 3:20).*

What of the lions and boars and other sensate animals? And what of the vine clinging to the earth or the elm reaching toward the sky, that edify us in their turn? There are many useful examples available to men. Read what is said in the appropriate books, and you will find out. *Speak to the earth, and it shall answer thee,* it is written, and *ask ... the beasts, and they shall teach thee; and the birds of the air, and they shall tell thee ... and the fishes of the sea shall tell (Job 12:7–8).* The meaning of this passage is indeed useful, and it is clear to

some who know it. For there is one Creator and Restorer. He has seen fit to choose man before all the other beings to be in charge of them, according to a certain poet. As he says in his verses:

A virgin, he created the earth; a virgin, he
    created a virgin man,
And he was later made man of another virgin.
Alas, oh grief! The virgin man was corrupted
Oh grief, alas!—the virgin woman was
    corrupted,
Yielding, both of them, to the serpent.[5]

Likewise the same poet:

On that account he will leave his father and
    mother,
And will cleave to his wife.
The two will be one flesh,
Commanding all that is subject to them,
Raising their estate by the use of reason.

And again:

He who gave to man all the things
That heaven and earth and sea generate
In sky and stream and field
Whatever the eye can see or hand feel
This he set under their sway, and they under
    his. (*Prudentius, Cathemerinon 3:36–40*)

The meaning of this, my son William, is that the Highest, the omnipotent one, saw fit that man be fashioned out of the mud of the earth to replenish the number of his angels and to be joined to their high rank. Granting to man the use of all things, God chose him to enjoy the great glory of eternity in his Lord's company. For man God willed that he be born, suffer, rise again, ascend to heaven, so that according to the measure of their goodness he might join great and lesser men to himself and bring them to his heavenly kingdom.

What more could I or might I say to you by way of example of those who are of differing status—subjects or equals or even those of low estate—but joined together by love? With God's help, you know this already, and you will always be able

---

5   Presumably an unknown Carolingian poet. Only the final verse quoted here is by Prudentius.

to learn more concerning the standard of him who made all life. Great and greatly to be praised (*Augustine, Confessions 1.1; compare Ps. 144:3*), granting his bounty to the mighty and the small, may he cause you and all those mentioned above, as well as those who like them adhere to Christ, to be joined to him. And then may you come to that Lord who holds the mighty in his embrace and gathers in the small, praising them in saying, *Suffer the little children to come unto me ... for of such is the kingdom of* heaven (*Mark 10:14*). And may this happen with the help and grace of him who reigns without end in heaven. Amen.

11. On respect for priests.

Priests are to be revered, my son, because they have been chosen for God's ministry and because, in holding sacred orders, they intercede for our sins. So fear God and honor his priests with all your soul. Love them and revere them. It is they who bless the chrism and the oil. It is they who baptize the people in the faith of Holy Trinity, uniting them with the holy church of God. It is they who consecrate the bread and the wine in the likeness of the body and blood of our Lord Jesus Christ, preparing the table and giving us communion *unto remission of sins (Matt. 26:28)* and for the health of the body.

They are called sacerdotes, "priests," in order to sanctify or consecrate them after the example of him who said, Be holy because I am holy (*Lev. 11:44*). And again, *Follow peace with all men, and holiness: without which ... (Heb. 12:14)* and so forth. They are called priests, for the Prophet says, *You shall be called the priests of the Lord* our God (*Isa. 61:6*). They will wear down the Gentiles' strength, and *they shall eat the sins of my people (Hosea 4:8)*. They are the shepherds who do not fail to feed the flock of the Lord through words and examples and who invite the people to the kingdom of God so that they do not hesitate to enter, but say with the Psalmist: *Come let us adore and fall down: and weep before the Lord that made us. For he is the Lord our God: and we are the people* and the sheep *of his pasture (Ps. 94:6–7)*.

Priests are also called *presbyteri* for the reason that they are ready and prepared for the work of God; for in this word we use *prae* for *ante*, "before," as the Psalmist says: I have seen the Lord before (*compare Ps. 15:8*), that is through the contemplation of the mind I have seen him in advance. We mean something similar when we say "precursor," that is, one who goes before and precedes, or takes his place before. Thus it is the priests among us who—on account of their worthy merits—approach the altar, warning us to have a ready heart and that *our conversation is in heaven (Phil. 3:20)*. They are the path through the example of whose preaching we travel confidently toward our heavenly fatherland through the practice of good works.

Bishops are called *episcopi* and "overseers" because they admonish us always to be alert in our direction and goal. For *epi* in Greek is *super*, "over," in Latin. *Scopon* in Greek, in the same fashion, is *intuitio* or *destinatio*, "sight" or "objective," in Latin. And so it is the responsibility of bishops to reveal each man to others, and our responsibility to observe and to obey those bishops. For priests are also called *pontifices* because we cross to our fatherland through them as on a *pons*, a "bridge," across a river. That is, we cross and do not tarry in the malice of the heart as in churning mud. We are corrected through penance and amends, and with God's help we touch upon no foreign shore. It is written, *they went back another way into their country (Matt, 2:12)*.

Bishops, after the model of the true and sublime Lord, are the bearers of authority above, below, within, and outside. They have authority above for the reason that they give protection by looking out afar, as they take up a point of observation at a distance. For through their learning and by the example of their chastisement, the Lord gathers us together from far-off lands. And bishops have authority below because they are the feet that bring peace, announce good tidings, preach salvation, and speak to Sion (*compare Isa. 52:7*). They have authority within because we are imbued with the example of their worth and wisdom; we are made learned and satisfied by them. And they have authority outside because through their constant prayer, staying as they do close to God, we are found worthy to be surrounded, fortified, protected, and kept safe, so that evil spirits do not seize us. Only thus we are able to direct ourselves toward him who appeared in the world and who was made our salvation and our support, so that he might recall fallen man to the heavenly fatherland.

And what may I say of those who are so worthy of reverence? My spirit shrinks from this task. It is priests who, according to the example of the holy apostles, bind and loose (*compare Matt. 18:18*) and *they eat the sins of the people (Osee 4:8)*. They are closer and nearer to God. They are the fishermen and the hunters, as the Prophet says, *Behold I will send my fishers … and they shall fish them: and … I will send my hunters, and they shall hunt them (Jer. 16:16)*. They seize the prize from the hands of others, that is from unclean spirits, and by penance they join those they have captured to the company of their heavenly fatherland. These priests fashion and assemble the holy altar to stand in its proper place. For Scripture says: and the priests and Levites brought in the altar of the Lord into its place, *into the holy of holies under the wings of the cherubim (3 Kings 8:6)*. For such are the properties of priests' titles. Although the names applied to them vary according to their rank and activity, still they are properly called priests or keepers of vessels, that is, of the souls that belong to God. For what better can we call the ranks of the priesthood than the company to be joined with the ranks of the angels and of the citizens of heaven? For they are called angels, as the prophet Zacharias says, *the lips of the priest … keep knowledge, and* the people *seek the law at his mouth: because he is the angel of the Lord,* and not just an angel but the angel *of hosts (Mal. 2:7)*.

What can be more sublime than the angels and archangels? Because of their merits they are so agile as to reach the sacred windows in their flight (*compare Isa. 60:8*) as do the watchful doves. Glorying in their worthy virtues, deservedly—in a fashion that is clear to understand—they are called the friends of God. Why? Because they are filled with the fervor of charity. Their living example never ceases to inform the many. As Scripture says, they are clothed in justice (*compare Ps. 131:9*), joined with the company of the saints. Joyful and holy and flourishing in Christ, they are found worthy, with the acquisition of a double treasure, to reach the sublime kingdom of heaven.

Since priests have so many and such great names and virtues that their dignity in the secular world is so brilliant, I urge you to render them, worthy as they are, as much honor as you can. As for those whose personal merit is not adequate to their sacred office—even if you realize this about them—do not hastily judge them but shrink from condemning their way of life, as many do. Think on David. When he cut the border of Saul's cloak he was sorry (*compare 1 Kings 24:5–6*). And so we should not condemn priests, my son. God knows their hearts and the hearts of all who struggle in the secular world. Their fruit and their achievement are known to be worthy from their appearance, their speech, their understanding, and their life. As it is written, *by their fruits you shall know them (Matt. 7:16)*.

What more shall I say? The Lord knows his own (*compare 2 Tim. 2:19*). Still, take as your models those priests whom you find to be the better among them, more clearheaded in word and deed. Such men, even more than others, announce to us the word of God; they are the people chosen for his holy inheritance (*compare Ps. 32:12*). Listen to what they say, consider it, accomplish it, and think back upon it often. Wherever you encounter such priests, act humbly toward them and revere them—not only them but also the angels who go before them. For as sacred Scripture says, their angels always see the face of the Father (*compare Matt. 11:10*). May you dine often, if you can, with them and with hungry pilgrims. As I have said above, do not hesitate to entrust yourself into the hands of honorable priests. Find in them, among all those loyal to you, counselors when you have need. Listen to those who you see are especially close to God. Let them give food and drink to the poor from your hand and your table, and you will receive your reward in the aftermath.

So, my son William, as I have already said, revere those worthy priests who are God's servants. They are the chosen of God, and they are his helpers and his worshipers. If their behavior is not as it should be, do not—as is written—revile them. The sacred Scripture says in part of them: *touch ye not my anointed*, that is, those touched by my chrism; *do not evil to my prophets (Ps. 104:15)*, that is, my priests. For in the house of the Lord *there are many mansions (John 14:2)*, and the stars of heaven do not gleam so brightly. For *star differeth from star in glory (1 Cor. 15:41)*, and the just are brighter than the others because of the variety of their merits. In the same way there are differences among priests. Some *instruct many* through the example of their good works, drawing laymen along with them to Christ *as stars for all eternity (compare Dan. 12:3)*, as we believe. And this is God's gift. But revere them, my son, as I have said, and if you are remiss in something, correct it. *For there is no man who sinneth not (3 Kings 8:46)* even if his life is as short as a single day *(compare Job 14:5)*. But there is only one creator, shaper, ruler, and governor. On account of God and as his gift, the Lord's words come forth from the priest, for he grants this to us not according to our sins but according to his ancient mercy. In offering us this release, the Lord is called good, gentle, and merciful; he is, he has been, he will always be. May you know that it is he in whom, always and everywhere, true and learned priests find their understanding.

Offer them your true confession as best you know how—in privacy, with sighing and with tears. As the learned authors say, true confession liberates the soul from death *(compare Isidore, Synonyma 1.53, PL 83:839)* and prevents it from going to hell. Do not hesitate, I urge you, to entrust your mind and body to the hands of priests. When you are busy or at rest, or whatever you do or is done to you, always ask and pray that they deign to pray for you, interceding with that God who chose them as his people's intercessors in this world. Then you may deserve to be found worthy, as you devote half your days to penance *(compare Ps. 54:24)* through true amends and worthy reparation, to be granted what he has promised to his saints.

May that true priest who is pontifex for eternity *(compare Heb. 5:6)* bring you to true and worthy progress as you study and struggle in earthly service and as you follow the good examples of the ministers of his holy church. Through the help and grace of that God who reigns through all time, amen.

21. CLUNIAC CHARTERS

THE MONASTERY OF CLUNY received gifts of land, churches, and monasteries throughout the tenth, eleventh, and twelfth centuries. These and other property transactions were preserved in written form, i.e. in charters. The charters from the tenth century that were preserved at Cluny are among the richest primary sources for that period. Although unprecedented in number, the charters of Cluny are not unlike those made for other monasteries. Except for the Foundation Charter of Cluny, the following were all drawn up for members of one family, later known as the Grossi.[1] The family relationships were as follows:

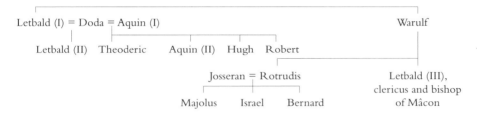

(The Majolus of this family was *not* the same person as the Majolus who was abbot of Cluny 954–994.)

The documents presented here illustrate the ways in which a pious family and a monastery related to one another through the medium of land. These charters raise numerous issues connected with the history of religion; the meaning of property; the uses of written instruments; the uses of land and dependents; the memories that people had of families, land, crimes, and acts of piety; ideas about the Church; and the gift-exchange system of the early Middle Ages.

Sources: E.F. Henderson (ed.), *Select Historical Documents of the Middle Ages* (London: George Bell, 1892), 176–89; A. Bruel, *Recueil des Chartes de l'Abbaye de Cluny* (Paris: Imprimerie Nationale, 1876–84), trans. Barbara Rosenwein.

Further Reading: Barbara H. Rosenwein, *To Be the Neighbor of Saint Peter: The Social Meaning of Cluny's Property, 909–1049* (Philadelphia: University of Pennsylvania Press, 1989).

The Foundation Charter of Cluny[2]

To all right thinkers it is clear that the providence of God has so provided for certain rich men that, by means of their transitory possessions, if they use them well, they may be able to merit everlasting rewards. As to which thing, indeed, the divine word, showing it to be possible

---

1   This family is discussed by Georges Duby, in both *La société* and in his article "Lineage, Nobility, and Knighthood" in *The Chivalrous Society*. The Grossi are also studied most recently in Constance Bouchard's *Sword, Mitre and Cloister*.

2   September 11, 910.

and altogether advising it, says: "The riches of a man are the redemption of his soul" (Prov. xiii.). I, William, count and duke by the grace of God, diligently pondering this, and desiring to provide for my own safety while I am still able, have considered it advisable—nay, most necessary, that from the temporal goods which have been conferred upon me I should give some little portion for the gain of my soul. I do this, indeed, in order that I who have thus increased in wealth may not, perchance, at the last be accused of having spent all in caring for my body, but rather may rejoice, when fate at last shall snatch all things away, in having reserved something for myself. Which end, indeed, seems attainable by no more suitable means than that, following the precept of Christ: "I will make his poor my friends" (Luke xvi. 9) and making the act not a temporary but a lasting one, I should support at my own expense a congregation of monks. And this is my trust, this my hope, indeed, that although I myself am unable to despise all things, nevertheless, by receiving despisers of the world, whom I believe to be righteous, I may receive the reward of the righteous. Therefore be it known to all who live in the unity of the faith and who await the mercy of Christ, and to those who shall succeed them and who shall continue to exist until the end of the world, that, for the love of God and of our Savior Jesus Christ, I hand over from my own rule to the holy apostles, Peter, namely, and Paul, the possessions over which I hold sway, the town of Cluny, namely, with the court and demesne manor, and the church in honor of St. Mary the mother of God and of St. Peter the prince of the apostles, together with all the things pertaining to it, the vills, indeed, the chapels, the serfs of both sexes, the vines, the fields, the meadows, the woods, the waters and their outlets, the mills, the incomes and revenues, what is cultivated and what is not, all in their entirety. Which things are situated in or about the country of Mâcon, each one surrounded by its own bounds. I give, moreover, all these things to the aforesaid apostles—I, William, and my wife Ingelberga—first for the love of God; then for the soul of my lord king Odo, of my father and my mother; for myself and my wife—for the salvation, namely, of our souls and bodies;—and not least for that of Ava who left me these things in her will; for the souls also of our brothers and sisters and nephews, and of all our relatives of both sexes; for our faithful ones who adhere to our service; for the advancement, also, and integrity of the Catholic religion. Finally, since all of us Christians are held together by one bond of love and faith, let this donation be for all,—for the orthodox, namely, of past, present or future times.

I give these things, moreover, with this understanding, that in Cluny a regular monastery shall be constructed in honor of the holy apostles Peter and Paul, and that there the monks shall congregate and live according to the rule of St. Benedict, and that they shall possess, hold, have and order these same things unto all time. In such wise, however, that the venerable house of prayer which is there shall be faithfully frequented with vows and supplications, and that celestial converse shall be sought and striven after with all desire and with the deepest ardor; and also that there shall be sedulously directed to God prayers, beseechings and exhortations as well for me as for all, according to the order in which mention has been made of them above. And let the monks themselves, together with all the aforesaid possessions, be under the power and dominion of the abbot Berno, who, as long as he shall live, shall preside over them regularly according to his knowledge and ability. But after his death, those same monks shall have power and permission to elect any one of their order whom they please as abbot and rector, following the will of God and the rule promulgated by St. Benedict,—in such wise that neither by the intervention of our own nor of any other power may they be impeded from making a purely canonical election. Every five years, moreover, the aforesaid monks shall pay to the church of the apostles at Rome ten shillings to supply them with lights; and they shall have the protection of those same apostles and the defense of the Roman pontiff; and those monks may, with their whole heart and soul, according to their ability and knowledge, build up the aforesaid place. We will, further, that in our times and in those of our successors, according as the opportunities and possibilities of that place shall allow, there shall daily, with the greatest zeal to be performed there works of mercy towards the poor, the needy, strangers, and pilgrims. It has pleased us also to insert in this document that, from this day, those same monks there congregated shall be subject neither to our yoke, nor to that of our relatives, nor to the sway of any earthly power. And, through God and all his saints, and by the awful day of judgment, I warn and abjure that no one of the secular princes, no count, no bishop whatever, not the pontiff of the aforesaid Roman see, shall invade the property of these servants of God, or alienate it, or diminish it, or exchange it, or give it as a benefice to any one, or constitute any prelate over them against their will. And that such unhallowed act may be more strictly prohibited to all rash and wicked men, I subjoin the following, giving force to the warning. I adjure ye, o holy apostles and glorious princes of the world, Peter and Paul, and thee, o supreme pontiff of the apostolic see, that, through the canonical and apostolic authority which ye have received from God, ye do remove from participation in the holy church and in eternal life, the robbers and invaders and alienators of these possessions which I do give to ye with joyful heart and ready will; and be ye protectors and defenders of the aforementioned place of Cluny and of the servants of God abiding there, and of all these possessions— on account of the clemency and mercy of the most holy Redeemer. If any one—which Heaven forbid, and which, through the mercy of the God and the protection of the apostles I do not think will happen—whether he be a neighbor or a stranger, no matter what his condition or power, should, through any kind of wild attempt to do any act of violence contrary to this deed of gift which we have ordered to be drawn up for the love of almighty God and for reverence of the chief apostles Peter and Paul; first, indeed, let him incur the wrath of almighty God, and let God remove him from the land of the living and wipe out his name from the book of life, and let his portion be with those who said to the Lord God: Depart from us; and, with Dathan and Abiron whom the earth, opening its jaws, swallowed up, and hell absorbed while still alive, let him incur everlasting damnation. And being made a companion of Judas let him be kept thrust down there with eternal tortures, and, lest it seem to human eyes that he pass through the present world with impunity, let him experience in his own body, indeed, the torments of future damnation, sharing the double disaster with Heliodorus and Antiochus, of whom one being coerced with sharp blows and scarcely escaped alive; and the

other, struck down by the divine will, his members putrefying and swarming with vermin, perished most miserably. And let him be a partaker with other sacrilegious persons who presume to plunder the treasure of the house of God; and let him, unless he come to his senses, have as enemy and as the one who will refuse him entrance into the blessed paradise, the key-bearer of the whole hierarchy of the church, and, joined with the latter, St. Paul; both of whom, if he had wished, he might have had as most holy mediators for him. But as far as the worldly law is concerned, he shall be required, the judicial power compelling him, to pay a hundred pounds of gold to those whom he has harmed; and his attempted attack, being frustrated, shall have no effect at all. But the validity of this deed of gift, endowed with all authority, shall always remain inviolate and unshaken, together with the stipulation subjoined. Done publicly in the city of Bourges. I, William, commanded this act to be made and drawn up, and confirmed it with my own hand.

(*Signed by Ingelberga and a number of bishops and nobles.*)

Charters of the Grossi Family

Charter # 802 (March 951)

To all who consider the matter reasonably, it is clear that the dispensation of God is so designed that if riches are used well, these transitory things can be transformed into eternal rewards. The Divine word showed that this was possible, saying "Wealth for a man is the redemption of his soul," and again, "Give alms and all things are yours."[3]

We, that is, I, Doda, a woman, and my son Letbald [II], carefully considering this fact, think it necessary that we share some of the things that were conferred on us, Christ granting, for the benefit of our souls. We do this to make Christ's poor our friends, in accordance with Christ's precept and so that He may receive us, in the end, in the eternal tabernacle.

Therefore, let it be known to all the faithful that we—Doda and my son Letbald—give some of our possessions, with the consent of lord Aquin [I], my husband, for love of God and his

---

3   Luke 12:33.

holy apostles, Peter and Paul,[4] to the monastery of Cluny, to support the brothers [i.e. monks] there who ceaselessly serve God and His apostles. [We give] an allod[5] that is located in the *pagus*[6] of Mâcon, called Nouville.[7] The serfs [*servi*] that live there are: Sicbradus and his wife, Robert, Eldefred and his wife and children, Roman and his wife and children, Raynard and his wife and children, Teutbert and his wife and children, Dominic and his wife and children, Nadalis with her children, John with his wife and children, Benedict with his wife and children, Maynard with his wife and children, another Benedict with his wife and children, and a woman too …[8] with her children.

And we give [land in] another *villa*[9] called Colonge and the serfs living there: Teotgrim and his wife and children, Benedict and his wife and children, Martin and his children, Adalgerius and his wife and children, [and] Sicbradus.

And [we give] a *mansus*[10] in Culey and the serfs there: Andrald and his wife and children, Eurald and his wife and children. And [we give] whatever we have at Chazeux along with the serf Landrad who lives there. We also give a little harbor on the Aar river[11] and the serfs living there: Agrimbald and Gerald with their wives and children.

In addition, we give an allod in the *pagus* of Autun, in the *villa* called Beaumont and the serfs living there, John, Symphorian, Adalard and their wives and children, in order that [the monks] may, for the love of Christ, receive our nephew, Adalgysus, into their society.[12]

[We give] all the things named above with everything that borders on them: vineyards, fields, buildings, serfs of every sex and age, ingress and egress, with all mobile and immobile property already acquired or to be acquired, wholly and completely. We give all this to God omnipotent and His apostles for the salvation of our souls and for the soul of Letbald [I], the father of my son, and for the salvation of Aquin [I], my husband, and of all our relatives and finally for all the faithful in Christ, living and dead.

Moreover, I, the aforesaid Letbald, unbuckle the belt of war, cut off the hair of my head and beard for divine love, and with the help of God prepare to receive the monastic habit in the monastery [of Cluny]. Therefore, the property that ought to come to me by paternal inheritance I now give [to Cluny] because of the generosity of my mother and brothers. [I do so] in such a way that while [my mother and brothers] live, they hold and possess it. I give a *mansus* in Fragnes, along with the serf Ermenfred and his wife and children, to [my brother] Theoderic, *clericus*,[13] and after his death let it revert to [Cluny]. And I give another *mansus* at Verzé with the serf Girbald and his wife and children to my brother Hugo. In the *pagus* of Autun I give to [my brother] Aquin [II] the allod that is called Dompierre-les-Ormes, and the serf Benedict and his wife and their son and daughter. [I give Aquin also] another allod in Vaux, and the serfs Teutbald and his wife and children and Adalgarius. [I give all this] on condition that, if these brothers of mine [Hugh and Aquin], who are laymen, die without legitimate offspring, all these properties will go to the monastery as general alms.

If anyone (which we do not believe will happen) either we ourselves (let it not happen!) or any other person, should be tempted to bring a claim in bad faith against this charter of donation, let him first incur the wrath of God, and let him suffer the fate of Datan and Abiran and of Judas, the traitor of the Lord. And unless he repents, let him have the apostles [Peter and Paul] bar him from the celestial kingdom. Moreover, in accordance with earthly law, let him be forced to pay

---

4   Cluny was dedicated to the apostles Peter and Paul.

5   An allod was land that was owned outright, in contrast to land held in fief, for example.

6   A Roman administrative subdivision.

7   Almost all the places mentioned in these charters are within about ten miles of the monastery of Cluny.

8   Effaced in the manuscript.

9   In this region a *villa* was normally not a great estate nor a village, but rather a small district in which many landowners held land.

10   A *mansus* (plural: *mansi*) was, strictly speaking, a farming unit. In the context of Doda's charter, she is probably thinking of a "demesne mansus," an outsize farming unit that included the *mansi* of dependents.

11   A tributary of the Rhin (*not* the Rhine) river.

12   Possibly Adalgysus is to become a monk, but it is more likely that he is to become a special "friend" of the monastery for whom prayers will be said.

13   *I.e.*, a priest.

ten pounds. But let this donation be made firm by us, with the stipulation added. S[ignum][14] of Doda and her son Letbald, who asked that it be done and confirmed. S. of Aquin, who consents. S. of Hugo. S. of Evrard. S. of Walo. S. of Warembert. S. of Maingaud. S. of Giboin. S. of Leotald. S. of Widald. S. of Hemard. S. of Raimbald. Dated in the month of March in the 15th year of the reign of King Louis.[15] I, brother Andreas, *levite*,[16] undersign at the place for the secretary.

Charter # 1460 (November 12, 978—November 11, 979)[17]

I, Majolus, humble abbot [of Cluny] by the will of God, and the whole congregation of brothers of the monastery of Cluny. We have decided to grant something from the property of our church to a certain cleric, named Letbald [III] for use during his lifetime, and we have done so, fulfilling his request.

The properties that we grant him are located in the *pagus* of Mâcon, in the *ager*[18] of Grevilly, in a *villa* called Colonge: *mansi*, vineyards, land, meadows, woods, water, and serfs of both sexes and whatever else we have in that place, which came to us from Raculf.[19] And we grant two *mansi* at Boye and whatever we have there. And in Massy, one *mansus*. And in "Ayrodia,"[20] in a place called Rocca, we give *mansi* with vineyards, land, woods, water, and serfs of every sex and age; and we grant all the property of Chassigny [a place near Lugny that has disappeared]: vineyards, land, meadows, woods, water, mills and serfs and slaves. And at "Bussiacus" [near St-Huruge], similarly [we grant] *mansi*, vineyards, lands, meadows, and woods. And at "Ponciacus"[21] [we give]

mansi, vineyards, land. Just as Raculf gave these things to us in his testament, so we grant them to [Letbald] on the condition that he hold them while he lives and after his death these things pass to Cluny. And let him pay 12 denars every year to mark his taking possession (*in vestitura*).

We also grant to him other property that came from lord Letbald [I], his uncle: a *mansus* at La Verzée and another at Bassy and another at Les Légères, and again another in Fragnes and another in Chazeux. And again a *mansus* in the *pagus* of Autun, at Dompierre-les-Ormes and another in Vaux and the serfs and slaves of both sexes that belong to those *mansi*. Let him hold and possess these properties as listed in this *precaria*[22] for as long as he lives. And when his mortality prevails—something no man can avoid—let this property fall to [Cluny] completely and without delay. [Meanwhile] let him pay 12 denars every year, on the feast day of apostles Peter and Paul.

I have confirmed this decree with my own hand and have ordered the brethren to corroborate it, so that it will have force throughout his lifetime. S. of lord Majolus, abbot. S. of Balduin, monk. S. of Vivian. S. of John. S. of Arnulf. S. of Costantinus. S. of Tedbald. S. of Joslen. S. of Grimald. S. of Hugo. S. of Rothard. S. of Ingelbald. S. of Achedeus. S. of Vuitbert. S. of Ingelman. Dated by the hand of Rothard, in the 25th year of the reign of King Lothar.

Charter # 1577 (November 12, 981—November 11, 982)

To this holy place, accessible to our prayers [et cetera].[23] I, Rotrudis, and [my husband] Josseran, and my sons, all of us give to God and his holy

---

14 Usually laymen did not sign charters; rather they made marks or signs (their *signum*) which was copied by the scribe in front of their name. The S refers to this sign.

15 A Carolingian king of the area that would later become France between 936–954.

16 I.e., a deacon.

17 This charter is dated in this way because the scribe dated it in the 25th year of the reign of King Lothar, the son of King Louis, whose rule began on November 12, 954.

18 The *pagus* of Mâcon was divided into subdivisions called *agri* (singular: *ager*). There were perhaps ten or more *villae* in each *ager*.

19 Raculf was probably a member of this family whose precise relationship has not been established.

20 Not identified.

21 Not identified.

22 This document is in fact an excellent example of a precarial donation. It was a conditional grant of land *by* the monastery to someone outside of the monastery for his (or her) lifetime.

23 A formula considered so commonplace that it did not need to be fully written out. Consider the formula today, "Sincerely yours," which is so familiar that the full sentence, "Be assured that I remain sincerely yours" (or something on that order), is usually left out.

apostles, Peter and Paul, and at the place Cluny, half of a church[24] that is located in the *pagus* of Mâcon, named in honor of St. Peter, with everything that belongs to it, wholly and completely, and [property in] the *villa* that is called Curtil-sous-Buffières. There [we give] a field and a meadow that go together and have the name *ad Salas*. This land borders at the east on a *via publica*[25] and a man-made wall; at the south on a meadow; at the west on a *via publica*, and similarly at the north. [I make this gift] for the salvation of the soul of my husband Josseran, and [for the soul of my son] Bernard. Done at Cluny. Witnesses: Rotrudis, Josseran, Bernard, Israel, Erleus, Hugo, Odo, Raimbert, Umbert. Ingelbald wrote this in the 28th year of the reign of King Lothar.

Charter # 1845 (990–991)

By the clemency of the Savior a remedy was conceded to the faithful: that they could realize eternal returns on His gifts if they distributed them justly. Wherefore, I, Majolus,[26] in the name of God, give to God and his holy apostles Peter and Paul and at the place Cluny some of my property which is located in the county of Lyon, in the *villa* "Mons." It consists of a *mansus indominicatus*[27] with a serf named Durannus and his wife, named Aldegard, and their children, and whatever belongs or appears to belong to this *mansus*, namely fields, vineyards, meadows, woods, pasturelands, water and water courses, that is already acquired or will be acquired, whole and complete. I make this donation first for my soul and for my burial [in Cluny's cemetery] and for the soul of my father Josseran and of my mother Rotrudis and of my brothers, and for the souls of my *parentes*[28] and for the salvation of all the departed faithful, so that all may profit in common. [I give it] on the condition that I may hold and possess it while I

live, and that every year I will pay a tax of 12 denars on the feast day of the Prince of the Apostles [i.e. St. Peter]. After my death, let [the property] go to Cluny without delay.

But if anyone wants to bring any bad-faith claim against this donation, let him first incur the wrath of the Omnipotent and all His saints; and unless he returns to his senses, let him be thrust into hell with the Devil. As in the past, let this donation remain firm and stable, with the stipulation added. Done publicly at Cluny. S. of Majolus, who asks that it be done and confirmed. S. of Bernard, S. of Israel, S. of Arleius, S. of Bernard, S. of Hubert. Aldebard, *levite* wrote this in the 4th year of the reign of Hugh [Capet].

Charter # 2508 (994–1030?)[29]

Notice of a quitclaim that took place at Cluny in the presence of lord Rainald, venerable prior at that place; and of other monks who were there, namely Walter, Aymo, Amizon, Warner, Lanfred, Locerius, Giso; and of noblemen: Witbert, Robert, Ildinus, Gislebert, Bernard, and Hugo. In the first place, let all, present and future, know that a long and very protracted quarrel between the monks of Cluny and Majolus[30] finally, by God's mercy, came to this end result: first that he [Majolus] quit his claim to the land which Oddo and Teza [Oddo's] daughter[31] destined for us and handed over by charter: the woods in *Grandi Monte* with its borders [as follows]: on the east [it borders on] its own inheritance [namely] passing between mountains and through wasteland and across the castle of Teodoric; on the south [it borders on] *terra francorum*;[32] on the west and north [it borders on] land of St. Peter. [Majolus] draws up this notice at this time so that he may reunite himself with the favor of St. Peter and the brothers, and so that he may persevere in future as a faithful servant in the

---

24 Churches could be given in whole or in part, and with or without their tithes (which often belonged not to the holder of the church but to the local bishop).
25 A dirt road. There was a very extensive network of roads in the area around Cluny, left from the Roman period.
26 *Not* the abbot.
27 This is the "demesne mansus" referred to above.
28 Meaning much more than a nuclear family, but perhaps not quite as much as a clan.
29 The scribe did not give a date. But we know that Rainald was prior at Cluny beginning in 994, and that Majolus died c. 1030; these give us, respectively, the *terminus post quem* and the *terminus ante quem* of the document.
30 The same man as the donor above.
31 These were probably relatives of Majolus.
32 Probably land of free peasants.

service of St. Peter. S. Hugo, S. Witbert, S. Robert, S. Ildinus, S. Gislebert, S. Bernard.

Charter # 2946 (?1018—1030)[33]

In the name of the incarnate Word. I, Raimodis, formerly the wife of the lord Wichard, now dead, and now joined in matrimony to lord Ansedeus, my husband; with the consent and good will [of Ansedeus], I give or rather give again some land which is called Chazeux to St. Peter and Cluny. [I give it] for the soul of my husband Wichard. This land once belonged to St. Peter and Cluny. But the abbot and monks gave it as a precarial gift to lord Letbald [III], a certain cleric who afterwards became bishop of Mâcon. Letbald, acting wrongly, alienated [the land] from St. Peter and gave it to Gauzeran to make amends for killing Gauzeran's relative, Berengar.

Therefore I give it again to St. Peter for the soul of my husband Wichard, and for Gauzeran, Wichard's father. I also give a slave named Adalgarda and her children, and [I give] the whole inheritance for the soul of my husband Wichard, and of my daughter Wiceline, and for my own soul.

If anyone wants to bring false claim against this donation, let him not prevail, but let him pay a pound of gold into the public treasury. S. of Raimodis, who asked that this charter be done and confirmed. S. of Ansedeus. S. of another Ansedeus. S. of Achard. S. of Walter. S. of Costabulus. S. of Ugo.

33 This date is suggested, on the basis of other charters elsewhere that tell us at what date Raimodis, the donor in this charter, became a widow.

22. MIRACLES OF SAINT FOY

SAINT FOY (FAITH) WAS traditionally reputed to have been a girl of twelve martyred at Agen in 303. In the ninth century, monks from the monastery of Conques stole her relics, parts of her body that were thought to be imbued with high levels of holiness, and brought them to their monastery where they became the object of a major pilgrimage from the tenth century. The body of the saint was kept in a case reliquary while the head was venerated in a golden statue that represented the young woman seated in glory.

Bernard of Angers, a student of Fulbert of Chartres (ca. 960–1028) and later director of the episcopal school in Angers, made three pilgrimages to Conques and, although at first skeptical of the cult, was entirely won over to the saint. His book of her miracles helped to spread the cult of Saint Foy across Europe and also served as a model for hagiographical dossiers for other cults.

Source: A. Bouillet (ed.), *Liber miraculorum Sancte Fidis* (Paris: Alphonse Picard, 1897).

Further Reading: Kathleen Ashley and Pamela Sheingorn, *Writing Faith: Text, Sign and History in the Miracles of Sainte Foy* (Chicago: University of Chicago Press, 1999).

I. Concerning Vuitbert whose eyes, having been gouged out, were restored by Saint Foy

In the region of Rouergue where reposes the blessed virgin Foy, in the vicus of Conques, there lived a priest named Gerald, who is still alive. He had a godson who was attached to him both by kinship and by episcopal confirmation named Vuitbert, who was his domestic servant and a competent administrator of his property. Once this Vuitbert went to Conques to celebrate the feast. When the solemn vigil was completed the next morning, that is the very day of the feast, as he was returning home, by bad fortune he encountered his lord who had been moved against him by an inexplicable evil zeal. This priest, when he saw him in the garb of a pilgrim, began with words of peace, but then was roused to aggressive abuse: "Well, Vuitbert, I see you have become a Roman." (This was the way the people of the area called pilgrims). He answered, "Yes, master, I am returning from the feast of Saint Foy." Then after speaking amicably of various things, the priest gave him permission to depart. But after he had gone on a little way, looking over his back this priest of the Jewish treason, if one can call one contaminated by such a sacrilege a priest, ordered his servant to wait a bit for him. Vuitbert

complied and suddenly the priest ordered him to be encircled and held by his men.

When he saw this, shaking with fear, he asked of what crime he was accused, but the evil man gave only this response: "You did me wrong and are planning even worse things. This is why I want for reparations nothing less than your own eyes," and would not describe any more openly the nature of the offense as if from modesty. It is unjust for a priest to make judgment based on his own jealousy since the cause of this evil had arisen from the suspicion of debauchery with women. Vuitbert, since he was ignorant of the affair, confidently offered to vindicate himself of all culpability. "My lord," he said, "if you would openly indicate all the crimes of which you suspect me, I am prepared to refute them legally. I am unable to determine by what law I ought to incur your wrath and that of your followers." The priest replied, "Enough, enough, of your superficial excuses; the sentence has been pronounced: your eyes will be torn out."

But Vuitbert, seeing the priest stand firm in his gladiatorial resolve and seeing the hour of his irreparable destruction imminent, and discerning no other opportunity of defending himself but prayer, although despairing of his safety, made this plea: "Lord, pardon me! If not for my innocence, at least for the love of God and of Saint Foy for the love of whom I am now wearing the holy habit of a pilgrim."

At these words the wild monster, not taking seriously either God or his saint, contorted by rage, vomited forth the poison of blasphemy which he had in his heart: "Neither God nor Saint Foy will save you today! You will not be able to escape my hands by invoking them. And don't expect that out of reverence for the habit of a pilgrim I would consider you worthy and inviolable since you have so evilly harmed me." This said, he ordered the man be thrown down and that his eyes be torn out. But when he could force none of his three men whose names we omit because of the horror of this barbarity, to carry out such a deed, ordering them at least to hold him down and descending from his horse, he tore out the eyes of his godson with the same fingers which were consecrated to holding the body of Christ and tossed them away.

These things did not happen without the presence of the heavenly power, which does not abandon men who call upon divine assistance and is always near those calling on it in truth and which passes judgment for those enduring injury. Those who were present immediately saw a snow white dove, or as the doer of this evil deed claimed, a magpie. This magpie or dove took up the bloody eyes of the poor unfortunate and rising high above the earth carried them toward Conques.

Nor should one wonder if God entrusted magpies with the task of protecting the eyes in this desert of a place since he had preserved the life of Elias in the desert by means of ravens. Or by chance, as the divinity wished, unknown birds may have come, which could be thought of neither as magpies nor as doves. In truth there is no ambiguity between the two types of birds since the servants saw a white dove, but the priest was unable to see anything but a pie which is distinctive by its black and white. But because God shows himself terrible to the evildoer and mild to the just, it may be that for the innocent and for those grieving with a clear conscience at the sight of such evil a white species of bird was seen while it appeared mixed to the evil doer. Nevertheless when the wicked priest saw this, he was overcome with remorse and began to cry profusely, at which one of his companions told him that it was too

late and in vain to act in such a way. After he departed, he never again celebrated the mass either because he did not dare to do so having perpetrated such a crime or, as is more likely, because he altogether neglected it because of worldly concerns.

The mother of this Gerald, profoundly upset by the great wrong done to an innocent person, received Vuitbert into her home and provided for everything he needed with great charity until he was well. For during this same time he had gone before her, not on the order of his lord but rather to show her the more severe than usual atrocity which on her word her son had caused, by which false zeal she felt wounded in her heart. Once he was well in the same year he sought his food in the art of a public entertainer and so well accepted his injury that as he was accustomed to say he did not worry about not having eyes, so much did the desire for gain and the pleasure of amusing delight him.

A year passed. The day before the vigil of Saint Foy, he had fallen to sleep when he saw before him a young girl of indescribable beauty. Her appearance was like that of an angel. Her face shone and appeared with droplets of rose and scarlet. Her expression surpassed all human beauty. Her size was as had been read that it was in the time of her passion, that of an adolescent, not yet of mature age. She wore majestic clothing entirely brocaded of gold and surrounded by a variety of subtle colors. Her wide sleeves, carefully pleated, fell to her feet. She wore on her head a diadem decorated with four gems from which radiated extraordinary light. The smallness of her body seems to me to have signified nothing more than that at the time of her passion, as we have said, one reads that she had been a youth.

The beauty of her mouth, in so far as it was given to the one to which this vision appeared to see, and her marvelous clothing, were not, I believe, without cause, for these were in themselves glorious symbols. We can see that the so to speak too large clothes represented the armor or protection of overflowing faith. The golden radiance properly represents the illumination of spiritual grace. What could the delicacy of the colors and the pleated sleeves mean unless they offered the trace of divine wisdom? On the most important part of the body, that is the head, were seen four gems, which remind us of the four principal virtues, prudence, fortitude, justice and temperance. Since Saint Foy had the knowledge and perfection of these virtues and, deeply filled with the Holy Spirit, she cultivated in the depths of her loving heart those other virtues derived from these, she was altogether pleasing to the Most-High. Moreover, not ignorant of the greatest good she offered herself to holy martyrdom as a willing and pure sacrifice to Christ. There remains the beauty of her face. We mentioned it first according to the order of our account, reserving its mystery for the end because it presents us with the culmination and the end of all life, that is, charity. It is right that charity be represented by white which surpasses all the colors by its brilliance. It is right to understand charity, the most perfect of virtues, which we place before the ruddiness which suggests martyrdom. This is not absurd because no one obtains the grace of martyrdom without the eminence of charity. Saint Foy heroically protected this virtue when for His love she faced with bravery a horrible death.

Thus the saint, leaning on the bedpost, softly touched the right cheek of the sleeper and whispered to him, "Vuitbert, are you asleep?" He answered, "Who is there?" "I am Saint Foy," she replied. "My lady, why have you come to me?" "Simply to see you." Vuitbert thanked her, and Saint Foy replied, "Do you know me?" He recognized her as if he had already seen her and answered, "Yes, I see you well, my lady, and I recognize you perfectly." "Tell me how you are and how your affairs are doing." "Very well, my Lady, and all is going very well. Everything succeeds for me by the grace of God." "What," she said, "how can all be going well when you cannot see the light of the heavens?" But he, as happens in dreams, thought that he could see although he could not. This last question reminded him of his torn out eyes. "How could I see," he asked, "when, last year, while returning from your feast, alas, I lost my eyes by the brutality of an unjust master?" The saint said, "He offended God too much and raised the anger of the Creator, he who harmed you so seriously in your body without your having merited it. But if tomorrow, on the vigil of my martyrdom, you go to Conques, and you buy two candles and place one before the altar of the Holy Savior, the other before the altar where my bodily

clay is placed, you will merit to enjoy the complete restoration of your eyes. For with a great supplication concerning the injury done you I moved the piety of the divine Judge to mercy. I bothered God by my incessant prayers until I obtained for you this cure." After these words she still insisted and urged him to go to Conques and encouraged him because he hesitated before the expense. "A thousand people, whom you have never before seen," she said, "will give to you. Besides, so that you can easily complete the present business, go quickly at dawn to the church of this parish, (this was the parish of he who had deprived him of his eyes which since ancient times was called Espeyrac) and hear Mass there, and you will receive six pence." He thanked her as a benefactor deserved and the celestial power left him.

He awoke immediately and went to the church where he told his vision. People thought that he was delirious. But not at all discouraged, he went through the crowd asking each in order to obtain twelve pence. Finally a certain Hugo, moving apart from the others, opened his purse and offered him six pence and one obole, that is, a little more than the vision had announced. This first success increased his confidence. What more can I say? He arrived at Conques, told his vision to the monks, bought the candles, presented them to the altar, and started the vigil before the golden statue of the holy martyr.

Around midnight it seemed to him that he could see as though two small glowing berries, no larger than the fruit of a laurel, came from above and buried themselves deeply into his gouged eye sockets. At the shock, his thoughts became muddled and he fell asleep. But at the hour of lauds the chanting of the psalms awoke him and he seemed to see spots of light and the silhouettes of people moving about, but he had an unbelievable headache and only half conscious he thought that he was dreaming. Gradually coming out of his stupor, he began to distinguish more clearly forms and finally himself again he recalled the vision he had seen. He raised his hands to his eyes and touched those windows of his flesh returned to the light and entirely reconstituted. He went to tell his neighbors and broke forth in praises for the immeasurable magnificence of Christ. This caused an indescribable rejoicing. Each person asked himself if he was dreaming or if he had actually seen an extraordinary miracle. The most amazed were those who had known him the longest.

Among these things something ridiculous and worthy of applause happened. Since he was a man of the purest simplicity, the fear entered his heart that perhaps that Gerald who had torn out his eyes might come to the public feast and again if he should by chance encounter him he might once more by the force of his hand remove the glory of his eyes in his wrath. Therefore amongst the confusion of the common crowd he attempted to slip away unseen. Since he was not yet certain of the gift of recovering his sight a great bewilderment took over him when by chance hurrying with the tightly packed crowd to the church he came opposite an ass which he saw as clear as day. When he had admired it, rebuking its owner with severity, he said, "You, whoever you are, you fool, move your ass so that you do not block travelers." When the former was absolutely certain of what had happened, he withdrew quickly and hurried to find a certain knight known to him whose city (castle) was situated on a high cliff whence it was protected by nature such that it appeared inaccessible to all sorts of siege machines, not further from Conques than sixteen miles. After he had fled to this castle because of the protection of its impregnable valleys, with difficulty he at last returned (to Conques) because of the many entreaties and promises of security made by the monks. When many people coming from far and near hurried there desiring to see him because of this unheard-of miracle, as they left rejoicing they gave him many gifts. And this is what Saint Foy had said to him in the vision as we said, "A thousand men whom you have never seen will give to you," naming a finite number, as is customary in the Scriptures, for an infinite one.

Next, so that he might be better known and established in the place, abbot Arlaldus of happy memory who has recently died, with the common agreement of the brothers, gave him the task of selling wax which was extremely abundant here by the hand of God. From whence, when he had gathered together with many complaints he began, as is the nature of men, to become swollen with pride, and when there appeared in his soul the desire of a woman, he immediately forgot the dignity of the miracle worked in him. But in order that this might not be borne unavenged, suddenly the revenge of the holy virgin caused the misfortune that one of the man's eyes was blinded, not totally, and when he was led to the remedy of penance, she entirely restored his vision. Later on he again and again fell into the habit of wallowing in lust, and pursued by divine vengeance, he lost the vision of one eye, and recovered it when he repented. We could write as many chapters of miracles as often as this happened, were our purpose not to avoid excess. At last, when this had happened to him without cease, he lost the use of both his eyes. For this reason, in order to do more perfect penance, after cutting his beard and receiving the tonsure, he bound himself over to the clerical order. Although this ignorant and illiterate layman did this, nevertheless it was founded in love of God and thus he merited to recover his eyesight. Thus finally after so many lashings of correction, the impatience of his lust which could be said to have heaped up filth in him, was not punished corporally any further. Now this old man, reduced by evil actions to the lowest value and poverty, now is nourished by the public alms of the brothers, and he is content with his diminished condition and for the most part the support offered him in his twilight years. He rejoices in the fame of such a restoration, altogether secure from the fickleness of frivolity.

Thus I, a witness of the truth of divine providence, have painted without any falsification, as is contained in this writing, what I received from the mouth of this Vuitbert. Nor did I add anything for a more decorative effect nor do I think that I can escape unpunished if I think to celebrate in a lying style this eternal friend and beloved of God Saint Foy, who it is known suffered the deadly sentence of martyrdom for truth which is Christ. Finally, since many whose authority is sufficiently accepted have accepted prodigious things even though they happened much before their own time only based on the testimony of those who were not present at the events and who were intent to describe them in the most elegant manner, why should I allow things which took place in my own time and which I saw with my own eyes, and concerning which the people of the Auvergne, Rouergue, the Toulousin, and other regions present indisputable testimony, which pertain to our duty of teaching, disappear from memory? Especially since this thing which we have just finished describing with such little adornment almost violently forces such an insignificant person as myself to presume to present a subject so dangerous and arduous.

In this region there are few people trained in writing, I do not know whether by sloth or ignorance (since there are many who glory in the profession of learning who never show themselves learned by their works), but these writers, ungrateful for their gifts, have either wilfully neglected these great events or been entirely ignorant of them. Therefore I declare that it is better to be accused of audacity than to incur the guilt of negligence provided that I attempt to write down in letters what by no means he can do if writing for posterity is to be served without having the reproach of doubt or the condemnation of truth. So that there should be no doubt that this above mentioned Vuitbert was not immediately cured by divine mercy there, but in truth as was said above lost his eyes, he was without health for a whole year. Moreover he showed the taking of his eyes by evil means to many of his neighbors and when this had been recognized by all He cured him at last. Thus this miracle was no less than that of the man born blind in the Gospel possibly even more astonishing. But we recall what the Truth had promised: "He who believes in me, the works which I do he too will do, and he will even do greater things because I go to the Father." …

XI Concerning those who, robbing Saint Foy, suddenly perished in the collapse of a roof

There was another miracle of divine vengeance, but in a time before my arrival, which encourages the ecclesiastics and those devotedly serving the divine cult in the house of God and which terrified those who violently rob the goods of the holy church of God or who claim the inheritance of the saints as their own right. For in this time there are many whom we can justly term antichrists, who are so blinded by ambition that they dare to invade church rights, that they not only do not revere the offices of sacred ministry but they even attack them not only with invective and with beatings, but even afflict them with death. We have seen canons, monks and abbots despoiled of their honor and deprived of their goods and destroyed by death. We have seen bishops, some condemned by proscription, others expelled from their bishopric without cause, others cut down with the sword, and even burned by Christians in terrible flames for the defense of ecclesiastical rights, if in truth one can call those people Christians, who attack the order of Christian religion, they who stand opposed to Christ and to truth in all things. Because these undergo no punishment in the present life, they are not terrified by celestial vengeance. Rather they hope that there will never be any vengeance and there are even those who do not believe in a future judgment because in doing evil they have always enjoyed success and in following their own wills they have always escaped punishment. They have never experienced any hint of vengeance and therefore what they hear about vengeance of Christ they consider to be fables. Therefore it is necessary that the divine avenger punish some of them even in this world, lest they becomes so elated by their impunity that it appear a trivial thing to irritate God. It is also needed so that prowling folly, which rejects the sweet yoke of Christ and disdains the warnings of holy correction might be so bridled by the suffering of present punishments so that it will impose a limit on its own malice lest it be more severely punished or that it might repent altogether and return to health. Then those who prepared their soul similarly for a like deed might be terrified by such an example and might repent of their intended evil, and might hurry in penance to the society of the sons of light. But having spoken about these things first, let us come now to that end toward which we hurry.

There was in the region of Cahors a noble woman, Doda, lord of Castelnau on the Dordogne. She had unjustly occupied an estate of Saint Foy which is called Alans. At the moment of her death, concerned about the salvation of her soul, she returned this property to the monastery of Conques. Hildegar, the son of her daughter, succeeded her, rich in the abundance of wealth as well as in the honor of office. He ruled from this famous castle in the territory of Albi called Penne, and he again dared to invade once more the same property and to take it from the monastery of Conques. For this reason the monks, in order to recover their property through the justice of the divine judge from the hand of this most violent robber, as was their custom, decided to go to in procession with the populace carrying as was the custom, the venerable effigy of the holy virgin. I shall explain later my feelings about this image, which might appear to be an object of superstition. There it happened that a knight of Hildegar (the grandson of Doda), whose name we forget and right now we are not able to return to Conques in order to ask for it, was reveling on Christmas, was dining in the midst of splendid knights and a succession of servants. Having consumed more wine than he was accustomed, among other things bodily abused the servants of Saint Foy, called them vile manure, protesting that he was amused to see the monks carrying their statue, a mask or sham worthy of ridicule and spittle, onto the contested estate. He would not be scared away by this nor would he defend his lord's rights any less violently and strenuously. Rather it seemed simple if he were to show how altogether vile this statue was by trampling it under foot. It would be tedious to tell how many times, three and four or more, he repeated such insults and laughter, when suddenly, the terrible sound of a divine storm was heard. It suddenly destroyed the balcony, the structure of the upper story collapsed, and all of the roof fell in. However, of the whole multitude who were present, only the blasphemer, his wife, and his five servants were killed. And so that no one might think that the house collapsed and that these men were killed by chance; the seven bodies were found thrown far out of the windows. Their remains lie in the cemetery of Saint-Antoin in the region of Albi.

Listen, robbers and devastators of Christian estates: the punishments of God are ineluctable and just are his judgments. His vengeance cedes place to no power; if it hold back for a time, it will strike with more force in the future. If you escape it in the present, a harsher punishment awaits you: that of eternal fire.

XII The processions of Saint Foy

There are many and undeniable indications that divine justice exercises a terrible judgment upon those who speak against Saint Foy. We will tell about one most extraordinary event when we speak about the image of the holy martyr. It is an ancient custom in all of Auvergne, Rodez, Toulouse and the neighboring regions that the

local saint has a statue of gold, silver, or some other metal according to their means. This statue serves as a reliquary for the head of the saint or for a part of his body. The learned might see in this a superstition and a vestige of the cult of demons, and I myself who am but an ignoramus had the same impression the first time that I saw the statue of Saint Gerard enthroned on the altar resplendent with gold and stones, with an expression so human that the simple people sense that they are being watched by the gaze of an inquisitor and they pretend that it winks at pilgrims whose prayers it answers. I admit to my shame that turning to my friend Bernerius and laughing I whispered to him in Latin, "What do you think of the idol? Wouldn't Jupiter or Mars be happy with it?" And Bernerius was inspired to add rather ingenuous pleasantries and to revile the statue. We were not wrong: when one adores the true God, it is inappropriate and absurd to make images of plaster, wood or bronze except for the image of the Lord crucified that Christian piety makes with love to celebrate the memory of the passion of the Lord and which all of the holy Church has adopted. As for saints, it is sufficient that the truthful books or frescoes on walls recall their memory. For we do not tolerate statues of saints for any reason, unless as an ancient abuse and an eradicable and inborn custom of the ignorant. In certain regions these images take on such an importance that if, for example, I had the misfortune to express my reflections on the image of St. Gerard out loud, I would have had to pay dearly for my crime.

Three days later we arrived at Saint Foy. At the moment that we entered the monastery it happened by chance that the back of the sanctuary where the holy image is kept was open. We approached but the crowd was such that we could not prostrate ourselves like so many others already lying on the floor. Unhappy, I remained standing, fixing my view on the image and murmuring this prayer, "Saint Foy, you whose relics rest in this sham, come to my assistance on the day of judgment." And this time again I looked at my companion the scholastic Bernerius from out of the corner because I found it outrageous that all of these rational beings should be praying to a mute and inanimate object. My idle talk or little understanding nevertheless did not come from a clean conscience, because I should not have disrespectfully called a sacred image, which is not consulted for divination by means of sacrifices like an idol but is rather for revering the memory of a martyr in honor of the highest God, a sham like those of Venus of Diana. Later I greatly regretted to have acted so stupidly toward the saint of God. This was because among other miracles Don Adalgerius, at that time dean and later as I have heard, abbot (of Conques and Figeac), told me a remarkable account of a cleric named Oldaric. One day when the venerable image had to be taken to another place, because he thought himself smarter than the others, his heart was so twisted that he restrained the crowd from bringing offerings and he insulted and belittled the image of the saint with various insults. The next night, a lady of imposing severity appeared to him: "You," she said, "how dare you insult my image?" Having said this, she flogged her enemy with a staff which she was seen to carry in her right hand. He survived only long enough to tell the vision in the morning.

Thus there is no place left for arguing whether the effigy of Saint Foy ought to be venerated since it is clear that he who reproached the holy martyr nevertheless retracted his reproach, nor is it a spurious idol where nefarious rites of sacrifice or of divination are conducted, but rather a pious memorial of the holy virgin before which great numbers of faithful decently and eloquently implore her efficacious intercession for their sins. And what is more wisely to be recognized, the container of the relics of the saints was made as a votive offering of the craftsman in the form of that person and is by far a more precious treasure than the ark of the covenant was of old. In the statue of Saint Foy her whole head is preserved, which is surely one of the most noble pearls of the celestial Jerusalem. Out of consideration of her merits, the divine goodness effects such prodigies that I have never heard the like concerning any other saint in our time. Therefore the image of Saint Foy is not something which ought to be destroyed or vituperated, especially since it has never led anyone to fall back into the error of paganism nor has it lessened the virtues of the saints nor caused the slightest harm to religion....

XXVIII That Saint Foy performs great miracles at synods and concerning the boy in whom a fourfold miracle was worked

Nor do I think it should be omitted that among the many bodies of saints which are carried to councils as is the custom of the region, Saint Foy, holding as it were the first place, shows forth the glory of miracles. Among the many of these there are two which we do not think tedious to recount in this book. The most reverend Arnaldus, bishop of Rodez [1025–31] convoked a synod in his dioceses to which the various bodies of the saints were carried from the various communities of monks and canons. The battle lines of the saints were arranged in tents and pavilions in the field of St. Felix which is about one mile from the town. The golden majesty of Saint Amantius, likewise confessor and bishop, the golden reliquary of Saint Saturninus, martyr, and the golden image of Mary, the mother of God, and the golden majesty of Saint Foy especially adorned the field. There was present in addition many relics of the saints whose number will not be estimated in the present writing. Here one famous and miraculous event was chosen by the All-powerful to glorify his faithful follower. A boy born blind and lame, deaf and mute, was carried by his kinsmen and placed below the image which occupied the sublime position of honor. After remaining here for about one hour, he merited divine medicine. And made entirely well by the gift of grace, he rose up speaking, hearing, seeing and happily walking about on his feet without difficulty. When the cries of the vulgar masses went up at such a wonder, the lords in attendance at the council, who were deliberating a bit removed, began to ask each other saying, "What does this cry from the people mean?" The countless Bertilda [of Rouergue, d. ca. 1015] answered them, "What else could this be, unless it is Saint Foy joking around as usual." Then, when the event had been investigated, filled with wonder and joy, everyone urged the whole assembly to the praise of God, contemplating frequently with great joy that the venerable lady had said that Saint Foy was playing.

23. ANSELM

Proslogion

ANSELM OF CANTERBURY (CA. 1033/34–1109) was born in Aosta in northern Italy but came to the Norman monastery of Bec to study with his fellow countryman Lanfranc. He succeeded his teacher in 1063 as abbot and then, in 1093, as archbishop of Canterbury. He was the outstanding teacher and writer in the tradition of what has been termed the "old scholasticism," that is, the pursuit of a rational foundation to Augustinian theology based on elementary dialectics, persuasive argument based on classical models. His *Proslogion* is his attempt to prove the existence of God using the "ontological argument," a proof based entirely on the concept of being.

Source: S.N. Deane (ed. and trans.), *Anselm: Basic Writings* (La Salle, IL: Open Court Publishing Company, 1962), 47–80.

Further Reading: Gillian Rosemary Evans, *Anselm and Talking about God* (Oxford: Clarendon Press, 1978).

Preface

After I had published, at the solicitous entreaties of certain brethren, a brief work [the *Monologium*] as an example of meditation on the grounds of faith, in the person of one who investigates, in a course of silent reasoning with himself, matters of which he is ignorant; considering that this book was knit together by the linking of many arguments, I began to ask myself whether there might be found a single argument which would require no other for its proof than itself alone; and alone would suffice to demonstrate that God truly exists, and that there is a supreme good requiring nothing else, which all other things require for their existence and well-being; and whatever we believe regarding the divine Being.

Although I often and earnestly directed my thought to this end, and at times that which I sought seemed to be just within my reach, while again it wholly evaded my mental vision, at last in despair I was about to cease, as if from the search for a thing which could not be found. But when I wished to exclude this thought altogether, lest, by busying my mind to no purpose, it should keep me from other thoughts, in which I might be successful; then more and more, though I was unwilling and shunned it, it began to force itself upon me, with a kind of importunity. So, one day, when I was exceedingly wearied with resisting its

importunity, in the very conflict of my thoughts, the proof of which I had despaired offered itself, so that I eagerly embraced the thoughts which I was strenuously repelling.

Thinking, therefore, that what I rejoiced to have found, would, if put in writing, be welcome to some readers, of this very matter, and of some others, I have written the following treatise, in the person of one who strives to lift his mind to the contemplation of God, and seeks to understand what he believes. In my judgment, neither this work nor the other, which I mentioned above, deserved to be called a book, or to bear the name of an author; and yet I thought they ought not to be sent forth without some title by which they might, in some sort, invite one into whose hands they fell to their perusal. I accordingly gave each a title, that the first might be known as, An Example of Meditation on the Grounds of Faith, and its sequel as, Faith Seeking Understanding. But after both had been copied by many under these titles, many urged me, and especially Hugo, the reverend Archbishop of Lyons, who discharges the apostolic office in Gaul, who instructed me to this effect on his apostolic authority—to prefix my name to these writings. And that this might be done more fitly, I named the first, *Monologium*, that is, A Soliloquy; but the second, *Proslogium*, that is, A Discourse.

Chapter I.

Exhortation of the mind to the contemplation of God.—It casts aside cares, and excludes all thoughts save that of God, that it may seek Him. Man was created to see God. Man by sin lost the blessedness for which he was made, and found the misery for which he was not made. He did not keep this good when he could keep it easily. Without God it is ill with us. Our labors and attempts are in vain without God. Man cannot seek God, unless God himself teaches him; nor find him, unless he reveals himself. God created man in his image, that he might be mindful of him, think of him, and love him. The believer does not seek to understand, that he may believe, but he believes that he may understand; for unless he believed he would not understand.

Up now, slight man! flee, for a little while, thy occupations; hide thyself, for a time, from thy disturbing thoughts. Cast aside, now, thy burdensome cares, and put away thy toilsome business. Yield room for some little time to God; and rest for a little time in him. Enter the inner chamber of thy mind; shut out all thoughts save that of God, and such as can aid thee in seeking him; close thy door and seek him. Speak now, my whole heart! speak now to God, saying, I seek thy face; thy face, Lord, will I seek (Psalms 27: 8). And come thou now, O Lord my God, teach my heart where and how it may seek thee, where and how it may find thee.

Lord, if thou art not here, where shall I seek thee, being absent? But if thou art everywhere, why do I not see thee present? Truly thou dwellest in unapproachable light. But where is unapproachable light, or how shall I come into it? Or who shall lead me to that light and into it, that I may see thee in it? Again, by what marks, under what form, shall I seek thee? I have never seen thee, O Lord, my God; I do not know thy form. What, O most high Lord, shall this man do, an exile far from thee? What shall thy servant do, anxious in his love of thee, and cast out afar from thy face? He pants to see thee, and thy face is too far from him. He longs to come to thee, and thy

dwelling-place is inaccessible. He is eager to find thee, and knows not thy place. He desires to seek thee, and does not know thy face. Lord, thou art my God, and thou art my Lord, and never have I seen thee. It is thou that hast made me, and hast made me anew, and hast bestowed upon me all the blessings I enjoy; and not yet do I know thee. Finally, I was created to see thee, and not yet have I done that for which I was made.

O wretched lot of man, when he hath lost that for which he was made! O hard and terrible fate! Alas, what has he lost, and what has he found? What has departed, and what remains? He has lost the blessedness for which he was made, and has found the misery for which he was not made. That has departed without which nothing is happy, and that remains which, in itself, is only miserable. Man once did eat the bread of angels, for which he hungers now; he eateth now the bread of sorrows, of which he knew not then. Alas! for the mourning of all mankind, for the universal lamentation of the sons of Hades! He choked with satiety, we sigh with hunger. He bounded, we beg. He possessed in happiness, and miserably forsook his possession; we suffer want in unhappiness, and feel a miserable longing, and alas! we remain empty.

Why did he not keep up for us, when he could so easily, that whose lack we feel so heavily? Why did he shut us away from the light, and cover us over with darkness? With what purpose did he rob us of life, and inflict death upon us? Wretches that we are, whence have we been driven out; whither are we driven on? Whence hurled? Whither consigned to ruin? From a native country into exile, from the vision of God into our present blindness, from the joy of immortality into the bitterness and horror of death. Miserable exchange of how great a good, for how great an evil! Heavy loss, heavy grief, heavy all our fate!

But alas! wretched that I am, one of the sons of Eve, far removed from God! What have I undertaken? What have I accomplished? Whither was I striving? How far have I come? To what did I aspire? Amid what thoughts am I sighing? I sought blessings, and lo! confusion. I strove towards God, and I stumbled on myself. I sought calm in privacy, and I found tribulation and grief, in my inmost thoughts. I wished to smile in the joy of my mind, and I am compelled to frown by the sorrow of my heart. Gladness was hoped for, and lo! a source of frequent sighs!

And thou too, O Lord, how long? How long, O Lord, dost thou forget us; how long dost thou turn thy face from us? When wilt thou look upon us, and hear us? When wilt thou enlighten our eyes, and show us thy face? When wilt thou restore thyself to us? Look upon us, Lord; hear us, enlighten us, reveal thyself to us. Restore thyself to us, that it may be well for us,—thyself, without whom it is so ill with us. Pity our toilings and strivings toward thee, since we can do nothing without thee. Thou dost invite us; do thou help us. I beseech thee, O Lord, that I may not lose hope in sighs, but may breathe anew in hope. Lord, my heart is made bitter by its desolation; sweeten thou it, I beseech thee, with thy consolation. Lord, in hunger I began to seek thee; I beseech thee that I may not cease to hunger for thee. In hunger I have come to thee; let me not go unfed. I have come in poverty to the Rich, in misery to the Compassionate; let me not return empty and despised. And if, before I eat, I sigh, grant, even after sighs, that which I may eat. Lord, I am bowed down and can only look downward; raise me up that I may look upward. My iniquities have gone over my head; they overwhelm me; and, like a heavy load, they weigh me down. Free me from them; unburden me, that the pit of iniquities may not close over me.

Be it mine to look up to thy light, even from afar, even from the depths. Teach me to seek thee, and reveal thyself to me, when I seek thee, for I cannot seek thee, except thou teach me, nor find thee, except thou reveal thyself. Let me seek thee in longing, let me long for thee in seeking; let me find thee in love, and love thee in finding. Lord, I acknowledge and I thank thee that thou hast created me in this thine image, in order that I may be mindful of thee, may conceive of thee, and love thee; but that image has been so consumed and wasted away by vices, and obscured by the smoke of wrong-doing, that it cannot achieve that for which it was made, except thou renew it, and create it anew. I do not endeavor, O Lord, to penetrate thy sublimity, for in no wise do I compare my understanding with that; but I long to understand in some degree thy truth, which my heart believes and loves. For I do not seek to understand that I may believe, but I believe in order to understand. For this also I believe,—that unless I believed, I should not understand.

Chapter II.

Truly there is a God, although the fool hath said in his heart, There is no God.

And so, Lord, do thou, who dost give understanding to faith, give me, so far as thou knowest it to be profitable, to understand that thou art as we believe; and that thou art that which we believe. And, indeed we believe that thou art a being than which nothing greater can be conceived. Or is there no such nature, since the fool hath said in his heart, there is no God? (Psalms xiv. 1). But, at any rate, this very fool, when he hears of this being of which I speak—a being than which nothing greater can be conceived—understands what he hears, and what he understands is in his understanding; although he does not understand it to exist.

For, it is one thing for an object to be in the understanding, and another to understand that the object exists. When a painter first conceives of what he will afterwards perform, he has it in his understanding, but he does not yet understand it to be, because he has not yet performed it. But after he has made the painting, he both has it in his understanding, and he understands that it exists, because he has made it.

Hence, even the fool is convinced that something exists in the understanding, at least, than which nothing greater can be conceived. For, when he hears of this, he understands it. And whatever is understood, exists in the understanding. And assuredly that, than which nothing greater can be conceived, cannot exist in the understanding alone. For, suppose it exists in the understanding alone: then it can be conceived to exist in reality; which is greater.

Therefore, if that, than which nothing greater can be conceived, exists in the understanding alone, the very being, than which nothing greater can be conceived, is one, than which a greater can be conceived. But obviously this is impossible. Hence, there is no doubt that there exists a being, than which nothing greater can be conceived, and it exists both in the understanding and in reality.

Chapter III.

God cannot be conceived not to exist.—God is that, than which nothing greater can be conceived.—That which can be conceived not to exist is not God.

And it assuredly exists so truly, that it cannot be conceived not to exist. For, it is possible to conceive of a being which cannot be conceived not to exist; and this is greater than one which can be conceived not to exist. Hence, if that, than which nothing greater can be conceived, can be conceived not to exist, it is not that, than which nothing greater can be conceived. But this is an irreconcilable contradiction. There is, then, so truly a being than which nothing greater can be conceived to exist, that it cannot even be conceived not to exist; and this being thou art, O Lord, our God.

So truly, therefore, dost thou exist, O Lord, my God, that thou canst not be conceived not to exist; and rightly. For, if a mind could conceive of a being better than thee, the creature would rise above the Creator; and this is most absurd. And, indeed, whatever else there is, except thee alone, can be conceived not to exist. To thee alone, therefore, it belongs to exist more truly than all other beings, and hence in a higher degree than all others. For, whatever else exists does not exist so truly, and hence in a less degree it belongs to it to exist. Why, then, has the fool said in his heart, there is no God (Psalms xiv. 1), since it is so evident, to a rational mind, that thou dost exist in the highest degree of all? Why, except that he is dull and a fool?

Chapter IV.

How the fool has said in his heart what cannot be conceived.—A thing may be conceived in two ways: (1) when the word signifying it is conceived; (2) when the thing itself is understood. As far as the word goes, God can be conceived not to exist; in reality he cannot.

But how has the fool said in his heart what he could not conceive; or how is it that he could not conceive what he said in his heart? since it is the same to say in the heart, and to conceive.

But, if really, nay, since really, he both conceived, because he said in his heart; and did not say in his heart, because he could not conceive; there is more than one way in which a thing is said in the heart or conceived. For, in one sense, an object is conceived, when the word signifying is conceived; and in another, when the very entity, which the object is, is understood.

In the former sense, then, God can be conceived not to exist; but in the latter, not at all. For no one who understands what fire and water are can conceive fire to be water, in accordance with the nature of the facts themselves, although this is possible according to the words. So, then, no one who understands what God is can conceive that God does not exist; although he says these words in his heart, either without any, or with some foreign, signification. For, God is that than which a greater cannot be conceived. And he who thoroughly understands this, assuredly understands that this being so truly exists, that not even in concept can it be non-existent. Therefore, he who understands that God so exists, cannot conceive that he does not exist.

I thank thee, gracious Lord, I thank thee; because what I formerly believed by thy bounty, I now so understand by thine illumination, that if I were unwilling to believe that thou dost exist, I should not be able not to understand this to be true.

Chapter V.

God is whatever it is better to be than not to be; and he, as the only self-existent being, creates all things from nothing.

What art thou, then, Lord God, than whom nothing greater can be conceived? But what art thou, except that which, as the highest of all beings, alone exists through itself, and creates all other things from nothing? For, whatever is not this is less than a thing which can be conceived of. But this cannot be conceived of thee. What good, therefore, does the supreme Good lack, through which every good is? Therefore, thou art just, truthful, blessed, and whatever it is better to be than not to be. For it is better to be just than not just; better to be blessed than not blessed.

Chapter VI.

How God is sensible (*sensibilis*) although he is not a body.—God is sensible, omnipotent, compassionate, passionless; for it is better to be these than not be. He who in any way knows, is not improperly said in some sort to feel.

But, although it is better for thee to be sensible, omnipotent, compassionate, passionless, than not to be these things; how art thou sensible, if thou art not a body; or omnipotent, if thou hast not all powers; or at once compassionate and passionless? For, if only corporeal things are sensible, since the senses encompass a body and are in a body, how art thou sensible, although thou art not a body, but a supreme Spirit, who is superior to body? But, if feeling is only cognition, or for the sake of cognition,—for he who feels obtains knowledge in accordance with the proper functions of his senses; as through sight, of colors; through taste, of flavors,—whatever in any way cognizes is not inappropriately said, in some sort, to feel.

Therefore, O Lord, although though art not a body, yet thou art truly sensible in the highest degree in respect of this, that thou dost cognize all things in the highest degree; and not as an animal cognizes, through a corporeal sense.

Chapter VII.

How he is omnipotent, although there are many things of which he is not capable.—To be capable of being corrupted, or of lying, is not power, but impotence. God can do nothing by virtue of impotence, and nothing has power against him.

But how art thou omnipotent, if thou art not capable of all things? Or, if thou canst not be corrupted, and canst not lie, nor make what is true, false—as, for example, if thou shouldest make what has been done not to have been done, and the like—how art thou capable of all things? Or

else to be capable of these things is not power, but impotence. For, he who is capable of these things is capable of what is not for his good, and of what he ought not to do; and the more capable of them he is, the more power have adversity and perversity against him; and the less has he himself against these.

He, then, who is thus capable is so not by power, but by impotence. For, he is said to be able because he is able of himself, but because his impotence gives something else power over him. Or, by a figure of speech, just as many words are improperly applied, as when we use "to be" for "not to be," and "to do" for what is really "not to do," or "to do nothing." For, often we say to a man who denies the existence of something: "It is as you say it to be," though it might seem more proper to say, "It is not, as you say it is not." In the same way, we say: "This man sits just as that man does," or, "This man rests just as that man does"; although to sit is not to do anything, and to rest is to do nothing.

So, then, when one is said to have the power of doing or experiencing what is not for his good, or what he ought not to do, impotence is understood in the word power. For, the more he possesses this power, the more powerful are adversity and perversity against him, and the more powerless is he against them.

Therefore, O Lord, our God, the more truly art thou omnipotent, since thou art capable of nothing through impotence, and nothing has power against thee.

Chapter VIII.

How he is compassionate and passionless. God is compassionate, in terms of our experience, because we experience the effect of compassion. God is not compassionate, in terms of his own being, because he does not experience the feeling (*affectus*) of compassion.

But how art thou compassionate, and, at the same time, passionless? For, if thou art passionless, thou dost not feel sympathy; and if thou dost not feel sympathy, thy heart is not wretched from sympathy for the wretched; but this it is to be compassionate. But if thou art not compassionate, whence cometh so great consolation to the wretched? How, then, art thou compassionate and not compassionate, O Lord, unless because thou art compassionate in terms of our own experience, and not compassionate in terms of thy being.

Truly, thou art so in terms of our experience, but thou art not so in terms of thine own. For, when thou beholdest us in our wretchedness, we experience the effect of compassion, but thou dost not experience the feeling. Therefore, thou art both compassionate, because thou dost save the wretched, and spare those who sin against thee; and not compassionate, because thou art affected by no sympathy for wretchedness.

Chapter IX.

How the all-just and supremely just God spares the wicked, and justly pities the wicked. He is better who is good to the righteous and the wicked than he who is good to the righteous alone. Although God is supremely just, the source of his compassion is hidden. God is supremely compassionate, because he is supremely just. He saveth the just, because justice goes with them; he frees sinners by the authority of justice. God spares the wicked out of justice; for it is just that God, than whom none is better or more powerful, should be good even to the wicked, and should make the wicked good. If God ought not to pity, he pities unjustly. But this it is impious to suppose. Therefore, God justly pities.

But how dost thou spare the wicked, if thou art all just and supremely just? For how, being all just and supremely just, dost thou augur that it is not just? Or, what justice is that to give him who merits eternal death everlasting life? How, then, gracious Lord, good to the righteous and the wicked, canst thou save the wicked, if this is not just, and thou dost not aught that is not just? Or, since thy goodness is incomprehensible, is this hidden in the unapproachable light wherein thou dwellest? Truly, in the deepest and most secret parts of thy goodness is hidden the fountain whence the stream of thy compassion flows.

For thou art all just and supremely just, yet thou art kind even to the wicked, even because thou art all supremely good. For thou wouldst be less good if thou wert not kind to any wicked being. For, he who is good, both to the righteous and the wicked, is better than he who is good to be good alone; and he who is good to the wicked, both by punishing and sparing them, is better than he who is good by punishing them alone. Therefore, thou art compassionate, because thou art all supremely good. And, although it appears why thou dost reward the good with goods and the evil with evils; yet this, at least, is most wonderful, why thou, the all and supremely just, who lackest nothing, bestoweth goods on the wicked and on those who are guilty toward thee.

The depth of thy goodness, O God! The source of thy compassion appears, and yet is not clearly seen! We see whence the river flows, but the spring whence it arises is not seen. For, it is from the abundance of thy goodness that thou art good to those who sin against thee; and in the depth of thy goodness is hidden the reason for this kindness.

For, although thou dost reward the good with goods and the evil with evils, out of goodness, yet this the concept of justice seems to demand. But, when thou dost bestow goods on the evil, and it is known that the supremely Good hath willed to do this, we wonder why the supremely Just has been able to will this.

O compassion, from what abundant sweetness and what sweet abundance dost thou well forth to us! O boundless goodness of God, how passionately should sinners love thee! For thou savest the just, because justice goeth with them; but sinners thou dost free by the authority of justice. Those by the help of their deserts; these, although their deserts oppose. Those by acknowledging the goods thou hast granted; these by pardoning the evils thou hatest. O boundless goodness, which dost so exceed all understanding, let that compassion come upon me, which proceeds from thy so great abundance! Let it flow upon me, for it wells forth from thee. Spare, in mercy; avenge not, in justice.

For, though it is hard to understand how thy compassion is not inconsistent with thy justice; yet we must believe that it does not oppose justice at all, because it flows from goodness, which is no goodness without justice; nay, that it is in true harmony with justice. For, if thou art compassionate only because thou art supremely good, and supremely good only because thou art supremely just, truly thou art compassionate even because thou art supremely just. Help me, just and compassionate God, whose light I seek; help me to understand what I say.

Truly, then, thou art compassionate even because thou art just. Is, then, thy compassion born of thy justice? And dost thou spare the wicked, therefore, out of justice? If this is true, my Lord, if this is true, teach me how it is. Is it because it is just, that thou shouldst be so good that thou canst not be conceived better; and that thou shouldst work so powerfully that thou canst not be conceived more powerful? For what can be more just than this? Assuredly it could not be that thou shouldst be good only by requiting (*retribuendo*) and not by sparing, and that thou shouldst make good only those who are not good, and not the wicked also. In this way, therefore, it is just that thou shouldst spare the wicked, and make good souls of evil.

Finally, what is not done justly ought not to be done; and what ought not to be done is done unjustly. If, then, thou dost not justly pity the wicked, thou oughtest not to pity them. And, if thou oughtest not to pity them, thou pityest them unjustly. And if it is impious to suppose this, it is right to believe that thou justly pityest the wicked.

Chapter X.

How he justly punishes and justly spares the wicked.—God, in sparing the wicked, is just, according to his own nature, because he does what is consistent with his goodness; but he is not just, according to our nature, because he does not inflict the punishment deserved.

But it is also just that thou shouldst punish the wicked. For what is more just than that the good should receive goods, and the evil, evils? How, then, is it just that thou shouldst punish the wicked, and, at the same time, spare the wicked? Or, in one way, dost thou justly punish, and in another, justly spare them? For, when thou punishest the wicked, it is just, because it is consistent with their deserts; and when, on the other hand, thou sparest the wicked, it is just, not because it is compatible with their deserts, but because it is compatible with thy goodness.

For, in sparing the wicked, thou art just, according to thy nature, but not according to ours, as thou art compassionate, according to our nature, and not according to thine; seeing that, as in saving us, whom it would be just for thee to destroy, thou art compassionate, not because thou feelest an affection (*affectum*), but because we feel the effect (*effectum*); so thou art just, not because thou requitest us as we deserve, but because thou dost that which becomes thee as the supremely good Being. In this way, therefore, without contradiction thou dost justly punish and justly spare.

Chapter XI.

How all the ways of God are compassion and truth; and yet God is just in all his ways. We cannot comprehend why, of the wicked, he saves these rather than those, through his supreme goodness; and condemns those rather than these through his supreme justice.

But, is there any reason why it is not also just, according to thy nature, O Lord, that thou shouldst punish the wicked? Surely it is just that thou shouldst be so just that thou canst not be conceived more just; and this thou wouldst in no wise be if thou didst only render goods to the good, and not evils to the evil. For, he who requiteth both good and evil according to their deserts is more just than he who so requites the good alone. It is, therefore, just, according to thy nature, O just and gracious God, both when thou dost punish and when thou sparest.

Truly, then, all the paths of the Lord are mercy and truth (Psalms xxv. 10); and yet the Lord is righteous in all his ways (Psalms cxlv. 17). And assuredly without inconsistency: For, it is not just that those whom thou dost will to punish should be saved, and that those whom thou dost will to spare should be condemned. For that alone is just which thou dost will; and that alone unjust which thou dost not will. So, then, thy compassion is born of thy justice.

For it is just that thou shouldst be so good that thou art good in sparing also; and this may be the reason why the supremely Just can will goods for the evil. But if it can be comprehended in any way why thou canst will to save the wicked, yet by no consideration can we comprehend why, of those who are alike wicked, thou savest some rather than others, through supreme goodness; and why thou dost condemn the latter rather than the former, through supreme justice.

So, then, thou art truly sensible (*sensibilis*), omnipotent, compassionate, and passionless, as thou art living, wise, good, blessed, eternal: and whatever it is better to be than not to be.

Chapter XII.

God is the very life whereby he lives; and so of other like attributes.

But undoubtedly, whatever thou art, thou art through nothing else than thyself. Therefore, thou art the very life whereby thou livest; and the wisdom wherewith thou art wise; and the very goodness whereby thou art good to the righteous and the wicked; and so of other like attributes.

Chapter XIII.

How he alone is uncircumscribed and eternal, although other spirits are uncircumscribed and eternal.—No place and time contain God. But he is himself everywhere and always. He alone not only does not cease to be, but also does not begin to be.

But everything that is in any way bounded by place or time is less than that which no law of place or time limits. Since, then, nothing is greater than thou, no place or time contains thee; but thou art everywhere and always. And since this can be said of thee alone, thou alone art uncircumscribed and eternal. How is it, then, that other spirits also are said to be uncircumscribed and eternal?

Assuredly thou art alone eternal; for thou alone among all beings not only dost not cease to be, but also dost not begin to be.

But how art thou alone uncircumscribed? Is it that a created spirit, when compared with thee, is circumscribed, but when compared with matter, uncircumscribed? For altogether uncircumscribed is that which, when it is wholly in one place, cannot at the same time be in another. And this is seen to be true of corporeal things alone. But uncircumscribed is that which is, as a whole, at the same time everywhere. And this is understood to be true of thee alone. But circumscribed, and, at the same time, uncircumscribed is that which, when it is anywhere as a whole, can at the same time be somewhere else as a whole, and yet not everywhere. And this is recognized as true of created spirits. For, if the soul were not as a whole in the separate members of the body, it would not feel as a whole in the separate members.

Therefore, thou, Lord, art peculiarly uncircumscribed and eternal; and yet other spirits also are uncircumscribed and eternal.

Chapter XIV.

How and why God is seen and yet not seen by those who seek him.

Hast thou found what thou didst seek, my soul? Thou didst seek God. Thou hast found him to be a being which is the highest of all beings, a being than which nothing better can be conceived; that this being is life itself, light, wisdom, goodness, eternal blessedness and blessed eternity; and that it is everywhere and always.

For, if thou hast not found thy God, how is he this being which thou hast found, and which thou hast conceived him to be, with so certain truth and so true certainty? But, if thou hast found him, why is it that thou dost not feel thou hast found him? Why, O Lord, our God, does not my soul feel thee, if it hath found thee? Or, has it not found him whom it found to be light and truth? Or, could it understand anything at all of thee, except through thy light and thy truth?

Hence, if it has seen light and truth, it has seen thee; if it has not seen thee, it has not seen light and truth. Or, is what it has seen both light and truth; and still it has not yet seen thee, because it has seen thee only in part, but has not seen thee as thou art? Lord my God, my creator and renewer, speak to the desire of my soul, what thou art other than it hath seen, that it may clearly see what it desires. It strains to see thee more; and sees nothing beyond this which it hath seen, except darkness. Nay, it does not see that it cannot see farther, because of its own darkness.

Why is this, Lord, why is this? Is the eye of the soul darkened by its infirmity, or dazzled by thy glory? Surely it is both darkened in itself, and dazzled by thee. Doubtless it is both obscured by its own insignificance, and overwhelmed by thy infinity. Truly, it is both contracted by its own narrowness and overcome by thy greatness.

For how great is that light from which shines every truth that gives light to the rational mind? How great is that truth in which is everything that is true, and outside which is only nothingness and the false? How boundless is the truth which sees at one glance whatsoever has been made, and by whom, and through whom, and how it has been made from nothing? What purity, what certainty, what splendor where it is? Assuredly more than a creature can conceive.

Chapter XV.

He is greater than can be conceived.

Therefore, O Lord, thou art not only that than which a greater cannot be conceived, but thou art a being greater than can be conceived. For, since it can be conceived that there is such a being, if thou art not this very being, a greater than thou can be conceived. But this is impossible.

Chapter XVI.

Thus is the unapproachable light wherein he dwells.

Truly, O Lord, this is the unapproachable light in which thou dwellest; for truly there is nothing else which can penetrate this light, that it may see thee there. Truly, I see it not, because it is too bright for me. And yet, whatsoever I see, I see through it, as the weak eye sees what it sees through the light of the sun, which in the sun itself it cannot look upon. My understanding cannot reach that light, for it shines too bright. It does not comprehend it, nor does the eye of the soul endure to gaze upon it long. It is dazzled by the brightness, it is overcome by the greatness, it is overwhelmed by the infinity, it is dazed by the largeness, of the light.

O supreme and unapproachable light! O whole and blessed truth, how far art thou from me, who am so near to thee! How far removed art thou from my vision, though I am so near to thine! Everywhere thou art wholly present, and I see thee not. In thee I move, and in thee I have my

being; and I cannot come to thee. Thou art within me, and about me, and I feel thee not.

Chapter XVII.

In God is harmony, fragrance, sweetness, pleasantness to the touch, beauty, after his ineffable manner.

Still thou art hidden, O Lord, from my soul in thy light and thy blessedness; and therefore my soul still walks in its darkness and wretchedness. For it looks, and does not see thy beauty. It hearkens, and does not hear thy harmony. It smells, and does not perceive thy fragrance. It tastes, and does not recognize thy sweetness. It touches, and does not feel thy pleasantness. For thou hast these attributes in thyself, Lord God, after thine ineffable manner, who hast given them to objects created by thee, after their sensible manner; but the sinful senses of my soul have grown rigid and dull, and have been obstructed by their long listlessness.

Chapter XVIII.

God is life, wisdom, eternity, and every true good.—Whatever is composed of parts is not wholly one; it is capable, either in fact or in concept, of dissolution. In God wisdom, eternity, etc., are not parts, but one, and the very whole which God is, or unity itself, not even in concept divisible.

And lo, again confusion; lo, again grief and mourning meet him who seeks for joy and gladness. My soul now hoped for satisfaction; and lo, again it is overwhelmed with need. I desired now to feast, and lo, I hunger more. I tried to rise to the light of God, and I have fallen back into my darkness. Nay, not only have I fallen into it, but I feel that I am enveloped in it. I fell before my mother conceived me. Truly, in darkness I was conceived, and in the cover of darkness I was born. Truly, in him we all fell, in whom we all sinned. In him we all lost, who kept easily, and wickedly lost to himself and to us that which when we wish to seek it, we do not find; when we find, it is not that which we seek.

Do thou help me for thy goodness' sake! Lord, I sought thy face; thy face, Lord, will I seek; hide not thy face far from me (Psalms xxvii. 8). Free me from myself toward thee. Cleanse, heal, sharpen, enlighten the eye of my mind, that it may behold thee. Let my soul recover its strength, and with all its understanding let it strive toward thee, O Lord. What art thou, Lord, what art thou? What shall my heart conceive thee to be?

Assuredly thou art life, thou art wisdom, thou art truth, thou art goodness, thou art blessedness, thou art eternity, and thou art every true good. Many are these attributes: my straitened understanding cannot see so many at one view, that it may be gladdened by all at once. How, then, O Lord, art thou all these things? Are they parts of thee, or is each one of these rather the whole, which thou art? For, whatever is composed of parts is not altogether one, but is in some sort plural, and diverse from itself; and either in fact or in contempt is capable of dissolution.

But these things are alien to thee, than whom nothing better can be conceived of. Hence, there are no parts in thee, Lord, nor art thou more than one. But thou art so truly a unitary being, and so identical with thyself; rather thou art unity itself, indivisible by any conception. Therefore, life and wisdom and the rest are not parts of thee, but all are one; and each of these is the whole, which thou art, and which all the rest are.

In this way, then, it appears that thou hast no parts, and that thy eternity, which thou art, is nowhere and never a part of thee or of thy eternity. But everywhere thou art as a whole, and thy eternity exists as a whole forever.

Chapter XIX.

He does not exist in place or time, but all things exist in him.

But if through thine eternity thou hast been, and art, and wilt be; and to have been is not to be destined to be; and to be is not to have been, or to be destined to be; how does thine eternity exist as a whole forever? Or is it true that nothing of thy eternity passes away, so that it is not now; and that nothing of it is destined to be, as if it were not yet?

Thou wast not, then, yesterday, nor wilt thou be to-morrow; but yesterday and to-day and to-morrow thou art; or, rather, neither yesterday nor to-day nor to-morrow thou art; but simply, thou art, outside all time. For yesterday and to-day and to-morrow have no existence, except in time; but thou, although nothing exists without thee, nevertheless dost not exist in space or time, but all things exist in thee. For nothing contains thee, but thou containest all.

Chapter XX.

He exists before all things and transcends all things, even the eternal things.—The eternity of God is present as a whole with him; while other things have not yet that part of their eternity which is still to be, and have no longer that part which is past.

Hence, thou dost permeate and embrace all things. Thou art before all, and dost transcend all. And, of a surety, thou art before all; for before they were made, thou art. But how dost thou transcend all? In what way dost thou transcend those beings which will have no end? Is it because they cannot exist at all without thee; while thou art in no wise less, if they should return to nothingness? For so, in a certain sense, thou dost transcend them. Or, is it also because they can be conceived to have an end; but thou by no means? For so they actually have an end, in a certain sense; but thou, in no sense. And certainly, what in no sense has an end transcends what is ended in any sense. Or, in this way also dost thou transcend all things, even the eternal, because thy eternity and theirs is present as a whole with thee; while they have not yet that part of their eternity which is to come, just as they no longer have that part which is past? For so thou dost ever transcend them, since thou art ever present with thyself, and since that to which they have not yet come is ever present with thee.

Chapter XXI.

Is this the age of the age, or ages of ages?—The eternity of God contains the ages of time themselves, and can be called the age of the age or ages of ages.

Is this, then, the age of the age, or ages of ages? For, as an age of time contains all temporal things, so thy eternity contains even the ages of time themselves. And these are indeed an age, because of their indivisible unity; but ages, because of their endless immeasurability. And, although thou art so great, O Lord, that all things are full of thee, and exist in thee; yet thou art without all space, that neither midst, nor half, nor any part, is in thee.

Chapter XXII.

He alone is what he is and who he is.—All things need God for their being and their well-being.

Therefore, thou alone, O Lord, art what thou art; and thou art he who thou art. For, what is one thing in the whole and another in the parts, and in which there is any mutable element, is not altogether what it is. And what begins from non-existence, and can be conceived not to exist, and unless it subsists through something else, returns to non-existence; and what has a past existence, which is no longer, or a future existence, which is not yet,—this does not properly and absolutely exist.

But thou art what thou art, because, whatever thou art at any time, or in any way, thou art as a whole and forever. And thou art he who thou art, properly and simply; for thou hast neither a past existence nor a future, but only a present existence; nor canst thou be conceived as at any time non-existent. But thou art life, and light, and wisdom, and blessedness, and many goods of this nature. And yet thou art only one supreme good; thou art all-sufficient to thyself, and needest none; and thou art he whom all things need for their existence and well-being.

Chapter XXIII.

This good is equally Father, and Son, and Holy Spirit. And this is a single, necessary Being, which is every good, and wholly good, and the only good.—Since the Word is true, and is truth itself, there is nothing in the Father, who utters it, which is not accomplished in the Word by which he expresses himself. Neither is the love which proceeds from the Father and Son unequal to the Father or the Son, for Father and Son love themselves and one

another in the same degree in which what they are is good. Of supreme simplicity nothing can be born, and from it nothing can proceed except that which is this, of which it is born, or from which it proceeds.

This good thou art, thou, God the Father; this is thy Word, that is, thy Son. For nothing, other than what thou art, or greater or less than thou, can be in thy Word by which thou dost express thyself; for thy Word is true, as thou art faithful. And hence it is truth itself, just as thou art; no other truth than thou; and thou art of so simple a nature, that of thee nothing can be born other than what thou art. This very good is the one love common to thee and to thy Son, that is, the Holy Spirit proceeding from both. For this love is not unequal to thee or to thy Son; seeing that thou dost love thyself and him, and he, thee and himself, to the whole extent of thy being and his. Nor is there aught else proceeding from thee and from him, which is not unequal to thee and to him. Nor can anything proceed from the supreme simplicity, other than what this, from which it proceeds, is.

But what each is, separately, this is all the Trinity at once, Father, Son, and Holy Spirit; seeing that each separately is none other than the supremely simple unity, and the supremely unitary simplicity, which can neither be multiplied nor varied. Moreover, there is a single necessary Being. Now, this is that single, necessary Being, in which is every good; nay, which is every good, and a single entire good, and the only good.

Chapter XXIV.

Conjecture as to the character and the magnitude of this good.—If the created life is good, how good is the creative life!

And now, my soul, arouse and lift up all thy understanding, and conceive, so far as thou canst, of what character and how great is that good. For, if individual goods are delectable, conceive in earnestness how delectable is that good which contains the pleasantness of all goods; and not such as we have experienced in created objects, but as different as the Creator from the creature. For, if the created life is good, how good is the creative life! If the salvation given is delightful, how delightful is the salvation which has given all salvation! If wisdom in the knowledge of the created world is lovely, how lovely is the wisdom which has created all things from nothing! Finally, if there are many great delights in delectable things, what and how great is the delight in him who has made these delectable things.

Chapter XXV.

What goods, and how great, belong to those who enjoy this good.—Joy is multiplied in the blessed from the blessedness and joy of others.

Who shall enjoy this good? And what shall belong to him, and what shall not belong to him? At any rate, whatever he shall wish shall be his, and whatever he shall not wish shall not be his. For, these goods of body and soul will be such as eye hath not seen nor ear heard, neither has the heart of man conceived (Isaiah lxiv. 4; 1 Corinthians ii. 9).

Why, then, dost thou wander abroad, slight man, in thy search for the goods of thy soul and thy body? Love the one good in which are all goods, and it sufficeth. Desire the simple good which is every good, and it is enough. For, what dost thou love, my flesh? What dost thou desire, my soul? There, there is whatever ye love, whatever ye desire.

If beauty delights thee, there shall the righteous shine forth as the sun (Matthew xiii. 43). If swiftness or endurance, or freedom of body, which naught can withstand, delight thee, they shall be angels of God,—because it is sown a natural body; it is raised a spiritual body (1 Corinthians xv. 44)—in power certainly, though not in nature. If it is a long and sound life that pleases thee, there a healthful eternity is, and an eternal health. For the righteous shall live forever (Wisdom v. 15), and the salvation of the righteous is of the Lord (Psalms xxxvii. 39). If it is satisfaction of hunger, they shall be satisfied when the glory of the Lord hath appeared (Psalms xvii. 15). If it is quenching of thirst, they shall be abundantly satisfied with the fatness of thy house (Psalms xxxvi. 8). If it is melody, there the choirs of angels sing forever, before God. If it is any not impure, but pure,

pleasure, thou shalt make them drink of the river of thy pleasures, O God (Psalms xxxvi. 8).

If it is wisdom that delights thee, the very wisdom of God will reveal itself to them. If friendship, they shall love God more than themselves, and one another as themselves. And God shall love them more than they themselves; for they love him, and themselves, and one another, through him, and he, himself and them, through himself. If concord, they shall all have a single will.

If power, they shall have all power to fulfil their will, as God to fulfil his. For, as God will have power to do what he wills, through himself, so they will have power, through him, to do what they will. For, as they will not will aught else than he, he shall will whatever they will; and what he shall will cannot fail to be. If honor and riches, God shall make his good and faithful servants rulers over many things (Luke xii. 42); nay, they shall be called sons of God, and gods; and where his Son shall be, there they shall be also, heirs indeed of God, and joint-heirs with Christ (Romans viii. 17).

If true security delights thee, undoubtedly they shall be as sure that those goods, or rather that good, will never and in no wise fail them; as they shall be sure that they will not lose it of their own accord; and that God, who loves them, will not take it away from those who love him against their will; and that nothing more powerful than God will separate him from them against his will and theirs.

But what, or how great, is the joy, where such and so great is the good! Heart of man, needy heart, heart acquainted with sorrows, nay, overwhelmed with sorrows, how greatly wouldst thou rejoice, if thou didst abound in all these things! Ask thy inmost mind whether it could contain its joy over so great a blessedness of its own.

Yet assuredly, if any other whom thou didst love altogether as thyself possessed the same blessedness, thy joy would be doubled, because thou wouldst rejoice not less for him than for thyself. But, if two, or three, or many more, had the same joy, thou wouldst rejoice as much for each one as for thyself, if thou didst love each as thyself. Hence, in that perfect love of innumerable blessed angels and sainted men, where none shall love each other less than himself, every one shall rejoice for each of the others as for himself.

If, then, the heart of man will scarce contain his joy over his own so great good, how shall it contain so many and so great joys? And doubtless, seeing that every one loves another so far as he rejoices in the other's good, and as, in that perfect felicity, each one should love God beyond compare, more than himself and all the others with him; so he will rejoice beyond reckoning in the felicity of God, more than in his own and that of all the others with him.

But if they shall so love God with all their heart, and all their mind, and all their soul, that still all the heart, and all the mind, and all the soul shall not suffice for the worthiness of this love; doubtless they will so rejoice with all their heart, and all their mind, and all their soul, that all the heart, and all the mind, and all the soul shall not suffice for the fullness of their joy.

Chapter XXVI.

Is this joy which the Lord promises made full?—The blessed shall rejoice according as they shall love; and they shall love according as they shall know.

My God and my Lord, my hope and the joy of my heart, speak unto my soul and tell me whether this is the joy of which thou tellest us through thy Son: Ask and ye shall receive, that your joy may be made full (John xvi. 24). For I have found a joy that is full, and more than full. For when heart, and mind, and soul, and all the man, are full of that joy, joy beyond measure will still remain. Hence, not all of that joy shall enter into those who rejoice; but they who rejoice shall wholly enter into that joy.

Show me, O Lord, show thy servant in his heart whether this is the joy into which thy servants shall enter, who shall enter into the joy of their Lord. But that joy, surely, with which thy chosen ones shall rejoice, eye hath not seen nor ear heard, neither has it entered into the heart of man (Isaiah lxiv. 4; 1 Corinthians ii. 9). Not yet, then, have I told or conceived, O Lord, how greatly those blessed ones of thine shall rejoice. Doubtless they shall rejoice according as they shall love; and they shall love according as they shall know. How far they will know thee, Lord, then! and how much they will love thee! Truly, eye hath not seen, nor ear heard, neither has it entered into the heart of man in this life, how far they shall know thee, and how much they shall love thee in that life.

I pray, O God, to know thee, to love thee, that I may rejoice in thee. And if I cannot attain to full joy in this life, may I at least advance from day to day, until that joy shall come to the full. Let the knowledge of thee advance in me here, and there be made full. Let the love of thee increase, and there let it be full, that here my joy may be great in hope, and there full in truth. Lord, through thy Son thou dost command, nay, thou dost counsel us to ask; and thou dost promise that we shall receive, that our joy may be full. I ask, O Lord, as thou dost counsel through our wonderful Counselor. I will receive what thou dost promise by virtue of thy truth, that my joy may be full. Faithful God, I ask. I will receive, that my joy may be full. Meanwhile, let my heart meditate upon it; let my tongue speak of it. Let my heart love it; let my mouth talk of it. Let my soul hunger for it; let my flesh thirst for it; let my whole being desire it, until I enter into thy joy, O Lord, who art the Three and the One God, blessed for ever and ever. Amen.

24. BERNARD OF CLAIRVAUX

Sermons on the Song of Songs

BERNARD OF CLAIRVAUX (CA. 1090–1153) was the dominant personality of the first half of the twelfth century. As abbot of the Cistercian monastery of Clairvaux, which he founded, he was constantly involved in the political, religious, and philosophical issues of his time, including the expansion of the Cistercian order through the establishment of monasteries, and the adjudication of a papal schism in 1130. His intellectual productions represent the tradition of monastic spirituality, and he was a sharp and constant critic of the new philosophical movements based on Aristotelian logic. In his *Sermons on the Song of Songs* one sees the allegorical method of scriptural exegesis applied to the most beloved book of the Bible in the monastic tradition.

Source: Kilian Walsh, O.C.S.O., *The Works of Bernard of Clairvaux*, vol. 2, *Song of Songs I* (Kalamazoo, MI: Kalamazoo Publications Inc., 1981).

Further Reading: Gillian Rosemary Evans, *Bernard of Clairvaux* (Oxford: Oxford University Press, 2000).

Sermon 1: On the Title of the Book

The instructions that I address to you, my brothers, will differ from those I should deliver to people in the world, at least the manner will be different. The preacher who desires to follow St. Paul's method of teaching will give them milk to drink rather than solid food, and will serve a more nourishing diet to those who are spiritually enlightened: "We teach," he said, "not in the way philosophy is taught, but in the way that the Spirit teaches us: we teach spiritual things spiritually." And again: "We have a wisdom to offer those who have reached maturity," in whose company, I feel assured, you are to be found, unless in vain have you prolonged your study of divine teaching, mortified your senses, and meditated day and night on God's law. Be ready then to feed on bread rather than milk. Solomon has bread to give that is splendid and delicious, the bread of that book called the Song of Songs. Let us bring it forth then if you please, and break it.

2. Now, unless I am mistaken, by the grace of God you have understood quite well from the book of Ecclesiastes how to recognize and have done with the false promise of this world. And then the book of Proverbs—has not your life and your conduct been sufficiently amended and enlightened by the doctrine it inculcates? These are two loaves of which it has been your pleasure to taste, loaves you have welcomed as coming from the cupboard of a friend. Now approach for this third loaf that, if possible, you may always recognize what is best. Since there are two evils that comprise the only, or at least the main, enemies of the soul: a misguided love of the world and an excessive love of self, the two books previously mentioned can provide an antidote to each of these infections. One uproots pernicious habits of mind and body with the hoe of self-control. The other, by the use of enlightened reason, quickly perceives a delusive tinge in all that the world holds glorious, truly distinguishing between it and deeper truth. Moreover, it causes the fear of God and the observance of his commandments to be preferred to all human pursuits and worldly desires. And rightly so, for the former is the beginning of wisdom, the latter its culmination, for there is no true and consummate wisdom other than the avoidance of evil and the doing of good, no one can successfully shun evil without the fear of God, and no work is good without the observance of the commandments.

3. Taking it then that these two evils have been warded off by the reading of those books, we may

suitably proceed with this holy and contemplative discourse which, as the fruit of the other two, may be delivered only to well-prepared ears and minds.

II.

Before the flesh has been tamed and the spirit set free by zeal for truth, before the world's glamor and entanglements have been firmly repudiated, it is a rash enterprise on any man's part to presume to study spiritual doctrines. Just as a light is flashed in vain on closed or sightless eyes, so "an unspiritual person cannot accept anything of the Spirit of God." For "the Holy Spirit of instruction shuns what is false," and that is what the life of the intemperate man is. Nor will he ever have a part with the pretensions of the world, since he is the Spirit of Truth. How can there be harmony between the wisdom that comes down from above and the wisdom of the world, which is foolishness to God, or the wisdom of the flesh which is at enmity with God? I am sure that the friend who comes to us on his travels will have no reason to murmur against us after he has shared in this third loaf.

4. But who is going to divide this loaf? The Master of the house is present, it is the Lord you must see in the breaking of the bread. For who else could more fittingly do it? It is a task that I would not dare to arrogate to myself. So look upon me as one from whom you look for nothing. For I myself am one of the seekers, one who begs along with you for the food of my soul, the nourishment of my spirit. Poor and needy, I knock at that door of his which, "when he opens, nobody can close," that I may find light on the profound mystery to which this discourse leads. Patiently all creatures look to you, O Lord. "Little children go begging for bread; no one spares a scrap for them"; they await it from your merciful love. O God most kind, break your bread for this hungering flock, through my hands if it should please you, but with an efficacy that is all your own.

III.

5. Tell us, I beg you, by whom, about whom and to whom it is said: "Let him kiss me with the kiss

of his mouth." How shall I explain so abrupt a beginning, this sudden irruption as from a speech in mid-course? For the words spring upon us as if indicating one speaker to whom another is replying as she demands a kiss—whoever she may be. But if she asks for or demands a kiss from somebody, why does she distinctly and expressly say *with the mouth*, and even with *his own* mouth, as if lovers should kiss by means other than the mouth, or with mouths other than their own? But yet she does not say: "Let him kiss me *with his mouth*"; what she says is still more intimate: "with the kiss of his mouth." How delightful a ploy of speech this, prompted into life by the kiss, with Scripture's own engaging countenance inspiring the reader and enticing him on, that he may find pleasure even in the laborious pursuit of what lies hidden, with a fascinating theme to sweeten the fatigue of research. Surely this mode of beginning that is not a beginning, this novelty of diction in a book so old, cannot but increase the reader's attention. It must follow too that this work was composed, not by any human skill but by the artistry of the Spirit, difficult to understand indeed but yet enticing one to investigate.

IV.

6. So now what shall we do? Shall we bypass the title? No, not even one iota may be omitted, since we are commanded to gather up the tiniest fragments lest they be lost. The title runs: "The beginning of Solomon's Song of Songs." First of all take note of the appropriateness of the name "Peaceful," that is, Solomon, at the head of a book which opens with the token of peace, with a kiss. Take note too that by this kind of opening only men of peaceful minds, men who can achieve mastery over the turmoil of the passions and the distracting burden of daily chores, are invited to the study of this book.

7. Again, the title is not simply the word "Song," but "Song of Songs," a detail not without significance. For though I have read many songs in the Scriptures, I cannot recall any that bear such a name. Israel chanted a song to Yahweh celebrating his escape from the sword and the tyranny of Pharaoh, and the twofold good fortune that simultaneously liberated and avenged him in the

Red Sea. Yet even though chanted, this has not been called a "Song of Songs"; Scripture, if my memory serves me right, introduces it with the words: "Israel sang this song in honor of Yahweh." Song poured from the lips of Deborah, of Judith, of the mother of Samuel, of several of the prophets, yet none of these songs is styled a "Song of Songs." You will find that all of them, as far as I can see, were inspired to song because of favors to themselves or to their people, songs for a victory won, for an escape from danger or the gaining of a boon long sought. They would not be found ungrateful for the divine beneficence, so all sang for reasons proper to each, in accord with the Psalmist's words: "He gives thanks to you, O God, for blessing him." But King Solomon himself, unique as he was in wisdom, renowned above all men, abounding in wealth, secure in his peace, stood in no need of any particular benefit that would have inspired him to sing those songs. Nor does Scripture in any place attribute such a motive to him.

8. We must conclude then it was a special divine impulse that inspired these songs of his that now celebrate the praises of Christ and his Church, the gift of holy love, the sacrament of endless union with God. Here too are expressed the mounting desires of the soul, its marriage song, an exultation of spirit poured forth in figurative language pregnant with delight. It is no wonder that like Moses he put a veil on his face, equally resplendent as it must have been in this encounter, because in those days few if any could sustain the bright vision of God's glory. Accordingly, because of its excellence, I consider this nuptial song to be well deserving of the title that so remarkably designates it, the Song of Songs, just as he in whose honor it is sung is uniquely proclaimed King of kings and Lord of lords.

V.

9. Furthermore if you look back on your own experience, is it not in the victory by which your faith overcomes the world, in "your exit from the horrible pit and out of the slough of the marsh," that you yourselves sing a new song to the Lord for all the marvels he has performed? Again, when he purposed to "settle your feet on a rock

and to direct your steps," then too, I feel certain, a new song was sounding on your lips, a song to our God for his gracious renewal of your life. When you repented that he not only forgave your sins but even promised rewards, so that rejoicing in the hope of benefits to come, you sing of the Lord's ways: how great is the glory of the Lord! And when, as happens, texts of Scripture hitherto dark and impenetrable at last become bright with meaning for you, then, in gratitude for this nurturing bread of heaven you must charm the ears of God with a voice of exultation and praise, a festal song. In the daily trials and arising from the flesh, the world and the devil, that are never wanting to those who live devout lives in Christ, you learn by what you experience that man's life on earth is a ceaseless warfare, and are impelled to repeat your songs day after day for every victory won. As often as temptation is overcome, an immoral habit brought under control, an impending danger shunned, the trap of the seducer detected, when a passion long indulged is finally and perfectly allayed, or a virtue persistently desired and repeatedly sought is ultimately obtained by God's gift; so often, in the words of the prophet, let thanksgiving and joy resound. For every benefit conferred, God is to be praised in his gifts. Otherwise when the time of judgment comes, that man will be punished as an ingrate who cannot say to God: "Your statutes were my song in the land of exile."

10. Again I think that your own experience reveals to you the meaning of those psalms, which are called not Song of Songs but Song of the Steps, in that each one, at whatever stage of growth he be, in accord with the upward movements of his heart may choose one of these songs to praise and give glory to him who empowers you to advance. I don't know how else these words could be true: "There are shouts of joy and victory in the tents of the just." And still more that beautiful and salutary exhortation of the Apostle: "With psalms and hymns and spiritual canticles, singing and chanting to the Lord in your hearts."

VI.

11. But there is that other song which, by its unique dignity and sweetness, excels all those I

have mentioned and any others there might be; hence by every right do I acclaim it as the Song of Songs. It stands at a point where all the others culminate. Only the touch of the Spirit can inspire a song like this, and only personal experience can unfold its meaning. Let those who are versed in the mystery revel in it; let all others burn with desire rather to attain to this experience than merely to learn about it. For it is not a melody that resounds abroad but the very music of the heart, not a trilling on the lips but an inward pulsing of delight, a harmony not of voices but of wills. It is a tune you will not hear in the streets, these notes do not sound where crowds assemble; only the singer hears it and the one to whom he sings—the lover and the beloved. It is pre-eminently a marriage song telling of chaste souls in loving embrace, of their wills in sweet concord, of the mutual exchange of the heart's affections.

12. The novices, the immature, those but recently converted from a worldly life, do not normally sing this song or hear it sung. Only the mind disciplined by persevering study, only the man whose efforts have borne fruit under God's inspiration, the man whose years, as it were, make him ripe for marriage—years measured out not in time but in merits—only he is truly prepared for nuptial union with the divine partner, a union we shall describe more fully in due course. But the hour has come when both our rule and the poverty of our state demand that we go out to work. Tomorrow,[1] with God's help, we shall continue to speak about the kiss, because today's discourse on the title sets us free to resume where we had begun.

Sermon 2: Various Meanings of the Kiss

During my frequent ponderings on the burning desire with which the patriarchs longed for the incarnation of Christ, I am stung with sorrow and shame. Even now I can scarcely restrain my tears, so filled with shame am I by the lukewarmness, the frigid unconcern of these miserable times. For which of us does the consummation of that event fill with as much joy as the mere promise of it inflamed the desires of the holy men of pre-Christian times? Very soon now there will be great rejoicing as we celebrate the feast of Christ's birth.[2] But how I wish it were inspired by his birth! All the more therefore do I pray that the intense longings of those men of old, their heartfelt expectation, may be enkindled in me by these words: "Let him kiss me with the kiss of his mouth." Many an upright man in those far-off times sense within himself how profuse the graciousness that would be poured upon those lips. And intense desire springing from that perception impelled him to utter: "Let him kiss me with the kiss of his mouth," hoping with every fiber of his being that he might not be deprived of a share in a pleasure so great.

2. The conscientious man of those days might repeat to himself: "Of what use to me the wordy effusions of the prophets? Rather let him who is the most handsome of the sons of men, let him kiss me with the kiss of his mouth. No longer am I satisfied to listen to Moses, for he is a slow speaker and not able to speak well. Isaiah is 'a man of unclean lips,' Jeremiah does not know how to speak, he is a child; not one of the prophets makes an impact on me with his words. But he, the one whom they proclaim, let him speak to me, 'let him kiss me with the kiss of his mouth.' I have no desire that he should approach me in their person, or address me with their words, for they are 'a watery darkness, a dense cloud'; rather in his own person, 'let him kiss me with the kiss of his mouth'; let him whose presence is full of love, from whom exquisite doctrines flow in streams, let him become 'a spring inside me, welling up to eternal life.' Shall I not receive a richer infusion of grace from him whom the Father has anointed with the oil of gladness above all his rivals, provided that he will bestow on me the kiss of his mouth? For his living, active word is to me a kiss, not indeed an adhering of the lips that can sometimes belie a union of hearts, but an unreserved infusion of joys, a revealing of mysteries, a marvelous and indistinguishable mingling of the divine light with the enlightened mind, which, joined in truth to God, is one spirit with him. With good reason then I avoid trucking with visions and dreams; I

---

1   The early Cistercians gathered daily in chapter after prime to receive instruction from the abbot.

2   Bernard places this sermon in the context of Advent, whose liturgy has undoubtedly influenced its thought.

want no part with parables and figures of speech; even the very beauty of the angels can only leave me wearied. For my Jesus utterly surpasses these in his majesty and splendor. Therefore I ask of him what I ask of neither man nor angel: that he kiss me with the kiss of his mouth.

II.

Note how I do not presume that it is with his mouth I shall be kissed, for that constitutes the unique felicity and singular privilege of the human nature he assumed. No, in the consciousness of my lowliness I ask to be kissed with the kiss of his mouth, an experience shared by all who are in a position to say: 'Indeed from his fullness we have, all of us, received.'"

3. I must ask you to try to give your whole attention here. The mouth that kisses signifies the Word who assumes human nature; the nature assumed receives the kiss; the kiss however, that takes its being both from the giver and the receiver, is a person that is formed by both, none other than "the one mediator between God and mankind, himself a man, Christ Jesus." It is for this reason that none of the saints dared say: "let him kiss me with his mouth," but rather, "with the kiss of his mouth." In this way they paid tribute to that prerogative of Christ, on whom uniquely and in one sole instance the mouth of the Word was pressed, that moment when the fullness of the divinity yielded itself to him, as the life of his body. A fertile kiss therefore, a marvel of stupendous self-abasement that is not a mere pressing of mouth upon mouth; it is the uniting of God with man. Normally the touch of lip on lip is the sign of the loving embrace of hearts, but this conjoining of natures brings together the human and divine, shows God reconciling "to himself all things, whether on earth or in heaven." "For he is the peace between us, and he has made the two into one." This was the kiss for which just men yearned under the old dispensation, foreseeing as they did that in him they would "find happiness and a crown of rejoicing," because in him were hidden "all the jewels of wisdom and knowledge." Hence their longing to taste that fullness of his.

4. You seem to be in agreement with this explanation, but I should like you to listen to another.

III.

Even the holy men who lived before the coming of Christ understood that God had in mind plans of peace for the human race. "Surely the Lord God does nothing without revealing his secret to his servants, the prophets." What he did reveal however was obscure to many. For in those days faith was a rare thing on the earth, and hope but a faint impulse in the heart even of many of those who looked forward to the deliverance of Israel. Those indeed who foreknew also proclaimed that Christ would come as man, and with him, peace. One of them actually said: "He himself will be peace in our land when he comes." Enlightened from above they confidently spread abroad the message that through him men would be restored to the favor of God. John, the fore-runner of the Lord, recognizing the fulfillment of that prophecy in his own time, declared: "Grace and truth have come through Christ Jesus." In our time every Christian can discover by experience that this is true.

5. In those far-off days however, while the prophets continued to foretell the covenant, and its author continued to delay his coming, the faith of the people never ceased to waver because there was no one who could redeem or save. Hence men grumbled at the postponements of the coming of the Prince of Peace so often proclaimed by the mouth of his holy prophets from ancient times. As doubts about the fulfillment of the prophecies began to recur, all the more eagerly did they make demands for the kiss, the sign of the promised reconcilement. It was as if a voice from among the people would challenge the prophets of peace: "How much longer are you going to keep us in suspense? You are always foretelling a peace that is never realized; you promise a world of good but trouble on trouble comes. At various times in the past and in various different ways this same hope was fostered by angels among our ancestors, who in turn have passed the tidings on to us. 'Peace! Peace!' they say, 'but there is no peace.' If God desires to convince me of that benevolent will of his, so often vouched for by the prophets but not yet

revealed by the event, then let him kiss me with the kiss of his mouth, and so by this token of peace make my peace secure. For how shall I any longer put my trust in mere words? It is necessary now that words be vindicated by action. If those men are God's envoys let him prove the truth of their words by his own advent, so often the keynote of their predictions, because unless he comes they can do nothing. He sent his servant bearing a staff, but neither voice nor life is forthcoming. I do not rise up, I am not awakened, I am not shaken out of the dust, nor do I breathe in hope, if the Prophet himself does not come down and kiss me with the kiss of his mouth."

6. Here we must add that he who professes to be our mediator with God is God's own Son, and he is God. But what is man that he should take notice of him, the son of man that he should be concerned about him? Where shall such as I am find the confidence, the daring, to entrust myself to him who is so majestic? How shall I, mere dust and ashes, presume that God takes an interest in me? He is entirely taken up with loving his Father, he has no need of me nor of what I possess. How then shall I find assurance that if he is my mediator he will never fail me? If it be really true, as you prophets have said, that God has determined to show mercy, to reveal himself in a more favorable light, let him establish a covenant of peace, an everlasting covenant with me by the kiss of his mouth. If he will not revoke his given word, let him empty himself, let him humble himself, let him bend to me and kiss me with the kiss of his mouth. If the mediator is to be acceptable to both parties, equally dependable in the eyes of both, then let him who is God's Son become man, let him become the Son of Man, and fill me with assurance by this kiss of his mouth. When I come to recognize that he is truly mine, then I shall feel secure in welcoming the Son of God as mediator. Not even a shadow of mistrust can then exist, for after all he is my brother, and my own flesh. It is impossible that I should be spurned by him who is bone from my bones, and flesh from my flesh.

7. We should by now have come to an understanding how the discontent of our ancestors displayed a need for this sacrosanct kiss, that is, the mystery of the incarnate Word, for faith, hard-pressed throughout the ages with trouble upon trouble, was ever on the point of failing, and a fickle people, yielding to encouragement, murmured against the promises of God. Is this a mere improvisation on my part? I suggest that you will find it to be the teaching of the Scriptures: for instance, consider the burden of complaint and murmuring in those words: "Order on order, order on order, rule on rule, rule on rule, a little here, a little there." Or those prayerful exclamations, troubled yet loyal: "Give those who wait for you their reward, and let your prophets be proved worthy of belief." Again: "Bring about what has been prophesied in your name." There too you will find those soothing promises, full of consolation: "Behold the Lord will appear and he will not lie. If he seems slow, wait for him, for he will surely come and he will not delay." Likewise: "His time is close at hand when he will come and his days will not be prolonged." Speaking in the name of him who is promised the prophet announces: "Behold I am coming towards you like a river of peace, and like a stream in spate with the glory of the nations." In all these statements there is evidence both of the urgency of the preachers and of the distrust of those who listened to them. The people murmured, their faith wavered, and in the words of Isaiah: "the ambassadors of peace weep bitterly." Therefore because Christ was late in coming, and the whole human race in danger of being lost in despair, so convinced was it that human weakness was an object of contempt with no hope of the reconciliation with God through a grace so frequently promised, those good men whose faith remained strong eagerly longed for the more powerful assurance that only his human presence could convey. They prayed intensely for a sign that the covenant was about to be restored for the sake of a spiritless, faithless people.

8. Oh root of Jesse, that stands as a signal to the peoples, how many prophets and kings wanted to see what you see, and never saw it!

IV.

Happy above them all is Simeon, by God's mercy still bearing fruit in old age! He rejoiced to think that he would see the long-desired sign. He saw it and was glad; and having received the kiss of peace he is allowed to go in peace, but not before he had told his audience that Jesus was born to be a sign that would be rejected. Time proved how true this was. No sooner had the sign of peace arisen than it was opposed, by those, that is, who hated peace; for his peace is with men of good-will, but for the evil-minded he is "a stone to stumble over, a rock to bring men down." Herod accordingly was perturbed, and so was the whole of Jerusalem. Christ "came to his own domain, and his own people did not accept him." Those shepherds, however, who kept watch over their flocks by night, were fortunate for they were gladdened by a vision of this sign. Even in those early days he was hiding these things from the learned and the clever, and revealing them to mere children. Herod, as you know, desired to see him, but because his motive was not genuine he did not succeed. The sign of peace was given only to men of good-will, hence to Herod and others like him was given the sign of the prophet Jonah. The angel said to the shepherds: "Here is a sign for you," you who are humble, obedient, not given to haughtiness, faithful to prayer and meditating day and night on God's law. "This is a sign for you," he said. What sign? The sign promised by the angels, sought after by the people, foretold by the prophets; this is the sign that the Lord Jesus has now brought into existence and revealed to you, a sign by which the incredulous are made believers, the dispirited are made hopeful and the fervent achieve security. This therefore is the sign for you. But as a sign what does it signify? It reveals mercy, grace, peace, the peace that has no end. And finally, the sign is this: "You will find a baby, wrapped in swaddling clothes and lying in a manger." God himself, however, is in this baby, reconciling the world to himself. He will be put to death for your sins and raised to life to justify you, so that made righteous by faith you may be at peace with God. This was the sign of peace that the Prophet once urged King Achez to ask of the Lord his God, "either from the depths of Sheol or from the heights above." But the ungodly king refused. His wretched state blinded him to the belief that in this sign the highest things above would be joined to the lowest things below in peace. This was achieved when Christ, descending into Sheol, saluted its dwellers with a holy kiss, the pledge of peace, and then going up to heaven, enabled the spirits there to share in the same pledge in joy without end.

9. I must end this sermon. But let me sum up briefly the points we have raised. It would seem that this holy kiss was of necessity bestowed on the world for two reasons. Without it the faith of those who wavered would not have been strengthened, nor the desires of the fervent appeased. Moreover, this kiss is no other than the Mediator between God and man, himself a man, Christ Jesus, who with the Father and Holy Spirit lives and reigns as God for ever and ever. Amen.

Sermon 3: The Kiss of the Lord's Feet, Hands and Mouth

Today the text we are to study is the book of our own experience. You must therefore turn your attention inwards, each one must take note of his own particular awareness of the things I am about to discuss. I am attempting to discover if any of you has been privileged to say from his heart: "Let him kiss me with the kiss of his mouth." Those to whom it is given to utter these words sincerely are comparatively few, but any one who has received this mystical kiss from the mouth of Christ at least once, seeks again that intimate experience, and eagerly looks for its frequent renewal. I think that nobody can grasp what it is except the one who receives it. For it is "a hidden manna," and only he who eats it still hungers for more. It is "a sealed fountain" to which no stranger has access; only he who drinks still thirsts for more. Listen to one who has had the experience, how urgently he demands: "Be my savior again, renew my joy." But a soul like mine, burdened with sins, still subject to carnal passions, devoid of any knowledge of spiritual delights, may not presume to make such a request, almost totally unacquainted as it is with the joys of the supernatural life.

2. I should like however to point out to persons like this that there is an appropriate place for them on the way of salvation. They may not rashly aspire to the lips of a most benign Bridegroom, but let them prostrate with me in fear at the feet

of a most severe Lord. Like the publican full of misgiving, they must turn their eyes to the earth rather than up to heaven. Eyes that are accustomed only to darkness will be dazzled by the brightness of the spiritual world, overpowered by its splendor, repulsed by its peerless radiance and whelmed again in a gloom more dense than before. All you who are conscious of sin, do not regard as unworthy and despicable that position where the holy sinner laid down her sins, and put on the garment of holiness. There the Ethiopian changed her skin, and, cleansed to a new brightness, could confidently and legitimately respond to those who insulted her: "I am black but lovely, daughters of Jerusalem." You may ask what skill enabled her to accomplish this change, or on what grounds did she merit it? I can tell you in a few words. She wept bitterly, she sighed deeply from her heart, she sobbed with a repentance that shook her very being, till the evil that inflamed her passions was cleansed away. The heavenly physician came with speed to her aid, because "his word runs swiftly." Perhaps you think the Word of God is not a medicine? Surely it is, a medicine strong and pungent, testing the mind and the heart. "The Word of God is something alive and active. It cuts like any double-edged sword but more finely. It can slip through the place where the soul is divided from the spirit, or the joints from the marrow: it can judge the secret thoughts." It is up to you, wretched sinner, to humble yourself as this happy penitent did so that you may be rid of your wretchedness. Prostrate yourself on the ground, take hold of his feet, soothe them with kisses, sprinkle them with your tears and so wash not them but yourself. Thus you will become one of the "flock of shorn ewes as they come up from the washing." But even then you may not dare to lift up a face suffused with shame and grief, until you hear the sentence: "Your sins are forgiven," to be followed by the summons: "Awake, awake, captive daughter of Sion, awake, shake off the dust."

II.

3. Though you have made a beginning by kissing the feet, you may not presume to rise at once by impulse to the kiss of the mouth; there is a step to be surmounted in between, an intervening kiss on the hand for which I offer the following explanation. If Jesus says to me: "Your sins are forgiven," what will it profit me if I do not cease from sinning? I have taken off my tunic, am I to put in on again? And if I do, what have I gained? If I soil my feet again after washing them, is the washing of any benefit? Long did I lie in the slough of the marsh, filthy with all kinds of vices; if I return to it again I shall be worse than when I first wallowed in it. On top of that I recall that he who healed me said to me as he exercised his mercy: "Now you are well again, be sure not to sin any more, or something worse may happen to you." He, however, who gave me the grace to repent, must also give me the power to persevere, lest by repeating my sins I should end up by being worse than I was before. Woe to me then, repentant though I be, if he without whom I can do nothing should suddenly withdraw his supporting hand. I really mean nothing; of myself I can achieve neither repentance nor perseverance, and for that reason I pay heed to the Wise Man's advice: "Do not repeat yourself at your prayers." The Judge's threat to the tree that did not yield good fruit is another thing that makes me fearful. For these various reasons I must confess that I am not entirely satisfied with the first grace by which I am enabled to repent of my sins; I must have the second as well, and so bear fruits that befit repentance, that I may not return like the dog to its vomit.

4. I am now able to see what I must seek for and receive before I may hope to attain to a higher and holier state. I do not wish to be suddenly on the heights, my desire is to advance by degrees. The impudence of the sinner displeases God as much as the modesty of the penitent gives him pleasure. You will please him more readily if you live within the limits proper to you, and do not set your sights at things beyond you. It is a long and formidable leap from the foot to the mouth, a manner of approach that is not commendable. Consider for a moment: still tarnished as you are with the dust of sin, would you dare touch those sacred lips? Yesterday you were lifted from the mud, today you wish to encounter the glory of his face? No, his hand must be your guide to that end. First it must cleanse your stains, then it must raise you up. How raise you? By giving you the grace

to dare to aspire. You wonder what this may be. I see it as the grace of the beauty of temperance and the fruits that befit repentance, the works of the religious man. These are the instruments that will lift you from the dunghill and cause your hopes to soar. On receiving such a grace then, you must kiss his hand, that is, you must give glory to his name, not to yourself. First of all you must glorify him because he has forgiven your sins, secondly because he has adorned you with virtues. Otherwise you will need a bold front to face reproaches such as these: "What do you have that was not given to you? And if it was given, how can you boast as though it were not?"

III.

5. Once you have had this twofold experience of God's benevolence in these two kisses, you need no longer feel abashed in aspiring to a holier intimacy. Growth in grace brings expansion of confidence. You will love with greater ardor, and knock on the door with greater assurance, in order to gain what you perceive to be still wanting to you. "The one who knocks will always have the door opened to him." It is my belief that to a person so disposed, God will not refuse that most intimate kiss of all, a mystery of supreme generosity and ineffable sweetness. You have seen the way that we must follow, the order of procedure: first, we cast ourselves at his feet, we weep before the Lord who made us, deploring the evil we have done. Then we reach out for the hand that will lift us up, that will steady our trembling knees. And finally, when we shall have obtained these favors through many prayers and tears, we humbly dare to raise our eyes to his mouth, so divinely beautiful, not merely to gaze upon it, but—I say it with fear and trembling—to receive its kiss. "Christ the Lord is a Spirit before our face," and he who is joined to him in a holy kiss becomes through his good pleasure, one spirit with him.

6. To you, Lord Jesus, how truly my heart has said: "My face looks to you. Lord, I do seek your face." In the dawn you brought me proof of your love, in my first approach to kiss your revered feet you forgave my evil ways as I lay in the dust. With the advancement of the day you gave your servant reason to rejoice when, in the kiss of the hand, you imparted the grace to live rightly. And now what remains, O good Jesus, except that suffused as I am with the fullness of your light, and while my spirit is fervent, you would graciously bestow on me the kiss of your mouth, and give me unbounded joy in your presence. Serenely lovable above all others, tell me where will you lead your flock to graze, where will you rest it at noon? Dear brothers, surely it is wonderful for us to be here, but the burden of the day calls us elsewhere. These guests, whose arrival has just now been announced to us, compel me to break off rather than to conclude a talk that I enjoy so much. So I go to meet the guests, to make sure that the duty of charity, of which we have been speaking, may not suffer neglect, that we may not hear it said of us: "They do not practice what they preach." Do you pray in the meantime that God may accept the homage of my lips for your spiritual welfare, and for the praise and glory of his name.

25. GUIBERT OF NOGENT

Memoirs

GUIBERT OF NOGENT (CA. 1064–1121), came from a family of minor nobility in Picardy (northern France). He entered the monastery of Flay and in 1104 became abbot of the small monastery of Nogent in Picardy. His writings include a history of the first crusade, a treatise critical of the veneration of relics, and various theological and exegetical works. His autobiography, written in 1115 and modeled in part on Augustine's *Confessions*, is the first full autobiography in the Middle Ages and contains revealing information on Guibert, his family, and monastic mentality.

Source: C.C. Swinton Bland, rev. John F. Benton, *Self and Society in Medieval France: The Memoirs of Abbot Guibert of Nogent* (New York: Harper and Row, 1970).

Further Reading: Jay Rubenstein, *Guibert of Nogent: Portrait of a Medieval Mind* (London: Routledge, 2002).

Book 1

Chapter 1

I confess to Thy Majesty, O God, my endless wanderings from Thy paths, and my turning back so often to the bosom of Thy Mercy, directed by Thee in spite of all. I confess the wickedness I did in childhood and in youth, wickedness that yet boils up in my mature years, and my ingrained love of crookedness, which still lives on in the sluggishness of my worn body. Whenever I call to mind my persistence in unclean things, O Lord, and how Thou didst always grant remorse for them, I am amazed at the long-suffering of Thy compassion, which is beyond all that man can conceive. If repentance and a prayerful mind cannot exist without the entrance of Thy Spirit, how dost Thou so graciously suffer them to creep into the hearts of sinners, how dost Thou grant so much favor to those who turn away from Thee, indeed, even to those who provoke Thee to wrath? Thou knowest, Almighty Father, how stubbornly we set our hearts against those who incur our anger and with how much difficulty we forgive those who have offended us often or even once, either by a look or a word.

But Thou art not only good but truly goodness itself, even its very source. And since Thy aid goes out to all in general, shalt Thou not be able also to succor each single being? Why not? When the world lay in ignorance of God, when it was wrapped in darkness and the shadow of death, when, as night went on its course, a universal silence prevailed, by whose merit, by whose cry could Thy Almighty Word be summoned to come forth from Thy royal seat? When all mankind gave no heed to Thee, Thou couldst not even then be turned from pity on them; no wonder that Thou shouldst show Thy compassion on one single sinner, great sinner though he be! It is not for me to say that Thou art merciful more readily to individual men than to men in general, for in either case there is no halting in Thy willingness, because there is nothing more willing than Thee. Since Thou art the fountain, and since Thou owest to all what flows forth from Thee, manifestly Thou dost not withhold from any what belongs to all.

I am forever sinning, and between sins ever returning to Thee, fleeing from goodness and forsaking it. When I turn back to goodness, will goodness lose its essence and, overwhelmed by manifold offenses, will it then be different? Is it not said of Thee that Thou wilt not "in Thy anger shut up Thy mercies"? The same psalmist sings that this mercy shall abide both now and forever. Thou knowest that I do not sin because I see that Thou art merciful, but I do confidently avow that Thou art called merciful because Thou art at hand for all who seek Thy indulgence. I am not abusing Thy mercy whenever I am driven to sin by the necessity of sinning, but it would indeed be an impious abuse if I ever took delight in the waywardness of sin because the return to Thee after sinning is so easy. I sin, it is true, but when reason returns, I repent that I yielded to the lust of my heart and that my soul, with unwilling heaviness, bedded itself in baskets full of dung.

In the midst of these daily afflictions of a fall followed by a sort of resurrection, what was I to do? Is it not far wiser to struggle toward Thee for a time, to take breath in Thee even for a moment, than to forget all healing and to despair of Thy grace? And in what does despair consist, if not in throwing oneself deliberately into the pigsty of every outrageous lust? For when the spirit no longer resists the flesh, the very substance of the unhappy soul is wasted in the profligacy of pleasure. As a man who is drowning in a tempest of waters is sucked down into the deep, so one's judgment is drawn down from the mouth of the pit to the depths of evil.

Holy God, while my wits, recovering from the drunkenness of my inner being, come back to Thee, although at other times I do not go forward, yet at least meanwhile I am not turning from knowledge of myself. How could I catch even a glimpse of Thee if my eyes were blind to see myself? If, as Jeremiah says, "I am the man that sees my poverty," it surely follows that I should shrewdly search for those things by which my lacks may be supplied. And on the contrary, if I do not understand what is good, how shall I be able to know evil, much less to forswear it? If I know beauty, I shall never be frightened by foulness. Both matters are therefore apparent, that I should seek knowledge of myself, and, enjoying that, I should consequently not fail in self-knowledge. It is a worthy act and singularly for my soul's good that through these confessions the darkness of my understanding should be dispersed by the searching rays Thy light often casts upon it, by which, being lastingly illuminated, it may forever know itself.

Chapter 2

The first thing to do is to acknowledge Thee the benefits Thou hast conferred on me, O God, that Thy servants who shall read of them may weigh exactly the cruelty of my ingratitude. For hadst Thou bestowed on me only what Thou dost allot to other men, wouldst Thou not have exceeded all that I merit? But Thou didst add many more things that redound to Thy praise and not at all to mine, and still other things about which I think I should remain silent. For if my birth, wealth, and appearance, to mention no other things (if there are any), are the gifts of Thy hand, O Lord, good men do not praise them, except when those to whom Thou hast given them guard under the rule of honor; otherwise they are regarded as utterly contemptible because they are subject to the flaw of changeableness. What have I to do with those things which only serve the interests of lust and pride with their outward show and reputation? They are of such a neutral nature that according to the quality of the mind they may be turned to good or evil, and the more changeable they are, the more suspect their inconstancy renders them. If no other reason could be found, it is sufficient to observe that no one achieves by his own efforts his parentage or good looks, and of these things in particular all that he has was a gift to him.

Human effort may play a part in the acquisition of some other things, such as wealth and skill; as Solomon testifies, "When the iron be blunt, with much labor it shall be sharpened." Yet even all that is confuted by the ready answer that unless the "light which enlighteneth every man that cometh into this world" be shed on him, and unless Christ shall open to him the doors of learning with the key of knowledge, there is no doubt that every teacher shall spend himself in vain or dull ears. Therefore any sensible man would be foolish to claim anything as his own except his sin.

But, leaving these matters, let us return to the subject with which we began. I said, O Good and Holy One, that I thanked Thee for Thy gifts. First and above all, I render thanks to Thee because Thou didst bestow on me a mother who was beautiful, yet chaste, modest, and steeped in the fear of the Lord. Without doubt I would have proclaimed her beauty in a worldly and foolish fashion if I had not austerely declared beauty to be but an empty show. Still, just as the obligatory fasting of the utterly poor is less praiseworthy, since they cannot choose their food, while the abstinence of rich men takes its value from their abundance, in the same way beauty has the higher title to praise of every sort the more desirable it is, so long as it hardens itself against the temptations of lust. If Sallust Crispus had not thought beauty devoid of morality worthy to be praised, he would never have said of Aurelia Orestilla, "In whom good men never found aught to praise except her beauty."[1] If he declares that her good looks alone were to be praised by the good, but that in all else she was foul, I confidently affirm that this was Sallust's meaning: it is as if he had said that she was deservedly approved for a gift of nature from God, although it appears that she was defiled by added impurities. In the same way, we praise beauty in an idol which is justly proportioned, and although, where faith is concerned, an idol is called "nothing" by the apostle, and nothing more profane could be imagined, yet it is not unreasonable to commend the true modeling of its members.[2]

Certainly however transitory may be the nature of beauty, which is liable to change through the instability of the blood, yet following the usual standard of symbolic goodness, it cannot be denied to be good. For if whatever has been eternally established by God is beautiful, then all that is temporarily fair is, as it were, the reflection of that eternal beauty. "The invisible things of God are clearly seen, being understood by the things that are made," says the apostle. Angels have always presented countenances of shining beauty when they appear to men. Hence, the wife of Manue says, "There came a man of God to me having the countenance of an angel." On the contrary, according to the first Peter, devils are "reserved in a mist" till the day of the great judgment; they usually appear in an extremely ugly form, except when they deceitfully "transform themselves into angels of light." And not unjustly so, since they have revolted from the splendor of their noble peers.

Furthermore, we are told that the bodies of the elect ought to conform to the glory of the body of Christ, so that the vileness that is contracted by accident or natural decay is amended to the pattern of the Son of God as transfigured on the Mount.

If their internal models are beautiful and good, those who manifest their image, especially if they do not depart from their measure, are beautiful, and hence they are good. Augustine himself, in his book *On Christian Doctrine*, if I am not mistaken, is known to have said, "He who has a beautiful body and an ugly soul is less to be mourned than if he had an ugly body, too." If therefore a blemished exterior is rightly a matter for sorrow, without any doubt a thing is good which can be spoiled by combination with something bad, or improved by a quality of respectability.

Thanks to Thee, O God, that Thou didst infuse her beauty with virtue. The seriousness of her manner was such as to make evident her scorn for all vanity; the gravity of her eyes, the restraint of her speech, and the modesty of her expression gave no encouragement to light looks. Thou knowest, Almighty God, Thou didst put into her in earliest youth the fear of Thy name and into her heart rebellion against the allurements of the flesh. Take note that never or hardly ever was she to be found in the company of women who made much of themselves, and just as she kept Thy gift unto herself, so she was sparing in blame of those who were incontinent, and when sometimes a scandalous tale was circulated by strangers or those of her own household, she would turn away and take no part in it, and she was as much annoyed by such whisperings as if she had been slandered in her own person. God of Truth, Thou knowest it is not something personal, such as my love for my mother, that prompts me to say these things. The power of my words should have the more force, since the rest of my race are in truth mere animals ignorant of God, or brutal fighters and murderers, who must surely become outcast from Thee unless Thou shouldst with the greatness of Thy accustomed mercy pity them. But a better opportunity will occur in this work to speak of her. Let us now turn to my own life.

Chapter 3

To this woman, as I hope and believe truest to me of all whom she bore, Thou granted that this worst sinner should be born. In two senses I was her last

---

1   For Sallust (Roman historian, 86–34 BCE), a beautiful but evil woman married to the conspirator Cataline. Sall. Cat. 15.2–15.3.
2   By idols, Guibert means classical statues.

child, for while the others have passed away with the hope of a better life, I am left with a life of utter despair. Yet, through her merit next to Jesus and His Mother and the Saints, while I still live in this evil world there remains to me the hope of that salvation which is open to all. Certainly I know, and it is wrong to disbelieve, that, as in the world she showed me a greater love and brought me up in greater distinction (with a mother's special affection for her last-born), she remembers me the more now that she is in the presence of God. From her youth she was full of God's fire in Zion, since the concern she had for me in her heart did not cease whether she was asleep or awake. And now that she is dead, the wall of her flesh being broken away, I know that in Jerusalem that furnace burns with greater heat than words can express, the more that, being filled there with the Spirit of God, she is not ignorant of the miseries in which I am entangled, and, blessed as she is, she bewails my wanderings when she sees my feet go astray from the paths of goodness marked out by her recurrent warnings.

O Father and Lord God, Who didst give being to me (I who am bad in such manner and measure as Thou knowest) from her so truly and really good, Thou didst also grant me hope in her merit, a hope which I should not dare to have at all if I were not for a little near Thee relieved of the fear of my sins. Likewise Thou didst bring into my wretched heart perhaps not hope so much as the shadow of hope, in that Thou didst vouchsafe to me birth, and rebirth also, on the day that is the highest of all days and best-loved by Christian people. My mother had passed almost the whole of Good Friday in excessive pain of childbirth (in what anguish, too, did she linger, when I wandered from the way and followed slippery paths!) when at last came Holy Saturday, the day before Easter.

Racked by pains long-endured, and her tortures increasing as her hour drew near, when she thought I had at last in natural course come to birth, instead I was returned within the womb. By this time my father, friends, and kinsfolk were crushed with dismal sorrowing for both of us, for while the child was hastening the death of the mother, and she her child's in denying him deliverance, all had reason for compassion. It was a day

on which, with the exception of that solemn office which is celebrated exclusively and at its special time, the regular services for the household were not taking place. And so they asked counsel in their need and fled for help to the altar of the Lady Mary, and to her (the only Virgin that ever was or would be to bear a child) this vow was made, and in the place of an offering this gift laid upon the gracious Lady's altar: that should a male child be born, he should be given up to the religious life in the service of God and the Lady, and if one of the inferior sex, she should be handed over to the corresponding calling. At once a weak little being, almost an abortion, was born, and at that timely birth there was rejoicing only for my mother's deliverance, the child being such a miserable object. In that poor mite just born, there was such a pitiful meagerness that he had the corpse-like look of a premature baby; so much so that when reeds (which in that region are very slender when they come up—it being then the middle of April—) were placed in my little fingers, they seemed stouter in comparison. On that very day when I was put into the baptismal font—as I was so often told as a joke in boyhood and even in youth— a certain woman tossed me from hand to hand. "Look at this thing," she said. "Do you think such a child can live, whom nature by a mistake has made almost without limbs, giving him something more like an outline than a body?"

All these things, my Creator, were signs of the state in which I seem now to live. Could truth in Thy service be found in me, O Lord? I have shown no firmness toward Thee, no constancy. If to the eye any work of mine has appeared good, many times crooked motives have made it slight. God of supreme love, I have said that Thou gavest me hope, or a faint likeness of some little hope, out of the promise of that joyous day on which I was born and reborn and offered, too, to her who is Queen of all next to God. O Lord God, I do not realize with what reason Thou hast given me that the day of birth brings nothing better than the day of death to those who live an unprofitable life? It is denied beyond dispute that no merits can exist prior to the day we are born but can exist on the day of our death; if it should be our chance not to live in goodness, then I confess that famous days, whether for birth or death, can do us no good.

For if it is true that He made me, and not I myself, and that I did not fix the day, and had no right to the choice of it, its bestowal on me by God affords me neither hope for honor unless my life, imitating the holiness of the day, justifies its promise. Certainly my birthday would then be brightened by the joyous character of the season if the purpose of my life were controlled by virtue searching for uprightness; and the glory of a man's entry into the world would appear a favor granted to his merit if his spirit continuing in righteousness should glorify his end. Whether I be named Peter or Paul, whether Remi or Nicolas, I shall not profit, in the words of the poet, "by the name that has been derived from great Iulus"[3] unless I carefully copy the examples of those whom Providence or fortune has made my namesakes. Behold, O God, how my swelling heart puffs up again, how a feather's weight will be magnified into a matter of pride!

O Lady who rules Earth and Heaven after thy only Son, how good was the thought of those who placed me under bondage to thee! And how much better would my thoughts have been if in later years I had bent my heart to that vow's resolve! Behold, I declare that I was given to be especially thy own, nor do I deny that sacrilegiously and knowingly I took myself from thee. Did I not rob thee of myself when I preferred my stinking willfulness to thy sweet odor? But although many times by such deceit I stole myself away from thee, yet to thee, and through thee to God the Father and the only Son, I returned more fearlessly when I contemplated that offering. And when, recurring a thousand times to my sins, I pined again, then out of thy never-failing compassion my sureness was born again, and I was encouraged to hope by the gift of thy earlier mercy. But why that word "earlier"? I have so often known, and continue to know daily, the constancy of thy mercy, I have escaped so often from the prison of my fall when thou didst set me free, that on those old matters I would gladly keep utter silence when such a wealth of freedom rules. As often as the repetition of sin begets in me a cruel hardening of the heart, then my resort to thee, as by a natural instinct, softens it again; and after looking at myself, after

considering my misfortunes, when I come close to fainting in despair, almost involuntarily I feel springing up in my unhappy soul a certainty of recovery in thee. It lies so close to my thought that in whatever ills I am entangled, thou canst not, if I dare to say it, be a defaulter in my need. To thee in particular shall I lay the due cause of my ruin if thou hast no regard in his perversity for him who was taken straight from the womb to thee, and if thou givest him no welcome when he turns to thee again. Since clearly the power is thine at will, and the authority of the Son is known to overflow to the mother, from whom may I rather demand salvation than from thee to whom I cry out "I am thine" by right of the bondage that began at my birth? At another time how gladly will I reflect upon these things with thee! But first let us touch upon other matters.

Chapter 4

After birth I had scarcely learned to cherish my rattle when Thou, Gracious Lord, henceforth my Father, didst make me an orphan. For when about eight months had passed, the father of my flesh died. Great thanks are due to Thee that Thou didst allow that man to depart in a Christian state. If he had lived, he would undoubtedly have endangered the provision Thou hadst made for me. Because my young body and a certain natural quickness for one of such tender age seemed to fit me for worldly pursuits, no one doubted that when the proper time had come for beginning my education, he would have broken the vow which he had made for me. O Gracious Provider, for the well-being of us both Thou didst determine that I should not miss the beginning of instruction in Thy discipline and that he should not break his solemn promise for me.

And so with great care that widow, truly Thine, brought me up, and at last she chose the day of the festival of the Blessed Gregory for putting me in school. She had heard that that servant of Thine, O Lord, had been eminent for his wonderful understanding and had abounded in extraordinary wisdom. Therefore she strove with bountiful almsgiving to win the good word

---

3   Virgil, *Aeneid*, I:267.

of Thy Confessor, that he to whom Thou hadst granted understanding might make me zealous in the pursuit of knowledge. Put to my book, I had learned the shapes of the letters, but hardly yet to join them into syllables, when my good mother, eager for my instruction, arranged to place me under a schoolmaster.

There was a little before that time, and in a measure there was still in my youth, such a scarcity of teachers that hardly any could be found in the towns, and in the cities there were very few, and those who by good chance could be discovered had but slight knowledge and could not be compared with the wandering scholars of these days. The man in whose charge my mother decided to put me had begun to learn grammar late in life, and he was the more unskilled in the art through having imbibed little of it when he was young. Yet he was of such character that what he lacked in letters he made up for in honesty.

Through the chaplains who conducted the divine services in her house, my mother approached this teacher, who was in charge of the education of a young cousin of mine and was closely bound to some of my relatives, at whose court he had been raised. He took into consideration the woman's earnest request and was favorably impressed by her honorable and virtuous character, but he was afraid to give offense to those kinsmen of mine and was in doubt whether to come into her house. While thus undecided, he was persuaded by the following vision:

At night when he was sleeping in his room, where I remember he conducted all the instruction in our town, the figure of a white-headed old man, of very dignified appearance, seemed to lead me in by the hand through the door of the room. Halting within hearing, while the other looked on, he pointed out his bed to me and said, "Go to him, for he will love you very much." When he dropped my hand and let me go, I ran to the man, and as I kissed him again and again on the face, he awoke and conceived such an affection for me that putting aside all hesitation, and shaking off all fear for my kinsfolk, on whom not only he but everything that belonged to him was dependent, he agreed to go to my mother and live in her house.

Now, that boy whom he had been educating so far was handsome and of good birth, but he was so eager to avoid proper studies and unsteady under all instruction, a liar and a thief, as far as his age would allow, that he never could be found in productive activity and hardly ever in school, but almost every day played truant in the vineyards. Since my mother's friendly advances were made to him at the moment when the man was tired of the boy's childish folly, and the meaning of the vision fixed still deeper in his heart what he had already desired, he gave up his companionship of the boy and left the noble family to which he was attached. He would not have done this with impunity, however, if their respect for my mother, as well as her power, had not protected him.

Chapter 5

Placed under him, I was taught with such purity and checked with such honesty from the vices which commonly spring up in youth that I was kept from ordinary games and never allowed to leave my master's company, or to eat anywhere else than at home, or to accept gifts from anyone without his leave; in everything I had to show self-control in word, look, and deed, so that he seemed to require of me the conduct of a monk rather than a clerk. While others of my age wandered everywhere at will and were unchecked in the indulgence of such inclinations as were natural at their age, I, hedged in with constant restraints and dressed in my clerical garb,[4] would sit and look at the troops of players like a beast awaiting sacrifice. Even on Sundays and saints' days I had to submit to the severity of school exercises. At hardly any time, and never for a whole day, was I allowed to take a holiday; in fact, in every way and at all times I was driven to study. Moreover, he devoted himself exclusively to my education, since he was allowed to have no other pupil.

He worked me hard, and anyone observing us might have thought that my little mind was being exceedingly sharpened by such perseverance, but the hopes of all were disappointed. He was, in fact, utterly unskilled in prose and verse composition. Meanwhile I was pelted almost every day

---

4   Guibert here puns on *infulsa*, which in classical Latin sometimes means a woolen headdress worn by a victim about to be sacrificed.

with a hail of blows and harsh words while he was forcing me to learn what he could not teach.

In this fruitless struggle I passed nearly six years with him, but got no reward worth the time it took. Yet otherwise, in all that is supposed to count for good training, he devoted himself completely to my improvement. Most faithfully and lovingly he instilled in me all that was temperate and modest and outwardly refined. But I clearly perceived that he had no consideration or restraint in the trial he put me to, urging me on without intermission and with great pain under the pretense of teaching me. By the strain of undue application, the natural powers of grown men, as well as of boys, are blunted, and the hotter the fire of their mental activity in unremitting study, the sooner is the strength of their understanding weakened and chilled by excess, and its energy turned to apathy.

It is therefore necessary to treat the mind with greater moderation while it is still burdened with its bodily covering. If there is to be silence in heaven for half an hour, so that while it continues the unremitting activity of contemplation cannot exist, in the same way what I may call perseverance will not stay fresh while struggling with some problem. Hence we believe that when the mind has been fixed exclusively on one subject, we ought to give it relaxation from its intensity, so that after dealing in turn with different subjects we may with renewed energy, as after a holiday, fasten upon that one with which our minds are most engaged. In short, let wearied nature be refreshed at times by varying its work. Let us remember that God did not make the world without variety, but in day and night, spring and summer, winter and autumn, He has delighted us by temporal change. Let everyone who has the name of master see in what manner he may moderate the teaching of boys and youths, since such men think their students should be treated like old men who are completely serious.

Now, my teacher had a harsh love for me, for he showed excessive severity in his unjust floggings, and yet the great care with which he guarded me was evident in his acts. Clearly I did not deserve to be beaten, for if he had the skill in teaching which he professed, it is certain that I, though a boy, would have been well able to grasp anything that he taught. But because he stated his thoughts poorly and what he strove to express was not at all clear to him, his talk rolled ineffectively on and on in a banal but by no means obvious circle, which could not be brought to any conclusion, much less understood. He was so uninstructed that he retained incorrectly, as I have said before, what he had once learned badly late in life, and if he let anything slip out (incautiously, as it were), he maintained and defended it with blows, regarding all his own opinions as firmly established. I think he certainly should have avoided such folly, for indeed, a learned man says, "before one's nature has absorbed knowledge, it is less praiseworthy to say what you know than to keep silent about what you do not know."

While he took cruel vengeance on me for not knowing what he did not know himself, he ought certainly to have considered that it was very wrong to demand from a weak little mind what he had not put into it. For as the words of madmen can be understood by the sane with difficulty or not at all, so the talk of those who are ignorant but say they know something and pass it on to others will be the more darkened by their own explanations. You will find nothing more difficult than trying to discourse on what you do not understand, so that your subject is obscure to the speaker and even more to the listener, making both look like blockheads. I say this, O my God, not to put a stigma on such a friend, but for every reader to understand that we should not attempt to teach as a certainty every assertion we make, and that we should not involve others in the mists of our own conjectures.

It has been my purpose here, in consideration of the poorness of my subject to give it some flavor by reasoning about things, so that if the one deserves to be reckoned of little value, the other may sometimes be regarded as worthwhile.

Chapter 6

Although he crushed me by such severity yet in other ways he made it quite plain that he loved me as well as he did himself. With such watchful care did he devote himself to me, with such foresight did he secure my welfare against the spite of others and teach me on what authority I should beware of the dissolute manners of some who paid court to me, and so long did he argue with my mother about the elaborate richness of my dress, that he was thought to guard me as a parent, not as a master, and not my body alone but my soul as well. As for me, considering the dull sensibility of my age and my littleness, I conceived much love for him in response, in spite of the many weals with which he furrowed my tender skin, so that not through fear, as is common in those of my age, but through a sort of love deeply implanted in the heart, I obeyed him in utter forgetfulness of his severity. Indeed, when my master and my mother saw me paying due respect to both alike, they tried by frequent tests to see whether I would dare to prefer one or the other.

At last, without any intention on the part of either, an opportunity occurred for a test which left no room for doubt. Once I had been beaten in school—the school being no other than the dining hall of our house, for he had given up the charge of others to take me alone, my mother having wisely required him to do this for a higher wage and a better position. When my studies, such as they were, had come to an end about the time of vespers, I went to my mother's knee after a more severe beating than I had deserved. And when, as often happened, she began to ask me repeatedly whether I had been whipped that day, I, not to appear a telltale, entirely denied it. Then against my will she threw off my inner garment (which is called a shirt or *chemise*) and saw my little arms blackened and the skin of my back everywhere puffed up with the cuts from the twigs. Grieved to the heart by the very savage punishment inflicted on my tender body, troubled, agitated, and weeping with sorrow, she said: "You shall never become a clerk, nor any more suffer so much to get an education." At that, looking at her with what reproach I could, I replied: "If I had to die on the spot, I would not give up studying my lessons and becoming a clerk." I should add that she had promised that if I wished to become a knight, when I reached the age for it she would give me the arms and equipment of knighthood.

When I had declined all these offers with a good deal of scorn, she, Thy servant, O Lord, accepted this rebuff so gladly, and was made so cheerful by my disdain of her proposal, that she repeated to my master the reply with which I had opposed her. Then both rejoiced that I had such an eager longing to fulfill my father's vow. I was eager to pursue my lessons more quickly, although I was poorly taught. Moreover, I did not shirk the church offices; indeed, when the hour sounded or there was occasion, I did not prefer even my meals to that place and time. That is how it was then: but Thou, O God, knowest how much I afterward fell away from that zeal, how reluctantly I went to divine services, hardly consenting even when driven to them by blows. Clearly, O Lord, the impulses that animated me then were not religious feelings begotten by thoughtfulness, but only a child's eagerness. But after adolescence had exhausted itself in bringing forth wickedness within me, I hastened toward the loss of all shame and that former zeal entirely faded away. Although for a brief space, my God, good resolve seemed to shine forth, it came to pass that it soon vanished, overshadowed by the storm clouds of my evil imagination.

Chapter 7

At length my mother tried by every means to get me into a church living. Now, the first opportunity for placing me was not only badly but abominably chosen. My adolescent brother, a knight and defender of the castle of Clermont (which, I should say, is situated between Compiègne and Beauvais), was expecting some money from the lord of that stronghold, either as largess or as a moneyfief, I do not know which.[5] And when he deferred payment, probably through want of ready money, by the advice of some of my kinsmen it was suggested to him that he should give me a canonry, called a prebend, in the church of that place (which, contrary to canon law, was subject to his authority)[6] and that he should then cease to be troubled for what he owed.

---

5   The lord of Clermont-en-Beauvais was Renaud I, who fought at the battle of Mortemer in 1054 and was still alive in 1084. Guibert refers to his brother as *municeps*, an ambiguous word which probably means that he was one of the nobles of the castle.

6   The collegiate church attached to the castle of Clermont was consecrated to the Virgin and St. Arnoul, and came to be known as Notre-Damedu-Chatel. Although church reformers of the late eleventh century condemned lay presentation to canonries and other ecclesiastical benefices, the practice remained common. While it would have been improper for a boy not yet twelve to be given a benefice, this abuse, too, was not uncommon.

At that time the apostolic see was making a fresh attack on married priests; this led to an outburst of rage against them by people who were so zealous about the clergy that they angrily demanded that married priests should either be deprived of their benefices or should cease to perform their priestly duties. Thereupon a certain nephew of my father, a man conspicuous for his power and knowledge but so bestial in his debauchery that he had no respect for any woman's conjugal ties, now violently inveighed against the clergy because of this canon, as if exceptional purity of heart drove him to horror of such practices. A layman himself, he refused to be bound by a layman's laws, their very laxity making his abuse of them more shameful. The marriage net could not hold him; he never allowed himself to be entangled in its folds. Being everywhere in the worst odor through such conduct, but protected by the rank which his worldly power gave him, he was never prevented by the reproach of his own unchastity from thundering persistently against the holy clergy.

Having found a pretext by which I might profit at the expense of a priest with a benefice, he begged the lord of the castle, with whom, as one of his intimates, he had more than sufficient influence, to summon me and invest me with that canonry, on the ground that the cleric was an absentee and utterly unsuitable for the office. For, contrary to all ecclesiastical law and right, he held the office of abbot by permission of the bishop, and, not being under rule himself, he demanded obedience to rule from those who were.[7] At this time not only was it treated as a serious offense for the members of the higher orders[8] and the canons to be married, but it was also considered a crime to purchase ecclesiastical offices involving pastoral care, such as prebends and the offices of precentor, provost, etc., not to speak of the higher dignities. Consequently, those who were empowered to transact the affairs of the church, those who favored the side of the cleric who had lost his prebend, and many of my contemporaries began to stir up a whispering campaign about simony

and excommunication, which recently the cleric had talked of publicly.

Now, married priest as he was, although he would not be separated from his wife by the suspension of his office, at least he had given up celebrating mass. Because he treated the divine mysteries as of less importance than his own body, he was rightly caught in that punishment which he thought to escape by the renunciation of the Sacrifice. And so, being stripped of his canonry, because there was no longer anything to restrain him, he now began freely to celebrate mass, while keeping his wife. Then a rumor grew that at this service he was daily repeating the excommunication of my mother and her family. My mother, always fearful in religious matters, dreading the punishment of her sins and therefore the giving of offense, thereupon surrendered the prebend which had been wickedly granted, and, in the expectation of some cleric's death, bargained with the lord of the castle for another for me. Thus "we flee from weapons of iron and fall before a bow of brass," for to grant something in anticipation of another's death is nothing else than a daily incentive to murder.

O Lord my God, at that time I was wrapped up in these evil hopes and in no wise occupied with waiting for Thy gifts, which I had not yet learned to know. This woman, Thy servant, did not yet understand the hope, the certainty, she ought to have of my sustenance in Thee and had not learned what benefits had already been won for me from Thee. Since while still in the world she had for a short time thoughts that were of the world, it is no wonder that she sought to obtain for me those things which she had chosen to get for herself, believing that I, too, would desire the things of the world. Later, however, after perceiving the peril of her own soul, when she burdened the many secret places of her heart with sorrow for her past life, then she thought it the worst madness to practice for others what she scorned for herself, as though she had said, "What I do not wish to be done to me, I will not do to another," and what she had ceased to seek for herself, she

---

7 That is, with the authorization of the bishop of Beauvais the lord of Clermont had the right of presentation and oversight over the canons of the church in his castle.

8 Priest, deacon, and subdeacon.

thought it a wicked thing to desire for someone else, if he should be injured by it. Far different is the practice of many, whom we see with a show of poverty casting away their own advantages but too eager to secure the advancement of others not only of their own family, which is bad enough, but of those unrelated to them, which is worse....

Chapter 12

After these lengthy accounts I return to Thee, my God, to speak of the conversion of that good woman, my mother. When hardly of marriageable age, she was given to my father, a mere youth, by the provision of my grandfather, since she was of the nobility, had a very pretty face, and was naturally and most becomingly of sober mien. She had, however, conceived a fear of God's name at the very beginning of her childhood. She had learned to be terrified of sin, not from experience but from dread of some sort of blow from on high, and—as she often told me herself—this dread had so possessed her mind with the terror of sudden death that in later years she grieved because she no longer felt in her maturity the same stings of righteous fear as she had in her unformed and ignorant youth.

Now, it so happened that at the very beginning of that lawful union conjugal intercourse was made ineffective through the bewitchments of certain persons. It was said that their marriage drew upon them the envy of a stepmother, who had some nieces of great beauty and nobility and who was plotting to slip one of them into my father's bed. Meeting with no success in her designs, she is said to have used magical arts to prevent entirely the consummation of the marriage. His wife's virginity thus remained intact for three years, during which he endured his great misfortune in silence; at last, driven to it by those close to him, my father was the first to reveal the facts. In all sorts of ways, his kinsmen endeavored to bring about a divorce, and by their constant pressure upon my father, who was then young and dull-witted, they tried to induce him to become a monk, although at that time there was little talk

of this order. They did not do this for his soul's good, however, but with the purpose of getting possession of his property.

When their suggestion produced no effect, they began to hound the girl herself, far away as she was from her kinsfolk and harassed by the violence of strangers, into voluntary flight out of sheer exhaustion under their insults, and without waiting for divorce. She endured all this, bearing with calmness the abuse that was aimed at her, and if out of this rose any strife, she pretended ignorance of it. Besides this, certain rich men, perceiving that she was not in fact a wife, began to assail the heart of the young girl; but Thou, O Lord, the builder of inward chastity, didst inspire her with purity stronger than her nature or her youth. Thy grace it was that saved her from burning, though set in the midst of flames, Thy doing that her weak soul was not hurt by the poison of evil talk, and that when enticements from without were added to those impulses common to our human nature, like oil poured upon the flames yet the young maiden's heart was always under her control and never won from her by any allurements. Are not such things solely Thy doing, O Lord? When she was in the heat of youth and continually engaged in wifely duties, yet for seven whole years[9] Thou didst keep her in such continence that, in the words of a certain wise man, even "rumor dared not speak lies about her."

O God, Thou knowest how hard, how almost impossible it would be for women of the present time to keep such chastity as this; whereas there was in those days such modesty that hardly ever was the good name of a married woman sullied by evil rumor. Ah! how wretchedly have modesty and honor in the state of virginity declined from that time to this our present age, and both the reality and the show of a married woman's protection fallen to ruin. Therefore coarse mirth is all that may be noted in their manners and naught but jesting heard, with sly winks and ceaseless chatter. Wantonness shows in their gait, only silliness in their behavior. So much does the extravagance of their dress depart from the old simplicity that in the enlargement of their sleeves, the

---

9   Since earlier in the chapter Guibert says that consummation was delayed for three years, this and the following reference to seven years may be figurative and intended to call to mind the seven-year periods Jacob served for Rachel.

tightness of their dresses, the distortion of their shoes of Cordovan leather with their curling toes, they seem to proclaim that everywhere modesty is a castaway. A lack of lovers to admire her is a woman's crown of woe, and on her crowds of thronging suitors rests her claim to nobility and courtly pride. There was at that time, I call God to witness, greater modesty in married men, who would have blushed to be seen in the company of such women, than there is now in brides. By such shameful conduct they turn men into greater braggarts and lovers of the market place and the public street.

What is the end of all this, Lord God, but that no one blushes for his own levity and licentiousness, because he knows that all are tarred with the same brush, and, seeing himself in the same case as all others, why then should he be ashamed of pursuits in which he knows all others engage? But why do I say "ashamed" when such men feel shame only if someone excels them as an example of lustfulness? A man's private boastfulness about the number of his loves or his choice of a beauty whom he has seduced is no reproach to him, nor is he scorned for vaunting his love affairs before Thee. Instead, his part in furthering the general corruption meets with the approval of all. Listen to the cheers when, with the inherent looseness of unbridled passions which deserve the doom of eternal silence, he shamelessly noises abroad what ought to have been hidden in shame, what should have burdened his soul with the guilt of ruined chastity and plunged him in the depths of despair. In this and similar ways, this modern age is corrupt and corrupting, distributing evil ideas to some, while the filth thereof, spreading to others, goes on increasing without end.

Holy God, scarcely any such thing was heard of in the time when Thy handmaid was behaving as she did; indeed, then shameful things were hidden under the cloak of sacred modesty and things of honor had their crown. In those seven years, O Lord, that virginity which Thou didst in wondrous fashion prolong in her was in agony under

countless wrongs, as frequently they threatened to dissolve her marriage with my father and give her to another husband or to send her away to the remote houses of my distant relatives. Under such grievous treatment she suffered bitterly at times, but with Thy support, O God, she strove with wonderful self-control against the enticements of her own flesh and the inducements of others.

I do not say, gracious Lord, that she did this out of virtue, but that the virtue was Thine alone. For how could that be virtue that came of no conflict between body and spirit, no straining after God, but only from concern for outward honor and to avoid disgrace? No doubt a sense of shame has its use, if only to resist the approach of sin, but what is useful before a sin is committed is damnable afterward. What prostrates the self with the shame of propriety, holding it back from sinful deeds, is useful at the time, since the fear of God can bring aid, giving holy seasoning to shame's lack of savor, and can make that which was profitable at the time (that is, in the world) useful not for a moment but eternally. But after a sin is committed a sense of shame which leads to vanity is the more deadly the more it obstinately resists the healing of holy confession. The desire of my mother, Thy servant, O Lord God, was to do nothing to hurt her worldly honor, yet following Thy Gregory, whom, however, she had never read or heard read, she did not maintain that desire, for afterward she surrendered all her desires into Thy sole keeping. It was therefore good for her at that time to be attached to her worldly reputation.

Since the bewitchment by which the bond of natural and lawful intercourse was broken lasted seven years and more, it is all too easy to believe that, just as by prestidigitation the faculty of sight may be deceived so that conjurers seem to produce something out of nothing, so to speak, and to make certain things out of others, so reproductive power and effort may be inhibited by much less art; and indeed it is now a common practice, understood even by ignorant people.[10] When that bewitchment was broken by a certain old woman,

---

10 Writing early in the eleventh century, Burchard of Worms proposed that priests hearing confessions might ask, "Hast thou done what some adulteresses are wont to do? When first they learn that their lovers wish to take legitimate wives, they thereupon by some trick of magic extinguish the male desire, so that they are impotent and cannot consummate their union with their legitimate wives. If thou hast done or taught others to do this, thou shouldst do penance for forty days on bread and water." See *Medieval Handbooks of Penance*, trans. John T. McNeill and Helena M. Gamer (New York, 1938), 340.

my mother submitted to the duties of a wife as faithfully as she had kept her virginity when she was assailed by so many attacks. In other ways she was truly fortunate, but she laid herself open not so much to endless misery as to mourning when she, whose goodness was ever growing, gave birth to an evil son who (in my own person) grew worse and worse. Yet Thou knowest, Almighty One, with what purity and holiness in obedience to Thee she raised me, how greatly she provided me with the care of nurses in infancy and of masters and teachers in boyhood, with no lack even of fine clothes for my little body, so that I seemed to equal the sons of kings and counts in indulgence.

And not only in my mother, O Lord, didst Thou put this love for me, but Thou didst inspire with it other, far richer persons, so that rather because of the grace Thou didst grant me than under the obligations of kinship, they lavished on me careful tending and nurture.

O God, Thou knowest what warnings, what prayers she daily poured into my ears not to listen to corrupting words from anyone. Whenever she had leisure from household cares, she taught me how and for what I ought to pray to Thee. Thou alone knowest with what pains she labored so that the sound beginning of a happy and honorable childhood which Thou hadst granted might not be ruined by an unsound heart. Thou didst make it her desire that I should without ceasing burn with zeal for Thee, that above all Thou might add to my outward comeliness inner goodness and wisdom. Gracious God, Gracious Lord, if she had known in advance under what heaps of filth I should blot out the fair surface of Thy gifts, bestowed by Thee at her prayer, what would she have said? What would she have done? How hopeless the lamentations she would have uttered! How much anguish she would have suffered! Thanks to Thee, sweet and temperate Creator, "Who hath made our hearts." If, indeed, her vision had pierced the secret places of my heart, unworthy of her pure gaze, I wonder if she would not there and then have died.

Chapter 13

After introducing these comments by way of anticipation, let us return to what we left further

back. I have learned that this woman had such a fear of God's name, even while she was serving the world, that in her obedience to the church, in almsgiving, in her offerings for masses, her conduct was such as to win respect from all. Full belief in my story will, I know, be made difficult by a natural suspicion that the partiality of a son has exaggerated her virtues. If to praise one's mother be thought a cautious, disingenuous way of glorifying oneself, I dare to call Thee to witness, O God, Who knowest her soul, in which Thou didst dwell, that I have truthfully asserted her surpassing merit. And indeed, since it is clearer than daylight that my life has strayed from the paths of the good and that my pursuits have always been an affront to any sensible person, of what avail will the reputation of my mother and father or ancestors be to me when all their grandeur will be squeezed out of their wretched offspring? I, who through lack of will and deed fail to make their behavior live again, am riding posthaste to infamy if I claim their praise for myself.

While she was still a young married woman, something happened which gave no slight impulse to the amendment of her life. The French in the time of King Henri were fighting with great bitterness against the Normans and their Count William, who afterward conquered England and Scotland, and in that clash of the two nations it was my father's fate to be taken prisoner. It was the custom of this count never to hold prisoners for ransom, but to condemn them to captivity for life. When the news was brought to his wife (I put aside the name of mother, for I was not yet born, nor was I for a long time after), she was struck down half dead with wretched sorrow; she abstained from food and drink, and sleep was still more difficult through her despairing anxiety, the cause of this being not the amount of his ransom but the impossibility of his release.

In the dead of the night, as she lay in her bed full of deep anxiety, since it is the habit of the Devil to invade souls weakened with grief, suddenly, while she lay awake, the Enemy himself lay upon her and by the burden of his weight almost crushed the life out of her. As she choked in the agony of her spirit and lost all use of her limbs, she was unable to make a single sound; completely silenced but with her reason free, she awaited aid from God alone. Then suddenly from the head of her bed a spirit, without doubt a good one, began to cry out in loud and kindly tones, "Holy Mary, help her." After the spirit had spoken out in this fashion for a bit, and she had fully understood what he was saying and was aware that he was thoroughly outraged, he sallied forth burning with anger. Thereupon he who lay on her rose up, and the other met and seized him and by the strength of God overthrew him with a great crash, so that the room shook heavily with the shock of it, and the maidservants, who were fast asleep, were rudely awakened. When the Enemy had thus been driven out by divine power, the good spirit who had called upon Mary and routed the Devil turned to her whom he had rescued and said, "Take care to be a good woman." The attendants, alarmed by the sudden uproar, rose to see how their mistress was and found her half dead, with the blood drained from her face and all the strength crushed out of her body. They questioned her about the noise and heard about the causes of it from her, and they were scarcely able by their presence and talk and by the lighting of a lamp to revive her.

Those last words of her deliverer—nay, Thy words, O Lord God, through the mouth of Thy messenger—were stored up forever in the woman's memory and she stood ready to be guided to a greater love, if with God's help the opportunity should occur later. Now, after the death of my father, although the beauty of her face and form remain undimmed, and I, scarcely half a year old, gave her reason enough for anxiety, she resolved to continue in her widowhood. With what spirit she ruled herself and what an example of modesty she set may be gathered from the following event. When my father's kinsmen, eager for his fiefs and possessions, strove to take them all by excluding my mother, they fixed a day in court for advancing their claims. The day came and the barons were assembled to deliver justice. My mother withdrew into the church, away from the avaricious plotters, and was standing before the image of the crucified Lord, mindful of the prayers she owed. One of my father's kinsmen, who shared the views of the others and was sent by them, came to request her presence to hear their decision, as they were waiting for her. Whereupon she said, "I will take part in this matter only in the presence of my Lord." "Whose lord?" said he. Then, stretching out her hand toward the image of the crucified Lord, she replied, "This is my Lord, the advocate under whose protection I will plead." At that the man reddened and, not being very subtle, put on a wry smile to hide his evil intent and went off to tell his friends what he had heard. And they, too, were covered with confusion at such an answer, since they knew that in the face of her utter honesty they had no just grounds, and so they ceased to trouble her.

Shortly after that, one of the leading men of that place and province, my father's nephew, who was as greedy as he was powerful, addressed the woman in the following terms: "Madame," said he, "since you have sufficient youth and beauty, you ought to marry, so that your life in this world would be more pleasant, and the children of my uncle would come under my care to be brought up by me in a worthy fashion, and finally his possessions would devolve to my authority, as it is right they should."[11] She replied, however, "You know that your uncle was of very noble descent. Since God has taken him away, Hymen shall not repeat his rites over me, my lord, unless a marriage with some much greater noble shall offer itself." Now, the woman was quite crafty in speaking of marrying a greater noble, knowing that could hardly, if at all, come to pass. Consequently, since he bristled at her talk of a higher noble, she, who was wholly set against nobles and commoners alike, put an end to all expectation of a second marriage. When he set down to overweening pride her talk of a greater noble, she replied, "Certainly either a greater noble or no husband at all." Perceiving the resolution with which the lady spoke, he desisted from his designs, and never again sought anything of the kind from her.

In great fear of God and with no less love of all her kin and especially of the poor, this woman wisely ruled our household and our property. That loyalty which she had given her husband in

---

11   By the law of succession being applied here, if a widow remarried, her dower was held in trust by the family of her first husband to be administered for the children of that marriage.

his lifetime she kept unbroken and with double constancy to his spirit, since she did not break the ancient union of their bodies by a substitution of other flesh on his departure, and almost every day she endeavored to help him by the offering of her life-bringing sacrifice. Friendly to all the poor in general, to some in her great pity she was generous and courtly to the full extent of her means. The sting of remembering her sins could not have been sharper if she had been given up to all kinds of wickedness and dreaded the punishment of every ill deed that is done. In plainness of living there was nothing else she could do, for her delicacy and her customary sumptuous diet did not accord with frugality. In other matters her behavior was completely unexpected. I personally have both seen and made certain by touch that although on certain occasions she wore outer garments of rich material, next to her skin she was covered with the roughest haircloth. Although her delicate skin was completely unaccustomed to it, she wore this cloth throughout the day and even went to bed in it at night.

She never or hardly ever missed the night offices, while she regularly attended the assemblies of God's people in holy seasons, in such fashion that scarcely ever in her house was there rest from the singing of God's praises by her chaplains, who were always busy at their office. So constantly was her dead husband's name on her lips that her mind seemed to turn on no other subject, and in her prayers, in giving alms, even in the midst of ordinary business, she continually spoke of the man, because she could do nothing without thinking of him. For when the heart is full of love for someone, the mouth shapes his name whether one wants to or not.

Chapter 14

Passing over those matters in which she showed her goodness, but not her most admirable qualities, let us proceed with what is left. When I had passed about twelve years, as I was told, after my father's death, and his widow had managed her house and children while wearing a laywoman's clothes, she now made haste to bring to happy birth a resolve with which she had long been in labor. While she was still pondering this idea,

discussing it with no one but that master and teacher of mine whom I discussed before, I heard a certain devil-possessed dependent of hers, who was rambling on under the Devil's influence about other matters, shouting out these words, "The priests have placed a cross in her loins." Nothing indeed could have been truer, although I did not then understand what he was intimating, for thereafter she submitted not to one but to many crosses. Soon afterward, while her intention was still unknown to anyone but the person I have mentioned, who was then a sort of steward in her house and who himself a little later followed her in her conversion by renouncing the world, she saw the following vision in a dream: she seemed to be marrying a man and celebrating her nuptials, much to the amazement and even stupefaction of her children, friends, and kinsfolk. The next day when my mother went into the country for a walk attended by the man who was my teacher and her steward, he explained what she had seen. My mother did not need to be a skilled interpreter in such matters. One look at my master's face, and without speech from him she knew that the vision pointed to the subject of their many conversations about the love of God, to Whom she longed to be united. Making haste with what she had begun and overcome by the burning zeal within her, she withdrew from the life of the town in which she lived.

At the time of this withdrawal, she stayed with the owner's permission at a certain manor belonging to the lord of Beauvais, Bishop Guy. This Guy was a man of courtly manner and noble birth, in person well-fitted for the office he held. After conferring notable benefits on the church of Beauvais, such as laying the first stone of a church for regular canons dedicated to St. Quentin, he was charged before Archbishop Hugues of Lyon, the papal legate, with simony and other crimes by those who owed their training and advancement to him. Because he did not appear when summonsed, he was declared deposed by default, and, being at Cluny and afraid of the sentence pronounced against him, he retired into the monastery there. Since he seemed to cherish my mother and my family and loved me most of all with a special affection, as one who had received from him every sacrament of benediction except that of the priesthood, when members of my mother's household asked him to live for a while in his property adjoining the church of that place, he gladly consented. Now, this manor, named Catenoy, was about two miles distant from our town.

While staying there, she resolved to retire to the monastery of Fly. After my master had a little house built for her there near the church, she then came forth from the place where she was staying. She knew that I should be utterly an orphan with no one at all on whom to depend, for great as was my wealth of kinsfolk and connections, yet there was no one to give me the loving care a little child needs at such an age; though I did not lack for the necessities of food and clothing. I often suffered from the loss of that careful provision for the helplessness of tender years that only a woman can provide. As I said, although she knew that I would be condemned to such neglect, yet Thy love and fear, O God, hardened her heart. Still, when on the way to that monastery she passed below the stronghold where I remained, the sight of the castle gave intolerable anguish to her lacerated heart, stung with the bitter remembrance of what she had left behind. No wonder indeed if her limbs seemed to be torn from her body, since she knew for certain that she was a cruel and unnatural mother. Indeed, she heard this said aloud, as she had in this way cut off her heart and left bereft of succor such a fine child, made worthy, it was asserted, by so much affection, since I was held in high regard not only by our own family but by outsiders. And Thou, good and gracious God, didst by Thy sweetness and love marvelously harden her heart, the tenderest in all the world, that it might not be tender to her own soul's harm. For tenderness would then have been her ruin, if she, neglecting her God, in her worldly care for me had put me before her own salvation. But "her love was strong as death," for the closer her love for Thee, the greater her composure in breaking from those she loved before.

Coming to the cloister, she found an old woman in the habit of a nun whom she compelled to live with her, declaring that she would submit to her discipline, as she gave the appearance of great piety. "Compelled," I say, because once she had tested the woman's character, she exerted all her powers of persuasion to get her companionship.

And so she began gradually to copy the severity of the older woman, to imitate her meager diet, to choose the plainest food, to give up the soft mattress to which she had been accustomed, to sleep in contentment with only straw and a sheet. And since she still had much beauty and showed no sign of age, she purposely strove to assume the appearance of age with an old woman's wrinkles and bowed form. Her long flowing locks, which usually serve as a woman's crowning beauty, were frequently cut short with the scissors; her dress was black and unpleasant-looking, its unfashionable width adorned with countless patches; her cloak was undyed and her shoes were pierced with many a hole past mending, for there was within her one whom she tried to please with such mean apparel.

Since she had learned the beginning of good deeds from the confession of her old sins, she repeated her confessions almost daily. Consequently, her mind was forever occupied in searching out her past deeds, what she had thought or done or said as a maiden of tender years, or in her married life, or as a widow with a wider range of activities, continually examining the seat of reason and bringing what she found to the knowledge of a priest, or rather to God through him. Then you might have seen the woman praying with such sharp sighs, pining away with such anguish of spirit that as she worshiped, there was scarcely ever a pause in the heart-rending sobs that went with her entreaties. She had learned the seven penitential psalms from the old woman I mentioned before, not by sight but by ear, and day and night she turned them over in her mind, chewing them with such savor, one might say, that the sighs and groans of those sweet angel songs never ceased to echo in Thy ears, O Lord. But whenever assemblies of people from outside disturbed her beloved solitude—for all who were acquainted with her, especially men and women of noble rank, took pleasure in conversing with her because of her wondrous wit and forbearance—on their departure, every untrue, idle, or thoughtless word she had uttered during their talk begat in her soul indescribable anguish until she reached the familiar waters of penitence or confession.

Whatever the zeal and anxiety she showed in such matters, she could win for her soul no confidence, no composure to stay her unceasing lamentations, her earnest and tearful questionings whether she could ever earn pardon for her offenses. Thou knowest, O Lord, the extent of her sins, and I have some knowledge of it. How small was their whole sum compared with those of others who neither sorrow nor sigh! Thou knowest, O Lord, how well I was able to assess the condition of her thoughts, because I never saw her heart grow cold in the fear of punishment and in her love for Thee.

Chapter 15

Why go on? While she was divorcing herself from the world in the manner I have described, I was left without a mother, teacher, and master. For he who after my mother had so faithfully trained and taught me, fired by my mother's example, love, and counsel, himself entered the monastery of Fly. Possessing a perverted liberty, I began without any self-control to abuse my power, to mock at churches, to detest school, to try to gain the company of my young lay cousins devoted to knightly pursuits by cursing the appearance of a clerk, to promise remission of sins, and to indulge in sleep, in which formerly I was allowed little relaxation, so that by unaccustomed excess of it my body began to degenerate. Meanwhile my mother heard the agitating news of my doings and was struck half dead by what she heard, surmising my immediate ruin. For the fine clothing which I had for the church processions, provided by her in the hope that I might be the more eager for the clerk's life, I wore everywhere on wanton pursuits which my age did not permit; I emulated older boys in their juvenile rowdiness, and I was completely bereft of responsibility and discretion.

The more restrained and chastened I had been before, the worse my looseness, or even madness, now became. Unable to endure what she heard, my mother therefore went to the abbot and begged him and the brotherhood that my master might be allowed to resume my training. The abbot, brought up by my grandfather and under obligation for benefits received at his court, was amenable; he gave me a ready welcome and followed up his kind reception with still kinder treatment thereafter. I call Thee to witness, Holy God and my Provider, that from the moment I entered the monastery church and saw the monks sitting there, at that sight I was seized by a longing for the monk's life which never grew cold, and my spirit had no rest until its desire was fulfilled. Since I lived with them in the same cloister and observed their whole existence and condition, as the flame increases when fanned by the wind, so by contemplation of them my soul, yearning continually to be like them, could not but be on fire. Lastly, with redoubled entreaties the abbot of the place daily urged me to become a monk there, and although I passionately desired to do so, my tongue could not be loosened by any of the demands of those who desired me to make such a promise. Although now that I have grown older it would be very hard for me to keep silent with such a full heart, as a boy I was able to maintain that silence without much difficulty.

After some time I brought up the matter with my mother, and she, fearing the instability of boyhood, rejected my proposal with a great many arguments, which made me very sorry that I had revealed my intention. When I also told my master, he opposed it still more. Deeply annoyed at the opposition of both, I determined to turn my mind elsewhere; and so I began to act as if I had never had such a desire. After putting the matter off from the week of Pentecost until Christmas, and being both eager and anxious to bring the matter to an end, I was unable to bear Thy incitement within me, O Lord, and threw off my respect for my mother and my fear of my master. I went to the abbot, who greatly desired this to happen but had failed to draw any promise from me, and cast myself at his feet, tearfully imploring him, using these very words, to receive a sinner. He gladly granted my prayer and provided the necessary habit as soon as he could—that is, on the next day—and invested me with it while my mother watched in tears from afar, and he ordered that alms should be offered on that day.

Meanwhile my former master, who was unable to teach me any longer because of the stricter rule, at least took care to urge me to subject to close interrogation those holy books which I was reading, to reflect upon those discourses less known by more learned men, and to compose short pieces of prose and verse, warning me to apply myself the more closely because less care was being expended by others on my instruction. O Lord, True Light, I well remember the inestimable bounty Thou didst then bestow on me. For as soon as I had taken Thy habit at Thy invitation, a cloud seemed to be removed from the face of my understanding and I soon began to find my way through those things in which earlier I had wandered blindly and in error. Besides, I was suddenly inspired with such a love of learning that I yearned for it above all else and thought the day was lost on which I did not engage in some such work. How often they thought I was asleep and resting my little body under the coverlet when my mind was really concentrated on composition, or I was reading under a blanket, fearful of the rebuke of the others.

And Thou, Holy Jesus, didst know with what motive I did this, chiefly to win glory and so that greater honor in this present world might be thine. My friends were clearly my enemies, for although they gave me good advice, yet they often plied me with talk of fame and literary distinction and, through these things, the winning of high status and wealth. They put into my shortsighted mind hopes worse than the eggs of asps, and since I believed that all their promises would quickly come to pass, they deceived me with the vainest expectations. What they said might come to pass in the fullness of age, I thought I would surely attain in adolescence or early manhood. They proclaimed my learning (which by Thy gift was daily increasing) and good birth according to worldly standards and good looks, but they did not remember that by such steps a man "shall not go up unto Thy altar, lest his nakedness be discovered." For he that "climbeth up another way, the same is a thief and a robber," which is nakedness.

But in these beginnings of mine under Thy inspiration, if it had any wisdom at all, my mind ought to have been prepared for temptation. In truth my wisdom at that time was to some degree foolishness. Although I was moved by the childish emotions of joy or anger, would that I now, O Lord, so hated my great sins as then I feared Thy judgment and hated sins that were minor or scarcely sins at all. Sensibly and with great eagerness, I imitated those whom I saw weeping bitterly for their sins, and whatever came from Thee gave delight to my sight and hearing. And I who now search the Scriptures for vocabulary and matter for display, and even store in my mind the disreputable sayings of pagan writers to make mere babbling, in those days got from them tears and matter for sorrow, and thought my reading vain if I found in it no matter for meditation, nothing leading to repentance. So, unknowingly, I acted wisely.

But that old Foe, who has learned from ages of experience how to deal with the varying conditions of heart and age, he, I say conceived new conflicts for me, according to the measure of my mind and little body. He presented to my gaze in sleep many visions of dead men, especially those whom I had seen or heard of as slain with swords or by some such death, and by such sights he so terrified my spirit when it was relaxed in sleep that but for the watchful protection of that master of mine, I could not have been kept in my bed at night, or prevented from calling out, and I would have nearly gone out of my mind. Although this trouble may seem childish and ridiculous to those who have not felt it, it is regarded as a great calamity by those who are oppressed by it, so that fear itself, which most men consider absurd, can be held in check by no reasoning or counsel. Although the sufferer himself cares not at all for what he suffers, his spirit, when once for a brief moment it is plunged in sleep, has no power to shake off the horrid sights; indeed, the mind, deeply disturbed by its terrors, dreads the return of sleep itself. To this emotion, crowds or solitude are the same, since the company of others is no defense against such fear, and dwelling alone either leaves it as bad as before or makes it worse.

My condition, Lord God, was then far different from my present state. Then I clearly had great respect for Thy law and unbounded loathing for all sin, and I eagerly drank in all that could be said or heard or known from Thee. I know, Heavenly Father, that by such childish application the Devil was savagely enraged, although later he was appeased by the surrender of all my pious fervor. One night, in winter, I believe, kept awake by my wretched anxiety, I was lying in my bed, thinking I was safer with a lamp close by that gave a bright light, when suddenly and apparently close above my head there arose the tumult of many voices, although it was the dead of night. One voice uttered no words, but only a howl of distress. Shaken by these nightmarish events, I lost my senses and seemed to see a certain dead man who, someone cried out, had been killed at the baths. Struck with the terror of the phantasy, I leaped screaming from my bed, and, looking around as I leaped, I saw the lamp extinguished and through the shadows of a high cloud of darkness I saw standing near me a demon in his own shape. At that horrible sight I should have gone almost mad, had not my master, who very frequently stayed on guard to control my terrors, adroitly soothed my perturbed and terror-struck wits.

Even in the tender years of childhood, I was aware that the desire for a good endeavor which burned in my heart enraged the Devil in no small measure to stir up wickedness in me. Gracious God, what victories, what crowns for victories I would deserve today if I had stood fast to the end in that struggle! I have concluded from many tales I have heard that devils are most fiercely embittered against recent converts or those who continually aspire to this manner of life. I remember that in the time of Bishop Guy of Beauvais, whom I mentioned before, there was a certain young knight in his household whom the bishop cared more for than almost all his retainers. This man, repenting with horror of his vices, resolved at all costs to fly from contact with the world. While torn with anxious thoughts about this return to a pristine state, he was sleeping one night in the bishop's chamber along with the bishop and a God-fearing man named Ivo, a native of Saint-Quentin, I think, who was very famous for his writing and distinguished for his almost more famous eloquence, and who was a monk of Cluny who filled the office of prior there for a long time under Abbot Hugues of blessed memory. Some other men who were equally outstanding in the holy life were there as well. One of the chief nobles from a neighboring town, a very courtly and discreet man, kept watch while the rest slept in the dead of night. As his thoughts wandered at will and his eyes roved hither and thither, suddenly the figure of a chief devil with a small head and a hunched back appeared advancing toward the man, and, looking at each of the beds in turn, he proceeded to walk slowly around the room. When the great Deceiver came to the mattress of

the young man whom I mentioned as being most beloved by the bishop, he halted and, turning his gaze on the sleeper, said: "This man troubles me bitterly and worst of all those who sleep here." After saying that, he headed for the door of the latrine and went in. The man who was looking on, while paying attention to all this, was oppressed with a burden which made speech or movement impossible. But when the Adversary went out, both faculties returned to him, and in the morning, on relating his vision to the wiser men and inquiring with them into the condition and disposition of the young man, he found that his heart was earnestly set on entering a holier life. If there is more joy in heaven over one sinner that is converted than over ninety just men who need not penance, then without doubt we may fully believe that the enemies of the human race are vexed with the most bitter hatred at the rescue of those who change for the better. And just as I, after a good beginning, have clearly followed a pestilent course, so he, after accepting the Devil's testimony, henceforward gradually fell away and grew cold, returning to his worldly interests. Still, one may believe how painfully that sudden stirring of our good intentions must sting the hearts of devils. And no wonder that the Devil is grieved by the sudden and transient emotions of any penitent, since even the shallow self-abasement of that wicked king Ahab brought him to the attention of God before that of men. Hence the Lord said to Elias, if I am not mistaken, "Hast thou not seen Ahab humbled before me? Therefore, because he has humbled himself for my sake, I will not bring the evil in his days."

Chapter 16

With the gradual growth of my young body, as the life of this world began to stir my itching heart with fleshly longings and lusts to suit my stature, my mind repeatedly fell to remembering and dwelling on what and how great I might have been in the world, in which my imaginings often traveled beyond the truth. These thoughts, Gracious God Who cares for all, Thou didst reveal to Thy servant, my mother. Whatever the state, healthy or diseased, to which my unstable heart changed, an image of it came to her in a vision of Thy will,

O God. But since dreams are said to follow many cares, and that is indeed true, yet her cares were not aroused by the heat of greed, but were created by a real eagerness for inward holiness. Soon after the troubling vision was impressed on her most pious mind, as she was very subtle and clear-sighted in the interpretation of such matters, when she had perceived what trouble was betokened by her dream, she soon summoned me and in private questioned me about my activities, what I was doing, and how I was behaving. Since I was in such submission to her that my will was one with hers, I readily confessed all those things in which my mind seemed to grow slack, following the content of the dreams which I had feared, and after she had warned me to improve, with true affection I at once promised to do so.

O my God, she often spoke to me in enigmas concerning that state in which I now suffer, and what she believed I had done or should do in that state in which I was then, so that every day I now experience in the secret places of my heart the truth of her statements and contemplate their fulfillment. Since my master was also moved by an incessant and heartfelt solicitude, enlightened by Thee, he saw through many kinds of figures what was happening at the time and what might come to pass in the future. By God's gift, both foretold adversity and success, on the one hand terrifying me, on the other comforting me, so that whether I would or not, I abstained from hidden weaknesses, because by Thy wonder-working so much was revealed to those who loved me, and sometimes I rejoiced in the promise of a better hope.

At a time when I was swayed by a spirit of sullenness because of the envy which I suffered from my superiors and equals, I hoped with the aid of my relatives to be able to transfer to some other monastery. Some of our brotherhood, seeing me once far below them both in age and learning, in ability and understanding, and afterward perceiving that I equaled them, or, if I may say so, altogether surpassed them—since He Who is the key to all knowledge had by His gift alone stimulated in me a hunger for learning—raged against me with such burning and evil wrath that, wearied with everlasting disputes and quarrels, I often regretted I had ever seen or known letters. They so greatly disturbed my work and, when an occasion arose over some matter of learning, so often started disputes with their constant questions that they seemed to have as their sole object to make me change my resolve and to impede my talents. But as when oil is poured on a fire a livelier flame creeps forth from what was supposed to put it out, the more my ingenuity was overtaxed in such labors, the better it became, like an oven rendered stronger by its own heat. The questions by which they thought to crush me gave great keenness to my intelligence, and the difficulty of their objections, which required much pondering to find answers and the turning over of many books, brought about a strengthening of my wits and ability in debate. Although I was thus bitterly hated by them, yet Thou knowest, O Lord, how little, if at all, I hated them, and when they could not put any stigma on me, as they wished, in disparagement they told everyone that I was too proud of my little learning.

Although from difficulties of this sort abundant good was produced, yet my spirit grew weak, languishing under the endless torture of its thoughts and surrounded by these annoyances, which affected me bitterly. With a fearful heart and failing powers of reason, I did not consider what profit there was in hardship, but eagerly decided to seek the solution which the weakness of my flesh suggested. When I therefore proposed to leave the place, not so much with the kindly permission of my abbot as at the suggestion and demand of my kinsfolk, my mother gave her assent, too, believing that I was doing this from pious motives, for the place to which I wished to retire was considered very holy. Then the following vision appeared to her to witness to the good and evil in me.

She thought she was in the church of that monastery; that is, of Saint-Germer of Fly. When she looked at the church more closely, she saw it was foresaken in a most lonely fashion; the monks, too, were not only ragged and covered with cassocks huge beyond belief, but all alike were shortened to a cubit in height like those commonly called dwarfs. But since "where your treasure is, there is your heart, and where your gaze is turned, there is your love," she fixed a long look on me, and saw that I stood no higher than the rest and was covered with no better apparel.

While she was mourning my plight and that of such a church, suddenly a woman of beauty and majesty beyond measure advanced through the midst of the church right up to the altar, followed by one like a young girl whose appearance was in its deference appropriate to her whom she followed. Being very curious to know who the lady was, my mother was told that she was the Lady of Chartres. At once she interpreted this to mean the Blessed Mother of God, whose name and relics at Chartres are venerated throughout almost all the Latin world. Going up to the altar, the lady knelt in prayer and the noble attendant who in the vision was following her did the same behind her. Then, rising and stretching out her hand with the appearance of great reproof, she said, "I founded this church. Why should I permit it to be deserted?" Then this standard-bearer of piety turned her tranquil gaze on me and, pointing with her shining hand, said, "I brought him here and made him a monk. By no means will I permit him to be taken away." After this the attendant repeated these same words in like fashion. No sooner had that powerful one spoken than in a moment all that ruin and waste was changed and appeared as it had before, and the dwarf stature of the rest and of myself, too, was amended and made normal by the power that attended her command. When my prudent mother had given me an orderly narrative of this dream, I received such a story with such remorse and tears, and, influenced by the meaning of so desirable a dream, I so restrained my indulgence in thoughts of wandering that I was never again drawn by a desire for another monastery.

O Lady, Mother of Heaven, this and other things like it gave me the opportunity to return to you, rising above the horror of my sins and the countless apostasies by which I rebelled from your love and service, while my heart prophesies that the wide bosom of Thy mercies cannot be closed against me even by mountains of my ill deeds. I shall always remember, too, Lady of Heaven, that when, as a boy, I was eager to put on this habit, one night in a vision I was in the church dedicated to you and I thought I was carried from it by two devils. And when they had taken me to the roof of the church, they fled away and let me go uninjured within the walls of that church. I often recall these things when I consider my incorrigibility, and the

more often I repeat those sins, or rather add to them sins which get worse and worse, I turn back to you, most holy one, as a refuge from the peril of despair, abusing my little hope or faith.

Although I am forever sinning, compelled by my weakness and not through the willfulness of pride, yet I in no wise lose the hope of amendment. Clearly "a just man falls seven times and rises again." If the number seven here stands for an entirety, as it usually does, then no matter how many ways a man falls by sin and although his flesh is weak, if he resolves to rise again to righteousness, if he shows the grief of a penitent, he does not at all lose the name of a just man. Why would we cry aloud to God to deliver us from our necessities if the corruption of our nature did not condemn us, whether we will or no, to the servitude of sin? "I see it," the apostle says, "leading me captive in the law of sin, that is in my members; for I do not that good which I will; but the evil which I hate, that I do."

There is a depth of certain evils which a wicked man despises when he enters. Moreover, concerning certain other depths a cry is made to God, and the petitioner does not doubt that his voice is heard. There is a scorn of despair begotten by excess of sinning, which can be of this depth, where "there is no sure standing," in which misery does not stand. There is lastly the depth out of which Jeremiah was drawn by a rope of rags, and although that be deep, yet farther on it has a bottom; for despite the loosening of the understanding through much sinning, yet reason gives some little check, so that it is not swallowed up in the bottomless gulf without any knowledge of all its iniquity.

Chapter 17

After steeping my mind unduly in the study of versemaking, with the result that I put aside for such ridiculous vanities the matters of universal importance in the divine pages, I was so far guided by my folly as to give first place to Ovid and the pastoral poets and to aim at a lover's urbanity in distributions of types and in a series of letters. Forgetting proper severity and abandoning the modesty of a monk's calling, my mind was led away by these enticements of a poisonous license, and I considered only if I could render the conversation of the courts in the words of some poet, with no thought of how much the toil which I loved might hurt the aims of our holy profession. By love of it I was doubly taken captive, being snared both by the wantonness of the sweet words I took from the poets and by those which I poured forth myself, and I was caught by the unrestrained stirring of my flesh through thinking on these things and the like. Since my unstable mind, unaccustomed now to discipline, was grinding out these things, no sound could come from my lips but that which my thought prompted.

Hence it came to pass that, from the boiling over of the madness within me, I was carried along to words which were a bit obscene and composed some sort of little compositions, irresponsible and indiscreet, in fact bereft of all decency. When this came to the attention of the master I have mentioned, he took it very bitterly, and while he was provoked by his distaste, he fell asleep. As he slept, there appeared to him the following vision: an old man with beautiful white hair—in fact that very man, I dare say, who had brought me to him at the beginning and had promised his love for me in the future—appeared to him and said with great severity, "I wish you to give account to me for the writings that have been composed; however, the hand which wrote them is not his who wrote." When my master had related this to me, he and I gave much the same interpretation to the dream. We mourned and were joyful in Thy hope, on the one hand seeing Thy displeasure in that fatherly rebuke, and on the other thinking from the meaning of the vision that confidence in some amendment of my frivolity was to come. For when the hand that wrote the letters was said not to be his who write them, without doubt it meant that the hand would not continue in such shameful activity. It was mine and is not, as it is written, "Turn the wicked and they shall not be," and that which was mine in the practice of vice, when applied to the pursuit of virtue, lost all the efficacy of that utterly worthless ownership.

And yet Thou knowest, O Lord, and I confess, that at that time my life was chastened neither by fear of Thee, nor by shame, nor by respect for that holy vision. I put no check on that irreverence I had within me, and did not refrain from the vain jests of frivolous writers. I hammered out these verses in secret and dared to show them to no one, or at least only to a few like myself, but I often recited those which I could, inventing an author for them. I was delighted when those which I thought it inconvenient to acknowledge as mine were praised by those who shared such studies, and what did not produce the profit of any praise for their author still left him to enjoy the profit, or rather the shamefulness, of sin. But Thou didst punish these acts, O Father, in Thy own good time. Thou didst fence in my wandering soul with rising misfortune against me for such work and with great adversity, and Thou didst hold me down with bodily infirmity. Then "the sword reached even to the soul," and vexation touched my understanding.

When the punishment of sin had brought understanding to my hearing, then at last the folly of useless study withered away. Since I could not bear to be idle, as if by some necessity I rejected these fancies of mine, took up the spiritual life again, and turned to more appropriate exercises. All too late I began to pant for the knowledge that had repeatedly been distilled for me by many good scholars: to busy myself, that is, with commentaries on the Scriptures, to study frequently the works of Gregory, in which are to be found the best keys to that art, and, according to the rules of ancient writers, to treat the words of the prophets and the Gospels in their allegorical, their moral, and finally their anagogical meaning. In this work I had the special encouragement of Anselm, the abbot of Bec, afterward archbishop of Canterbury, who was born across the Alps in the region of Aosta, a man of sublime example and holiness of life. While he was still prior at Bec, he admitted me to his acquaintance, and though I was a mere child of most tender age and knowledge, he readily offered to teach me to manage the inner self, how to consult the laws of reason in the government of the body. Both before he became abbot and as abbot, he was a familiar visitor at the abbey of Fly where I was, welcomed for his piety and his teaching. He bestowed on me so assiduously the benefits of his learning and with such ardor labored at this that it seemed as if I alone were the unique and special reason for his frequent visits.

His teaching was to divide the mind in a

threefold or fourfold way, to treat the operations of the whole interior mystery under the headings of appetite, will, reason, and intellect. By a resolution, based on clear analyses, of what I and many others thought to be one, he showed that appetite and will are not identical, although it is established by evident assertions that in the presence of reason or intellect they are practically the same.[12] He discussed with me certain chapters of the Gospels on this principle, and most clearly explained the difference between willing and being subject to appetite; it was plain, however, that he did not originate this, but got it from books at hand which did not so explicitly deal with these matters. I then began to endeavor to equal his methods in similar commentaries, so far as I could, and to search carefully with all the keenness of my mind everywhere in the Scriptures to see if anything accorded on the moral level with these thoughts.

It came to pass that when I was traveling with my former abbot to a certain monastery in our province, I suggested to him as a man of great piety that on coming to the chapter meeting he should preach a sermon there. He turned over to me what he was asked to do, exhorting and ordering me to do it in his place. Now, the birth of Mary Magdalene is celebrated on that day. Taking the text of my sermon from the Book of Wisdom, I contented myself with that single word for the homily I was asked to give: "Wisdom," that is, "overcomes evil; she reaches therefore from end to end mightily, and orders all things sweetly." When I had explained this with such oratory as I could, and had pleased my audience with the suitability of these remarks, the prior of the church, who was no mean student of sacred literature within the limits of his understanding, in a friendly way asked me to write something which would give him the material for preparing sermons on any subject. Since I knew that my abbot, in whose presence I had said this, would be annoyed by my writings, I approached the man

with caution and, acting as if I came on behalf of his friend and did not care much about it myself, I begged him to grant what I was asking for the sake of the prior, whom he professed to love. Supposing that I would write very briefly, he consented. When I had snatched his consent from his mouth, I began to work at what I had in mind.

I proposed to undertake a moral commentary on the beginning of Genesis, that is, the Six Days of Creation. To the commentary, I prefixed a treatise of moderate length showing how a sermon ought to be composed. I followed up this preface with a tropological[13] exposition at length of the Six Days, with poor eloquence but such as I was capable of. When my abbot saw that I was commenting on the first chapter of that sacred history, he no longer took a favorable view of the matter and warned me with great reproof to put an end to these writings.[14] I saw that such works only put thorns in his eyes, and by avoiding both his presence and that of anyone who might report it to him, I pursued my task in secret. For the composition and writing of this or my other works, I did not prepare a draft on the wax tablets, but committed them to the written page in their final form as I thought them out. In that abbot's time my studies were carried on in complete secrecy. But when he was gone, finding my opportunity when the pastoral office was vacant, at last I attacked and quickly finished my work. It consisted of ten books which followed the four activities of the inner man mentioned before, and I so carried out the moral treatment in all of them that they went from beginning to end with absolutely no change in the order of the passages. Whether in this little work I helped anyone, I do not know, although I have no doubt that most learned men were greatly pleased with it. This much is certain, that I gained no little profit from it myself, seeing that it saved me from idleness, that servant of vice.

Since then, I wrote a little book in chapters on various meanings in the Gospels and the

---

12 Augustine described the three faculties of the soul as memory, intelligence, and will. Anselm's novelty was to replace memory with reason and add appetite or desire; this allowed him to argue that the will was always free, since appetite was a separate function. Under the control of reason, will and appetite could be one.

13 That is, an analysis on the moral level.

14 Origen and Jerome refer to a Hebrew tradition that no one under thirty should read the beginning of Genesis, the beginning and end of Ezekiel, and the Song of Songs.

prophets, including some things from the books of Numbers, Joshua, and Judges. I am putting off the completion of this because after finishing what I have in hand, I propose, if I am still alive and God prompts me, to engage at times in similar exercises. As I did in treating Genesis, I mostly followed the tropological approach, and the allegorical in a few instances. In Genesis, I therefore gave my attention chiefly to morals, not that there was wanting matter for thought on the allegorical level, had I equally worked that out, but because in my opinion moral meanings are in these times more useful than allegories, since faith is established unchanged by God but morals are almost universally debased by the many forms of vice, and because I had neither the freedom nor the wish to enlarge my book to excessive length.

Chapter 18

As much as my mother esteemed my success in learning, she was greatly perturbed by her dread of the excesses of a dangerous time of life. How earnestly she begged me to follow her example! Although God had given her such great good looks, she thought little of that in her which won praise, as though she were unaware of her beauty, and she cherished her widowhood as if, unable to bear them, she had always loathed a wife's bedtime duties. Yet Thou knowest, O Lord, how much loyalty, how much love she rendered to her dead husband, how with almost daily masses, prayers, and tears, and much almsgiving, she strove without ceasing to release his soul, which she knew was fettered by his sins. By the wonderful dispensation of God, it came about that in frequent visions she saw in the clearest images what pains he endured in his purgation. Without doubt such visions come from God; for when no perverse sense of security is falsely caused by the assumption of the beauty of light,[15] but a stimulus is given to prayer and almsgiving by the sight of suffering and punishment, and when the remedies of the divine office are clearly demanded by the dead, or rather by the angels, who care for dead Christians, it is proof enough that these things come from God, because devils never seek the salvation of any man's soul. The anxious mind of that good woman was kindled again by these signs and was inflamed by the intimation of his soul's torments to constant efforts to intercede for her former husband.

One summer night, for instance, on a Sunday after matins, after she had stretched out on her narrow bench and had begun to sink into sleep, her soul seemed to leave her body without her losing her senses. After being led, as it were, through a certain gallery, at last she issued from it and began to approach the edge of a pit. After she was brought close to it, suddenly from the depth of that abyss men with the appearance of ghosts leaped forth, their hair seemingly eaten by worms, trying to seize her with their hands and to drag her inside. From behind the frightened woman, who was terribly distressed by their attack, suddenly a voice cried out to them, saying, "Touch her not." Compelled by that forbidding voice, they leaped back into the pit. Now, I forgot to say that as she passed through the gallery, as she knew she had left her mortal being, her one prayer to God was to be allowed to return to her body. After she was rescued from the dwellers in the pit and was standing by its edge, suddenly she saw that my father was there, appearing as he did when he was young. When she looked hard at him and piteously asked of him whether he was called Evrard (for that had been his name), he denied that he was.

Now, it is no wonder that a spirit should refuse to be called by the name which he had as a man, for spirit should give no reply to a spirit which is inconsistent with its spiritual nature. Moreover, that spirits should recognize each other by their names is too absurd to be believed; otherwise in the next world it would be rare to know anyone except those close to us. Clearly it is not necessary for spirits to have names, since all their vision, or rather their knowledge of vision, is internal.

Although he denied that he was called by that name, and yet nonetheless she felt that it was he, she then asked him where he was staying. He indicated that the place was located not far away, and that he was detained there. She also asked how he was. Baring his arm and his side, he showed both of them so torn, so cut up with many wounds,

---

15 That is, by the Devil.

that she felt great horror and emotional distress as she looked. The figure of a little child was also there, crying so bitterly that it troubled her greatly when she saw it. Moved by its cries, she said to him, "My lord, how can you endure the wailing of this child?" "Whether I like it or not," said he, "I endure it." Now, the crying of the child and the wounds on his arm and side have this meaning. When my father in his youth was separated from lawful intercourse with my mother through the witchcraft of certain persons, some evil counselors appealed to his youthful spirit with the vile advice to find out if he could have intercourse with other women. In youthful fashion he took their advice, and, having wickedly attempted intercourse with some loose woman unknown to me, he begat a child which at once died before baptism. The rending of his side is the breaking of his marriage vow; the cries of that distressed voice indicate the damnation of that evilly begotten child. Such, O Lord, O Inexhaustible Goodness, was Thy retribution on the soul of Thy sinner, who yet lives by faith. But let us return to the orderly narrative of the vision.

When she asked him whether prayer, almsgiving, or the mass gave him any relief (for he was aware that she frequently provided these things for him), he replied that they did, adding, "But among you there lives a certain Liégearde." My mother understood that he named this woman so that she would ask her what memory of him she had. This Liégearde was very poor in spirit, a woman who lived for God alone apart from the customs of the world.

Meanwhile, bringing her talk with my father to an end, my mother looked toward the pit, above which was a picture, and in the picture she saw a certain knight named Renaud, of no mean reputation among his countrymen. After dinner on that very day, which as I said before was a Sunday, this Renaud was treacherously killed at Beauvais by those close to him. In that picture he was kneeling with his neck bent down, puffing to blow up a fire in a heap of fuel. This vision was seen in the early morning, whereas he perished at midday, doomed to descend into those flames which he had kindled by his deserts. In the same picture she saw a brother of mine who was helping, but he died long afterward. He was taking a dreadful

oath by the sacrament of God's body and blood. The significance of this is precisely that by false swearing and by taking the holy name of God and His sacred mysteries in vain, he earned both his punishment and the place of his punishment.

In the course of the same vision, she also saw that old woman who, as I said, lived with her at the beginning of her conversion, a woman who clearly was always mortifying her body with crosses on the outside, but, it was said, was not enough on her guard against a hunger for vainglory. She saw this woman carried off by two coal-black spirits, her form a mere shadow. Moreover, while that old woman was alive and the two were living together, when they were talking of the state of their souls and the coming of death, they once took a mutual pledge that the one who died first should, through the grace of God, appear to the survivor and make known to her the nature of her condition, whether good or bad. They confirmed this by prayer, earnestly beseeching God that after the death of either the other should be allowed to discover by the revelation of some vision her happy or unhappy state. When the old woman was about to die, she had seen herself in a vision deprived of her body and going with others like her to a certain temple, and, as she went, she seemed to be carrying a cross on her shoulders. Coming to the temple with that company, she was compelled to stay outside, the doors being barred against her. Finally, after her death she appeared to someone else in the midst of a great stench to express her gratitude for giving prayers which had saved her from decay and pain. While the old woman was dying, at the foot of the bed she saw standing a horrible devil with eyes of dreadful and monstrous size. When she adjured him by the holy sacraments to flee in confusion from her and seek nothing of her, with that frightful charge she drove him off.

My mother drew her conclusions about the cries of the infant, of whose existence she had been aware, from the exact way in which the vision agreed with the facts, when she put them together, and from the immediate prophecy of the impending slaying of the knight, whom she had seen assigned to the place of punishment below. Having no doubt about these things, she devoted herself wholly to bringing help to my father.

Setting like against like, she chose to take on the raising of a little child only a few months old that had lost its parents. But since the Devil hates good intentions no less than faithful actions, the baby so harassed my mother and all her servants by the madness of its wailing and crying at night—although by day it was very good, by turns playing and sleeping—that anyone in the same little room could get scarcely any sleep. I have heard the nurses whom she hired say that night after night they could not stop shaking the child's rattle, so naughty was he, not through his own fault, but made so by the Devil within, and that a woman's craft failed entirely to drive him out. The good woman was tormented by extreme pain; amid those shrill cries no contrivance relieved her aching brow, nor could any sleep steal over her sorely tried and exhausted head, since the frenzy of the child goaded from within and by the Enemy's presence caused continual disturbance. Although she passed her sleepless nights in this way, she never appeared listless at the performance of the night offices. Since she knew that these troubles were to purge away those of her husband, which she had seen in her vision, she bore them gladly, because she rightly thought that by sharing his suffering herself she was lessening the pains of the other sufferer. Yet she never shut the child out of her house, never appeared less careful of him. Indeed, the more she perceived that the Devil was cruelly blazing against her to destroy her resolve, the more she chose to submit with equanimity to any inconvenience rising from it; and the more she happened to experience the eagerness of the Devil in the irritation of the child, the more she was assured that his evil sway over the soul of her husband was being countered.

26. FULBERT OF CHARTRES

Letter to William of Aquitaine

IN 1020, BISHOP FULBERT of Chartres (ca. 960–1028), who is known both for his writings (primarily letters) as well as for his rebuilding of the cathedral at Chartres in north-central France and his theological innovations, wrote to Duke William V of Aquitaine (ca. 960–1030) a letter on the duties of lords and vassals, at the duke's insistence. This ideal image of feudal relations can be contrasted with the brutal realities in the two documents that follow.

Source: L. Delisle (ed.), *Recueil des historiens des Gaules et de la France* (Paris, 1904), vol. 10, p. 463.

Further Reading: Giles Constable, "The Orders of Society in the Eleventh and Twelfth Centuries," in Constance Hoffman Berman (ed.), *Medieval Religion: New Approaches* (New York: Routledge, 2005), 68–94.

Fulbert, bishop, to the glorious duke of the Aquitanians William.

Invited to write something concerning the form of fealty, I have briefly noted for you the following things from the authority of books. He who swears fealty to his lord must always remember these six things: harmless, safe, honorable, useful, easy, possible. Harmless, that is, he must not harm his lord in his body. Safe, he must not harm him in his secrets or in the fortifications by which he is able to be safe. Honorable, so that he must not harm him in his justice or in other affairs which are seen to pertain to his honor. Useful, that he might not be harmful to him in his possessions. Easy or possible, so that he not make difficult any good which his lord could easily do nor make anything impossible that is difficult. It is just that the vassal avoid these evils, but he does not merit his holding for so doing, for it is not enough that he abstain from evil unless he does what is good.

Therefore it remains that he should give his lord counsel and aid in these same six above-mentioned things if he wishes to be seen worthy of his benefice and to be safe in the fealty he has sworn. The lord should act toward his vassal reciprocally in all these things. If he does not do so, he deserves to be considered of bad faith, just as the vassal, if he were caught in collusion or in doing or in consenting to them, would be perfidious or perjured.

I would have written to you at greater length if I had not been occupied with many other things, both the restoration of our city and of our church which have recently been totally consumed by a horrendous fire. Although for a time we could not be turned away from this loss, through the hope in the consolation of God and of you we once more breathe.

27. HUGH OF LUSIGNAN

Agreement between Lord and Vassal

AROUND 1020–1025 HUGH OF Lusignan, a powerful and ambitious chatelain in Poitou, wrote or dictated his account of his relations with William V of Aquitaine over the previous decades. Hugh contended that he had been unjustly deprived of lands and castles that had belonged to his ancestors. His description of his treatment at the hands of his lord provides unique glimpses into the realities of feudal relationships in the eleventh century.

Source: Jane Martindale (ed.), "Hugh of Lusignan, Agreement Between Lord and Vassal," *English Historical Review* 84 (1969): 528–48. Trans. George Beech.

Further Reading: George T. Beech, "The Lord/Dependant (Vassal) Relationship: a Case Study from Aquitaine c. 1030," *Journal of Medieval History* 24 (1998): 1–30.

William Count of the Aquitanians had an agreement with Hugh the Chiliarch to the effect that when Viscount Roso dies he [William] would give him his honor in commendation. Roho the bishop saw and heard this and he kissed the arm of the count. Then Viscount Savary seized from Hugh land which he [Hugh] held from Count William and when the viscount died the count promised Hugh that he would make no agreement or accord with Ralph the dead man's brother until the land had been restored. This he said in the presence of all, but afterwards he secretly gave him [Ralph] the land. Hugh had an agreement with Viscount Ralph that he would marry his [Ralph's] daughter in return for that estate or for a larger one, or for other things. When the count heard of this he was greatly angered and went humbly to Hugh and said to him, "Don't marry Ralph's daughter, I will give you whatever you want from me and you will be my friend before everyone else except my son." And Hugh did what the count ordered him to do and out of love and fidelity he secretly rejected the woman. At the same time it happened that Joscelin of Parthenay Castle died, and the count said that he would turn over his [Joscelin's] honor and wife to Hugh, but that if he [Hugh] refused to accept them, he would no longer have confidence in him. In this affair Hugh did not encourage the count at all in his own behalf or in anyone else's, nor did he discourage him. Thinking it over, he said to the count, "I will do everything you order me to do." Making an agreement with Count Fulk, the count promised to give him [Fulk] something from his own benefices in place of that one. Fulk then promised that he would give to Hugh those things which belonged to him. As a part of this agreement the count called for Viscount Ralph and said to him, "Hugh will not keep the agreement which he has with you because I forbid him to. But Fulk and I have an agreement that we will give him [Hugh] the honor and wife of Joscelin and we do this to punish you because you don't keep faith with me." And when Ralph heard this he was deeply sorry and said to the count, "For the sake of God do not do that," and the count said, "Make a pledge to me that you will not give him your daughter nor keep your agreement with him and I likewise will see that he does not possess the honor or the wife of Joscelin." And they did thus so that Hugh got neither the one nor the other. Ralph left to go to Count William who was in Montreuil Castle, sending a message to Hugh that they should talk with one another. This was done and Ralph said to Hugh, "I tell you these things in advance in the faith that you will not reveal me; give me a pledge that you will aid me against Count William and I will keep your agreement and I will aid you against all men." But out of love for Count William, Hugh refused to do this and Hugh and Ralph parted angrily. Then Ralph started war with Count William and out of love for the count, Hugh went to war with Ralph and suffered greatly.

When Ralph died Hugh asked the count to restore to him the land which Ralph had seized from him. The count said to Hugh, "I will not make an agreement with Viscount Josfred, the nephew of Ralph, nor with the men of Thouars Castle, until I return your land." But the count by no means did this but left and made an agreement with Viscount Josfred and with the men of Thouars Castle and did not make an agreement with Hugh; and Hugh did not get his land but on account of the evil deed which Hugh did for the count. Josfred started a war with Hugh and burned Mouzeuil Castle and seized Hugh's knights and cut off their hands and did enough else. The count in no way aided Hugh nor did he make an honest agreement between them, but Hugh in addition to this lost his land and on account of his assistance to the count he lost still another which he was holding peacefully. And when Hugh saw that he was not going to get his land he seized 43 of the best knights of Thouars and he could have had justice and peace and his land back. And if he had been willing to accept a ransom he could have had 40,000 *solidi*. When the count heard of this he ought to have been happy but he was angry and sent for Hugh saying to him, "Give me the men." And Hugh answered him, "Why do you ask these things of me my lord? It is only your fidelity [i.e., your lack of it] which causes me to lose things." The count then said, "I don't ask you for them in order to do you wrong but because you are mine [i.e., my vassal] to do my will [i.e., to act according to my wishes] and so that everyone may know as a result of our agreement according to which I will get the men, that I will make an agreement with you that you will get your lands back and be repaid for the evil done you or else I will return the men to you. Believe and trust me and if anything should turn out badly for you, you will know because it was I who betrayed you." Then Hugh trusted in him and in God and handed over the men to the count under such an agreement. Later on Hugh lost his land and got neither justice nor the men back.

The Count of the Poitevins and Bishop Gilbert had an agreement among themselves with Hugh's uncle Joscelin. It concerned Vivonne Castle to the effect that after the death of Bishop Gilbert the castle should go to Joscelin. While still alive the bishop had the men of that castle commend themselves to [i.e., become vassals of] Joscelin and turned over the tower to him; after the death of both men the count made an agreement between Bishop Isembert and Hugh to the effect that half of the castle should be Hugh's, half from the demesne and two parts from the fiefs of the vassals. Therefore the count had Hugh commend himself to Bishop Isembert. Then he took the best estate from them.

A tribune named Aimery seized the castle called Civray from his lord Bernard and this castle was rightfully Hugh's as it had been his father's. Because of his anger at Aimery, Count William urged Hugh to become the vassal of Bernard for that part of the castle which had belonged to his father so that both [Bernard and Hugh] could do war with Aimery. But Hugh did not want to be the vassal of Bernard. The count let this request wait for a year and then, growing angrier, he urged Hugh all the more to become the vassal of Bernard. When a year had passed the count came with great wrath to Hugh and said to him, "Why don't you make an agreement with Bernard? You owe so much to me that if I should tell you to make a peasant into a lord you should do it. Do what I tell you and if it should turn out badly for you, come and see me about it." Hugh believed him and became the man [i.e., vassal] of Bernard for the fourth part of the said castle. As his pledge to Hugh, Bernard gave the count four hostages. The count said to Hugh, "Commend those hostages to me under such conditions that if Bernard should not keep those agreements made to you on faith, I will turn them over to you to custody and by my faith will be your helper." The count promised this very strongly to Hugh [how strongly he himself well knows]. And Hugh trusted in his lord and took up a just war on account of the above castle and suffered great losses in men and other things. And the count started to build a castle for him called Couhe but did not finish it, but he spoke with Aimery and gave up the castle to him [Aimery] and in no way aided Hugh.

Later the count became upset with Aimery on account of the castle called Chize which Aimery had seized, and Hugh and the count went to war together against him. He [the count] besieged the castle of Malavallis in return for the evil deed which Aimery had done to him and captured it, and Hugh aided him as best he could. Before Hugh left the count the latter promised him, just as a lord ought to promise satisfaction to his vassal, that he would make no agreement with Aimery nor have anything to do with him without Hugh, and that Malavallis would not be built without his [Hugh's] advice. But the count did make an agreement with Aimery and permitted him to build Malavallis without the advice of Hugh. As long as Aimery lived Hugh got nothing back with respect to the aforesaid matters.

After the death of Aimery a great war began between the son of Aimery [also named Aimery] and Hugh. At the same time Hugh came to the count and said to him, "Things are going badly for me now, my Lord, in that I have no part of the fief which you caused me to acquire." The count answered him, "I am going to make a pact with them [Aimery's son and his men] which, if they keep it well, should be fine: if not, I will build the castle which I started." And the castle was constructed on the advice of Bernard, who hitherto had assisted Hugh in the war. Then the men of Civray, when they saw how Hugh was oppressing them, were no longer able to hold out and made an agreement with Bernard giving him the castle and admitting him into it without consulting Hugh. Now both Bernard and Aimery were at war against Hugh and he was alone against them. Coming to the count, Hugh said to him, "My Lord, I am doing very badly because the lord of whom I became a vassal at your advice has just taken away my fief. I beg and urge you through the faith which a lord ought to render to his vassal that you see to it that I get either a favorable pact or my fief as you pledged to me, or that you turn over to me the hostages which I commended to you, and that in addition you aid me as you pledged to me." The count, however, neither aided him nor made an agreement with him nor gave over his hostages, but gave them back to Bernard with no strings attached.

After this a war started between Bernard, Aimery, and Hugh. And when Hugh saw that the count aided him in no way he went to seek the advice of Gerald the Bishop of Limoges, and they both left to move against Bernard in La Marche where they built a castle. But the count who ought to have aided Hugh seized the castle from him and burned it. And he [the count] and his son ordered all their men that no one should help Hugh unless he wished to die. Then Bernard in consultation with his men decided that they should do evil to Hugh on the advice of the count and

they [Bernard and his men] appointed a deadline fifteen days away. During those fifteen days the count arranged a truce between Bernard and Hugh. Three days before the end of the truce the count took Hugh along with his host to Apremont Castle and a meeting was held in his castle. From there the count went to Blaye where he was to have a meeting with Count Sancho, and he told Hugh that he should come along. And Hugh responded, "My Lord, why do you ask me to go with you? You yourself know how short is the truce which I have with Bernard and he is threatening to do me ill." The count said to him, "Don't fear that they will do anything to you as long as you are with me," and he [the count] took him along with him for force and against his wishes. And while they were staying at the meeting place Hugh's men heard that Bernard was attacking him. They sent a message to Hugh that he should come. Then Hugh said to the count, "Bernard is attacking me." And the count said, "Do not fear that they should have dared to attack you. Besides you would have needed that they attack in order that I might put them [Bernard and his men] to confusion and give you assistance." And in the very same hour the count sent directions to Hugh through his own men that he should go on ahead and then he [the count] followed him. When Hugh reached Lusignan, Bernard was at Confolens Castle and had captured the *burg* and the *barrium* [i.e., the cleared area and houses around the *burg*] and had burned everything except the spoils and the men taken prisoners, and had done enough other evil deeds. A messenger ran up to Hugh and said to him, "Bernard has your wife besieged in the old castle which is left over from the fire." Coming to the count, Hugh said to him, "My Lord, now help me because my wife is besieged." But the count gave him no aid nor advice at all, and Bernard and his men turned back and did much harm to Hugh and his men, more than he could bear, fifty thousand *solidi* worth. And Hugh suffered this damage during the truce which the count offered him at Blaye.

Not long after this, Hugh went to Gencay Castle and burned it and seized the men and women and took everything with him; and proceeding to the count he said to him, "My Lord, give me permission to build the castle which I burned." And the count said to him, "How can you build a castle when you are Fulk's vassal? He will demand it from you and you won't be able to keep it unless you turn it over to him." Hugh said, "My Lord, when I became the vassal of Fulk I told him that his men were seizing things which belonged to me and that if I was able to regain possession of them I would do it, but that I want to do this in such a way as to remain his vassal. And Fulk said to me, 'If you get angry at them, don't get angry at me.'" And when the count heard that Fulk and Hugh had such an agreement he was pleased and said to Hugh, "Build the castle under such an agreement that if I am able to buy your share and mine from Count Fulk, one part [i.e., of the castle] will be mine and the other yours." And Hugh built the castle. Then Fulk asked the count for it, and the count responded, "Ask Hugh for it." Then Fulk did this and Hugh responded, "When I became your vassal, I told you that if I was able to seize the castles from my enemies I would do it and that I would hold it [sic] from you, and I want to do this because this castle which you are demanding belonged to my relatives and I have a better right to it than those who were holding it." And Fulk said to him, "How can you, who are my vassal, hold something which I did not give you, against my will?" Then Hugh sought again the advice of the count. The count told him, "If he is willing to give you pledges that your enemies will not have the castle then you can't keep it; if not, keep it, because he will not be able to accuse you [i.e. of breaking feudal custom]." Hugh then asked Fulk to give him hostages, but he gave none saying, "I am going to see the count and I will give him the hostages, and he can give you some of his own," and then the conference turned into an angry one. Fulk demanded Hugh's castle of the count. "I will never give it up without pledges," said Hugh. Then the count said to him, "I will give you a pledge; tell me which ones you want." Hugh said, "Get the ones you want from Count Fulk and give me what I'm asking for. Give me the man who has custody of the tower of Melle so that if Aimery should get the castle without my advice and evil should happen to me, that man will turn the tower over to me." The count said to him, "I will not do this because it is not in my power to do it." Then Hugh said, "If you don't want to do this with Melle, make the same agreement with regard to Chize." But the count was willing to do neither

the one nor the other; and Hugh and his men saw that the count was dealing badly with them, and they parted in anger. Then Hugh sent all kinds of necessities into the castle and intended to hold it against all comers if they would not give him pledges. Then the count came outside his *civitas* [presumably Poitiers] and asked Hugh to come to him and through Count William of Angoulême ordered him to submit himself to the mercy of the count because he [the count] could not change the situation which called for him to aid Fulk, and he was fearful of losing [the friendship of] either Fulk or Hugh. Then Hugh committed himself to the friendship and trust of the count his Lord and did this out of love for him [the count] because he [the count] was certain that Fulk had not been badly led. And the count said, "Let Hugh do this for me and I will give him my faith just as a Lord ought to do to his vassal, and if evil should happen to him he will know that it was I who betrayed him and he will never trust in me again." And Hugh responded, "My Lord has spoken to me in such a way about many things and as a result has led me away [i.e., from my original opposition to him]." And not a single one of Hugh's men would advise him to trust the count. But the count reminded Hugh of all the good things which he had done for him and pressed him with his love and requests and appeals; then Hugh said to the count, "I will trust every thing to you, but watch out lest you do me evil, for if you do, I will not be faithful to you nor will I serve you, nor will I render fidelity to you; but on account of the fact that I will be separated from you and you are not able to give me pledges, I want you to give me my fief as a hostage that [in case of your violation] I will never serve you and [I want you to] release me from that oath which I made to you." And the Court answered, "Gladly." And Hugh against the wishes of his men had turned the castle over to the count under such an agreement that Aimery would not get possession of it without his [Hugh's] advice and that evil should not happen to him. When these reservations had been heard, Hugh accepted [and the count gave] his fief as a pledge under such an agreement that if the count should mislead him with regard to the agreement about Gencay, he would never again render service to him [as a vassal]. And the count released him from the oaths so that he would never observe them and without any malevolence [on the part of the count]. And the count handed over Gencay without consulting Hugh and was given money and some domaine land. And it went very badly for Hugh with men killed, houses burned, booty taken, lands seized, and many other things which in truth cannot be enumerated. When this had ended the count gave Hugh a respite and promised that he would give him a benefice either of something which was his by right or of something which would be pleasing to him. But when this period passed the count did nothing for Hugh but sent an order to him, "Don't wait because I am not going to do anything for you. If all the world were mine I would not give you as much as a finger could hold with regard to this matter." When Hugh heard this he went to the court of the count and informed him of his rights but it profited him not a bit. This saddened Hugh and in the presence of all who were there he renounced his allegiance to the count except what he owed for the city [i.e., Poitiers] and his own person.

Before either Hugh or his men did any evil the men of the count seized a benefice from Hugh's men in the name of war. When Hugh saw this he went to Chize Castle, which had been his uncle's but which Peter was holding unjustly, and whence much harm was being done to Hugh. He seized the tower and threw out Peter's men. And Hugh did this because he thought he had a right to it since it had belonged to his father or others of his relatives and he was losing that right. And when the count heard of this he was greatly saddened and sent an order to Hugh that the latter should turn over to him the tower which he had taken away from Peter. Hugh sent back to the count that he [the count] should turn over to him [Hugh] his father's honor and the other things which he had seized in it, and in addition the entire honor which had belonged to Joscelin and which the count had given him. The count thought this over and then they arranged for a conference. The count said to Hugh, "I will not give you those honors which you ask of me, but I will give you that honor which was your uncle's— the castle, the tower, and the entire honor—under such an agreement that you no longer demand of me that honor which was your father's, or others of your relatives, nor anything which you claim as your right." When he heard this Hugh greatly

mistrusted the count in that the latter with evil intent had taken much away from him in the past, and he said to the count, "I don't dare to do this because I'm afraid that you'll threaten me with evil as you have done with regard to many other things." The count said to Hugh, "I will make such pledges to you that you will no longer distrust me." Hugh asked him, "What kind of pledges?" The count said, "I will produce a serf who will undergo an ordeal for you so that you will not doubt that the agreement which we make among ourselves will be kept nor that harm will ever again be done to you with regard to those affairs of the past, but the agreement will be kept firmly without any evil intent." When Hugh heard the count speak in this manner he said, "You are my Lord, I will not accept a pledge from you, but I will simply rely on the mercy of God and of yourself." The count said to Hugh, "Give up all those claims over which you have quarreled with me in the past and swear fidelity to me and my son and I will give you your uncle's honor or something else of equal value in exchange for it." Then Hugh said, "My Lord, I beg you through God and this blessed crucifix which is made in the figure of Christ that you do not make me do this if you and your son were intending to threaten me with trickery." And the count said, "On my honor my son and I will do this without trickery." Hugh then said, "And when I shall have sworn fidelity to you, you will demand Chize Castle of me, and if I should not turn it over to you, you will say that it is not right that I deny you the castle which I hold from you, and if I should turn it over to you, you and your son will seize it [and keep it] because you will have given nothing in pledge except the mercy of God and yourself." The count said, "We will not do that, but if we should demand it of you, don't turn it over to us." Under the terms of such an agreement, or *finis* as it was also called, that the count and his son should render fidelity to Hugh with no evil intentions, they received Hugh as their vassal in faith and trust. And they had Hugh abandon everything which he claimed from the past. And he swore fidelity to them and they gave him the honor of his uncle Joscelin just as the latter held it one year before he died.

Here end the agreements between the count and Hugh.

28. GALBERT OF BRUGES

The Murder of Charles the Good

GALBERT, A NOTARY OF Bruges, recorded as an eye-witness the events prior and subsequent to the murder of Count Charles the Good of Flanders in 1127. This account shows the judicial measures by which the count had attempted to consolidate his county at the expense of the lesser nobility and chatelains who had gained power following the dissolution of the Carolingian state. Although the account is extremely favorable to Charles to the point of being hagiographic, the description of his murder by the Emerbald family and the subsequent disintegration of his centralizing efforts indicates the strength of centrifugal forces in twelfth-century society.

Source: James Bruce Ross, *The Murder of Charles the Good Count of Flanders* (New York: Harper and Row, 1967).

Further Reading: Jeff Rider, *God's Scribe: The Historiographical Art of Galbert of Bruges* (Washington, DC: The Catholic University of America Press, 2001).

---

[1] Charles becomes count of Flanders in 1119; his concern for peace and justice, 1119–24

Charles, son of Canute, king of Denmark, and born of a mother who was descended from the blood of the counts of the land of Flanders,[1] because of this relationship grew up from boyhood to manly strength of body and mind in our fatherland. After he was armed with the honors of knighthood[2] he fought with distinction against his enemies and gained a fine reputation and glory for his name among the rulers of the earth. Our barons had for many years shown a preference for him as prince if by chance such a possibility should occur.[3] Therefore when Count Baldwin, that extraordinary brave youth, was dying, he, together with the barons,[4] handed the realm over to his cousin Charles and commended it to him under oath. The pious count, acting with the prudence of his predecessor, now took such measures to strengthen the peace, to reaffirm the laws and rights of the realm, that little by little public order was restored in all parts, and by the fourth year of his reign, thanks to his efforts, everything was flourishing, everything was happy, and joyful in the security of peace and justice. When he saw that such a great boon of peace made everyone happy, he gave orders that throughout the limits of the realm all who frequented markets or dwelt in towns should live together in quiet and security without resort to arms; otherwise they would be punished by the very arms they bore. To enforce this, bows and arrows and subsequently all arms were laid aside not only in those places already

---

1   The marriage of Adele by her father, Robert the Frisian, count of Flanders (1071–93), to Canute IV of Denmark was intended to strengthen a Flemish-Danish alliance against William the Conqueror which crumbled in 1086 on Canute's assassination; following this event Adele fled to Flanders with her young son, Charles. Neither the exact date of the marriage nor of Charles's birth has been established, but he must have been born between ca. 1080 and 1086. He was still a "very small boy" (*parvulus*) on his arrival in Flanders, according to Walter of Therouanne's *Vita Karoli*, c. 2, MGH, SS XII, 540 (hereafter cited as Walter, giving only the chapter number).

2   That is, after he had undergone the ceremony of induction into the knightly order, when the candidate was girded with the sword and "dubbed" by his knightly sponsor.

3   If, that is, his cousin Count Baldwin VII (1111–19) should die without heirs, as it so happened. Baldwin, born in 1093, was injured on the Norman border while serving in the host of his feudal lord, Louis VI of France, in September 1118, and died on June 19, 1119.

4   This was the normal procedure of succession in Flanders at the time, designation by the reigning count and confirmation by the barons.

protected by the count's peace but in other places as well.

Thanks to this boon of peace, men governed themselves in accordance with laws and justice, devising by skill and study every kind of argument for use in the courts, so that when anyone was attacked he could defend himself by the strength and eloquence of rhetoric, or when he was attacking, he might ensnare his enemy, who would be deceived by the wealth of his oratory. Rhetoric was now used both by the educated and by those who were naturally talented, for there were many illiterate people, endowed by nature herself with the gift of eloquence and rational methods of inference and argument, whom those who were trained and skilled in the rhetorical art were not able to resist or refute. But, on the other hand, because these by their deceits brought action in the courts against the faithful and the lambs of God, who were less wary, God, who sees all from on high, did not fail to chastise the deceivers so that He might reach by scourges those whom He had endowed with the gift of eloquence for their salvation because they had used this gift for their own perdition.

[2] God desolates Flanders by famine, 1124–25

Therefore God inflicted the scourge of famine and afterwards of death on all who lived in our realm, but first He deigned by the terror of omens to recall to penitence those whom He had foreseen as prone to evil. In the year 1124 from the Incarnation of our Lord, in the month of August, there was visible to all the inhabitants of the lands an eclipse[5] on the body of the sun at about the ninth hour of the day,[6] and an unnatural failure of light so that the eastern part of the sun, darkened little by little, poured forth strange clouds on the other parts, not darkening the whole sun at the same time, however, but only partially. Nevertheless, the same cloud wandered over the whole circle of the sun, moving across from east to west, but only within the circle of the solar essence. Consequently, those who observed the condition of the peace and the wrongs in the courts, threatened everyone with the peril of famine and death. But when men were not corrected in this way, neither lords nor serfs, there came the hunger of sudden famine,[7] and subsequently the scourges of death attacked them. As it is said in the Psalms: "He called for a famine upon the land, and broke the whole staff of bread."

During this time no one was able to sustain himself by eating and drinking in his usual way, but, contrary to habit, a person ate as much bread in one meal as he had been accustomed to consume in several days before this time of famine. So he was glutted by this unusual quantity, and since all the natural passages of the organs were distended by the excess of food and drink, he fell ill. Men were wasting away from repletion and indigestion and yet they suffered from hunger until they drew the last breath. Many swelled up, and food and drink were loathsome to them although they had plenty of both. In this time of famine, in the middle of Lent,[8] the men of our land living near Ghent and the Leie and Scheldt rivers ate meat because bread was completely lacking. Some who tried to make their way to the cities and towns where they could buy bread[9] perished of hunger along the road, choking to death before they were halfway. Near the manors and farms[10] of the rich and the strongholds and castles, the poor,

---

5   Scientists have demonstrated that this solar eclipse was visible in Europe, at noon on the meridian of Paris on August 11, 1124. It is puzzling that Galbert describes the obscuration as moving from east to west; actually in a solar eclipse the moon travels across the sun from west to east.

6   Since the day was divided into two periods, each of twelve hours, beginning respectively at sunset and sunrise, the hours were variable.

7   This great famine is mentioned in many contemporary records. It is best explained in terms of a long, extremely cold and snowy winter in 1123–24, a late, cold, and rainy summer, followed by another bitter winter in 1124–25 and again in 1125–26.

8   That is, about March 4, 1125.

9   It is clear that grain was stored and could therefore be purchased not in the country but in the towns. The granaries of the counts, where the produce of the domain and payments in kind were assembled, were generally located in the "castles" (*castra*) of the counts, close to which mercantile settlements such as Bruges and Ghent had sprung up. A charter of Charles in 1123 refers to "my granary" at Veurne.

10 By *villas et curtes* Galbert probably refers to larger and smaller units of agrarian exploitation. The older great domain or villa was now breaking up into smaller units, manors or farms of various sizes and kinds. In the area around Bruges and Ghent the domanial disintegration began early, probably in the tenth century.

bent low in their misery as they came for alms, fell dead in the act of begging. Strange to say, no one in our land retained his natural color but all bore a pallor like that of death. Both the well and the ill languished because those who were sound in body became ill on seeing the misery of the dying.

[3] Count Charles takes steps to relieve the poor

But the impious were not corrected in this way, for it is said that at this very time they had plotted the death of the most pious count Charles.[11] The count tried in every way possible to take care of the poor, distributing alms in the towns and throughout his domain, both in person and by his officials. At the same time he was feeding one hundred paupers in Bruges every day; and he gave a sizable loaf of bread to each one of them from before Lent until the harvests of the same year.[12] And likewise in his other towns he had made the same provision.[13] In the same year the lord count had decreed that whoever sowed two measures of land in the sowing time should sow another measure in peas and beans,[14] because these legumes yield more quickly and seasonably and therefore could nourish the poor more quickly if the misery of famine and want should not end in that year. He had also ordered this to be done throughout the whole county, in this way making provision for the poor in the future as well as he could.[15] He reprimanded those men of Ghent who had allowed poor people whom they could have fed to die of hunger on their doorsteps.

He also prohibited the brewing of beer because the poor could be fed more easily and better if the townspeople and country-people refrained from making beer in this time of famine. For he ordered bread to be made out of oats so that the poor could at least maintain life on bread and water. He ordered a fourth of a measure of wine to be sold for six pennies and not more dearly so that the merchants would stop hoarding and buying up wine and would exchange their wares, in view of the urgency of the famine, for other foodstuffs which they could acquire more quickly and which could be used more easily to nourish the poor. From his own table he took daily enough food to sustain one hundred and thirteen paupers. In addition he provided daily for one of the poor a set of new garments, including a shirt, tunic, cloak, breeches, hose, and shoes, from the beginning of that Lent and of his devout fasting (during which, betrayed, he fell asleep in the Lord) until the day when he died in Christ. And after he had seen to these arrangements and completed such a merciful distribution to the poor, he was in the habit of going to church where, kneeling in prayer, he would sing psalms to the Lord, and according to his custom would distribute pennies to the poor while prostrate before God.[16]

[4] Count Charles is offered and refuses the imperial crown, 1125

While the marquis Charles was reigning in his county of Flanders in the splendor of peace and fame, Henry, the Roman emperor, died, and the realm of that empire was made desolate and left without an heir to the throne. Therefore the leading men among the clergy and the people of the realm of the Romans and the Germans made a great effort to find someone for the office of

---

11 Evidence that this chapter was written after the murder of Charles, March 2, 1127. It also reveals the current belief that a plot against the count had sprung up earlier than his legal action (in 1126) against the Erembald clan, the villains of Galbert's story. The complex motivation of the crime is discussed more fully below.

12 Galbert's calculation of the yearly calendar from Christmas rather than from Easter is in accord with the general practice of the time in Flanders, where the "Paschal style" did not appear until late in the twelfth century and then only concurrently with the still predominant "Christmas style."

13 Walter, c. 11, also speaks of Charles's order that a daily stipend be given to the needy on every one of his many farms, and of his personal distribution of food, money, and clothing wherever he was, in town, stronghold or manor (*urbe, oppido, vel villa*). One day at Ypres he gave out 7,800 loaves of bread.

14 Galbert obviously means measures of land sown with bread grains, probably wheat. A "measure" probably refers to the Flemish *ghemet*; the *ghemet* of Bruges contained 4,426.38 square meters, a little more than the English statute acre (4,047 square meters). Peas and beans were essential foods, used in a variety of ways. In hard times flour ground from them was mixed with the usual bread cereals.

15 This seems to imply that the original order affected only those parts of the count's domain which he exploited directly as a landlord.

16 The evidence of the use of money supports the theory that coins, especially in the form of silver pennies, were an indispensable instrument of daily life, even among the poor, at this time.

emperor who was noble both in ancestry and character. After weighing the merits of rulers of various lands and kingdoms, those wise and powerful men of the realm decided, after due consideration, that they would formally send suitable delegates, namely, the chancellor of the archbishop of Cologne and with him Count Godfrey, to the count of Flanders, Charles the Pious, on behalf of the whole clergy and people of the kingdom and empire of the Germans, to beg and entreat him by virtue of his power and piety to assume the honors of empire and the regal dignities with their appurtenances, if only for the sake of charity. For all the best men among both clergy and people were hoping, ardently and rightly, that he would be elected so that if, God willing, he deigned to come to them, they could elevate him unanimously by the imperial coronation and establish him as king by the law of the preceding Catholic emperors. When Count Charles had heard the embassy and their urgent request, he took counsel with the nobles and peers of his land[17] as to what he should do. But those who had rightly cherished and loved him, and who venerated him as a father, began to grieve and to lament his departure, predicting that it would prove the ruin of the fatherland if he should desert it. Those evil traitors, however, who were threatening his life, advised him to assume the German kingship and its dignities, pointing out to him how much glory and fame would be his as king of the Romans. Those wretches were trying by this guile and trickery to get rid of him; later when they had been unable to remove him while he was alive, they betrayed him while he was contending with them on behalf of the law of God and men.

And so Count Charles remained in his county because of the insistence of those who loved him, seeking and establishing for all, so far as possible, the peace and well-being of the fatherland; he was a Catholic, good and devout worshiper of God and a prudent ruler of men. When he wanted to perform good deeds of knighthood, he had no enemies around his land, either in the marches or on the frontiers and borders, either because his neighbors feared him or because, united to him in the bond of peace and love, they preferred to exchange offerings and gifts with him. So he undertook chivalric exploits for the honor of his land and the training of his knights in the lands of the counts or princes of Normandy or France, sometimes even beyond the kingdom of France; and there with two hundred knights on horseback he engaged in tourneys, in this way enhancing his own fame and the power and glory of his county. Whatever sin he committed by his worldliness he redeemed with God many times by almsgiving.

[5] Count Charles is offered but refuses the crown of the kingdom of Jerusalem, 1123

During his lifetime it happened that the king of Jerusalem was taken captive by the Saracens, and the city of Jerusalem sat desolate without her king. As we have learned, the Crusaders who were pursuing the course of Christian knighthood there hated that captive king because he was grasping and penurious, and had not governed the people of God well. Therefore they took counsel and by general consent sent a letter to Count Charles asking him to come to Jerusalem and receive the kingdom of Judaea, and in that place and in the holy city take possession of the crown of the Catholic realm and the royal dignity. But he was unwilling, after consulting his vassals, to desert the fatherland of Flanders, which in his lifetime he was to govern well, and would have ruled even better if those evil traitors, full of the demon, had not slain their lord and father, who was imbued with the spirit of piety and wisdom and courage. Alas, what sorrow, that they should rob the Church of God of such a great man whom the church and the people of the Eastern Empire, and the holy city of Jerusalem and its Christian population, had preferred and chosen, and even demanded to have as a king!

[6] In praise of Count Charles

Strength of mind and memory and even reason, the greater virtue of the mind, fail me in praising the good Count Charles; in comparison with him all you earthly princes are less worthy and less powerful, lacking experience and judgment, and

---

17   Galbert doubtless refers to a convoking of the count's *curia* or feudal court, a body of variable size, composed primarily of the great officials of his household, his more important direct vassals who came to fulfill one of their essential feudal functions, that of giving "counsel" to their lord, and other vassals who happened to be present.

disorderly in habits. For Count Charles held such a place among the devout sons of the Church that in his merits he excelled the leaders and many philosophers of the Christian faith; and although he had once been a sinner and guilty, at the end of his good life, from the fruit of penance, all things worked together for his good and for the eternal salvation of his soul. As it is said,

> And none be counted happy till his death,
> Till his last funeral rites are paid.

And, according to the apostle, "We know that to them who love God all things work together for good, even to them that are called according to his purpose." For in a holy place and in holy prayer, and in holy devoutness of heart, and in the holy time of Lent, and in the holy act of alms-giving, and before the sacred altar and the sacred relics of Saint Donatian, archbishop of Rheims, and Saint Basil the Great, and Saint Maximus, the one who raised three dead, those foul dogs, full of the demon, those serfs, murdered their lord! Certainly there is no one so senseless, so stupid and obtuse, as not to sentence those traitors to the vilest and most unheard-of punishments, those serfs who by unheard-of treachery did away with their lord, the very one whom they should most have protected.

It is certainly a marvelous and memorable fact that among the many emperors, kings, dukes, and counts whom we have seen, we have never yet seen or heard of any one whom it so well became to be lord and father, and advocate[18] of the churches of God. That he knew how to be lord, father, advocate, to be pious, gentle, compassionate, an honor to God and an ornament to the Church, cannot be doubted, for after the death of such a great man, everyone bore witness to his merits.

Friends and enemies, foreigners and neighbors, nobles and common people, and the inhabitants of every land whatsoever, were convinced that he would be held worthy of great merit by God and men, because he died like a Christian ruler, seeking the justice of God and the welfare of those over whom he ruled. But the men whom he trusted tripped him up and betrayed him, as it is said in the Psalm: "Why, my own intimate friend, who shared my bread, has lifted his heel to trip me up."

[7] The discovery of the servile origin of the Erembald clan, 1126

Now after the clemency of God had withdrawn the scourges[19] and completely removed the troubles of the time, He began in His mercy to bestow plenty on the land, and He ordered the granaries to be filled with the produce of the fields and the earth to abound in wine and other foodstuffs, and by divine order the whole land flourished again in the loveliness of the seasons. The pious count, wishing to reestablish proper order in his realm, sought to find out who belonged to him, who were servile and who were free men in the realm. When cases were being heard in the courts,[20] the count was often present, and he learned from the judgments concerning secular liberty and the status of serfs that in important cases and general pleas free men scorned to answer charges made by servile ones. Those whom the count had been able to identify as belonging to him, he now set about trying to claim for himself. A certain provost, that Bertulf of Bruges, and his brother the castellan of Bruges, with their nephews Borsiard, Robert, Albert, and other leading members of that clan, were striving by every device of craft and guile to find a way by which they could slip out of servitude and cease belonging to the count;

---

18   "Advocate" may be used here in the general sense of "protector" (as it seems to be in Galbert's Introduction and in c. 6) but it also possesses a specific meaning since the counts of Flanders were the "superior-advocates" of almost all the abbeys in their realm. This function of military protection and limited judicial authority, which they exercised at the expense of the abbots and their officials, as well as of the lesser lay advocates, gave them a substantial control over these great and rich religious establishments.

19   "The scourges" doubtless refer to the famine of chapters 2 and 3. What follows seems to be a direct continuation of those chapters and therefore it is likely that chapters 4, 5, and 6 were a later interpolation.

20   Galbert is probably referring to the count's local tribunals or judicial assemblies exercising common law jurisdiction within most of the great territorial units of the domain, the castellanies, and hence called in French *tribunaux de châtellenie*. They were presided over by the count's key local official and vassal, the castellan, and were composed of a variable number of *scabini* (*échevins*) or "judges," named by the count, free men of standing in the area, probably often knights of the petty nobility; they are often referred to as *échevinages*. These tribunals possessed a broad competence, both civil and penal, over free men, but none in cases of a strictly feudal nature or over the persons of vassals of the count.

for they belonged to him, being of servile status. Finally, after due consideration, the provost gave his marriageable nieces, whom he had reared in his home, in wedlock to free knights, resorting to this policy of intermarriage as a means by which he and his kin might gain a certain measure of secular liberty.

But it happened that a knight who had married a niece of the provost challenged to single combat in the presence of the count another knight, who was free according to the descent of his family; and the latter replied vigorously with an indignant refusal, asserting that by birth he was not of servile status but rather of free rank, according to his family lineage, and for this reason he would not contend as an equal in single combat with his challenger. For, according to the law of the count, a free man who had taken to wife a female serf was no longer free after he had held her for a year, but had come to be of the same status as his wife. And so that knight mourned who had lost his liberty on account of his wife, through whom he had believed he could become freer[21] when he married her; and the provost and his kin mourned, and for that reason kept on trying in every way possible to free themselves from servitude to the count. Therefore when the count had learned from the judgment of the courts and the report of the elders of the realm that they—the Erembald clan—belonged to him beyond doubt, he set about trying to claim them as his serfs. Nevertheless, because the provost and his kin had not heretofore been molested or accused of servile status by the predecessors of the count, this would have been consigned to oblivion, having been laid to rest, as it were, and disregarded for so long, if it had not been brought to the attention of the courts by the challenge to combat.

[8] Bertulf and his nephew become desperate, 1127

But the provost, who with the whole line of his nephews was more powerful than anyone in the realm except the count and more eminent in reputation and in religion,[22] asserted that he himself was free, as were both his predecessors and successors in the clan, and he insisted that this was so with a certain irrationality and arrogance. And so he endeavored by laying plans and using influence to extract himself and his family from the possession and ownership of the count, and he often attacked the count in these terms:

"That Charles of Denmark[23] would never have succeeded to the countship if I had not been willing. But now, although he became count by my efforts, he does not remember how much I did for him but instead seeks to cast me and all my line back into serfdom, trying to find out from the elders whether we are his serfs.

"But let him try as much as he wants, we shall be free and we are free, and there is no man on earth who can make us into serfs!" He talked so boastfully in vain, however, for the count, on his guard, had found out that they were slandering him and had heard of their deceit and also of their treachery. And when the provost and his kin realized that they could not succeed in defending themselves but were, on the contrary, about to be deprived of their usurped liberty, he preferred to perish together with the whole line of his nephews rather than be handed over in servitude to the count. At last, in the guile of abominable deliberation, they began secretly to plot the death of the most pious count, and finally to fix on a place and an opportunity for killing him.

[9] Private war breaks out between Borsiard and Thancmar, 1127

When strife and conflict broke out between his nephews and those of Thancmar, whose side the count justly favored, the provost was delighted because it gave him an opportunity to betray the count, for he had called to the aid of his nephews all the knights of our region, using money, influence, and persuasion. They besieged Thancmar on all sides in the place where he had entrenched

---

21 "Freer" here probably means more "noble."

22 Walter, c. 14, stresses above all the wealth of Bertulf as a source of his power and pride. "Religion" here probably refers to Bertulf's ecclesiastical position rather than to his piety.

23 Derogatory, stressing the fact that Charles in his eyes was a foreigner, and perhaps implying some weakness in Charles's right to the succession. Bertulf's claim to have supported Charles when his succession was challenged by Clemence, the mother of Baldwin VII, is not sustained by any other evidence in the sources.

himself, and finally with a considerable force strongly attacked those within.[24] Breaking the bolts of the gates, they cut down the orchards and hedges of their enemies. Though the provost did not take part and acted as if he had done nothing, he actually did everything by direction and deception. He pretended in public that he was full of good will and told his enemies that he grieved to see his nephews engaged in so much strife and killing, although he himself had incited them to all these crimes. In that conflict many on both sides fell on that day wounded or dead. When the provost had learned that this fight was going on, he himself went to the carpenters who were working in the cloister of the brothers and ordered that their tools, that is, their axes, should be taken to that place for use in cutting down the tower and orchards and houses of his enemies.[25] Then he sent around to various houses in the town to collect axes which were quickly taken to that place. And when in the night his nephews had returned with five hundred knights and squires[26] and innumerable foot-soldiers, he took them into the cloister and refectory of the brothers where he entertained them all with various kinds of food and drink and was very happy and boastful about the outcome.

And while he was harassing his enemies in this way, spending a great deal in support of those who were helping his nephews, first the squires and then the knights began to plunder the peasants, even seizing and devouring the flocks and cattle of the country people. The nephews of the provost were forcibly seizing the belongings of the peasants and appropriating them for their own use. But none of the counts from the beginning of the realm had allowed such pillaging to go on in the realm, because great slaughter and conflict came to pass in this way.

[10] The count takes measures against the nephews of Bertulf, February 27–28, 1127, and returns to Bruges

When the country people heard that the count had come to Ypres, about two hundred of them went to him secretly and at night, and kneeling at his feet begged him for his customary paternal help. They entreated him to order their goods to be returned to them, that is, their flocks and herds, clothes and silver, and all the other furniture of their houses which the nephews of the provost had seized together with those who had fought with them continuously in that attack and siege. After listening solemnly to the complaints of those appealing to him, the count summoned his counselors, and even many who were related to the provost, asking them by what punishment and with what degree of severity justice should deal with this crime. They advised him to burn down Borsiard's house without delay because he had plundered the peasants of the count; and therefore strongly urged him to destroy that house because as long as it stood, so long would Borsiard indulge in fighting and pillaging and even killing, and would continue to lay waste the region. And so the count, acting on this advice, went and burned the house and destroyed the place to its foundations. Then that Borsiard and the provost and their accomplices were beside themselves with anxiety both because in this act the count had clearly lent aid and comfort to their enemies and because the count was daily disquieting them about their servile status and trying in every way to establish his rights over them.

After burning the house the count went on to Bruges. When he had settled down in his house, his close advisers came to him and warned him, saying that the nephews of the provost would betray him because now they could claim as pretext the burning of the house, although even if the count had not done this they were going to betray

---

24 According to Walter, c. 17, the count had forced the unwilling adversaries to accept a truce (*treuga*) and thus halted their feud; the Erembalds now violate this peace and thus catch Thancmar off guard.

25 Adding Walter's account, c. 17, a clearer picture of Thancmar's country stronghold emerges. An enclosure, probably of wood, which his enemies break into through gates, contains orchards and hedges, forming an outer or lower courtyard, where everything is cut down or demolished in the first assault. Thancmar is driven into his upper or inner defense, a tower, probably wooden, since axes were to be used against it. Just where the "houses" were located is not clear.

26 Galbert, who is an accurate observer in so many respects, and who as a notary might be expected to be careful in the use of numbers, here follows a common medieval habit of inaccuracy in dealing with large numbers. It would have been difficult to feed more than five hundred men in the quarters of the canons!

him anyway. After the count had eaten, mediators came and appealed to him to behalf of the provost and his nephews, begging the count to turn his wrath from them and to receive them mercifully back into his friendship. But the count replied that he would act justly and mercifully toward them if they would henceforth give up their fighting and pillaging; and he assured them, moreover, that he would certainly compensate Borsiard with a house that was even better. He swore, however, that as long as he was count, Borsiard should never again have any property in that place where the house had been burned up, because as long as he lived there near Thancmar he would never do anything but fight and feud with his enemies, and pillage and slaughter the people.

The mediators, some of whom were aware of the treachery, did not bother the count very much about the reconciliation, and since the servants were going about offering wine they asked the count to have better wine brought in. When they had drunk this, they kept on asking to be served again still more abundantly, as drinkers usually do, so that when they had finally received the very last grant from the count they could go off as if to bed. And by the order of the count everyone present was abundantly served with wine until, after receiving the final grant, they departed.[27]

[11] The Erembalds seal the plot against the count, during the night of March 1, 1127

Then Isaac and Borsiard, William of Wervik, Ingran, and their accomplices, after receiving the assent of the provost, made haste to carry out what they were about to do, by the necessity of divine ordination, through free will. For immediately those who had been mediators and intercessors between the count and the kinsmen of the provost went to the provost's house and made known the count's response, that is, that they had not been able to secure any mercy either for the nephews or their supporters, and that the count would treat them only as the opinion of the leading men of the land had determined in strict justice.[28]

Then the provost and his nephews withdrew into the inner room and summoned those whom they wanted. While the provost guarded the door, they gave their right hands to each other as a pledge that they would betray the count, and they summoned the young Robert to join in the crime, urging him to pledge by his hand that he would share with them what they were about to do and what they had pledged by their hands. But the noble young man, forewarned by the virtue of his soul and perceiving the gravity of what they were urging upon him, resisted them, not wishing to be drawn unwittingly into their compact until he could find out what it was they had bound themselves to do; and while they were pressing him, he turned away and hurried toward the door. But Isaac and William and the others called out to the provost guarding the door not to let Robert leave until by the pressure of his authority Robert should do what they had demanded. The young man, quickly influenced by the flattery and threats of the provost, came back and gave his hand on their terms, not knowing what he was supposed to do with them, and, as soon as he was pledged to the traitors he inquired what he had done. They said:

"We have now sworn to betray that Count Charles who is working for our ruin in every way and is hastening to claim us as his serfs, and you must carry out this treachery with us, both in word and in deed."

Then the young man, struck with terror and dissolved in tears, cried out:

"God forbid that we should betray one who is our lord and the count of the fatherland. Believe me, if you do not give this up, I shall go and openly reveal your treachery to the count and to everyone, and, God willing, I shall never lend aid and counsel to this pact!"

But they forcibly detained him as he tried to flee from them, saying:

"Listen, friend, we were only pretending to you that we were in earnest about that treachery so that we could try out whether you want to stay by us in a certain serious matter; for there is

---

27 Galbert gives here a revealing picture of the count's "day," his conference with the intimates while eating, his audience to others later, his hospitality to all in the evening. The importance of wine in the social life of the time is clear; mass drinking was probably the chief indoor diversion of the fighting class. Some formalities in the drinking ceremony seem to be observed.

28 Galbert is referring to the judgment of the count's court at Ypres.

something we have concealed from you up to this point, in which you are bound to us by faith and compact, which we shall tell you about in good time."

And so turning it off as a joke, they concealed their treachery.

Now each one of them left the room and went off to his own place. When Isaac had finally reached home, he pretended to go to bed, for he was awaiting the silence of the night, but soon he remounted his horse and returned to the castle.[29] After stopping at Borsiard's lodgings and summoning him and the others whom he wanted, they went secretly to another lodging, that of the knight, Walter. As soon as they had entered, they put out the fire that was burning in the house so that those who had been awakened in the house should not find out from the light of the fire who they were and what sort of business they were carrying on at that time of night, contrary to custom. Then, safe in the darkness, they took counsel about the act of treason to be done as soon as dawn came, choosing for this crime the boldest and rashest members of Borsiard's household, and they promised them rich rewards. To the knights who would kill the count they offered four marks and to the servingmen who would do the same, two marks, and they bound themselves by this most iniquitous compact. Then Isaac returned to his home about daybreak, after he had put heart into them by his counsel and made them ready for such a great crime.

[12] Borsiard and his accomplices slay the count on March 2, 1127; the news spreads

Therefore when day had dawned, so dark and foggy that you could not distinguish anything a spear's length away, Borsiard secretly sent several serfs out into the courtyard of the count[30] to watch for his entrance into the church. The count had arisen very early and had made offerings to the poor in his own house, as he was accustomed to do, and so was on his way to church. But as his

chaplains reported, the night before, when he had settled down in bed to go to sleep, he was troubled by a kind of anxious wakefulness; perplexed and disturbed in mind, he was so disquieted by the many things on his mind that he seemed quite exhausted, even to himself, now lying on one side, now sitting up again on the bed. And when he had set out on his way toward the church of Saint Donatian, the serfs who had been watching for his exit ran back and told the traitors that the count had gone up into the gallery[31] of the church with a few companions. Then that raging Borsiard and his knights and servants, all with drawn swords beneath their cloaks, followed the count into the same gallery, dividing into two groups so that not one of those whom they wished to kill could escape from the gallery by either way, and behold! they saw the count prostrate before the altar, on a low stool, where he was chanting psalms to God and at the same time devoutly offering prayers and giving out pennies to the poor.

Now it should be known what a noble man and distinguished ruler those impious and inhuman serfs betrayed! His ancestors were among the best and most powerful rulers who from the beginning of the Holy Church had flourished in France, or Flanders, or Denmark, or under the Roman Empire. From their stock the pious count was born in our time and grew up from boyhood to perfect manhood, never departing from the noble habits of his royal ancestors or their natural integrity of life. And before he became count, after performing many notable and distinguished deeds, he took the road of holy pilgrimage to Jerusalem. After crossing the depths of the sea and suffering many perils and wounds for the love of Christ, he at last fulfilled his vow and with great joy reached Jerusalem. Here he also fought strenuously against the enemies of the Christian faith. And so, after reverently adoring the sepulcher of the Lord, he returned home. In the hardship and want of this pilgrimage the pious servant of the Lord learned, as he often related when he was count, in what extreme poverty the poor labor, and with what pride

---

29 That is, the fortified enclosure of the "castle" which contained numerous buildings besides the count's house proper.

30 That is, the courtyard of the count's house within the castle.

31 The *solarium* was probably an open colonnaded gallery encircling the hexagonal core or "choir" of the church as in the tomb-chapel of Charlemagne at Aachen. From the narrative which follows, it seems to have been accessible only from the stairs in the two smaller towers which flanked the great "tower" or west-work. To the east it opened out into a chapel, directly over the apse or sanctuary, and to the west probably into another chapel over the "porch."

the rich are exalted, and finally with what misery the whole world is affected. And so he made it his habit to stoop to the needy, and be strong in adversity, not puffed up in prosperity; and as the Psalmist teaches, "The king's strength loves judgment," he ruled the country according to the judgment of the barons and responsible men.

When the life of such a glorious prince had undergone martyrdom, the people of all lands mourned him greatly, shocked by the infamy of his betrayal. Marvelous to tell, although the count was killed in the castle of Bruges on the morning of one day, that is, the fourth day of the week, the news of this impious death shocked the citizens of London, which is in England, on the second day afterwards about the first hour; and towards evening of the same day it disturbed the people of Laon who live far away from us in France.[32] We learned this through our students who at that time were studying in Laon, as we also learned it from our merchants who were busy carrying on their business on that very day in London. For no one could have spanned these intervals of time or space so quickly either by horse or by ship!

[13] Bertulf's past: his ambition, pride and simony

It was ordained by God that bold and arrogant descendants of Bertulf's ancestors should be left behind to carry out the crime of treachery. The others, prevented by death, were influential men in the fatherland in their lifetime, persons of eminence and of great wealth, but the provost passed his life among the clergy, extremely severe and not a little proud. For it was his habit when someone whom he knew perfectly well came into his presence, to dissemble, in his pride, and to ask disdainfully of those sitting near him, who that could be, and then only, if it pleased him, would he greet the newcomer. When he had sold a canonical prebend to someone he would invest him with it not by canonical election but rather by force, for not one of his canons dared to oppose him either openly or secretly. In the house

of the brothers in the church of Saint Donatian the canons had formerly been deeply religious men and perfectly educated, that is, at the beginning of the provostship of this most arrogant prelate. Restraining his pride, they had held him in check by advice and by Catholic doctrine so that he could not undertake anything unseemly in the church. But after they went to sleep in the Lord, the provost, left to himself, set in motion anything that pleased him and toward which the force of his pride impelled him. And so when he became head of his family, he tried to advance beyond everyone in the fatherland his nephews who were well brought up and finally girded with the sword of knighthood. Trying to make their reputation known everywhere, he armed his kinsmen for strife and discord; and he found enemies for them to fight in order to make it known to everyone that he and his nephews were so powerful and strong that no one in the realm could resist them or prevail against them. Finally, accused in the presence of the count himself of servile status, and affronted by the efforts of the count himself to prove that he and all his lineage were servile, he tried, as we have said, to resist servitude by every course and device and to preserve his usurped liberty with all his might. And when, steadfast in his determination, he could not succeed otherwise, he himself, with his kinsmen, carried through the treachery, which he had long refused to consider, with frightful consequences involving both his own kinsmen and the peers of the realm.

[14] Omens and predictions of the crime; the character of Galbert's work

But the most pious Lord thought fit to recall His own by the terror of omens, for in our vicinity bloody water appeared in the ditches, as a sign of future bloodshed. They could have been called back from their crime by this if their hardened hearts had not already entered into a conspiracy for betraying the count. They often asked themselves, if they killed the count, who would avenge him? But they did not know what they were

---

32 Galbert uses *Francia* here in the more restricted sense of the royal domain or Isle de France; the county of Flanders was, of course, a fief of the French crown and therefore part of "France" in the larger sense. If a courier with urgent news could double the average rate of 30 to 40 kilometers a day by land, it is not impossible that the word could reach Laon, about 200 kilometers away as the crow flies, on the second day.

saying, for "who," an infinite word, meant an infinite number of persons, who cannot be reckoned in a definite figure; the fact is that the king of France with a numerous army and also the barons of our land with an infinite multitude came to avenge the death of the most pious count! Not even yet has the unhappy consequence of this utterance reached an end, for as time goes on they do not cease to avenge the death of the count upon all the suspect and the guilty and those who have fled in all directions and gone into exile. And so we, the inhabitants of the land of Flanders, who mourn the death of such a great count and prince, ever mindful of his life, beg, admonish, and beseech you, after hearing the true and reliable account of his life and death (that is, whoever shall have heard it), to pray earnestly for the eternal glory of the life of the soul and his everlasting blessedness with the saints. In this account of his passion, the reader will find the subject divided by days and the events of those days, up to the vengeance, related at the end of this little work, which God alone wrought against those barons of the land whom He has exterminated from this world by the punishment of death, those by whose aid and counsel the treachery was begun and carried through to the end.

[15] The murder of Count Charles, Tuesday, March 2, 1127

In the year one thousand one hundred and twenty-seven, on the sixth day before the Nones of March,[33] on the second day, that is, after the beginning of the same month, when two days of the second week of Lent had elapsed, and the fourth day was subsequently to dawn,[34] on the fifth Concurrent,[35] and the sixth Epact,[36] about dawn, the count at Bruges was kneeling in prayer in order to hear the early Mass in the church of Saint Donatian, the former archbishop of Rheims. Following his pious custom he was giving out alms to the poor, with his eyes fixed on reading

the psalms, and his right hand outstretched to bestow alms; for his chaplain who attended to this duty had placed near the count many pennies which he was distributing to the poor while in the position of prayer.

The office of the first hour was completed and also the response of the third hour,[37] when "Our Father" is said, and when the count, according to custom, was praying, reading aloud obligingly; then at last, after so many plans and oaths and pacts among themselves, those wretched traitors, already murderers at heart, slew the count, who was struck down with swords and run through again and again, while he was praying devoutly and giving alms, humbly kneeling before the Divine Majesty. And so God gave the palm of the martyrs to the count, the course of whose good life was washed clean in the rivulets of his blood and brought to an end in good works. In the final moment of life and at the onset of death, he had most nobly lifted his countenance and his royal hands to heaven, as well as he could amid so many blows and thrusts of the swordsmen; and so he surrendered his spirit to the Lord of all and offered himself as a morning sacrifice to God. But the bloody body of such a great man and prince lay there alone, without the veneration of his people and the due reverence of his servants. Whosoever has heard the circumstances of his death has mourned in tears his pitiable death and has commended to God such a great and lamented prince, brought to an end by the fate of the martyrs.

[16] The murders continue; the flight of the count's friends and the panic of the merchants, March 2, 1127

They also killed the castellan of Bourbourg. First wounding him mortally, they afterward dragged him ignobly by his feet from the gallery into which he had gone up with the count, to the doors of the church and dismembered him outside with their swords. This castellan, however,

---

33   The Nones fell on the seventh day of the month in March, as in May, July, and October, not on the fifth as in the other months.

34   The days of the week were counted from Sunday as the first day, and so Tuesday, the day of the murder, was the "third" day.

35   The Concurrents were a series of numbers used in determining the date of Easter, using March 24 and Friday as key days.

36   The Epacts are a feature of the Lunar Year, the calculation of which was essential in the determination of Easter. The age of the Moon on January 1 is called the Epacts (adiectiones lunae); if the number is 1 in a given year, it is 12 in the next and 23 in the third. The year was reckoned for this purpose as beginning on September 1 preceding the current year.

37   That is, Prime and Tierce, the canonical hours or offices which the clergy were chanting before the celebration of the Mass.

after making confession of his sins to the priests of that very church, received the body and blood of Christ according to the Christian custom. For immediately after killing the count, the swordsmen, leaving the corpse of the count and the castellan at the point of death in the gallery, went out to attack those of their enemies who happened to be present at the court of the count, so that they could slay them at will as they moved about in the castle. They pursued into the count's house a certain knight named Henry whom Borsiard suspected of the death of his brother Robert. He threw himself at the feet of the castellan, Hacket, who had just gone into the house with his men to take possession of it and who now took Henry and the brother of Walter of Loker under his protection and saved them from their attackers.

At the same moment, there fell into the hands of the traitors two sons of the castellan of Bourbourg who meanwhile was confessing his sins to the priests in the gallery of the church; these sons of his were praised by everyone for their knighthood and also for their character. Walter and Gilbert they were called, brothers in blood, peers in knighthood, handsome in appearance, worthy to be loved by all who knew them. As soon as they had heard of the murder of the count and their father they tried to flee, but the wretched traitors, going after them on horseback, pursued them to the Sands at the exit of the town. A wicked knight named Eric, one of those who had betrayed the count, pulled one of the brothers off the horse on which he was fleeing and then together with the pursuers slew him. The other brother, who was rushing in flight to the threshold of his lodgings, they came upon face to face and pierced him through with their swords. As he fell, one of our citizens named Lambert Benkin cut him down as if he were a piece of wood. And so they sent those slaughtered brothers to the holy beatitude of the celestial life.

They also pursued for a mile Richard of Woumen, the mighty master of that stronghold whose daughter had married a nephew of Thancmar, against whom the provost and his nephews formerly stirred up strife and conflict. He with his vassals had gone up to the court of the count, like many of the barons who on the same day were getting ready to go to court.

The traitors, frustrated in their pursuit, returned to the castle where the clergy and people of our place had poured in and were wandering around, stunned by what had happened. Those who were known to have been friends of the count as long as he lived, were now, without doubt, in a state of fear, and, lying low for the time, they were avoiding being seen by the traitors; while those in the count's court who depended on his friendship quickly took flight and got away while the people were in a state of confusion. Gervaise, a chamberlain of the count, whom the hand of God armed first to avenge the death of his lord, fled on horseback toward those Flemings who were his kinsmen. A certain John, a servant of the count who looked after his room, and whom the count had loved most among his serving men, fled at dawn on horseback, riding by side paths until noon, and at noon reached Ypres where he broke the news of the death of the count and his men. At this time merchants from all the kingdoms around Flanders had come together at Ypres,[38] on the feast of Saint Peter's Chair, where the market and all the fairs were going on; they were in the habit of carrying on their business safely under the peace and protection of the most pious count. At the same time merchants from the kingdom of the Lombards had come to the same fair;[39] the count had bought from them for twenty-one marks a silver vessel which was marvelously made so that the liquid which it held disappeared as one looked at it.[40] When the news reached all these people from various places who had come together at the fair, they packed up their goods and fled by day and by night, bearing with them word of the disgrace of our land and spreading it everywhere.

---

38 One of several Flemish fairs, international, long-term, as distinguished from local, weekly markets, which seem to date from the late eleventh century. Their appearance was probably due to the initiative of the counts, and was one of several measures undertaken to create a powerful economic bond across Flanders, from the Scheldt to the sea, and thus unify their lands.

39 The commercial expansion of the north Italian merchants (coming probably from the smaller cities such as Asti and Piacenza rather than Genoa) was even more precocious than that of England, but Galbert's reference is the first sure evidence of their presence at the Flemish fairs.

40 Probably a false bottom!

29. FOUR ACCOUNTS

THE FOLLOWING FOUR TEXTS reflect the impressions of the first Crusade (1096–99) from the Christian, Jewish, Muslim, and Byzantine perspectives.

Fulcher of Chartres

FULCHER OF CHARTRES WAS a priest and the chaplain of Baldwin I, Count of Edessa and first king of Jerusalem. Fulcher lived in Jerusalem from 1100 until at least 1127. Part of his account is based on his own experience traveling to and in the Levant, and part is drawn from other eye-witness chronicles. Although loyal to his lord, he remains relatively objective in describing the events of the twelfth century.

Source: Harold S. Fink (ed.), *A History of the Expedition to Jerusalem 1095–1127,* trans. Frances Rita Ryan, S.S.J. (Knoxville: University of Tennessee Press, 1969).

Further Reading: Jonathan Riley-Smith, *The First Crusade and the Idea of Crusading* (Philadelphia: University of Pennsylvania Press, 1986).

Here Beginneth the First Book Concerning the Deeds of the Franks, Pilgrims to Jerusalem

I The Council Held at Clermont.

1. In the year 1095 after the Incarnation of Our Lord, while Henry the so-called emperor was reigning in Germany[1] and King Philip in France,[2] evils of all kinds multiplied throughout Europe because of vacillating faith. Pope Urban II[3] then ruled in the city of Rome. He was a man admirable in life and habits who strove prudently and vigorously to raise the status of Holy Church ever higher and higher.

2. Moreover he saw the faith of Christendom excessively trampled upon by all, by the clergy as well as by the laity, and peace totally disregarded, for the princes of the lands were incessantly at war quarreling with someone or other. He saw that people stole worldly goods from one another, that many captives were taken unjustly and were most barbarously cast into foul prisons and ransomed for excessive prices, or tormented there by three evils, namely hunger, thirst and cold, and secretly put to death, that holy places were violated, monasteries and villas consumed by fire, nothing mortal spared, and things human and divine held in derision.

---

1 Henry IV (1054–1106), German king and antagonist of the Cluny reform papacy, had been crowned emperor of the Romans by antipope Clement III in 1084. Fulcher's sympathies with the reform party are apparent here and below.

2 Philip I (1060–1108), already in trouble with the church for his bigamous relations with Bertrada of Montfort, was re-excommunicated at Clermont in November 1095.

3 Urban II (1088–1100) was the friend and disciple of Gregory VII (1073–85), the great champion of the Cluny reform movement.

3. When he heard that the interior part of Romania had been occupied by the Turks and the Christians subdued by a ferociously destructive invasion, Urban, greatly moved by compassionate piety and by the prompting of God's love, crossed the mountains and descended into Gaul and caused a council to be assembled in Auvergne at Clermont, as the city is called. This council, appropriately announced by messengers in all directions, consisted of 310 members, bishops as well as abbots carrying the crozier.

4. On the appointed day Urban gathered them around himself and in an eloquent address carefully made known the purpose of the meeting. In the sorrowing voice of a suffering church he told of its great tribulation. He delivered an elaborate sermon concerning the many raging tempests of this world in which the faith had been degraded as was said above.

5. Then as a suppliant he exhorted all to resume the powers of their faith and arouse in themselves a fierce determination to overcome the machinations of the devil, and to try fully to restore Holy Church, cruelly weakened by the wicked, to its honorable status as of old.

II The Decree of Urban in the Same Council.

1. "Dearest brethren," he said, "I, Urban, supreme pontiff and by the permission of God prelate of the whole world, have come in this time of urgent necessity to you, the servants of God in these regions, as a messenger of divine admonition. I hope that those who are stewards of the ministry of God shall be found to be good and faithful, and free from hypocrisy [I Cor. 4:1–2].

2. "For if anyone is devious and dishonest, and far removed from the moderation of reason and justice, and obstructs the law of God, then I shall endeavor with divine help to correct him. For the Lord has made you stewards over His household so that when the time comes you may provide it with food of modest savour. You will be blessed indeed if the Lord of the stewardship shall find you faithful [Matt. 24:45–46].

3. "You are called shepherds; see that you do not do the work of hirelings. Be true shepherds always holding your crooks in your hands; and sleeping not, guard on every side of the flock entrusted to you [John 10:12–13].

4. "For if through carelessness or neglect a wolf carries off a sheep you will certainly not only lose the reward prepared for you by our Lord, but after first having been beaten by the rods of the lictor you will be summarily hurled into the abode of the damned.

5. "In the words of the Gospel, 'You are the salt of the earth' [Matt. 5:13]. But if you fail how will the salting be accomplished? Oh how many men must be seasoned! [Matt. 5:13; Mark 9:50; Luke 14:34]. It is needful for you to salt with the corrective salt of your wisdom the ignorant who gape overmuch after the lusts of the world. Otherwise they will be putrefied by their transgression and be found unseasoned when the Lord speaks to them.

6. "For if He shall find in them worms, that is sins, because of your slothful performance of duty He will forthwith order them, despised, cast into the abyss of filth [Mark 9:44–48]. And because you will not be able to restore such loss to Him He will straightway banish you, damned in His judgment, from the presence of His love.

7. "But one that salteth ought to be prudent, farseeing, modest, learned, peacemaking, truth-seeking, pious, just, equitable, and pure. For how can the unlearned make others learned, the immodest others modest, and the impure others pure? If one hates peace how can one bring about peace? Or if one has soiled hands how can he cleanse those who are soiled of other pollution? For it is read, 'If a blind man leads a blind man, both will fall into a pit' [Matt. 15:14; Luke 6:39].

8. "Accordingly first correct yourself so that then without reproach you can correct those under your care. If you truly wish to be the friends of God then gladly do what you know is pleasing to Him.

9. "Especially see to it that the affairs of the church are maintained according to its law so that simoniacal heresy in no way takes root among you. Take care that sellers and buyers, scourged by the lash of the Lord [Matt. 21:12; Mark 11:15; Luke 19:45; John 2:15], be miserably driven out through the narrow gates to utter destruction [Matt. 7:13; Luke 13:24].

10. "Keep the church in all its ranks entirely free from secular power, cause a tithe of all the fruits of the earth to be given faithfully to God, and let them not be sold or retained.

11. "Whoever shall have seized a bishop, let him be accursed. Whoever shall have seized monks or priests or nuns, and their servants, or pilgrims and traders, and despoiled them, let him be accursed. Let thieves and burners of houses, and their accomplices, be banished from the church and excommunicated.

12. "'Thereafter we must consider especially,' said Gregory, 'how severely punished will be he who steals from another, if he is infernally damned for not being generous with his own possessions.' For so it happened to the rich man in the familiar gospel story [Luke 16:19–31]. He was not punished for stealing from another, but because having received wealth he used it badly.

13. "By these evils it has been said, dearest brethren, that you have seen the world disturbed for a long time and particularly in some parts of your own provinces as we have been told. Perhaps due to your own weakness in administering justice scarcely anyone dares to travel on the road with hope of safety for fear of seizure by robbers by day or thieves by night, by force or wicked craft, indoors or out.

14. "Wherefore the truce commonly so-called, which was long ago established by the holy fathers, should be renewed. I earnestly admonish each of you to strictly enforce it in your own diocese. But if anyone, smitten by greed or pride, willingly infringes this truce, let him be anathema by virtue of the authority of God and by sanction of the decrees of this council."

III Urban's Exhortation Concerning a Pilgrimage to Jerusalem.[4]

1. When these and many other matters were satisfactorily settled, all those present, clergy and people alike, spontaneously gave thanks to God for the words of the Lord Pope Urban and promised him faithfully that his decrees would be well kept. But the pope added at once that another tribulation not less but greater than that already mentioned, even of the worst nature, was besetting Christianity from another part of the world.

2. He said, "Since, oh sons of God, you have promised Him to keep peace among yourselves and to faithfully sustain the rights of Holy Church more sincerely than before, there still remains for you, newly aroused by godly correction, an urgent task which belongs to both you and God, in which you can show the strength of your good will. For you must hasten to carry aid to your brethren dwelling in the East, who need your help for which they have often entreated.

3. "For the Turks, a Persian people, have attacked them, as many of you already know, and have advanced as far into Roman territory as that part of the Mediterranean which is called the Arm of St. George. They have seized more and more of the lands of the Christians, have already defeated them in seven times as many battles, killed or captured many people, have destroyed churches, and have devastated the kingdom of God. If you allow them to continue much longer they will conquer God's faithful people much more extensively.

4. "Wherefore with earnest prayer I, not I, but God exhorts you as heralds of Christ to repeatedly urge men of all ranks whatsoever, knights as well as foot-soldiers, rich and poor, to hasten to

---

4   This heading does not fit chap. iii because the chapter does not mention Jerusalem, the Holy Sepulcher, or the Holy Land. The chapter is broad in scope and includes the rescue of the Byzantines as a large part of the purpose of the crusade. As this and some other chapter headings do not fit the chapters they entitle, it is probable that the divisions in the text were made and titled by a later scribe, not by Fulcher.

exterminate this vile race from our lands and to aid the Christian inhabitants in time.

5. "I address those present; I proclaim it to those absent; moreover Christ commands it. For all those going thither there will be remission of sins if they come to the end of this fettered life while either marching by land or crossing by sea, or in fighting the pagans. This I grant to all who go, through the power vested in me by God.

6. "Oh what a disgrace if a race so despicable, degenerate, and enslaved by demons should thus overcome a people endowed with faith in Almighty God and resplendent in the name of Christ! Oh what reproaches will be charged against you by the Lord Himself if you have not helped those who are counted like yourselves of the Christian faith!

7. "Let those," he said, "who are accustomed to wantonly wage private war against the faithful march upon the infidels in a war which should be begun now and be finished in victory. Let those who have long been robbers now be soldiers of Christ. Let those who once fought against brothers and relatives now rightfully fight against barbarians. Let those who have been hirelings for a few pieces of silver [Matt. 27:3] now attain an eternal reward. Let those who have been exhausting themselves to the detriment of body and soul now labor for a double glory. Yea on the one hand will be the sad and the poor, on the other the joyous and the wealthy; here the enemies of the Lord, there His friends.

8. "Let nothing delay those who are going to go. Let them settle their affairs, collect money, and when winter has ended and spring has come, zealously undertake the journey under the guidance of the Lord."

IV Concerning the Bishop of Le Puy and Subsequent Events.

1. After these words were spoken and the audience inspired to enthusiasm, many of them, thinking that nothing could be more worthy, at once promised to go and to urge earnestly those who were not present to do likewise. Among them was a certain Bishop of Le Puy, Adhemar by name, who afterwards acting as vicar apostolic prudently and wisely governed the entire army of God and vigorously inspired it to carry out the undertaking.

2. So when these matters which we have mentioned were decided in the council and firmly agreed upon by all, the blessing of absolution was given and all departed. After they had returned to their homes they told those who were not informed of what had been done. When the edict of the council had been proclaimed everywhere through the provinces, they agreed under oath to maintain the peace which is called the Truce [of God].

3. Indeed finally many people of varied calling, when they discovered that there would be remission of sins, vowed to go with purified soul whither they had been ordered to go.

4. Oh how fitting, and how pleasing it was to us all to see those crosses made of silk, cloth-of-gold, or other beautiful material which these pilgrims whether knights, or other laymen, or clerics sewed on the shoulders of their cloaks. They did this by command of Pope Urban once they had taken the oath to go. It was proper that the soldiers of God who were preparing to fight for His honor should be identified and protected by this emblem of victory. And since they thus decorated themselves with this emblem of their faith, in the end they acquired from the symbol the reality itself. They clad themselves with the outward sign in order that they might obtain the inner reality.

5. It is evident that because a good intention brings about the accomplishment of a good work, a good work brings about the salvation of the soul. If it is well to have good intentions it is still better after meditation to carry them out. Therefore it is best to lay up a store of good works so that through worthy deeds one acquires nourishment for the soul. Therefore let each one intend [to do] good so that he will finish by doing better and at length by deserving attain the best, which will not diminish in eternity.

6. In such a manner Urban, a wise man and
   reverenced
Meditated a labour whereby the world
   flowered.

For he restored peace and re-established the rights of the church in their former condition. He also made a vigorous effort to drive out the pagans from the lands of the Christians. And since he endeavored in every way to glorify everything which was of God, nearly everyone freely submitted in obedience to his paternal authority.

V Concerning the Dissension Between Pope Urban and Guibert.

1. But the Devil, who always seeks man's destruction and goes about like a lion, seeking whom he may devour [I Pet. 5:8], stirred up, to the confusion of the people, a certain rival to Pope Urban, Guibert by name.[5] This man, incited by pride and supported for a while by the impudence of the aforesaid emperor of the Bavarians,[6] began to usurp the apostolic office while Urban's predecessor Gregory, that is Hildebrand, rightfully held the see and excluded Gregory himself from the limits of St. Peter's Basilica.

2. And because Guibert acted thus perversely, the better people did not care to recognize him. Since Urban after the death of Hildebrand was legally elected and consecrated by the cardinal bishops,[7] the greater and more pious part of the people were in favor of obedience to him.

3. Guibert, however, urged on by the support of the said emperor and by the passion of most of the Roman citizens, kept Urban a stranger to the Monastery of the Blessed Peter as long as possible. But Urban during the time that he was excluded

from his church traveled about the country reconciling to God the people who had gone somewhat astray.

4. Guibert even as he was puffed up by his primacy in the church showed himself to be a pope indulgent to sinners. He exercised the papal office, albeit unjustly, amongst his adherents and ridiculed the acts of Urban as invalid.

5. But Urban, in the year in which the Franks first passed through Rome on their way to Jerusalem,[8] obtained the whole apostolic power with the aid of a certain most noble matron, Mathilda by name, who was then very powerful in her native region about Rome.

6. Guibert was then in Germany. Thus there were two popes over Rome, but whom to obey many did not know, nor from whom to seek counsel or who should heal the sick. Some favored one, some the other.

7. But it was clear to the intelligence of men that Urban was the better; for he is rightly considered better who controls his passions just as if they were his enemies.

8. Guibert as the archbishop of the city of Ravenna was very rich. He was resplendent in pomp and wealth. It was remarkable that such riches did not satisfy him. Ought he to be considered by all an exemplar of right living who, a lover of ostentation, boldly presumes to usurp the sceptre of God's authority? Certainly this office is not to be seized by force but accepted with fear and humility.

9. Nor is it a wonder that the whole world was disquieted and disturbed. For if the Church of Rome,

---

5   Guibert had been the Archbishop of Ravenna. In the famous investiture controversy between the Emperor Henry IV and Pope Gregory VII [Hildebrand], Guibert sided with Henry and as a result was chosen (anti-)pope in 1080, taking the name of Clement III. He died in 1100.

6   Fulcher sarcastically refers to Henry IV not as emperor of the Romans but of the Bavarians. Henry had become duke of Bavaria in 1055 and drew much of his strength from that area.

7   Gregory died in 1085, and his successor, Victor III, reigned briefly from 1086 to 1087. Then the former Cluny monk, the Frenchman Odo de Lagny, Cardinal Bishop of Ostia, was elected pope in 1088, taking the name of Urban II.

8   Fulcher, in referring to the year (1096) when the Franks first passed through Rome, must have been writing after they had passed through again, that is, after the members of the Crusade of 1101 went through. By "Franks" Fulcher meant "crusaders," because most crusaders at that time (though by no means all) were Frenchmen.

the source of correction for all of Christianity, is troubled by any disorder, then immediately the members subject to it derive the malady through the chief nerves and are weakened by suffering along with it.

10. Yes, truly this church, which is indeed our mother, at whose bosom we were reared, by whose example we profited, and by whose counsel we were strengthened, was rudely smitten by that proud Guibert. And when the head is thus struck the members are hurt immediately.

If the head is afflicted the other members suffer.

11. Moreover when the head was sick in this way the members were enfeebled with pain because in all parts of Europe peace, virtue, and faith were brutally trampled upon by stronger men and lesser, inside the church and out. It was necessary to put an end to all these evils and, in accordance with the plan initiated by Pope Urban, to turn against the pagans the fighting which up to now customarily went on among the Christians.

12. Now therefore I must turn my pen to history in order to tell clearly the uninformed about the journey of those going to Jerusalem, what happened to them, and how the undertaking and the labor gradually came to a successful conclusion with the help of God. I, Fulcher of Chartres, who went with the other pilgrims, afterwards diligently and carefully collected all this in my memory for the sake of posterity, just as I saw it with my own eyes.[9]

VI The Time of Departure of the Christians Together with the Names of the Leaders of the Pilgrims.

1. In the year of 1096 of the Lord's Incarnation and in the month of March following the council, which, as has been said, Pope Urban held during November in Auvergne, some who were more speedy in their preparation than others began to set out on the holy journey. Others followed in April or May, in June or in July, or even in August or September or October as they were able to secure the means to defray expenses.

2. In that year peace and a very great abundance of grain and wine existed in all countries by the grace of God, so that there was no lack of bread on the trip for those who had chosen to follow Him with their crosses in accordance with His commands.

3. Since it is fitting to remember the names of the leaders of the pilgrims at that time I mention Hugh the Great, the brother of King Philip of France, the first of the heroes to cross the sea. Hugh landed with his men near Durazzo, a city in Bulgaria,[10] but rashly advancing with a small force was captured there by the citizens and conducted to the emperor at Constantinople. Here he stayed for some time, being not entirely free.

4. After him Bohemond of Apulia, a son of Robert Guiscard, of the nation of the Normans, passed with his army over the same route.

5. Next Godfrey, Duke of Lorraine, traveled through Hungary with a large force.

6. Raymond, Count of the Provençals, with Goths and Gascons, and also Adhemar, Bishop of Le Puy, crossed through Dalmatia.

7. A certain Peter the Hermit, having gathered to himself a crowd of people on foot but only a few knights, was the first to pass through Hungary. Afterwards Walter the Penniless, who was certainly a very good soldier, was the commander of these people. Later he was killed with many of his companions between Nicomedia and Nicaea by the Turks.

8. In the month of October, Robert, Count of the Normans, a son of William, King of the English, began the journey, having collected a great army

---

9   Fulcher here identifies himself by name and as a member of the First Crusade. The phrase "successful conclusion" indicates that he wrote it at some time after, and not before, the conclusion of that crusade in 1099.

10 The reference to Durazzo, Albania, as a part of Bulgaria dates back to the great Bulgarian monarchy of Czar Samuel (d. 1014), destroyed by the Byzantine emperor Basil by 1018.

of Normans, English, and Bretons. With him went Stephen, the noble Count of Blois, his brother-in-law, and Robert, Count of the Flemings, with many other nobles.

9. Therefore since such a multitude came from all Western countries, little by little and day by day the army grew while on the march from a numberless host into a group of armies. You could see a countless number from many lands and of many languages. However, they were not gathered into a single army until we reached the city of Nicaea....

XV The Arrival of the Franks at Antioch and the Vicissitudes of the Siege.

1. In the month of October the Franks came to Antioch in Syria, a city founded by Seleucus, son of Antiochus. Seleucus made it his capital. It was previously called Reblata. Moreover it lay on the other side of the river which they called the Fernus or Orontes.[11] Our tents were ordered pitched before the city between it and the first milestone. Here afterwards battles were very frequently fought which were most destructive to both sides. When the Turks rushed out from the city they killed many of our men, but when the tables were turned they grieved to find themselves beaten.

2. Antioch is certainly a very large city, well fortified and strongly situated. It could never be taken by enemies from without provided the inhabitants were supplied with food and were determined to defend it. There is in Antioch a much-renowned church dedicated to the honor of Peter the Apostle where he, raised to the episcopate, sat as bishop after he had received from the Lord Jesus the primacy of the church and the keys to the Kingdom of Heaven.

3. There is another church too, circular in form, built in honor of the Blessed Mary, together with others fittingly constructed. These had for a long time been under the control of the Turks, but God, foreseeing all, kept them intact for us so that one day He would be honored in them by ourselves.

4. The sea is, I think, about thirteen miles from Antioch. Because the Fernus River flows into the sea at that point, ships filled with goods from distant lands are brought up its channel as far as Antioch. Thus supplied with goods by sea and land, the city abounds with wealth of all kinds.

5. Our princes when they saw how hard it would be to take the city swore mutually to cooperate in a siege until, God willing, they took it by force or stratagem.

6. They found a number of boats in the aforesaid river. These they took and fashioned into a pontoon bridge over which they crossed to carry out their plans. Previously they had been unable to ford the river.

7. But the Turks, when they had looked about anxiously and saw that they were beset by such a multitude of Christians, feared that they could not possibly escape them. After they had consulted together, Aoxianus, the prince and Amir of Antioch, sent his son Sanxado to the sultan, that is the emperor of Persia, urging that he should aid them with all haste. The reason was that they had no hope of other help except from Mohammed their advocate. Sanxado in great haste carried out the mission assigned to him.

8. Those who remained within the city guarded it, waiting for the assistance for which they had asked while they frequently concocted many kinds of dangerous schemes against the Franks. Nevertheless the latter foiled the stratagems of the enemy as well as they could.

9. On a certain day it happened that seven hundred Turks were killed by the Franks, and thus those who had prepared snares for the Franks were by snares overcome.[12] For the power of God was manifest there. All of our men returned safely except one who was wounded by them.

10. Oh how many Christians in the city, Greeks, Syrians, and Armenians, did the Turks kill in

---

11 The Franks arrived at Antioch on October 20–21, 1097.

12 This refers to a demonstration against a neighboring Turkish fortress called Hârim (Harene, Aregh) in mid-November 1097. Fulcher's figure, seven hundred, is hearsay.

rage and how many heads did they hurl over the walls with *petrariae* and *fundibula*[13] in view of the Franks! This grieved our men very much. The Turks hated these Christians, for they feared that somehow the latter might assist the Franks against a Turkish attack.

11. After the Franks besieged the city for some time and had scoured the country roundabout in search of food for themselves and were unable to find even bread to buy, they suffered great hunger. For this reason all were very much discouraged, and many secretly planned to withdraw from the siege and to flee by land or by sea.

12. But they had no money on which to live. They were even obliged to seek their sustenance far away and in great fear by separating themselves forty or fifty miles from the siege, and there in the mountains they were often killed by the Turks in ambush.

13. We felt that misfortunes had befallen the Franks because of their sins and that for this reason they were not able to take the city for so long a time. Luxury and avarice and pride and plunder had indeed vitiated them.

14. Then the Franks, having again consulted together, expelled the women from the army, the married as well as the unmarried, lest perhaps defiled by the sordidness of riotous living they should displease the Lord. These women then sought shelter for themselves in neighboring towns.

15. The rich as well as the poor were wretched because of starvation as well as of the slaughter, which daily occurred. Had not God, like a good pastor, held His sheep together, without doubt they would all have fled thence at once in spite of the fact that they had sworn to take the city. Many though, because of the scarcity of food, sought for many days in neighboring villages what was necessary for life; and they did not afterward return to the army but abandoned the siege entirely.

16. At that time we saw a remarkable reddish glow in the sky and besides felt a great quake in the earth, which rendered us all fearful. In addition many saw a certain sign in the shape of a cross, whitish in color, moving in a straight path toward the East.[14]

XVI The Miserable Poverty of the Christians and the Flight of the Count of Blois.

1. In the year of our Lord 1098, after the area around Antioch had been stripped completely bare by the large number of our people, both the old and the young were increasingly distressed by excessive hunger.

2. Then the starving people devoured the stalks of beans still growing in the fields, many kinds of herbs unseasoned with salt, and even thistles which because of the lack of firewood were not well cooked and therefore irritated the tongues of those eating them. They also ate horses, asses, camels, dogs, and even rats. The poorer people ate even the hides of animals and the seeds of grain found in manure.

3. The people for the love of God endured cold, heat, and torrents of rain. Their tents became old and torn and rotten from the continuous rains. For this reason many people had no cover but the sky.

4. Just as gold is thrice tried in the fire and seven times purified [Psalms 12:7], so I believe the elect were tried by the Lord and by such suffering were cleansed of their sins. For although the sword of the Assassin did not fail to do its deadly work, many of the people suffered long agony and gladly ran the full course of martyrdom. Perhaps they took consolation from the example of Holy Job who purging his soul by torments of the body always remembered God [Job 2:12]. When they struggled against the pagans they labored for God.

5. Although God, who creates all, orders all that He has created and sustains what he has ordered,

---

13 *Fundibula*, like *petrariae*, were machines for hurling stones. The two types seem to have been much the same.

14 The auroral display and earthquake were on December 30, 1097, according to Raymond of Aguilers. The "sign in the sky" may have been something imagined in the auroral display.

governs with vigor and is able to destroy or repair whatever He wishes, I feel that at the cost of suffering to the Christians He wills that the pagans shall be destroyed, they who have so many times foully trod underfoot all which belongs to God although with His permission and as the people deserved. In truth He has permitted the Christians to be slain for the augmentation of their salvation, the Turks, however, for the damnation of their souls. But those of the Turks predestined to salvation it pleased God to have baptized by our priests. "For those whom He predestined, them He called and also glorified" [Rom. 8:30].

6. What then? Some of our men as you have heard about withdrew from a siege which was so difficult, some from want, some from cowardice, some from fear of death, first the poor, then the rich.

7. Then Stephen, Count of Blois, left the siege and went home to France by sea. We all grieved on this account because he was a very noble man and was mighty in arms. On the day following his departure the city of Antioch was surrendered to the Franks. If he had persevered he would have greatly rejoiced with the rest, for what he did was a disgrace to him. For a good beginning does not profit one if one does not end well. In things regarding God I shall be brief lest I might go astray, for in these matters I must be careful not to wander from the truth.

8. From this month of October, as was said, the siege of the city continued throughout the following winter and spring until the month of June. The Turks and Franks alternately staged many attacks and counterattacks. They conquered and were conquered. We, however, won more often than they. Once it happened that many Turks in fleeing fell into the Fernus River and miserably drowned.[15] On this side of the river and on the other side both people fought many times.

9. Our princes constructed forts in front of the city. By frequent sallies from them our men sturdily held back the Turks. As a result they often denied pasturage to the animals of the enemy.

Nothing was brought in from the Armenians of the outlying areas; yet they often acted to our detriment.

XVII The Surrender of the City of Antioch.

1. When, however, God, appeased no doubt by their prayers, was pleased to end the labor of His people who had daily poured forth beseeching supplications to Him, in His love He granted that through the treachery of these same Turks the city should be secretly delivered up and restored to the Christians. Hear therefore of a treachery, and yet not a treachery.

2. Our Lord appeared to a certain Turk predestined by His grace and said to him, "Arise, you who sleep! I command you to return the city to the Christians." Although wondering about it the man kept the vision a secret.

3. Again the Lord appeared to him. "Return the city to the Christians," He said, "for I who command this am Christ indeed." Wondering therefore what he should do the man went to his master, the prince of Antioch, and made known the vision to him. The latter replied, "Do you wish, stupid man, to obey a ghost?" The man returned, and remained silent.

4. Again the Lord appeared unto him, saying, "Why have you not done what I have commanded? It is not for you to hesitate, for I who command this am the Lord of all." The Turk no longer doubting discreetly made a plot with our men by which they should obtain the city.

5. When this agreement was made, the Turk gave his son as a hostage to the Lord Bohemond to whom this plan had first been proposed and whom he had first influenced. On the appointed night the Turk admitted over the wall twenty of our men by means of rope ladders. At once, without delay, the gate was opened. The Franks, who were ready, entered the city. Forty more of our soldiers who had already entered by means of the ropes slew sixty Turks whom they found guarding

---

15   This may refer to skirmishes of November 18, 1097, or March 6, 1098.

the towers. Then all the Franks shouted together in a loud voice, "God wills it! God wills it!" For this was our signal cry when we were about to accomplish any good enterprise.

6. Hearing this the Turks were all extremely terrified. The Franks immediately began to attack the city, the dawn then growing lighter. When the Turks first noticed Bohemond's red banner, now waving aloft, the great tumult already raging round about, the trumpets of the Franks sounding from the top of the wall, and the Franks running about through the streets with drawn swords and savagely killing people, they were bewildered and began to flee here and there. As many Turks as could fled to the citadel situated on a lofty cliff.

7. Our common people indiscriminately seized whatever they found in the streets and houses, but the knights, who were experienced in the business of warfare, continued to seek out and kill the Turks.

8. The amir of Antioch, Aoxianus by name, was beheaded while fleeing by an Armenian peasant, who at once brought the severed head to the Franks.

XVIII The Discovery of the Lance.

1. It happened moreover that after the city was taken a certain man found a lance in a hole in the ground under the Church of the blessed Apostle Peter. When it was discovered the man asserted that it was the very lance with which Longinus had, according to the Scriptures, pierced Christ in the right side [John 19:34]. He said that this had been revealed to him by St. Andrew the Apostle.

2. And when it had been discovered and the man himself told the Bishop of Le Puy and Count Raymond, the Bishop thought the story false, but the count hoped that it was true.

3. All the people when they heard this exulted and glorified God. For almost a hundred days[16] the lance was held in great veneration and was carried gloriously by Count Raymond, who guarded it. Then it happened that many of the priests and laity hesitated, thinking that this was not the Lord's lance but another one dishonestly found by that doltish man.

4. Wherefore after three days of fasting and prayers had been decided upon and finished by all, they lighted a heap of wood in the middle of the field in front of the town of Archas in the eighth month after the capture of Antioch; the bishops made the judicial benediction over the same fire; and the finder of the lance quickly ran clear through the midst of the burning pile to prove his honesty, as he had requested. When the man passed through the flames and emerged, they saw that he was guilty, for his skin was burned and they knew that within he was mortally hurt. This was demonstrated by the outcome, for on the twelfth day he died, seared by the guilt of his conscience.

5. And since everyone had venerated the lance for the honor and love of God, when the ordeal was over those who formerly believed in it were now incredulous and very sad. Nevertheless Count Raymond preserved it for a long time afterward....

XXVI The Site of Jerusalem.

1. The city of Jerusalem is located in a mountainous region which is devoid of trees, streams, and springs excepting only the Pool of Siloam, which is a bowshot from the city. Sometimes it has enough water, and sometimes a deficiency due to a slight drainage. This little spring is in the valley at the foot of Mount Zion in the course of the Brook Kedron which, in winter time, is accustomed to flow through the center of the Valley of Jehoshaphat.

2. The many cisterns inside the city, reserved for winter rains, have a sufficiency of water. More, at which men and beasts are refreshed, are also found outside the city.

3. It is generally conceded that the city is laid out in such proper proportion that it seems neither

---

16 *I.e.*, until late in September 1098.

too small nor too large. Its width from wall to wall is that of four bowshots. To the west is the Tower of David with the city wall on each flank; to the south is Mount Zion a little closer than a bowshot; and to the east, the Mount of Olives a thousand paces outside the city.

4. The aforesaid Tower of David is of solid masonry half-way up, of large squared blocks sealed with molten lead. Fifteen or twenty men, if well supplied with food, could defend it from all assaults of an enemy.

5. In the same city is the Temple of the Lord, round in shape, built where Solomon in ancient times erected the earlier magnificent Temple. Although it can in no way be compared in appearance to the former building, still this one is of marvelous workmanship and most splendid appearance.

6. The Church of the Lord's Sepulcher is likewise circular in form. It was never closed in at the top but always admits the light through a permanent aperture ingeniously fashioned under the direction of a skillful architect.

7. I cannot, I dare not, I know not how to enumerate the many objects which it now contains or contained in the past lest in some way I deceive those reading or hearing about the matter. In the middle of the Temple, when we first entered it and for fifteen years thereafter, was a certain native rock. It was said that the Ark of the Lord's Covenant along with the urn and tables of Moses was sealed inside of it, that Josiah, King of Judah, ordered it to be placed there saying, "You shall never carry it from this place" [II Chronicles 35:3]. For he foresaw the future Captivity.

8. But this contradicts what we read in the descriptions of Jeremiah, in the second book of the Maccabees, that he himself hid it in Arabia, saying that it would not be found until many peoples should be gathered together. Jeremiah was a contemporary of King Josiah; however, the king died before Jeremiah [II Macc. 2:4–9].

9. They said that the angel of the Lord had stood upon the aforesaid rock [II Chronicles 3:1; II Sam. 24:18–25] and destroyed the people because of the enumeration of the people foolishly made by David and displeasing to the Lord [II Sam. 24:1–2, 15–17; I Chronicles 21:15]. Moreover this rock because it disfigured the Temple of the Lord was afterwards covered over and paved with marble. Now an altar is placed above it, and there the clergy have fitted up a choir. All the Saracens held the Temple of the Lord in great veneration. Here rather than elsewhere they preferred to say the prayers of their faith although such prayers were wasted because offered to an idol set up in the name of Mohammed. They allowed no Christian to enter the Temple.

10. Another temple, called the Temple of Solomon, is large and wonderful, but it is not the one that Solomon built. This one, because of our poverty, could not be maintained in the condition in which we found it. Wherefore it is already in large part destroyed.

11. There were gutters in the streets of the city through which in time of rain all filth was washed away.

12. The Emperor Aeilus Hadrian[17] decorated this city magnificently and fittingly adorned the streets and squares with pavements. In his honor Jerusalem was called Aelia. For these and many other reasons Jerusalem is a most renowned and glorious city.

XXVII The Siege of the City of Jerusalem.

1. When the Franks beheld the city and realized that it would be difficult to take, our leaders ordered wooden ladders to be made. By carrying these to the wall and erecting them, and climbing with fierce energy to the top of the wall, they hoped with the help of God to enter the city.

2. These ladders were made, and on the seventh day after the arrival our leaders gave the command for the attack. At the sound of the trumpets

17 The Roman emperor Hadrian (r. 117–38).

at daybreak our men attacked the city on all sides with remarkable energy. But when they had continued the attack up to the sixth hour of the day and were not able to enter by means of the ladders which they had prepared because the ladders were too few, they reluctantly gave up the assault.

3. Then after consultation our leaders ordered the engineers to make machines of war. They hoped when these were moved up to the walls to attain the desired result with the help of God. Therefore this was done.

4. Meanwhile, however, our men did not suffer from lack of bread or meat. Yet because the area was dry, unwatered, and without streams our men as well as their beasts suffered for lack of water to drink. Wherefore, because necessity demanded it, they brought water daily to the siege from four or five miles away, laboriously carrying it in the skins of animals.

5. When the machines were ready, namely battering rams and *scrofae*, our men again prepared to attack the city. Among those contrivances they put together a tower made of short pieces of timber because there was no large stuff in that area. When the command was given they transported the tower, in sections, by night to a corner of the city. In the morning they quickly erected it, all assembled, not far from the wall, together with *petrariae* and other auxiliary weapons which they had prepared. After they had set it up and well protected it on the outside with hides, they pushed it little by little nearer the wall.

6. Then some soldiers, few it is true but brave, climbed upon the tower at a signal from the trumpet. The Saracens nevertheless set up a defense against them. With *fundibula* they hurled small burning brands soaked in oil and grease against the tower and the soldiers in it. Therefore many on both sides met sudden death in this fighting.

7. From the side where they were located, namely Mount Zion, Count Raymond and his men launched a heavy attack with their machines. From the other side where Duke Godfrey, Count Robert of Normandy, and Robert of Flanders were

stationed there was still greater assault upon the wall. These were the events of that day.

8. The next day at the sound of the trumpets they undertook the same task with still more vigor. As a result they made a breach in the wall by battering it in one place with rams. The Saracens had suspended two timbers in front of the battlements and tied them there with ropes as a protection against the stones hurled at them by their assailants. But what they did for their advantage later turned to their detriment, by Divine Providence. For when the Franks had moved the aforesaid tower up to the wall they used falchions to cut the ropes by means of which the two beams were suspended. With these timbers they contrived a bridge and skillfully extended it from the tower to the top of the wall.

9. Already one stone tower on the wall, at which those working our machines had thrown flaming brands, was afire. This fire, gradually fed by the wooden material in the tower, caused so much smoke and flame that none of the city guards could remain there any longer.

10. Soon therefore the Franks gloriously entered the city at noon on the day known as Dies Veneris, the day in which Christ redeemed the whole world on the Cross. Amid the sound of trumpets and with everything in an uproar they attacked boldly, shouting "God help us!" At once they raised a banner on the top of the wall. The pagans were completely terrified, for they all exchanged their former boldness for headlong flight through the narrow streets of the city. The more swiftly they fled the more swiftly they were pursued.

11. Count Raymond and his men, who were strongly pressing the offensive in another part of the city, did not notice this until they saw the Saracens jumping off from the top of the wall. When they noticed it they ran with the greatest exultation as fast as they could into the city and joined their companions in pursuing and slaying their wicked enemies without cessation.

12. Some of the latter, Arabs as well as Ethiopians, fled into the Tower of David, and others shut

themselves up in the Temples of the Lord and of Solomon. In the courts of these buildings a fierce attack was pressed upon the Saracens. There was no place where they could escape our swordsmen.

13. Many of the Saracens who had climbed to the top of the Temple of Solomon in their flight were shot to death with arrows and fell headlong from the roof. Nearly ten thousand were beheaded in this Temple. If you had been there your feet would have been stained to the ankles in the blood of the slain. What shall I say? None of them were left alive. Neither women nor children were spared.

XXVIII The Spoils Taken by the Christians.

1. How astonishing it would have seemed to you to see our squires and footmen, after they had discovered the trickery of the Saracens, split open the bellies of those they had just slain in order to extract from the intestines the coins which the Saracens had gulped down their loathsome throats while alive! For the same reason a few days later our men made a great heap of corpses and burned them to ashes in order to find more easily the above-mentioned gold.

2. And also Tancred rushed into the Temple of the Lord and seized much gold and silver and many precious stones. But he restored these things, putting them or their equivalent back into the holy place. This was in spite of the fact that no divine services were conducted there at that time. The Saracens had practiced their rule of idolatry there with superstitious rite and moreover had not allowed any Christian to enter.

3. With drawn swords our men ran through the city
   Not sparing anyone, even those begging for mercy.
   The crowd fell just as rotten apples fall
   From shaken branches and acorns from swaying oaks.

Solomon Bar Simson

LITTLE IS KNOWN ABOUT Solomon Bar Simson, a member of the Jewish community of Mainz, who wrote a *Chronicle* after 1140 about the Jewish communities in Germany, although he also used earlier accounts of attacks on Jewish populations. Subsequent additions were made to the *Chronicle*, including lists of martyrs of Speyer, Worms, and Mainz and details of the self-immolations of Jewish communities.

Source: Shlomo Eidelberg (ed. and trans.), *The Jews and the Crusaders: Hebrew Chronicles of the First and Second Crusades* (Madison: University of Wisconsin Press, 1977).

Further Reading: Jonathan Riley-Smith, *The First Crusade and the Idea of Crusading* (Philadelphia: University of Pennsylvania Press, 1986).

I will now recount the event of this persecution in other martyred communities as well—the extent to which they clung to the Lord, God of their fathers, bearing witness to His Oneness to their last breath.

In the year four thousand eight hundred and fifty-six, the year one thousand twenty-eight of our exile, in the eleventh year of the cycle Ranu, the year in which we anticipated salvation and solace, in accordance with the prophecy of Jeremiah: "Sing with gladness for Jacob, and shout at the head of the nations," etc.—this year turned instead to sorrow and groaning, weeping and outcry. Inflicted upon the Jewish People were the many evils related in all the admonitions; those enumerated in Scripture as well as those unwritten were visited upon us.

At this time arrogant people, a people of strange speech, a nation bitter and impetuous, Frenchmen and Germans, set out for the Holy

City, which had been desecrated by barbaric nations, there to seek their house of idolatry and banish the Ishmaelites and other denizens of the land and conquer the land for themselves. They decorated themselves prominently with their signs, placing a profane symbol—a horizontal line over a vertical one—on the vestments of every man and woman whose heart yearned to go on the stray path to the grave of their Messiah. Their ranks swelled until the number of men, women, and children exceeded a locust horde covering the earth; of them it was said: "The locusts have no king [yet they go forth all of them by bands]."[18] Now it came to pass that as they passed through the towns where Jews dwelled, they said to one another: "Look now, we are going a long way to seek out the profane shrine and to avenge ourselves on the Ishmaelites, when here, in our very midst, are the Jews—they whose forefathers murdered and crucified him for no reason. Let us first avenge ourselves on them and exterminate them from among the nations so that the name of Israel will no longer be remembered, or let them adopt our faith and acknowledge the offspring of promiscuity."[19]

When the Jewish communities became aware of their intentions, they resorted to the custom of our ancestors, repentance, prayer, and charity. The hands of the Holy Nation turned faint at this time, their hearts melted, and their strength flagged. They hid in their innermost rooms to escape the swirling sword. They subjected themselves to great endurance, abstaining from food and drink for three consecutive days and nights, and then fasting many days from sunrise to sunset, until their skin was shriveled and dry as wood upon their bones. And they cried out loudly and bitterly to God.

But their Father did not answer them; He obstructed their prayers, concealing Himself in a cloud through which their prayers could not pass, and He abhorred their tent, and He removed them out of His sight—all of this having been decreed by Him to take place "in the day when I visit"; and

this was the generation that had been chosen by Him to be His portion, for they had the strength and the fortitude to stand in His Sanctuary, and fulfill His word, and sanctify His Great Name in His world. It is of such as these that King David said: "Bless the Lord, ye angels of His, ye almighty in strength, that fulfil His word," etc.

That year, Passover fell on Thursday, and the New Moon of the following month, Iyar, fell on Friday and the Sabbath. On the eighth day of Iyar, on the Sabbath, the foe attacked the community of Speyer and murdered eleven holy souls who sanctified their Creator on the holy Sabbath and refused to defile themselves by adopting the faith of their foe. There was a distinguished, pious woman there who slaughtered herself in sanctification of God's Name. She was the first among all the communities of those who were slaughtered. The remainder were saved by the local bishop[20] without defilement [i.e., baptism], as described above.

On the twenty-third of Iyar they attacked the community of Worms. The community was then divided into two groups; some remained in their homes and others fled to the local bishop seeking refuge.[21] Those who remained in their homes were set upon by the steppe-wolves who pillaged men, women, and infants, children and old people. They pulled down the stairways and destroyed the houses, looting and plundering; and they took the Torah Scroll, trampled it in the mud, and tore and burned it. The enemy devoured the children of Israel with open maw.

Seven days later, on the New Moon of Sivan— the very day on which the Children of Israel arrived at Mount Sinai to receive the Torah—those Jews who were still in the court of the bishop were subject to great anguish. The enemy dealt them the same cruelty as the first group and put them to the sword. The Jews, inspired by the valor of their brethren, similarly chose to be slain in order to sanctify the Name before the eyes of all, and exposed their throats for their heads to be severed for the glory of the Creator. There were also those who took their own lives, thus fulfilling

18 Proverbs 30:27.
19 Bar Simson's derogatory references to the Holy Family were influenced by an earlier work known as *Ma'aseh Yeshu*, and also as *Toldot Yeshu*.
20 Bishop John of Speyer (1090–1104).
21 The name of the bishop of Worms of this period was Adalbert or Allenbrand.

the verse: "The mother was dashed in pieces with her children."[22] Fathers fell upon their sons, being slaughtered upon one another, and they slew one another—each man his kin, his wife and children; bridegrooms slew their betrothed, and merciful women their only children. They all accepted the divine decree wholeheartedly and, as they yielded up their souls to the Creator, cried out: "Hear, O Israel, the Lord is our God, the Lord is One." The enemy stripped them naked, dragged them along, and then cast them off, sparing only a small number whom they forcibly baptized in their profane waters. The number of those slain during the two days was approximately eight hundred—and they were all buried naked. It is of these that the Prophet Jeremiah lamented: "They that were brought up in scarlet embrace dunghills." I have already cited their names above.[23] May God remember them for good.

When the saints, the pious ones of the Most High, the holy community of Mainz, whose merit served as shield and protection for all the communities and whose fame had spread throughout the many provinces, heard that some of the community of Speyer had been slain and that the community of Worms had been attacked a second time,[24] and that the sword would soon reach them, their hands became faint and their hearts melted and became as water. They cried out to the Lord with all their hearts, saying: "O Lord, God of Israel, will You completely annihilate the remnant of Israel? Where are all your wonders which our forefathers related to us, saying, 'Did You not bring us up from Egypt and from Babylonia and rescue us on numerous occasions?' How, then, have You now forsaken and abandoned us, O Lord, giving us over into the hands of evil Edom so that they may destroy us? Do not remove Yourself from us, for adversity is almost upon us and there is no one to aid us."

The leaders of the Jews gathered together and discussed various ways of saving themselves. They said, "Let us elect elders so that we may know how to act, for we are consumed by this great evil." The elders decided to ransom the community by generously giving of their money and bribing the various princes and deputies and bishops and governors. Then, the community leaders who were respected by the local bishop[25] approached him and his officers and servants to negotiate this matter. They asked: "What shall we do about the news we have received regarding the slaughter of our brethren in Speyer and Worms?" They [the Gentiles] replied: "Heed our advice and bring all your money into our treasury. You, your wives, and your children, and all your belongings shall come into the courtyard of the bishop until the hordes have passed by. Thus will you be saved from the errant ones."

Actually, they gave this advice so as to herd us together and hold us like fish that are caught in an evil net, and then to turn us over to the enemy, while taking our money. This is what actually happened in the end, and "the outcome is proof of the intentions." The bishop assembled his ministers and courtiers—mighty ministers, the noblest in the land—for the purpose of helping us; for at first it had been his desire to save us with all his might, since we had given him and his ministers and servants a large bribe in return for their promise to help us. Ultimately, however, all the bribes and entreaties were of no avail to protect us on the day of wrath and misfortune.

It was at this time that Duke Godfrey [of Bouillon], may his bones be ground to dust, arose in the hardness of his spirit, driven by a spirit of wantonness to go with those journeying to the profane shrine, vowing to go on this journey only after avenging the blood of the crucified one by shedding Jewish blood and completely eradicating any trace of those bearing the name "Jew," thus assuaging his own burning wrath. To be sure, there arose someone to repair the breach—a God-fearing man who had been bound to the most holy of altars—called Rabbi Kalonymos, the *Parnass* of the community of Mainz.[26] He

---

22   Hosea 11:6.

23   This is an allusion to the register of martyrs which preceded Bar Simson's account.

24   It seems that Emicho ignored the order of Emperor Henry and attacked Speyer on May 3, 1096. The same troops assaulted the Jews in Worms on May 18. A second attack on the Worms community by a local mob occurred on May 25.

25   Archbishop Ruthard of Mainz (1089–1109).

26   The official leader of the community—an office generally reserved for men of unquestionable character and piety.

dispatched a messenger to King Henry in the kingdom of Pula, where the king had been dwelling during the past nine years, and related all that had happened.

The king was enraged and dispatched letters to all the ministers, bishops and governors of all the provinces of his realm, as well as to Duke Godfrey, containing words of greeting and commanding them to do no bodily harm to the Jews and to provide them with help and refuge. The evil duke then swore that he had never intended to do them harm. The Jews of Cologne nevertheless bribed him with five hundred *zekukim* of silver, as did the Jews of Mainz. The duke assured them of his support and promised them peace.

However, God the maker of peace, turned aside and averted His eyes from His people, and consigned them to the sword. No prophet, seer, or man of wise heart was able to comprehend how the sin of the people infinite in number was deemed so great as to cause the destruction of so many lives in the various Jewish communities. The martyrs endured the extreme penalty normally inflicted only upon one guilty of murder. Yet, it must be stated with certainty that God is a righteous judge, and we are to blame.

Then the evil waters prevailed.[27] The enemy unjustly accused them of evil acts they did not do, declaring: "You are the children of those who killed our object of veneration, hanging him on a tree; and he himself had said: 'There will yet come a day when my children will come and avenge my blood.' We are his children and it is therefore obligatory for us to avenge him since you are the ones who rebel and disbelieve in him. Your God has never been at peace with you. Although He intended to deal kindly with you, you have conducted yourselves improperly before Him. God has forgotten you and is no longer desirous of you since you are a stubborn nation. Instead, He has departed from you and has taken us for His portion, casting His radiance upon us."

When we heard these words, our hearts trembled and moved out of their places. We were dumb with silence, abiding in darkness, like those long dead, waiting for the Lord to look forth and behold from heaven.

And Satan—the Pope of evil Rome—also came and proclaimed to all the nations[28] believing in that stock of adultery—these are the stock of Seir—that they should assemble and ascend to Jerusalem so as to conquer the city, and journey to the tomb of the superstition whom they call their god. Satan came and mingled with the nations, and they gathered as one man to fulfill the command, coming in great numbers like the grains of sand upon the seashore, the noise of them clamorous as a whirlwind and a storm. When the drops of the bucket had assembled, they took evil counsel against the people of the Lord and said: "Why should we concern ourselves with going to war against the Ishmaelites dwelling about Jerusalem, when in our midst is a people who disrespect our god—indeed, their ancestors are those who crucified him. Why should we let them live and tolerate their dwelling among us? Let us commence by using our swords against them and proceed upon our stray path."

The heart of the people of our God grew faint and their spirit flagged, for many sore injuries had been inflicted upon them and they had been smitten repeatedly. They now came supplicating to God and fasting, and their hearts melted within them. But the Lord did as He declared, for we had sinned before Him, and He forsook the sanctuary of Shiloh—the Temple-in-Miniature—which He had placed among His people who dwelt in the midst of alien nations. His wrath was kindled and He drew the sword against them, until they remained but as the flagstaff upon the mountain-top and as the ensign on the hill, and He gave over His nation into captivity and trampled them underfoot. See, O Lord, and consider to whom Thou hast done thus: to Israel, a nation despised and pillaged, Your chosen portion! Why have You uplifted the shield of its enemies, and why have they gained in strength? Let all hear, for I cry out in anguish; the ears of all that hear me shall be seared: How has the staff of might been broken, the rod of glory—the sainted community comparable to fine gold, the community of Mainz! It was caused by the Lord to test those that fear Him, to have them endure the yoke of His pure fear.

One day a Gentile woman came, bringing a

---

27 The "evil waters" refer to baptism.
28 This is a reference to the speech of Pope Urban II at Clermont on November 27, 1095.

goose which she had raised since it was newborn. The goose would accompany her wherever she went. The Gentile woman now called out to all passersby: "Look, the goose understands my intention to go straying and desires to accompany me."

At that time, the errant ones gathered against us, and the burghers and peasants said to us: "Where is He in Whom you place your trust? How will you be saved? Now you shall see that these are the wonders which the crucified one works for them [the Crusaders] to signal that they should exact vengeance from their enemies." And they all came with swords to destroy us. But some of the leading burghers stood up to them, and prevented them from harming us.

At this point, the errant ones all united and battled the burghers, and the Gentiles fought with each other, until a Crusader was slain. Seeing this the Crusaders cried out: "The Jews have caused this," and nearly all of them reassembled, reviling and deriding them with the intention of falling upon them.

When the holy people saw this, their hearts melted. Upon hearing their words, the Jews, old and young alike, said: "Would that our death might be by the hands of the Lord, so that we should not perish at the hands of the enemies of the Lord! For He is a Merciful King, the sole sovereign of the universe."

They abandoned their houses; neither did they go to the synagogue save on the Sabbath preceding the month of Sivan—the final Sabbath before the evil decree befell us—when a small number of them entered the synagogue to pray. Rabbi Judah, son of Rabbi Isaac, also came there to pray with that *minyan*.[29] They wept exceedingly, to the point of exhaustion, for they saw that it was a decree of the King of Kings, not to be nullified.

A venerable student, Baruch, son of Isaac, was there, and he said to us: "Know in truth and honesty this decree has been issued against us, and we cannot be saved; for this past night I and my son-in-law Judah heard the souls praying in the synagogue in a loud voice, like weeping. When we heard the sound, we thought at first that perhaps some of the community had come from the court

of the bishop to pray in the synagogue at midnight. In our anguish and bitterness of heart we ran to the door of the synagogue to see who was praying. The door was closed. We heard the sound and the loud wailing, but we did not understand a word of what was being said. We returned dismayed to our house—for it was close to the synagogue. Upon hearing this, we cried out: 'Ah Lord God! Wilt Thou make a full end of the remnant of Israel?'" Then they went and reported the occurrence to their brethren who were concealed in the court of the count and in the bishop's chambers, and all knew that this decree was of God. Thereupon, they, too, wept exceedingly, declaring themselves ready to accept God's judgment, saying: "Righteous art Thou, O Lord, and upright are Thy judgments."

On the New Moon of Sivan, Count Emicho,[30] the oppressor of all the Jews—may his bones be ground to dust between iron millstones—arrived outside the city with a mighty horde of errant ones and peasants. They encamped in tents, since the gates of the city were closed, for he, too, had said: "I desire to follow the stray course." He was made leader of the hordes and concocted a tale that an apostle of the crucified one had come to him and made a sign on his flesh to inform him that when he arrived at Magna Graecia, he [Jesus] himself would appear and place the kingly crown upon his head, and Emicho would vanquish his foes. This man was chief of our oppressors. He showed no mercy to the aged, or youths, or maidens, babes or sucklings—not even the sick. And he made the people of the Lord like dust to be trodden underfoot, killing their young men by the sword and disemboweling their pregnant women. They encamped outside the city for two days.

At this time, when the evildoer arrived at Mainz on his way to Jerusalem, the elders of the Jewish community approached their bishop, Ruthard, and bribed him with three hundred *zekukim* of silver. Ruthard had intended to journey to the villages that were subject to the authority of the bishops, but the Jewish community came and bribed and entreated him, until they persuaded him to remain in Mainz, and he took the entire community into his inner chamber, with the

---

29　A reference to the quorum of ten adult male Jews required for congregational prayer.

30　Emicho, count of Leiningen, commanded a band of Crusaders.

words: "I have agreed to aid you." The count, too, declared: "I also wish to remain here in order to help you, but you will have to provide all our needs until those who bear the symbol have passed"; and the community agreed to these terms.

The two of them—the bishop and the count—thereupon acceded to the request of the Jews and said: "We shall die with you or remain alive with you." The community then said: "Since these two who are close to us have granted our request, let us now send out money to the evildoer Emicho, and give him letters of safe conduct so that the communities along the route will honor him. Perhaps the Lord will intercede in His abundant grace and cause him to refrain from his present intentions. It is for this very purpose that we have generously expended our money, giving the bishop, his officers, his servants, and the burghers about four hundred *zekukim* of silver." We dispatched seven pounds of gold to the evil Emicho—so as to aid ourselves, but it was of no avail whatever, and up to the present time we have had no respite from our affliction. We were not even comparable to Sodom and Gomorrah; for in their case they were offered reprieve if they could produce at least ten righteous people, whereas in our case not twenty, not even ten, were sought.

On the third day of Sivan,[31] a day of sanctification and abstinence for Israel in preparation for receiving the Torah, the very day on which our Master Moses, may he rest in peace, said: "Be ready against the third day"—on that very day the community of Mainz, saints of the Most High, withdrew from each other in sanctity and purity, and sanctified themselves to ascend to God all together. Those who had been "pleasant in their lives … in their death they were not divided," for all of them were gathered in the courtyard of the bishop. God's wrath was kindled against His people, and He fulfilled the intention of the errant ones, who succeeded in their purpose; and all our wealth did not avail us, nor did our fasting, self-affliction, lamenting, or charity, and no one was found to stand in the breach—neither teacher nor prince—and even the holy Torah did not shelter its scholars. "And the daughter of Zion was shorn of all her splendor"—this refers to Mainz. Silenced were the voices of the leaders of

the flock, "those who wage war," they that sway the many to righteousness; and silenced was the city of praise, the metropolis of joy, which had generously distributed great sums of money to the poor. An iron stylus writing upon a folio would not suffice to record her numerous good deeds extending back to ancient times—the city in which there were to be found simultaneously Torah and greatness and riches and glory and wisdom and modesty and good deeds, where "prohibition was added upon prohibition" so as to assure scrupulous adherence to the teaching of the Talmud: now this wisdom was completely destroyed, as happened to the dwellers of Jerusalem at the time of its destruction.

At midday the evil Emicho, oppressor of the Jews, came to the gate with his entire horde. The townspeople opened the gate to him, and the enemies of the Lord said to one another: "See, they have opened the gate for us; now let us avenge the blood of the crucified one."

When the people of the Holy Covenant, the saints, the fearers of the Most High, saw the great multitude, a vast horde of them, as the sand upon the seashore, they clung to their Creator. They donned their armor and their weapons of war, adults and children alike, with Rabbi Kalonymos, the son of Rabbi Meshullam, the *Parnass*, at their head. But, as a result of their sufferings and fasts, they did not have the strength to withstand the onslaught of the foe. The troops and legions surged in like a streaming river until finally Mainz was completely overrun from end to end. Emicho had it rumored that the enemy was to be driven from the city, and the Lord's panic was great within the city.

The Jews armed themselves in the inner court of the bishop, and they all advanced toward the gate to fight against the errant ones and the burghers. The two sides fought against each other around the gate, but as a result of their transgressions the enemy overpowered them and captured the gate. The hand of the Lord rested heavily on His people, and all the Gentiles assembled against the Jews in the courtyard to exterminate them. Our people's strength flagged when they saw that the hand of evil Edom was prevailing against them. The bishop's people, who had promised to help them, being

---

31 Corresponding to May 27, 1096.

as broken reedstaffs, were the first to flee, so as to cause them to fall into the hands of the enemy. The bishop himself fled from his church, for they wanted to kill him, too, because he had spoken in favor of the Jews. The enemy entered the courtyard on the third day of the week—a day of darkness and gloom, a day of clouds and thick darkness; let darkness and the shadow of death claim it for their own. Let God not inquire after it from above, nor let the light shine upon it. Alas for the day on which we saw the torment of our soul! O stars—why did you not withhold your light? Has not Israel been compared to the stars and the twelve constellations, according to the number of Jacob's sons? Why, then, did you not withhold your light from shining for the enemy who sought to eradicate the name of Israel?

When the people of the Sacred Covenant saw that the Heavenly decree had been issued and that the enemy had defeated them and were entering the courtyard, they all cried out together—old and young, maidens and children, menservants and maids—to their Father in Heaven. They wept for themselves and for their lives and proclaimed the justness of the Heavenly judgment, and they said to one another: "Let us be of good courage and bear the yoke of the Holy Creed, for now the enemy can only slay us by the sword, and death by the sword is the lightest of the four deaths. We shall then merit eternal life, and our souls will abide in the Garden of Eden in the presence of the great luminous speculum forever."

All of them declared willingly and wholeheartedly, "After all things, there is no questioning the ways of the Holy One, blessed be He and blessed be His Name, Who has given us His Torah and has commanded us to allow ourselves to be killed and slain in witness to the Oneness of His Holy Name. Happy are we if we fulfill His will, and happy is he who is slain or slaughtered and who dies attesting the Oneness of His Name. Such a one is destined for the World-to-Come, where he will sit in the realm of the saints—Rabbi Akiba and his companions, pillars of the universe, who were killed in witness to His Name. Moreover—for such a one a world of darkness is exchanged for a world of light, a world of sorrow for one of joy, a transitory world for an eternal world."

Then in a great voice they all cried out as one: "We need tarry no longer, for the enemy is already upon us. Let us hasten and offer ourselves as a sacrifice before God. Anyone possessing a knife should examine it to see that it is not defective, and let him then proceed to slaughter us in sanctification of the Unique and Eternal One, then slaying himself—either cutting his throat or thrusting the knife into his stomach."

Upon entering the courtyard, the enemy encountered some of perfect piety, including Rabbi Isaac, son of Rabbi Moses, uprooter of mountains. He extended his neck and was the first to be decapitated. The others wrapped themselves in their fringed prayer shawls and sat in the courtyard waiting to expedite the will of their Creator, not wishing to flee within the chambers just to be saved for temporal life, for lovingly they accepted Heaven's judgment. The foe hurled stones and arrows at them, but they did not scurry to flee; the enemy smote all whom they found there with their swords, causing slaughter and destruction.

Those Jews in the chambers, seeing what the enemy had inflicted upon the saints, all cried out: "There is none like our God unto whom it would be better to offer our lives." The women girded their loins with strength and slew their own sons and daughters, and then themselves. Many men also mustered their strength and slaughtered their wives and children and infants. The most gentle and tender of women slaughtered the child of her delight. They all arose, man and woman alike, and slew one another. The young maidens, the brides, and the bridegrooms looked out through the windows and cried out in a great voice: "Look and behold, O Lord, what we are doing to sanctify Thy Great Name, in order not to exchange You for a crucified scion who was despised, abominated, and held in contempt in his own generation, a bastard son conceived by a menstruating and wanton mother."

Thus the precious children of Zion, the people of Mainz, were tested with ten trials as was our Father Abraham, and as Hananiah, Mishael, and Azariah were. They, too, bound their children in sacrifice, as Abraham did his son Isaac, and willingly accepted upon themselves the yoke of fear of Heaven, of the King of Kings, the Blessed Holy One. Refusing to gainsay their faith and replace the fear of our King with an abominable stock, bastard son of a menstruating and wanton mother, they extended their necks for slaughter and offered up their pure souls to their Father in Heaven. The saintly and pious women acted in a similar manner, extending their necks to each other in willing sacrifice in witness to the Oneness of God's name—and each man likewise to his son and brother, brother to sister, mother to son and daughter, neighbor to neighbor and friend, bridegroom to bride, fiancé to his betrothed; each first sacrificed the other and then in turn yielded to be sacrificed, until the streams of blood touched and mingled, and the blood of husbands joined with that of their wives, the blood of fathers with that of their sons, the blood of brothers with that of their sisters, the blood of teachers with that of their pupils, the blood of bridegrooms with that of their brides, the blood of community deacons with that of their scribes, the blood of babes and sucklings with that of their mothers—all killed and slaughtered in witness to the Oneness of the Venerated and Awesome Name.

Let the ears hearing this and its like be seared, for who has heard or seen the likes of it? Inquire and seek: was there ever such a mass sacrificial offering since the time of Adam? Did it ever occur that there were a thousand and one offerings on one single day—all of them comparable to the sacrifice of Isaac, the son of Abraham? The earth trembled over just one offering that occurred on the myrrh mountain—it is said: "Behold, the valiant ones cry without," and the heavens are darkened. What have they [the martyrs] done? Why did the heavens not darken and the stars not withhold their radiance, why did not the sun and the moon turn dark? On a single day—the third

of Sivan, the third day of the week—one thousand and one hundred[32] holy souls were killed and slaughtered, babes and sucklings who had not sinned or transgressed, the souls of innocent poor people. Wilt Thou restrain Thyself for these things, O Lord? It was for You that innumerable souls were killed! May You avenge the spilt blood of your servants, in our days and before our very eyes—Amen—and speedily!

The day the diadem of Israel fell, the students of the Torah fell, and the outstanding scholars passed away. The glory of the Torah fell, as it is written: "He hath cast down from heaven unto the earth the splendor of Israel." Gone were the sin-fearers, gone were the men of virtuous deed; ended were the radiance of wisdom and purity and abstinence; [ended was] the glory of the priesthood and of the men of perfect faith—repairers of the breach, nullifiers of evil decrees, and placaters of the wrath of their Creator; diminished were the ranks of those who give charity in secret. Gone was truth; gone were the explicators of the Word and the Law; fallen were the people of eminence and the sage—all on this day, on which so many sorrows befell us and we could turn neither to the right nor to the left from the fury of the oppressor. For since the day on which the Second Temple was destroyed, their like had not arisen, nor shall there be their like again—for they sanctified and bore witness to the Oneness of God's Name with all their heart and with all their soul and with all their might. Happy are they and happy is their lot, for all of them are destined for life eternal in the World-to-Come—and may my place be amongst them!

Ibn Al-Athir

IBN AL-ATHIR (1160–1233) WAS a Mesopotamian intellectual who wrote a history of the Muslim world primarily from Mosul (in present-day Iraq), although later in life worked under Saladin (1138–93) and lived in Damascus. His account of the First Crusade is drawn from earlier sources and is colored by his own experience of later wars against the Latins, especially those of Saladin.

Source: Francesco Gabrieli [Italian translation], *Arab Historians of the Crusades*, trans. E.J. Costello (Berkeley: University of California Press, 1969).

Further Reading: Jonathan Riley-Smith, *The First Crusade and the Idea of Crusading* (Philadelphia: University of Pennsylvania Press, 1986).

32 Rabbi Eliezer bar Nathan reports that 1,300 were killed in Mainz.

The Franks Seize Antioch (X, 185–88)

The power of the Franks first became apparent when in the year 478/1085–86[33] they invaded the territories of Islam and took Toledo and other parts of Andalusia, as was mentioned earlier. Then in 484/1091 they attacked and conquered the island of Sicily and turned their attention to the African coast. Certain of their conquests there were won back again but they had other successes, as you will see.

In 490/1097 the Franks attacked Syria. This is how it all began: Baldwin, their king, a kinsman of Roger the Frank who had conquered Sicily, assembled a great army and sent word to Roger saying: "I have assembled a great army and now I am on my way to you, to use your bases for my conquest of the African coast. Thus you and I shall become neighbors."

Roger called together his companions and consulted them about these proposals. "This will be a fine thing both for them and for us!" they declared, "for by this means these lands will be converted to the Faith!" At this Roger raised one leg and farted loudly, and swore that it was of more use than their advice. "Why?" "Because if this army comes here it will need quantities of provisions and fleets of ships to transport it to Africa, as well as reinforcements from my own troops. Then, if the Franks succeed in conquering this territory they will take it over and will need provisioning from Sicily. This will cost me my annual profit from the harvest. If they fail they will return here and be an embarrassment to me here in my own domain. As well as all this Tamïm will say that I have broken faith with him and violated our treaty, and friendly relations and communications between us will be disrupted. As far as we are concerned, Africa is always there. When we are strong enough we will take it."

He summoned Baldwin's messenger and said to him: "If you have decided to make war on the Muslims your best course will be to free Jerusalem from their rule and thereby win great honor. I am bound by certain promises and treaties of allegiance with the rulers of Africa." So the Franks made ready and set out to attack Syria.

Another story is that the Fatimids of Egypt were afraid when they saw the Seljuqids extending their empire through Syria as far as Gaza, until they reached the Egyptian border and Atsiz invaded Egypt itself. They therefore sent to invite the Franks to invade Syria and so protect Egypt from the Muslims.[34] But God knows best.

When the Franks decided to attack Syria they marched east to Constantinople, so that they could cross the straits and advance into Muslim territory by the easier, land route. When they reached Constantinople, the emperor of the east refused them permission to pass through his domains. He said: "Unless you first promise me Antioch, I shall not allow you to cross into the Muslim empire." His real intention was to incite them to attack the Muslims, for he was convinced that the Turks, whose invincible control over Asia Minor he had observed, would exterminate every one of them. They accepted his conditions and in 490/1097 they crossed the Bosphorus at Constantinople. Iconium and the rest of the area into which they now advanced belonged to Qilij Arslan ibn Sulaiman ibn Qutlumísh, who marred their way with his troops. They broke through in rajab[35] 490/July 1097, crossed Cilicia, and finally reached Antioch, which they besieged.

When Yaghi Siyan, the ruler of Antioch, heard of their approach, he was not sure how the Christian people of the city would react, so he made the Muslims go outside the city on their own to dig trenches, and the next day sent the Christians out alone to continue the task. When they were ready to return home at the end of the day he refused to allow them. "Antioch is yours," he said, "but you will have to leave it to me until I see what happens between us and the Franks." "Who will protect our children and our wives?" they said. "I shall look after them for you." So they resigned themselves to their fate, and lived in the Frankish camp for nine months, while the city was under siege.

Yaghi Siyan showed unparalleled courage and wisdom, strength and judgment. If all the Franks who died had survived they would have overrun

---

33 Dates are given in AH (After the Hijira) as well as according to the Common Era.
34 The Fatimids were also Muslims, but they were heretics and so opposed to the rest of *sunni* Islam.
35 Seventh month of the Islamic calendar.

all the lands of Islam. He protected the families of the Christians in Antioch and would not allow a hair of their heads to be touched.

After the siege had been going on for a long time the Franks made a deal with one of the men who were responsible for the towers. He was a cuirass-maker called Ruzbih whom they bribed with a fortune in money and lands. He worked in the tower that stood over the riverbed, where the river flowed out of the city into the valley. The Franks sealed their pact with the cuirass-maker, God damn him! and made their way to the water-gate. They opened it and entered the city. Another gang of them climbed the tower with ropes. At dawn, when more than 500 of them were in the city and the defenders were worn out after the night watch, they sounded their trumpets. Yaghi Siyan woke up and asked what the noise meant. He was told that trumpets had sounded from the citadel and that it must have been taken. In fact the sound came not from the citadel but from the tower. Panic seized Yaghi Siyan and he opened the city gates and fled in terror, with an escort of thirty pages. His army commander arrived, but when he discovered on enquiry that Yaghi Siyan had fled, he made his escape by another gate. This was of great help to the Franks, for if he had stood firm for an hour, they would have been wiped out. They entered the city by the gates and sacked it, slaughtering all the Muslims they found there. This happened in jumada I[36] (491/April/May 1098). As for Yaghi Siyan, when the sun rose he recovered his self control and realized that his flight had taken him several *farsakh*[37] from the city. He asked his companions where he was, and on hearing that he was four *farsakh* from Antioch he repented of having rushed to safety instead of staying to fight to the death. He began to groan and weep for his desertion of his household and children. Overcome by the violence of his grief he fell fainting from his horse. His companions tried to lift him back into the saddle, but they could not get him to sit up, and so left him for dead while they escaped. He was at his last gasp when an Armenian shepherd came past, killed him, cut off his head and took it to the Franks at Antioch.

The Franks had written to the rulers of Aleppo and Damascus to say that they had no interest in any cities but those that had once belonged to Byzantium. This was a piece of deceit calculated to dissuade these rulers from going to the help of Antioch.

The Muslim Attack on the Franks, and its Results (X, 188–90)

When Qawam ad-Daula Kerbuqa heard that the Franks had taken Antioch he mustered his army and advanced into Syria, where he camped at Marj Dabiq. All the Turkish and Arab forces in Syria rallied to him except for the army from Aleppo. Among his supporters were Duqaq ibn Tutush, the Ata-beg Tughtikin, Janah ad-Daula of Hims, Arslan Tash of Sanjar, Sulaiman ibn Artuq and other less important amirs. When the Franks heard of this they were alarmed and afraid, for their troops were weak and short of food. The Muslims advanced and came face to face with the Franks in front of Antioch. Kerbuqa, thinking that the present crisis would force the Muslims to remain loyal to him, alienated them by his pride and ill-treatment of them. They plotted in secret anger to betray him and desert him in the heat of battle.

After taking Antioch the Franks camped there for twelve days without food. The wealthy ate their horses and the poor ate carrion and leaves from the trees. Their leaders, faced with this situation, wrote to Kerbuqa to ask for safe-conduct through his territory but he refused, saying "You will have to fight your way out." Among the Frankish leaders were Baldwin, Saint-Gilles, Godfrey of Bouillon, the future Count of Edessa, and their leader Bohemond of Antioch. There was also a holy man who had great influence over them, a man of low cunning, who proclaimed that the Messiah had a lance buried in the Qusyan, a great building in Antioch: "And if you find it you will be victorious and if you fail you will surely die." Before saying this he had buried a lance in a certain spot and concealed all trace of it. He exhorted them to fast and repent for three days, and on the

---

36 Fifth month of the Islamic calendar.

37 One *farsakh* (parasang) is about four miles.

fourth day he led them all to the spot with their soldiers and workmen, who dug everywhere and found the lance as he had told them. Whereupon he cried "Rejoice! For victory is secure." So on the fifth day they left the city in groups of five or six. The Muslims said to Kerbuqa: "You should go up to the city and kill them one by one as they come out; it is easy to pick them off now that they have split up." He replied: "No, wait until they have all come out and then we will kill them." He would not allow them to attack the enemy and when some Muslims killed a group of Franks, he went himself to forbid such behavior and prevent its recurrence. When all the Franks had come out and not one was left in Antioch, they began to attack strongly, and the Muslims turned and fled. This was Kerbuqa's fault, first because he had treated the Muslims with such contempt and scorn, and second because he had prevented their killing the Franks. The Muslims were completely routed without striking a single blow or firing a single arrow. The last to flee were Suqman ibn Artuq and Janah ad-Daula, who had been sent to set an ambush. Kerbuqa escaped with them. When the Franks saw this they were afraid that a trap was being set for them, for there had not even been any fighting to flee from, so they dared not follow them. The only Muslims to stand firm were a detachment of warriors from the Holy Land, who fought to acquire merit in God's eyes and to seek martyrdom. The Franks killed them by the thousand and stripped their camp of food and possessions, equipment, horses and arms, with which they re-equipped themselves.

The Franks Take Ma'arrat an-Nu'man (X, 190)

After dealing this blow to the Muslims the Franks marched on Ma'arrat an-Nu'man and besieged it. The inhabitants valiantly defended their city. When the Franks realized the fierce determination and devotion of the defenders they built a wooden tower as high as the city wall and fought from the top of it, but failed to do the Muslims any serious harm. One night a few Muslims were seized with panic and in their demoralized state thought that if they barricaded themselves into

one of the town's largest buildings they would be in a better position to defend themselves, so they climbed down from the wall and abandoned the position they were defending. Others saw them and followed their example, leaving another stretch of wall undefended, and gradually, as one group followed another, the whole wall was left unprotected and the Franks scaled it with ladders. Their appearance in the city terrified the Muslims, who shut themselves up in their houses. For three days the slaughter never stopped; the Franks killed more than 100,000 men and took innumerable prisoners. After taking the town the Franks spent six weeks shut up there, then sent an expedition to 'Arqa, which they besieged for four months. Although they breached the wall in many places they failed to storm it. Munqidh, the ruler of Shaizar, made a treaty with them about 'Arqa and they left it to pass on to Hims. Here too the ruler Janah ad-Daula made a treaty with them, and they advanced to Acre by way of an-Nawaqir. However they did not succeed in taking Acre.

The Franks Conquer Jerusalem (X, 193–95)

Taj ad-Daula Tutush was the Lord of Jerusalem but had given it as a fief to the amir Suqman ibn Artuq the Turcoman. When the Franks defeated the Turks at Antioch the massacre demoralized them, and the Egyptians, who saw that the Turkish armies were being weakened by desertion, besieged Jerusalem under the command of al-Afdal ibn Badr al-Jamali. Inside the city were Artuq's sons, Suqman and Ilghazi, their cousin Sunij and their nephew Yaquti. The Egyptians brought more than forty siege engines to attack Jerusalem and broke down the walls at several points. The inhabitants put up a defense, and the siege and fighting went on for more than six weeks. In the end the Egyptians forced the city to capitulate, in sha'ban 489/August 1096.[38] Suqman, Ilghazi and their friends were well treated by al-Afdal, who gave them large gifts of money and let them go free. They made for Damascus and then crossed the Euphrates. Suqman settled in Edessa and Ilghazi went on into Iraq. The Egyptian governor of Jerusalem was a

---

38　The date given here is wrong; the Egyptians took Jerusalem in August 1098. Sha'ban is the eighth month of the Islamic calendar.

certain Iftikhar ad-Daula, who was still there at the time of which we are speaking.

After their vain attempt to take Acre by siege, the Franks moved on to Jerusalem and besieged it for more than six weeks. They built two towers, one of which, near Sion, the Muslims burnt down, killing everyone inside it. It had scarcely ceased to burn before a messenger arrived to ask for help and to bring the news that the other side of the city had fallen. In fact Jerusalem was taken from the north on the morning of Friday 22 sha'ban 492/15 July 1099. The population was put to the sword by the Franks, who pillaged the area for a week. A band of Muslims barricaded themselves into the Oratory of David and fought on for several days. They were granted their lives in return for surrendering. The Franks honored their word, and the group left by night for Ascalon. In the Masjid al-Aqsa the Franks slaughtered more than 70,000 people, among them a large number of imams and Muslim scholars, devout and ascetic men who had left their homelands to live lives of pious seclusion in the Holy Place. The Franks stripped the Dome of the Rock[39] of more than forty silver candelabra, each of them weighing 3,600 drams, and a great silver lamp weighing forty-four Syrian pounds, as well as a hundred and fifty smaller silver candelabra and more than twenty gold ones, and a great deal more booty. Refugees from Syria reached Baghdad in ramadan, among them the qadi Abu sa'd al-Harawi. They told the Caliph's ministers a story that wrung their hearts and brought tears to their eyes. On Friday they went to the Cathedral Mosque and begged for help, weeping so that their hearers wept with them as they described the sufferings of the Muslims in that Holy City: the men killed, the women and children taken prisoner, the homes pillaged. Because of the terrible hardships they had suffered, they were allowed to break the fast.

*   *   *

It was the discord between the Muslim princes, as we shall describe, that enabled the Franks to overrun the country. Abu l-Muzaffar al-Abiwardi composed several poems on this subject, in one of which he says:

We have mingled blood with flowing tears,
    and there is no room left in us for pity (?)
To shed tears is a man's worst weapon when
    the swords stir up the embers of war. Sons
    of Islam, behind you are battles in which
    heads rolled at your feet.
Dare you slumber in the blessed shade of
    safety, where life is as soft as an orchard
    flower?
How can the eye sleep between the lids at a
    time of disasters that would waken any
    sleeper?
While your Syrian brothers can only sleep on
    the backs of their chargers, or in vultures'
    bellies!
Must the foreigners feed on our ignominy,
    while you trail behind you the train of a
    pleasant life, like men whose world is at
    peace?
When blood has been spilt, when sweet girls
    must for shame hide their lovely faces in
    their hands!
When the white swords' points are red with
    blood, and the iron of the brown lances is
    stained with gore!
At the sound of sword hammering on lance
    young children's hair turns white.
This is war, and the man who shuns the
    whirlpool to save his life shall grind his
    teeth in penitence.
This is war, and the infidel's sword is naked
    in his hand, ready to be sheathed again in
    men's necks and skulls.
This is war, and he who lies in the tomb at
    Medina seems to raise his voice and cry:
    "O sons of Hashim![40]
I see my people slow to raise the lance against

---

39 The rock from which, the Muslims believe, Muhammad ascended into heaven. Over it was built the so-called 'Mosque of 'Umar', the chief Islamic monument in Jerusalem. It was from this Mosque that the conquerors took their booty. Nearby, but separate from it, is the 'Farthest Mosque' (al-Masjid al-Aqsa), where according to Ibn al-Athir the armies of the Cross showed even greater barbarity. The two sanctuaries are often confused in both Arabic and European sources.

40 The Prophet, who from the tomb raises his voice to rebuke his descendants (the sons of Hashim), that is, the unworthy caliphs whose opposition to the Crusades is only half-hearted.

the enemy: I see the Faith resting on feeble
pillars.
For fear of death the Muslims are evading the
fire of battle, refusing to believe that death
will surely strike them."
Must the Arab champions then suffer with
resignation, while the gallant Persians shut
their eyes to their dishonor?

The Capture of Bohemond of Antioch (X, 203–4)

In dhu l-qa'da[41] of this year (493/September
1100) Kumushtikin ibn ad-Danishmand Tailu,
Prince of Malatia, Siwas and other territories, met
Bohemond the Frank, one of the Frankish leaders,
near Malatia. The former governor of Malatia had
a treaty of friendship with Bohemond and asked
for his help. Bohemond came with 5,000 men, but

was defeated in battle by Ibn ad-Danishmand and
taken prisoner. Then seven Frankish Counts came
from across the sea to seek Bohemond's release.
They came to a fortress called Ankuriyya, took it
and killed the Muslims they found there, before
passing it on to another fort, which they besieged.
Isma'il ibn ad-Danishmand, who was defending
the fort, mustered his great army, set an ambush
for the Franks and then challenged them to battle.
Battle was joined, the ambush sprung and of the
300,000 Franks only 3,000 escaped, during the
night, and even they were wounded and exhausted. Ibn ad-Danishmand attacked Malatia, took it
and imprisoned the governor. The Frankish army
from Antioch came out to challenge him, but he
fought and defeated them. All this happened in
the space of a few months.

Anna Comnena

ANNA COMNENA (1083–CA.1148), WAS the daughter of the Byzantine emperor Alexius.
She composed *The Alexiad*, a history of her father's reign, toward the end of her life, after she had left Constantinople following a failed attempt to place her husband, Nicephorus
Bryennios, upon the Byzantine throne. Although *The Alexiad* is a glorification of her father's
reign and is occasionally inaccurate in detail, it is generally a reliable and vivid description
of her time.

Source: F.R.A. Sewter, *The Alexiad of Anna Comnena* (Harmondsworth: Penguin, 1969).

Further Reading: Jonathan Riley-Smith, *The First Crusade and the Idea of Crusading* (Philadelphia: University
of Pennsylvania Press, 1986).

[Alexius] had no time to [rest] before he heard a
rumor that countless Frankish armies were approaching. He dreaded their arrival, knowing as
he did their uncontrollable passion, their erratic
character and their irresolution, not to mention
the other peculiar traits of the Kelt, with their
inevitable consequences; their greed for money,
for example, which always led them, it seemed, to
break their own agreements without scruple for
any clear reason. He had consistently heard this
said of them and it was abundantly justified. So

far from despairing, however, he made every effort to prepare for war if need arose. What actually happened was more far-reaching and terrible
than rumor suggested, for the whole of the west
and all the barbarians who lived between the
Adriatic and the Straits of Gibraltar migrated in
a body to Asia, marching across Europe country
by country with all their households. The reason
for this mass-movement is to be found more or
less in the following events. A certain Kelt, called
Peter, with the surname Koukoupetros,[42] left to

41 Eleventh month of the Islamic calendar.
42 He was known to his contemporaries as Peter the Little, but we know him as Peter the Hermit.

worship at the Holy Sepulcher and after suffering much ill-treatment at the hands of the Turks and Saracens who were plundering the whole of Asia, he returned home with difficulty. Unable to admit defeat, he wanted to make a second attempt by the same route, but realizing the folly of trying to do this alone (worse things might happen to him) he worked out a clever scheme. He decided to preach in all the Latin countries. A divine voice, he said, commanded him to proclaim to all the counts in France that all should depart from their homes, set out to worship at the Holy Shrine and with all their soul and might strive to liberate Jerusalem from the Agarenes.[43] Surprisingly, he was successful. It was as if he had inspired every heart with some divine oracle. Kelts assembled from all parts, one after another, with arms and horses and all the other equipment for war. Full of enthusiasm and ardor they thronged every highway, and with these warriors came a host of civilians, outnumbering the sand of the sea shore or the stars of heaven, carrying palms and bearing crosses on their shoulders. There were women and children, too, who had left their own countries. Like tributaries joining a river from all directions they streamed towards us in full force, mostly through Dacia. The arrival of this mighty host was preceded by locusts, which abstained from the wheat but made frightful inroads on the vines. The prophets of those days interpreted this as a sign that the Keltic army would refrain from interfering in the affairs of Christians but bring dreadful affliction on the barbarian Ishmaelites, who were the slaves of drunkenness and wine and Dionysos. The Ishmaelites are indeed dominated by Dionysos and Eros; they indulge readily in every kind of sexual licence, and if they are circumcised in the flesh they are certainly not so in their passions. In fact, the Ishmaelites are nothing more than slaves—trebly slaves—of the vices of Aphrodite.[44] Hence they reverence and worship Astarte and Ashtaroth, and in their land the figure of the moon and the golden image of Chobar[45] are considered of major importance.

Corn, because it is not heady and at the same time is most nourishing, has been accepted as the symbol of Christianity. In the light of this the diviners interpreted the references to vines and wheat. So much for the prophecies. The incidents of the barbarians' advance followed in the order I have given and there was something strange about it, which intelligent people at least would notice. The multitudes did not arrive at the same moment, nor even by the same route—how could they cross the Adriatic *en masse* after setting out from different countries in such great numbers?—but they made the voyage in separate groups, some first, some in a second party and others after them in order, until all had arrived, and then they began their march across Epirus. Each army, as I have said, was preceded by a plague of locusts, so that everyone, having observed the phenomenon several times, came to recognize locusts as the forerunners of Frankish battalions. They had already begun to cross the Straits of Lombardy in small groups when the emperor summoned certain leaders of the Roman forces and sent them to the area round Dyrrachium and Avlona, with instructions to receive the voyagers kindly and export from all countries abundant supplies for them along their route; then to watch them carefully and follow, so that if they saw them making raids or running off to plunder the neighboring districts, they could check them by light skirmishes. These officers were accompanied by interpreters who understood the Latin language; their duty was to quell any incipient trouble between natives and pilgrims. I would like here to give a clearer and more detailed account of the matter.

The report of Peter's preaching spread everywhere, and the first to sell his land and set out on the road to Jerusalem was Godfrey.[46] He was a very rich man, extremely proud of his noble birth, his own courage and the glory of his family. (Every Kelt desired to surpass his fellows.) The upheaval that ensued as men *and* women took to the road was unprecedented within living memory. The simpler folk were in very truth led on by

---

43 Another name (like Ishaelites) for the Turks, i.e., descendants of Hagar.

44 Anna is unfair to the Muslims, but other authors accuse them of excessive wine-bibbing. She seems to be unaware that Aphrodite, Astarte and Ashtaroth are identical goddesses of love.

45 Chobar (or Chabar), meaning "The Great," was the name given by the Saracens to the goddess of love.

46 Godfrey of Bouillon, Duke of Lower Lorraine.

a desire to worship at Our Lord's tomb and visit the holy places, but the more villainous characters (in particular Bohemond and his like) had an ulterior purpose, for they hoped on their journey to seize the capital itself, looking upon its capture as a natural consequence of the expedition. Bohemond disturbed the morale of many nobler men because he still cherished his old grudge against the emperor. Peter, after his preaching campaign, was the first to cross the Lombardy Straits, with 80,000 infantry and 100,000 horsemen. He reached the capital via Hungary.[47] The Kelts, as one might guess, are in any case an exceptionally hotheaded race and passionate, but let them once find an inducement and they become irresistible.

The emperor knew what Peter had suffered before from the Turks and advised him to wait for the other counts to arrive, but he refused, confident in the number of his followers. He crossed the Sea of Marmora and pitched camp near a small place called Helenopolis. Later some Normans, 10,000 in all, joined him but detached themselves from the rest of the army and ravaged the outskirts of Nicaea, acting with horrible cruelty to the whole population; they cut in pieces some of the babies, impaled others on wooden spits and roasted them over a fire; old people were subjected to every kind of torture. The inhabitants of the city, when they learnt what was happening, threw open their gates and charged out against them. A fierce battle ensued, in which the Normans fought with such spirit that the Nicaeans had to retire inside their citadel. The enemy therefore returned to Helenopolis with all the booty. There an argument started between them and the rest (who had not gone on the raid)—the usual quarrel in such cases—for the latter were green with envy. That led to brawling, whereupon the daredevil Normans broke away for a second time and took Xerigordos by assault. The sultan's reaction was to send Elkhanes with a strong force to deal with them. He arrived at Xerigordos and captured it; of the Normans some were put to the sword and others taken prisoner. At the same time Elkhanes made plans to deal with the remainder, still with

Koukoupetros. He laid ambushes in suitable places, hoping that the enemy on their way to Nicaea would fall into the trap unawares and be killed. Knowing the Keltic love of money he also enlisted the services of two determined men who were to go to Peter's camp and there announce that the Normans, having seized Nicaea, were sharing out all the spoils of the city. This story had an amazing effect on Peter's men; they were thrown into confusion at the words "share" and "money"; without a moment's hesitation they set out on the Nicaea road in complete disorder, practically heedless of military discipline and the proper arrangement which should mark men going off to war. As I have said before, the Latin race at all times is unusually greedy for wealth, but when it plans to invade a country, neither reason nor force can restrain it. They set out helter-skelter, regardless of their individual companies. Near the Drakon they fell into the Turkish ambuscade and were miserably slaughtered. So great a multitude of Kelts and Normans died by the Ishmaelite sword that when they gathered the remains of the fallen, lying on every side, they heaped up, I will not say a mighty ridge or hill or peak, but a mountain of considerable height and depth and width, so high was the mass of bones. Some men of the same race as the slaughtered barbarians later, when they were building a wall like those of a city, used the bones of the dead as pebbles to fill up the cracks. In a way the city became their tomb. To this very day it stands with its encircling wall built of mixed stones and bones. When the killing was over, only Peter with a handful of men returned to Helenopolis. The Turks, wishing to capture him, again laid an ambush, but the emperor, who had heard of this and indeed of the terrible massacre, thought it would be an awful thing if Peter also became a prisoner. Constantine Euphorbenus Catacalon (already mentioned often in this history) was accordingly sent with powerful contingents in warships across the straits to help him. At his approach the Turks took to their heels. Without delay Catacalon picked up Peter and his companions (there were only a few) and brought them in safety to Alexius, who reminded

---

47   The Crusaders arrived at Constantinople on August 1, 1096. They crossed the Bosphorus on August 6. The attack on Nicaea, which
      was the headquarters of the Seljuq sultan (Kilij Arslan), took place in September.

Peter of his foolishness in the beginning and added that these great misfortunes had come upon him through not listening to his advice. With the usual Latin arrogance Peter disclaimed responsibility and blamed his men for them, because (said he) they had been disobedient and followed their own whims. He called them brigands and robbers, considered unworthy therefore by the Savior to worship at His Holy Sepulcher. Some Latins, after the pattern of Bohemond and his cronies, because they had long coveted the Roman Empire and wished to acquire it for themselves, found in the preaching of Peter an excuse and caused this great upheaval by deceiving more innocent people. They sold their lands on the pretence that they were leaving to fight the Turks and liberate the Holy Sepulcher.

A certain Hugh,[48] brother of the king of France, with all the pride of a Nauatos in his noble birth and wealth and power, as he was about to leave his native country (ostensibly for a pilgrimage to the Holy Sepulcher) sent an absurd message to the emperor proposing that he [Hugh] should be given a magnificent reception: "Know, Emperor, that I am the King of Kings, the greatest of all beneath the heavens. It is my will that you should meet me on my arrival and receive me with the pomp and ceremony due to my noble birth." When this letter reached Alexius, John the son of Isaac the sebastocrator[49] happened to be Duke of Dyrrachium, and Nicolas Mavrocatacalon, commander of the fleet, had anchored his ships at intervals round the harbor there. From this base he made frequent voyages of reconnaissance to prevent pirate ships sailing by unnoticed. To these two men the emperor now sent urgent instructions: the duke was to keep watch by land and sea for Hugh's arrival and inform Alexius at once when he came; he was also to receive him with great pomp; the admiral was exhorted to keep a constant vigil—there must be no relaxation or negligence whatever. Hugh reached the coast of Lombardy safely and forthwith despatched envoys to the Duke of Dyrrachium. There were twenty-four of them in all, armed with breastplates and greaves of gold and accompanied by Count William the Carpenter[50] and Elias (who had deserted from the emperor at Thessalonica). They addressed the duke as follows: "Be it known to you, Duke, that our Lord Hugh is almost here. He brings with him from Rome the golden standard of St. Peter.[51] Understand, moreover, that he is supreme commander of the Frankish army. See to it then that he is accorded a reception worthy of his rank and yourself prepare to meet him." While the envoys were delivering this message, Hugh came down via Rome to Lombardy, as I have said, and set sail for Illyricum from Bari, but on the crossing he was caught by a tremendous storm. Most of his ships, with their rowers and marines, were lost. Only one ship, his own, was thrown up on the coast somewhere between Dyrrachium and a place called Pales, and that was half-wrecked. Two coastguards on the lookout for his arrival found him, saved by a miracle. They called to him, "The duke is anxiously waiting for your coming. He is very eager to see you." At once he asked for a horse and one of them dismounted and gave him his own gladly. When the duke saw him, saved in this way, and when he had greeted him, he asked about the voyage and heard of the storm which had wrecked his ships. He encouraged Hugh with fine promises and entertained him at a magnificent banquet. After the feasting Hugh was allowed to rest, but he was not granted complete freedom. John the duke had immediately informed the emperor of the Frank's adventures and was now awaiting further instructions. Soon after receiving the news Alexius sent Boutoumites to Epidamnos (which we have on numerous occasions called Dyrrachium) to escort Hugh, not by the direct route but on a detour through Philippopolis to the capital. He was afraid of the armed Keltic hordes coming on behind him. Hugh was welcomed with honor by the emperor, who soon persuaded him by generous largess and every proof of friendship to become his liege-man and take the customary oath of the Latins.

---

48 Hugh of Vermandois, younger son of Henry I of France and Anne of Kiev. Despite his extraordinary bombast he had made little mark in French politics.
49 Honorific title created by Emperor Alexius for his brother Isaac.
50 William of Melun. Apparently surnamed "the Carpenter" because of his strength.
51 Given by the pope to soldiers leaving to fight the infidels.

This affair was merely the prelude. Barely fifteen days later Bohemond made the crossing to the coast of Kabalion. Hard on his heels came the Count Richard of the Principate. He too when he reached the Lombardy coast wanted to cross over to Illyricum. A three-masted pirate vessel of large tonnage was hired for 6,000 gold staters. She carried 200 rowers and towed three ship's boats. Richard did not make for Avlona, as the other Latin armies had done, but after weighing anchor changed direction a little and with a favorable wind sailed straight for Chimara (he was fearful of the Roman fleet). However, in escaping the smoke he fell into the fire: he avoided the ships lying in wait at different points in the Lombardy straits but crossed the path of the commander-in-chief of the whole Roman fleet, Nicolas Mavrocatacalon himself. The latter had heard of this pirate vessel some time before and had detached biremes, triremes and some fast cruisers from the main force; with these he moved from his base at Ason to Kabalion and there took up station. The so-called "second count" was sent with his own galley (*Excussaton* to the ordinary seamen) to light a torch when he saw the rowers loose the stern-cables of the enemy ship and throw them into the sea. Without delay the order was carried out and Nicolas, seeing the signal, hoisted sail on some of his ships, while others were rowed with oars—they looked like millipedes—against Richard, who was now at sea. They caught him before he had sailed three stades from the land, eager to reach the opposite shore by Epidamnos. He had 1,500 soldiers on board, plus eighty horses belonging to the nobles. The helmsman, sighting Nicolas, reported to the Frank: "The Syrian fleet is on us. We're in danger of being killed by dagger and sword." The count at once ordered his men to arm and put up a good fight. It was midwinter—the day sacred to the memory of Nicolas, greatest of pontiffs—but there was a dead calm and the full moon shone more brightly than in the spring. As the winds had fallen completely the pirate ship could no longer make progress under sail; it lay becalmed on the sea. At this point in the history I should like to pay tribute to the exploits of Marianus. He immediately asked the Duke of the Fleet, his father, for some of the lighter vessels and then steered straight for Richard's ship. He fell upon the prow and tried to board her. The marines soon rushed there when they saw that he was fully armed for battle, but Marianus, speaking in their language, told the Latins there was no need for alarm; he urged them not to fight against fellow-Christians. Nevertheless one of them fired a cross-bow and hit his helmet. The arrow drove clean through the top of it without touching a hair on his head—Providence thwarted it. Another arrow was quickly fired at the count, striking him on the arm; it pierced his shield, bored through his breastplate of scale-armor and grazed his side. A certain Latin priest who happened to be standing in the stern with twelve other fighting-men saw what had occurred and shot several times with his bow at Marianus. Even then Marianus refused to give up; he fought bravely himself and encouraged his men to follow his example, so that three times the priest's comrades had to be relieved because of wounds or fatigue. The priest, too, although he had been hit again and again and was covered with streams of blood from his wounds, still was undaunted. After a bitter contest which went on from evening till the next mid-day the Latins yielded much against their will to Marianus, when they had asked for and obtained an amnesty from him. The warrior-priest, however, even when the armistice was being arranged, did not cease from fighting. After emptying his quiver of arrows, he picked up a sling-stone and hurled it at Marianus, who protected his head with a shield, but that was broken into four and his helmet was shattered. The blow stunned him; he lost consciousness at once and for some time lay speechless, just as the famous Hector lay almost at his last gasp when struck by Ajax's stone. With difficulty he recovered his senses, pulled himself together and firing arrows against his enemy wounded him three times. The polemarch[52] (he was more that than a priest) was far from having had his fill of battle, although he had exhausted the stones and arrows and was at a loss what to do and how to defend himself against his adversary. He grew impatient, on fire with rage, gathering himself for the spring like a wild animal. He was ready to use whatever

---

52   An army rank—a commander-in-chief of soldiers.

came to hand and when he found a sack full of barley-cakes, he threw them like stones, taking them from the sack. It was as if he were officiating at some ceremony or service, turning war into the solemnization of sacred rites. He picked up one cake, hurled it with all his might at Marianus' face and hit him on the cheek. So much for the story of the priest, the ship and its marines. As for Count Richard, he put himself in the hands of Marianus, together with his ship and her crew, and thereafter gladly followed him. When they reached land and were disembarking, the priest kept on making inquiries about Marianus; he did not know his name, but described him by the color of his garments. When at last he found him, he threw his arms round him and with an embrace boasted, "If you had met me on dry land, many of you would have died at my hands." He drew out a large silver cup, worth 130 staten, and as he gave it to Marianus and uttered these words, he died.

It was at this time that Count Godfrey made the crossing with some other counts and an army of 10,000 horsemen and 70,000 infantry. When he reached the capital he quartered his men in the vicinity of the Propontis, from the bridge nearer the Kosmidion[53] as far as the Church of St. Phocas. But when the emperor urged him to go over to the far side of the Propontis he put off the decision from day to day; the crossing was deferred with a series of excuses. In fact, of course, he was waiting for Bohemond and the rest of the counts to arrive. Peter had in the beginning undertaken his great journey to worship at the Holy Sepulcher, but the others (and in particular Bohemond) cherished their old grudge against Alexius and sought a good opportunity to avenge the glorious victory which the emperor had won at Larissa. They were all of one mind and in order to fulfil their dream of taking Constantinople they adopted a common policy. I have often referred to that already: to all appearances they were on pilgrimage to Jerusalem; in reality they planned to dethrone Alexius and seize the capital. Unfortunately for them, he was aware of their perfidy, from long experience. He gave written orders to move the auxiliary forces

with their officers from Athyra to Philea *en masse* (Philea is a place on the coast of the Black Sea). They were to lie in wait for envoys from Godfrey on their way to Bohemond and the other counts coming behind him, or *vice versa*; all communications were thus to be intercepted. Meanwhile the following incident took place. Some of the counts who accompanied Godfrey were invited by the emperor to meet him. He intended to give them advice: they should urge Godfrey to take the oath of allegiance. The Latins, however, wasted time with their usual verbosity and love of long speeches, so that a false rumor reached the Franks that their counts had been arrested by Alexius. Immediately they marched in serried ranks on Byzantium, starting with the palaces near the Silver Lake; they demolished them completely. An assault was also made on the city walls, not with helepoleis[54] (because they had none), but trusting in their great numbers they had the effrontery to try to set fire to the gate below the palace, near the sanctuary of St. Nicolas. The vulgar mob of Byzantines, who were utterly craven, with no experience of war, were not the only ones to weep and wail and beat their breasts in impotent fear when they saw the Latin ranks; even more alarmed were the emperor's loyal adherents. Recalling the Thursday on which the city was captured,[55] they were afraid that on that day[56] (because of what had occurred then) vengeance might be taken on them. All the trained soldiers hurried to the palace in disorder, but the emperor remained calm: there was no attempt to arm, no buckling on of scaled cuirass, no shield, no spear in hand, no girdling on of his sword. He sat firmly on the imperial throne, gazing cheerfully on them, encouraging and inspiring the hearts of all with confidence, while he took counsel with his kinsmen and generals about future action. In the first place he insisted that no one whatever should leave the ramparts to attack the Latins, for two reasons: because of the sacred character of the day (it was the Thursday of Holy Week, the supreme week of the year, in which the Savior suffered an ignominious death on behalf of the whole world);

---

53 The Monastery of St. Kosmas.
54 A heavy catapult.
55 A reference to the revolt of the Comneni.
56 April 2, 1097 (also a Thursday).

and secondly because he wished to avoid blood-shed between Christians. On several occasions he sent envoys to the Latins advising them to desist from such an undertaking. "Have reverence," he said, "for God on this day was sacrificed for us all, refusing neither the Cross, nor the Nails, nor the Spear—proper instruments of punishment for evil-doers—to save us. If you must fight, we too shall be ready, but after the day of the Savior's res-urrection." They, far from listening to his words, rather reinforced their ranks, and so thick were the showers of their arrows that even one of the emperor's retinue standing near the throne, was struck in the chest. Most of the others ranged on either side of the emperor, when they saw this, be-gan to withdraw, but he remained seated and un-ruffled, comforting them and rebuking them in a gentle way—to the wonder of all. However, as he saw the Latins brazenly approaching the walls and rejecting sound advice, he took active steps for the first time. His son-in-law Nicephorus (my Caesar) was summoned. He was ordered to pick out the best fighters, expert archers, and post them on the ramparts; they were to fire volleys of arrows at the Latins, but without taking aim and mostly off-target, so as to terrify the enemy by the weight of the attack, but at all costs to avoid kill-ing them. As I have remarked, he was fearful of desecrating that day and he wished to prevent fratricide. Other picked men, most of them carry-ing bows, but some wielding long spears, he or-dered to throw open the gates of St. Romanus and make a show of force with a violent charge against the enemy; they were to be drawn up in such a way that each lancer had two peltasts[57] to protect him on either side. In this formation they would advance at a walking pace, but send on ahead a few skilled archers to shoot at the Kelts from a distance and alter direction, right or left, from time to time; when they saw that the space be-tween the two armies had been reduced to a nar-row gap, then the officers were to signal the ar-chers accompanying them to fire thick volleys of arrows at the horses, not at the riders, and gallop at full speed against the enemy. The idea was part-ly to break the full force of the Keltic attack by wounding their mounts (they would not find it

easy to ride in this condition) and partly (this was more important) to avoid the killing of Christians. The emperor's instructions were gladly followed. The gates were flung open; now the horses were given their head, now reined in. Many Kelts were slain, but few of the Romans on that day were wounded. We will leave them and return to the Caesar, my lord. Having taken his practised bow-men, he set them on the towers and fired at the barbarians. Every man had a bow that was accu-rate and far-shooting. They were all young, as skilled as Homer's Teucer in archery. The Caesar's bow was truly worthy of Apollo. Unlike the fa-mous Greeks of Homer he did not "pull the bow-string until it touched his breast and draw back the arrow so that the iron tip was near the bow"; he was making no demonstration of the hunter's skill, like them. But like a second Hercules he shot deadly arrows from deathless bows and hit the target at will. At other times, when he took part in a shooting contest or in a battle, he never missed his aim: at whatever part of a man's body he shot, he invariably and immediately inflicted a wound there. With such strength did he bend his bow and so swiftly did he let loose his arrows that even Teucer and the two Ajaxes were not his equal in archery. Yet, despite his skill, on this occasion he respected the holiness of the day and kept in mind the emperor's instructions, so that when he saw the Franks recklessly and foolishly coming near the walls, protected by shield and helmet, he bent his bow and put the arrow to the bow-string, but purposely shot wide, shooting sometimes beyond the target, sometimes falling short. Although, for the day's sake, he refrained from shooting straight at the Latins, yet whenever one of them in his foolhardiness and arrogance not only fired at the defenders on the ramparts, but seemingly poured forth a volley of insults in his own language as well, the Caesar did bend his bow. "Nor did the dart fly in vain from his hand," but pierced the long shield and cleft its way through the corselet of mail, so that arm and side were pinned togeth-er. "Straightway he fell speechless to the ground," as the poet says, and a cry went up to heaven as the Romans cheered their Caesar and the Latins bewailed their fallen warrior. The battle broke out

---

57 Light infantrymen.

afresh, their cavalry and our men on the walls both fighting with courage; it was a grim, dour struggle on both sides. However, when the emperor threw in his guards, the Latin ranks turned in flight. On the next day Hugh advised Godfrey to yield to the emperor's wish, unless he wanted to learn a second time how experienced a general Alexius was. He should take an oath, he said, to bear his true allegiance. But Godfrey rebuked him sternly. "You left your own country as a king," he said, "with all that wealth and a strong army; now from the heights you've brought yourself to the level of a slave. And then, as if you had won some great success, you come here and tell me to do the same." "We ought to have stayed in our own countries and kept our hands off other peoples'," replied Hugh. "But since we've come thus far and need the emperor's protection, no good will come of it unless we obey his orders." Hugh was sent away with nothing achieved. Because of this and reliable information that the counts coming after Godfrey were already near, the emperor sent some of his best officers with their troops to advise him once more, even to compel him to cross the straits. No sooner were they in sight when the Latins, without a moment's hesitation, not even waiting to ask them what they wanted, launched an attack and began to fight them. In this fierce engagement many on both sides fell and all the emperor's men who had attacked with such recklessness were wounded. As the Romans showed greater spirit the Latins gave way. Thus Godfrey not long after submitted; he came to the emperor and swore on oath as he was directed that whatever cities, countries or forts he might in future subdue, which had in the first place belonged to the Roman Empire, he would hand over to the officer appointed by the emperor for this very purpose. Having taken the oath he received generous largess, was invited to share Alexius' hearth and table, and was entertained at a magnificent banquet, after which he crossed over to Pelekanum and there pitched camp. The emperor then gave orders that plentiful supplies should be made available for his men.

In the wake of Godfrey came Count Raoul, with 15,000 cavalry and foot-soldiers. He encamped with his attendant counts by the Propontis near the Patriarch's Monastery; the rest he quartered as far as Sosthenion along the shore. Following Godfrey's example he procrastinated, waiting for the arrival of those coming after him, and the emperor who dreaded it (guessing what was likely to happen) used every means, physical and psychological, to hurry them into crossing the straits. For instance, Opus was summoned—a man of noble character, unsurpassed in his knowledge of things military—and when he presented himself before the emperor he was despatched overland with other brave men to Raoul. His instructions were to force the Frank to leave for the Asian side. When it was clear that Raoul had no intention of going, but in fact adopted an insolent and quite arrogant attitude to the emperor, Opus armed himself and set his men in battle order, maybe to scare the barbarian. He thought this might persuade him to set sail. But the Keltic reaction was immediate: with his available men he accepted the challenge, "like a lion who rejoices when he has found a large prey." There and then he started a violent battle. At this moment Pegasios arrived by sea to transport them to the other side and when he saw the fight on land and the Kelts throwing themselves headlong at the Roman ranks, he disembarked and himself joined in the conflict, attacking the enemy from the rear. In this fight many men were killed, but a far greater number were wounded. The survivors, under the circumstances, asked to be taken over the straits; reflecting that if they joined Godfrey and told him of their misfortunes he might be stirred to action against the Romans, the emperor prudently granted their request; he gladly put them on ships and had them transported to the Savior's tomb, especially since they themselves wanted this. Friendly messages, offering great expectations, were also sent to the counts whom they were awaiting. Consequently, when they arrived, they willingly carried out his instructions. So much for Count Raoul. After him came another great contingent, a numberless heterogeneous host gathered together from almost all the Keltic lands with their leaders (kings and dukes and counts and even bishops). The emperor sent envoys to greet them as a mark of friendship and forwarded politic letters. It was typical of Alexius: he had an uncanny prevision and knew how to seize a point of vantage before his rivals. Officers appointed for this particular task were ordered to provide victuals on the journey—the pilgrims must have no excuse for complaint for any reasons whatever. Meanwhile they were eagerly pressing on to the capital. One might have compared them for number to the stars of heaven or the grains of sand poured out over the shore; as they hurried towards Constantinople they were indeed "numerous as the leaves and flowers of spring" (to quote Homer). For all my desire to name their leaders, I prefer not to do so. The words fail me, partly through my inability to make the barbaric sounds—they are so unpronounceable—and partly because I recoil before their great numbers. In any case, why should I try to list the names of so enormous a multitude, when even their contemporaries became indifferent at the sight of them? When they did finally arrive in the capital, on the emperor's orders they established their troops near the monastery of Saint Cosmas and Saint Damian, reaching as far as the Hieron. It was not nine heralds, after the old Greek custom, who "restrained them with cries," but a considerable number of soldiers who accompanied them and persuaded them to obey the emperor's commands. With the idea of enforcing the same oath that Godfrey had taken, Alexius invited them to visit him separately. He talked with them in private about his wishes and used the more reasonable among them as intermediaries to coerce the reluctant. When they rejected advice—they were anxiously waiting for Bohemond to come—and found ingenious methods of evasion by making new demands, he refuted their objections with no difficulty at all and harried them in a hundred ways until they were driven to take the oath. Godfrey himself was invited to cross over from Pelekanum to watch the ceremony. When all, including Godfrey, were assembled and after the oath had been sworn by every count, one nobleman dared to seat himself on the emperor's throne. Alexius endured this without a word, knowing of old the haughty temper of the Latins, but Count Baldwin went up to the man, took him by the hand and made him rise. He gave him a severe reprimand: "You ought never to have done such a thing, especially after promising to be the emperor's liege-man. Roman emperors

don't let their subjects sit with them. That's the custom here and sworn liege-men of His Majesty should observe the customs of the country." The man said nothing to Baldwin, but with a bitter glance at Alexius muttered some words to himself in his own language: "What a peasant! He sits alone while generals like these stand beside him!" Alexius saw his lips moving and calling one of the interpreters who understood the language asked what he had said. Being told the words he made no comment to the man at the time, but kept the remark to himself. However, when they were all taking their leave of him, he sent for the arrogant, impudent fellow and asked who he was, where he came from and what his lineage was. "I am a pure Frank," he replied, "and of noble birth. One thing I know: at a cross-roads in the country where I was born is an ancient shrine; to this any one who wishes to engage in single combat goes, prepared to fight; there he prays to God for help and there he stays awaiting the man who will dare to answer his challenge. At that cross-roads I myself have spent time, waiting and longing for the man who would fight—but there was never one who dared." Hearing this the emperor said, "If you didn't get your fight then, when you looked for it, now you have a fine opportunity for many. But I strongly recommend you not to take up position in the rear of the army, nor in the van; stand in the centre with the *hemilochitae*.[58] I know the enemy methods. I've had long experience of the Turk." The advice was not given to him alone, but as they left he warned all the others of the manifold dangers they were likely to meet on the journey. He advised them not to pursue the enemy too far, if God gave them the victory, lest falling into traps set by the Turkish leaders they should be massacred.

So much for Godfrey, Raoul and those who came with them. Bohemond arrived at Apros with the other counts. Knowing that he himself was not of noble descent, with no great military following because of his lack of resources, he wished to win the emperor's goodwill, but at the same time to conceal his own hostile intentions against him. With only ten Kelts he hurried to reach the capital before the rest. Alexius understood his

---

58   Junior officers in the army.

schemes—he had long experience of Bohemond's deceitful, treacherous nature—and desired to talk with him before his companions arrived; he wanted to hear what Bohemond had to say and while he still had no chance of corrupting the rest (they were not far away now) he hoped to persuade him to cross over to Asia. When Bohemond came into his presence, Alexius at once gave him a smile and inquired about his journey. Where had he left the counts? Bohemond replied frankly and to the best of his knowledge to all these questions, while the emperor politely reminded him of his daring deeds at Larissa and Dyrrachium; he also recalled Bohemond's former hostility. "I was indeed an enemy and foe then," said Bohemond, "but now I come of my own free will as Your Majesty's friend." Alexius talked at length with him, in a somewhat discreet way trying to discover the man's real feelings, and when he concluded that Bohemond would be prepared to take the oath of allegiance, he said to him, "You are tired now from your journey. Go away and rest. Tomorrow we can discuss matters of common interest." Bohemond went off to the Cosmidion, where an apartment had been made ready for him and a rich table was laid full of delicacies and food of all kinds. Later the cooks brought in meat and flesh of animals and birds, uncooked. "The food, as you see, has been prepared by us in our customary way," they said, "but if that does not suit you here is raw meat which can be cooked in whatever way you like." In doing and saying this they were carrying out the emperor's instructions. Alexius was a shrewd judge of a man's character, cleverly reading the innermost thoughts of his heart, and knowing the spiteful, malevolent nature of Bohemond, he rightly guessed what would happen. It was in order that Bohemond might have no suspicions that he caused the uncooked meat to be set before him at the same time, and it was an excellent move. The cunning Frank not only refused to taste any of the food, but would not even touch it with his finger-tips; he rejected it outright, but divided it all up among the attendants, without a hint of his own secret misgivings. It looked as if he was doing them a favor, but that was mere pretence: in reality, if one considers the matter rightly, he was mixing them a cup of death. There was no attempt to hide his treachery, for it was his habit to treat servants with utter indifference. However, he told his own cooks to prepare the raw meat in the usual Frankish way.

On the next day he asked the attendants how they felt. "Very well," they replied and added that they had suffered not the slightest harm from it. At these words he revealed his hidden fear: "For my own part," he said, "when I remembered the wars I have fought with him, not to mention the famous battle, I was afraid he might arrange to kill me by putting a dose of poison in the food." Such were the actions of Bohemond. I must say I have never seen an evil man who in all his deeds and words did not depart far from the path of right; whenever a man leaves the middle course, to whatever extreme he inclines he takes his stand far from virtue. Bohemond was summoned then and required, like the others, to take the customary Latin oath. Knowing what his position was he acquiesced gladly enough, for he had neither illustrious ancestors nor great wealth (hence his forces were not strong—only a moderate number of Keltic followers). In any case Bohemond was by nature a liar. After the ceremony was over, Alexius set aside a room in the palace precincts and had the floor covered with all kinds of wealth: clothes, gold and silver coins, objects of lesser value filled the place so completely that it was impossible for anyone to walk in it. He ordered the man deputed to show Bohemond these riches to open the doors suddenly. Bohemond was amazed at the sight. "If I had had such wealth," he said, "I would long ago have become master of many lands." "All this," said the man, "is yours today—a present from the emperor." Bohemond was overjoyed. After accepting the gift and thanking him for it, he went off to rest at his lodging-place. Yet when the things were brought to him, although he had expressed such admiration before, he changed. "I never thought I should be so insulted by the emperor," he said. "Take them away. Give them back to the sender." Alexius, familiar with the Latins' characteristic moodiness, quoted a popular saying: "His mischief shall return upon his own head." Bohemond heard about this, and when he saw the servants carefully assembling the presents to carry them away, he changed his mind once more; instead of sending them off in anger he smiled on them, like a sea-polyp which transforms itself in a minute.

The truth is that Bohemond was an habitual rogue, quick to react to fleeting circumstance; he far surpassed all the Latins who passed through Constantinople at that time in rascality and courage, but he was equally inferior in wealth and resources. He was the supreme mischief-maker. As for inconstancy, that followed automatically—a trait common to all Latins. It was no surprise then that he should be overjoyed to receive the money he had formerly refused. When he left his native land, he was a soured man, for he had no estates at all. Apparently he left to worship at the Holy Sepulcher, but in reality to win power for himself—or rather, if possible, to seize the Roman Empire itself, as his father had suggested. He was prepared to go to any length, as they say, but a great deal of money was required. The emperor, aware of the man's disagreeable, ill-natured disposition, cleverly sought to remove everything that contributed to Bohemond's secret plans. When therefore Bohemond demanded the office of domestic of the east, he was not granted his request; he could not "out-Cretan the Cretan,"[59] for Alexius was afraid that once possessed of authority he might use it to subjugate all the other counts and thereafter convert them easily to any policy he chose.

At the same time, because he did not wish Bohemond to suspect in any way that his plans were already detected, he flattered him with fine hopes. "The time for that is not yet ripe, but with your energy and loyalty it will not be long before you have even that honor." After a conversation with the Franks and after showing his friendship for them with all kinds of presents and honors, on the next day he took his seat on the imperial throne. Bohemond and the others were sent for and warned about the things likely to happen on their journey. He gave them profitable advice. They were instructed in the methods normally used by the Turks in battle; told how they should draw up a battle-line, how to lay ambushes; advised not to pursue far when the enemy ran away in flight. In this way, by means of money and

good advice, he did much to soften their ferocious nature. Then he proposed that they should cross the straits. For one of them, Raymond the Count of Saint-Gilles,[60] Alexius had a deep affection, for several reasons: the count's superior intellect, his untarnished reputation, the purity of his life. He knew moreover how greatly Raymond valued the truth: whatever the circumstances, he honored truth above all else. In fact, Saint-Gilles outshone all Latins in every quality, as the sun is brighter than the stars. It was for this that Alexius detained him for some time. Thus, when all the others had taken their leave of him and made the journey across the straits of the Propontis to Damalion,[61] and when he was now relieved of their troublesome presence, he sent for him on many occasions. He explained in more detail the adventures that the Latins must expect to meet with on their march; he also laid bare his own suspicions of their plans. In the course of many such conversations on this subject he unreservedly opened the doors of his soul, as it were, to the count; he warned him always to be on his guard against Bohemond's perfidy, so that if attempts were made to break the treaty he might frustrate them and in every way thwart Bohemond's schemes. Saint-Gilles pointed out that Bohemond inherited perjury and guile from his ancestors—it was a kind of heirloom. "It will be a miracle if he keeps his sworn word," he said. "As far as I am concerned, however, I will always try to the best of my ability to observe your commands." With that he took his leave of the emperor and went off to join the whole Keltic army. Alexius would have liked to share in the expedition against the barbarians, too, but he feared the enormous numbers of the Kelts. He did think it wise, though, to move to Pelekanum. Making his permanent headquarters near Nicaea, he could obtain information about their progress and at the same time about Turkish activities outside the city, as well as about the condition of the inhabitants inside. It would be shameful, he believed, if in the meantime he did not himself win some military success. When

---

59   An allusion to the reputation of Cretans as liars.
60   Anna calls him Isangeles. He was Count of Toulouse and Marquis of Provence, hoped to lead the crusaders in the field and was a
      rival of Bohemond.
61   In April 1097.

a favorable opportunity arose, he planned to capture Nicaea himself; that would be preferable to receiving it from the Kelts (according to the agreement already made with them). Nevertheless he kept the idea to himself. Whatever dispositions he made, and the reasons for them, were known to himself alone, although he did entrust this task to Boutoumites (his sole confidant). Boutoumites was instructed to suborn the barbarians in Nicaea by all kinds of guarantees and the promise of a complete amnesty, but also by holding over them the prospect of this or that retribution—even massacre—if the Kelts took the city. He had long been assured of Boutoumites' loyalty and he knew that in such matters he would take energetic measure. The history of the foregoing events has been set out in chronological order from the beginning.

30. *CANONS* OF THE FOURTH LATERAN COUNCIL, 1215

THE COUNCIL CALLED BY Pope Innocent III in 1215 was the greatest ecclesiastical assembly of the century. It was attended by over four hundred bishops, eight hundred priests, and representatives of all the princes of Europe. The canons of the council, given below, attempted to address the essential doctrinal issues of Christianity as well as the problem of clerical and lay disciplines and issues ranging from the aftermath of the Crusades to the disposition of relics.

Source: Harry Rothwell (ed.), *English Historical Documents 1189–1327* (London: Eyre and Spottiswoode, 1975).

Further Reading: John C. Moore, *Pope Innocent III (1160/61–1216): To Root Up and to Plant* (Leiden: Brill, 2003).

1. We firmly believe and simply confess, that there is one only true God, eternal, without measure, omnipotent, unchangeable, incomprehensible and ineffable, the Father, the Son, and the Holy Spirit: three persons indeed, but one simple essence, substance, or nature altogether; the Father of none, the Son of the Father alone, and the Holy Spirit proceeding; consubstantial, and co-equal, co-omnipotent, and co-eternal; one principle of all things; the creator of all things visible and invisible, spiritual and corporal, who by His omnipotent virtue at once from the beginning of time established out of nothing both forms of creation, spiritual and corporal, that is the angelic and the mundane, and afterwards the human creature, composed as it were of spirit and body in common. For the devil and other demons were created by God naturally good, but they became evil by their own doing. Man, however, sinned by the suggestion of the devil.

This Holy Trinity, undivided as regards common essence, and distinct in respect of proper qualities of person, in accordance with the perfectly ordered plan for the ages, gave the teaching of salvation to the human race first by means of Moses and the holy prophets and others His servants. Finally the only-begotten son of God, Jesus Christ, incarnate of the whole Trinity in common, being conceived of Mary ever Virgin by the cooperation of the Holy Spirit, made very man, compounded of a reasonable soul and human flesh, one person in two natures, shewed the way of life in all its clearness. He, while as regards His divinity He is immortal and incapable of suffering, nevertheless, as regards His humanity, was made capable of suffering and mortal. He also, having suffered for the salvation of the human race upon the wood of the cross and died, descended to hell, rose again from the dead, and ascended into heaven; but descended in spirit and rose again in flesh, and ascended in both alike to come at the end of the world to judge the quick and the dead, and to render to every man according to his works, both to the reprobate and to the elect, who all shall rise again with their own bodies which they now wear, that they may receive according to their works, whether they be good or bad, these perpetual punishment with the devil, and those everlasting glory with Christ.

There is moreover one universal church of the faithful, outside which no man at all is saved, in which the same Jesus Christ is both the priest and the sacrifice, whose body and blood are truly contained in the sacrament of the altar under the species of bread and wine, the bread being transubstantiated into the body and the wine into the blood by the divine power, in order that, to accomplish the mystery of unity, we ourselves may receive of His that which He received of ours. This sacrament no one can perform but a priest, who has been duly ordained, according to the keys of the church, which Jesus Christ Himself granted to the apostles and their successors.

But the sacrament of baptism, which is consecrated in water by invoking the indivisible Trinity, that is the Father, and the Son, and the Holy Spirit, is profitable to the salvation of children and adults alike when duly conferred in proper church fashion by anyone, whosoever he be. And if anyone, after receiving baptism, has fallen into sin, he can always be redeemed by true penitence. Not only virgins and the continent, but married people too, find favor with God by right faith and good works and deserve to attain eternal blessedness.

2. We condemn therefore and reject the little book or treatise which the abbot Joachim has put out against Mr. Peter Lombard on the unity or essence of the Trinity, calling him a heretic and madman because he said in his *Sentences*, "There is a supreme reality which is Father, Son and Holy Ghost and it does not beget, neither is it begotten, nor does it proceed," from which he asserts that Peter Lombard makes God not so much a Trinity as a quaternity, that is to say three persons and the common essence, a sort of fourth, declaring plainly that there is no reality which is Father, Son and Holy Ghost, neither is it essence, substance or nature, although he concedes that Father, Son and Holy Ghost are one essence, one substance, and one nature. He professes, however, that such a unity is not true and proper, but, as it were, a collective and analogous unity in the way many

men are called one people and many believers one church, according to "The multitude of them that believed were of one heart and one soul,"[1] and "He that is joined unto the Lord is one spirit with him"[2]; also "He that planteth and he that watereth are one,"[3] and all of us "are one body in Christ"[4]: again, in the book of Kings, "My people and thy people are one."[5] But to establish this opinion he adduces above all what Christ says in the Gospel about believers: "I wish, Father, that they may be one in us, even as we are one, that they may be made perfect in one."[6] For (so he says) Christians are not one, i.e. a single reality common to all: they are one in this way, i.e., one church because of the unity of the Catholic faith and finally one kingdom because of the indissoluble union of charity. Thus one reads in the canonical epistle of John, "For there are three that bear record in heaven, the Father, the Word, and the Holy Ghost, and these three are one,"[7] and immediately the author adds, "And there are three that bear witness in earth, the spirit, the water, and the blood, and these three are one,"[8] according to certain manuscripts.

But we, with the approbation of the holy and universal council, believe and confess with Peter [Lombard] that there is one single supreme reality, incomprehensible indeed and ineffable, who truly is Father, Son and Holy Ghost, the three persons together and each of them separately, and therefore in God there is a Trinity only, not a quaternity, because each of the three persons is that reality, that is to say essence, substance or divine nature, which alone is the principle of all things, apart from which another cannot be found, and that reality does not beget, neither is it begotten, nor does it proceed, but it is the Father who begets, the Son who is begotten, and the Holy Ghost which proceeds, so there are distinctions of person and unity of nature. Although therefore one person is the Father, another is the Son, another the Holy Ghost, there is not another, but that

---

1   Acts 4:32.
2   1 Corinthians 6:17.
3   1 Corinthians 3:7.
4   Romans 12:5.
5   1 Kings 3:9.
6   John 17:21.
7   John 5:7.
8   John 5:8.

which is the Father is the Son and the Holy Ghost, altogether the same, so, according to the orthodox and Catholic faith, they are believed to be consubstantial. For the Father by begetting everlastingly the Son gave him his substance, as he himself testifies, "What the Father gave me is greater than all," and it cannot be said that he gave part of his substance to him and kept part for himself, as the substance of the Father is indivisible inasmuch as it is utterly simple; but neither can it be said that the Father transferred his substance to the Son in begetting him, as if he so gave it to the Son that he did not keep it himself, otherwise he would have ceased to be substance. It is clear therefore that in being born the Son received the substance of the Father without any diminution of it, and so the Father and the Son have the same substance and thus the Father and the Son and the Holy Ghost proceeding from both are the same reality. When therefore Truth prays to the Father for those believing in him, saying, "I wish that they may be one in us, as we also are one," this word "one" is taken to mean in the case of believers the union of charity in grace, in the case of divine persons the unity of identity in nature, as Truth says elsewhere, "Be ye perfect even as your heavenly Father is perfect," as if it were to say more plainly, "Be ye perfect" with the perfection of grace "as your heavenly Father is perfect" with the perfection of nature—each, that is, after his fashion, for between the Creator and a creature there can be remarked no similarity so great that a greater dissimilarity cannot be seen between them.

If therefore anyone ventures to defend or approve the opinion or teaching of the said Joachim on this matter, he is to be refuted by all as a heretic. By this however we do not wish to do anything at all to the detriment of the monastery of Fiore, of which Joachim was the founder, because there the foundation is according to rule and the observance is in a healthy state; particularly as this same Joachim ordered all his writings to be sent to us for approval or correction at the judgment of the apostolic see and composed a letter, signed by his own hand, in which he firmly confesses that he holds the faith held by the Roman church, the mother and teacher, by the divine plan, of all believers. We reject and condemn also the utterly perverse opinion of the impious Aymer whose mind the father of lies has blinded to such an extent that his teaching must be reckoned not so much heretical as insane.

3. We excommunicate and anathematise every heresy setting itself up against this holy, orthodox, Catholic faith which we have expounded above, and condemn all heretics by whatever names they go under: they have various faces indeed, but tails tied one to another, for they have vanity in common. Those condemned as heretics shall be handed over to the secular authorities present or to their bailiffs for punishment by the penalty deserved, clerks first being degraded from their orders. The goods of these condemned are, if they are laymen, to be confiscated, if clerks, assigned to the churches from which they drew their stipend. Those found no more than suspect of heresy shall, unless they prove their innocence by a suitable purgation having regard to the reasons for suspicion and the character of the person, be struck by the sword of anathema, and until adequate satisfaction has been made they shall be avoided by everybody, so that if they continue under excommunication for a year they shall be condemned as heretics forthwith. Secular authorities, whatever functions they discharge, shall be instructed, exhorted and, if necessary, compelled by ecclesiastical censure, as they wish to be reputed Christian and treated as such, to take for the defense of the faith public oath that they will concern themselves and do their utmost in good faith to expel from lands under their jurisdiction all heretics pointed out by the church: accordingly from now on whenever anyone is raised to a position of authority spiritual or temporal he shall be bound to confirm this chapter on oath. If however a temporal lord, required and instructed by the church, neglects to purge his land of this heretical filth he shall be bound by the metropolitan and the other bishops of the same province with the bond of excommunication, and if he disdains to render satisfaction within the year it shall be reported to the supreme pontiff in order that he may forthwith declare his vassals absolved from their fealty to him, and make the land available for occupation by Catholics, who when they have evicted the heretics are to have possession of it without opposition and keep it in the purity of

the faith—saving the right of the principal lord, provided that in this matter he opposes no obstacle and puts no impediment in the way. The same rule is to be no less observed for those who do not have principal lords. Catholics who having taken the cross undertake to expel heretics shall enjoy the indulgence and be protected by the holy privilege allowed to those going to the help of the Holy Land. We decree that adherents of, besides receivers, defenders and helpers of heretics are liable to excommunication and firmly ordain that if any such, after being marked with excommunication refuses to render satisfaction within the year he shall forthwith be *ipso facto* branded with infamy, not to be admitted to public office or advisory functions or the electing of anyone to such, and his testimony shall not be acceptable; he shall also be *intestabilis*, i.e., he shall not have the right to make a will and he may not enter upon the succession to an inheritance; no one moreover shall be forced to answer to him about any matter whatever, but he shall answer to others. If he chances to be a judge, his sentence shall have no force, nor shall any causes be brought to his court; if he is an advocate his pleading shall not be listened to at all; if a notary, documents drawn up by him shall have no weight whatever, but be condemned with their condemned author; other cases we order to be treated similarly. If however he is a clerk he shall be deprived of every office and benefice, so that the heavier punishment may be employed against him whose fault is the greater. If any refuse to avoid heretics after they have been pointed out by the church they shall be struck by the sentence of excommunication until proper satisfaction has been made. Clerks shall not, of course, administer the church's sacraments to such pestilent folk or presume to give them Christian burial or accept their alms or offerings; otherwise they shall be deprived of their office and never be restored to it without a special indult of the apostolic see. Similarly with regulars of whatever sort, and on them this too shall be inflicted—that their privileges are not to be respected in the diocese in which they have presumed to commit such excesses. Because some "under a form of godliness denying (as the apostle says) the power thereof"

claim for themselves the authority to preach when the same apostle says, "How shall they preach except they be sent?", all who are prohibited or not yet sent but presume to usurp publicly or privately the office of preaching without having received the authority of the apostolic see or the Catholic bishop of the place shall be bound by the bond of excommunication, and unless they repent very promptly shall be punished by another appropriate penalty. We add moreover that every archbishop or bishop shall personally or through his archdeacon or other suitable and upright persons visit twice or at least once a year any parish of his in which there are said to be heretics and there compel three or more men of good reputation, or even if it seems expedient the whole neighborhood, to swear that if anyone knows of heretics there or of any who hold secret conventicles or any whose life and habits differ from the normal way of living of Christians he will make it his business to point them out to the bishop. He, the bishop, shall summon the accused to his presence and if they do not clear themselves[9] of the accusation, or if after clearance they relapse into their former errors of faith, they shall be punished in accordance with canon law. If any of them, however, refuse with damnable obstinacy to be bound by oath and will not swear, they shall be from that very fact reckoned as heretics. We will command and strictly order, on the strength of their obedience, bishops to see carefully to the effective execution of these things all over their dioceses, if they wish to escape canonical punishment; for if any bishop is negligent or slack over clearing the ferment of heresy from his diocese when it shows itself by unmistakable signs he shall be deposed from his office as bishop and in his place another suitable person substituted who has the will and the power to overthrow heresy.

4. Although we should like to cherish and honor the Greeks, who in our time are returning to the obedience of the apostolic see, by maintaining as much as we can under the Lord their customs and rites, we neither want to nor should defer to them in things which breed danger to souls and detract from the decorum of the church. For after the

---

9   *I.e.*, by compurgation or ordeal.

Greek church withdrew with certain associates and supporters from the obedience of the apostolic see the Greeks began to loathe the Latins so much that, among other wicked things they did out of contempt for them, they would not, when Latin priests had celebrated on their altars, themselves sacrifice on them before they had washed them, as if by this they had been defiled. Also, those baptized by Latins these Greeks had the temerity to rebaptize and there are some still, we are told, who do not fear to do it. Wishing therefore to do away with such a scandal in the church of God, we on the advice of the holy council strictly command them not to venture to do such things in future and to conform like obedient sons to the holy Roman church, their mother, so that there may be "one fold and one shepherd." If anyone does venture to do such a thing he shall be struck with the sword of excommunication and deprived of every ecclesiastical office and benefice.

5. Renewing the ancient privileges of the patriarchal see, we decree with the approbation of the holy universal council that, after the Roman church, which by the divine plan, has as mother and ruler of all Christians the primacy of ordinary power over all other churches, the churches of Constantinople shall have the first place, that of Alexandria the second, that of Antioch the third, that of Jerusalem the fourth, each of them keeping its own authority—so that after their pontiffs have received the pallium, which is the distinguishing mark of the plenitude of the pontifical office, from the Roman pontiff and taken the oath of fealty and obedience to him, they may lawfully confer the pallium on their own suffragans and receive from them for themselves the canonical profession and for the Roman church the promise of obedience. They shall have the standard of the divine cross carried before them everywhere save in Rome or wherever the pope (or his legate) is present wearing the insignia of apostolic dignity. In all provinces under their jurisdiction appeal, when necessary, shall be made to them, except for appeals lodged with the apostolic see, to which all must humbly defer.

6. As is known to have been ordained of old by the holy fathers, metropolitans should not fail to hold provincial councils every year with their suffragans to consider diligently and in the fear of God the correction of excesses and the reform of morals, especially in the clergy, reciting the canonical rules (particularly those laid down by the present general council) to secure their observance, inflicting on transgressors the punishment due. In order that this may be the more effectively achieved, they are to set up in each diocese suitable persons, discreet that is and honest, who throughout the year shall carefully find out simply and summarily without any jurisdiction what things deserve correction or reform and faithfully report those things to the metropolitan and suffragans and others at the ensuing council, that they after careful deliberation may proceed against these things and others suitably and decently. What they decree, they shall cause to be observed, making it known in diocesan synods, which shall be held annually in each diocese. Whoever neglects to act upon this salutary statute is to be suspended from his benefices and his office until he is released by the decision of his superior.

7. By an irrevocable decree we ordain that persons in authority over churches shall prudently and diligently give their minds to correcting the excesses and reforming the morals of those, especially the clergy, subject to them, lest the blood of these be required at their hands. So that they can perform the task of correcting and reforming freely, we decree that no custom or appeal can impede the execution of their [sentences], unless they have exceeded the rules to be observed in such things. Let, however, the excesses of canons of a cathedral church which by custom have been corrected by the chapter be corrected by it, in churches which have had such a custom until now, at the instance and on the orders of the bishop within a sufficient time-limit, which the bishop shall fix. If this is not done, then the bishop, mindful of God and putting a stop to all opposition, shall not delay to correct them by ecclesiastical censure as the care of souls requires, and not omit to correct their other excesses too as the charge of souls requires, due order nevertheless being observed in all things. For the rest, if canons stop celebrating divine service without manifest and reasonable

cause, particularly in contempt of the bishop, the bishop may celebrate in the cathedral church notwithstanding if he wishes, and on complaint from him the metropolitan as our delegate for this may, when he has established the truth of the matter, chastise them with ecclesiastical censure in such fashion that for fear of the punishment they shall not venture such action in future. Let those in authority over churches carefully see to it therefore that they do not turn this salutary decree into a way of getting money or other exaction, but operate it zealously and faithfully if they wish to avoid canonical punishment, since the apostolic see will, with divine authority, watch over these things most particularly.

8. "By what right and in what way a prelate ought to proceed to enquire into and punish the excesses of subordinates is clearly shown from the testimony assembled in the New and Old Testament, from which the subsequent canon law sanctions derive," as we said distinctly some time ago and now with the approbation of the holy council confirm. For one reads in the Gospel that the bailiff who was "denounced to his lord for having wasted his goods" heard from him, "What is this I hear of thee? Give an account of thy bailiwick for now thou canst no more be bailiff."[10] And in Genesis God says, "I will go down now, and see whether they have done altogether according to the cry of it which is come to me."[11] From which authorities it is clearly proved that not only when a subordinate but even a prelate commits some excess and through complaint and rumor it reaches the ears of his superior, not from the ill-disposed and slanderous but from prudent and honest people, not just once but often (which complaint implies and rumour is manifest proof of), he, the superior, ought in the presence of senior people of the church to enquire into the truth and if the case demands it canonical distress shall smite the fault of the offender—not as if he were accuser and judge but with rumor informing and complaint denouncing, as one carrying out the duty of his office. While this is to be done in the case of subordinates, it must still more carefully be done in

the case of prelates, who are set "as a mark for the arrow." And because they cannot please everybody since they are bound *ex officio* not only to reprove but also to blame, nay even at times to suspend, sometimes to bind, they frequently incur the hatred of many people and are liable to ambushes. For this reason the holy fathers wisely decreed that accusation of prelates is not to be allowed easily, for fear that if the columns are shaken the building may fall, unless there is careful provision for shutting the door against not only false but also malicious accusation. They wished so to provide for prelates not to be accused unjustly that they would take care all the same not to offend out of arrogance and they found a suitable preventative for either evil, viz, that a criminal accusation, which entails the *diminutio capitis*, i.e., degradation, shall in no wise be allowed unless it is preceded by the *inscriptio legitima*.[12] But when anyone is so notorious for his excesses that complaint now cannot be ignored any longer without scandal or without danger allowed to continue, action is to be taken without the slightest hesitation to enquire into and punish his excesses, not out of hate but out of charity; with the condition that if it is a matter of grave excess, though not one involving his degradation, he shall be deprived of all office, in accordance with the gospel sentence that the bailiff is to be removed from his bailiwick who cannot give a proper account of it. He ought therefore to be present about whom enquiry is to be made, unless out of contumacy he absents himself, and the points to be enquired into should be set out before him so that he can be in a position to defend himself, and not only the depositions of the witnesses but also their names, in order that he may know what has been said and who said it, are to be revealed to him, also legitimate exceptions and replications are to be allowed, lest through the suppression of names the audacious may prefer false charges or through the barring of exceptions, bear false witness. A prelate ought to be all the more zealous to correct the excesses of his subordinates, the more to blame he would be for leaving their offenses unpunished. Against them, notorious cases aside,

---

10   Luke 16:2–3.

11   Genesis 18:21.

12   The accuser is named and he will be liable to a penalty if his accusation is not sustained.

although three procedures are possible, viz, by accusation, denunciation and inquest, let careful precautions nevertheless be taken in all cases lest for the sake of a slight gain grave loss may be incurred: just as the *legitima inscriptio* ought to precede the accusation, so a kindly warning ought to come before denunciation and entry of complaint before inquest, always with the rule applied that the method of pronouncing sentence shall be according to the mode of trial. This order, however, need not in our view be observed in all respects as regards regulars, who can at need be more easily and freely removed from their offices.

9. Since in many parts peoples of different languages with various rites and usages within the common faith are mixed together in the same city and diocese, we strictly command the bishops of cities or dioceses of this sort to appoint suitable men to celebrate divine service for them in the various rites and languages, administer the ecclesiastical sacraments to them and instruct them by word and by example alike. We utterly forbid one and the same city or diocese to have more than one bishop, like a body with more than one head as if it were a monster, yet if for the reasons aforesaid necessity requires it, the bishop of the place may after careful deliberation set up a Catholic bishop appropriate for those nations as vicar for himself in the aforesaid matters, who will in all respects be under and obedient to him—as to which, if anyone behaves otherwise he shall know he is smitten by the sword of excommunication, and if he does not then recover his senses he is to be deposed from all ecclesiastical office, the help of the secular arm being invoked if necessary to curb such presumption.

10. Among the other things pertaining to the saving of Christian souls the bread of the Gospel is recognized as the most necessary of all, for as the body is nourished by material food so is the soul by spiritual, because "Man does not live by bread alone, but by every word that proceedeth out of the mouth of God." Hence, since it often happens that bishops because of their manifold occupations or bodily ailments or enemy attacks or other

reasons—not to mention lack of learning, in them a most grievous fault, not to be tolerated in future—are unable themselves to do all the preaching of the Gospel to the people that is needed, especially in large and scattered dioceses, we by a general constitution decree that bishops are to choose men effective in action and speech, suitable for executing the office of sacred preaching to advantage, to visit zealously the peoples committed to them in their place when they themselves cannot and edify them by word and example, and they are to furnish these men, when they need them, with what is appropriate and necessary lest for lack of the things necessary they be forced to abandon an undertaking. We order, in consequence, suitable men to be appointed as well in cathedral as in other conventual churches for the bishops to have as coadjutors and cooperators not only in preaching but also in hearing confessions and enjoining penances and everything else pertaining to the saving of souls. If any one neglects to carry this out, he shall be subject to rigorous punishment.

11. As because of their poverty some have neither the opportunity to study nor chance of advancement, the Lateran council[13] provided by pious decree that "in each cathedral church some competent benefice should be given to a master, whose duty it should be to instruct for nothing the clerks of that church and other poor scholars, thus at once relieving the need of the teacher and opening up the path of knowledge to those who are learning." Since, however, this decree is very little observed in many churches, we confirm it, adding that not only in every cathedral church but also in others, whose resources are adequate, a suitable master, elected by the chapter or the greater and sounder part of the chapter, shall be established by the prelate. He is to instruct for nothing the clerks of those churches and of others in grammar and in other branches of study as far as possible. The metropolitan church shall maintain nonetheless a theologian to teach holy writ to priests and others and above all instruct them in those things which are recognized as having to do with the cure of souls. To each of the masters there is to

---

13   Third Lateran Council, 1179.

be assigned by the chapter the income of a single prebend, and just as much by the metropolitan for the theologian, without his being made on that account a canon, though he shall get the revenues of one as long as he remains prepared to teach. If the metropolitan church finds the two a burden, let it provide for the theologian in the way stated, but for the grammarian get adequate provision made in another church of the city or diocese.

12. In each kingdom or province let there be held every three years, saving the right of diocesan bishops, a general chapter of abbots and of priors without an abbot of their own who have not been accustomed to hold one. They should all attend, if there is no canonical impediment, at one of the monasteries which is suitable for the purpose, with this limitation—that none of them shall bring with him more than six mounts and eight persons. Let them call in as a favor at the start of this innovation two neighboring Cistercian abbots to furnish appropriate counsel and assistance, as they have long been accustomed to holding such chapters and are very knowledgeable. They, with no opposition, shall coopt two they think would be a help from their own order, and these four shall preside over the general chapter, in such a way that from this no one of them assumes leadership; so, if need be, they can, after careful deliberation, be changed. This kind of chapter shall last several consecutive days, as is Cistercian practice, and in it there is to be careful consideration of the reform of the order and the observance of the rule, and what is decided with the approval of those four is to be inviolably observed by all, without any excuse, opposition or appeal. It shall be settled as well where the chapter is to be held next time. Those attending are to lead a common life and divide between them, proportionately, the common expenses. If they cannot all be put up in the same house, let them stay many together at least in several houses. In the same chapter too let there be appointed discreet religious who will make it their business to visit, in the way prescribed for them and on our behalf, every abbey of monks and of nuns of the kingdom or province to correct and reform what in their view needs correction and reform. If they consider that the superior of the place should be

removed outright from the running of it, they shall denounce him to his bishop, that he may remove him, and if he does not do it, the visitors shall refer the matter to the consideration of the papal see. This same thing we will and command canons regular to observe according to their order. If any difficulty arises out of this innovation which cannot be resolved by the said visitors, let it be referred without fuss to the judgment of the papal see, the rest of what after careful discussion they have agreed upon being observed without being called in question again. On the other hand, diocesan bishops shall make it their business so to reform the monasteries under their jurisdiction that when the said visitors come they find more in them worthy of commendation than of correction; and shall be most careful lest the said monasteries are oppressed by them with undue burdens, for, just as we wish the rights of superiors to be upheld, we do not wish to support wrongs done to inferiors. Furthermore, we strictly command both diocesan bishops and those who preside at chapters to restrain by ecclesiastical censure, with no appeal from it, advocates, patrons, vidames, rectors and consuls, magnates and knights, or any others, from presuming to commit offenses against monasteries in respect of their persons or their things, and should they have committed such an offense they shall without fail force them to give satisfaction, so that monasteries may serve Almighty God freely and quietly.

13. For fear too great a diversity of religious orders should lead to grave confusion in the church of God, we firmly forbid anyone in future to invent a new religious order: whoever wishes to become a religious must adopt one of the approved orders. Similarly, anyone wishing to found a new religious house must accept the rule and constitutions of one of the approved religious orders. We forbid also anyone to presume to have a place as a monk in more than one monastery.

14. That the morals and conduct of clerks may be improved, let all strive to live continently and chastely, especially those established in holy orders; let them seek to avoid completely the sin of lust—particularly that on account of which the anger of God comes down from heaven upon the

sins of disobedience—in order that they may be able to minister in the sight of Almighty God with a pure heart and clean body. Lest too easy a pardon afford an incentive to sin, we decree that they who are caught giving way to the sin of incontinence shall in proportion to the degree of their sin be punished according to the rules of canon law, which we wish to be most effectively and rigorously observed in order that those whom the fear of God does not hold back from evil temporal punishment at least may restrain from sin. If anyone, therefore, suspended because of this, presumes to celebrate the divine service he shall not only be deprived of ecclesiastical benefices but also for this twofold transgression be forever deposed from office. Prelates who venture to support such in their wickednesses, especially for money or other temporal advantage, shall be subject to like punishment. Those who, in the manner of their country, have not renounced the marriage bond shall if they fall into sin be punished more severely, since they can avail themselves of lawful matrimony.

15. All clerks shall carefully abstain from gluttony and drunkenness, by which means they may temper the wine to themselves and themselves to the wine; and let no one be urged to drink, as drunkenness both causes the loss of one's senses and rouses the temptation to lust. Accordingly we decree that that abuse is to be utterly abolished whereby in certain parts drinkers bind each other to drink measure for measure and he in their judgment is most praised who has made most people drunk and drained the deepest cups. If anyone shows himself to blame in these things, unless he makes suitable satisfaction when warned by his superior he is to be suspended from his benefice or office. Hunting and bird-catching we forbid for all clerks, hence let them not presume to have either hunting dogs or falcons.

16. Clerks are not to practice secular callings or business, especially if they are dishonorable, not to watch mimes, entertainers and actors and not to frequent taverns at all, unless compelled of necessity to do so on a journey. They are not to play at dice or the little dice [*taxillos*] or be present at such games. They are to have a suitable crown and

tonsure and apply themselves to the divine services and other good pursuits. They are to wear outer garments that are closed, not noticeable by being too short or too long; they are not to indulge in red or green cloths, long sleeves or shoes with embroidery or with curved toes, bridles, pectorals and spurs that are gilded or have other unnecessary ornamentation. Priests and those in minor dignities are not to wear cloaks with sleeves at divine service inside the church, and not even elsewhere, unless a justifiable fear requires a change of dress. They are not to wear buckles or belts ornamented with gold or silver, or even rings except those whose dignity it befits to have them. All bishops are to wear outer garments of linen in public and in church unless they are monks, when they should wear the monastic habit: they are not to wear their cloaks loose in public, but fastened on either side behind the neck or at the chest.

17. We grieve to relate that not only certain lesser clerks but also some prelates spend nearly half the night in unnecessary feasting and forbidden conversation, not to mention other things, and leaving for sleep what is left of the night, they are barely roused at the dawn chorus of the birds and doze away the whole morning. There are also others who celebrate mass barely four times a year or, what is worse, do not bother to attend it, and if they are present while it is being celebrated, they flee the silence of the choir and pay attention to the conversation of the laity outside and, while they are listening to things being said that they are not required to, their ears are not intent on the service. These things and the like we utterly forbid therefore on pain of suspension and strictly command them on the strength of their obedience to celebrate the divine service, day and night alike, as far as God allows them, with zeal and devotion.

18. No clerk may decree or pronounce a sentence of death; nor may he carry out a punishment which involves blood or be there when it is carried out. If anyone presumes to inflict injury on churches or ecclesiastical persons by transgressing this decree he shall be restrained by ecclesiastical censure. Nor shall any clerk write or dictate letters requiring a punishment which involves blood: in the courts of princes let this responsibility be given

to laymen, not clerks. Also let no clerk be put in command of mercenaries, crossbowmen or such-like men of blood; and no subdeacon, deacon, or priest is to practise the art of surgery, which involves burning and cutting; and none is to bestow any blessing or consecration on a purgation by ordeal of boiling water or of cold water or of the red-hot iron, saving nevertheless previously promulgated prohibitions concerning single combats or duels.

19. We do not wish it to be left uncorrected that certain clerks store their own furniture, and that of others, in churches, so that they look more like lay houses than houses of God, regardless of the fact that God would not suffer a vessel to be carried through the temple. There are others too who not only let churches fall into neglect, but also leave the sacred vessels and the liturgical vestments and the altarcloths too and the very communion-cloths so dirty that at times they horrify some people. Now because the zeal of God's house has eaten us up, we firmly prohibit such furniture to be allowed into churches unless on account of enemy attacks or sudden fire or other emergencies they have to be taken in; yet so that when the emergency is over things are taken back to where they were. We command too that oratories, vessels, communion-cloths and the aforementioned vestments be kept clean and fresh. For it seems too absurd to neglect an uncleanness in sacred things which would be disgraceful even in profane.

20. We order the chrism and the eucharist in all churches to be kept locked away in a safe place so that no audacious hand can reach them to do anything horrible or impious. If he who is responsible for keeping them is careless and leaves them about he shall be suspended from office for three months, and if through his carelessness anything unspeakable happens to them he shall be subject to greater punishment.

21. Every Christian of either sex after reaching the years of discretion shall confess all his sins at least once a year privately to his own priest and try as hard as he can to perform the penance imposed on him; and receive with reverence the sacrament of the eucharist at least at Easter, unless for some

reasonable cause, on the advice of his own priest, he thinks he should temporarily refrain from taking it. Otherwise he shall be barred from entering a church in his lifetime and at death shall not have Christian burial. This salutary decree shall be published frequently in churches, so that no one can find the veil of an excuse in the blindness of ignorance. Should, however, anyone for good reasons wish to confess his sins to another priest, let him first ask for and get the permission of his own priest, otherwise the other will not be able to absolve him or bind him. As for the priest, he should be discerning and prudent so that like a practised doctor he can pour wine and oil on the wounds of the injured, diligently enquiring into the circumstances both of the sinner and of the sin, from which to choose intelligently what sort of advice he ought to give him and what sort of remedy to apply, various means availing to heal the sick. Let him take the utmost care not to betray the sinner in some measure by word or sign or any other way whatever, but if he needs sage advice, let him seek it cautiously without mentioning the person: he who presumes to reveal a sin disclosed in the confessional we decree is to be not only deposed from his priestly office but also shut up to do penance for life in a monastery of strict observance.

22. As physical illness is sometimes the result of sin—the Lord said to a sick man whom he had cured, "Go and sin no more, lest worse befall you,"—we by the present decree ordain and strictly command doctors, when it happens before anything else to call in doctors of souls, so that after his spiritual health has been seen to, the sick man may respond better to the bodily medicine—for when the cause ceases, the effect ceases. This among other things has occasioned this decree: that some on a sickbed, when advised by doctors to arrange for the good of their souls, fall into a state of despair, whereby they incur more easily the danger of death. If any doctor shall transgress this our decree, after it has been published by the local prelates, he shall be barred from entering a church more, until he has performed the appropriate penance for this sort of transgression. Furthermore, as the soul is much more precious than the body, we forbid on pain of eternal

anathema any doctor to prescribe anything for a sick man for his bodily health which might endanger his soul.

23. Lest for lack of a shepherd a rapacious wolf attack the Lord's flock and a bereaved church suffer grave injury to its goods and wishing in this matter to counteract the danger to souls and provide protection for churches, we decree that a cathedral or monastic church may not be without a prelate for more than three months, and if, there being no lawful impediment, an election is not made within that time, those who should have elected shall be for that occasion deprived of the power to elect and it shall devolve upon him who is recognized as the immediate superior. He on whom the power has devolved shall, ever mindful of the Lord, not delay more than three months in supplying, with the counsel of his chapter and of other discreet men, the bereaved church canonically with a suitable person from that church or another church if one is not to be found in that, if he wishes to escape canonical penalty.

24. Owing to the various forms of election which some try to invent, both many impediments are produced and great dangers threaten bereaved churches. Because of this we decree that when an election is to be made, with all present who ought, want to and conveniently can be there, there shall be chosen three worthy of trust from the college who shall carefully find out in confidence one by one everybody's vote, and having written them down, shall quickly make known the result of this voting [*publicent in communi*],[14] and no appeal shall be allowed to obstruct it, so that after scrutiny he shall be elected on whom the whole or the greater or sounder part of the chapter agrees. Or else the power of electing shall be committed to some suitable men, who acting for everybody shall provide the bereaved church with a pastor. Otherwise no election made shall be valid, unless perchance it was made by all unanimously as if by divine inspiration and without flaw. Those who attempt to elect contrary to the aforesaid forms shall be deprived of the power of electing on that occasion. What we absolutely forbid is that anyone should appoint a proxy in the business of election

unless he is away from the place where he ought to receive the summons and, detained by a lawful impediment, cannot come—as to which, if need be, he shall take an oath—and that if he wishes he may commission someone from the electoral college in his stead. We condemn also clandestine elections and decree that as soon as an election has taken place it be solemnly published.

25. Whoever consents to election of himself by misuse of secular power contrary to canonical freedom shall both be deprived of the advantage of having been elected and be rendered ineligible; nor can he without a dispensation be elected to any dignity. Those who presume to take part in this sort of election, which we declare *ipso jure*, invalidated, shall be suspended completely from their offices and benefices for three years and during that time deprived of the power to elect.

26. There is nothing more harmful to the church of God than the elevation of unworthy prelates to the government of souls. Wishing therefore to apply the necessary medicine for this malady, we ordain by an irrevocable decree that when anyone is raised to the government of souls he who has the right to confirm him shall diligently examine both the election procedure and the character of the person elected, so that if everything is in order he may give him his confirmation, because if it were incautiously given in advance and everything was not in order, not only would the one unworthily promoted have to be rejected but also the one who promoted unworthily would have to be punished. The latter, we decree, is to suffer this punishment: if it is clearly a matter of negligence on his part, especially if he has confirmed the election of a man of insufficient learning or disgraceful life or uncanonical age, not only shall he be deprived of the power of confirming the first one to follow that man, but also (lest by any chance he escapes punishment) be debarred from receiving the fruits of his own benefice until he can justly obtain a pardon; if convicted of having intentionally transgressed in the matter, let him suffer a heavier penalty. Bishops too shall endeavor to promote to holy orders and ecclesiastical dignities such as are able to discharge worthily the office

---

14 *I.e.*, totals, not the individual votes.

committed to them, if they themselves wish to escape canonical penalty. For the rest, those who are immediately under the Roman pontiff shall, to get confirmation of their office, appear personally before him if it can be conveniently done or send suitable persons, by means of whom careful inquiry into election procedure and into those who are elected can be made, so that in the end, on the strength of his informed judgment, they may attain the full authority of their office, when nothing in the canon law stands in their way—provided meanwhile that those who are in very distant posts, that is outside Italy, may by dispensation, if they were elected peaceably, where it meets the church's needs or is to its advantage administer in things spiritual and temporal, but shall alienate nothing whatever belonging to the church. They may be given the customary consecration or benediction.

27. As the governing of souls is the art of arts, we strictly command bishops carefully to prepare those who are to be promoted to the priesthood and instruct them, either personally or through other suitable men, in the divine services and the sacraments of the church, in order that they may know how to celebrate them properly: since if they presume in future to ordain the ignorant and unskilled (which could indeed be easily detected) we decree that both those who ordain and those who are ordained are to be subject to punishment. For it is better, particularly in the ordaining of priests, to have a few good than many bad ministers, because if the blind leads the blind both will fall into the ditch.

28. Certain people persistently demand leave to resign and having got it omit to do so. But in demanding such resignation they would seem to have in mind either the good of the churches over which they preside or their own wellbeing, neither of which things do we wish to be impeded by the advice of those seeking their own or even by any fickleness of purpose: we therefore decree that they are to be compelled to resign.

29. With great foresight it was prohibited in the [Third] Lateran council for anyone to receive divers ecclesiastical dignities and several parish churches contrary to the ordinances of canon law

on pain both of the receiver losing what he has thus received and of the one bestowing being deprived of the power to bestow. But as, owing to the presumption and greed of some, the said statute has borne no fruit, or very little, we, wishing to counter with a surer and stronger remedy, ordain by the present decree that whoever receives a benefice with cure of souls attached, if he already has such a benefice shall automatically be deprived of that and if perchance he tries to keep it let him be deprived of the other one also. Also he who has the giving of the first benefice shall freely bestow it, after the receiving of the second, on a person on whom he considers it can worthily be bestowed, but if he delays more than three months over bestowing it not only shall the bestowal of it devolve upon another in accordance with the statute of the Lateran council but also he shall be forced to assign for the use of the church of the benefice in question as much from his own income as is established was obtained from it while it was vacant. The very same we decree is to be done with regard to minor dignities, adding that no one shall presume to have several dignities or minor dignities in one and the same church even if they do not have cure of souls. As to men of birth and lettered persons, who should be honored by greater benefices, they when reason demands it can be dispensed by the apostolic see.

30. It is very serious and improper that certain heads of churches, when they could promote serious men to ecclesiastical benefices, fear not to adopt unworthy people recommended neither by upright living nor by learning, following the inclination of their heart, not the judgment of their reason. How much churches lose by this every man of right mind knows. Wishing therefore to cure this malady, we order them to pass over the unworthy and choose suitable people, who have both the desire and the ability to serve God and churches well, and let careful enquiry be made about this each year in provincial council, so that he who is found guilty after a first and a second correction shall be suspended by that council from conferring benefices, and a prudent and honest person appointed in that same council to take the place of the one suspended in conferring benefices; and the very same is to be done with regard to chapters who offend in these things. An

offense by a metropolitan shall however be left by the council to be reported to the judgment of a superior. So that this salutary provision shall have its full effect, a sentence of suspension of this kind shall definitely not be lifted without the authority of the Roman pontiff or of the appropriate patriarch—that in this too the four patriarchal sees may be specially honored.

31. To abolish a very bad corruption indeed which has been on the increase in many churches, we firmly prohibit sons of canons, particularly as they are bastards, being made canons in secular churches where their fathers are established; and if in spite of this it is attempted, we decree it not valid. And they who, as has been said, venture to make canons of such shall be suspended from their benefices.

32. A vicious custom that ought to be uprooted has established itself in some parts, namely that patrons of parish churches, and certain other persons, claim the incomes from them wholly for themselves, leaving the priests deputed to serve them so small a portion that they cannot fittingly live on it. We have learnt for certain that in some regions parish priests get for their support only a quarter of a quarter, that is a sixteenth, of the tithes. Whence it is said that in these regions scarcely any parish priest can be found who has even a modicum of education. As the ox ought not to be muzzled when it treadeth out the corn, and he who serves the altar ought to live from the altar, we decree therefore, any custom of a bishop or patron or anyone else notwithstanding, that a sufficient portion shall be assigned to the priests. He who has a parish church shall serve it not by a vicar but personally in the due form which the care of that church requires, unless perchance the parish church is annexed to a prebend or a dignity. In which case we allow that he who has such a prebend or dignity should, as he must serve in a greater church, make it his business to have in the parish church a suitable, canonically instituted perpetual[15] vicar, who, as has been said, shall have a fitting portion from the revenues of that church: otherwise, he shall know that by the authority of this decree he is deprived of that church and it is

to be given freely to someone else who is willing and able to do as we have said. What we utterly forbid is that anyone should presume deceitfully to confer from the revenues of a church which has to maintain its own priest a pension on another as it were as a benefice.

33. Procurations due, by reason of visitation, to bishops, archdeacons, or anyone else, also to legates or nuncios of the apostolic see, should by no means, without manifest and necessary cause, be exacted, save when they actually incur the expense of visitation, and then they shall observe the moderation in transport and retinue decreed in the [Third] Lateran council. We add this modification as regards legates and nuncios of the apostolic see, that when they must necessarily stay in some place, so that this place may not be excessively burdened because of them they may receive moderate procurations from other churches or persons who have not yet been burdened with their procurations, on condition that the number of procurations shall not exceed the number of days they stayed in that place, and when any person has not sufficient means on his own, two or more may be combined into one. Rather, those performing the office of visitation shall not seek their own but the things which are Jesus Christ's, by devoting themselves to preaching, exhortation, correction, and reformation, that they may bring back the fruit which does not perish. He who presumes to contravene this shall both restore what he has received and pay the same amount as compensation to the church he has thus burdened.

34. Many prelates, to meet the cost of a procuration or some service to a legate or some other person, extort more from their subordinates than they pay out, and trying to gain from their loss, seek booty rather than aid from those under them. This we forbid to be done in future. And if perchance anyone ventures to do it let him both restore what has been thus extorted and be forced to distribute an equivalent amount to the poor. A superior with whom a complaint has been lodged about this shall, if he is negligent in executing this decree, suffer canonical punishment.

---

15   *I.e.*, with security of tenure, not removable.

35. In order that due honor be paid to judges and thought taken for litigants in the matter of trouble and expense, we decree that when anybody sues an adversary before the competent judge, he shall not before judgment has been given appeal to a superior judge without reasonable cause, but proceed with his suit before that one and it shall not be open to him to obstruct by saying that he has sent a messenger to a superior judge or even procured letters from him before they were remitted to the judge delegate. When, however, in his view he has reasonable cause for appealing, and has stated before that same judge the grounds of the appeal and these are such that if they were proved they would be reckoned legitimate, the superior judge shall take cognizance of the appeal. If he finds it not reasonable he shall send the appellant back to the inferior judge and sentence him to bear the costs of the other party; otherwise he shall proceed with the case, saving the constitutions about referring major cases to the apostolic see.

36. As when the cause ceases the effect ceases, we decree that if a judge ordinary or a judge delegate has pronounced a comminatory or interlocutory sentence on anything, an order for the execution of which would prejudice one of the parties and on good advice refrains from putting it into effect, he shall proceed freely with the hearing of the case, notwithstanding any appeal made against such comminatory or interlocutory sentence (provided his action is not open to question on any other legal ground), in order that the action may not be held up for frivolous reasons.

37. Some abusing the grace of the holy see try to sue out writs from it to distant judges so that the one sued, tired of the trouble and expense of the action, shall have to give in to or come to terms with the bringer of the action. But since a way should not be opened by a court of justice for wrongs which observance of the law forbids, we decree that nobody can be dragged outside his diocese, unless it was procured with the assent of both parties and it expressly mentions this constitution. There are others, too, who, turning to a new kind of trade, to revive complaints that are dormant or to introduce new questions invent causes, for which they sue out writs from

the apostolic see without authority from their superiors and offer them for sale, either to the party sued that he may not be vexed by an outlay of trouble and expense because of them, or to the bringer of the action that he through them may tire out the adversary with undue vexations. But since lawsuits should be shortened rather than prolonged, we by this general edict decree that if anybody on any question presumes in future to sue out papal writs without special mandate from his superior, both the writs shall be invalid and he himself punished as a maker of false documents, unless he happens to be one of those from whom a mandate rightly ought not to be required.

38. Against a false assertion of an unjust judge an innocent litigator is never at any time able to prove the truth by a denial, as the act of denying is not in the nature of things at all a direct proof. So, lest the false should prejudice the truth or iniquity prevail over equity, we decree that in both ordinary and extraordinary judicial proceedings the judge shall always employ either a public official [*publica persona*, i.e., a notary], if he can get one, or two suitable men to draw up faithfully all judicial acts (that is to say, citations, adjournments, objections and exceptions, petitions and answers, interrogations, confessions, depositions of witnesses, productions of documents, interlocutions, appeals, renunciations, final decisions and the rest of the things that call for proper drafting) specifying places, times and persons; and everything thus written is to be given to the parties on condition that the originals are kept by the writers, so that if dispute arises over the handling of the case by the judge the truth can be established from them. With the application of this measure such deference will be paid to upright and experienced judges that justice will not be impaired for the innocent by imprudent and wicked judges. A judge who neglects to observe this decree shall, if any difficulty results from his neglect, be punished by a superior judge with the punishment he deserves, nor shall there be a presumption in favor of his procedure save to the extent that it accords with the legal documents.

39. It often happens that a man unjustly deprived of something loses in effect the right to it, because of the difficulty of proof when the one who

deprived him of it has transferred it to a third party, there being no remedy at law for the deprived by means of an action for restitution against the possessor, the advantage of possession having changed hands. Wherefore, notwithstanding the strict civil law, we decree that if anyone in future knowingly receives such a thing (taking over as it were, too, the fault of the depredator because there is not much difference, particularly as regards peril to the soul, between unjustly withholding and seizing the property of another), as a help against this sort of possessor the deprived is to have the benefit of restitution.

40. It sometimes happens that a plaintiff who, on account of the contumacy of the opposing party, has the possession of a thing adjudged to him to look after, is not able to get it into his possession within a year because of force or fraud over it, or having got it loses it, and thus, since in the opinion of many he does not qualify as the true possessor at the end of the year, the defendant profits by his wickedness. Therefore so that a contumacious party shall not be in a better position than one who obeys a citation, we decree in the name of canonical equity that in the case aforesaid the plaintiff shall when a year has elapsed be accepted as the true possessor. Furthermore, we prohibit generally submission of spiritual matters to the arbitration of a layman, because it is not fitting for a layman to arbitrate in such things.

41. As "Whatsoever is not of faith is sin," we define by synodal decree that no prescription, canonical or civil, is valid without good faith, since generally any statute or custom is to be discounted which cannot be observed without committing mortal sin. So that it behooves one who claims a prescriptive right to have had no knowledge at any stage that the thing was someone else's.

42. Just as it is our will that laymen should not usurp the rights of clerks, so it ought to be our will that clerks should not lay claim to the rights of laymen. For which reason we forbid every clerk in future on the pretext of ecclesiastical freedom to extend his jurisdiction to the detriment of

secular justice: let him be content with the written laws and the customs up to now approved, in order that by a right distribution "the things that are Caesar's" may be rendered unto Caesar and "the things that are God's" rendered unto God.

43. Some laymen try to encroach too far upon divine right when they force churchmen who hold nothing temporal from them to take oaths of fealty to them. Because, according to the apostle, a servant "to his own master standeth or falleth," we prohibit by the authority of holy council such clerks to be compelled to take an oath of this sort to secular persons.

44. Laymen, however devout, have no power to dispose of church property: their lot is to obey, not to be in command. We deplore it, then, when in some of them charity grows so cold that the freedom of the church, which not only the holy fathers but secular rulers too have buttressed by many privileges, they do not fear to attack by their decrees, or rather their devices; by not only alienating fiefs and other ecclesiastical possessions and usurping jurisdictions but also illegally appropriating mortuaries as well as other things connected with spiritual property. It being our wish to ensure the immunity of churches from these things and to provide against such great injuries, we pronounce, with the approval of holy council, such decrees and the claiming of fiefs or other ecclesiastical goods appropriated under a decree of a lay power without the lawful assent of the ecclesiastical authorities, not valid, as it could be termed not a decree but a deprivation or molestation. Those who expropriate the church are to be curbed by its censures.

45. In certain provinces, patrons or vidames[16] and advocates of churches display so much arrogance that they not only create difficulties and snares when vacant churches have to be provided with suitable pastors but also presume to dispose of church possessions and other church goods as they like, and, dreadful to relate, fear does not deter them from murdering prelates. Since therefore what has been devised as a protection ought not

---

16   A secular official chosen to perform duties on behalf of the church.

to be turned into a roundabout way of oppression, we expressly forbid patrons or advocates or vidames in future to appropriate the aforesaid things to a greater extent than they are entitled to by law; and if contrary to this they do presume, they are to be curbed with the utmost severity of the canon law. Equally, with the approbation of the sacred council we decree that if patrons or advocates or feudatories or vidames or others with benefices venture with unspeakable daring either in person or through others to kill or maim the rector of any church or other clerk of that church they shall surrender completely, patrons the right of patronage, feudatories the fief, vidames the dignity of vidame, the beneficed their benefice. And lest the punishment be less well remembered than the offense, not only shall nothing from the aforesaid things pass to their heirs, but also their posterity to the fourth generation shall by no means be admitted into a college of clerks or attain a position of any authority in houses of regulars, save when out of compassion they are given dispensation.

46. With regard to consuls and rulers of cities and others who endeavor to oppress churches and churchmen by tallages or levies or other exactions, the [Third] Lateran council, wishing to preserve ecclesiastical immunity, strictly forbade such presumption on pain of anathema, ordering offenders and their abettors to be subject to excommunication until they give suitable satisfaction. If, however, when for instance the bishop and his clergy together foresee a necessity or advantage so great that without any coercion, for the common good or the common need when the resources of laymen do not suffice, they consider churches should give subsidies, the aforesaid laymen shall humbly and devoutly receive them and give thanks. But as some are imprudent, let the Roman pontiff, whose business it is to see to the common good, be consulted beforehand. We decree further that, since as things now stand the malice of certain people towards the church of God has not abated, decrees and sentences promulgated by those excommunicated on this score or at their command shall be deemed null and void and never at any time to be valid. Besides, as fraud and guile ought not to protect anyone,

let no one be duped by foolish error into resisting anathema during his time of authority as if after it he would not be compelled to give due satisfaction; for we decree that both he who has refused to give satisfaction and his successor (if he has not satisfied within a month) are to remain bound by ecclesiastical censure until suitable satisfaction is given, since he who succeeds to an office succeeds to its responsibilities.

47. With the approbation of the holy council we forbid anybody to venture to promulgate sentence of excommunication on anyone save after sufficient warning in the presence of suitable persons, who can if necessary testify to this warning. If anybody does contravene this, even if the sentence of excommunication is just, he shall know that entry to a church is forbidden him for a month and he shall nonetheless be punished with another penalty if that seems expedient. Let him also be careful not to proceed to the excommunication of anyone without manifest and reasonable cause. If perchance he does so proceed and, on being humbly requested, does not take the trouble to revoke the process without imposing punishment, the injured party may put in a complaint of unjust excommunication to a superior judge. This superior, if he can do it without danger from the delay, shall send him back to the one who excommunicated him with orders for him to be absolved by some suitably appointed date, otherwise he, the superior, will, either personally or through another as shall be expedient, on receiving sufficient security give him absolution. Whenever a case of unjust excommunication is made out against an excommunicator, he shall be condemned to pay the excommunicated compensation for damages, and be nonetheless punished in another way at the will of the superior judge if the nature of the offense calls for it—for it is not a light offense to inflict so great a punishment on someone innocent—unless it can be shown that he acted in error, particularly if he is of praiseworthy reputation. If, however, against the sentence of excommunication nothing reasonable is proved by the complainant, it is he who for the trouble caused by an unjustified complaint shall be condemned to be punished by having to pay compensation or in another way at the discretion of the superior

judge, unless in his case it can be shown that there is the excuse of error, and moreover he shall be compelled upon security to give satisfaction for that for which he was justly excommunicated or be subjected once more to the initial sentence until fully adequate satisfaction without remission has been given. Should, however, the judge of first instance acknowledge his error and be prepared to revoke the sentence but he for whose benefit it was passed appeals, for fear it may be revoked without satisfaction being exacted, appeal shall not be admitted in this regard unless the error is such that there can properly be doubt about it; in this case the judge, giving sufficient security that he will stand trial before the judge appealed to or one delegated by him, shall absolve the excommunicate and thus not be subject at all to the prescribed punishment—every precaution being taken that he does not wish with the wicked purpose of harming somebody pretend to have erred, if he wishes to escape strict canonical punishment.

48. As there is a special provision forbidding anybody to venture to promulgate sentence of excommunication on anyone save after sufficient warning[17] and as we wish to provide against the possibility of the one warned being able, by means of a fraudulent objection or appeal, to avoid examination by the giver of the warning, we decree that if he alleges he considers the judge suspect he shall, before this same judge, bring an action of just suspicion, and he himself in agreement with his adversary (or, if he happens not to have an adversary, with the judge) shall choose the arbiters or if it happens that they cannot reach agreement they shall choose without evil intent he one and the other another to take cognizance of the action of suspicion. If they, the arbiters, cannot reach an agreed decision they shall call in a third, so that what two of them decree shall have binding force. They are to know also that this they are bound, in accordance with the command strictly enjoined by us in virtue of obedience under the testimony of the divine judgment, faithfully to give effect to. If the action of suspicion is not legally established before them within a sufficient time the judge shall exercise his jurisdiction. If on the other hand it is legally established, with the assent of the objector

the judge objected to shall commit the matter to a suitable person or transmit it to a superior judge that he may conduct it as it should be conducted. Furthermore, if a person warned is resorting to appeal and his transgression is manifest from the evidence or by his confession or in some other lawful way—as the remedy of appeal has not been established to defend iniquity but to protect innocence—such an appeal is not to be allowed. If his transgression is in any doubt, the appellant, in order that he may not by the subterfuge of a frivolous appeal, impede the action of the judge, shall set out before him the verifiable grounds of the appeal, such that if they were verified would have to be considered legitimate. Then if he has an adversary, by a date to be fixed by the same judge according to the distance between places, the circumstances, and the nature of the business, he shall proceed with the appeal, and if he does not trouble to proceed with it, forthwith the judge himself shall proceed, notwithstanding the appeal. If no adversary appears, the judge shall proceed *ex officio* and once the grounds of the appeal have been verified before the superior judge, the superior shall exercise his office as judge. But if the appellant fails to get the grounds of his appeal verified he shall be sent back to him from whom it has been established he appealed maliciously. We do not however wish the above two constitutions to apply to regulars, who have their own special observances.

49. Under the threat of divine judgment we absolutely forbid anyone out of cupidity to dare to bind someone with the bond of excommunication or to absolve anyone so bound, especially in those regions where by custom when an excommunicate is absolved he is punished by a money penalty; and we decree that when it is established that a sentence of excommunication was unjust he who imposed it shall be compelled by ecclesiastical censure to restore the money thus extorted, and, unless he demonstrably acted in error, he shall pay his victim as much again and if perchance he cannot pay he shall be punished in another way.

50. It should not be judged reprehensible if men's decrees are varied at some time or other in

---

17   The reference is to the preceding canon, No. 47.

accordance with changing circumstances, especially when urgent necessity or evident advantages requires it, since God himself, of the things he decreed in the Old Testament, has changed some in the New. Since therefore the prohibitions about contracting marriage in the second or third degree of affinity and about uniting the offspring of a second marriage to the kindred of the first husband frequently lead to difficulty and sometimes endanger souls, we, inasmuch as when the prohibition ceases the effect ceases, revoke with the approval of the holy council decrees published on this subject and by the present constitution decree that contracting parties connected in these ways may in future be freely united. Also the prohibition of marriage shall not in future exceed the fourth degree of the consanguinity and affinity, since in grades beyond that such prohibition cannot now be generally complied with without grave harm. The number four agrees well with bodily marriage—of which the apostle says, "The husband hath not power of his own body, but the wife, neither has the wife power of her own body, but the husband"—because there are four humors in the body, which is composed of the four elements. As the prohibition of marriage is now restricted to the fourth degree it is our will that it should be unqualified, notwithstanding decrees published before on this subject whether by others or by us, so that if any presume to be united contrary to this prohibition they shall not be protected by length of time, since lapse of time does not diminish a sin but increases it, and the graver offenses are, the longer they keep the unfortunate soul in bondage.

51. As the prohibition of marriage in the three remotest degrees is repealed, we wish it to be strictly observed in the others. Hence, following in the steps of our predecessors, we absolutely prohibit clandestine marriages, forbidding also any priest to presume to be present at such. For which reason we extend the particular custom of certain countries to countries generally, decreeing that when marriages are to be contracted they shall be published in the churches by the priests, a suitable period being fixed beforehand within which whoever wants and is able to may adduce a lawful impediment. Those priests shall nevertheless find out whether any impediment exists. When

it seems probable that there is an impediment to contracting a union, the contract shall be expressly forbidden, until it is clear from documents produced what ought to be done about it. If any presume to enter into such clandestine marriages or forbidden marriages in a prohibited degree even in ignorance, the issue begotten of such union shall be reckoned truly illegitimate with no help to be had from the ignorance of the parents, since they by contracting such unions could be regarded as not devoid of knowledge or at least as affecting ignorance. Likewise the offspring shall be reckoned illegitimate if both parents, knowing of a lawful impediment, presume to contract marriage in the presence of the church, contrary to every prohibition. Certainly a parish priest who does not trouble to forbid such unions or any regular also, whatever his order, who ventures to be present at them, shall be suspended from office for three years, and more severely punished if the nature of the office demands it. And for those too who presume to be united in such fashion, even in a permitted degree, an adequate penance shall be enjoined. If however any one, to impede a legitimate union, alleges out of wickedness an impediment, he shall not escape ecclesiastical punishment.

52. Although, contrary to normal practice, it was at one time of a certain necessity decided that in reckoning degrees of consanguinity and affinity hearsay evidence should be valid seeing that owing to the short life of man witnesses cannot testify from personal knowledge in a reckoning as far as the seventh degree, nevertheless, because from numerous instances and definite proofs we have learnt that many dangers for lawful unions have arisen from this, we decree that in this matter witnesses from hearsay are not to be admitted in future (since the prohibition does not now go beyond the fourth degree) unless there exist persons of weight who are trustworthy and who testified before the cause was begun to things they learnt from their elders: not merely from one of them, since he alone if he were alive would not suffice, but from at least two, and they not of bad repute and suspect, but trustworthy and quite unexceptionable, since it would seem rather absurd to admit those whose actions would be rejected; nor if one got from a number what he testifies to, or if a

number with bad reputations got what they testify to from men with good, should he be admitted as if he were more than one, or they as if they were suitable witnesses, since, according to normal legal practice, the assertion of a single witness is not sufficient even if he were resplendent with authority, and legal actions are forbidden to those of bad repute. Such witnesses shall declare on oath that in bearing witness in the cause they do not act from hate or fear or love or for advantage; shall indicate persons by their exact names or by gesture or by sufficient description; shall distinguish by clear reckoning every degree of relationship on either side; and, finally, shall include in their oath the statement that what they depose in evidence they got from their forefathers and they believe it to be correct. Still, they shall not be sufficient unless they declare on oath that to their knowledge the persons belonging to at least one of the aforesaid degrees regard each other as blood-relations. For it is preferable to allow some unions that are contrary to the laws of man than to contravene the law of God by parting those lawfully joined.

53. In some regions there are mingled certain peoples who in accordance with their rites by custom do not pay tithes, although they are counted as Christians. To these people some landed lords assign their lands to be cultivated in order, by cheating churches of the tithes, to get greater revenues from them. Wishing therefore to provide for the immunity of churches from these things, we ordain that, when lords make over their lands for cultivation to such persons in such a way, they shall pay the tithes to the churches without objection and in full, themselves, and if necessary be compelled to do so by ecclesiastical censure. Those tithes are of necessity payable inasmuch as they are due by divine law and accepted local custom.

54. It is not in man's power for the seed to answer to the hopes of the sower, since in the words of the apostle, "Neither is he that planteth anything, neither he that watereth, but God that giveth the increase," he who from the dead seed bringeth forth much fruit, and some from excess of greed endeavor to cheat over the tithes, deducting from the crops and first-fruits the rents and dues, which meanwhile are got by untithed. But since

as a sign of universal dominion, and by a certain special title as it were, the Lord has reserved tithes to himself, we, wishing to prevent both injury to churches and danger to souls, decree that in virtue of this general dominion payment of tithes is to precede payment of dues and rents, or at least those who receive untithed rents and dues shall, seeing that a thing carries with it its burden, be forced by ecclesiastical censure to tithe them for the churches to whom by right they are due.

55. Lately abbots of the Cistercian order assembled in general chapter wisely decreed at our instance that brothers of that order shall not in future buy property from which tithes are due to churches, unless it might be for founding new monasteries. And if such property is conferred on them by the pious devotion of the faithful or bought for founding new monasteries, they shall assign them for cultivation to others by whom the tithes shall be paid to churches, lest because of their privileges churches be permanently deprived. We accordingly decree that on lands assigned to others and on future acquisitions, even if they cultivate them with their own hands or at their own expense, they shall pay tithes to the churches to which because of the lands they were previously paid, unless they think fit to compound with those churches. Considering this sort of statute as acceptable and right, we will that it be extended to other regulars who enjoy like privileges and we command prelates of churches to be readier and prompter in affording them full justice with regard to those who wrong them and to be at pains to maintain their privileges more carefully and completely.

56. Many regulars, we understand, and sometimes secular clerks, in letting houses or granting fiefs add, to the prejudice of parish churches, a covenant that the tenants and vassals should pay them the tithes and choose burial in their ground. Since it springs from avarice, we utterly disapprove of such a pact and decree that whatever is received because of such a pact shall be surrendered to the parish church.

57. In order that charters which the Roman church has granted to certain religious may

remain intact, we have come to the conclusion that certain things in them should be clarified, lest through being not well understood they lead to abuse, on which account they could justly be revoked, for he deserves to lose his charter who abuses power granted to him.

The apostolic see has rightly given an indult[18] to certain regulars that Christian burial shall not be denied to those who have become members of their fraternity if perchance the churches they belong to are under interdict and they happen to die, unless they are excommunicate or interdicted by name, and they may carry away members of their fraternity whom heads of churches will not permit to be buried in their churches to their own churches for burial, unless they were excommunicate or interdicted by name. But by members of their fraternity we understand this: either those who while still in this world have offered themselves to their order and changed their secular habit, or those who in their lifetime have given them their property, keeping for as long as they live the usufruct of it. They are only to be buried in the churches of these regulars or in churches not under interdict belonging to others which they have elected to be buried in, for if it were understood of anybody acquiring membership of their fraternity by paying them twopence or threepence a year ecclesiastical discipline would be at the same time loosened and cheapened, though even they may get a certain remission allowed them by the apostolic see.

Another indult has been given to such regulars: that if any of their brothers sent by them to receive dues or fraternity—money come to any city, castle or place which happens to be under an interdict, churches shall be opened once a year at their "joyous advent" for divine services to be celebrated there, the excommunicate being excluded. This we wish to be understood thus—that in the same city or castle or place one church only shall be opened to the brothers of that order as has been said once a year. Because although it is said in the plural "churches shall be opened at their joyous advent," this on a rational explanation refers not to churches of one place but churches of the said places as a whole: for if in this way they

visited all the churches of one place the sentence of interdict would incur too much contempt.

They who venture to usurp anything for themselves contrary to the above-written explanations shall undergo severe punishment.

58. The indult which has been given to some religious we extend to bishops in respect of their episcopal office, granting that when a country is under a general interdict they can sometimes—the excommunicate and persons interdicted being excluded—behind closed doors, in a lowered voice, and without the ringing of bells celebrate divine service, unless this has been expressly forbidden them. We grant this, however, to those who have not in any way occasioned the interdict, lest they introduce any guile or fraud and turn the gain into a wicked loss.

59. What to certain religious is forbidden by the apostolic see we will and command to be extended to all: that no religious may without the leave of his abbot and the majority of his chapter be surety for anyone or accept a loan from another for a sum bigger than that decided on by the common opinion. Otherwise the community shall not be held at all responsible for these things, unless perchance the matter has manifestly redounded to the advantage of the house. And he who presumes to contravene this statute shall be subject to the severest discipline.

60. From complaints we get from bishops in various parts of the world, we have become aware of grave and great excesses committed by certain abbots, who not content with the frontiers of their own authority reach out to those of the episcopal dignity, taking cognizance of matrimonial causes, enjoining public penances, granting even letters of indulgence and like presumptions, from which it sometimes happens that for many episcopal authority is cheapened. Wishing therefore to provide in these things for both the dignity of bishops and the well-being of abbots, we by the present decree strictly forbid any of the abbots to presume to reach for such things, if he wishes to avoid danger for himself, unless perchance any

---

18 Permission granted by a church authority for an exemption from a canon law requirement.

of them by special concession or other legitimate cause is able to defend himself in respect of such things.

61. For any regulars to presume to receive churches or tithes from lay hands without the consent of the bishops or to admit to any divine services those under excommunication or those interdicted by name is known to have been prohibited under the [Third] Lateran Council. We now prohibit it more strongly and will see that the offenders are punished by penalties which are adequate. We confirm, nevertheless, that in churches which do not fully belong to them they shall, in accordance with the statutes of that council, present priests who are to be instituted to the bishops for examination by them about the care of the people: to themselves they are to avoid evidence of sufficient sense in things temporal. They shall not dare to remove them once they are instituted without first consulting the bishops; indeed we add that they shall try to present those who are either noted for their way of life or recommended on verifiable grounds by the bishops.

62. Because some put up saints' relics for sale and display them indiscriminately the Christian religion is very often disparaged. So, in order that it may not be disparaged in future, we ordain by the present decree that ancient relics from now on are not to be shown outside the reliquary or put up for sale. As for newly-discovered relics, let no one venture to venerate them publicly without their having first been approved by the authority of the Roman pontiff. Neither should prelates in future allow those who come to their churches in order to venerate to be deceived by vain fictions or false documents, as has commonly happened in many places for the getting of alms. We forbid, too, questors of alms, some of whom deceive one another, advancing in their preaching a number of errors, to be recognized unless they show genuine letters from the pope or the diocesan bishop. Even then they shall be allowed to put forward to the people nothing beyond what is contained in those letters. We have indeed thought it well to give a copy of the form of letter which the apostolic see generally

grants to such persons, in order that diocesan bishops may model their own letters on it. It is thus:

Since, as the apostle says, "we shall all stand before the judgment seat of Christ" to receive as we have "done in the body, whether it be good or bad,"[19] it behooves us to prepare for the day of the last judgment by works of mercy and for the sake of eternity to sow on earth what, God giving us it back multiplied, we should collect in heaven—keeping a firm hope and confidence, since "He that soweth sparingly shall reap also sparingly, and he that soweth in blessings, of blessings shall also reap for life eternal."[20] To support the brethren and the indigent who flock into such and such hospital its own resources do not suffice. We therefore admonish and exhort you all in the Lord and for the remission of your sins enjoin you from the goods God has conferred upon you to bestow pious alms and to give them grateful charitable assistance so that through your help their need may be cared for and you, by these and other good things which, God inspiring you, you have done, can attain eternal happiness.

Let those who are sent in quest of alms be modest and discreet, they are not to put up in taverns or other unsuitable places or incur unnecessary expense, being careful above all not to bear the garb of false religion. Moreover, because of indiscriminate and excessive indulgences, which certain heads of churches are not afraid to grant, the keys of the church are brought into contempt and at the same time penitential satisfaction loses force; we accordingly decree that when a church is dedicated the indulgence shall be not for more than a year, whether it is dedicated by one bishop or by more than one, and then for the anniversary of the dedication the remission granted shall not exceed forty days of the penance imposed. We order the letters of indulgence which are granted for various reasons at different times to fix this number of days also, since the Roman pontiff himself, who possesses the plenitude of power, generally observes this moderation in such things.

63. As we have learnt for certain, shameful and wicked exactions and extortions are levied in many places and by many persons, sellers of doves

---

19   Romans 14:10.
20   2 Corinthians 9:6.

in the temple as it were, for the consecration of bishops, the blessing of abbots and the ordaining of clerks, and it is fixed how much is to be paid for this or that and how much for another or yet another, and, verging on the utterly damnable, there are some who strive to defend such base and crooked conduct on the grounds of old-established custom. Wishing to abolish so great an abuse, we thoroughly reject a custom such as this, which should rather be termed a corruption, and firmly decree that no one shall presume to exact anything under any pretext whatever for conferring things or for things conferred; otherwise both he who receives and he who gives so absolutely condemned a payment as this shall be condemned with Gehazi and Simon.

64. The stain of simony has discolored many nuns to such an extent that they admit scarcely any as sisters without payment—wishing to cover this vice with the pretext of poverty. We absolutely forbid this to happen in future and ordain that whoever commits such wickedness in future, both she who admits and she who is admitted, whether she is just a nun or in authority, shall be expelled from her convent without hope of reinstatement and thrust into a house of stricter observance to do perpetual penance. As to those who have thought fit to provide that they be removed from the convents they entered wrongly and placed in other houses of the same order. But if perchance there are too many of them to be conveniently placed elsewhere they are, by dispensation, so as not to roam about and perhaps imperil their souls in the world, to be admitted afresh to the same convent, with a change of superior and of the inferior offices of the houses. This, we decree, is to be observed with regard to monks and other regulars also. Yet, that they may not be able to excuse themselves on grounds of simplicity or ignorance, we command diocesan bishops to have this published all over their dioceses each year.

65. We have heard that certain bishops on the death of rectors of churches put these churches under an interdict and do not allow anyone to be instituted to them until they themselves have had a certain sum of money paid to them. Further, when a knight or a clerk enters a house of religion or chooses burial with religious, although he may have left nothing to the house, they cunningly make difficulties until their hand touches something in the way of a present. Therefore, since one should abstain not only from evil but also, according to the apostle, "from all appearance of evil," we absolutely forbid exactions of this sort: and any transgressor shall restore double what was exacted, this to be faithfully used for the benefit of places prejudiced by the exactions.

66. It comes frequently to the ears of the pope that certain clerks exact and extort payments for funeral rites for the dead, the blessing of those being married, and the like, and if it happens that their greed is not satisfied they deceitfully set up false impediments. In retaliation some laymen, from a ferment of heretical wickedness, try to break with what is for holy church a laudable custom introduced by the pious devotion of the faithful, on the pretext of canonical scruples. For which reason we alike forbid the wicked exactions to be made in these matters and order the pious customs to be kept, ordaining that the sacraments of the church are to be given freely, but also that those who maliciously try to alter a laudable custom are, when the truth is known, to be restrained by the bishop of the place.

67. The more Christianity is restrained from exacting interest that much more strongly does the dishonesty of the Jews in these matters grow, so that in a short time they exhaust the means of Christians. Wanting therefore in this business to see that Christians are not savagely opposed by Jews, we ordain by conciliar decree that if in future on any pretext whatever Jews extort oppressive and excessive interest from Christians they shall be allowed no contact with Christians until they have made suitable amends for the excessive burden. Christians too, if need be, shall be compelled by ecclesiastical censure without appeal to abstain from dealings with them. We enjoin upon rulers not to be hostile to Christians on this account, but, rather, zealous in restraining Jews from such great oppression. And by the same penalty Jews shall, we decree, be compelled to compensate churches for tithes and offerings due to them which they used to receive from Christians

for houses and other possessions before these went by whatever title to the Jews, so that churches may be preserved from loss.

68. In some provinces a difference of dress distinguishes Jews or Saracens from Christians, but in certain others such confusion has developed that they are indistinguishable. Whence it sometimes happens that by mistake Christians unite with Jewish or Saracen women and Jews or Saracens with Christian. Therefore, in order that so reprehensible and outrageous a mixing cannot for the future spread under cover of the excuse of an error of this kind, we decree that such people of either sex in every Christian province and at all times shall be distinguished from other people by the character of their dress in public, seeing that in addition one finds that this was enjoined upon them by Moses himself. On the days of Lamentation and on Passion Sunday they shall not appear in public at all, because some of them on such days, so we have heard, do not blush to parade in their most elegant clothes and are not afraid to ridicule the Christians, who exhibit a memorial of the most holy Passion and display signs of grief. What we most strictly forbid is for them to venture to burst out at all in derision of the Redeemer. And as we ought not to ignore the insulting of Him who atoned for our sins, we order secular rulers to inflict condign punishment upon those who so venture, to restrain them from daring at all to blaspheme Him who was crucified for us.

69. It would be too absurd for a blasphemer of Christ to be in a position of authority over Christians and what the council of Toledo[21] providently laid down on this we, because of the boldness of transgressors, here renew, forbidding Jews to be appointed to public office, since with such authority they are very hostile to Christians. Whoever commits such office to them shall by the provincial council—which we order to be held annually—be first admonished then curbed by an appropriate sanction. The officer so appointed shall be denied communion with Christians in

business and in other things as long as whatever he has got from Christians by reason of his office thus acquired is not converted in accordance with the stipulations of the diocesan bishop to the use of poor Christians, and the office he disrespectfully assumed he shall surrender out of shame. We extend this same thing to pagans.

70. Some, we have learnt, who have come voluntarily to the water of holy baptism do not wholly cast off the old man to put on completely the new, when, keeping parts of their old rite, they upset by such mixing the decorum of the Christian religion. But since it is written "Woe unto the man who goes into a land two ways" and "A garment ought not to be put on woven of linen and wool together," we decree that such persons shall be completely stopped by heads of churches from observing their old rite, in order that those who freely offered themselves to the Christian religion may by a salutary coercion be kept from its observance, for it is a lesser evil not to know the way of the Lord than to go back on it after knowing it.

71. It being our ardent aspiration to liberate the Holy Land from infidel hands, we decree, on the advice of men of experience who are fully aware of the circumstances of time and place and with the approbation of the holy council, that crusaders are to make ready so that all who have arranged to go by sea shall assemble in the kingdom of Sicily on the calends of June after next,[22] some as necessary and fitting at Brindisi, the others at Messina and places neighboring it on either side, where we too have arranged to be in person at that time, God willing, in order that by our counsel and aid the Christian army may be in good order for setting out with divine and apostolic benediction. By the same date also they should take care to be ready who have decided to go by land. These shall forewarn us meanwhile, in order that we may grant them a suitable legate *a latere* for counsel and aid. Priests and other clerks, subordinates and prelates as well, who may be in the Christian army shall devote themselves to prayer and exhortation, teaching the troops by word and

---

21 Third Council of Toledo (589) canon 14 forbade Jews to have Christian wives, concubines, or slaves and forbid them to hold public offices in which they might punish Christians.

22 *I.e.*, on June 1, 1217.

example alike to have always before their eyes the fear and love of God and to say or do nothing which might offend the divine majesty. And if ever they fall into sin they shall through true penitence soon rise again, humble of mind and body and observing moderation in way of life and of dress, avoiding all discord and rivalry, having put completely aside all bitterness and envy, so that thus armed with spiritual and material weapons they shall fight the enemies of the faith more safely, relying not on their own power but on that of God. To these clerks we grant that they may receive the fruits of their benefices in full for three years as if they were resident in the churches and, if necessary, have power to put them in pawn for that length of time. To prevent this holy purpose being hindered or delayed, we strictly enjoin on all heads of churches each in his own jurisdiction diligently to warn and induce those who have given up the cross to resume it, and them and others who have taken the cross and those who will take it to fulfil their vows to God, and if necessary compel them to do so without further demur by sentences of excommunication against their persons and of interdict on their lands—those only being excepted who find themselves faced with an obstacle of such a sort that their vow may, in accordance with regulations laid down by the apostolic see, rightly be commuted or postponed.

Furthermore, to prevent anything connected with this matter of Jesus Christ being left undone, we will and command that patriarchs, archbishops, bishops, abbots and others who have cure of souls shall make it their business to preach the cross to those in their charge, earnestly entreating in the name of the Father, the Son and the Holy Ghost, one only true and eternal God, kings, dukes, princes, margraves, counts, barons and other magnates, also the communities of cities, vills and towns, that those who do not go in person to help of the Holy Land should contribute, according to their means, the appropriate number of fighting men with their necessary expenses for three years, for the remission of their sins as is explained in encyclicals and for greater assurance will also be explained below. We wish not only those who furnish their own ships but also those who are zealous enough to build ships for this purpose to participate in this remission. To

those who refuse, if there chance to be any so ungrateful to the Lord our God, we firmly declare in the name of the apostle they are to know they will be answerable to us before the awful judge at the latter day of strict judgment for this and let them ask themselves beforehand with what conscience, with what composure they can confess before the only-begotten Son of God Jesus Christ, to whom "the Father gave all things into his hands," if in this matter which is as it were peculiarly his they refuse to serve Him who was crucified for sinners, by whose beneficence they are sustained, nay more, by whose blood they are redeemed. Lest, however, we appear to put on men's shoulders heavy and unbearable burdens which we are unwilling to move a finger for, like those who say "by all means" but do not do, behold we from what we have been able to save over and above necessary and moderate expenses do grant and give to this work thirty thousand pounds, besides the ship which we are providing for the crusaders of Rome and neighboring districts, and will nonetheless appropriate to this same purpose three thousand marks of silver which we have left over from the alms of certain faithful, the rest having been faithfully distributed for the needs and benefit of the said Land by the hands of Albert, patriarch of Jerusalem, of blessed memory, and the masters of the Temple and the Hospital. But desiring to have other heads of churches and all clerks participate and share in both the merit and the reward, we, with the general approbation of the council, have decreed that all clerks, subordinate as well as prelates, shall give a twentieth part of their ecclesiastical revenues for three years in aid of the Holy Land by means of those appointed for the purpose by apostolic provision, the only exceptions being that certain religious are rightly to be exempted from this taxation, likewise those who have taken or will take the cross and are to go in person.

As for us and our brethren the cardinals of the holy Roman church, we shall pay a full tenth. And let them all know that they are obliged to observe this faithfully on pain of excommunication: so that those who knowingly commit fraud in this matter shall incur sentence of excommunication. Because those who continue in the service of the ruler of heaven ought certainly in justice to enjoy special privilege and as the date of departure is somewhat more than a year ahead, crusaders shall be exempt from levies, tallages and other burdens, and we take their persons and goods under the protection of St. Peter and ourselves once the cross has been taken, ordaining that they are to be safeguarded by the archbishops, bishops and all prelates of the church, deputies to be specially appointed *ad hoc* for their protection so that until there is certain knowledge of their death or of their return their goods may remain intact and undisturbed. If anyone contravenes this he shall be curbed by ecclesiastical censure. If any of those setting out are bound by oath to pay interest, we command their creditors to be compelled by the same punishment to release them from the oath they have taken and to desist from exacting interest. But if any of the creditors does force them to pay interest we order him to be compelled by similar punishment to restore it. Jews we order to be compelled by the secular power to remit interest and until they do so all intercourse shall be refused them by Christians on pain of excommunication. For the benefit of those who are unable at present to pay off their debts to Jews, secular rulers shall so provide for them that from the start of their journey until there is certain knowledge of their death or return they shall not be subject to the inconvenience of interest, the Jews being compelled, after deduction of necessary expenses, to reckon the revenue they have received meanwhile from property held as security towards reduction of the debt: such a benefit does not seem to do much harm in that it defers payment in a way which does not devour the debt. Heads of churches who are negligent in doing justice to crusaders and their families are to know that they will be severely punished.

Furthermore, because corsairs and pirates greatly hinder help to the Holy Land by capturing and plundering those going to or returning from it, we bind with the chain of excommunication those who help and support them. We forbid under threat of anathema anyone to be knowingly party to any contract of sale or purchase with them. We enjoin rulers of cities and their territories to restrain and constrain them from this iniquity: otherwise, because to be unwilling to overthrow wrongdoers is none other than to encourage them and he is not without a touch of

secret complicity who does not oppose a manifest crime, it is our wish and command that ecclesiastical discipline be used against their persons and lands by heads of churches. Furthermore, we excommunicate and anathematise those false and impious Christians who affronting Christ himself and Christian people carry arms and iron and timber for galleys to the Saracens. Those too who sell them galleys or ships and those who pilot Saracen pirate ships or give them any advice or help with machines or anything else to the detriment of the Holy Land we decree are to be punished by being deprived of their possessions and are to be the slaves of those who capture them; and we order such a sentence to be renewed on Sundays and feast-days in every maritime city and the bosom of the church not to be opened for them unless they send in aid of the Holy Land the whole of what they have received of such damnable wealth and the same amount of their own so that they get a punishment proportionate to their offense. But if, perchance, they cannot pay, those guilty of such things shall be punished otherwise in order that through their punishment the audacity to attempt like things may be crushed in others. In addition we prohibit and on pain of anathema forbid all Christians for four years to send or take their ships across to the lands of Saracens in eastern parts, in order that by this a greater supply of shipping may be got ready for those wanting to cross to the help of the Holy Land and the said Saracens deprived of the not inconsiderable help they have been used to getting from it. Although tournaments have been forbidden on pain of a certain penalty in various councils in a general way, we, because the business of a crusade is greatly impeded by them at the present time, strictly forbid them to be held for three years. Because it is of the utmost necessity for the accomplishment of this business that rulers of Christian peoples should keep peace with each other, we ordain on the advice of the holy universal council that a general peace shall be kept throughout Christendom for at least four years, so that heads of churches may bring those at variance to conclude a peace or observe firmly and inviolably a truce. Those who refuse to agree shall be most strictly compelled to do so by excommunication of their persons and an interdict on their lands, unless their wrongdoing is so great that they ought not to have the enjoyment of such peace; but if perchance they make light of the church's censure they can, not without cause, dread the invocation by ecclesiastical authority of the secular arm against them as disturbers of the business of Him who was crucified. We therefore trusting in the mercy of Almighty God and the authority of the blessed apostles Peter and Paul, by that power of binding and unbinding which God has given us, though unworthy, grant to all who in person and at their own expense go on this journey full pardon of their sins about which they are profusely contrite in heart and have spoken in confession and at the retribution of the just we promise the further benefit of eternal salvation. To those who do not go there in person but send entirely at their own expense according to their means and status men suitably equipped, and similarly to those who although at others' expense, go in person, we grant full pardon of their sins. We will and grant that all those shall participate too in this remission in proportion to the nature of their help and the intensity of their piety who contribute suitably from their goods to the support of the Holy Land or give useful advice and assistance. Likewise, the universal synod gives its full support and blessing to all starting out on this common enterprise that it may contribute worthily to their salvation.

31. *THE RULE OF SAINT FRANCIS OF ASSISI*

FRANCIS OF ASSISI (1182–1226) was the most important religious figure of the thirteenth century. Francis's dedication to a life of poverty and simplicity caught the imagination of Europeans and resulted in the rapid increase of his followers in his growing religious community. In 1210 Pope Innocent III approved a simple rule for Francis and his followers, which was simply a collection of gospel precepts emphasizing poverty and preaching. By the 1220s, when the Franciscans numbered in the thousands, a more formal rule was needed. The following, written by Francis in 1223 and approved by the papacy, became the official rule of the Franciscans.

Source: E.F. Henderson (ed.), *Select Historical Documents* (London: George Bell, 1894).

Further Reading: Michael Robson, *St Francis of Assisi. The Legend and the Life* (London: Geoffrey Chapman, 1997).

1. This is the rule and way of living of the minorite brothers: namely to observe the holy Gospel of our Lord Jesus Christ, living in obedience, without personal possessions, and in chastity. Brother Francis promises obedience and reverence to our lord pope Honorius, and to his successors who canonically enter upon their office, and to the Roman Church. And the other brothers shall be bound to obey brother Francis and his successors.

2. If any persons shall wish to adopt this form of living, and shall come to our brothers, they shall send them to their provincial ministers; to whom alone, and to no others, permission is given to receive brothers. But the ministers shall diligently examine them in the matter of the Catholic faith and the ecclesiastical sacraments. And if they believe all these, and are willing to faithfully confess them and observe them steadfastly to the end; and if they have no wives, or if they have them and the wives have already entered a monastery, or if they shall have given them permission to do so—they themselves having already taken a vow of continence by the authority of the bishop of the diocese, and their wives being of such age that no

suspicion can arise in connection with them:— the ministers shall say unto them the word of the holy Gospel, to the effect that they shall go and sell all that they have and strive to give it to the poor. But if they shall not be able to do this, their good will is enough. And the brothers and their ministers shall be on their guard and not concern themselves for their temporal goods; so that they may freely do with those goods exactly as God inspires them. But if advice is required, the ministers shall have permission to send them to some God-fearing men by whose counsel they shall dispense their goods to the poor. Afterwards there shall be granted to them the garments of probation; namely two gowns without cowls and a belt, and hose and a cape down to the belt; unless to these same ministers something else may at some time seem to be preferable in the sight of God. But, when the year of probation is over, they shall be received into obedience; promising always to observe that manner of living, and this Rule. And, according to the mandate of the lord pope, they shall never be allowed to break these bonds. For according to the holy Gospel, no one putting his hand to the plow and looking back is fit for the kingdom of God. And those who have now promised obedience shall have one gown with a cowl, and another, if they wish it, without a cowl. And those who are compelled by necessity, may wear shoes. And all the brothers shall wear humble garments, and may repair them with sack cloth and other remnants, with the benediction of God. And I warn and exhort them lest they despise or judge men whom they shall see clad in soft garments and in colors, using delicate food and drink; but each one shall the rather judge and despise himself.

3. The clerical brothers shall perform the divine service according to the order of the holy Roman Church; excepting the psalter, of which they may have extracts. But the lay brothers shall say twenty-four Paternosters at matins, five at the service of praise, seven each at the first, third, sixth, and ninth hour, twelve at vespers, seven at compline and they shall fast from the feast of All Saints to the Nativity of the Lord; but as to the holy season of Lent, which begins from the Epiphany of the Lord and continues forty days, which the Lord consecrated with his holy fast— those who fast during it shall be blessed of the Lord, and those who do not wish to fast shall not be bound to do so; but otherwise they shall fast until the Resurrection of the Lord. But at other times the brothers shall not be bound to fast save on the sixth day (Friday); but in time of manifest necessity the brothers shall not be bound to fast with their bodies. But I advise, warn and exhort my brothers in the Lord Jesus Christ, that, when they go into the world, they shall not quarrel, nor contend with words, nor judge others. But they shall be gentle, peaceable and modest, merciful and humble, honestly speaking with all, as is becoming. And they ought not to ride unless they are compelled by manifest necessity or by infirmity. Into whatever house they enter they shall first say: peace be to this house. And according to the holy Gospel it is lawful for them to eat of all the dishes which are placed before them.

4. I firmly command all the brothers by no means to receive coin or money, of themselves or through an intervening person. But for the needs of the sick and for clothing the other brothers, the ministers alone and the guardians shall provide through spiritual friends, as it may seem to them that necessity demands, according to time, place and cold temperature. This one thing being always regarded, that, as has been said, they receive neither coin nor money.

5. Those brothers to whom God has given the ability to labor, shall labor faithfully and devoutly; in such way that idleness, the enemy of the soul, being excluded, they may not extinguish the spirit of holy prayer and devotion; to which other temporal things should be subservient. As a reward, moreover, for their labor, they may receive for themselves and their brothers the necessaries of life, but not coin or money; and this humbly, as becomes the servants of God and the followers of most holy poverty.

6. The brothers shall appropriate nothing to themselves, neither a house, nor a place, nor anything; but as pilgrims and strangers in this world, in poverty and humility serving God, they shall confidently go seeking for alms. Nor need they be ashamed, for the Lord made Himself poor for us in this world. This is the height of most lofty poverty, which has constituted you my most beloved brothers heirs and kings of the kingdom of heaven, has made you poor in possessions, has exalted you in virtues. This be your portion, which leads on to the land of the living. Adhering to it absolutely, most beloved brothers, you will wish to have for ever in heaven nothing else than the name of our Lord Jesus Christ. And wherever the brothers are and shall meet, they shall show themselves as of one household; and the one shall safely manifest to the other his necessity. For if a mother loves and nourishes her son in the flesh, how much more zealously should one love and nourish one's spiritual brother? And if any of them fall into sickness, the other brothers ought to serve him, as they would wish themselves to be served.

7. But if any of the brothers at the instigation of the enemy shall mortally sin: for those sins concerning which it has been ordained among the brothers that recourse must be had to the provincial ministers, the aforesaid brothers must be

bound to have recourse to them, as quickly as they can, without delay. But those ministers, if they are priests, shall with mercy enjoin penance upon them. But if they are not priests, they shall cause it to be enjoined upon them through others, priests of the order; according as it seems to them to be most expedient in the sight of God. And they ought to be on their guard lest they grow angry and be disturbed on account of the sin of any one; for wrath and indignation impede love in themselves and in others.

8. All the brothers shall be bound always to have one of the brothers of that order as general minister and servant of the whole fraternity, and shall be firmly bound to obey him. When he dies, the election of a successor shall be made by the provincial ministers and guardians, in the chapter held at Pentecost; in which the provincial ministers are bound always to come together in whatever place shall be designated by the general minister. And this, once in three years; or at another greater or lesser interval, according as shall be ordained by the aforesaid minister. And if, at any time, it shall be apparent to the whole body of the provincial ministers and guardians that the aforesaid minister does not suffice for the service and common utility of the brothers: the aforesaid brothers to whom the right of election has been given shall be bound, in the name of God, to elect another as their guardian. But after the chapter held at Pentecost the ministers and the guardians can, if they wish it and it seems expedient for them, in that same year call together, once, their brothers, in their districts, to a chapter.

9. The brothers may not preach in the bishopric of any bishop if they have been forbidden to by him. And no one of the brothers shall dare to preach at all to the people, unless he have been examined and approved by the general minister of this fraternity, and the office of preacher have been conceded in him. I also exhort these same brothers that, in the preaching which they do, these expressions shall be chaste and chosen, to the utility and edification of the people; announcing to them vices and virtues, punishment and glory, with briefness of discourse; for the words were brief which the Lord spoke upon earth.

10. The brothers who are the ministers and servants of the other brothers shall visit and admonish their brothers and humbly and lovingly correct them; not teaching them anything which is against their soul and against our Rule. But the brothers who are subjected to them shall remember that, before God, they have discarded their own wills. Wherefore I firmly command them that they obey their ministers in all things which they have promised God to observe, and which are not contrary to their souls and to our Rule. And wherever there are brothers who know and recognize that they can not spiritually observe the Rule, they may and should have recourse to their ministers. But the ministers shall receive them lovingly and kindly, and shall exercise such familiarity towards them, that they may speak and act towards them as masters to their servants; for so it ought to be, that the ministers should be the servants of all the brothers. I warn and exhort, moreover, in Christ Jesus the Lord, that the brothers be on their guard against all pride, vainglory, envy, avarice, care and anxiety for this world, detraction and murmuring. And they shall not take trouble to teach those ignorant of letters, but shall pay heed to this that they desire to have the spirit of God and its holy workings; that they pray always to God with a pure heart; that they have humility, patience, in persecution and infirmity; and that they love those who persecute, revile and attack us. For the Lord saith: "Love your enemies, and pray for those that persecute you and speak evil against you; Blessed are they that suffer persecution for righteousness' sake, for of such is the kingdom of Heaven; He that is steadfast unto the end shall be saved."[1]

11. I firmly command all the brothers not to have suspicious intercourse or to take counsel with women. And, with the exception of those whom special permission has been given by the apostolic chair, let them not enter nunneries. Neither may they become fellow godparents with men or women, lest from this cause a scandal may arise among the brothers or concerning brothers.

---

1   Matthew 5:44.

12. Whoever of the brothers by divine inspiration may wish to go among the Saracens and other infidels, shall seek permission to do so from their provincial ministers. But to none shall the ministers give permission to go, save to those whom they shall see to be fit for the mission.

Furthermore, through their obedience I enjoin on the ministers that they demand from the lord pope one of the cardinals of the holy Roman Church, who shall be the governor, corrector and protector of that fraternity, so that, always being subjected and lying at the feet of that same holy Church, steadfast in the Catholic faith, we may observe poverty and humility, and the holy Gospel of our Lord Jesus Christ; as we have firmly promised.

32. CLARE OF ASSISI

Testament

BORN IN ASSISI TO a devout family, Clare (1194–1253) had already acquired a reputation for piety when, upon hearing Francis preach in 1212, she determined to imitate his life. Despite concerted opposition from her family, she and a few companions established a life somewhat similar to that of Francis at San Damiano. Although she and Francis had initially hoped that she might provide leadership to women wishing to lead a life similar to his, ecclesiastical opposition made this impossible. The rule imposed on the order set up by Clare, known as the Poor Clares, by Pope Innocent III was essentially that of the Benedictines, who followed the rule of St. Benedict. Under Innocent's successor Honorius III, the Poor Clares were required to lead a strictly cloistered life.

Clare's *Testament* emphasizes the fundamental principles of her religious orientation: poverty, humility, and penance in the tradition of Francis to the extent permitted women by the thirteenth-century Church.

Source: Ignatius Brady, *The Legend and Writings of Saint Clare of Assisi* (New York: St. Bonaventure, 1953).

Further Reading: Joan Mueller, *The Privilege of Poverty: Clare of Assisi, Agnes of Prague, and the Struggle for a Franciscan Rule for Women* (University Park: Pennsylvania State University Press, 2006).

In the Name of the Lord, Amen.

1. Among the many graces which we have received and continue daily to receive from the liberality of the Father of mercies and for which we must give deepest thanks to our glorious God, our vocation holds first place. Indeed, because it is the more perfect and the greater among these graces, so much the more does it claim our gratitude. Therefore the Apostle says: "Know your vocation"[1]

2. The Son of God became for us the Way[2] and that Way our Blessed Father Francis, His true lover and imitator, has shown and taught us by word and example.

3. Therefore, beloved Sisters, we must consider the immense benefits which God has conferred upon us, but especially those which He has deigned to work in us through His beloved servant, our Father the Blessed Francis, not only after our conversion but even while we yet dwelt among the vanities of the world.

4. For when the saint as yet had neither friars nor companions and, shortly after his conversion, was repairing the Church of San Damiano and there, filled completely with divine consolation, was led to abandon the world wholly and forever, in great joy and in the illumination of the Holy Spirit he prophesied concerning us what the Lord later fulfilled. For at that time he mounted the wall of the church and cried with a loud voice in the French tongue to certain poor folk of the neighborhood: "Come and help me in building the Monastery of San Damiano; for here will dwell ladies whose good name and holy life will glorify our Heavenly Father throughout His holy Church."

5. In this therefore we can behold the great kindness of God toward us, who of the abundance of His mercy and love deigned to speak thus through His saint of our vocation and election. And it

---

1   1 Cor. 1:26.
2   John 14:16.

was not of us alone that our most blessed Father prophesied these things, but of all others likewise who were about to enter the holy calling to which God has called us.

6. With what solicitude, therefore, and fervor of mind and body must we not observe the commandments of God and of our Father, that with the help of God we may return to Him with increase the talent He has given us! For the Lord has placed us as an example and mirror not only for other men, but also for our sisters whom God has called to our way of life, that they in turn should be a mirror and an example to those living in the world.

Since therefore the Lord has called us to such heights of holiness that in us our other sisters may behold themselves who are to be an example to mankind, we are truly bound to bless the Lord and praise Him and to be strengthened in Him more and more to do good. Wherefore if we live according to the pattern given us, we shall leave others a noble example and after life's short labor gain the prize of eternal happiness.

7. After the most high celestial Father had deigned to enlighten my heart by His mercy and grace to do penance after the example and teaching of our most Blessed Father Francis shortly after his own conversion, I voluntarily promised him obedience with the few sisters whom the Lord had given me soon after my conversion, according to the light of His grace which the Lord had given us by the holy life and teaching of His servant.

8. But when the Blessed Father saw that though we were weak and frail of body, we shirked neither privation nor poverty, hardship, tribulation, ignominy, nor the contempt of the world, but rather, as he and his friars often saw for themselves, that after the example of the saints and his friars we accounted all these as great delight, he rejoiced in the Lord. And moved to love for us, he bound himself always to have, in his own person or through his Order, the same diligent care and special solicitude for us as for his own friars.

9. And thus by the will of God and of our most blessed Father Francis we came to dwell at the church of San Damiano. There in a short time

the Lord by His mercy and grace increased our number that what He had prophesied through His saint might come to pass. Before this we had dwelled in another place, but for a little while only.

10. Afterwards he wrote for us a form of life, especially that we should persevere always in holy poverty. Nor was he content while living to exhort us by many words and examples to the love and observance of most holy poverty, but also gave us many writings that after his death we would in no wise turn aside from it, even as the Son of God while He lived in this world wished never to desert this same holy poverty. And our most blessed Father Francis, following the footsteps of Christ, never while he lived departed in example or in teaching from His holy poverty, which he had chosen for himself and for his friars.

11. And I, Clare, the unworthy handmaid of Christ and of the Poor Sisters of the Monastery of San Damiano, and the little plant of the holy Father, considered with my sisters our most high calling and the command of so great a Father, and the frailty of the other sisters, which we feared in ourselves after the death of our holy Father Francis, who was our pillar of strength, and after God our one consolation and our support. Therefore we have bound ourselves again and again to our Lady most holy Poverty, that after my death the sisters present and to come may never in any way abandon her.

12. And as I have ever been zealous and careful to observe and have the others observe the holy poverty which we have promised the Lord and our Holy Father Francis, so the other abbesses who shall follow me in my office are bound always to observe holy poverty unto the end and to cause it to be observed by their sisters.

Indeed, for greater surety I took care to have our profession of holy poverty, which we promised our Father, strengthened by the privileges granted us by the Lord Pope Innocent, in whose pontificate we had our beginning, and by his successors, that at no time or in any fashion we might ever depart from it.

13. Wherefore on bended knees and prostrate in body and soul I recommended all my sisters present and to come to our holy Mother, the Roman Church, to the Supreme Pontiff, and especially to the Lord Cardinal who has been appointed for the religion of the friars minor and for us. And for love of that Lord who was poor in the crib, who lived a poor life, and who hung naked on the gibbet of the Cross, may the Lord Cardinal always cause his little flock to observe the holy poverty which we have promised God and our most blessed Father Francis, and may he always strengthen and preserve them in this poverty. For this is the little flock which the Lord and Father had begotten in His holy Church by the word and example of the blessed Father Francis, who followed the poverty and humility of His beloved Son and of the glorious Virgin, His Mother.

14. The Lord gave us our most blessed Father Francis as founder, planter and helper in the service of Christ and in those things which we have promised God and him our Father; and in his lifetime he was ever solicitous in word and in work to cherish and foster us, his little plants. Wherefore I also recommend and entrust my sisters, present and to come, to the successor of our blessed Father Francis and to the whole Order, that they may always help us to advance to better things in the service of God and above all to observe most holy poverty in a more perfect way.

15. If it should ever happen that the aforesaid Sisters leave this place and go elsewhere, they are bound nevertheless, wherever they may be after my death, to observe the aforesaid manner of poverty which we have promised God and our most blessed Father Francis.

16. In such an event, let that Sister who fills my office and the other Sisters be ever careful and prudent not to acquire or receive more land around such a place than strict necessity demands for a garden wherein to grow vegetables. But if at any time it should be expedient for the proper solitude of the monastery to have more land beyond the limits of the garden, they may not permit more to be acquired than strict necessity demands. And this land shall not be cultivated nor sown but is to remain always untouched and uncultivated.

17. I admonish and exhort in the Lord Jesus Christ all my sisters present and to come that they strive always to follow the way of holy simplicity, humility and poverty and to live worthily and holily, as we have been taught by our blessed Father Francis from the beginning of our conversion to Christ. Thereby, though not by our own merits but only through the mercy and bounteous grace of the Father of mercies, they may always diffuse the fragrance of their good name to our other sisters near and afar off.

18. Love one another with the charity of Christ, and let the love which you have in your hearts be shown outwardly by your deeds that, inspired by this example, the sisters may always grow in the love of God and in mutual charity.

19. And I beseech that sister who shall be entrusted with the care of the sisters to govern others more by her virtues and holy life than by her office, so that, encouraged by her example, they may obey her not only out of duty but rather out of love. Let her be prudent and watchful toward her Sisters as a good Mother toward her daughters; and from the alms which the Lord shall give her let her take care to provide for them according to the needs of each one. Let her also be so kind and approachable that they may reveal their necessities without fear and have recourse to her at any hour with all confidence as may seem good to them for themselves or for their sisters.

20. But the sisters who are under her should remember that they have renounced their own wills for God's sake. Therefore I will that they obey their Mother as they have of their own free will promised the Lord; and thus the Mother, seeing their charity and humility and the unity that exists among them, will carry more lightly the burdens of her office, and what is painful and bitter will, by their holy living, be turned to sweetness for her.

21. And because straight is the way and the path one walks, and narrow the gate by which one enters into life, so few there are that walk thereon and enter through it (cf. Matt. 7, 13:14); and if there are some that walk that way for a time, how few indeed are those who persevere thereon. Happy

those to whom it is given to walk that way and to persevere to the end! (cf. Matt. 10:22).

22. Let us take care, therefore, if we have entered the way of the Lord, lest by our own fault or negligence or ignorance at any time and in any way we turn aside therefrom and so do injury to so great a Lord and His Virgin Mother, and to our blessed Father Francis and to the Church Triumphant and the Church Militant. For it is written: "Cursed are they who turn aside from Thy commandments!" (Ps. 118:21).

23. For this reason I bend my knees to the Father of our Lord Jesus Christ (Eph. 3:14), that through the prayers and merits of the glorious and holy Virgin Mary, His Mother, and of our most blessed Father Francis and all the saints, the Lord Himself who has given us a good beginning will give also the increase (cf. 1 Cor. 3, 7), and likewise constant perseverance to the end. Amen.

24. This writing, that it may be better observed, I leave to you, my most beloved and dearest sisters present and to come, as a sign of the blessing of the Lord and of our most blessed Father Francis, and of my blessing, who am your mother and handmaid.

33. CANONIZATION PROCESS OF ST. DOMINIC

DOMINIGO DE GUZMAN (1170–1221) began his religious career as a regular canon of the cathedral of Osma, Spain, in 1206 but within ten years was preaching against the Albigensian heretics of southern France. Like Francis, he attracted numerous followers who formed a mendicant preaching order, the Order of Preachers known as the Dominicans. The following texts were part of the testimony presented in the course of his canonization process, which resulted in his canonization as a saint in 1234.

Source: Simon Tugwell, O.P., *Early Dominicans: Selected Writings* (New York: Paulist Press, 1987), 133–36.

Further Reading: M.-H. Vicaire, *St. Dominic and His Times* (London: Darton, Longman & Todd, 1964).

Testimony of Brother Ventura (August 6)

(2) Brother Ventura of Verona, prior of the convent of the Order of Preachers in Bologna, said on oath that it was thirteen years and more since he entered the Order of Preachers on the advice and encouragement of the blessed father Dominic, the founder of the Order of Preachers and its first master, and made profession in his hand and received the habit from him. At that time the blessed father Dominic had, after the pope, full authority over the whole Order of Friars Preachers, to shape and organize and correct it. "In the same year," he said, "the first General Chapter of the Order was held at Bologna, and I was present at it."

He also said that he was with the blessed father Dominic and enjoyed great intimacy with him in his comings and goings throughout the province of Lombardy, being associated with him in his traveling and when he was staying somewhere, and in eating, drinking, sleeping and praying.

(3) He also said that on a journey or wherever he was, he wanted to be always preaching or talking or arguing about God, either in person or through his companions. He was also persistent in prayer, and said mass every day if he could find a church, though he never did so without weeping. When he arrived at a hostel, if there was a church there he would go there first. When he was staying somewhere other than one of the convents, when he heard others saying matins he would get up at once and recite matins devoutly with his companions. After compline, when he was on a journey, wherever he was, he observed silence with his companions and with everybody else, and did not want it to be broken until the hour of Terce the next day. When he was traveling, he would lie down at night on some straw, fully clothed, barely even taking his shoes off.

(4) He also said that when he was traveling he observed to the full the Order's fasts, from the feast of Holy Cross until Easter, that is, and every Friday in summer. He was content to eat whatever food was set before him, except that he would not eat any meat whatsoever. It made him very happy if the provision of food was coarse and poor, as the witness testifies he had often observed. As soon as he arrived at any convent of the Order, he called the brethren together and preached to them, bringing them all no little consolation.

(5) He also said that when he was stopping in any convent, he conformed to the common usage of the others in what he ate and in everything else, and he wanted them all to do likewise.

He never saw him doing or saying anything different from this.

He never saw him speaking ill of anyone, or ever saw him utter an idle word.

He said that the blessed Dominic was wise, sensible, patient, kind and very compassionate; he thinks he never saw any mortal man so endowed with virtues, although he has seen many religious people in different parts of the world.

He also said that he heard his general confession at the time of his death in Bologna, and he reckoned from this that he had never sinned mortally, and that he had kept his virginity all his life, because the blessed father accused himself to him in confession of once revealing to some people that he was a virgin, though he did so to be useful to them.

(6) When he came to any place where there were any religious houses, he visited them all, preaching and encouraging them to regular observance. There was no one so troubled that he would not go away comforted if he came and listened to his words. He did this particularly in parts of Lombardy like Milan and the Cistercian monastery of Colomba. He also said that he preached nearly every day unless he was prevented, or gave the brethren a conference, during which he would weep a lot and make others weep too. He was strict in punishing the faults of the brethren, and was a great enthusiast for the Rule, but at the same time his words were so pleasant that the brethren endured the penances imposed by their loving father with the utmost patience and eagerness. He was constant in his attendance at the Divine Office, and used to spend the night in prayer, weeping a lot. When the witness was asked how he knew this, he said that he often found him in church praying and weeping, and sometimes overcome by sleep. Sometimes when he was tired because of his vigils, he would go to sleep at table.

(7) He also said that when the blessed Dominic had been visiting the lord Ugolino, cardinal of Ostia and papal legate, in Venice, he returned to Bologna in very hot weather, late at night, and then spent a long time talking with the witness and with brother Rudolph about the affairs of the Order, and these fathers urged him to go and rest, but he refused and went into the church and prayed, and then said matins with the brethren at the proper time. It was from his staying up that night that he got the pain in his head and the sickness which resulted in his going to the Lord. When he was ill, he refused to lie in a bed, but lay on some sacking instead. He had the novices called to him and gave them advice about their salvation. He appeared to be, and indeed he really was, cheerful and happy in his sickness.

(8) When his illness got worse, the blessed father had himself carried to Santa Maria del Monte, which was said to be a healthier place. There he sent for the prior, who came with twenty brethren from the community; he gave them a long talk. When he had received the holy oil there, the prior of Santa Maria said, "I shall bury him in this church, and I will not allow him to be taken away." When the blessed Dominic realized this, he said to those of his brethren who were standing by, "Quick, take me away from here. God forbid that I should be buried anywhere except under the feet of my brethren." So he was taken back to the church of St. Nicholas, and the brethren were actually afraid he was going to die on the way.

An hour later, he called the witness and said to him, "Make yourselves ready." When he, the prior, and the other brethren had got ready in the proper way for the commendation of his soul and had gathered around him, the holy father said to the prior and the brethren, "Wait a little longer." While this was going on, the prior said to him, "Father, you know that you are leaving us desolate and sad. Remember to pray for us to the Lord." And brother Dominic lifted his hands to heaven and said, "Holy Father, you know that I have gladly persevered in your will, and I have watched over and kept those whom you gave me. Now I commend them back to you. Watch over them and keep them." He said that the brethren had told him that when they asked about themselves, he replied, "I shall be more useful to you and more fruitful after my death than I was in my life." After this, saint Dominic said to the prior and the brethren, "Begin." And during the office of the commendation of his soul, the blessed father was saying the words with the brethren, because his lips were moving. While the brethren were saying, "Come to help him, you saints of God, and receive his soul," he breathed his last.

His funeral was attended by lord Ugolino, cardinal of Ostia, who is now the pope, and by the lord patriarch of Aquileia and by many venerable bishops and abbots. The mass was sung at the funeral by the lord Ugolino.

(9) That year everybody noticed an extraordinary fragrance in the whole church, especially near the tomb, and the witness in particular says that he noticed it himself. There were also a lot of miracles worked that year and in the following years

for people who came to the tomb of the blessed Dominic, bringing wax images and all kinds of things. When several people tried to present silk cloths to cover the tomb of the blessed Dominic, the brethren would not allow them to, for fear they would be accused of greed.

(10) When the body of the blessed Dominic was due to be moved, for several days the *podestà* of Bologna and many noble citizens guarded it to prevent it from being stolen. When the tomb was opened, in the presence of the *podestà* and many citizens of Bologna and other noble men, including religious, bishops and laymen, the brethren found a wooden coffin, shut with iron nails; and such a fragrance came out that they were all amazed, saying that they had never smelled anything like it. So the body was moved by the archbishop and other prelates to the new tomb, and the extraordinary fragrance remained the whole time. Master Jordan held the holy body in his hands and gave it to the three hundred or so brethren who had come to the General Chapter to kiss. When the witness was asked how he knew all this, he said that he was present at all of it.

(11) He also said that the blessed Dominic had such charity that he wanted to extend it to everybody, even the damned, and he used sometimes to weep for them.

Testimony of Brother William of Monferrato (August 7)

(12) The second sworn witness was brother William of Monferrato, of the Order of Preachers, whose disposition was as follows.

"Going to Rome once," he said, "when I was still in the world, I went to stay in the house of the bishop of Ostia, who is now the pope, to spend Lent there, and there I consorted with brother Dominic who used to come and see the cardinal frequently, and I recognized him as a holy man and I liked his way of life. I began to love him and I often spoke with him about the salvation of others, and, though I have lived with many people, I never met anyone more holy.

"I went to Paris to study theology for two years, and there I received the habit of the Preachers

from the blessed Dominic, although we had previously agreed to go and convert unbelievers.

"I accompanied him when he was going to Rome and elsewhere. Whether he was ill or well, I always found him remarkably strict in his observance. He gave dispensations to the other brethren, but not to himself. Even when he was ill, he kept the Order's fasts. When he had an attack of dysentery on his way to Rome, he would not break the Order's fasts or eat meat or take anything extra with his food except some herbs or a bit of turnip." When the witness was asked how he knew this, he replied that he was with him and saw it all, especially at Viterbo where he had been very ill.

(13) "When he was badly treated in any place where he was staying, in the way of food and drink and bedding and such things, I never saw him complaining, but only his extraordinary patience. When he settled down to rest, he prayed for a long time and wept so much that he used to wake his companions up. He spent more time in prayer than asleep. He slept in his tunic and cappa, with his stockings and belt on. He always slept without a mattress, and more often on a plank than on bedding.

"He always observed silence at the times laid down in the Order, and he avoided idle words and spoke always with God or about God." Asked how he knew this, the witness said that, as one of the blessed Dominic's principal companions, he lived with him by day and by night, whether he was traveling or staying somewhere, and he saw and heard all this.

(14) "I must also say, and I believe it to be true, because of his holy way of life, that the blessed father always preserved his virginity; another reason why I believe it is that I have heard it from many reliable people, especially the bishop of Osma, with whom he had been for a long time, and from some of the bishop's canons, with whom he had also lived; I do not remember their names."

(15) He also says that he was present at the translation of the blessed Dominic, when his body was moved from its previous burial place into the church, to the place where it is now. The brethren,

including the provincial, did not want any seculars to be present, because they were afraid it would stink, since water had already seeped into that tomb; but they could not prevent the *podestà* at Bologna and twenty-four noble citizens from being there, and some of them guarded the tomb for several days before it was opened. When the stone was taken away, a wooden coffin was revealed, in which the body of the saint was lying, and then a pleasant, sweet smell came out and none of them could decide what it smelled like.

(16) After this translation, many people of various states of life said that they had received graces of healing. "But I do not remember their names, because I was a diffinitor[1] at the Chapter and was too caught up in other things to pay attention to them."

Testimony of Brother Amizo of Milan (August 8)

(17) The third sworn witness was brother Amizo of Milan, the prior of Padua, whose deposition was as follows.

Master Dominic, he said, was a humble man, gentle, patient, kind, quiet, peaceful, modest and very balanced in everything he did and said. He was a loyal comforter of other people, particularly his own brethren. He was an outstanding enthusiast for regular observance, a great lover of poverty, both in the food and in the clothing of the brethren of his Order, and also in their buildings and churches and in the style and ornamentation of their church vestments. During his lifetime he was very keen on this and took great pains to see that the brethren did not use purple or silk vestments in their churches on themselves or on the altars, and that they did not have vessels of gold or silver, except chalices.

(18) He also said that he was persistent in prayer, by day and by night. He followed the Order's observance fully in choir and in the refectory and elsewhere. He was very fervent in prayer and in preaching, and, because he was zealous for souls, he encouraged his brethren most insistently to be

the same. He loved other religious and spoke most highly of them.

(19) He preserved his virginity up to the time of his death, as nearly everybody said. He also said that he was present when the *podestà* of Bologna, with the master of the Order of Preachers and many others, had the new tomb and the coffin of the blessed Dominic's body opened, and how they all smelled a wonderful fragrance, such as they had never smelled before.

Testimony of Brother Buonviso (August 9)

(20) The fourth sworn witness was brother Buonviso of the Order of Preachers. He was with the blessed Dominic, as he says, at Bologna, in the cloister of St. Nicholas, and at Rome and at Milan, and he looked after him when he was ill. So he said that when the brethren left the church in the evening to go and rest, the blessed Dominic used to remain secretly in the church to pray, and the witness used to watch him and sometimes heard him praying with shouts and groans. He had no place of his own to lie down; if drowsiness ever overcame him, he would go to sleep on a board or a bench or on the bier they used for the dead. He used to lie down at night exactly as he was, as he had been walking about during the day.

(21) When the blessed Dominic went to Rome with the witness, whenever he left a city or village he always took his shoes off and carried them under his arm, though his companion was quite willing to carry them for him, and when he approached a town or village he would put them on again. When they came to a particular path which was full of stones, the blessed father said to his companion, "Here, poor wretch that I am, I was once forced to put my shoes on when I was coming along this path." When his companion asked him why, he said, "Because the rain had made these stones so sharp that I could not bear it." Also on one occasion when it rained very heavily while they were traveling and St. Dominic was caught in it, he quite happily began to sing a hymn; the witness saw this and heard it, because

---

1   Member of the governing council or chapter.

he was traveling with him. When he came to the rivers that were swollen because of the heavy rain, he beat them down with the sign of the cross and went over, encouraging his nervous companions to cross too.

During the celebration of Mass and during the psalmody, tears used to flow in great abundance from his eyes.

(22) When they were in a hostel, he never asked for provision to be made to suit his own taste, but always that of the others. And when he was badly treated, he showed all the signs of being particularly pleased. When the blessed Dominic was ill at Milan with a fever, the witness says that when the fever came on, he became quite lifted up to God and afterwards he had someone read to him.

"When I, brother Buonviso, was procurator at Bologna, once when there was no bread for the brethren at lunch time, St. Dominic sat down at table with them and lifted up his hands in prayer, looking towards heaven, and then two extremely handsome young men came into the refectory with two baskets, with the purest white bread in one, and some figs in the other, and they distributed the bread and the figs to each one of the brethren. I write this and I know this because I was there when it happened and saw it."

He also said that the blessed father was very humble, loving, kind, compassionate, patient, sober, zealous for poverty and for the salvation of souls, and a lover of all religious and religious orders. In himself he kept the Rule strictly. He never returned curse for curse, but blessed those who cursed.

(23) When the *podestà* of Bologna and a great number of the citizens of Bologna together with the master of the Order and the provincial of Lombardy opened the new tomb and the coffin where the bones of the blessed Dominic were, a wonderful fragrance came out, such that they all said that nobody had ever smelled anything like it. "I smelled it myself and was present when this happened."

(24) The witness said that when he was a novice and had no skill in preaching, because he had not yet studied scripture, the holy father told him to go to Piacenza to preach. He excused himself, but he spoke so charmingly that he induced him to go, saying that the Lord would be with him and would put words in his mouth. God did in fact give him such grace in his preaching that many people were converted and three entered the Order.

Testimony of John of Spain (August 10)

(25) The fifth sworn witness was brother John of Spain of the Order of Preachers, who was received into the Order by the blessed Dominic in Toulouse, at the church of St. Romain, at the time of the council of Innocent III. He lived with brother Dominic on his journeys and in various places, by day and night.

He also said that he prayed more persistently than all the other brethren. He used to take the discipline with a triple chain, particularly at night, either giving it to himself or getting someone else to give it to him, and there are many brethren who can attest this, who beat him at his request. He punished people who broke the Rule severely yet mercifully. He was very upset whenever he punished anyone for any fault.

(26) He was zealous for souls and used to send his brethren out to preach, bidding them look to the salvation of others. He had such confidence in God's goodness that he even sent unlearned men out to preach, saying to them, "Do not be afraid; the Lord will be with you and will put power in your mouths." And it turned out as he said.

When the blessed Dominic was at Toulouse, in the church already referred to, he sent the witness to Paris with five other clerical brethren and one lay brother, to study and preach there and to establish a convent. This was contrary to the wishes of Count Simon de Montfort and the archbishop of Narbonne and the bishop of Toulouse and several other prelates, but he told the prelates, the Count and the brethren, "Do not contradict me. I know quite well what I am doing." He told the witness and the others not to have any fear, because everything would work out well. He also sent some others to Spain with similar instructions.

While the witness and his companions were studying in Paris and applying themselves to the salvation of souls, they were given the church of St. Jacques, situated in the gate of Orléans, by Master John, the dean of St. Quentin, who was at that time a regent master in theology in Paris, and by the masters and students of the whole University of Paris. There they established a convent. Many brethren were received into the Order, and they were given a great many properties and revenues and some estates, particularly in the regions of Toulouse and Albi. The witness said that in the days when the Order of Preachers owned estates and many properties in these places and used to carry money with them when they traveled and ride on horseback and wear surplices, brother Dominic worked hard to get the brethren of the Order to abandon and make light of all such temporal things and to devote themselves to poverty and to give up riding on horseback and take nothing with them when they traveled. So their properties in the kingdom of France were given to some nuns belonging to the Cistercian Order, and other properties were given to other people.

To allow the brethren to devote themselves more energetically to study and preaching, brother Dominic wanted them to have uneducated laybrothers, who would be in charge of the educated brethren in the administration and provision of all worldly goods; but the clerical brethren refused to have laybrothers in charge of them, in case what happened to the brethren of Grandmont at the hands of their laybrothers should happen to them too.

(27) St. Dominic was loved by everybody, rich and poor, Jew and pagan (there were many of these in Spain), in fact by everybody except for the heretics and the enemies of the church whom he pursued and refuted in debate and in preaching.

He lay down at night just as he was during the day, except that he took his shoes off. When he was travelling from one land to another, he took his shoes off, and when he arrived anywhere he put them on again, and he did this in all the towns and villages he came to. He refused to have anyone help him carry his shoes. He used to get great delight from anything untoward that happened to him on the way. For example, if he tripped over a stone his face would light up as he said, "This is doing penance!"

He had a great love of poverty, and he encouraged the brethren to love it too. He exulted in cheap clothes, though he liked them to be clean.

(28) He was most sparing in what he ate and drank. He hardly ever took anything extra, if he was offered it, and he observed the Rule strictly himself, though he gave dispensations to others.

When he was walking about in a city or town, he barely lifted his eyes from the ground.

He did not have any place of his own to lie down in, as the other brethren did. (Asked how he knew this, he said that if he had a place of his own, he would have discovered it, because he had been most persistent in trying to find out.)

He was elected bishop two or three times, but always refused, preferring to live in poverty with his brethren to having any bishopric. The sees he refused were those of Béziers and Comminges.

(29) He rarely spoke except about God or with God in prayer, and he encouraged the brethren to do likewise. He was happy when he was with other people, but in prayer he sobbed and wept.

He remained a virgin all his life, and this was what everybody said.

He often said that it was his desire to be whipped and cut up for the name of Christ, and finally to die.

In letters and in his spoken words he encouraged the brethren to apply themselves to the study of the New and Old Testaments more than to any other reading. He always carried round with him the gospel of Matthew and the letters of Paul, and he read them so often that he knew them by heart.

The canons with whom he had lived before the Order was founded related that when the blessed Dominic was still in the world, as a student at Palencia, he sold his books and furniture to feed the poor during a time of famine. At his example many other people began to do the same thing.

Testimony of Brother Rudolph of Faenza (August 11)

(30) The sixth sworn witness was brother Rudolph of Faenza of the Order of Preachers, who was the priest in charge of the church of St. Nicholas of the Vines in Bologna, and who gave this church to

the brethren, with the permission of the bishop of Bologna, at the request of the lord Ugolino, bishop of Ostia, who was papal legate at the time and is now the Pope.

The witness says that he was with the blessed Dominic in Bologna, in church, at the office, in the dormitory, in the refectory, by day and by night, because he, the witness, was procurator for the brethren and had entered the Order many years before and had made profession before the blessed Dominic came to Bologna, and so he knew him well.

(31) "The blessed father Dominic," the witness says, "nearly always spent the night in church, praying and weeping there, as I saw by the light of the lamp which is in the church, and sometimes I saw him standing on the tip of his toes with his hands stretched up. Because of the intimacy I had with him I sometimes went and prayed beside him, and I saw in him a fervor in prayer such as I have never seen the like of.

"The blessed father wore an iron chain next to the skin. When I stripped him after his death, I took this chain as a great treasure, but eventually I gave it to Master Jordan at his urgent request.

"At night he used to lie down dressed just as he was for walking about during the day. He would lie down on some planks or on the ground or sometimes on a trellis, and he did not take anything off except his shoes. Because of his long vigils in church, he sometimes used to go to sleep at table. He was regularly there with the brethren in choir and in the refectory, and he took the same food as the others.

"When I was procurator for the brethren in Bologna," the witness says, "I once prepared an extra dish for the brethren, and he came to me after lunch and said, 'Why are you killing the brethren by giving them extra dishes?' When we were short of bread or other food, I often went to him to tell him what we needed. He used to say, 'Go to church and pray.' He would do the same, and I found that God provided whatever we were short of. Even a little supply of bread put out at his command for a whole lot of brethren was abundantly sufficient for them all. He kept the Rule completely in every respect, with regard to food and fasting and everything else, and he took care to see that it was observed by the others.

(32) "Finally, I never saw a man whose service of God pleased me more than did that of the blessed Dominic. He longed for the salvation of all men, including Christians and Saracens, and especially the Cumans,[2] to whom he wanted to go.

"He was happy, kind, patient, cheerful, compassionate, and a comforter of the brethren. If he saw any of the brethren offending in any point, he walked past as if he had not seen it, but later, looking perfectly calm, he would address him with soothing words and say to him, 'Brother, you have done wrong; do penance.' In this kind way he led them all to do penance and to make amends; and though his words were humble when he spoke to offenders, he still punished their offenses severely.

"He had a supreme love of poverty and encouraged the others to practice poverty too. For instance, Signor Oderico Gallicani once gave the brethren in Bologna a certain piece of property worth five hundred Bolognese pounds; when the blessed Dominic arrived, he tore up the title deeds and returned the property, saying, 'Preachers ought to live by alms.' If ever they had enough in the house to support the brethren for the day, he would not let them beg on that day, and if anyone gave them any alms, he ordered them to return it. He wanted them to have small houses and cheap clothes and even cheap vestments in church. He did not want the brethren to concern themselves with temporal affairs, except those who had been made responsible for them. When he saw that anyone was suitable to be a preacher, he did not want him to be given any other job.

"Whether he was traveling or at home, he always wanted to talk about God or the salvation of souls. I never heard an idle or harmful word from his mouth, or anything derogatory.

(33) "He was very fervent in his preaching and often used to weep while preaching, which made the people weep too.

"At the first General Chapter in Bologna, in the presence of the brethren, he said that he deserved to be deposed and that they ought to depose him. But the fathers refused to do this, so he appointed

---

2   A nomadic steppe people.

diffinitors who were to have the authority to do this for the duration of the Chapter. 'I am slack,' he said, 'and useless, so put me out of office.'

"When he was sick at Bologna, the time he died, the brethren stood round him, in tears. Then the blessed Dominic exhorted them to keep the observances of their religious life, and told them not to be afraid, because he would be more useful to them after his death. 'I was holding his head with a towel,' the witness says, 'wiping away the sweat from his face. One of the brethren came to the blessed Dominic and said, "Father, where do you want your body to be buried?" He said, "Under the feet of my brethren."' While the brethren were saying the commendation of his soul, the blessed father said the words with them. But when they got to 'Come to help him, you saints of God, come to meet him, you angels of the Lord, and receive his soul and present it before the Most High,' he breathed his last. All this took place in one of the cells at St. Nicholas. I never saw him sleeping in a bed with a feather mattress, or even on sacking except when he died, because he was on sacking then. When he breathed his last, he lifted his hands toward heaven."

(34) He also said that he prepared his tomb and the wooden coffin, since he was procurator. His body was shut in with iron nails and he guarded it carefully until it was put in the tomb. Nor did anyone put any perfumes there, because the witness was present the whole time. He also said that he was one of those who opened the tomb in which the blessed father had been buried first, when his body was moved to the place where it is now. It was he who broke the wall of the tomb with iron hammers; the wall was very strong and was sealed with strong, hard cement. He also raised the stone which was on top, with an iron bar, because the tomb was protected by large stones and sealed with cement. He had had all this done most carefully at the outset, to make sure that people did not steal the body. And when the witness raised the stone that was on top with the iron bar, and the tomb was opened, a great fragrance came out, an overwhelming fragrance, very pleasant and sweet; he did not recognize it. All those who smelled it agreed that there had never been any fragrance like it. It still remains in the bones of the blessed Dominic.

Testimony of Brother Stephen of Spain (August 9)

(35) The seventh sworn witness was brother Stephen of the Order of Preachers, the provincial of Lombardy. He said that "it is fifteen years since I first knew Master Dominic, the founder of the Order of Preachers and its first master; before I knew him personally I heard from reliable people that while he was still a student he sold his books and fed the poor during a time of famine. He said, 'I refuse to study dead skins while men are dying of hunger.' At his example, other men of great authority did the same sort of thing."

Round about this time, he began to preach in the district of Toulouse against the heretics there, with the bishop of Osma, and he started the Order of Preachers.

(36) He also said that when he, the witness, was a student at Bologna, the blessed Dominic came to Bologna and preached there. "After I had confessed my sins to him, one evening when I was at dinner with some friends in the house where we were staying, the blessed Dominic sent two of the brethren to me to say, 'Brother Dominic says you are to come to him.' I told them to go away and said I would come when I had finished my dinner, but they said, 'He says you are to come now.' So I left everything and went to him. I found him with many of the brethren at the church of St. Nicholas." He said to the brethren who were standing by, "Quick, show him how to do a *venia*." When he had done a *venia*, he put himself in his hands. Then the blessed Dominic received him into the Order, saying, "I am giving you arms with which you will be able to fight the devil all the days of your life." The witness was surprised at the time and afterwards, wondering what had prompted Dominic to summon him and clothe him in the habit of the Friars Preachers, because he had not discussed his conversion with him beforehand. He thought that it must have been because of some divine revelation and inspiration that he did it.

(37) He also said that the blessed Dominic was a great comforter of the brethren and of other people who were in distress. "For instance," the witness says, "When I was a novice, I suffered a great

many trials, but I endured them all at the encouragement of the holy man. The same thing happened to many of the novices, as they told me."

The witness was with the blessed Dominic at Bologna for a whole year, in the cloister of St. Nicholas, and became very intimate with him there, and he never heard him speak a single malicious or idle word. When he preached, his words were so moving that they made both him and his hearers weep with compunction. Whether he was at home or on a journey, he always spoke about God or other profitable subjects, and he urged the others to do the same.

After compline, when the common prayer was finished, he made the brethren go to the dormitory, while he remained in the church to pray. And while he prayed, he used to reach such a pitch of groaning and lamenting that the brethren who were nearby were woken up by it. He often used to spend the whole night in church, up to the time of matins. At matins he would go round both sides of choir, urging and encouraging the brethren to sing loudly and with devotion. The holy man was so devoted to his vigils of prayer "that I never saw him leave the church and go to any place of his own to sleep, only to the bier."

(38) When he was celebrating mass, particularly during the words of the canon, he used to weep and show all the signs of a most intensely fervent love. He was enthusiastic for regular life and was a great observer of the Rule of the Order. He had a supreme love of poverty, and encouraged the brethren to imitate him in this, so he would not accept any properties he was offered nor did he want the brethren to accept them. He had cheap clothes made out of coarse, though clean material, and he wore a very cheap, short scapular, and would never hide it with his cappa, even in the presence of important people. When brother Rudolph raised the cells by an arm's length, because the brethren used to have poor, mean, low cells, and this was in the absence of the blessed Dominic, when the holy father came back, he said, "Do you so quickly want to abandon poverty and build great palaces?" So he ordered them to abandon the work, and it duly remained unfinished as long as he was alive. He put it in his Rule that the brethren were to use cheap clothes and

buildings and that they were not to take money with them when they traveled, but were to live off alms. He was most sparing in food and drink, to such an extent that when the brethren had two dishes, he contented himself with one. While the brethren went on eating after he had finished, he used to go to sleep, because of the long vigils he kept in church.

(39) It was generally said that he preserved his virginity until the end of his life. "I heard his confession several times and could never discover that he had committed a mortal sin." He was patient and happy in all trials. When he was in need, or the brethren lacked anything, in food or in clothing, he showed every sign of happiness.

Since brother John of Vicenza announced to the people in a sermon a revelation he had received about the blessed Dominic, and since he, the witness, began to think about moving his body, great graces in increasing abundance have been seen plainly both in the brethren and in the people who listened to the life and miracles of the blessed Dominic. In the cities of Lombardy a huge number of heretics has been burned, and more than a hundred thousand people who did not know whether they ought to belong to the Roman church or to the heretics have been sincerely converted to the Catholic faith of the Roman church by the preaching of the friars preachers. Their sincerity is shown by the fact that these converts, who had previously been defending the heretics, are now pursuing them and detest them, and in almost all the cities of Lombardy and the Marches the statutes which were opposed to the church have been handed over to the friars preachers to correct and emend and bring into line with Catholic truth. They have eradicated feuds and established peace between many cities, they have subdued usury and arranged for repayments, ever since the life and miracles of the blessed Dominic began to be famous.

(40) The witness also said that he was present when the body of the blessed Dominic was moved from the tomb under the ground to the marble tomb, and he says that they broke the limestone and the very hard cement with picks and other iron instruments, and then opened the tomb,

on which there was a thick, strong stone; inside they found a wooden coffin, from which a marvelous fragrance was coming. The master of the Order took the bones and put them in a new coffin, in the presence of many of the brethren and the archbishop of Ravenna and many other bishops and prelates and the *podestà* of Bologna with many noble citizens, and they put the new coffin in a stone monument, where it is now. The fragrance lasted for many days afterwards in the hands of those who had touched the relics.

Testimony of Brother Paul of Venice (August 16)

(41) The eighth sworn witness was brother Paul of Venice of the Order of Preachers, who received the habit at Bologna fourteen years ago and made profession in the hands of Master Reginald. After his profession, when the blessed Dominic came to Bologna, the witness was very intimate with him and walked with him round the Marches of Treviso and was with him in eating and drinking, when he was staying anywhere and when he was traveling, in the Divine Office, by day and by night, for about two years. "In all this time, I never heard from him an idle word or a derogatory or flattering word or any damaging word." On the contrary, when he was traveling, he saw him either praying or preaching or giving his time to prayer or meditation. When he was travelling, he would tell his companions to go on ahead, saying, "Let us think about our Savior." Wherever he was, he always spoke either about God or to God, and he encouraged the brethren to do the same, and put it in his Rule. He was never seen to be angry or upset or worried by the toil of traveling, but was patient and happy in all adversities.

(42) He had a supreme love of poverty for himself and for his Order. When some of the people of Bologna wanted to give the brethren certain properties, he refused them, saying that he wanted his brethren to live off alms. And he put it in the constitutions that properties should not be accepted in the Order.

When he left any town he used to take his shoes off and walk barefoot. He wore the cheapest of habits. "I sometimes saw the blessed Dominic seeking alms from door to door and receiving bread like any pauper. For example, at Dugliolo one day when he was begging for alms, someone offered him a whole loaf of bread, and the father knelt down and took it with great humility and devotion.

"When he was traveling, I never saw him lie in a bed, though he did sometimes lie on some bedding. Once when I visited the church of Porto Legnago with him, the father had a place prepared for his companions to lie down, but he went into the church and spent the night there until matins, and then he said matins with the clergy. When he was traveling, he kept the Order's fasts, though he made his companions eat because of the labor of the journey. In the convent of St. Nicholas in Bologna I looked for a long time to see if he had any place of his own to lie down in, and I found that he had not; he slept either on the ground or on a wicker trellis or on a wooden board, and very often he spent the night in church. When he prayed he wept a great deal, because sometimes when I went to fetch him from prayer I saw his face wet with tears. Every day, even when he was traveling, he wanted to sing mass, if he could find a convenient church for it.

(43) "He longed jealously for the salvation of believers and unbelievers alike. He sometimes said to me, 'When we have established our Order, we shall go to the Cumans and preach the faith of Christ to them and win them for the Lord.'

He wanted the Rule to be observed strictly by himself and by the others. He reprimanded offenders justly and so affectionately that no one was ever upset by his correction and punishment. He conformed to the community in his food and in the Office. When he spent the night in church, he was still always there with the rest to celebrate matins. He used to encourage the brethren in choir, now on one side, now on the other, to sing well and excellently and to recite the psalms with devotion.

"He was patient, kind, compassionate, sober, loving, humble and chaste, and he was always a virgin. I never knew anyone to compare with him in holiness of life.

"When he was traveling, he preached to the people who joined his party and urged them on to follow the good.

(44) "I was present at Bologna when his body was moved, when such a delightful fragrance came from it that everyone prostrated themselves on the ground and gave thanks to God. The whole church was filled with the fragrance.

(45) "When I was coming to Bologna from Venice to give evidence about the life of the blessed Dominic, my usual kidney pains attacked me so severely that I thought I would not be able to give evidence at the time appointed. I went to the tomb of the blessed Dominic and when I had prayed about this, I was completely freed from the pain."

Testimony of Brother Frugerio of Pennabilli (August 17)

(46) The ninth sworn witness was brother Frugerio of Pennabilli of the Order of Preachers, who had been in the Order for fourteen years and had made profession in the hands of Master Reginald and received the habit from him in the church of Mascarella, which was the first place in Bologna where the Order of Preachers was established. After his profession, with permission from Master Reginald, the witness went to visit his family, and when he returned to Bologna he found the blessed Dominic at the church of St. Nicholas, where the brethren had moved. He lived with him there for more than four months. He was also with him in the convent of Florence and in the convent in Rome, and also traveling to Rome and through various other towns, being with him in the Office, in eating and talking, hearing his confession, in prayer and in discussing God with him, by day and by night.

The blessed Dominic was very devoted in his prayer, both when he was traveling and when he was in a convent, so much so that he, the witness, could not see that he ever slept in a bed, although one was sometimes prepared for him. But sometimes when he was tired, as a result of keeping vigil too long at night, he would go to sleep on the ground or on a piece of wood. When he was celebrating mass he wept a good deal.

(47) When he was talking to the brethren he used to weep and he made them weep too.

"I never heard an idle or harmful word from him, whether of flattery or of detraction." He always spoke about God or with God, and he used to preach to anyone he met on the way when he was traveling, and he urged the brethren to do the same. This was why he wanted to put this in his Rule. He was zealous for souls, not only those of Christians, but also Saracens and other unbelievers. As evidence of this, he proposed to go to the pagans and die there for the faith, once he had organized his brethren.

He treated himself roughly and observed the Order's fasts very strictly when he was traveling, and would not eat before the set time, even though he made his companions eat. He used a single tunic in winter and in summer. He exhorted the brethren to practice the poverty which he himself loved so much. He used a cheap tunic. He was quick to rebuke and correct any of the brethren who were wearing clothes that were at fault. This was why he directed that they should not accept properties, but should live off alms, and he put this in the Rule. He wanted the brethren to have cheap houses and cheap reading desks, so that they would display poverty in everything.

(48) He himself observed the Rule strictly and wanted it to be observed by the others. He convicted and corrected offenders with gentleness and kindness in such a way that no one was upset, even though the penances were sometimes very severe.

"He was never defiled by any mortal sin, as far as I could tell from his confession, which I heard. He was kind and patient in all trials, rejoicing in adversities, loving, compassionate, a comforter of the brethren and of others. He was adorned with all the virtues to such a degree that I never saw anyone like him."

(49) *I, Aldrovando, son of the late Tebaldo, notary by imperial authority, received these witnesses, on the instructions of Master Tancred, archdeacon of Bologna, Dom Thomas, prior of Santa Maria di Reno, and brother Palmiero of Campagnola, the judges appointed by the lord pope, and I put them in official form and wrote them out in the year of our Lord 1233 in the sixth indiction, in the earlier part of August.*

34. THOMAS OF CANTIMPRÉ

Defense of the Mendicants

THOMAS OF CANTIMPRÉ (1210–1263/80) was born in the area of Brussels. He became an Augustinian canon in Cantimpré before joining the Dominican order in Louvain. He studied in Cologne and Paris and was the author of lives of contemporary saints and a compilation of natural history, and was also recognized during his life as a persuasive and eloquent preacher. The following text is a description and defense of his fellow mendicants against other forms of religious life.

Source: Simon Tugwell, O.P., *Early Dominicans: Selected Writings* (New York: Paulist Press, 1974).

Further Reading: M.-H. Vicaire, *St. Dominic and His Times* (London: Darton, Longman & Todd, 1964).

I had often heard of the ways in which the friars had to do without things, sometimes in considerable hardship, but I wanted to try it for myself, and will tell you simply what happened to me with the friars in my own native land. I arrived on foot in some town which I did not know, so tired from the journey that I thought my heart would soon fail from my excessive weakness. The friars went to the priest's house, but could not even get a crust of the very black bread which the servants of his household were using. From there they went far and wide through the town and got nothing, except a piece of bran bread from a poor little lady who lived on the edge of the town—a large gift indeed, in fact a huge benefaction! So we sat down in the open air and ate the bread. And though the husks in the bread pricked our mouths as we ate, I never in my life enjoyed such a delicious meal. This made me reflect, not without a certain depression of spirit, on what those blessed men had been enduring all over the place, often in much worse situations than this, while I could not sustain such discomfort for even a single day. So I shall keep quiet about this kind of thing, which is constantly happening to them.

But there is just one thing which I do want to mention here. It is possible to distinguish three different kinds of way of life followed by our clergy. The secular clergy work at their studies, the canons, whether secular or regular, devote themselves to the celebration of the Divine Office, and the monks and other religious apply all their energy to the careful practice of their regular observances. But the friars, both the preachers and the minors, in accordance with the requirements of their Orders, seem to follow all three ways of life at one and the same time. They study with the clerics, they devote themselves to the Divine Office with the canons, and, in common with the monks and other religious, they practice community life with its accusations and beatings and fasting, and, in part, they also practice silence, and almost every day they all take the discipline after compline; in addition to that, they have certain observances of their own, so that, for instance, the preachers wear a rough rope next to the skin round their loins, and wear woolen clothes which get prickly with all their sweat as they travel round on foot. And apart from all that, they have chosen to live without owning any properties at all. What a labor it is for the friars minor to beg their bread every day! And what a labour it is for all the preachers who go out generally to beg after August, to collect enough bread for the rest of the year, so that their study will not be hindered or prevented!

You most faithful and long-suffering men, do not be ashamed to beg your bread; Christ the Lord begged for a drink of water from a Samaritan woman. Do not be afraid to be called and to be beggars; Christ himself, who is the Truth, declared that the poor are blessed. This is attested to by both the New and Old Testaments.

Christ is my witness in saying all of this. I am not seeking any special glory for these two orders.

They have their judge and it is he who seeks glory for them. I am simply constrained to reply to their critics, who consider these new religious orders to be superstitious and silly, and reckon their traveling ground to be frivolous; to use their own word, they call the friars "gyrovagues."[1] Well, my brethren, you need not be ashamed to be called or to be gyrovagues. You are in the company of Paul, the teacher of the nations, who completed the preaching of the gospel all the way from Spain to Illyria. While they sit home in their monasteries—and let us hope that it is with Mary—you go touring round with Paul, doing the job you have been given to do. And I am hopeful that if you suffer oppression in the world, you will still have peace in Christ, perhaps even as much peace or more than they have who sit grumbling in their place of quiet, stirring up quarrels among themselves or with their superiors. And if they are free from quarrels, as they will perhaps claim, let them sit there if they want to, with all their warm clothes on, enjoying their peace, but then they should allow the friars, whom they call gyrovagues, to travel round the world in their meager tunics and in rags, rescuing from the jaws of the demons souls that were redeemed by the life-giving death of Christ, while they, in their peaceful and carefree existence, turn a blind eye while such souls go down to Hell. If they were real religious and real lovers of Christ, these people who malign and criticize and ridicule the friars like this, what a welcome they would give them, how glad they would be to rejoice with the friars, who apply themselves to rescuing and saving the souls Christ thought it worthwhile to ransom with his own precious Blood, valuing them so much that he made nothing of doing whatever he could for the sake of their salvation.

While we are on the subject, let me record a vision seen by a Cistercian monk who was so holy that it would appear wicked and impious not to believe him. Caught up in spirit, he saw the patroness of the Cistercian Order, the loving Mother of Jesus Christ. The blessed Virgin said to him, "I commend to your charity my brethren and my sons, so that you will love them truly and pray for them all the more earnestly." He agreed to

this happily, confident that she meant the brethren of his own Order. But she said, "I have other brethren too whom I take to myself, to be cherished and protected by my patronage." With these words, she drew back her cloak and revealed the brethren of the Order of Preachers gathered safely there, and she said to him, "These are men whose life's work it is to make sure that my beloved Son's blood was not shed in vain."

Brother Walter of Trier, of the Order of Preachers, told me a similar story. There was a lady in Saxony, a recluse with a high reputation for sanctity. When she heard of the Order of Preachers, in its early days, she was very excited by its name and passionately wanted to see some of the friars. Eventually, when the opportunity offered, she did see two young friars. She was amazed and said to the Lord, "What is this, Lord? Has the preaching of your word been usurped by such unskilled babies as these?" Soon after she had said this, the Mother of Christ appeared to her and drew back her cloak and showed her the brethren of the Order, saying, "Do not despise any such as these, because I am the one who guides and protects them, and I direct their feet into the way of peace."

Now, reader, see how truly the Mother of Truth said this. Particularly in the beginning of the Order, but also in our own day, we have seen young men with no experience, delicately brought up, only recently converted from the world, touring round the world in pairs, not overthrown even though they are among wicked people, innocent among the harmful, simple as doves among the cunningly malicious, but at the same time prudent as serpents in their care of themselves. Who would not be amazed at boys like this, now even more than before, not being burned though they are in the thick of the blazing furnace, while religious who belong to other Orders which are very strictly kept away from the turmoil of the world can hardly win through without tremendous difficulty, as we have, alas, seen and heard all too often? The friars are tormented by work, distracted by all kinds of different business, and yet they survive unbroken; but these others have nothing else to attend to except their own mental and bodily

---

1   Wandering or itinerant monks.

health, and yet they still wobble. To what are we to ascribe this? To their own strength? Surely not. Rather to the Mother of Christ. If there are some who fall, because they are flesh as well as spirit, it is because they have idly tried to support themselves on a broken reed of Egypt instead of on Mary, the pillar of heaven.

So let our evil-mouthed and impious detractors beware of going against the patronage of the Mother of Christ by persecuting her children; if they do, they are liable to incur her anger, because she supports and defends her children. A certain pope in our days, whose name we pass over in silence, out of respect for the Holy See, issued letters against the privileges which had been granted by himself and the four previous popes to these two orders, one of which is called by the Creator from all eternity "Beauty," through the prophet Zechariah, and that is the Order of Preachers, the other of which is called "Rope," by which we may obviously understand the minors. We have it from people who were in the Roman court at the time, and there can be no doubt about it, that on the same day that he wrote these letters he was struck down by paralysis and lost his ability to talk; nor did he ever again regain his health or leave his bed. What is more, he was seen after his death by a certain holy man living outside the walls of Rome, being handed over to the two saints of God, Francis and Dominic, to be judged.

35. ST. THOMAS AQUINAS

On the Proofs of God's Existence

THOMAS AQUINAS (1224/5–74), FROM a comital family in Aquino, Italy, was a Dominican philosopher and theologian who sought to defend Aristotelian philosophy within the Christian tradition and thus drew the ire of both traditionalists and radical interpreters of Aristotle. As an Aristotelian, he was certain that all knowledge began with sense perception and thus rejected arguments for God's existence such as that posited by Anselm of Canterbury (see p. 329). In this excerpt from his unfinished *Summa Theologica* (or *Summa Theologicae*), he offers other proofs of God's existence presented in the standard scholastic form of premise, objections, solution, and responses to each objection.

Source: St. Thomas Aquinas, *Summa Theologiae*, ([Cambridge]: Blackfriars; New York, McGraw-Hill, [1964–<c1969>]), 5–17.

Further Reading: Anthony Kennedy, *The Five Ways: Saint Thomas Aquinas' Proofs of God's Existence* (London: Routledge & Kegan Paul, 1969).

Question 2. Whether there is a God

Under the first of these questions there are three points of inquiry:

1. Is it self-evident that there is a God?
2. Can it be made evident?
3. Is there a God?

Article I. is it self-evident that there is a God?

THE FIRST POINT: 1. It seems self-evident that there is a God. For things are said to be self-evident to us when we are innately aware of them, as, for example, first principles. Now as Damascene[1] says when beginning his book, *the awareness that God exists is implanted by nature in everybody.* That God exists is therefore self-evident.

2. Moreover, a proposition is self-evident if we perceive its truth immediately upon perceiving the meaning of its terms: a characteristic, according to Aristotle *[Posterior Analytics I, 2. 72a7–8],* of first principles of demonstration. For example, when we know what wholes and parts are, we know at once that wholes are always bigger than their parts. Now once we understand the meaning of the word 'God' it follows that God exists. For the word means 'that than which nothing greater can be meant.' Consequently, since existence in thought and fact is greater than existence in thought alone, and since, once we understand the word 'God,' he exists in thought, he must also exist in fact.[2] It is therefore self-evident that there is a God.

3. Moreover, it is self-evident that truth exists, for even denying it would admit it. Were there no such thing as truth, then it would be true that there is no truth; something then is true, and therefore there is truth. Now God is truth itself; *I am the way, the truth and the life (John 14:6).* That there is a God, then, is self-evident.

ON THE OTHER HAND, nobody can think the opposite of a self-evident proposition, as Aristotle's discussion of first principles makes clear *[Metaphysics IV, 3. 1005b11; Posterior Analytics I, 10. 76b23–27].* But the opposite of the proposition 'God exists' can be thought, for *the fool* in the psalms *said in*

---

1 John of Damascus (ca. 676–749).
2 This is the argument of Anselm. See above, p. 329.

his heart: There is no God [Ps. 13(14):1; 52(53):1]. That God exists is therefore not self-evident.

REPLY: A self-evident proposition, though always self-evident in itself, is sometimes self-evident to us and sometimes not. For a proposition is self-evident when the predicate forms part of what the subject means; thus it is self-evident that man is an animal, since being an animal is part of the meaning of man. If therefore it is evident to everybody what it is to be this subject and what it is to have such a predicate, the proposition itself will be self-evident to everybody. This is clearly the case with first principles of demonstration, which employ common terms evident to all, such as 'be' and 'not be,' 'whole' and 'part.' But if what it is to be this subject or have such a predicate is not evident to some people, then the proposition, though self-evident in itself, will not be so to those to whom its subject and predicate are not evident. And this is why Boethius can say that *certain notions are* self-evident and *commonplaces only to the learned, as, for example, that only bodies can occupy space.*

I maintain then that the proposition 'God exists' is self-evident in itself, for, as we shall see later, its subject and predicate are identical, since God is his own existence. But, because what it is to be God is not evident to us, the proposition is not self-evident to us, and needs to be made evident. This is done by means of things which, though less evident in themselves, are nevertheless more evident to us, by means, namely, of God's effects.

Hence: 1. The awareness that God exists is not implanted in us by nature in any clear or specific way. Admittedly, man is by nature aware of what by nature he desires, and he desires by nature a happiness which is to be found only in God. But this is not, simply speaking, awareness that there is a God, any more than to be aware of someone approaching is to be aware of Peter, even should it be Peter approaching: many, in fact, believe the ultimate good which will make us happy to be riches, or pleasure, or some such thing.

2. Someone hearing the word 'God' may very well not understand it to mean 'that than which nothing greater can be thought,' indeed, some people have believed God to be a body. And even

if the meaning of the word 'God' were generally recognized to be 'that than which nothing greater can be thought,' nothing thus defined would thereby be granted existence in the world of fact, but merely as thought about. Unless one is given that something in fact exists than which nothing greater can be thought—and this nobody denying the existence of God would grant—the conclusion that God in fact exists does not follow.

3. It is self-evident that there exists truth in general, but it is not self-evident to us that there exists a First Truth.

Article 2. Can it be made evident?

THE SECOND POINT: 1. That God exists cannot, it seems, be made evident. For that God exists is an article of faith, and since, as St. Paul says, faith is concerned with *the unseen [Hebrews 11:1],* its propositions cannot be demonstrated, that is, made evident. It is therefore impossible to demonstrate that God exists.

2. Moreover, the central link of demonstration is a definition. But Damascene[3] tells us that we cannot define what God is, but only what he is not. Hence we cannot demonstrate that God exists.

3. Moreover, if demonstration of God's existence were possible, this could only be by arguing from his effects. Now God and his effects are incommensurable; for God is infinite and his effects finite, and the finite cannot measure the infinite. Consequently, since effects incommensurate with their cause cannot make it evident, it does not seem possible to demonstrate that God exists.

ON THE OTHER HAND, St. Paul tells us that *the hidden things of God can be clearly understood from the things that he has made [Romans 1:20].* If so, one must be able to demonstrate that God exists from the things that he has made, for knowing whether a thing exists is the first step towards understanding it.

REPLY: There are two types of demonstration.

---

3   *De Fide Orthodoxa* 1,4.

One, showing 'why,' follows the natural order of things among themselves, arguing from cause to effect; the other, showing 'that,' follows the order in which we know things, arguing from effect to cause (for when an effect is more apparent to us than its cause, we come to know the cause through the effect). Now any effect of a cause demonstrates that that cause exists, in cases where the effect is better known to us, since effects are dependent upon causes, and can only occur if the causes already exist. From effects evident to us, therefore, we can demonstrate what in itself is not evident to us, namely, that God exists.

Hence: 1. The truths about God which St. Paul says we can know by our natural powers of reasoning [*Romans 1:19–20*]—that God exists, for example—are not numbered among the articles of faith, but are presupposed to them. For faith presupposes natural knowledge, just as grace does nature and all perfections that which they perfect. However, there is nothing to stop a man accepting on faith some truth which he personally cannot demonstrate, even if that truth in itself is such that demonstration could make it evident.

2. When we argue from effect to cause, the effect will take the place of a definition of the cause in the proof that the cause exists; and this especially if the cause is God. For when proving anything to exist, the central link is not what that thing is (we cannot even ask what it is until we know that it exists), but rather what we are using the name of the thing to mean. Now when demonstrating from effects that God exists, we are able to start from what the word 'God' means, for, as we shall see, the names of God are derived from these effects.

3. Effects can give comprehensive knowledge of their cause only when commensurate with it: but, as we have said, any effect whatever can make it clear that a cause exists. God's effects, therefore, can serve to demonstrate that God exists, even though they cannot help us to know him comprehensively for what he is.

Article 3: Is there a God?

THE THIRD POINT: I. It seems that there is no God. For if, of two mutually exclusive things, one

were to exist without limit, the other would cease to exist. But by the word 'God' is implied some limitless good. If God then existed, nobody would ever encounter evil. But evil is encountered in the world. God therefore does not exist.

2. Moreover, if a few causes fully account for some effect, one does not seek more. Now it seems that everything we observe in this world can be fully accounted for by other causes, without assuming a God. Thus natural effects are explained by natural causes, and contrived effects by human reasoning and will. There is therefore no need to suppose that a God exists.

ON THE OTHER HAND, the book of *Exodus* represents God as saying, *I am who I am* [*Exodus 3, 14*].

REPLY: There are five ways in which one can prove that there is a God.

The first and most obvious way is based on change. Some things in the world are certainly in process of change: this we plainly see. Now anything in process of change is being changed by something else. This is so because it is characteristic of things in process of change that they do not yet have the perfection towards which they move, though able to have it; whereas it is characteristic of something causing change to have that perfection already. For to cause change is to bring into being what was previously only able to be, and this can only be done by something that already is: thus fire, which is actually hot, causes wood, which is able to be hot, to become actually hot, and in this *way* causes change in the wood. Now the same thing cannot at the same time be both actually x and potentially x, though it can be actually x and potentially y: the actually hot cannot at the same time be potentially hot, though it can be potentially cold. Consequently, a thing in process of change cannot itself cause that same change; it cannot change itself. Of necessity therefore anything in process of change is being changed by something else. Moreover, this something else, if in process of change, is itself being changed by yet another thing; and this last by another. Now we must stop somewhere, otherwise there will be no first cause of the change, and, as a result, no subsequent causes. For it is only when acted upon by the first cause that the intermediate causes will produce the change: if the hand does not move the stick, the stick will not move anything else. Hence one is bound to arrive at some first cause of change not itself being changed by anything, and this is what everybody understands by God.

The second way is based on the nature of causation. In the observable world causes are found to be ordered in series; we never observe, nor ever could, something causing itself, for this would mean it preceded itself, and this is not possible. Such a series of causes must however stop somewhere; for in it an earlier member causes an intermediate and the intermediate a last (whether the intermediate be one or many). Now if you eliminate a cause you also eliminate its effects, so that you cannot have a last cause, nor an intermediate one, unless you have a first. Given therefore no stop in the series of causes, and hence no first cause, there would be no intermediate causes either, and no last effect, and this would be an open mistake. One is therefore forced to suppose some first cause, to which everyone gives the name 'God.'

The third way is based on what need not be and on what must be, and runs as follows. Some of the things we come across can be but need not be, for we find them springing up and dying away, thus sometimes in being and sometimes not. Now everything cannot be like this, for a thing that need not be, once was not; and if everything need not be, once upon a time there was nothing. But if that were true there would be nothing even now, because something that does not exist can only be brought into being by something already existing. So that if nothing was in being nothing could be brought into being, and nothing would be in being now, which contradicts observation. Not everything therefore is the sort of thing that need not be; there has got to be something that must be. Now a thing that must be, may or may not owe this necessity to something else. But just as we must stop somewhere in a series of causes, so also in the series of things which must be and owe this to other things. One is forced therefore to suppose something which must be, and owes this to no other thing than itself; indeed it itself is the cause that other things must be.

The fourth way is based on the gradation observed in things. Some things are found to be more good, more true, more noble, and so on, and other things less. But such comparative terms describe varying degrees of approximation to a superlative; for example, things are hotter and hotter the nearer they approach what is hottest. Something therefore is the truest and best and most noble of things, and hence the most fully in being; for Aristotle says that the truest things are the things most fully in being [*Metaphysics II, 1. 993b30*]. Now *when many things possess some property in common, the one most fully possessing it causes it in the others: fire*, to use Aristotle's example, *the hottest of all things, causes all other things to be hot (Metaphysics II, 1. 993b25)*. There is something therefore which causes in all other things their being, their goodness, and whatever other perfection they have. And this we call 'God.'

The fifth way is based on the guidedness of nature. An orderedness of actions to an end is observed in all bodies obeying natural laws, even when they lack awareness. For their behavior hardly ever varies, and will practically always turn out well; which shows that they truly tend to a goal, and do not merely hit it by accident. Nothing however that lacks awareness tends to a goal, except under the direction of someone with awareness and with understanding; the arrow, for example, requires an archer. Everything in nature, therefore, is directed to its goal by someone with understanding, and this we call 'God'.

Hence: 1. As Augustine says, *Since God is supremely good, he would not permit any evil at all in his works, unless he were sufficiently almighty and good to bring good even from evil [Enchridion II]*. It is therefore a mark of the limitless goodness of God that he permits evils to exist, and draws from them good.

2. Natural causes act for definite purposes under the direction of some higher cause, so that their effects must also be referred to God as the first of all causes. In the same manner contrived effects must likewise be referred back to a higher cause than human reasoning and will, for these are changeable and can cease to be, and, as we have seen, all changeable things and things that can cease to be require some first cause which cannot change and of itself must be.

36. JACQUES FOURNIER

Inquisition Records

IN 1320 THE BISHOP of Pamiers, Jacques Fournier (ca. 1280–1342), later Pope Benedict XII, interrogated the inhabitants of the village of Montaillou in southern France on the supposition of Cathar heresy in the village. This extraordinarily detailed record allows one to see not only the procedures of the Inquisition and the nature of fourteenth-century heterodox belief, but also the private lives of ordinary villagers.

The following testimony is that of a member of the minor nobility, Béatrice de Planissoles.

Source: Jean Duvernoy, *Le registre d'inquisition de Jacques Fournier* (Paris: Mouton de Gruyter, 1978).

Further Reading: Emmanuel LeRoy Ladurie, *Montaillou: The Promised Land of Error*, trans. Barbara Bray (New York: George Braziller, 1978).

Witnesses against Béatrice, widow of Othon of Lagleize of Dalou

In the year of our lord 1320, the 19th of June. It came to the knowledge of the reverend father in Christ our lord Jacques, by the grace of God bishop of Pamiers, that Béatrice, widow of Othon, of Lagleize, of Dalou, who lives at Varilhes, had made comments that smelled of Manichean heresy or touched it, and especially against the sacrament of the altar, he wished, with the assistance of Gaillard of Pomiès, substitute for my lord the inquisitor of Carcassonne, to inform himself on the events which preceded, and he received the following witnesses:

Guillaume Roussel of Dalou, sworn witness and ordered to say the truth, said:

Ten years ago, it seems to me, but I do not remember exactly the period or the day, I was at the home of Béatrice, in her house near the church of Dalou, and two of her daughters were near Béatrice, one of whom was about six or seven years old and the other four or five, and some other people. I do not recall the names of these latter.

They started to talk about priests and the sacrament of the altar which is the business of priests. Béatrice said, I think, that she was astounded: "If God was in the sacrament of the altar how did he allow himself to be eaten by the priests (or by a priest)?" Hearing that, I left the house in confusion.

—Why did you hide this for so long?—Because I was not interrogated before and also because I did not think that I was doing wrong in not denouncing it myself.

—Did Béatrice say this as a joke?—It did not seem to me that she was joking, the more I paid attention to what came from her facial expression and her words.

—Did Béatrice go to church willingly?—No, not until she was reprimanded by Barthélemy, a priest vicar of this church. Afterwards, she went to church.

—Who were the people who were very intimate with this Béatrice, who might have known her secrets?—Grazide, widow of Bernard Pujol, of Dalou, Bernarde, wife of Garisot, who lives at Varilhes, Mabille, wife of Raimond Gouzey of Herm, Sibille, maid servant of Michel Dupont of Foix, Esperte, wife of Arnaud of Varilhes.

The same day and year as above, Guillaume of Montaut, rector of the church of Dalou, sworn witness and interrogated on what had preceded said:

> Twelve years ago, it seems to me, although I do not exactly recall the period or the day, I was at the church of Dalou, and there I found Mabille Vaquier, of Dalou, now deceased. She told me that she had reprimanded this Béatrice who was the wife of her uncle because she did not go to church and also because she had heard her say evil things which had upset her. What she had said was, "You believe that what the priests hold at the altar is the body of Christ? Surely, if it was the body of Christ, even if it was as large as this mountain, the priests would already have eaten it all themselves!" And for this reason, Jean had himself had insulting words with Béatrice.

And he said nothing else although he was diligently interrogated.

Confession of Béatrice, widow of Othon de Lagleize of Dalou

In the year of the Lord 1320, the Wednesday after the feast of Saint James the Apostle (July 23, 1320), the reverend father in Christ my lord Jacques, by the grace of God bishop of Pamiers, addressed a letter of citation against Béatrice, widow of Othon de Lagleize, living in Varilhes, the contents of which follows:

Brother Jacques, by the divine commiseration bishop of Pamiers, to his well-loved in Christ curate of Varilhes or his vicar, greetings in the Lord.

We order you to require immediately Béatrice, widow of Othon de Lagleize and Jeanne, wife of Guillaume de Reumaze the younger, to appear next Saturday before us in our seat of Pamiers in person, to answer certain facts touching the Catholic faith, about which we desire to know the truth and the reasons for it.

Given in the above mentioned seat, the Wednesday before the feast of Saint James the Apostle, the year of the Lord 1320. Return the letter sealed with your seal in evidence of having accomplished this order.

The designated Saturday the above-mentioned Béatrice cited by the curate of Varilhes, as is evident from the seal of the above-mentioned priest on the back of the above-mentioned letter of summons, appeared before my lord the bishop of the above-mentioned see, and my lord the bishop informed her that she was strongly suspected of heresy according to his sources, and that she had to speak the pure and simple truth on all of the points about herself as well as about others living and dead.

The above-mentioned Béatrice said nothing to the above order, neither about herself nor about others, and she did not wish to do so. My lord bishop, wishing to direct her to say the truth and not to hide it and not wishing to see her fall into perjury, asked her without demanding an oath, if she had ever affirmed that if the sacrament of the altar was the true body of Christ, he would not allow himself to be eaten by priests, and that if it was as large as Mount Margail, which is near Dalou, it would long ago have been eaten by the priests alone. She answered no.

He asked her if she had seen, received in her home, or had gone to see Pierre, Jacques, and Guillaume Authié or other heretics. She answered no, except that she had once seen Pierre Authié exercising his profession of notary and in this capacity he had prepared the act of sale of a property belonging to her husband. She had approved this sale by oath, and Pierre Authié had prepared the instrument of sale and of its ratification. He was not yet considered a heretic at this time, and she had not seen him since.

On the question of my lord bishop, she said that she had once received the late Gaillarde Cuq in her home for a night, but she did not hear from her spells, or see magic, or receive evil teachings from her.

My lord bishop, hearing that Béatrice did not wish to say or avow these things and without oath wishing to act with benevolence toward her and to listen more, assigned the following Tuesday for her to appear before the above-mentioned see, ordering her to be present that day in person and to be ready to answer these facts and all others concerning the faith under oath. Béatrice accepted this day willingly, promising by her own oath to appear before my lord the bishop as ordered and to answer these facts under oath and to do and accomplish all that would be necessary in this matter. She was thus graciously postponed until the Tuesday by my lord bishop.

On that Tuesday the above-mentioned Béatrice did not appear, although she was waited for all the day, and for this reason the lord bishop formally noted her absence and declared her defiant.

After this the above mentioned Béatrice, fleeing, was sought by the men of my lord bishop carrying his letters to all bailiffs, officers and judges and was found by them while she was hiding in Mas-Saintes-Puelles, in the diocese of Saint Papoul. She was taken prisoner by the men of my lord bishop and the sergeants of the court of Mas-Saintes-Puelles, to my lord bishop and presented to him the 1st of August of the above year. The below-listed objects were found on her person. These were all shown in the presence of my lord bishop and she recognized that they were all hers and that she had fled with them.

My lord bishop ordered that she be held strongly suspect concerning the Catholic faith, both because of the preceding information and by her flight and the objects found on her. Wishing to hear about her, he received from her an oath to say the pure, simple and entire truth both about herself and about others living and dead as witness, in matters concerning the Catholic faith. When she had sworn this oath, he asked her:

—Are you guilty of heresy? Have you had relations and intimacy with Pierre, Guillaume, Jacques Authié, the heretics, and with other heretics, by adoring them, seeing them, giving or sending them anything, or favoring them in any other manner?—No, on my oath, except that which I said about Pierre Authié, when I ratified the act of sale which my dead husband the knight Béof de Roquefort made.

When I contracted marriage with this Bérenger, at the wedding ceremony, I saw Guillaume Authié dancing. This was about twenty-four years ago.

—Do you know of other persons living or dead who had this sort of relations or intimacy or who committed anything of this sort?—No. But, when I was a little girl and I was at Celles, about six years before marrying my first husband, the people were hurrying one day to see the body of Christ at the church of this place. I heard a mason (I don't know his name but I think he was Oudin) ask where these people were going. They answered that they were going to see the body of Christ. He said, "They need not hurry so for that because if the body of Christ was as large as the Pech de Boulque, it would long ago have been eaten like a pasta!"

And I sometimes repeat these words that I heard this man say, without believing them, and I told them at Dalou. I do not recall if it was when the people were going to see the body of the Lord at Dalou or on other occasions. It seems to me that it was about fourteen years ago that I repeated these words.

—To whom, on presence of whom?—I do not recall.

(August 7, 1320, in the chamber before the bishop and Gaillard de Pomiès)

Twenty-six years ago during the month of August (I do not recall the day), I was the wife of the late knight Bérenger de Roquefort, castelain of Montaillou. The late Raimond Roussel, of Rades, was the intendant and the stewart of our household which we held at the castle of Montaillou. He often asked me to leave with him and to go to Lombardy with the good Christians who are there, telling me that the

Lord had said that man must quit his father, mother, wife, husband, son and daughter and follow him, and that he would give him the kingdom of heaven. When I asked him, "How could I quit my husband and my sons?" he replied that the Lord had ordered it and that it was better to leave a husband and sons whose eyes rot than to abandon him who lives for eternity and who gives the kingdom of heaven.

When I asked him "How is it possible that God created so many men and women if many of them are not saved?" he answered that only the good Christians will be saved and no others, neither religious nor priests, nor anyone except these good Christians. Because, he said, just as it is impossible for a camel to pass through the eye of a needle, it is impossible for those who are rich to be saved. This is why the kings and princes, prelates and religious, and all those who have wealth, cannot be saved, but only the good Christians. They remained in Lombardy, because they did not dare live here where the wolves and the dogs would persecute them. The wolves and the dogs were the bishops and the Dominicans, who persecute the good Christians and chase them from this country.

He said that he had listened to some of these good Christians. They were such that once one had heard them speak one could not do without them and if I heard them one time, I would be one of theirs for ever.

When I asked how we could flee together and go to the good Christians, because, when my husband found out, he would follow us and kill us, Raimond answered that when my husband took a long trip and was far from our country, we could leave and go to the good Christians. I asked him how we would live when we were there. He answered that they would take care of us and give us enough with which to live. "But," I told him, "I am pregnant. What could I do with the child that I am carrying when I leave with you for the good Christians?" "If you give birth to it in their presence, it will be an angel. With the help of God they will make a king and a holy thing of him because he will be born without sin, not having frequented the people of this world,

and they would be able to educate him perfectly in their sect, since he would know no other."

He also told me that all spirits sinned at the beginning with the sin of pride, believing that they could know more and be worth more than God, and for that they fell to earth. These spirits later take on bodies, and the world will not end before all of them have been incarnated into the bodies of men and women. Thus it is that the soul of a new-born child is as old as that of an old man.

They also said that the souls of men and women who were not good Christians, after leaving their bodies, enter the bodies of other men and women a total of nine times. If in these nine bodies they do not find the body of a good Christian, the soul is damned. If on the contrary, they find the body of a good Christian, the soul is saved.

I asked him how the spirit of a dead man or woman could enter the mouth of a pregnant woman and from there into the mouth of the fruit that she carries in her womb. He answered that the spirit could enter the fruit of the woman's womb by any part of her body. When I asked him why children do not speak from birth, since they have the old souls of other persons, he answered that God does not wish it. He also told me that the spirits of God which sinned lived wherever they could.

Thus he urged me to leave with him so that we could go together to the good Christians, mentioning various noble women who had gone there.

Alesta and Serena, women of Châteauverdun, painted themselves with colors which made them appear foreign so that they could not be recognized and went to Toulouse. When they arrived at an inn, the hostess wanted to know if they were heretics and gave them live chickens, telling them to prepare them because she had things to do in town, and left the house.

When she had returned she found the chickens still alive and asked them why they had not prepared them. They responded that if the hostess killed them, they would prepare them but that they would not kill them. The hostess heard that and went to tell the inquisitors that two heretics were in her establishment. They were arrested and burned. When it was time to go to the stake, they asked for water to wash their faces, saying that they would not go to God painted thus.

I told Raimond that they would have done better to abandon their heresy than to allow themselves to be burned, and he told me that the good Christians did not feel fire because fire with which they are burned cannot hurt them.

Raimond also told me that one of these two women, when she was leaving her house at Châteauverdun, had a child in a crib that she wanted to see before leaving. She kissed it, the child smiled, and as she was beginning to move away from the place where it lay, she returned toward it. The child began to laugh and this process began again so that she could not leave. Finally she ordered its nurse to take it, which she did. Thus she was able to leave.

And Raimond told me this to encourage me to do the same!

He told me that Stephanie, the wife of the late Guillaume Arnaud, one of the ladies of Châteauverdun, had abandoned everything and had gone to the good Christians. Prades Tavernier, who since has been accepted as a heretic and is called André, left with her. He told me all of this to convince me to leave, but I answered that if two or three women of my rank left with us, I would then have an excuse that I would not have if, still young, I left with him, because people would immediately say that we had left our country to satisfy our lust.

After having so often shared his heretical discourses with me in various times and places and invited me to leave with him, finally one evening after we had dined together, he secretly entered the bedroom where I slept and put himself under my bed.

I put the house in order and went to bed and when all was quiet and asleep and I was asleep myself, Raimond came out from under my bed and slipped into it in his night shirt and started to act as though he wished to lie with me carnally. "What is going on?" I said. He told me to be quiet. I answered, "What do you mean, be quiet, you peasant?" And I started to shout and to call my maid servants who slept beside me in this bedroom telling them that there was a man with me in my bed.

When he heard this he left the bed and the bedroom. The next day he said that he had acted badly in hiding near me. I answered, "I see now that your invitations to go to the good Christians were intended only to possess me and know me carnally. If I had not been afraid that my husband would believe that I did something dishonorable with you, I would immediately put you in the dungeon."

We did not speak further of heretical questions and shortly after Raimond left our house and returned home to Prades.

—Did you believe and do you still believe what he told you about the good Christians, about the sin of the spirits of heaven, about the reincarnation of souls?—No.

—Did you ever reveal the statements which you heard from this Raimond?—No, except to a Franciscan friar of the convent of Limoux in sacramental confession.

—Did anyone else hear the heretical statements which this Raimond made to you?—I do not recall that there was anyone else present.

Alazaïs Gonelle from Gébetz in the diocese of Alet often came to talk with me and she told me on behalf of Raimond that it would be good for us to leave for Lombardy and the good Christians to save our souls because no one could be saved except in their sect. If I wanted to go with Raimond she herself, Alazaïs, would go with us and she knew that if anyone left for Lombardy and the good Christians, Algée de Martre, from Camurac in the diocese of Alet, would leave with them.

This Alazaïs had been the concubine of Guillaume Clergue, the brother of the rector of Montaillou, and this Algée is the sister of the mother of this rector. But I did not see this Algée.

—What did you understand by these good Christians concerning whom Raimond and Alazaïs spoke constantly?—By good Christians I understood the heretics.

About 25 years ago, when I was living in Montaillou, one day during the month of July, Alazaïs, the wife of Bernard Ribas of

Montaillou, knocked at the door. I sent to see what she wanted. She said that she wanted some vinegar. I ordered some to be given her. She said that she did not want it, but that she wanted to speak with me. I replied that I could not, and she departed. The same day she returned and knocked at the door. I sent to find out what she wanted and she said that her daughter was in agony and she asked me to come down to her house because her daughter very much wanted to see me. I answered that I could not come down to her house because it had not been long enough since I had given birth. This Alazaïs returned again to me the same day asking and begging that I go see her daughter, which I could not do.

The same day I had made a candle which is called a "recolor" to go to the church of Sainte-Marie-de-Carnesses. I summoned a woman who lived at the home of the rector of Montaillou (this woman was from Limbrassac) and we both went to the church. Descending to Montaillou, we met this Alazaïs who was leading two geese; she told me to come to her home to see her daughter Guillemette (the wife of Pierre Clergue of Montaillou). I told her that I could not go and she told me that her brother Prades Tavernier was there and wished to speak with me because Stéphanie, the wife of Guillaume Arnaud de Châteauverdun, had given him a message which he wished to transmit to me.

But since it was notorious that this Prades Tavernier had left the country with this Stéphanie to go to the heretics, I said to Alazaïs to leave me alone because I did not wish to speak with Prades. She then left me and I did not see this Prades Tavernier, and I did not speak with him since his departure from the region with this Stéphanie.

About 21 years ago, a year after the death of my husband, I wanted to go to the church of Montaillou to confess during Lent. When I was there, I went to Pierre Clergue, the rector, who was hearing confessions behind the altar of Saint Mary. As soon as I had knelt before him, he embraced me, saying that there was no woman in the world that he loved as much as me. In my surprise, I left without having confessed.

Later, around Easter, he visited me several times, and he asked me to give myself to him. I said one day that he so bothered me in my home that I would rather give myself to four men than to a single priest because I had heard it said that a woman who gave herself to a priest could not see the face of God. To which he answered that I was an ignorant fool because the sin is the same for a woman to know her husband or another man, and the same whether the man were husband or priest. It was even a greater sin with a husband he said, because the wife did not think that she had sinned with her husband but realized it with other men. The sin was therefore greater in the first case.

I asked him how he, who was a priest, could speak like that, since the church said that marriage had been instituted by God, and that it was the first sacrament instituted by God between Adam and Eve, as a result of which it was not a sin when spouses know each other. He answered, "If it was God who instituted marriage between Adam and Eve and if he created them, why didn't he protect them from sin?" I understood then that he was saying that God did not create Adam and Eve and that he had not instituted marriage between them. He added that the Church taught many things which were contrary to truths. Ecclesiastics said these things because without them it would inspire neither respect nor fear. Because, except for the Gospels and the Lord's Prayer, all of the other texts of Scripture were only "affitilhas," a word in the vernacular which designates what one adds on one's own to what one has heard.

I answered that in this case ecclesiastics were throwing the people into error.

(August 8, 1320, in the Chamber of the bishop before the bishop and Gaillard de Pomiès)

Speaking of marriage, he told me that many of the rules concerning it do not come from divine will who did not forbid people to marry their sisters or other persons related by blood, since at the beginning brothers knew their sister. But when several brothers had one or two pretty sisters, each wanted to have her or them.

The result was many murders among them and this is why the Church had forbidden brothers to know their sisters or blood relatives carnally. But for God the sin is the same whether it is an outside woman, a sister, or another relative, because the sin is as great with one woman as with another, except that it is a greater sin between a husband and wife, because they do not confess it and they unite themselves without shame.

He added that the marriage was complete and consummated as soon as a person had promised his faith to the other. What is done at the church between spouses, such as the nuptial benediction, was only a secular ceremony which had no value and had been instituted by the Church only for secular splendor.

He further told me that a man and a woman could freely commit any sort of sin as long as they lived in this world and act entirely according to their pleasure. It was sufficient that at their death they be received into the sect or the faith of the good Christians to be saved and absolved of all the sins committed during this life. Because, he said, Christ said to his apostles to leave father, mother, spouse, and children, and all that they possessed, to follow him, in order to have the kingdom of heaven. Peter answered Christ, "If we, who have left everything and followed you, will have the kingdom of heaven, what will be the share of those who are ill and cannot follow you?" The Lord answered Peter that his "friends" would come and impose their hands on the heads of the ill. The ill would be healed, and healed they would follow him and have the kingdom of heaven.

The rector said that these "friends of God" were the good Christians, whom others call heretics. The imposition of the hands that they give to the dying saves them and absolves them of all their sins.

To prove that it was better for the world if brothers married sisters, he told me, "You see that we are four brothers. I am a priest and do not want a wife. If my brothers Guillaume and Bernard had married Esclarmonde and Guillemette, our sisters, our house would not have been ruined by the need of giving them a dowry. It would have remained whole. With a wife who would have been brought into the house for Raimond, our brother, we would have had enough spouses and our house would have been richer. It would therefore have been better if the brother married the sister or the sister the brother, because when she leaves her paternal house with great wealth in order to marry an outsider, the house is ruined."

And with these opinions and many others he influenced me to the point that in the octave of saints Peter and Paul I gave myself to him one night in my home. This was often repeated and he kept me like this for one and one half years, coming two or three times each week to spend the night in my house near the chateau of Montaillou.

I myself came two nights to his house so that he could unite himself with me. He even knew me carnally Christmas night and still this priest said the mass the next morning although there were other priests present.

And when, on this night of the Nativity, he wanted to have relations with me, I said to him, "How could you want to commit so great a sin on so holy a night?" He answered that the sin was the same to have intercourse with a woman on any other night or on Christmas night. Since this time and many others he said mass the morning after having known me the night before without having confessed since there was no other priest and since I often asked him how he could celebrate the mass after having committed such a sin the night before, he answered that the only valid confession is one which one makes to God, who knows the sin before it is committed, and who alone can absolve it. But the confession that one makes to a priest who is ignorant of the sin until it is revealed to him and who does not have the power to absolve sin has no value and is only made for the ostentation and the splendor of this world. Because only God can absolve sins, man cannot.

He added that I should not confess to another priest the sin which I committed with him but only to God, who knew it and who could absolve me, because a man could not do it. In order to incite me to believe that not even the sovereign pontiff nor the other bishops nor the priests who depend on them do not have this power, he alleged that Saint Peter was not a pope during his life but after his death and that his bones were thrown into a pit where they remained many years. When they were discovered, they were washed and placed in the chair on which the Roman pontiffs sit. But, since the bones of Saint Peter did not have the power to absolve when they were enthroned and apostolized, nor did Peter thus become "apostolic" nor did the Roman pontiffs who are made popes on this chair have the power to pardon. Only the good Christians who suffer persecution and death are able to do so, like saints Laurence, Stephen, and Barthélemy, but not the bishops and the priests subject to the Roman church, who are heretics and persecutors of the good Christians. God took this power from them and retained it for himself, and transmitted it only to the good Christians who he knew and announced in advance that they would suffer persecution.

I then asked him since confession to priests had no value, since they could not absolve, and since the penances that they imposed were without value, why he himself heard confessions, absolved, and imposed penances. This priest said that it was necessary for him and for other priests to do this, even though they meant nothing, because otherwise he would lose his income and no one would give them anything if they did not do what the Church ordered.

But only the good Christians and those who were received by them after having adored them could absolve all other people from their sins. And it was not necessary that those who wished to be absolved by them of their sins confess to them. It was sufficient to give themselves to God and to the good Christians, and they would absolve them simply by the imposition of hands.

He told me all this and what will follow in my home, sometimes near a window that looked out on the road, while I was delousing his head, sometimes near the fire, sometimes when I was in bed. We avoided being overheard by others as much as possible when we broached this subject. I do not recall if Sibille

my maid servant, the daughter of Arnaud Teisseyre of Montaillou, who became the concubine of Raimond Clergue, heard anything.

The priest told me that God only made the spirits and that which did not decay or corrode, because the works of God endure for ever. But all of the body which one sees and which one feels, that is to say the heaven and the earth and all that is in them, except only the spirits, were the work of the devil, who rules the world, who made them. It is because it is he who made them that all things are in the process of corruption, because he cannot make anything that is stable or solid.

He told me at this time that God, in the beginning, made a man who spoke and walked. Seeing it, the devil made the body of another man which could neither walk nor speak. God said to him, "Why did you make a sort of person that can neither walk nor speak?" The devil answered that he could not, and said to God to make his person walk and speak. God said that he would willingly do so, if what he put in this man would be for him, God. The devil agreed. God breathed into the mouth of the man that the devil had made and this man began to walk and to talk. Since then the soul of man belongs to God and the body to the devil.

He also told me that God had made all the spirits of heaven. These spirits sinned in their pride, wishing to equal God, and because of this sin they fell from heaven through the air and onto the earth. They live in and penetrate the bodies that they encounter, indifferently, when able, whether bodies of animals or animals of humans. And these spirits in the bodies of animals are as capable of reason and understanding as are those in human bodies, except that they cannot speak in the bodies of animals. And the fact that the spirits which are in the bodies of animals are endowed with reason and with understanding results, he said, in the fact that they flee from that which is dangerous for them and search what is good for them. This is why it is a sin to kill any animal or a person, because each has reason and understanding. He also said that it is necessary that all these spirits enter a human body to be able to do penance for this sin of pride, and this must be done before the end of the world. It is only in the bodies of humans, according to him, that these spirits can do penance for this sin. They cannot do it in the bodies of beasts.

He also told me that these spirits who sinned thus, if they can enter the body of a good Christian, rejoice greatly, and, as soon as they leave his body, they return to heaven from which they fell. If they do not enter the body of a good Christian but into the body of another man or another woman, when they leave they enter, if they can, into the body of another man or woman up to nine times, if they do not enter the body of a good Christian man or woman. If they do enter, as soon as they exit, they return to heaven from whence they had fallen.

But if in these nine bodies which they enter successively, there is no good Christian, when they leave the last body they are entirely lost and cannot do any further penance. He told me that all of this is true in general, but the spirits which consented to the betrayal of Christ, as was the case of Judas and some of the other Jews, as soon as they left their bodies, were immediately lost and could not do penance, and they did not enter the bodies of people to do penance. But those who were present at the betrayal of Christ without having consented to it, entered into nine other bodies like the others.

This priest also told me that only the spirits who enter the bodies of good Christians will be saved and no others, whether they be Christian, Jew or Saracen. According to him all of the good Christians, those who worship them believing in them and having been received into their sect, have been saved. And he said that for this reason his mother Mengarde was saved because she had done much good for the good Christians, and Roqua and Raimond Roché his son who were immured for heresy for a time received all of their subsistence from her house. Her mother was kind to these two people because they had been heretics and believers.

This priest also told me that these spirits which were in heaven and which had sinned in revolting against God divided. Some of them plotted and rebelled against God, and these were first to leave heaven. Their sin was so serious that later God did not wish to accept penance and they were sent to hell and are demons. But there were other spirits that did not plot the revolt against God and did not rebel openly but who wished to follow those who had planned this revolt. Those fell onto the earth and in the air and are incorporated into the bodies of men and animals, do penance, and are saved or damned as has been previously said.

He also said that the good Christians do not believe that God causes the seeds of things that multiply, flower, and ripen on the earth. Because if it were so, since God could also make things grow on bare rock as well as on fertile soil, the seeds thrown on stone would grow as well as those on earth. But this takes place, he said, because soil is rich, and God does not intervene.

He also told me that the good Christians do not believe that Christ took flesh from the holy Virgin nor did he descend to take flesh from her because, before she was born Christ had existed from all eternity. But he simply "adombrad" himself in Mary without taking anything from her. Explaining this word "adombration" this priest told me that, just as the wine that is in a cask is within its shadow without taking anything from it, but is only contained in it, in the same way Christ lived in the virgin Mary without taking anything from her, but was simply in her as is the contents in a container.

He also told me that Christ, although he dined with his disciples, never ate or drank, although he appeared to do so.

He told me that from the time that Christ was crucified on the cross, no one should venerate or adore it since an outrage against Christ had been committed on it.

He also told me that there was no church of God except there where there is a good Christian because he is the Church of God, but elsewhere there is no church of God and the other men are not the church of God.

He also told me that when the good Christians are burned for their faith they are the martyrs of Christ. He also told me that when these good Christians have received any-one into their sect, that person must no longer eat or drink except cold water, and he said that when the people thus die of weakness they be-come the saints of God.

He also told me that the fires in which they are burned do not make the good Christians suffer, because God assists them so that they will not suffer from this fire and that they will not have great pain.

The above-mentioned Raimond Roussel told me that a man was seriously ill and a priest came to him and asked him if he wanted to see and receive the body of the Lord. The man replied that he wanted to see the body of Christ more than anything else in the world. This priest went to get the body of the Lord and bring it to the sick man. He took it from the pix[1] and held it in his hands, showing it to the sick man, and questioned him on the ar-ticles of faith especially asking if he believed that it was the body of Christ. The indignant patient said to the priest, "You miserable whore of a peasant, if what you are holding were the body of Christ, and if it were as large as a great mountain, you and the other priests would long ago have eaten it all!" And he refused to receive the body of Christ.

Pierre Clergue, the rector, told me that this world which the devil had made is decaying and will totally destroy itself, and before this happens, God will assemble his friends and draw them to himself so that they do not see so great a catastrophe as that of the destruction of the world.

When I went down from the region of Alion to contract a marriage with my second hus-band, Othon de Lagleize of Dalou, this rector told me that he was very displeased that I was going down into that low country because no one would dare speak further with me about the good Christians or come see me to save my soul. I was going to live with wolves and dogs, of whom, he said, none would be saved. He called all the Catholics who are not good Christians wolves and dogs.

He nevertheless said that if one day my

heart told me to be received into the sect of good Christians, I should let him know early because he would do all that he could so that the good Christians would receive me into their sect and save my soul. I answered him that I did not want to be received into that sect but that I wanted to be saved in the faith in which I was, quoting my sister Gentille, who had first said this.

These heretical conversations continued be-tween us for around two years and this priest taught me all of this.

—Did you believe and do you still believe these heresies that this rector of the church of Montaillou, Pierre Clergue, told you and in which he instructed you?—The last year, when I left the region of Alion from Easter until the following August, I completely and fully be-lieved these errors to the point that I would not have hesitated to undergo any suffering to defend them. I believed that they were truth taught by the priest whom, because he was a priest, I believed what he said. But when I was at Crampagna with my second husband and I heard the preaching of the Dominicans and Franciscans and I visited with faithful Christians, I abandoned these errors and her-esies and I confessed at the penitential court of a Franciscan of the convent of Limoux in the Church of Notre Dame de Marseille where I had gone to see my sister Gentille, who lived at Limoux and who was the wife of the late Paga de Post. I made this confession fifteen years ago and I remained around five years without confessing heretical opinions that I had heard and believed, although I confessed my other sins during these five years.

At the time when I believed these heresies, I did not see (nor did I see before or after) any heretics that I knew to be heretics, although I believed that they were good men because they suffered martyrdom for God and this priest had taught me that it was only in their sect that one could be saved.

I greatly regret having ever heard these he-retical opinions and even more for having be-lieved these heresies, and I am ready to accept

---

1   A container in which Eucharistic wafers are kept.

the penance that my lord the bishop may wish to impose on me for them.

(August 9, 1320, in the chamber of the bishopric, before the bishop and Gaillard de Pomiès)

Nineteen years ago at the Assumption of Mary (August 15, 1301) I left Prades in the region of Alion where I lived in a house near the church and went to Crampagna to marry Othon de Lagleize. Before leaving Prades, Bernard Belot of Montaillou, who died on the wall of Carcassonne, came to see me and told me that the rector of Montaillou, Pierre Clergue, was very unhappy with me because I was going into the low country where I could not have good Christians to save my soul. Because these good Christians did not trust the people of the low country and that they did not dare to speak with them about their sect or their life. This is why this priest feared that I would lose my soul if I went down to the low country where there were no good Christians. This Bernard also told me that the good Christians, if they dared, would ask me to see them, because, he said, no one could be confirmed in their faith if he had not seen them and heard them speak. I answered that I did not wish to see them and that I did not have the heart to wish to do so. He told me to send them something as a sign of recognition in the same way that when a person received a benefit from another, he has the obligation to pray to God for that person. These good Christians, he told me, only pray for those from whom they receive something. I asked him, "What should I send them?" He answered that it was sufficient that I send them something if I wished that they pray to God for you. I gave him five Paris sous, the current coin, to take to the good Christians and I said, "I do not know who will have this money, but may it be for the love of God."

At the time that I lived in Montaillou and Prades, the rumor was circulating among the believers that the heretics were visiting the houses of the brothers Raimond and Bernard Belot, who lived together, those of Alazaïs den Riba, sister of the heretic Prades Tavernier, and of Guillaume Benet, brother of Arnaud Benet

of Ax, who were all from Montaillou. It was said that they served as guides for these heretics and that they knew their routes.

The same year that I sent this money to the heretics by the intermediary of Bernard Belot, I was at Crampagna with Guillaume Othon my second husband around the feast of St. Michael in September. Bernard Belot came to see me at Crampagna in the house or the estate called Carol, where I was then living, and told me that the rector of Montaillou sent greetings and also sent me by his intermediary an act of marriage concerning my marriage with my first husband in which was found the assignment of my dowry. I had deposited this act with the rector. Since I was not concerned about this act because I had already settled with the heirs of my first husband, I thought that Bernard was bringing me a message from the rector, and I spoke with him in secret. He said that the rector greeted me and asked me to remember the discussions we had about the sect and the stature and way of life of the good men. I answered that I did not wish to remember and that on the contrary it very much displeased me to have ever heard or to have spoken of them. I told him that it was better to hear the opinions of the Dominicans and Franciscans than to speak of the sect and the way of life of the heretics, and this Bernard told me that my heart had changed quickly and that the discussions that he and the rector had held with me were lost. He had thought right away, he said, that when I descended into the low country they had lost their good words. I answered that in the future he was not to send me such messages because if my husband knew something bad would happen. "In the future, do not return, because if you visit this house my husband will believe right away something evil about me, either dishonest conduct or some other evil."

Thus he left me, unhappy with my answer, and said that he did not believe that their good words could have been so quickly lost.

Twenty-two years ago, I was gravely ill at Varilhes in the house of my late husband Othon. This priest came one day to the synod at Pamiers and he entered my home to visit me. When he was with me he sat at the head of my bed where I lay and asked me how I was, gently stroking my hand and arm. I answered that I was seriously ill. He then said to my late daughter Béatrice who was there to leave the room because he wanted to speak to me in private. When she had left, he asked me how my heart was. I answered him that it was very weak and that I was afraid of the discussions that we had together (I meant by that the heretical opinions described above that the priest had told me). I was so afraid of them that I did not dare to confess these sins to any priest for fear that he would judge me of suspicious faith. He told me not to fear that because God knew my sin and alone could absolve the sins I had and that I need not confess to any priest. He also told me that I would soon be cured and that when he went down to Pamiers he would see me and that we would discuss these matters. This said, he left me and since then I have not seen him. He nevertheless sent me an engraved cup and some sugar.

About twenty-one years ago, I was at Montaillou after the death of my first husband. One day, around Christmas, I was in the home of Alazaïs Maury of Montaillou. We were warming ourselves by the fire and since we were there Gauzia, the wife of Bernard Clergue, arrived and in front of me asked this Alazaïs if Guillemette, the widow of Pierre Faure of Montaillou, was dead. Alazaïs answered yes and that she had been buried. Gauzia then said, "Did you do it well?" Alazaïs answered, "Yes, by my faith, well." Gauzia then said, "And you did it very, very well? You did not omit anything?" Alazaïs answered that it had been done "well" and that there had been no obstacle to doing it. Gauzia then said, "Thank God!" Having said this, she sat down by the fire. I did not understand why this discussion had taken place between these two women nor what they meant to say, but a few days later I met Alazaïs, I don't remember where, and I asked her what these words between her and Gauzia meant. She answered that they meant nothing. I said that on the contrary one did not say such things for nothing. Then she told me that she did not dare reveal to me what they meant because she

feared that I would denounce her. I promised on my faith to keep her secret. She then told me that the good Christians had come to the house of the ill woman, Guillemette, and she had been received into their sect to become a good Christian. After that, they had ordered her not to eat or to drink except for cold water, and she did so, neither eating not drinking anything but cold water. She stayed in this state for around fifteen days until her death.

From this time on Alazaïs began to visit me and she spoke to me about the good Christians, saying that they were holy and good people and that one should have more confidence in them than in the clergy because they bore many persecutions for Christ and that the clerics do not bear persecution but that they have the pleasures of this world.

She said that a person should not quit the sect of the good Christians for any danger or misfortune. She also said that one can only be saved in their sect and in their faith. Regardless of what sins one has committed in the present life, if one has been received by them at the end, those sins are remitted and one is saved.

She also said that these good Christians hide and do not dare show themselves because the Church persecutes and destroys them and that it is a great work of charity to do them good. She said that she and her husband Raimond Maury often did them good deeds taking on their poverty and depriving themselves of food to give it to them and often sending them flour and other things that they had, always of the best quality. I said, "These good Christians accept flour?" She answered yes, and I then gave her a quarter of a barrel of flour to give to the good persons on my behalf. I do not know if she gave them the flour or not.

Because of the opinions that I heard concerning these heretics from Raimond Roussel and the priest, I believed that what Alazaïs had told me was true concerning these good Christians. This is why I sent them flour through her. Afterwards I did not further speak with this Alazaïs about the heretics.

Around the same time Alazaïs, wife of Pens Azéma of Montaillou had a son named Raimond Azéma, who was said by some to frequent the heretics. One evening at nightfall I was at her home. Raimond arrived carrying a basket in which he seemed to have something and he quickly left. I asked Alazaïs where her son was going at such an hour. She answered me that he was going somewhere. I asked her to be more precise, and she answered that I was "chilarda" (that means I had big eyelids) and that she would not reveal where her son was going. I said, "And why not?" She said that I would not keep the secret. I assured her of the contrary and also asked her what her son was carrying in the basket. She said that actually her son was carrying food in the basket and that when I had insisted and asked her many times to whom he was carrying this food, she finally told me that he was taking it to the good persons whom the others called heretics, and yet these were good and holy people who underwent many persecutions for Christ. One must not abandon their faith out of any human fear because all that one sees in the world was made by the devil who rules the world and all will be destroyed like spider webs except for spirits which were made by God. She also told me that people cannot be saved except in their faith and belief, and that it is sufficient to have been received into their sect to be saved regardless of the sins that one has committed during one's life, and that it is a great thing that one can save one's soul by believing in these people and in dying in one's home. I only answered that her son would be in great trouble if he was stopped carrying this basket to the good Christians. Since then I did not speak with her about this subject. The above-mentioned Raimond drowned in the Douctuyre near the church of Notre-Dame de Vals.

About twenty years ago, when I was living in Prades, one day, I do not remember exactly, I was going to Cassou to visit my sister Ava, wife of Verèze, who was in labor. The following Sunday I went to the church of Unac which is the parish church of Cassou. When I was there Raimonde, widow of Guillaume-Bernard of Luzenac, who had also come, embraced and kissed me (because she was a member of my family), and told me near the entry of the church, "And you, my cousin who is in

this good region, you have not yet seen these good people? If I lived there, I would see them willingly." I asked her whom she called "good people." She answered that she meant the good Christians. I told her that I had not seen any and that I did not have the heart to see them. She told me that once I had seen them and listened to them, I would no longer want to hear anyone else, and that after having listened one time, I would always be in a good state, wherever I went. We said nothing more on this subject and we entered the church and heard mass.

(August 12, 1320, before the bishop and Gaillard de Pomiès)

During the life time of my husband, Raimond Clergue, alias Pathau, natural son of Guillaume Clergue (he himself brother of Pons Clergue who was the father of Pierre Clergue the curate of Montaillou) took me by force in the castle. A year later, at the death of my husband Bérenger de Roquefort, he kept me publicly. This did not prevent this curate, Pierre Clergue, from soliciting me, even though he knew that his cousin Raimond had possessed me.

"How can you ask this," I said to him. "You know very well that your cousin Raimond had me. He will reveal everything!" The rector answered me that this was neither necessary nor a problem. "I know well what has happened, but I can be of more use to you and give you more presents than this bastard!" He told me that they could both support me, he the curate and Raimond. I answered that I would not permit this at any cost because there would be bad feelings between them because of me and that both would revile me because of the other.

And after the priest possessed me, I had no further relations with this Raimond, although he tried from time to time. Since then Raimond and the priest shared a secret hatred because of that, but I did not know it.

When I was at Dalou, after having contracted marriage with my second husband, Othon de Lagleize, a marriage which took place at the Assumption of Mary, this priest came to Dalou to the following grape harvests and pretended to be from Limoux. Entering my house he told me that my sister Gentille, who lived in Limoux, sent greetings, and I allowed him to enter. We both went into the cellar and he knew me carnally, while Sibille, the daughter of the late Armaud Teisseyre, stayed at the door of the cellar.

The previous evening she had brought me a silk blouse of Barcelona workmanship which had one red and another yellow lace as a gift from this rector and she told me that he would come the following day so that no one would come and that if someone else did arrive he would not think that anything had happened between the rector and me because this servant was standing in the middle of the open cellar door in which the priest and I were coupling. Having committed this sin, I took him out of the house. When we were at the outside door, I told him that I had given five sous to Bernard Belot. "Did he tell you?" He answered that he had told him and that I had done a good thing to give him those five sous. I was thinking of the five sous that I had given this Bernard to take to the heretics on my behalf and I believe that this is what the priest understood.

When he came to see me at Varilhes, when I was ill, as has been said and when he told me to remember the discussions that we had at Montaillou about the good Christians, and that I should not confess, he also told me that he was holding the inquisition over the heads of the people of Montaillou. "How can that be! You now persecute the good Christians and their believers, you who usually wish them well?" He answered that he continued to wish them well, but that he wanted to revenge himself against many people of the place who hated him in whatever he could and that later he would arrange things with God.

Twelve years ago I was at Dalou. One day, a priest brought the body of the Lord to the bridge of Dalou where Pierre du Pont was who wished to receive communion. I went to this house and saw and heard the priest question the ill man on the articles of faith and also ask him if he believed that it was the true body of Christ by which we are saved. The sick person said that he believed and devotedly asked for the body of Christ with joined hands. I returned home with Grazide Pujol of Dalou. On the way I said that he had received the body of the Lord better than that man described above who said that if the body of the Lord was that which the priests say is the body of the Lord and if it were as large as a mountain, it would already have been eaten only by the priests. Grazida told me to be silent because if one heard me say such things, they would be taken badly. I answered that I did not say them evilly but that I was repeating the words that this bad man had said.

—Did you ever believe that the true body of the Lord was not in the sacrament of the altar?—No.

—Did you say to anyone else these words or their equivalent?—I do not remember, but if I do recall, I will admit it.

—Have you told others the heretical opinions that Raimond Roussel, this priest, and other above-mentioned people told you?—No.—Have you heard these heretical opinions from others than those named above by you?—No.

—Did anyone ever tell you that the devil was the principal and the maker of corporeal creatures in the sense that they were not made or produced by God or by anyone but that he made them by himself and of himself principally, in the same way that God is a principal not made or produced by another spirit?—I have not heard this. These people did not tell me either that God made the devil or the contrary.

—Did you ever hear from these people that there was a good God and a bad God?—No. They called God he who made the spirits, and the maker of the world they called the devil and the director of the world. I never heard them call him "Hylè [matter]."

—Have you heard these or others say that the good God made two worlds and the bad God ten other worlds, and that the bad God with his ten worlds and those who were in his worlds had fought the good God and his worlds, and that things which are in the worlds of God and that he had been in part the victor over the good God and had conquered a part of him?—No.

—Have you heard these or others say that the spirits were of the substance of God or part of God?—No, except for what I have already said.

(August 13, 1320, in the episcopal chamber, before the bishop)

—Have you heard these or others say that there are two souls in people, one of which inclines people to do evil (and that it is the one of the devil) and the other to do good (and that it is part of God)?—No.

—Have you heard them say that all of the spirits created by God were of the same nature and condition?—This priest told me that all the spirits were created by God in heaven of the same condition but that some adhered to God and remained in heaven with him and that others revolted against God (and those were put in hell and are demons) and others, although they did not rebel against God, still followed the rebels, and these fell on the earth and in the air. These are the spirits which enter the bodies of dumb beasts and of men and women, as has been said.

—Did you hear them say that the devil, moved by pride or envy against God, made this world and all that is in it except for the spirits, in order to seem the equal of God?—No, but only that the devil made all visible things. I did not hear why he made them.

—Did you hear them say that the scriptures of the Old Testament are not of the good God?—Only that the priest told me that all of the Scriptures, except for the Gospels and the Lord's Prayer, were "affitilhas" and lies.

—Did you hear them say that the Son descended in Mary and "adumbrated" himself in her?—I heard the priest say that it was not the Father who descended but that he sent the Holy Spirit, who "adumbrated" himself in Mary.

—Did they call Mary the mother of God if according to this priest the Holy Spirit did not take flesh in her?—Yes.

—Did you hear them or others say that Christ was dead?—This priest said that he had

been crucified but I do not recall hearing from him that he was dead.

—When he spoke to you of Jesus Christ, did you at times hear him called true man?—This priest called him true God but I do not recall having heard him call him true man.

—Did he say that Jesus Christ rose from the dead?—He said that Christ rose, but I do not recall if he said that he rose from the dead.

—Did you hear him say that Christ will judge the good and the bad at the last judgment?—Yes.

—That all the resurrected with their bodies will come to the last judgment of Christ?—He said "We will all come to the judgment of Christ, at which there will be many called but few chosen, and this few chosen was only the good Christians, and those who will be received by them at their deaths. No matter how much one believed in the good Christians during one's life, if one was not received into their sect at death, one is not saved."

He said also that no one, regardless of his order, state, or condition, except for the good Christians, and those whom they receive at their deaths, will be saved. And although he said that all would come to the judgment of Christ, I never heard him or the others who believe in the heretics say that persons will be raised or will come to the judgment of Christ with their own bodies.

—Did this priest or the other believers deny baptism by water, confession, the sacrament of the altar, holy orders, extreme unction?—I never heard them speak of other sacraments or deny them, except those of penance and marriage.

(She said nothing more about the Manichean sect)

(August 22, 1320, in the episcopal chamber, before the bishop and Brother Gaillard de Pomiès)

Mengarde, the widow of Pons Clergue, once told me after the death of my first husband, in her house, while we were speaking of Roqua and of his son Raimond Roché, who had been immured for heresy, that it was good that they had been done a good turn. I answered that it was good because she was a good woman. Mengarde told me, "If you well know, it is good to do good to this Roqua." Later paying attention to these words, I thought that this Mengarde had told me that with attention because she was in agreement with this Roqua about the heresy.

While I was living at Prades, after the death of my first husband, I was living in a small house between those of Jean Clergue, rector of Prades, and the inn of Pierre Guilhem of that place. Since this house touched that of the curate, everything which took place there could be heard by those in the other house. Pierre Clergue, curate of Montaillou, who had come to see me, told me that he would send Jean, his student, whose family name I do not know, to get me the next night to sleep with him. I accepted.

Therefore I was home when the first hour sounded, waiting for this student. He arrived and I followed him through a very dark night and we arrived at the church of St. Pierre de Prades, where we entered. We found Pierre Clergue who had prepared a bed in the church. I said, "O, how can we do such a thing in the church of Saint Pierre?" He answered, "What a great wrong it will do to St. Peter!" This said we went to bed together in the church and this night he knew me carnally in this church. Afterward, before dawn, he showed me out of the church himself and took me to the door of the house where I was living.

I had said to him at the beginning of our relations, "What will I do if I become pregnant by you? I will be dishonored and lost." He answered that he had a good herb which, if a man wears it when he is with a woman, he can not engender nor can a woman conceive. I said to him, "What is this herb? Is it not the one that the cheese makers put on their pots of milk into which they have put rennet and which prevents the milk from curdling as long as it is on the pot?" He told me not to bother trying to know what kind of herb it was but that it was a herb that had this power and that he had some.

Since that time when he wanted to take me, he wore something rolled up and tied in a piece of linen the thickness and length of an ounce or of the first digit of my little finger, with a long thread which he passed around my neck. And this thing which he said was this herb hung down between my breasts to the base of my stomach. He always placed it thus when he wanted to know me and it remained on my neck until he rose. And if sometimes during the same night this priest wanted to know me two or more times, he asked me, before we coupled, where this herb was. I would take it by finding it by the thread which I had at my neck and place it in his hand. He took it and placed it before the base of my stomach with the thread passing between my breasts. This is how he coupled with me and no other way. I asked him one day to leave this herb with me. He refused because he said that then I could give myself to another man without becoming pregnant. He would not give it to me so that I would refrain from so doing out of fear of the consequences. He did this in particular thinking of his cousin Raimond Clergue, alias Pathau, who had first kept me before this priest, his fraternal cousin, had me, because they were jealous of each other.

He again told me that he did not want me to have a child from him while my father, Philippe de Planissoles was alive, because the latter would have been too ashamed, but that after his death he wanted me to have his child.

After this, the same year, on the 25th of the month of August, the above-named Béatrice swore juridically before the bishop of Pamiers before my lord bishop, assisted by Brother Gaillard of Pomiès, substitute of my lord the inquisitor of Carcassonne, in presence of the religious person Brother Guillaume Séguier, prior of the convent of Preachers (Dominicans) of Pamiers, the discrete person master Bernard Gaubert, jurist, and me, the undersigned notary. Because she was very ill and in bed and her death was expected, my lord bishop told her that if she had hidden anything concerning heresy in the confession that she had made above about herself or others, or if she had accused a person against truth and justice, she should admit it and reveal it, or she should exonerate the persons she had unjustly accused. And my lord the bishop commanded this at the peril of her soul. She responded, exonerating the rector and accusing the above named Raimond Roussel concerning the following articles:

Although in her confession she had said that the above-mentioned rector had told her that God had only made the spirits and that the devil made all bodies that one sees and feels, such as the earth, the sky, and all found there, except for the spirits, and as a result spirits remain forever but corporeal things disintegrate and corrode, now, called to a better memory, she says that it was not the rector who told her this, but the above-named Raimond Roussel, and that he said this near the gate of the castle of Montaillou.

What she said that the rector had said, that Christ did not come down from heaven and did not take flesh of Mary but that the Holy Spirit "adumbrated" itself in her, in explaining the word adumbration in the above manner, it had not been the rector who said this but Raimond Roussel in the same place as in the previous article.

She said under her own oath and in peril of her soul, that all the rest, together and in parts, that she reported on the facts of heresy against herself, this rector, and other persons, both living and dead, and which is contained in the above confessions, were true.

The above was read to her so that she could understand them and the heretical articles that she had admitted in her previous confessions against herself, the rector, and Raimond Roussel were read to her in the vernacular language. She confirmed them entirely and fully and said that they were true, except what she had retracted in her previous confession (not the articles, but who had told them to her).

Asked if she had instructed any other person on these articles or on some of them, if it was not as she had stated, she answered no.

—Why did you flee when you were called by my lord bishop and you appeared on the accusation of heresy? Did someone advise you to flee or to absent yourself?—I fled out of the fear that I had of my lord the bishop because of the heresy that I had committed and above all because my lord, when I appeared before him the first time, called me by the name of my father Philippe who had been accused of this crime.

I realized some time before my lord the bishop called me that he was going to do so, and I sent to Barthelémy Amilhac, a priest who had conducted himself evilly with me for a certain time, to discuss it with him and to take council with him to know what I should do if I was accused of heresy by my lord the bishop. He came to Varlhes where I was living, but without entering the town, and we spoke. I told him that I had understood that my lord had interrogated witnesses against me concerning heresy and that I was afraid that I would be accused of this crime.—Did it seem more appropriate to him to flee than to appear on this accusation?—He asked me, "Do you consider yourself guilty?" I answered no, and that he could be sure that if I have committed anything of this sort I would have told him, whom I had loved so much.

This priest told me that then it was better to appear since I did not feel guilty because my lord the bishop, he told me, would not do me an injustice. Having said this he left.

Afterward I appeared, summoned by my lord, I was terrified, and returning to Varilhes, I dreamed of fleeing and I gathered all the things that I wanted to take with me. I said to no one that I wanted to flee. On the contrary, to my daughter Condors, I said that I was returning to my lord the bishop on the day that he had ordered me. I promised her this, embraced her, and then fled toward Belpech in the diocese of Mirepoix. As soon as I arrived there I sent word to Barthelémy, this priest, at Mézerville where he was staying. He came immediately to find me at Belpech.

Arriving and seeing my trousseau of clothes that I had carried with me he said, "Why have you come here? What do you intend to do, carrying so many clothes with you?" I took him aside and told me that I had been summoned by my lord the bishop and that I had appeared, and that he had told me that I had said that the body of the Lord was not in the sacrament of the altar, and that if he had been as large as a mountain, it would have already been eaten by the priests alone. He had also said that I had seen Pierre, Guillaume and Jacques Authié the heretics, that I had listened to them and that I had performed magic on their advice. Even though I did not feel guilty, as I said to this priest, because I had not seen the heretics Pierre and Guillaume Authié since they had become heretics, I wanted nevertheless to flee and to go to the home of my daughter Gentille at Limoux to hide.

He answered that I had done very wrong to flee, that it was necessary to return and to appear before my lord bishop. I said that I would not do so even if he gave me the whole bishopric of Pamiers. The priest said, "If that is how it is and I can not retain you, take this money," and he gave me eight *Tournois* of money. We ate together. He again told me that he would not abandon me unless I wanted him to do so before I was at Limoux, but that after the feast of the Invention of Saint Stephen (August 8), the feast when he had to go to Mézerville, because it was the feast of the altar of the church of that place, he would accompany me to Limoux. In the meantime he pawned or sold a book or otherwise obtained money so that we could make the trip to Limoux together. From there, he told me that we would go to Mas-Saintes-Puelles, which is on the outskirts, and where no one would look for me. After this feast, we would leave together. I was delighted to hear it, and we, this priest, I, and a sergeant of Belpech whose name I do not know, went to Mas-Saintes-Puelles, where I was arrested by the people of my lord the bishop and taken by them to him.

Likewise it was established that certain very suspect things that had been collected by her for witchcraft were found among her things and that she recognized them as hers, and that she had possessed them. These were: two umbilical cords of infants found in her purse; cloth stained by blood which seemed to be menstrual blood in a leather sack with a [roquette] seed and slightly burned incense grains; a mirror and a small knife wrapped in a piece of linen; the seed of a plant wrapped in muslin; a piece of dried bread which

is called "tinhol"; a number of written formulas, and pieces of linen. Since it was established that for these reasons there was a great suspicion that this Béatrice was a witch and used spells, my lord the bishop asked her why she possessed these items. She answered:

I had the cords of the male children of my daughters and I kept them because a Jewish woman, since baptized, had told me that if I carried them with me and I had a legal suit, I would not lose. This is why I took these from my grandchildren and kept them. I never had the occasion to verify their efficacy.

These clothes stained with blood are from the menstrual blood of my daughter Philippa and because this baptized Jew had told me that if I kept some of her first blood and that I gave it to her husband or to another man to drink he would never be interested in another woman. This is why, when a long time ago my daughter Philippa was young and had her first menses, I looked at her face and seeing that she was congested, I asked her what was wrong. She answered that she was bleeding from her vulva. I then remembered the words of this baptized Jew. I cut a piece of the slip of my daughter Philippa which was stained with this blood and since it seemed to me that there was not enough, I gave my daughter another piece of linen "blouset" so that, when she had her period, she could stain and impregnate this cloth. She did this and then I dried the cloth with the intention, when her husband married her, of giving it to him to drink, by extracting it from this cloth that I had stained. Philippa married this year and I had the intention of giving it to her fiancé to drink. But I thought that it would be better to wait until the marriage was consummated and that it should be Philippa herself who would give it to her husband to drink. And since, when I was arrested, the marriage had not yet been consummated between Philippa and her husband, and that they had not yet celebrated the wedding, I did not give it to him to drink.

I did not put these clothes with the incense grains in order to cast a spell. It was by chance. My daughter had a headache this year and someone told me that incense mixed with other things cures this illness. This is why some of the grains remained in my possession in this bag. I did not have any intention to do anything with them.

Neither the mirror, the wrapped knife, nor the pieces of linen cloth, were intended for magic or a spell.

As for the seed wrapped in muslin, it is a seed of a plant called the bugle. It was given to me by a pilgrim who said that it was efficacious against epilepsy. Since my grandson, the son of my daughter, Condors, suffers from it this year, I wanted to use it. But my daughter said that she had taken him to the church of Saint-Paul and that he had been cured of this illness, and that she did not want me to do anything to her son for his illness. Thus I did not use it.

—Have you made other spells, have you taught them, have you learned them from anyone?—No. At times however I believed that Barthelémy, this priest, had cast some sort of spell because I loved him too much and I too much wanted to be with him, even though, when I met him, I had already entered menopause. I often asked him but he always denied it.

In light of the fact that she had plainly confessed to in matters of heresy and witchcraft both about herself and others living or dead, that she had greatly repented having committed this and that she wanted to return to union with the Church and the Catholic faith; that she had asked absolution and was also ready to do the penance that my lord the bishop judged good to impose on her for the above listed acts; for these reasons my lord bishop, having received from her the abjuration of heresy and the promise under oath according to the formula of the Church, gave her absolution of the sentences which she had incurred for the crimes of heresy and witchcraft, if she had fully confessed and repented of what had preceded. If not it was not the intention of my lord bishop, as he told her, to absolve these sentences. The above named Béatrice promised nevertheless, if she should later remember anything concerning heresy, to report it both concerning herself and concerning others living or dead.

The formula of this abjuration and of this engagement under oath is the following:

I, Béatrice, appearing juridically before you, reverend father in Christ my lord Jacques, by the grace of God bishop of Pamiers, I entirely abjure all heresy raised against our lord Jesus Christ and the Holy Catholic Church, and all beliefs of heretics, of whatever sects condemned by the Roman Church, and especially the sect to which I had adhered and all complicity, participation, defense, and frequenting of these heretics, under the penalty of that which is due by law to one who has relapsed into heresy abjured by law.

Likewise, I abjure and promise to pursue according to my ability the heretics of any sect condemned by the Roman Church and especially the sect to which I adhered and the believers, frauds, dissimulators, and defenders of these heretics as well as those whom I know or believe to be in flight by reason of heresy and to have any of them arrested and handed over to my lord bishop or the inquisitors of heretical deviation to the extent of my power every time and in every place that I learn of the existence of one or more of them.

Likewise, I swear and promise to hold, guard and defend the Catholic faith that the Holy Roman Church preaches and observes.

Likewise, I promise to obey and to defer to the orders of the church, of my lord the bishop and of the inquisitors and to come on the day and days specified before them or their replacements every time and in every place that I receive the order or the demand from them by messenger or by letter or in other manners. I promise never to flee or to knowingly absent myself in a spirit of rebellion and to receive and to accomplish as far as I am able the penalties of the penance that they will have judged it good to impose on me. And to this end I obligate my person and my property.

After which the above year, the 5th of March, the above named Béatrice appeared juridically before my lord bishop and the religious person Brother Jean de Beaude of the Order of Preachers (Dominicans), inquisitor of heretical deviation in the kingdom of France commissioned by the apostolic see in the episcopal chamber. In fidelity to the oath that she had sworn, she confessed that the extract of her deposition was correct and she concluded in the present case, asking for sentencing on the facts and requesting that one act toward her with mercy. And my lord bishop concurred with her.

And my lords the bishop and the inquisitor assigned to the above named Béatrice a day to hear the definitive sentence on the preceding, that is, the following Sunday, March 8, before the third hour, in the house of the Preachers (Dominicans) of Pamiers.

Done in the year and day above, in the presence of the religious persons Brothers Gaillard of Pomiès, prior of the convent of the Brothers Preachers of Pamiers, Arnaud of Carla, of the same convent, Brother Pierre, companion of my lord the inquisitor, David and Bernard of Centelles, monks of Fontfroide of the Order of Citeaux, and of my lord Germain de Castelnau, archdeacon of the church of Pamiers, witnesses for these summoned, and us Guillaume Peyre-Barthe, notary of my lord the archbishop, and Barthelémy Adalbert, notary of the Inquisition, who have been present at what preceded and have received and written it.

And the Sunday assigned to the above-named Béatrice, she appeared in the cemetery of Saint-Jean-Martyr of Pamiers and was given the sentence by my lords the bishop and the inquisitor which reads as follows, "Know all ye, etc." See this sentence in the book of sentences of the Inquisition.[2]

And I, Rainaud Jabbaud, cleric of Toulouse, sworn in the matter of the Inquisition, on the order of my lord the bishop, have faithfully corrected this confession against the original.

---

2   She was sentenced to death on the walls of Carcassonne but the sentence was commuted to wearing a double cross (indicating a heretic) on her clothing for the remainder of her life.

37. MARSILIUS OF PADUA

Discourses

MARSILIUS OF PADUA (CA. 1275–1342), a secular scholar and rector of the University of Paris, dedicated his 1324 attack on ecclesiastical claims to political power to the Emperor Louis of Bavaria. His political ideology, which based political power on the consent of the people, entirely denied papal and episcopal claims to secular political authority and was extremely radical for the time. He was an equally ardent defender of the position of the Spiritual Franciscans, who insisted on the primacy of radical poverty in keeping with the tradition of Francis.

Source: Alan Gewirth, *Marsilius of Padua, The Defender of Peace* (New York: Columbia University Press, 1951).

Further Reading: Gerson Moreno-Riaño (ed.), *The World of Marsilius of Padua* (Turnhout: Brepols, 2006).

CHAPTER III: ON THE CANONIC STATEMENTS AND OTHER ARGUMENTS WHICH SEEM TO PROVE THAT COERCIVE RULERSHIP BELONGS TO BISHOPS OR PRIESTS AS SUCH, EVEN WITHOUT THE GRANT OF THE HUMAN LEGISLATOR, AND THAT THE SUPREME OF ALL SUCH RULERSHIPS BELONGS TO THE ROMAN BISHOP OR POPE

Having thus distinguished the meanings of these terms with which the largest part of our inquiry will deal, we now enter more securely upon our principal task. First of all, we shall adduce the authorities of the holy Scripture which might lead someone to think that the Roman bishop called pope is the supreme judge, in the third sense of "judge" or "judgment," over all the bishops or priests and other ecclesiastic ministers in the world, and also over all rulers, communities, groups, and individuals of this world, of whatever condition they may be.

2. Let us first quote the passage of Scripture in the sixteenth chapter of Matthew, where Christ says to St. Peter: "And I will give to thee the keys of the kingdom of heaven: and whatsoever thou shalt bind on earth, it shall be bound also in heaven: and whatsoever thou shalt loose on earth, it shall be loosed also in heaven." For through this passage, certain Roman bishops have assumed for themselves the authority of the supreme jurisdiction mentioned above. For by the "keys" given to St. Peter by Christ, they wish to understand plenitude of power over the whole regime of men; just as Christ had this plenitude of power over all kings and rulers, so did he grant it to St. Peter and his successors in the Roman episcopal seat, as Christ's general vicars in this world.

3. A second passage of Scripture in support of the same position is taken from the words of Christ in the eleventh chapter of Matthew, when he said: "All things are delivered to me by my father"; and again in the twenty-eighth chapter when he said: "All power is given to me in heaven and in earth." Since, therefore, St. Peter and his successors in the episcopal seat at Rome were and are Christ's vicars, as they say, it seems that all power or plenitude of power has been given to them, and consequently jurisdictional authority over everyone.

4. A third passage to the same effect is taken from the eighth chapter of Matthew and the fifth chapter of Mark, where it is written: "And the devils besought him," that is, Christ, "saying, If thou cast us out hence, send us into the herd of swine. And he said to them, Go. But they going out went into the swine: and, behold, the whole herd ran violently down a steep place into the sea, and they perished in the waters." From these words it appears that Christ disposed of temporal things as

if they were all his own; for otherwise he would have sinned in destroying the herd of swine. But it is wrong to say that Christ, whose flesh did not see corruption, sinned. Since, therefore, St. Peter and his successors the Roman bishops are and were the special vicars of Christ, as some say, they can dispose of all temporal things as judges in the third sense of the word, and they, like Christ, have plenitude of power and dominion over them all.

5. Again, the same is shown by what is written in the twenty-first chapter of Matthew, the eleventh of Mark, and the nineteenth of Luke: "Then Jesus sent two disciples, saying to them, Go ye into the village that is over against you, and immediately you shall find an ass tied, and a colt with her"; or, "a colt tied, upon which no man yet hath sat," as in Mark and Luke. "Loose them and bring them to me." From these words the same conclusion can be reached, and by the same mode of deduction, as from the passage quoted immediately above.

6. Moreover, the same point is proved from the twenty-second chapter of Luke, where these words are found: "Behold, here are two swords," said the apostles, replying to Christ. "And he," that is, Christ, "said to them: It is enough." By these words, according to some men's interpretation, it must be understood that there are in the present world two governments, one ecclesiastic or spiritual, the other temporal or secular. Since, therefore, Christ said to the apostles: "It is enough," namely, for you to have these two swords, he seems to have meant that both swords should belong to the authority of the apostles, and particularly to St. Peter as the leading apostle. For if Christ had not wanted the temporal sword to belong to them, he should have said: It is too much.

7. Again, it seems that the same must be believed from the twenty-first chapter of John, where Christ spoke to St. Peter as follows: "Feed my sheep, feed my lambs, feed my sheep," repeating the same phrase three times, just as we have quoted. From these words some draw the following interpretation: that St. Peter and his successors the Roman bishops ought absolutely to be in charge over all of Christ's faithful sheep, that is, the Christians, and especially over the priests and deacons.

8. Moreover, this clearly seems to be the view of St. Paul in the first epistle to the Corinthians, chapter 6, where he writes: "Know ye not that we shall judge angels? how much more secular things?" Therefore, judgments in the third sense over secular things seem to pertain to priests or bishops, and especially to the first of them, the Roman bishop. Again, the apostle seems to have thought the same in the first epistle to the Corinthians, chapter 9, when he said: "Have not we power to eat," etc. And the same in the second epistle to the Thessalonians, chapter 3. In these passages he seems explicitly to hold that God gave him power over the temporalities of the faithful, and consequently jurisdiction over them.

9. The same is again shown from the first epistle to Timothy, chapter 5, where the apostle wrote to Timothy: "Against a priest receive not an accusation, but under two or three witnesses." From this, then, it seems that the bishop has jurisdiction at least over priests, deacons, and other ministers of the temple, inasmuch as it pertains to him to hear accusations against them.

We shall omit to quote proofs in support of the proposed conclusion and its opposite from the Old Scripture or Testament, for a reason which we shall indicate in chapter IX of this discourse.

And so, from the aforesaid authorities of the holy Scripture, and other similar ones, and from such interpretations of them, someone might be led to think that the highest of all rulerships belongs to the Roman bishop.

10. Following upon these, it is fitting to adduce some quasi-political arguments which might perhaps lead men to fancy and believe the aforesaid conclusion. The first of these arguments is as follows. As the human body is to the soul, so is the ruler of bodies to the ruler of souls. But the body is subject to the soul with respect to rule. Therefore too the ruler of bodies, the secular judge, must be subject to the rule of the judge or ruler of souls, and especially of the first of them all, the Roman pontiff.

11. Again, another argument from almost the same root: As corporeals are to spirituals, so is the ruler of corporeals to the ruler of spirituals.

But it is certain that corporeals are by nature inferior and subject to spirituals. Therefore the ruler of corporeals, the secular judge, must be subject to the ruler of spirituals, the ecclesiastic judge.

12. Moreover, as end is to end, and law to law, and legislator to legislator, so is the judge or ruler in accordance with the one of these to the judge or ruler in accordance with the other. But the end toward which the ecclesiastic judge, the priest or bishop, directs, the law by which he directs, and the maker of that law, are all superior to and more perfect than the end, the law, and the maker to which and by which the secular judge directs. Therefore the ecclesiastic judge, bishop or priest, and especially the first of them all, is superior to every secular judge. For the end toward which the ecclesiastic judge directs is eternal life; the law by which he directs is divine; and its immediate maker is God, in whom neither error nor malice can lodge. But the end toward which the secular judge aims to direct is sufficiency of this worldly life; the law by which he directs is human; and the immediate maker of this law is man or men, who are subject to error and malice. Therefore, the latter are inferior to and less worthy than the former. Therefore, too, the secular judge, even the supreme one, is inferior to and less worthy than the ecclesiastic judge, the supreme priest.

13. Moreover, a person or thing is absolutely more honorable than another when the action of that first person or thing is absolutely more honorable than the action of the second. But the action of the priest or bishop, the consecration of the blessed body of Christ, is the most honorable of all the actions which can be performed by man in the present life. Therefore, any priest is more worthy than any non-priest. Since, therefore, the more worthy should not be subject to the less worthy, but rather above it, it seems that the secular judge should not be above the priest in jurisdiction, but rather subordinate to him, and especially to the first of them all, the Roman pontiff.

14. The same is again shown with more specific reference to the Roman ruler, called emperor. For any person who has the authority to establish this ruler's government and to transfer it at pleasure from nation to nation is superior to this ruler in judgment, in the third sense of "judgment." But the Roman pontiff proclaims that he is such a person, inasmuch as he transferred the Roman empire from the Greeks to the Germans, as was set forth in the seventh of his decretals, *On Oaths*; and the same is stated even more explicitly by the modern so-called bishop of the Romans, in an edict of his addressed to Ludwig, duke of Bavaria, elected king of the Romans.

15. Another argument to the same effect is that a great difficulty seems to arise if we assume that Christ's vicar, the Roman bishop, and the other bishops who are successors of the apostles, are subject to the sentence of any secular ruler. For since the secular ruler may sin against divine and human law, whereupon he must be corrected, as was said in chapter XVIII of Discourse I, and since he, being supreme over all laymen, does not have a superior or an equal, inasmuch as a plurality of governments was rejected in chapter XVII of Discourse I, it will seem that coercive jurisdiction over him belongs to the Roman bishop, and not conversely.

By the above, therefore, it might seem possible to prove that bishops or priests have coercive jurisdiction, and that to the supreme Roman pontiff belongs the supreme rulership of all in this world. We seem adequately to have set forth both the authorities of the holy Scripture and certain quasi-political and human arguments in support of this position.

CHAPTER IV: ON THE CANONIC SCRIPTURES, THE COMMANDS, COUNSELS, AND EXAMPLES OF CHRIST AND OF THE SAINTS AND APPROVED DOCTORS WHO EXPOUNDED THE EVANGELIC LAW, WHEREBY IT IS CLEARLY DEMONSTRATED THAT THE ROMAN OR ANY OTHER BISHOP OR PRIEST, OR CLERGYMAN, CAN BY VIRTUE OF THE WORDS OF SCRIPTURE CLAIM OR ASCRIBE TO HIMSELF NO COERCIVE RULERSHIP OR CONTENTIOUS JURISDICTION, LET ALONE THE SUPREME JURISDICTION OVER ANY CLERGYMAN OR LAYMAN; AND THAT, BY CHRIST'S COUNSEL AND EXAMPLE, THEY OUGHT TO REFUSE SUCH RULERSHIP, ESPECIALLY IN COMMUNITIES OF THE FAITHFUL, IF IT IS OFFERED TO THEM OR BESTOWED ON THEM

BY SOMEONE HAVING THE AUTHORITY TO DO SO; AND AGAIN, THAT ALL BISHOPS, AND GENERALLY ALL PERSONS NOW CALLED CLERGYMEN, MUST BE SUBJECT TO THE COERCIVE JUDGMENT OR RULERSHIP OF HIM WHO GOVERNS BY THE AUTHORITY OF THE HUMAN LEGISLATOR, ESPECIALLY WHERE THIS LEGISLATOR IS CHRISTIAN

We now wish from the opposite side to adduce the truths of the holy Scripture in both its literal and its mystical sense, in accordance with the interpretations of the saints and the expositions of other approved doctors of the Christian faith, which explicitly command or counsel that neither the Roman bishop called pope, nor any other bishop or priest, or deacon, has or ought to have any rulership or coercive judgment or jurisdiction over any priest or non-priest, ruler, community, group, or individual of whatever condition; understanding by "coercive judgment" that which we said in chapter II of this discourse to be the third sense of "judge" or "judgment."

2. The more clearly to carry out this aim, we must not overlook that in this inquiry it is not asked what power and authority is or was had in this world by Christ, who was true God and true man, nor what or how much of this power he was able to bestow on St. Peter and the other apostles and their successors, the bishops or priests; for Christian believers have no doubts on these points. But we wish to and ought to inquire what power and authority, to be exercised in this world, Christ wanted to bestow and in fact (de facto) did bestow on them, and from what he excluded and prohibited them by counsel or command. For we are bound to believe that they had from Christ only such power and authority as we can prove to have been given to them through the words of Scripture, no other. For it is certain to all the Christian believers that Christ, who was true God and true man, was able to bestow, not only on the apostles but also on any other men, coercive authority or jurisdiction over all rulers or governments and over all the other individuals in this world; and even more perhaps, as for example the power to create things, to destroy or repair heaven and earth and the things therein, and even to be in complete command of angels;

but these powers Christ neither bestowed nor determined to bestow on them. Hence Augustine, in the tenth sermon *On the Words of the Lord in Matthew*, wrote the following: "'Learn of me' not how to make a world, not how to create all visible and invisible things, nor how to do miracles in the world and revive the dead; but: 'because I am meek and humble of heart.'"

3. Therefore for the present purpose it suffices to show, and I shall first show, that Christ himself came into the world not to dominate men, nor to judge them by judgment in the third sense, nor to wield temporal rule, but rather to be subject as regards the status of the present life; and moreover, that he wanted to and did exclude himself, his apostles and disciples, and their successors, the bishops or priests, from all such coercive authority or worldly rule, both by his example and by his words of counsel or command. I shall also show that the leading apostles, as Christ's true imitators, did this same thing and taught their successors to do likewise; and moreover, that both Christ and the apostles wanted to be and were continuously subject in property and in person to the coercive jurisdiction of secular rulers, and that they taught and commanded all others, to whom they preached or wrote the law of truth, to do likewise, under pain of eternal damnation. Then I shall write a chapter on the power or authority of the keys which Christ gave to the apostles and their successors in office, bishops and priests, so that it may be clear what is the nature, quality, and extent of such power, both of the Roman bishop and of the others. For ignorance on this point has hitherto been and still is the source of many questions and damnable controversies among the Christian faithful, as was mentioned in the first chapter of this discourse.

4. And so in pursuit of these aims we wish to show that Christ, in his purposes or intentions, words, and deeds, wished to exclude and did exclude himself and the apostles from every office of rulership, contentious jurisdiction, government, or coercive judgment in this world. This is first shown clearly beyond any doubt by the passage in the eighteenth chapter of the gospel of John. For when Christ was brought before Pontius Pilate,

vicar of the Roman ruler in Judaea, and accused of having called himself king of the Jews, Pontius asked him whether he had said this, or whether he did call himself a king, and Christ's reply included these words, among others: "My kingdom is not of this world," that is, I have not come to reign by temporal rule or dominion, in the way in which worldly kings reign. And proof of this was given by Christ himself through an evident sign when he said: "If my kingdom were of this world, my servants would certainly fight, that I should not be delivered to the Jews," as if to argue as follows: If I had come into this world to reign by worldly or coercive rule, I would have ministers for this rule, namely, men to fight and to coerce transgressors, as the other kings have; but I do not have such ministers, as you can clearly see. Hence the interlinear gloss: "It is clear that no one defends him." And this is what Christ reiterates: "But now my kingdom is not from hence," that is, the kingdom about which I have come to teach....

8. Moreover, the same is shown very evidently by Christ's words and example in the following passage of the twelfth chapter of Luke: "And one of the multitude said to him, Master, speak to my brother, that he divide the inheritance with me. But he," that is Christ, "said to him, Man, who hath appointed me judge or divider over you?" As if to say: I did not come to exercise this office, nor was I sent for this, that is, to settle civil disputes through judgment; but this, however, is undoubtedly the most proper function of secular rulers or judges. Now this passage from the gospel contains and demonstrates our proposition much more clearly than do the glosses of the saints, because the latter assume that the literal meaning, such as we have said, is manifest, and have devoted themselves more to the allegorical or mystical meaning. Nevertheless, we shall now quote from the glosses for a stronger confirmation of our proposition, and so that we may not be accused of expounding Scripture rashly. These words of Christ, then, are expounded by St. Ambrose as follows: "Well does he who descended for the sake of the divine avoid the earthly, and does not deign to be judge over disputes and appraiser of wealth, being the judge of the living and the dead and the appraiser of their merits." And a little below he adds: "Hence not undeservedly is this brother rebuffed, who wanted the dispenser of the heavenly to concern himself with the corruptible." See, then, what Ambrose thinks about Christ's office in this world; for he says that "well does he avoid the earthly," that is, the judgment of contentious acts, "who descended for the sake of the divine," that is, to teach and minister the spiritual; in this he designated Christ's office and that of his successors, namely, to dispense the heavenly or spiritual; that spiritual of which Ambrose spoke in his gloss on the first epistle to the Corinthians, chapter 9, which we quoted in chapter II of this discourse under the third meaning of this word "spiritual."

9. It now remains to show that not only did Christ himself refuse rulership or coercive judgment in this world, whereby he furnished an example for his apostles and disciples and their successors to do likewise, but also he taught by words and showed by example that all men, both priests and non-priests, should be subject in property and in person to the coercive judgment of the rulers of this world. By his word and example, then, Christ showed this first with respect to property, by what is written in the twenty-second chapter of Matthew. For when the Jews asked him: "Tell us therefore, what dost thou think? Is it lawful to give tribute to Caesar, or not?" Christ, after looking at the coin and its inscription, replied: "Render therefore to Caesar the things that are Caesar's, and to God the things that are God's." Whereon the interlinear gloss says, "that is, tribute and money." And on the words: "Whose image and inscription is this?" Ambrose wrote as follows: "Just as Caesar demanded the imprinting of his image, so too does God demand that the soul be stamped with the light of his countenance." Note, therefore, what it was that Christ came into the world to demand. Furthermore, Chrysostom[1] writes as follows: "When you hear: 'Render to Caesar the things that are Caesar's,' know that he means only those things which are not harmful to piety, for if they were, the tribute would be not to Caesar but to the devil." So, then,

---

1   John Chrysostom (ca. 347–407), Archbishop of Constantinople.

we ought to be subject to Caesar in all things, so long only as they are not contrary to piety, that is, to divine worship or commandment. Therefore, Christ wanted us to be subject in property to the secular ruler. This too was plainly the doctrine of St. Ambrose, based upon this doctrine of Christ, for in his epistle against Valentinian, entitled *To the People,* he wrote: "We pay to Caesar the things that are Caesar's, and to God the things that are God's. That the tribute is Caesar's is not denied."

10. The same is again shown from the seventeenth chapter of Matthew, where it is written as follows: "They that received the didrachmas came to Peter, and said, Doth not your master pay the didrachmas?" and then, a little below, is written what Christ said to Peter: "But that we may not scandalize them, go to the sea and cast in a hook, and that fish which shalt first come up, take: and when thou hast opened its mouth, thou shalt find a piece of money: take that, and give it to them for me and thee." Nor did the Lord say only, "Give it to them," but he said, "Give it to them for me and thee." And Jerome on this passage says: "Our Lord was in flesh and in spirit the son of a king, whether we consider him to have been generated from the seed of David or the word of the Almighty Father. Therefore, being the son of kings, he did not owe tribute." And below he adds: "Therefore, although he was exempt, yet he had to fulfill all the demands of justice, because he had assumed the humility of the flesh." Moreover, Origen[2] on the words of Christ: "That we may not scandalize them," spoke more to the point and in greater conformity to the meaning of the evangelist, as follows: "It is to be understood," that is, from Christ's words, "that while men sometimes appear who through injustice seize our earthly goods, the kings of this earth send men to exact from us what is theirs. And by his example the Lord prohibits the doing of any offense, even to such men, either so that they may no longer sin, or so that they may be saved. For the son of God, who did no servile work, gave the tribute money, having the guise of a servant which he assumed for the sake of man."

How, then, is it possible, on the strength of the words of the evangelic Scripture, that the bishops and priests be exempt from this tribute, and from the jurisdiction of rulers generally, unless by the rulers' own gratuitous grant, when Christ and Peter, setting an example for others, paid such tribute? And although Christ, being of royal stock in flesh, was perhaps not obliged to do this, yet Peter, not being of royal stock, had no such reason to be exempt, just as he wanted none. But if Christ had thought it improper for his successors in the priestly office to pay tribute and for their temporal goods to be subject to the secular rulers, then without setting a bad example, that is, without subjecting the priesthood to the jurisdiction of secular rulers, he could have ordained otherwise and have made some arrangement about those tax collectors, such as removing from them the intention of asking for such tribute, or in some other appropriate way. But he did not think it proper to do so, rather he wanted to pay; and from among the apostles, as the one who was to pay with him the tribute, he chose Peter, despite the fact that Peter was to be the foremost teacher and pastor of the church, as will be said in chapter XVI of this discourse, in order that by such an example none of the others would refuse to do likewise.

11. The passage of Scripture which we quoted above from the seventeenth chapter of Matthew is interpreted in the way we have said by St. Ambrose in the epistle entitled *On Handing Over the Basilica,* where he writes as follows: "He," that is, the emperor, "demands tribute, it is not denied. The fields of the church pay tribute." And a little further on he says, more to the point: "We pay to Caesar the things that are Caesar's, and to God the things that are God's. The tribute is Caesar's, it is not denied." Expressing more fully this which we have called the meaning of the above-quoted passage of Scripture, St. Bernard in an epistle to the archbishop of Sens wrote as follows: "This is what is done by these men," namely, those who suggested that subjects rebel against their superiors. "But Christ ordered and acted otherwise. 'Render,' he said, 'to Caesar the things that are Caesar's, and to God the things that are God's.' What he spoke by word of mouth, he soon took care to carry out

---

2   Origen (ca. 185–254), Alexandrian theologian.

in deed. The institutor of Caesar did not hesitate to pay the tax to Caesar. For he thus gave you the example that you should do likewise. How, then, could he deny the reverence due to the priests of God, when he took care to show it even for the secular powers?"

And we must note what Bernard said, that Christ, in taking care to pay the tax to the secular powers, showed "due," and therefore not coerced, "reverence." For everyone owes such tax and tribute to the rulers, as we shall show in the following chapter from the words of the apostle in the thirteenth chapter of the epistle to the Romans, and the glosses thereon of the saints and doctors; although perhaps not every tax is owed everywhere by everyone, such as the entry tax[3] which was not owed by the inhabitants, although the custodians or collectors sometimes wrongly demanded and exacted it from simple inhabitants or natives, such as were the apostles. And therefore, in agreement with Origen, who I believed grasped the meaning of the evangelist on this point better than did Jerome, I say that it seemed customary and was perhaps commonly established in states, especially in Judaea, that entry taxes were not to be paid by inhabitants or natives, but only by aliens. And hence Christ said to Peter: "Of whom do the kings of the earth receive tribute?" etc., by "tribute" meaning that entry tax which the tax collectors were demanding. For Christ did not deny that the children of the earth, that is, natives, owe "tribute," taking the word as a common name for every tax; on the contrary, he later said of it, excepting no one: "Render to Caesar the things that are Caesar's"; and this was also expressed by the apostle in agreement with Christ, when he said, in the thirteenth chapter of the epistle to the Romans: "For this cause also you pay tribute," that is, to rulers, "for they are the ministers of God." By "children," therefore, Christ meant the children of kingdoms, that is, persons born or raised therein, and not the children of kings by blood; otherwise

his words would not seem to have been pertinent, for very often he spoke in the plural both for himself and for Peter, who was certainly not the child of such kings as those discussed by Jerome. Moreover, if Christ was of David's stock in flesh, so too were very many other Jews, although not perhaps Peter. Again, the tribute was not then being exacted by David or by anyone of his blood; why, therefore, should Christ have said, "The kings of the land ... then the children are free,"[4] saying nothing about the heavenly king? But it is certain that neither Christ nor Peter was a child of Caesar, either in flesh or in spirit. Moreover, why should Christ have asked the above question? For everyone certainly knows that the children of kings by blood do not pay tribute to their parents. Jerome's exposition, therefore, does not seem to have been as much in agreement with Scripture as was Origen's. But the above words of Scripture show that Christ wanted to pay even undue tribute in certain places and at certain times, and to teach the apostle and his successors to do likewise, rather than to fight over such things. For this was the justice of counsel and not of command which Christ, in the humility of the flesh which he had assumed, wanted to fulfill and to teach others to fulfill. And the apostle, like Christ, also taught that this should be done. Hence, in the first epistle to the Corinthians, chapter 6: "Why do ye not rather take wrong? why do ye not rather suffer yourselves to be defrauded?" than to quarrel with one another, as he had said before.

12. Moreover, not only with respect to property did Christ show that he was subject to the coercive jurisdiction of the secular ruler, but also with respect to his own person, than which no greater jurisdiction could be had by the ruler over him or over anyone else, for which reason it is called "capital jurisdiction" [*merum imperium*] by the Roman legislator.[5] That Christ was thus subject can be clearly shown from the twenty-seventh

---

3   This is the *pedagium*, a tax paid to the ruler of a territory by those who came into the territory from outside.

4   Matthew 17:24–25. The complete text, required to make sense of the fragment quoted by Marsilius, is as follows: "The kings of the earth, of whom do they receive tribute or custom? Of their own children, or of strangers? And he said: Of strangers. Jesus said to him: Then the children are free."

5   For this untranslatable phrase see *Corp. jur. civ., Digest* II. i. 3: "Capital jurisdiction is to have the power of the sword to punish criminal men, which jurisdiction is also called power" (*Merum est imperium habere gladii potestatem ad animadvertendum facinorosos homines, quod etiam potestas appellatur*).

chapter of Matthew; for there it is written that Christ allowed himself to be seized and brought before Pilate, who was the vicar of the Roman emperor, and he suffered himself to be judged and given the extreme penalty by Pilate as judge with coercive power; nor did Christ protest against him as not being a judge, although he perhaps indicated that he was suffering an unjust punishment. But it is certain that he could have undergone such judgment and punishment at the hands of priests, had he so desired, and had he deemed it improper for his successors to be subject to the secular rulers and to be judged by them.

But since this view is borne out at great length in the nineteenth chapter of John, I shall here adduce what is written there. When Christ had been brought before Pilate, vicar of Caesar, to be judged, and was accused of having called himself king of the Jews and son of God, he was asked by Pilate: "Whence art thou?" But having no reply from Jesus, Pilate spoke to him the following words, which are quite pertinent to our subject; here is the passage: "Pilate therefore saith to him, Speakest thou not to me? Knowest thou not that I have power to crucify thee, and I have power to release thee? Jesus answered: Thou shouldst not have any power against me, unless it were given thee from above." See, then, Jesus did not deny that Pilate had the power to judge him and to execute his judgment against him; nor did he say: This does not pertain to you of right (*de jure*) but you do this only in fact (*de facto*). But Christ added that Pilate had this power "from above." How from above? Augustine answers: "Let us therefore learn what he," that is, Christ, "said, and what he taught the apostle," that is, Paul, in the epistle to the Romans, chapter 13. What, then, did Christ say? What did he teach the apostle? "That there is no power," that is, authority of jurisdiction, "except from God," whatever be the case with respect to the act of him who badly uses the power. "And that he who from malice hands over an innocent man to the power to be killed, sins more than does the power itself if it kills the man from fear of another's greater power. But God had certainly given to him," that is, Pilate, "power in such manner that he was under the power of Caesar."

The coercive judicial power of Pilate over the person of Christ, therefore, was from God, as

Christ openly avowed, and Augustine plainly showed, and Bernard clearly said in his epistle to the archbishop of Sens: "For," as he wrote, "Christ avows that the Roman ruler's power over him is ordained of heaven," speaking of Pilate's power and with reference to this passage of Scripture. If, then, the coercive judiciary power of Pilate over Christ was from God, how much more so over Christ's temporal or carnal goods, if he had possessed or owned any? And if over Christ's person and temporal goods, how much more over the persons and temporal goods of all the apostles, and of their successors, all the bishops or priests?

Not only was this shown by Christ's words, but it was confirmed by the consummation of the deed. For the capital sentence was pronounced upon Christ by the same Pilate, sitting in the judgment seat, and by his authority that sentence was executed. Hence in the same chapter of John this passage is found: "Now when Pilate had heard these words, he brought Jesus forth, and sat down in the judgment seat"; and a little below is added: "Then therefore he delivered him," that is, Jesus, "to them to be crucified." Such was the Apostle's view regarding Christ, when he said in the third chapter of the epistle to the Galatians: "But when the fullness of the time was come, God sent his son, made of a woman, made under the law," and therefore also under the judge whose function it was to judge and command in accordance with the law, but who was not, however, a bishop or a priest.

13. Not only did Christ wish to exclude himself from secular rulership or coercive judicial power, but he also excluded it from his apostles, both among themselves and with respect to others. Hence in the twentieth chapter of Matthew and the twenty-second chapter of Luke this passage is found: "And there was also a strife among them," that is, the apostles, "which of them should seem to be the greater. And he," Christ, "said to them, The kings of the Gentiles lord it over them, and they that have power over them are called beneficent." (But in Matthew this clause is written as follows: "And they that are the greater exercise power upon them.") "But you not so: but he that is the greater among you, let him become as the younger; and he that is the leader, as he

that serveth." "But whosoever will be the greater among you shall be your servant: even as the Son of man is not come to be ministered unto, but to minister," that is, to be a servant in the temporal realm, not to lord it or rule, for in spiritual ministry he was first, and not a servant among the apostles. Whereon Origen comments: "'You know that the princes of the Gentiles lord it over them,' that is, they are not content merely to rule their subjects, but try to exercise violent lordship over them," that is, by coercive force if necessary. "But those of you who are mine will not be so; for just as all carnal things are based upon necessity, but spiritual things upon the will, so too should the rulership of those who are spiritual rulers," prelates, "be based upon love and not upon fear." And Chrysostom writes, among other remarks, these pertinent words:

> The rulers of the world exist in order to lord it over their subjects, to cast them into slavery and to despoil them [namely, if they deserve it] and to use them even unto death for their [that is, the rulers'] own advantage and glory. But the rulers [that is, prelates] of the church are appointed in order to serve their subjects and to minister to them whatever they have received from Christ, so that they neglect their own advantage and seek to benefit their subjects, and do not refuse to die for their salvation. To desire the leadership of the church is neither just nor useful. For what wise man is there who wants to subject himself of his own accord to such servitude and peril, as to be responsible for the whole church? Only he perhaps who does not fear the judgment of God and abuses his ecclesiastic leadership for secular purposes, so as to change it into secular leadership.

Why, then, do priests have to interfere with coercive secular judgments? for their duty is not to exercise temporal lordship, but rather to serve, by the example and command of Christ. Hence Jerome: "Finally he," that is, Christ, "sets forth his own example, so that if they," the apostles, "do not respect his words they may at least be ashamed of their deeds,"[6] that is, wielding temporal lordship. Hence Origen on the words: "And to give his life a redemption for many," wrote as follows:

> The rulers of the church should therefore imitate Christ, who was approachable, and spoke to women, and placed his hands upon the children, and washed the feet of his disciples, so that they might do the same for their brethren. But we are such [he is speaking of the prelates of his day] that we seem to exceed even the worldly rulers in pride, either misunderstanding or despising the commandment of Christ, and we demand fierce, powerful armies, just as do kings.

But since to do these things is to despise or be ignorant of Christ's commandment, the prelates must first be warned about it, which is what we shall do in this treatise, by showing what authority belongs to them; then, if they disregard this, they must be compelled and forced by the secular rulers to correct their ways, lest they corrupt the morals of others. These, then, are the comments made on the passage in Matthew. On Luke, Basil[7] writes: "It is fitting that those who preside should offer bodily service, following the example of the Lord who washed the feet of his disciples."

Christ, then, said: "The kings of the Gentiles lord it over them. But you," that is, the apostles, "not so." So Christ, king of kings and lord of lords, did not give them the power to exercise the secular judgments of rulers, nor coercive power over anyone, but he clearly prohibited this to them, when he said: "But you not so." And the same must consequently be held with respect to all the successors of the apostles, the bishops or priests. This too is what St. Bernard[8] clearly wrote to Eugene, *On Consideration*, book II, chapter IV, discussing the above words of Christ: "The kings of the Gentiles lord it over them," etc. For Bernard wrote, among other things:

---

6   Marsilius' misinterpretation of Jerome's meaning necessitates a mistranslation of this passage. What Jerome says is that the apostles "may at least be shamed to deeds" (*erubescant ad opera*), i.e., deeds such as Christ wanted them to perform, not the "wielding temporal lordship" with which Marsilius taxes them.

7   Basil of Caesarea (ca. 330–379), bishop of Caesarea Mazaca, theologian and monk.

8   Bernard of Clairvaux, Saint (ca.1090–1153), Cistercian abbot and theologian.

What the apostle [Peter] has, this did he give, namely, the guardianship, as I have said, of the churches. But not lordship? Hear him. "Neither as lording it over the clergy," he says, "but being made a pattern of the flock." And lest you think he spoke only from humility, but not with truth, the voice of the Lord is in the gospel: "The kings of the Gentiles lord it over them, and they that have power over them are called beneficent." And he adds: "But you not so." It is quite plain, then, that lordship is forbidden to the apostles. Go, then, if you dare, and usurp either the apostolate if you are a lord or lordship if you are an apostle. You are plainly forbidden to have both. If you wish to have both at once, you shall lose both. In any case, do not think you are excepted from the number of those about whom God complains in these words: "They have reigned, but not by me: they have been princes, and I knew not."

And so from the evangelic truths which we have adduced, and the interpretations of them made by the saints and other approved teachers, it should be clearly apparent to all that both in word and in deed Christ excluded and wished to exclude himself from all worldly rulership or governance, judgment, or coercive power, and that he wished to be subject to the secular rulers and powers in coercive jurisdiction.

CHAPTER XIII: ON THE STATUS OF SUPREME POVERTY, WHICH IS USUALLY CALLED EVANGELICAL PERFECTION; AND THAT THIS STATUS WAS HELD BY CHRIST AND HIS APOSTLES

Having thus distinguished the senses and meanings of the terms given above, we shall now infer some conclusions. The first of these is that no one can lawfully handle, individually or in common with others, some temporal thing, whether his own or someone else's, or something pertaining thereto, like the use or the usufruct, without right or without having a right to the thing or to something pertaining thereto—taking "right" in its first and second senses. For every deed which is not commanded or permitted to be done by right is not lawful, as everyone can clearly see from the definition of "lawful"; nor must we linger to prove this, since it is almost self-evident to all men.

2. The second conclusion which we can infer from what we have said is that one can handle a thing, or something pertaining thereto, lawfully according to one law, such as the divine, and unlawfully according to another, such as the human; and likewise conversely; and again, one can do the same thing lawfully or unlawfully according to each law. This is not difficult to see, since the commands, prohibitions, and permissions in these laws sometimes differ and disagree with one another and sometimes agree. Consequently, when one acts in accordance with the command or permission of one kind of law, one acts lawfully according to it; but if this act is prohibited by the other kind of law, one does it unlawfully according to that other law; if it is permitted by both kinds of law, one acts lawfully according to both. But if it is prohibited by both, one does it unlawfully according to both laws. Whether anything which is permitted to be done or omitted by divine law, is commanded or prohibited by human law, and conversely, still remains to be considered; for it does not pertain to our present inquiry. It is, however, certain that many things are permitted by human law, like fornication, drunkenness, and other sins, which are prohibited by divine law.

3. And now I wish to show that even apart from having any ownership, in the first three senses, of any temporal thing or of anything pertaining thereto, a person may lawfully handle it in private (in the third sense of "private") or even possess it in common with someone else (understanding the third sense of "possession"), and also lawfully destroy it. This is so, I maintain, regardless of whether that thing, or something pertaining thereto, be consumable in some one use or not; whether it be private to him (in the third sense of "private") or be common to him with another person or persons; whether it be his own, that is, rightfully acquired by him, or belong to someone else who, having rightfully (in the first sense) acquired it, consents to his handling it.

I demonstrate this proposition as follows. That temporal thing (or something pertaining thereto) which a person handles or holds apart from having ownership of it (in the first three senses of ownership), in accordance with divine law or human law or both, he can handle and destroy lawfully, apart from having ownership of it (in the above senses) whether in private or in common with others. But, regardless of whether a thing (or something pertaining thereto) be his own or belong to someone else who consents to his handling it, a person can, in accordance with these laws, handle the thing, as has been said, apart from having the aforementioned ownership of it. Therefore he can lawfully handle the thing without having ownership of it.

The first proposition of this deduction is self-evident from the definition of "lawful." The second I prove by an argument taken from induction, first with regard to a thing which belongs to a person privately or in common with someone else, or which he has rightfully acquired through his own act or someone else's, as by gift or legacy, by hunting, or fishing, or by some other lawful labor or deed of his. For suppose that a person has thus acquired a thing. It is then certain that he can use and handle it in accordance with the laws, as is plain from induction. Also it is clear that anyone who has the capacity can lawfully renounce a right introduced on his behalf, since, according to human and divine law, a benefit is not bestowed on an unwilling person. Therefore, a person who can by his own or by another's deed acquire ownership of a thing, or of its use, will be able to renounce such ownership. Since, therefore, the same person, if he wants to, acquires both the power lawfully to use a thing and the power to claim it and to prohibit another person from it, he can lawfully renounce the power of laying claim to the thing (or something pertaining thereto) or of prohibiting another therefrom (which power is none other than ownership taken in its first three legal senses), without renouncing the power of using the thing (or something pertaining thereto). This latter power falls under the right taken in its second sense, and is by some men called "simple use of a thing" (*simplex facti usus*) without the right of using (*jus utendi*), by "right of using" meaning "ownership" in any of its three senses given above.

4. Moreover, a thing which belongs to no one (*in nullius bonis est*) a person can lawfully use in accordance with the laws; but when someone has renounced the power to lay claim to a thing and to prohibit another person therefrom, that thing can then belong to no one; therefore a person can

lawfully use it. Since, therefore, a person who renounces the aforesaid power does not have the aforesaid ownership of the thing, it is apparent that one can lawfully handle and use a thing apart from having any of the aforesaid legal ownership.

5. Again, those things are separate from each other, of which one can for any time be given up by lawful vow, and the other not. But the aforesaid ownership of a thing, or the power to lay claim to and prohibit from a temporal thing or something pertaining thereto, can be given up for any time by lawful vow; while the lawful having or simple use of a thing cannot by lawful vow be given up for any time. Therefore these two cases are properly separate from each other. The first proposition of this deduction is self-evident from the definition of "lawful"; for the same thing cannot at once be lawful and unlawful according to the same law. The second proposition I shall prove with respect to each part. And first, that to give up for any time the aforesaid ownership by vow is lawful: for that vow is lawful which can be derived from the counsel of Christ. But such giving up is what Christ counseled, when in Matthew, chapter 20, he said: "And every one that hath forsaken house or lands … for my name's sake, shall receive an hundredfold, and shall inherit everlasting life." The same counsel is to be found in Matthew, chapter 5, and Luke, chapter 6, when Christ said: "And him that taketh away thy cloak, forbid not to take thy coat also." "And if any man will sue thee at the law, and take away thy coat, let him have thy cloak also." Whereon Augustine: "If he gives this command with regard to necessary things," that is, he counsels that one should not sue at law, "how much more so with regard to superfluities?" And in accordance with this teaching of Christ, the apostle said in I Corinthians, chapter 6: "Now therefore there is utterly a fault among you, because you go to law one with another. Why do ye not rather take wrong? Why do ye not rather suffer yourselves to be defrauded?" (supply: rather than sue someone at law, even justly, in order to lay claim to a temporal thing?). Whereon the gloss according to Augustine, after quoting the above passages of the gospel, adds: "This," that is, to sue at law justly, "the Apostle tolerates in the weak, since such judgments have to be made among brethren in the church with

brethren sitting as judges." And then, because of some doubts regarding Augustine's meaning, the gloss adds:

> Correctly to understand the above words of Augustine, where he says that "it is a sin to go to law with a brother," it must here be stated what is fitting for the perfect in such matters and what is not, and what is allowed to the weak and what is not. The perfect, then, are allowed to demand what is theirs simply, that is, without suit, litigation or judgment; but it is not fitting for them to have recourse to a lawsuit before a judge. The weak, however, are allowed to demand what is theirs both by starting a lawsuit before a judge and by having judgments against a brother.

Therefore, a lawful vow can be taken with respect to the giving up of ownership. But if it is not lawful for the perfect to sue before a coercive judge, then they do not have the power lawfully to lay claim to a thing, which power is the ownership discussed above; for they have renounced such power by a vow which they are allowed at no time to contravene, especially while it still stands.

And as for the other part of the second proposition, that the lawful having of a thing or of its use, or the simple use of a thing, cannot be given up for any time—this is clear enough: for nothing which is prohibited by divine law can lawfully fall under a vow. But such giving up is prohibited by divine law, because it is a species of homicide. For he who observed such a vow would knowingly kill himself from hunger or cold or thirst; which is explicitly prohibited by divine law, as in Matthew, chapter 19, Mark, chapter 10, and Luke, chapter 18, where Christ, confirming some commands of the old law, says: "Thou shalt not kill," etc. Therefore, the simple use of a thing, or the lawful having of it, is separate from all the afore-mentioned kinds of ownership, or the power of laying claim to and prohibiting from the thing or something pertaining thereto.

6. From this too it clearly follows of necessity that it is insane heresy to assert that a thing or its use cannot be had apart from the aforesaid ownership. For he who says this thinks nothing other than that Christ's counsel cannot be fulfilled; which is an open lie and, as we have said, must be shunned as vicious and heretical.

7. Nor is any difficulty presented by the objection that, while one may lawfully vow to give up an *act* of litigation, yet one cannot thus vow to give up the *habit* or the active legal *power* to claim the thing and prohibit it from someone else before a coercive judge, which power we have called ownership. For this statement is false, since every habit or legal power, acquired or acquirable, the act of which can be given up by lawful vow, can itself be given up in the same way, as is apparent by induction in all objects of deliberation which fall under vows. For he who vows chastity or obedience gives up by his vow not only the acts, but also the lawful power to perform these acts which had previously belonged to him by right (taken in the first sense). Again, it is inconsonant with the truth to say that a person has lawful power to perform acts all of which are unlawful, since a power is not called lawful or unlawful, nor is the difference between these known, otherwise than through the lawfulness or unlawfulness of the acts which emerge or can emerge from that power. Since, therefore, all the acts which emerge from the lawful power which a person had before his vow, are unlawful after the vow has been taken, it is clear that the person taking the vow has retained no lawful power to perform these acts.

8. Next I show that apart from having any ownership (in the senses given above), a person can have lawful use of something which belongs to another man, even to the extent of consuming the thing itself, if he exercises this use with the consent of the owner. For since the thing is assumed to be entirely in the ownership (or power to claim) of another person, it is certain that such ownership is not transferred to anyone else except by the deed and the express consent of its owner, and with no dissent on the part of the person to whom such ownership (or power to claim) of such a thing or of its use is to be transferred. Suppose, therefore, that the owner does not wish to transfer such ownership of a thing or of its use to some other person. Suppose, too, that this other person dissents from receiving such ownership, as for instance, because he has given up the ownership of all temporal things by an explicit vow, as befits

those who are perfect. Suppose, further, that an owner consents to have some perfect person use some thing of his, even to the extent of consuming the thing, and that the perfect person, who has given up ownership of every thing, wishes to use such thing with the owner's consent. I say, then, that the person who thus uses the thing, uses it lawfully, and that he nevertheless has no ownership whatsoever (in the senses given above) of the thing or of its use. That he has no ownership of the thing, or of its use, is apparent from the assumed conditions with regard both to the will of the owner and to the condition of the person who is to receive the use of the thing, who has completely given up such ownerships. That he uses the thing lawfully is apparent from the definition of "lawful," since everyone is permitted by law to use a thing belonging to someone else even to the extent of consuming it, if there intervenes the express consent of the owner of the thing.

9. Now if we take ownership or control in its last sense, as meaning the human will or freedom, with that natural motive power which is not acquired but innate in us, then I say that neither lawfully nor unlawfully can we freely handle a thing, or something pertaining thereto, without having such ownership or control, nor can we give up such ownership or control. And for the sake of brevity, I pass over this without proof, since it is almost self-evident, inasmuch as without these powers no one can continue to exist.

10. From these statements, then, it can be seen that not all lawful or rightful (in the first or second sense or both) power over a temporal thing or over its use is ownership, although conversely all lawful ownership (in the first three legal senses) of a thing or of its use or both, is lawful or rightful power. And hence, when one argues in this fashion: there is lawful or rightful power over a thing or its use, therefore there is lawful or rightful ownership of the thing or of its use— one makes an invalid inference. For a person can lawfully have and handle a thing, whether it is his in private or in common or whether it belongs to another—in which case the owner or the person

who has lawfully acquired it must give his consent—without acquiring any legal ownership of it.

11. Having set forth these premises, we now enter more fully upon our main task. We say first that the existence of poverty or of poor persons is almost self-evident, and is found in many passages of Scripture, from which it will suffice to quote one, in Mark, chapter 12, where Christ says: "Verily I say unto you, that this poor widow hath cast more in than all of them."

12. Next I show similarly by Scripture that poverty is meritorious as a means toward eternal life, for the Truth has said, in Luke, chapter 6: "Blessed be the poor: for yours is the kingdom of God," that is, you merit it, for in this life no one except Christ is actually blessed, but rather merits it.

13. And from this it necessarily follows that poverty is a virtue, if one becomes habituated thereto by many acts of thus willing to lack temporal goods; or else poverty is an act which is productive of a virtue or elicited from a virtue; for everything which is meritorious is a virtue or an act of virtue. Again, every counsel of Christ pertains essentially to virtue; but poverty is such a counsel, as is sufficiently clear from Matthew, chapters 5 and 19 and from many other passages of the evangelic Scripture.

14. From this it necessarily follows that the poverty to which we here refer as a virtue is that voluntary poverty which was defined in the third and fourth senses of poverty given above. For there is no virtue or deed of virtue without choice, and there is no choice without consent, as is sufficiently clear from the second and third books of the *Ethics* [of Aristotle]. This can be confirmed by Matthew, chapter 5, where Christ said: "Blessed are the poor in spirit," by "spirit" meaning will or consent, although some of the saints interpret "spirit" to mean pride, which interpretation is not, however, very appropriate, inasmuch as there immediately follow in the same chapter these words: "Blessed are the meek."[9] But whatever be the interpretation of this passage, there

---

9   Matthew 5:3,4. The saints referred to are Chrysostom and Augustine; in Thomas Aquinas, *Catena aurea* (XI, 55).

is no doubt, according to the views of the saints, that if poverty is deserving of the kingdom of the heavens, as Christ says, it must be not primarily the external lack of temporal goods, but an internal habit of the mind, whereby one freely wishes to be lacking in such goods for the sake of Christ. Whence on the words in Luke, chapter 6: "Blessed are the poor," etc., Basil writes: "Not everyone who is oppressed by poverty is blessed. For there are many persons who are poor in means, but most avaricious in desire, and these are not saved by their poverty, but damned by their desire. For nothing which is involuntary can be blessed, since every virtue is marked by free will." Poverty, then, is a meritorious virtue, and consequently voluntary. But external lack is not in itself a virtue, inasmuch as it does not lead to salvation without the proper desire; for a person might be lacking in temporal goods under coercion and against his will, and yet he would be condemned because of his inordinate desire for these goods. This was also the view of the apostle on this subject, when in II Corinthians, chapter 8, he said: "For if there be first a willing mind, it is accepted according to that a man hath"—"accepted," that is, meritorious.

15. Moreover, if this choice to be lacking in temporal goods is to be meritorious, it must be made for the sake of Christ. Hence the Truth says in Matthew, chapter 19: "And everyone that hath forsaken houses … for my name's sake." Whereon Jerome: "He who has forsaken carnal things for the sake of the Savior, will receive spiritual things, whose worth is to that of carnal things as the number one hundred is to a small number." And further on: "Those who because of faith in Christ have shunned all secular desires, riches, and pleasures in order to preach the gospel, will be benefited a hundredfold and will possess eternal life."

16. Again, since that which is opposed to avarice is essentially meritorious, it is essentially a virtue; such is voluntary poverty for the sake of Christ; for avarice is a vice. This virtue of voluntary poverty

bears an analogy to moral liberality, although it differs from it in its end and is of a more perfect species, at least so far as concerns the mean in the thing itself, as will be clear from what follows; and hence both of them cannot be placed in the same indivisible species.[10]

17. From these considerations, therefore, it can be seen that meritorious poverty is the virtue whereby a person wishes for the sake of Christ to be deprived of and to lack all the temporal goods, usually called riches, which are over and above what is necessary for his subsistence.

18. Whence too it manifestly follows that this virtue is not the habit or act of charity, as some seem to think. For poverty is not the habit or act which is essentially and primarily opposed to the actual or habitual hatred of God, because if it were, then more than one thing would be primarily opposed to one thing. For although the vice which is opposed to each theological virtue is incompatible with charity, yet from this it does not follow that charity is every theological virtue, since such vices are not opposed to charity primarily.

19. Nor is any difficulty presented by the argument that the virtue whereby we tend toward God through love, and the virtue whereby we recede from an inordinate desire for temporal things, are essentially the same virtue, just as the motion whereby a thing leaves some terminus and the motion whereby it tends in the opposite direction are essentially the same motion; and that since by charity we essentially tend toward God, therefore it is by this same virtue, and not by a different one, that we seem to depart from the love of temporal things.

20. The weakness of this argument can be seen primarily through our previous statement. For although by charity we essentially and primarily tend toward God through love, yet its opposite, from which we essentially and primarily depart, is hatred of God, not the unlawful love of

10   For the indivisible species, see Aristotle, *Posterior Analytics* II. 13. 96b 15 ff.; *Metaphysics* V. 10. 1018b 4. For the mean "in the thing itself," see Aristotle, *Nicomachean Ethics* II. 6. 1106a 25 ff., where it is pointed out that the "mean" in which the moral virtues consist is a mean "relatively to us" rather than a mean in terms of the thing or object with which the virtue is concerned. For liberality as a moral virtue, see *ibid.* IV. 1. 1119b 21 ff.

temporal things. This is so even though this latter departure sometimes is a consequence of charity, because when one departs from the love of temporal goods, there follows virtuous poverty, which is essentially and primarily such a voluntary giving up of temporal things as is necessarily followed by the departure from what is opposed to it essentially and primarily, namely, the unlawful love of temporal things. For if our opponent reasoned truly, the conclusion from true premises would be as follows: that charity is well-nigh every virtue, since charity is necessarily followed by most of the virtues, like faith and hope, whereby we essentially and primarily depart from heresy and despair, respectively.

21. Moreover, charity cannot fall under vow, because it is a command. But the afore-mentioned poverty, especially as taken in the fourth sense, falls under a vow. Therefore, charity is not essentially virtuous poverty, nor conversely, although poverty follows upon charity just as do most of the other theological virtues.

22. Moreover, I say that the highest mode or species of this virtue is the explicit vow of the wayfarer, whereby for the sake of Christ he renounces and wishes to be deprived of and to lack all acquired legal ownership, both in private and in common, or the power to claim and to prohibit another from temporal things (called "riches") before a coercive judge. And by this vow, also, the wayfarer wishes, for the sake of Christ, to be deprived of and to lack, both in private and in common, all power, holding, handling, or use of temporal things over and above what is necessary quantitatively and qualitatively for his present subsistence. Nor does he wish at one time to have such goods, however lawfully they may come to him, in an amount sufficient to supply several of the future needs or necessities either of himself alone or of himself together with a determinate other person or persons in common. Rather, he wishes to have at one time only what is necessary for a single need, as the immediately actual and present need of food and shelter; but with this sole exception, that the person who takes this vow should be in such place, time, and personal circumstance that he can acquire for himself, on

each successive day, a quantity of temporal things sufficient to supply his aforesaid individual need, but only one at a time, not more. This mode or species of meritorious poverty is the status which is considered to be necessary for evangelical perfection, as will clearly be seen from what follows. And this mode of meritorious poverty, or this status of a person who does not have possessions in private (in the third sense) or even in common with another (in the sense of "common" which is opposed to the above sense of "private"), we shall henceforth, for the sake of brevity, call "supreme poverty," and the person who wishes to have this status we shall call, in keeping with the custom of theologians, "perfect."

23. That this mode of meritorious poverty is the supreme one can be shown from this, that through it all the other meritorious counsels of Christ are observed. For in the first place, men give up by a vow all the temporal things which it is possible for a wayfarer to give up; secondly, most of the impediments to divine charity are removed for those who take this vow; thirdly, they are put in condition to endure many secular passions, humiliations, and hardships, and are willingly deprived of many secular pleasures and vanities; and in a word, they are put in the best condition to observe all the commands and counsels of Christ. That he who takes such a vow completely gives up temporal things to the extent that it is possible and lawful for the wayfarer to do so, is evident. For he wishes to have at one time nothing except what is necessary to supply a single present or almost present need of food and clothing; less than this no faithful wayfarer is allowed to have, since if he wished to have less than was necessary for sustenance of his life, he would knowingly be a homicide, which by divine law at least no one is allowed to be. Therefore, he who wishes to have temporal things in such quantity that he is not allowed to have less, wishes to have the minimum of them; and he who gives up such a quantity of them that he is not allowed to give up more, gives up the maximum. But this is what the wayfarer does in accordance with the aforesaid mode of meritorious poverty, which we have called the supreme mode. But that this is in accord with the counsel of Christ is evident. For he gave a counsel concerning this vow

in Luke, chapter 14, when he said: "So likewise, whosoever he be of you that forsaketh not all that he hath, he cannot be my disciple."

24. That the person who takes this vow removes from his path most of the impediments to divine charity, is evident. For the love and will to save temporal things turns a man toward them, and consequently turns him so much the more away from love or affection for God. Whence the Truth in Matthew, chapter 6: "Where your treasure is, there will your heart be also." To no avail is the excuse that the person who has these things does not turn his love toward them. For listen to Christ, who in Matthew, chapter 13, and Mark, chapter 4, says that "the deceitfulness of riches chokes the word." Whereon Jerome[11]: "Riches are flatterers which do one thing and promise another." And hence, Christ counseled complete renunciation of temporal things for the person who wishes to be perfect, in Luke, chapter 18: "Sell all that thou hast, and distribute unto the poor." Whereon Bede: "Whoever wishes to be perfect, then, must sell the things which he has: not partly, as Ananias and Sapphira did, but completely." And on the same passage, Theophylact[12] adds these pertinent words: "He urges supreme poverty. For if there remains anything," that is, any temporal things, "he is its slave," namely, the person who saves such things for himself. For such things by their very nature move inordinately the emotions of their possessors. Expounding the same counsel of Christ in Matthew, chapter 19, Raban[13] adds a remark in support of the same position which is quite pertinent. He writes: "There is a difference between having money and loving money. But it is safer neither to have nor to love riches." For, as Jerome says on the same passage: "It is difficult to despise riches when one possesses them." For "they are stickier than lime," as Thomas says, discussing the same counsel of Christ in Luke, chapter 18. Therefore, the person who gives up riches so far as it is possible and lawful for the wayfarer to do so, removes from his path the greatest impediments to charity.

25. Also he exposes himself to many secular passions, humiliations and hardships; he willingly deprives himself of many worldly pleasures and advantages. While this is self-evident from experience, let us quote the wise Solomon in Ecclesiastes, chapter 10: for "all things," he says, "obey money," that is, the person who has money. And on the other hand, as it is written in Proverbs, chapter 15: "All the days of the poor are evil"; for the poor man "has many afflictions," as the gloss thereon says. Again in Proverbs, chapter 19: "Wealth maketh many friends; but the poor man is separated from his neighbor." But that it is meritorious and advisable to bear sorrows in this world and to abstain from pleasures, is evident from Matthew, chapters 5 and 19, and Luke, chapter 6, where it is written with regard to the bearing of sorrows: "Blessed are the poor," "Blessed are they that mourn," "Blessed are they which are persecuted," "Blessed are ye that hunger," together with the other statements there added; and with regard to abstinence from pleasures: "Everyone that hath forsaken houses and brethren," with the other things there listed, "shall receive an hundredfold, and shall inherit everlasting life." This same position is expounded by the glosses of the saints thereon, which I have omitted to quote for the sake of brevity and because this matter is sufficiently well known. This too was the view of the apostle, in Romans, chapter 8: "For I reckon," he writes, "that the sufferings of this present time are not worthy to be compared with the glory which shall be revealed in us." And therefore the adversities of this world are meritorious for those who willingly bear them. The same view was taken in II Corinthians, chapter I, when the Apostle said "that as ye are partakers of the sufferings, so shall ye be also of the consolation." Whereon Ambrose: "For your hardships will be repaid with equal," that is, proportional, "glory." But groups of persons who have ownership of temporal things in common do not entirely put themselves in condition thus to bear secular sufferings and hardships: indeed, they do so in lesser degree than do many poor secular married couples who sometimes

---

11 Jerome (ca. 347 -420), theologian and biblical translator. All of the following patristic quotations are actually taken from Thomas Aquinas' *Catena Aurea.*, a compilation of patristic biblical commentaries.

12 Theophylact of Ohrid (1055–1107), Archbishop of Ohrid and biblical commentator.

13 Rabanus Maurus (ca. 780–856), monk, Archbishop of Mainz, and theologian.

have private possessions, and who nevertheless are more often in need of things required for sufficiency of life than are they who only possess such things in common.

26. Furthermore, that through this mode of meritorious poverty, which we have called the supreme mode, all the commands and counsels of Christ can be observed to the highest degree, will be apparent to anyone who reads the Gospel, especially the chapters we have indicated. For how can a person who has chosen to endure such poverty be avaricious or proud, incontinent or intemperate, ambitious, pitiless, unjust, timid, slothful, or jealous; why should he be mendacious or intolerant, for what reason malevolent toward others? On the contrary, he who has put himself in this condition seems to have an open door to all the virtues, and also to the serene fulfillment of all the commands and counsels. This is so plain to anyone who considers it that I omit the proof, for the sake of brevity.

27. Thus, therefore, the supreme mode or species of meritorious poverty is that which we have described above; for through it, all the commands and meritorious counsels of Christ can be more fully and more securely observed. And from this description it is apparent, first, that the perfect person ought, by an explicit vow, to renounce temporal things so far as their ownership is concerned, both because this is the counsel of Christ, as we have shown above from Luke, chapter 14, and because the perfect person by thus manifesting his poverty renders himself more contemptible in the sight of others and makes a fuller abandonment of secular honors. Whence in Luke, chapter 9: "If any man will come after me, let him deny himself." From this, moreover, it follows that no one can observe supreme poverty before attaining the complete use of reason. And from this description it also follows that the perfect person ought neither to have nor to acquire or save anything for himself, that is, for the purpose of supplying his future needs, but should look out only for the immediate present, except in the case which we have mentioned in the description above. Whence in Matthew, chapter 7: "Take therefore no thought for the morrow: for the morrow shall take thought for the things of itself." Whereon the gloss: "'for

the morrow,' that is, for the future; but he grants that thought must be taken with regard to the present. It is not proper to take thought for the future, since the divine ordinance provides for this; but gratefully accepting what the present offers, let us leave the care of the uncertain future to God, who takes care of us." And the same counsel is given in Matthew, chapter 7, when Christ said to his disciples: "Behold the fowls of the air: for they sow not, neither do they reap, nor gather into barns; yet your heavenly father feedeth them." And a little below he adds: "Therefore take no thought, saying, What shall we eat, or what shall we drink, or wherewith shall we be clothed? For after all these things do the Gentiles seek."

28. Now when we said that the perfect person is not allowed to provide for himself for the morrow, we did not mean that if anything remained from his lawful daily acquisitions, he ought to throw it away and in no manner save it, but that he ought to save it only with the firm intention of properly distributing it to any poor person or persons he met who were more needy than he. Whence in Luke, chapter 3: "He that hath two coats, let him impart to him that hath none: and he that hath meat, let him do likewise"; understanding by "two coats" and "meat" that which remains over and above one's own present needs.

We said that the surplus must be given to *any* poor person; for a community of men who save or have goods for certain definite persons only, such as the community of monks, canons, and the like, is not a perfect community; for the perfect community, like that of Christ and his apostles, extends to all the faithful, as is clear from Acts, chapter 4. And if it chanced to extend to infidels also, it would perhaps be still more meritorious, according to Luke, chapter 6: "Do good to them which hate you."

But the perfect person lawfully can and should keep surplus goods, so long as he has the firm intention of dealing with them as we have said. Whence in John, chapter 6: "Gather up the fragments that remain, that nothing be lost. Therefore they gathered them together, and filled twelve baskets with the fragments of the twelve barley loaves." This view was also expressed by the gloss on the words in Matthew, chapter 18: "Take that piece of money"; for the gloss says: "So great was the poverty of the Lord that he did not have wherewith to give tribute. Judas had the common goods in the bags, but he said that it was wrong to convert to one's own uses the goods of the poor." Which shows that what had been stored up belonged to the poor, that is, it was saved with that intention.

29. And from this it is clear that they are wrong who say that perfection is attained by vowing to accept nothing for distribution to the poor who are weak or otherwise incapable of acquiring for themselves the necessities of life. For, as is clear from II Corinthians, chapters 8 and 9, the apostle acquired goods with this purpose, and there is no doubt that he did so lawfully and meritoriously. And this is also apparent from the gloss on the words in John, chapter 21: "Feed my sheep," etc. But since the matter is quite evident, I omit to quote these passages, for the sake of brevity.

30. From our above description of supreme poverty it also necessarily follows that the perfect person neither can nor ought to save or keep in his power any real estate, like house or field, unless he has the firm intention of giving it away as soon as he can, or exchanging it for money or for something else which can immediately and conveniently be distributed to the poor. For since house or field could not as such be conveniently distributed to the poor without incurring the difficulty of giving too much to some and too little to others, we must follow the counsel of Christ, and do what he advised when he said, in Matthew, chapter 19, Luke, chapter 8, and Mark, chapter 10: "Go and sell." Nor did Christ say: Give to the poor everything that you have; nor did he say: Throw away everything that you have; but rather he said: "Go and sell," for by selling the distribution of wealth can be more conveniently made. Such too was the counsel of the apostles, and those to whom they gave this counsel followed it out, wishing to distribute their goods to the poor conveniently. Whence in Acts, chapter 4: "For as many as were possessors of lands or houses sold them, and brought the prices of the things that

were sold. And distribution was made unto every man according as he had need."

31. From the above it is also apparent that no perfect person can acquire the ownership (in the first, second, and third senses) of any temporal thing, as we have proved above from Matthew, chapter 5, and Luke, chapter 6. And we have confirmed this through the apostle in I Corinthians, chapter 6; and we made it sufficiently clear by the words of Augustine and the gloss on that scriptural passage. Since the matter is evident, I have omitted to quote these passages for the sake of brevity.

32. Nor should we pay attention to the argument that perfect men may lawfully save real estate in order to distribute the annual income thereof to the poor. For it is more meritorious because of love of Christ and pity for one's neighbor to distribute at once to the poor both the real estate and the income thereof, rather than the latter alone; and besides, it is more meritorious to give away the real estate alone rather than its income alone. For in this way help can be given to many poor and needy persons at once, who might perhaps through want become ill or die before the income became available, or commit an act of violence, theft, or some other evil. Again, a person who kept the real estate might die before the time when the income was distributed, and thus he would never have the merit therefrom that he could have had.

Entirely the same view must be held with respect to any kind of chattels, which similarly, when thus kept, naturally affect to an inordinate degree the desire of the person who holds them. But if the virtue here considered is believed to be charity, as some seem to think, then undoubtedly this mode of charity, that is, with supreme poverty, is more perfect than having private or common ownership of a temporal thing, as is plain from the preceding reasonings.

33. But now advancing to the principal proposition, we wish to show that Christ while he was a wayfarer observed the supreme species or mode of meritorious poverty.[14] For that which is first in

---

14 Marsilius here argues against the bull of John XXII, *Cum inter nonnullos*, of Nov. 12, 1323 (*Corp. jur can., Extravag. Joh. XXII* Tit. 14. cap. 4), which condemned the doctrine that Christ had absolute poverty. Marsilius' position on this and other issues is in turn condemned in John's bull, *Quia quorundam mentes*, of Nov. 10, 1324 (*ibid.* Tit. 14. cap. 5).

each sphere is greatest; but Christ under the New Law was the first of the wayfarers who merited eternal life; therefore he was the greatest of all in perfection; therefore observed this status with respect to temporal things, for without this it is impossible, according to the common law, to attain the greatest degree of meritoriousness. Again, if he had not observed this mode of poverty, then some other wayfarer could have been or might in the future be more perfect in merit than Christ according to the common law, which it is impious to believe. For Christ asserted that this status was required for perfection in merit, when he said: "If you wish to be perfect, sell all whatsoever that thou hast and distribute unto the poor"; nor did he add: the things that thou hast in private or in common, but he meant this to be taken universally, so that he stressed its universal meaning by saying: "all whatsoever." For he who has the ownership or keeping of temporal things in common with another person or persons, in a way other than the one described by us, has not given up all the temporal things which it is possible to give up, nor is he exposed to so many secular sufferings or deprived of so many advantages as is he who renounces temporal things both as private property and in common, nor is he thus free from solicitude for these things, nor does he observe all the counsels of Christ equally as much as does he who completely gives us temporal things.

34. And now I wish to show that while Christ observed supreme poverty, he did have some possessions both as private property and in common. That he had private property (in the third sense) is shown by the passage in Mark, chapter 2: "For there were many, and they followed him. And the scribes and sinners saw him eat with publicans and sinners." Now it is certain that he lawfully had as private or individual property that which he put to his mouth and ate. Moreover, his clothes were his private or individual property, as is sufficiently clear from Matthew, chapter 27, Mark, chapter 15, Luke, chapter 23, and John, chapter 19. Whence in Matthew, in the chapter mentioned: "They took the robe off from him, and put his own raiment on him." Thus too in John, in the chapter just mentioned: "Then the soldiers, when they had crucified Jesus, took his garments." Thus too

in Mark and Luke, whose passages are omitted for the sake of brevity. Christ, therefore, even while observing supreme poverty, lawfully or rightfully had temporal things as his private property, and wanted them and it was fitting that he want them; otherwise he would have sinned mortally, for being a true man he was subject to hunger, as is apparent from Matthew, chapter 21, and Mark, chapter 18, and hence he needed food, which he had to take when he was able to do so, for otherwise he would have gravely sinned, by knowingly starving himself to death.

35. Christ also lawfully had some things in common while observing supreme poverty. Whence in John, chapter 12: "This Judas said, not that he cared for the poor; but because he was a thief, and had the bags," that is, the common belongings of Christ and the apostles and the other poor persons. That these were held in common is apparent from the fact that Christ ordered some of them to be distributed to the hungry crowds of the poor, as is sufficiently clear from Matthew, chapter 14. The "bags" were the repositories wherein was kept the alms money which had been given to them. This is again shown by the fourteenth chapter of the same book: "For some of them thought that Judas had the bag." Also it is shown by the gloss on the passage in Matthew, chapter 18: "Take that piece of money," etc., whereon the gloss says: "Judas had the common goods in the bags." Thus too the apostles, while observing supreme poverty, had belongings in common among themselves and with other poor persons, after the resurrection of Christ. Whence in Acts, chapter 4: "But they had all things in common." And similarly they had some things as private property, namely, their own food and clothing, which they applied for their private use, just as did Christ.

36. Next I wish to give a necessary proof of what constitutes the principal thesis of this chapter and the ones immediately preceding and following, namely, that Christ the wayfarer, giving a pre-eminent manifestation of the height of perfection, had no acquired ownership (in the first, second, or third sense), in private or in common, of any temporal thing or of its use. For if he had assumed for himself such ownership, he would

not have observed all the counsels, and especially that form of poverty which is the highest one possible for the wayfarer. But Christ observed all these counsels in the most perfect manner of any wayfarer. Therefore, Christ did not have or want to have such ownership of temporal things, which the Scripture in many passages calls "possession," as in Luke, chapter 14: "Whosoever he be of you that forsaketh not all that he possesseth"; so too in Matthew, chapter 10: "Possess neither gold, nor silver, nor brass in your purses," that is, do not keep these unless perhaps for a lawful occasion, namely, for the purpose and needs mentioned above, such as for the sake of the powerless poor, as Paul did, or from urgent necessity of time, place, and personal condition; which cases will be made clearer in the following chapter. Although even in the afore-mentioned cases the person who has taken a vow of supreme poverty is not allowed to have ownership, for such ownership necessarily excludes the fulfillment of Christ's counsel regarding supreme poverty. Christ, therefore, did not have the aforesaid ownership of temporal things, nor can it be had by any imitator of him, that is, by anyone who wishes to observe supreme poverty.

37. In consequence of these considerations, I say that it cannot be proved from the holy Scripture that Christ, however condescending he may have been to the weak, had the aforesaid ownership or possession of temporal goods in private or in common, although some of the saints are believed to have held this view. For by parity of reasoning one might conclude that Christ did everything which was permitted lest he should seem to have condemned the status of persons who did such things. If this argument were sound, Christ would have accepted and exercised secular rulership or contentious jurisdiction over litigation, whereas the opposite of this was irrefutably shown in chapter IV of this discourse; so too, he would have married, would have engaged in lawsuits before a coercive judge, and would have done everything else that was permitted; but that Christ did these things no one can prove by Scripture, but rather the opposite. For it was not necessary or fitting for him to do such things in order that he should not seem to have condemned the status of those persons who did them, and who are called "weak." For it does not follow that because Christ was not married, therefore he seemed to be condemning the status of those who were married; and similarly in the other cases. For he himself sufficiently expressed the difference between the things which it is necessary to do or omit for salvation—the commands or prohibitions—and the things which are not necessary for salvation, which the saints call "supererogatory." For when someone asked Christ what things were necessary for eternal salvation, Christ replied: "If thou wilt enter into life, keep the commandments." And again when the person asked him what things were supererogatory, Christ did not reply: If thou wilt enter into life, but he said to him: "If thou wilt be perfect." In these words in Matthew, chapter 19, Luke, chapter 18, and Mark, chapter 10, Christ explicitly showed that for eternal life the observance of the commandments was sufficient, for he made no reply, to the person asking about this, other than to say: "Keep the commandments, if thou wilt enter into life." And hence it was not necessary or fitting for Christ to do all the things that were permitted, in order that he should not seem to have condemned the status of persons who did such things, for he had already made it clear that men can be saved by observing only the commandments or commands, taking "command" in its more general sense as both affirmative and negative; but it was more fitting for Christ to observe the counsels, as for example to maintain supreme poverty and not to marry, in order to afford to all others an example of such observance; which, as we read in Scripture, he actually carried out both in word and in deed. For speaking of his poverty in Matthew, chapter 8, and Luke, chapter 9, he said: "The foxes have holes, and the birds of the air have nests; but the Son of man hath not where to lay his head." Whereon the gloss: "I am so poor that I do not have a shelter of my own." For "so great was the poverty of the Lord that he did not have wherefrom to give tribute," as the gloss says on the words in Matthew, chapter 18: "Take that piece of money, and give to them for me and you." But we never read that Christ had a castle or fields or treasure chests in order that he might not seem to be condemning the status of those who did have such things.

38. But if Christ had done things that were permitted, he could none the less have equally obeyed all the counsels, for he, who was the legislator, was able to do such things in order that he should not seem to be condemning the status of those who did them. Hence he would not have wanted in an unqualified sense to do such things, as do the weak who want them for their own advantage; but he would have wanted to do such things for a different purpose, wanting them and at the same time, in a certain way, not wanting them, since he wanted them not for himself but for the aforesaid reason. But all other perfect men can in no way properly want such ownership, if they are to observe the counsels to the full. For they cannot want such ownership in order that they may not seem to be condemning the status of others, as it does not pertain to them to approve or condemn anyone's status, because they neither were nor are nor will be legislators. If therefore they wanted such ownership, they would want it as weak persons, not as perfect ones. So, then, it would have been lawful for Christ to do these things that were permitted, if he had wanted to, while at the same time observing all the counsels to the full; but it can be lawful for no one else to do so, for the reason already stated.

39. But if it be asked who can be so perfect as to wish to have, at one time, only such an amount of temporal goods as is merely sufficient for one's own present or immediate need, I reply that Christ and other men did so desire, although such men are few, because "strait is the gate, and narrow is the way ... and few there be that find it," as it is written in Matthew, chapter 7. And do you tell me, I beg: How many voluntary martyrs are there in these times, how many heroic men, how many Catos, Scipios, and Fabricii[15]?

---

15   The families of the Catos, Scipios, and Fabricii were held as models of Roman virtue.

38. *THE BOOK OF MARGERY KEMPE*

MARGERY KEMPE (1373–1439) WAS the daughter of a prosperous merchant of Lynne. At 20 she was married to John Kempe, and after bearing a large number of children she began a series of pilgrimages. Her writings comprise the first autobiography in English—although she herself was illiterate and dictated to two clerks—and reflect the tensions of her dual life: wife and mother on the one hand, and pilgrim and mystic on the other.

Source: W. Butler-Bowdon, *The Book of Margery Kempe* (New York: The Devin-Adair Company, 1944), 1–18, 28–68.

Further Reading: John H. Arnold and Katherine J. Lewis, *A Companion to the Book of Margery Kempe* (Woodbridge: D.S. Brewer, 2004).

The First Book

Chapter 1

Her marriage and illness after childbirth. She recovers.

When this creature was twenty years of age, or some deal more, she was married to a worshipful burgess [of Lynne] and was with child within a short time, as nature would. And after she had conceived, she was belabored with great accesses till the child was born and then, what with the labor she had in childing, and the sickness going before, she despaired of her life, weening[1] she might not live. And then she sent for her ghostly father, for she had a thing on her conscience which she had never shewn before that time in all her life. For she was ever hindered by her enemy, the devil, evermore saying to her that whilst she was in good health she needed no confession, but to do penance by herself alone and all should be forgiven, for God is merciful enough. And therefore this creature oftentimes did great penance in fasting on bread and water, and other deeds of alms with devout prayers, save she would not shew that in confession.

And when she was at any time sick or diseased, the devil said in her mind that she should be damned because she was not shriven of that default. Wherefore after her child was born, she, not trusting to live, sent for her ghostly father, as is said before, in full will to be shriven of all her lifetime, as near as she could. And when she came to the point for to say that thing which she had so long concealed, her confessor was a little too hasty and began sharply to reprove her, before she had fully said her intent, and so she would no more say for aught he might do. Anon, for the dread she had of damnation on the one side, and his sharp reproving of her on the other side, this creature went out of her mind and was wondrously vexed and labored with spirits for half a year, eight weeks and odd days.

And in this time she saw, as she thought, devils opening their mouths all inflamed with burning waves of fire, as if they would have swallowed her in, sometimes ramping at her, sometimes threatening her, pulling her and hauling her, night and day during the aforesaid time. Also the devils cried upon her with great threatenings, and bade her that she should forsake Christendom, her faith, and deny her God, His Mother and all the Saints in Heaven, her good works and all good virtues, her father, her mother and all her friends. And so she did. She slandered her husband, her friends and her own self. She said many a wicked word, and many a cruel word; she knew no virtue nor goodness; she desired all wickedness; like as the spirits tempted her to say and do, so she said and did. She would have destroyed herself many a time at their stirrings and have been damned with them in Hell, and in witness thereof, she bit her own hand so violently, that the mark was seen all her life after.

---

1   Thinking.

And also she rived the skin on her body against her heart with her nails spitefully, for she had no other instruments, and worse she would have done, but that she was bound and kept with strength day and night so that she might not have her will. And when she had long been labored in these and many other temptations, so that men weened she should never have escaped or lived, then on a time as she lay alone and her keepers were from her, Our Merciful Lord Jesus Christ, ever to be trusted, worshipped be His Name, never forsaking His servant in time of need, appeared to His creature who had forsaken Him, in the likeness of a man, most seemly, most beauteous and most amiable that ever might be seen with man's eye, clad in a mantle of purple silk, sitting upon her bedside, looking upon her with so blessed a face that she was strengthened in all her spirit, and said to her these words:—

"Daughter, why hast thou forsaken Me, and I forsook never thee?"

And anon, as He said these words, she saw verily how the air opened as bright as any lightning. And He rose up into the air, not right hastily and quickly, but fair and easily, so that she might well behold Him in the air till it was closed again.

And anon this creature became calmed in her wits and reason, as well as ever she was before, and prayed her husband as soon as he came to her, that she might have the keys of the buttery to take her meat and drink as she had done before. Her maidens and her keepers counseled him that he should deliver her no keys, as they said she would but give away such goods as there were, for she knew not what she said, as they weened.

Nevertheless, her husband ever having tenderness and compassion for her, commanded that they should deliver to her the keys; and she took her meat and drink as her bodily strength would serve her, and knew her friends and her household and all others that came to see how Our Lord Jesus Christ had wrought His grace in her, so blessed may He be, Who ever is near in tribulation. When men think He is far from them, He is full near by His grace. Afterwards, this creature did all other occupations as fell to her to do, wisely and soberly enough, save she knew not verily the call of Our Lord.

Chapter 2

Her worldly pride. Her attempt at brewing and milling, and failure at both. She amends her ways.

When this creature had thus graciously come again to her mind, she thought that she was bound to God and that she would be His servant. Nevertheless, she would not leave her pride or her pompous array, which she had used beforetime, either for her husband, or for any other man's counsel. Yet she knew full well that men said of her full much villainy, for she wore gold pipes on her head, and her hoods, with the tippets, were slashed. Her cloaks also were slashed and laid with divers colours between the slashes, so that they should be the more staring to men's sight, and herself the more worshipped.

And when her husband spoke to her to leave her pride, she answered shrewdly and shortly, and said that she was come of worthy kindred—he should never have wedded her—for her father was sometime mayor of the town of N...[2] and afterwards he was alderman of the High Guild of the Trinity in N.... And therefore she would keep the worship of her kindred whatever any man said.

She had full great envy of her neighbors, that they should be as well arrayed as she. All her desire was to be worshipped by the people. She would not take heed of any chastisement, nor be content with the goods that God had sent her, as her husband was, but ever desired more and more.

Then for pure covetousness, and to maintain her pride, she began to brew, and was one of the greatest brewers in the town of N... for three years or four, till she lost much money, for she had never been used thereto. For, though she had ever such good servants, cunning in brewing, yet it would never succeed with them. For when the ale was fair standing under barm as any man might see, suddenly the barm would fall down, so that all the ale was lost, one brewing after another, so that her servants were ashamed and would not dwell with her.

Then this creature thought how God had punished her aforetime—and she could not take heed—and now again, by the loss of her goods. Then she left and brewed no more.

---

2   Lynne, now King's Lynn, is evidently referred to. This anonymity is dropped later on.

Then she asked her husband's mercy because she would not follow his counsel aforetime, and she said that her pride and sin were the cause of all her punishing, and that she would amend and that she had trespassed with good will.

Yet she left not the world altogether, for she now bethought herself of a new housewifery. She had a horse-mill. She got herself two good horses and a man to grind men's corn, and thus she trusted to get her living. This enterprise lasted not long, for in a short time after, on Corpus Christi Eve, befell this marvel. This man, being in good health of body, and his two horses sturdy and gentle, had pulled well in the mill beforetime, and now he took one of these horses and put him in the mill as he had done before, and this horse would draw no draught in the mill for anything the man might do. The man was sorry and essayed with all his wits how he should make this horse pull. Sometimes he led him by the head, sometimes he beat him, sometimes he cherished him and all availed not, for he would rather go backward than forward. Then this man set a sharp pair of spurs on his heels and rode on the horse's back to make him pull, and it was never the better. When the man saw it would work in no way, he set up this horse again in the stable, and gave him corn, and he ate well and freshly. And later he took the other horse and put him in the mill, and like his fellow did, so did he, for he would not draw for anything the man might do. Then the man forsook his service and would no longer remain with the aforesaid creature. Anon, it was noised about the town of N… that neither man nor beast would serve the said creature.

Then some said she was accursed; some said God took open vengeance upon her; some said one thing and some said another. Some wise men, whose minds were more grounded in the love of Our Lord, said that it was the high mercy of Our Lord Jesus Christ that called her from the pride and vanity of the wretched world.

Then this creature, seeing all these adversities coming on every side, thought they were the scourges of Our Lord that would chastise her for her sin. Then she asked God's mercy, and forsook her pride, her covetousness, and the desire that she had for the worship of the world, and did great bodily penance, and began to enter the way of everlasting life as shall be told hereafter.

Chapter 3

Her vision of Paradise. She desires to live apart from her husband. Does penance and wears a haircloth.

On a night, as this creature lay in her bed with her husband, she heard a sound of melody so sweet and delectable, that she thought she had been in Paradise, and therewith she started out of her bed and said:—

"Alas, that ever I did sin! It is full merry in heaven."

This melody was so sweet that it surpassed all melody that ever might be heard in this world, without any comparison, and caused her, when she heard any mirth or melody afterwards, to have full plenteous and abundant tears of high devotion, with great sobbings and sighings after the bliss of heaven, not dreading the shames and the spites of this wretched world. Ever after this inspiration, she had in her mind the mirth and the melody that was in heaven, so much, that she could not well restrain herself from speaking thereof, for wherever she was in any company she would say oftentimes:—"It is full merry in heaven."

And they that knew her behavior before-time, and now heard her speaking so much of the bliss of heaven, said to her:—

"Why speak ye so of the mirth that is in heaven? Ye know it not, and ye have not been there, any more than we." And were wroth with her, for she would not hear nor speak of worldly things as they did, and as she did beforetime.

And after this time she had never desired to commune fleshly with her husband, for the debt of matrimony was so abominable to her that she would rather, she thought, have eaten or drunk the ooze and the muck in the gutter than consent to any fleshly communing, save only for obedience.

So she said to her husband:—"I may not deny you my body, but the love of my heart and my affections are withdrawn from all earthly creatures, and set only in God."

He would have his will and she obeyed, with great weeping and sorrowing that she might not live chaste. And oftentimes this creature counseled her husband to live chaste, and said that they often, she knew well, had displeased God by their inordinate love, and the great delectation they each had in using the other, and now it was good that they should, by the common will and consent of them both, punish and chastise themselves wilfully by abstaining from the lust of their bodies. Her husband said it was good to do so, but he might not yet. He would when God willed. And so he used her as he had done before. He would not spare her. And ever she prayed to God that she might live chaste; and three or four years after, when it pleased Our Lord, he made a vow of chastity, as shall be written afterwards, by leave of Jesus.

And also, after this creature heard this heavenly melody, she did great bodily penance. She was shriven sometimes twice or thrice on a day, and specially of that sin she so long had [hid], concealed and covered, as is written in the beginning of the book.

She gave herself up to great fasting and great watching; she rose at two or three of the clock, and went to church, and was there at her prayers unto the time of noon and also all the afternoon. Then she was slandered and reproved by many people, because she kept so strict a life. She got a hair-cloth from a kiln, such as men dry malt on, and laid it in her kirtle as secretly and privily as she might, so that her husband should not espy it. Nor did he, and she lay by him every night in his bed and wore the hair-cloth every day, and bore children in the time.

Then she had three years of great labour with temptations which she bore as meekly as she could, thanking Our Lord for all His gifts, and was as merry when she was reproved, scorned and japed for Our Lord's love, and much more merry than she was beforetime in the worship of the world. For she knew right well she had sinned greatly against God and was worthy of more shame and sorrow than any man could cause her, and despite of the world was the right way heavenwards, since Christ Himself had chosen that way. All His apostles, martyrs, confessors and virgins, and all that ever came to heaven, passed by the way of tribulation, and she, desiring nothing so much as heaven, then was glad in her conscience when she believed that she was entering the way that would lead her to the place she most desired.

And this creature had contrition and great compunction with plenteous tears and many boisterous sobbings for her sins and for her unkindness against her maker. She repented from her childhood for unkindness, as Our Lord would put it in her mind, full many a time. Then, beholding her own wickedness, she could but sorrow and weep and ever pray for mercy and forgiveness. Her weeping was so plenteous and continuing, that many people thought she could weep and leave off, as she liked. And therefore many men said she was a false hypocrite, and wept before the world for succor and worldly goods. Then full many forsook her that loved her before while she was in the world, and would not know her. And ever, she thanked God for all, desiring nothing but mercy and forgiveness of sin.

Chapter 4

Her temptation to adultery with a man, who, when she consents, rejects her.

The first two years when this creature was thus drawn to Our Lord, she had great quiet in spirit from any temptations. She could well endure to fast, and it did not trouble her. She hated the joys of the world. She felt no rebellion in her flesh. She was so strong, as she thought, that she dreaded no devil in hell, as she did such great bodily penance. She thought that she loved God more than He did her. She was smitten with the deadly wound of vainglory, and felt it not, for she many times desired that the crucifix should loosen His hands from the Cross, and embrace her in token of love. Our Merciful Lord Jesus Christ, seeing this creature's presumption, sent her, as is written before, three years of great temptations, one of the hardest of which I purpose to write as an example to those who come after, so that they should not trust in themselves, or have joy in themselves, as she had. For, no dread, our ghostly enemy sleepeth not, but he full busily searcheth our complexions and dispositions and where he findeth us most frail, there, by Our Lord's sufferance, he layeth his snare, which no man may escape by his own power.

So he laid before this woman the snare of lechery, when she believed that all fleshly lust had wholly been quenched in her. And so for a long time she was tempted with the sin of lechery, for aught that she could do. Yet she was often shriven, she wore her hair-cloth, and did great bodily penance and wept many a bitter tear, and prayed full often to Our Lord that He should preserve her and keep her, so that she should not fall into temptation, for she thought she would rather be dead than consent thereto. All this time she had no lust to commune with her husband; but it was very painful and horrible unto her.

In the second year of her temptation, it so fell that a man whom she loved well, said unto her on St. Margaret's Eve before evensong that, for anything, he would lie by her and have his lust of his body, and she should not withstand him, for if he did not have his will that time, he said he would anyhow have it another time; she should not choose. And he did it to see what she would do, but she thought that he had meant it in full earnest at that time, and said but little thereto. So they parted then and both went to hear evensong, for her church was that of Saint Margaret. This woman was so labored with the man's words that she could not hear her evensong, nor say her Paternoster, or think any other good thought, but was more troubled than ever she was before.

The devil put into her mind that God had forsaken her, or else she would not be so tempted. She believed the devil's persuasion, and began to consent because she could think no good thought. Therefore thought she that God had forsaken her, and when evensong was done, she went to the man aforesaid, so that he could have his lust, as she thought he had desired, but he made such simulation that she could not know his intent, and so they parted asunder for that night. This creature was so labored and vexed all that night, that she never knew what she might do. She lay by her husband, and to commune with him was so abominable to her that she could not endure it, and yet it was lawful unto her, in lawful time, if she would. But ever she was labored with the other man, to sin with him inasmuch as he had spoken to her. At last, through the importunity of such temptation, and lack of discretion, she was overcome and consented in her mind, and went to the man to know if he would then consent to her, and he said he never would, for all the gold in this world; he would rather be hewn as small as flesh for the pot.

She went away all shamed and confused in herself at seeing his stability and her own instability.

Then thought she of the grace that God had given her before; how she had two years of great quiet in her soul, repenting of her sin with many bitter tears of compunction, and a perfect will never again to turn to her sin, but rather to die. Now she saw how she had consented in her will to do sin, and then fell she half into despair. She thought she must have been in hell for the sorrow she felt. She thought she was worthy of no mercy, for her consent was so wilfully done, nor ever worthy to do Him service, because she was so false to Him. Nevertheless she was shriven many times and often, and did whatever penance her confessor would enjoin her to do, and was governed by the rules of the Church. That grace, God gave his creature, blessed may He be, but He withdrew not her temptation, but rather increased it, as she thought.

Therefore she thought He had forsaken her, and dared not trust to His mercy, but was afflicted with horrible temptations to lechery and despair all the next year following. But Our Lord, of His mercy, as she said herself, gave her each day for the most part two hours of sorrow for her sins, with many bitter tears. Afterwards, she was labored with temptation to despair as she was before, and was as far from feelings of grace, as they that never felt any, and that she could not bear, and so she gave way to despair. But for the time that she felt grace, her labors were so wonderful that she could evil fare with them, but ever mourned and sorrowed as though God had forsaken her.

Chapter 5

She speaks with Our Lord, Who orders her to abstain from flesh-meat, and to contemplate and meditate.

Then on the Friday before Christmas Day, as this creature was kneeling in a chapel of Saint John, within a Church of St. Margaret in N..., weeping wondrous sore, and asking mercy and forgiveness for her sins and trespasses, Our merciful Lord Christ Jesus, blessed may He be, ravished her spirit and said unto her:—

"Daughter, why weepest thou so sore? I am coming to thee, Jesus Christ Who died on the cross, suffering bitter pains and passions for thee. I, the same God, forgive thee thy sins to the uttermost point, and thou shalt never come to hell or purgatory, but when thou shalt pass out of this world, within a twinkling of an eye, thou shalt have the bliss of heaven, for I am the same God that hath brought thy sins to thy mind and made thee be shriven thereof. And I grant thee contrition to thy life's end. Therefore I bid thee and command thee, boldly call Me 'Jesus Christ, thy love,' for I am thy love, and shall be thy love without end. And, daughter, thou hast a haircloth on thy back. I will that thou put it away, and I shall give thee a haircloth in thy heart that shall please Me much better than all the haircloths in the world. Also, my dearworthy daughter, thou must forsake that which thou lovest best in this world, and that is the eating of flesh. Instead of that flesh, thou shalt eat of My flesh and My blood, that is the Very Body of Christ in the Sacrament of the Altar. This is My will, daughter, that thou receive My Body every Sunday, and I shall flow so much grace into thee, that all the world shall marvel thereof. Thou shalt be eaten and gnawed by the people of the world as any rat gnaweth stockfish. Dread thee nought, daughter, for thou shalt have victory over all thine enemies. I shall give thee grace enough to answer every clerk in the love of God. I swear to thee by My Majesty that I will never forsake thee in weel[3] or in woe. I shall help thee and keep thee, so that no devil in hell shall part thee from Me, nor angel in heaven, nor man on earth, for devils in hell may not, and angels in heaven will not, and man on earth shall not. And, daughter, I will thou leave thy bidding of many beads, and think such thoughts as I shall put into thy mind. I shall give thee leave to pray till six of the clock, saying what thou wilt. Then shalt thou be still and speak to Me in thought and I shall give to thee high meditation and very contemplation. I bid thee go to the anchorite at the preaching friars and shew him My secrets and My counsels which I shew to thee, and work after his counsel, for My Spirit shall speak in him to thee."

Then this creature went forth to the anchorite as she was commanded, and shewed him the revelations, as they were revealed to her. Then the anchorite, with great reverence and weeping, thanking God, said:—

"Daughter, ye suck even on Christ's breast, and ye have an earnest-penny of heaven. I charge you to receive such thoughts as God gives, as meekly and devoutly as ye can, and to come to me and tell me what they are, and I shall, with the leave of Our Lord Jesus Christ, tell you whether they are of the Holy Ghost or of your enemy the devil."

Chapter 6

The birth of Our Lady. Her speech with Saint Elizabeth. The birth of Our Lord.

Another day, she gave herself up to meditation as she had been bidden and lay still, not knowing what she might best think of. Then she said to Our Lord Jesus Christ:

"Jesus, of what shall I think?"

Our Lord answered to her mind:—"Daughter, think of My Mother, for she is the cause of all the grace that thou hast."

Then, anon, she saw Saint Anne, great with child, and she prayed Saint Anne that she might be her maiden, and her servant. And anon, Our Lady was born, and then she arranged to take the child to herself and keep it till it was twelve years of age, with good meat and drink, with fair white clothing and white kerchiefs.

Then she said to the blessed child:—"Lady, you shall be the Mother of God."

The blessed child answered and said:—"I would I were worthy to be the handmaiden of her that should conceive the Son of God."

The creature said:—"I pray you, Lady, if that grace befall, you renounce not my service."

The blissful child passed away for a certain time, the creature being quite quiet in contemplation, and afterwards came again and said:—

"Daughter, now am I become the Mother of God."

And then the creature fell down on her knees with great reverence and great weeping and said:—

"I am not worthy, Lady, to do you service."

"Yes, daughter," said she, "follow thou me, thy service liketh me well."

Then went she forth with Our Lady and with

---

3   Well.

Joseph, bearing with her a pottle[4] of wine and honey, and spices thereto. Then went they forth to Elizabeth, Saint John the Baptist's mother, and when they met together, each worshipped the other, and so they dwelt together, with great grace and gladness twelve weeks. And Saint John was born, and Our Lady took him up from the earth with all manner of reverence, and gave him to his mother, saying of him that he should be a holy man, and blessed him. Afterwards they took leave of each other with compassionate tears. Then the creature fell down on her knees to Saint Elizabeth, and begged her to pray for her to Our Lady that she might do her service and pleasure.

"Daughter," said Elizabeth, "me-seemeth thou dost right well thy duty."

Then went the creature forth with Our Lady to Bethlehem and purchased her shelter every night with great reverence, and Our Lady was received with glad cheer. Also she begged for Our Lady fair white cloths and kerchiefs to swathe her Son in, when He was born; and when Jesus was born, she provided bedding for Our Lady to lie in with her Blessed Son. Later she begged meat for Our Lady and her Blessed Child, and she swathed Him with bitter tears of compassion, having mind of the sharp death He would suffer for love of sinful men, saying unto Him:—

"Lord, I shall fare fair with You. I will not bind You tight. I pray You be not displeased with me."

Chapter 7

The adoration of the Magi. She accompanies Our Lady into Egypt.

And afterwards on the twelfth day, when three Kings came with their gifts, and worshipped Our Lord in His Mother's lap, this creature, Our Lady's handmaiden, beholding all the process in contemplation, wept wondrous sore.

And when she saw that they would take their leave to go home again into their country, she could not bear that they should go from the presence of Our Lord, and for wonder that they should go, she cried wondrous sore. Soon after came an angel, and bade Our Lady and Joseph to go from

the country of Bethlehem into Egypt. Then went this creature forth with Our Lady, day by day finding her harborage with great reverence and many sweet thoughts and high meditations, and also high contemplation, sometimes continuing in weeping two hours and often longer in mind of Our Lord's Passion without ceasing, sometimes for her own sin, sometimes for the sin of the people, sometimes for the souls in purgatory, sometimes for them that were in poverty and disease, for she desired to comfort them all.

Sometimes she wept full plenteously and full boisterously for desire of the bliss of heaven, and because she was so long deferred therefrom. She greatly coveted to be delivered out of this wretched world. Our Lord Jesus Christ said to her mind that she should abide and languish in love, "for I have ordained thee to kneel before the Trinity, to pray for all the world, for many hundred thousand souls shall be saved by thy prayers. So ask, daughter, what thou wilt, and I will grant thee thine asking."

The creature said:—"Lord, I ask mercy and preservation from everlasting damnation for me and all the world. Chastise us here how Thou wilt and in Purgatory also, and of Thy great mercy, keep us from damnation."

Chapter 8

She asks Our Lord to be her executor and to give Master N. half of the reward of her good deeds.

Another time, as this creature lay in her prayer, the Mother of Mercy, appearing to her, said:—

"Daughter, blessed may thou be, thy seat is made in heaven, before my Son's knee, and whom thou wilt have with thee."

Then asked her Blessed Son:—"Daughter, whom wilt thou have fellow with thee?"

"My dearworthy Lord, I ask for my ghostly father, Master N...."

"Why asketh thou more for him than thine own father or thine husband?"

"Because I may never requite him for his goodness to me, and the gracious labor he has taken over me in hearing my confession."

---

4   A pot or tankard holding two quarts.

"I grant thee thy desire for him; yet shall thy father be saved, and thy husband also, and all thy children."

Then this creature said:—"Lord, after Thou has forgiven me my sin, I make Thee mine executor of all the good works that Thou workest in me. In praying, in thinking, in weeping, in going on pilgrimage, in fasting, or in speaking any good word, it is fully my will, that Thou give Master N… half of it to the increase of his merit, as if he did them himself. And the other half, Lord, spread on Thy friends and Thine enemies, and on my friends and mine enemies, for I will have but Thyself for my share."

"Daughter, I shall be a true executor to thee and fulfil all thy will; and for the great charity that thou hast to comfort thy fellow Christians, thou shalt have double reward in heaven."

Chapter 9

Our Lord promises to slay her husband's lust. She is injured by falling stones and timber in church.

Another time, as she prayed to God that she might live chaste by leave of her husband, Christ said to her:—

"Thou must fast on Friday, both from meat and drink, and thou shalt have thy desire ere Whitsunday, for I shall suddenly slay (the fleshly lust) in thy husband."

Then on the Wednesday in Easter week, after her husband would have had knowledge of her, as he was wont before, and when he came nigh to her, she said:—"Jesus Christ, help me," and he had no power to touch her at that time in that way, nor ever after with any fleshly knowledge.

It befell on a Friday before Whitsun Eve, as this creature was in a church of Saint Margaret at N… hearing her mass, she heard a great noise, and a dreadful. She was sore amazed through fear of the voice of the people, who said God should take vengeance on her. She knelt on her knees, holding down her head, with her book in her hand, praying Our Lord Jesus Christ for grace and mercy.

Suddenly there fell down from the highest part of the church roof, from under the foot of the spar, on her head and back, a stone which weighed three pounds, and a short end of a beam weighing

six pounds, so that she thought her back was broken asunder, and she feared she would be dead in a little while.

Soon afterwards, she cried, "Jesus, mercy!" and anon, her pain was gone.

A good man, called John of Wyreham, seeing this wonder and supposing she had been greatly injured, came and pulled her by the sleeve and said:—

"Dame, how fare ye?"

The creature, whole and sound, then thanked him for his cheer and his charity, much marvelling and greatly a-wonder that she felt no pain, having had so much a little before. For twelve weeks afterwards, she felt no pain. Then the spirit of God said to her soul:—

"Hold this for a great miracle, and if the people will not believe this, I will work many more."

A worshipful doctor of divinity, named Master Aleyn, a white friar, hearing of this wonderful work, inquired of this creature all the details of the process. He, desiring the work of God to be magnified, got the same stone that fell on her back and weighed it, and then got the beam-end that fell on her head, which one of the keepers of the church had laid on the fire to burn. This worshipful doctor said it was a great miracle, and Our Lord was highly to be magnified for preserving this creature against the malice of her enemy, and told it to many people and many people magnified God much in this creature. Many also would not believe it, and thought it more a token of wrath and vengeance, rather than believe it was any token of mercy and kindness.

Chapter 10

She wishes to visit certain places for spiritual reasons and starts with her husband for York.

Soon after, this creature was urged in her soul to go and visit certain places for ghostly health, inasmuch as she was cured, but might not without the consent of her husband. She asked her husband to grant her leave, and he, full trusting it was the will of God, soon consenting, they went to such places as she was inclined.

Then Our Lord Jesus Christ said to her:—"My servants desire greatly to see thee."

Then she was welcomed and made much of in divers places, wherefore she had great dread of vainglory, and was much afraid. Our Merciful Lord Jesus Christ, worshipped be His Name, said to her:—

"Dread not, daughter, I will take vainglory from thee, for they that worship thee, worship Me; they that despise thee, despise Me and I will chastise them therefor. I am in thee and thou in Me, and they that hear thee, hear the voice of God. Daughter, there is no so sinful man living on earth, that, if he will forsake his sin and live after thy counsel, such grace as thou promisest him, I will confirm for thy love."

Then her husband and she went forth to York and divers other places.

Chapter 11

On the way back from York, she and her husband argue as to their carnal relationship to each other.

It befell on a Friday on Midsummer Eve in right hot weather, as this creature was coming from York-ward carrying a bottle with beer in her hand, and her husband a cake in his bosom, that he asked his wife this question:—

"Margery, if there came a man with a sword, who would strike off my head, unless I should commune naturally with you as I have done before, tell me on your conscience—for ye say ye will not lie—whether ye would suffer my head to be smitten off, or whether ye would suffer me to meddle with you again, as I did at one time?"

"Alas, sir," said she, "why raise this matter, when we have been chaste these eight weeks?"

"For I will know the truth of your heart."

And then she said with great sorrow:— "Forsooth, I would rather see you being slain, than that we should turn again to our uncleanness."

And he replied:—"Ye are no good wife."

She then asked her husband what was the cause that he had not meddled with her for eight weeks, since she lay with him every night in his bed. He said he was made so afraid when he would have touched her, that he dare do no more.

"Now, good sir, amend your ways, and ask God's mercy, for I told you nearly three years ago that ye[5] should be slain suddenly, and now is this the third year, and so I hope I shall have my desire. Good sir, I pray you grant me what I ask, and I will pray for you that ye shall be saved through the mercy of Our Lord Jesus Christ, and ye shall have more reward in heaven than if ye wore a hair-cloth or a habergeon.[6] I pray you, suffer me to make a vow of chastity at what bishop's hand God wills."

"Nay," he said, "that I will not grant you, for now may I use you without deadly sin, and then might I not do so."

Then she said to him:—"If it be the will of the Holy Ghost to fulfil what I have said, I pray God that ye may consent thereto; and if it be not the will of the Holy Ghost, I pray God ye never consent to it."

Then they went forth towards Bridlington in right hot weather, the creature having great sorrow and dread for her chastity. As they came by a cross, her husband sat down under the cross, calling his wife to him and saying these words unto her:—"Margery, grant me my desire, and I shall grant you your desire. My first desire is that we shall lie together in bed as we have done before; the second, that ye shall pay my debts, ere ye go to Jerusalem; and the third, that ye shall eat and drink with me on the Friday as ye were wont to do."

"Nay, sir," said she, "to break the Friday, I will never grant you whilst I live."

"Well," said he, "then I shall meddle with you again."

She prayed him that he would give her leave to say her prayers, and he granted it kindly. Then she knelt down beside a cross in the field and prayed in this manner, with a great abundance of tears:—

"Lord God, Thou knowest all things. Thou knowest what sorrow I have had to be chaste in my body to Thee all these three years, and now might I have my will, and dare not for love of Thee. For if I should break that manner of fasting which Thou commandest me to keep on the Friday, without meat or drink, I should now have my desire. But, Blessed Lord, Thou knowest that I will not contravene Thy will, and much now is my sorrow unless

---

5   *I.e.*, "your lust." See chapter 9, line 5.

6   A habergeon, or coat of mail, was worn as a penance, in addition to its primary purpose of bodily protection.

I find comfort in Thee. Now, Blessed Jesus, make Thy will known to me unworthy, that I may follow it thereafter and fulfil it with all my might."

Then Our Lord Jesus Christ with great sweetness, spoke to her, commanding her to go again to her husband, and pray him to grant her what she desired, "And he shall have what he desireth. For, my dearworthy daughter, this was the cause that I bade thee fast, so that thou shouldst the sooner obtain and get thy desire, and now it is granted to thee. I will no longer that thou fast. Therefore I bid thee in the Name of Jesus, eat and drink as thy husband doth."

Then this creature thanked Our Lord Jesus Christ for His grace and goodness, and rose up and went to her husband, saying to him:—

"Sir, if it please you, ye shall grant me my desire, and ye shall have your desire. Grant me that ye will not come into my bed, and I grant you to requite your debts ere I go to Jerusalem. Make my body free to God so that ye never make challenge to me, by asking any debt of matrimony. After this day, whilst ye live, I will eat and drink on the Friday at your bidding."

Then said her husband:—"As free may your body be to God, as it hath been to me."

This creature thanked God, greatly rejoicing that she had her desire, praying her husband that they should say three Paternosters in worship of the Trinity for the great grace that He had granted them. And so they did, kneeling under a cross, and afterwards they ate and drank together in great gladness of spirit. This was on a Friday on Midsummer's Eve. Then went they forth Bridlington-ward and also to many other countries and spoke with God's servants, both anchorites and recluses, and many others of Our Lord's lovers, with many worthy clerks, doctors of divinity and bachelors also, in divers places. And this creature, to many of them, shewed her feelings and her contemplations, as she was commanded to do, to find out if any deceit were in her feelings.

Chapter 16

She and her husband go to Lambeth to visit the Archbishop of Canterbury, whom she reproves for the bad behavior of his clergy and household.

Then went this creature forth to London with her husband unto Lambeth, where the archbishop lay at that time; and as they came into the hall in the afternoon, there were many of the archbishop's clerks and other reckless men, both squires and yeomen, who swore many great oaths and spoke many reckless words, and this creature boldly reprehended them, and said they would be damned unless they left off their swearing and other sins that they used.

And with that, there came forth another woman of the same town in a furred cloak, who forswore this creature, banned her, and spoke full cursedly to her in this manner:—

"I would thou wert in Smithfield, and I would bring a faggot to burn thee with. It is a pity thou art alive."

This creature stood still and answered not, and her husband suffered it with great pain, and was full sorry to hear his wife so rebuked.

Then the archbishop sent for this creature into his garden. When she came into his presence, she saluted him as best she could, praying him of his gracious lordship to grant her authority to choose her confessor and to be houseled[7] every Sunday, if God would dispose her thereto, under his letter and his seal through all his province. And he granted her full benignly all her desire without any silver or gold, nor would he let his clerks take anything for the writing or the sealing of the letter.

When this creature found this grace in his sight, she was well comforted and strengthened in her soul, and so she showed this worshipful lord her manner of life, and such grace as God wrought in her mind and in her soul, to find out what he would say thereto, and whether he found any default either in her contemplation or in her weeping.

And she told him also the cause of her weeping, and the manner of dalliance that Our Lord

---

7   To go to Holy Communion.

spoke to her soul; and he found no default in her, but praised her manner of living, and was right glad that Our Merciful Lord Christ Jesus showed such grace in our days, blessed may He be.

Then this creature boldly spoke to him for the correction of his household, saying with reverence:—

"My lord, Our Lord of all, Almighty God has not given you your benefice and great worldly wealth to keep His traitors and them that slay Him every day by great oaths swearing. Ye shall answer for them, unless ye correct them, or else put them out of your service."

Full benignly and meekly he suffered her to speak her intent, and gave her a fair answer, she supposing it would then be better. And so their dalliance continued till stars appeared in the firmament. Then she took her leave, and her husband also.

Afterwards they came again to London, and many worthy men desired to hear her dalliances and communication, for her communication was so much in the love of God that her hearers were often stirred thereby to weep right sadly.

And so she had there right great cheer, and her husband because of her, as long as they remained in the city.

Afterwards they came again to Lynne, and then went this creature to the anchorite at the preaching friars in Lynne and told him what cheer she had, and how she had sped whilst she was in the country. And he was right glad of her coming home, and held it was a great miracle, her coming and going to and fro.

And he said to her:—"I have heard much evil language of you since ye went out, and I have been sore counseled to leave you and no more to associate with you, and there are promised me great friendships, on condition that I leave you. And I answered for you thus:—

"'If ye were in the same plight as ye were when we parted asunder, I durst well say that ye were a good woman, a lover of God, and highly inspired by the Holy Ghost. And I will not forsake her for any lady in this realm, if speaking with the lady means leaving her. Rather would I leave the lady and speak with her, if I might not do both, than do the contrary.'"

Chapter 17

She visits Norwich and has an interview with the vicar, who believes in her, and later on helps her when under examination.

On a day, long before this time, while this creature was bearing children and she was newly delivered of a child, Our Lord Jesus Christ said to her that she should bear no more children, and therefore He bade her to go to Norwich.

And she said:—"Ah! dear Lord, how shall I go? I am both faint and feeble."

"Dread thee not. I shall make thee strong enough. I bid thee go to the vicar of Saint Stephen's and say that I greet him well, and that he is a highly chosen soul of Mine, and tell him he pleaseth Me much with his preaching and shew him thy secrets, and My counsels such as I shew thee."

Then she took her way Norwich-ward, and came into his church on a Thursday a little before noon. And the vicar went up and down with another priest, who was his ghostly father, who lived when this book was made. And this creature was clad in black clothing at that time.

She saluted the vicar, praying him that she might speak with him an hour or else two hours at afternoon, when he had eaten, in the love of God.

He, lifting up his hands and blessing her, said:—"Benedicite. How could a woman occupy an hour or two hours in the love of Our Lord? I shall never eat meat till I learn what ye can say of Our Lord God in the time of an hour."

Then he sat himself down in the church. She, sitting a little aside, showed him all the words that God had revealed to her in her soul. Afterwards she shewed him all her manner of life from her childhood, as nigh as it would come to her mind; how unkind she had been against Our Lord Jesus Christ, how proud and vain she had been in her behavior, how obstinate against the laws of God, and how envious against her fellow Christians. Later, when it pleased Our Lord Christ Jesus, how she was chastised with many tribulations and horrible temptations and afterwards how she was fed and comforted with holy meditations and specially in the memory of Our Lord's Passion.

And, while she conversed on the Passion of Our Lord Jesus Christ, she heard so hideous a melody that she could not bear it. Then this creature fell down, as if she had lost her bodily strength, and lay still a great while, desiring to put it away, and she might not. Then she knew well, by her faith, that there was great joy in heaven where the least point of bliss, without any comparison, passeth all the joy that ever might be thought or felt in this life.

She was greatly strengthened in her faith and more bold to tell the vicar her feelings, which she had by revelation both of the quick and the dead, and of his own self.

She told him how sometimes the Father of Heaven spoke to her soul as plainly and as verily as one friend speaks to another by bodily speech. Sometimes in the second person in Trinity, sometimes all three persons in Trinity, and one substance in godhead spoke to her soul, and informed her in her faith and in His love, how she should love Him, worship Him and dread Him, so excellently that she never heard of any book, either Hylton's book[8] or Bride's[9] book, or Stimulus Amoris[10], or Incendium Amoris[11], or any other that she ever heard read, that spoke so highly of the love of God. But she felt that, as highly working in her soul, as if she could have shewn what she felt.

Sometimes Our Lady spoke to her mind; sometimes St. Peter, sometimes St. Paul, sometimes St. Katherine, or whatever saint in heaven she had devotion to, appeared in her soul and taught her how she should love Our Lord, and how she should please Him. Her dalliance was so sweet, so holy and so devout, that this creature might not oftentimes bear it, but fell down and wrestled with her body, and made wondrous faces and gestures with boisterous sobbings, and great plenty of tears, sometimes saying "Jesus, Mercy," and sometimes, "I die."

And therefore many people slandered her, not believing that it was the work of God, but that some evil spirit vexed her in her body or else that she had some bodily sickness.

Notwithstanding the rumors and the grutching[12] of the people against her, this holy man, the vicar of Saint Stephen's Church of Norwich, whom God hath exalted, and through marvelous works shewn and proved for holy, ever held with her and supported her against her enemies, unto his power, after the time that she, by the bidding of God, had shewn him her manner of governance and living, for he trustfully believed that she was well learned in the law of God, and endued with the grace of the Holy Ghost, to Whom it belongeth to inspire where He will. And though His voice be heard, it is not known in the world from whence it cometh or whither it goeth.

This holy vicar, after this time, was confessor to this creature always when she came to Norwich, and houseled her with his own hands.

And when she was at one time admonished to appear before certain officers of the bishop, to answer to certain articles which would be put against her by the stirring of envious people, the good vicar, preferring the love of God before any shame of the world, went with her to hear her examination, and delivered her from the malice of her enemies. And then it was revealed to this creature that the good vicar would live seven years after, and then should pass hence with great grace, and he did as she foretold.

Chapter 18

At Norwich she visits a white friar, William Sowthfeld, and an anchoress, Dame Jelyan.

This creature was charged and commanded in her soul that she should go to a white friar, in the same city of Norwich, called William Sowthfeld, a good man and a holy liver, to shew him the grace that God wrought in her, as she had done to the good vicar before. She did as she was commanded and came to the friar on a forenoon, and was with him in a chapel a long time, and shewed him her meditations, and what God had wrought

---

8   Walter Hylton, *Ladder of Perfection*, a fifteenth-century devotional text.
9   *Revelations* by Saint Bridget of Sweden (1303–73).
10   *The Prick of Love*, a popular thirteenth-century devotional text.
11   *The Fire of Love*, a devotional text by Richard Rolle, a fourteenth-century mystic and hermit.
12   Grumbling.

in her soul, to find out if she were deceived by any illusion or not.

This good man, the white friar, ever whilst she told him her feelings, holding up his hands, said:—"Jesu Mercy and gramercy."

"Sister," he said, "dread not for your manner of living, for it is the Holy Ghost working plenteously His grace in your soul. Thank Him highly for His goodness, for we all be bound to thank Him for you, Who now in our days will inspire His grace in you, to the help and comfort of us all, who are supported by your prayers and by such others as ye be. And we are preserved from many mischiefs and diseases which we should suffer, and worthily, for our trespass. Never were such good creatures amongst us. Blessed be Almighty God for His goodness. And therefore, sister, I counsel you that ye dispose yourself to receive the gifts of God as lowly and meekly as ye can, and put no obstacle or objection against the goodness of the Holy Ghost, for He may give His gifts where He will, and of unworthy He maketh worthy, of sinful He maketh rightful. His mercy is ever ready unto us, unless the fault be in ourselves, for He dwelleth not in a body subject to sin. He flieth all false feigning and falsehood: He asketh of us a lowly, a meek and a contrite heart, with a good will. Our Lord sayeth Himself:—'My Spirit shall rest upon a meek man, a contrite man, and one dreading My words.'

"Sister, I trust to Our Lord that ye have these conditions either in your will or your affection, or else in both, and I believe not that Our Lord suffereth them to be deceived endlessly, that set all their trust in Him, and seek and desire nothing but Him only, as I hope ye do. And therefore believe fully that Our Lord loveth you and worketh His grace in you. I pray God to increase it and continue it to His everlasting worship, for His mercy."

The aforesaid creature was much comforted both in body and in soul by this good man's words, and greatly strengthened in her faith.

Then she was bidden by Our Lord to go to an anchoress in the same city, named Dame Jelyan, and so she did, and showed her the grace that God put into her soul, of compunction, contrition, sweetness and devotion, compassion with holy meditation and high contemplation, and full many holy speeches and dalliance that Our Lord spake to her soul; and many wonderful revelations, which she shewed to the anchoress to find out if there were any deceit in them, for the anchoress was expert in such things, and good counsel could give.

The anchoress, hearing the marvelous goodness of Our Lord, highly thanked God with all her heart for His visitation, counseling this creature to be obedient to the will of Our Lord God and to fulfil with all her might whatever He put into her soul, if it were not against the worship of God, and profit of her fellow Christians, for if it were, then it were not the moving of a good spirit, but rather of an evil spirit. "The Holy Ghost moveth ne'er a thing against charity, for if He did, He would be contrary to His own self for He is all charity. Also He moveth a soul to all chasteness, for chaste livers are called the temple of the Holy Ghost, and the Holy Ghost maketh a soul stable and steadfast in the right faith, and the right belief.

"And a double man in soul is ever unstable and unsteadfast in all his ways. He that is ever doubting is like the flood of the sea which is moved and borne about with the wind, and that man is not likely to receive the gifts of God.

"Any creature that hath these tokens may steadfastly believe that the Holy Ghost dwelleth in his soul. And much more when God visiteth a creature with tears of contrition, devotion, and compassion, he may and ought to believe that the Holy Ghost is in his soul. Saint Paul saith that the Holy Ghost asketh for us with mourning and weeping unspeakable, that is to say, He maketh us to ask and pray with mourning and weeping so plenteously that the tears may not be numbered. No evil spirit may give these tokens, for Saint Jerome saith that tears torment more the devil than do the pains of Hell. God and the devil are ever at odds and they shall never dwell together in one place, and the devil hath no power in a man's soul.

"Holy Writ saith that the soul of a rightful man is the seat of God, and so I trust, sister, that ye be. I pray God grant you perseverance. Set all your trust in God and fear not the language of the world, for the more despite, shame and reproof that ye have in the world, the more is your merit in the sight of God. Patience is necessary to you, for in that shall ye keep your soul."

Much was the holy dalliance that the anchoress and this creature had by communing in the love of Our Lord Jesus Christ the many days that they were together.

This creature shewed her manner of living to many a worthy clerk, to worshipful doctors of divinity, both religious men and others of secular habit, and they said that God wrought great grace with her, and bade her she should not be afraid—there was no deceit in her manner of living. They counseled her to be persevering, for their greatest dread was that she should turn and not keep her perfection. She had so many enemies and so much slander, that they thought she might not bear it without great grace and a mighty faith.

Others who had no knowledge of her manner of governance, save only by outward sight or else by jangling of other persons perverting the judgment of truth, spoke full evil of her and caused her much enmity and much distress, more than she would otherwise have had, had their evil language never been spoken. Nevertheless the anchorite of the preaching friars in Lynne, who was the principal ghostly father of this creature, as is written before, took it on charge of his soul that her feelings were good and sure, and that there was no deceit in them, and he by the spirit of prophecy, told her that, when she should go Jerusalemward, she would have much tribulation with her maiden, and how Our Lord would try her sharply and prove her full straitly.

Then said she to him:—"Ah! Good sir, what shall I do when I am far from home, and in strange countries, and my maiden is against me? Then is my bodily comfort gone, and ghostly comfort from any confessor such as ye be, I wot not where to get."

"Daughter, dread ye nothing, for Our Lord Himself shall comfort you His own self, Whose comfort surpasseth all other, and when all your friends have forsaken you, Our Lord will make a broken-backed man lead you forth whither ye will go."

And so it befell as the anchorite had prophesied in every point, and as, I trust, shall be written more fully afterwards.

Then this creature, in a manner complaining, said to the anchorite:—

"Good sir, what shall I do? He that is my confessor in your absence is right sharp with me; he

will not believe my feelings; he setteth naught by them; he holdeth them but trifles and japes, and that is great pain to me, for I love him well and would fain follow his counsel."

The anchorite answering her, said:—"It is no wonder, daughter, if he cannot believe in your feelings so soon. He knoweth well that ye have been a sinful woman, and therefore he weeneth that God would not be homely with you in so short a time. After your conversion, I would not for all this world be so sharp to you as he is. God, for your merit, hath ordained him to be your scourge, and he fareth with you as a smith with a file maketh the iron bright and clean to the sight, which before appeared rusty, dirty, and evil-colored. The more sharp he is to you the more clearly shineth your soul in the sight of God, and God hath ordained me to be your nurse and your comfort. Be ye lowly and meek and thank God for both one and the other."

On a time, before this creature went to her prayers to find out what answer she should give to the widow, she was commanded in her spirit to bid the widow leave her confessor that was, at that time if she would please God, and go the anchorite at the Preaching Friars in Lynne and show him her life.

When this creature gave this message, the widow would not believe her words, nor her ghostly father either, unless God should give her the same grace that He gave this creature, and she charged this creature that she should no more come to her place.

And because this creature told her that she had to feel love and affection for her ghostly father, therefore the widow said it had been good for this creature that her love and her affection were set as hers was.

Then Our Lord bade this creature write a letter and send it her. A master of divinity wrote a letter at her request and sent it to the widow with these clauses that follow:

One clause was that the widow should never have the grace that this creature had. Another was that, though this creature never came into her house, it would please God right well.

Our Lord soon after said to this creature: "It were better for her than all this world, if her love were set as thine is, and I bid thee go to her ghostly father and tell him that, as he will not believe thy words, they shall be parted asunder sooner than he thinketh, and they that be not of her counsel shall know it ere he does, whether he will or not. Lo! Daughter, here mayest thou see how hard it is to part a man from his own will."

And all this procedure was fulfilled in truth, as the creature had said, before twelve years after. Then this creature suffered much tribulation and great grief, because she said these words, as Our Lord bade her. And ever she increased in the love of God and was more bold than she was before.

Chapter 19

The lady whose husband is in purgatory.

Before this creature went to Jerusalem, Our Lord sent her to a worshipful lady, so that she should speak with her in counsel and do His errand to her. The lady would not speak with her unless her ghostly father were present, and she said she was well pleased. And then, when the lady's ghostly father had come, they went into a chapel, all three together, and then this creature said with great reverence and many tears:—

"Madam, Our Lord Jesus Christ bade me tell you that your husband is in purgatory, and that ye shall be saved, but that it shall be long ere ye come to heaven."

And then the lady was displeased, and said her husband was a good man—she believed not that he was in purgatory. Her ghostly father held with this creature, and said it might right well be as she said, and confirmed her words with many holy tales.

And then this lady sent her daughter, with many others of her household with her, to the anchorite who was principal confessor to this creature, so that he should forsake her or else he would lose her friendship. The anchorite said to the messengers that he would not forsake this creature for any man on earth, because to such creatures as would inquire of him her manner of governance and what he thought of her, he said she was God's own servant, and also he said that she was the tabernacle of God.

And the anchorite said unto her own person to strengthen her in her faith:—

"Though God take from you all tears and dalliance, believe nevertheless that God loveth you

and that ye shall be right sure of Heaven for what ye have had beforetime, for tears with love are the greatest gift which God may give on earth, and all men that love God ought to thank Him for you."

Also, there was a widow who prayed this creature to pray for her husband, and find out if he had any need of help. And as this creature prayed for him, she was answered that his soul would be thirty years in purgatory, unless he had better friends on earth. Thus she told the widow and said:—

"If ye will give alms, three pounds or four, in masses and alms-giving to poor folk, ye shall highly please God and give the soul great ease."

The widow took little heed of her words and let it pass.

Then this creature went to the anchorite and told him how she had felt, and he said the feeling was of God, and the deed in itself was good, even though the soul had no need thereof, and counseled that it should be fulfilled. Then this creature told this matter to her ghostly father, so that he should speak to the widow, and so for a long time this creature heard no more of this matter.

Afterwards Our Lord Jesus Christ said to this creature:—"That thing I bade should be done for the soul, it is not done. Ask now thy ghostly father."

And so she did, and he said it was not done.

She said again:—"My Lord Jesus Christ told me so right now."

Chapter 20

The Host flutters at the Consecration.

On a day as this creature was hearing her mass, a young man and a good priest was holding up the Sacrament in his hands, over his head, and the Sacrament shook and flickered to and fro, as a dove flickereth with her wings. And when he held up the chalice with the Precious Sacrament, the chalice moved to and fro, as if it would have fallen out of his hands. When the Consecration was done, this creature had great marvel of the stirring and moving of the Blessed Sacrament, desiring to see more consecrations, and watching if it would do so again.

Then said Our Lord Jesus Christ to the creature:—"Thou shalt no more see It in this manner; therefore thank God that thou hast seen. My daughter, Bride, saw Me never in this wise."

Then said this creature, in her thought:—

"Lord, what betokeneth this?"

"It betokeneth vengeance."

"Ah! Good Lord, what vengeance?"

Then said Our Lord again to her:—"There shall be an earthquake; tell it to whom thou wilt, in the name of Jesus. For I tell thee forsooth, right as I spoke to Saint Bride, right so I speak to thee, daughter, and I tell thee truly that it is true, every word that is written in Bride's book, and by thee it shall be known for very truth. And thou shalt fare well, daughter, in spite of all thine enemies; the more envy they have of thee for My grace, the better shall I love thee. I were not rightful God unless [I loved] thee, for I know thee better than thou dost thyself, [whatsoever men][13] say of thee. Thou sayest I have great patience in the sin of the people, and thou sayest truth, but if thou saw the sin of the people as I do, then wouldst thou have much more marvel in My patience and much more sorrow in the sin of the people than thou hast."

Then the creature said:—"Alas! dearworthy Lord, what shall I do for the people?"

Our Lord answered:—"It is enough to thee to do as thou dost."

Then she prayed:—"Merciful Lord Christ Jesus, in Thee is all mercy and grace and goodness. Have mercy, pity and compassion on them. Show Thy mercy and Thy goodness to them, help them, send them true contrition, and never let them die in their sin."

Our Merciful Lord said:—"I may no more, daughter, of My rightfulness do for them than I do. I send them preaching and teaching, pestilence and battles, hunger and famine, loss of their goods with great sickness and many other tribulations, and they will not believe My words, nor will they know My visitation. And therefore I shall say to them thus:—

"'I made My servants pray for you and ye despised their works and their living.'"

Chapter 21

Our Lord speaks on the merits of maidenhood, marriage and widowhood.

At the time that this creature had revelations, Our Lord said to her:—"Daughter, thou art with child."

She said to Him:—"Ah! Lord, what shall I do for the keeping of my child?"

Our Lord said:—"Dread thee not. I shall arrange for a keeper."

"Lord, I am not worthy to hear Thee speak, and thus to commune with my husband. Nevertheless, it is to me great pain and great disease."

"Therefore it is no sin to thee, daughter, for it is rather to thee reward and merit, and thou shalt have never the less grace, for I will that thou bring Me forth more fruit."

Then said the creature:—"Lord Jesus, this manner of living belongeth to Thy holy maidens."

"Yea, daughter, trow thou right well that I love wives also, and specially those wives who would live chaste if they might have their will, and do their business to please Me as thou dost; for, though the state of maidenhood be more perfect and more holy than the state of widowhood, and the state of widowhood more perfect than the state of wedlock, yet, daughter, I love thee as well as any maiden in the world. No man may hinder Me in loving whom I will, and as much as I will, for love, daughter, quencheth all sin. And therefore ask of Me the gifts of love. There is no gift so holy as is the gift of love, nor anything to be desired so much as love, for love may purchase what it can desire. And therefore, daughter, thou mayest no better please God than continually to think on His love."

Then this creature asked Our Lord how she should best love Him, and Our Lord said:—

"Have mind of thy wickedness and think of My goodness."

She said again:—"I am the most unworthy creature that ever Thou shewedest grace unto on earth."

"Ah! daughter," said Our Lord, "fear thee nothing. I take no heed what a man hath been, but I take

---

13   Words missing owing to damage to the MS.

heed what he will be. Daughter, thou hast despised thyself; therefore thou shalt never be despised of God. Have mind, daughter, what Mary Magdalene was, Mary of Egypt, Saint Paul, and many other saints that are now in heaven, for of unworthy, I make worthy, and of sinful, I make rightful. And so have I made thee worthy. To Me, once loved, and ever more loved by Me. There is no saint in heaven that thou wilt speak with, but he shall come to thee. Whom God loveth, they love. When thou pleasest God, thou pleasest His Mother, and all the saints in heaven. Daughter, I take witness of My Mother, of all the angels in heaven, and of all the saints in heaven, that I love thee with all My heart, and I may not forget thy love."

Our Lord said then to His Blissful Mother:—"Blessed Mother, tell ye My daughter of the greatness of the love I have unto her."

Then this creature lay still, all in weeping and sobbing as if her heart would have burst for the sweetness of speech that Our Lord spoke unto her soul.

Immediately afterwards, the Queen of Mercy, God's Mother, dallied to the soul of this creature, saying:—

"My dearworthy daughter, I bring thee sure tidings, as witness my sweet Son Jesus, with all the angels and all the saints in heaven who love thee full highly. Daughter, I am thy Mother, thy Lady and thy Mistress, to teach thee in all wise how thou shalt please God best."

She taught this creature and informed her so wonderfully, that she was abashed to say it or tell it to any—the matters were so high and so holy—save only to the anchorite who was her principal confessor, for he had most knowledge of such things. And he charged this creature, by virtue of obedience, to tell him whatever she felt, and so she did.

Chapter 22

Our Lord praises her and promises her eternal life.

As this creature lay in contemplation for weeping, in her spirit she said to Our Lord Jesus Christ:—

"Ah! Lord, maidens dance now merrily in Heaven. Shall not I do so? For, because I am no maiden, lack of maidenhood is to me now great

sorrow; me-thinketh I would I had been slain when I was taken from the font-stone, so that I should never have displeased Thee, and then shouldst Thou, blessed Lord, have had my maidenhood without end. Ah! dear God, I have not loved thee all the days of my life and that sore rueth me; I have run away from Thee, and Thou hast run after me; I would fall into despair, and Thou wouldst not suffer me."

"Ah! Daughter, how often have I told thee that thy sins are forgiven thee, and that we are united [in love] together without end. Thou art to Me a singular love, daughter, and therefore I promise thee thou shalt have a singular grace in Heaven, daughter, and I promise thee that I shall come to thine end at thy dying with My Blessed Mother, and My holy angels and twelve apostles, Saint Katherine, Saint Margaret, Saint Mary Magdalene and many other saints that are in heaven, who give great worship to Me for the grace that I give to thee, thy God, thy Lord Jesus. Thou needest dread no grievous pains in thy dying, for thou shalt have thy desire, that is to have more mind of My Passion than of thine own pain. Thou shalt not dread the devil of hell, for he hath no power in thee. He dreadeth thee more than thou dost him. He is wroth with thee because thou tormentest him more with thy weeping than doth all the fire in hell; thou winnest many souls from him with thy weeping. And I have promised thee that thou shouldst have no other Purgatory than the slander and speech of the world, for I have chastised thee Myself as I would, by many great dreads and torments that thou hast had with evil spirits, both asleep and awake for many years. And therefore I shall preserve thee at thine end through My mercy, so that they shall have no power over thee either in body or in soul. It is a great grace and miracle that thou hast thy bodily wits, for the vexation that thou hast had with them aforetime.

"I have also, daughter, chastised thee with the dread of My Godhead, and many times have I terrified thee with great tempests of winds, so that thou thoughtst vengeance would have fallen on thee for sin. I have proved thee by many tribulations, many great griefs, and many grievous sicknesses, insomuch that thou hast been anointed for death, and all, through my Grace, hast thou escaped. Therefore dread thee naught, daughter, for with Mine own hands which were nailed to the Cross, I will take thy soul from thy body with great mirth and melody, with sweet smells and good odors, and offer it to My Father in Heaven, where thou shalt see Him face to face, living with Him without end.

"Daughter, thou shalt be right welcome to My Father, and My Mother, and to all My saints in heaven, for thou hast given them drink full many times with the tears of thine eyes. All My holy saints shall rejoice at thy coming home. Thou shall be full filled with all manner of love that thou covetest. Then shalt thou bless the time that thou wert wrought, and the Body that thee hath dearly bought. He shall have joy in thee and thou in Him without end.

"Daughter, I promise thee the same grace that I promised Saint Katherine, Saint Margaret, Saint Barbara, and Saint Paul, insomuch that what creature on earth unto the Day of Doom asketh thee any boon and believeth that God loveth thee, he shall have his boon or else a better thing. Therefore they that believe that God loveth thee, they shall be blessed without end. The souls in purgatory shall rejoice in thy coming home, for they know well that God loveth thee specially. And men on earth shall rejoice in God for thee, for He shall work much grace for thee and make all the world to know that God loveth thee. Thou hast been despised for My love and therefore thou shalt be worshipped for My love.

"Daughter, when thou art in heaven, thou shalt be able to ask what thou wilt, and I shall grant thee all thy desire. I have told thee before-time that thou art a singular lover, and therefore thou shalt have a singular love in heaven, a singular reward, and a singular worship. And, forasmuch as thou art a maiden in thy soul, I shall take thee by the one hand in heaven, and My Mother by the other hand, and so shalt thou dance in heaven with other holy maidens and virgins, for I may call thee dearly bought, and Mine own dearworthy darling. I shall say to thee, Mine own blessed spouse:—'Welcome to Me with all manner of joy and gladness, here to dwell with Me and never to depart from Me without end, but ever to dwell with Me in joy and bliss, which no eye may see, nor ear hear, nor tongue tell, nor heart think, that I have ordained for thee and all My servants who desire to love and please Me as thou dost.'"

Chapter 23

The vicar who thought of leaving his benefice. Margery's revelations as to the fate of departed souls, and of sick people.

There came once a vicar to this creature, praying her to pray for him, and to find out whether he would more please God by leaving his cure and his benefice, or by keeping it still, for he thought he profited not among his parishioners. The creature being at her prayers, having mind of this matter, Christ said unto her spirit:—

"Bid the vicar keep still his cure and his benefice, and be diligent in preaching and teaching them in person, and sometimes to procure others to teach them My laws and My commandments, so that there be no default on his part, and if they do never the better, his merit shall be never the less."

So she gave her message as she was commanded, and the vicar still kept his cure.

As this creature was in a church of Saint Margaret in the choir, where a corpse was present, and he that was husband of the same corpse, whilst she lived, was there in good health to offer her mass-penny, as was the custom of the place, Our Lord said to the aforesaid creature:—

"Lo! Daughter, the soul of this corpse is in purgatory, and he that was her husband is now in good health, and yet he shall be dead in a short time."

And so it befell, as she felt by revelation.

Also, as this creature lay in the choir at her prayers, a priest came to her and prayed her to pray for a woman who lay at point of death. As this creature began to pray for her, Our Lord said to her:—

"Daughter, there is great need to pray for her, for she hath been a wicked woman, and she shall die."

And she answered:—"Lord, as thou lovest me, save her soul from damnation."

Then she wept with plenteous tears for that soul, and Our Lord granted her mercy for the soul, commanding her to pray for her.

This creature's ghostly father came to her, moving her to pray for a woman who lay at point of death, to man's sight, and anon Our Lord said she should live and fare well, and so she did.

A good man, who was a great friend of this creature and helpful to the poor people, was very sick for many weeks together. And much mourning was made for him, for men thought he would never have lived, his pain was so amazing in all his joints and all his body. Our Lord Jesus said to her spirit:—

"Daughter, be not afraid for this man, he shall live and fare right well."

And so he lived many years after, in good health and prosperity.

Another good man, who was a reader, lay sick also, and when this creature prayed for him, it was answered to her mind that he should linger a while, and later would be dead of the same sickness, and so he was a short time after.

Also a worshipful woman, and as men believed, a holy woman, who was a special friend of this creature, was right sick, and many people thought she should have been dead. Then, this creature praying for her, Our Lord said:—

"She shalt not die these ten years, for ye shall, after this, make full merry together, and have full good communication as ye have had before."

And so it was, in truth. This holy woman lived many years after.

Many more such revelations this creature had in feeling; to write them all would be hindrance, peradventure, of more profit.

These are written to show the homeliness and goodliness of Our Lord Jesus Christ, and for no commendation of this creature.

These feelings and many more than are written, both of living and of dying, of some to be saved, of some to be damned, were to this creature great pain and punishment. She would rather have suffered any bodily penance than these feelings, if she might have put them away, for the dread she had of illusions and deceits of her ghostly enemies. She had sometimes such great trouble with such feelings when they fell not true to her understanding, that her confessor feared that she would have fallen into despair therewith. And then, after her trouble and her great fears, it would be shewn unto her soul how the feelings should be understood.

Chapter 24

The priest who wrote the book proves Margery's revelations to be true. The man who tried to borrow money. The other who tried to sell a breviary.

The priest who wrote this book, to prove this creature's feelings many and divers times asked her questions, and information of things that were to come, unknown and uncertain at that time to any creature as to what would be the outcome, praying her, though she was loath and unwilling to do such things, to pray to God therefore, and ascertain, when Our Lord would visit her with devotion, what would be the outcome, and truly, without any feigning, tell him how she felt, or else he would not gladly write the book.

And so this creature, compelled somewhat for fear that he would not otherwise have followed her intent to write this book, did as he prayed her, and told him her feelings as to what would befall in such matters as he asked her, if her feelings were truth. And thus he proved them for very truth. And yet he would not always give credence to her words, and that hindered him in the manner that followeth.

It befell on a time, that there came a young man to this priest, which young man the priest had never seen before, complaining to the priest of poverty and distress into which he had fallen by misfortune, explaining the cause of the misfortune, saying also that he had taken holy orders to be a priest. For a little hastiness, defending himself, as he had no choice unless he was to be dead through the pursuit of his enemies, he smote a man, or perhaps two, where-through, as he said, they were dead or likely to die.

And so he had fallen into irregularities and might not execute his orders without dispensation of the Court of Rome, and for this reason he fled from his friends, and dared not go into his country for dread of being taken for their death.

The aforesaid priest, giving credence to the young man's words inasmuch as he was an amiable person, fair featured, well favored in cheer and countenance, sober in his language and dalliance, priestly in his gesture and vesture, having compassion on his distress, purposing to get him friends unto his relief and comfort, went to a worshipful burgess in Lynne, a mayor's equal, and a merciful man, who lay in great sickness, and long had done so, complaining to him and his wife, a full good woman, of the misfortune of this young man, trusting to have fair alms as he oftentimes had for others that he asked for.

It happened that the creature, of whom this book is written, was present there and heard how the priest pleaded for the young man, and how the priest praised him. And she was sore moved in her spirit against that young man, and said they had many poor neighbors who, they knew well enough, had great need of being helped and relieved, and it should rather be alms to help them that they knew well for well disposed folk, and their own neighbors, than strangers that they knew not, for many speak and seem full fair outwardly to the sight of the people. God knoweth what they are in their souls!

The good man and his wife thought she spoke right well, and therefore they would grant him no alms.

At that time the priest was evil-pleased with this creature, and when he met her alone, he repeated how she had hindered him so that he could get no alms for the young man, who was a well-disposed man, as he thought, and much commended his behavior.

The creature said:—"Sir, God knoweth what his behavior is, for, as far as I know, I have never seen him and yet I have understanding what his behavior should be; and therefore, Sir, if ye will act by my counsel, and after what I feel, let him choose and help himself as well as he can, and meddle ye not with him, for he will deceive you at the last."

The young man resorted always to the priest, flattering him and saying that he had good friends in other places, who would help him if they knew where he was, and that in a short time; and also they would thank those persons who had supported him in his distress. The priest, trusting it would be as this young man told him, lent him silver, with good will, to help him. The young man prayed the priest to hold him excused if he saw him not for two days or three, for he would go a little way, and come again in a short time and bring him back his silver right well and truly. The priest, having confidence in his promise, was well content, granting him good love and leave unto

the day on which he had promised to come again.

When he was gone, the aforesaid creature, understanding by feeling in her soul that Our Lord would show that he was an untrue man, and would come back no more, she, to prove whether her feeling was true or false, asked the priest where the young man was, that he had praised so much.

The priest said he had walked a little way and he trusted that he would come again. She said she supposed he would no more see him, and no more he did ever after. And then he repented that he had not done after her counsel.

A short time after this was past, there came another false rascal, an old man, to the same priest and proffered him a breviary, a good little book, for sale. The priest went to the aforesaid creature, praying her to pray for him, and find out whether God willed that he should buy the book or not, and while she prayed, he cheered the man as well as he could, and then came again to this creature and asked how she felt.

"Sir," she said, "buy no book from him, for he is not to be trusted, and that ye will well know if ye meddle with him."

Then the priest prayed the man that he might see his book. The man said he had not got it on him. The priest asked how he came by it. He said he was executor to a priest who was of his kindred, and he charged him to sell it, and dispose of it for him.

"Father," said the priest—because of reverence—"why do ye offer me this book rather than other men or other priests, when there are so many more thriftier and richer priests in this church than I am, and I wot well ye had no knowledge of me before this time?"

"Forsooth, Sir," he said, "no more I had. Nevertheless I have good will toward your person, and also it was his will, who owned it before, that, if I knew any young priest that me-thought quiet and well-disposed, he should have this book before any other man, and for less price than any other man, that he might pray for him, and these causes make me come to you rather than to another."

The priest asked him where he dwelt.

"Sir," he said, "but five miles from this place in Penteney Abbey."

"There have I been," said the priest, "but I have not seen you."

"No, Sir," said he again, "I have been there but a little while, and now have I there an allowance of food, thanks be to God."

The priest prayed him that he might have a sight of the book and see if they might agree.

He said:—"Sir, I hope to be here again next week and to bring it with me, and, Sir, I promise you, ye shall have it before any other man, if ye like it." The priest thanked him for his good will and so they parted asunder, but the man never came to the priest afterwards, and the priest knew well that the aforesaid creature's feeling was true.

Chapter 25

The dispute between the church and the chapels regarding the font.

Furthermore, here followeth a right notable matter of the creature's feeling, and it is written here for convenience inasmuch as it is, in feeling, like the matters that be written before, notwithstanding that it befell long after the matters which follow.

It happened in a worshipful town where there was one parish church and two chapels annexed, the chapels having and administering all the Sacraments, except only christening and purifications, through sufferance of the parson, who was a monk of Saint Benedict's Order, sent from the house of Norwich, keeping residence with three of his brethren in the worshipful town before written.

Through some of the parishioners desiring to make the chapels like the parish church by pursuance of a bull from the Court of Rome, there befell great dispute and great trouble between the prior, who was their parson and curate, and the aforesaid parishioners, who desired to have fonts and purifications in the chapels, as there were in the parish church. And especially in the one chapel which was the greater and fairer, they would have a font.

There was pursued a bull, under which a font was granted to the chapel, provided that it was no derogation to the parish church. The bull was put in plea and divers days were spent in form of law to prove whether the font, if it were put in, would be derogatory to the parish church or not. The parishioners who pursued were right strong, and had great help of lordship, and also, most of all, they were rich men, worshipful merchants, and had gold enough, that can speed in every need; and it is ruth that need should speed ere truth.

Nevertheless, the prior who was their parson, though he was poor, manfully withstood them with the help of some of his parishioners who were his friends, and love the worship of their parish church. So long was this matter in plea that it began to irk them on both sides, and it was never the nearer an end.

Then was the matter put to my Lord of Norwich—Alnewyk—to see if he might by treaty bring it to an end. He labored this matter diligently; and to set it at rest and peace, he proffered the aforesaid parishioners much of their desire with certain conditions, insomuch that they that held with the parson and with their parish church, were full sorry, dreading greatly that they that sued to have a font would obtain and get their intent and so make the chapel equal to the parish church.

Then the priest who afterwards wrote this book, went to the creature of whom this treatise maketh mention, as he had done before in time of plea, and asked her how she felt in her soul on this matter, whether they should have a font in the chapel or not.

"Sir," said the creature, "dread ye not, for I understand in my soul, though they should give [even][14] a bushel of nobles[15] they could not have it."

"Ah! Mother," said the priest, "my lord of Norwich hath offered it to them on certain conditions, and they have a time for consideration to say nay or yea, whichever they will, and therefore I am afraid they will not refuse it, but be right glad to have it."

This creature prayed to God that His will might be fulfilled, and, forasmuch as she had the revelation that they would not have it, she was the

---

14 Word missing in MS.
15 The value of a noble was six shillings and eight-pence.

more bold to pray Our Lord to withstand their intent and slacken their boasting.

And so, as Our Lord willed, they obeyed not nor liked the conditions which were offered them, for they trusted fully to get their intent by lordship and process of law; and, as God willed, they were deceived of their intent, and because they would have all, they lost all.

And so, blessed may God be, the parish church stood fast in their worship and her degree, as she had done for two hundred years before and more, and the inspiration of Our Lord was by experience proved very true and sure in the aforesaid creature.

Chapter 26

She starts from Yarmouth on her way to the Holy Land. She has trouble with her companions owing to her weeping and piety. She reaches Constance.

When the time came that this creature should visit those holy places where Our Lord was quick and dead, as she had by revelation years before, she prayed the parish priest of the town where she was dwelling, to say for her in the pulpit, that, if any man or woman claimed any debt from her husband or herself, they should come and speak with her ere she went, and she, with the help of God would make a settlement with each of them, so that they should hold themselves content. And so she did.

Afterwards, she took her leave of her husband and of the holy anchorite, who had told her, before, the process of her going and the great disease that she would suffer by the way, and when all her fellowship forsook her, how a broken-backed man would lead her forth in safety, through the help of Our Lord.

And so it befell indeed, as shall be written afterward.

Then she took her leave of Master Robert, and prayed him for his blessing, and so, forth of other friends. Then she went forth to Norwich, and offered at the Trinity, and afterwards she went to Yarmouth and offered at an image of Our Lady, and there she took her ship.

And next day they came to a great town called Zierikzee, where Our Lord of His high goodness visited this creature with abundant tears of contrition for her own sins, and sometime for other men's sins also. And especially she had tears of compassion in mind of Our Lord's Passion. And she was houseled each Sunday where there was time and place convenient thereto, with great weeping and boisterous sobbing, so that many men marveled and wondered at the great grace that God had wrought in His creature.

This creature had eaten no flesh and drunk no wine for four years ere she went out of England, and so now her ghostly father charged her, by virtue of obedience, that she should both eat flesh and drink wine. And so she did a little while; afterwards she prayed her confessor that he would hold her excused if she ate no flesh, and suffer her to do as she would for such time as pleased him.

And soon after, through the moving of some of her company, her confessor was displeased because she ate no flesh, and so were many of the company. And they were most displeased because she wept so much and spoke always of the love and goodness of Our Lord, as much at the table as in other places. And therefore shamefully they reproved her, and severely chid her, and said they would not put up with her as her husband did when she was at home and in England.

And she answered meekly to them:—"Our Lord, Almighty God, is as great a Lord here as in England, and as good cause have I to love Him here as there, blessed may He be."

At these words, her fellowship was angrier than before, and their wrath and unkindness to this creature was a matter of great grief, for they were held right good men and she desired greatly their love, if she might have it to the pleasure of God.

And then she said to one of them specially:—"Ye cause me much shame and great grievance."

He answered her anon:—"I pray God that the devil's death may overcome thee soon and quickly," and many more cruel words he said to her than she could repeat.

And soon after some of the company in whom she trusted best, and her own maiden also, said she could no longer go in their fellowship. And they said that they would take away her maiden from her, so that she should no strumpet be, in her company. And then one of them, who had her gold in keeping, left her a noble with great anger and vexation to go where she would and help herself as she might, for with them, they said, she should no longer abide; and they forsook her that night.

Then, on the next morning, there came to her one of their company, a man who loved her well, praying her that she would go to his fellows and meeken herself to them, and pray them that she might go still in their company till she came to Constance.

And so she did, and went forth with them till she came to Constance with great discomfort and great trouble, for they did her much shame and much reproof as they went, in divers places. They cut her gown so short that it came but little beneath her knee, and made her put on a white canvas, in the manner of a sacken apron, so that she should be held a fool and the people should not make much of her or hold her in repute. They made her sit at the table's end, below all the others, so that she ill durst speak a word.

And, notwithstanding all their malice, she was held in more worship than they were, wherever they went.

And the good man of the house where they were hosteled, though she sat lowest at the table's end, would always help her before them all as well as he could, and sent her from his own table such service as he had, and that annoyed her fellowship full evil.

As they went by the way Constance-ward, it was told them that they would be robbed and have great discomfort unless they had great grace.

Then this creature came to a church and went in to make her prayer, and she prayed with all her heart, with great weeping and many tears, for help and succor against their enemies.

Then Our Lord said to her mind:—"Dread thee naught, daughter, thy fellowship shall come to no harm whilst thou art in their company."

And so, blessed may Our Lord be in all His works, they went forth in safety to Constance.

Chapter 27

At Constance, the papal legate befriends her. She meets William Wever of Devonshire. She goes to Bologna and Venice.

When this creature and her fellowship had come to Constance, she heard tell of an English friar, a master of divinity, and the pope's legate, who was in that city. Then she went to that worshipful man and shewed him her life from the beginning to that hour, as nigh as she might in confession, because he was the pope's legate and a worshipful clerk.

And afterwards she told him what discomfort she had with her fellowship. She told him also what grace God gave her of contrition and compunction, of sweetness and devotion and of many divers revelations that God had revealed to her, and the fear that she had of illusions and deceits of her ghostly enemies, of which she lived in great dread, desiring to put them away, and to feel none, if she might withstand them.

And when she had spoken, the worshipful clerk gave her words of great comfort, and said it was the work of the Holy Ghost, commanding and charging her to obey them and receive them when God should give them and to have no doubts, for the devil hath no power to work such grace in a soul. And also he said that he would support her against the evil will of her fellowship.

Afterwards, when it pleased her fellowship, they prayed this worthy doctor to dinner, and the doctor told the aforesaid creature, warning her to sit at the meat in his presence as she did in his absence, and to keep the same manner of behavior as she kept when he was not there.

When the time had come for them to sit at meat, every man took his place as he liked; the worshipful legate and doctor sat first, and then the others, and, at the last, the said creature at the board's end, sitting and speaking no word, as she was wont to do, when the legate was not there.

Then the legate said to her:—

"Why are ye no merrier?"

And she sat still and answered not, as he himself had commanded her to do.

When they had eaten, the company made great complaint against this creature to the legate, and said that, utterly, she could no longer be in their company, unless he commanded her to eat flesh as they did and stop her weeping, and that she should not talk so much of holiness.

Then the worshipful doctor said:—"Nay, sirs, I will not make her eat flesh whilst she can abstain and be the better disposed to Our Lord. If one of you made a vow to go to Rome barefoot, I would not dispense him of his vow whilst he could fulfil it, nor will I bid her to eat flesh whilst our Lord giveth her strength to abstain. As for her weeping, it is not in my power to restrain it, for it is the gift of the Holy Ghost. As for her speaking, I will pray her to cease till she cometh where men will hear her with better will than ye do."

The company was wroth, and in great anger. They gave her over to the legate and said utterly that they would no more associate with her. He full benignly and kindly received her as though she had been his mother, and received her gold, about twenty pounds, and yet one of them withheld wrongfully about sixteen pounds.

And they withheld also her maiden, and would not let her go with her mistress, notwithstanding that she had promised her mistress and assured her that she would not forsake her for any need.

And the legate made arrangements for this creature and made her his charge as if she had been his mother.

Then this creature went into a church and prayed Our Lord that He would provide her with a leader.

And anon Our Lord spoke to her and said:—

"Thou shalt have right good help and a good leader."

Immediately afterwards there came to her an old man with a white beard. He was from Devonshire, and said:—

"Damsel, will ye pray me for God's love, and for Our Lady's, to go with you and be your guide, for your countrymen have forsaken you?"

She asked, what was his name?

He said:—"My name is William Wever."

She prayed him, by the reverence of God and of Our Lady, that he would help her at her need, and she would well reward him for his labor, and so they agreed.

Then went she to the legate and told him how well Our Lord had ordained for her, and took her leave of him and of her company who so unkindly had rejected her, and also of her maiden who was bounden to have gone with her. She took her leave with full heavy face and rueful, having great grief in as much as she was in a strange country, and knew not the language, or the man who would lead her, either.

And so the man and she went forth in great dread and gloom. As they went together, the man said to her:—

"I am afraid thou wilt be taken from me, and I shall be beaten for thee, and lose my jacket."

She said:—"William, dread you not. God will keep us right well."

And this creature had every day mind of the Gospel which telleth of the woman that was taken in adultery, and brought before Our Lord.

And she prayed:—"Lord, as thou drove away her enemies, so drive away mine enemies, and keep well my chastity that I vowed to Thee, and let me never be defiled, for if I am, Lord, I make my vow, that I will never come back to England whilst I live."

Then they went forth day by day and met with many jolly men. And they said no evil word to this creature, but gave her and her man meat and drink, and the good wives where they were housed, laid her in their own beds for God's love, in many places where they came.

And Our Lord visited her with great grace of ghostly comfort as she went by the way. And so God brought her forth till she came to Bologna. And after she had come there, there came thither also her other fellowship, which had forsaken her before. And when they heard say that she had come to Bologna ere they had, then had they great wonder, and one of their fellowship came to her praying her to go to his fellowship and try if they would receive her again into their fellowship. And so she did.

"If ye will go in our fellowship, ye must make a new covenant, and that is this—ye shall not speak of the Gospel where we are, but shall sit still and make merry, as we do, both at meat and at supper."

She consented and was received again into their fellowship. Then went they forth to Venice and dwelt there thirteen weeks; and this creature was houseled every Sunday in a great house of nuns, and had great cheer among them, where Our Lord Jesus Christ visited this creature with great devotion and plenteous tears, so that the good ladies of the place were much marveled thereof.

Afterwards, it happened, as this creature sat at meat with her fellowship, that she repeated a text of the Gospel that she had learnt before-time with other good words, and then her fellowship said she had broken covenant. And she said:—

"Yea, sirs, forsooth I may no longer keep your covenant, for I must needs speak of My Lord Jesus Christ, though all this world had forbidden it to me."

Then she took to her chamber and ate alone for six weeks, unto the time that Our Lord made her so sick that she weened to have been dead, and then suddenly He made her whole again. And all the time her maiden let her alone and made the company's meat and washed their clothes, and, to her mistress, under whom she had taken service, she would no deal attend.

Chapter 28

She sails from Venice and reaches Jerusalem. Much trouble owing to her crying.

Also this company, which had put the aforesaid creature from their table, so that she should no longer eat amongst them, engaged a ship for themselves to sail in. They bought vessels for their wine, and obtained bedding for themselves, but nothing for her. Then she, seeing their unkindness, went to the same man where they had been, and bought herself bedding as they had done, and came where they were and shewed them what she had done, purposing to sail with them in that ship which they had chartered.

Afterwards, as this creature was in contemplation, Our Lord warned her in her mind that she should not sail in that ship, and He assigned her to another ship, a galley, that she should sail in. Then she told this to some of the company, and they told it forth to their fellowship, and then they durst not sail in the ship they had chartered. So they sold away their vessels which they had got for their wines, and were right fain to come to the galley where she was, and so, though it was against her will, she went forth with them in their company, for they durst not otherwise do.

When it was time to make their beds, they locked up her clothes, and a priest, who was in their company, took away a sheet from the aforesaid creature, and said it was his. She took God

to witness that it was her sheet. Then the priest swore a great oath, by the book in his hand, that she was as false as she might be, and despised her and strongly rebuked her.

And so she had ever much tribulation till she came to Jerusalem. And ere she came there, she said to them that she supposed they were grieved with her.

"I pray you, Sirs, be in charity with me, for I am in charity with you, and forgive me that I have grieved you by the way. And if any of you have in anything trespassed against me, God forgive it you, and I do."

So they went forth into the Holy Land till they could see Jerusalem. And when this creature saw Jerusalem, riding on an ass, she thanked God with all her heart, praying Him for His mercy that, as He had brought her to see His earthly city of Jerusalem, He would grant her grace to see the blissful city of Jerusalem above, the city of heaven. Our Lord Jesus Christ, answering her thought, granted her to have her desire.

Then for the joy she had, and the sweetness she felt in the dalliance with Our Lord, she was on the point of falling off her ass, for she could not bear the sweetness and grace that God wrought in her soul. Then two pilgrims, Duchemen,[16] went to her, and kept her from falling; one of whom was a priest, and he put spices in her mouth to comfort her, thinking she had been sick. And so they helped her on to Jerusalem, and when she came there, she said:—

"Sirs, I pray you be not displeased though I weep sore in this holy place where Our Lord Jesus Christ was quick and dead."

Then went they to the temple in Jerusalem and they were let in on the same day at evensong time, and abode there till the next day at evensong time. Then the friars lifted up a cross and led the pilgrims about from one place to another where Our Lord suffered His[17] ... and His Passion, every man and woman bearing a wax candle in one hand. And the friars always, as they went about, told them what Our Lord suffered in every place. The aforesaid creature wept and sobbed as plenteously as though she had seen Our Lord with her bodily eye, suffering His Passion at that time.

---

16 Dutchmen.
17 Word missing in MS.

Before her in her soul she saw Him verily by contemplation, and that caused her to have compassion. And when they came up on to the Mount of Calvary, she fell down because she could not stand or kneel, and rolled and wrestled with her body, spreading her arms abroad, and cried with a loud voice as though her heart would have burst asunder; for, in the city of her soul, she saw verily and clearly how Our Lord was crucified. Before her face, she heard and saw, in her ghostly sight, the mourning of Our Lady, of Saint John, and Mary Magdalene and of many others that loved Our Lord.

And she had such great compassion and such great pain, at seeing Our Lord's pain that she could not keep herself from crying and roaring though she should have died for it. And this was the first cry[18] that ever she cried in any contemplation. And this manner of crying endured many years after this time, for aught any man might do, and therefore, suffered she much despite and much reproof. The crying was so loud and so wonderful that it made the people astounded unless they had heard it before, or unless they knew the cause of the crying. And she had them so often that they made her right weak in her bodily might, and especially if she heard of Our Lord's Passion.

And sometimes, when she saw the crucifix, or if she saw a man with a wound, or a beast, whichever it were, or if a man beat a child before her, or smote a horse or other beast with a whip, if she saw it or heard it, she thought she saw Our Lord being beaten or wounded, just as she saw it in the man or the beast either in the field or the town, and by herself alone as well as amongst the people.

First when she had her cryings in Jerusalem, she had them often, and in Rome also. And when she came home to England, first at her coming home, it came but seldom, as it were once a month, then once a week, afterwards daily, and once she had fourteen in one day, and another day she had seven, and so on, as God would visit her, sometimes in church, sometimes in the street, sometimes in her chamber, sometimes in the fields, whenever God would send them, for she never knew the time nor the hour when they would come. And they never came without

passing great sweetness of devotion and high contemplation. And as soon as she perceived that she would cry, she would keep it in as much as she might that the people should not hear it, to their annoyance. For some said that a wicked spirit vexed her; some said it was a sickness; some said she had drunk too much wine; some banned her; some wished she was in the harbor; some wished she was on the sea in a bottomless boat; and thus each man as he thought. Other ghostly men loved her and favored her the more. Some great clerks said Our Lady cried never so, nor any saint in Heaven, but they knew full little what she felt, nor would they believe that she could not stop crying if she wished.

And therefore when she knew that she would cry, she kept it in as long as she might, and did all she could to withstand it or put it away, till she waxed as livid as any lead, and ever it would labor in her mind more and more till the time it broke out. And when the body might no longer endure the ghostly labor, but was overcome with the unspeakable love that wrought so fervently in her soul, then she fell down and cried wondrous loud, and the more she labored to keep it in or put it away, so much the more would she cry, and the louder. Thus she did on the Mount of Calvary, as is written before.

Thus she had as very contemplation in the sight of her soul, as if Christ had hung before her bodily eye in His manhood. And when through the dispensation of the high mercy of Our Sovereign Savior Christ Jesus, it was granted to this creature to behold so verily His precious tender body, all rent and torn with scourges, fuller of wounds than ever was a dove-house of holes, hanging on the Cross with the crown of thorns upon His head, His beautiful hands, His tender feet nailed to the hard tree, the rivers of blood flowing out plenteously from every member, the grisly and grievous wound in His precious side shedding blood and water for her love and her salvation, then she fell down and cried with a loud voice, wonderfully turning and wresting her body on every side, spreading her arms abroad as if she would have died, and could not keep herself from crying, and from these bodily movements for the fire of love

---

18 Outcry; scream.

that burnt so fervently in her soul with pure pity and compassion.

It is not to be marveled at, if this creature cried and made wondrous faces and expressions, when we may see each day with the eye both men and women, some for the loss of worldly goods, some for affection of their kindred, or worldly friendships, through over much study and earthly affection, and most of all for inordinate love and fleshly affection, if their friends are parted from them, they will cry and roar and wring their hands as if they had no wits or senses, and yet know they well that they are displeasing God.

And, if a man counsel them to leave or cease their weeping and crying, they will say that they cannot; they loved their friend so much, and he was so gentle and so kind to them, that they may in no way forget him. How much more might they weep, cry, and roar, if their most beloved friends were with violence taken in their sight and with all manner of reproof, brought before the judge, wrongfully condemned to death, and especially so spiteful a death as Our Merciful Lord suffered for our sake. How would they suffer it? No doubt they would both cry and roar and avenge themselves if they might, or else men would say they were no friends.

Alas! Alas! for sorrow that the death of a creature, who hath often sinned and trespassed against their maker, shall be so immeasurably mourned and sorrowed. And it is an offense to God, and a hindrance to the souls beside them.

And the compassionate death of Our Savior by which we are all restored to life, is not kept in mind by us unworthy and unkind wretches, nor do we support Our Lord's own secretaries whom He hath endued with love, but rather detract and hinder them as much as we may.

Chapter 29

She visits the Holy Sepulcher, Mount Sion and Bethlehem.

When this creature with her fellowship came to the grave where Our Lord was buried, anon, as she entered that holy place, she fell down with her candle in her hand, as if she would have died for sorrow. And late she rose up again with great weeping and sobbing, as though she had seen Our Lord buried even before her.

Then she thought she saw Our Lady in her soul, how she mourned and how she wept for her Son's death, and then was Our Lady's sorrow her sorrow.

And so, wherever the friars led them in that holy place, she always wept and sobbed wonderfully, and especially when she came where Our Lord was nailed on the Cross. There cried she, and wept without measure, so that she could not restrain herself.

Also they came to a stone of marble that Our Lord was laid on when He was taken down from the Cross, and there she wept with great compassion, having mind of Our Lord's Passion.

Afterwards she was houseled on the Mount of Calvary, and then she wept, she sobbed, she cried so loud that it was a wonder to hear it. She was so full of holy thoughts and meditations and holy contemplations on the Passion of Our Lord Jesus Christ, and holy dalliance that Our Lord Jesus Christ spoke to her soul, that she could never express them after, so high and so holy were they. Much was the grace that Our Lord shewed to this creature whilst she was three weeks in Jerusalem.

Another day, early in the morning, they went again amongst great hills, and their guides told her where Our Lord bore the Cross on His back, and where His Mother met with Him, and how she swooned and fell down and He fell down also. And so they went forth all the forenoon till they came to Mount Sion. And ever this creature wept abundantly, all the way that she went, for compassion of Our Lord's Passion. On Mount Sion is a place where Our Lord washed His disciples' feet and, a little therefrom, He made His Maundy with His disciples.

And therefore this creature had great desire to be houseled in that holy place where Our Merciful Lord Christ Jesus first consecrated His precious Body in the form of bread, and gave it to His disciples. And so she was, with great devotion and plenteous tears and boisterous sobbings, for in this place is plenary remission, and so there is in four other places in the Temple. One is on the Mount of Calvary; another at the grave where Our Lord was buried; the third is at the marble stone that His precious Body was laid on, when It was taken from the Cross; the fourth is where the Holy Cross was buried; and in many other places in Jerusalem.

And when this creature came to the place where the apostles received the Holy Ghost, Our Lord gave her great devotion. Afterwards she went to the place where Our Lady was buried, and as she knelt on her knees the time of two masses, Our Lord Jesus Christ said to her:—

"Thou comest not hither, daughter, for any need except merit and reward, for thy sins were forgiven thee ere thou came here and therefore thou comest here for the increasing of thy reward and thy merit. And I am well pleased with thee, daughter, for thou standest under obedience to Holy Church, and because thou wilt obey thy confessor and follow his counsel who, through authority of Holy Church, hath absolved thee of thy sins and dispensed thee so that thou shouldst not go to Rome and Saint James unless thou wilt thine own self. Notwithstanding all this, I command thee in the Name of Jesus, daughter, that thou go visit these holy places and do as I bid thee, for I am above Holy Church, and I shall go with thee and keep thee right well."

Then Our Lady spoke to her soul in this manner, saying:—

"Daughter, well art thou blessed, for my Son Jesus shall flow so much grace into thee that all the world shall wonder at thee. Be not ashamed, my dearworthy daughter, to receive the gifts that my Son shall give thee, for I tell thee in truth, they shall be great gifts that He shall give thee. And therefore, my dearworthy daughter, be not ashamed of Him that is thy God, thy Lord and thy love, any more than I was, when I saw Him hanging on the Cross—my sweet Son, Jesus—to cry and to weep for the pain of my sweet Son Jesus Christ. Mary Magdalene was not ashamed to cry and weep for my Son's love. Therefore, daughter, if thou will be partaker in our love, thou must be partaker in our sorrow."

This sweet speech and dalliance had this creature at Our Lady's grave, and much more than she could ever repeat.

Afterwards she rode on an ass to Bethlehem, and when she came to the temple and the crib where Our Lord was born, she had great devotion, much speech and dalliance in her soul, and high

ghostly comfort with much weeping and sobbing, so that her fellows would not let her eat in their company, and therefore she ate her meat by herself alone.

And then the Grey Friars, who had led her from place to place, received her to them and set her with them at the meat so that she should not eat alone. And one of the friars asked one of her fellowship if she were the woman of England whom, they had heard said, spoke with God. And when this came to her knowledge, she knew well that it was the truth that Our Lord said to her, ere she went out of England:—

"Daughter, I will make all the world to wonder at thee, and many a man and many a woman shall speak of Me for love of thee, and worship Me in thee."

Chapter 30

She visits the Jordan, Mount Quarentyne, Bethania and Rafnys. Starts for Rome, and at Venice meets Richard, the broken-backed man, and goes on in his company.

Another time, this creature's fellowship would go to the Flood of Jordan and would not let her go with them. Then this creature prayed Our Lord that she might go with them, and He bade that she should go with them whether they would or not. Then she went forth by the grace of God, and asked no leave of them.

When she came to the Flood of Jordan, the weather was so hot that she thought her feet would have burnt for the heat that she felt.

Afterwards she went with her fellowship to Mount Quarantyne. There Our Lord fasted forty days, and there she prayed her fellowship to help her up on to the Mount. And they said, "Nay," for they could not well help themselves. Then had she great sorrow, because she might not come on to the hill. And anon, happed a Saracen, a well-favored man, to come by her, and she put a groat into his hand, making him a sign to bring her on to the Mount. And quickly the Saracen took her under his arm and led her up on to the high Mount, where Our Lord fasted forty days.

Then was she sore athirst, and had no comfort in her fellowship. Then God, of His great goodness, moved the Grey Friars with compassion, and they comforted her, when her countrymen would not know her.

And so she was ever more strengthened in the love of Our Lord and the more bold to suffer shame and reproof for His sake in every place where she came, for the grace that God wrought in her of weeping, sobbing, and crying, which grace she might not withstand when God would send it. And ever she proved her feelings true, and those promises that God had made her while she was in England and other places also. They befell her in effect just as she had felt before, and therefore she durst the better receive such speeches and dalliance, and the more boldly work thereafter.

Afterwards, when this creature came down from the Mount, as God willed, she went forth to the place where Saint John the Baptist was born. And later she went to Bethania, where Mary and Martha dwelt, and to the grave where Lazarus was buried and raised from death into life. And she prayed in the chapel where Our Blessed Lord appeared to His blissful Mother on Easter Day at morn, first of all others. And she stood in the same place where Mary Magdalene stood when Christ said to her:—

"Mary, why weepest thou?"

And so she was in many more places than be written, for she was three weeks in Jerusalem and the country thereabout, and she had ever great devotion as long as she was in that country.

The friars of the temple made her great cheer and gave her many great relics, desiring that she should have dwelt still amongst them if she would, for the faith they had in her. Also the Saracens made much of her, and conveyed her, and led her about the country wherever she would go; and she found all people good to her and gentle, save only her own countrymen.

And as she came from Jerusalem unto Rafnys, then would she have turned again to Jerusalem for the great grace and ghostly comfort that she felt when she was there, and to purchase herself more pardon.

Then Our Lord commanded her to go to Rome and, so, forth home to England, and said to her:—

"Daughter, as oftentimes as thou sayest or thinkest 'Worshipped be those Holy Places in Jerusalem that Christ suffered bitter pain and Passion in,' thou shalt have the same pardon as if thou wert there with thy bodily presence, both to thyself and to all that thou wilt give it to."

And as she went forth to Venice, many of her fellowship were right sick, and Our Lord said to her:—

"Dread thee not, daughter, no man shall die in the ship that thou art in."

And she found her feelings right true. When Our Lord had brought them again to Venice in safety, her countrymen forsook her and went away from her, leaving her alone. And some of them said that they would not go with her for a hundred pound.

When they had gone away from her, then Our Lord Jesus Christ, Who ever helpeth at need, and never forsaketh His servants who truly trust in His mercy, said to this creature:—

"Dread thee not, daughter, for I will provide for thee right well, and bring thee in safety to Rome and home again into England without any villainy to thy body, if thou wilt be clad in white clothes, and wear them as I said to thee whilst thou wert in England."

Then this creature, being in great grief and distress, answered Him in her mind: ...

"If Thou be the spirit of God that speaketh in my soul, and I may prove Thee for a true spirit with the counsel of the Church, I shall obey Thy will; and if Thou bringest me to Rome in safety, I shall wear white clothes, though all the world should wonder at me, for Thy love."

"Go forth, daughter, in the Name of Jesus, for I am the spirit of God, which shall help thee in all thy need, go with thee, and support thee in every place, and therefore mistrust Me not. Thou foundest Me never deceivable, and I bid thee nothing do, but that which is worship to God, and profit to thy soul. If thou will do thereafter, then I shall flow on thee great plenty of grace."

Then anon, as she looked on one side, she saw a poor man sitting, who had a great hump on his back. His clothes were all clouted and he seemed a man of fifty winters' age. Then she went to him and said:—

"Good man, what aileth your back?"

He said:—"Damsel, it was broken in a sickness."

She asked, what was his name, and what countryman he was. He said his name was Richard, and he was of Ireland. Then thought she of her confessor's words, who was a holy anchorite, as is written before, who spoke to her whilst she was in England in this manner:—

"Daughter, when your fellowship hath forsaken you, God will provide a broken-backed man to lead you forth, wherever you will go."

Then she, with a glad spirit, said to him:—

"Good Richard, lead me to Rome, and you shall be rewarded for your labor."

"Nay, damsel," said he, "I wot well thy countrymen have forsaken thee, and therefore it were hard on me to lead thee. Thy countrymen have both bows and arrows with which they might defend both thee and themselves, and I have no weapons save a cloak full of clouts, and yet I dread me that mine enemies will rob me, and peradventure take thee away from me and defile thy body, and therefore I dare not lead thee, for I would not, for a hundred pounds, that thou hadst a villainy in my company."

And she said again:—"Richard, dread you not; God shall keep us both right well and I shall give you two nobles for your labor."

Then he consented and went forth with her. Soon after, there came two grey friars and a woman that came with them from Jerusalem, and she had with her an ass, which bore a chest and an image therein, made after Our Lord.

Then said Richard to the aforesaid creature:— "Thou shalt go forth with these two men and the woman and I will meet thee morning and evening, for I must get on with my job and beg my living."

So she did after his counsel and went forth with the two friars and the woman. And none of them could understand her language, and yet they provided for every day, meat, drink, and harborage as well as they did for themselves and rather better, so that she was ever bounden to pray for them.

Every evening and morning, Richard with the broken back came and comforted her as he had promised.

The woman who had the image in the chest, when they came into good cities, took the image out of her chest and set it in worshipful wives' laps; and they would put shirts thereon, and kiss it as if it had been God Himself.

When the creature saw the worship and reverence that they gave to the image, she was taken with sweet devotion and sweet meditations, so that she wept with great sobbing and loud crying; and she was moved so much the more, because while she was in England, she had high meditations on the birth and the childhood of Christ, and she thanked God forasmuch as she saw these creatures having as great faith in what she saw with her bodily eye, as she had had before with her ghostly eye.

When these good women saw this creature weeping, sobbing and crying so wonderfully and mightily that she was nearly overcome therewith, then they arranged a good soft bed and laid her thereon, and comforted her as much as they could for Our Lord's sake, blessed may He be.

Chapter 31

Her ring is stolen and recovered. She reaches Assisi, and meets Dame Margaret Florentyne, with whom she goes on to Rome.

The aforesaid creature had a ring, which Our Lord had commanded her to have made whilst she was at home in England, and she had engraved thereon, "Jesus Christ est amor meus."[19] She had much thought how she should keep this ring from thieves and stealing, as she went about the countries, for she thought she would not have lost the ring for a thousand pounds and much more, because she had it made by the bidding of God; and also, she wore it by His bidding, for she purposed beforetime, ere she had it by revelation, never to have worn a ring.

So it happed her to be harbored in a good man's house, and many neighbors came in to cheer her for her perfection and her holiness, and she gave them the measure of Christ's grave which they received full kindly, having great joy thereof, and thanked her highly therefor.

Afterwards this creature went to her chamber and let her ring hang by her purse-string, which she bore at her breast. In the morning on the next day, when she would have taken her ring, it was

---

19   Latin: Jesus Christ is my love.

gone. She could not find it. Then had she great grief, and complained to the good wife of the house, saying in this wise:—

"Madam, my good wedding ring to Jesus Christ, as one might say, it is away."

The good wife, understanding what she meant, prayed her to pray for her, and she changed her face and countenance strangely, as though she had been guilty. Then this creature took a candle in her hand and sought all about her bed where she had lain all night, and the good wife of the house took another candle in her hand and busied herself seeking also about the bed; and at last she found the ring under the bed on the boards. And with great joy she told the good wife that she had found her ring. Then the good wife, submitting herself, prayed this creature for forgiveness, as well as she could. "Good Christian, pray for me."

Afterwards this creature came to Assisi, and there she met with a friar minor, an Englishman; and a devout clerk, he was held to be. She told him of her manner of living, of her feelings, of her revelations, and of the grace that God wrought in her soul by holy inspirations and high contemplations, and how Our Lord dallied to her soul in a manner of speaking. Then the worshipful clerk said she was much beholden to God, for he said he had never heard of anyone living in this world, who was so homely with God by love and homely dalliance, as she was, thanked be God for His gifts, for it is His goodness, and no man's merit.

Upon a time, as this creature was in church at Assisi, there was shewn Our Lady's kerchief which she wore here on earth, with many lights and great reverence. Then this creature had great devotion. She wept, she sobbed, she cried with great plenty of tears and many holy thoughts. She was also there on Lammas Day, when there is great pardon with plenary remission, to purchase grace, mercy and forgiveness for herself, for all her friends, for all her enemies, and for all the souls in purgatory.

And there was a lady who had come from Rome to purchase her pardon. Her name was Margaret Florentyne, and she had with her many knights of Rhodes, many gentlewomen, and much good baggage.

Then Richard, the broken-backed man, went to her, praying her that this creature might go with her to Rome, and himself also, so as to be kept from the peril of thieves. And then that worshipful lady received them into her company and let them go with her to Rome, as God willed. When the aforesaid creature had come into Rome, they that were her fellows aforetime, who had put her out of their company were in Rome also, and having heard that such a woman had come thither, they had great wonder how she came there in safety.

Then she went and got her white clothes and was clad all in white, as she was commanded to do, years before, in her soul by revelation, and now it was fulfilled in effect.

Then was this creature received into the Hospital of Saint Thomas of Canterbury in Rome, and she was houseled every Sunday with great weeping, boisterous sobbing, and loud crying, and was highly beloved by the master of the hospital and all his brethren. And then, through the stirring of her ghostly enemy, there came a priest, that was held a holy man in the hospital and also in other places of Rome, who was one of her fellows, and one of her own countrymen. And notwithstanding his holiness, he spoke so evil of this creature and slandered so her name in the hospital that, through his evil language, she was put out of the hospital, so that she might no longer be shriven or houseled therein.

39. LIUDPRAND OF CREMONA

A Chronicle of Otto's Reign

LIUDPRAND (LIUDBRAND) OF CREMONA (ca. 920–972) was raised in the court of King Hugo of Italy before becoming chancellor of King Berengar II. After breaking with Berengar, he found favor with his rival, Otto I, who would soon become king of Italy. In the service of Otto, Liudprand became bishop of Cremona and was sent on various diplomatic missions. He was the author of a history of Italy, Germany, and Byzantium between 888 and 949 directed against Berengar, which he called *Antapodosis* (Retaliation), an account of his unsuccessful attempt to arrange a marriage for Otto II with a Byzantine princess, and the following text, a justification of Otto I's Italian policy.

Source: F.A. Wright, *The Works of Liudprand of Cremona* (London: George Routledge and Sons, Ltd., 1930).

Further Reading: Robert Levine, "Liudprand of Cremona: History and Debasement in the Tenth Century," *Mittellateinisches Jahrbuch* 26 for 1991 (1992): 70–84.

Ch. I. Berengar and Adalbert were reigning, or rather raging, in Italy, where, to speak the truth, they exercised the worst of tyrannies, when John, the supreme pontiff and universal pope, whose church had suffered from the savage cruelty of the aforesaid Berengar and Adalbert, sent envoys from the holy church of Rome, in the persons of the cardinal deacon John and the secretary Azo, to Otto, at that time the most serene and pious king and now our august emperor, humbly begging him, both by letters and a recital of facts, for the love of God and the holy apostles Peter and Paul, whom he hoped would remit his sins, to rescue him and the holy Roman church entrusted to him from their jaws, and restore it to its former prosperity and freedom. While the Roman envoys were laying these complaints, Waldpert, the venerable archbishop of the holy church of Milan, having escaped half-dead from the mad rage of the aforesaid Berengar and Adalbert, sought the powerful protection of the above-mentioned Otto, at that time king and now our august emperor, declaring that he could no longer bear or submit to the cruelty of Berengar and Adalbert and Willa, who contrary to all human and divine law had appointed Manasses bishop of Arles to the see of Milan. He said that it was a calamity for his church thus to intercept a right that belonged to him and to his people. After Waldpert came Waldo bishop of Como, crying out that he also had suffered a like insult at the hands of Berengar, Adalbert and Willa. With the apostolic envoys there also arrived some members of the laity, among them the illustrious marquess Otbert, asking help and advice from his most sacred majesty Otto, then king now emperor.

Ch. II. The most pious king was moved by their tearful complaints, and considered not himself but the cause of Jesus Christ. Therefore, although it was contrary to custom, he appointed his young son Otto as king, and leaving him in Saxony collected his forces and marched in haste to Italy. There he drove Berengar and Adalbert from the realm at once, the more quickly inasmuch as it is certain that the holy apostles Peter and Paul were fighting under his flag. The good king brought together what had been scattered and mended what had been broken, restoring to each man his due possessions. Then he advanced on Rome to do the same again.

Ch. III. There he was welcomed with marvelous ceremony and unexampled pomp, and was anointed as emperor by John the supreme bishop and universal pope. To the church he not only gave back her possessions but bestowed lavish gifts of jewels, gold and silver. Furthermore Pope John and all the princes of the city swore solemnly on the most precious body of Saint Peter that they would never give help to Berengar and Adalbert. Thereupon Otto returned to Pavia with all speed.

Ch. IV. Meanwhile Pope John, forgetful of his oath and the promise he had made to the sacred emperor, sent to Adalbert asking him to return and swearing that he would assist him against the power of the most sacred emperor. For the sacred emperor had so terrified this Adalbert, persecutor of God's churches and of Pope John, that he had left Italy altogether and had gone to Fraxinetum and put himself under the protection of the Saracens. The righteous emperor for his part could not understand at all why Pope John was now showing such affection to the very man whom previously he had attacked in bitter hatred. Accordingly he called together some of his intimates and sent off to Rome to inquire if this report was true. On his messengers' arrival they got this answer, not from a few chance informants, but from all the citizens of Rome:—"Pope John hates the most sacred emperor, who freed him from Adalbert's clutches, for exactly the same reason that the devil hates his creator. The emperor, as we have learned by experience, knows, works and loves the things of God: he guards the affairs of church and state with his sword, adorns them by his virtues, and purifies them by his laws. Pope John is the enemy of all these things. What we say is a tale well known to all. As witness to its truth take the widow of Rainer his own vassal, a woman with whom John has been so blindly in love that he has made her governor of many cities and given to her the golden crosses and cups that are the sacred possessions of St. Peter himself. Witness also the case of Stephana, his father's

mistress, who recently conceived a child by him and died of an effusion of blood. If all else were silent, the palace of the Lateran, that once sheltered saints and is now a harlot's brothel, will never forget his union with his father's wench, the sister of the other concubine Stephania. Witness again the absence of all women here save Romans: they fear to come and pray at the thresholds of the holy apostles, for they have heard how John a little time ago took women pilgrims by force to his bed, wives, widows and virgins alike. Witness the churches of the holy apostles, whose roof lets the rain in upon the sacrosanct altar, and that not in drops but in sheets. The woodwork fills us with alarm, when we go there to ask God's help. Death reigns within the building, and, though we have much to pray for, we are prevented from going there and soon shall be forced to abandon God's house altogether. Witness the women he keeps, some of them fine ladies who, as the poet says, are as thin as reeds by dieting, others everyday buxom wenches. It is all the same to him whether they walk the pavement or ride in a carriage and pair. That is the reason why there is the same disagreement between him and the holy emperor as there is of necessity between wolves and lambs. That he may go his way unchecked, he is trying to get Adalbert, as patron, guardian and protector."

Ch. V. When the envoys on their return gave this report to the emperor, he said:—"He is only a boy, and will soon alter if good men set him an example. I hope that honorable reproof and generous persuasion will quickly cure him of these vices; and then we shall say with the prophet:—'This is a change which the hand of the Highest has brought.'" He added:—"The first thing required by circumstances is that we dislodge Berengar from his position on Montefeltro. Then let us address some words of fatherly admonition to the lord pope. His sense of shame, if not his own wishes, will soon effect a change in him for the better. Perchance if he is forced into good ways, he will be ashamed to get out of them again."

Ch. VI. This done, the emperor went on board ship and sailed down the Po to Ravenna. Thence he advanced to Montefeltro, sometimes called St Leo's Mountain, and besieged the fort in which Berengar and Willa had taken refuge. Thereupon the aforesaid Pope John sent Leo, then the venerable chief notary of the holy Roman church and now in that same see successor to Saint Peter chief of the apostles, together with Demetrius, one of the most illustrious of the Roman princes, as envoy to the holy emperor. By their mouths he declared that it was not surprising if in the heat of youth he had hitherto indulged in childish follies; but now the time had come when he would fain live in a different fashion. He also cunningly alleged that the holy emperor had sheltered two of his disloyal subordinates, Bishop Leo and the cardinal deacon John, and that he was now breaking his sworn promise by letting them take an oath of allegiance not to the pope but to the emperor. To the envoys the emperor gave this answer: "I thank the pope for the change and improvement in his ways that he promises. As for the violation of pledges that he charges me with, judge yourselves if the accusation be true. We promised to restore all the territory of Saint Peter that might fall into our hands: and for that reason we are now striving to drive Berengar with all his household from yonder fort. How can we restore this territory to the pope, if we do not first wrest it from the hands of violent men and bring it under our control? As for Bishop Leo and the cardinal deacon John, his disloyal subordinates, whom he accuses us of having welcomed, we have neither seen them in these days nor welcomed them. The lord pope sent them to Constantinople to do us damage, and on their way, we are told, they were taken prisoners at Capua. We are also informed that with them was arrested a certain Saleccus, a Bulgarian by birth and an Hungarian by training, who is an intimate friend of the lord pope, and also a reprobate named Zacheus, a man quite ignorant of all literature sacred or profane, whom the lord pope has recently consecrated as bishop, with the intention that he should preach to the Hungarians a campaign against us. We would not have believed that the lord pope would have acted thus, whoever told us; but his letter, sealed with leaden seals and bearing his signature, compels us to think that it is true."

Ch. VII. This done, the emperor sent Landohard the Saxon bishop of Minden and Liudprand the Italian bishop of Cremona to Rome in company with the pope's envoys, to satisfy the lord pope that no blame attached to him. Furthermore the righteous emperor bade the soldiers of their guard to prove the truth of his words in single combat if the pope refused to believe him. The aforesaid bishops Landohard and Liudprand came before the lord pope at Rome, and although they were received with all due honor they saw clearly with what scorn and indifference he was prepared to treat the holy emperor. They explained everything in order, as they had been told to do, but the pope refused to be satisfied either with an oath or with a single combat and persisted in being obdurate. Still, a week later he craftily sent John, bishop of Narni, and Benedict, cardinal deacon, back to the lord emperor with his envoys, thinking that by their tricks he could delude a man whom it is exceptionally difficult to deceive. Before they got back, however, Adalbert at the pope's invitation had left Fraxinetum and reached Civita Vecchia; whence he set out for Rome and there, so far from being repudiated by the pope, as he should have been, received from him an honorable welcome.

Ch. VIII. While these things were going on, the fierce heat of the dog days kept the emperor away from the hills of Rome. But when the sun had entered the sign of the Virgin and brought a temperate change, he collected his forces, and at the secret invitation of the Romans drew near to the city. Yet why do I say "secret," when the greater part of the Roman princes forced their way into the castle of St. Paul and giving hostages invited the holy emperor to enter. Why make a long tale? When the emperor pitched his camp in the vicinity, the pope and Adalbert made their escape together from Rome. The citizens welcomed the holy emperor and all his men into their town, promising again to be loyal and adding under a strong oath that they would never elect or ordain a pope except with the consent and approval of the august Caesar Otto the lord emperor and his son King Otto.

Ch. IX. Three days later at the request of the bishops and people of Rome a synod was held in the church of St Peter, attended by the emperor and the Italian archbishops. The deacon Rodalf acted in place of Ingelfred patriarch of Aquileia, who had been seized by a sudden sickness in that city; Waldpert came from Milan, Peter from Ravenna; Archbishop Adeltac and Landohard, bishop of

Minden, represented Saxony; Otker, bishop of Spires, France. The Italian bishops were Hubert of Parma, Liudprand of Cremona, Hermenard of Reggio; the Tuscans, Conrad of Lucca, Everard of Arezzo, the bishops of Pisa, Sienna, Florence, Pistoia, Peter of Camerino, the bishop of Spoleto; the Romans, Gregory of Albano, Sico of Ostia, Benedict of Porto, Lucidus of Gavio, Theophylact of Palestrina, Wido of Selva Candida, Leo of Velletri, Sico of Bieda, Stephen of Cerveteri, John of Nepi, John of Tivoli, John of San Liberato, Romanus of Ferentino, John of Norma, John of Veroli, Marinus of Sutri, John of Narni, John of Sabina, John of Gallese, the bishops of Civita, Castellana, Alatri, Orte, John of Anagni, the bishop of Trevi, Sabbatinus of Terracina. There were also present: Stephen cardinal archpriest of the parish Balbina, Dominic of the parish Anastasia, Peter of the parish Damascus, Theophylact of the parish Chrysogonus, John of the parish Equitius, Peter of the parish Pamachius, Adrian of the parish Caecilia, Adrian of the parish Lucina, Benedict of the parish Sixtus, Theophylact of the parish Four Crowned Saints, Stephen of the parish Sabina, Benedict cardinal archdeacon, John deacon, Bonofilius chief cardinal deacon, George second cardinal deacon, Stephen assistant, Andrew treasurer, Sergius chief warden, John sacristan, Stephen, Theophylact, Adrian, Stephen, Benedict, Azo, Adrian, Romanus, Leo, Benedict, Leo, Leo, Leo notaries, Leo chief of the school of singers, Benedict subdeacon in charge of the offertories, Azo, Benedict, Demetrius, John, Amicus, Sergius, Benedict, Urgo, John, Benedict subdeacon and steward, Stephen arch-acolyte with all the acolytes and district deacons. Representing the princes of Rome were Stephen son of John, Demetrius Meliosi, Crescenti de Caballo Marmoreo, John Mizina, Stephen de Imiza, Theodore de Rufina, John de Primicerio, Leo de Cazunuli, Rihkard, Pietro de Canapanaria, and Benedict with his son Bulgamin. The commoner Peter, also called Imperiola, together with the whole body of Roman soldiery was in attendance.

Ch. X. When all had taken their seats and complete silence was established, the holy emperor began thus: "How fitting it would have been for the lord pope John to be present at this glorious holy synod. I ask you, holy fathers, to give your opinion why he has refused to attend this great gathering, for you live as he does and share in all his interests." Thereupon the Roman bishops and the cardinal priests and deacons together with the whole population said:—"We are surprised that your most holy wisdom deigns to ask us this question: even the inhabitants of Iberia and Babylonia and India know the answer to it. John is not now even one of those who come in sheep's clothing and within are ravening wolves: his savageness is manifest, he is openly engaged in the devil's business, and he makes no attempt at disguise." The emperor replied:—"It seems to us right that the charges against the pope should be brought forward seriatim, and that the whole synod should then consider what course we should adopt." Thereupon the cardinal priest Peter got up and testified that he had seen the pope celebrate mass without himself communicating. John bishop of Narni and John cardinal deacon then declared that they had seen the pope ordain a deacon in a stable and at an improper season. Benedict cardinal deacon with his fellow deacons and priests said that they knew the pope had been paid for ordaining bishops and that in the city of Todi he had appointed a bishop for ten years. On the question of his sacrilege, they said, no inquiries were necessary; knowledge of it was a matter of eyesight not of hearsay. As regards his adultery, though they had no visual information, they knew for certain that he had carnal acquaintance with Rainer's widow, Stephana his father's concubine, the widow Anna, and his own niece, and that he had turned the holy palace into a brothel and resort for harlots. He had gone hunting publicly: he had blinded his spiritual father Benedict who died of his injuries: he had caused the death of cardinal subdeacon John by castrating him: he had set houses on fire and appeared in public equipped with sword, helmet and cuirass. To all this they testified; while everyone, clergy and laity alike, loudly accused him of drinking wine for love of the devil. At dice, they said, he asked the aid of Jupiter, Venus, and the other demons; he did not celebrate matins nor observe the canonical hours nor fortify himself with the sign of the cross.

Ch. XI. When he had heard this, as the Romans could not understand his native Saxon tongue, the emperor bade Liudprand bishop of Cremona to deliver the following speech in the Latin language to all the Romans. Accordingly he got up and began thus: "It often happens, and we know it by experience that men set in high positions are besmirched by the foul tongue of envy: the good displease the bad, even as the bad displease the good. For this reason we still regard as doubtful the charge against the pope which the cardinal Benedict read out and communicated to you, and we are uncertain whether it originated from zeal for righteousness or from impious envy. Therefore, unworthy as I am, by the authority of the position that has been granted me I call upon you all by the Lord God, whom no one, even if he wishes, can deceive, and by his holy mother the pure virgin Mary, and by the most precious body of the chief of apostles, in whose church this is now being read, cast no foul words against the lord pope nor accuse him of anything that he has not really done and that has not been witnessed by men on whom we can rely." Thereupon the bishops, the priests, the deacons, the rest of the clergy, and the whole Roman people cried out as one man:—"If Pope John has not committed all the shameful crimes that the deacon Benedict read out to us and done things even worse and more disgusting than those, may the most blessed Peter, whose verdict closes the gates of heaven against the unworthy and opens them for the righteous, never free us from the chains of our sins: may we be held fast in the bonds of anathema and at the last day be set on the left hand with those who said to the Lord God: 'Depart from us, we would have no knowledge of thy ways.' If you do not give us credence, at least you ought to believe the army of our lord the emperor, against whom the pope advanced five days ago, equipped with sword, shield, helmet and cuirass. It was only the intervening waters of the Tiber that saved him from being taken prisoner in that garb." Then the holy emperor said:— "There are as many witnesses to that as there are fighting men in our army." So the holy synod pronounced: "If it please the holy emperor, let a letter be sent to the lord pope, that he come here and purge himself from all these charges." Thereupon a letter was sent to him as follows:—

Ch. XII. "To the supreme pontiff and universal pope lord John, Otto, august emperor by the grace of God, together with the archbishops and bishops of Liguria, Tuscany, Saxony and France, sends greeting in the name of the Lord. When we came to Rome in God's service and inquired of your sons, the Roman bishops, cardinal priests and deacons, and the whole body of the people besides, concerning your absence, and asked them what was the reason that you were unwilling to see us, the defenders of your church and your person, they brought out such foul and filthy tales about you that we should be ashamed of them, even if they were told about actors. That your highness may not remain in complete ignorance we set down some of them briefly here; for though we would fain give them all seriatim, one day is not enough. Know then that you are charged, not by a few men but by all the clergy and laity alike, of homicide, perjury, sacrilege and of the sin of unchastity with your own kinswoman and with two sisters. They tell me too something that makes me shudder, that you have drunk wine for love of the devil, and that in dice you have asked the help of Jupiter, Venus and the other demons. Therefore we earnestly beg your paternal highness not to refuse under any pretense to come to Rome and clear yourself of all these charges. If perchance you fear the violence of a rash multitude, we declare under oath that no action is contemplated contrary to the sanction of the holy canons."

Ch. XIII. After reading this letter, the pope sent the following reply: "Bishop John, servant of God's servants, to all the bishops. We hear say that you wish to make another pope. If you do, I excommunicate you by Almighty God, and you have no power, to ordain no one or celebrate mass."

Ch. XIV. When this answer was read in the holy synod, the following clergy, who had been absent at the previous meeting, were present: from Lorraine, Henry archbishop of Trèves; from Aemilia and Liguria, Wido of Modena, Gezo of Tortona, Sigulf of Piacenza. The synod returned the following reply to the lord pope:—"To the supreme pontiff and universal lord pope John, Otto, august emperor by the grace of God, and the holy synod assembled at Rome in God's service, send greeting in the Lord's name. At our last meeting of the sixth of November we sent you a letter containing the charges made against you by your accusers and their reasons for bringing them. In the same letter we asked your highness to come to Rome, as is only just, and to clear yourself from these allegations. We have now received your answer, which is not at all of a kind suited to the character of this occasion but is more in accordance with the folly of rank indifference. There could be no reasonable excuse for not coming to the synod. But messengers from your highness ought certainly to have put in an appearance here, and assured us that you could not attend the holy synod owing to illness or some such insuperable difficulty. There is furthermore a sentence in your letter more fitting for a stupid boy than a bishop. You excommunicated us all if we appointed another bishop to the see of Rome, and yet gave us power to celebrate the mass and ordain clerical functionaries. You said:—'You have no power to ordain no one.' We always thought, or rather believed, that two negatives make an affirmative, if your authority did not weaken the verdict of the authors of old. However, let us reply, not to your words, but to your meaning. If you do not refuse to come to the synod and to clear yourself of these charges, we certainly are prepared to bow to your authority. But if—which Heaven forbid!—under any pretense you refrain from coming and defending yourself against a capital charge, especially when there is nothing to stop you, neither a sea voyage, nor bodily sickness, nor a long journey, then we shall disregard your excommunication, and rather turn it upon yourself, as we have justly the power to do. Judas, who betrayed, or rather who sold, Our Lord Jesus Christ, with the other disciples received the power of binding and loosing from their master in these words:—'Verily I say unto you, Whatsoever ye shall bind on earth shall be bound in heaven: and whatsoever ye shall loose on earth shall be loosed in heaven.' As long as Judas was a good man with his fellow disciples, he had the power to bind and loose. But when he became a murderer for greed and wished to destroy all men's lives, whom then could he loose that was bound or bind that was loosed save himself, whom he hanged in the accursed noose?" This letter was written on the twenty-second day of November and sent by the hand of the cardinal priest Adrian and the cardinal deacon Benedict.

Ch. XV. When these latter arrived at Tivoli, they could not find the pope: he had gone off into the country with bow and arrows, and no one could tell them where he was. Not being able to find him they returned with the letter to Rome and the holy synod met for the third time. On this occasion the emperor said: "We have waited for the pope's appearance, that we might complain of his conduct towards us in his presence: but since we are now assured that he will not attend, we beg you earnestly to listen to an account of his treacherous behavior. We hereby inform you, archbishops, bishops, priests, deacons, clerics, counts, judges and people, that Pope John being hard pressed by Berengar and Adalbert, our revolted subjects, sent messengers to us in Saxony, asking us for the love of God to come to Italy and free him and the church of St. Peter from their jaws. We need not tell you how much we did for him with God's assistance: you see it to-day for yourselves. But when by my help he was rescued from their hands and restored to his proper place, forgetful of the oath of loyalty which he swore to me on the body of St. Peter, he got Adalbert to come to Rome, defended him against me, stirred up tumults, and before my soldiers' eyes appeared as leader in the campaign equipped with helmet and cuirass. Let the holy synod now declare its decision." Thereupon the Roman pontiffs and the other clergy and all the people replied: "A mischief for which there is no precedent must be cauterized by methods equally novel. If the pope's moral corruption only hurt himself and not others, we should have to bear with him as best we could. But how many chaste youths by his example have become unchaste? How many worthy men by association with him have become reprobates? We therefore ask your imperial majesty that this monster, whom no virtue redeems from vice, shall be driven from the holy Roman church, and another be appointed in his place, who by the example of his goodly conversation may prove himself both ruler and benefactor, living rightly himself and setting us an example of like conduct." Then the emperor said: "I agree with what you say; nothing will please me more than for you to find such a man and to give him control of this holy universal see."

Ch. XVI. At that all cried with one voice:—"We elect as our shepherd Leo, the venerable chief notary of the holy Roman church, a man of proved worth deserving of the highest sacerdotal rank. He shall be the supreme and universal pope of the holy Roman church, and we hereby reprobate the apostate John because of his vicious life." The whole assembly repeated these words three times, and then with the emperor's consent escorted the aforesaid Leo to the Lateran Palace amid acclamations, and later at the due season in the church of St. Peter elevated him to the supreme priesthood by holy consecration and took the oath of loyalty towards him.

Ch. XVII. When this had been arranged the most holy emperor, hoping that he could stay at Rome with a few men and not wishing the Roman people to be burdened with a great army, gave many of his soldiers leave to return home. John, the so-called pope, hearing of this and knowing how easily the Romans could be bribed, sent messengers to the city, promising the people all the wealth of St. Peter and the churches, if they would fall upon the pious emperor and the lord pope Leo and impiously murder them. Why make a long tale? The Romans encouraged, or rather ensnared by the fewness of the emperor's troops and animated by the promised reward, at once sounded their trumpets and rushed in hot haste upon the emperor to kill him. He met them on the bridge over the Tiber, which the Romans had barricaded with wagons. His gallant warriors, well trained in battle with fearless hearts and fearless swords, leaped forward among the foe, like hawks falling on a flock of birds, and drove them off in panic without resistance. No hiding place, neither basket nor hollow tree trunk nor filthy sewer, could protect them in their flight. Down they fell, and as usually happens with such gallant heroes, most of their wounds were in the back. Who of the Romans then would have escaped from the massacre, had not the holy emperor yielded to the pity, which they did not deserve, and called off his men still thirsting for the enemies' blood.

Ch. XVIII. After they were all vanquished and the survivors had given hostages, the venerable pope Leo fell at the emperor's feet and begged him to give the hostages back and rely on the people's loyalty. At the request of the venerable pope Leo the holy emperor gave back the hostages, although he knew that the Romans would soon start the trouble I am about to relate. He also commended the pope to the Romans' loyalty, a lamb entrusted to wolves; and leaving Rome hastened towards Camerino and Spoleto where he had heard that Adalbert was to be found.

Ch. XIX. Meanwhile the women, with whom the so-called pope John was accustomed to carry on his voluptuous sports, being many in numbers and noble in rank, stirred up the Romans to overthrow Leo, whom God and they themselves had chosen as supreme and universal pope, and bring John back again into Rome. This they did; but by the mercy of God the venerable pope Leo escaped from their clutches and with a few attendants made his way to the protection of the most pious emperor Otto.

Ch. XX. The holy emperor was bitterly grieved at this insult, and to avenge the expulsion of the lord pope Leo and the foul injuries done by the deposed John to the cardinal deacon John and the notary Azo, one of whom had his right hand cut off, and the other his tongue, two fingers and his nose, he got his army together again and prepared to return to Rome. But before the holy emperor's forces were all assembled, the Lord decreed that every age should know how justly Pope John had been repudiated by his bishops and all the people, and how unjustly afterwards he had been welcomed back. One night when John was disporting himself with some man's wife outside Rome, the devil dealt him such a violent blow on the temples that he died of the injury within a week. Moreover at the prompting of the devil, who had struck the blow, he refused the last sacraments, as I have frequently heard testified by his friends and kinsmen who were at his death bed.

Ch. XXI. At his death the Romans, forgetful of the oath they had taken to the holy emperor, elected Benedict cardinal deacon as pope, swearing moreover that they would never abandon him but would defend him against the emperor's might. Thereupon the emperor invested the city closely and allowed no one to get out with a whole skin. Siege engines and famine completed the work, and finally in spite of the Romans he got possession of the city again, restored the venerable Leo to his proper place, and bade Benedict the usurper to appear before him.

Ch. XXII. Accordingly the supreme and universal pope the lord Leo took his seat in the church of the Lateran and with him the most holy emperor Otto, together with the Roman and Italian bishops, the archbishops of Lorraine and Saxony, the bishops, priests, deacons and the whole Roman people whose names will be given later. Before them appeared Benedict, the usurper of the apostolic chair, brought in by the men who had elected him and still wearing the pontifical vestments. To him the cardinal archdeacon Benedict addressed the following charge: "By what authority or by what law, O usurper, are you now wearing this pontifical raiment, seeing that our lord the venerable pope Leo is alive and here present, whom you and we elected to the supreme apostolic office when John had been accused and disowned? Can you deny that you swore to our lord the emperor here present that you and the other Romans would never elect nor ordain a pope without the consent of the emperor and his son King Otto?" Benedict replied:—"Have mercy upon my sin." Then the emperor, revealing by his tears how inclined he was to mercy, asked the synod not to pass hasty judgment upon Benedict. If he wished and could, let him answer the questions and defend his case: if he had neither the wish nor the power but confessed his guilt, then let him for the fear of God have some mercy shown to him. Thereupon Benedict flung himself in haste at the feet of the lord pope Leo and the emperor, and cried out: "I have sinned in usurping the holy Roman see." He then handed over the papal cloak and gave the papal staff which he was holding to pope Leo, who broke it in pieces and showed it to the people. Next the pope bade Benedict to sit down on the ground and took from him his chasuble and stole. Finally he said to all the bishops: "We hereby deprive Benedict, usurper of the holy Roman apostolic chair, of all pontifical and priestly office: but by reason of the clemency of the lord emperor Otto, by whose help we have been restored to our proper place, we allow him to keep the rank of deacon, not at Rome but in exile, which we now adjudge against him."

40. POPE GREGORY VII AND KING HENRY IV

The Investiture Controversy

ALTHOUGH THE INVESTITURE CONTROVERSY was a pan-European phenomenon, the critical eleventh-century phase most affected the development of the Empire. The contest between Pope Gregory VII (1073–85) and Emperor Henry IV (1056–1106)[1] was largely a propaganda war fought for the allegiance of the German episcopate and nobility nominally over which power had the right to install bishops and abbots. This series of letters by Gregory and Henry presents the positions of each side and their attempts to best their opponents in public opinion.

Sources: Theodor E. Mommsen and Karl F. Morrison, *Imperial Lives and Letters of the Eleventh Century* (New York: Columbia University Press, 1962); Ephraim Emerton, *The Correspondence of Pope Gregory VII* (New York: Columbia University Press, 1932).

Further Reading: Uta-Renate Blumenthal, *The Investiture Controversy: Church and Monarchy from the Ninth to the Twelfth Century* (Philadelphia, University of Pennsylvania Press, 1988).

The Correspondence of Pope Gregory VII

Book III, 3 (July 20, 1075)

Gregory ... to King Henry, greeting ...

Among other praiseworthy actions, my beloved son, to which you are reported to have risen in your efforts at self-improvement, there are two that have specially commended you to your holy mother, the Roman church: first, that you have valiantly withstood those guilty of simony; and second, that you freely approve, and strenuously desire to enforce, the chastity of the clergy as servants of God. For these reasons you have given us cause to expect of you still higher and better things with God's help. Wherefore we earnestly pray that you may hold fast by these, and we beseech our Lord God that he may deign to increase your zeal more and more.

But now, as regards the church of Bamberg, which according to the ordinance of its founder [King Henry II] belongs to the holy and apostolic see as the shoulder to the head, that is, as a most intimate member, by a certain special bond of duty, we are greatly disturbed and we are forced by the obligation of our office to come to the rescue of its distress with all our powers. That simoniac so-called bishop Hermann, summoned to a Roman synod this present year, failed to appear. He came within a short distance of Rome, but there halted and sent forward messengers with ample gifts, trying, with his well-known trickery, to impose upon our innocence and, if possible, to corrupt the integrity of our colleagues by a pecuniary bargain. But when this turned out contrary to his hopes, convinced of his own damnation he hastily retreated and, soothing the minds of the clergy who were with him by smooth and deceitful promises, declared that if he were able to regain his own country he would resign his bishopric and enter the monastic life.

How he kept these promises Your Highness, beloved son, well knows. With increasing audacity he plundered the clergy who were upholding the welfare and the honor of their church, and had not your royal power restrained him, as we are informed, he would have completely ruined them. After careful consideration of these outrages we removed him from his episcopal and

---

1   Henry was crowned king in 1054 before the death of his father Henry III. He was crowned emperor in 1084 by Antipope Clement III.

priestly office. Further, as he dared to oppress the church of Bamberg, under the apostolic patronage of St. Peter, more cruelly and more harshly than before, we placed him in the bonds of anathema until he should lay down his usurped dignity and, nevertheless, present himself for trial before the apostolic see.

Now, therefore, most excellent son, we ask Your Highness and urge you by our dutiful obligation to take counsel with men of piety and so to regulate the affairs of that church according to God's order, that you may be worthy of divine protection through the intercession of St. Peter, in whose name and under whose patronage the church was founded.

What I have written regarding this case to our colleague Siegfried, bishop of Mainz, and the clergy and people of Bamberg, you may learn with certainty from the letters dispatched to them.[2]

To King Henry IV, Admonishing Him to Show
More Deference to the Holy See and Its Decrees
Book III, 10, p. 263 (Dec. 8, 1075 [or Jan. 8, 1076])

Gregory, bishop, servant of God's servants, to King Henry, greeting and the apostolic benediction—but with the understanding that he obeys the apostolic see as becomes a Christian king.

Considering and weighing carefully to how strict a judge we must render an account of the stewardship committed to us by St. Peter, prince of the apostles, we have hesitated to send you the apostolic benediction, since you are reported to be in voluntary communication with men who are under the censure of the apostolic see and of a synod. If this is true, you yourself know that you cannot receive the favor of God nor the apostolic blessing unless you shall first put away those excommunicated persons and force them to do penance and shall yourself obtain absolution and forgiveness for your sin by due repentance and satisfaction. Wherefore we counsel Your Excellency, if you feel

yourself guilty in this matter, to make your confession at once to some pious bishop who, with our sanction, may impose upon you a penance suited to the offense, may absolve you and with your consent in writing may be free to send us a true report of the manner of your penance.

We marvel exceedingly that you have sent us so many devoted letters and displayed such humility by the spoken words of your legates, calling yourself a son of our Holy Mother Church and subject to us in the faith, singular in affection, a leader in devotion, commending yourself with every expression of gentleness and reverence, and yet in action showing yourself most bitterly hostile to the canons and apostolic decrees in those duties especially required by loyalty to the Church. Not to mention other cases, the way you have observed your promises in the Milan affair, made through your mother and through bishops, our colleagues, whom we sent to you, and what your intentions were in making them is evident to all. And now, heaping wounds upon wounds, you have handed over the sees of Fermo and Spoleto—if indeed a church may be given over by any human power to persons entirely unknown to us, whereas it is not lawful to consecrate anyone except after probation and with due knowledge.

It would have been becoming to you, since you confess yourself to be a son of the Church, to give more respectful attention to the master of the Church, that is, to Peter, prince of the apostles. To him, if you are of the Lord's flock, you have been committed for your pasture, since Christ said to him: "Peter, feed my sheep," and again: "To thee are given the keys of heaven, and whatsoever thou shalt bind on earth shall be bound in Heaven and whatsoever thou shalt loose on earth shall be loosed in heaven." Now, while we, unworthy sinner that we are, stand in his place of power, still whatever you send to us, whether in writing or by word of mouth, he himself receives, and while we read what is written or hear the voice of those who speak, he discerns with subtle insight from

---

2   In December 1075, almost six months to the day after Henry's great victory on the Unstrut over the Saxons, Gregory, prosecuting the policy he had begun at his Lenten Synod earlier in 1075, threatened to excommunicate Henry should he not shun the company of the bishops excommunicated at the Synod, obey the synodal edict against lay investiture, and conform to papal orders in regard to imperial churches in Italy. Henry received Gregory's letters early in 1076 and vigorously accepted their implicit challenge, dispatching at once the first four letters reprinted here and summoning the Synod of Brixen, where the majority of German bishops joined him in pronouncing Gregory's deposition.

what spirit the message comes. Wherefore Your Highness should beware lest any defect of will toward the apostolic see be found in your words or in your messages and should pay due reverence, not to us but to Almighty God, in all matters touching the welfare of the Christian faith and the status of the Church. And this we say although our Lord deigned to declare: "He who heareth you heareth me; and he who despiseth you despiseth me."

We know that one who does not refuse to obey God in those matters in which we have spoken according to the statutes of the holy fathers does not scorn to observe our admonitions even as if he had received them from the lips of the apostle himself. For if our Lord, out of reverence for the chair of Moses, commanded the apostles to observe the teaching of the scribes and pharisees who sat thereon, there can be no doubt that the apostolic and gospel teaching, whose seat and foundation is Christ, should be accepted and maintained by those who are chosen to the service of teaching.

At a synod held at Rome during the current year, and over which Divine Providence willed us to preside, several of your subjects being present, we saw that the order of the Christian religion had long been greatly disturbed and its chief and proper function, the redemption of souls, had fallen low and through the wiles of the Devil had been trodden under foot. Startled by this danger and by the manifest ruin of the Lord's flock we returned to the teaching of the holy fathers, declaring no novelties nor any inventions of our own, but holding that the primary and only rule of discipline and the well-trodden way of the saints should again be sought and followed, all wandering paths to be abandoned, for we know that there is no other way of salvation and eternal life for the flock of Christ and their shepherds except that shown by him who said: "I am the door and he who enters by me shall be saved and shall find pasture." This was taught by the apostles and observed by the holy fathers and we have learned it from the Gospels and from every page of Holy Writ.

This edict [against lay investiture], which some who place the honor of men above that of God call an intolerable burden, we, using the right word, call rather a truth and a light necessary for salvation, and we have given judgment that it is to be heartily accepted and obeyed, not only by you

and your subjects but by all princes and peoples who confess and worship Christ—though it is our especial wish and would be especially fitting for you, that you should excel others in devotion to Christ as you are their superior in fame, in station and in valor.

Nevertheless, in order that these demands may not seem to you too burdensome or unfair we have sent you word by your own liegemen not to be troubled by this reform of an evil practice but to send us prudent and pious legates from your own people. If these can show in any reasonable way how we can moderate the decision of the holy fathers [at the Council] saving the honor of the eternal king and without peril to our own soul, we will condescend to hear their counsel. It would in fact have been the fair thing for you, even if you had not been so graciously admonished, to make reasonable inquiry of us in what respect we had offended you or assailed your honor, before you proceeded to violate the apostolic decrees. But how little you cared for our warnings or for doing right was shown by your later actions.

However, since the long-enduring patience of God summons you to improvement, we hope that with increase of understanding your heart and mind may be turned to obey the commands of God. We warn you with a father's love that you accept the rule of Christ, that you consider the peril of preferring your own honor to his, that you do not hamper by your actions the freedom of that Church which he deigned to bind to himself as a bride by a divine union, but, that she may increase as greatly as possible, you will begin to lend to Almighty God and to St. Peter, by whom also your own glory may merit increase, the aid of your valor by faithful devotion.

Now you ought to recognize your special obligation to them for the triumph over your enemies which they have granted you, and while they are making you happy and singularly prosperous, they ought to find your devotion increased by their favor to you. That the fear of God, in whose hand is all the might of kings and emperors, may impress this upon you more than any admonitions of mine, bear in mind what happened to Saul after he had won a victory by command of the prophet, how he boasted of his triumph, scorning the prophet's admonitions, and how he was rebuked by the Lord, and also what favor followed David the King as a reward for his humility in the midst of the tokens of his bravery.

Finally, as to what we have read in your letters and do not mention here we will give you no decided answer until your legates, Radbod, Adalbert and Odescalcus, to whom we entrust this, have returned to us and have more fully reported your decision upon the matters which we commissioned them to discuss with you.

The Roman Lenten Synod of 1076
Book III, 10(a) (Feb. 14–20, 1076)

In the year of the Incarnation 1075, our lord Pope Gregory held a synod at Rome in the church of Our Savior which is called the Constantiniana. A great number of bishops and abbots and clergy and laymen of various orders were present.

At this synod, among the decrees promulgated was the excommunication of Siegfried, archbishop of Mainz, in the following form:

In accordance with the judgment of the Holy Spirit and by authority of the blessed apostles Peter and Paul, we suspend from every episcopal function, and exclude from the communion of the body and blood of the Lord, Siegfried, archbishop of Mainz, who has attempted to cut off the bishops and abbots of Germany from the Holy Roman Church, their spiritual mother—unless perchance in the hour of death, and then only if he shall come to himself and truly repent. Those who voluntarily joined his schism and still persist in their evil deeds, we also suspend from all episcopal functions. Those, however, who consented against their will we allow time until the feast of St. Peter; but if within that term they shall not have given due satisfaction in person or by messengers in our presence, they shall thenceforth be deprived of their episcopal office.

Excommunication of the Bishops of Lombardy

The bishops of Lombardy who, in contempt of canonical and apostolic authority, have joined in a sworn conspiracy against St. Peter, prince of the apostles, we suspend from their episcopal functions and exclude them from the communion of Holy Church.

[Here follows a list of excommunications of prelates and laymen beyond the Alps, ending with the proclamation against King Henry IV.]

Excommunication of Henry IV

O blessed Peter, prince of the apostles, mercifully incline thine ear, we [*sic*] pray, and hear me, thy servant, whom thou hast cherished from infancy and hast delivered until now from the hand of the wicked who have hated and still hate me for my loyalty to thee. Thou art my witness, as are also my Lady, the Mother of God, and the blessed Paul, thy brother among all the saints, that thy Holy Roman Church forced me against my will to be its ruler. I had no thought of ascending thy throne as a robber, nay, rather would I have chosen to end my life as a pilgrim than to seize upon thy place for earthly glory and by devices of this world. Therefore, by thy favor, not by any works of mine, I believe that it is and has been thy will, that the Christian people especially committed to thee should render obedience to me, thy especially constituted representative. To me is given by thy grace the power of binding and loosing in heaven and upon earth.

Wherefore, relying upon this commission, and for the honor and defense of thy Church, in the name of Almighty God, Father, Son and Holy Spirit, through thy power and authority, I deprive King Henry, son of the emperor Henry, who has rebelled against thy Church with unheard-of audacity, of the government over the whole kingdom of Germany and Italy, and I release all Christian men from the allegiance which they have sworn or may swear to him, and I forbid anyone to serve him as king. For it is fitting that he who seeks to diminish the glory of thy Church should lose the glory which he seems to have.

And, since he has refused to obey as a Christian should or to return to the God whom he has abandoned by taking part with excommunicated persons, has spurned my warnings which I gave him for his soul's welfare, as thou knowest, and has separated himself from thy Church and tried to rend it asunder, I bind him in the bonds of anathema in thy stead and I bind him thus as commissioned by thee, that the nations may know and be convinced that thou art Peter and that upon thy rock the son of the living God has built his Church and the gates of hell shall not prevail against it.

A General Apology to All the Faithful in Germany
Epistolae collectae, Book IV, 14 (1076)

Gregory … to all bishops, dukes, counts and other loyal defenders of the faith in Germany, greeting …

We hear that certain among you are in doubt regarding our excommunication of the king and are asking whether he was lawfully condemned; also whether our sentence was pronounced with due deliberation and under authority of a legal right of inquiry. We have therefore taken pains to make clear to the understanding of all by what motives, as our conscience bears witness, we were led to this act of excommunication. And we do this, not so much in order to make public by our own complaint the several cases which, alas! are only too well known, as to silence the accusations of those who feel that we took up the sword of the spirit rashly and were moved rather by our own impulses than by a holy fear and a zeal for justice.

While we were still in the office of deacon, sinister and dishonorable rumors came to us regarding the conduct of the king, and we sent him frequent admonitions both by letter and by legates, for the sake of the imperial station and personal character of his father and mother as well as from our hope and wishes for his improvement, warning him to desist from his evil ways and, mindful of his noble birth and station, so to order his life as would be fitting for a king and, God willing, for an emperor. And later, when we had reached the dignity of supreme pontiff—unworthy as we were—and he had grown in years and in vice, we, knowing that God would require his soul at our hands the more strictly now that authority and freedom were given to us above all others, besought him the more earnestly in every way, by argument, by persuasion and by threats, to amend his life. He replied with frequent letters of devotion, pleading his frail and fickle youth and the evil counsels of those in power at his court and promising from day to day that he would comply with our instructions—he promised in words, but

in fact he trampled them under foot with ever-increasing misbehavior.

In the meantime we summoned to repentance certain of his intimates by whose intrigues and advice he had profaned bishoprics and many monasteries, for money installing wolves instead of shepherds. We ordered them, while there was still time, to give back the church property, which they had received with sacrilegious hand through this accursed commerce, to its rightful owners and to give satisfaction to God for their sins by penitential service. But when we learned that they refused to do this after due time and continued in their accustomed evil ways, we cut them off from the communion and body of the whole Church as guilty of sacrilege and as servants and members of the Devil, and we warned the king to banish them from his household and from his counsels and to desist from all association with them as persons under excommunication.

But again, when the Saxon uprising against the king was gaining strength and he saw that the resources and defenses of the kingdom were failing him to a great extent, he wrote us a letter of supplication full of humility. In this letter he confessed his fault before Almighty God and St. Peter and ourself and besought us by our apostolic authority to correct his offenses in church affairs against the canon law and the decrees of holy fathers. He also promised to obey us in all respects and to give us his faithful aid and counsel. And afterward, being admitted to penance by our colleagues and legates, Humbert, bishop of Palestrina, and Gerald, bishop of Ostia, whom we had sent to him, he reaffirmed all these promises in their hands, taking his oath by the sacred scarfs which they wore around their necks.

Then some time later, after a battle with the Saxons, he performed his sacrifices of gratitude to God for his victory by promptly breaking his vows of amendment, fulfilling none of his promises, receiving the excommunicated persons into his intimate counsels and bringing ruin upon the churches as he had done before.

With the greatest grief, then, although we had lost almost all hope of his improvement after he had treated with scorn the gifts of the heavenly king, we decided to make a further attempt, desiring rather that he should listen to apostolic gentleness than that he should suffer from our severity. We therefore wrote warning him to remember his promises and consider to whom they had been made; not to imagine that he could deceive God, whose anger when he begins to give judgment is the more severe the longer his patience has endured; and not to dishonor God, who has honored him, or use his power in contempt of God and in despite of apostolic authority, knowing as he does that God resists the proud but shows favor to the humble.

Besides this, we sent to him three clergymen, his own subjects, through whom we gave him private warnings to do penance for his crimes, horrible to describe, but known to many and published through many lands and for which the authority of law, human and divine, commands that he should not only be excommunicated until he should give due satisfaction, but should be deposed from his royal office without hope of restitution.

Finally we warned him that, unless he should exclude the excommunicated persons from his intimacy, we could pass no other sentence upon him but that, being cut off from the Church, he should join the fellowship of the condemned, with whom, rather than with Christ, he has chosen to take his part. And yet, if he were willing to listen to our warnings and reform his conduct, we called upon God—and we call upon him still—to bear witness how greatly we should rejoice in his honor and his welfare, and with what affection we should welcome him into the bosom of Holy Church as one who, being the chief of a nation and ruling over a widespread kingdom, is bound to be the defender of the Catholic peace and righteousness.

On the other hand, his actions prove how little he cares either for our written words or for the messages sent by our legates. He was angered that anyone should reprove or correct him, and could not be led back to any improvement, but, carried away by a still greater fury of self-confidence, he did not stop until he had caused almost all the bishops in Italy and as many as he could in Germany to suffer shipwreck of their faith and had compelled them to refuse the obedience and honor which they owed to St. Peter and the apostolic see and which had been granted to these by Our Lord Jesus Christ.

When, therefore, we saw that we had reached the limit: namely, first, that he refused to give up his relations with those who had been excommunicated for sacrilege and the heresy of simony; second, because he was not willing, I will not say to perform, but even to promise repentance for his crimes, for the penance which he had sworn to in the hands of our legates was a fraudulent one; finally, because he had dared to divide the body of Christ, that is, the unity of the Church—for all these crimes, I say, we excommunicated him through the decision of a council. Since we could not bring him back to the way of salvation by gentle means, we tried, with God's help, to do so by severity, and if—which God forbid!—he should not be afraid even of the severest penalty, our soul should at least be free from the charge of negligence or timidity.

If, then, anyone thinks that this sentence was imposed illegally or without reason, if he is willing to apply common sense to the sacred law he will take our part, will listen patiently to what is taught, not by ourself but by divine authority, and is sanctioned by the unanimous opinion of the holy fathers, and he will agree with us. We do not believe that any true believer who knows the canon law can be caught by this error and can say in his heart, even though he dare not openly proclaim it, that this action was not well taken. Nevertheless, even if—which God forbid!—we had bound him with this chain without due cause or in irregular form, the judgment is not to be rejected on this ground, as the holy fathers declare, but absolution is to be sought in all humility.

Now do you, my beloved, who have not desired to forsake the righteousness of God on account of the wrath of the king or of any danger, take no thought of the folly of those who "shall be consumed for their cursing and lying," but stand fast like men and comfort yourselves in the Lord. Know that you are on the side of him who, as unconquered king and glorious victor, will judge the living and the dead, rendering to each one according to his works. Of his manifold rewards you may be assured if you remain faithful to the end and stand firm in his truth. For this we pray God without ceasing, that he may give you strength to be established by the Holy Spirit in his name. May he turn the heart of the king to repentance and cause him to understand that we and you love him far more truly than those who now favor and support his evil doing.

And if, under God's blessing, he shall return to his senses, no matter what he may be plotting against us, he shall find us always ready to receive him back into holy communion in accordance with your affectionate counsel.

To All in Authority in Germany, Urging Their Support in His Struggle with Henry IV
Book IV, 1 (July 25, 1076)

Gregory ... to all his brethren in Christ, bishops, abbots and priests, dukes, princes and knights, all dwellers in the Roman Empire who truly love the Christian faith and the honor of St. Peter, greeting ...

We render thanks to Almighty God, who for the exceeding love he bore to us did not spare his own son, but gave him for us all, to protect and govern his Church, beyond all our deserts, beyond the expectation even of good men. You know, beloved brethren, that in this time of peril when Antichrist is busy everywhere by means of his members, scarce one is to be found who truly loves God and his honor, or who prefers his commands rather than earthly profit and the favor of the princes of this world. But he who rejects not his own and daily changes sinners from his left side to his right has looked upon you with calm and favoring countenance and has set you up against his enemies to the healing of many nations, that it might please you rather to be steadfast in the perils of this present life than to set the favor of men above the glory and honor of the eternal king. So doing you will not pass over with deaf ears that saying of the prince of the apostles, "Ye are a chosen generation, a royal priesthood," and also, "We ought to obey God rather than men."

You well know, my brethren, for how long a time our Holy Church has had to bear the unheard-of wickedness and manifold wrongdoing of the king—would that I could call him Christian or [truly] your king—and what misfortunes it has suffered at his hands under the lead of our ancient enemy. Already during our diaconate we sent him words of warning out of our affection for him and

our devotion to his parents, and after we came to the priestly office—unworthy as we are—frequently and earnestly have we striven, with the help of pious men, to bring him to his senses. But how he has acted against all this, how he has rendered evil for good, and how he has raised his heel against St. Peter and striven to rend in twain the Church which God entrusted to him you know, and it has been spread abroad throughout the world. But, since it belongs to our office to regard men and not their vices, to resist the wicked that they may repent, and to abhor evil but not men, we admonish you by authority of St. Peter, prince of the apostles, and call upon you as our beloved brethren to endeavor in every way to snatch him from the hand of the Devil and rouse him to a true repentance, that we may be able with God's help to bring him back in brotherly love into the bosom of that Church which he has sought to divide. This, however, in such ways that he may not be able by some fraud to disturb the Christian faith and trample our Holy Church under his feet.

But if he will not listen to you and shall choose to follow the Devil rather than Christ and shall prefer the counsel of those who have long been under excommunication for simoniacal heresy to yours, then we shall find ways under divine inspiration to rescue the already declining Church Universal by serving God rather than man.

Now do you, my brethren and fellow priests, by authority of St. Peter, receive and bring back into the bosom of our Holy Mother Church as many as shall repent of those who have not been ashamed to set the king above Almighty God and to deny the law of Christ, if not in words, at least by their deeds—as the apostle says, "They profess that they know God; but in works they deny him"—these receive, that you may be worthy to rejoice in Heaven with the angels of God. In all things keep before your eyes the honor of your holy father, the prince of the apostles. But all those, bishops or laymen, who, led astray by fear or the favor of men, have not withdrawn from association with the king, but by favoring him have not feared to hand over the king's soul and their own to the Devil—have no dealings or friendship with these unless they shall repent and perform the proper acts of penance. For these are they who hate and slay their own souls and the king's as well, and are not ashamed to throw the kingdom, their fatherland and the Christian faith into confusion. For, as we are subject to the word of the prophet: "If thou speakest not to warn the wicked from his wicked way ... his soul will I require at thine hand," and again, "Cursed be he that shall hold back his sword from blood," that is, shall hold back the word of reproof from smiting those of evil life, so they, unless they obey, are subject to the wrath of the divine judgment and to the penalties of idolatry, as Samuel bears witness. And God is our witness that we are moved against evil princes and faithless priests by no question of worldly advantage, but by our sense of duty and by the power of the apostolic see which continually weighs upon us. It were better for us, if need were, to pay the debt of mortality at the hands of tyrants rather than to consent in silence to the ruin of the Christian law through fear or for any advantage. We know what our fathers said: "He who does not oppose evil men out of regard for his station gives his consent; and he who removes not that which ought to be cut out is guilty of the offense."

May Almighty God, from whom all good things proceed, guard and strengthen your hearts through the merits of Our Lady, the Queen of Heaven, and the intercession of the blessed apostles Peter and Paul, and may he always pour upon you the grace of his Holy Spirit that you may do what is pleasing to him. May you be worthy to rescue his Bride, our Mother, from the jaws of the wolf, and may you attain to his supreme glory, cleansed of all your sins.

To Bishop Hermann of Metz, in Defense of the Excommunication of Henry IV
Book IV, 2 (Aug. 25, 1076)

Gregory ... to Hermann, bishop of Metz, greeting ...

You have asked a great many questions of me, a very busy man, and have sent me an extremely urgent messenger. Wherefore I beg you to bear with me patiently if my reply is not sufficiently ample.

The bearer will report to you as to my health and as to the conduct of the Romans and the Normans in regard to me. As to the other matters about which you inquire—would that the blessed Peter himself, who is many times honored or wronged in me his servant, such as I am, might give the answers!

There is no need to ask me who are the excommunicated bishops, priests or laymen; since beyond a doubt they are those who are known to be in communication with the excommunicated king Henry—if, indeed, he may properly be called king. They do not hesitate to place the fear and favor of men before the commands of the eternal King nor to expose their king to the wrath of Almighty God by giving him their support.

He too feared not to incur the penalty of excommunication by dealing with followers who had been excommunicated for the heresy of simony nor to draw others into excommunication through their dealings with him. How can we think of such things but in the words of the psalmist: "The fool hath said in his heart there is no God," or again: "They are all gone astray in their wills."

Now to those who say: "A king may not be excommunicated," although we are not bound to reply to such a fatuous notion, yet, lest we seem to pass over their foolishness impatiently we will recall them to sound doctrine by directing their attention to the words and acts of the holy fathers. Let them read what instructions St. Peter gave to the Christian community in his ordination of St. Clement in regard to one who had not the approval of the pontiff. Let them learn why the apostle said, "Being prompt to punish every disobedience"; and of whom he said, "Do not even take food with such people." Let them consider why Pope Zachary deposed a king of the Franks and released all his subjects from their oaths of allegiance. Let them read in the records [*registra*] of St. Gregory how in his grants to certain churches he not merely excommunicated kings and dukes who opposed him but declared them deprived of their royal dignity. And let them not forget that St. Ambrose not only excommunicated the emperor Theodosius but forbade him to stand in the room of the priests within the church.

But perhaps those people would imagine that when God commended his Church to Peter three times saying, "Feed my sheep," he made an exception of kings! Why do they not see, or rather confess with shame that, when God gave to Peter as leader the power of binding and loosing in heaven and on earth he excepted no one, withheld no one from his power? For if a man says that he cannot be bound by the ban of the Church, it is evident that he could not be loosed by its authority, and he who shamelessly denies this cuts himself off absolutely from Christ. If the holy apostolic see, through the princely power divinely bestowed upon it, has jurisdiction over spiritual things, why not also over temporal things? When kings and princes of this world set their own dignity and profit higher than God's righteousness and seek their own honor, neglecting the glory of God, you know whose members they are, to whom they give their allegiance. Just as those who place God above their own wills and obey his commands rather than those of men are members of Christ, so those of whom we spoke are members of Antichrist. If then spiritual men are to be judged, as is fitting, why should not men of the world be held to account still more strictly for their evil deeds?

Perchance they imagine that royal dignity is higher than that of bishops; but how great the difference between them is, they may learn from the difference in their origins. The former came from human lust of power; the latter was instituted by divine grace. The former constantly strives after empty glory; the latter aspires ever toward the heavenly life. Let them learn what Anastasius the pope said to Anastasius the emperor regarding these two dignities, and how St. Ambrose in his pastoral letter distinguished between them. He said: "If you compare the episcopal dignity with the splendor of kings and the crowns of princes, these are far more inferior to it than lead is to glistening gold." And knowing this, the emperor Constantine chose, not the highest, but the lowest seat among the bishops; for he knew that God resists the haughty, but confers his grace upon the humble.

Meantime, be it known to you, my brother, that, upon receipt of letters from certain of our clerical brethren and political leaders we have given apostolic authority to those bishops to absolve such persons excommunicated by us as have dared to cut themselves loose from the king. But as to the king himself, we have absolutely forbidden anyone to dare to absolve him until we shall have been made certain by competent witnesses of his sincere repentance and reparation; so that at the same time we may determine, if divine grace shall have visited him, in what form we may grant him absolution, to God's glory and his own salvation. For it has not escaped our knowledge that there are some of you who, pretending to be authorized by us, but really led astray by fear or the favor of men, would presume to absolve him if I [sic] did not forbid them, thus widening the wound instead of healing it. And if others, bishops in very truth, should oppose them, they would say that these were actuated, not by a sense of justice, but by personal hostility.

Moreover ordination and consecration by those bishops who dare to communicate with an excommunicated king become in the sight of God an execration, according to St. Gregory. For since they in their pride refuse to obey the apostolic see, they incur the charge of idolatry, according to Samuel. If he is said to be of God who is stirred by divine love to punish crime, certainly he is not of God who refuses to rebuke the lives of carnal men so far as in him lies. And if he is accursed who withholds his sword from blood—that is to say, the word of preaching from destroying the life of the flesh—how much more is he accursed who through fear or favor drives his brother's soul into everlasting perdition! Furthermore you cannot find in the teaching of any of the holy fathers that men accursed and excommunicated can convey to others that blessing and that divine grace which they do not fear to deny by their actions.

Meanwhile, we order you to ask our brother, the venerable archbishop of Trier, to forbid the bishop of Toul to interfere in the affairs of the abbess of Remiremont and, with your assistance, to annul whatever action he has taken against her.

But, concerning Matilda, daughter to us both and faithful servant of St. Peter, I will do as you wish. I am not yet quite clear as to her future status—*deo gubernante*. I wish you, however, clearly to understand that although I remember her late husband Godfrey as a frequent offender against God, I am not affected by his enmity toward me nor by any other personal feeling, but moved by my fraternal affection for you and by Matilda's prayers I pray God for his salvation.

May Almighty God, through the mediation of Mary, Queen of Heaven, ever virgin, and the authority of the blessed apostles Peter and Paul granted by him to them, absolve you and all our brethren who uphold the Christian faith and the dignity of the apostolic see from all your sins, increase your faith, hope and charity and strengthen you in your defense of his law that you may be worthy to attain to everlasting life.

To All the Faithful in Germany, Counseling Them to Choose a New King in the Event that Henry IV Cannot Be Brought to Repentance
Book IV, 3 (Sept. 3, 1076)

Gregory ... to all the beloved brethren in Christ, fellow bishops, dukes, counts and all defenders of the Christian faith dwelling in the kingdom of Germany, greeting and absolution from all their sins through the apostolic benediction.

If you weigh carefully the decree in which Henry, king so-called, was excommunicated in a holy synod by judgment of the Holy Spirit, you will see beyond a doubt what action ought to be taken in his case. It will there be seen why he was bound in the bondage of anathema and deposed from his royal dignity, and that every people formerly subject to him is released from its oath of allegiance.

But because, as God knows, we are not moved against him by any pride or empty desire for the things of this world, but only by zeal for the Holy See and our common mother, the Church, we admonish you in the Lord Jesus and beg you as beloved brethren to receive him kindly if with his whole heart he shall turn to God, and to show toward him not merely justice which would prohibit him from ruling, but mercy which wipes out many crimes. Be mindful, I beg you, of the frailty of our common human nature and do not forget the pious and noble memory of his father and his mother, rulers the like of whom cannot be found in this our day.

Apply, however, the oil of kindness to his wounds in such a way that the scars may not grow foul by neglect of the wine of discipline and thus the honor of Holy Church and of the Roman Empire fall in widespread ruin through our indifference. Let those evil counselors be far removed from him, who, excommunicated for the heresy of simony, have not scrupled to infect their master with their own disease and by diverse crimes have seduced him into splitting our Holy Church in twain and have brought upon him the wrath of God and of Saint Peter. Let other advisors be given him who care more for his advantage than their own and who place God above all earthly profit. Let him no longer imagine that Holy Church is his subject or his handmaid but rather let him recognize her as his superior and his mistress. Let him not be puffed up with the spirit of pride and defend practices invented to check the liberty of Holy Church, but let him observe the teaching of the holy fathers which divine power taught them for our salvation.

But if he shall have given you reliable information as to these and other demands which may properly be made upon him, we desire that you give us immediate notice by competent messengers so that, taking counsel together, we may with God's help decide upon the right course of action. Above all, we forbid, in the name of St. Peter, that any one of you should venture to absolve him from excommunication until the above-mentioned information shall have been given to us and you shall have received the consent of the Apostolic See and our renewed answer. We are distrustful of the conflicting counsels of different persons and have our suspicions of the fear and favor of men.

But now, if through the crimes of many [others]—which God forbid!—he shall not with whole heart turn to God, let another ruler of the kingdom be found by divine favor, such an one as shall bind himself by unquestionable obligations to carry out the measures we have indicated and any others that may be necessary for the safety of the Christian religion and of the whole empire. Further, in order that we may confirm your choice—if it shall be necessary to make a choice—and support the new order in our time, as we know was done by the holy fathers before us, inform us at the earliest possible moment as to the person, the character and the occupation of the candidate. Proceeding thus with pious and practical method you will deserve well of us in the present case and will merit the favor of the apostolic see by divine grace and the blessing of St. Peter, prince of the apostles.

As to the oath which you have taken to our best beloved daughter, the empress Agnes, in case her son should die before her, you need have no scruples, because, if she should be led by over-fondness for her son to resist the course of justice or, on the other hand, should defend justice and consent to his deposition, you will know how to do the rest. This, however, would seem to be advisable: that when you have come to a firm decision among yourselves that he shall be removed, you should take counsel with her and with us as to the person to be entrusted with the government of the kingdom. Then either she will give her assent to the common judgment of us all, or the authority of the apostolic see will release all bonds which stand in the way of justice.

With regard to the excommunicated persons, I remind you that I have already given to those of you who defend the Christian faith as bishops authority to absolve them, and I hereby confirm this—provided only that they truly repent and with humble hearts apply for penance.

To the German Princes, Giving an Account of Canossa
Book IV, 12 (End of January 1077)

Whereas, for love of justice you have made common cause with us and taken the same risks in the warfare of Christian service, we have taken special care to send you this accurate account of the king's penitential humiliation, his absolution and the course of the whole affair from his entrance into Italy to the present time.

According to the arrangement made with the legates sent to us by you we came to Lombardy about twenty days before the date at which some of your leaders were to meet us at the pass and waited for their arrival to enable us to cross over into that region. But when the time had elapsed and we were told that on account of the troublous times—as indeed we well believe—no escort could be sent to us, having no other way of coming to you we were in no little anxiety as to what was our best course to take.

Meanwhile we received certain information that the king was on the way to us. Before he entered Italy he sent us word that he would make satisfaction to God and St. Peter and offered to amend his way of life and to continue obedient to us, provided only that he should obtain from us absolution and the apostolic blessing. For a long time we delayed our reply and held long consultations, reproaching him bitterly through messengers back and forth for his outrageous conduct, until finally, of his own accord and without any show of hostility or defiance, he came with a few followers to the fortress of Canossa where we were staying. There, on three successive days, standing before the castle gate, laying aside all royal insignia, barefooted and in coarse attire, he ceased not with many tears to beseech the apostolic help and comfort until all who were present or who had heard the story were so moved by pity and compassion that they pleaded his cause with prayers and tears. All marveled at our unwonted severity, and some even cried out that we were showing, not the seriousness of apostolic authority, but rather the cruelty of a savage tyrant.

At last, overcome by his persistent show of penitence and the urgency of all present, we released him from the bonds of anathema and received him into the grace of Holy Mother Church, accepting from him the guarantees described below, confirmed by the signatures of the abbot of Cluny, of our daughters, the Countess Matilda and the Countess Adelaide, and other princes, bishops and laymen who seemed to be of service to us.

And now that these matters have been arranged, we desire to come over into your country at the first opportunity, that with God's help we may more fully establish all matters pertaining to the peace of the Church and the good order of the land. For we wish you clearly to understand that, as you may see in the written guarantees, the whole negotiation is held in suspense, so that our coming and your unanimous consent are in the highest degree necessary. Strive, therefore, all of you, as you love justice, to hold in good faith the obligations into which you have entered. Remember that we have not bound ourselves to the king in any way except by frank statement—as our custom is—that he may expect our aid for his safety and his honor, whether through justice or through mercy, and without peril to his soul or to our own.

To Hermann of Metz, in Defense of the Papal Policy toward Henry IV
Book VIII, 21 (March 15, 1081)

Gregory ... to his beloved brother in Christ, Hermann, bishop of Metz, greeting ...

We know you to be ever ready to bear labor and peril in defense of the truth, and doubt not that this is a gift from God. It is a part of his unspeakable grace and his marvelous mercy that he never permits his chosen ones to wander far or to be completely cast down; but rather, after a time of persecution and wholesome probation, makes them stronger than they were before. On the other hand, just as among cowards one who is worse than the rest is broken down by fear, so among the brave one who acts more bravely than the rest is stirred thereby to new activity. We remind you of this by way of exhortation that you may stand more joyfully in the front ranks of the Christian host, the more confident you are that they are the nearest to God the conqueror.

You ask us to fortify you against the madness of those who babble with accursed tongues about the authority of the holy apostolic see not being able to excommunicate King Henry as one who despises the law of Christ, a destroyer of churches and of the empire, a promoter and partner of heresies, nor to release anyone from his oath of fidelity to him; but it has not seemed necessary to reply to this request, seeing that so many and such convincing proofs are to be found in Holy Scripture. Nor do we believe that those who abuse and contradict the truth to their utter damnation do this as much from ignorance as from wretched and desperate folly. And no wonder! It is ever the way of the wicked to protect their own iniquities by calling upon others like themselves; for they think it of no account to incur the penalty of falsehood.

To cite but a few out of the multitude of proofs: Who does not remember the words of our Lord and Savior Jesus Christ: "Thou art Peter and on this rock I will build my Church, and the gates of hell shall not prevail against it. And I will give thee the keys of the kingdom of heaven and whatsoever thou shalt bind on earth shall be bound in heaven and whatsoever thou shalt loose on earth shall be loosed in heaven." Are kings excepted here? Or are they not of the sheep which the Son of God committed to St. Peter? Who, I ask, thinks himself excluded from this universal grant of the power of binding and loosing to St. Peter unless, perchance, that unhappy man who, being unwilling to bear the yoke of the Lord, subjects himself to the burden of the Devil and refuses to be numbered in the flock of Christ? His wretched liberty shall profit him nothing; for if he shakes off from his proud neck the power divinely granted to Peter, so much the heavier shall it be for him in the day of judgment.

This institution of the divine will, this foundation of the rule of the Church, this privilege granted and sealed especially by a heavenly decree to St. Peter, chief of the Apostles, has been accepted and maintained with great reverence by the holy fathers, and they have given to the Holy Roman Church, as well in general councils as in their other acts and writings, the name of "universal mother." They have not only accepted her expositions of doctrine and her instructions in [our] holy religion, but they have also recognized her judicial decisions. They have agreed as with one spirit and one voice that all major cases, all especially important affairs and the judgments of all churches ought to be referred to her as to their head and mother, that from her there shall be no appeal, that her judgments may not and cannot be reviewed or reversed by anyone.

Thus Pope Gelasius, writing to the emperor Anastasius, gave him these instructions as to the right theory of the principate of the holy and apostolic see, based upon divine authority:

Although it is fitting that all the faithful should submit themselves to all priests who perform their sacred functions properly, how much the more should they accept the judgment of that prelate who has been appointed by the supreme divine ruler to be superior to all priests and whom the loyalty of the whole later Church has recognized as such. Your wisdom sees plainly that no human capacity [*concilium*] whatsoever can equal that of him whom the word of Christ raised above all others and whom the reverend Church has always confessed and still devotedly holds as its head.

So also Pope Julius, writing to the eastern bishops in regard to the powers of the same holy and apostolic see, says:

You ought, my brethren, to have spoken carefully and not ironically of the Holy Roman and Apostolic Church, seeing that our Lord Jesus Christ addressed her respectfully [*decenter*], saying, "Thou art Peter and upon this rock I will build my church, and the gates of hell shall not prevail against it; and I will give thee the keys of the kingdom of heaven." For it has the power, granted by a unique privilege, of opening and shutting the gates of the celestial kingdom to whom it will.

To whom, then, the power of opening and closing in heaven is given, shall he not be able to judge the earth? God forbid! Do you remember what the most blessed apostle Paul says: "Know ye not that we shall judge angels? How much more things that pertain to this life?"

So Pope Gregory declared that kings who dared to disobey the orders of the apostolic see should forfeit their office. He wrote to a certain senator and abbot in these words:

If any king, priest, judge or secular person shall disregard this decree of ours and act contrary to it, he shall be deprived of his power and his office and shall learn that he stands condemned at the bar of God for the wrong that he has done. And unless he shall restore what he has wrongfully taken and shall have done fitting penance for his unlawful acts he shall be excluded from the sacred body and blood of our Lord and Savior Jesus Christ and at the last judgment shall receive condign punishment.

Now then, if the blessed Gregory, most gentle of doctors, decreed that kings who should disobey his orders about a hospital for strangers should be not only deposed but excommunicated and condemned in the last judgment, how can anyone blame us for deposing and excommunicating Henry, who not only disregards apostolic judgments, but so far as in him lies tramples upon his mother the Church, basely plunders the whole kingdom and destroys its churches—unless indeed it were one who is a man of his own kind?

As we know also through the teaching of St. Peter in his letter touching the ordination of Clement, where he says: "If any one were friend to those with whom he [Clement] is not on speaking terms, that man is among those who would like to destroy the Church of God and, while he seems to be with us in the body, he is against us in mind and heart, and he is a far worse enemy than those who are without and are openly hostile. For he, under the forms of friendship, acts as an enemy and scatters and lays waste the Church." Consider then, my best beloved, if he passes so severe a judgment upon him who associates himself with those whom the pope opposes on account of their actions, with what severity he condemns the man himself to whom the pope is thus opposed.

But now, to return to our point: Is not a sovereignty invented by men of this world who were ignorant of God subject to that which the providence of Almighty God established for his own glory and graciously bestowed upon the world? The Son of God we believe to be God and man, sitting at the right hand of the Father as high priest, head of all priests and ever making intercession for us. He despised the kingdom of this world wherein the sons of this world puff themselves up and offered himself as a sacrifice upon the cross.

Who does not know that kings and princes derive their origin from men ignorant of God who raised themselves above their fellows by pride, plunder, treachery, murder—in short, by every kind of crime—at the instigation of the Devil, the prince of this world, men blind with greed and intolerable in their audacity? If, then, they strive to bend the priests of God to their will, to whom may they more properly be compared than to him who is chief over all the sons of pride? For he, tempting our high priest, head of all priests, son of the Most High, offering him all the kingdoms of this world, said: "All these will I give thee if thou wilt fall down and worship me."

Does anyone doubt that the priests of Christ are to be considered as fathers and masters of kings and princes and of all believers? Would it not be regarded as pitiable madness if a son should try to rule his father or a pupil his master and to bind with unjust obligations the one through whom he expects to be bound or loosed, not only on earth but also in heaven? Evidently recognizing this the emperor Constantine the Great, lord over all kings and princes throughout almost the entire earth, as St. Gregory relates in his letter to the emperor Mauritius, at the holy synod of Nicaea took his place below all the bishops and did not venture to pass any judgment upon them but, even addressing them as gods, felt that they ought not to be subject to his judgment but that he ought to be bound by their decisions.

Pope Gelasius, urging upon the emperor Anastasius not to feel himself wronged by the truth that was called to his attention said: "There are two powers, O august emperor, by which the world is governed, the sacred authority of the priesthood and the power of kings. Of these the priestly is by so much the greater as they will have to answer for kings themselves in the day of divine judgment"; and a little further: "Know that you are subject to their judgment, not that they are to be subjected to your will."

In reliance upon such declarations and such authorities, many prelates have excommunicated kings or emperors. If you ask for illustrations: Pope Innocent excommunicated the emperor Arcadius because he consented to the expulsion of St. John Chrysostom from his office. Another Roman pontiff deposed a king of the Franks, not so much on account of his evil deeds as because he was not equal to so great an office, and set in his place Pippin, father of the emperor Charles the Great, releasing all the Franks from the oath of fealty which they had sworn to him. And this is often done by Holy Church when it absolves fighting men from their oaths to bishops who have been deposed by apostolic authority. So St. Ambrose, a holy man but not bishop of the whole Church, excommunicated the emperor Theodosius the Great for a fault which did not seem to other prelates so very grave and excluded him from the Church. He also shows in his writings that the priestly office is as much superior to royal power as gold is more precious than lead. He says: "The honor and dignity of bishops admit of no comparison. If you liken them to the splendor of kings and the diadem of princes, these are as lead compared to the glitter of gold. You see the necks of kings and princes bowed to the knees of priests, and by the kissing of hands they believe that they share the benefit of their prayers." And again: "Know that we have said all this in order to show that there is nothing in this world more excellent than a priest or more lofty than a bishop."

Your fraternity should remember also that greater power is granted to an exorcist when he is made a spiritual emperor for the casting out of devils, than can be conferred upon any layman for the purpose of earthly dominion. All kings and princes of this earth who live not piously and in their deeds show not a becoming fear of God are ruled by demons and are sunk in miserable slavery. Such men desire to rule, not guided by the love of God, as priests are, for the glory of God and the profit of human souls, but to display their intolerable pride and to satisfy the lusts of their mind. Of these St. Augustine says in the first book of his Christian doctrine: "He who tries to rule over men—who are by nature equal to him—acts with intolerable pride." Now if exorcists have power over demons, as we have said, how much more over those who are subject to demons and are limbs of demons! And if exorcists are superior to these, how much more are priests superior to them!

Furthermore, every Christian king when he approaches his end asks the aid of a priest as a miserable suppliant that he may escape the prison of hell, may pass from darkness into light and may appear at the judgment seat of God freed from the bonds of sin. But who, layman or priest, in his last moments has ever asked the help of any earthly king for the safety of his soul? And what king or emperor has power through his office to snatch any Christian from the might of the Devil by the sacred rite of baptism, to confirm him among the sons of God and to fortify him by the holy chrism? Or—and this is the greatest thing in the Christian religion—who among them is able by his own word to create the body and blood of the Lord? or to whom among them is given the power to bind and loose in Heaven and upon earth? From this it is apparent how greatly superior in power is the priestly dignity.

Or who of them is able to ordain any clergyman in the Holy Church—much less to depose him for any fault? For bishops, while they may ordain other bishops, may in no wise depose them except by authority of the apostolic see. How, then, can even the most slightly informed person doubt that priests are higher than kings? But if kings are to be judged by priests for their sins, by whom can they more properly be judged than by the Roman pontiff?

In short, all good Christians, whomsoever they may be, are more properly to be called kings than are evil princes; for the former, seeking the glory of God, rule themselves rigorously; but the latter, seeking their own rather than the things that are of God, being enemies to themselves, oppress others tyrannically. The former are the body of the true Christ; the latter, the body of the Devil. The former rule themselves that they may reign forever with the supreme ruler. The power of the latter brings it to pass that they perish in eternal damnation with the prince of darkness who is king over all the sons of pride.

It is no great wonder that evil priests take the part of a king whom they love and fear on account of honors received from him. By ordaining any person whomsoever, they are selling their God at a bargain price. For as the elect are inseparably united to their Head, so the wicked are firmly bound to him who is head of all evil—especially against the good. But against these it is of no use to argue, but rather to pray God with tears and groans that he may deliver them from the snares of Satan, in which they are caught and after trial may lead them at last into knowledge of the truth.

So much for kings and emperors who, swollen with the pride of this world, rule not for God but for themselves. But since it is our duty to exhort everyone according to his station, it is our care with God's help to furnish emperors, kings and other princes with the weapons of humility that thus they may be strong to keep down the floods and waves of pride. We know that earthly glory and the cares of this world are wont especially to cause rulers to be exalted, to forget humility and, seeking their own glory, strive to excel their fellows. It seems therefore especially useful for emperors and kings, while their hearts are lifted up in the strife for glory, to learn how to humble themselves and to know fear rather than joy. Let them therefore consider carefully how dangerous, even awesome is the office of emperor or king, how very few find salvation therein, and how those who are saved through God's mercy have become far less famous in the Church by divine judgment than many humble persons. From the beginning of the world to the present day we do not find in all authentic records [seven] emperors or kings whose lives were as distinguished for virtue and piety as were those of a countless multitude of men who despised the world—although

we believe that many of them were saved by the mercy of God. Not to speak of apostles and martyrs, who among emperors and kings was famed for his miracles as were St. Martin, St. Antony and St. Benedict? What emperor or king ever raised the dead, cleansed lepers or opened the eyes of the blind? True, Holy Church praises and honors the emperor Constantine, of pious memory, Theodosius and Honorius, Charles and Louis, as lovers of justice, champions of the Christian faith and protectors of churches, but she does not claim that they were illustrious for the splendor of their wonderful works. Or to how many names of kings or emperors has Holy Church ordered churches or altars to be dedicated or masses to be celebrated?

Let kings and princes fear lest the higher they are raised above their fellows in this life, the deeper they may be plunged in everlasting fire. Wherefore it is written: "The mighty shall suffer mighty torments." They shall render unto God an account for all men subject to their rule. But if it is no small labor for the pious individual to guard his own soul, what a task is laid upon princes in the care of so many thousands of souls! And if Holy Church imposes a heavy penalty upon him who takes a single human life, what shall be done to those who send many thousands to death for the glory of this world? These, although they say with their lips, *mea culpa*, for the slaughter of many, yet in their hearts they rejoice at the increase of their glory and neither repent of what they have done nor regret that they have sent their brothers into the world below. So that, since they do not repent with all their hearts and will not restore what they have gained by human bloodshed, their penitence before God remains without the fruits of a true repentance.

Wherefore they ought greatly to fear, and they should frequently be reminded that, as we have said, since the beginning of the world and throughout the kingdoms of the earth very few kings of saintly life can be found out of an innumerable multitude, whereas in one single chair of successive bishops—the Roman—from the time of the blessed apostle Peter nearly a hundred are counted among the holiest of men. How can this be, except because the kings and princes of the earth, seduced by empty glory, prefer their own interests to the things of the Spirit, whereas pious pontiffs, despising vainglory, set the things of God above the things of the flesh. The former readily punish offenses against themselves but are not troubled by offenses against God; the latter quickly forgive those who sin against them but do not easily pardon offenders against God. The former, far too much given to worldly affairs, think little of spiritual things; the latter, dwelling eagerly upon heavenly subjects, despise the things of this world.

All Christians, therefore, who desire to reign with Christ are to be warned not to reign through ambition for worldly power. They are to keep in mind the admonition of that most holy pope Gregory in his book on the pastoral office: "Of all these things what is to be followed, what held fast, except that the man strong in virtue shall come to his office under compulsion? Let him who is without virtue not come to it even though he be urged thereto." If, then, men who fear God come under compulsion with fear and trembling to the apostolic see where those who are properly ordained become stronger through the merits of the blessed apostle Peter, with what awe and hesitation should men ascend the throne of a king where even good and humble men like Saul and David become worse! What we have said above is thus stated in the decrees of the blessed pope Symmachus—though we have learned it by experience: "He, that is St. Peter, transmitted to his successors an unfailing endowment of merit together with an inheritance of innocence"; and again: "For who can doubt that he is holy who is raised to the height of such an office, in which if he is lacking in virtue acquired by his own merits, that which is handed down from his predecessor is sufficient. For either he [Peter] raises men of distinction to bear this burden or he glorifies them after they are raised up."

Wherefore let those whom Holy Church, of its own will and with deliberate judgment, not for fleeting glory but for the welfare of multitudes, has called to royal or imperial rule—let them be obedient and ever mindful of the blessed Gregory's declaration in that same pastoral treatise: "When a man disdains to be the equal of his fellow men, he becomes like an apostate angel. Thus Saul, after his period of humility, swollen with pride, ran into excess of power. He was raised in humility, but rejected in his pride, as God bore witness, saying: 'Though thou wast little in thine own sight, wast thou not made the head of the tribes of Israel?'" and again: "I marvel how, when he was little to himself he was great before God, but when he seemed great to himself he was little before God." Let them watch and remember what God says in the Gospel: "I seek not my own glory," and, "He who would be first among you, let him be the servant of all." Let them ever place the honor of God above their own; let them embrace justice and maintain it by preserving to everyone his right; let them not enter into the counsels of the ungodly, but cling to those of religion with all their hearts. Let them not seek to make Holy Church their maidservant or their subject, but recognizing priests, the eyes of God, as their masters and fathers, strive to do them becoming honor.

If we are commanded to honor our fathers and mothers in the flesh, how much more our spiritual parents! If he that curseth his father or his mother shall be put to death, what does he deserve who curses his spiritual father or mother? Let not princes, led astray by carnal affection, set their own sons over that flock for whom Christ shed his blood if a better and more suitable man can be found. By thus loving their own son more than God they bring the greatest evils upon the Church. For it is evident that he who fails to provide to the best of his ability so great and necessary an advantage for our holy mother, the Church, does not love God and his neighbor as befits a Christian man. If this one virtue of charity be wanting, then whatever of good the man may do will lack all saving grace.

But if they do these things in humility, keeping their love for God and their neighbor as they ought, they may count upon the mercy of him who said: "Learn of me, for I am meek and lowly of heart." If they humbly imitate him, they shall pass from their servile and transient reign into the kingdom of eternal liberty.

The Letters of Henry IV

Henry declares to the Roman clergy and people that Hildebrand is his enemy. He sends them a copy of his decree of deposition (Letter 11) and exhorts them to take a new pope after forcing Hildebrand (that is, Gregory VII) to step down (1076).

Henry, king by the grace of God, sends grace, greeting, and every good thing to the clergy and people of the entire holy Roman Church:

That fidelity is believed firm and unshaken which is always kept unchanged for one whether he is present or absent—fidelity altered neither by the extended absence of him to whom it is owed nor through the wearisome passage of a long time. We know that this is the sort of fidelity which you keep for us; we are thankful, and we ask that it continue unchanged. Specifically, we ask that just as you act now, so in the future you will steadfastly be friends of our friends and enemies of our enemies.

Noting particularly among the latter the monk Hildebrand, we urge you to enmity against him, since we have found him to be an assailant and an oppressor of the Church, as well as a waylayer of the Roman commonwealth, and of our kingdom, as may be known clearly from the following letter sent to him by us:

[In the original of Letter 10, the full text of Letter 11 is given here. Letter 10 continues:]

This is the text of our letter to the monk Hildebrand, which we have also written to you so that our will may be both yours and ours—nay rather, so that your love may bring satisfaction to God and to us. Rise up against him, therefore, O most faithful, and let the man who is first in the faith be first in his condemnation. We do not say, however, that you should shed his blood, since after his deposition life would indeed be a greater penalty for him than death. We say rather that if he prove unwilling to descend, you should force him to do so and receive into the apostolic see another, elected by us with the common counsel of all the bishops and of yourselves, one who will be willing and able to cure the wounds which that man has inflicted upon the Church.

Henry charges Hildebrand with having stolen his hereditary privileges in Rome, striven to alienate Italy, abused the bishops, and threatened his office and his life. He reports the sentence of deposition issued by the Diet of Worms, and as patrician of the Romans, he commands him to descend from the throne of St. Peter (1076).

Henry, king by the grace of God, to Hildebrand:

Although hitherto I hoped for those things from you which are expected of a father and obeyed you in all respects to the great indignation of our vassals,[3] I have obtained from you a requital suitable from one who was the most pernicious enemy of our life and kingly office. After you had first snatched away with arrogant boldness all the hereditary dignity owed me by that see, going still further you tried with the most evil arts to alienate the kingdom of Italy.[4] Not content with this, you have not feared to set your hand against the most reverend bishops, who are united to us like most cherished members and have harassed them with most arrogant affronts and the bitterest abuses against divine and human laws. While I let all these things go unnoticed through patience, you thought it not patience but cowardice and dared to rise up against the head itself, announcing, as you know, that (to use your own words) you would either die or deprive me of my life and kingly office.

Judging that this unheard-of defiance had to be confuted not with words, but with action, I held a general assembly of all the foremost men of the kingdom, at their supplication. When they had made public through their true declaration (which you will hear from their own letter) those things which they had previously kept silent through fear and reverence, they took public action to the

---

3 The Latin original is *fidelis*, a word which appears frequently throughout Henry IV's letters. At the risk of imprecision, the requirements of translation have forced a rendering as either "vassal" or "subject." The reader should not be misled, however, by the modern meaning of "vassal": *fidelis* denoted no servile status, but, to the contrary, indicated a man who had taken an oath of "fealty" (*fidelitas*) to an overlord—and invariably, therefore, a *fidelis* was a person of high station within feudal political society.

4 A reference to Gregory's denial of Henry's right to name Tedald archbishop of Milan and to fill the sees of Fermo and Spoleto.

end that you could no longer continue in the apostolic see. Since their sentence seemed just and righteous before God and men, I also give my assent, revoking from you every prerogative of the papacy which you have seemed to hold, and ordering you to descend from the throne of the city whose patriciate is due me through the bestowal of God and the sworn assent of the Romans.

Renunciation of Gregory VII by the German Bishops (Synod of Worms, 1076)

Siegfried, archbishop of Mainz, Udo of Trier, William of Utrecht, Herman of Metz, Henry of Liège, Ricbert of Verdun, Bido of Toul, Hozeman of Speier, Burchard of Halberstadt, Werner of Strassburg, Burchard of Basel, Otto of Constance, Adalbero of Würzburg, Rupert of Bamberg, Otto of Regensburg, Egilbert of Freising, Ulric of Eichstätt, Frederick of Münster, Eilbert of Minden, Hezilo of Hildesheim, Benno of Osnabrück, Eppo of Naumburg, Imadus of Paderborn, Tiedo of Brandenburg, Burchard of Lausanne, and Bruno of Verona, to Brother Hildebrand:

When you had first usurped the government of the Church, we knew well how, with your accustomed arrogance, you had presumed to enter so illicit and nefarious an undertaking against human and divine law. We thought, nevertheless, that the pernicious beginnings of your administration ought to be left unnoticed in prudent silence. We did this specifically in the hope that such criminal beginnings would be emended and wiped away somewhat by the probity and industry of your later rule. But now, just as the deplorable state of the universal Church cries out and laments, through the increasing wickedness of your actions and decrees, you are woefully and stubbornly in step with your evil beginnings.

Our Lord and Redeemer impressed the goodness of peace and love upon his Faithful as their distinctive character, a fact to which there are more testimonies than can be included in the brevity of a letter. But by way of contrast, you have inflicted wounds with proud cruelty and cruel pride, you are eager for profane innovations, you delight in a great name rather than in a good one, and with unheard-of self-exaltation, like a standard bearer of schism, you distend all the limbs of the Church which before your times led a quiet and tranquil life, according to the admonition of the apostle. Finally, the flame of discord, which you stirred up through terrible factions in the Roman church, you spread with raging madness through all the churches of Italy, Germany, Gaul, and Spain. For you have taken from the bishops, so far as you could, all that power which is known to have been divinely conferred upon them through the grace of the Holy Spirit, which works mightily in ordinations. Through you all administration of ecclesiastical affairs has been assigned to popular madness. Since some now consider no one a bishop or priest save the man who begs that office of Your Arrogance with a most unworthy servility, you have shaken into pitiable disorder the whole strength of the apostolic institution and that most comely distribution of the limbs of Christ, which the Doctor of the Gentiles so often commends and teaches. And so through these boastful decrees of yours—and this cannot be said without tears—the name of Christ has all but perished. Who, however, is not struck dumb by the baseness of your arrogant usurpation of new power, power not due you, to the end that you may destroy the rights due the whole brotherhood? For you assert that if any sin of one of our parishioners comes to your notice, even if only by rumor, none of us has any further power to bind or to loose the party involved, for you alone may do it, or one whom you delegate especially for this purpose. Can anyone schooled in sacred learning fail to see how this assertion exceeds all madness?

We have judged that it would be worse than any other evil for us to allow the Church of God to be so gravely jeopardized—nay rather, almost destroyed—any longer through these and other presumptuous airs of yours. Therefore, it has pleased us to make known to you by the common counsel of all of us something which we have left unsaid until now: that is, the reason why you cannot now be, nor could you ever have been, the head of the apostolic see.

In the time of the emperor Henry [III] of good memory, you bound yourself with a solemn oath that for the lifetime of that emperor and for that of his son, our lord the glorious king who now presides at the summit of affairs, you would neither obtain the papacy yourself nor suffer another to obtain it, insofar as you were able, without the consent and approbation either of the father in his lifetime or of the son in his. And there are many bishops today who were witnesses of this solemn oath, who saw it then with their own eyes and heard it with their own ears. Remember also that in order to remove jealous rivalry when ambition for the papacy tickled some of the cardinals, you obligated yourself with a solemn oath never to assume the papacy both on the plea and on the condition that they did the same thing themselves. We have seen in what a holy way you observed each of these solemn vows. Again, when a synod was celebrated in the time of Pope Nicholas [II], in which one hundred twenty-five bishops sat together, it was decided and decreed under anathema that no one would ever become pope except by the election of the cardinals and the approbation of the people, and by the consent and authority of the king. And of this council and decree, you yourself were author, advocate, and subscriber.

In addition to this, you have filled the entire Church, as it were, with the stench of the gravest of scandals, rising from your intimacy and cohabitation with another's wife who is more closely integrated into your household than is necessary. In this affair, our sense of decency is affected more than our legal case, although the general complaint is sounded everywhere that all judgments and all decrees are enacted by women in the apostolic see, and ultimately that the whole orb of the Church is administered by this new senate of women. For no one can complain adequately of the wrongs and the abuse suffered by the bishops, whom you call most undeservedly sons of whores and other names of this sort.

Since your accession was tainted by such great perjuries, since the Church of God is imperiled by so great a tempest arising from abuse born of your innovations, and since you have degraded your life and conduct by such multifarious infamy, we declare that in the future we shall observe no longer the obedience which we have not promised to you. And since none of us, as you have publicly declared, has hitherto been a bishop to you, you also will now be pope to none of us.

Henry charges Hildebrand with having thrown the whole Church into confusion and with having threatened his life and office. He declares that Hildebrand was not ordained of God, but is damned by the precept of St. Paul and by the judgment of all Henry's bishops; and he commands him to descend from the apostolic see (1076).

Henry, king not by usurpation, but by the pious ordination of God, to Hildebrand, now not pope, but false monk:

You have deserved such a salution as this because of the confusion you have wrought; for you left untouched no order of the Church which you could make a sharer of confusion instead of honor, of malediction instead of benediction.

For to discuss a few outstanding points among many: Not only have you dared to touch the rectors of the holy Church—the archbishops, the bishops and the priests, anointed of the Lord as they are—but you have trodden them under foot like slaves who know not what their lord may do. In crushing them you have gained for yourself acclaim from the mouth of the rabble. You have judged that all these know nothing, while you alone know everything. In any case, you have sedulously used this knowledge not for edification, but for destruction, so greatly that we may believe Saint Gregory, whose name you have arrogated to yourself, rightly made this prophesy of you when he said: "From the abundance of his subjects, the mind of the prelate is often exalted, and he thinks that he has more knowledge than anyone else, since he sees that he has more power than anyone else."

And we, indeed, bore with all these abuses, since we were eager to preserve the honor of the apostolic see. But you construed our humility as fear, and so you were emboldened to rise up even against the royal power itself, granted to us by God. You dared to threaten to take the kingship away from us—as though we had received the kingship from you, as though kingship and empire were in your hand and not in the hand of God.

Our Lord, Jesus Christ, has called us to kingship, but has not called you to the priesthood. For you have risen by these steps: namely, by cunning, which the monastic profession abhors, to money; by money to favor; by favor to the sword. By the sword you have come to the throne of peace, and from the throne of peace you have destroyed the peace. You have armed subjects against their prelates; you who have not been called by God have taught that our bishops who have been called by God are to be spurned; you have usurped for laymen the bishops' ministry over priests, with the result that these laymen depose and condemn the very men whom the laymen themselves received as teachers from the hand of God, through the imposition of the hands of bishops.

You have also touched me, one who, though unworthy, has been anointed to kingship among the anointed. This wrong you have done to me, although as the tradition of the holy fathers has taught, I am to be judged by God alone and am not to be deposed for any crime unless—may it never happen—I should deviate from the faith. For the prudence of the holy bishops entrusted the judgment and the deposition even of Julian the Apostate not to themselves, but to God alone. The true pope Saint Peter also exclaims, "Fear God, honor the king." You, however, since you do not fear God, dishonor me, ordained of Him.

Wherefore, when Saint Paul gave no quarter to an angel from heaven if the angel should preach heterodoxy, he did not except you who are now teaching heterodoxy throughout the earth. For he says, "If anyone, either I or an angel from heaven, preach any other gospel unto you than that which we have preached unto you, let him be accursed." Descend, therefore, condemned by this anathema and by the common judgment of all our bishops and of ourself. Relinquish the apostolic see which you have arrogated. Let another mount the throne of Saint Peter, another who will not cloak violence with religion but who will teach the pure doctrine of Saint Peter.

I, Henry, king by the grace of God, together with all our bishops, say to you: Descend! Descend!

In this encyclical letter to his bishops, Henry admonishes them to help the beleaguered Church against Hildebrand, who has destroyed the peace between the kingship and the priesthood and has recently abused royal envoys. He invites them to participate in an assembly at Worms on Whitsun (1076).

Henry, king by the grace of God, sends to A., the grace, greeting, and love which he sends not to all men, but only to a few:

In the greatest affairs there is need for the greatest counsels of the greatest men, who externally should have power and within should not be lacking in good will, so that they may be both willing and able to deliberate well about that matter for which they wish well. For in the advancement of any enterprise, neither power without good will nor good will without power is useful. O most faithful subject, you possess, we think, each of these in equal proportion. To tell the truth, although as one of the great, you possess great power, your good will for our advantage and for that of our kingdom grows even greater than this great power—if we know you well and have properly noted your fidelity. From past actions faithfully done, the hope grows that future actions will be done yet more faithfully. We trust to your love, however, that your fidelity may not fall short of our hope, since from the fidelity of none of the kingdom's princes do we hope for greater things than from yours. Thus until this very time, we have rejoiced not only in what past affairs reveal but also in your promise of things still to be hoped for.

Let your good will stand by us, therefore, together with your power at this opportune time, the good will for which not only our need is earnestly longing, but also that of all your fellow bishops and brethren, nay rather, that of the whole oppressed Church. Certainly, you are not ignorant of this oppression. Only see to it that you do not withdraw assistance from the oppressed Church, but rather that you give your sympathy to the kingship and to the priesthood. Just as hitherto the Church was exalted by each of these offices, so now, alas, it is laid low, bereft of each; since one man has arrogated both for himself, he has injured both, and he who has neither wanted nor was able to be of benefit in either has been useless in each.

To keep you in suspense no longer as to the name of the man under discussion, learn of whom we speak: it is the monk Hildebrand (a monk indeed in habit), so-called pope who, as you yourself know clearly, presides in the apostolic see not with the care of a pastor but with the violence of a usurper and from the throne of peace dissolves the bond of the one catholic peace. To cite a few things among many: without God's knowledge he has usurped for himself the kingship and the priesthood. In this deed he held in contempt the pious ordinance of God, which especially commanded these two—namely, the kingship and the priesthood—should remain, not as one entity, but as two. In his Passion, the Savior Himself meant the figurative sufficiency of the two swords to be understood in this way: When it was said to him, "Lord, behold there are two swords here," He answered, "It is enough," signifying by this sufficient duality, that the spiritual and the carnal swords are to be used in the Church and that by them every hurtful thing is to be cut off. That is to say, He was teaching that every man is constrained by the priestly sword to obey the king as the representative of God but by the kingly sword both to repel enemies of Christ outside and to obey the priesthood within. So in charity the province of one extends into the other, as long as neither the kingship is deprived of honor by the priesthood nor the priesthood is deprived of honor by the kingship. You yourself have found out, if you have wanted to discover it, how the Hildebrandine madness has confounded this ordinance of God; for in his judgment, no one may be a priest unless he begs that [honor] from his arrogance. He has also striven to deprive me of the kingship—me whom God has called to the kingship (God,

however, has not called him to the priesthood)—since he saw that I wished to hold my royal power from God and not from him and since he himself had not constituted me as king. And further, he threatened to deprive me of kingship and life, neither of which he had bestowed.

Although he often contrived these outrages against us, and others like them, as you yourself know, nonetheless he was not satisfied unless from day to day he cast new and coarse sorts of affliction upon us, as he recently showed in dealing with our envoys. This paper is not sufficiently long to set forth how he handled those messengers of ours; how demeaningly he afflicted them; how cruelly he imprisoned them; and when they had been imprisoned, how he harmed them with nakedness, cold, hunger and thirst, and blows. Finally, he ordered them to be led about through the middle of the city to offer a spectacle to all, after the example of the martyrs. So you may believe and say that in common with the tyrant Decius[5] he rages and torments the saints.

Wherefore, be not ashamed, most cherished friend, be not ashamed to satisfy the petition we make in common with your fellow bishops: that you come to Worms at Pentecost and hear many things there with the other princes, a few of which this letter mentions, and advise us what is to be done. For you are besought by the love of your fellow bishops, admonished through the advantage of the Church, and bound by the honor of our life and of the whole kingdom.

The Promise of Henry IV to Gregory VII (Promissio Oppenheimensis, 1076)

Admonished by the counsel of our vassals, I promise to maintain a due obedience in all things to the apostolic see and to you, Pope Gregory.[6] I

---

5   Roman Emperor (249–51) remembered for his persecution of Christians.

6   In joining battle with Gregory, Henry severely miscalculated his strength. While most of the German bishops supported him against Gregory, a great number of temporal princes led by his old enemies Welf of Bavaria, Rudolf of Swabia, and Berthold of Carinthia took the opportunity to rebel against their excommunicate king. The threat of revolt in Saxony also revived immediately. In October 1076, Henry's army gathered at Oppenheim, facing the rebel army at Tribur just opposite them across the Rhine. Fearing the results of open battle, Henry offered this promise to the papal legates who were with his enemies; it was accepted and, with the understanding that points at issue between Henry and Gregory's partisans would be settled at a future meeting, both armies disbanded. In the 1076 letter to the princes reprinted here, Henry declared his altered policy to his supporters and urged them to conform themselves to it. For their part, the rebellious princes sent a legation to Gregory, asking him to go to Germany the next February to arbitrate the conflict between them and their king. Gregory accepted these proposals and was making his way toward Germany when Henry intercepted him at Canossa and, after making his submission, was released from excommunication.

shall take care to emend with dutiful reparation whatever diminution of the honor of that see or of your own honor is seen to have arisen through us.

Since certain rather serious schemes which I am supposed to have against that same see and Your Reverence are now at issue, at a fitting time, either I shall clear them away through the prayer of innocence or through the help of God or at that very time I shall gladly undertake suitable penance for them.

It is also altogether fitting, however, for Your Sanctity not to ignore those things which have been spread abroad about you and which bear scandal to the Church. But after this scruple has also been removed from the public conscience, it is fitting that the universal tranquility of the Church as well as that of the kingdom be made firm through your wisdom.

Henry declares to his princes that he wishes to obey and to render satisfaction to Pope Gregory; he exhorts them to follow his example and to obtain release from excommunication (1076).

Henry, king by the grace of God, sends the glorious esteem of his good will to archbishops, bishops, dukes, margraves, counts, and to every order of dignity:

We have learned by the assertion of our vassals that on behalf of Our Mercy some men have detracted from the apostolic see and its venerable pontiff, the lord pope Gregory. For this reason, it has pleased us, on beneficial counsel, to change our former position and after the fashion of our predecessors and ancestors to reserve in all respects due obedience to that same sacrosanct see and to the lord pope Gregory, who is known to serve as its head. It has also pleased us to make amends with fitting reparation if anything serious has been done against him.

We wish that you also admonished by the example of Our Serenity, like us, will not refuse to show solemn [obedience] to Saint Peter and to his vicar. And may whosoever know that they are bound by his ban strive to be absolved formally by this same lord pope Gregory.

Henry informs his mother, the empress-dowager Agnes, that at a recent diet he was persuaded to allow the case of the bishops who had deserted him to be discussed at another assembly in the near future. He grants her petition (1074–76).

To the mother of blessing and well-being, Henry, king by the grace of God, sends love from his whole heart and whatever is better and beyond:

Since it is right for you to know well how we progress, we want to send you word, inasmuch as you are our dearest mother, of what this Curia and assembly has ordered and ratified. After much consideration of our case, we were finally overcome by the apostolic legation and by the counsel and persuasion of all our vassals, many of whom were present, and we granted and permitted the restitution of the deserter-bishops. Nonetheless, we did this in such a fashion that in whatever manner we wish, we may continue warily to watch these men in the interests of our side until the day we have set to consider their case. Know that those same legates of the pope are awaiting that day and time here.

But for the sake of that good faith which we have in you, ask earnestly of God that our cause may receive its long-expected outcome. As for that, however, which you have asked of us, most certainly you will receive it on that condition which you wish and of which you have notified us. In addition [you will receive] whatever we can grant to your love.

The Vow of Henry IV to Gregory VII at Canossa (1077)

Oath of Henry, king of the Germans.

Before the date the lord pope Gregory is to set, I, King Henry, shall bring about justice according to his judgment or harmony according to his counsel with regard to the complaint and objection now being made against me by archbishops, bishops, dukes, counts, the other princes in the realm of the Germans, and those who follow them by reason of the same objection. If a concrete obstacle hinder me or him, I shall be ready to do the same when that hindrance has been overcome. Also, if the same lord pope Gregory should wish to go beyond the mountains to other lands, he, those who are among his retainers or guards, and those who are sent by him or come to him from any region, will be safe in coming, staying, and going thence, from any harm to life and limb and from capture by me and by those whom I can control. Moreover, no other difficulty prejudicial to his honor will occur with my assent; and should any person create one for him, I shall help him [Gregory] in good faith, according to my ability.

Done at Canossa, January 28, the fifteenth Indiction.

Decree of the Synod of Brixen (1080)

In the year of the incarnation of the Lord 1080, with the most serene King Henry IV as moderator, in the twenty-sixth year of his reign, on the seventh day before the Kalends of July, on the fifth day of the week, in the third indiction, when an assembly of thirty bishops and of the leaders of the army, not only of Italy but also of Germany, was gathered at Brixen in Bavaria by royal order, of one accord a voice came forth as though from the mouth of all complaining terribly against the cruel madness of one false monk, Hildebrand, also called Pope Gregory VII. It complained that the ever-unconquered king suffered this madness to rage untouched for so long, when Paul, the vessel of election, witnesses that the prince does not carry a sword without cause and Peter, the first of the apostles, cries out that the king not only is supreme but that governors are to be sent by him specifically for the punishment of evildoers and for the praise of the good. In fulfillment of these sayings it seemed just to this most glorious king and to his princes that the judgment of the bishops with the sentence of divine censure ought to issue against this Hildebrand before the material sword went forth against him, with the consequence that the royal power might resolve to prosecute him with greater freedom after the prelates of the Church had first deposed him from his proud prelacy.

Which of the faithful knowing him would fear to let fly the shaft of damnation against him? From the time he entered the world, this man strove to procure position for himself[7] over men through vain glory, without the support of any merits; to

set dreams and divinations, his own and those of others, ahead of divine dispensation; to appear a monk in habit and not to be one by profession; to judge himself exempt from ecclesiastical discipline, subject to no master; to devote himself more than laymen to obscene theatrical shows; publicly for the sake of filthy lucre, to attend to the tables of the money changers on the porch of them who do business? And so from these pursuits, he garnered his money and, supplanting the abbot, usurped the abbacy of Saint Paul.

Thereafter, seizing the archdiaconate, he led a certain man named Mancius astray by guile so that man sold him his own office. And against the will of Pope Nicholas, a popular tumult attending his action, he forced his advancement to the stewardship of Saint Peter's. Finally, he is convicted of having murdered four Roman pontiffs with violent deaths. His instrument was poison administered at the hands of one of his intimates, namely, John Braciutus. Although he repented too late, while others still kept silent this ministrant of death himself bore witness to these deeds with dire cries, pressed by the nearness of his own death. And then, on the same night in which the funeral rites of Pope Alexander were lovingly performed in the basilica of the Savior, this oft-mentioned plague-bearer fortified the gates of the Roman city and the bridges, the towers and the triumphal arches, with detachments of armed men. When a military force had been brought together, like an enemy he occupied the Lateran Palace. And lest the clergy should dare oppose him, since no one wished to elect him, he terrified them by threatening them with death upon the unsheathed swords of his followers. He sprang upon the long-occupied throne before the body of the dead man reached its tomb. But when certain of the clergy wanted to remind him of the decree of Pope Nicholas (which was promulgated with the threat of anathema by one hundred twenty-five bishops and with the approval of this same Hildebrand and which stated that if anyone presumed to be pope without the assent of the Roman prince, he should be considered by all not pope, but an apostate), he denied that he knew there was a king anywhere, and he asserted that he could adjudge the decrees of his predecessors void.

What more? Not only Rome, indeed, but the

---

7   *Se commendare*, in the feudal sense of commending oneself to a lord in order to gain lands and position.

Roman world itself, bears witness that he has not been elected by God but that he has most impudently thrust himself upward through force, fraud, and money. His fruits reveal his root; his words show his intent. He it was who subverted ecclesiastical order, who threw the rule of the Christian empire into turmoil, who plotted death of body and soul for the catholic and pacific King, who defended a king who was a breaker of vows and a traitor, who sowed discord among those in concord, strife among the peaceful, scandals among brothers, divorce among the married, and who shook whatever was seen to stand in quiet amidst those who lived piously.

Wherefore, as was said before, we who have been gathered together through the agency of God, supported by the legates and letters of the nineteen bishops who assembled at Mainz on the holy day of last Pentecost, pass judgment against that same most insolent Hildebrand: for he preaches acts of sacrilege and arson; he defends perjuries and murders; long a disciple of the heretic Berenger, he places in question the Catholic and apostolic Faith in regard to the body and blood of the Lord; he is an open devotee of divinations and dreams, and a necromancer working with an oracular spirit;[8] and therefore he wanders beyond the limits of the true Faith. We judge that canonically he must be deposed and expelled and that, unless he descends from this See after hearing these words, he is forever damned.

I, Hugh Candidus,[9] cardinal priest of the holy Roman Church, from the Title of Saint Clement in the third district of the city, have assented to this decree promulgated by us, and I have subscribed it in the name of all the Roman cardinals.

I, Diepold, archbishop of Milan, have subscribed.

I, Kuono, bishop of Brescia, have subscribed.

I, Otto, bishop-elect of Tortona, have subscribed.

I, William, bishop of Pavia, have subscribed.

I, Reginald, bishop of Belluno, have subscribed.

I, Sigebod, bishop of Verona, have subscribed.

I, Dionysius, bishop of Piacenza, have subscribed.

Udo, bishop of Asti. I have subscribed.

I, Hugh, bishop-elect of Firmo, have subscribed.

Milo of Padua has subscribed.

I, Conrad, bishop of Utrecht, have subscribed.

Henry, the patriarch [of Aquileia], has subscribed.

Didald, bishop of Vicenza, has subscribed.

Regenger, bishop of Vercelli, has subscribed.

Rupert, bishop of Bamberg, has subscribed.

Norbert, bishop of Chur, has subscribed.

Eberhard, bishop of Parma, has subscribed.

Roland, by the grace of God, bishop of Treviso, most willingly has subscribed.

Arnold, bishop of Cremona, has subscribed.

Arnold, bishop of Bergamo, has subscribed.

I, Diedo, bishop of Brandenburg, have subscribed.

Leomar, archbishop of the holy church of Hamburg.

---

8 Probably a reference to the prophecy Gregory made at the Lenten Synod of 1080, after he had excommunicated Henry for the second time: "Be it known to all of you, that if he does not repent before the feast of St. Peter, he will be killed or deposed. If it does not happen thus, no one need believe me ever again." Bonizo, *Liber ad Amicum*, chap. 9, MGH Ldl., I, 616. Sigebert of Gembloux (*Chronicon*, MGH SS., VI, 369) reports, "Pope Hildebrand predicted, as though it had been divinely revealed to him, that the false king was to die in this year. Indeed, he predicted the truth; but the conjecture about the false king deceived him, since, according to his construction, the prediction referred to King Henry." Sigebert refers to the death of Rudolf of Rheinfelden.

9 At first a supporter of Gregory, he turned to the royalists within a year of Gregory's election, charging that it was uncanonical, and became a leader of the Synod of Worms (1076).

I, Werner, by the grace of God, bishop of Bobbio, have subscribed.

I, Altwin, bishop of Brixen, have subscribed.

I, Meginward, bishop of Freising, have subscribed.

I, Burchard, bishop of Lausanne, have subscribed.

I, Conrad, bishop of Genoa, have subscribed.

Henry, king by the grace of God. I have subscribed.

Henry praises the constancy of the clergy and people of Rome and announces his imminent arrival at Rome to assume his hereditary dignity (the Imperial office), to remove the conflicts of kingship and priesthood and to restore all things to peace and unity (1081).[10]

Henry, king by the grace of God, sends to the clergy and the Roman people, to the greater and lesser [feudatories], his affection in the most sincere expression of his favor and best wishes:

From many accounts of the elder nobles of our empire we have learned with what great fidelity and benevolence you honored our father of sacrosanct memory and with what great acts of honor he advanced publicly and privately both the dignity of your church and the universal grandeur of the Roman name. Nor, indeed, after his death did you cherish us in our infancy with less love and reverence. On all counts you stood beside us with faithful constancy as far as was possible in the face of the wickedness of certain pestilential and proud men. The helplessness of our youth was at

first our plea for not responding to your enduring love with due requital by granting you our favor. And after we put on the man, so great a madness of tyrannical perfidy swelled up against us that supreme necessity forced us to direct the entire concern of our effort toward crushing it.

But now since we have cut off with the sword both the life and the pride of those most bitter enemies, not by our power but by that of God, and in large part have set in order the members of the disrupted and sundered Empire, we intend to come to you. Our specific aim is to receive from you, by the common assent and favor of you all, our due and hereditary dignity and to bestow with every kind of honor the thanks which you deserve. We are surprised, however, that when our approach became better known, no legation from you came to us in the customary manner. For that reason we have refrained from sending our envoys to you. You yourselves know with what infamous abuse our envoys, honored and venerable men, were afflicted in the last year by him from whom such conduct was least fitting, in a manner exceeding the inhumanity of all barbarians.

This is the very thing with which those disturbers of peace and concord charge us. They scatter word among you that we come meaning to diminish the honor of Saint Peter, the prince of the apostles, and through our own power to overturn the commonwealth of you all. Indeed, these tactics accord with their usual conduct. But we tell the truth to you in good faith, for it is altogether our will and resolve to visit you peacefully, as far as is within us, and then, having considered the advice of all of you especially, and of our other vassals, to remove from our midst the long-lasting discord of the kingship and the priesthood, and to recall all things to peace and unity in the name of Christ.

---

10   Between Canossa and Gregory's Lenten Synod of 1080, the papacy took no major part in German affairs. Toward the end of this period, however, Gregory gave his support openly to the antiking Rudolf of Rheinfelden, whom Henry defeated and killed in battle in January 1080. This defeat and Henry's steadfast refusal to obey Gregory's edicts against lay investiture led to Gregory's second excommunication of the king at his Lenten Synod two months after Rudolf's death. Henry's position in Germany was then quite strong, and, in addition, the greater part of the German and Lombard bishops declared for him in this new crisis, rejecting Gregory as pope at the Synods of Bamberg and Mainz and electing Archbishop Wibert of Ravenna as his successor at the Synod of Brixen. With ample forces, Henry entered Italy early in 1080 to execute the judgments of his bishops; he then sent this letter to the people of Rome. Armed resistance to his march through the lands of his cousin, Mathilda of Tuscany, a stanch supporter of the reformed papacy, kept him from Rome almost a year. Late in 1082 he withdrew from Tuscany, and in 1083 he began his brief and victorious siege of Rome.

41. THE CONCORDAT OF WORMS

THE FIRST PHASE OF the investiture controversy ended in September 1122 with a compromise between Calixtus II and Henry V—the Concordat of Worms of September 1122.

Source: Henry Bettenson (ed.), *Documents of the Christian Church* (London: Oxford University Press, 1963).

Further Reading: Maureen Miller, *Power and the Holy in the Age of the Investiture Conflict: A Brief History with Documents* (Boston: Bedford/St. Martin's, 2005).

Agreement of Pope Calixtus II.

I, Calixtus, Bishop, servant of the servants of God, do grant to thee, beloved son, Henry—by the grace of God emperor of the Romans, Augustus—that the elections of bishops and abbots of the German kingdom, who belong to that kingdom, shall take place in thy presence, without simony or any violence; so that if any dispute shall arise between the parties concerned, thou, with the counsel or judgement of the metropolitan and the co-provincial bishops, shalt give consent and aid to the party which has the more right. The one elected shall receive the regalia from thee by the scepter and shall perform his lawful duties to thee on that account. But he who is consecrated in the other parts of thy empire [i.e., Burgundy and Italy] shall, within six months, and without any exaction, receive the regalia from thee by the scepter, and shall perform his lawful duties to thee on that account (saving all rights which are known to belong to the Roman Church). Concerning matters in which thou shalt make complaint to me, and ask aid—I, according to the duty of my office, will furnish aid to thee. I give unto thee true peace, and to all who are or have been of thy party in this conflict.

Edict of the Emperor Henry V

In the name of the holy and indivisible Trinity I, Henry, by the grace of God emperor of the Romans, Augustus, for the love of God and of the Holy Roman Church and of our lord pope Calixtus, and for the salvation of my soul, do surrender to God, and to the holy apostles of God, Peter and Paul, and to the Holy Catholic Church, all investiture through ring and staff; and do grant that in all the churches that are in my kingdom or empire there may be canonical election and free consecration. All the possessions and regalia of St. Peter which, from the beginning of this discord unto this day, whether in the time of my father or in mine have been seized, and which I hold, I restore to that same Holy Roman Church. And I will faithfully aid in the restoration of those things which I do not hold. The possessions also of all other churches and princes, and of all other persons lay and clerical which have been lost in that war: according to the counsel of the princes, or according to justice, I will restore, as far as I hold them; and I will faithfully aid in the restoration of those things which I do not hold. And I grant true peace to our lord pope Calixtus, and to the Holy Roman Church, and to all those who are or have been on its side. And in matters where the Holy Roman Church shall ask aid I will grant it; and in matters concerning which it shall make complaint to me I will duly grant to it justice. All these things have been done by the consent and counsel of the princes. Whose names are here adjoined: Adalbert archbishop of Mainz; F. archbishop of Cologne; H. bishop of Ratisbon; O. bishop of Bamberg; B. bishop of Spires; H. of Augsburg; G. of Utrecht; Ou. of Constance; E. abbot of Fulda; Henry, duke; Frederick, duke; S. duke; Pertolf, duke; Margrave Teipold; Margrave Engelbert; Godfrey, count Palatine; Otto, count Palatine; Berengar, count.

I, Frederick, archbishop of Cologne and arch-chancellor, have ratified this.

42. OTTO OF FREISING

The Deeds of Frederick Barbarossa

OTTO OF FREISING (1115–58) was the uncle of Frederick Barbarossa. After studying in Paris with Abelard, Hugh of St. Victor, and others, he entered the Cistercian Order and became bishop of Freising in 1138. Although best known for his writings, through his position and his familial connections he played an important role in strengthening the Church after the investiture controversy, acted as intermediary between monarchs, and even went on crusade. His greatest work is *Two Cities*, a world chronicle to 1146 which combines his philosophical and historical interests. His *Deeds of Frederick Barbarossa*, begun ten years later but left incomplete at his death, presents a glorified vision of the reign of his nephew as a period of peace. The selection below describes Frederick's election, his disposition of internal German affairs, and the beginnings of his first campaign against Milan and the Lombard League.

Source: C.C. Mierow, *The Deeds of Frederick Barbarossa* (New York: W.W. Norton, 1953).

Further Reading: Marcel Pacaut, *Frederick Barbarossa*, trans. Arnold J. Pomerand (New York: Charles Scribner's Sons, 1970).

Here Begins the Prologue of the Book that Follows

I am not unaware, O paragon of emperors and kings, that while I am attempting to portray the magnificence of your exploits, my pen will prove unequal to the material, as your victories increase. Yet of the two evils, so to speak, I have thought it better that my work should be surpassed by the subject (through my deficiency in expression) than that your glorious deeds should be veiled in silence and perish, were I to say nothing of them.

But because I brought my previous little book to an end with the beginning of your rule as king and emperor, at the death of your most glorious uncle, King Conrad, may this second book, that is to vie with the glory of your principate, now, with God's favor, take its beginning.

Here Ends the Prologue.

Here Begins the Second Book

i. In the year 1800 since the founding of the City,[1] but 1154 [1152] from the incarnation of the Lord,

the most pious King Conrad departed this life in the springtime, on the fifteenth day before the Kalends of March—that is, on the Friday following Ash Wednesday—in the city of Bamberg, as has been said. Wonderful to relate, it was possible to bring together the entire company of the princes, as into a single body, in the town of Frankfort, from the immense extent of the transalpine kingdom (as well as certain barons from Italy), by the third [fourth] day before the Nones of March [March 4]—that is, on Tuesday after *Oculi mei semper*. When the chief men took counsel together there concerning the choice of a prince—for this is the very apex of the law of the Roman empire, namely, that kings are chosen not by lineal descent but through election by the princes (this right it claims for itself as though by unique prerogative)—finally Frederick, duke of the Swabians, the son of Duke Frederick, was sought by all. By the favor of all he was raised to the rank of king.

ii. The explanation of this support, the reason for so unanimous an agreement upon that person,

---

1 Otto dated the birth of Christ in the year 752 from the founding of the City of Rome (*Two Cities* III.vi), or 2 BCE, so that this date should read 1904 rather than 1800.

was, as I recall, as follows. There have been hitherto in the Roman world, within the borders of Gaul and Germany, two renowned families: one that of the Henrys of Waiblingen,[2] the other that of the Welfs of Altdorf. The one was wont to produce emperors, the other great dukes. These families, eager for glory as is usually the case with great men, were frequently envious of each other and often disturbed the peace of the state. But by the will of God (as men believe), providing for the peace of his people in time to come, it came about that Duke Frederick, the father of this Frederick, who was a descendant of one of the two families (that is, of the family of the kings), took to wife a member of the other, namely, the daughter of Henry, duke of the Bavarians, and by her became the father of the Frederick who rules at the present time.

The princes, therefore, considering not merely the achievements and the valor of the youth already so frequently mentioned, but also this fact, that being a member of both families, he might—like a cornerstone—link these two separate walls, decided to select him as head of the realm. They foresaw that it would greatly benefit the state if so grave and so long-continued a rivalry between the greatest men of the empire for their own private advantage might by this opportunity and with God's help be finally lulled to rest. So it was not because of dislike for King Conrad, but (as has been said) in the interest of a universal advantage that they preferred to place this Frederick ahead of Conrad's son (likewise named Frederick), who was still a little child. By reason of such considerations and in this way the election of Frederick was celebrated.

iii. When, therefore, all the princes who had thronged to that place had been bound by oath of fealty and homage, the king with a few men whom he considered suitable for the purpose, having dismissed the rest in peace, took ship, amid great rejoicing, on the fifth day of the week. He sailed by the Main and the Rhine, and disembarked at the royal seat at Sinzig. There taking horse, he came the next Saturday to Aachen.

On the following day, that is, on that Sunday on which *Laetare Ierusalem* is sung,[3] he was escorted by the bishops from the palace to the church of the blessed Mary ever virgin. With the greatest applause of all who were present, he was crowned by Arnold, archbishop of Cologne, the others assisting, and was seated on the throne of the realm of the Franks that was placed in that same church by Charles the Great. Not a few marveled that in so short a space of time not only had so great a throng of princes and of nobles of the kingdom flocked together, but that some also had arrived from western Gaul, whither the report of this event was supposed not yet to have arrived.

I think I ought not to omit the fact that while the diadem was being placed on Frederick's head, after the completion of the sacramental anointing, one of his retainers, from whom for certain grave offenses he had withdrawn his favor before he was king, cast himself at his feet in the center of the church, hoping to turn the latter's spirit from the rigor of justice on so happy an occasion. But Frederick maintained his previous severity and remained unmoved and thus gave to all of us not small proof of his firmness, declaring that it was not from hatred but out of regard for justice that this man had been excluded from his patronage. Nor did this fail to win the admiration of many, that pride could not dissuade the young man (already, as it were, in possession of an old man's judgment) from virtuous firmness to the fault of laxity. What more need be said? Neither the intercession of the princes, nor the favor of smiling fortune, nor the present joy of so great a festival could help that poor wretch. He departed from the inexorable prince unheard.

But this, too, should not be veiled in silence, that on the same day and in the same church the bishop-elect of Münster (also named Frederick) was consecrated by those same bishops who consecrated the king. So it was believed that the Highest King and Priest was actually participating in the present rejoicing: and this was the sign, that in one church one day beheld the anointing of the two persons who alone are sacramentally anointed according to the ordinance of the New

2   That is, the Hohenstaufen, so-called from the village of Waiblingen in Swabia; the Italians turned Waiblingen into "Ghibelline."
3   The fourth Sunday in Lent, March 9, 1152.

and of the Old Testament, and are rightly called the anointed of Christ the Lord.

iv. When all that pertains to the dignity of the crown had been duly performed, the prince retired to the private apartments of the palace and summoned the more prudent and powerful of the assembled nobles. After consulting them concerning the condition of the state, he arranged to have ambassadors sent to the Roman pontiff, Eugenius, to the City, and to all Italy, to carry the tidings of his elevation to the rank of king. Therefore, Hillin, archbishop-elect of Trier, and Eberhard, bishop of Bamberg, prudent and learned men, were sent. Then the prince advanced upon the lower regions of the Rhine, to punish the people of Utrecht for the arrogance which, as has previously been related, they had shown toward his uncle Conrad. After he had punished them by the imposition of a fine and confirmed Herman as bishop, moving back up the Rhine he celebrated holy Easter at Cologne. Thence he passed through Westphalia and entered Saxony.

v. In the kingdom of the Danes there arose at that time a serious controversy concerning the rule, between the two kinsmen Peter (who is also called Svein) and Knut. The king summoned them before him and held a great assembly in Martinopolis, a city of Saxony which is also called Merseburg, with a large number of princes. The aforesaid young men came there and humbly yielded themselves to his command. Their case is said finally to have been settled by the judgment or advice of the chief men as follows: that Knut (to whom certain provinces were left) should abdicate the royal title by surrendering his sword—for it is the custom of the court that kingdoms are bestowed by the prince or taken back again by the sword, provinces by the military standard—but that Peter, receiving the royal power at the sovereign's hand, should be bound to him by fealty and homage. So the crown of the realm was placed on his head

by the hand of the prince, on Whitsunday, and he himself, wearing the crown, bore the sword of the king who marched in state wearing his crown. Waldemar, also, who was a member of the same family, received a certain duchy of Denmark.[4]

vi. At about the same time the church of Magdeburg (which is known to be the metropolis of Saxony), being bereft of its shepherd, determined to hold an election. And since some were for choosing Gerhard, the provost of that church, and others the dean, individuals being divided on this side and on that, they decided to approach the king, who was still tarrying in Saxony. The prince endeavored in many ways to lead them back to unity and the bond of peace. As he could not accomplish this, he persuaded one party—that is, the dean and his followers—to choose Wichmann, the bishop of Zeitz, a man still young but of noble blood, and having summoned him, invested him with the regalia of that church. For the court holds and declares that when the controversy between the empire and the papacy concerning the investiture of bishops was settled, under Henry V,[5] it was granted by the Church that when bishops died, if there happened to be a division in the choice of a successor, it should be the prerogative of the prince to appoint as bishop whomsoever he might please, with the advice of his chief men; and that no bishop-elect should receive consecration before having obtained the regalia from the prince's hand through the scepter.

The king, having brought all matters in Saxony into good order and inclined to his own will all the princes of that province, entered Bavaria and wore his crown in Regensburg, the metropolis of that duchy, at the festival of the apostles,[6] in the monastery of St. Emmeram; for the cathedral had burned down, together with certain quarters of the city. The ambassadors sent to the City, to Pope Eugenius, and to the other cities of Italy returned to that same diet with glad tidings. There indeed did the prince, having displayed a strong will in

---

4   The emperors enjoyed a rather shadowy control over the states to the north and east: Denmark, Poland, Bohemia, Hungary. Though Otto's account leaves the impression that this settlement of the Danish throne was definitive, its actual effect seems to have been negligible. The struggle between Svein and Knut continued, and the former (Frederick's candidate) was driven into exile within two years. Svein had Knut killed in 1157, but the result was to put on the throne his cousin Waldemar, whom Otto had just mentioned.

5   The Concordat of Worms, 1122. See doc. 41, above.

6   The apostles Peter and Paul, June 29.

arranging all to his satisfaction within the confines of his empire, think to display abroad a stout arm. He wished to declare war on the Hungarians and to bring them under the might of the monarchy. But being for certain obscure reasons unable to secure the assent of the princes in this matter, and thus being powerless to put his plans into effect, he postponed them until a more opportune time.

vii. However, though all was prospering in his kingdom, the most serene prince was indeed very anxious to end without bloodshed that dispute over the duchy of Bavaria between his own relatives, that is, Duke Henry, his paternal uncle, and Duke Henry, his maternal uncle's son.[7] (For the latter was the son of the former Duke Henry of Bavaria, whom King Conrad had compelled to remain in Saxony after he had been outlawed, as has been told elsewhere. His duchy he had bestowed first upon Leopold, the son of Margrave Leopold, and then upon this Henry, the younger Leopold's brother.) The king, therefore, to decide the aforesaid strife by judicial decree or by his counsel, appointed for them a diet at the city of Würzburg in autumn, during the month of October. Inasmuch as the one (that is, the son of Duke Henry) appeared there and the other absented himself, the latter was summoned again and again.

At that same diet exiles from Apulia, whom Roger had driven out from their native land, made tearful lament and cast themselves pitifully at the feet of the prince. Both because of the affliction of these people and that he might receive the crown of empire, it was solemnly agreed that an expedition into Italy should be undertaken within a little less than two years.

viii. Next, the provost Gerhard hastened to Rome and applied to Pope Eugenius. Setting forth the case of the church of Magdeburg, he charged Wichmann (who, as has been narrated above, had been installed in office by the prince after his election by the second party) with usurpation, on many counts. How greatly disturbed the Roman pontiff was by this matter we have learned both from the letter he sent (in reply to certain bishops

who had written to the Roman Church on his [Wichmann's] behalf, out of love for the king) and by word of mouth from the cardinals who were afterward sent across the Alps. Now the content of the letter was as follows:

"Bishop Eugenius, the servant of the servants of God, to his venerable brothers, the archbishops Eberhard of Salzburg, Hartwig of Bremen, and Hillin of Trier, and the bishops Eberhard of Bamberg, Herman of Constance, Henry of Regensburg, Otto of Freising, Conrad of Passau, Daniel of Prague, Anselm of Havelberg, and Burchard of Eichstädt, greeting and apostolic benediction.

"The letter which Your Prudence dispatched on behalf of the church of Magdeburg we received in all due kindness. But in reading it and learning its contents we were filled with great surprise and amazement, because we perceived them to be far other than beseems you, in consideration of your office of bishop. For though you have by Divine Providence been set at the head of the Church, to remove from its midst such things as are harmful and to preserve with zealous care the things that are useful, in the present case (as has become known to us from the contents of your letter) you have heeded not what is expedient for the Church of God, what is in accord with the sanction of the sacred canons, what accordingly would be approved by the will of heaven, but rather that which is pleasing to earthly princes. And you, who ought to turn aside their hearts from their unrighteous intent and show where the way of the Lord is, have not advised them what is right, nor stood as a wall before the house of Israel. Nay even, as the prophet says, when men were building a wall you 'daubed it with untempered mortar'; a thing that we can scarcely say without great bitterness of spirit. Not so did the prince of the apostles judge, who in consequence of the confession of his faith obtained the promise that he should be the foundation of the whole Church; but when the sons of this world menaced the apostles and threatened destruction and death if they

---

7   Henry Jasomirgott, brother of Bishop Otto, half-brother of Conrad III, and paternal uncle of Frederick, who had received the duchy of Bavaria from Conrad, and Henry the Lion, son of Henry the Proud (Frederick's mother, Judith, was the latter's sister).

preached in the name of Jesus, he made answer: 'We ought to obey God rather than men.'

"But you, lest you should appear to disagree with earthly princes, bestow your favor upon that cause to which both the authority of ecclesiastical enactment and the test of the will of heaven is surely believed to be opposed. For whereas the expression of divine law does not permit the transferring of bishops without a proof of evident advantage and necessity, and whereas also a far greater harmony of clergy and people should precede [in such a transfer] than in other elections, in the transfer of our venerable brother Wichmann, bishop of Zeitz, we find none of these circumstances, but only the anticipated favor of the prince. Without investigating the needs of the Church, or considering the usefulness of the person, the clergy unwilling—nay more, with the majority of them, it is said, protesting it—you declare that he must be moved to the church of Magdeburg.

"We marvel the more at this, as we know from past experience how much weight and wisdom that person [Frederick] has, and likewise are not entirely ignorant of how useful he is to that church. Now whoever else may be moved by the breezes of temporal favor, we who are founded upon the stability of that rock which was worthy to be established as the foundation of the Church, both should not and desire not to be tossed about by 'every wind of doctrine,' or to wander because of some impulse from the right way of the sacred canons. We charge you, therefore, by this present writing that you no longer lend your favor to that cause, and that you endeavor by your exhortations so to influence our very dear son Frederick (whom God has exalted at this time to the eminence of royal authority to preserve the liberty of the Church) that he himself desist from his purpose in this matter, and no longer bestow his favor upon that same cause in opposition to God, in opposition to the sacred canons, in opposition to demands of his royal dignity; but that he relinquish to

the church of Magdeburg—as also to the other churches of the realm entrusted to him by God—the free privilege of choosing whomsoever it wishes, in accordance with God's will, and sustain that same election thereafter by his favor, as is seemly for royal majesty. For if we could see that what he is endeavoring to do concerning our aforesaid brother is supported by reason, we would not think that either his will or your request should at all be opposed. But there is no petition whatever to which we can grant our consent in opposition to God and the sanctions of the sacred canons.

"Given at Segni, on the sixteenth day before the Kalends of September [August 17, 1152]."

ix. Now the king, when he wore the crown in Bamberg the following Easter, had with him two cardinals, namely, the priest Bernard and the deacon Gregory, sent by the apostolic see for the deposing of certain bishops. So, while celebrating the next Whitsunday at Worms, he deposed through the instrumentality of the same cardinals Henry, archbishop of the see of Mainz (a man often reproved for weakening his Church, but never improved)[8] and replaced him by his chancellor, Arnold,[9] through election by certain of the clergy and people who had come thither. To the aforesaid court came the dukes previously mentioned, the two Henrys, contending for the duchy of Bavaria, as has been said. But as the one alleged that he had not been summoned in proper form, the matter could not there reach a due conclusion. Moreover, the same cardinals with the permission of the prince likewise removed Burchard of Eichstädt, a man weighed down by years, giving as their reason his inefficiency. And when, after this, they were thinking of passing sentence upon the archbishop of Magdeburg and certain others, they were prevented by the prince and bidden to return home [ad propria redire].

x. At that time Pope Eugenius, a just man and notable for his piety, departed this life [July 8, 1153] and left the see to Anastasius, who was of

---

8   Archbishop Henry seems to have raised the only dissenting voice at Frederick's election as king, and this is probably the reason for his removal.

9   Arnold of Selenhofen, later murdered in a communal uprising at Mainz in 1160, and afterward canonized.

advanced age and experienced in the customs of the court.[10] When a certain cardinal, Gerard by name, had been sent by him to end the case of the archbishop-elect of Magdeburg, he had approached the prince in that same city while he was celebrating the Lord's Birthday.[11] As he tried to do certain things there against the will of the prince, he incurred the latter's anger and was compelled by stern command to return ingloriously, leaving unfinished the business for which he had come; indeed, he died on the road. But the prince sent messengers to Anastasius, together with Wichmann, and secured not only the ratification of his action but also the pallium for Wichmann, not without offending certain persons who had heard (from their own lips) that the Romans were immovably determined that this should never happen. Since that time the authority of the prince has very greatly increased in the administration not only of secular but also of ecclesiastical affairs.

xi. At about the same time, in the month of September [1153], the princes and the leading men of Bavaria were called together by the king at Regensburg. But nothing could be settled there with reference to the blessing of peace in that province, on account of the strife between the two dukes. Now the king, because he had been separated from his wife by legates of the apostolic see not long before, on the ground of consanguinity, was negotiating for another marriage. Both on this account and for the overthrow of William of Sicily, who had recently succeeded his deceased father, Roger, the enemy of both empires, he arranged to send ambassadors to Manuel, emperor of the Greeks. And so, by the advice of his chief men, that mission was undertaken by Anselm, bishop of Havelberg, and Alexander, once count of Apulia, but expelled by Roger with other nobles of that same province under suspicion of seeking the throne.

Then, in the following month of December [1153], both the dukes (Henry and the other Henry) attended the prince's judgment seat in the city of

Speyer. But the case was postponed, because the one for the second time claimed that he had not been summoned in due legal form. Frederick had now striven for almost two years to terminate the strife between the two princes so close to him, as has been said, by blood relationship. Therefore, being at length moved by the insistence of the one who desired to return to the land he had inherited from his father, from which he had long been debarred, Frederick was compelled to make an end of the matter because of the imminent task of the expedition in which he needed that same youth as a knight and companion of his journey. Accordingly, holding court at Goslar, a town of Saxony, he summoned both dukes by issuing edicts. Since the one came and the other absented himself, the duchy of Bavaria was thereby decision of the princes, adjudged to the former, that is, to Duke Henry of Saxony. After this the prince, betaking himself from Saxony into Bavaria and thence proceeding through Swabia, in the third year of his reign assembled a military force on the plains of the river Lech, the boundary of Bavaria, opposite the city of Augsburg, in order to enter Italy. This was at about the beginning of the month of October, almost two years having elapsed since the expedition had first been vowed. Nor, by the judgment recently proclaimed against so great a prince of the empire and the no little murmuring of other princes arising therefrom, was it possible to distract the illustrious spirit from so great a deed, but disregarding all those things that were behind, and entrusting himself to God, he pressed on to the things that were before. Therefore after crossing the passes of the Alps and passing through Brixen and the valley of the Trent, he encamped on the plains of Verona, near Lake Garda. When he was there taking counsel with his princes concerning their further advance, he determined he must first of all win the favor of the Prince of Heaven. In short, the army, being unable on its passage through the mountain barriers to find things necessary for the support of life, on account of the barrenness of the country, while suffering great want (a

---

10 Anastasius IV, elected in July 1153, and died December 3, 1154.
11 Frederick celebrated Christmas of 1153 at Speyer; the meeting with the cardinal seems to have occurred at Magdeburg on the following Easter (April 4, 1154).

thing that is always very grievous for troops) had violated certain holy places. To atone for this—although they seemed to have the aforesaid excuse of necessity—the king ordered a collection to be taken from the entire army. He decided that the not inconsiderable sum of money thus amassed should be taken back by certain holy men to the two bishops (of Trent, that is, and of Brixen) and divided among the various places of the saints which had suffered loss. Thus he provided nobly for the common good, fulfilling nobly a leader's task. For being about to enter upon very great undertakings, he decided that before all else he must placate the Ruler and Creator of all, without Whom nothing is well begun, nothing successfully completed, and that His wrath must be averted from his people.

xii. Then, breaking camp, Frederick halted in the month of November on the plain of Roncaglia, on the Po, not far from Piacenza. Now it is the custom of the kings of the Franks (who are also called kings of the Germans), that as often as they have assembled a military force to cross the Alps in order to assume the crown of the Roman empire, they make a halt on the aforesaid plain. There a shield is suspended on a wooden beam that is raised aloft, and all the knights that are his vassals are summoned by the herald of the court to stand watch over their prince the ensuing night. Accordingly the princes who are in his company each likewise calls out his own feudatories, by heralds. The next day anyone discovered to have absented himself from the night watch is again summoned into the presence of the king and the other princes and illustrious men. Thus all the vassals, both of the sovereign and of the princes, who have remained at home without the full consent of their lords are punished [by confiscation of] their fiefs. The prince followed this custom, and not only the fiefs of some laymen but also the regalia of certain bishops (namely, Hartwig of Bremen and Ulrich of Halberstadt) were taken away from them: only from these individuals, however, because they were bestowed in perpetuity by the princes upon the churches but not upon individuals.

Now since mention has been made of this country, I shall say a few words concerning its location and customs, and by whom it was previously inhabited, by what name it was called, by whom it was afterward possessed, by what appellation it was distinguished.

xiii. This land, shut in on this side and on that by the Pyrenees [Alps] and the Apennines, very high and rugged mountains that extend for a long distance, like the navel of these mountains—or rather of this range of mountains—extends as a very garden of delights from the Tyrrhenian Sea to the shore of the Adriatic Sea. It has to the north the Pyrenees mountains (as has been said); on the south the Apennines which presently, changing their name, are commonly called the Mount of Bardo; on the west the Tyrrhenian; on the east the Adriatic Sea. It is watered by the course of the Po, or *Eridanus* River, which topographers rate as one of the three most famous rivers of Europe,[12] and of other streams, and by reason of the pleasantness of the soil and the moderate climate it is productive of wine and oil, to such a degree, indeed, that it brings forth fruit-bearing trees, especially chestnuts, figs, and olives, like forest groves.

The colony of the Romans, once called Farther Italy, was separated into three provinces: Venetia, Aemilia, and Liguria. Aquileia was the metropolis of the first, Ravenna of the second, and Milan of the third. The district in the Apennines themselves—where the city of Rome also is known to be situated—which is now called Tuscany, was quite properly termed Inner Italy because, being surrounded by the Apennines, it holds in its lap the City itself as well. But that plain which succeeds when the mountains run out, and is for this reason still customarily called Campania, was once termed Hither Italy or Greater Greece; now it is named Apulia and Calabria. It extends to Faro di Messina, an arm of the sea unfavorable for ships on account of the sandbanks; for Sicily, the boundary of Europe, is counted with Sardinia and the other islands of Italy. But some, who count this and mid-Italy as one, have preferred to call Hither Italy and Greater Greece "Italy," enumerating not three (as aforesaid) but only two Italies: Farther and Hither.

12   The others being the Danube and the Rhone.

Some, indeed, hold that the aforesaid mountains, the Apennines and the Pyrenees, are one mountain range. For approximately where the city of Genoa (well versed in naval warfare) is situated, on the Tyrrhenian Sea, they enclose the aforesaid province by drawing close together. As a proof of their statement they declare that, according to Isidore, Pannonia received its name from being enclosed by the Apennines; however, not the Apennines (now called the Mount of Bardo) but the Pyrenees Mountains touch it. It is evident, I think, why I have previously called this land the navel of two ranges or of the one range.

But as it began to be subject to the invasions and the domination of the barbarians who, coming from the island of Scandza [Scandinavia] with their leader Alboin, first inhabited the Pannonias, from them it began to be called Lombardy. For to increase their army [by the drafting of women] they twisted the women's hair about the chin in such a way as to imitate a manly and bearded face, and for that reason they were called Lombards [*Longobardi*], from their long beards. Hence it came to pass that as the ancient inhabitants of that province were crowded together around the exarchate of Ravenna, that part of Italy (which was formerly called Aemilia) is commonly called even today Romaniola, which is known to be a diminutive, derived from "Rome."

But [the Lombards] having put aside crude, barbarous ferocity, perhaps from the fact that when united in marriage with the natives they begat sons who inherited something of the Roman gentleness and keenness from their mothers' blood, and from the very quality of the country and climate, retain the refinement of the Latin speech and their elegance of manners. In the governing of their cities, also, and in the conduct of public affairs, they still imitate the wisdom of the ancient Romans. Finally, they are so desirous of liberty that, avoiding the insolence of power, they are governed by the will of consuls rather than rulers. There are known to be three orders among them: captains, vavasors,[13] and commoners.[14] And in order to suppress arrogance, the aforesaid

consuls are chosen not from one but from each of the classes. And lest they should exceed bounds by lust for power, they are changed almost every year. The consequence is that, as practically that entire land is divided among the cities, each of them requires its bishops to live in the cities, and scarcely any noble or great man can be found in all the surrounding territory who does not acknowledge the authority of his city. And from this power to force all elements together they are wont to call the several lands of each [noble, or magnate] their contado [*comitatus*].[15] Also, that they may not lack the means of subduing their neighbors, they do not disdain to give the girdle of knighthood or the grades of distinction to young men of inferior station and even some workers of the vile mechanical arts, whom other peoples bar like the pest from the more respected and honorable pursuits. From this it has resulted that they far surpass all other states of the world in riches and in power. They are aided in this not only, as has been said, by their characteristic industry, but also by the absence of their princes,[16] who are accustomed to remain on the far side of the Alps. In this, however, forgetful of their ancient nobility, they retain traces of their barbaric imperfection, because while boasting that they live in accordance with law, they are not obedient to the laws. For they scarcely if ever respect the prince to whom they should display the voluntary deference of obedience or willingly perform that which they have sworn by the integrity of their laws, unless they sense his authority in the power of his great army. Therefore it often happens that although a citizen must be humbled by the laws and an adversary subdued by arms in accordance with the laws, yet they very frequently receive in hostile fashion him whom they ought to accept as their own gentle prince, when he demands what is rightfully his own. From this arises a twofold loss to the common weal: the prince is obliged to assemble an army for the subjugation of his people, and the people (not without great loss of their own possessions) are forced to obey their prince. Accordingly, by the same process of reasoning

13   Lesser subvassals.
14   This is a sketchy attempt by Otto to indicate the class structure of the northern Italian towns. The captains are the great nobles.
15   Otto is here trying to describe the north Italian city state, with its extensive control over the surrounding territories.
16   That is, the emperors.

whereby impetuosity accuses the people for this situation, so should necessity excuse the prince in the sight of God and men.

xiv. Among all the cities of this people Milan now holds chief place. It is situated between the Po and the Pyrenees, and between the Ticino and the Adda, which take their source from the same Pyrenees and drain into the Po, thereby creating a certain very fertile valley, like an island. Located midway, it is rightly called *Mediolanum*, although some think it was named *Mediolanum* by its founders from a certain portentous sow that had bristles on one side and wool on the other. Now this city is considered (as has been said) more famous than others not only because of its size and its abundance of brave men, but also from the fact that it has extended its authority over two neighboring cities situated within the same valley, Como and Lodi. Furthermore—as usually happens in our transitory lot when favoring fortune smiles—Milan, elated by prosperity, became puffed up to such audacious exaltation that not only did it not shrink from molesting its neighbors, but recently even dared incur the anger of the prince, standing in no awe of his majesty. From what causes this situation arose I shall afterward briefly set forth.

xv. Meanwhile, it seems necessary to say a few words concerning the jurisdiction over the realm. For it is an old custom, maintained from the time that the Roman empire passed over to the Franks even down to our own day, that as often as the kings have decided to enter Italy they send ahead certain qualified men of their retinue to go about among the individual cities and towns to demand what pertains to the royal treasury and is called by the natives *fodrum*. Hence it comes about that, on the prince's arrival, most of the cities, towns, and strongholds that attempt to oppose this right by absolute refusal or by not making full payment are razed to the ground to give evidence of their impudence to posterity. Likewise, another right is said to have found its source in ancient custom. When the prince enters Italy all dignities and magistracies must be vacated and everything administered by his nod, in accordance with legal decrees and the judgment of those versed in the law. The judges are said also to accord him so great authority over the land that they think it just to supply for the use of the king as much as he needs from all that the land customarily produces that is essential for his use and may be of advantage to the army, only excepting the cattle and the seed devoted to the cultivation of the soil.

xvi. Now the king abode, it is said, for five days [November 30–December 6, 1154] at Roncaglia and held a diet, with the princes, consuls, and elders of almost all the cities assembled there, and diverse things became known from the complaints of this party or of that. Among them were William, marchese of Montferrat, a noble and great man, and practically the only one of the barons of Italy who could escape from the authority of the cities, and also the bishop of Asti. They made serious charges: one, concerning the insolence of the people of Asti; the other (that is, the marchese), concerning that of the inhabitants of Chieri.

(But we do not think that, in comparison with his other valiant exploits, it contributes much to the prince's claim to glory if, while hastening on to more important things, we speak of the fortified places, rocky strongholds, towns, and great estates destroyed since his coming, not only by those of knightly order but even by the assault of the unbridled sergeants.)[17]

There were present also the consuls of Como and of Lodi, making mournful lament over the arrogance of the people of Milan. They bewailed their long-continued misery of mistreatment in the presence of two consuls of that very city, Oberto de Orto and Gerardo Negri. Therefore, as the prince was about to visit the upper regions of Italy and wished to pass through the Milanese territory he kept the aforesaid consuls with him to guide his way and to make arrangements for suitable places for encampments.

There came also to the same court ambassadors of the people of Genoa, who not long before this time had captured Almeria and Lisbon,[18]

---

17   This paragraph, seemingly out of place here, may be a later addition to the text.
18   A Genoese fleet had operated in Spanish waters in 1147–48, and had assisted in the capture of Almeria and Tortosa. Lisbon also fell to the Christians in 1147, but the Genoese played no part in that enterprise. For the capture of Lisbon, see C.W. David, *De expugnatione Lyxbonensi: The Conquest of Lisbon*, "Records of Civilization," No. 34 (New York, 1926).

renowned cities in Spain, very famous for their workmanship of silk cloths, and returned laden with spoils of the Saracens. They presented the prince with lions, ostriches, parrots, and other valuable gifts.

xvii (xiii b). Frederick, therefore, being (as has been said) about to set out for the upper regions of Farther Italy, led his forces from Roncaglia and pitched camp in the territory of the Milanese. And as he was conducted by the aforesaid consuls through wastelands where provisions [*stipendia*] could neither be found nor secured by purchase, he was moved to anger and turned his arms against the people of Milan, having first ordered the consuls to return home. Another circumstance aggravated his wrath. The whole army is said to have been so exasperated by a heavy downpour of rain that in consequence of this double annoyance—hunger and the inclement weather—all aroused the prince against the consuls as much as they could. There was likewise another by no means trivial cause for this high feeling. The prince had already perceived their swollen insolence in the fact that they were not only unwilling to rebuild the cities which they had destroyed, but were even trying to bribe and to corrupt his noble and hitherto untarnished spirit to acquiesce in their iniquity. The king, moving his camp from the barren region, betook himself to fertile places of this land, not far from the city, and refreshed his weary soldiers.

43. THE *SAXON MIRROR (SACHSENSPIEGEL)*

THE *SACHSENSPIEGEL*, COMPILED IN 1235 by Eike von Repgow, is the earliest compilation of customary law in the German language. Although originally compiled for Saxony, the text spread throughout the German-speaking regions of Europe and beyond, undergoing numerous revisions, each manuscript providing a flexible guide adapted to the needs of a particular region or community. The following excerpt from Book I, dealing with inheritance and kinship, is translated from the illuminated Wolfenbüttel manuscript of the fourteenth century.

Source: Maria Dobozy (ed.), *The Saxon Mirror: A Sachsenspiegel of the Fourteenth Century* (Philadelphia: University of Pennsylvania Press, 1999), 67–74.

Further Reading: Maria Dobozy "From Oral Custom to Written Law: the German *Sachsenspiegel*," in Gerhard Jaritz and Michael Richter (eds.), *Oral History of the Middle Ages: The Spoken Word in Context* (Budapest: Central European University, 2001), 154–63.

FIRST PROLOGUE. May the love of the Holy Spirit sharpen my mind so that I may pronounce what is lawful and unlawful among the Saxons for the grace of God and the benefit of the world. I cannot accomplish this project alone. Therefore, I request the support of all law-abiding people who desire justice. Should they encounter a juridical dispute that I have omitted from this book because of my limited knowledge, I request that they reach a just determination to their best knowledge and discretion. No one should let himself be diverted from the law, not for love or jealousy, wrath or gain. God is Law itself; therefore, justice is dear to him. Consequently, all those to whom God has given the task of judging shall strive to reach judgments in such a manner that God in His wrath and judgment may treat them mercifully.

SECOND PROLOGUE. God who is the beginning and the end of all worthwhile things created heaven and earth first, then formed man on earth and placed him in paradise. Man broke the commandment to the ruin of us all. That is why we all went astray like shepherdless sheep until the day He saved us with His martyrdom. But now that we have been converted, and God has summoned us, we keep His law and His commandments—the ones His prophets and pious spiritual people taught us, and also the ones the Christian kings, Constantine and Charlemagne, provided—in Saxony to the advancement of His law.

Book I

God left behind on earth two swords for the protection of Christianity: To the pope he gave the spiritual sword, and to the emperor, the temporal one. Now the pope is also required to ride a white horse at a specified time, and on this occasion the emperor shall hold his stirrup so that the saddle will not slip. The meaning is this: Any [entity] resisting the pope in a way that he cannot control by ecclesiastical jurisdiction needs to be compelled by the emperor and his use of secular law to obey the pope. So, too, shall the spiritual jurisdiction assist the secular power when necessary.

2 Once he has come of age, every Christian is duty-bound to attend the ecclesiastical court three times a year in the bishopric where he resides. There are three levels of obligation. Those belonging to the class eligible to be Schöffen[1] shall attend the episcopal court; the king's tenants attend the dean's court, and [the other] tenants, the archpriest's court. Everyone also owes attendance at the secular court in the same manner. The Schöffen attend

---

1   Lay judge or juror.

the count's court every eighteen weeks held under the king's legal jurisdiction. Should a court be called into session because of a crime within a fortnight after the regular session, then the Schöffen are required to attend this hearing as well, so that the crime may be judged. With these actions they maintain their allodial land free of encumbrance before the judge. The king's tenants are also duty-bound to attend the court of the Schultheiss² because of their heritable land. Whenever the local officer of the court (bailiff) dies, another must be chosen from among this group. The tenants who have no hereditary interest in their land attend the court of the local district judge every six weeks. In addition, each advocate must hold court and each village headman must raise the hue and cry and make an indictment for each bloody wound inflicted by one person on another, for each sword drawn to inflict harm on another, for each person who fails to attend court when he is duty-bound to do so, and for each crime that is punishable with loss of hand or life if the complaint has not yet been made before the court. He may not bring a suit in any other way.

3 Origen foretold long ago that there would be six ages, each age calculated to last a thousand years, and in the seventh, the world is expected to end. Now we know from the Holy Scriptures that the first age began with Adam. The second began with Noah, with Abraham the third, with Moses the fourth, with David the fifth, and with God's birth the sixth. We are now in the seventh age without certainty of its duration. The orders of nobility eligible to bear arms are organized in the same way. Within this hierarchy, the king belongs to the first order, the bishops, abbots, and abbesses to the second, the lay princes to the third since they became vassals to the bishops, the free lords belong to the fourth, the Schöffen class and the vassals of the free lords to the fifth, and their vassals to the sixth order. Just as Christianity has no secure knowledge of the seventh age or how long it will last, it is likewise unclear whether the seventh order can participate in either the right to bear arms or in feudal law. The lay princes extended the sixth

order into the seventh when they became vassals of the bishops, which had not been the case earlier. Just as the hierarchy of shields extends to the seventh order, likewise blood relations also continue to the seventh degree. Now note how and where kinship begins and ends. At the head are man and wife who have come together lawfully. The neck is the next generation of family members. They are the children born of the union and not outside of it. A child born of one of the couple, related by half-blood, cannot be considered part of the same degree. In fact, this child is removed into the next level of membership. If two brothers marry two sisters and the third brother an unrelated woman, their children are all of equal degree of kinship, equally removed, equally close, so that each can assume the other's inheritance as long as they are of equal birth. The children of legitimate brothers are located at the level where the arm connects to the shoulder. The same holds for children of sisters. These people are related in the very next level; that is, in the first degree of consanguinity. They are the children of brothers and sisters. The level of the elbow marks the second degree, the wrist the third, the first joint of the middle finger the fourth, the second joint the fifth, and the third joint the sixth. At the seventh level there is no joint; only a fingernail marks the degree and therefore the kinship ends with the nail members. Those persons between head and fingernail who stand at the same level of consanguinity share the inheritance in equal parts. The heir who can be placed closest to [the head of] the clan lays first claim to the estate. Kin share legitimately in the estate up to the seventh degree although the pope permits marriage to a woman of one's own kin to the fifth degree only. This is permissible because the pope cannot promulgate any law that would weaken our land or feudal law. Neither tenancy nor hereditary property can devolve upon the feebleminded, dwarfs, or cripples. The actual heirs and their next of kin are, however, responsible for their care.

4 A child born dumb, blind, or lacking hand or foot is a legitimate heir according to the territorial

2   Count's appointed judge.

law but not according to feudal law. If he has been granted a fief before this [disability] occurred, then he forfeits nothing. A leper cannot succeed to feudal tenancy or hereditary property, but if he was invested before the illness and becomes ill afterwards, then he does not forfeit it.

5 If a son marries a woman of equal birth during his father's lifetime, has sons by her and dies before his father has divided the inheritance, then the sons succeed to the grandfather's estate in their father's stead equally with their paternal uncles. They all receive the portion due to males. It is not possible for the children of a daughter to partake equally in the inheritance from their grandfather or grandmother as their mother can. A daughter who lives in the [parent's] house without a dowry does not divide the mother's personal belongings with the daughter who already possesses a dowry. However, she must divide with her sister whatever belongs to the estate. A woman can damage her reputation through unchaste conduct, but she does not thereby lose either her legal rights or her parental inheritance. A lay priest inherits the mother's personal belongings in equal portion to his sister, and the allod and heritable property in equal portion to his brother. No one can be called a priest who lacks the education of the clergy and who has not also been ordained as a priest before the mother's personal belongings devolve on him. But if a woman has only one brother, and he is a priest, then she and he share equally in both the mother's personal property and the inheritance. When a priest dies, one does not distinguish the mother's endowment because everything he leaves is considered one estate. The sister without trousseau does not share her mother's personal belongings with a priest who has a church or prebend.

6 Whatever property a man has at the time of his death is called his heritable estate. Whoever inherits the property must pay the outstanding debts of the deceased up to the value of his movable goods. However, he is not responsible for theft, robbery, or gambling debts, just as he is not liable for debts for which the deceased either did not receive compensation or was not a guarantor. The heir must discharge the debt if, as the law provides, proof of the outstanding debt is brought forth by seventy-two men, all of whom are either of legitimate birth or of the Schoen class.[3] If the person knows of a debt, then proof with witnesses is not necessary as long as the creditor is willing to forego the witnesses and makes his claim because the heir knows of the debt according to land and feudal law. The heir should acknowledge and discharge the debt or deny it with an oath. Debtors shall pay the heir what they owed the deceased person. The debts that the man [heir] himself has incurred may not be proven through compurgators. He must admit or deny them.

7 Whoever offers surety or a pledge is required to fulfill it, and whatever he promises, he must keep reliably. Should he wish to void it later, he can withdraw from the other party with an oath whatever had not been arranged in court. In contrast, whatever he carried out before the court can be proven against him by the party initiating the case with two men swearing on the relics, and the judge shall be the third.

8 In cases where a person alienates or transfers his allodial land or when he tries to prosecute a man in a court [case] that requires forfeiture of the defendant's rights, life, or health because of what that man had pledged in court or lost as a result of a court decision, then the judge must be a witness along with six others who hand down a judgment for him. In cases where the oath of seven is required, the oath of the bailiff is equal to that of two men when he is needed. The bailiff's compensation payment is also double, as is his wergeld as determined by his birth at the time he is selected. An oath of reconciliation as well as an oath of truce that a person vows before the court, however, is witnessed by the judge and two men. Should this oath occur outside a court, then he must bear witness with six other men to the man to whom he vowed reconciliation or truce.

9 If one person pledges his allodial land to another person in court, and the recipient gives his

---

3   Honorable rank.

silver or other property in return, and if the latter dies before the transfer is confirmed, then one must accord to the heir what one would accord the deceased as long as he had paid for it in full. One must treat movable property in the same way. Further, if a person pledges his property holdings to another with a promise to convey it in the presence of his lord, and when he has discharged this, and the other has paid him in part or entirety, then if the recipient who made the contract dies before he could be invested with the promised property, the transferor is responsible for transferring it to the heir to the fief whether he is of equal birth or not. And if there is no successor to the fief, he is required to convey it to the legal heir, whoever he may be, just as he had been required originally to transfer it to the first person [the deceased], provided that he had been paid in full. Otherwise, he must pay to the successor to the fief the amount that had been paid to him. A lord shall follow the same procedure when a man pays him for a piece of land which he must enfeoff him with or make available to him, and the man dies before the enfeoffment. However, if the man who is supposed to transfer the land swears that he is obtaining the property for the tenancy of another person, and if he does so and declares to the recipient before witnesses that he may come and take possession, and if the recipient refuses without just cause, then if the lord hereafter refuses to bestow the property or dies, and the transferor can no longer procure it as before, he is then released from riding in to transfer possession, but not of relinquishing the property if the other is still able to acquire it. Whoever places real property in another's possession should, before he transfers it, first represent him in his right of possession whenever he requires this warranty, as long as the property has not yet been conveyed. Should the court deny right of possession to the person holding the property or to the person to whom the property is to be transferred, then the property holder should return it to the person who had [originally] placed it in his possession. If the person transferring the property dies, then his son is not required to transfer it unless he himself had pledged it or given security to do so.

10 If a father gives his son clothing, a charger and riding horse, and a mail coat when he needs them and is able to use them, and the father has them to give, then afterwards, if the father dies, the son is not required to share them with his brothers, nor to turn them over to his father's lord, nor to his father's heir if he is not of equal birth to the father, just as if he had never received any separate settlement from his father.

11 A father who also retains guardianship of his children after the death of their mother must, when the children separate from him, return and transfer their mother's entire property to them unless it was lost through misfortune for which he was not responsible. The wife should do the same for the father's children if the father dies, and so should every man who is the guardian of children.

12 When brothers or other people own property jointly and they improve it either through expenditure or through their own labor, the gain belongs to them jointly. The same holds for losses. But whatever a man gains from his wife [in marriage], he does not share with his brothers. If a man gambles away his property, or squanders it through debauchery, or wastes it on gifts or expenses to which his brothers or those with whom he stands in joint ownership have not agreed, then the resulting losses are his alone and not those of his brothers or peers with whom he owns property jointly.

13 It is possible for a father or a mother to give one of the sons or one of the daughters the rightful share of inheritance from his or her own property whether the offspring continue to share in the household expenses or not. If, after the death of the father or after the death of the mother, they claim their part of the inheritance, either the brother from his brothers or the married sister from her unendowed sisters, they must with an oath return for partitioning all the property that they had been given if it was movable goods with the exception of a dowry. But if the property is of a type that one must prove, then it cannot be forsworn. If, however, they have renounced their share of the inheritance, then they shall remain without it unless they rescind with an oath on the relics; but should they have sworn to abandon

[their claim] in court, then it is easier to bring a judgment against them with witnesses than for them to be acquitted. In such cases the village headman is witness concerning the peasants within his jurisdiction in place of the judge.

14 Only according to feudal law may the lord bestow a father's fief to no more than one son. It is not consistent with general territorial law that one son alone retain it without compensating his brothers for the portion legally due them. It is equally unacceptable according to territorial law for the father to dispose of his fief to his son and transfer it to him immediately so that he may possess it already at the time of the father's death and, in addition, receive equal shares of another landholding with his brothers. Even if the brothers cannot deny him according to feudal law, it still does not hold for territorial law. And if they bring a suit against him according to territorial law, they easily force him to divide the inheritance justly with a court decision.

15 Whoever gives his movable goods to another in loan, pledge or in safe-keeping either for a specified or unspecified period, and if afterwards the other person, or his heir after his death, contests [the agreement], the lender who transferred the property is closer to winning with his oath and that of two oath-helpers than the property holder is to proving his [case] using witnesses or his heritable property, or even if he has a guarantor for it. When a man accuses another of possessing something that he does not have, he can clear himself with a cleansing oath, but whatever can be proven, he must answer for without an oath.

16 No one can acquire any legal status other than that with which he was born. Should he deny his legal rank and rights before a court of law and claim for himself a different legal status that he cannot substantiate, he loses both. The exception is the bondman who has been freed. He attains the legal status of a free tenant.

17 An offspring who is free and legitimate retains the legal rank of the father, but if the father or the mother is a servant, the child has the legal status of its birth. If a man dies without issue, his father succeeds to his estate. If he has no father, then his mother succeeds with more justification than his brother. The son and not the daughter inherits from father and mother, sister and brother. But when an inheritance is divided among more distant family members such as brothers and sisters, then all who can count themselves at the same level inherit equally, whether man or woman. The Saxons call these people common heirs. However, the offspring of a son or daughter precedes the father or mother and sister or brother [of the deceased] in sequence of inheritance for the following reason: Nothing may break the direct line of descent as long as such members are alive. Whoever is not equal in birth to the decedent may not succeed to the inheritance. A Swabian cannot inherit from the woman's side since the women in their tribe have all been disinherited because of the transgression of their [female] ancestors.

44. EMPEROR CHARLES IV

Autobiography

IN THE FOURTEENTH CENTURY the Luxemburg emperor Charles IV (r. 1355–78) made his kingdom of Bohemia an artistic and intellectual center. Charles, who was born Wenceslas in 1316 and educated in the French court, took an active role in the cultivation of both Latin and Czech letters. His autobiography, which describes the life of the pan-European aristocracy during his time, is one of the first true autobiographies of a layperson in the West.

Source: Bede Jarrett, O.P., *The Emperor Charles IV* (New York: Sheed & Ward, 1935).

Further Reading: Albrecht Classen, "Autobiography as a Late Medieval Phenomenon," *Medieval Perspectives* 3.1 (1990): 89–104.

II

Henry VII, emperor of the Romans, begat my father, John by name, by Margaret, daughter of Wenceslaus II of Bohemia, and succeeded to the kingdom with her because of failure in the royal house of the Bohemians. He expelled Henry Duke of Carinthia, who had married the elder sister of his wife (who died later without children), who on account of his wife had obtained the kingdom of Bohemia before him, as can be seen in chronicles of the Bohemians. John, king of Bohemia, begat of Elizabeth the queen his first-born Wenzel,[1] 1316, on May 14, at one in the morning in Prague. Then another son, Ottokar, who died in childhood. Then a third son, John. The above king had two marriageable sisters; one he gave to Charles I, king of the Hungarians. She died without children. The other he gave to Charles IV, king of the Franks, reigning in France, 1323. My said father sent me to the same king of France in the seventh year of my boyhood. The said king had me confirmed by the pope and imposed on me his own name of Charles, and gave me to wife the daughter of his uncle, Charles of Valois, Margaret by name, called Blanche. That year, his wife, my father's sister, died without children; the king then married again.

He loved me very much, and ordered my chaplain to teach me letters a little, though he himself was ignorant of letters. Thus I learned to read the hours of the glorious Virgin the Blessed Mary, and, understanding them a little every day, I gladly read all through my boyhood, because my guardians were told by the king to impel me to do this. The king was no avaricious lover of gold, he had good counsellors, and his court shone with a group of elder statesmen, spiritual and secular.

But soon a great dissension came between the king of England and the king of France. The king of England, Edward II, had as his wife the sister of the king of France, Isabella, and expelled her from England together with her son Edward. She came to France to her brother, and remained there with her firstborn. But the king of France, indignant at the expulsion of his sister and his nephew, asked my father-in-law, his uncle, that he should avenge the insult offered to one of his family. He led an army into Aquitaine, and took all of it except Bordeaux and some strongholds of castles. Then Charles, coming back in triumph to France, gave his daughter's daughter, Philippa, the countess of Hainault, niece of my wife, in marriage to the son of the king of England, Edward, then in exile. Further, giving him a company of men, he sent him into England. He prevailed against his father, captured him, deprived him of his kingdom, and took his crown. The same year his father was murdered in prison [1327].

---

1   This is himself, to whom, as he says, the name Charles was subsequently given instead of Wenzel.

In the very same year [1325][2] Charles my father-in-law died, and left an eldest son, Philip. Also the same year [1328] died King Charles, on the feast of the Purification [February 2], leaving his wife with child, a daughter. And because it is not the custom of the kingdom of France for daughters to succeed, Philip, the son of my father-in-law, was made king of the Franks, because he was the nearest of the male line. Philip continued the same counselors as the late king, but agreed little with their counsels and took greedily to wealth. One of these counselors, a most prudent man, was Peter, abbot of Fécamp, a native of Limoges, gracious and literary, endowed with all moral virtues, who on Ash Wednesday in the first year of Philip during the celebration of mass preached with such studied care that he was commended by all. At that time I was at the court of Philip, whose sister I had married (it was after the death of King Charles, with whom I was for five years). The abbot's facility of speech or eloquence so pleased me that day, and seeing him and hearing him gave me such devout and peaceful prayerfulness, that I began to think "Why is it that so much grace is poured into me from that man?" At once I acquainted myself with him, and he treated me kindly and fatherly, often teaching me the sacred Scriptures.

I remained at the court of Philip two years after the death of King Charles. After these two years the king sent me and my wife (his sister Blanche) to my father, John, king of Bohemia, to the city of Luxemburg, which earldom my father inherited by succession from his father, Henry the emperor of holy memory, who, being count of Luxemburg, was elected king of the Romans, as is to be found more fully in the chronicles; also how and for how long he reigned.

Having come back from France [1330], I found my father in Luxemburg, Lewis of Bavaria being then emperor, styling himself "Lewis IV," who after the death of my grandfather, Henry VII, was (in a disputed election) chosen king of the Romans against Frederick, duke of Austria. These whose names follow elected him and stood by him till his triumph when he captured his rival Frederick, duke of Austria; namely John, king of

Bohemia, my father, the archbishops of Mainz and Treves, and Wildemar, the last Brandenburger: on Frederick's side were the archbishop of Cologne, the duke of Saxony, and the count Palatine. Lewis afterwards went to Rome and received his crown and consecration from a bishop of the Venetians against the will of Pope John XXII. Afterwards he created an antipope, Nicholas by name, a Franciscan, who was later handed over to the pope and died in penance.

Already Lewis had returned to Germany, as is clear from the chronicles of the Romans.

When I got back from France at that time and had found my father [1330], Duke Frederick of Austria was besieging Colmar in Alsace, and Lewis could not relieve it. My father went to them and made the two come into concord. Then he went to the county of Tyrol to the duke of Carinthia, whom he had expelled from Bohemia. His first wife, my mother's sister, was dead. However, he had married a second wife, the sister of the Duke of Brunswick, by whom he had one daughter, Margaret [Maultasch]. Her he joined in marriage to my brother John. At his death he bequeathed to her the rule of the principality. Then my father went to Trent; at that time [Sept. 28] my mother died in Prague on the feast of B. Wenceslaus the martyr. While he was staying in Trent these Lombard cities offered themselves to him, Brescia, Bergamo, Cremona, Pavia, Parma, Reggio, Modena. Also Lucca in Tuscany with all the districts belonging to it gave itself to him. Drawing near to them, my father took up his abode in Parma [March 1331], and Azzo Visconti took them over from him as vicar, accepting his vicariate from my father.

It was then my father sent for me to Luxemburg. I came through the city of Metz, the dukedom of the Lorraine, through Burgundy and Savoy to the city of Lausanne on its lake. Then I crossed the mountains of Brega and came to the territory of Novara, and thence on Good Friday to the city of Pavia, which my father held. On Easter day, the third day after my arrival, my family were poisoned—which hurt, by divine grace, I escaped. For the high mass was so prolonged and I wanted to go to communion at it so that I did not wish to

---

2   It will be seen that these dates given by Charles are often not exact.

eat before mass was over. When at last I sat down to dinner, I was told that my family had suddenly been taken ill, and precisely those who had eaten the dinner. Sitting down at table, I did not wish to eat, so frightened was I. Then, looking about, I saw a beautiful man, very agile, whom I did not know, who walked by the table, pretending to be dumb. In my suspicion I had him seized. After three days of torture he confessed that he had put poison in the food by the order of Azzo Visconti of Milan. From that poison died John lord of Berge, master of my court, John of Hokrem, Simon of Kail, who waited on my table, and many others. But I remained there in Pavia in the monastery of St. Augustine, where his body lay, from which monastery Lewis of Bavaria had expelled the abbot and the canons regular. I recalled them and installed them in the abbey, which after the death of these brethren [1349], Pope John gave to the Augustinians who now have it; it was during my father's rule that I gave them possession of it. Then I went to my father at Parma; I was sixteen years old.

My father gave the rule of all these cities and my guardianship to Ludovico of Savoy, who was father-in-law of Azzo Visconti and governor of Milan. Leaving Parma, he went to France, and gave his second daughter, my sister, Guta [Bona] by name, to John, the eldest son of Philip of France. The eldest Margaret was already married to Henry duke of Bavaria. At the time that I remained with the said Lord Ludovico of Savoy in Italy, there were secretly leagued against my father and me, Robert king of Apulia [Naples], the Florentines, Lord Azzo, governor of Milan, the lord of Verona, who then held Padua, Trevico, Vicenza, Feltre and Belluno, the governor of Mantua, who had already sworn fealty to us, and the governor of Ferrara. Secretly they divided between them the cities I held. To Verona were to go Brescia and Parma, to Mantua Reggio, to Ferrara Modena, to Milan Pavia, Bergamo and Cremona, to Florence Lucca. Thus suddenly revolting, before we knew they had all broken faith with us, they attacked us who were in no wise expecting this, since they had vowed loyalty to us and had sworn to us and had confirmed in writing that they would faithfully assist my father and me.

Verona entered Brescia, Milan besieged Bergamo and took it suddenly. The Pavians, in whom I had greater confidence than in any other of the cities, rebelled against us, and accepted Beccaria as their tyrant. All these joined together to make a violent war against me. But the lord Ludovico of Savoy, my vicar and guardian, though he had already foreseen some of these dangers, put no remedy to them, and moved I do not know by what (but perhaps by love of his son-in-law Azzo), the said lord withdrew from the country, leaving me to face the trouble. But the leading citizens of Parma, the Rossi, and the Fogliani and Manfredi of Reggio, and the Pii of Modena, and the Ponzoni, and Siena, and Cremona, and the lord Simone Filippi of Pistoja, captain of Lucca, took my side and gave all the help and advice they could, as the following pages will make clear.

Then the allies above named gathered a strong army before our own city of Modena and stayed there six weeks, to wit, men from Milan, Verona, Ferrara and Mantua. After six weeks, when they had devastated the districts and countries of Modena and Reggio, they retired and stationed their forces and arms before the castle of San Felice. And when they had been there a long time they made an agreement with the garrison that if I did not succor them within a month, namely by the feast of St. Catherine, which expired in a month's time, they would surrender the castle. But the men of Parma, Cremona, Modena and Reggio, hearing this, gathered their forces and sent to me, saying, "Sir, we must destroy before we are destroyed." Then, taking counsel, I went out into the country, and I fortified the castles, and on the feast of St. Catherine I came from the city of Parma to the castle which was on that day to surrender. And at nine o'clock with 1,200 armed knights and 6,000 foot I attacked the enemy, who were as numerous or more numerous than we. The battle lasted till sunset. Almost all the horses were killed on both sides and we were almost defeated, even the horse on which I sat was killed under me. Held up by my men, and standing and looking about and seeing we were almost destroyed, I was well aware how desperate was our state. But at that very moment the enemy began to fly with their standards, first those of Mantua and then the rest. So only by the grace of God we obtained the victory, capturing eighty armed knights in flight and killing 5,000[?] foot.

By this victory our castle of San Felice was freed. In this battle, along with 200 others, I received the dignity of knighthood. The next day we returned with great joy to Modena with booty and captives. Dismissing my people, I returned to Parma, where I then held my court. Afterwards I passed through to Lucca in Tuscany, and marshaled the war against the Florentines. There I built a fine castle with a fortified wall around it on the crest of a hill, ten miles from Lucca towards the Val de Nievole, and called it Monte Carlo. After this I returned to Parma, leaving its rule to the lord Simone Pistoja, who had previously ruled well for us and had won the city of Barga from the enemy and had done many other good things in his rule. When I reached Parma, our enemies were gathered from everywhere strongly against us. But the severity of the winter helped us, for it was so fierce that no one could stay in their camps.

At the same time a treaty was made between Verona and our enemies on one side and on the other by Marsiglio dei Rossi, Gilbert dei Fogliani and the Manfredi of Reggio, who were nobles respectively of Parma, Reggio and Modena, and were almost rulers of their own cities. They went with very strong forces to a little church in the diocese of Reggio and agreed to unite together against me and destroy me, and they had Mass said, wishing to swear on the Eucharist to hold firm their agreements. But it happened that when the priest had consecrated, darkness came over the church and a high wind, so that all were terrified. And when it grew light again the priest could not find the host on the altar before him. Then, standing amazed, and looking at one another in distress, they saw the host lying at the feet of Marsiglio dei Rossi, who was the head and leader of the treaty. Then all said together: "What we have determined to do does not please God." So the council broke up and each went home. Then the priest who had said the Mass went to the city of Reggio and told the bishop what had happened. The bishop sent him to the cardinal of Ostia [Bertrand de Poiet, nephew of John XXII], then legate in Lombardy, who was in Bologna at the time. The legate and bishop told it to my vicar, Egidio de Berlario Francigene, in the city of Reggio, that he should warn me of the conspiracy, so as to put me on my guard against them. However, these who had tried to

conspire against me were so moved by contrition that they came to me and gave me every possible aid, keeping my cause in their hearts. One day Gilberto Septimo Fogliani said to me, "I should always have been distressed if the Body of Christ had been found before my feet as It was before the feet of Marsiglio dei Rossi, and well hath God saved us from doing those things which we should rather have died than done." But I kept silence, as though I knew nothing at all.

In those days my father, hearing how hard beset I was, made arrangements with many in France, chief of whom were the bishop of Beauvais, count of Eu, constable of the kingdom of France, Count St. Cesar, and many other counts and barons. They came from France into Savoy, thence through the Alps to the marquisate of Montserrat, and from thence to Lombardy up to Cremona, and from Cremona to Parma. There were about 600 armed knights in all who came to our aid. Thus our father with this assembled army came to succor the castle of Pavia, which still held out in my name against the city. We joined our camp with them and besieged the city of Pavia; then we were fully 3,000 armed knights. We destroyed the suburbs and the monasteries of the suburbs and we filled the castle, to the aid of which we had come, with provisions and food. But we could not capture the city from the castle, because the citizens placed trenches and ramparts between the castle and the city so that we could not get in. They had 1,000 armed knights from Milan to aid them. After ten days I left them, turning towards Milan and ravaging the country and district of Milan. Then I went to Bergamo, where I had an agreement with some friends of ours that they should open a gate to us. It was arranged that at dawn some of our people should enter and that a great regiment should follow them in and hold the city, till my father and I with all his army should arrive, which we promised to do that same day. It happened as we had agreed; our friends, the conspirators, opened the gates, and the first company of our men went in. But for some reason that I do not know the main force would not follow them. So the first comers had to retreat again, as they could not fight the whole city by themselves. Many of our friends in the city managed to escape with them. But the rest who remained were captured and hanged on the walls, more than fifty of them. When my father and I arrived and saw what had been done and what not done, we were frightened, and after some days we crossed the river Ada with our whole army and returned through the territory of Cremona to the city of Parma.

After this [1334] my father went to Bologna to the cardinal of Ostia, Bertrand of Poiet, then legate-a-latere[3] in the Lombardy, who ruled Bologna and other places, Piacenza, Ravenna, the Romagna and the march of Ancona, and discussed matters with him, for he was in treaty with us, and was thus the enemy of our enemies. But even already he was in enmity with the lord of Ferrara for the sake of Holy Church and his own sake, for the lord of Ferrara was allied with his enemies, each undertaking to support the other. The cardinal gave us men and money, and he put a force and built a tower against the enemy in the suburbs of Ferrara, the captain of which was later the count of Armagnac.

That same summer after Pentecost my father gathered a great army and sent me on ahead to Cremona from Parma beyond Padua, with 500 armed knights, whom he sent to the city of Pizzighetone, which had revolted from us and was being helped by Pavia and Milan. We remained with scarcely twenty armed knights at Cremona. Suddenly our enemies strengthened themselves and grew in such force that I began to look about for help. At the same time from Mantua and Ferrara they sent ships through Padua to Cremona, and sank all our ships, so that my father and his troops could neither help us nor send us word what to do. Thus in Cremona we were in great peril of destruction, being so few. Hence I was disheartened, for neither could my father aid me nor I him.

Happily, however, our enemies, who were besieging us on the river Po, quarreled amongst themselves. Hearing this, my father came from Parma to the river, ordered the ships to be recovered from the river, and with a few crossed over to Cremona. Joining forces next day with us, we went to help those who were besieging Pizzighetone. By the grace of God we were now so strengthened as to be stronger than all our enemies, for we had 3,000 armed knights. When, however, I saw that nothing could be done against the fort, I wished to proceed to Pavia. Knowing this, the enemy sent councillors who deceitfully treated with my father and made a league with him: they gave all sorts of undertakings, under which we promised to withdraw. We did so, but they never kept their promises, and so we lost Pavia and, winter coming on, we could do no more. Thus was the proverb exemplified, delays are dangerous.

At that time the men of Ferrara, Verona, Mantua and Milan captured the captain of the Legate [the Count of Armagnac] in the suburbs of Ferrara and killed many of his army and drowned others in the Po, so that the legate could not recover his position.

Then my father, at last seeing that his resources were failing and that the war was making no progress, determined to return home and to leave his cities to their inhabitants and tyrants, Parma to the Rossi, Reggio to the Fogliani, Modena to the Pii, Cremona to the Ponzoni, who had given these cities to my father and to whom he wished to give them again. Lucca he wished to sell to Florence, but prevented by our advice and that of his councillors, he handed it over to the Rossi who ruled Parma.

At that time when I was in Lucca, the devil, who always seeks whom he may devour and offers men honey in which gall lurks, then tempted me, but by the grace of God I was not vanquished. For he instigated wicked men (since he could not do it himself), the councillors of my father, by bribery to lead me from the right way to the snares of impurity, so that with the perverse I might be perverse. Then my father not long after took me towards Parma, where I stayed at a village called Tarenzo in the diocese of Parma, on a Sunday which was the feast of the Assumption of Our Lady. Here I had a vision at night. An angel appeared to strike me on the left side and say, "Arise and come with us." I answered, "Lord, I know neither whither nor how to go with you." Taken by my hair through the air, I saw a great force of horsemen drawn up in front of a castle ready to fight. Holding me in the air over them, the angel said, "Look and see." Another angel

---

3   Specially appointed representative of the pope.

with a flaming sword then appeared, and struck the leader of the host on the thigh. In great agony with the wound he still sat his horse. The angel asked me, "Do you know who he is who is struck by the angel and wounded to death?" "Lord," said I, "I neither know him nor the place where he is." "Know, then," answered he, "this is the Dauphin of Vienne, who on account of his sins of impurity is stricken by God. Beware, then, and tell your father that he too should beware of the same sin, or worse will befall him and you." I was sorry for that Dauphin of Vienne called Bigon [Guiges, 1318–33], whose grandmother was the sister of our grandfather, and who was the son of the sister of King Charles I of Hungary. I asked the angel, "Shall he be able to confess before he dies?" so sad was I. "He will confess and live a few days," was the answer. Then I saw on my left a group of many in white, men of great reverence and holiness, talking to each other, looking at the horseman, and I noted them well. However, I had not the grace to ask, nor did the angel tell me who or what they were. Suddenly I found myself back, and dawn was breaking as I woke. Thomas of Villeneuve, the chamberlain of my father, a knight of Liège, came and woke me, saying: "Sir, why do you not get up? Your father is up and ready on horseback." Then I got up, and found I was quite tired out, as though after a great labor. I said to him, "Where shall I go, for this night I have suffered much, and I do not know what I ought to do?" "Why, Sir?" said he. I answered, "The dauphin is dead; now my father wants to gather an army and go to the dauphin's support, who is at war with the count of Savoy: our aid will not profit him, for he is dead." But he laughed at me, and when we got to Parma told my father what I had said. Then my father called me and asked if it were true. To whom I answered, "Yes, sir, I know for sure that the dauphin is dead." My father upbraided me, saying, "Never believe in dreams." To these two I had not told all that I had seen, but only that the dauphin was dead. After some days news arrived that as the dauphin was besieging a castle of the count of Savoy he was hit by a great arrow in the thigh, and after some time confessed and died. My father was astonished and said so. But no one spoke of my vision to those who brought the news.

My father, seeing that he was losing money and making no headway against the said lords of Lombardy, determined to go away and leave me in charge of the cities and the war. But I refused, because I could not honorably accept the charge. Then, giving me leave to go, he sent me ahead of him to Bohemia. So, making treaties with all our enemies, I went through the territory of Mantua to Verona, and thence to the county of Tyrol, where I found my brother John, whom my father had married to the daughter of the duke of Carinthia and count of Tyrol. This duke, father-in-law to my brother, had, as we have said, as his first wife Anna, the sister of my mother. After her death he had Adelaide as wife, the sister of the duke of Brunswick, by whom he had a daughter, Margaret Maultasch. With her, since he had no male heirs, he undertook to bequeath Carinthia and Tyrol to my brother. So peace was made between him and my father, for there had been trouble between them since my father expelled him from Bohemia, as I have already said. From the Tyrol I went through Bavaria, where I found my eldest sister Margaret, who had one son, John, by Henry duke of Bavaria. Then I came to Bohemia after an absence of eleven years.

I found that my mother, Elizabeth, had died some years before. While she yet lived, my second sister Guta [Bona] was sent to France and married to John, the eldest son of Philip, king of France, whose sister named Blanche was my wife. My third and last sister, Anne, was with her sister in France. So when I came to Bohemia I found neither father nor mother nor brother nor sister nor any one I knew. Also I had completely forgotten Bohemian, which later I relearnt, so that I now speak and understand it like any other Bohemian. By divine grace not only can I speak and read and write Bohemian, but French, Lombard, German and Latin. I am equally apt in all. Then my father went to Luxemburg on account of a war he had with the duke of Brabant, he and his partners, the bishop of Liège, the marquis of Juliers, the Graf von Geldern and others. He gave me therefore a commission over Bohemia in his absence. I found that kingdom desolate. Not a castle free that was not pledged, so I had nowhere to lodge except in houses in cities like any other citizen. Prague had been desolated and destroyed since the days of King Ottokar. So I decided to build a new palace which should be large and handsome. It was built at a high cost, as is evident today to whoever looks at it. I then sent for my wife, who was still in Luxemburg. After she came she had her first daughter, Margaret. At that time my father, out of love for me, gave me the title of Margrave of Moravia, and that title I always used. But when the great council of Bohemia remembered that I belonged to the ancient house of Bohemia, they gave me help to recover the castles and royal possessions. With much labor and cost I repaired the castles of Burglitz, Tyrzow, Lichtenburg, Luze, Greiz, Piesek, Nechanic, Zbirow, Tachau and Trautenau in Bohemia, but in Moravia Luckow, Telcz, Weverzy, Olmuzc, Brünn, Znoymo, I recovered all sorts of other pawned goods, alienated from the kingdom. I had many knights serving me, and the kingdom prospered from day to day, and the great council was devoted to me. Evil was afraid and desisted from evil. Justice only in part prevailed in the kingdom, for the barons were often tyrannous and did not fear the king as they should have done, and the kingdom was thus divided. But for two years we held the captaincy of the kingdom, and things improved daily. I gave my sister Anne to Otto, duke of Austria, as wife.

In those days died the duke of Carinthia [April 2, 1335], my brother's father-in-law. Though my brother ought to have taken possession of the dukedom of Carinthia and the county of Tyrol, Lewis, who called himself emperor, made league secretly with the dukes of Austria [to wit Albert and Otto] to divide my brother's lordship falsely and secretly between them. Thus was Louis forgetful and ungrateful to my father, who had supported him for the empire, as I have already said. The duke of Austria, though he had my sister to wife, immediately after the death of the duke of Carinthia, by a conspiracy with the lord of Aufstein, who on the duke's behalf was captain of all Carinthia, took possession of it with his brother. It was fully made over to him by the same Aufstein. Thus my brother lost Carinthia. But the Tyrolese did not want to have Lewis, and remained loyal to my brother. Meanwhile, my father came to Bohemia with Beatrice, his second queen, the daughter of the duke of Bourbon, of the race of the kings of France, by whom he begat Wenzel, the only son of this marriage.

At this time false and wicked counsellors prevailed against me with my father, thinking to secure their own good, both Bohemians and Luxemburgers. They went to my father saying: "Look you, Sire, your son has many castles in your kingdom and a large following of your people. Hence if he holds sway for long, he will be able to expel you when he wants to, for he is heir and of the blood royal of Bohemia, and much loved by the Bohemians, whereas you are a stranger." This they said to get profit and place by getting him to give them the said castles and goods. So far my father gave way as to lose confidence in me, and he took away all the castles and administration in Bohemia from me and the march of Moravia, so I had only the title of margrave of Moravia, but not the powers.

At that time I went on horseback one day from Burglitz to Prague, wishing to visit my father, who was then in Moravia, and so we came late to the city of Prague, to an old burgh-house, where we stayed for some time before the great palace was built. At night we went to bed. Buscho of Willhartiscz the elder lay in another bed at the end of my bed. A big fire burnt in the room because it was winter, and many candles were also alight in the room, so that there was a good light in it. The windows and doors were shut. When we began to sleep we both heard something or other walking across the room, so that we both woke, and I made Buscho get up to see what it was. Getting up, he went round the room and saw nothing and could find nothing. Then he made the fire larger and lit even more candles and went to the jugs that were full of wine and stood on benches. He drank from one and replaced it near a great burning candle. When he had finished his drink he returned to bed. I sat up with my cloak around me, and could still hear someone walking round my bed, but could see no one. As I looked with Buscho at the jugs and the candles, we both saw the jug he had used thrown by some one or other beyond the bed of Buscho from one corner of the room to the opposite wall, hitting the wall and falling broken into the middle of the room. Seeing this, we were both terrified. All the while we heard some one ceaselessly walking, yet could see no one. Making the sign of the cross and calling on the name of Christ, we slept till morning. In the morning we found the jug lying broken in the middle of the room and showed it to our servants.

My father then sent me to the duke of Silesia, Polcon by name, lord of Munsterberg, with a fine army. For that duke was not an independent prince but the vassal of my father and of the kingdom of Bohemia. My father had acquired the city of Warsaw through Lord Henry VII, duke of Warsaw, who had no heirs. The same duke accepted Glaz for his life in exchange for its sovereignty; the duke preferred that it should go to my father and the kingdom of Bohemia rather than to his brother Bodeslaus, with whom he was at enmity. But after my father acquired Warsaw, all the dukes of Silesia and Oppeln subjected themselves for ever to his rule and to the crown of Bohemia, to the end that they should be defended by the kings of Bohemia except the lord of Schweidnitz and Polcon of Munsterberg. We devastated Polcon's territory, as you can read in the chronicles. So badly was it devastated that he had to surrender to my father and to the crown of Bohemia like the other dukes.

This done, I set out for Hungary to my father, whom I found at Blindenburg on the Danube with King Charles I, whose first wife was my father's sister, and who after her death had married the sister of King Casimir of Cracow, by whom he had three sons, Lewis the first-born, Andrew, and Stephen the third. King Charles made peace between my father and the King of Cracow, so that my father renounced his rights in Lower Poland—to wit, Gnesen and Kalisz and the other provinces of Poland. The king of Cracow in his turn renounced to my father and the crown of Bohemia for himself and his successors, for ever, the kingdoms of Lower Poland, the dukedoms of Silesia and Oppeln and the city of Warsaw. For before there was strife between them, since my grandfather, Wenzel II, king of Bohemia, possessed Lower Poland with the kingdoms of Cracow and Sandomierz through the sole heiress, daughter of Premysl, king of Lower Poland, and duke of Cracow and Sandomierz, whom he had for wife. Premysl gave to my father and the crown of Bohemia for ever both the kingdom and the dukedom. But Casimir was uncle of the girl, and said he had rights over Lower Poland, since a woman could not inherit the kingdom. Hence war for a long time was waged between the kings of Bohemia, and Casimir and his father Ladislaus, once kings of Lower Poland and Cracow. Peace was made by the king of Hungary, who in return

for this promised to ally himself with my father and help him against the duke of Austria, who had taken Carinthia from my brother, and against Lewis. These were, then, in the league: my father, the king of Hungary and Duke Henry of Bavaria, who had married my sister. At the same time, my father sent me to the Tyrol to govern it, as my brother and his wife were children. So I went there at my father's bidding and took part in every thing, and was admitted to rule over the place by the inhabitants of the said county.

On the day after Easter [April 1336] I gathered an army from the Tyrol and entered the valley of Pusterthal in the diocese of Brixen against the count of Gorz [he had fiefs in Friuli and possessed Pusterthal in the valley of the Drave], and took the castle of Mount St. Lambert, and I went further against the same count, and devastated his land up to the fortress which is called Lienz. There I stayed three weeks, ravaging because he was an ally of the dukes of Austria, our enemies. The day after the feast of St. George [April 23] my father drove Duke Otto beyond the Danube and took many castles in Austria. Lewis who called himself emperor was helping the dukes of Austria, so too was all Germany, and the governors of the cities of Lombardy, and specially Mastino della Scala, lord of Verona, Vicenza, Padua, Treviso, Brescia, Parma and Lucca. All these invaded us and the county of Tyrol; so that Trent and the whole valley of Etschthal was in great danger from the Lombards, and the valley of the Inn was threatened by the Swabians and Bavarians. Hence the Tyrol was in much danger on every side. Then I made Nicholas Brünn our chancellor bishop of Trent, and Mathew, my brother's chaplain, bishop of Brixen, for both bishoprics were vacant.

The same summer Lewis led a great army with all the princes of Germany against Henry duke of Bavaria, my brother-in-law, who was with us. The duke of Austria came through Passau to help the same Lewis: my father came to Henry's aid, and they pitched camp near a stream close to Landau. Lewis and the duke of Austria came against them with a big army, but since they could not cross the river, they ravaged Bavaria for a month: and though Henry's army was smaller, Lewis and Austria were not able to work their will, and returned home. At the same time, I wished to come to my father's aid and Henry's with a large army of foot and horse from the Tyrol, but I could not get any further than Kuffstein, where Lewis' son was, whom we besieged with all his forces during the whole time that the princes lay opposite each other's camp. When they separated I returned to the Tyrol.

After this, about the feast of St. Michael, peace was made between my father and the duke of Austria, who gave back the city of Znoymo, which my father had given as dowry with his daughter. Also a large sum of money was paid him, and some castles on the Drave were given to the county of Tyrol for my brother. But he, Otto, was allowed to keep the dukedom of Carinthia.

That winter my father and I went to Prussia against the Lithuanians. With us were the young William of Holland, de Monte, young de Lo and many other earls and barons. The winter was so mild that there was no ice: so we could not cross the river to attack the Lithuanians, so each returned home.

Since a great war had broken out amongst the Lombards (which I had prepared for before I left the Tyrol) on account of the league made between Venice, Florence, Milan, Ferrara, Mantua, Bologna, etc., against Mastino della Scala, governor of Verona and Padua, who was our enemy, as will have been already seen, in April I went through Moravia to Austria, wanting to enter Lombardy, but the duke of Austria would not give me leave. So, going on board ship, I went to the king of Hungary, who gave me leave to go through Croatia and Dalmatia, to the city of Zengg on the sea-shore, where we embarked. The Venetian captains, knowing this through their friends, wanted to capture us. So they surrounded our galley with their galleys in such a way that our galley could not escape. So when on the ninth day we came to their city of Grado, agreeing to the counsel given me by Bartholomew, count of Veglia and Zengg, who was with us in the galley, I ordered that one of my men should say, "Behold, my lords, we see that we cannot escape your hands, so please go ahead of us to the city, and treat with them so that they may be willing to receive us." Then secretly, while he spoke these friendly words, I climbed

down from the prow of the galley into a little fishing-smack with Bartie and John de Lipa; and so, hidden by sacks and nets, we went through their galleys and came to the harbor amongst the reeds, and so, escaping their hands, walked to Aquileia. But they captured our galley and all my family, whom they held captive a few days and then set free.

When I was in Aquileia I notified my host who I was. He took the news to the patriarch. He came at once to the city and to the ringing of bells, with great pomp of clergy and people, took us into his palace, and so for four weeks I and my family (when they had been set free) received his hospitality. He safeguarded us, taking us through Cadore to the Tyrol, which then I ruled for my brother, who was little more than a boy.

In June the Venetians, Florentines, Milanese, Mantuans, people of Ferrara and their other accomplices besieged Padua with enormous forces, about 10,000 armed knights and an infinite number of foot, and some part of them besieged also the city of Feltre with the bishop Siccone de Caldinacio, the earls of Siena and the lords of the house of Camino.[4] For a long while they held to the siege with 500 armed knights and foot, because the city of Padua belonged to Mastino della Scala, lord of Verona, who also owned the other city named above. Already the Venetians had got hold of Tinglam, Saravalle and Bassano, which were part of Mastino's dominions; moreover, Count Collalto, advocate of Treviso, and a number of others had also revolted from Mastino and made cause with Venice. On this account a certain citizen of the city of Belluno, named Sudracio de Bongagio, fearing lest in this way Feltre would be lost and fall into the hands of Venice, which especially he hated, and seeing it surrounded on every side, bethought himself of Jacopo Anoschano, who with certain castles and some mountains belonging to Belluno had put himself under my rule, and came to me secretly in a little boat, so that neither the Venetians nor Mastino should know, since he was acting against both of them, and said to us, "If you can put to flight the enemies round the city of Feltre, one door of the city shall be opened to you by me, for I would rather that you

---

4   The Camini were lords Treviso, Feltre and Belluno earlier in the century.

had the city than any one else at all." I listened to what he said and proposed a day on which I would come secretly as he asked. I was able to collect a force of men prudently because of a duel between two noblemen in the diocese of Neumarkt (between Bozen and Trent). On this excuse I gathered many nobles round me, pretending that their friends were causing a dissension, and this that none should know the reason for my having so many forces with me and yet that I should be able to go near Feltre secretly. As a matter of fact, we knighted the victor who killed his adversary. Then I asked the troops present if they would follow me where I wished. They agreed to come with me. We rode our horses through the Val di Fieme all night. The next day I rode through the desolate mountain ranges near Castrozza, where men are not wont to ride. When we came to a grove between Castrozza and Primiero I could not find any road on account of the fallen trees. My army was in despair. Then on foot with the other foot-soldiers I scouted till I found a way down sheer cliffs and broken roads, and till at last we got beyond the forest. Happily the forest wardens had gone at sunset, not expecting any trouble that night. Thus we got through the hills. With my following I came to Primiero, which was also besieged by the Venetians, and setting them to flight I captured it. These routed enemies went to their allies at Feltre and said that a huge army under someone or other whom they did not know had overwhelmed them. Hearing this they fled during the night. Passing the castle next day from Primiero to Agordo, we hurried to Belluno. I sent word to Sudracio that we had come with a large army. He at once got hold of the captains and magistrates and told them that he had received news that the counts of Clermont, allies of Mastino della Scala, had come to their aid and scattered their foe. These joyously opened their gates, thinking us to be friends. I entered on the feast of St. Procopius, the 4th of July. When we had all entered I unfurled the banner of the king of Bohemia and the count of Tyrol. When they saw we were enemies, they were amazed, and knew not how to resist our power. So by the grace of God I obtained the city, though the castle held out against us a few days; but when we had laid mines to the castle, those in it surrendered it to us. Then we encamped before

Feltre. But because the lord of Verona was busy with the Venetians and they with him, neither was able to do us harm. Indeed, both entered into treaty with us, desiring to have us as allies. When we had sat in front of Feltre six weeks, we made a treaty with the Venetians. They agreed to help us by every means in their power against Mastino. At their own expense they sent us 700 armed knights and many foot.

Leaving my brother with the army, I went to Venice, where I was received with much honor and reverence, and I confirmed the treaty. Thence returning, we captured Feltre by starvation. Also the Carrara, Lords of Padua, treated with us and took Padua and captured Alberto, the elder brother of Mastino, whom they gave to the Venetians to imprison; and remaining our subjects, held Padua. But we, scattering our followers, installed them in the cities of Belluno and Feltre and in their castles as captains; Volcmar de Burchstal, a noble of the Tyrol, in Feltre, Sudracio de Bongagio in Belluno, and as captain against Verona John de Lipa, who died seven days after his appointment. In his place I named Lepor.

So I returned to the Tyrol by the valley of Inn and thence into the kingdom of Bohemia. I made an alliance with the dukes of Austria (with whom before I was not friends). That winter in Septuagesima I gave my eldest daughter, Margaret, to the eldest son of Charles the Great, king of Hungary, named Lewis; and I made a treaty with him against all comers. Next day I had invited my brother-in-law to dine with me, but one of the servants woke me at dawn saying: "The last day has come; get up, the world is covered with locusts." So, getting up and going on my horse, I rode hurriedly out, wishing to see where they were. They were as far as Pultava, where they stretched seven miles long, but the width of them I could not gauge at all. Their noise was like a riot. Their wings seemed covered with black letters. They were in such numbers that the sun's light was obscured. A terrible stench preceded them. They divided, some to Bavaria, some to Lombardy, some in every direction all over the world. They were prolific: in a night two became twenty. At first they were very small, but grew very big. They were to be found for three years after. Within two months both our sister and her husband, the duke of Austria, died. We never saw the locusts again from that time.

When we had come to Bohemia, we happened to reach Tauschim in Bunzlau, and when we were asleep we had by chance in a dream a picture of the Gospel which says, "The kingdom of heaven is like to a treasure hidden in a field," which is read on the feast of St. Limila.[5] And so beginning to picture it I began in my sleep the exposition of the Gospel. Waking, I remembered the opening concept of the first part of the Gospel, and so by divine help I learnt its meaning: Dear Brethren: no one can understand the words of the Holy Gospels …

[Here for four chapters of the Vita, Charles gives in detail a commentary on the parables of the kingdom from Matthew 13 …]

That same summer, coming to Muta, I broke the castle of Chocyn and many other castles of the lord of Pottenstein, as I was at that time at war with him. Afterwards we came to terms. At the same time a silver mine was found in Vresnik.

I left Bohemia with my barons, wishing to go to Luxemburg to my father, who had sent for me. From Frankfurt I came back again, and coming back I inaugurated the college of All Saints in the royal chapel of the castle of Prague.

I went on then to the king of Hungary, who was sick. Before I got back to Bohemia, as I was leaving Hungary, my father went to Lewis who acted as emperor to make peace with him. Now, Lewis had promised me that he would make no treaties with my father without me, but that, thanks to my advice, he would deal kindly with my father. But Lewis, unmindful of his promises and of his plighted word, deceived my father into making terms with him by saying that he had already made a treaty with me. Thus he occasioned a difference between us; and because of this treaty and the one he said he had made with me, my father agreed to hold his territories from him as emperor. Also he came to terms with him and agreed to many things that he would not have done had he known that I had no treaty with him. Knowing nothing of this, I hurried to Miltenburg in the diocese of Mainz to meet him, and told him that the whole affair that he had negotiated with the same Lewis of Bavaria was fraudulently reached, and so I with the barons of Bohemia refused to seal or confirm the treaty he had made, and held it to be null and void.

Then I went to Presburg on the frontiers of Hungary and Austria and persuaded the king of Hungary and the duke of Austria to come to peace. Then my father went towards Moravia, wishing to destroy Nicholas, duke of Troppau and Ratibor, whom with difficulty I reconciled to my father. Then we went to the siege of the castle of Pottenstein, which had rebelled against me and the king of Bohemia and had done much damage; and although it seemed inaccessible, within nine weeks I captured it and had thrown to the ground both the tower and the baron whose castle it was. I also razed the walls and the whole castle all by myself. Then I went with my father to Warsaw. The bishop of it was disobedient to my father because my father, in anger, had taken away from him the castle of Militsch. For this reason he excommunicated my father. This trouble between my father and the said cleric lasted two years.

Thence my father went to Budweis; and so to France to the aid of the king of France, because the war between the kings of France and England was then beginning. He sent me in his place into his kingdom. But in my place I put Peter von Rosinberk and followed him into Bavaria. There I found that Henry, duke of Bavaria, my sister's husband, was dead and had left an only son by my sister Margaret as his heir, aged ten years old, whose guardian and the guardian of the land Lewis, the supposed emperor, made himself, on the grounds of a treaty he had previously made with the boy's father. He repudiated the daughter of Rudolph I, duke of Bavaria, and Count Palatine, the son of his brother, who had been promised and vowed to the said boy, and gave him instead his own daughter, who could not speak yet, saying that he would promise her for her till she could speak. By the permission of God she remained dumb all her life.

Thence passing through Bavaria I came to my father in the county of Luxemburg. There I wished to go to the aid of the king of France, for the English

---

5 St. Limila, patroness of Bohemia, was Charles' great-grandmother. Her feast is kept on Sept. 16.

king was besieging the city of Cambrai before his enemy had time to collect his forces. Then he went to the city of St. Quentin, then to Ribemont, and finally to Laon. Then he returned to the county of Hainault, whither the French king followed him to its frontiers. Both pitched their camps on the frontiers of Hainault. But after the French king had waited for him a whole day and had his troops all in line, the King of England retreated, leaving his camp to the French king, although he had many German princes with him, the duke of Brabant, the marquis of Juliers and de Monti and the earl of Flanders from Lower Germany, while from Upper Germany he had the margrave of Meissen, the margrave of Brandenburg, the son of the Bavarian, and many other of Lewis' forces: for Lewis had nominated the king of England his vicar imperial through Germany.

In those days, since for a long while my father had already lost the sight of one eye, the other eye began to get affected. He went to Montpellier secretly to doctors to see if he could get cured. From that time, however, he went completely blind. Meanwhile I intended to go to the king of Spain to his aid against the king of Granada, Yussuf I [1333–54], and so sent forward my people and my siege engine to Montauban. But my father held me secretly at Montpellier and would not let me go beyond the passes. Since he could not get cured, I went with him to Pope Benedict XII at Avignon to treat with him about the Peter's pence which had been given by the diocese of Warsaw. But we made no settlement with the bishop of Warsaw at the time, and affairs were left at variance. However, later on peace was made between us and the Church of Rome and the diocese of Warsaw over the money. When I was there I told the pope my vision of the death of the dauphin as I have written it above. But I still at the time judged it better to keep from telling my father the whole story, for various reasons. But while we were with the pope we found that Peter, late abbot of Fécamp, of the diocese of Limoges, had meanwhile become bishop of Orleans, then archbishop of Sens, after that archbishop of Rouen, and at that time was actually cardinal priest of the title of saints Nereo and Achilleo. I have already spoken of him, saying that he was a councillor of King Philip, and had said mass in his presence one Ash Wednesday.

At Avignon he took me to his house, I being then margrave of Moravia and visiting Pope Benedict. One day when I was in his house he said to me, "You will yet be king of the Romans." I answered him, "Before that happens you will be pope." Both of these things came to pass.

After that I returned with my father to France. Then my father sent me to my sister [Margaret], the relict of Henry, duke of Bavaria, who was oppressed by Lewis, in order to give her counsel and aid. When I got there, I found she had made peace with him. So I turned to go through the archbishopric of Salzburg by the Alps that are called Hohen Tauern. As at day I came through the valley of Gerlostal, I remembered the miracle or vision which had come to me on the Assumption of Our Lady in Tarenzo in the Parma diocese. From that moment I got the idea of ordering the hours of the glorious Virgin Mary to be sung daily in her honor in the Church of Prague, and that her life and miracles and the account of her should be proclaimed in new lessons in the office. This took place as I shall describe below. Then I went to visit my brother at Innsbrück, sending the duke of Trent to act as captain in the county of the Tyrol; my brother came with me to Bohemia, thence to the king of Cracow, and thence to Charles of Hungary, with whom and his son Lewis, my son-in-law, he bound himself firmly by a treaty and league.

When he was there, news reached him that his wife with the barons of his county of the Tyrol had conspired against him. So he had to return post haste through Bavaria and Bohemia to the Tyrol. In a short while I followed him into the same county into the valley of the Inn. There I learnt secretly that Albert, the natural brother of his wife, and a certain baron who was master of the court to my brother, had, with her consent and that of the other barons of the county, decided to divorce my brother and marry her to Lewis, son of the Bavarian, the alleged emperor, and that the barons wanted to have him for their lord, and that she wanted to be his wife. Anxious to be certain of this, I laid a trap for Albert through Buschko the Younger, and captured him and took him through a wood to the castle which is called Sonnenburg, south of Innsbrück. Under torture he confirmed everything that had already been told me. After that I tried to capture my brother's master of the court, but he then escaped me: but his castle I destroyed. Later on his friends gave him to me with leave to do whatever I liked to him so long as I spared his life. I told my brother all this, who was grateful to me and followed my advice in this campaign. We besieged his wife in a castle of the Tyrol.

Then I went to my sister in Bavaria, who needed me; thence I returned through Salzburg and the bishopric of Brixen to the castle of Taufers. Thence I went to the valley of Cordevole to Belluno, and by night went to the suburbs of the strong castle of Zumelles on the vigil of the feast of St. Wenceslaus. I besieged and possessed it from Count Czenench, who was lord of Camerino, a city of the Venetians, who were then my enemies. It remained in my hands after the peace. Then I came to Trent. Coming into the county of Tyrol I was there till the vigil of St. Catherine. I besieged the castle Penede on Lake Garda, defended by the Milanese and the lord of Arco. This army after a secret treaty with the bishop of Trent I put to flight; and on the feast of St. Catherine the castle was put into my hands. I gave it to the church of Trent. Then I came to the castle of Belvicino, in the diocese of Vicenza, which city with all the county was held by Mastino. I had to go to the bishop secretly by night with great danger to defend him from his people. Thence I went on to Trent, and from Trent to Belluno. When I was there, the patriarch of Aquileia, who was overpowered by the duke of Austria and the lord of Verona near Frejus, whom he could not resist, sent me this letter:—

"To you, illustrious Prince Charles, of the royal house of Bohemia, margrave of Moravia, and to your army I notify that the house of the queen of queens and virgin of virgins at Aquileia is grievously oppressed by her enemies. These knightly princes who are pledged to defend maidens and women should rather have defended it. But I ask you and all your princes that by the love of this maiden of maidens you do not allow her house and property to be violated."

When we got this letter, we marched with our troops of nearly 200 armed knights and 1,000 foot over mountains which have seldom been crossed. Thus the Lord prepared our way over Serravalle, south of Belluno, near Ceneda, and after much difficulty we got to Aquileia, and the next day to the patriarch. He had collected his people and had pitched his camp near a river opposite the enemy, who lay on the farther side of it. They learnt that night of our arrival and fled, and their army broke up. We followed them and besieged part of them in a castle. There we halted some time and often attacked the castle but lost many men wounded.[6]

A little after [June 1341] King John and Charles returned to Bohemia; and King John gave the administration of the whole kingdom to Charles, on this condition that Charles on the one side should undertake to give the king 5,000 pounds of money, and that King John on the other should promise not to come to Bohemia for two years nor within that time ask any money from Bohemia. The money was speedily collected for Charles and given to King John, who left for France. Once he had gone, Charles happily and with great diligence ruled the kingdom, and by recovering what had been dissipated, reduced the debt and administered the wealth of the kingdom well.

After the two years were over King John returned to Bohemia and persuaded Charles to march with him against the Lithuanians in Prussia. Quickly getting together what was necessary for their journey, they went to Warsaw, where were also the king of Hungary, the count of Holland, and many other princes, dukes and notables come for the same purpose from all over Christendom. While these were waiting at Warsaw, amongst other pastimes which the kings used for their amusement, they played at the evil and foolish game of dice. The king of Hungary and the count of Holland played the game so eagerly against each other that the count won 600 florins from the king. When he saw the king was angry and furious, he shouted with arrogance: "O lord king, it is a wonderful thing that a prince so magnificent as you, whose land abounds in gold, should be so irritated by the loss of so small a sum and should be so disturbed in mind. That you all

---

6   After this point the narrative is not in the first person and would appear therefore not to be Charles' own account but an account nevertheless by an eye-witness. The style of the Latin is different now from Charles' usual style.

may see clearly that I do not want money so obtained and shall not use it for myself, I freely let it slip." So saying he threw it amongst the people. This made the king even more furious, but he was wise enough to hide it. Not long after all these princes and great men left Warsaw for Prussia. And when they had remained there a long time, waiting for the frost, the winter was so warm and mild that they could not cross the ice as they had done in other years. Thus these great men failed of their purpose, and lost their labors and at much expense too to themselves. The said lords went back, each to his own place.

But the king of Cracow and the Duke Polco made a deceitful agreement to capture King John and Charles on their return from Prussia, and after much hurt to squeeze the last farthing out of them. Ignorant of these wiles, King John, taking passage by the march of Brandenburg and Lusatz, went to Luxemburg. But Charles could not help going through the territory of the king of Cracow towards Warsaw. Thus he came to Kalisch, where the king of Cracow had him caught, not openly like a public enemy, but by having the city gates shut once he was within the city. This Charles saw, but he pretended not to notice it, and asked to stay there a few days. However, he managed to send out a messenger on foot to the captain of Warsaw to explain what had happened. At once he came with 300 horsemen to within a mile of Kalisch and stationed a fine horse outside the city gate. Charles, instructed by the messenger whom he had sent, very cleverly managed to have the horse brought to him to show to the magistrates. At the open gate as the horse was led in he got on it and scampered off to join his men from Warsaw. When the king of Cracow saw that Charles had escaped, he imprisoned his whole family; but after a while he let them all go.

After this the said King Casimir besieged and took the city of Skiernienice, near the Warsaw territory, when he committed many enormities, dishonoring maidens and wives. When King John of Bohemia, who then was waiting on the banks of the Rhine, heard this, he at once returned to Bohemia and gathering an army besieged Schweidnitz and butchered its suburbs and devastated its lands; he attacked and took the

city of Landshut. Moreover, because they knew that the duke of Schweidnitz had arranged the trap whereby Charles had been held at Kalisch, King John and Charles remained seven weeks there in his land, doing damage in revenge for the crime, and then returned to Bohemia. Not long after Lewis the Bavarian, who called himself emperor, with the king of Hungary, the duke of Austria, the king of Cracow, the margrave of Meissen and the Duke of Schweidnitz, all made a lasting treaty against King John of Bohemia and Charles Margrave of Moravia, in one week calling all their forces, intending to invade these two and pursue them to death. Frightened by this news, King John sent a solemn embassy, to wit, Lord Nicholas of Luxemburg, his intimate councillor, and Lord Henry the treasurer, his protonotary in Neuenberg, to Lewis to draw up some treaty or concord with him. Lewis refused absolutely to have anything to do with drawing up any treaty or truce with him. John, hearing this, said, "In the Lord's name, the larger the host of enemies we have, the more the loot and booty will there be. I swear by the Lord Jesus Christ that whoever first invades me I shall so root up as to terrify all the rest."

Not long after this Casimir, king of Cracow, attacked the city of Nicholas, duke of Troppau, Sohr by name, and besieged it, who straightway sent the news to John at Prague, asking that he should send him sufficient armed men to save him from King Casimir, who had surrounded him. King John, hearing this, answered gladly that he would not send him men, but that within four days he would come himself with a huge army. At once King John, having called together all the barons of Bohemia, addressed them thus: "Behold, nobles, faithful, loyal and beloved, we must defend our country against those who insult us with swords and arms. And since Casimir, king of Cracow, has held us and our kingdom of Bohemia in such despite as to attack Nicholas, duke of Troppau, our vassal and prince, he thus has offended our majesty gravely, for we cannot bear it lightly that those who submit to our peace and grace should suffer trouble. Lest this should be ascribed to our laziness and drowsy lethargy, we wish and order that each and all of you should at once take arms and follow us to war without delay to lower his pride who has presumed to invade our prince and vassal. Aided by our power he shall rejoice in peace and tranquility." The barons, however, answered the king: "Lord king: it is our oath, and has been inviolably observed from ancient times, that outside the limits of the kingdom we should not set forth armed, but that within the limits of the kingdom we should defend the kingdom from all aggression." So the king answered them: "The duchy of Troppau, like the other duchies of Poland, is within the kingdom, since it is known to belong to the king of Bohemia and to the crown of the kingdom. Hence I will go to this war, and I shall see which of you will be bold enough or presumptuous enough to remain behind." So that night King John with 500 armed knights came down from Mount Kutno, where he had made this speech to his barons, and hurried off to Nicholas, duke of Troppau, in a day and a night. Immediately all the barons and notables of the kingdom followed him, and before they reached the duke they numbered 2,000 armed knights, besides archers and others heavily armed. These Zdenko de Lipa quickly despatched with 300 armed men, and attacked fiercely the Hungarians and others whom King Casimir had ordered to besiege the city of the duke. These they pursued in flight to the walls of Cracow. In this flight 300 Hungarians were killed and sixty nobles captured. But the rest he pursued with such fury that he and most of his men burst into the city. The portcullis was instantly lowered and they were caught in the city. King John was furious at not being present at the fight, as he believed he could have captured the city with a single blow. However, he advanced to Cracow and besieged it with a large army and devastated all its suburbs and county round. Then King Casimir of Cracow sent word that to avoid useless slaughter they should engage in single combat, and whoever won should have his will. But since King John was quite blind, he sent word that if Casimir would first blind himself he would very gladly give him combat with equal arms. After this Casimir asked and got a seven weeks' treaty. During it the whole cause of the trouble was settled, so that Charles went to the march of Moravia free and at peace,

having received 10,000 marks from Casimir. The cause of the trouble ended, there was peace between them. In which peace all these princes who had first opposed King John and Charles margrave of Moravia were included.

After this Lewis the Bavarian sent an embassy to King John and Charles asking anxiously that they should have a talk with him, for he said that he wanted to indemnify the king and his son John for all that the latter had suffered in the taking away of his wife Margaret and the county of Tyrol, and to make complete amends. This was arranged to take place on a certain day at Treves before the archbishop of Treves, who was the uncle of King John. To it came many lords and magnificent princes on behalf of King John, because of the greatness of the injury done him by the wicked and execrable crime of the divorce. For it had not been heard of for a century that a great and generous prince and lord, by the evil of his own councillors and by their betrayal, should be deprived of his land and wife. After much discussion it was publicly agreed that John, who had been deceitfully ejected and expelled from the Tyrol and other lordships, could not honorably be indemnified by the restoration of the Tyrol, nor could he honorably take back his wife, whom, because of her adultery, he could no longer caress or love again. It came, however, to this, that Lewis of Bavaria should give instead to King John and to his son, who had both been deprived of their lordships, the land of Lusatz [i.e., Gorlitz and Budweis] and that these and all their lordships should be incorporated in the kingdom of Bohemia for ever; moreover, that 20,000 marks of pure silver should be given to King John and his son John; and that they should hold Berlin, Brandenburg and Stendal with all profits and fines until the money should be paid. This King John accepted. But when he had shown this to his sons, Charles margrave of Moravia and John, they refused to agree to it: "If our father gets that money he will spend it amongst his Rhine troopers, and so we shall remain deceived and betrayed." When Lewis understood that the sons of King John would not accept the arrangement nor confirm it, the whole treaty stood null and void. At this Lewis the Bavarian was amazed and stupefied; and thought it an evil that the treaty made after mature counsel by great princes and with much wisdom should be fiercely and proudly rejected by the sons of King John.

After this King John went to the court at Avignon to Pope Benedict, and with him made arrangements that he should persuade all the electors that Lewis of Bavaria was not the emperor, since he was opposed to the Holy Roman Church, the mother of Christendom, and had created a pope to crown him, namely, a certain friar minor. And so at once the electors proceeded to a new election and chose Charles, margrave of Moravia, as king of the Romans, with most happy auguries.

The Golden Bull

IN 1356, THE GOLDEN Bull of Emperor Charles IV established the process by which emperors would be selected and confirmed the autonomy of the German princes. The provisions largely formalized the structure that the Empire had taken on its own by the fourteenth century, a form characterized by extreme fragmentation and a lack of universally accepted principles of legitimacy.

Source: E.F. Henderson (ed.), *Select Historical Documents* (London: George Bell, 1894).

Further Reading: Henry J. Cohn, "The Electors and Imperial Rule at the End of the Fifteenth Century," in Björn Weiler and Simon MacLean (eds.), *Representations of Power in Medieval Germany, 800–1500* (Turnhout: Brepols, 2006), 295–318.

The Golden Bull of the Emperor Charles IV. 1356 A.D.

Eternal, omnipotent God, in whom the
    sole hope of the world is,
Of Heaven the Maker Thou, of earth, too,
    the lofty Creator:
Consider, we pray Thee, Thy people, and
    gently, from out Thy high dwelling,
Look down lest they turn their steps to
    the place where Erinis[7] is ruler;
There where Allecto[8] commands,
    Megaera[9] dictating the measures.
But rather by virtue of him, this emperor
    Charles whom Thou lovest,
O most beneficent God, may'st Thou
    graciously please to ordain it,
That, through the pleasant glades of
    forests ever in flower,
And through the realms of the bless'd,
    their pious leader may bring them

Into the holy shades, where the heavenly
    waters will quicken
The seeds that were sown in the life,
    and where the ripe crops are made
    glorious,
Cleansed in supernal founts from all of
    the thorns they have gathered.
Thus may the harvest be God's, and great
    may its worth be in future,
Heaping a hundred fold the corn in the
    barns overflowing.

In the name of the holy and indivisible Trinity felicitously amen. Charles the Fourth, by favor of the divine mercy emperor of the Romans, always august, and king of Bohemia; as a perpetual memorial of this matter. Every kingdom divided against itself shall be desolated. For its princes have become the companions of thieves. Wherefore God has mingled among them the spirit of dizziness, that

7 The furies.
8 The fury responsible for castigating moral crimes.
9 The fury responsible for punishing jealousy.

they may grope in midday as if in darkness; and He has removed their candlestick from out of His place, that they may be blind and leaders of the blind. And those who walk in darkness stumble; and the blind commit crimes in their hearts which come to pass in time of discord. Tell us, pride, how would'st thou have reigned over Lucifer if thou had'st not had discord to aid thee? Tell us, hateful Satan, how would'st thou have cast Adam out of Paradise if thou had'st not divided him from his obedience? Tell us, luxury, how would'st thou have destroyed Troy, if thou had'st not divided Helen from her husband? Tell us, wrath, how would'st thou have destroyed the Roman republic had'st thou not, by means of discord, spurred on Pompey and Caesar with raging swords to internal conflict? Thou, indeed, oh envy, hast, with impious wickedness, spued with the ancient poison against the Christian empire which is fortified by God, like to the holy and indivisible Trinity, with the theological virtues of faith, hope, and charity; whose foundation is happily established above in the very kingdom of Christ. Thou hast done this, like a serpent, against the branches of the empire and its nearer members; so that, the columns being shaken, thou mightest subject the whole edifice to ruin. Thou hast often spread discord among the seven electors of the holy empire, through whom, as through seven candlesticks throwing light in the unity of a septiform spirit, the holy empire ought to be illuminated.

Inasmuch as we, through the office by which we possess the imperial dignity, are doubly—both as emperor and by the electoral right which we enjoy—bound to put an end to future danger of discords among the electors themselves, to whose number we, as king of Bohemia are known to belong: we have promulgated, decreed and recommended for ratification, the subjoined laws for the purpose of cherishing unity among the electors, and of bringing about a unanimous election, and of closing all approach to the aforesaid detestable discord and to the various dangers which arise from it. This we have done in our solemn court at Nuremberg, in session with all the electoral princes, ecclesiastical and secular, and amid a numerous multitude of other princes, counts, barons, magnates, nobles and citizens; after mature deliberation, from the fullness of our imperial power; sitting on the throne of our imperial majesty, adorned with the imperial bands, insignia and diadem; in the year of our Lord 1356, in the 9th Indiction, on the 4th day before the Ides of January, in the 10th year of our reign as king, the 1st as emperor.

1. What sort of escort the electors should have, and by whom furnished.

1 We decree, and, by the present imperial and ever valid edict, do sanction of certain knowledge and from the plenitude of the imperial power: that whenever, and so often as in future, necessity or occasion shall arise for the election of a king of the Romans and prospective emperor, and the prince electors, according to ancient and laudable custom, are obliged to journey to such election,—each prince elector, if, and whenever, he is called upon to do this, shall be bound to escort any of his fellow prince electors or the envoys whom they shall send to this election, through his lands, territories and districts, and even as much beyond them as he shall be able; and to lend them escort without guile on their way to the city in which such election is to be held, and also in returning from it. This he shall do under pain of perjury and the loss, for that time only, of the vote which he was about to have in such election; which penalty, indeed, we decree that he or they who shall prove rebellious or negligent in furnishing the aforesaid escort shall, by the very act, incur.

2 We furthermore decree, and we command all other princes holding fiefs from the holy Roman empire, whatever the service they have to perform,—also all counts, barons, knights, noble and common followers, citizens and communities of castles, cities and districts of the holy empire: that at this same time—when, namely, an election is to take place of king of the Romans and prospective emperor—they shall, without guile, in the manner aforesaid, escort through their territories and as far beyond as they can, any prince elector demanding from them, or any one of them, help of this kind, or the envoys whom, as has been explained before, he shall have sent to that election. But if any persons shall presume to run counter to this our decree they shall, by the act itself, incur

the following penalties: all princes and counts, barons, noble knights and followers, and all nobles acting counter to it, shall be considered guilty of perjury and deprived of all the fiefs which they hold of the holy Roman empire and of any lords whatever, and also of all their possessions no matter from whom they hold them. All cities and guilds, moreover, presuming to act counter to the foregoing, shall similarly be considered guilty of perjury, and likewise shall be altogether deprived of all their rights, liberties, privileges and favors obtained from the holy empire, and both in their persons and in all their possessions shall incur the imperial bann and proscription. And any man, on his own authority and without trial or the calling in of any magistrate, may henceforth with impunity attack those whom we, by the act itself, deprive, from now or from a past time on, of all their rights. And, in attacking them, he need fear no punishment on this account from the empire or any one else; inasmuch as they, rashly negligent in so great a matter, are convicted of acting faithlessly and perversely, as disobedient and perfidious persons and rebels against the state, and against the majesty and dignity of the holy empire, and even against their own honor and safety.

3 We decree, moreover, and command, that the citizens and guilds of all cities shall be compelled to sell or cause to be sold to the aforesaid prince electors, or to any one of them who demands it, and to their envoys, when they are going to said city for the sake of holding said election, and even when they are returning from it: victuals at the common and current price for the needs of themselves or the said envoys and their followers. And in no way shall they act fraudulently with regard to the foregoing. We will that those who do otherwise shall, by the act itself, incur those penalties which we, in the foregoing, have seen fit to decree against citizens and guilds. Whoever, moreover, of the princes, counts, barons, knights, noble or common followers, citizens or guilds of cities shall presume to erect hostile barriers or to prepare ambushes for a prince elector going to hold the election of a king of the Romans or returning from it,—or to attack or disturb them or any one of them in their persons or in their property, or in the persons of said envoys sent by them or any

one of them, whether they have sought escort or have not considered it worth while to demand it: we decree that he, together with all the accomplices of his iniquity, shall, by the act itself, have incurred the above penalties; in such wise, namely, that each person shall incur the penalty or penalties which, according to what precedes, we have thought best, relatively to the rank of those persons, to inflict.

4 But if any prince elector should be at enmity with any one of his co-electors, and any contention, controversy, or dissension should be going on between them;—notwithstanding this, one shall be bound, under penalty of perjury and loss, for this one time, of his vote in the election, as has been stated above, to escort in said manner the other, or the envoys of the other who shall be sent in said manner to such election.

5 But if any princes, counts, barons, knights, noble or common followers, citizens, or guilds of cities, should bear ill-will to one or more of the prince electors, or any mutual discord, or war, or dissension should be going on between them: nevertheless, all opposition and fraud being laid aside, they ought to furnish such escort to this or to these prince electors, or to his or their envoys dispatched to or returning from such election, according as they each and all desire to avoid the said punishments declared by us against them; punishments which those who act counter shall, we decree, by the act itself incur. Moreover, for the ampler security and certitude of all the above, we command and we will that all the prince electors and other princes, also the counts, barons, nobles, cities or guilds of the same, shall confirm all the aforesaid through their writings and through their oaths, and shall efficaciously bind themselves to fulfill them with good faith and without guile. But whoever shall refuse to give writings of this kind, shall, by the act itself, incur such punishment as we, by the above, have seen fit to inflict on each person according to his rank.

6 But if any prince elector or other prince of whatever condition or standing, or any count, baron, or noble, or the successors or heirs of such, holding a fief or fiefs from the holy empire, be not

willing to fulfill our imperial constitutions and laws above and below laid down, or shall presume to act counter to them: if such a one, indeed, be an elector prince, his co-electors shall, from that time on, exclude him from association with themselves, and he shall lose both his vote in the election and the position, dignity and privileges possessed by the other electors; nor shall he be invested with the fiefs which he shall obtain from the holy empire or from any one otherwise, and shall, in addition, incur by the act itself all the aforesaid penalties concerning his person.

7 Although, indeed, we have willed and decreed in general terms that all princes, counts, barons, nobles, knights, followers, and also cities and guilds of the same, are bound, as has been said, to furnish the aforesaid escort to any prince elector or his envoys: nevertheless, we have thought best to designate for each one of them special escorts and conductors who will be best suited for them according to the nearness of their lands and districts, as will directly be made clearer from what follows.

8 For first the king of Bohemia, the arch-cupbearer of the holy empire, shall be escorted by the archbishop of Mainz, the bishops of Bamberg and Wurzburg, the burgraves of Nuremberg; likewise by those of Hohenlohe, of Wertheim, of Bruneck and of Hohenau; likewise by the cities of Nuremburg, Rothenburg, and Windesheim.

9 Then the archbishop of Cologne, the arch-chancellor of the holy empire for Italy, shall be escorted—they being bound to furnish such escort—by the archbishops of Mainz and Treves, the count palatine of the Rhine, the landgrave of Hesse; likewise by the counts of Katzenellenbogen, of Nassau, of Dietz; likewise of Ysenburg, of Westerburg, of Runkel, of Limburg and Falkenstein; likewise by the cities of Wetzlar, Gelnhausen and Friedberg.

10 In like manner the archbishop of Treves, arch-chancellor of the holy empire for the Gallic provinces and for the kingdom of Arles, shall be escorted by the archbishop of Mainz, the count palatine of the Rhine; likewise the counts of Sponheim, of Veldenz; likewise the Raugraves and Wiltgraves

of Nassau, of Ysenburg, of Westerburg, of Runkel, of Dietz, of Katzenellenbogen, of Eppenstein, of Falkenstein; likewise the city of Mainz.

11 Then the count palatine of the Rhine, arch-steward of the holy empire, ought to be escorted by the archbishop of Mainz.

12 But the duke of Saxony, the arch-marshal of the holy empire, shall, by right, be escorted by the king of Bohemia, the archbishops of Mainz and Magdeburg; likewise by the bishops of Bamberg and Wurzburg, the margrave of Meissen, the landgrave of Hesse; likewise the abbots of Fulda and Hersfeld, the burgraves of Nuremburg; likewise those of Hohenlohe, of Wertheim, of Bruneck, of Hohenau, of Falkenstein; likewise the cities of Erfurt, Mülhausen, Nuremburg, Rothenburg and Windesheim. And all of these last named shall likewise be bound to escort the margrave of Brandenburg, arch-chamberlain of the holy empire.

13 We will, moreover, and do expressly decree that each prince elector who shall wish to have such escort shall make known this fact and the way by which he is to pass, and shall demand this escort in such good time that those who have been deputed to furnish such escort, and from whom it shall thus have been demanded, may be able to prepare themselves for this in good time and conveniently.

14 We declare, moreover, that the foregoing decrees promulgated concerning the matter of escort shall, indeed, be so understood that each person named above—or perhaps not expressed—from whom, in the aforesaid case, escort may happen to be demanded, shall be bound to furnish it at least through his lands and territories, and as far beyond as he can, without fraud, under the penalties contained above.

15 Moreover we decree, and also ordain, that he who shall be archbishop of Mainz at the time shall intimate this same election to the different princes, ecclesiastical and secular, his co-electors, by letters patent, through his envoys. In which letters, indeed, the day and the term shall be expressed

within which those letters may probably reach each of those princes. And letters of this sort shall state that, within three successive months from the day expressed in the letters themselves, each and all of the prince electors ought to be settled at Frankfort on the Main, or to send their lawful envoys, at that time and to that place, with full and diverse power, and with their letters patent, signed with the great seal of each of them, to elect a king of the Romans and prospective emperor. How, moreover, and under what form such letters ought to be drawn up, and what formality ought to be immutably observed with regard to them, and in what form and manner the prince electors should arrange what envoys are to be sent to such election, and the power, mandate, or right of procuration that they are to have: all this will be found clearly and expressly written at the end of the present document. And we command and decree, through the plenitude of the imperial power, that the form there established be preserved unto all time.

16 Moreover we ordain and decree that when the death of the emperor or king of the Romans shall come to be known for certain in the diocese of Mainz,—within one month of that time, counting continuously from the day of the notice of such death, the death itself and the summons of which we have spoken shall be announced by the archbishop of Mainz through his letters patent. But if this same archbishop should chance to be negligent or remiss in carrying out this and in sending the summons,—thereupon those same princes of their own accord shall, even without summons, by virtue of the fealty which they owe to the holy empire, come together in the oft-mentioned city of Frankfort within three months after this, as is contained in the decree immediately preceding, being about to elect a king of the Romans and future emperor.

17 Moreover any one prince elector or his envoys should, at the time of the aforesaid election, enter the said city of Frankfort with not more than two hundred mounted followers, among which number he may be allowed to bring in with himself only fifty armed men or fewer, but not more.

18 But a prince elector, called and summoned to such election, and neither coming to it nor sending lawful envoys with letters patent, sealed with his greater seal and containing empowerment, full, free and of every kind, for the election of king of the Romans and prospective emperor; or one who comes, or perchance sends envoys, to the same, but who, afterwards, himself—or the aforesaid embassy—goes away from the place of election before a king of the Romans and prospective emperor, has been elected, and does not formally substitute a lawful procurator and leave him there: shall forfeit for that time the vote or right which he had in that election and which he abandoned in such a manner.

19 We command, moreover, and enjoin on the citizens of Frankfort, that they, by virtue of the oath which we decree they shall swear on the gospel concerning this, shall, with faithful zeal and anxious diligence, protect and defend all the prince electors in general and each one of them in particular from the invasion of the other, if any quarrel shall arise between them; and also from the invasion of any other person. And the same with regard to all the followers whom they or any one of them shall have brought into the said city among the said number of two hundred horsemen. Otherwise they shall incur the guilt of perjury, and shall also lose all their rights, liberties, privileges, favors and grants which they are known to hold from the holy empire, and shall, by the act itself, fall under the bann of the empire as to their persons and all their goods. And, from that time on, every man on his own authority and without judicial sentence may, with impunity, invade as traitors and as disloyal persons and as rebels against the empire, those citizens whom we, in such a case, from now or from a former time on, deprive of all their rights. And such invaders need in no way fear any punishment from the holy empire or from any one else.

20 The said citizens of Frankfort, moreover, throughout all that time when the oft-mentioned election is being treated of and carried on, shall not admit, or in any way permit any one, of whatever dignity, condition or standing he may be, to enter the aforesaid city: the prince electors and

their envoys and the aforesaid procurators alone being excepted; each of whom shall be admitted, as has been said, with two hundred horsemen. But if, after the entry of these same prince electors, or while they are present, any one shall chance to be found in the said city, the citizens themselves shall, effectually and without delay, straightway bring about his exit, under penalty of all that has above been promulgated against them, and also by virtue of the oath concerning this that those same citizens of Frankfort must, by the terms of this present decree, swear upon the gospel, as has been explained in the foregoing.

2. Concerning the election of a king of the Romans.

1 After, moreover, the oft-mentioned electors or their envoys shall have entered the city of Frankfort, they shall, straightway on the following day at dawn, in the church of St. Bartholomew the apostle, in the presence of all of them, cause a mass to be sung to the Holy Spirit, that the Holy Spirit himself may illumine their hearts and infuse the light of his virtue into their senses; so that they, armed with his protection, may be able to elect a just, good and useful man as king of the Romans and future emperor, and as a safeguard for the people of Christ. After such mass has been performed all those electors or their envoys shall approach the altar on which that mass has been celebrated, and there the ecclesiastical prince electors, before the gospel of St. John: "In the beginning was the word," which must there be placed before them, shall place their hands with reverence upon their breasts. But the secular prince electors shall actually touch the said gospel with their hands. And all of them, with all their followers, shall stand there unarmed. And the archbishop of Mainz shall give to them the form of the oath, and he together with them, and they, or the envoys of the absent ones, together with him, shall take the oath in common as follows:

2 "I, archbishop of Mainz, arch-chancellor of the holy empire throughout Germany, and prince elector, do swear on this holy gospel of God here actually placed before me, that I, through the faith which binds me to God and to the holy Roman empire, do intend by the help of God, to the utmost extent of my discretion and intelligence, and in accordance with the said faith, to elect one who will be suitable, as far as my discretion and discernment can tell, for a temporal head of the Christian people,—that is, a king of the Romans and prospective emperor. And my voice and vote, or said election, I will give without any pact, payment, price, or promise, or whatever such things may be called. So help me God and all the saints."

3 Such oath having been taken by the electors or their envoys in the aforesaid form and manner, they shall then proceed to the election. And from now on they shall not disperse from the said city of Frankfort until the majority of them shall have elected a temporal head for the world and for the Christian people; a king, namely, of the Romans and prospective emperor. But if they shall fail to do this within thirty days, counting continuously from the day when they took the aforesaid oath: when those thirty days are over, from that time on they shall live on bread and water, and by no means leave the aforesaid city unless first through them, or the majority of them, a ruler or temporal head of the faithful shall have been elected, as was said before.

4 Moreover after they, or the majority of them, shall have made their choice in that place, such election shall in future be considered and looked upon as if it had been unanimously carried through by all of them, no one dissenting. And if any one of the electors or their aforesaid envoys should happen for a time to be detained and to be absent or late, provided he arrive before the said election has been consummated, we decree that he shall be admitted to the election in the stage at which it was at the actual time of his coming. And since by ancient approved and laudable custom what follows has always been observed inviolately, therefore we also do establish and decree by the plenitude of the imperial power that he who shall have, in the aforesaid manner, been elected king of the Romans, shall, directly after such election shall have been held, and before he shall attend to any other cases or matters by virtue of his imperial office, without delay or contradiction, confirm and approve, by his letters and seals, to each

and all of the elector princes, ecclesiastical and secular, who are known to be the nearer members of the holy empire, all their privileges, charters, rights, liberties, ancient customs, and also their dignities and whatever they shall have obtained and possessed from the empire before the day of the election. And he shall renew to them all the above after he shall have been crowned with the imperial adornments. Moreover, the elected king shall make such confirmation to each prince elector in particular, first as king, then, renewing it, under his title as emperor; and, in these matters, he shall be bound by no means to impede either those same princes in general or any one of them in particular, but rather to promote them with his favor and without guile.

5 In a case, finally, where three prince electors in person, or the envoys of the absent ones, shall elect as king of the Romans a fourth from among themselves or from among their whole number—an elector prince, namely, who is either present or absent:—we decree that the vote of that person who has been elected, if he shall be present, or of his envoys if he shall chance to be absent, shall have full vigor and shall increase the number of those electing, and shall constitute a majority like that of the other prince electors.

3. Concerning the seating of the bishops of Treves, Cologne and Mainz.

In the name of the holy and indivisible Trinity felicitously amen. Charles the Fourth, by favor of the divine mercy emperor of the Romans, always august, and king of Bohemia. As a perpetual memorial of this matter. The splendor and glory of the holy Roman empire, and the imperial honor, and the cherished advantage of the state are fostered by the concordant will of the venerable and illustrious prince electors, who, being the chief columns as it were, sustain the holy edifice by the vigilant piety of circumspect prudence; by whose protection the right hand of the imperial power is strengthened. And the more they are bound together by an ampler benignity of mutual favor, so much more abundantly will the blessings of peace and tranquility happily flow for the people of Christ. In order, therefore, that between the venerable archbishops of Mainz, Cologne and Treves,

prince electors of the holy empire, all causes of strife and suspicion which might arise in future concerning the priority or dignity of their seats in the imperial and royal courts may be for all time removed, and that they, remaining in a quiet state of heart and soul, may be able, with concordant favor and the zeal of virtuous love, to meditate more conveniently concerning the affairs of the holy empire, to the consolation of the Christian people: we, having deliberated with all the prince electors, ecclesiastical as well as secular, do decree from the plenitude of the imperial power, by this law, in the form of an edict, to be forever valid,—that the aforesaid venerable archbishops can, may, and ought to sit as follows in all public transactions pertaining to the empire; namely, in courts, while conferring fiefs, when regaling themselves at table, and also in councils and in all other business on account of which they happen or shall happen to come together to treat of the honor or utility of the empire. He of Treves, namely, shall sit directly opposite and facing the emperor. But at the right hand of the emperor of the Romans shall sit he of Mainz when in his own diocese and province; and also, outside of his province, throughout his whole arch-chancellorship of Germany, excepting alone the province of Cologne. And he of Cologne, finally, shall sit there when in his own diocese and province, and, outside of his province, throughout all of Italy and Gaul. And we will that this form of seating, in the same order as is above expressed, be extended forever to the successors of the aforesaid archbishops of Cologne, Treves and Mainz; so that at no time shall any doubt whatever arise concerning these matters.

4. Concerning the prince electors in common.

We decree, moreover, that, as often as an imperial court shall henceforth chance to be held, in every assembly,—in council, namely, at table or in any place whatsoever where the emperor or king of the Romans shall happen to sit with the prince electors, on the right side of the emperor or king of the Romans there shall sit immediately after the archbishop of Mainz or the archbishop of Cologne—whichever, namely, shall happen at that time, according to the place or province, following the tenor of his privilege, to sit at the right hand of the emperor—first, the king of Bohemia, as he is a crowned and anointed prince, and secondly, the count palatine of the Rhine. But on the left side, immediately after whichever of the aforesaid archbishops shall happen to sit on the left, the duke of Saxony shall have the first, and, after him, the margrave of Brandenburg the second place.

But so often and whenever the holy empire shall hereafter happen to be vacant, the archbishop of Mainz shall then have the right, which he is known from of old to have had, of convoking the other princes, his aforesaid companions in the said election. And when all of them, or those who can will be present, are assembled together at the term of the election, it shall pertain to the said archbishop of Mainz and to no other to call for the votes of these his co-electors, one by one in the following order. First, indeed, he shall interrogate the archbishop of Treves, to whom we declare that the first vote belongs, and to whom, as we find, it hitherto has belonged. Secondly, the archbishop of Cologne, to whom belongs the dignity and also the duty of first imposing the royal diadem on the king of the Romans. Thirdly, the king of Bohemia, who, rightly and duly, on account of the prestige of his royal dignity, has the first place among the lay electors. Fourthly, the count palatine of the Rhine. Fifthly, the duke of Saxony. Sixthly, the margrave of Brandenburg. Of all these the said archbishop of Mainz shall call for the votes in the aforesaid order. This being done, the aforesaid princes his companions, shall, in their turn, call on him to express his own intention and to make known to them his vote. Moreover, when an imperial court is held, the margrave of Brandenburg shall present the water for washing the hands of the emperor or king of the Romans. And the king of Bohemia shall be the first to offer drink; but, according to the tenor of the privileges of his kingdom, he shall not be bound to offer it with his royal crown on, except of his own free will. The count palatine of the Rhine, moreover, shall be obliged to offer food, and the duke of Saxony shall perform the office of marshal, as has been the custom from of old.

5. Concerning the right of the count palatine and also of the duke of Saxony.

Whenever, moreover, as has been said before, the throne of the holy empire shall happen to be vacant, the illustrious count palatine of the Rhine, arch-steward of the holy empire, the right hand of the future king of the Romans in the districts of the Rhine and of Swabia and in the limits of Franconia, ought, by reason of his principality or by privilege of the county palatine, to be the administrator of the empire itself, with the power of passing judgments, of presenting to ecclesiastical benefices, of collecting returns and revenues and investing with fiefs, of receiving oaths of fealty for and in the name of the holy empire. All of these acts, however, shall, in due time, be renewed by the king of the Romans who is afterwards elected, and the oaths shall be sworn to him anew. The fiefs of princes are alone excepted, and those which are commonly called banner-fiefs: the conferring of which, and the investing, we reserve especially for the emperor or king of the Romans alone. The count palatine must know, nevertheless, that every kind of alienation or obligation of imperial possessions, in the time of such administration, is expressly forbidden to him. And we will that the illustrious king of Saxony, arch-marshal of the holy empire, shall enjoy the same right of administration in those places where the Saxon jurisdiction prevails, under all the modes and conditions that have been expressed above.

And although the emperor or king of the Romans, in matters concerning which he is called to account, has to answer before the count palatine of the Rhine and prince elector—as is said to have been introduced by custom:—nevertheless the count palatine shall not be able to exercise that right of judging otherwise than in the imperial court, where the emperor or king of the Romans shall be present.

6. Concerning the comparison of prince electors with other, ordinary princes.

We decree that, in holding an imperial court, whenever in future one shall chance to be held, the aforesaid prince electors, ecclesiastical and secular, shall immutably hold their positions on the right and on the left—according to the prescribed order and manner. And no other prince, of whatever standing, dignity, pre-eminence or condition he may be, shall in any way be preferred to them or anyone of them, in any acts relating to that court; in going there, while sitting or while standing. And it is distinctly declared that especially the king of Bohemia shall, in the holding of such courts, in each and every place and act aforesaid, immutably precede any other king, with whatsoever special prerogative of dignity he may be adorned, no matter what the occasion or cause for which he may happen to come or to be present.

7. Concerning the successors of the princes.

Among those innumerable cares for the wellbeing of the holy empire over which we, by God's grace, do happily reign—cares which daily try our heart,—our thoughts are chiefly directed to this: that union, desirable and always healthful, may continually flourish among the prince electors of the holy empire, and that the hearts of those men may be preserved in the concord of sincere charity, by whose timely care the disturbances of the world are the more easily and quickly allayed, the less error creeps in among them, and the more purely charity is observed, obscurity being removed and the rights of each one being clearly defined. It is, indeed, commonly known far and wide, and clearly manifest, as it were, throughout the whole world, that those illustrious men the king of Bohemia and the count palatine of the Rhine, the duke of Saxony and the margrave of Brandenburg, have—the one by reason of his kingdom, the others of their principalities,—together with the ecclesiastical princes their co-electors, their right, vote and place in the election of the king of the Romans and prospective emperor. And, together with the spiritual princes, they are considered and are the true and lawful prince electors of the holy empire. Lest, in future, among the sons of these same secular prince electors, matter for scandal and dissension should arise concerning the above right, vote and power, and the common welfare be thus jeopardized by dangerous delays, we, wishing by God's help to wholesomely obviate future dangers, do establish with imperial authority and decree, by the present ever-to-be-valid law, that when these same secular prince electors, or any of them, shall die, the right, vote and power of thus electing shall, freely and without the contradiction of any one, devolve on his first born, legitimate, lay son; but, if he be not living, on the son of this same first-born son,

if he be a layman. If, however, such first-born son shall have departed from this world without leaving male legitimate lay heirs,—by virtue of the present imperial edict, the right, vote and aforesaid power of electing shall devolve upon the elder lay brother descended by the true paternal line, and thence upon his first born lay son. And such succession of the first born sons, and of the heirs of these same princes, to their right, vote and power, shall be observed in all future time; under such rule and condition, however, that if a prince elector, or his first born or eldest lay son, should happen to die leaving male, legitimate, lay heirs who are minors, then the eldest of the brothers of that elector, or of his first born son, shall be their tutor and administrator until the eldest of them shall have attained legitimate age. Which age we wish to have considered, and we decree that it shall be considered, eighteen full years in the case of prince electors; and, when they shall have attained this, the guardian shall straightway be obliged to resign to them completely, together with his office, the right, vote and power, and all that these involve. But if any such principality should happen to revert to the holy empire, the then emperor or king of the Romans should and may so dispose of it as of a possession which has lawfully devolved upon himself and the empire. Saving always the privileges, rights and customs of our kingdom of Bohemia concerning the election, through its subjects, of a king in case of a vacancy. For they have the right of electing the king of Bohemia; such election to be made according to the contents of those privileges obtained from the illustrious emperors or kings of the Romans, and according to long observed custom; to which privileges we wish to do no violence by an imperial edict of this kind. On the contrary we decree that, now and in all future time, they shall have undoubted power and validity as to all their import and as to their form.

8. Concerning the immunity of the king of Bohemia and his subjects.

Inasmuch as, through our predecessors the divine emperors and kings of the Romans, it was formerly graciously conceded and allowed to our progenitors and predecessors the illustrious kings of Bohemia, also to the kingdom of Bohemia and to the crown of that same kingdom; and was introduced, without hindrance of contradiction or interruption, into that kingdom at a time to which memory does not reach back, by a laudable custom preserved unshaken by length of time, and called for by the character of those who enjoy it; that no prince, baron, noble, knight, follower, burgher, citizen—in a word no person belonging to that kingdom and its dependencies wherever they may be, no matter what his standing, dignity, pre-eminence, or condition—might, or in all future time may, be cited, or dragged or summoned, at the instance of any plaintiff whatsoever, before any tribunal beyond that kingdom itself other than that of the king of Bohemia and of the judges of his royal court: therefore of certain knowledge, by the imperial authority and from the plenitude of imperial power, we renew and also confirm such privilege, custom and favor; and by this our imperial forever-to-be-valid edict do decree that if, contrary to the said privilege, custom, or favor, any one of the foregoing—namely, any prince, baron, noble, knight, follower, citizen, burgher, or rustic, or any afore-mentioned person whatever—at any time be cited in any civil, criminal, or mixed case, or concerning any matter, before the tribunal of any one outside the said kingdom of Bohemia, he shall not at all be bound to appear when summoned, or to answer before the court. But if it shall chance that, against any such person or persons not appearing, by any judge outside of that kingdom of Bohemia, no matter what his authority, judicial proceedings are instituted, a trial is carried on, or one or more intermediate or final sentences are passed and promulgated: by the aforesaid authority, and also from the plenitude of the aforesaid imperial power, we declare utterly vain, and do annul such citations, commands, proceedings and sentences, also the carrying out of them and everything which may in any way be attempted or done in consequence of them or any one of them. And we expressly add and, by the same authority and from the fullness of the aforesaid power, do decree by an ever-to-be-valid imperial edict that, just as it has been continually observed from time immemorial in the aforesaid kingdom of Bohemia, so, henceforth, no prince, baron, noble, knight, follower, citizen, burgher, or

rustic—in short no person or inhabitant of the oft-mentioned kingdom of Bohemia, whatever be his standing, pre-eminence, dignity, or condition—may be allowed to appeal to any other tribunal from any proceedings, provisional or final sentences, or ordinances of the king of Bohemia or of his judges, instituted or promulgated, or henceforth to be instituted or promulgated against him, in the royal court or before tribunals of the king, the kingdom or the aforesaid judges. Nor may he appeal against the putting into execution of the same provocations or appeals of this kind, moreover, if any, contrary to this edict, should chance to be brought, shall of their own accord be invalid; and those appealing shall know that, by the act itself, they have incurred the penalty of loss of their case.

9. Concerning mines of gold, silver and other specie.

We establish by this ever-to-be-valid decree, and of certain knowledge do declare that our successors the kings of Bohemia, also each and all future prince electors, ecclesiastical and secular, may justly hold and lawfully possess—with all their rights without exception, according as such things can be, or usually have been possessed—all the gold and silver mines and mines of tin, copper, lead, iron and any other kind of metal, and also of salt: the king, those which have been found, and which shall at any future time be found, in the aforesaid kingdom and the lands and dependencies of that kingdom,—and the aforesaid electors in their principalities, lands, domains and dependencies. And they may also have the Jew taxes and enjoy the tolls which have been decreed and assigned to them in the past, and whatever our progenitors the kings of Bohemia of blessed memory, and these same prince electors and their progenitors and predecessors shall have legally possessed until now; as is known to have been observed by ancient custom, laudable and approved, and sanctioned by the lapse of a very long period of time.

10. Concerning money.

(1) We decree, moreover, that our successor, the king for the time being of Bohemia, shall have the

same right which our predecessors the kings of Bohemia of blessed memory are known to have had, and in the continuous peaceful possession of which they remained: the right, namely, in every place and part of their kingdom, and of the lands subject to them, and of all their dependencies—wherever the king himself may have decreed and shall please—of coining gold and silver money and of circulating it in every way and manner observed up to this time in this same kingdom of Bohemia in such matters. (2) And, by this our imperial ever-to-be-valid decree and favor we establish, that all future kings of Bohemia forever shall have the right of buying or purchasing, or of receiving in gift or donation for any reason, or in bond, from any princes, magnates, counts or other persons, any lands, castles, possessions, estates or goods, under the usual conditions with regard to such lands, castles, possessions, estates, or goods: that, namely, alods shall be bought or received as alods, freeholds as freeholds; that holdings in feudal dependency shall be bought as fiefs, and shall be held as such when bought. In such wise, however, that the kings of Bohemia shall themselves be bound to regard and to render to the holy empire its pristine and customary rights over these things (lands, etc.) which they shall, in this way, have bought or received, and have seen fit to add to the kingdom of Bohemia. (3) We will, moreover, that the present decree and favor, by virtue of this our present imperial law, be fully extended to all the elector princes, ecclesiastical as well as secular, and to their successors and lawful heirs, under all the foregoing forms and conditions.

11. Concerning the immunity of the prince electors.

We also decree that no counts, barons, nobles, feudal vassals, knights of castles, followers, citizens, burghers—indeed, no male or female subjects at all of the Cologne, Mainz and Treves churches, whatever their standing, condition or dignity—could in past times, or may or can in future be summoned at the instance of any plaintiff whatsoever, beyond the territory and boundaries and limits of these same churches and their dependencies, to any other tribunal or the court of any other person than the archbishops of Mainz, Treves and Cologne and their judges. And this

we find was the observance in the past. But if, contrary to our present edict, one or more of the aforesaid subjects of the Treves, Mainz or Cologne churches should chance to be summoned, at the instance of any one whatever, to the tribunal of any one beyond the territory, limits or bounds of the said churches or of any one of them, for any criminal, civil or mixed case, or in any matter at all; they shall not in the least be compelled to appear or respond. And we decree that the summons, and the proceedings, and the provisional and final sentences already sent or passed, or in future to be sent or passed against those not appearing, by such extraneous judges,—furthermore their ordinances, and the carrying out of the above measures, and all things which might come to pass, be attempted or be done through them or any one of them, shall be void of their own accord. And we expressly add that no count, baron, noble, feudal vassal, knight of a castle, citizen, peasant—no person, in short, subject to such churches or inhabiting the lands of the same, whatever be his standing, dignity or condition—shall be allowed to appeal to any other tribunal from the proceedings, the provisional and final sentences, or the ordinances—or the putting into effect of the same—of such archbishops and their churches, or of their temporal officials, when such proceedings, sentences or ordinances shall have been, or shall in future be held, passed or made against him in the court of the archbishops or of the aforesaid officials. Provided that justice has not been denied to those bringing plaint in the courts of the aforesaid archbishops and their officials. But appeals against this statute shall not, we decree, be received; we declare them null and void. In case of defect of justice, however, it is allowed to all the aforementioned persons to appeal, but only to the imperial court and tribunal or directly to the presence of the judge presiding at the time in the imperial court. And, even in case of such defect, those to whom justice has been denied may not appeal to any other judge, whether ordinary or delegated. And whatever shall have been done contrary to the above shall be void of its own accord. And, by virtue of this our present imperial law, we will that this statute be fully extended, under all the preceding forms and conditions, to those illustrious men the count palatine of the Rhine, the duke of Saxony, the margrave of

Brandenburg,—the secular or lay prince electors, their heirs, successors and subjects.

12. Concerning the coming together of the princes.

In view of the manifold cares of state with which our mind is constantly distracted, after much consideration our sublimity has found that it will be necessary for the prince electors of the holy empire to come together more frequently than has been their custom, to treat of the safety of that same empire and of the world. For they, the solid bases and immovable columns of the empire, according as they reside at long distances from each other, just so are able to report and confer concerning the impending defects of the districts known to them, and are not ignorant how, by the wise counsels of their providence, they may aid in the necessary reformation of the same. Hence it is that, in the solemn court held by our highness at Nuremburg together with the venerable ecclesiastical and illustrious secular prince electors, and many other princes and nobles, we, having deliberated with those same prince electors and followed their advice, have seen fit to ordain, together with the said prince electors, ecclesiastical as well as secular, for the common good and safety: that these same prince electors, once every year, when four weeks, counting continuously from the Easter feast of the Lord's resurrection, are past, shall personally congregate in some city of the holy empire; and that when next that date shall come round, namely, in the present year, a colloquium, or court, or assembly of this kind, shall be held by us and these same princes in our imperial city of Metz. And then, and henceforth on any day of an assembly of this kind, the place where they shall meet the following year shall be fixed upon by us with their counsel. And this our ordinance is to endure just so long as it may be our and their good pleasure. And, so long as it shall endure, we take them under our imperial safe conduct when going to, remaining at, and also returning from said court. Moreover, lest the transactions for the common safety and peace be retarded, as is sometimes the case, by the delay and hindrance of diversion or the excessive frequenting of feasts, we have thought best to ordain, by concordant desire, that henceforth, while the

said court or congregation shall last, no one may be allowed to give general entertainments for all the princes. Special ones, however, which do not impede the transaction of business, may be permitted in moderation.

13. Concerning the revocation of privileges.

Moreover we establish, and by this perpetual imperial edict do decree, that no privileges or charters concerning any rights, favors, immunities, customs or other things conceded, of our own accord or otherwise, under any form of words, by us or our predecessors of blessed memory the divine emperors or kings of the Romans, or about to be conceded in future by us or our successors the Roman emperors and kings, to any persons of whatever standing, pre-eminence or dignity, or to the corporation of cities, towns, or any places: shall or may, in any way at all, derogate from the liberties, jurisdictions, rights, honors or dominions of the ecclesiastical and secular prince electors; even if in such privileges and charters of any persons, whatever their preeminence, dignity or standing, as has been said, or of corporations of this kind, it shall have been, or shall be in future, expressly cautioned that they shall not be revokable unless, concerning these very points and the whole tenor included in them, special mention word for word and in due order shall be made in such revocation. For such privileges and charters, if, and in as far as, they are considered to derogate in any way from the liberties, jurisdictions, rights, honors or dominions of the said prince electors, or any one of them, in so far we revoke them of certain knowledge and cancel them, and decree, from the plenitude of our imperial power, that they shall be considered and held to be revoked.

14. Concerning those from whom, as being unworthy, their feudal possessions are taken away.

In very many places the vassals and feudatories of lords unseasonably renounce or resign, verbally and fraudulently, fiefs or benefices which they hold from those same lords. And, having made such resignation, they maliciously challenge those same lords, and declare enmity against them, subsequently inflicting grave harm upon them. And, under pretext of war or hostility, they again invade and occupy benefices and fiefs which they had thus renounced, and hold possession of them. Therefore we establish, by the present ever-to-be-valid decree, that such renunciation or resignation shall be considered as not having taken place, unless it shall have been freely and actually made by them in such way that possession of such benefices and fiefs shall be personally and actually given over to those same lords so fully that, at no future time, shall they, either through themselves or through others, by sending challenges, trouble those same lords as to the goods, fiefs or benefices resigned; nor shall they lend counsel, aid or favor to this end. He who acts otherwise, and in any way invades his lords as to benefices and fiefs, resigned or not resigned, or disturbs them, or brings harm upon them, or furnishes counsel, aid or favor to those doing this: shall, by the act itself, lose such fiefs and benefices, shall be dishonored and shall underlie the bann of the empire; and no approach or return to such fiefs or benefices shall be open to him at any time in future, nor may the same be granted to him anew under any conditions; and a concession of them, or an investiture which takes place contrary to this, shall have no force. Finally, by virtue of this present edict, we decree that he or they who, not having made such resignation as we have described, acting fraudulently against his or their lords, shall knowingly invade them—whether a challenge has previously been sent or has been omitted,—shall, by the act itself, incur all the aforesaid punishments.

15. Concerning conspiracies.

Furthermore we reprobate, condemn, and of certain knowledge declare void, all conspiracies, detestable and frowned upon by the sacred laws and conventicles, or unlawful assemblies in the cities and out of them, and associations between city and city, between person and person or between a person and a city, under pretext of clientship, or reception among the citizens, or of any other reason; furthermore the confederations and pacts—and the usage which has been introduced with regard to such things, which we consider to be corruption rather than any thing else—which cities or persons, of whatever dignity, condition or standing, shall have thus far made and shall

presume to make in future, whether among themselves or with others, without the authority of the lords whose subjects or serving-men they are, those same lords being expressly excluded. And it is clear that such are prohibited and declared void by the sacred laws of the divine emperors our predecessors. Excepting alone those confederations and leagues which princes, cities and others are known to have formed among themselves for the sake of the general peace of the provinces and lands. Reserving these for our special declaration, we ordain that they shall remain in full vigor until we shall decide to ordain otherwise concerning them. And we decree that, henceforth, each individual person who, contrary to the tenor of the present decree, and of the ancient law issued regarding this, shall presume to enter into such confederations, leagues, conspiracies and pacts, shall incur, besides the penalty of that law, a mark of infamy and a penalty of ten pounds of gold. But a city or community similarly breaking this our law shall, we decree, by the act itself incur the penalty of a hundred pounds of gold, and also the loss and privation of the imperial liberties and privileges; one half of such pecuniary penalty to go to the imperial fisc, the other to the territorial lord to whose detriment the conspiracies, etc., were formed.

16. Concerning pfalburgers.

Moreover since some citizens and subjects of princes, barons and other men—as frequent complaint has shown us,—seeking to cast off the yoke of their original subjection, nay, with bold daring despising it, manage, and frequently in the past have managed to be received among the citizens of other cities; and, nevertheless, actually residing in the lands, cities, towns and estates of the former lords whom they so fraudulently presume or have presumed to desert, succeed in enjoying the liberties of the cities to which they thus transfer themselves and in being protected by them—being what is usually called in common language in Germany "pfalburgers": therefore, since fraud and deceit ought not to shelter any one, from the plenitude of the imperial power and by the wholesome advice of all the ecclesiastical and secular prince electors, we establish of certain knowledge, and, by the present ever-to-be-valid law do decree, that in all territories, places, and provinces of the holy empire, from the present day on, the aforesaid citizens and subjects thus eluding those under whom they are, shall in no way possess the rights and liberties of those cities among whose citizens they contrive, or have contrived, by such fraudulent means to be received; unless, bodily and actually going over to such cities and there taking up their domicile, making a continued, true and not fictitious stay, they submit to their due burdens and municipal functions in the same. But if any, contrary to the tenor of our present law, have been, or shall in future be received as citizens, their reception shall lack all validity, and the persons received, of whatever condition, dignity or standing they may be, shall, in no case or matter whatever, in any way exercise or enjoy the rights and liberties of the cities into which they contrive to be received. Any rights, privileges, or observed customs, at whatever time obtained, to the contrary notwithstanding; all of which, in so far as they are contrary to our present law, we, by these presents, revoke of certain knowledge, decreeing from the plenitude of the aforesaid imperial power that they lack all force and validity. For in all the aforesaid respects, the rights of the princes, lords and other men who chance, and shall in future chance, to be thus deserted, over the persons and goods of any subjects deserting them in the oft-mentioned manner, shall always be regarded. We decree, moreover, that those who, against the ordering of our present law, shall presume, or shall in the past have presumed, to receive the oft-mentioned citizens and subjects of other men, if they do not altogether dismiss them within a month after the present intimation has been made to them, shall, for such transgression, as often as they shall hereafter commit it, incur a fine of a hundred marks of pure gold, of which one half shall be applied without fail to our imperial fisc, and the rest to the lords of those who have been received as citizens.

17. Concerning challenges of defiance.

We declare that those who, in future, feigning to have just cause of defiance against any person, unseasonably challenge them in places where they do not have their domicile, or which they do not inhabit in common, cannot with honor inflict any harm through fire, spoliation or rapine, on the challenged ones. And, since fraud and deceit should not shelter any one, we establish by the present ever-to-be-valid decree that challenges of this kind, thus made, or in future to be made by any one against any lords or persons to whom they were previously bound by companionship, familiarity or any honest friendship, shall not be valid; nor is it lawful, under pretext of any kind of challenge, to invade any one through fire, spoliation or rapine, unless the challenge, three natural days before, shall have been intimated personally to the challenged man himself, or publicly in the place where he has been accustomed to reside, where full credibility can be given, through suitable witnesses, to such an intimation. Whoever shall presume otherwise to challenge any one and to invade him in the aforesaid manner, shall incur, by the very act, the same infamy as if no challenge had been made; and we decree that he be punished as a traitor by his judges, whoever they are, with the lawful punishments.

We prohibit also each and every unjust war and feud, and all unjust burnings, spoliations and rapines, unlawful and unusual tolls and escorts, and the exactions usually extorted for such escorts, under the penalties by which the sacred laws prescribe that the foregoing offenses, and any one of them, are to be punished.

18. Letter of intimation.

To you, illustrious and magnificent prince, lord margrave of Brandenburg, arch-chamberlain of the holy empire, our co-elector and most dear friend, we intimate by these presents the election of the king of the Romans, which is about to take place on account of rational causes. And, as a duty of our office, we duly summon you to said election, bidding you within three months, counting continuously, from such and such a day, yourself, or in the person of one or more envoys or procurators having sufficient mandates, to be careful and come to the rightful place, according to the form of the holy laws issued concerning this, ready to deliberate, negotiate and come to an agreement with the other princes, yours and our co-electors, concerning the election of a future king of the Romans and, by God's favor, future emperor. And be ready to remain there until the full consummation of such election, and otherwise to act and proceed as is found expressed in the sacred laws carefully promulgated concerning this. Otherwise, notwithstanding your or your envoys' absence, we, together with our other co-princes and co-electors, shall take final measures in the aforesaid matters, according as the authority of those same laws has sanctioned.

19. Formula of representation sent by that prince elector who shall decide to send his envoys to carry on an election.

We ... such a one by the grace of God, etc., of the holy empire, etc., do make known to all men by the tenor of these presents, that since, from rational causes, an election of a king of the Romans is about to be made, we, desiring to watch with due care over the honor and condition of the holy empire, lest it be dangerously subjected to so grave harm, inasmuch as we have the great confidence, as it were of an undoubted presumption, in the faith and circumspect zeal of our beloved ... and ..., faithful subjects of ours: do make, constitute and ordain them and each one of them, completely, in every right, manner and form in which we can or may do it most efficaciously and effectually, our true and lawful procurators and special envoys—so fully that the condition of him who is acting at the time shall not be better than that of the other, but that what has been begun by one may be finished and lawfully terminated by the other. And we empower them to treat wherever they please with the others, our co-princes and co-electors, ecclesiastical as well as secular, and to agree, decide and settle upon some person fit and suitable to be elected king of the Romans, and to be present, treat and deliberate in the transactions to be carried on concerning the election of such a person, for us and in our place and name; also, in our stead and name, to nominate such a person, and to consent to him, and also to raise him to be king of the Romans, to elect him to the holy empire, and to take, upon our soul, with regard to the foregoing or any one of the foregoing, whatever oath shall be necessary, requisite or customary. And we empower them to substitute altogether, as well as to recall, one or more other procurators who shall perform each and every act, included in

and concerning the foregoing matters, that may be needful, useful, or even in any way convenient, even to the consummation of such negotiations, nomination, deliberation and impending election. Even if the said matters, or any one of them, shall require a special mandate; even if they shall turn out to be greater or more especial than the above mentioned; provided that we could have performed them ourselves had we been present personally at the carrying on of such negotiations, deliberation, nomination and eventual election. And we consider, and wish to consider, and firmly promise that we always will consider satisfactory and valid any thing done, transacted or accomplished, or in any way ordained, in the aforesaid matters or in any one of them, by our aforesaid procurators or envoys, or their substitutes, or by those whom the latter shall substitute.

20. Concerning the unity of the electoral principalities and of the rights connected with them.

Since each and all the principalities, by virtue of which the secular prince electors are known to hold their right and vote in the election of the king of the Romans and prospective emperor, are so joined and inseparably united with such right of election, also with the offices, dignities and other rights connected with each and every such principality and dependent from it, that the right, vote, office and dignity, and all other privileges belonging to each of these same principalities may not devolve upon any other than upon him who is recognized as possessing that principality itself, with all its lands, vassalages, fiefs and domains, and all its appurtenances: we decree, by the present ever-to-be-valid imperial edict, that each of the said principalities, with the right and vote and duty of election, and with all other dignities, rights and appurtenances concerning the same, ought so to continue and to be, indivisibly and for all time, united and joined together, that the possessor of any principality ought also to rejoice in the quiet and free possession of its right, vote and office, and dignity, and all the appurtenances that go with it, and to be considered prince elector by all. And he himself, and no one else, ought at all times to be called in and admitted by the other prince electors, without any contradiction whatever, to the election and to all other transactions to be carried on for the honor or welfare of the holy empire. Nor, since they are and ought to be inseparable, may any one of the said rights, etc., be divided from the other, or at any time be separated, or be separately demanded back, in court or out of it, or dis-trained, or, even by a decision of the courts, be separated; nor shall any one obtain a hearing who claims one without the other. But if, through error or otherwise, any one shall have obtained a hearing, or proceedings, judgment, sentence or any thing of the kind shall have taken place, or shall chance in any way to have been attempted, contrary to this our present decree: all this, and all consequences of such proceedings, etc., and of any one of them, shall be void of their own accord.

21. Concerning the order of marching, as regards the archbishops.

Inasmuch as we saw fit above, at the beginning of our present decrees, fully to provide for the order of seating of the ecclesiastical prince electors in council, and at table and elsewhere, whenever, in future, an imperial court should chance to be held, or the prince electors to assemble together with the emperor or king of the Romans—as to which order of seating we have heard that in former times discussions often arose: so, also, do we find it expedient to fix, with regard to them, the order of marching and walking. Therefore, by this perpetual imperial edict, we decree that, as often as, in an assembly of the emperor or king of the Romans and of the aforesaid princes, the emperor or king of the Romans shall be walking, and it shall happen that the insignia are carried in front of him, the archbishop of Treves shall walk in a direct diametrical line in front of the emperor or king, and those alone shall walk in the middle space between them, who shall happen to carry the imperial or royal insignia. When, however, the emperor or king shall advance without those same insignia, then that same archbishop shall precede the emperor or king in the aforesaid manner, but so that no one at all shall be in the middle between them; the other two archiepiscopal electors always keeping their places—as with

regard to the seating above explained, so with regard to walking—according to the privilege of their provinces.

22. Concerning the order of proceeding of the prince electors, and by whom the insignia shall be carried.

In order to fix the order of proceeding, which we mentioned above, of the prince electors in the presence of the emperor or king of the Romans when he is walking, we decree that, so often as, while holding an imperial court, the prince electors shall, in the performance of any functions or solemnities, chance to walk in procession with the emperor or king of the Romans, and the imperial or royal insignia are to be carried: the duke of Saxony, carrying the imperial or royal sword, shall directly precede the emperor or king, and shall place himself in the middle, between him and the archbishop of Treves. But the count palatine, carrying the imperial orb, shall march in the same line on the right side, and the margrave of Brandenburg, bearing the scepter, on the left side of the same duke of Saxony. But the king of Bohemia shall directly follow the emperor or king himself, no one intervening.

23. Concerning the benedictions of the archbishops in the presence of the emperor.

Furthermore, so often as it shall come to pass that the ceremony of the mass is celebrated in the presence of the emperor or king of the Romans and that the archbishops of Mainz, Treves and Cologne, or two of them, are present,—in the confession which is usually said before the mass, and in the presenting of the gospel to be kissed, and in the blessing to be said after the "Agnus Dei," also in the benedictions to be said after the end of the mass, and also in those said before meals, and in the thanks to be offered after the food has been partaken of, the following order shall be observed among them, as we have seen fit to ordain by their own advice: namely, on the first day each and all of these shall be done by the first of the archbishops, on the second, by the second, on the third, by the third. But we will that first, second and third shall be understood in this case, according as each one of them was consecrated at an earlier or later date. And, in order that they may mutually make advances to each other with worthy and becoming honor, and may give an example to others of mutual respect, he whose turn it is according to the aforesaid, shall, without regard to that fact, and with charitable intent, invite the other to officiate; and, not till he has done this, shall he proceed to perform the above, or any of the above functions.

24.

(1) If any one, together with princes, knights or privates, or also any plebian persons, shall enter into an unhallowed conspiracy, or shall take the oath of such conspiracy, concerning the death of our and the holy Roman empire's venerable and illustrious prince electors, ecclesiastical as well as secular, or of any one of them—for they also are part of our body; and the laws have decided that the intention of a crime is to be punished with the same severity as the carrying out of it:— he, indeed, shall die by the sword as a traitor, all his goods being handled over to our fisc. (2) But his sons, to whom, by special imperial lenity, we grant their life—for those ought to perish by the same punishment as their father, whose portion is the example of a paternal, that is of a hereditary crime—shall be without share in any inheritance or succession from the mother or grandparents, or even from relatives; they shall receive nothing from other people's wills, and shall be always poor and in want; the infamy of their father shall always follow them, and they shall never achieve any honor or be allowed to take any oath at all; in a word they shall be such that to them, groveling in perpetual misery, death shall be a solace and life a punishment. (3) Finally we command that those shall be made notorious, and shall be without pardon, who shall ever try to intervene with us for such persons. (4) But to the daughters, as many of them as there are, of such conspirators, we will that there shall go only the "falcidia"— the fourth part of the property of the mother if she die intestate; so that they may rather have the moderate alimony of a daughter, than the entire emolument or name of an heir;—for the sentence ought to be milder in the case of those who, as we trust, on account of the infirmity of their sex, are less likely to make daring attempts. (5) Deeds of gift, moreover, made out to either sons or daughters by the aforesaid persons, after the passing of this law, shall not be valid. (6) Dotations and donations of any possessions; likewise, in a word, all transfers which shall prove to have been made, by any fraud or by right, after the time when first the aforesaid people conceived the idea of entering into a conspiracy or union, shall, we decree, be of no account. (7) But the wives of the aforesaid conspirators, having recovered their dowry—if they shall be in a condition to reserve for their children that which they shall have received from their husbands under the name of a gift,— shall know that, from the time when their usufruct ceases, they are to leave to our fisc all that which, according to the usual law, was due to their children. (8) And the fourth part of such property shall be put aside for the daughters alone, not also for the sons. (9) That which we have provided concerning the aforesaid conspirators and their children, we also decree, with like severity, concerning their followers, accomplices and aiders, and the children of these. (10) But if any one of these, at the beginning of the formation of a conspiracy, inflamed by zeal for the right kind of glory, shall himself betray the conspiracy, he shall be enriched by us with reward and honor; he, moreover, who shall have been active in the conspiracy, if, even late, he disclose secret plans which were, indeed, hitherto unknown,—shall nevertheless be deemed worthy of absolution and pardon. (11) We decree, moreover, that if anything be said to have been committed against the aforesaid prince electors, ecclesiastical or secular,—even after the death of the accused that charge can be instituted. (12) Likewise in such a charge, which regards high treason against his prince electors, slaves shall be tortured even in a case concerning the life of their master. (13) We will, furthermore, and do decree by the present imperial edict, that even after the death of the guilty persons this charge can be instituted, and, if some one already convicted die, his memory shall be condemned and his goods taken away from his heirs. (14) For from the time when any one conceived so wicked a plot, from then on he has to some extent been punished mentally; but from the time when any one drew down upon himself such a charge, we decree that

he may neither alienate nor release, nor may any debtor lawfully make payment to him. (15) For in this case we decree that slaves may be tortured in a matter involving the life of their master; that is, in the case of a damnable conspiracy against the prince electors, ecclesiastical and secular, as has been said before. (16) And if any one should die, on account of the uncertain person of his successor his goods shall be held, if he be proved to have died in a case of this kind.

25.

If it is fitting that other principalities be preserved in their entirety, in order that justice may be enforced and faithful subjects rejoice in peace and quiet: much more ought the magnificent principalities, dominions, honors and rights of the elector princes to be kept intact—for where greater danger is imminent a stronger remedy should be applied,—lest, if the columns fall, the support of the whole edifice be destroyed. We decree, therefore, and sanction, by this edict to be perpetually valid, that from now on unto all future time the distinguished and magnificent principalities, viz.: the kingdom of Bohemia, the county palatine of the Rhine, the duchy of Saxony and the margravate of Brandenburg, their lands, territories, homages or vassalages, and any other things pertaining to them, may not be cut, divided, or under any condition dismembered, but shall remain forever in their perfect entirety. The first born son shall succeed to them, and to him alone shall jurisdiction and dominion belong; unless he chance to be of unsound mind, or idiotic, or have some other marked and known defect on account of which he could not or should not rule over men. In which case, he being prevented from succeeding, we will that the second born, if there should be one in that family, or another elder brother or lay relative, the nearest on the father's side in a straight line of descent, shall have the succession. He, however, shall always show himself clement and gracious to the others, his brothers and sisters, according to the favor shown him by God, and according to his best judgment and the amount of his patrimony,—division, partition or dismemberment of the principality and its appurtenances being in every way forbidden to him.

26.

On the day upon which a solemn imperial or royal court is to be held, the ecclesiastical and secular prince electors shall, about the first hour, come to the imperial or royal place of abode, and there the emperor or king shall be clothed in all the imperial insignia; and, mounting their horses, all shall go with the emperor or king to the place fitted up for the session, and each one of them shall go in the order and manner fully defined above in the law concerning the order of marching of those same prince electors. The arch-chancellor, moreover, in whose arch-chancellorship this takes place, shall carry, besides the silver staff, all the imperial or royal seals and signets. But the secular prince electors, according to what has above been explained, shall carry the scepter, orb and sword. And immediately before the archbishop of Treves, marching in his proper place, shall be carried first the crown of Aix and second that of Milan: and this directly in front of the emperor already resplendent with the imperial adornments; and these crowns shall be carried by some lesser princes, to be chosen for this by the emperor according to his will. The empress, moreover, or queen of the Romans, clad in her imperial insignia, joined by her nobles and escorted by her maids of honor, shall proceed to the place of session after the king or emperor of the Romans, and also, at a sufficient interval of space, after the king of Bohemia, who immediately follows the emperor.

27. Concerning the offices of the prince electors in the solemn courts of the emperors or kings of the Romans.

We decree that whenever the emperor or king of the Romans shall hold his solemn courts, in which the prince electors ought to serve or to perform their offices, the following order shall be observed in these matters. First, then, the emperor or king having placed himself on the royal seat or imperial throne, the duke of Saxony shall fulfil his office in this manner: before the building where the imperial or royal session is being held, shall be placed a heap of oats so high that it shall reach to the breast or girth of the horse on which the duke himself shall sit; and he shall have in his hand a silver staff and a silver measure, which, together, shall weigh 12 marks of silver; and, sitting upon his horse, he shall first fill that measure with oats, and shall offer it to the first slave who appears. This being done, fixing his staff in the oats, he shall retire; and his vice-marshal, namely, he of Pappenheim, approaching—or, in his absence, the marshal of the court,—shall further distribute the oats. But when the emperor or king shall have gone into table, the ecclesiastical prince electors—namely the archbishops,—standing before the table with the other prelates, shall bless the same according to the order above prescribed; and, the benediction over, all those same archbishops if they are present, otherwise two or one, shall receive from the chancellor of the court the imperial or royal seals and signets, and he in whose arch-chancellorship this court happens to be held advancing in the middle, and the other two joining him on either side, shall carry those seals and signets—all touching with their hands the staff on which they have been suspended—and shall reverently place them on the table before the emperor or king. The emperor or king, however, shall straightway restore the same to them, and he in whose arch-chancellorate this takes place, as has been said, shall carry the great seal appended to his neck until the end of the meal, and after that until, riding from the imperial or royal court, he shall come to his dwelling place. The staff, moreover, that we spoke of shall be of silver, equal in weight to twelve marks of silver; of which silver, and of which price, each of those same archbishops shall pay one third; and that staff afterwards, together with the seals and signets, shall be assigned to the chancellor of the imperial court to be put to what use he pleases. But after he whose turn it has been, carrying the great seal, shall, as described, have returned from the imperial court to his dwelling place, he shall straightway send that seal to the said chancellor of the imperial court. This he shall do through one of his servants riding on such a horse as, according to what is becoming to his own dignity, and according to the love which he shall bear to the chancellor of the court, he shall be bound to present to that chancellor.

Then the margrave of Brandenburg, the arch-chamberlain, shall approach on horseback, having in his hands silver basins with water, of the weight of twelve marks of silver, and a beautiful towel; and, descending from his horse, he shall present the water to the lord emperor or king of the Romans to wash his hands.

The count palatine of the Rhine shall likewise enter on horseback, having in his hands four silver dishes filled with food, of which each one shall be worth three marks; and, descending from his horse, he shall carry them and place them on the table before the emperor or king.

After this, likewise on horseback, shall come the king of Bohemia, the arch-cupbearer, carrying in his hands a silver cup or goblet of the weight of twelve marks, covered, filled with a mixture of wine and water; and, descending from his horse, he shall offer that cup to the emperor or king of the Romans to drink from.

Moreover, as we learn it to have hitherto been observed, so we decree, that, after their aforesaid offices have been performed by the secular prince electors, he of Falkenstein, the sub-chamberlain, shall receive for himself the horse and basins of the margrave of Brandenburg; he of Northemburg, master of the kitchen, the horse and dishes of the count palatine; he of Limburg, the vice-cupbearer, the horse and cup of the king of Bohemia; he of Pappenheim, the vice-marshal, the horse, staff and aforesaid measure of the duke of Saxony. That is, if these be present at such imperial or royal court, and if each one of them minister in his proper office. But if they, or any one of them, should see fit to absent themselves from the said court, then those who daily minister at the imperial or royal court shall, in place of the absent ones,—each one, namely, in place of that absent one with whom he has his name and office in common,—enjoy the fruits with regard to the aforesaid functions, inasmuch as they perform the duties.

28.

Moreover the imperial or royal table ought so to be arranged that it shall be elevated above the other tables in the hall by a height of six feet. And at it, on the day of a solemn court, shall sit no one at all except alone the emperor or king of the Romans.

But the seat and table of the empress or queen shall be prepared to one side in the hall, so that that table shall be three feet lower than the imperial or royal table, and as many feet higher than the seats of the prince electors; which princes shall have their seats and tables at one and the same altitude among themselves.

Within the imperial place of session tables shall be prepared for the seven prince electors, ecclesiastical and secular,—three, namely, on the right, and three others on the left, and the seventh directly opposite the face of the emperor or king, as has above been more clearly defined by us in the chapter concerning the seating and precedence of the prince electors; in such wise, also, that no one else, of whatever dignity or standing he may be, shall sit among them or at their table.

Moreover it shall not be allowed to any one of the aforesaid secular prince electors, when the duty of his office has been performed, to place himself at the table prepared for him so long as any one of his fellow prince electors has still to perform his office. But when one or more of them shall have finished their ministry, they shall pass to the tables prepared for them, and, standing before them, shall wait until the others have fulfilled the aforesaid duties; and then, at length, one and all shall place themselves at the same time before the tables prepared for them.

29.

We find, moreover, from the most renowned accounts and traditions of the ancients that, from time immemorial, it has been continuously observed, by those who have felicitously preceded us, that the election of the king of the Romans and future emperor should be held in the city of Frankfort, and the first coronation in Aix, and that his first imperial court should be celebrated in the town of Nuremburg. Wherefore, on sure grounds, we declare that the said usages should also be observed in future, unless a lawful impediment should stand in the way of them or any one of them. Whenever, furthermore, any prince elector, ecclesiastical or secular, detained by a just impediment, and not able to come when summoned to the imperial court, shall send an envoy or procurator, of whatever dignity or standing,—that

envoy, although, according to the mandate given him by his master, he ought to be admitted in the place of him who sends him, shall, nevertheless, not sit at the table or in the seat intended for him who sent him.

Moreover, when those matters shall have been settled which were at that time to be disposed of in any imperial or royal court, the master of the court shall receive for himself the whole structure or wooden apparatus of the imperial or royal place of session, where the emperor or king of the Romans shall have sat with the prince electors to hold his solemn court, or, as has been said, to confer fiefs on the princes.

30. Concerning the rights of the officials when princes receive their fiefs from the emperor or king of the Romans.

We decree by this imperial edict that the prince electors, ecclesiastical and secular, when they receive their fiefs or regalia from the emperor or king, shall not at all be bound to give or pay anything to anybody. For the money which is paid under such a pretext is due to the officials; but since, indeed, the prince electors themselves are at the head of all the offices of the imperial court, having also their substitutes in such offices, furnished for this by the Roman princes, and paid,—it would seem absurd if substituted officials, under cover of any excuse whatever, should demand presents from their superiors; unless, perchance, those same prince electors, freely and of their own will, should give them something.

On the other hand, the other princes of the empire, ecclesiastical or secular,—when, in the aforesaid manner, any one of them receives his fiefs from the emperor or king of the Romans,—shall give to the officials of the imperial or royal court 63 marks of silver and a quarter, unless any one of them can protect himself by an imperial or royal privilege or grant, and can prove that he has paid or is exempt from such, or also from any other, payments usually made when receiving such fiefs. Moreover the master of the imperial or royal court shall make division of the 63-¼ marks as follows: first reserving, indeed, 10 marks for himself, he shall give to the chancellor of the imperial or royal court 10 marks; to the masters, notaries, copyists, 3 marks; and to the sealer, for wax and parchment, one quarter. This with the understanding that the chancellor and notaries shall not be bound to do more than to give the prince receiving the fief a testimonial to the effect that he has received it, or a simple charter of investiture.

Likewise, from the aforesaid money, the master of the court shall give to the cupbearer, him of Limburg, 10 marks; to the master of the kitchen, him of Northemburg, 10 marks; to the vice-marshal, him of Pappenheim, 10 marks; and to the chamberlain, him of Falkenstein, 10 marks: under the condition, however, that they and each one of them are present and perform their offices in solemn courts of this kind. But if they or any one of them shall have been absent, then the officials of the imperial or royal court who perform these same offices, shall carry off the reward and the perquisites of those whose absence they make good, individual for individual, according as they fill their place, and bear their name, and perform their task.

When, moreover, any prince, sitting on a horse or other beast, shall receive his fiefs from the emperor or king, that horse or beast, of whatever kind he be, shall be the due of the highest marshal—that is, of the duke of Saxony if he shall be present; otherwise of him of Pappenheim, his vice-marshal; or, in his absence, of the marshal of the imperial or royal court.

31.

Inasmuch as the majesty of the holy Roman empire has to wield the laws and the government of diverse nations distinct in customs, manner of life, and in language, it is considered fitting, and, in the judgment of all wise men, expedient, that the prince electors, the columns and sides of that empire, should be instructed in the varieties of the different dialects and languages: so that they who assist the imperial sublimity in relieving the wants of very many people, and who are constituted for the sake of keeping watch, should understand, and be understood by, as many as possible. Wherefore we decree that the sons, or heirs and successors of the illustrious prince electors, namely of the king of Bohemia, the count palatine of the Rhine, the duke of Saxony and the margrave of Brandenburg—since they are expected in all likelihood to have naturally acquired the German language, and to have been taught it from their infancy,—shall be instructed in the grammar of the Italian and Slavic tongues, beginning with the seventh year of their age; so that, before the fourteenth year of their age, they may be learned in the same according to the grace granted them by God. For this is considered not only useful, but also, from the aforementioned causes, highly necessary, since those languages are wont to be very much employed in the service and for the needs of the holy empire, and in them the more arduous affairs of the empire are discussed. And, with regard to the above, we lay down the following mode of procedure to be observed: it shall be left to the option of the parents to send their sons, if they have any—or their relatives whom they consider as likely to succeed themselves in their principalities,—to places where they can be taught such languages, or, in their own homes, to give them teachers, instructors, and fellow youths skilled in the same, by whose conversation and teaching alike they may become versed in those languages.

45. *THE DEEDS OF THE PRINCES OF THE POLES*

THE ANONYMOUS AUTHOR OF the first history of Poland was a monk from Western Europe writing some time in the first decades of the twelfth century. The selection below deals with the reign of Bolesław Chrobry (967–1025) and contains legendary as well as historical information about this ruler. In particular, it presents a Polish version of his meeting with Emperor Otto III at Gniezno at which, according to the *Deeds*, Otto crowned Bolesław king. The earlier German account by Thietmar of Merseburg (see doc. 46, below) provides a different account of this meeting and is entirely silent about the putative coronation of Bolesław.

Source: Paul W. Knoll and Frank Shaer (ed. and trans.), *Gesta Principum Polonorum: The Deeds of the Princes of the Poles*, Central European Medieval Texts 3 (Budapest/New York: Central European Press, 2003), 31–71.

Further Reading: Thomas N. Bisson, "On Not Eating Polish Bread in Vain: Resonance and Conjuncture in the Deeds of the Princes of Poland (1109–1113)," *Viator* 29 (1998): 279–88.

6. Bolesław The First, Who Was Called The Glorious or Chrabri

So, thanks to his devout wife, Mieszko [I, ca. 920/45–92] was the first duke of Poland to receive the grace of baptism. And it is fully enough to say to his praise and glory that in his days and through him the dayspring from on high visited the kingdom of Poland. For the glorious Bolesław was born to him of that holy woman, and after his death Bolesław governed the kingdom valiantly, and with God's favor so grew in courage and strength that, if I may put it so, his virtues gilded the whole of Poland. For who could do full justice in speaking of his brave deeds or his battles against the peoples all around, to say nothing of setting them down in written record? Did not he conquer Moravia and Bohemia and win the seat of the duchy in Prague and appointed his suffragans to it; was it not he who time and again defeated the Hungarians in battle and made himself master of all their lands as far as the Danube? The indomitable Saxons were not a match for his valor: hence in the middle of their country an iron boundary sign in the River Saale marked Poland's boundaries. What need is there then to list by name his victories and triumphs over heathen nations, nations which, one may say, he trampled under his feet? For when Selencia, Pomorania, and Prussia persisted in their perfidy he crushed them, and when they converted he strengthened them in their faith, indeed he established through the pope many churches and bishops there, or rather the pope established them through him. Moreover, when St. Adalbert [c. 956–997; Bishop of Prague] came to him on his long wanderings after suffering many indignities through his rebellious Czech people, Bolesław received him with great veneration and paid faithful attention to his instructions and his sermons. Then, once he saw that the faith had begun to blossom in Poland and the holy church was growing, the holy martyr, alight with the fire of love and zeal for preaching, fearlessly entered Prussia; and there he met with martyrdom and brought his holy struggle to consummation. Afterwards Bolesław obtained his body from the Prussians for a weight of gold and laid him to rest in the metropolitan see of Gniezno with all the honor befitting him. One further matter seems to me worthy of record. In his time the emperor Otto Rufus [Otto III, 980–1002] went to visit St. Adalbert to pray and seek reconciliation, and at the same time to learn more of what was reported of the glorious Bolesław (the story can be read at greater length in the book of his martyrdom), and Bolesław received him with the honor and ceremony with which such a distinguished guest, a king and Roman emperor, should fittingly be received. Marvelous and wonderful sights Bolesław set before the emperor when he arrived: the ranks first of the knights in all their variety, and then of the princes, lined up on a spacious plain like choirs, each separate unit set apart by the distinct and varied colors of its apparel, and no garment there was of inferior quality, but of the most precious stuff that might anywhere be found. For in Bolesław's time every knight and every lady of the court wore robes instead of garments of linen or wool, nor did they wearprecious furs, however new, without orphrey.[1] For gold in his days was held by all to be as common as silver, and silver deemed as little worth as straw. So when the Roman emperor beheld his glory and power and richness, he exclaimed in admiration, "By the crown of my empire, the things I behold are greater than I had been led to believe," and after taking counsel with his magnates he added before the whole company, "Such a great man does not deserve to be styled duke or count like any of the princes, but to be raised to a royal throne and adorned with a diadem in glory." And with these words he took the imperial diadem from his own head and laid it upon the head of Bolesław in pledge of friendship. And as a triumphal banner he gave him as a gift one of the nails from the cross of our Lord with the lance of St. Maurice, and in return Bolesław gave to him an arm of St. Adalbert. And in such love were they united that day that the emperor declared him his brother and partner in the empire, and called him a friend and ally of the Roman people. And what is more, he granted him and his successors authority over whatever ecclesiastical honors belonged to the empire in any part of the kingdom of Poland or other territories he had conquered or might conquer among the barbarians, and a decree about this arrangement was confirmed by Pope Sylvester in a privilege of the holy Church of Rome. So Bolesław was thus gloriously raised to kingship by the emperor, and he gave an example of the liberality innate in him when for the three days following his coronation he celebrated a feast in style fit for a king or emperor. Every day the plate and the tableware were new, and many different ones were given out, ever richer again. For at the end of the feast he ordered the waiters and the cupbearers to gather the gold and silver vessels—for there was nothing made of wood there—from all three days' courses, that is, the cups and goblets, the bowls and plates and the drinking-horns, and he presented them to the emperor as a token of honor, and not as a princely tribute. His servants were likewise told to collect the wall-hangings and the coverlets, the carpets and tablecloths and napkins and everything that had been provided for their needs and take them to the emperor's quarters. In addition he presented many other vessels, of gold and silver and of diverse workmanship, and robes of various hues and ornaments never seen before, precious stones and so many other marvelous things that the emperor regarded such presents as a miracle. Each of his princes was given presents of such magnificence that from being friendly they now became closest friends. But who could count what and how many presents he gave to all the lords, so that not a single servant out of all the multitude went away without a gift? The emperor returned home, delighted with the lavish gifts. Bolesław for his part returned to the business of the kingdom, and summoned up again his old anger against his foes.

7. How Bolesław Entered the Land of Rus' in Force

A story specially worth including in our account is how gloriously and splendidly Bolesław avenged the injury done to him by the king of the Ruthenians when he refused to give him the hand of his sister in marriage.[2] Enraged at this, King Bolesław with boundless courage burst upon the kingdom of the Ruthenians. At first they would have attempted resistance, but they did not dare to meet him in battle, and he scattered them

---

1   Embroidery.
2   Iaroslav the Wise, grand prince of Kiev 1015–16 and 1019–54.

before his face as dust before the wind. Instead of slowing his advance in the usual way of armies by taking cities or exacting tribute, he sped directly to Kiev, the capital of the kingdom, so as to seize the citadel of the kingdom and its king at one and the same time. But at that particular time the king of the Ruthenians, with the simplicity of his nation, happened to be sitting in a little boat with a hook and line fishing, when out of nowhere came the news that King Bolesław was at hand. The king could scarcely believe his ears, but when report after report confirmed the story, at last horror seized him. Thereupon, the story goes, he brought his thumb and forefinger to his lips and spat on the fishhook the way fishermen do, and to his people's shame he uttered the memorable words: "As Bolesław has not practiced this art but is used to bearing arms as a soldier, God has therefore ordained that this city and the kingdom of the Ruthenians and their wealth should pass into his hands." These were his only words, and without further ado he took to his heels. Bolesław thus met with no resistance when he entered this grand and rich city. As he did, he drew his sword and struck it upon the Golden Gate, to his followers' amazement. When they asked the reason for this, he laughed gleefully and explained: "Just as my sword pierces the Golden Gate of the city at this hour, so on the night to come the sister of this most cowardly king, whose hand had earlier been refused me, will be ravished. And she will not be joined to Bolesław as his lawful wife, but as his concubine and on one occasion only, that with this act the insult done to our people may be avenged, and shame and disgrace be brought upon the Ruthenians." So said Bolesław, and what he said he did. Then for ten months the richest city of the Ruthenians and their powerful kingdom was in King Bolesław's hands, and he never rested from shipping money back to Poland. But by the eleventh month, as he was now lord of numerous realms and he had not seen the boy Mieszko, who was now old enough to rule, he left a Ruthenian who was related to him as ruler in his place, and taking what treasure remained he set off back to Poland. But the king of the Ruthenians, the same who fled previously, had meanwhile gathered the forces of the Ruthenian dukes, including Cumans and Pechenegs, and followed Bolesław from

behind as he was marching home in great joy with all his money; and when Bolesław was nearly at the boundaries of Poland, the king sought to join battle with him at the river Bug, feeling certain of victory. For he reasoned that after their great victory and with their plunder to boast of, the Poles like other men would be hurrying to return each to his own home, now that they were approaching the boundaries of their land in triumph and had been so long away from their country and separated from their wives and children. In fact, his thinking was not unreasonable, for a large part of the Polish army had indeed drifted away without the king's knowledge. Bolesław now realized how few his soldiers were, and the enemy a hundred times greater in number. It was not like Bolesław to be fearful or cowardly, but to be bold and foresightful. So he addressed his troops with the following words. "You, tried soldiers and true, need no long rousing speech, nor to make delay to seize a triumph that is present for our taking. What the hour calls for are strength of body and a courageous spirit. For what is the use of having won so many great victories or to have reduced so many realms to our rule or to have taken so much wealth from others if now we risk being defeated and losing what we won and even what we had before? But I have confidence in God's mercy and in your proven courage, and if you fight like men in this contest today, if you attack as bravely as you always have, if you call to mind the boasts and promises which you made at my banquets and when the booty was being divided, I have no doubt that you will carry the day and bring our long struggles to an end, and win a triumphant victory and undying renown. But on the other hand, should you be defeated—which I cannot believe—you and your sons will become the slaves of the Ruthenians you were masters of, and you will suffer the most humiliating penalties for the injuries you have done to them." Such and similar were the words Bolesław addressed to them. As he did so, all his men of one accord brandished their spears and answered that they would rather have the triumph than slink home in shame with the booty. Then, calling upon each of his followers by name and urging them on, King Bolesław plunged like a thirsting lion into the thickest of the foe. I have not the skill to relate the slaughter he made of those who barred his path, nor can anyone set a sure figure on how many thousands of the enemy were slain, but they say that of the untold numbers who joined the battle very few survived to slip away and escape. Many people, who days later came from far parts to look for friends and relatives on the battlefield, stated as a fact that there was such blood and gore that they could not walk anywhere over the whole field without stepping in blood or over bodies, and the whole course of the Bug looked more like a stream of blood than a river. Thereafter and for a long time to come Rus' was forced to pay tribute to Poland.

8 The Power and Magnificence of Bolesław the Glorious

The deeds Bolesław performed are greater and more numerous than I can describe or tell in plain words. No clever arithmetician could with any certainty set a figure on the numbers of his iron-clad ranks, let alone to set down in writing the victories or the triumphs won by so great a host. From Poznań, 1,300 mailed knights and 4,000 footsoldiers; from Gniezno, 1,500 mailed knights and 5,000 footsoldiers; from the stronghold of Wloclawek, 800 mailed knights and 2,000 footsoldiers; from Giecz, 300 mailed knights and 2,000 footsoldiers—these were the forces mustered in the days of Bolesław the Great. These were all the bravest of warriors, fully trained for war. How many came from other cities and castles would be a long and endless labor for us to list, and perhaps tedious for you to listen to. But not to weary you with countless numbers, I shall recount the number of his forces without a count of numbers: King Bolesław had more knights in armor than all Poland now has men bearing shields; in his time there were almost as many knights in Poland as there are people of any kind in our time.

9 The Virtues and Nobility of the Glorious Bolesław

Such was the military might of King Bolesław. But the king in no way fell short in the virtue of spiritual obedience. For he held his bishops and chaplains in such veneration that he would never presume to remain seated when they were standing, and he always addressed them as "My lords." He worshipped God with the greatest piety and promoted the holy Church and honored her with kingly gifts. Furthermore, he had such a great sense of justice and a special humility that if some poor peasant or some ordinary woman came with a complaint against any duke or count, no matter how important the matters he was engaged in, amid the throng and press of his lords and officers, he would not stir from the spot before he had heard the full account of the complaint and sent a chamberlain to fetch the lord against whom the complaint had been made. Meanwhile he left the aggrieved person in the care of one of his retainers, who would take his part and would help him with his plea while the adversary was coming. And so he would advise the peasant as a father would his son, so that he would not make a groundless accusation against the absent party, nor by complaining unjustly load upon himself the anger he was directing against the other. Moreover, the accused would never fail to come with all speed when he was summoned and never for any reason neglect to appear on the day appointed by the king. When the great man who had been sent for arrived, Bolesław would never show him anger or ill-will, but would welcome him in a warm and friendly way and invite him to a meal, and wait till the second or even the third day before broaching the matter of contention. So he treated a poor man's problem with as much concern as if he had been a great prince. What great wisdom, what great accomplishment of Bolesław! He passed judgement regardless of person, he governed the people with such justice, and he set the dignity of the Church and the state of the country above all else. His sense of justice and fairness raised Bolesław to such glory and dignity—the virtues by which the Romans in the beginning rose to power and empire. Such was the prowess, the power, and the victories which Almighty God bestowed on Bolesław in recognition of the goodness and justice which Bolesław showed to Him and to his fellow men! Bolesław enjoyed all the glory, abundance, and happiness that his worthiness and generosity deserved.

10 Bolesław's Battle With the Ruthenians

But let us defer these themes to a later page, and turn to the story of a battle with some unusual features that make it quite memorable. From it we will be able draw a lesson that humility is better than pride. It came about that, unbeknown to each other, King Bolesław and the king of the Ruthenians invaded each other's countries at one and the same time. The two armies camped on the banks of a river, each in the other's territory, with the river [presumably the Bug] running between them. The king of the Ruthenians had received word that Bolesław had crossed the river and his army was encamped within the boundaries of his own kingdom, and foolishly he imagined that he and his great host had Bolesław trapped like a netted animal. It is said that the king sent a message memorable in its pride, which was to redound upon his own head: "Let Bolesław know that my dogs and my hunters have caught him like a pig wallowing in the mire." To this the Polish king sent the following reply: "A pig in the mire? Well put, indeed! The hoofs of my horses shall wallow in the blood of the hunters and the dogs, that is, your captains and soldiers, and I shall savage your land and your cities like a wild boar." So passed this exchange between them. The next day a festival was due to be held, and in order to celebrate it King Bolesław put off joining battle till the third day. Now on that day great numbers of animals were being slaughtered as usual in preparation for the king's table at the coming holiday, when he was planning to eat with all his princes. So all the army's cooks, kitchen-hands, servants and camp-followers were gathered on the riverbank cleaning the carcasses and purging the offal. Meanwhile on the other bank the men-at-arms and retainers of the Ruthenians jeered and hurled abuse, trying to provoke them to anger with their gibes and mockery. They made no reply to the taunts, but instead repaid the insults by hurling in their eyes offal and excrement from the intestines. But when the Ruthenians grew more and more provocative in their taunts, and even began to harry them in earnest with arrows, they left what they were handling to their dogs and birds. They borrowed the arms of the soldiers sleeping in the midday heat, and swimming over the river, Bolesław's army of camp-followers defeated the very sizeable host of the Ruthenians. The shouting and the din of the fighting woke the king and the rest of the army, who wondered what ever was going on. When they found out, they doubted that this had been intentional. So they drew up in battle array and went in pursuit of the enemy who were now fleeing in all directions. Thus in the end the glory of the victory did not go solely to the camp-followers, nor were they the sole ones to suffer bloodshed. But the number of soldiers who then crossed the river was so huge that from downstream the river did not seem to be water but a dry road. But let this little episode suffice on the subject of his wars, that the record of his life may serve as a model and be of benefit to the listeners.

11 The Arrangements for the Churches in Poland, and Bolesław's Virtues

King Bolesław was deeply devoted to religion, building churches and establishing episcopal sees and granting endowments; so much indeed, that in his days Poland had two metropolitans along with their suffragans. He was always well-disposed towards them and he was so obedient to them in everything, that if, for example, one of the great men happened to open a lawsuit against a cleric or a bishop, or seized any ecclesiastical property, with a wave of his hand Bolesław would call for general silence, and then as patron and advocate he would defend the interests of the bishops and the church. With the neighboring barbarian peoples whom he defeated he was more concerned for the increase of the true faith than to force them to pay tribute. Indeed, he even built churches there from his own means and appointed bishops with all honors and clerics canonically among the unbelievers, supplying them with all necessaries. Such were the virtues which set Bolesław apart—justice, fairness, fear and affection, and such was the wisdom with which he managed the realm and the commonwealth. The light of Bolesław's many virtues and good qualities shone far and wide, but it was by three in particular—justice, fairness, and piety—that he attained the heights of greatness. Justice, in that he decided cases in law without respect to persons;

fairness, for his concern and tact extended to both princes and commoners; and piety, for he honored Christ and His bride in every way. And since he exercised justice and respected all men equally and exalted the Mother Church and the men of the Church, the Lord in answer to the prayers of the holy Mother Church and the intercessions of his prelates exalted his horn in honor, and all went well for him and all his ventures prospered. Yet for all Bolesław's piety in matters divine, it was in earthly affairs that he won even greater glory.

12 How Bolesław Would Travel Across His Lands Without Causing Harm to the Poor

In Bolesław's time not only comites, but all the nobles used to wear enormously heavy gold necklaces, for they had money in such abundance and excess. The women of the court wore golden crowns, necklaces, chains, bracelets, gold brocade, and jewels, so heavy that without others to support them they were unable to walk under the weight of the metal. Moreover, God endowed Bolesław with such charm, and all were so attracted to the sight of him, that if ever he banished anyone from his presence even for a short time because of a minor transgression, even if the person continued to enjoy his possessions and liberty, he would feel as though he was dying rather than alive, and not free but cast into a dungeon until he was readmitted to the king's grace and presence. He did not treat his peasants like a lord and exact forced labor from them, but cared for them as a kind-hearted father and left them to live in peace. For everywhere he had his stations and defined services, and did not like to live in tents like a Numidian or in the open country but more commonly stayed in cities and in castles. And when he moved his station from one city to another he would dismiss some at the boundary and would replace others of his officers and stewards. When he traveled by, no one on the road or at work would ever hide his sheep and cattle, but rich and poor alike would smile upon him as he passed and the whole country would come hurrying up to see him.

13 The Goodness and Compassion of the Wife Of Bolesław the Glorious

The king loved his dukes, comites, and princes as if they were his brothers or his sons, and as far as his dignity permitted he honored them as a wise master would. If any complaint was made against them, he never would rashly believe it; while for those who had been sentenced he would temper judgment with mercy. For often his wife the queen,[3] a wise and discreet woman, would rescue those condemned to death for some crime from the hands of the executioners and save them at the last minute from the threat of death. She would leave them under guard in the prison, their lives preserved through her mercy. At times the king did not know of this, and at times he would pretend not to. The king had twelve friends as counselors, and regularly, once free of all his cares and deliberations, he would enjoy their company, dining with them and their wives and discussing the secrets of the realm and council in a more intimate atmosphere. While they were feasting together and in high spirits, as the conversation turned to different matters it might chance that the occasion would arise to recall the family of those who had been condemned. Recalling their parents' goodness, King Bolesław would express sorrow at their deaths and regret having ordered their execution. Then the venerable queen, stroking the king's merciful breast with a gentle hand, would ask him if it would please him if some saint should raise them from the dead. To which the king would reply that he possessed nothing so precious that he would not give it if someone could call them back to life from the grave and save their offspring from the stain of infamy. Hearing this his wise and faithful queen would admit her guilt and her well-intentioned trickery, and then she and the twelve friends and their wives would all throw themselves at the king's feet and plead pardon for themselves and the condemned. The king would embrace her fondly and kiss her and take her hands and raise her from the ground and speak in warm terms of her truehearted trickery—indeed, of her works of mercy.

---

3   It is not clear whether the author is referring to Bolesław's first wife Emnilde (987–1017), to his second wife Oda (ca. 996 –1023) or indeed if this is simply a story of an ideal queen.

So that very hour messengers and a team of horses would be sent to fetch the prisoners whose lives had been spared thanks to a woman's wit, and a time would be set for their return. Then the guests at the banquet would burst into joy and delight that the queen had shown such wisdom in guarding the interests of the country while respecting the king's honor, and that the king had taken the advice of his friends and listened to her and her petitions. When those who had been sent for arrived, they were not presented to the king first but to the queen. She would rebuke them with both sharp and mild words, and then have them taken to the king's bath. There King Bolesław would bathe with them as a father would with his children, berating them and dwelling on the praises of their forebears. "It was unworthy of you, who are descended from such a distinguished family, to stoop to such things." The older ones he would merely rebuke either personally or through others, while for the younger ones the words would be accompanied by the switch. After this paternal reprimand he would dress them in royal garments, give them presents and honors, and send them home with joy. Such was King Bolesław's way of treating the people and the princes, and thus through his wise ways he caused himself to be both feared and loved by all who were subject to him.

14 Bolesław's Lavish Table and his Liberality

His table was maintained in such magnificent array that every non-festal day there were forty main courses laid out (not counting the minor ones)—all supplied not at other persons' expense, but at his own. He had fowlers and hunters from all nations who by their special skills could catch birds and animals of every kind, and at his table there would be at least one dish served every day with each kind of animal and bird.

15 Bolesław's Arrangements Concerning the Castles and Cities in his Realm

Also, when the great Bolesław, who was many times occupied with the defense of his borders against enemies about, was asked by his stewards and governors what should be done about the garments or about the food and drink prepared for the annual festivals in the different cities, he used to say something memorable that would go down as an example to posterity. He would say: "For me it is better and more honorable to safeguard a single chicken here from the enemy than to feast idly in one city or another while my enemies get a chance to do me injury. For I do not regard losing a chicken in a brave fight as the loss of a chicken but as the loss of a castle or a city." And he would summon those of his companions whom he pleased to, and send them each to a city or castle, and have them hold in his stead banquets in the castle or city, and present his faithful men with clothes and other royal gifts which the king was in the habit of giving. When they heard or saw him do such things everyone expressed admiration for the wisdom and intelligence of this great man. They would confer among themselves and say: "He is truly the father of our country, our defender, our lord—not the squanderer of other people's money but the honest steward of the commonwealth. He treats the violence and damage inflicted on a peasant by the enemy as equal to the loss of a castle or the city." What need is there to go on? If we wished to write down separately every memorable deed or saying of the great Bolesław, it would be as great a task for my pen as draining the ocean drop by drop. But what does it hurt my leisured readers to hear this, which the writer of history could only laboriously find out?

16 The Tragic Death of the Glorious Bolesław

So, as mentioned, King Bolesław had abundance of wealth and fine warriors in numbers beyond any other king. And yet he was always lamenting that knights were the one thing he lacked. If any doughty foreigner was at his court proving his worth in martial skills, he would be not be called a warrior but the king's son. And if the king ever heard that any of them had suffered some mishap on horseback or otherwise, as happens on occasion, he would give him endless gifts and confide in the bystanders: "If I could save this fine warrior from death by my wealth, just as I can relieve his misfortunes or his poverty by my resources, then I would ply greedy death with riches to preserve this fine, brave warrior in my service." The successors of such a great man should therefore strive to copy his qualities, so that they might rise to the heights of glory and power that he did. Any man, who seeks to win such fame after his life, let him win such a palm for his virtues while he is alive. If anyone wants to equal Bolesław in memory and renown, let him strive to pattern his life on that man's venerable life. Valor in warlike deeds will find due praise when a man's life is graced by many honorable qualities. Such was the glory of the great Bolesław, worthy to be remembered; let his valor be told and remembered, and imitated by those who come after him. For it was not for naught that God heaped on him grace upon grace, nor without reason did He set him before so many dukes and kings, but because he loved God in everything and above all else, and because love for his people abounded within him, as in a father towards his sons. Because of this everyone, but especially the archbishops and bishops, abbots, monks, and clerks whom he venerated, never ceased to commend him to God in their prayers; while his dukes, comites, and other great nobles ever wished and prayed that he would survive them and be victorious for ever. So the glorious Bolesław brought a felicitous life to a praiseworthy end. For when he realized that he was due to render the debt that all flesh must pay, he summoned to him all his princes and friends from all parts, and gave instructions in private for the governance and disposition of the realm. And with the voice of prophecy he foretold that many woes were to befall them after he had gone. "O my brothers," he said, "whom I have fostered and spoilt as a mother her sons, if only the harm that I foresee in my great anguish might turn to good for you, and that those who light the fire of sedition might have regard for God and man! Alas, alas, now as through a glass darkly I see our line of kings in exile, wandering afar and begging piteously from those very foes that I have trodden beneath my feet. I see, too, afar that from my loins comes as it were a glowing ruby attached to the hilt of my sword, that makes all of Poland ablaze with its light." Then indeed grief and woe gripped to the very hearts those who stood about and heard these words, and their pain was so great that the minds of all were quite numb. When they had contained their grief for a moment, they asked Bolesław how long should they commemorate his passing and wear mourning. He told them in truth: "I set you no limits of months and years to your grief; but let every one who knew me and enjoyed my favor weep every single day in memory of me. And not only those who knew me and have gained my goodwill, but their sons and their sons' sons shall hear the story from others and lament King Bolesław's passing." So Bolesław passed from the company of this world, and the age of gold became an age of lead. Poland, once queen and crowned with radiant gold and gems, sits in the dust wrapped in the garments of her widowhood. Her harp is turned to mourning, her joy to sorrow, and her organ music to sighs. For all through that year no one celebrated a public feast in Poland, no noble man or woman dressed in formal attire, no clapping or sound of stringed instruments was heard in the taverns, no girls sang songs, nor did any voice of happiness echo in the streets. This year of mourning was universally observed by all, but noble men and women never ceased to weep for Bolesław till the day of their death. So when King Bolesław passed from the world of men, it seemed as if peace and happiness and abundance departed from Poland at the same time.

46. THE *CHRONICLE* OF THIETMAR OF MERSEBURG

BISHOP THIETMAR OF MERSEBURG (975–1018) was a Saxon noble raised to the episcopacy by Henry II. His *Chronicle* draws on written sources such as necrologies, as well as personal knowledge and his wide contacts within the Saxon aristocracy. This section of the *Chronicle*, which describes Otto III's actions during the year 1000, indicates his animosity toward the Polish prince Bolesław Chrobry.

Source: David A. Warner (ed. and trans.), *Ottonian Germany: The Chronicon of Thietmar of Merseburg* (Manchester/New York: Manchester University Press, 2001), 182–86.

Further Reading: Andrzej Pleszczyński, "Poland as an Ally of the Holy Ottonian Empire," in Przemysław Urbańczyk (ed.), *Europe Around the Year 1000* (Warsaw: Wydawnictwo DiG, 2001), 409–25.

Chapter Forty-Four

Afterwards, the emperor went before the Roman synod and accused Archbishop Giselher of holding two dioceses, ordering through a legal judgment that he be suspended from office and summoned there by the pope's envoys. Giselher had suffered a stroke and, as he was prevented from coming there, sent the cleric Rotman who was to justify him by oath should he not be believed. At this point, discussion of the issue was postponed until the emperor could meet with the bishops of Giselher's province. Afterwards, the emperor heard of the miracles which God was performing through his beloved martyr Albert and made haste to go there for the sake of prayer. When he arrived at Regensburg, the emperor was received with great honor by Gebhard, bishop of that church [ca. January 20, 1000]. The imperial entourage included the patrician Ziazo, the oblationarius[1] Robert, and the cardinals. Indeed, no emperor ever exited from Rome or returned there with greater glory. Giselher went to meet him and obtained his peace, though not permanently, and also accompanied him.

Chapter Forty-Five

When he arrived at Zeitz, the emperor was received in a manner appropriate to an emperor by Hugh II, third pastor of that see [ca. February 10]. Then he went by a direct route to Meißen where he was honorably received by Eid, the venerable bishop of this church, and by Margrave Ekkehard whom he regarded highly. Then, having traversed the territories of the Milzeni, he was met as he arrived at the district of Diadesi by Bolesław whose name is interpreted as "greater praise" not by merit but by old custom. With great rejoicing, Bolesław offered the emperor hospitality at a place called Eulau. It would be impossible to believe or describe how the emperor was then received by him and conducted to Gniezno. Seeing the desired city from afar, he humbly approached barefoot. After being received with veneration by Bishop Unger, he was led into the church where, weeping profusely, he was moved to ask the grace of Christ for himself through the intercession of Christ's martyr. Without delay, he established an archbishopric there, as I hope legitimately, but without the consent of the aforementioned bishop to whose diocese this whole region is subject. He committed the new foundation to Radim, the martyr's brother, and made subject to him Bishop Reinbern of Kolberg, Bishop Poppo of Kraków, and Bishop John of Wrocław, but not Unger of

---

1   An ecclesiastical officer responsible for collecting offerings.

Poznań. And with great solemnity, he also placed holy relics in an altar which had been established there.

Chapter Forty-Six

After all issues had been settled, the duke honored Otto with rich presents and, what was even more pleasing, three hundred armored warriors. When the emperor departed, Bolesław and an illustrious entourage conducted him to Magdeburg where they celebrated Palm Sunday with great festivity [March 24–25]. On Monday, the archbishop of that church was enjoined, by imperial edict, to resume his previous see but barely managed to have the issue postponed until the assembly at Quedlinburg by offering a great deal of money to certain intermediaries. At Quedlinburg, a great assembly of the nobility convened in conjunction with the joyful celebration of Easter [March 31]. On Monday, Giselher was again summoned before the synod. His absence, due to a still serious illness, was again excused by Rotman, and Walthard, then provost of the cathedral, presented many arguments on his behalf. A council was arranged for him at Aachen, to which he himself came with his supporters and where once again he was addressed by an archdeacon of the Roman see

[May 19]. Following wise council, he demanded to present his case before a general council and all of these matters were therefore postponed, without discussion, until God deigned to bring them to a favorable resolution in our time.

Chapter Forty-Seven [1000]

Because the emperor wished to renew the ancient custom of the Romans, now mostly obliterated, he did many things which received a rather mixed reaction. He dined alone at a semicircular table which, moreover, was elevated above the others. As he had doubts regarding the location of the bones of Emperor Charles, he secretly had the pavement over their supposed resting place ripped up and excavations carried out until they were discovered, on the royal throne. After taking a gold cross which hung around the emperor's neck and part of his clothing, which remained uncorrupted, he replaced everything with great veneration. But how should I recall each of his comings and goings through all of his bishoprics and counties? With everything well disposed north of the Alps, Otto betook himself to the Roman Empire and, arriving at the Romulan citadel, was received with great honor by the pope and his fellow bishops [August 14].

FRANCE

47. JOINVILLE

Life of St. Louis

Under king louis ix (1226–70) the French monarchy perfected not only truly sovereign powers but also an efficient bureaucracy that made the king's presence felt throughout the kingdom. Louis was an extraordinary figure: a saint, a crusader, and a king sincerely concerned with justice. Jean de Joinville (ca. 1227–1317) was seneschal (equivalent to bailiff) of Champagne and close companion and advisor to Louis. He wrote his life of Louis (of which few manuscripts survive, the earliest from the fourteenth century) when he was in his eighties, both as a tribute to the memory of Louis and as a lesson for Louis's grandson, King Philip IV. Thus it can be compared with Einhard's life of Charlemagne.

Source: Frank Marziais (trans.), *Memoirs of the Crusades by Villehardhouin and de Joinville* (London: J.M. Dent, 1908).

Further Reading: Jacques LeGoff, *Saint Louis*, trans. Gareth Evan Gollrad (South Bend, IN: University of Notre Dame Press, 2009).

Beginning of the First Book: Principal Virtues of St. Louis

In the name of God Almighty, I, John, Lord of Joinville, seneschal of Champagne, dictate the life of our holy King Louis; that which I saw and heard by the space of six years that I was in his company on pilgrimage oversea, and that which I saw and heard after we returned. And before I tell you of his great deeds, and of his prowess, I will tell you what I saw and heard of his good teachings and of his holy words, so that these may be found here set in order for the edifying of those who shall hear thereof.

This holy man loved God with all his heart, and followed Him in His acts; and this appeared in that, as God died for the love He bore His people, so did the king put his body in peril, and that several times, for the love He bore to his people; and such peril he might well have avoided, as you shall be told hereafter.

The great love that he bore to his people appeared in what he said during a very sore sickness that he had at Fountainebleau, unto my Lord Louis, his eldest son. "Fair son," he said, "I pray thee to make thyself beloved of the people of thy kingdom; for truly I would rather that a Scot should come out of Scotland and govern the people of the kingdom well and equitably than that thou shouldest govern it ill in the sight of all men." The holy king so loved truth, that, as you shall hear hereafter, he would never consent to lie to the Saracens as to any covenant that he had made with them.

Of his mouth he was so sober, that on no day of my life did I ever hear him order special meats, as many rich men are wont to do; but he ate patiently whatever his cooks had made ready, and was set before him. In his words he was temperate; for on no day of my life did I ever hear him speak evil of any one; nor did I ever hear him name the Devil—which name is very commonly spoken throughout the kingdom, whereby God, as I believe, is not well pleased.

He put water into his wine by measure, according as he saw that the strength of the wine would suffer it. At Cyprus he asked me why I put no water into my wine; and I said this was by order of the physicians, who told me I had a large head and a cold stomach, so that I could not get drunk. And he answered that they deceived me; for if I did not learn to put water into my wine in my youth, and wished to do so in my old age, gout and diseases of the stomach would take hold upon me, and I should never be in health; and if I drank pure wine in my old age, I should get drunk every night, and that it was too foul a thing for a brave man to get drunk.

He asked me if I wished to be honored in this world, and to go into paradise at my death? And I said "Yes." And he said: "Keep yourself then from knowingly doing or saying anything which, if the whole world heard thereof, you would be ashamed to acknowledge, saying 'I did this,' or 'I said that.'" He told me to beware not to contradict or impugn anything that was said before me—unless indeed silence would be a sin or to my own hurt—because hard words often move to quarreling, wherein men by the thousand have found death.

He said that men ought to clothe and arm their bodies in such wise that men of worth and age would never say, this man has done too much, nor young men say, this man has done too little. And I repeated this saying to the father of the king that now is, when speaking of the embroidered coats of arms that are made nowadays; and I told him that never, during our voyage oversea, had I seen embroidered coats, either belonging to the king or to any one else. And the king that now is told me that he had such suits, with arms embroidered, as he had cost him eight hundred pounds parisis. And I told him he would have employed the money to better purpose if he had given it to God, and had had his suits made of good taffeta [satin] ornamented with his arms, as his father had done.

St. Louis's Horror of Sin—his Love For the Poor

He called me once to him and said: "Because of the subtle mind that is in you I dare not speak to you of the things relating to God; so I have summoned these two monks that are here, as I want to ask you a question." Now the question was this: "Seneschal," said he, "what manner of thing is God?" And I said: "Sire, it is so good a thing that there cannot be better." "Of a truth," said he, "you have answered well; for the answer that you have given is written in this book that I hold in my hand."

"Now I ask you," said he, "which you would the better like, either to be a leper, or to have committed a mortal sin?" And I, who never lied to him, made answer that I would rather have committed thirty mortal sins than be a leper. And when the monks had departed, he called me to him alone, and made me sit at his feet, and said, "How came you to say that to me yesterday?" And I told him that I said it again. And he answered, "You spoke hastily and as a fool. For you should know that there is no leprosy so hideous as the being in mortal sin, inasmuch as the soul that is in mortal sin is like unto the Devil; wherefore no leprosy can be so hideous. And sooth it is that, when a man dies, he is healed of the leprosy in his body; but when a man who has committed mortal sin dies, he cannot know of a certainty that he has, during his lifetime, repented in such sort that God has forgiven him; wherefore he must stand in great fear lest that leprosy of sin should last as long as God is in paradise. So I pray you," said he, "as strongly as I can, for the love of God, and for the love of me, so to set your heart that you prefer any evil that can happen to the body, whether it be leprosy, or any other sickness, rather than that mortal sin should enter into your soul."

He asked me if I washed the feet of the poor on Holy Thursday. "Sire," said I, "it would make me sick! The feet of these villains will I not wash." "In truth," said he, "that was ill said; for you should never disdain what God did for our teaching. So I pray you, for the love of God first, and then for the love of me, that you accustom yourself to wash the feet of the poor."

Regard of St. Louis for Worth and Uprightness

He so loved all manner of people who had faith in God and loved Him, that he gave the constableship of France to my Lord Giles Le Brun, who was not of the kingdom of France, because men held him in so great repute for his faith and for love to God. And verily I believe that his good repute was well deserved.

He caused Master Robert of Sorbon to eat at his table, because of the great repute in which he was held as a man of uprightness and worth. One day it chanced that Master Robert was eating at my side, and we were talking to one another. The king took us up, and said: "Speak out, for your companions think you are speaking ill of them. If you talk at table of things that can give us pleasure, speak out, and, if not, hold your peace."

When the king would be mirthful he would say to me: "Seneschal, tell me the reasons why a man of uprightness and worth [prud'homme] is better than a friar?" Then would begin a discussion between me and Master Robert. When we had disputed for a long while, the king would give sentence and speak thus: "Master Robert, willingly would I bear the title of upright and worthy (prud'-homme) provided I were such in reality—and all the rest you might have. For uprightness and worth are such great things and such good things that even to name them fills the mouth pleasantly."

On the contrary, he said it was an evil thing to take other people's goods. "For," he said, "to restore is a thing so grievous, that even in the speaking the word restore scratches the throat by reason of the rs that are in it, and these rs are like so many rakes with which the Devil would draw to himself those who wish to 'restore' what they have taken from others. And very subtly does the Devil do this; for he works on great usurers and great robbers in such sort that they give to God what they ought to 'restore' to men."

He told me to warn King Thibaut, from him, to beware of the house of the preachers of Provins, which he was building, lest he should encumber his soul on account of the great sums he was spending thereon. "For wise men," said he, "should, while they live, deal with their possessions as executors ought to do. Now the first thing a good executor does is to satisfy all the claims upon the dead, and pay back to others what is due to them, and it is only after having done this that he should spend in alms what remains of the dead man's possessions."

How St. Louis Thought Men Ought to Clothe Themselves

The holy king was at Corbeil one Pentecost day, and there were there eighty knights. The king came down after dinner into the court below the chapel, and was talking, at the entrance of the door, to the count of Brittany, the father of the count that now is—whom may God preserve!—when Master Robert of Sorbon came to fetch me thither, and took me by the skirt of my mantle and led me to the king; and all the other knights came after us. Then I said to Master Robert, "Master Robert, what do you want with me?" He said, "I wish to ask you whether, if the king were seated in this court, and you were to seat yourself on his bench, and at a higher place than he, ought you to be greatly blamed?" And I said, "Yes." And he said, "Then are you to be blamed when you go more nobly appareled than the king, for you dress yourself in fur and green cloth, and the king does not do so." And I replied: "Master Robert, saving your grace, I do nothing blameworthy when I clothe myself in green cloth and fur, for this garment was left to me by my father and mother. But you are to blame, for you are the son of a common man and a common woman, and you have abandoned the vesture worn by your father and mother, and wear richer woolen cloth than the king himself." Then I took the skirt of his surcoat, and of the surcoat of the king, and said, "See if I am not speaking sooth." Then the king set himself to defend Master Robert and all his power.

After this my lord the king called my lord Philip, his son, the father of the king that now is, and King Thibaut, and sat himself at the entrance to his oratory, and put his hand to the ground and said: "Sit yourselves down here, quite close to me, so that we be not overheard." "Ah! Sire," they replied, "we should not dare to sit so close to you." And he said to me, "Seneschal, sit you here." And I did so—so close that my robe touched his. And he made them sit after me, and said to them: "You have done very ill, seeing you are my sons, and have not, at the first word, done what I commanded you. See, I pray you, that this does not happen again." And they said it should not so happen. Then he said to me that he had so called us together to confess that he had wrongly defended Master Robert against me. "But," said he, "I saw that he was so discouraged that he had great need of my help. Nevertheless, you must not attach import to anything I may have said to defend Master Robert; for, as the seneschal says, you ought to clothe yourselves well and suitably, so that your wives may love you the better, and your people hold you in the greater honor. For, as the sage tells us, our garments should be of such fashion as neither to cause the aged and worthy to say that too much has been spent upon them, nor the young to say that too little has been spent."

The Warnings of God—How They Are to Be Turned to Advantage

You shall be told here of one of the lessons he taught me at sea, when we were returning from the lands oversea. It chanced that our ship struck before the island of Cyprus, when a wind was blowing which is called *garban*; and this wind is not one of the four great winds. And at the shock that our ship received, the mariners so despaired that they rent their garments and tore their beards. The king sprang from his bed, barefoot, for it was night, and having on no more than his tunic, and went and placed himself crosswise before the body of our Lord, as one who expected nothing but death. The day after this happened, the king called me to him alone, and said: "Seneschal, God has just showed us a portion of His great power; for one of these little winds, a wind so little that one can scarcely give it a name, came near to drown the king of France, his children, his wife, and his men. Now St. Anselm says that such are warnings from our Lord, as if God meant to say to us, 'See how easily I could have compassed your death, had it been my will.' 'Lord God,' says the saint, 'why dost Thou thus threaten us? For when Thou dost threaten us, it is not for Thine own profit, nor for Thine advantage—seeing that if Thou hadst caused us all to be lost, Thou wouldst have been none the poorer, and if Thou hadst caused us all to be saved, Thou wouldst have been none the richer. Therefore, this Thy warning is not for Thine own advantage, but for ours, if so be that we suffer it do its work.' Let us therefore take the warning that God has given us in such sort that, if we feel that we have, in our

hearts or bodies, anything displeasing to God, we shall remove it hastily, and if there by anything we think will please Him, let us try hastily to do it. If we so act, then our Lord will give us blessings in this world, and in the next blessings greater than we can tell. And if we do not act thus, He will deal with us as the good lord deals with his wicked servant; for if the wicked servant will not amend after warning given the lord punishes him with death, or with other great troubles that are worse than death."

Let the king that now is beware; for he has escaped from peril as great as that in which we then were, or greater. Therefore let him amend from his evil deeds in such sort that God smite him not grievously, either in himself or in his possessions.

What St. Louis Thought about Faith

The holy king endeavored with all his power—as you shall here be told—to make me believe firmly in the Christian law, which God has given us. He said that we ought to believe so firmly the articles of faith that neither from fear of death, nor for any mischief that might happen to the body, should we be willing to go against them in word or deed. And he said that the Enemy is so subtle that, when people are dying, he labors all he can to make them die doubting as to some points of the faith. For he knows that he can in no wise deprive a man of the good works he has done; and he knows also that the man is lost to him if he dies in the faith.

Wherefore we should so guard and defend ourselves from this snare, as to say to the Enemy, when he sends such a temptation: "Away!" Yes, "Away!" must one say to the Enemy. "Thou shalt not tempt me so that I cease to believe firmly all the articles of the faith. Even if thou didst cause all my members to be cut off, yet would I live and die in the faith." And whosoever acts thus, overcomes the Enemy with the very club and sword that the Enemy desired to murder him withal.

He said that the Christian faith and creed were things in which we ought to believe firmly, even though we might not be certain of them except by hearsay. On this point he asked me what was my father's name? And I told him his name was Simon. And he asked how I knew it. And I said I thought I was certain of it, and believed it firmly, because my mother had borne witness thereto. Then he said, "So ought you to believe all the articles of the faith, to which the apostles have borne witness, as also you chant of a Sunday in the Creed."

William, Bishop of Paris, Comforts a Certain Theologian

He told me that the bishop, William of Paris, had related how a great master of divinity had come to him and told him he desired to speak with him. And the bishop said to him: "Master, say on." And when the master thought to speak to the bishop, he began to weep bitterly. And the bishop said: "Master, say on; be not discomfited; no one can sin so much but that God can forgive him more." "And yet I tell you," said the master, "that I cannot choose but weep; for I fear me I am a miscreant, inasmuch as I cannot so command my heart as to believe in the sacrifice of the altar, like as Holy Church teaches; and yet I know well that this is a temptation of the Enemy."

"Master," said the bishop, "pray tell me, when the Enemy sends you this temptation, does it give you pleasure?" And the master said: "Sir far from it; it troubles me as much as anything can trouble me." "Now," said the bishop, "I will ask you whether, for gold or silver you would utter anything out of your mouth that was against the sacrament of the altar, or the other holy sacraments of the Church?" "Sir!" said the master, "be it known to you that there is nothing in the world that would induce me so to do; I would much rather that every member were torn from my body than that I should say such a thing."

"Now I will say something more," said the bishop. "You know that the king of France is at war with the king of England, and you know too that the castle that lies most exposed in the border-land between the two is the castle of la Rochelle in Poitou. Now I will ask you a question: If the king had set you to guard la Rochelle, which is in the dangerous border-land, and had set me to guard the castle of Montlhéri, which is in the heart of France, where the land is at peace, to whom, think you, would the king owe most at the end of the war—to you who had guarded la Rochelle without loss, or to me, who had guarded the castle of Montlhéri without loss?" "In God's name, sir," said the master, "to me, who had guarded la Rochelle without losing it."

"Master," said the bishop, "my heart is like the castle of Montlhéri; for I have neither temptation nor doubt as to the sacrament of the altar. For which thing I tell you that for the grace that God owes to me because I hold this firmly, and in peace, He owes to you four-fold, because you have guarded your heart in the war of tribulation, and have such good-will towards Him that for no earthly good, nor for any harm done to the body, would you relinquish that faith. Therefore I tell you, be of good comfort, for in this your state is better pleasing to our Lord than mine." When the master heard this, he knelt before the bishop, and held himself for well appeased.

Faith of the Count of Montfort—One Must Not Enter into Controversy with Jews

The sainted king told me that several people among the Albigenses came to the count of Montfort, who was then guarding the land of the Albigenses for the king, and asked him to come and look at the body of our Lord, which had become blood and flesh in the hands of the priest. And the count of Montfort said, "Go and look at it yourselves, you who do not believe it. As for me, I believe it firmly, holding as Holy Church teaches of the sacrament of the altar. And do you know what I shall gain," said the count, "in that during this mortal life I have believed as Holy Church teaches? I shall have a crown in the heavens, above the angels, for the angels cannot but believe, inasmuch as they see God face to face."

He told me that there was once a great disputation between clergy and Jews at the monastery of Cluny. And there was at Cluny a poor knight to whom the abbot gave bread at that place for the love of God; and this knight asked the abbot to suffer him to speak the first words, and they suffered him, not without doubt. So he rose, and leant upon his crutch, and asked that they should bring to him the greatest clerk and most learned master among the Jews; and they did so. Then he asked the Jew a question, which was this: "Master," said the knight, "I ask you if you believe that the Virgin Mary, who bore God in her body and in her arms, was a virgin mother, and is the mother of God?"

And the Jew replied that of all this he believed nothing. Then the knight answered that the Jew had acted like a fool when—neither believing in her, nor loving her—he had yet entered into her monastery and house. "And verily," said the knight, "you shall pay for it!" Whereupon he lifted his crutch and smote the Jew near the ear, and beat him to the earth. Then the Jews turned to flight, and bore away their master, sore wounded. And so ended the disputation.

The abbot came to the knight and told him he had committed a deed of very great folly. But the knight replied that the abbot had committed a deed of greater folly in gathering people together for such a disputation; for there were a great many good Christians there who, before the disputation came to an end, would have gone away misbelievers through not fully understanding the Jews. "And I tell you," said the king, "that no one, unless he be a very learned clerk, should dispute with them; but a layman, when he hears the Christian law missaid, should not defend the Christian law, unless it be with his sword, and with that he should pierce the mis-sayer in the midriff, so far as the sword will enter."

The Devotions of St. Louis—How He Did Justice in his Land

The rule of his land was so arranged that every day he heard the hours sung, and a *Requiem* mass without song; and then, if it was convenient, the mass of the day, or of the saint, with song. Every day he rested in his bed after having eaten, and when he had slept and rested, he said, privily in his chamber—he and one of his chaplains together—the office for the dead; and after he heard vespers. At night he heard complines.

A gray friar [Franciscan] came to him at the castle of Hyères, there where we disembarked; and said in his sermon, for the king's instruction, that he had read the Bible, and the books pertaining to heathen princes, and that he had never found, either among believers or misbelievers, that a kingdom had been lost, or had changed lords, save there had first been failure of justice.

"Therefore let the king, who is going into France, take good heed," said he, "that he do justice well and speedily among his people, so that our Lord suffer his kingdom to remain in peace all the days of his life." It is said that the right worthy man who thus instructed the king, lies buried at Marseilles, where our Lord, for his sake, performs many a fine miracle. He would never consent to remain with the king, however much the king might urge it, for more than a single day.

The king forgot not the teaching of the friar, but ruled his land very loyally and godly, as you shall hear. He had so arranged that my lord of Nesle, and the good count of Soissons, and all of us who were about him, should go, after we had heard our masses, and hear the pleadings at the gate which is now called the gate of Requests.

And when he came back from church, he would send for us and sit at the foot of his bed, and make us all sit round him, and ask if there were any whose cases could not be settled save by himself in person. And we named the litigants; and he would then send for such and ask: "Why do you not accept what our people offer?" And they would make reply, "Sire, because they offer us very little." Then would he say, "You would do well to accept what is proposed, as our people desire." And the saintly man endeavored thus, with all his power, to bring them into a straight path and a reasonable.

Ofttimes it happened that he would go, after his mass, and seat himself in the wood of Vincennes, and lean against an oak, and make us sit round him. And all of those who had any cause in hand came and spoke to him, without hindrance of usher, or of any other person. Then would he ask, out of his own mouth, "Is there any one who has a cause in hand?" And those who had a cause in hand stood up. Then would he say, "Keep silence all, and you shall be heard in turn, one after the other." Then he would call my lord Peter of Fontaines and my lord Geoffry of Villette, and say to one of them, "Settle me this cause."

And when he saw that there was anything to amend in the words of those who spoke on his behalf, or in the words of those who spoke on behalf of any other person, he would himself, out of his own mouth, amend what they had said. Sometimes have I seen him, in summer, go to do justice among his people in the garden of Paris, clothed in a tunic of camlet, a surcoat of tartan without sleeves, and a mantle of black taffeta about his neck, his hair well combed, no cap, and a hat of white peacock's feathers upon his head. And he would cause a carpet to be laid down, so that we might sit round him, and all the people who had any cause to bring before him stood around. And then would he have their causes settled, as I have told you afore he was wont to do in the wood of Vincennes.

St. Louis Refuses an Unjust Demand Made by the Bishops

I saw him, yet another time, in Paris, when all the prelates of France had asked to speak with him, and the king went to the palace to give them audience. And there was present Guy of Auxerre, the son of my lord William of Mello, and he spoke to the king on behalf of all the prelates, after this manner: "Sire, the lords who are here present, archbishops and bishops, have directed me to tell you that Christendom, which ought to be guarded and preserved by you, is perishing in your hands." The king crossed himself when he heard that word, and he said, "Tell me how that may be."

"Sire," said Guy of Auxerre, "it is because excommunications are at the present day so lightly thought of that people suffer themselves to die before seeking absolution, and will not give satisfaction to the Church. These lords require you therefore, for the sake of God, and because it is your duty, to command your provosts and bailiffs to seek out all such as suffer themselves to remain excommunicated for a year and day, and constrain them, by seizure of their goods, to have themselves absolved."

And the king replied that he would issue such commands willingly whensoever it could be shown to him that the excommunicate persons were in the wrong. The bishops said they would accept this condition at no price whatever, as they contested his jurisdiction in their causes. Then the king told them he would do no other; for it would be against God and reason if he constrained people to seek absolution when the clergy were doing them wrong. "And of this," said the king, "I will give you an example, viz.,

that of the count of Brittany, who, for seven years long, being excommunicated pleaded against the prelates of Britanny, and carried his cause so far that the apostle [the pope] condemned them all. Wherefore, if I had constrained the count of Brittany, at the end of the first year, to get himself absolved, I should have sinned against God and against him." Then the prelates resigned themselves; nor did I ever hear tell that any further steps were taken in the aforesaid matters.

The Uprightness of St. Louis

The peace that he made with the king of England was made against the advice of his council, for the council said to him: "Sire, it seems to us that you are giving away the land that you make over to the king of England; for he has no right thereto, seeing that his father lost it justly." To this the king replied that he knew well that the king of England had no right to the land, but that there was a reason why he should give it to him, "for," said he, "we have two sisters to wife, and our children are cousins-german; wherefore it is fitting that there should be peace between us. Moreover a very great honor accrues to me through the peace that I have made with the king of England, seeing that he is now my liegeman, which he was not aforetime."

The uprightness of the king may be seen in the case of my lord Renaud of Trie, who brought to the saintly man a charter stating that the king had given to the heirs of the countess of Boulogne, lately deceased, the county of Dammartin in Gouelle. The seal on the charter was broken, so that naught remained save half the legs of the image on the king's seal, and the stool on which the king set his feet. And the king showed the seal to all those who were of his council, and asked us to help him to come to a decision. We all said, without a dissentient, that he was not bound to give effect to the charter. Then he told John Sarrasin, his chamberlain, to give him a charter which he had asked him to obtain. When he held this charter in his hands, he said: "Lords, this is the seal I used before I went overseas, and you can see clearly from this seal that the impression on the broken seal is like unto that of the seal that is whole; wherefore I should not dare, in good conscience, to keep the said county." So he called to him my lord Renaud of Trie, and said, "I give you back the county."

Second Book

Birth and Coronation of St. Louis

In the name of God Almighty, we have, hereinbefore, written out a part of the good words and of the good teachings of our saintly King Louis, so that those who read may find them set in order, the one after the other, and thus derive more profit therefrom than if they were set forth among his deeds. And from this point we begin, in the name of God and in his own name, to speak of his deeds.

As I have heard tell he was born on the day of St. Mark the Evangelist, after Easter (April 25, 1214). On that day crosses are, in many places, carried in procession, and, in France, these are called black crosses; and this was as it were a prophecy of the great number of people who were to die in the two Crusades, viz., that of Egypt, and the other, in which he himself died, at Carthage, whereby there were great mournings in this world, and many great rejoicings in paradise for such as in these two pilgrimages died true crusaders.

He was crowned on the first Sunday in Advent (November 29, 1226). The beginning of the mass for that Sunday runs: *Ad te levavi animam meam* and what follows after; and this means, "Fair Lord God, I have lifted up my soul to thee, I put my confidence in thee." In God had he great confidence from his childhood to his death; for when he died, in his last words, he called upon God and His saints, and specially upon my lord St. James and my lady St. Genevieve.

First Troubles in the Reign of St. Louis

God, in whom he put his trust, kept him all his days from childhood unto the end; and specially, in his youth, did he keep him, when great need was, as you shall shortly hear.

As to his soul, God kept it through the good teachings of his mother, who taught him to believe in God and to love Him, and to gather round himself all good people of religion. And, child as he was, she made him recite all the Hours, and listen to the sermons on festival days. He recorded that his mother had sometimes given him to understand that she would rather he were dead than have committed a mortal sin.

Good need had he of God's help in his youth, for his mother, who came from Spain, had neither relations nor friends in all the kingdom of France. And because the barons of France saw that the king was but a child, and the queen, his mother, a foreign woman, they made the count of Boulogne, who was uncle to the king, their chief, and held him as their lord. After the king was crowned, there were certain barons who demanded of the queen that she should give them great lands, and because she would none of it, all the barons assembled at Corbeil.

And the saintly king told me that neither he, nor his mother, who were at Montlhéri, dared return to Paris till those in Paris came in arms to fetch them. And he told me that all the way, from Montlhéri to Paris, was filled with people, armed and unarmed, and that all cried to our Saviour to give him a good life and a long, and to defend and guard him from his enemies. And this God did, as you shall presently hear.

In this parliament which the barons held at Corbeil, the barons there present decided, so it is said, that the good knight, the Count Peter of Brittany, should rebel against the king, and they agreed besides that they would each in person, and with two knights only, attend the count when he obeyed the summons which the king would address to him. And this they did to see if the count of Brittany would be able to master the queen, who was a foreign woman, as you have heard. And many people say that the count would have mastered the queen and the king too, if God had not helped the king in this his hour of need, as He never failed to do.

The help God gave him was such that Count Thibaut of Champagne, who was afterwards the king of Navarre, came there to serve the king with three hundred knights; and through the help that the count gave to the king, the count of Britanny had to yield to the king's mercy, and when making that peace, as it is said, to surrender to the king the county of Anjou and the county of the Perche.

Crusade of Richard Coeur-de-lion—Rights of Alice, Queen of Cyprus, over Champagne

Inasmuch as there are certain things of which you should have knowledge, I hold it fitting here to depart somewhat from my subject. We will tell you here, therefore, that the good Count Henry the Large had by the Countess Mary—who was sister to the king of France and sister to King Richard of England—two sons, of whom the elder was called Henry and the other Thibaut. This Henry, the elder, went as a crusader on pilgrimage to the Holy Land at the time when King Philip and King Richard besieged Acre and took it.

So soon as Acre was taken, King Philip returned to France, for which he was greatly blamed; but King Richard remained in the Holy Land, and did there such mighty deeds that the Saracens stood in great fear of him; so much so, as it is written in the book of the Holy Land, that when the Saracen children cried, their mothers called out, "Wisht! here is King Richard," in order to keep them quiet. And when the horses of the Saracens and Bedouins started at tree or bush, their masters said to the horses, "Do you think that is King Richard?"

This King Richard wrought to such effect that he gave for wife to Count Henry of Champagne, who had remained with him, the queen of Jerusalem, who was direct heiress to the kingdom. By the said queen Count Henry had two daughters of whom the first was queen of Cyprus, and the other did my lord Everard of Brienne have to wife, and from them sprang a great lineage, as is known in France and Champagne. Of the wife of my lord Everard of Brienne I will say nothing to you at this present; but I will speak to you of the queen of Cyprus, seeing she is related to the matter I have in hand; and I speak, therefore, as follows.

The Barons Attack Thibaut IV, Count of Champagne

After the king had foiled Count Peter of Brittany, all the barons of France were so wroth with Count Thibaut of Champagne that they settled to send for the queen of Cyprus, who was the daughter of the eldest son of Champagne, so as to disinherit Count Thibaut, who was the son of the second son of Champagne.

But some took steps to reconcile Count Peter with Count Thibaut, and the matter was discussed to such effect that Count Thibaut promised to take to wife the daughter of Count Peter of Brittany. A day was fixed on which the count of Champagne should espouse the damsel; and she was to be taken, for the marriage, to an abbey of Premontre near Chateau-Thierry, and called as I believe, Val-Secret. The barons of France, who were nearly all related to Count Peter, undertook this duty, and conducted the damsel to Val-Secret to be married, and advised thereof the count of Champagne, who was at Chateau-Thierry.

And while the count of Champagne was coming for the marriage, my lord Geoffry of la Chapelle came to him on the part of the king, with a letter of credence, and spoke thus: "My lord count of Champagne, the king has heard that you have covenanted with Count Peter of Brittany to take his daughter in marriage. Now the king warns you that, unless you wish to lose everything you possess in the kingdom of France, you will not do this thing, for you know that the count of Brittany has done more evil to the king than any man living." Then the count of Champagne, by the advice of those he had with him, returned to Chateau-Thierry.

When Count Peter and the barons of France, who were expecting him at Val-Secret, heard this, they were all like men distraught, with anger at what he had done to them, and they at once sent to fetch the queen of Cyprus. And as soon as she was come, they entered into a common agreement to gather together as many men-at-arms as they could, and enter into Brie and Champagne, from the side of France; and the duke of Burgundy, who had to wife the daughter of Count Robert of Dreux, was to enter into Champagne from the side of Burgundy. And they fixed a day on which they should assemble before the city of Troyes, to take the city of Troyes if they could accomplish it.

The duke collected all the people he could, and the barons also. The barons came burning and wasting everything on one side, and the duke of Burgundy on another, and the king of France came on yet another side to fight against them. The evil plight of the count of Champagne was such that he himself burned his cities before the arrival of the barons, so that they might not find supplies therein. Among the other cities that the count of Champagne burned, he burned Epernay, and Vertus, and Sézanne.

Simon of Joinville Defends Troyes—Peace between the Count of Champagne and the Queen of Cyprus

The citizens of Troyes, when they perceived that they had lost the help of their lord, asked Simon, lord of Joinville, and father of the lord of Joinville that now is, to come to their help. And he, who had gathered together all his men-at-arms, moved from Joinville by night, so soon as the tidings were brought to him, and came to Troyes before it was day. And thus were the barons foiled of their intent to take the said city; wherefor the barons passed before Troyes without doing aught, and went and encamped in the meadow of l'Isle— there where the duke of Burgundy already was.

The king of France, who knew they were there, at once addressed himself to go thither and at-tack them; and the barons sent and begged him to withdraw in person from the field, and then they would go and fight against the count of Champagne and the duke of Lorraine and the rest of the king's people, with three hundred knights less than the count and duke had in their force. But the king told them they should not so fight without him, for he would remain with his peo-ple in person. Then the barons sent back to the king and said that, if it so pleased him, they would willingly incline the queen of Cyprus to make peace. The king replied that he would agree to no peace, nor suffer the count of Champagne to agree to any peace, till they had retired from the county of Champagne.

They retired in such sort that from Isle, where they were, they went and encamped before Jully, and the king encamped at Isle, from which he had driven them. And when they knew that the king had come to Isle, they went and encamped at Chaource, and not daring to wait for the king, they went and encamped at Laignes, which belonged to the count of Nevers, who was of their party. So the king caused the count of Champagne and the queen of Cyprus to come to terms, and peace was made in such sort that the count of Champagne

gave to the queen of Cyprus about two thousand livres (yearly) in land, and forty thousand livres, which latter sum the king paid for the count of Champagne. And the count of Champagne sold to the king, for the said forty thousand livres, the fiefs hereinafter names, viz.—the fief of the coun-ty of Blois, the fief of the county of Chartres, the fief of the county of Sancerre, the fief of the coun-ty of Châteaudun. Now there are certain people who say that the king only holds the said fiefs in pledge; but this is not so, for I asked our saintly king of it when we were oversea.

The land that Count Thibaut gave to the queen of Cyprus is held by the count of Brienne that now is, and by the count of Joigny, because the great-grandmother of the count of Brienne was daugh-ter to the queen of Cyprus and wife to the great Count Walter of Brienne.

Of Henry I, Called the Large-hearted, Count of Champagne

In order that you may learn whence came the fiefs that the count of Champagne sold to the king, you must know that the great Count Thibaut, who lies buried at Lagny, had three sons. The first was called Henry, the second Thibaut, and the third Stephen. The aforesaid Henry was count of Champagne and of Brie, and was called Count Henry the Large-hearted; and rightly was he so called, for he was large-hearted both in his dealings with God and the world: large-hearted towards God as appears in the Church of St. Stephen of Troyes and the other fair churches which he founded in Champagne, and large-hearted towards the world as appeared in the case of Artaud of Nogent, and on many other occasions, of which I would tell you if I did not fear to interrupt my story.

This Artaud of Nogent was the citizen of all the world in whom the count had the great-est faith; and he became so rich that he built the castle of Nogent L'Artaud with his moneys. Now it happened that Count Henry was coming down from his halls at Troyes to go and hear mass at St. Stephen's on the day of Pentecost. At the foot of the steps there came before him a poor knight and knelt down before him and spoke thus: "Sire, I pray you, for the love of God, to give me of what is yours, so that I may marry my two daughters whom you see here." Artaud, who went behind him, said to the poor knight: "Sir knight, it is not courteous on your part to beg of my lord, for he has given away so much that he has nothing left to give." The large-hearted count turned towards Artaud and said: "Sir villain, you speak not sooth when you say I have nothing left to give; I have you left. There, take him, sir knight, for I give him to you, and moreover, I pledge myself for him." The knight was not abashed, but took hold of Artaud's cloak, and said he would not leave him till they had done business together. And before he escaped, Artaud had done business with him to the tune of five hundred livres.

The second brother of Count Henry was called Thibaut and was count of Blois. The third brother was called Stephen, and was count of Sancerre. And these two brothers held from Count Henry all their heritages, and their counties, and the appurtenances thereof; and they held them afterwards from the heirs of Count Henry who held the county of Champagne, until such time as Count Thibaut sold them to the king of France, as has been related above.

St. Louis Holds a Full Court at Saumur in 1241

Now let us return to our subject and tell how, after these things, the king held a full court at Saumur in Anjou, and I was there and can testify that it was the best-ordered court that ever I saw. For at the king's table ate, after him, the count of Poitiers, whom he had newly made knight at the feast of St. John; and after the count of Poitiers, ate the count of Dreux, whom he had also newly made knight; and after the count of Dreux the count of la Marche; and after the count of la Marche the good Count Peter of Brittany; and before the king's table, opposite the count of Dreux, ate my lord and the king of Navarre, in tunic and mantle of samite well bedight with a belt and a clasp, and a cap of gold; and I carved before him.

Before the king the count of Artois, his brother, served the meat, and before the king the good Count John of Soissons carved with the knife. In order to guard the king's table there were there my lord Imbert of Beaujeu, who was afterwards constable of France, and my lord Enguerrand of Coucy, and my lord Archamband of Bourbon.

Behind these three barons stood some thirty of their knights, in tunics of silken cloth, to keep guard over them; and behind these knights there were a great quantity of sergeants bearing on their clothing the arms of the count of Poitiers embroidered in taffeta. The king was clothed in a tunic of blue satin, and surcoat and mantle of vermeil samite[1] lined with ermine, and he had a cotton cap upon his head, which suited him very badly, because he was at that time a young man.

The king held these banquets in the halls of Saumur which had been built, so it was said, by the great King Henry of England [Henry II.] in order that he might hold his great banquets therein; and this hall is built after the fashion of the cloisters of the white monks of the Cistercian order. But I think there is none other hall so large, and by a great deal. And I will tell you why I think so—it is because by the wall of the cloister, where the king ate, surrounded by his knights and sergeants who occupied a great space, there was also room for a table where ate twenty bishops and archbishops, and yet again, besides the bishops and archbishops, the Queen Blanche, the king's mother, ate near the table, at the head of the cloister, on the other side from the king.

And to serve the queen there was the count of Boulogne, who afterwards became king of Portugal, and the good Count Hugh of St. Paul, and a German of the age of eighteen years, who was said to be the son of St. Elizabeth of Thuringia, for which cause it was told that Queen Blanche kissed him on the forehead, as an act of devotion, because she thought that his mother must ofttimes have kissed him there.

At the end of the cloister, on the other side, were the kitchens, the cellars, the pantries and the butteries; from this end were served to the king and to the queen meats, and wine, and bread. And in the wings and in the central court ate the knights, in such numbers, that I knew not how to count them. And many said they had never, at any feast, seen together so many surcoats and other garments, of cloth of gold and of silk; and it was said also that no less than three thousand knights were there present.

---

1   A woolen cloth interwoven with gold and silver.

Battle of Taillebourg in 1242

After this feast the king led the count of Poitiers to Poitiers, so that his vassals might do homage for his fiefs. And when the king came to Poitiers, he would gladly have been back in Paris, for he found that the count of la Marche, who had eaten at his table on St. John's day, had assembled as many men-at-arms as he could collect, at Lusignan near Poitiers. The king remained at Poitiers nearly a fortnight, nor did he dare to depart therefrom till he had come to terms—how, I know not—with the count of la Marche.

Ofttimes I saw the count of la Marche come from Lusignan to speak to the king at Poitiers, and always he brought with him the queen of England, his wife, who was mother to the king of England. And many people said that the king and the count of Poitiers had made an evil peace with the count of la Marche.

No long time after the king had returned from Poitiers, the king of England came into Gascony to wage war against the king of France. Our saintly king rode forth to fight against him with as many people as he could collect. Then came the king of England and the count of la Marche to do battle before a castle called Taillebourg, seated on an evil river called La Charente, at a point where one cannot pass except over a stone bridge, very narrow.

So soon as the king came to Taillebourg, and the hosts came in sight of one another, our people, who had the castle behind them, bestirred themselves mightily and passed over the stream with great peril, in boats, and on pontoons, and fell upon the English. Then began a battle grim and fierce. When the king saw this, he put himself in peril, with the others; and for every man that the king had with him when he passed the stream, the English had, on their side, at least twenty. Nevertheless, as God willed, it so befell that when the English saw the king pass over, they fled, and took refuge in the city of Saintes, and several of our people entered into the city, mingled with them, and were taken prisoners.

Those of our people who were taken at Saintes reported that they heard great discord arise between the king of England and the count of la Marche; and the king of England said that the count of la Marche had sent for him on the plea that he would find great help in France. That very night the king of England had left Saintes and went away into Gascony.

Submission of the Count of La Marche

The count of la Marche, as one who could do no better for himself, came to the king's prison, and brought with him to the prison his wife and his children; and the king, in making peace with the count, obtained a great deal of his land, but how much I know not, for I had nothing to do with that matter, seeing I had never then worn a hauberk [i.e., was not yet a knight]. But I heard tell that besides the land which the king thus gained, the count of la Marche made over to him ten thousand livres parisis, which were in the king's coffers, and the same sum every year.

When we were at Poitiers I saw a knight, my lord Geoffry of Rancon by name, who, for some great wrong that the count of la Marche had done him, so it was said, had sworn on holy relics that he would never have his head shorn, as knights are wont, but would wear his hair in woman's tresses until such time as he should see vengeance done on the count of la Marche, either by himself or by some other. And when my lord Geoffry saw the count of la Marche, his wife, and his children, kneeling before the king and crying for mercy, he caused a trestle to be brought, and his tresses cut off, and had himself immediately shorn in the presence of the king, of the count of la Marche, and of all those there present.

In this expedition against the king of England, and against the barons, the king gave great gifts, as I have heard tell by those who returned thence. But neither on account of such gifts, nor of the expenses incurred in this expedition, nor in other expeditions, whether beyond the seas or this side of the seas, did he ever demand, or take, any [money] aid from his barons, or his knights, or his men, or his good cities, in such sort as to cause complaint. Nor is this to be wondered at; for he ruled himself by the advice of the good mother who was with him—and whose counsel he took—and of the right worthy men who had remained by him from the time of his father and of his grandfather.

St. Louis Falls Ill, and Takes the Cross in 1244

After the things related above, it happened, as God so willed, that a very grievous sickness came upon the king in Paris, and brought him to such extremity, so it was said, that one of the ladies who were tending him wished to draw the cloth over his face, saying he was dead; but another lady, who was on the other side of the bed, would not suffer it, and said the soul was still in his body.

And as he listened to the debate between these two ladies, our Lord wrought within him, and soon sent him health, for before that he had been dumb and could not speak. And as soon as he was in case to speak, he asked that they should give him the cross, and they did so. When the queen, his mother, heard say that speech had come back to him, she made as great joy thereof as ever she could. But when she knew that he had taken the cross—as also he himself told her—she made as great mourning as if she had seen him dead.

After he had taken the cross, so also took the cross, Robert, count of Artois, Alfonse, count of Poitiers, Charles, count of Anjou, who afterwards was king of Sicily—all three brothers of the king;—and there also took the cross, Hugh, duke of Burgundy, William, count of Flanders, and brother of Count Guy of Flanders lately deceased, the good Hugh, count of St. Paul, and my lord Gaucher, his nephew, who did right well oversea, and would have done much good service if he had lived.

With them also took the cross, the count of la Marche and my lord Hugh LeBrun, his son, the count of Sarrebruck and my lord Gobert of Apremont, his brother—in whose company I, John, lord of Joinville, passed over the sea in a ship which we hired because we were cousins—and we passed over with twenty knights, of whom he was over ten, and I over ten.

Joinville Prepares to Join the Crusade

At Easter, in the year of grace that stood at 1248, I summoned my men, and all who held fiefs from me, to Joinville, and on the vigil of the said Easter, when all the people that I had summoned were assembled, was born my son John, lord of Ancerville, by my first wife, the sister of the count of Grandpré. All that week we feasted and danced, and my brother, the lord of Vaucouleurs, and the other rich men who were there, gave feasts on the Monday, the Tuesday, the Wednesday and the Thursday.

On the Friday I said to them: "Lords, I am going oversea, and I know not whether I shall ever return. Now come forward; if I have done you any wrong, I will make it good, as I have been used to do, dealing, each in turn, with such as have any claim to make against me, or my people." So I dealt with each, according to the opinions of the men on my lands; and in order that I might not weigh upon their debate, I retired from the council, and agreed, without objection raised, to what they recommended.

Because I did not wish to take away with me any penny wrongfully gotten, therefore I went to Metz, in Lorraine, and placed in pawn the greater part of my land. And you must know that on the day when I left our country to go to the Holy Land, I did not hold more than one thousand livres a year in land, for my lady mother was still alive; and yet I went, taking with me nine knights and being the first of three knights-banneret. And I bring these things to your notice, so that you may understand that if God, who never yet failed me, had not come to my help, I should hardly have maintained myself for so long a space as the six years that I remained in the Holy Land.

As I was preparing to depart, John, lord of Apremont and count of Sarrebruck in his wife's right, sent to tell me he had settled matters to go oversea, taking ten knights, and proposed, if I so willed, that we should hire a ship between him and me; and I consented. His people and mine hired a ship at Marseilles.

Of a Clerk Who Killed Three of the King's Sergeants

The king summoned all his barons to Paris, and made them take oath that, if anything happened to him while away, they would give faith and loyalty to his children. He asked me to do the same; but I would not take the oath, because I was not his liegeman.

While I was on my way to Paris, I found three men dead upon a cart, whom a clerk had killed;

and I was told they were being taken to the king. When I heard this, I sent one of my squires after, to know what befell. And my squire, whom I had sent, told me that the king, when he came out of his chapel, went to the entrance steps to look at the dead, and inquired of the provost of Paris how this thing had happened.

And the provost told him that the dead men were three of his sergeants of the Chatelet, who had gone into unfrequented streets to rob people. "And they found," said he to the king, "this clerk, whom you see here, and robbed him of all his clothes. The clerk, being only in his shirt, went to his lodging, and took his crossbow, and caused a child to bring his falchion [one-edged sword]. Then when he saw them again he cried out upon them, and said they should die. So the clerk drew his crossbow, and shot, and pierced one of the men through the heart. The two others made off flying. And the clerk took the falchion which the child handed to him, and followed them in the moonlight, which was fine and clear. The one man thought to pass through a hedge into a garden, and the clerk struck him with his falchion," said the provost, "and cut right through his leg, in such sort that it only holds to the boot, as you may see here. The clerk then followed the other, who thought to go down into a strange house, where the people were still awake; but the clerk struck him in the middle of the head with his falchion, so that he clove his head to the teeth, as you may see here," said the provost to the king. "Sire," continued he, "the clerk showed what he had done to the neighbors in the street, and then came and made himself your prisoner. And now sire, I have brought him to you to do with him what you will. Here he is."

"Sir clerk," said the king, "you have forfeited your priesthood by your prowess; and for your prowess I take you into my service, and you shall go with me overseas. And this thing I do for you, because I would have my men to fully understand that I will uphold them in none of their wickedness."

When the people there assembled heard this, they cried out to our Savior, and prayed God to give the king a good and a long life, and bring him back in joy and health.

Joinville Leaves his Castle

After these things I returned to our county, and we agreed, the count of Sarrebruck and I, that we should send our baggage in carts to Ausonne, thence to be borne on the river Saone, and to Arles by the Saone and the Rhone.

How the King Reformed his Bailiffs, Provosts, and Mayors—and How he Instituted New Ordinances—and How Stephen Boileau Was his Provost of Paris

After King Louis had returned to France from overseas, he bore himself very devoutly towards our Savior, and very justly towards his subjects; wherefore he considered and thought it would be a fair thing, and a good, to reform the realm of France. First he established a general ordinance for all his subjects throughout the realm of France, in the manner following:

"We, Louis, by the grace of God king of France, ordain that Our bailiffs, viscounts, provosts, mayors, and all others, in whatever matter it may be, and whatever office they may hold, shall make oath that, so long as they hold the said office, or perform the functions of bailiffs, they shall do justice to all, without acceptation of persons, as well to the poor as to the rich, and to strangers as to those who are native-born; and that they shall observe such uses and customs as are good and have been approved.

"And if it happens that the bailiffs, or viscounts, or others, as the sergeants or foresters, do aught contrary to their oaths, and are convicted thereof, We order that they be punished in their goods, or in their persons, if the misfeasance so require; and the bailiffs shall be punished by Ourselves, and others by the bailiffs.

"Henceforward the other provosts, the bailiffs and the sergeants shall make oath to loyally keep and uphold Our rents and Our rights, and not to suffer Our rights to lapse or to be suppressed or diminished; and with this they shall swear not to take or receive, by themselves or through others, gold, nor silver, nor any indirect benefit, nor any other thing, save fruit, or bread, or wine, or other present, to the value of ten sous, the said sum not being exceeded.

"And besides this they shall make oath not to take, or cause to be taken, any gift, of whatever kind, through their wives, or their children, or their brothers, or their sisters, or any other persons connected with them; and so soon as they have knowledge that any such gifts have been received, they will cause them to be returned as soon as may be possible. And, besides this, they shall make oath not to receive any gift, of whatever kind, from any man belonging to their bailiwicks, nor from any others who have a suit or may plead before them.

"Henceforth they shall make oath not to bestow any gift upon any men who are of Our council, nor upon their wives, or children, or any person belonging to them; nor upon those who shall receive the said officers' accounts on Our behalf, nor to any persons who We may send to their bailiwicks, or to their provost-ships, to enquire into their doings. And with this they shall swear to take no profit out of any sale that may be made of Our rents, Our bailiwicks, Our coinage, or aught else to Us belonging.

"And they shall swear and promise, that if they have knowledge of any official, sergeant, or provost, serving under them, who is unfaithful, given to robbery and usury, or addicted to other vices whereby he ought to vacate Our service, then they will not uphold him for any gift, or promise, or private affection, or any other cause, but punish and judge him in all good faith.

"Henceforward Our provosts, Our viscounts, Our mayors, Our foresters, and Our other sergeants, mounted and dismounted, shall make oath not to bestow any gift upon their superiors, nor upon their superiors' wives, nor children, nor upon any one belonging to them.

"And because We desire that these oaths be fairly established, We order that they be taken in full assize, before all men, by clerks and laymen, knights and sergeants, notwithstanding that any such may have already made oath before Us; and this We ordain so that those who take the oaths may avoid the guilt and the sin of perjury, not only from the fear of God and of Ourselves, but also for shame before the world.

"We will and ordain that all Our provosts and bailiffs abstain from saying any word that would bring into contempt God, or our Lady, or the saints; and also that they abstain from the game of dice and keep away from taverns. We ordain that the making of dice be forbidden throughout Our realm, and that lewd women be turned out of every house; and whosoever shall rent a house to a lewd woman shall forfeit to the provost, or the bailiff, the rent of the said house for a year.

"Moreover, We forbid Our bailiffs to purchase wrongfully, or to cause to be purchased, either directly, or through others, any possession or lands that may be in their bailiwick, or in any other, so long as they remain in Our service, and without Our express permission; and if any such purchases are made, We ordain that the lands in question be, and remain, in Our hands.

"We forbid Our bailiffs, so long as they shall be in Our service, to marry any sons or daughters that they may have, or any other person belonging to them, to any other person in their bailiwick, without Our special sanction; and moreover We forbid that they put any such into a religious house in their bailiwick, or purvey them with any benefice of Holy Church, or any other possession; and moreover We forbid that they obtain provisions or lodgings from any religious house, or nearby, at the expense of the religious. This prohibition as concerns marriages and the acquisition of goods, as stated above, does not apply to provosts, or mayors, nor to others holding minor offices.

"We order that no bailiff, provost, or any other, shall keep too many sergeants or beadles, to the burdening of our people; and We ordain that the beadles be appointed in full assize, or else be not regarded as beadles. When sergeants are sent to a distant place, or to a strange county, We ordain that they be not received without letters from their superiors.

"We order that no bailiff or provost in Our service shall burden the good people in his jurisdiction beyond what is lawful and right; and that none of Our subjects be put in prison for any debt save in so far as such debt may be due to Ourselves only.

"We ordain that no bailiff levy a fine for a debt due by any of Our subjects, or for any offense, save in full and open court, where the amount of such fine may be adjudged and estimated, with the advice of worthy and competent persons, even when the fine has already been considered by them [informally? passage obscure]. And if it happens that the accused will not wait for the judgment of Our court, which is offered him, but offers for the fine a certain sum of money, such as has been commonly received aforetime, we ordain that the court accept such sum of money if it be reasonable and convenient; and, if not, we ordain that the fine be adjudicated upon, as aforesaid, even though the delinquent place himself in the hands of the court. We forbid that the bailiffs, or the mayors, or the provosts, should compel Our subjects, either by threats, or intimidation, or any chicanery, to pay a fine in secret or in public or accuse any save for reasonable cause.

"And We ordain that those who hold the office of provost, viscount, or any other office, do not sell such office to others without Our consent; and if several persons buy jointly any of the said offices, We order that one of the purchasers shall perform the duties of the office for all the rest, and alone enjoy such of its privileges in respect of journeyings, taxes, and common charges, as have been customary aforetime.

"And We forbid that they sell the said offices to their brothers, nephews, or cousins, after they have bought them from Us; and that they claim any debts that may be due to themselves, save such debts as appertain to their office. As regards their own personal debts, they will recover them by authority of the bailiff, just as if they were not in Our service.

"We forbid Our bailiffs and provosts to weary our subjects, in the causes brought before them, by moving the venue from place to place. They shall hear the matters brought before them in the place where they have been wont to hear them, so that Our subjects may not be induced to forego their just rights for fear of trouble and expense.

"From henceforth we command that Our provosts and bailiffs dispossess no man from the seisin which he holds, without full enquiry, or Our own especial order; and that they impose upon Our people no new exactions, taxes and imposts; and that they compel no one to come forth to do service in arms, for the purpose of exacting money from him; for We order that none who owes Us service in arms shall be summoned to join the host without sufficient cause, and that those who would desire to come to the host in person should

not be compelled to purchase exemption by money payment.

"Moreover, we forbid Our bailiffs and provosts to prevent corn, wine and other merchandise from being taken out of Our Kingdom, save for sufficient cause; and when it is convenient that these goods should not be taken out of the kingdom, the ordinance shall be made publicly, in the council of worthy and competent elders, and without suspicion of fraud or misdoing.

"Similarly We ordain that all bailiffs, viscounts, provosts, and mayors do remain, after they have left office, for the space of forty days in the land where such office has been exercised— remaining there in person or by deputy—so that they may answer to the new bailiffs in respect of any wrong done to such as may wish to bring a complaint against them."

By these ordinances the king did much to improve the condition of the kingdom.

Reform of the Provostship of Paris

The provostship of Paris was at that time sold to the citizens of Paris, or indeed any one; and those who bought the office upheld their children and nephews in wrongdoing; and the young folk relied in their misdoings on those who occupied the provostship. For which reason the mean people were greatly downtrodden; nor could they obtain justice against the rich, because of the great presents and gifts that the latter made to the provosts.

Whenever at that time any one spoke the truth before the provost, and wished to keep his oath, refusing to perjure himself regarding any debt, or other matter on which he was bound to give evidence, then the provost levied a fine upon that person, and he was punished. And because of the great injustice that was done, and the great robberies perpetrated in the provostship, the mean people did not dare to sojourn in the king's land, but went and sojourned in other provostships and other lordships. And the king's land was so deserted that when the provost held his court, no more than ten or twelve people came thereto.

With all this there were so many malefactors and thieves in Paris and the country adjoining that all the land was full of them. The king, who was very diligent to enquire how the mean people were governed and protected, soon knew the truth of this matter. So he forbade that the office of provost in Paris should be sold; and he gave great and good wages to those who henceforward should hold the said office. And he abolished all the evil customs harmful to the people; and he caused enquiry to be made throughout the kingdom to find men who would execute good and strict justice, and not spare the rich any more than the poor.

Then was brought to his notice Stephen Boileau, who so maintained and upheld the office of provost that no malefactor, no thief, nor murderer dared to remain in Paris, seeing that if he did, he was soon hung or exterminated: neither parentage, or lineage, nor gold, nor silver could save him. So the king's land began to amend, and people resorted thither for the good justice that prevailed. And the people so multiplied, and things so amended, that sales, seisines, purchases, and other matters were doubled in value, as compared with what the king had received aforetime.

A further ordinance issued by the king did much to bring about a better state of things in the kingdom of France, as many wise and venerable persons have testified. It ran as follows:

"In all these matters which We have ordained for the advantage of Our subjects, and of Our realm, We reserve to Ourselves the right to elucidate, amend, adjust, or diminish, according as We may determine."

By this ordinance also the king did much to reform the kingdom of France, as many wise and ancient persons bear witness.

Love of St. Louis for the Poor—of his Alms and Pious Foundations

From the time of his childhood, the king had pity on the poor suffering; and the custom was that, wherever the king went, six score poor persons were always fed every day, in his house, with bread and wine, and meat or fish. In Lent and Advent the number of the poor was increased; and ofttimes it happened that the king served them, and set their food before them, and carved the meat before them, and gave them money with his own hand at their departing.

Particularly at the great vigils, before the solemn festivals, he served the poor in all matters as aforesaid, before he himself either ate or drank. Besides all this he had, every day, to dine or sup near him, old and broken men, and caused them to be fed with the same meats of which he himself partook; and when they had eaten they took away a certain sum of money.

Besides all this the king gave, day by day, large and great alms to the poor religious, to the poor in hospitals, to the poor sick, and to poor communities, also to poor gentlemen and ladies, and girls, and to fallen women, and to poor widows and to women who were lying in, and to poor workmen, who through age or sickness could no longer work at their crafts; so that hardly would it be possible to number his alms. Therefore may it well be said that he was more fortunate than Titus, the Emperor of Rome of whom old writings tell that he was sad and discomforted for any day on which he had not been able to confer some benefit.

From the first that he came to his kingdom and knew where he stood he began to erect churches, and many religious houses, among which the abbey of Royaumont bears the palm for honor and magnificence. He caused many almshouses to be erected: the almshouse for Paris, that of Pontoise, that of Compiegne and of Vernon, and assigned to them large rents. He founded the abbey of St. Matthew at Rouen, where he set women of the order of the Preaching Brothers; and he founded that of Longchamp, where he set women of the order of the Minorist Brothers, and assigned to them large rents for their livelihood.

And he allowed his mother to found the abbey of the Lis near Melun-sur-Seine, and the abbey near Pontoise, which is called Maubuisson, and there assigned to them large rents and possessions. And he caused to be built the House of the Blind, near Paris, for the reception of the poor blind of the city; and caused a chapel to be built for them, so that they might hear the service of God. And the good king caused the house of the Carthusians, which is called Vauvert, to be built outside Paris, and assigned sufficient rents to the monks who there served our Savior.

Pretty soon after he caused another house to be built outside Paris, on the way to St. Denis, and it was called the house of Filles-Dieu; and he caused to be placed there a great multitude of women, who, through poverty, had lapsed into the sin of incontinence; and he gave them, for their maintenance, four hundred livres a year. And in many places of his kingdom he instituted houses for beguines, and gave them rents for their livelihood, and commanded that any should be received therein who were minded to live in chastity.

There were some of his familiars who murmured at his giving such large alms, and because he expended so much; and he would say: "I like better that the great and excessive expenditure which I incur should be incurred in almsgiving for the love of God, than in pomp and splendor and for the vainglory of this world." Yet, notwithstanding that the king spent so largely in almsgiving, he did not forbear to incur daily great expenditure in his household. Largely and liberally did the king behave to the parliaments and assemblies of his barons and knights; and he caused his court to be served courteously, and largely, and without stint, and in more liberal fashion than aforetime in the court of his predecessors.

Of the Religious Orders That the King Established in France

The king loved all people who set themselves to serve God, and took on them the religious habit; nor did any come to him but he gave them what they needed for a living. He provided for the brothers of Carmel, and bought them land on the Seine, towards Charenton, and caused a house to be built for them, and purchased for them vestments, chalices, and such other things as are needful for the service of our Savior. And after he provided for the brothers of St. Augustine, and bought them the grange of a citizen of Paris, and all its appurtenances, and caused a church to be built for them outside the gate of Montmartre.

The brothers of the "Sacks"[2] he provided for, and he gave them a site on the Seine, towards Saint-Germain des Prés, where they established themselves; but they remained there no long time, for they were shortly suppressed. After the brothers of the "Sacks" had been lodged came another kind of brothers, who were called the order of the "White Mantles,"[3] and they begged the king to give them help so that they might remain in Paris. The king bought them a house and certain old buildings lying round where they might lodge near the old gate of the Temple of Paris, rather near to the Weavers' house. These "White Mantles" were suppressed at the Council of Lyons, held by Gregory X.

Afterward came yet another kind of brothers, who had themselves called brothers of the Holy Cross, and wore a cross upon their breasts; and they asked the king to help them. The king did so willingly, and lodged them into a street called the Cross-roads of the Temple, and now called the street of the Holy Cross.

Thus did the good king surround the city of Paris with people of religion.

---

2 Ordre du Sac et de la Pénitence de Jésus Christ established by King Louis.
3 Knights Templar.

48. *ENQUÊTS* OF KING LOUIS

THE *QUERIMONIAE NORMANORUM* WERE collected when Louis IX (St. Louis, 1226–70) sought to reform royal administration in thirteenth-century France on the eve of a crusade. The conquest of Normandy in 1204 by Philip Augustus brought a large territory under French rule. Wishing to impose his personal standards of justice and piety on a growing administration, St. Louis dispatched special judges (*enquêteurs*) in 1247 to hear the complaints (*querimoniae*) of his Norman subjects against royal officers. The 64 cases in this selection are drawn from the diocese of Séez in the viscounty of Falaise (an administrative district). The cases form a unified group, very long or repetitive examples have been excluded. A few terms recur throughout the cases. *Baillis* were the most important royal officials in Normandy; they served as judges in lawsuits involving the king's rights and were responsible for the king's revenues. Subordinate to them were *firmarii*, the revenue farmers or collectors of rents. Awarded a particular region after a successful bid, a *firmarius* was permitted to "farm" a certain source of revenue in the region for a specified term, usually one year. Income that exceeded his bid constituted his profit. The currency prevalent in thirteenth-century Normandy and France was the pound, either the *livre* (l.) *parisis* or *livre* (l.) *tournois*; smaller amounts were expressed in shillings (*solidii*), abbreviated as s., and pennies (*denarii*), abbreviated as d. References to pounds alone are assumed to be to *livres parisis*.

Source: L. Delisle (ed.), *Recueil des historiens des Gaules et de la France* (Paris, 1904), vol. 4, pp. 1–73, trans. Jonathan M. Elukin, with the assistance of Professor William Chester Jordan.

Further Reading: William Chester Jordan, *Louis IX and the Challenge of the Crusade: A Study in Rulership* (Princeton: Princeton University Press, 1979).

Querimoniae Normanorum de Domino Rege in Vicecomitati Falesiae in Dyocesi Sagiensi

[Complaints of the Normans concerning the lord king in the Viscounty of Falaise in the Diocese of Séez]

355. R ... de Clerdoit, Richard Flori, ... Herberti, Hugues Herberti, Guillaume, son of Hugh de Clerdoit, of Saint Jacques de ... t, complain that both they and all others from the said parish for whom they similarly complain, were forced by the *baillis* and revenue farmers of the lord king to pay a customs duty on all things they sell and purchase, wherever they sell or purchase them, just as they had been accustomed to do when there was a market at Montpinçon ... on the Tuesday of each week, at the time when Raoul de Grandvilliers, knight and baron, held peaceful possession of his land before he went to England with King John; at which time he forfeited the land. And they say that they paid the said customs duty unjustly because, from the time when the land of the said baron came to the hand of King Philip, there has been no market in the village of Montpinçon, as there had been at the aforesaid time; and nevertheless, they have paid the said customs duty from that time till the present and are still compelled to pay it.

356. Robert, called "the Passionate," of Le Renouard ..., complains that Girard de La Boiste wrested from him a certain mill, found in the aforesaid parish, which he used to hold in fief from the lord king for 2 measures of oats and 6 hens, because he [Robert] did not wish to provide all the components of the said mill; and although he was only supposed to provide the millstone and the iron implements that hold the millstone, he has not been able to recover the said mill for the past 6 years.

358. Geoffroy *de Ponte Malveisin*, of the parish of Saint-Pierre-de-Chapelle, complains that the

lord king keeps in his hand his mother's marriage portion, which, located in the parish of *Roonnai* of the diocese of Séez, is currently worth 4-½ l. *tournois* annually to the lord king, because her husband had crossed over to England at the time of the conquest of Normandy and did not come to the peace of Philip, king of France, of illustrious memory. Geoffroy's mother had died before the death of her husband, who died beyond the sea as a Hospitaller. The said husband had neither sons nor daughters from the said woman, so [Geoffroy] says, for he was not Geoffroy's father but his stepfather.

359. Mabel, widow of Richard, son of Fulk, the knight, of Vieuxpont-en-Auge, complains that Girard de La Boiste acquired for the lord king land lying in the parish of Castillon, of the diocese of Lisieux, and worth approximately 100s. annually, because the brother of the said woman, a lay person, after the death of his brother the priest, also died in England. It is the priest who had given the said land to Mabel, on the condition that he peacefully and with no interference hold the aforesaid land at farm from Mabel and her heirs throughout his lifetime for one pair of gloves worth 6d. The land was acquired by the lord king last year on the previous Nativity of the Lord.

361. Agnes, a minor, daughter of Raoul Taquel of Saint-Georges-en-Auge, complains that about 12 years ago, the revenue farmers of the lord king acquired for him 6 acres of land, consisting of pasturage, wood, and cultivated fields, found in the parish of Le Tilleul. [They took the land], worth 20s., 2 loaves, 2 hens, and 20 eggs annually to the lord king, on account of Agnes' youth and helplessness. However, she was supposed to hold it in fief from the lord king for the aforesaid rent, namely the specified moneys, eggs, hens, and breads.

362. Robin *de Ripparia*, of Saint-Martin-de-Fresnay, complains that 24 years ago, Renaud de Ville-Thierri acquired for the lord king in the aforesaid parish 1 acre of wood, which is next to the wood of the lord king, upon the single statement of Robert Hirauth, a sergeant of the king, who said such things because he did not wish to lose the 1 pound of pepper which [Robinus] used to pay him annually.

364. Gilbert de Vaudeloges, *de Tot Ysembert*, complains that Pierre du Thillai, a *bailli* of the lord king, seized from his father a certain sergeanty [consisting] of a plot, which is between La Dive and La Vie, and placed it in the hand of the lord king 28 years ago; for he claimed that his father was not an enfeoffed sergeant, because he was not able to show [Pierre] a written charter to this effect. [Gilbert claims the charter] had been burned in a certain house, and he is prepared to seek an investigation by a jury[1] about this. And [Gilbert complains], the said Pierre, about 15 years ago, seized the patronage of the church of Heurtevent from his mother after the death of his father, and placed it in the hand of the lord king, because his mother did not want to give the church[2] according to Pierre's wish.

366. Emeline, daughter of Alain of Bretteville-sur-Dive, complains that the revenue farmers of the lord king acquired for the king 1-½ acres of land, which lie in the aforesaid parish. She was not able to recover them after the death of her father, who used to hold them from the said lord king in fief for 3 capons, 3 hens, and 3 loaves to be paid annually; and the land was taken into the king's hand approximately 12 years ago. Nor in this matter was the lord king injured.

367. Guillaume Pipart, a knight, of Escoz, complains that 4 years ago Jean de Vignes extracted 100l. *tournois*, which went to the lord king as [Jean] acknowledged before the said lord king. He was not supposed to extract [the money] unless [Guillaume] went to England, as was acknowledged before the king. Therefore, since he did not cross over to England at that time, Guillaume moves that the aforesaid money be returned to him.

---

1   Latin: *Inquisitio patriae*; literally, the investigation of the country. Under Norman law, this meant the sworn testimony of local men. In several cases below, *inquisitio* appears alone but also refers to a jury.

2   Latin: *dare ecclesiam*; appoint the parson, or parish priest.

368. Hugues d'Abbeville, of Vendeuvre, complains that King Philip, of good memory, ordered the land of Robert Louvel, of Morteaux-Couliboeuf, to be seized, land which the said Robert had given in pledge to Hugues for 22l. *tournois*, because Robert had gone to England and did not come to [the king's] peace. Hugues has since extracted nothing from the said land in the parish of Vendeuvre, nor was he able to recover afterwards the said money, which he had given to Robert. The land was taken into the lord king's possession at the time of the conquest of Normandy, so [Hugues] says.

369. Robert *de Senonis*, a clerk, of Condé-sur-Laison, complains that the servants or revenue farmers of the lord king of France, at the time of the conquest of Normandy, wrested from his uncle, his father, and from himself 3 measures of oats, customarily worth 15s., beyond the rent that his ancestors were accustomed to pay to the king of England, before the said conquest, from a certain piece of land, in the said parish, which he holds in fief from the lord king. The aforesaid ancestors used to pay only 2s. annually from the land, so he says.

370. Richard, called "the Englishman" of Saint-Pierre-sur-Dive, complains that Guillaume [*de Oilleio*], archdeacon of Angers, whose land came into the possession of the lord king 16 years ago, owed him 100s., which he has not been able to recover; for the said land came to the hand of the said lord king because his [Guillaume's] heirs remained in England.

371. Adam, son of Beatrice, of Saint-Pierre-sur-Dive, complains that Guillaume, archdeacon of Angers, whose land came into the possession of the lord king 16 years ago because his heirs remained in England, owed her 17l. from his accounts, which he has not been able to recover since the death of that individual.

372. Robert *de Fel*, of Saint-Pierre-sur-Dive, complains that lord king Philip, at the time of the conquest of Normandy, took the land of Robert Louvel of Cesny-aux-Vignes, a knight; which land [Louvel] has handed over to [*De Fel*] in pledge for

8l. *tournois*, which money he has not been able to recover.

374. Robert, called "the Blockhead" of Eraines, complains on behalf of his wife, since she is ill, saying that 20 years ago the lord king retained in his possession the 3 quarts of barley that his wife used to collect in a certain land lying in the parish of Aubigny; for the *baillis* of the king did not wish to return the land to his wife's mother nor to her after the year and a day that it had been held in the hand of the king. [It was held] because of the outlawry of one of her men, who had been holding that land from [his wife's] mother; although it ought to have been returned after a year and a day.

377. Hugues, the priest, rector of the church of Saint-Loup-Canivet, complains that Pierre du Thillai, formerly a *bailli* of the lord king, 30 years ago disseized him of 2 sheaves of the tithe of the said parish, which are worth 3 measures of barley at the Falaise measure annually to lord king, in whose hand they have been held unjustly from that time; for [Pierre] disseized him without cause, as was discovered through 2 investigations [by jury] made about this matter, so he says. The first one, conducted by the venerable father in Christ, the Bishop of Séez, was made known before the lord king, and the other one was made by Girard de La Boiste, who was then *bailli*.

378. Raoul Viethe and Robert *de Porta*, Nicholas le Fornier, Laurence Belebarbe, Etienne *de Furno* and Robert le Daneis, of Epaney, complain that the service of a wagon is being exacted from them to carry the timber of the mill of Jort, which they and their ancestors never did of old. And they have fallen into this evil custom because they used to give a little something every year to the servants of the king who had demanded the aforesaid service from them, so they would be quit from the said service. They have fallen into performing that service for 2 years.

382. Guillaume des Loges, squire, of the parish of Aubigny, complains that at the time of the conquest of Normandy, King Philip, of illustrious memory acquired land, worth 18l. a year and lying in the parishes of Martigny, Pierrepont, Tassilly,

and Les Loges-Saulces, which Guillaume, called "the Blockhead," the knight, had wrested from his father. [The king received the said land] with all the land of the aforesaid knight, who, on account of his forfeiture by going to England and not coming to the king's peace, had given up his land. And it now remains in the hands of the present king. And although [Guillaume des Loges] works the land for the lord king and has the homage of the men, he is still not able to recover the aforesaid rents. And his mother, by inquiry, has a third portion from the said land in dower, which goes to the king after her death.

385. Leceline, widow of G. Ferant, and Guillaume, her son, of the parish of Saint-Loup-Canivet, complain that they are not able to recover 4 acres of land, lying next to a certain field, which they hold from the lord king, and which the lord king gave 8 years ago to the aforesaid Leceline to hold for herself and her heirs in return for 20s. to be paid annually for the said acres and the said field. And Girard de La Boiste was commanded to transfer the property to her, but he refused even though Jean de Vignes had commanded him to do it.

388. Giroth *de Treperel*, of the parish of Martigny, complains that Girard de La Boiste acquired for the lord king 1 acre of land that Morel [de Falaise] the Jew had purchased in his fief during the life of his father [but] without the assent and permission of the said father. Giroth is not able to recover [the land] for the price that the Jew had given for the land.

390. Robert Hultauth, of Bernieres-sur-Dive, complains that about 15 years ago Jean de Vignes wrested from his father and received for the lord king a certain piece of land, lying in the aforesaid parish and worth 11 quarts of barley at the measure of Saint-Pierre-sur-Dive, because a certain brother, a clerk, of the said father had died in England before the aforesaid time, where he had been staying because he had an ecclesiastical benefice there.

391. Heudeart, widow of Michel *de Bohon*, of the same parish, complains that her husband died in the service of the lord king 5 years ago at Saint-Jean-d'Angely in Acquitaine. He died before payment was made to the king's workers, for which reason he was not able to have 40s., which were owed to him from his wages. And therefore she seeks that they be given to her.

392. Matthieu de Bu, of the parish of Sainte-Trinité-de-Falaise, complains that 22 years ago Jean le Guerrier acquired for the lord king 7 acres of land, lying in the parish of Saint-Pierre-du-Bu and 1 acre of wood also found in the same parish, [the whole] worth 7 measures of barley. Matthew was supposed to receive the land after the death of his nephew, who was the son of an illegitimate sister, as he says. And let it be known that the said Jean received the said land because Matthew was born from a legitimate union, but his sister was born out of the fornication of concubinage. But Matthew seeks the land because his nephew was born from a legitimate marriage. Jean [also] wrested land worth 1 measure of oats and 1 goose from his wife's father, asserting that a certain brother of his had died in England; nor was an investigation [by jury], which [Matthew] sought, made about this. The land lies in the parish of Saint-Pierre-du-Bu, nor is there another heir except his wife.

393. Pierre le Peletier of Saint-Philbert-sur-Orne complains that Jean de Vignes acquired for the lord king 1 acre of garden, lying in the parish of Saint-Philbert-sur-Orne and worth 20s. annually, which Enguerrand de Saint-Philbert-sur-Orne, a knight, had wrested from [Pierre]. All of Enguerrand's land along with the said garden returned to the king because Enguerrand did not wish to appear before the justice of the king. [The king] gave the garden to Simon le Cornu, castellan of Falaise, in whose hand it is held. And likewise, the lord king gave another garden, worth 30s. annually, which the said Enguerrand had wrested from Pierre's brother, to the same castellan, and [Pierre] seeks on behalf of Raoul, son of Ami and W., his brother, and his three other brothers, and his nephews, that it be returned to them.

394. Robert Tison and Hugues, his brother, of Damblainville, complain that the revenue farmers of the lord king, out of greed, acquired for the lord

king 3 virgates of land lying in the aforesaid parish and worth 1 quart of oats yearly, and they are now retained in the possession of the lord king; for [the revenue farmers] arranged for an oath to be made [concerning the royal] demesne, without the viscount[3] or *bailli*, they being absent and uninformed.

395. Nicholas, rector of the church of Ussy, and Jean de Soulangy, priest, and Hugues, called "the Englishman," a clerk of the lord king, complain for themselves and for all parsons and vicars of the churches of the deanery of Aubigny, saying that the *prévôts*[4] of Falaise exact a duty from them on those things, pertaining to [their] livelihood, which they buy for their own use—if they exceed the price of 5 pennies; briefly, on all the things that they purchase for their use and the use of their churches, just as from lay dues payers, so they say. The dean of Falaise and Thomas of Morteaux-Couliboeuf, a priest, make a similar complaint for all the priests of the aforesaid deanery.

396. Robert l'Ardant, of Crocy, complains that Jean le Guerrier acquired for the king land valued at 15s. per year lying in the aforesaid parish [Aubigny], which was supposed to come into his wife's possession by hereditary right and to a certain blood relative of hers by the name of Erremborch, wife of Auberic le Brun. And he took the land 22 years ago, after the death of Renaud Bordon, because a certain son of the said Renaud, 6 years before the death of his father, went to England as a pilgrim and there, after 2 years, entered the Cistercian order.

399. W. d'Olendon complains that Guillaume le Cras (the "Blockhead"), in the year before he left for England during the conquest of Normandy, seized by his brute force a *vavassoria*[5] of land, containing about 30 acres, which Robert d'Olendon used to hold from [Le Cras]. And there was no fault or forfeiture on the part of the said Robert, whose closest heir the said W. says he is; but the lord king retained the said land from that time and still keeps it, with other lands and rents of the

said Guillaume le Cras.

402. Jean Sapience, of Evesqueville, complains that the king retains in his possession a certain piece of land at Evesqueville, worth 1 quart of oats valued at 2s., which he and the ancestors of his line had possessed 10 years ago, and up to this time he pays the rent of the said land with all his other lands, although a certain man from the said village received it from the revenue farmers of the king because Jean did not cultivate it.

403. Guillaume de Falaise, of Saint-Pierre-Canivet, complains that Pierre du Thillai, *bailli* of the lord king disseized him of a certain rent, which he used to collect for 15 years in the *prévôté* of Falaise, for the guard of the gate of the castle of Falaise. Renaud de Ville-Thierri had given the rent to him by the command of the lord king Louis. Nor did [Pierre] command that the said money that he was supposed to collect in the said *prévôté* be returned to him—for each year he would have had 61s. and would have them till now, as he says—as a result of which he was injured to the value of 45l. and 15s. And John, king of England, when he farmed the castle, did not render to him 21l. of annual rent, which he was supposed to have from the site of the said castle of Falaise, nor did he give anything in exchange for it, because at the time he was supposed to make an exchange for it, [John] lost the land of Normandy. [Guillaume] was not able to recover anything later from any king of France for the said rent, which he used to collect at the site of the moat-battlements of the castle.

404. Jean *de Mool*, knight, of Barberry, of the diocese of Bayeux, complains that at the time of the conquest of Normandy, a certain man who was holding a *vavassoria* from his father went to England. On account of which he lost the land and it fell into the king's possession, and at that time the said father was not able to obtain the services owed from the aforesaid *vavassoria*, such as the reliefs, the [military] services, the pleas, and the three aids of Normandy. The said Jean, after

---

3   A royal official immediately subordinate to the *baillis* with important duties in supervising commerce and routine judicial work.
4   Subordinate royal officials, with duties roughly equivalent to the viscounts, who were usually active in urban areas.
5   The amount of land comprising a subordinate type of fief and not carrying the full spectrum of feudal obligations.

the death of his father, is till now not able to recover the said *vavassoria*—which lies in the parish of Fourches near Vignats—from the prioress of Parthenon Sainte-Marguerite de Vignats, of the diocese of Séez, to whom the lord king had given it, as a result of which, he and his father had been injured to the value of 10l.

407. Robert Guillaume, of the parish of Morteaux-Couliboeuf, complains that the lord king at the time of the conquest of Normandy acquired 15 acres of land that the father of his wife had handed over, as a result of coercion and violence, to Guillaume le Cras, to whom [the father] used to make an annual payment because he held it from [him] in fief. The acres lie in the parish of Saint-Loup-Canivet and are worth annually more than the rent that the said father used to pay, to the value of 60s.

409. Raoul Garnier and Pierre *de Ponte Oilleii*, Jean his brother, a cleric, and their mother, the widow of Jean *de Ponte Oilleii*, and Bienvenue, widow of Pierre le Petit, *de Ponte Oilleii*, and his four sons and a certain daughter of his complain that Jean de Vignes threw Raoul, and the said Jean and Pierre [Le Petit], now dead, into prison because Pierre *de Ponte Oilleii* had said that they had had him arrested by Richard Suarth, a knight, (the castellan of Caen, at the time of the war in Brittany), and he was prepared to prove this. And they were not able to get out of prison until they had promised to pay the lord king 1800l. *tournois*, which they did and afterward were freed from the prison. And of the 1800l., the said Raoul paid 600l., Jean, 900l., and Pierre le Petit, 300l. And although the ones noted above who had been put in prison had sought an investigation [by jury] about this, they were not able to procure it.

411. Agnes *de Veilleio*, of Falaise, complains that King Philip, of illustrious memory, 2 years after the conquest of Normandy acquired possession of 2 plots, worth 48s. annually, and there fortified the castle of Falaise with moat-battlements and other structures; nor did he exchange [anything for them] with her, although the said plots had been given to her as a marriage portion.

414. Robert Ansere, of Sainte-Marguerite-de-Viette, of the diocese of Lisieux, complains that 22 years ago Renaud de Ville-Thierri acquired for the lord king a certain virgate of land lying in the parish of Bretteville-sur-Laize near Saint-Pierre-sur-Dive and worth 10s. annually to the lord king, on account of the poverty and helplessness of the said Robert. And the lord king was in no way injured by this, since he only paid 3s. for that [land], so [Robert] says, and 2 hens.

415. Acelin le Telier, of the parish of Aubigny, complains that 28 years ago, Pierre du Thillai took his son, W. Acelini into the king's hand, on account of land lying in the aforesaid parish and worth to the lord king 5 bushels of barley at the Falaise measure to the lord king. Pierre claimed that a certain cousin of [Acelin's], whose land it had been, had gone into Poitou against the king, but [in fact] before he had left his province to set out for Poitou, the said cousin had sold the land to Acelin, so he says.

416. Raoul *de Cantepie* and Pierre, his brother, of Beaumais, complain that 40 years ago, Jean le Guerrier acquired for the king 20 acres of land and 1 fishpond, lying in the aforesaid parish and worth 40s. per year to the king, by asserting that their father owed one-third of 18l. to Morel [de Falaise] the Jew. However, King Philip, of illustrious memory, had quit him of that third part and had returned to him that land which he had handed over to Morellus in pledge, so they say.

417. Raoul *de Fago*, of the parish of Sainte-Trinité-de-Falaise, complains that Richard Clerc, a revenue farmer of the king, acquired for the said lord king 7 acres of land lying in the parish of Le Mesnil-Hermier and worth 5s. annually to the lord king—[land] which his father had granted in fief to a certain female blood relative of his for 2s.—because the said Raoul was not in the country, but on pilgrimage when the said relative died; and he might have had the said land if Jean de Vignes, who was conducting an investigation into this matter through his viscount, had not died so quickly. And the land was kept in the hand of the lord king about 9 years.

419. Jeanne la Porcelle, of the parish of Saint-Gervais-de-Falaise, complains that King Philip, of illustrious memory, caused her orchard to be destroyed 40 years ago when he had a large tower made at the castle of Falaise, and he did not offer anything to her or to her husband in exchange, and it was worth a full 12s. each year.

420. Andre *de Plessiaco*, of the parish of Sainte-Trinité-de-Falaise, complains that King Philip took into his own hand 2 plots, lying in the aforesaid parish and worth 32s. annually, when he constructed the moat-battlement next to the "Aaliz" gate of the castle of Falaise 42 years ago. [The land] had been given as a marriage portion to Bienvenue, his wife, and he had nothing in exchange for them, so he says.

421. Robert Caffrei, of Olendon, complains that 6 years ago, Girard de La Boiste took in the lord king's hand a certain *vavassoria* lying in the aforesaid parish and worth 10s. annually to [Robert], after the death of a certain man who was holding the said *vavassoria* from him [Robert]—because the son of that man had acknowledged the lordship of the king after the death of [his] father; however, through an investigation [by jury] made about this it was discovered that the said *vavassoria* should have been held from the said Robert. And the said Girard had [collected] for the relief, 32s., for the aid of the host, 13s., and 10s. from [Robert] for bailing himself out of jail—in which [Girard] had put him for claiming the said *vavassoria*.

423. Guillaume Martin, cleric, Guillaume de Villeray, Geoffroy *de Hamello*, Nicolas Chaperon, Roger Tustain, and Elnaud *de Fonte*, of Beaumais, complain that the revenue farmers of the lord king refuse to help them pay the 36s. of aid for the host, which they were accustomed to pay for the demesne of the king. And they make the complaint for themselves and for their fellows. For the revenue farmers have not paid the said money for 3 years, although they [Guillaume Martin and company] have paid the aid for the host each year.

425. Nicolas *de Hamello*, of Cordey, Guillaume Fuchier, [and] Guillaume Eemelench complain on behalf of the entire parish, saying that they were accustomed to have a certain quittance, such that they did not pay the duty in Falaise on either wood or fields, for 1 penny, which each bordar of those [aforesaid] men used to pay to the *prévôt* of Falaise annually at the Circumcision of the Lord. Nevertheless, for the past 9 years the duty on forests and fields is demanded from them, although they are quit from the said rent.

430. Hugues le Boeuf, of Olendon, and Guillaume *de Long Prato*, of Aubigny, complain that King Philip, of illustrious memory, acquired possession of land lying in the parish of Soulangy—namely 3 acres of land worth 4 measures of barley a year to the king—which had belonged to the father of Hugues' wife and the father of the said Guillaume [*de Long Prato*], and which Guillaume le Cras had wrested from the said fathers. [Philip acquired] all the land of the aforesaid knight [Guillaume le Cras] on account of his forfeit. [Guillaume le Cras] had wrested the said land from the fathers, when a certain bastard brother of theirs gave [him] the portion [this brother] used to have in that land. But since he was a bastard, he was supposed to have no part of that land. It was received into the king's hand at the time of the conquest of Normandy, so they say.

432. W. Sibille de Soulangy, complains about 7-½ acres of land, which is found in the parish of Saint-Loup-Canivet and is worth 7 measures (*sextarii*) and 1 measure (*mina*) of oats at the Falaise measure to the lord king. Guillaume, called "the Blockhead," had wrested [the land] from his [W.'s] wife's father, accusing him of poorly caring for his pigs, because they died; when he had, in fact, taken good care of them. At the conquest of Normandy, King Philip, of illustrious memory, took possession of all the land of the aforesaid knight [Guillaume].

436. Guillaume *de Cerez*, Robert Guiart and Guillaume de Breuil, of Bellou-en-Houlme, complain on behalf of the whole parish that the Lady of La Ferté, at the time when King Philip, of illustrious memory, fought at the bridge of Bouvines, exacted from them payment for the right to pasture—worth 60s. annually to the lord

king—which they had never paid and yet had had the right to pasture their flocks. After the death of the said lady, whose land came into the king's possession two years after the said battle, the revenue farmers of the lord king demanded the said payment for pasturage from the same men. And for 22 years, they have not had the full pasturage because, since the aforesaid time, the revenue farmers of the lord king had put the land in which they used to have pasturage partially under cultivation. Nor however did they reduce the rent of pasturage; and the revenue farmers demand from the men each year 13s. and 4d. as a payment of wethers, but they still do not receive the dead wood that they used to have in the forest of Bellou in return for the payment, which they used to pay to the Lord of Ferté, whose land came to the king completely after the death of the aforesaid lady. And they demand from the men a dry multure [duty] worth 40s. annually in case the mills stop on account of the failure of water or anything else. But they are not responsible for the repair of the mills because the *seneschals* of the said Lord of Ferté imposed on them such a milling due without the knowledge of the lord, who then was staying in England, nor did he come to the king's peace at the time of the conquest of Normandy, for which reason his land went to the king's hand.

437. Pierre *de Hamello*, and Guillaume, his brother, of Bellou-en-Houlme, complain concerning a certain piece of land, which their mother had gained in the court of the lord king through a jury of the country. After the death of the mother, revenue farmers of the lord king, 22 years ago, wrested away 10 acres from them, which they then placed in the possession of the lord king. And the said acres are found in the aforesaid parish and are worth 10s. annually to the lord king. [The acres] were placed under the hand of the lord king on account of the default of the said brothers.

439. Sybil, widow of Enguerrand de Saint-Philbert-sur-Orne, the knight, complains that Jean de Vignes, at the time of the war at Saint-James-de-Beuvron, had claimed that her husband had harbored the enemies of the king [and] that he was

aware of the capture of Pierre *de Ponte*, mayor of Falaise, whom Richard Suarth, brother of the said Sybil, had taken. He [Enguerrand] sought an investigation [by jury] about this through the abbot *de Fonteneto* and through many others, but was not able to procure one: for Enguerrand did not dare to appear before him [Jean] lest he be imprisoned, because he was old, infirm and ill; and because he did not appear, his land was taken into the king's possession, and the lord king then gave [it] to Simon le Cornu, the castellan of Falaise, for an annual rent of 31l. and 8s., which the same Simon holds till now because the said Enguerrand, not daring to appear, as was said above, went to England and there he died. Thus, the said Sybil petitions the king, if it should so please him, to act compassionately and benignly to her sons, the children of the said Enguerrand.

442. Robert Guiart, of Bellou-en-Houlme, complains that the revenue farmers of the lord king, 25 years ago, exacted 36s. every year both from his father as well as from himself from 3 *vavassoriae*, which he holds from the lord king and which his ancestors held before him, for which the said ancestors made payment both to the Lord of La Ferté and to King Philip amounting to 18s. for three mounted sergeants;[6] and they complain that King Philip acquired at the time of the conquest of Normandy 1-½ acres of field, which the Lord of La Ferté—by the oath of three men whom he made swear to his lordship, although a fourth did not agree with the others—had wrested from his father, together with the land of the aforesaid knight, and still he [Robert] pays the rent for the land to the lord king.

443. Thomas Faber, of Bellou-en-Houlme, complains that Bertrand de Fresnay, knight, and revenue farmer of the lord king has not rendered to him for the past 16 years his supply of firewood and coal for his forge, and his quittance, which he had concerning the forest of Bellou and the other forests of the Lord of La Ferté such that he would be allowed to pasture pigs in these woods; and regarding his duty to provide hospitality, he was quit from providing food if the said lord were

---

6   [?] Latin: *pro tribus servitiis equi.*

present in the aforesaid village of Bellou, on the condition that he would shoe all the lord's horses, as well as those of his knights, squires, and other servants. And nevertheless, [Bertrand] demanded from him that he shoe all of his horses and those of his servants since the time specified; as a result of which he was damaged for every year of the 16 years to the amount of 50s., since beyond the aforesaid rent he was supposed to have a squire's robe, which he [Bertrand] has not rendered to him since the aforesaid time, so he says.

445. The lepers of Moulin Seranz, of Saint-Andre-de-Messei, complain that the sergeants of the lord king acquired for the king 2 acres of land lying in the parish of Bellou-en-Houlme. They have been retained since the time of the conquest of Normandy despite the fact that they were seized of them at the time of said conquest, and they fell into the hand of the lord king on account of their helplessness and …

447. Hugues de Saint André, of Briouze-Saint-Gervais, complains [for the sons] of Richard de Plessiaco, namely Rob[ert] … that 21 years ago, the lord king retained in his hand land of the said Richard, worth 100s. annually to the lord king and lying in the aforesaid parish of Briouze-Saint-Gervais, because Renaud de Ville-Thierri, by the act of certain knights, had the said Richard hanged unjustly, on the charge of theft. He was not found in possession of anything nor has Hugues been able to secure an investigation by a jury, which he was seeking.

450. Guillaume, called "the king," of Les Rotours, complains that about 35 years ago, Pierre du Thilai acquired for the king the land of a certain man, who used to render annually to his father 5s., which he has not been able to recover since from the said Pierre or from any other *baillis*, and the land remains in the hand of the king.

451. Robert, called "the Strong," of Écouché, a cleric, complains that 4 years ago, Jean de Vignes caused a millstream to be made through the field of the said Robert for the king's mill, which is called the "Choisel," at Tanquiez. He promised to make an exchange [with regard to] the said field,

which he did not do; whence he reckons to have been damaged to the amount of 30s. annual rent for the aforesaid millstream of the king.

452. Richard Corneth and two of his brothers, of Falaise, complain that 10 years after the conquest, Pierre du Thillai acquired for the king land, worth approximately 7l. *tournois* annually to the king and lying in the parish of Aubigny, which their father had handed over in pledge to Guillaume le Cras, and which King Philip, of illustrious memory, returned to the said brothers after the conquest of Normandy. Pierre du Thillai claimed that the said land had not been given in pledge to Guillaume but had been sold; nevertheless, it was discovered through an investigation [by jury] that it had been pledged, so they say.

453. Jean L'esveille, of Briouze-Saint-Gervais, complains that Raoul le Cordoanier, who 30 years ago was a revenue farmer of the lord king in Briouze-Saint-Gervais, imposed on his fief 10s. of annual rent, which his ancestors had never paid before and Robert *de Poteria*, a knight, who was the revenue farmer 10 years ago, imposed another 10s. on the same fief. Jean himself and his brother have paid the 20s., unjustly, to other revenue farmers from then on.

455. Gautier, son of Guillaume, called "the Old Man," of Ifs-sur-Laizon, complains that King Philip acquired a certain house and 3 acres of land lying in the said parish—and worth 6s. annually and 3 measures of oats at the Falaise measure—which Guillaume le Cras had wrested from his father before the conquest of Normandy on account of the father's helplessness. King Philip took the land at the time of the conquest along with the land of the said knight [Guillaume le Cras], because he did not wish to come to the lord king's peace.

456. Guillaume Poucin, of Saint Ouen, complains that 20 years ago Jean de La Porte acquired for the lord king land belonging to his man, lying in the said parish, and in which he used to collect annually 5s. and services worth another 5s. Jean claimed that the said man, who died without heirs, had died in England, but no investigation

[by jury] was begun into this matter, and the said Guillaume was not able to recover the rent from the sergeants of the lord king since the aforesaid time.

457. Richard Gronneit, of the parish of Sainte-Trinité-de-Falaise, complains that before the conquest of Normandy, John, king of England, took the land of his father—worth 100s. annually to him—so that he could build the moat-battlements of the castle of Falaise on it, for which he did not give him anything in return, because at the time he was supposed to make restitution, he lost the land of Normandy, nor did the father have any recompense from any king of France, nor he himself after the death of his father.

458. Robert Louvel, of Bellou-en-Houlme, complains that about 14 years ago, Elnaud le Flamench acquired for the king 3 virgates of land, which lie in the aforesaid parish next to the woods of the lord king, because the said woods had overgrown that land; before the seizure, he [Robert] used to take his firewood from that land, which he has not been able to recover since the aforesaid time.

461. Guillaume le Batard and Hugues *de Fonte* and Jean *de Capella*, of Habloville, complain for themselves and their fellows, saying that Jean de Vignes and Girard de La Boiste forced them to rebuild the mill of Habloville, which they were not responsible to repair, for they had never done it before in the time of the lord and lady of Ferté, from whom the mill had come into the possession of the lord king; by which they were injured to the amount of 9l. Nor did the said Jean, 3 years ago, wish to have an investigation [by jury] made about this matter although he had received a command from the court of the lord king that he should do so, so they say.

462. Alexander le Testu and Richard le Testu, of Ifs-sur-Laizon, complain that 15 acres of land lying in the aforesaid parish, which Guillaume le Cras had wrested from their fathers by his own power, were taken by King Philip, of illustrious memory, with the land of the aforesaid knight [Guillaume le Cras] at the time of the conquest of Normandy because he did not come to [the king's] peace; and afterwards those lands were given as a gift of the lord king to Simon le Cornu, who is now the castellan of Falaise; and they are worth annually 7-½ measures of oats at the Falaise measure, and 7s., 2 capons, 1 hen, 30 eggs, and 12d. Still the said fathers, who used to hold the land in fief from the said Guillaume, only made payment of 4s., 3 capons, and 30 eggs.

464. Baudouin *de Montibus*, a knight, complains that when compelled, he had gone to the Albigensian regions in the king's pay, [but] the clerks who were responsible for paying out on behalf of the king had kept out from his wages 100s., because of the debt that Thomas *de Colunchis*, a knight, owed to them. Baudouin was not of his retinue, nor did he act as pledge on Thomas' behalf, nor was he present at the lending or at the receiving of the aforesaid debt 4 years ago when Lord Imbert de Beaujeu, right after Jean de Beaumont, left for the aforesaid regions.

465. The abbot and convent of Silli-en-Gouffern complain that the king exacts the *tiers*[7] from the sale of [wood from] the forests of Blanefosse in the parishes of Saint-Martin-sur-Vivre and of Belhotel. [The abbey] used to sell [this wood] without the said *tiers* at the time of King Philip, of illustrious memory, and at the time of the father, of illustrious memory, of [the present] king. In addition, they seek the patronage of the church of Marigny, which Nicolas *de Sancto Lothario*, a clerk, had granted to them, and which Jean de La Porte acquired for the lord king; for through an investigation [by jury] made about the said patronage, he [Jean] found out that the lord of Marigny had presented the last [parson]; yet he did not wish to inquire nor hear from the jurors how the said lord had presented the said parson. But if he had done it, they would have acquired the said patronage, since the said clerk had received the patronage in the court of the lord king against the [claim of the] the aforesaid lord, after the presentation of the last parson.

---

7   A payment made to the King by landowners for the privilege of selling timber from their own forests.

49. JEAN FROISSART

Chronicles

JEAN FROISSART (1337–CA. 1410) is the principal chronicler of the first phase of the series of campaigns between England and France known as the Hundred Years' War. Froissart served in the entourage of Edward III, in the household of the counts of Flanders, Wenceslas of Bohemia, the count of Blois, and others. For the earlier parts of his *Chronicle* he depended on the writings of Jean Le Bel, who had been a participant in much of the early fighting. Most of his later material was collected orally, by being present at important events, and by talking with principal participants on both sides.

The following selections describe the Campaign of Crécy (1356) and the near anarchy in the aftermath of the capture of the French king John II at Poitiers in 1356, which included the communal revolt of Étienne Marcel and the peasant uprising known as the Jacquerie.

Source: Geoffrey Brereton, *Froissart: Chronicles* (Harmondsworth: Penguin, 1968).

Further Reading: Peter F. Ainsworth, *Jean Froissart and the Fabric of History: Truth, Myth, and Fiction in the Chroniques* (Oxford: Clarendon Press, 1990).

The Campaign of Crécy (1346)

Edward formally terminates the truce with Philip, alleging French violations. He sends one of his commanders, Thomas Dagworth, to Brittany, where the local struggle is still raging. At the request of the pro-English Gascon nobles, he sends a larger force to Bordeaux, under Henry of Derby, to repel French encroachments in Aquitaine. (The duchy had already been declared confiscate by Philip VI, after Edward's retraction of his homage.) Derby is at first highly successful, but in 1346 a powerful French army under the duke of Normandy wipes out many of his gains and lays siege to the English-held castle of Aiguillon.

Froissart's statement that Edward's campaign in northern France which followed, and led to Crécy and the acquisition of Calais, was originally planned as a relief expedition to Gascony, is not discounted by responsible historians and has documentary support (Rymer, Foedera).

When the king of England heard how hard pressed his men were in the castle of Aiguillon and learnt that his cousin, the earl of Derby, who was at Bordeaux, was not strong enough to take the field and raise the siege, he decided to assemble a large army and lead it to Gascony. He gave orders for full preparations to be made, mobilized men from his own kingdom and engaged mercenaries in other countries where they could be found.

At that time Sir Godfrey of Harcourt, having been banished from France, arrived in England. He went straight to the king and queen, who were than at Chertsey, a town on the Thames some fifteen miles from London. He was received with open arms and was immediately made a member of the king's household and council. A large estate was assigned to him in England to enable him to maintain himself and his followers on a lavish scale. Soon after this the king completed the first stage of his preparations. A large fleet was brought together in Southampton harbor, and all kinds of men-at-arms and archers were assembled there.

At about midsummer 1346 the king took leave of the queen, whom he left in the care of his cousin, the earl of Kent. He appointed Lord Percy and Lord Neville to be guardians of his kingdom together with four prelates, the archbishops of Canterbury and York and the bishops of Lincoln and Durham. He left sufficient forces in England to defend it if need be, then rode down to Southampton to wait for a favorable wind. When it came, he boarded his ship, as did his son the

Prince of Wales, Sir Godfrey of Harcourt, and the other lords, earls and barons, according to the order of embarkment. There must have been four thousand men-at-arms and ten thousand archers, without counting the Irish and Welsh who followed his army on foot....

They set sail in accordance with the will of God, the wind and the sailors, and made a good start towards Gascony, where the King intended to go. But on the third day the wind changed and drove them back to the coasts of Cornwall, where they lay at anchor for six days. At this point the king held a new council at the suggestion of Sir Godfrey, whose advice was that it would be a better venture to make a landing in Normandy. "Normandy," said Sir Godfrey, "is one of the richest countries in the world. I promise you, on my life, that once you reach it, it will be easy to land there. There will be no serious resistance, for the inhabitants have no experience of arms and the whole cream of the Norman knights are at the siege of Aiguillon with the duke. You will find large towns and fortresses completely undefended, in which your men will win enough wealth to make them rich for twenty years to come. Your fleet will be able to follow you almost as far as Caen. If you see fit to take my advice, you and all of us will profit by it. We shall have gold, silver, food supplies and everything else in abundance."

The king of England, who was then in his prime and desired nothing better than to meet the enemy and see action, readily agreed with Sir Godfrey, whom he called his cousin. He ordered his seamen to change course for Normandy and, taking the admiral's flag from the earl of Warwick, made himself admiral and led the fleet for that voyage. With the wind now in their favor, they sailed to the port of La Hogue in the Cotentin Peninsula. The news that the English had arrived soon spread and the townships of Cotentin sent messengers at all speed to the king of France in Paris. King Philip already knew that the English king had been assembling a large army and that his fleet had been seen passing the coasts of Normandy and Brittany, but it was not known where he was making for. So as soon as he received the news of the landing in Normandy, he summoned his commander-in-chief, the count of Guines, and the count of Tancarville, who

had both recently arrived from Gascony, and ordered them to go to Caen to be ready to defend the town and its approaches against the English. They promised to do their utmost and set out from Paris accompanied by a large force of men-at-arms, whose ranks were constantly swollen by new arrivals. Reaching Caen, they were greeted with joy by the citizens and the people from the surrounding country who had taken refuge there. They began to put the town in a state of defense (it was not walled at that period) and to see that the inhabitants were armed and equipped each according to his standing.

To return to the English fleet which had entered La Hogue: when it was drawn up and anchored on the shore, the king came off his ship. But as his foot touched the ground, he stumbled and fell so heavily that the blood gushed from his nose. The knights who were round him took this for a bad omen and begged him to go back on board for that day. "Why?" retorted the King without hesitation. "It's a very good sign for me. It shows that this land is longing to embrace me." They were all greatly cheered by this answer. So the King encamped on the beach for that day and night and the whole of the next.

Meanwhile the horses were unloaded from the ships with all their gear and a council was held to decide how they should proceed. The king appointed Sir Godfrey of Harcourt and the earl of Warwick to be marshals of the army, with the earl of Arundel as commander-in-chief. The earl of Huntingdon was directed to remain with the fleet with a hundred men-at-arms and four hundred archers. At a second council they decided their order of march. The men were divided into three columns, one to take the right flank and follow the coast, another the left, while the third marched in the center under the king and the Prince of Wales. Each night the flanking columns led by the two marshals were to join up again with the king.

Following this plan, the English army began its advance. The fleet sailed along the coast, seizing every vessel, large or small, that they fell in with. Archers and foot-soldiers marched near them within sight of the sea, robbing, pillaging and carrying off everything they came across. They moved forward by land and sea until they reached Barfleur, a seaport and fortified town which they took immediately because the inhabitants surrendered in the hope of saving their lives, though this did not prevent the town from being emptied of its gold, silver and jewelry. They found so much of it there that the very servants in the army turned up their noses at fur-lined gowns. All the men in the town were taken and put on board the ships so that there should be no danger of their rallying afterwards and harassing them in the rear.

After capturing and plundering Barfleur, though without burning it, they spread out over the country, though they still kept near the coast. They did whatever they pleased, for no one resisted them. They came in time to a large wealthy town and port called Cherbourg. They sacked and burnt part of it, but found the citadel too strongly defended to be taken, so they went on towards Montbourg and Valogne. This last they sacked completely and then set fire to it. They did the same to a number of other towns in the region, taking so much valuable booty that it would have been an impossible task to count it.

Continuing from Valogne, the earl of Warwick's column takes and sacks the fortified town of Carentan. The other two columns meet with similar success, amassing huge quantities of plunder in the form of household possessions and the livestock in which Normandy abounds.

So was the good, fat land of Normandy ravaged and burnt, plundered and pillaged by the English, until news of the havoc they were wreaking reached the king of France in Paris. When he heard of it, King Philip swore that they should not go home without being brought to battle and made to pay dearly for the misery and destruction they were inflicting on his subjects. He immediately caused a number of letters to be written. The first were to his friends in the empire because they were the most distant from him: to the good king of Bohemia, who was very dear to him, and also to his son Charles of Bohemia, who at that time styled himself king of Germany, and by general consent was its king thanks to the influence and support of his father and of the king of France. Indeed, he had already assumed the arms of the empire.

King Philip urgently requested them to join him with all their available forces in the campaign he was preparing against the English who were ravaging his country. They made no excuses, but assembled men from Germany, Bohemia and Luxemburg and came to France in strength to aid its king. The latter also wrote to the duke of Lorraine, who brought more than four hundred lances to serve him. The count of Salm, the count of Saarbrück, the count of Flanders and count William of Namur came also, each with a very handsome company. King Philip sent another letter with a special summons to Sir John of Hainault[1] who had recently become his ally through the influence of his son-in-law, Count Louis of Blois, and of the lord of Fagnolle. Sir John responded by bringing a large and splendidly equipped force of good knights from Hainault and elsewhere. His arrival so delighted the king that he attached him to his personal service and made him a member of his inner council. In this way the king of France summoned fighting men from every possible quarter and assembled one of the largest forces of great lords, dukes, counts, barons and knights that had been seen in France for a hundred years. But he had to bring them from such distant countries that it took a long time to collect them; and meanwhile the king of England had devastated the whole region of Cotentin and Normandy.

The tale of plunder continues. The inhabitants, who have never experienced war, flee at the mere mention of the English, leaving their houses and barns filled with provisions for the taking. The army find an abundance of everything they need except wine, and there are reasonable stocks even of that. They capture Saint-Lô, where they acquire such quantities of cloth that "they would have let it go cheap if they had had anyone to sell it to."

When the king of England and his men had done as they pleased with the town of Saint-Lô, they marched on towards Caen, which was three times larger and full of wealth in the form of cloth and other goods, with rich citizens, noble ladies and very fine churches. In particular, there are two big

---

1   The same man who had assisted Queen Isabella and the young Edward III in 1326–27.

and extremely wealthy abbeys, that of St. Stephen and that of the Trinity, situated at either end of the town. One of them housed a hundred and twenty nuns, all fully endowed. Besides this, one of the strongest and finest castles in Normandy lies on one side of the town. Its captain at that time was a gallant Norman knight called Sir Robert de Wargnies, commanding a garrison of three hundred Genoese.

In the town itself were the count of Eu and Guines, constable of France, and the count of Tancarville with a large number of good fighting men. The king of England advanced cautiously towards them, ordered his columns to join up, and encamped that night in open country five miles from the town. His fleet kept constantly near him and came to a port called Ouistreham, some six miles from Caen on the River Orne, which flows through Caen. The constable of France and the other lords with him kept good watch over the town that night and were not over concerned about the English. The next morning they armed themselves, ordering their men and all the townspeople to do the same, and then held a council to decide their plan of action. The constable and the count of Tancarville wished to keep all their forces in the town to hold the gates, the bridge and the river, and to abandon the outskirts to the English because they were not fortified. It would be difficult enough to hold the main part of the town, since the river was its only line of defense.

The townspeople refused to agree and insisted on marching out to the fields to meet the English there, saying that they were numerous and strong enough to fight them. When the constable heard their decision, he replied: "So be it then, and God be with us. If you fight, I and my men will fight with you." They marched out of the town in good enough order at the beginning. They seemed ready to risk their lives courageously and to put up a good defense.

On that day the English rose very early and made ready to advance. The king heard mass before sunrise, then mounted his horse, as did his son the prince and Sir Godfrey of Harcourt, on whose advice the king largely relied. They moved forward in perfect order, with the marshals' banner-bearers in the van, until they came close to the town of Caen and its defenders. These were waiting drawn up in the fields, apparently in excellent shape. But

no sooner did the townsmen see the English advancing upon them in three solid, close-ordered divisions and catch sight of the banners and the innumerable pennons waving and fluttering in the wind and hear the shouting of the archers—all things of which they had had no previous experience—than they were so filled with dismay that nothing in the world could have stopped them taking to their heels. They turned and fled in confusion, in spite of everything the constable could do. In a few moments their whole order of battle had broken up and they were rushing in terror to reach the safety of the town. Many of them stumbled and fell in the struggle to escape, while others piled on top of them in their panic.

The constable and the count of Tancarville with a few knights reached a gate at the entry to the bridge in safety. Since their men had broken, they could see that the battle was already lost. The English were now among them, killing as they liked without mercy. A few knights and squires and others who knew the way managed to reach the castle, where they were admitted by Sir Robert de Wargnies, who had plenty of room and provisions. There they were out of danger. Meanwhile the English, men-at-arms and archers, were continuing the slaughter of the fugitives, sparing none. Looking out from the gate-tower where they had taken refuge and seeing the truly horrible carnage which was taking place in the street, the constable and the count began to fear that they themselves might be drawn into it and fall into the hands of archers who did not know who they were. While they were watching the massacre in dismay, they caught sight of a gallant English knight with only one eye, called Sir Thomas Holland, and five or six other knights with him. They recognized him because they had campaigned together in Granada and Prussia and on other expeditions, in the way in which knights do meet each other. They were much relieved when they saw him and called out to him as he passed: "Sir Thomas, come and speak to us." On hearing his own name the knight stopped dead and asked: "Who are you, sirs, who seem to know me?" They gave their names, saying: "We are so-and-so. Come to us in this gate-tower and make us your prisoners."

When he heard this Sir Thomas was delighted, not only because he could save their lives but also because their capture meant an excellent day's work and a fine haul of valuable prisoners, enough to bring in a hundred thousand gold *moutons*. So he brought the whole of his troop to the spot as quickly as possible and went up with sixteen of his men into the gate-tower, where he found the lords who had called to him and at least twenty-five knights with them, all looking very uneasy at the slaughter they could see in the town. They surrendered immediately and pledged themselves to be Sir Thomas' prisoners. Leaving sufficient of his men to guard them, the knight rode on through the streets. He was able that day to prevent many cruel and horrible acts which would otherwise have been committed, thus giving proof of his kind and noble heart. Several gallant English knights who were with him also prevented a number of evil deeds and rescued many a pretty townswoman and many a nun from rape.

Fortunately for the English, the river which flows through Caen and which can float large ships was so low and sluggish that they could easily pass it without troubling about the bridge. In this way the king of England became master of Caen, though at a heavy price in men. For some of the inhabitants went up to the garrets overhanging the narrow streets and flung down stones and beams and masonry, killing and injuring several hundred of the English. The king was enraged when this was reported to him in the evening and gave orders for the whole population to be put to the sword on the next day and the town to be set on fire. Sir Godfrey of Harcourt forestalled this order by saying to him:

"Beloved sire, be a little less impetuous and content yourself with what you have done. You still have a long way to go before you reach Calais, as you intend. There are large numbers of people in this town who will defend themselves from house to house if they are attacked. To destroy the place might cost you dear and cripple your expedition. Remember that your enemy King Philip is certain to march against you in full strength and engage you, for good or ill, so there is still plenty of fighting before you, for which you will need all the forces you have and more. We can be masters of this town without further killing. Both men and women will be quite ready to give up everything they have to us."

Sir Godfrey sent his banner through all the streets and had it proclaimed, in the king's name, that none should dare, on pain of the gallows, to start a fire, kill a man or rape a woman.

This proclamation reassured the townspeople and they allowed some of the English into their homes, without attempting to harm them. Some opened their chests and strongboxes and gave up all they had, on condition that their lives were spared. But notwithstanding this and the orders of the king and the marshal, there were many ugly cases of murder and pillage, of arson and robbery, for in an army such as the king of England was leading it was impossible that there should not be plenty of bad characters and criminals without conscience.

For three days the English remained in possession of Caen, where they won an amazing quantity of wealth for themselves. They used the time to put their affairs in order and sent boats and barges laden with their gains—clothes, jewelry, gold and silver plate and many other valuable things—down the river to Ouistreham where their main fleet lay. They decided after long deliberation to send the fleet back to England with the booty and the prisoners. The earl of Huntingdon remained in command of it, with two hundred men-at-arms and four hundred archers. The king of England bought the count of Guines, constable of France, and the count of Tancarville from Sir Thomas Holland and his companions for twenty thousand nobles in cash.

So the king sent back his fleet full of conquered spoils and of good prisoners, including more than sixty knights and three hundred wealthy citizens, with a host of loving greetings to his wife, my lady Philippa, the gracious queen of England.

The English ravage the country west of the Seine, but without attacking the fortified places, "because the King wished to husband his men and artillery [i.e., siege-engines]." They follow the left bank of the river as far as Poissy, some twenty miles from the capital.

They found all the bridges over the Seine destroyed, so went on until they came to Poissy. Here the bridge had also been broken down, but the piles and cross-beams were still in the river. The king halted there for five days until the bridge had been rebuilt strongly enough for his army to cross with ease and safety. His marshals made forays nearly to Paris, burning Saint-Germain-en-Laye and La Montjoie, Saint-Cloud, Boulogne and Bourg-le-Reine. At this the people of Paris grew alarmed, for the city was not fortified at that time and they were afraid that the English would come right into it.

King Philip bestirred himself and had all the penthouses in Paris removed to make it easier for his men to ride through the streets. Then he prepared to leave for Saint-Denis, where the king of Bohemia, Sir John of Hainault, the duke of Lorraine, the counts of Flanders and Blois and many barons and knights were waiting.

When the people of Paris saw that their king was leaving, they were more alarmed than ever. They came and knelt before him, saying: "Beloved sire and noble king, what are you about to do? Will you abandon your good city of Paris in this way? The enemy are only five miles from us. When they hear that you have gone they will be here in an instant, and we shall have no one to defend us against them. Sire, we beg you to stay and help protect your loyal city."

The king answered: "My good people, you have nothing to fear. The English will come no nearer. I am going to Saint-Denis to be with my soldiers, for I mean to march against the English and fight them, whatever the outcome."

In this way the king of France calmed the people of Paris, who were in great fear of being attacked and destroyed, so suffering the same fate as Caen. But the king of England lodged in the Abbey of Poissy-les-Dames and held his solemn state on the Feast of the Assumption, in the middle of August. He sat at table in a sleeveless scarlet gown trimmed with ermine.

The English leave Poissy on August 16 and move rapidly north. They skirt Beauvais, burning the suburbs, and take several smaller places before they reach Vimeu, the district west of Amiens and Abbeville. King Philip is now in close pursuit with a much superior army. On his orders the bridges over the Somme have either been destroyed or are so strongly defended that the English probe in vain to find a way across. They are in danger of being hemmed in against the river. At this point in the narrative, the French are at Amiens and the English have just decamped from the neighboring town of Airaines to move to Oisemont, a few miles farther on. King Philip has sent a detachment under Sir Godemar du Fay to guard the last remaining crossing of the Somme, the ford of Blanchetaque, below Abbeville.

Having given these orders, King Philip, who was eager to come up with the English and engage them, left Amiens with his whole force. At about noon he reached Airaines, which the king of England had quitted in the early morning. The French found that large quantities of provisions had been left behind. There was meat on the spits, there were loaves and pies in the ovens, barrels and kegs of wine, and many tables ready laid, for the English had left in great haste.

At Airaines King Philip's advisers said to him: "Sire, you should halt here and wait for the rest of your army. It is certain now that the English cannot escape you." So the king took up his quarters in the town and, as the various lords arrived, they were lodged there also.

To return to the king of England, who was in the town of Oisemont and well aware that the king of France was following him in full strength thirsting for battle. He would have given much to be across the River Somme with his men. When his two marshals returned in the evening, after ranging the country as far as the gates of Abbeville and reaching Saint-Valery-sur-Somme, where there had been a sharp skirmish, he called together his council and, sending for some prisoners from Vimeu and Ponthieu, he said to them in a kindly voice:

"Do any of you know of a crossing—it must be below Abbeville—by which we and our army can pass safely? If anyone can guide us to it, we will set him free with twenty of his comrades."

There was a certain groom called Gobin Agace who knew the ford of La Blanchetaque as well as any man, having been born and bred near it and having crossed over it several times that year. This man came forward and said:

"Yes indeed, sire. I promise you on my life that I can take you to a place where you can cross quite safely. There are some shallows wide enough for twelve men to walk over abreast, with the water no higher than their knees. When the tide is in, the river is too deep to ford. But when it goes out, which happens twice a day, it is low enough to be crossed on horseback or on foot. That is the only place where it can be done, except by the bridge at Abbeville, but that is a fortified town with a strong garrison. The ford I am telling you about, my lord, has a firm bottom of white gravel which will bear the weight of carts. That is why it is called Blanchetaque."

When the king heard this, he was as pleased as if he had won a fortune, and he said: "Well, friend, if what you tell me proves to be true, I will set you free with all your comrades and give you a hundred gold nobles."

"On my life I swear it," said Gobin Agace. "But make your arrangements now to be on the bank before sunrise."

"Certainly," said the king. He gave orders for the whole army to be armed and ready to move on again at the sound of the trumpets.

He slept little that night, but rose at midnight and had the trumpeters sound the signal to strike camp. Soon everything was ready, the pack-horses loaded and the wagons filled. Leaving Oisemont at first light, they made such good progress guided by the groom that by sunrise they were near to the ford. But the tide was in and they could not cross, so the king was obliged to wait for the rest of his men to catch up with him. When the tide had gone out it was mid-morning and by that time Sir Godemar du Fay, the knight whom King Philip had sent to guard the crossing, had appeared with a large force on the opposite bank.

King Philip had given him a thousand men-at-arms and five thousand foot-soldiers, including the Genoese, and he had been joined on the way by large numbers of local men, so that they were at least twelve thousand strong when they drew up along the bank to dispute the crossing.

This brought no change to the king of England's plans. He ordered his marshals to strike at once into the water and his archers to shoot steadily at the French opposite. The two marshals of England sent their banner-bearers forward, in the name of God and St. George, and followed closely themselves. The bravest knights hurled their horses into the water, with the best mounted in the lead. There were many jousts in the river and many unhorsings on both sides, for Sir Godemar and his men defended the crossing bravely. A number of

his knights, with others from Artois and Picardy, had decided not to wait on the bank but to ride into the ford and fight there in order to win greater distinction. So there was, as I have said, many a joust and many a skilled piece of fighting, for the knights sent to defend the shallows were picked men who stood in good order at the neck of the crossing and clashed fiercely with the English as these came up out of the water. The Genoese also did much damage with their cross-bows, but the English archers shot so well together that it was an amazing sight to see. And while they were harassing the French, the mounted men got through.

When the English were finally across, though not without considerable losses, they spread out over the fields, with the king, the Prince of Wales and all their nobles. After this, the French order was broken and those who could get away from the ford made off like defeated men. Some went towards Abbeville, others towards Saint-Riquier. There was great slaughter among them because those on foot had no means of escape. The pursuit went on for more than three miles and many from Abbeville, Montreuil, Rue and Saint-Riquier were killed or captured. On the other hand, some of the English were attacked before they could get over the river by squires from the French army who had come out looking for a fight. These belonged in particular to the empire, to the king of Bohemia and to Sir John of Hainault. They captured some horses and equipment and killed or wounded a number in the English rear who were still trying to cross.

King Philip had left Airaines that morning and was riding rapidly forward when news was brought him of the English crossing and Sir Godemar's defeat. He was extremely angry, for he had been expecting to find the English on the bank of the Somme and fight them there. He halted in open country and asked his marshals what was the best thing to do. They replied: "Sire, you cannot cross the river yourself because the tide is in again now." So the king turned back in fury and took up his quarters in Abbeville with all his people.

When the English had scattered the enemy and cleared the ground, they formed up in excellent order, assembled their supply-train and moved off in their habitual way. Knowing that the Somme was behind them they were full of confidence. The king of England thanked and praised God many times that day for bringing him safely over the water and making him overcome his enemies in battle. He then sent for the groom who had guided him to the ford, set him free with all his comrades, and gave him a hundred gold nobles and a good horse. I do not know what became of him afterwards.

As the king and his army rode slowly and joyfully along, they thought of quartering for the night in the nearby town of Noyelle. But when they learnt that it belonged to the Countess of Aumale, the sister of the late Robert of Artois, they spared the town and the lady's lands for his sake—an act of friendship for which she thanked them warmly. The king halted instead in open country near La Broye, while the marshals made an incursion to Crotoy, on the coast, which they took and burnt to the ground. In the harbor they found a number of ships and barges laden with Poitou wines which belonged to merchants from Saintonge and La Rochelle. They quickly bought up the lot and the marshals had some of the best of them sent to the king's army encamped a few miles away.

Early the next day the king struck camp and moved towards Crécy in Ponthieu. The marshals led their forces on either side of him. One pushed forward as far as the gates of Abbeville, then turned away towards Saint-Riquier, burning and devastating the country. The other kept near the coast and reached the town of Rue. Then at noon on that Friday the three divisions joined up again and the whole army came to halt not far from Crécy.

Knowing that the king of France was close behind him and eager for battle, King Edward said to his men:

"I will take up my position here and go no further until I have a sight of the enemy. I have good reason to wait for him, for I am on the land I have lawfully inherited from my royal mother, which was given to her as her marriage portion. I am ready to defend my claim to it against my adversary Philip of Valois."

The king encamped in the open fields with his army and, since he was willing to risk the fortunes of battle with numbers which he knew were only an eighth of those of the king of France, he had to give urgent thought to his dispositions. He ordered his marshals, the earl of Warwick and Sir Godfrey of Harcourt, and with them that stout and gallant knight Sir Reginald Cobham, to consider the best place in which to draw up their forces. The three commanders rode round the fields and carefully studied the terrain to find the most advantageous position. Then they brought the king to it, with many others as well. Meanwhile, scouts had been sent out towards Abbeville, where they knew the king of France would cross the Somme, to discover if he was leaving that day to take the field. They reported that there was no sign of this.

So King Edward stood down his men for the day, with orders to assemble early next morning at the sound of the trumpets, in readiness to fight at once on the chosen positions. They all went to their quarters and busied themselves in checking and polishing their arms and armor.

The King of France spends the same day (Friday, August 25) in Abbeville, also preparing for battle. His scouts have reconnoitered the position of the English and reported that they are evidently waiting for him. He moves some troops out of the town in readiness to march the next day. In the evening he gives a supper for the principal nobles, at which they pledge themselves to behave as brothers-in-arms. King Edward also gives a supper for his commanders and then retires to his oratory. Froissart continues:

He knelt before his altar, devoutly praying God to grant that, if he fought the next day, he should come through the business with honor. He rose fairly early in the morning and heard mass with his son the Prince of Wales. They took communion and most of their men also confessed and put themselves in a state of grace.

The King then gave orders for every man to go to the positions decided upon the day before. Close to a wood in the rear he had a large park set up, in which all the wagons and carts were put. All the horses were led into this park, leaving every man-at-arms and archer on foot. The park had only one entrance.

He caused his constable and his marshals to divide the army into three bodies. In the first was his son the young prince, and to fight beside him he chose the earl of Warwick, the earl of Oxford, Sir Godfrey of Harcourt, Sir Reginald Cobham, Sir Thomas Holland, Sir Richard Stafford, the Lord of Man, the Lord Delawar, Sir John Chandos, Sir Bartholomew Burghersh, Sir Robert Neville, Sir Thomas Clifford, the Lord Bourchier, the Lord Latimer and many other brave knights and squires, whom I cannot name in full. In the Prince's division there would have been about eight hundred men-at-arms, two thousand archers and a thousand light infantry including the Welsh. This body moved on to its positions in good order, each knight marching beneath his banner or pennon, or among his men.

In the second division were the earls of Northampton and Arundel, the Lord Ros, the Lord Lucy, the Lord Willoughby, the Lord Basset, the Lord St. Aubin, Sir Lewis Tufton, the Lord Multon, the Lord Alasselle and a number of others. This body consisted of about five hundred men-at-arms and twelve hundred archers.

The third division was the king's and was made up, as was fitting, of numerous good knights and squires, amounting to seven hundred men-at-arms and two thousand archers. When the three divisions had taken up their positions and each earl, knight and squire knew what he had to do, the king mounted a small riding-horse and, holding a white baton in his hand, rode slowly round the ranks escorted by his marshals, encouraging his men and asking them to stand up for his honor and help defend his rights. He spoke to them in such a smiling, cheerful way that the most disheartened would have plucked up courage on hearing him. When he had gone round the whole army it was about midday. Returning to his own division, he gave orders for all the men to stand down and eat and drink at their ease. Having done this and packed up the pots, kegs and provisions in the carts again, they went back to their battle-positions. They sat down on the ground with their helmets and bows in front of them, so as to be fresh and rested when the enemy arrived.

That Saturday morning the king of France rose early and heard mass in the Abbey of St Peter in Abbeville, where he had his quarters. All the great lords and commanders who were in Abbeville,

the king of Bohemia, the count of Alençon, the count of Blois, the count of Flanders and others followed his example. It should be said that not all had been quartered in Abbeville, for there would not have been room for them. Some had lodged in the surrounding villages and a large number at Saint-Riquier, which is a fortified town. The king moved out of Abbeville after sunrise with such a great force of fighting men as has been rarely seen. Accompanied by the king of Bohemia and Sir John of Hainault, he rode very slowly to allow his men to catch up with him. When he had advanced about six miles in the direction of the enemy, his officers said to him:

"Sire, it would be advisable to put your divisions in order and to let all the foot-soldiers go forward to avoid being trampled down by the horsemen. And you should send some of your knights ahead to reconnoiter the enemy's position."

The king readily agreed and sent forward four gallant knights, Le Moine de Bazeilles, the lord of Noyers, the lord of Beaujeu and the lord of Aubigny, who approached so near to the English that they obtained a very good view of their disposition. The English saw clearly what they were doing, but they made no move and let them ride off unmolested.

The four returned towards the king of France and his commanders, who had been walking their horses until they came back and halted when they saw them. The knights pushed through the crowd to reach the king, who called to them: "Well, my lords, what news?" They looked at each other without answering, for none of them wished to be the first to speak, as a matter of courtesy towards his companions. At last the king turned to Le Moine de Bazeilles, who was esteemed as one of the bravest and most chivalrous of knights and one of the most experienced in war, and formally commanded him to give his opinion. This knight was a dependent of the king of Bohemia, who always felt more secure when he had him with him.

"Sire," said Le Moine de Bazeilles, "I will speak since it is your wish, subject to correction by my companions. We rode forward. We viewed the English lines. I have to report that they are drawn up in three divisions, very prettily disposed, and show no sign of intending to retreat. They are obviously waiting for you. So my advice—always subject to a better opinion—is that you should halt all your men now and encamp in the open for today. Before the rear can come up with you and you can put your divisions in some order, it will be getting late. Your men will be tired and in no sort of shape and you will find that the enemy are fresh and rested and in no doubt of the way they plan to fight. In the morning you will be able to give more thought to your battle-order and make a closer study of the enemy's position to see which is the best line of attack. You can be sure that they will still be there."

The king fully approved this advice and ordered his marshals to put it into execution. One of them rode forward and the other back, shouting to the standard-bearers: "Halt banners on the king's orders, in the name of God and St. Denis!" At this command the leaders halted, but those behind continued to advance, saying that they would not stop until they had caught up with the front ranks. And when the leaders saw the others coming they went on also. So pride and vanity took charge of events. Each wanted to outshine his companions, regardless of the advice of the gallant Le Moine and with the disastrous consequences of which you shall shortly hear. Neither the king nor his marshals could restrain them any longer, for there were too many great lords among them, all determined to show their power.

They rode on in this way, in no order or formation, until they came within sight of the enemy. For what they did then the leaders were much to blame. As soon as they saw the English they reined back like one man, in such disorder that those behind were taken by surprise and imagined they had already been engaged and were retreating. Yet they still had room to advance if they wished to. Some did, while others stopped where they were.

The countryside was also covered with countless volunteers from the district. They crowded the roads between Abbeville and Crécy, and when they came within ten miles of the enemy they drew their swords and shouted: "Kill! Kill!" Yet they hadn't seen a soul.

There is no one, even among those present on that day, who has been able to understand and relate the whole truth of the matter. This was especially so on the French side, where such confusion reigned. What I know about it comes chiefly from the English, who had a good understanding of their own battle-plan, and also from some of Sir John of Hainault's men, who were never far from the king of France.

The English, who were drawn up in their three divisions and sitting quietly on the ground, got up with perfect discipline when they saw the French approaching and formed their ranks, with the archers in harrow-formation[2] and the men-at-arms behind. The Prince of Wales's division was in front. The second, commanded by the earls of Northampton and Arundel, was on the wing, ready to support the Prince if the need arose.[3]

It must be stressed that the French lords—kings, dukes, counts and barons—did not reach the spot together, but arrived one after another, in no kind of order. When King Philip came near the place where the English were and saw them, his blood boiled, for he hated them. Nothing could now stop him from giving battle. He said to his marshals: "Send forward our Genoese and begin the battle, in the name of God and St. Denis."

He had with him about fifteen thousand[4] Genoese bowmen who would sooner have gone to the devil than fight at that moment, for they had just marched over eighteen miles, in armor and carrying their crossbows. They told their commanders that they were not in a state to fight much of a battle just then. These words came to the ears of the count of Alençon, who grew very angry and said: "What is the use of burdening ourselves with this rabble who give up just when they are needed!"

While this argument was going on and the Genoese were hanging back, a heavy storm of rain came on and there were loud claps of thunder, with lightning. Before the rain, huge flocks of crows had flown over both armies, making a deafening sound in the air. Some experienced knights said that this portended a great and murderous battle.

2　The most plausible interpretation of this phrase, *en manière de herse*, is that the archers formed hollow wedges pointed towards the enemy, at each end of a body of foot-soldiers and positioned slightly in advance of these.

3　The king's division remained in reserve and, according to Froissart's account, took no part in the battle, as appears later.

4　Modern authorities put their numbers at six thousand at most, and perhaps much fewer.

Then the sky began to clear and the sun shone out brightly. But the French had it straight in their eyes and the English at their backs. The Genoese, having been marshaled into proper order and made to advance, began to utter loud whoops to frighten the English. The English waited in silence and did not stir.[5] The Genoese hulloa'd a second time and advanced a little farther, but the English still made no move. Then they raised a third shout, very loud and clear, leveled their crossbows and began to shoot.

At this the English archers took one pace forward and poured out their arrows on the Genoese so thickly and evenly that they fell like snow. When they felt those arrows piercing their arms, their heads, their faces, the Genoese, who had never met such archers before, were thrown into confusion. Many cut their bowstrings and some threw down their crossbows. They began to fall back.

Between them and the main body of the French there was a hedge of knights, splendidly mounted and armed, who had been watching their discomfiture and now cut off their retreat. For the king of France, seeing how miserably they had performed, called out in great anger: "Quick now, kill all that rabble. They are only getting in our way!" Thereupon the mounted men began to strike out at them on all sides and many staggered and fell, never to rise again. The English continued to shoot into the thickest part of the crowd, wasting none of their arrows. They impaled or wounded horses and riders, who fell to the ground in great distress, unable to get up again without the help of several men.

So began the battle between La Broye and Crécy in Ponthieu at four o'clock on that Saturday afternoon.

The noble and gallant king of Bohemia, also known as John of Luxemburg because he was the son of the emperor Henry of Luxemburg, was told by his people that the battle had begun. Although he was in full armor and equipped for combat,

he could see nothing because he was blind. He asked his knights what the situation was and they described the rout of the Genoese and the confusion which followed King Philip's order to kill them. "Ha," replied the king of Bohemia. "That is a signal for us." He then asked for news of his son Charles, king of Germany, and was told: "My lord, we have none. We believe he must be fighting on some other part of the field." Then the king said a very brave thing to his knights: "My lords, you are my men, my friends and my companions-in-arms. Today I have a special request to make of you. Take me far enough forward for me to strike a blow with my sword."

Because they cherished his honor and their own prowess, his knights consented. Among them was Le Moine de Bazeilles, who rode beside him and would never willingly have left him, and there were several other good knights from the county of Luxemburg. In order to acquit themselves well and not lose the king in the press, they tied all their horses together by the bridles, set their king in front so that he might fulfil his wish, and rode towards the enemy.

It is true that too few great feats of arms were performed that day, considering the vast number of fine soldiers and excellent knights who were with the king of France. But the battle began late and the French had had a long and heavy day before they arrived. Yet they still went forward and preferred death to a dishonorable flight. There present were the count of Alençon, the count of Blois, the count of Flanders, the duke of Lorraine, the count of Harcourt,[6] the count of Saint-Pol, the count of Namur, the count of Auxerre, the count of Aumale, the count of Sancerre, the count of Saarbrück and many other lords, barons and knights.

There also was Lord Charles of Bohemia, who bore the title and arms of king of Germany, and who brought his men in good order to the battlefield. But when he saw that things were going badly for his side, he turned and left. I do not know which way he went.

Not so the good king his father, for he came

---

5   In one manuscript this sentence runs: "And the English kept quite still and fired off some cannons which they had in their battle-formation, to frighten the Genoese." The *Chroniques Abrégées*, an abridgement of the *Chronicles* of late date attributed to Froissart, also mentions the firing of "two or three bombards."

6   Brother of the English commander, Sir Godfrey of Harcourt. Froissart later records that he was killed in the battle, as were nearly all the other nobles listed here.

so close to the enemy that he was able to use his sword several times and fought most bravely, as did the knights with him. They advanced so far forward that they all remained on the field, not one escaping alive. They were found the next day lying round their leader, with their horses still fastened together.

The king of France was in great distress when he saw his army being destroyed piecemeal by such a handful of men as the English were. He asked the opinion of Sir John of Hainault, who was at his side. "Well, sire," Sir John answered, "the only advice I can give you now is to withdraw to some place of safety, for I see no hope of recovery. Also, it will soon be dark and you might just as easily fall in with your enemies and meet disaster as find yourself among friends."

The king, shaking with anger and vexation, made no immediate reply, but rode on a little farther as though to reach his brother the count of Alençon, whose banners he could see at the top of a small rise. The count was launching a very well-ordered attack on the English, as was the Count of Flanders from another quarter. They moved their forces along the flank of the archers and reached the Prince of Wales's division, which they engaged fiercely for a long time. King Philip would gladly have joined them had it been possible, but there was such a throng of archers and men-at-arms in front of him that he could not get through. The farther he advanced, the smaller his numbers grew....

The lateness of the hour harmed the French cause as much as anything, for in the dark many of the men-at-arms lost their leaders and wandered about the field in disorder only to fall in with the English, who quickly overwhelmed and killed them. They took no prisoners and asked no ransoms, acting as they had decided among themselves in the morning when they were aware of the huge numbers of the enemy.

Yet some French knights and squires, and with them Germans and Savoyards, succeeded in breaking through the Prince of Wales's archers and engaging the men-at-arms in hand-to-hand combat with swords. There was much brave and skilful fighting. On the English side, Sir Reginald Cobham and Sir John Chandos distinguished

themselves, as well as others too numerous to be named, for all the flower of the English knighthood was there with the prince. At that point the earls of Northampton and Arundel, commanding the second division on the wing, sent support over to the prince's division. It was high time, for otherwise it would have had its hands full. And because of the danger in which those responsible for the prince found themselves, they sent a knight to King Edward, who had his position higher up on the mound of a windmill, to ask for help.

When he reached the king, the knight said: "Sire, the earls of Warwick and Oxford and Sir Reginald Cobham, who are with the prince, are meeting a very fierce attack by the French. So they ask you to bring your division to their support, because if the attack grows any heavier, they fear it will be about as much as your son can deal with." The king asked the knight, whose name was Sir Thomas of Norwich: "Is my son dead or stunned, or so seriously wounded that he cannot go on fighting?" "No, thank God," replied the knight, "but he is very hard pressed and needs your help badly."

"Sir Thomas," the King answered, "go back to him and to those who have sent you and tell them not to send for me again today, as long as my son is alive. Give them my command to let the boy win his spurs, for if God has so ordained it, I wish the day to be his and the honor to go to him and to those in whose charge I have placed him."

The knight went back to his commanders and gave them the king's message. It heartened them greatly and they privately regretted having sent him. They fought better than ever and must have performed great feats of arms, for they remained in possession of the ground with honor.

Late in the evening, as it was growing dark, King Philip left the field in despair, accompanied by five lords only. These were Sir John of Hainault, the first and nearest to him, and the lords of Montmorency, Beaujeu, Aubigny, and Montsault. The king rode lamenting and mourning for his men until he came to the castle of La Broye. He found the gate shut and the drawbridge up, for it was now fully night and pitch-dark. He called for the captain of the castle, who came to the look-out turret and shouted down: "Who comes knocking at this hour?" "Open your gate, captain," King Philip answered. "It is the unfortunate king of France."

The captain came out at once, recognizing the king's voice and having already heard of the defeat from fugitives who had passed the castle. The drawbridge was lowered and the king entered with his whole troop, but he was warned that it would be unwise to stay shut up inside there. So he and his men took a drink and left the castle again at about midnight, taking guides with them who knew the country. They rode so hard that by daybreak they reached Amiens, where the king stopped and lodged in an abbey, saying he would go no farther until he had news of the fate of all his army.

It must be said that fearful losses had been inflicted on the French and that the kingdom of France was greatly weakened by the death of so many of her brave nobility. If the English had mounted a pursuit, as they did at Poitiers, they would have accounted for many more, including the king himself. But this did not happen. On the Saturday they never once left their lines to pursue the enemy, but stayed on their positions to defend themselves against attack.

Froissart insists again on the part played by the English archers, and repeats that a decisive factor was the discomfiture of the Genoese crossbowmen at the beginning, with the confusion into which this threw the French horsemen. He says his last word on the actual battle:

However, among the English there were pillagers and irregulars, Welsh and Cornishmen armed with long knives, who went out after the French (their own men-at-arms and archers making way for them) and, when they found any in difficulty, whether they were counts, barons, knights or squires, they killed them without mercy. Because of this, many were slaughtered that evening, regardless of their rank. It was a great misfortune and the king of England was afterwards very angry that none had been taken for ransom, for the number of dead lords was very great.

When night had fully come and no more shouting or whooping or rallying-cries could be heard, the English concluded that the enemy were routed and the field was theirs. So they lit great numbers of lanterns and torches because it was very dark. King Edward, who had not put on his battle-helmet all that day, came down with his whole division to his son the Prince. He embraced him and said: "Dear son, God grant that you may long go on in this way. You are indeed my son, for you have done your duty most loyally this day. You have proved yourself worthy to rule a land." The prince bowed very low and humbly did honor to his father, as was right.

It was natural that the English should be filled with joy when they realized that they had won the day. They hailed it as a glorious victory and were full of praise for their leaders and veteran captains. And several times that night they gave thanks to God for showing them such great mercies.

On the king's orders there were no noisy celebrations, and the night passed quietly. When Sunday morning dawned there was a heavy mist, making it impossible to see farther than about fifty yards. So the king and his marshals sent out a force of some five hundred men-at-arms and two thousand archers, who were to ride round and see if any of the French had reassembled. Levies of townsmen from Rouen and Beauvais had set out that morning from Abbeville and Saint-Riquier, knowing nothing of the previous day's defeat. To their misfortune they fell in with the English and went right up to them, thinking they were their own people. When the English recognized them, they charged down on them fiercely. There was a sharp engagement and the French were soon fleeing in disorder. More than seven thousand of them were killed in the open fields or under hedges and bushes. If the weather had been clear not a man would have escaped.

Not long after, the English ran into a force led by the archbishop of Rouen and the grand prior of France, who also knew nothing of the defeat and had heard that the king of France would not fight until that Sunday. These also mistook the English for their own side and went towards them, and once again the English attacked lustily. There was another fierce engagement, for the two French lords had some good men-at-arms with them. But they could not hold out long and soon nearly all were killed, including the two leaders.

No prisoners were taken for ransom.

So the English rode about that morning looking for adventures. They came across a good many French who had lost touch with their leaders the day before and had slept out in the open. These met with short shrift at their hands, being all put to the sword. I was told that the number of levies from the cities and towns who were killed on that Sunday morning was over four times greater than the number who died in the main battle on the Saturday.

The king of England was just coming away from mass when his horsemen and archers returned from their reconnaissance. They reported all they had seen and done and said that there was no sign that the French were reforming. The King therefore decided to have the dead examined to find out what nobles had fallen. Two gallant knights, Sir Reginald Cobham and Sir Richard Stafford, were instructed to go out, taking with them three heralds to identify the dead by their arms and two clerks to write down their names. They were amazed at the number they found. They searched all the fields as thoroughly as they could, working on until late evening. Returning just as the king was about to go to supper, they gave him an exact report of what they had seen. Eleven princes lay dead on the field, eighty bannerets, twelve hundred ordinary knights and about thirty thousand other men....[7]

The English remained there for that night and prepared to leave on the Monday morning. As an act of grace the king caused the bodies of all the chief nobles to be taken up and buried in consecrated ground in the nearby church at Maintenay. He accorded the people of the district a three days' truce to go over the battlefield and bury the other dead. He then made for Montreuil-sur-mer, while his marshals went towards Hesdin and burnt Waben and Beaurain. But the castle at the last place was too strong for them to do any damage to it. They camped that Monday by the river which runs through Hesdin, on the Blangy side,

and went on towards Boulogne the next day. On their way they burnt Saint-Josse and Neufchâtel, and then Étables and Rue and the country round Boulogne. They passed between the woods of Boulogne and the Forest of Hardelot until they came to the large town of Wissant. There the king, the prince and the whole army took up their quarters and rested for one day. On the Thursday they left it and came before the fortified town of Calais.

Consequences of Poitiers

The Three Estates; The Free Companies

If the English and their allies were jubilant at the capture of King John, the kingdom of France was deeply disturbed by it. There was cause enough, for it brought loss and suffering to people of all conditions, and the wiser heads predicted that greater evils were to come. Their sovereign was a prisoner and all the best of their knights were also in prison or dead, and the three princes who had escaped, Charles, Louis and John, were very young in age and experience, so there was little chance of recovery through them.

In addition, those knights and squires who had returned from the battle were so blamed and detested by the commons that they were reluctant to go into the big towns. There was much intriguing and mutual recrimination, until some of the wiser ones realized that things could not be allowed to go on in this way, but that something must be done about it. There was a force of English and Navarrese in the Cotentin, under Sir Godfrey of Harcourt, which was ranging over the whole region and laying it waste.

So all the prelates of the Church, bishops and abbots, all the nobility, lords and knights, the Provost of the merchants of Paris [Étienne Marcel] and the burgesses, and the councillors of the French towns, met together in Paris to consider how the realm should be governed until their king should be set free. They also wanted to find out what had happened to the vast sums

---

7 Froissart's total of 1,291 for the dead nobility is reasonably close to the figure of "1,541 good men-at-arms" given by an English eyewitness, Michael de Northburgh, in a letter written a few days after the battle. Northburgh gives no figure for what he calls "the commons and foot-soldiers," but Froissart's "thirty thousand" for these other ranks is usually considered to be at least three times too high. In the Amiens MS he has "fifteen to sixteen thousand."

which had been raised in the past through tithes, levies on capital, forced loans, coinings of new money and all the other extortionate measures by which the population had been tormented and oppressed while the soldiers remained underpaid and the country inadequately protected. But of these matters no one was able to give an account.

It was therefore agreed that the prelates should elect twelve good men from among them, with powers, as representatives of the clergy, to devise suitable means of dealing with the situation described. The barons and knights also elected twelve of the wisest and shrewdest of their number to attend to the same matters, and the burgesses twelve in the same way. It was then decided by common consent that these thirty-six persons should meet frequently in Paris to discuss the affairs of the realm and put them in order. Questions of all kinds were to be referred to these Three Estates. Their acts and ordinances were to be binding on all the other prelates, nobles and common people of the cities and towns. Nevertheless, even at the beginning, several of those elected were viewed unfavorably by the duke of Normandy[8] and his council.

As a first measure, the Three Estates stopped the coining of the money then being minted and took possession of the dies. Secondly, they required the duke to arrest his father's Chancellor, with Sir Robert de Lorris, Sir Simon de Bucy, Jean Poillevilain [master of the mint] and the other financial officers and former counsellors of the king, in order that they should render a true account of all the funds which had been levied and collected on their advice. When these high officials heard of this, they completely disappeared and were wise to do so. They left the kingdom of France as quickly as they could and went to live in other countries until the situation should have changed.

Next, they appointed on their own authority officials with the duty of raising and collecting all the levies, taxes, tithes, loans and other duties payable to the crown and they had new coinage of fine gold minted, called *moutons*.[9] They would also

have liked to have the king of Navarre[10] released from the castle of Arleux in the Cambrésis, where he was held prisoner, for many of them felt that, provided he was willing to be loyal and cooperative, the kingdom would be strengthened by such a measure, since after the defeat of Poitiers there were very few great lords who could act as leaders. They therefore requested the duke of Normandy to set him free, saying that he appeared to have been greatly wronged and they did not know why he was held in prison. The duke very prudently replied that he dared not release him nor advocate doing so, since it was his father the king who had put him there for reasons which he did not know. The king of Navarre was consequently not released just then.

At that time a knight called Sir Regnault de Cervoles, commonly known as the archpriest, took command of a large company of men-at-arms assembled from many countries. These found that their pay had ceased with the capture of King John and could see no way of making a living in France. They therefore went towards Provence, where they took a number of fortified towns and castles by assault and plundered the whole country as far as Avignon under the sole leadership of Sir Regnault. Pope Innocent VI and his cardinals who were at Avignon at that date were in such fear of them that they hardly knew where to turn and they kept their household servants armed day and night. After the archpriest and his men had pillaged the whole region, the pope and his college opened negotiations with him. He entered Avignon with most of his followers by friendly agreement, was received with as much respect as if he had been the king of France's son, and dined several times at the palace with the pope and the cardinals. All his sins were remitted him and when he left he was given forty thousand crowns to distribute among his companions. The company left the district but still remained under the command of the archpriest.

At that time also there arose another company of men-at-arms and irregulars from various countries, who subdued and plundered the

8   King John's eldest son, later Charles V. He assumed the powers of regent within a fortnight of the defeat of Poitiers.
9   So called because one side represented the "Lamb of God." The coin had been current in earlier reigns.
10   Charles "the Bad," king of Navarre, had been seized and imprisoned by King John a few months before Poitiers.

whole region between the Seine and the Loire. As a result, no one dared to travel between Paris and Vendôme, or Paris and Orléans, or Paris and Montargis, and no one dared to remain there. All the inhabitants of the country districts fled to Paris or Orléans. This company had a Welsh captain called Ruffin,[11] who had himself made a knight and became so powerful and rich that his wealth was uncountable. These companions often carried their raids almost to Paris, or at other times towards Orléans or Chartres. No place was safe from being attacked and pillaged unless it was very strongly defended.... They ranged the country in troops of twenty, thirty or forty and they met no one capable of putting up a resistance to them. Elsewhere, along the coast of Normandy, there was a larger company of English and Navarrese pillagers and marauders commanded by Sir Robert Knollys, who conquered towns and castles in the same way and also found no one to oppose them. This Sir Robert Knollys had been following this practice for a long time and had acquired at least a hundred thousand crowns. He had a large number of mercenaries at his command and paid them so well that they followed him eagerly.

These activities of what were known as the Free Companies, who attacked all travelers carrying valuables, began under the administration of the Three Estates. The nobles and the prelates began to grow tired of the institution of the Estates and left the provost of the merchants and some of the burgesses of Paris to go their own way, finding that these were interfering more than they liked with the conduct of affairs.

It happened one day, when the duke of Normandy was at the palace with a large company of nobles, knights and prelates, that the provost of the merchants also assembled a great crowd of the common people of Paris who supported him, all wearing similar caps by which they could recognize each other. He went to the palace surrounded by his men and entered the duke's room, where he asked him very sharply to shoulder responsibility for the affairs of the realm and give some thought to them, so that the kingdom—which would

eventually be his—should be properly protected from the depredations of the Free Companies. The duke replied that he would be quite ready to do so if he had the means at his disposal, but that it should be done by whoever collected the revenue and taxes belonging to the realm.

I do not know exactly how it happened, but such an angry argument arose that there, in the presence of the duke of Normandy, three of the chief members of his council were killed, so close to him that his robe was splashed with blood and he himself was in great danger. But he was given one of the people's caps to put on his head and was forced to pardon the murder of his three knights, two of them soldiers and the third a legal officer. The first were Sir Robert de Clermont, a nobleman of high standing, and the lord of Conflans. The lawyer was master Regnault d'Acy, the advocate general.

On the initiative of the provost, the king of Navarre is released from prison and brought to Paris. (Although Froissart places this after the killings just described, it occurred in fact some three months before them.)

When the king of Navarre had been in Paris for a short time, he called together a variety of people, prelates, knights, clerks of the University of Paris and any others who wished to attend, and delivered a speech to them. Speaking at first in Latin, with the duke of Normandy present, he complained very temperately and reasonably of the wrongs and violence which had been done to him without good cause. He said that no one should feel any fear of him, since he was ready to live and die defending the kingdom of France—as indeed he was bound to, for he was descended in the direct line on both his father's and his mother's side. And he let it be understood clearly enough that, if he ever wished to lay claim to the French crown, he could show that he had a better right to it than the king of England. His speech and his arguments were listened to with approval, and in such ways he gradually acquired great popularity among the Parisians, until they came to prefer him to the regent, the duke of Normandy. The

---

11   Also known as "Griffon," so perhaps "Griffith" or "Gruffydd."

same thing happened in a number of other French cities and towns.

The Jacquerie (1358)

Not long after the king of Navarre had been set free, there were very strange and terrible happenings in several parts of the kingdom of France. They occurred in the region of Beauvais, in Brie and on the Marne, in Valois, in Laonnais, in the fief of Coucy and round Soissons. They began when some of the men from the country towns came together in the Beauvais region. They had no leaders and at first they numbered scarcely a hundred. One of them got up and said that the nobility of France, knights and squires, were disgracing and betraying the realm, and that it would be a good thing if they were all destroyed. At this they all shouted: "He's right! He's right! Shame on any man who saves the gentry from being wiped out!"

They banded together and went off, without further deliberation and unarmed except for pikes and knives, to the house of a knight who lived near by. They broke in and killed the knight, with his lady and his children, big and small, and set fire to the house. Next they went to another castle and did much worse; for, having seized the knight and bound him securely to a post, several of them violated his wife and daughter before his eyes. They killed the wife, who was pregnant, and the daughter and all the other children, and finally put the knight to death with great cruelty and burned and razed the castle.

They did similar things in a number of castles and big houses, and their ranks swelled until there were a good six thousand of them. Wherever they went their numbers grew, for all the men of the same sort joined them. The knights and squires fled before them with their families. They took their wives and daughters many miles away to put them in safety, leaving their houses open with their possessions inside. And those evil men, who had come together without leaders or arms, pillaged and burned everything and violated and killed all the ladies and girls without mercy, like mad dogs. Their barbarous acts were worse than anything that ever took place between Christians and Saracens. Never did men

commit such vile deeds. They were such that no living creature ought to see, or even imagine or think of, and the men who committed the most were admired and had the highest places among them. I could never bring myself to write down the horrible and shameful things which they did to the ladies. But, among other brutal excesses, they killed a knight, put him on a spit, and turned him at the fire and roasted him before the lady and her children. After about a dozen of them had violated the lady, they tried to force her and the children to eat the knight's flesh before putting them cruelly to death.

They had chosen a king from among them who came, it was said, from Clermont in Beauvaisis; and they elected the worst of the bad. This king was called Jack Goodman. Those evil men burned more than sixty big houses and castles in the Beauvais region round Corbie and Amiens and Montdidier. If God had not set things right by His grace, the mischief would have spread until every community had been destroyed and Holy Church afterwards and all wealthy people throughout the land, for men of the same kind committed similar acts in Brie and in Pertois. All the ladies of the region, with their daughters, and the knights and squires, were forced to flee one after another to Meaux in Brie as best they could, in no more than their tunics. This happened to the duchess of Normandy and the duchess of Orléans and to a number of other great ladies, like the humbler ones, as their only alternative to being violated and then murdered.

Other wicked men behaved in just the same way between Paris and Noyon, and between Paris and Soissons and Ham in Vermandois, and throughout the district of Coucy. That was where the worst violators and evil-doers were. In that region they pillaged and destroyed more than a hundred castles and houses belonging to knights and squires, killing and robbing wherever they went. But God by His grace provided a remedy—for which He is devoutly to be thanked—in the manner of which you shall now hear.

When the gentry of the Beauvaisis and of the other districts where those wicked men assembled and committed their barbarous deeds saw their houses destroyed and their friends killed, they sent to their friends in Flanders, Hainault, Brabant and Hesbaye to ask for help. Soon they arrived in considerable numbers from all sides. The foreign noblemen joined forces with those of the country who guided and led them, and they began to kill those evil men and to cut them to pieces without mercy. Sometimes they hanged them on the trees under which they found them. Similarly the king of Navarre put an end to more than three thousand of them in one day, not far from Clermont in Beauvaisis. But by then they had increased so fast that, all taken together, they easily amounted to a hundred thousand men. When they were asked why they did these things, they replied that they did not know; it was because they saw others doing them and they copied them. They thought that by such means they could destroy all the nobles and gentry in the world, so that there would be no more of them….

At the time when these evil men were plaguing the country, the count of Foix and his cousin the captal de Buch came back from Prussia. On the road, when they were about to enter France, they heard of the dreadful calamities which had overtaken the nobility, and were filled with horror. They rode on so fast that they reached Châlons in Champagne in a single day. Here there were no troubles from the villeins, for they were kept out from there. They learnt in that city that the duchess of Normandy and the duchess of Orléans and at least three hundred other ladies and their daughters, as well as the duke of Orléans, were waiting at Meaux in a state of great anxiety because of the *Jacquerie*. The two gallant knights decided to visit the ladies and take them whatever support they could, although the captal de Buch was English. But at that time there was a truce between the kingdoms of France and of England, so that the captal was free to go wherever he wished. Also he wanted to give proof of his knightly qualities, in company with the count of Foix. Their force was made up of about forty lances and no more, for they were on their way back from a journey abroad, as I said.

They rode on until they came to Meaux in Brie. There they went to pay their respects to the duchess of Normandy and the ladies, who were overjoyed to see them arrive, for they were in constant danger from the Jacks and villeins of Brie, and no

less from the inhabitants of the town, as it soon became plain. When those evil people heard that there were a large number of ladies and children of noble birth in the town, they came together and advanced on Meaux, and were joined by others from the County of Valois. In addition, those of Paris, hearing of this assembly, set out one day in flocks and herds and added their numbers to the others. There were fully nine thousand of them altogether, all filled with the most evil intentions. They were constantly reinforced by men from other places who joined them along the various roads which converged on Meaux. When they reached that town, the wicked people inside did not prevent them from entering, but opened the gates and let them in. Such multitudes passed through that all the streets were filled with them as far as the market-place.

Now let me tell you of the great mercy which God showed to the ladies, for they would certainly have been violated and massacred, great ladies though they were, but for the knights who were in the town, and especially the count of Foix and the captal de Buch. It was these two who made the plan by which the villeins were put to flight and destroyed.

When these noble ladies, who were lodged in the marketplace—which is quite strong, provided it is properly defended, for the River Marne runs round it—saw such vast crowds thronging towards them, they were distracted with fear. But the count of Foix and the captal de Buch and their men, who were ready armed, formed up in the market-place and then moved to the gates of the market and flung them open. There they faced the villeins, small and dark and very poorly armed, confronting them with the banners of the count of Foix and the duke of Orléans and the pennon of the captal de Buch, and holding lances and swords in their hands, fully prepared to defend themselves and to protect the market-place.

When those evil men saw them drawn up in this warlike order—although their numbers were comparatively small—they became less resolute than before. The foremost began to fall back and the noblemen to come after them, striking at them with their lances and swords and beating them down. Those who felt the blows, or feared to feel them, turned back in such panic that they fell over each other. Then men-at-arms of every kind burst out of the gates and ran into the square to attack those evil men. They mowed them down in heaps and slaughtered them like cattle; and they drove all the rest out of the town, for none of the villeins attempted to take up any sort of fighting order. They went on killing until they were stiff and weary and they flung many into the River Marne.

In all, they exterminated more than seven thousand Jacks on that day. Not one would have escaped if they had not grown tired of pursuing them. When the noblemen returned, they set fire to the mutinous town of Meaux and burnt it to ashes, together with all the villeins of the town whom they could pen up inside.

After that rout at Meaux, there were no more assemblies of the Jacks, for the young lord de Coucy, whose name was Sir Enguerrand, placed himself at the head of a large company of knights and squires who wiped them out wherever they found them, without pity or mercy.

The Last Days of Étienne Marcel (1358)

Meanwhile the burghers of Paris under Étienne Marcel have acquired control of the city and completed its fortifications. They are virtually besieged by the regent, who has withdrawn to the outskirts from which he harries the capital with a strong force of mercenaries. The king of Navarre also leaves the capital and installs himself at Saint-Denis with his own army of mercenaries. These are ostensibly maintained for the protection of the Parisians, who are providing their pay. But, while pretending to support the burghers, the king enters into a secret pact with the regent.

The provost of the merchants and his faction, knowing that they had incurred the resentment and hatred of their sovereign lord the duke of Normandy, began to feel uneasy. They often visited the king of Navarre at Saint-Denis, pointing out to him gently but plainly that he was the cause of the danger in which they found themselves; for they had freed him from prison and brought him to Paris and would gladly have made him their lord and king had they been able to, and had indeed connived at the killing of the three councillors in the palace because they were opposed to

him. They entreated him not to fail them or to place too much trust in the duke of Normandy and his council. The king of Navarre, realizing that the provost and his supporters were growing anxious and reassured them as well as he could by saying: "My dear sirs and friends, you will never suffer any harm from me. Now, while you are in control of Paris with no one daring to thwart you, I would advise you to make provision for the future by building up a fund of gold and silver in some place where you can lay hands on it in case of need. If you send it here to Saint-Denis and entrust it to me, I will keep it for you and use it secretly to maintain a force of men-at-arms with whom you can fight your enemies if necessary." The provost of the merchants agreed to this. Twice a week from then on he sent two pack-horses laden with florins to Saint-Denis to the king of Navarre, who received them with jubilation.

Now it happened that inside Paris itself there had remained a large number of English and Navarrese mercenaries who had been retained by the provost and the commons to help defend them against the duke of Normandy. As long as the fighting lasted these men had behaved loyally and well. When peace was made between them and the duke, some of them left, but not all. Those who left went to the king of Navarre, who took them on his strength, but more than three hundred stayed on in Paris, enjoying themselves and spending their money freely, as soldiers do in such towns. A disturbance arose between them and the Parisians, in which more than sixty of the soldiers were killed, either in the streets or in their lodgings. The provost of the merchants was highly incensed by this and blamed the Parisians bitterly. But nevertheless, to appease the people, he took some hundred and fifty of the soldiers and imprisoned them in the Louvre, telling the citizens, who were clamoring to kill them, that he would punish them according to their crimes. This quietened the Parisians and after nightfall the provost, who wished to propitiate those English mercenaries, released them from prison and sent them on their way. They all joined the king of Navarre at Saint-Denis....

When they were all assembled at Saint-Denis, they decided to avenge their comrades and the treatment inflicted on themselves. They sent a declaration of war to the Parisians and began to rove about outside the city killing and hacking to pieces any of the inhabitants who were bold enough to venture out. These were in such fear of the English that soon no one dared to go outside the gates. For this the provost was held responsible and, afterwards, openly accused.

When the people of Paris found themselves harried like this by the English soldiers, they were frantic with rage and demanded that the provost should arm some of their community and send them out to fight. He agreed and said he would go with them, so one day they set out, over two thousand strong. Hearing that the English were somewhere near Saint-Cloud, they decided to divide into two bodies and take two separate roads, so as to make sure that the enemy should not escape them. They were to meet again at a certain spot not far from Saint-Cloud. So the two forces parted company, the provost taking the smaller one, and spent most of the day circling around Montmartre[12] and finding no trace of what they were looking for.

About mid-afternoon the provost, having accomplished nothing and growing tired of wandering about the country, returned to Paris by the Porte Saint-Denis. The other body knew nothing of this and stayed out longer; if they had known, they would have gone back also. In the evening they did make for home, marching without order, like men who had no expectation of meeting the enemy. They moved along in groups, looking thoroughly sick and tired of the whole business. Some carried their helmets in their hands or let them hang from their necks, some, through weariness and apathy, trailed their swords along the ground or wore them slung from their shoulders. Slouching along in this way, they took the road leading into Paris through the Porte Saint-Honoré. Suddenly at a turning of the road they were attacked by the English soldiers, who were at least four hundred strong and all of one sort and one mind. They dashed in shouting among the French, striking out at them lustily. Over two hundred were accounted for at the first onslaught.

Taken completely by surprise, the French were too shaken to attempt an organized resistance. They took to flight and let themselves be cut to pieces like cattle. Those who could fled back into Paris, but over seven hundred were killed in the pursuit which continued as far as the barriers of the city. The provost was fiercely blamed for this occurrence, many saying that he had betrayed them.

The next morning, the relatives and friends of those who had been killed went out with carts and wagons to fetch their bodies and give them burial. But on the way they were ambushed by the English and over a hundred more of them were killed or wounded. The people of Paris fell into such distress and confusion that they no longer knew whom to trust. They began to murmur and be suspicious of everyone. The king of Navarre was growing cool towards them, both because of the pact with his brother-in-law the duke of Normandy and because of the way they had attacked the English mercenaries who had remained in Paris. He was quite willing for them to be punished and so pay more dearly for that evil deed. The duke of Normandy for his part would not intervene as long as the Parisians were still ruled by the provost of the merchants. He sent them a public notification in writing that he would not make peace with them unless twelve of the citizens, to be chosen by himself, were surrendered to him at discretion. It is easy to understand why the provost and others who knew that they were inculpated were filled with alarm. They saw clearly enough, on considering the situation, that things could not continue as they were for long, for the people of Paris were beginning to cool in their enthusiasm for them and their party. They spoke of them contemptuously, and this was known to them.

Finally they concluded that if the choice lay between remaining alive and prosperous and being destroyed, it would be better for them to kill than to be killed. On that conclusion they based their whole plan of action and entered into secret

---

12 The apparent illogicality of looking for the enemy in the wrong direction—Montmartre was north of Paris, Saint-Cloud west— seems explained by the fact, not recorded by Froissart, that the king of Navarre helped to lead the expedition and had no desire to clash with the English mercenaries.

negotiations with the English soldiers who were harrying Paris. A pact was made between the two parties, according to which the provost and his supporters were to seize possession of the Porte Saint-Honoré and the Porte Sainte-Antoine and to open those two gates at midnight to a combined force of English and Navarrese, who would come ready armed to ravage and destroy Paris. These plunderers were to spare neither man nor woman, of high or low degree, but to put everyone to the sword, except for some who would be recognized by marks on their doors and windows.[13]

On the very night when this was to happen, an inspiration from God awoke some of the citizens who had an understanding with the duke of Normandy and whose leaders were Sir Pepin des Essarts and Sir Jean de Charny. These by divine inspiration—for so it must be supposed—learnt that Paris was to be plundered and destroyed. They immediately armed themselves and all their friends and caused the news to be whispered around secretly, so as to gain more supporters.

Pepin des Essarts and others, well armed and numerous, raised the banner of France to the cry of: "Up with the King and the Duke!" and were followed by the people. They went to the Porte Saint-Antoine, where they found the provost of the merchants with the keys of the gate in his hands. There they met Jean Maillart, who had had a quarrel earlier that day with the provost and with Josseran de Maçon[14] and had come over to the Duke of Normandy's party. Bitter accusations were hurled at the Provost and he was attacked and forced back. The people were in a tumult, clamouring and hooting. They shouted: "Death to the Provost and his friends! They have betrayed us! Kill them!"

In the midst of the commotion the provost, who was standing on the steps of the Saint-Antoine blockhouse, would gladly have escaped had he been able to, but was so close-pressed that he could not. Sir Jean de Charny hit him on the head with an ax and stretched him on the

ground. There he was struck by master Pierre de Fouace and others, who did not leave off until he was dead, together with six others of his faction, including Philippe Guiffart, Jean de Lille, Jean Poiret, Simon Le Paonnier and Gilles Marcel. Several other traitors were caught and put in prison. A search was made through the streets and the city was put in a state of defense and strong guards posted over it for the remainder of the night.

As soon as the provost and his supporters had been killed or caught, which took place on the evening of Tuesday, July 31, 1358, messengers were sent in haste with the news to the duke of Normandy, who was at Meaux. He was naturally delighted and prepared to come to Paris. But before his arrival, the king of Navarre's treasurer, Josseran de Maçon, and Charles Toussac, an alderman of Paris, were executed as traitors on the Place de Grève. The bodies of the provost and the others killed with him were dragged to the courtyard of St. Catherine's Church in the Val des Écoliers. Gashed and naked as they were, they were laid in front of the cross in the courtyard and left there for a long time, so that any who wished to see them could do so. Afterwards they were thrown into the Seine.

Brigandry, Warfare and Predictions

Acclaimed by his supporters, the duke of Normandy re-enters Paris and takes up residence in the Louvre. For a time Charles of Navarre continues his campaign of brigandage round Paris, but finally makes peace with the regent. His brother Philip, however, continues to pillage the country, in connivance with the English. Elsewhere also English, or so-called English, bands maintain a reign of terror, virtually paralysing trade and agriculture.

The kingdom of France was plundered and pillaged in every direction, so that it became impossible to ride anywhere without being attacked.

---

13 In Froissart's account the villain of the piece is Étienne Marcel, and too little is made of the dubious part played by the king of Navarre in these events. In spite of his secret understanding with the regent, he seems to have been anxious to gain possession of Paris for himself and was at least rumored to have intended pressing on with his claim to the French throne, to the exclusion both of the regent and of the captive King John.

14 The king of Navarre's treasurer. According to another source, the *Grandes Chroniques de France*, Étienne Marcel had ordered the keys of one of the gates to be handed over to him, but Jean Maillart, the captain of the guard, had refused.

Sir Eustace d'Aubrecicourt maintained himself in Champagne, of which he was the virtual master. Whenever he liked he could assemble at a day's notice seven hundred to a thousand fighting men. He or his men made raids almost daily, sometimes towards Troyes, sometimes towards Provins, or as far as Château-Thierry or Châlons. The whole of the low country was at their mercy, on both sides of the Seine and the Marne. This Sir Eustace performed many fine feats of arms and no one could stand up to him, for he was young and deeply in love and full of enterprise. He won great wealth for himself through ransoms, through the sale of towns and castles, and also through the redemption of estates and houses and the safe-conducts which he provided. No one was able to travel, either merchants or others, or venture out from the cities and towns without his authority. He had a thousand soldiers in his pay and held ten or twelve fortresses.

Sir Eustace at that time was very sincerely in love with a young lady of high breeding, and she with him. There is no harm in giving her name, since she later became his lawful wife. She was Madame Isabel de Juliers, daughter of the count of Juliers by one of the daughters of the count of Hainault. The queen of England was her aunt, and as a girl she had been married in England to the earl of Kent, but he died young. This lady was still young and she had fallen in love with Sir Eustace for his great exploits as a knight, of which accounts were brought to her every day. While he was in Champagne, she sent him several hackneys and chargers, with love-letters and other tokens of great affection, by which the knight was inspired to still greater feats of bravery and accomplished such deeds that everyone talked of him.

Sir Eustace d'Aubrecicourt is defeated and captured in a skirmish, to be ransomed later. As a result, the English evacuate a number of castles, but still hold others.

Sir Peter Audley remained none the less at Beaufort and Jean de Ségur at Nogent and Albrecht at Gyé-sur-Seine. At that time there departed this life in rather strange circumstances, in the castle of La Hérelle which he held, ten miles from Amiens, Sir Jean de Picquigny, strangled, it was said, by his chamberlain. One of his most trusted knights, called Sir Lus de Bethisi, also died in the same way. May God have mercy on their souls and forgive them their misdeeds.

A very strange thing happened at about the same time to an English squire belonging to the troop of Sir Peter Audley and Albrecht. They had gone raiding one day to a village called Ronay and began plundering it just as the priest was chanting high mass. This squire entered the church and went up to the altar and, seizing the chalice in which the priest was about to consecrate the blood of Our Lord, he spilt the wine on the ground. When the priest protested, he gave him a back-hand blow with his gauntlet, so hard that the blood spurted on to the altar. After this, they all left the village and, while they were riding across the country, with the robber who had committed the outrage carrying the chalice, the plate and the communion cloth against his breast, this thing suddenly happened which I will relate; it was a true example of God's anger and vengeance and a warning to all other pillagers. His horse and he on it began whirling madly about in the fields and raising such an outcry that none dared to go near them; until at last they fell in a heap with their necks broken and were immediately turned to dust and ashes. All this was witnessed by the comrades who were present and who were so terrified that they swore before God and Our Lady that they would never again violate a church, or rob one. I do not know whether they kept their promise.

In the autumn of 1359 Edward III led an expedition from Calais through north-eastern France with the object of bringing the regent to heel and enforcing a peace treaty which would consolidate the gains of Poitiers. He besieged Rheims unsuccessfully before finally reaching Chartres.

While Rheims was being besieged, the English nobles were dispersed about the neighboring country, where they could live more easily and could guard the roads to stop supplies from entering the city. That fine soldier and great English baron, Lord Bartholomew Burghersh, had his quarters with his whole contingent of men-at-arms and archers in the town of Cormicy, where there was an excellent castle belonging to the archbishop of Rheims. The archbishop had entrusted its defence to a knight from Champagne called Sir Henry de Vaulx, who had a number of good soldiers with him. The castle seemed safe from all assaults, having a great square tower with thick walls and strong battlements.

When Lord Burghersh, having invested the castle and considered its strong construction, had seen that he could not take it by assault, he summoned a band of miners whom he had in his service and ordered them to do their work of mining the fortress, adding that they would be well paid for it. "Right," they said. They started their mine and by digging continually night and day they made such progress that they came right under the great tower. All the time they were mining they were putting in props, but the men in the castle did not know they were working. When the tower was directly over the mine, so that it could be brought down at any moment, the miners went to Lord Burghersh and said: "Sir, we've pushed on so far with the job that the big tower can be dropped whenever you give the word." "That's good," said the knight, "but do nothing more until you have my orders." "Right," they said.

Lord Burghersh mounted his horse and, taking one of his companions, Jean de Ghistelles, with him, he rode up to the castle and signalled that he wished to speak with the men inside. Sir Henry came on to the battlements and asked him what he wanted. "What I want," said Lord Burghersh, "is for you to surrender. If not, you will all be dead men before long." "What?" said the French knight, beginning to laugh. "We are all safe and sound in here and well supplied with everything we need, and you ask us to surrender like that! No sir, never." "Come, Sir Henry," said the English knight, "if you knew what a mess you were in, you would surrender at once without arguing." "And what mess are we in, sir?" asked the French commander. "Just come outside and I'll show you," said Lord Burghersh, "on condition that if you want to go back into your tower I'll let you. You have my promise of that."

Sir Henry took the English knight at his word and accepted the offer. He came out of his fortress with only three companions and joined Lord Burghersh and Sir Jean de Ghistelles outside. They took him at once to their mine and let him see that the great tower was only supported by wooden props. When the French knight realized the danger they were in, he said to Lord Burghersh: "Certainly, sir, you were quite right and it was a really gentlemanly act to do what you did. We put ourselves at your disposal with everything we have with us."

Lord Burghersh accepted them as his prisoners and brought all their men out of the tower together with their possessions. Then he had fire set to the mine. When the props burnt through, the huge square tower split down the middle and collapsed. "Look at that," said Lord Burghersh to Sir Henry de Vaulx and the rest of the garrison. "Didn't I tell you?" "Yes, sir," they replied. "We will remain prisoners at your discretion and we are grateful for your courteous dealing. If the Jack Goodmans who were once uppermost in this district had got the better of us as you did just now, they would never have treated us in this generous way."

That was how the garrison of Cormicy was captured and the castle demolished.

You may like to know that on this campaign the great English lords and men of substance took with them tents of various sizes, mills for grinding corn, ovens for baking, forges for shoeing the horses and all other necessities. To carry all this, they had fully eight thousand wagons, each drawn by four good, strong rounseys which they had brought over from England. They also carried on the wagons a number of skiffs and other small boats so skillfully made from leather that they were a sight worth seeing. Each could take three men over the biggest lake or pond to fish whatever part of it they liked. This was a great standby for them at all seasons, including Lent, at least for the lords and the royal household, but the common soldiers had to manage with what they found. In addition, the king had for his personal use thirty mounted falconers and their loads of birds and sixty couples of big hounds and as many coursing-dogs, with which he went either hunting or wild-fowling every day. Many of the nobles and wealthy men also had their hounds and hawks like the king. Their army was always divided into three bodies, each moving independently

with its own vanguard and rearguard and halting for the night three miles behind the preceding one. The prince commanded one division, the
duke of Lancaster another, and the king the third
and largest. They kept this formation the whole
way from Calais until they reached the city of
Chartres.

In those days there was a Franciscan friar at
Avignon, a very learned and intelligent man,
called Brother Jean de la Rochetaillade. He was
kept imprisoned by Pope Innocent VI in the castle
of Bagnols because of the extraordinary misfortunes which he predicted, firstly for the prelates
and princes of the Church, on account of the excessive luxury and pomp in which they lived; and
also for the Kingdom of France and the great lords
of Christendom, because of the way in which they
oppressed the common people. This Friar John
claimed to prove his utterances by the Apocalypse
and the ancient books of the holy prophets, whose
sense was made clear to him, he said, by the grace
of the Holy Spirit. Many of his predictions were
hard to believe, yet some came true within the period in which he placed them. He did not speak as
a prophet, but knew about them through the old

Scriptures and by the grace of the Holy Spirit—as
one says—who had granted him understanding to
make clear all those ancient prophecies and writings, so as to announce to all Christians the year
and the date when the troubles were to come. He
composed several books, well written and based
on sound theological knowledge, one of which
appeared in the year 1356. In it he described so
many strange events for the years 1356 to 1360 that
they seemed incredible, although several of them
in fact occurred. And when he was asked about
the war between the French and the English he
replied that what had been seen so far was nothing beside what was to come, and that there would
be no peace nor end before the realm of France
had been wasted and destroyed in every district
and region. That came true, for France was indeed
ravaged, wasted and destroyed, and in particular
during the time which the friar predicted, in '56,
'57, '58 and '59, in all its regions, so savagely that
none of the princes or nobles dared to show his
face before those people of low degree, drawn
from many different countries, coming one after
another, with no highly placed leaders at all. And
the realm was defenseless before them, as you
have already heard.

50. *THE TRIAL OF JOAN OF ARC*

JOAN OF ARC (1412–31) was thirteen years old when she began to hear voices urging her to help the Dauphin, later Charles VII of France, defeat the English and claim the crown. In 1429 she convinced the Dauphin and a board of theologians of the veracity of her mission. Given an army, she decisively defeated the English at Orleans and paved the way for Charles's coronation at Rheims. Subsequently, she continued to fight the English and their Burgundian allies and in 1430 was captured at the battle of Compiegne. Tried in the English-held city of Rouen by clerical allies of the English, she was condemned as a heretic for wearing masculine clothing and claiming that she was directly responsible to God. She signed a confession but was tricked into again dressing in men's clothing, upon which she was retried as a lapsed heretic and burned at the stake on May 30, 1431. Twenty-five years later the church retried the case and found her innocent. The following excerpts from the transcript from her first trial cover questions of her childhood and early experiences of the voices and visions that led her on her extraordinary mission.

Source: *The Trial of Joan of Arc*: Being the verbatim report of the proceedings from the Orleans Manuscript, translated with an introduction and notes by W.S. Scott (Westport, CT: Associated Booksellers, n.d. [1956]). First published in 1956 by the Folio Society, London.

Further Reading: Bonnie Wheeler and Charles T. Wood (eds.), *Fresh Verdicts on Joan of Arc* (New York: Garland, 1996).

First Public Session

The following day, which was Wednesday the twenty-first day of February, in the chapel royal of the castle of Rouen, in the presence of the bishop and of my lords and masters, my lord Gilles, Abbot of Fécamp, Jean Beaupère, Jean de Châtillon, Jacques le Tessier, Nicolas Midi, Gerard Feuillet, Guillaume Haiton, Thomas de Courcelles and Maître Richard Praty, were read the letters of the king of England wherein he commanded the ordinary judges of Rouen to hand over and deliver the Pucelle to the bishop to be tried; the letters of the Chapter of Rouen showing that they had given permission to the bishop to hold the trial within the territory of Rouen; and the citation to the Pucelle to appear before him, together with the account of him who had cited her.

These being read, Maître Jean Estivet, appointed promoter at the trial by the bishop, required the Pucelle to be brought and questioned in accordance with law. Which was granted by the bishop.

And since Jeanne had made a supplication that she might be allowed to hear mass, the bishop said that he had consulted with several wise and notable persons, on whose advice he had come to the conclusion that, in view of the crimes of which she was accused, and of the fact that she wore man's dress, they ought to defer this request: and thus he declared it.

Very soon after, Jeanne was led in to the presence of the bishop and the assessors aforementioned.

She being present, the judge spoke to her and explained that she had been taken within the boundaries of his diocese. And since there was common report of a number of her deeds which were contrary to our faith, not only within the realm of France but in all the states in which they were known and published, and since she was accused of heresy, she had been handed over to him to be tried in a matter of faith.

After these words, the promoter showed how at his request she had been cited and convened to answer in a matter of faith, as appeared from the letters and acts which he then exhibited, begging that she should be adjured to speak the truth, and then questioned upon the accusations that he would deliver.

This was granted by the bishop and the court.

This request being granted, as has been said, the bishop caused Jeanne to come before him, and charitably admonished her.

And told her that she should tell the truth concerning the things which would be asked her, as much for the shortening of her trial as for the unburdening of her conscience, without subterfuge or craft; and that she should swear on the Holy Gospels to tell the truth concerning everything she should be asked.

Jeanne answered: I do not know on what you may wish to question me. Perhaps you may ask such things as I will not answer.

Whereupon the bishop said to her:

You will swear to tell the truth about whatever you are asked concerning the Catholic faith, and all else that you may know.

To which Jeanne answered that concerning her father and mother, and concerning everything she had done since she took the road for France,[1] she would willingly swear. But as for revelations sent her from God, never had she told or revealed them save to Charles, who she said was her king. And if they cut her head off, she would not reveal them; for she knew from her visions that she must keep them secret. But within eight days she would know if she ought to reveal them.

After these words the bishop admonished her, and asked her to take the oath to tell the truth concerning the faith.

Jeanne knelt down, her two hands on the book, that is to say a missal, and swore that she would tell the truth in all matters asked her concerning the faith. But that, about the aforesaid revelations, she would not tell anyone.

The same day, after several questions had been put to her concerning the name of her father and mother, the place where she was born, and her age, Jeanne complained of the fetters which she had on her legs.

She was told by the bishop that several times she had endeavored to escape from her prisons, wherefore, in order that she might be kept the more securely, he had ordered that she should be fettered.

To which Jeanne answered that it was true that on these previous occasions she would have much liked to escape from prison, as was lawful for every prisoner. She said further that if she had been able to escape, no one could have said that she had broken faith, for she had never given her parole to anyone.

On account of this answer, the bishop ordered John Rice, John Bernard, and William Talbot,[2] to whom the guardianship of Jeanne was committed, that they should guard her strictly, and that they should not allow anyone to speak to her unless they had his express permission; and made the guards place their hands on the missal, upon which they took a solemn oath to do all that they had been ordered.

The same day, Jeanne, being questioned as to her name and surname,

Answered that, in the place where she was born, she was called Jeannette, and in France, Jeanne; of a surname she knew nothing.

Questioned as to the place of her birth,

She answered that she was born in a village called Domremy de Greux, and in Greux is the principal church.

Questioned as to the name of her father and mother,

She answered that her father was named Jacques Tart and her mother Ysabeau.

Questioned as to where she had been baptized,

She answered that it was in the church of Domremy.

Questioned as to who were her godfathers and godmothers,

She answered that they were a woman named Agnes and another called Jeanne; and a man called Jean Bavent was her godfather. She said also that she had heard her mother say that she had other godfathers and godmothers as well as these.

Questioned as to who was the priest who baptized her,

She answered that he was called Messire Jean Nynet [Minet], to the best of her belief.

Questioned as to whether the said Nynet was still alive,

She answered yes, to the best of her belief.

---

1   France here refers to the parts of the country owing allegiance to Charles II.

2   The officer in command of the guard was John Gray, a gentleman in the household of the Duke of Bedford, who was afterwards knighted. He was assisted by John Berwoit and William Talbot. Four soldiers were engaged in the actual work of surveillance: Nicholas Bertin, Julian Flocquet, William Mouton, and another whose name is not known.

Questioned as to how old she was,

She answered that she was nineteen or thereabouts. She said also that her mother taught her the *Pater Noster*, *Ave Maria* and *Credo*; and that no one else save her mother taught her her faith.

Being required to repeat the *Pater Noster* and *Ave Maria*,

She answered that she would say it willingly, provided that my lord bishop of Beauvais, who was present, would hear her confession. And although she was several times required to say the *Pater Noster* and *Ave Maria*, she answered that she would not say them unless the bishop would hear her in confession.

And then the bishop said: I will give you one or two notable persons of this company to whom you will say your *Pater Noster* and *Ave Maria*,

To which she answered: I will not say them at all, if they do not hear me in confession.

Second Session

The year one thousand four hundred and thirty, the twenty-second day of February. The bishop showed how he had summoned and required Le Maître, as general inquisitor of the faith, to join in the trial of Jeanne, offering to communicate to him everything that had been done at the trial.

To which Le Maître answered that he was only commissioned in the city and diocese of Rouen; and since the trial was held before the bishop, not as ordinary of the diocese of Rouen, but as of borrowed jurisdiction, he was doubtful of joining in the matter. And although he had been doubtful as to joining in the trial, nevertheless, as much in order that the trial should not be null and void, as for the unburdening of his conscience, he was content to be present at the trial since he had inquisitorial powers.

This offer being made, Jeanne was first admonished and required to take the oath that she had taken the day before to tell the truth concerning all that would be asked her of the crimes and evils of which she was accused,

To which Jeanne answered that she had already taken the oath, and this should suffice.

And she was again ordered to swear to tell the absolute truth concerning everything that would be asked her; assuring her that there was not a prince who could or should refuse to take the oath to tell the truth in a matter of faith.

To which she answered: I did so yesterday. You are burdening me too much.

Finally she took the oath in the form in which she had taken it the day before.

The oath being taken, the bishop ordered Maître Jean Beaupère to question her. In obedience to his orders Beaupère questioned her as follows:

Firstly he asked her if she would tell the truth.

To which she replied: You may well ask me such things that as to some I shall tell the truth, as to others, not. She said further: If you are well informed about me, you would wish that I were out of your hands. I have done nothing save by revelation.

Questioned as to what age she was when she left her father's house,

She said that she did not know the answer.

Questioned as to whether she had learned any craft or trade,

She said yes; and that her mother had taught her to sew; and that she did not believe there was any woman in Rouen who could teach her anything in this matter.

She said also that she had left her father's house partly for fear of the Burgundians; and that she went to Neufchâteau with a woman named La Rousse;[3] where she stayed a fortnight. In this house she did the household tasks, and did not go into the fields to keep the sheep or other animals.

Asked whether she made her confession every year,

She said yes, to her own curé. And if he were prevented, she confessed to another priest, with her curé's leave. And she also said that she had confessed two or three times to mendicant friars. And that she received the Body of Our Lord every year at Easter.

Asked whether she had not received the Body of Our Lord at other feasts than Easter,

She answered: Go to the next question. And she said that, from the age of thirteen, she received revelation from Our Lord by a voice which taught her how to behave. And the first time she was greatly afraid. And she said that the voice

---

3   The widow of one Jean Waldaires. She was nicknamed La Rousse on account of her red hair.

came that time at noon, on a summer's day, a fast day, when she was in her father's garden, and that the voice came on her right side, in the direction of the church. And she said that the voice was hardly ever without a light, which was always in the direction of the voice.

She said further that, after she had heard it three times, she knew that it was the voice of an angel.

She said also that this voice had always taken good care of her.

Questioned as to what teaching this voice gave her as to the salvation of her soul,

She answered that it taught her how to behave. And it said to her that she ought to go often to church. And later it said to her that it was necessary that she should go into France.

And it said to her two or three times a week that she must leave and go into France. And that her father knew nothing of her going.

And with this, it said to her that she must hurry and go and raise the siege of Orleans; and that she should go to Robert de Baudricourt, captain of Vaucouleurs; and that he would give her men to accompany her.

To which she answered that she was only a poor woman, who knew nothing of riding or of making war.

And after these words, she went to an uncle's house, where she stayed a week, after which her uncle brought her to Robert de Baudricourt, whom she recognized, although she had never seen him before.

And she said that she recognized him by her voices, which had told her that it was he.

She said further that de Baudricourt refused her twice. The third time he received her, and gave her people to conduct her to France, as the voice had told her.

[She said also that before she received her king's commands, the duke of Lorraine asked for her to be sent to him. She went, and told him that she wished to be sent into France. He questioned her concerning his health, of which she told him she knew nothing. She said to him little about her journey, but asked him to lend her his son and some others to conduct her to France, and then she would pray God for his restoration to health. She went to him with a safe conduct, and returned to the town of Vaucouleurs.]

She said further that when she left Vaucouleurs, she took man's dress, and also a sword which de Baudricourt gave her, but no other armor. And she said she was accompanied by a knight and four other men; and that day they spent the night in the town of Saint Urbain, where she slept in the abbey.[4]

She said also that as for her route, she passed through Auxerre, where she heard mass in the great church; and that she often had her voices with her.

Questioned as to who advised her to take male dress,

[To this question I have found in one book that her voices had commanded her to take man's dress; and in the other I found that, although she was several times asked, she never made any other reply than "I charge nobody." And I found in this book that several times she answered variously.]

She said further that Robert de Baudricourt made her escort swear that they would conduct her well and safely.

She also said that when they left, de Baudricourt said to her: Go, and let come what may.

She said that she was well assured that God greatly loved the duke of Orleans, and that she had more revelations concerning him than any man in France, except her king.

She said further that it was absolutely essential for her to change her dress.

Questioned as to what letters she sent the English and what they contained,

She said that she sent letters to the English, who were before Orleans, wherein she wrote to them that they must leave. And she said that in these letters, as she had heard it said, they have altered two or three words; for example, Render to the Pucelle, where it should be Render to the king; and where there is Body for body, and Chieftain of war; this was not in the letters.

She said also that she went to her king without hindrance.

Further, she said that she found her king at Chinon, where she arrived about noon, and

---

4 Women were allowed to stay in the guest-house of the monastery, which stood beside the great gateway. This gateway is the only portion of the original buildings to remain standing.

lodged at an inn, and after dinner went to the king who was in the castle.

She said that she went right into the room where the king was; whom she recognized among many others by the advice of the voice.

She said that she told the king that she wished to make war on the English.

Questioned whether, when the voice pointed the king out to her, there was any light,

She answered: Go on to the next question.

Questioned if she saw an angel above the king,

She answered: Forgive me. Pass on to the next.

She said also that before the king set her to work, he had several apparitions and glorious revelations.

Questioned as to what revelations,

She answered: I shall not tell you yet; go to the king and he will tell you.

She said further that the voice promised her that very soon after she arrived the king would receive her.

She said also that those of her party well knew that the voice came from God; and that they saw and knew the voice; and that she knows this well.

She said that the king and several members of his council heard and saw the voices who came to her; and amongst others, Charles, duke of Bourbon.

She said also that she never asked anything of the voice save at the last the salvation of her soul.

She said further that the voice told her that she should stay at Saint Denis in France; and there she wished to remain. But the lords were not willing to leave her there, because she was wounded; otherwise she would not have left. And she said that she was wounded in the moat of Paris; of which wound she was cured within five days.

She said that she had made a great assault on Paris.

Asked whether the day she made this assault were a feast day,

She answered, after being questioned several times, that she believed it was a feast.

Asked if she thought it a good thing to make an assault on a feast day,

She replied: Go on to the next question.

These questions and answers being done, the bishop of Beauvais postponed the matter until the following Saturday.

Third Session

The following Saturday, which was the twenty-fourth of February, those who were there the previous day were convoked and called together by the dean of the Christendom of Rouen.

The bishop of Beauvais directed and admonished Jeanne to swear absolutely and without condition to tell the truth. Three times she was thus admonished and required.

To which she answered: Give me leave to speak.

And then said: By my faith, you might ask me such things as I will not tell you.

She further said: It could be that there are many things you might ask me of which I would not tell you the truth, especially concerning the revelations; for you would perhaps force me to say by mistake something that I have sworn not to say. Thus I should be perjured, which you ought not to wish.

Addressing my lord of Beauvais, she said: Beware of saying that you are my judge. For you take upon yourself great responsibility, and you overburden me.

She also stated that she thought it was enough to have taken the oath twice.

Questioned again and again as to whether she would take the oath simply and absolutely,

She answered: You can well do without it. I have sworn twice; that is enough. And I believe that all the clergy of Rouen and Paris would not condemn me save in error.

And she added that she would not have told all in a week.

She said also that, of her coming into France she will willingly tell the truth, but not everything.

As to what was told her, that she should take the advice of those present as to whether or no she should take the oath,

She answered that she would willingly tell the truth as to her coming, but nothing more. And that she should not be spoken to any more concerning the matter.

And being admonished and told that she would make herself suspect by her unwillingness to take the oath,

She answered as before.

The bishop ordering and requiring her to swear precisely and absolutely,

She answered: I shall willingly tell you what I know, but not all.

She also said that she came from God, and ought not to be here; and said that they should remit her into the hands of God, from Whom she came.

After being again and again ordered and required to take the oath and admonished to do so on pain of being found guilty of the acts imputed to her,

She answered: I have sworn enough. Leave the matter.

And when time and again she was admonished to tell the truth in what concerned her trial, it being explained to her that she was endangering herself,

She answered: I am ready to swear and to say all that I know concerning my trial. But I will not say all that I know.

After saying which, she took the oath.

These things being done, she was questioned by Maître Jean Beaupère. Firstly he asked her when she had last eaten or drunk,

To which she answered: yesterday afternoon.

Questioned since when had she heard her voice,

She answered that she had heard it both yesterday and to-day.

Questioned at what time she had heard it yesterday,

She said that she had heard it three times; once in the morning; again at the hour of Vespers; and yet again at the hour of the Ave Maria; sometimes she heard it more often than [this], she said.

Questioned as to what she was doing yesterday morning when she heard this voice,

She answered that she was asleep, and that the voice awoke her.

Asked whether the voice woke her by its sound, or by touching her on the arms or elsewhere,

She answered that she was wakened by the voice without being touched.

Questioned as to whether the voice was still in her room,

She replied that she thought not, but that it was in the castle.

Asked if she did not thank the voice, and kneel down,

She answered that she thanked it, being seated on her bed. And she said that she joined her hands together, and begged and prayed that it might help and advise her in what she had to do.

To which the voice told her to answer boldly.

Asked what the voice told her when she was awake,

She answered that it said that she must ask advice from Our Lord.

Asked whether it had said anything before she questioned it,

She said that before she was awake, the voice had said several words to her that she did not understand. But when she had wakened, she understood that the voice had told her that she must answer boldly.

She said several times to the bishop, You say that you are my judge; consider well what you do; for in truth I am sent from God, and you are putting yourself in great peril.

Asked if this voice had ever varied in its advice,

She answered that she had never found in it two contradictory words.

Asked whether it were an angel coming direct from God,[5] or if it were a saint,

She answered that it came from God.

And added, I am not telling you all I know, for I am greatly afraid of saying something displeasing to it in my answers to you.

And she said further: In this questioning I beg you that I may be allowed a delay.

Asked if she believed that God would be displeased if she told the truth,

She answered my lord of Beauvais that the voices had told her to say some things to the king and not to him.

She also said that the voice told her that night things concerning the king's good; things that she wished the king to know immediately; and that she would drink no wine till Easter, wherefore he would be happier when he dined.

Asked if she could make this heavenly voice obey her and carry a message to her king,

She answered that she did not know whether it would be willing to obey her, unless it were the will of God, and that Our Lord agreed.

And that, if it pleased God, it would be able to reveal it to the king; if so [she added] I would be very happy.

5 *Interroguée si c'est un angèle de Dieu, sans moyen.* Courcelles writes: *Sit unus angelus, velutrum sit a Deo, immediate.*

Questioned as to why she cannot now speak with her king, as she used to do in his presence,

She said that she did not know if it were God's will.

She said further that if she were not in the grace of God she could do nothing.

Asked if her counsel [her voices] had not revealed to her that she should escape,

She answered: I have [yet] to tell you this.

Asked if this voice has not now given her advice and counsel as to what she should answer,

She replied that if it had revealed or said anything to her [about this], she had not well understood it. Questioned as to whether, on the last two days that she heard her voices, a light had appeared,

She answered that the light comes before the voice.

Asked if with the voice she sees something,

She answered: I am not going to tell you everything, for I have not permission; and also my oath does not touch that; but I do say to you that it is a beautiful voice, righteous and worthy; otherwise I am not bound to answer you.

For this reason she asked to see in writing the points upon which they desired to question her.

Asked if the voice could see; that is to say, whether it had eyes,

She answered: You may not know that yet.

She said also that there is a saying among little children that people are often hanged for telling the truth.

Asked if she knew whether she were in the grace of God,

She answered: If I am not, may God put me there; if I am, may He keep me there.

She said further that if she knew she were not in the grace of God, she would be the most miserable person in the world. She said also that if she were in mortal sin, the voice would not come to her. And she would that everyone might hear them as well as she did.

She also said that she thought she was thirteen years of age when the voice came to her the first time.

Asked whether in her childhood she used to go and play in the fields with the others,

She said she did so sometimes. But she did not know at what age.

Asked if the people of Domremy sided with the Burgundians or the Armagnacs,

She answered that she only knew one Burgundian, whose head she would like to see chopped off, that is if it had pleased God.

Asked whether at Maxey they were Burgundians or Armagnacs,

She said they were Burgundians.

Questioned as to whether her voice told her in her childhood to hate the Burgundians,

She answered that ever since she learned that the voices were for the king of France, she did not love the Burgundians.

She added that the Burgundians would have war, if they did not do as they ought; she knew this from the voice.

Asked if the voice told her in her childhood that the English should come into France,

She said they were already in France when the voice first spoke to her.

Asked if she were ever with the other children when they played at fights between English and French,

She said no, as far as she could remember. But she had often seen those of her village fighting against those of Maxey, and sometimes coming back wounded and bleeding.

Asked if in her youth she had a great desire to defeat the Burgundians,

She answered that she had a great desire that the king should have his kingdom.

Asked if she had wanted to be a man when she knew that she had to come [into France],

She said that she had answered elsewhere.

Asked if she ever used to lead the animals to pasture,

She replied that she had already answered; and that, since she had grown up and reached years of understanding, she did not look after them; but she did help to drive them to the meadows, and to a castle called de l'Ile, for fear of the soldiers; but as to whether she looked after them or not in her childhood, she did not remember.

Questioned concerning the tree,

She answered that quite close to Domremy there was a tree which was called the Ladies' tree; others called it the Fairies' tree; and near it there was a spring; and she had heard it said that persons suffering from fever drank of it; and she has seen them going to it to be cured. But she did not know whether they were cured or not.

She said also that she had heard that the sick, when they could get up, went to the tree to walk about; and she said it was a large tree called a beech, from whence comes the *beau mai*;[6] and it belonged to Messire Pierre de Bourlémont.[7]

She said that she sometimes went there with the other girls in summer time, and made wreaths for Notre Dame de Domremy.

She had heard several old folk say, not of her family, that the fairies frequented it; and she had heard her godmother Jeanne, wife [of the mayor of the village of Domremy], say that she had seen them there. Whether this was true, she does not know.

She said that she herself had never seen a fairy, as far as she knew, either at the tree or anywhere else.

She said further that she had seen garlands hung on the branches of the tree by the girls; and she herself had hung them there with the other girls. Sometimes they took them away, and sometimes they left them.

She also said that ever since she learned that she must come into France, she played very little, the least that she could. And she did not know whether, since she had reached years of discretion, she had danced near the tree. Sometimes she may have danced there with the children, but she more often sang than danced.

She also said that there was a wood called the Bois Chesnu that one could see from her father's house, not more than a league away; but she was unaware and had never heard it said that the fairies frequented it.

She had heard from her brother that it was said in the neighborhood that she received her revelations at the tree and from the fairies. But she had not. And she told him quite the contrary.

She said further that when she came before the king, many people asked whether in her country there was not a wood called the Bois Chesnu, for

there was a prophecy saying that from the Bois Chesnu should come a maiden who would perform marvellous acts; but she put no faith in it.[8]

Questioned as to whether she wanted a woman's dress.

She answered: If you give me permission, give me one, and I will take it and go. Otherwise no. I am content with this one, since it is God's will that I wear it.

After these questions were done, the following Tuesday was appointed, at eight o'clock. And the assessors were requested to assemble on that day at the said hour, under pain of displeasure.

Fourth Session

The following Tuesday, which was the twenty-seventh day of the month of February, following the Sunday of Reminiscere, in the year one thousand four hundred and thirty, for the fifth session.[9]

Firstly the assessors were convoked; and in their presence Jeanne was required by my lord the Bishop of Beauvais to swear and take the oath concerning what touched her trial.

To which she answered that she would willingly swear as to what touched her trial, but not as to everything she knew.

Many times she was requested by the bishop to answer the truth concerning everything that would be asked her,

To which she answered as before: It seems to me you ought to be satisfied; I have sworn enough.

By order of my lord of Beauvais, Maître Jean Beaupère began to interrogate Jeanne, and asked her how she had been since Saturday.

She answered: You can see that I am as well as I can be.

Questioned as to whether she fasted every day of this Lent,

She replied: What has that to do with your trial?

To which Beaupère said: Yes, indeed, it belongs to the trial.

---

6   The *beau mai* was a branch from a beech tree, traditionally used for decoration.

7   The family of de Bourlémont were seigneurs of Domremy. The château of Bourlémont still stands not far from the village.

8   This refers to a prophecy attributed to Merlin, current in the courntryside. It was to the effect that a marvellous maid should come \ from the *Nemus Canutum* (*bois chesnu*) for the healing of nations.

9   The Orleans manuscript puts the fourth and fifth sessions into one, by reason of its omission of a long passage of interrogation [here supplied from d'Estivet]. This Sunday was the second Sunday in Lent.

She replied: Yes, certainly, I have fasted the whole time.

Asked whether she had heard her voice since Saturday,

She answered: Yes, indeed, many times.

Questioned as to whether she heard it in this hall on Saturday,

She answered: That has nothing to do with your trial; and afterwards said, yes.

Asked what it said to her on Saturday,

She answered: I did not well understand it; I understood nothing that I could tell you until my return to my room.

Asked what it said to her when she was back in her room,

She replied: That I should answer you boldly.

And she said further that she asked advice concerning the things that were asked her.

She said also that when she has leave of Our Lord to reveal it, she will tell it willingly; but touching the revelations concerning the king of France, she will not tell without permission from her voice.

Asked if the voice forbade her to tell everything,

She answered that she had still not quite understood.

Asked what the voice said to her,

She said that she asked advice from it as to certain questions that had been asked her.

Asked whether the voice had given her advice as to these matters, She replied that on certain points she had received advice.

She said also that as to certain questions, they might demand an answer, but she would not give it without leave; and if by chance she answered without permission, she would not have them for warrant. But [she said] when I have Our Lord's leave, then I shall not be afraid to answer, for I shall have a good warrant.

Questioned as to whether it were the voice of an angel, or of a saint, or directly from God,

She answered that the voices were those of Saint Catherine and of Saint Margaret. And their heads are crowned with beautiful crowns, most richly and preciously. And [she said] for [telling you] this I have leave from Our Lord. If you doubt it, send to Poitiers where I have been previously examined.

Asked how she knew that it was these two saints, and if she could tell the one from the other,

She answered that she was certain that it was these; and that she well knew the one from the other.

Asked how she knew the one from the other,

She replied that she knew them by the greeting they gave her.

She also said that it was seven years since they first began to guide her.

She also said she knows them because they tell her their names.

Asked whether they are dressed in the same cloth,

She answered: I shall not now tell you anything else. She also said that she had not leave to reveal it. And if you do not believe me [she added], go to Poitiers.

She said further: there are some revelations which were intended for the king of France, and not for those who question me.

Asked if they are of the same age,

She said: I have not leave to tell you that.

Asked if they talked at the same time, or one after the other,

She replied: I have not leave to tell you that; nevertheless I always receive advice from both of them.

Asked which [appeared] first,

She answered: I do not recognize them at once. I used to know well enough, but now I have forgotten. If she has leave, she will willingly say; and it is in the register of Poitiers.

She said also that she received counsel from Saint Michael.

Questioned which came first,

She said it was Saint Michael.

Asked if it were long ago,

She answered: I do not speak of Saint Michael's voice, but of the great comfort [he brought me].

Asked which was the first voice that came to her when she was thirteen,

She said it was Saint Michael whom she saw before her eyes; and he was not alone, but was accompanied by angels from heaven.

She said also that she would not have come into France had it not been for God's command.

Asked if she saw Saint Michael and the angels corporeally and in reality,

She answered: I saw them with my bodily eyes, as well as I am seeing you.

And when they left her, she wept and greatly longed that they should have taken her with them.

Asked in what form was Saint Michael,

I have not yet answered you this; and have not yet leave to tell it.

Questioned as to what Saint Michael said to her the first time,

She answered: You will not have any other answer.

[She also said that the voices told her to answer boldly.]

She said further that she had not yet leave to reveal what Saint Michael told her; and greatly wished that her examiner had a copy of the book which is at Poitiers, provided that was pleasing to God.

Asked whether Saint Michael and the other saints had told her not to tell her revelations without their permission,

She answered: I will not answer you further about that. And, concerning what I have leave to tell you, I will gladly answer. And [she added] that if they had forbidden her, she did not so understand it.

Asked what sign she gives whereby it might be known that they come from God, and that they are Saint Catherine and Saint Margaret,

She replied: I have told you often enough that they are Saint Catherine and Saint Margaret. Believe me if you will.

Asked how she is able to make a distinction between answering certain points, and not others,

She replied that on some points she had asked leave, and on some, she had obtained it.

She said furthermore that she would rather be torn asunder by horses than come into France without God's leave.

Asked if the voice ordered her to wear a man's dress,

She answered that the dress is but a small matter; and that she had not taken it by the advice of any living man; and that she did not take this dress nor do anything at all save by the command of Our Lord and the angels.

Questioned as to whether it seemed to her that this command to take male dress was a lawful one,

She answered that everything she had done was at Our Lord's command, and if He had ordered Jeanne to take a different dress, she would have done so, since it would have been at God's command. Nor had she ever taken this dress at the order of Robert [de Baudricourt].

Asked if she had done well to take man's dress,

She said that everything she had done at our Lord's command she considered well done, and from it she expected good surety and good support.

She said also that she had a sword which she obtained at Vaucouleurs.

Questioned as to whether in this particular case of taking male dress she considered she had done rightly,

She answered that without God's command she had not done so; and that she had done nothing in the world save by His command.

Asked whether, when she saw the voice, there was a light with it,

She said that there was a great deal of light on all sides as was fitting.

Asked whether there was an angel over her king's head when first she saw him,

She answered: By Saint Mary, if there were any, I did not know, nor did I see one.

Asked whether there was a light there,

She said that there were more than three hundred knights and fifty torches, not counting the spiritual light; and that she rarely received revelations without there being a light.

Asked how her king gave credence to her words,

She replied that he had good signs; and through the clergy.

Asked what revelations the king had,

She answered: You will not learn them from me, this year.

She said also that the ecclesiastics of her party were of this opinion, that there seemed to be nothing but good in her.

Asked whether she had been to Saint Catherine de Fierbois,

She answered yes. And there she heard three masses in one day, and then went to the town of Chinon.

She said that she told her king on one occasion that it had been revealed to her that she should go to him.

She said also that she had sent letters to her king, saying that she was writing to know whether she should enter the town where he was, and that she had already traveled a good hundred and fifty leagues to come to his aid, and that she had much good news for him; and she thought that the letter also said that she would be able to recognize him amongst all others.

She said further that she had a sword, which, when she was in Tours or in Chinon, she sent to be looked for at Saint Catherine de Fierbois. This sword was in the ground, behind the altar of Saint Catherine, and it was immediately found there, all rusted.

Asked how she knew the sword was there,

She said it was in the ground, all rusted, and upon it were five crosses. This she knew from her voices, saying that she never saw the man who was sent to look for the sword. She wrote to the clergy of the place asking that it might please them to let her have the sword, which they sent her. It was not deep in the ground behind the altar, so she thought, although in truth she was not certain whether it were in front of it or behind, but she believed that she wrote that it was behind [the altar].

She added that as soon as the sword was found, the clergy of the place rubbed it, and the rust fell off without any effort; and that it was an armorer of Tours who went to find the sword.[10] And the clergy of Saint Catherine and the citizens of Tours both gave her sheaths for it. They made two sheaths, one of crimson velvet and the other of cloth of gold. She herself had another made of very strong leather.

She also stated that when she was taken prisoner she no longer had this sword; but that she had always worn it until her departure from Saint Denis.

Asked whether she had ever said or caused to be said a blessing upon this sword,

She said no, nor would she have known how to do so.

She said also that she greatly prized this sword, since it was found in the church of Saint Catherine, whom she much loved.

Asked whether she had placed her sword upon any altar,

She said no, as far as she knew, nor had she done so in order that it might have better fortune.

Asked if she had her sword when she was taken prisoner,

She said no, but that she had one which was taken from a Burgundian.

She added that she had this sword at Lagny, and from Lagny to Compiègne she wore the Burgundian's sword, because it was a good sword for war, useful for giving hard clouts.

She said also that as to where she lost this sword, this had nothing to do with the trial, and she would not reply now.

Asked whether, when she was before the city of Orleans, she had a standard, and of what color it was,

She replied that it had a field sown with fleurs-de-lis, and showed a world with an angel on either side, white in color, of linen or *boucassin*; and she thought that the names JESUS MARIA were written on it; and it had a silk fringe.

Asked if these names JESUS MARIA were written at the top or the bottom, or along the side,

She answered that she thought they were along the side.

Asked which she preferred, her sword or her standard,

She replied that she was forty times fonder of her standard than she was of her sword.

Asked who persuaded her to have this design on her standard,

She said: I have told you often enough that I have done nothing save by God's command.

She said moreover that she herself bore her standard during an attack, in order to avoid killing anyone. And she added that she had never killed anyone at all.

Asked what forces her king gave her when he set her to work,

She answered, ten or twelve thousand men; and that at Orleans she went first to the fort of Saint Loup and then to that at the bridge [the Tourelles].

Asked at which fort she ordered her men to retire,

She said that she did not remember.

She said also that, through the revelation made to her, she was quite certain that she would relieve

---

10 This probably refers to the armorer from Tours who made Jeanne's armor, Colin de Montbazon.

Orleans; adding that she had so informed her king before she went there.

Asked whether, in launching her attack before Orleans, she told her men that she would receive arrows, missiles and stones from the bombards,

She said no; there were a good hundred wounded, and maybe more. But she had told her men to have no fear, and they would raise the siege.

She also said that during the attack on the fort at the bridge she was wounded in the neck by an arrow, but she was greatly comforted by Saint Catherine, and was well again in a fortnight; nor did she give up either riding or her military command on account of this wound.

Asked whether she knew beforehand that she would be wounded,

She said that she well knew it, and had informed her king of it; but that notwithstanding she would not give up her work. And this was revealed to her by the voices of Saint Catherine and Saint Margaret.

She said also that she herself was the first to plant the ladder against the fort at the bridge; and it was while she was raising it that she was wounded in the neck by an arrow.

Asked why she had not concluded a treaty with the captain of Jargeau,

She said that the lords of her party had told the English that they would not have the delay of a fortnight for which they had asked, but that they must go away immediately, and take their horses with them. And for her own part, she told them that they might go if they wished, in their doublets and tunics, safe and sound; if they did not, they would be taken by assault.

Asked whether she had any conversation with her counsel, that is to say her voices, as to whether or no to grant a delay,

She answered that she did not remember.

Fifth Session

Asked whether she had letters from the Comte d'Armagnac, asking her which of the three claimants to the Papacy should be obeyed,[11]

She answered that the count wrote a letter to this effect, to which she replied, amongst other matters, that when she was in Paris or anywhere else, when she had some time [to spare], she would give him a reply. She was just about to mount her horse when she gave this answer.

After this the letters from the count and from Jeanne were read, and she was asked whether it was her own letter in reply,

To which she said that she thought she had given such an answer, at any rate in part, if not the whole.

Questioned as to whether she said that she knew by the counsel of the King of kings what he ought to believe in this matter,

She answered that she knew nothing about it.

Asked if she were in any doubt as to whom the count should obey,

She said she did not know what to tell him as to whom he ought to obey, for he desired to know whom Our Lord wished him to obey. But as for herself, she held and believed that one ought to obey our lord the pope at Rome.

She added that she had said other things to the messenger than what is contained in the letter. If he had not gone away so hurriedly he would have been thrown into the water, though not through her.

She said also that with reference to his inquiry as to whom it pleased God that he should obey, she answered that she did not know, but sent him many messages which were not put into writing. As for herself, she believed in the pope at Rome.

Asked why she had written that she would give him a further answer, since she believed in the pope at Rome,

She replied that the answer she had given referred to another matter than the three popes.

Asked if she had ever said she would have counsel concerning the three popes,

She said that she had never written or caused to be written anything concerning the three popes. And she swore on oath that on this subject she had neither written nor caused to be written anything at all.

She said also that before seven years are past the English will have lost a greater stake than they

---

11 Martin V was then pope; there were also two antipopes. Armagnac was a supporter of one of these, for which he had been excommunicated by Pope Martin.

did before the town of Orleans, for they will have lost all they hold in France.

She added, as before, that she knew this by revelation, as well as she knew that we, the bishop of Beauvais, were there present before her, saying in the French tongue: *Je le sçay aussi bien comme vous estes ici.*[12]

And this she knew by the revelation given her; and that it would come to pass before seven years are past; and she was much grieved that it should be so long delayed.

Asked in what year,

She answered: You will not yet learn this; but I hope it may be before Saint John's Day.

Asked whether she had said it would come to pass before Saint Martin's Day in winter,

She replied that she had said that many events would be seen before Saint Martin's Day; and it might be that the English would be overthrown.

Asked what she had said to John Grey, her jailer in the prison, concerning Saint Martin's Day,

She answered: I have already told you.

Questioned as to through whom she knew that this would come to pass,

She replied that it was through Saint Catherine and Saint Margaret.

Asked whether, since the previous Tuesday, she had often spoken with Saint Catherine and Saint Margaret,

She said yes, both yesterday and to-day; but she does not know at what time; and there is no day when she does not hear them.

Asked whether the saints always appeared to her in the same dress,

She answered that she [always sees them] in the same form; and their heads are richly crowned; of their other clothing she does not speak, and of their robes she knows nothing.

Asked how she knows whether it is a man or woman who appears to her,

She answered that she was certain it was those saints by their voices, and by what they told her.

Asked what part of them she saw,

She answered, the face.

Asked whether they had hair,

She replied: Assuredly; in the French tongue, *Il est bon a savoir.*

Asked if there was anything between their crowns and their hair,

She answered, no.

Asked if their hair were long and hung down,

She replied: I do not know.

She added that she did not know if they had anything in the nature of arms or other members.

She said moreover that they spoke most excellently and beautifully; and that she understood them perfectly.

Asked how they spoke, when they had no other members,

She answered: I leave that to God.

She said that the voice was lovely, sweet and low in tone, and spoke in French.

Asked if that voice, that is to say Saint Margaret, spoke English,

She answered: Why should she speak English? She is not on the side of the English.

Asked who gave her the ring which the Burgundians have,

She answered, her father or mother; and she thought that JESUS MARIA was written on it. But she did not know who had had this written; she did not think there was any stone in it; and it was given to her at Domremy.

She said also that her brother had given her a ring which we, the bishop, now have; and she requested us to give it to the church.

She said further that she had never cured anyone with any of her rings.

Asked whether Saint Catherine and Saint Margaret had spoken to her beneath the tree,

She answered: I do not know.

Being repeatedly asked if the saints had spoken to her at the aforementioned spring,

She replied yes; and she had heard them there. But what they then said to her she does not know.

Being again asked if they had made any promises to her there or elsewhere,

She replied that they did not make any promise to her, except by leave of Our Lord.

Asked what promises Saint Catherine and Saint Margaret made her,

She answered: This does not concern your trial at all.

Amongst other things, they told her that her

---

12 The whole of this passage, being taken from d'Estivet, was originally in Latin.

king would be reestablished in his kingdom, whether his enemies wished it or no.

She said also that the saints promised to bring her to Paradise, as she had asked them.

Asked whether they had promised her anything else, as well as to bring her to Paradise,

She replied that they had made her other promises, but she will not tell them. She said this did not concern her trial.

She said further that within three months she will reveal another promise.

Asked whether the saints had told her that within three months she would be freed from prison,

She answered: That is not in your trial. But she does not know when she will be freed.

She said also that those who wished to remove her from this world might well themselves go first.

Asked whether her counsel had told her that she would be freed from prison,

She answered: Ask me in three months' time, and I will then give you my reply.

She also requested that the assessors should give their opinions on oath as to whether this concerns the trial.

And afterwards, when the assessors had deliberated and come to the conclusion that it did concern the trial,

She said: I have always told you that you cannot know all.

And she added: One day I must be freed. And I wish to have leave to tell you [when]. And for this she begged a delay.

Asked if the saints forbade her to tell the truth,

She answered: Do you wish me to tell you the affairs of the king of France?

She said that there were many matters which did not concern the trial.

She said also that she was well assured that her king would regain his kingdom; this she knows as well as she knows us [the bishop] to be present here.

She said also that she would be dead, were it not for the revelation which comforts her each day.

Asked what she has done with her mandrake,[13]

She answered that she never had one; but that she had heard it said that there was one near her village; but that she had never seen it.

She had heard it said that it was a dangerous and evil thing to him who keeps it; but she does not know its purpose.

Asked where is the place where this thing of which she has heard [is to be found],

She replied that she had heard that it is in the ground near the tree, but she does not know the spot. But she has heard it said that over the place grows a tree called a hazel.

Asked what purpose this mandrake serves,

She answered that she had heard it said that it attracts money, but she does not believe it, and on this matter her voices have never told her anything at all.

Asked in what form Saint Michael appeared,

She answered that she did not see his crown; and as to his clothing, she knew nothing.

Asked if he were naked,

She answered: Do you think that Our Lord has not wherewithal to clothe him?

Questioned as to whether Saint Michael had his scales,[14]

She replied: I do not know.

She said that she had great joy when she saw him; and said also that he told her, when she saw him, that she was not in a state of mortal sin.

She said further that Saint Catherine and Saint Margaret gladly heard her confession, each in turn.

She also said that if she is in mortal sin, she is not aware of it.

Asked whether, when she made her confession, she ever thought she was in mortal sin,

She replied that she did not know if she were, but she did not believe that she had ever committed such sins. And please God [she added], I never did so, nor will I act in such a way that my soul should be guilty of mortal sin.

Asked what sign she gave her king to show him that she came from God,

She answered: I have always told you that you

---

13 A mandrake (*mandragora officinarum*) is a plant of the potato family. Little images made of this root, which often looked like the lower limbs of a man, were cherished as oracles, and used in witchcraft and enchantments. The mandrake was believed to shriek when torn out of the earth.

14 A pair of scales is the emblem of the archangel.

will not drag that out of me. Go and ask him.

Asked whether she has sworn not to reveal what has been asked her touching the trial,

She said: I have told you before that I will not tell you anything concerning the king: but that which concerns the trial and the faith, I will tell you.

Asked if she did not know the sign,

She answered: You will not know that from me.

Being told that this concerns the trial,

She said: I will willingly tell you [other matters]; but the things I have promised to keep secret, I will not tell you.

And I have promised, so I cannot tell you without being forsworn.

Asked to whom she made this promise,

She said, to Saint Catherine and Saint Margaret; and it [the sign] was shown to the king.

She said also that she promised them without them asking her, and at her own request; and she said that too many people would have asked her if she had not promised.

Questioned whether, when she showed the sign, there was anyone present save the king,

She answered: I think there was no one but he, although there were a number of people fairly near.

Asked if she saw any crown on the king's head, when she showed him the sign,

She answered: I cannot tell you without perjuring myself.

Asked if he had a crown at Rheims,

She answered that she thinks that the one he found at Rheims he took with pleasure. But a very rich one was brought later. And he did so to hasten [his coronation] at the request of the citizens of the town, to avoid the cost of the men-at-arms; and if he had waited, he would have been crowned with one a thousand times richer.

Asked whether she had seen this richer crown,

She answered: I cannot tell you without being forsworn; and although I have not seen it, I have heard that it was so rich.

And after these questions were done, the following Saturday was appointed, at the hour of eight in the morning. And the assessors were requested to assemble on this day at the said hour under certain penalties.

51. *DOMESDAY BOOK*

IN 1085 WILLIAM THE Conqueror ordered a survey of his kingdom in order to provide him with an exact record of the local contributions to royal taxation. In addition, the inquest was designed to inform him of the manner in which England had been divided among his vassals and to settle issues of land disputes that had been continuing since the Norman Conquest twenty years before. The result was an extraordinarily rich and detailed survey that is an invaluable source for understanding English social, economic, and political structures in the eleventh century.

The survey of Huntingdonshire is fairly typical of the entries. In general, each entry describes the assessment of the manor in hides to the geld. These "hides" are not actual units of land but units of tax assessment. It then states the number of "ploughs," that is, the amount of arable land that can be ploughed each year by a team of eight oxen. Finally, it states the number of ploughs on the demesne of the manor and the number in the peasant tenures. It may also add miscellaneous information about the manor's other resources and its value at the death of Edward the Confessor in 1066 (abbreviated T.R.E., tempore Regis Edwardi, below) and in 1086.

Source: David C. Douglas and George W. Greenaway (eds.), *English Historical Documents 1042–1189*, vol. II (London: Eyre & Spottiswoode, 1953), 854–63.

Further Reading: V.H. Galbraith, *The Making of Domesday Book* (Oxford: Clarendon Press, 1961).

Huntingdonshire

In the borough of Huntingdon there are 4 quarters.

In 2 quarters there were *T.R.E.*, and are now, 116 burgesses rendering all customs and the king's geld, and under them there are 100 bordars[1] who help them to pay the geld. Of these burgesses St. Benedict of Ramsey had 10 with sake and soke[2] and every custom except that they paid geld *T.R.E.* Eustace took them away wrongfully from the abbey and they are, with the others, in the king's hand. Ulf Fenisc had 18 burgesses, now Gilbert of Ghent has them with sake and soke except for the king's geld.

The abbot of Ely has 1 toft[3] with sake and soke except for the king's geld.

The bishop of Lincoln had in the site of the castle a messuage[4] with sake and soke which has now disappeared.

Earl Siward had a messuage with a house with sake and soke, quit from all custom, which the Countess Judith has now.

In the site of the castle there were 20 messuages assessed to all customs, and rendering yearly 16 shillings and 8 pence to the king's "farm." These do not exist now.

In addition to these, there were and are 60 waste messuages within these quarters. These gave and give their customs. And in addition to

---

1 A serf who provided menial service in return for his cottage.
2 The right to hold a judicial court and retain the fines imposed.
3 Farmstead.
4 A dwelling including outbuildings, orchard, court-yard and garden.

these there are 8 waste messuages which *T.R.E.* were fully occupied. These gave all customs.

In the other 2 quarters there were and are 140 burgesses, less half a house, assessed to all customs and the king's geld, and these had 80 haws for which they gave and give all customs. Of these St. Benedict of Ramsey had 22 burgesses *T.R.E.* Two of these were quit of all customs, and 30 rendered 10 pence yearly each. All other customs belonged to the abbot, apart from the king's geld.

In these quarters Aluric the sheriff *T.R.E.* had 1 messuage which King William afterwards granted to his wife and sons. Eustace has it now, and the poor man, with his mother, is claiming it. In these 2 quarters there were and are 44 waste messuages which gave and give their customs. And in these 2 quarters Borred and Turchil *T.R.E.* had 1 church with 2 hides of land and 22 burgesses with houses belonging to the same church with sake and soke; Eustace has all this now. Wherefore these men claim the king's mercy; nevertheless these 22 burgesses give every custom to the king.

Geoffrey the bishop has 1 church and 1 house from the aforesaid which Eustace took away from St. Benedict, and the same saint is still claiming them.

In this borough Gos and Hunef had 16 houses *T.R.E.* with sake and soke and toll and team.[5] The Countess Judith has them now.

The borough of Huntingdonshire used to defend itself towards the king's geld for 50 hides as the fourth part of Hurstingstone hundred,[6] but now it does not so pay geld in that hundred, after the king set a geld of money on the borough. From this whole borough 10 pounds came out *T.R.E.* by way of "Landgable" of which the earl had the third part, and the king two-thirds. Of this rent 16 shillings and 8 pence, divided between the earl and the king, now remain upon 20 messuages where the castle is. In addition to these payments the king had 20 pounds and the earl 10 pounds from the "farm" of the borough more or less according as each could make disposition of his part. One mill rendered 40 shillings to the king and 20 shillings to the earl. To this borough there belong 2 ploughlands and 40 acres of land and 10 acres of meadow, of which the king with two parts, and the earl with the third part, divide the rent. The burgesses cultivate this land and take it on lease through the servants of the king and the earl. Within the aforesaid rent there are 3 fishermen rendering 3 shillings. In this borough there were 3 moneyers paying 40 shillings between the king and the earl, but now they are not there. *T.R.E.* it rendered 30 pounds; now the same.

In Hurstingstone hundred demesne ploughlands are quit of the king's geld. Villeins and sokemen pay geld according to the hides written in the return, apart from Broughton where the abbot of Ramsey pays geld for 1 hide with the others.

Here are noted those holding lands in Huntingdonshire

1. King William.
2. The bishop of Lincoln.
3. The bishop of Coutances.
4. The abbey of Ely.
5. The abbey of Crowland.
6. The abbey of Ramsey.
7. The abbey of Thorney.
8. The abbey of Peterborough.
9. Count Eustace.
10. The count of Eu.
11. Earl Hugh.
12. Walter Giffard.
13. William of Warenne.
14. Hugh of Bolbec.
15. Eudo, son of Hubert.
16. Sweyn of Essex.
17. Roger of Ivry.
18. Arnulf of Hesdins.
19. Eustace the sheriff.
20. The Countess Judith.
21. Gilbert of Ghent.
22. Aubrey "de Vere."
23. William, son of Ansculf.
24. Rannulf, the brother of Ilger.
25. Robert Fafiton.
26. William "Ingania."
27. Ralph, son of Osmund.
28. Rohais, the wife of Richard.
29. The king's thegns.

---

5   The privilege of having a market, and jurisdiction of serfs.
6   The division of a shire for administrative, military and judicial purposes.

1. The land of the king

Hurstingstone hundred

A manor. In Hartford King Edward had 15 hides assessed to the geld. There is land for 17 ploughs. Rannulf the brother of Ilger keeps it now. There are 4 ploughs now on the demesne; and 30 villeins and 3 bordars have 8 ploughs. There is a priest; 2 churches; 2 mills rendering 4 pounds; and 40 acres of meadow. Woodland for pannage, 1 league in length and half a league in breadth. *T.R.E.* it was worth 24 pounds; now 15 pounds.

Normancross hundred

A manor. In Bottlebridge King Edward had 5 hides assessed to the geld. There is land for 8 ploughs. The king has 1 plough now on the demesne; and 15 villeins have 5 ploughs. There is a priest and a church; 60 acres of meadow and 12 acres of woodland for pannage in Northamptonshire. *T.R.E.* it was worth 100 shillings; now 8 pounds. Rannulf keeps it.

In this manor belonging to the king, and in other manors, the enclosure of the abbot of Thorney is doing harm to 300 acres of meadow.

In Stilton the king's sokemen of Norman-cross have 3 virgates[7] of land assessed to the geld. There is land for 2 ploughs, and there are 5 ploughing oxen.

In Orton the king has soke over 3-½ hides of land in the land of the abbot of Peterborough which was Godwine's.

Toseland hundred

A manor. In Gransden Earl Alfgar had 8 hides of land assessed to the geld. There is land for 15 ploughs. There are 7 ploughs now on the demesne; and 24 villeins and 8 bordars have 8 ploughs. There is a priest and a church; 50 acres of meadow; 12 acres of underwood. From the pasture come 5 shillings and 4 pence. *T.R.E.* it was worth 40 pounds; now 30 pounds. Rannulf keeps it.

Leightonstone hundred

A manor. In Alconbury, and in Gidding, which is an outlying estate, there were 10 hides assessed to the geld. There is land for 20 ploughs. There are now 5 ploughs belonging to the hall on 2 hides of this land; and 35 villeins have 13 ploughs there; 80 acres of meadow. *T.R.E.* it was worth 12 pounds; now the same. Rannulf, the brother of Ilger, keeps it.

A manor. In Keyston King Edward had 4 hides of land assessed to the geld. There is land for 12 ploughs. There are 2 ploughs now on the demesne; and 24 villeins and 8 bordars have 10 ploughs; 86 acres of meadow. Scattered woodland for pannage 5 furlongs in length and 1-½ furlongs in breadth. *T.R.E.* it was worth 10 pounds; now the same. Rannulf, the brother of Ilger, keeps it.

A manor. In Brampton King Edward had 15 hides assessed to the geld. There is land for 15 ploughs. There are 3 ploughs now on the demesne; and 36 villeins and 2 bordars have 14 ploughs. There is a church and a priest; 100 acres of meadow. Woodland for pannage half a league in length and 2 furlongs in breadth. Two mills rendering 100 shillings. *T.R.E.* it was worth 20 pounds; now the same. Rannulf, the brother of Ilger, keeps it.

Soke.[8] In Graffham there are 5 hides assessed to the geld. There is land for 8 ploughs. The soke is in Leightonstone hundred. There 7 sokemen and 17 villeins have 6 ploughs now and 6 acres of meadow. Woodland for pannage 1 league in length and 1 league in breadth. *T.R.E.* it was worth 5 pounds; now 10 shillings less.

A manor. In Godmanchester King Edward had 14 hides assessed to the geld. There is land for 57 ploughs. There are 2 ploughs now on the king's demesne on 2 hides of this land; and 80 villeins and 16 bordars have 24 ploughs. There is a priest and a church; 3 mills rendering 100 shillings; 160 acres of meadow; and 50 acres of woodland for pannage. From the pasture come 20 shillings. From the meadows come 70 shillings. *T.R.E.* it was worth 40 pounds; now it is worth the same "by tale."

---

7   A land measurement equivalent to the amount of land a team of oxen could plough in a single season.

8   This term prefixed to estates in this survey indicates "a group of tenements—united to some manor by the ties of rent, the homage of the peasant landholders, and in most cases their suit of court to the manorial centre."

2. The land of the bishop of Lincoln

Toseland hundred

A manor. In "Cotes" the bishop of Lincoln had 2 hides assessed to the geld. There is land for 3 ploughs. There are 2 ploughs now on the demesne; and 3 villeins have 2 oxen; 20 acres of meadow. *T.R.E.* it was worth 40 shillings; now the same. Thurstan holds it of the bishop.

A manor. In Staughton the bishop of Lincoln had 6 hides assessed to the geld. There is land for 15 ploughs. There are 2-½ ploughs on the demesne; and 16 villeins and 4 bordars have 8 ploughs. There is a priest and a church; 24 acres of meadow; 100 acres of underwood. *T.R.E.* it was worth 10 pounds; now the same. Eustace holds it of the bishop. The abbot of Ramsey claims this manor against the bishop.

A manor. In Diddington the bishop of Lincoln had 2-½ hides assessed to the geld. There is land for 2 ploughs. There are now 2 ploughs on the demesne and 5 villeins have 2 ploughs. A church, and 18 acres of meadow. Woodland for pannage half a league in length and half in breadth. *T.R.E.* it was worth 60 shillings; now 70 shillings. William holds it of the bishop.

A manor. In Buckden the bishop of Lincoln had 20 hides assessed to the geld. There is land for 20 ploughs. There are now 5 ploughs on the demesne; and 37 villeins and 20 bordars have 14 ploughs. There is a church and a priest; 1 mill worth 30 shillings; 84 acres of meadow. Woodland for pannage 1 league in length and 1 league in breadth. *T.R.E.* it was worth 20 pounds; now 16 pounds and 10 shillings.

Normancross hundred

A manor. In Denton Godric had 5 hides assessed to the geld. There is land for 2 ploughs. There is 1 plough on the demesne; and 10 villeins and 2 bordars have 5 ploughs. There is a church and a priest; 24 acres of meadow and 24 acres of underwood. *T.R.E.* it was worth 100 shillings; now 4 pounds. Thurstan holds it of the bishop.

A manor. In Orton Leuric had 3 hides and 1 virgate of land assessed to the geld. There is land for 2 ploughs and 1 ox. There is now 1 plough on the demesne; and 2 villeins and 9 acres of meadow. *T.R.E.* it was worth 20 shillings; now 10 shillings. John holds it of the bishop. The king claims the soke of this land.

A manor. In Stilton Tovi had 2 hides assessed to the geld. There is land for 2 ploughs and 7 oxen. There is now 1 plough on the demesne; and 6 villeins have 3 ploughs; 16 acres of meadow and 5 acres of underwood. *T.R.E.* it was worth 40 shillings; now the same. John holds it of the bishop. This land was given to Bishop Wulfwig *T.R.E.*

Leightonstone hundred

A manor. In Leighton Bromswold Turchil the Dane had 15 hides assessed to the geld. There is land for 17 ploughs. There are now 6 ploughs on the demesne; and 33 villeins and 3 bordars have 10 ploughs. One mill rendering 3 shillings; 3 knights hold 3 hides less 1 virgate of this land: they have 3 ploughs and 3 villeins with half a plough. There are 30 acres of meadow and 10 acres of underwood. *T.R.E.* the bishop's demesne was worth 20 pounds and it is worth the same now. The land of the knights is worth 60 shillings. Earl Waltheof gave this manor in alms to St. Mary of Lincoln.

In Pertenhall Alwin had 1 virgate of land assessed to the geld. There is land for half a plough. This land is situated in Bedfordshire but renders geld and service in Huntingdonshire. The king's servants claim this land for his use. *T.R.E.* it was worth 5 shillings; now the same. William holds it of Bishop Remigius and ploughs it with his own demesne.

3. The land of the bishop of Coutances

In Hargrave Semar had 1 virgate of land assessed to the geld. There is land for 2 oxen. The soke belongs to Leightonstone hundred. The same man himself holds it of the bishop of Coutances and ploughs there with 2 oxen and has 2 acres of meadow. *T.R.E.* it was worth 5 shillings; now the same.

4. The land of the abbey of Ely

Hurstingstone hundred

A manor. In Colne the abbey of Ely had 6 hides assessed to the geld. There is land for 6 ploughs and in demesne the abbey has land for 2 ploughs apart from the 6 hides. There are now 2 ploughs on the demesne, and 13 villeins and 5 bordars have 5 ploughs; 10 acres of meadow. Woodland for pannage 1 league in length and half a league in breadth; marsh of the same extent. *T.R.E.* it was worth 6 pounds; now 100 shillings.

A manor. In Bluntisham the abbey of Ely had 6-½ hides assessed to the geld. There is land for 8 ploughs, and, apart from these hides, the abbey has land for 2 ploughs in demesne. There are now 2 ploughs on the demesne; and 10 villeins and 3 bordars have 3 ploughs. There is a priest and a church; 20 acres of meadow. Woodland for pannage 1 league in length and 4 furlongs in breadth. *T.R.E.* it was worth 100 shillings; now the same.

A manor. In Somersham the abbey of Ely had 8 hides assessed to the geld. There is land for 12 ploughs, and, apart from these hides, the abbey had land for 2 ploughs in demesne. There are now 2 ploughs on the demesne; and 32 villeins and 9 bordars have 9 ploughs. There are 3 fisheries rendering 8 shillings, and 20 acres of meadow. Woodland for pannage 1 league in length and 7 furlongs in breadth. *T.R.E.* it was worth 7 pounds; now 8 pounds.

A manor. In Spaldwick the abbey of Ely had 15 hides assessed to the geld. There is land for 15 ploughs. There are now 4 ploughs on the demesne on 5 hides of this land; and 50 villeins and 10 bordars have 25 ploughs. There is 1 mill rendering 2 shillings; and 160 acres of meadow; and 60 acres of woodland for pannage. *T.R.E.* it was worth 16 pounds; now 22 pounds.

A manor. In Little Catworth, outlying estate of Spaldwick, there are 4 hides assessed to the geld. Land for 4 ploughs; 7 villeins have 2 ploughs there now.

5. The land of the abbey of Crowland

A manor. In Morborne the abbey of Crowland has 5 hides assessed to the geld. There is land for 9 ploughs. There are now 2 ploughs on the demesne on 1 hide of this land; and 16 villeins and 3 bordars have 7 ploughs. There is a church and a priest; 40 acres of meadow; 1 acre of underwood. *T.R.E.* it was worth 100 shillings; now the same.

In Thurning there are 1-½ hides assessed to the geld. There is land for 1-½ ploughs. The soke belongs to the king's manor of Alconbury. Eustace holds it now from the abbot of Crowland, and had 1 plough there and 1 villein with half a plough and 6 acres of meadow. *T.R.E.* it was worth 20 shillings; now the same.

6. The land of St. Benedict of Ramsey

[This is similarly described as lying in Stukeley; Abbot's Ripton; Broughton; Wistow; Upwood; Holywell; St. Ives; Houghton; Wyton; Warboys; Sawtry; Elton; Lutton; Yelling; Hemingford Abbots; Offord; Dillington; Gidding; Bythorn; Bringtin; Old Weston; Ellington.]

7. The land of St. Mary of Thorney

[This is similarly described as lying in Yaxley; Stanground; Woodstone; Haddon; Water Newton; Sibson; Stibbington.]

8. The land of St. Peter of Peterborough

[This is similarly described as lying at Fletton; Alwalton; Orton Waterville.]

9. The land of Count Eustace

[This is similarly described as lying at Glatton; Chesterton; Sibson.]

10. The land of the Count of Eu

[This is similarly described as lying at Buckworth.]

11. The land of Earl Hugh

[This is similarly described as lying in Upton; Coppingford.]

12. The land of Walter Giffard

[This is similarly described as lying at Folksworth.]

13. The land of William of Warenne

[This is similarly described as lying at Kimbolton; Keysoe; Catworth.]

14. The land of Hugh of Bolbec

[This is similarly described as lying at Wood Walton.]

15. The land of Eudo, son of Hubert

[This is similarly described as lying at Hamerton.]

16. The land of Sweyn of Essex

[This is similarly described as lying at Waresley.]

17. The land of Roger of Ivry

[This is similarly described as lying at Covington.]

18. The land of Arnulf of Hesdins

[This is similarly described as lying in Offord Cluny.]

19. The land of Eustace the sheriff

[This is similarly described as lying in Sawtry; Caldecot; Washingley; Orton Longueville; Stilton; Chesterton; Bottlebridge; Swineshead; Catworth; Hargrave; Gidding; Winwick; Thurning; Luddington; Weston; Wooley; Hemingford; Offord; Waresley; Hail Weston; Southoe; Perry; Catworth.]

20. The land of the Countess Judith

[This is similarly described as lying in Conington; Sawtry; Stukeley; Molesworth; "Cotes"; Eynesbury; Offord; Diddington; Paxton.]

21. The land of Gilbert of Ghent

[This is similarly described as lying in Fen Stanton.]

22. The land of Aubrey "de Vere"

[This is similarly described as lying in Yelling; Hemingford.]

23. The land of William, son of Ansculf

[This is similarly described as lying in Waresley.]

24. The land of Rannulf, brother of Ilger

[This is similarly described as lying in Everton.]

25. The land of Robert Fafiton

[This is similarly described as lying in Hail Weston; Southhoe.]

26. The land of William "Ingania"

[This is similarly described as lying in Gidding.]

27. The land of Ralph, son of Osmund

[This is similarly described as lying in Hemingford.]

28. The land of Rohais, wife of Richard fitz Gilbert

Toseland hundred

A manor. In Eynesbury Robert, son of Wimarc, had 15 hides assessed to the geld. There is land for 27 ploughs. Rohais, the wife of Richard, has 7 ploughs on the demesne there now. In the same place St. Neot has from her 3 ploughs on the demesne, and in the same village 19 villeins and 5 bordars have 7 ploughs. There is 1 mill worth 23 shillings, and 1 fishery which is valued with the manor; 65-½ acres of meadow. *T.R.E.* it was worth 24 pounds; now it is worth 21 pounds apart from that which is assigned to the food of the monks, which is valued at 4 pounds. William "Brito" holds 2 hides and 1 virgate of this land from Rohais and has half a plough on the demesne; and 3 villeins and 4 bordars have 1 plough. It is worth 30 shillings.

29. The land of the king's thegns

A manor. In Washingley, Chetelebert had 2-½ hides assessed to the geld. There is land for 4 ploughs. He himself holds from the king and has 1 plough there; and 10 villeins have 4 ploughs. There is a church and a priest; 12 acres of meadow. Woodland for pannage 7 furlongs in length and 10-½ furlongs in breadth. *T.R.E.* it was worth 10 shillings; now the same.

Leightonstone hundred

In Keysoe Alwine had 1 virgate of land assessed to the geld with sake and soke. There is land for 2 oxen. It belongs to Bedfordshire, but gives geld in Huntingdonshire. He himself holds now of the king and has 1 villein there with 2 oxen in a plough. *T.R.E.* it was worth 16 pence; now the same.

A manor. In Catworth Avic had 3 hides assessed to the geld. There is land for 4 ploughs. Eric holds it now of the king. And the same man has under the king 1 hide assessed to the geld. There is land for 1 plough. He has 2 villeins there, and 6 acres of meadow. *T.R.E.* it was worth 40 shillings; now 20 shillings.

In Brampton Elric has 1 hide and 1 virgate of land assessed to the geld. There is land for 10 oxen. There are 3 bordars and 1 plough. It is worth 30 shillings.

A manor. In Wooley Golde and Uluric, his son, had 3 hides assessed to the geld. There is land for 6 ploughs. They themselves now have it from the king. There is 1 plough on the demesne; and 14 villeins have 5 ploughs; 20 acres of meadow. *T.R.E.* it was worth 60 shillings; now the same.

In Sawtry Alwine had half a carucate[9] assessed to the geld. There is land for 6 oxen. His wife holds it now of the king, and has 1 plough there and 2 acres. *T.R.E.* it was worth 10 shillings; now the same.

[Claims]

The jurors of Huntingdon say that the church of St. Mary of the borough and the land which is annexed to it belonged to the church of Thorney, but the abbot gave it in pledge to the burgesses. Moreover, King Edward gave it to Vitalis and Bernard, his priests, and they sold it to Hugh, chamberlain to King Edward. Moreover, Hugh sold it to two priests of Huntingdon, and in respect of this they have the seal of King Edward. Eustace has it now without livery, without writ, and without seisin.

Eustace took away wrongfully the house of Leveve and gave it to Oger of London.

They bear witness that the land of Hunef and Gos was under the hand of King Edward on the day when he was alive and dead and that they held of him and not of the earl. But the jurors say that they heard that King William was said to have given it to Waltheof.

Touching the 5 hides of Broughton the jurors say that it was the land of sokemen *T.R.E.*, but that the same king gave the land and the soke over the men to St. Benedict of Ramsey in return for a service which Abbot Alwin did for him in Saxony, and ever afterwards the saint had it.

The shire bears witness that the land of Bricmer "Belehorne" was "reeveland" *T.R.E.* and belonged to the king's "farm."

They bear witness that the land of Alwin the priest was to the abbot….

They bear witness that Aluric's land of Yelling and Hemingford belonged to St. Benedict and that it was granted to Aluric for the term of his life on the condition that after his death it ought to return to the church, and "Bocstede" with it. But this same Aluric was killed in the battle of Hastings, and the abbot took back his lands and held them until Aubrey "de Vere" deprived him of possession.

Touching 2 hides which Ralph, son of Osmund, holds in Hemingford, they say that one of them belonged to the demesne of the church of Ramsey in King Edward's day, and that Ralph holds it against the abbot's will. Touching the other hide, they say that Godric held it from the abbot, but

---

9   A unit of assessment for taxes equivalent to the amount of land a team of eight oxen could till in a season.

when the abbot was in Denmark, Osmund, Ralph's father, seized it from Sawin the fowler, to whom the abbot had given it for love of the king.

Touching Summerlede they say that he held his land from Turulf who gave it to him, and afterwards from the sons of Turulf, and they had sake and soke over him.

The jurors say that the land of Wulwine Chit of Weston was a manor by itself, and did not belong to Kimbolton, but that nevertheless he was a man of Earl Harold.

Touching a hide and a half of land which was Ælget's, the jurors say that this Ælget held them from Earl Tosti with sake and soke and afterwards of Waltheof.

Godric the priest likewise held 1 hide of land from Earl Waltheof *T.R.E.*, and Eustace holds it now.

They say that the land of Godwine of Weston in no way belonged to Saxi, Fafiton's predecessor.

The men of the shire bear witness that King Edward gave Swineshead to Earl Siward with sake and soke, and so Earl Harold had it, except that the men paid geld in the hundred, and performed military service with them.

Touching the land of Fursa, the soke was the king's. King Edward had soke over 1 virgate of land of Alwin Deule in Pertenhall.

The jurors say that the hide of land which Wulwine Chit had in Catworth was in the king's soke and that Earl Harold did not have it.

In Little Catworth the same Wulwine had 1 hide over which King Edward always had sake and soke. But Wulwine could give and sell the land to whom he wished. But the men of the countess say that the king gave the land to Earl Waltheof.

The shire bears witness that the third part of half a hide which lies in Easton and pays geld in Bedfordshire belongs to the abbot of Ely's manor of Spaldwick. The abbot of Ely thus held it *T.R.E.*, and for five years after the coming of King William. Eustace seized this land wrongfully from the church, and kept it.

The jurors say that Keystone was and is of the "farm" of King Edward, and although Aluric the sheriff resided in that village, he nevertheless always paid the king's "farm" therefrom, and his sons after him, until Eustace took the sheriffdom. They have never seen or heard of a seal of King Edward that he put it outside his "farm."

Alwold and his brother claim that Eustace took away their land from them, and the men of the shire deny that they have ever seen a seal, or seen anyone who gave Eustace seisin of it.

On the day when King Edward was alive and dead, Gidding was an outlying estate of Alconbury in the king's "farm."

The men of the shire bear witness that Buckworth was an outlying estate of Paxton *T.R.E.*

They say that 36 hides of land in Brampton which Richard "Ingania" claims to belong to the forest were of the king's demesne "farm," and did not belong to the forest.

They say that Graffham was and is the king's sokeland, and that they have not seen the writ, or anyone who gave legal possession of this to Eustace.

Touching 6 hides in Conington they said they had heard that these formerly belonged to the church of Thorney, and that they were granted to Turchill on condition that after [his] death they ought to return to the church with the other 3 hides in the same village. The jurors said that they had heard this, but they had not seen evidence of it, nor were they present when the arrangement was made.

Touching the land of Tosti of Sawtry, they say that Eric, his brother, bequeathed it to the church of Ramsey after his death and after the death of his brother and sister.

Touching Fletton the jurors say that *T.R.E.* the whole belonged to the church of Peterborough, and so it should.

Touching Leuric's land the jurors say that it was in the king's soke, but Bishop Remigius shows the writ of King Edward by which he gave Leuric with all his land to the bishopric of Lincoln with sake and soke.

52. RICHARD FITZ NIGEL

Dialogue of the Exchequer

THE *DIALOGUE OF THE EXCHEQUER*, written between 1177 and 1179 by Richard fitz Nigel, the treasurer for Henry II, presents in dialogue form the system by which the accounts of sheriffs were audited and enrolled by royal officials. This accounting system gave the English kings the most efficient form of financial control and hence ready wealth in Europe.

Sources: E.F. Henderson, *Select Historical Documents* (London: George Bell, 1894); David C. Douglas and George W. Greenaway (eds.), *English Historical Documents 1042–1189*, vol. II (London: Eyre & Spottiswoode, 1953), 578–83.

Further Reading: W.L. Warren, *The Governance of Norman and Angevin England, 1086–1272* (Stanford, CA: Stanford University Press, 1987).

First Book

In the twenty-third year of the reign of King Henry II, while I was sitting at the window of a tower next to the River Thames, a man spoke to me impetuously, saying: "master, hast thou not read that there is no use in science or in a treasure that is hidden?" when I replied to him, "I have read so," straightway he said: "why, therefore, dost thou not teach others the knowledge concerning the exchequer which is said to be thine to such an extent, and commit it to writing lest it die with thee?" I answered: "lo, brother, thou hast now for a long time sat at the exchequer, and nothing is hidden from thee, for thou art painstaking. And the same is probably the case with the others who have seats there." But he, "just as those who walk in darkness and grope with their hands frequently stumble,—so many sit there who seeing do not perceive, and hearing do not understand." Then I, "thou speakest irreverently, for neither is the knowledge so great nor does it concern such great things; but perchance those who are occupied with important matters have hearts like the claws of an eagle, which do not retain small things, but which great ones do not escape." And he, "so be it: but although eagles fly very high, nevertheless they rest and refresh themselves in humble places; and therefore we beg thee to explain humble things which will be of profit to the eagles themselves." Then I; "I have feared to put together a work concerning these things because

they lie open to the bodily senses and grow common by daily use; nor is there, nor can there be in them a description of subtle things, or a pleasing invention of the imagination." And he, "those who rejoice in imaginings, who seek the flight of subtle things, have Aristotle and the books of Plato; to them let them listen. Do thou write not subtle but useful things." Then I; "of those things which thou demandest it is impossible to speak except in common discourse and in ordinary words." "But," said he, as if aroused to ire,—for to a mind filled with desire nothing goes quickly enough,—"writers on arts, lest they might seem to know too little about many things, and in order that art might less easily become known, have sought to appropriate many things, and have concealed them under unknown words: but thou dost not undertake to write about an art, but about certain customs and laws of the exchequer; and since these ought to be common, common words must necessarily be employed, so that the style may have relation to the things of which we are speaking. Moreover, although it is very often allowable to invent new words, I beg, nevertheless, if it please thee, that thou may'st not be ashamed to use the customary names of the things themselves which readily occur to the mind, so that no new difficulty from using unfamiliar words may arise to disturb us." Then I; "I see that thou art angry; but be calmer; I will do what thou dost urge. Rise, therefore, and sit opposite to me; and ask me concerning those things that occur to thee. But if thou shalt propound something unheard of, I shall not blush to say 'I do not know.' But let us both, like discreet beings, come to an agreement." And he; "thou respondest to my wish. Moreover, although an elementary old man is a disgraceful and ridiculous thing, I will nevertheless begin with the very elements."

I. What the Exchequer is, and what is the reason of this name.

Disciple. What is the exchequer?

Master. The exchequer is a quadrangular surface about ten feet in length, five in breadth, placed before those who sit around it in the manner of a table, and all around it it has an edge about the height of one's four fingers, lest any thing placed upon it should fall off. There is placed over the top of the exchequer, moreover, a cloth bought at the Easter term, not an ordinary one but a black one marked with stripes, the stripes being distant from each other the space of a foot or the breadth of a hand. In the spaces moreover are counters placed according to their values; about these we shall speak below. Although, moreover, such a surface is called exchequer, nevertheless this name is so changed about that the court itself which sits when the exchequer does is called exchequer; so that if at any time through a decree any thing is established by common counsel, it is said to have been done at the exchequer of this or that year. As, moreover, one says today "at the exchequer," so one formerly said "at the tallies."

D What is the reason of this name?

M No truer one occurs to me at present than that it has a shape similar to that of a chess board.

D Would the prudence of the ancients ever have called it so for its shape alone, when it might for a similar reason be called a table [tabularium]?

M I was right in calling thee painstaking. There is another, but a more hidden reason. For just as, in a game of chess, there are certain grades of combatants and they proceed or stand still by certain laws or limitations, some presiding and others advancing: so, in this, some preside, some assist by reason of their office, and no one is free to exceed the fixed laws; as will be manifest from what is to follow. Moreover, as in chess the battle is fought between kings, so in this it is chiefly between two that the conflict takes place and the war is waged,—the treasurer, namely, and the sheriff who sits there to render account; the others sitting by as judges, to see and to judge.

D Will the accounts be received then by the treasurer, although there are many there who, by reason of their power, are greater?

M That the treasurer ought to receive the account from the sheriff is manifest from this, that the same is required from him whenever it pleases the king: nor could that be required of him which he had not received. Some say, nevertheless, that the treasurer and the chamberlains should be bounden alone for what is written in the rolls in the treasury, and that for this an account should be demanded of them. But it is believed with more truth that they should be responsible for the whole writing of the roll, as will be readily understood from what is to follow.

II. That there is a lower one and an upper one; both have the same origin however.

D Is that exchequer, in which such a conflict goes on, the only one?

M No. For there is a lower exchequer which is also called the Receipt, where the money is handed over to be counted, and is put down in writing and on tallies, so that afterwards, at the upper exchequer, an account may be rendered of them; both have the same origin however, for whatever is declared payable at the greater one is here paid; and whatever has been paid here is accounted for there.

III. As to the nature or arrangement of the lower one according to the separate offices.

D What is the nature or arrangement of the lower exchequer?

M As I see, thou canst not bear to be ignorant of any of these things. Know then that that lower exchequer has its persons, distinct from each other by reason of their offices, but with one intent devoted to the interests of the king, due regard, nevertheless, being paid to equity; all serving, moreover, not in their own names but in the names of their masters; with the exception of two knights, he, namely, who conducts the assays, and the melter. Their offices depend on the will of our king; hence they seem to belong rather to the upper than to the lower exchequer, as will be explained below. The clerk of the treasurer is there with his seal. There are also two knights of the chamberlains. There is also a certain knight who may be called the silverer, for, by reason of his office, he presides at the testing of silver. There are also four tellers to count the money. There is also the usher of the treasury and the watchman. These, moreover, are their offices: The clerk of the treasurer, when the money has been counted and put in boxes by the hundred pounds, affixes his seal and puts down in writing how much he has received, and from whom, and for what cause; he registers also the tallies which have been made by the chamberlains concerning that receipt. Not only, moreover, does he place his seal on the sacks of money, but also, if he wishes, on the chests and on the separate boxes in which the rolls and tallies are placed, and he diligently supervises all the offices which are under him, and nothing is hidden from him. The office of the knights, who are also called chamberlains because they serve in the name of the chamberlains, is this: they carry the keys of the chests; for each chest has two locks of a different kind, that is, to neither of which the key of the other can be fitted; and they carry the keys of them. Each chest, moreover, is girded with a certain immovable strap, on which, in addition, when the locks are closed the seal of the treasurer is placed; so that neither of the chamberlains can have access except by common consent. Likewise it is their duty to weigh the money which has been counted and placed by the hundred shillings in wooden receptacles, so that there be no error in the amount; and then, at length, to put them in boxes by the hundred pounds as has been said. But if a receptacle is found to have any deficiency, that which is thought to be lacking is not made

good by calculation, but straightway the doubtful one is thrown back into the heap which is to be counted. And take note that certain counties from the time of King Henry I and in the time of King Henry II could lawfully offer for payment coins of any kind of money provided they were of silver and did not differ from the lawful weight; because indeed, by ancient customs, not themselves having moneyers, they sought their coins from on all sides; such are Northumberland and Cumberland. Coins thus received, moreover, although they came from a farm, were nevertheless set apart from the others with some marks placed on them. But the remaining counties were accustomed to bring only the usual and lawful coin of the present money as well from farms as from pleas. But after the illustrious king whose renown shines the brighter in great matters, did, in his reign, institute one weight and one money for the whole kingdom, each county began to be bound by one necessity of law and to be constrained by the manner of payment of a general commerce. All, therefore, in whatever manner they are bounden, pay the same kind of money; but nevertheless all do not sustain the loss which comes from the testing by combustion. The chamberlains likewise make the tallies of receipts, and have in common with the clerk of the treasurer to disburse the treasure received when required by writs of the king or an order of the barons; not, however, without consulting their masters. These three, all together or by turns, are sent with treasure when it is necessary. These three have the principal care of all that is done in the lower exchequer.

D Therefore, as I perceive, these men are allowed to disburse the treasure received, in consequence of a royal writ or of an order from those who preside—after consultation with their masters, however.

M They are allowed, I say; in so far as they are entrusted with the payment of the servants of the lower exchequer, and with buying the small necessaries of the exchequer, such as the wooden receptacles, and other things which will be mentioned below; but not otherwise. When any one brings a writ or order of the king for money, by command of their masters that sum which is expressly named in the writ may be paid, with the understanding that, before he go out, he shall count the money received. But if anything be lacking, he who received it shall return to the exchequer and shall give an oath to this effect: that he has brought back as much as he received, adding this, *upon his conscience*, as is done in other things; and this being done the rest shall be paid him, it being first counted in the presence of all by the regular tellers. But if, the conditions being known to him, he shall have gone out of the door of the treasury, whoever the person, or however great the loss, no heed shall be paid to him. The offices of the knight silverer and of the melter are conjoined and belong rather to the upper exchequer, and therefore will be explained there with the other offices. The office of the four tellers is the following: When the money is sent to the exchequer to be counted, one of them diligently mixes the whole together, so that the better pieces may not be by themselves and the worse by themselves, but mixed, in order that they may correspond in weight; this being done, the chamberlain weighs in a scale as much as is necessary to make a pound of the exchequer. But if the number shall exceed 20 shillings by more than six pence in a pound, it is considered unfit to be received; but if it shall restrict itself to six pence or less, it is received, and is counted diligently by the tellers by the hundred shillings as has been said. But if the coins are from a farm and are to be tested, 44 shillings from the heap, being mixed together, are placed in a compartment by themselves, and on this the sheriff puts a mark; so that there may be afterwards a testing, which is commonly called assaying, of them, as will be made clear further on. It shall, moreover, be the care of those who preside over the Receipt by virtue of their masters—that is of the clerks of the treasurer and of the chamberlains—when the money is received, to put aside weights of the tested silver and coins from a farm, placing certain marks on the bags that contain them, so that, if the king wishes silver vessels to be made for the uses of the house of God, or for the service of his own palace, or perchance money for beyond seas, it may be made from this.

D There is something in what thou hast said that strikes me.

M Speak then.

D Thou said'st, if I remember rightly, that sometimes money is brought to be paid into the exchequer which is judged unfit to be received, if, indeed, being weighed against a pound weight of the exchequer, a deficiency is found of more than six pence. Inasmuch, then, as all money of this kingdom ought to have the stamped image of the king, and all moneyers are bound to work according to the same weight, how can it happen that all their work is not of one weight?

M That is a great question which thou askest, and one which requires further investigation; but it can happen through forgers and clippers or cutters of coin. Thou knowest, moreover, that the money of England can be found false in three ways: false, namely, in weight, false in quality, false in the stamping. But these kinds of falsification are not visited by an equal punishment. But of this elsewhere.

D If it please thee, continue concerning the offices as thou hast begun.

M It is the duty of the usher to exclude or admit as is necessary, and to be diligent in guarding every thing which is shut in by the door; wherefore, as door-money, he shall have two pence from each writ of exit. He furnishes the boxes to put the money in, and the rolls and the tallies, and the other things which become necessary during the year; and for each box he has two pence. He furnishes the whole Receipt with wood suitable for the tallies of receipts and of accounts, and once, that is at the Michaelmas term, he receives five shillings for the wood of the tallies. He furnishes the wooden receptacles, the knives, the compartments, and the straps and the other minute necessaries of the fisc. At that same term are due two shillings for furnishing the ink of the whole year to both exchequers, and this amount, by ancient right, the sacristan of the greater church of Westminster claims for himself. The office of the watchman is the same there as elsewhere; most diligent guarding, namely, at night, chiefly of the treasure and of all those things which are placed in the treasury building. Thus thou hast the various offices of those who serve in the lower exchequer. And they have fixed payments while the exchequer is in progress, that is from the day on which they are called together, to the day on which there is a general departure. The clerk of the treasurer who is below, has five pence a day. The scribe of the same treasurer in the upper exchequer has likewise five. The scribe of the chancellor, five. The two knights who bear the keys have each eight, by reason of their knighthood. For they claim that they are bound to be ready with the necessary horses and weapons, so that when they are sent with the treasure they may thus more readily execute what pertains to their office. The knight-silverer has twelve pence a day. The melter, five. The usher of the greater exchequer, five. The four tellers, each three pence, if they are at London; if at Winchester each one has two, since they are generally taken from there. The watchman has one penny. For the light of each night at the treasury one halfpenny.

D For what reason does the usher of the treasury alone receive no pay?

M I do not exactly know. But, however, perhaps he does not receive any pay because he is seen to receive something as door-money, and for furnishing the boxes and tallies; or perchance because he seems to serve, not the king, but the treasurer and the chamberlains in guarding the door of their building. In this way, then, has the arrangement of the lower exchequer or Receipt been made.

D I have been so well satisfied in this regard that nothing seems to be wanting. Proceed now, if it please thee, concerning the greater exchequer.

IV. What is the competency of the Upper Exchequer, and whence it takes its origin.

M Although the offices of those who have seats at the greater exchequer seem to differ in certain functions, the purpose, nevertheless, of all the offices is the same, to look out for the king's advantage; with due regard for equity, however, according to the fixed laws of the exchequer. The arrangement or ordering of the latter is confirmed by its antiquity and by the authority of the nobles who have their seats there. It is said to have begun with the very conquest of the kingdom made by King William, the arrangement being taken, however, from the exchequer across the seas; but they differ in very many and almost the most important points. Some believe it to have existed under the Anglo-Saxon kings, taking their argument in this matter from the fact that the peasants and already decrepit old men of those estates which are called of the crown, whose memory is gray in these matters, knew very well, having been taught by their fathers, how much extra money they are bound to pay on the pound for the blanching of their farm. But this argument applies to the payment of the farm, not to the session of the exchequer. The fact also seems to be against those who say that the blanching of the farm began in the time of the Anglo-Saxon kings, that in the Domesday book, in which a diligent description of the whole kingdom is contained, and in which the value is expressed of the different estates as well of the time of King Edward as of the time of King William, under whom it was made,—there is no mention at all of the blanching of the farm: from which it seems probable that, after the time when that survey was made in the reign of the aforementioned king, the blanching of the farm was fixed upon by his investigators on account of causes which are noted below. But at whatever time it came into use, it is certain that the exchequer is confirmed by the authority of the great, so that it is allowed to no one to infringe its statutes or to resist them by any kind of rashness. For it has this in common with the court itself of the lord king [Curia Regis], in which he in his own person administers the law, that no one is allowed to contradict a record or a sentence passed in it. The authority, moreover, of this court is so great, as well on account of the pre-eminence of the royal image, which, by a special prerogative, is kept on his seal of the treasury, as on account of those who have their seats there, as has been said; by whose watchfulness the condition of the whole kingdom is kept safe. For there sits the chief justice of the lord king by reason of his judicial dignity, as well as the greatest men of the kingdom, who share familiarly in the royal secrets; so that whatever has been established or determined in the presence of such great men subsists by an inviolable right. In the first place, there sits, nay also presides, by reason of his office, the first man in the kingdom,—namely, the Chief Justice. With him sit, solely by command of the sovereign, with momentary and varying authority, indeed, certain of the greatest and most discreet men in the kingdom, who may belong either to the clergy or to the court. They sit there, I say, to interpret the law and to decide upon the doubtful points which frequently arise from incidental questions. For not in its reckonings, but in its manifold judgments, does the superior science of the exchequer consist. For it is easy when the sum required has been put down, and the sums which have been handed in are placed under it for comparison, to tell by subtraction if the demands have been satisfied or if anything remains. But when one begins to make a many-sided investigation of those things which come into the fisc in varying ways, and are required under different conditions, and are not collected by the sheriffs in the same way,—to be able to tell if the latter have acted otherwise than they should, is in many ways a grave task. Therefore the greater science of the exchequer is said to consist in these matters. But the judgments on doubtful or doubted points which frequently come up can not be comprehended under one form of treatment; for all kinds of doubts have not yet come to light. Certain, however, of the matters which we know to have been brought up and settled, we shall note below in their proper place.

53. ACCOUNTS OF THE EXCHEQUER: AN EXAMPLE

THE ACCOUNTS OF THE Exchequer were recorded in the Pipe rolls. The following brief example is that of Henry II for Staffordshire from 1186.

Source: David C. Douglas and George Greenaway (eds.) *English Historical Documents 1042–1189*, volume II (London: Eyre & Spottiswoode, 1953).

Thomas Noel[1] accounts for the "farm" of Staffordshire. He has paid in the Treasury 88 pounds and 6 pence "blanch."[2]

He has disbursed:

In fixed alms 1 mark to the knights of the Temple.

In fixed liveries half a mark to the canons of Llanthony for the keeping of the king's houses at Cannock.

In lands granted to the monks of Bordesley 10 pounds "blanch" in Tardebigg. And in Trentham 30 pounds "blanch" concerning which Geoffrey Savage accounts below. And in Meertown 8 pounds "blanch" concerning which Roger Muisson accounts below. And to William "de Herovilla" 60 shillings "blanch" in Wednesbury.

And he is quit.[3]

Concerning purprestures[4] and escheats[5]

The same sheriff accounts for 33 shillings and 4 pence for the "farm" of Broom; and for 1 mark for the "farm" of Rowley Regis. He has made payment in the Treasury by means of 2 tallies. And he is quit.

Geoffrey Savage accounts for 30 pounds "blanch" in respect of the "farm" of Trentham. He has paid into the Treasury 14 pounds and 23 pence "blanch".

He has disbursed:

In lands given to the knights of the Temple in Keele, 43 shillings and 7 pence.

To John the chaplain, 100 shillings.

In fixed liveries to ten serjeants, 9 pounds, 2 shillings and 6 pence.

In pasture which the king granted to John Lestrange, 8 shillings and 8 pence. And he is quit. The same Geoffrey renders account for 8 pounds "blanch" for the "farm" of Meretown. He has paid into the Treasury. And he is quit. Robert "de Broc" accounts for 3 marks in respect of rent for the forest of Cannock for the third year. He has paid this in the Treasury. And he is quit.

The same Robert accounts for 6 pounds, 13 shillings and 4 pence for rent for the same forest of Cannock for this year. He has paid in the Treasury. And he is quit.

The same Robert accounts for 116 shillings and 3 pence in respect of the pannage of the forest of Cannock. He has paid in the Treasury. And he is quit.

[The same sheriff] accounts for 6 pounds in respect of the increase of Walsall. And for 3 shillings and 6 pence in respect of the house of Walter the reeve in the cemetery of Stafford. He has paid in the Treasury by means of 2 tallies. And he is quit.

---

1 The sheriff.
2 *I.e.*, by weight.
3 *I.e.*, released from further obligations.
4 Wrongful encroachment on another's land.
5 Property that had reverted to the king.

The same sheriff accounts for 3 shillings in respect of the profits of the mill at Cradley. And for 13 shillings and 4 pence for the prebend of Penkridge. He has made payment in the Treasury by means of 2 tallies. And he is quit.

[William], son of Guy, owes 2 war-horses in respect of the amercement of the king in connexion with the forest.

[Gervase] Paynel accounts for 14 pounds, 13 shillings and 4 pence that he may be quit of the pledge made by the earl of Leicester to Aaron the Jew, and that he may not be distrained for that pledge. He has paid 5 marks in the Treasury. And he owes 11 pounds, 6 shillings and 8 pence.

The same sheriff owes 21 shillings in respect of the wastes, the assarts,[6] the purprestures and the pleas of the forest of Staffordshire through Thomas, son of Bernard.

Ernald the priest owes 1 mark for false pleading. Richard Miles the forester owes half a mark for default.

Robert of Beaumais accounts for 1 mark for the sale of wood in the forest. He has paid half a mark into the Treasury. And he owes half a mark.

Concerning pleas of the court

Alice who was the wife of Robert of Bec accounts for 10 pounds for the recognition of 1 knight's fee against Robert of Stafford by the pledge of Geoffrey Savage. She has paid 6 pounds in the Treasury. And she owes 4 pounds.

Alina of Darlaston owes 2 marks in respect of the right given her in the king's court against Walter of Caverswall concerning the land of Olnea. But she has not yet had right.

[Geoffrey] Savage accounts for 100 pounds for goods distrained by the sheriff. By writ of the king the said Geoffrey has been pardoned 100 pounds. And he is quit.

[Robert] "Pulerefice" owes half a mark for making a false charge.

Concerning the offerings of the court

[William, son of] Turkill, owes 20 shillings for right in respect of 10 marks which he claims against the prior of Staines.

William of Sandford owes 1 mark for right concerning 5 marks against Robert of Tamhorn by the pledge of John of Sandford. But he has not yet had right.

New pleas and new agreements through Robert Marmion, Ralph of Arden, Hugh Pantulf, William, son of Stephen, and Thomas Noel

The same sheriff[7] accounts for 1 mark from Totmonslow for murder.[8]

And for 1 mark from Eitroph Hasting because he first denied what he afterwards admitted. And for 40 shillings from William of Birmingham because he did not have what he had pledged.

He has made payment in the Treasury by means of 3 tallies. And he is quit.

The same sheriff accounts for 2 marks from Gerard of Stafford in respect of the pledge of Robert the Frenchman. And for 1 mark from William the Frenchman for the same. And for 1 mark from Margaret "de la Barre" for false accusation.

And for 1 mark from Hereward of "Huneswurth" for false witness.

The king has granted by his writ 5 marks from the amercements of the above to the brethren of the Hospital of Jerusalem.
And he is quit.

---

6   Land cleared for farming.
7   Thomas Noel; see above.
8   The *murdrum* or murder-fine.

The same sheriff accounts for 20 shillings from "Pirhulle" hundred for murder. He has paid 18 shillings in the Treasury. And he owes 2 shillings.

The same sheriff accounts for 1 mark from Cuttleston hundred for murder. He has paid 12 shillings and 8 pence in the Treasury. And he owes 8 pence.

Hugh of Comberford accounts for 10 marks for "novel disseisin." He has paid 44 shillings and 4 pence in the Treasury. And he owes 4 pounds and 9 shillings.

Simon, son of Ailwin, accounts for 2 marks for the same. He has paid half a mark into the Treasury. And he owes 20 shillings.

Concerning those who have paid in full

The same sheriff accounts for 10 pounds and 3 shillings and 4 pence in respect of petty amercements from those men whose names and debts and delinquencies are noted in the roll of the aforesaid, and which they have paid in the Treasury. He has made payment in the Treasury by means of 30 tallies. And he is quit. Gamel of "Deruereslawa" owes half a mark because he did not have "Suanhilda" whom he had pledged.

Godwin, son of Chilla, owes half a mark for "novel disseisin."

Richard Wagtail accounts for half a mark because he withdrew from his appeal. He has paid 12 pence in the Treasury. And he owes 5 shillings and 8 pence.

Concerning the pleas of the forest through Robert "de Broc," William of Stanton and Robert of "Haselea"

John of Perton accounts for 20 shillings for keeping dogs in the forest without a warrant. He has paid this in the Treasury. And he is quit.

Concerning those who have paid in full in respect of pleas of the forest

The same sheriff accounts for 66 shillings in respect of petty amercements for the forest. He has paid in the Treasury, and he is quit.

Robert of Walton owes 2 shillings for new purpresture.

The same sheriff accounts for 63 shillings and 4 pence in respect of petty amercements for the forest. He has paid in the Treasury by means of 9 tallies. And he is quit.

The same sheriff accounts for 4 pounds, 2 shillings and 3 pence in respect of the assarts of Staffordshire. He has paid in the Treasury 40 shillings and 9 pence. And he owes 41 shillings and 6 pence.

Concerning the pleas of the court

Guy of Swinfen renders account for 1 mark for making his complaint against Henry of Perry in the king's court instead of in the shire court. He has paid in the Treasury. And he is quit.

Concerning the tallage of the demesne lands of the king and of those lands which were then in the king's hands; through Robert Marmion and his associates as aforesaid

The same sheriff accounts as follows:

For 15 pounds, 4 shillings and 8 pence for the gift of Newcastle.[9] He has paid 8 pounds and 10 shillings in the Treasury. And he owes 6 pounds, 13 shillings and 8 pence.

For 13 pounds for the gift of the borough of Stafford. He has paid 6 pounds and 10 shillings in the Treasury. And he owes 6 pounds and 10 shillings.

For 55 shillings in respect of the gift of Meretown. He has paid 53 shillings. And he owes 2 shillings.

9   Newcastle-under-Lyme.

For 103 shillings and 8 pence for the gift of Penkridge. He has paid 52 shillings in the Treasury. And he owes 51 shillings and 8 pence.

For 46 shillings and 8 pence for the gift of Cannock. He has paid 23 shillings and 4 pence in the Treasury. And he owes 23 shillings and 4 pence.

For 4 pounds and 17 shillings for the gift of Kinver. He has paid this in the Treasury. And he is quit.

For 71 shillings for the gift of Rugeley. He has paid 35 shillings and 6 pence into the Treasury. And he owes 35 shillings and 6 pence.

For 58 shillings and 4 pence for the gift of Clent. He has paid 29 shillings and 2 pence in the Treasury. And he owes 29 shillings and 2 pence.

For 34 shillings for the gift of Wolverhampton. He has paid 17 shillings in the Treasury. And he owes 17 shillings.

For 36 shillings for the gift of Bilston. He has paid 18 shillings in the Treasury. And he owes 18 shillings.

For 17 shillings for the gift of Willenhall. He has paid this into the Treasury. And he is quit.

For 63 shillings and 8 pence for the gift of Tettenhall. He has paid 31 shillings and 10 pence in the Treasury. And he owes 31 shillings and 10 pence.

For 40 shillings for the gift of Bromley. He has paid 20 shillings in the Treasury. And he owes 20 shillings.

For 42 shillings for the gift of Walsall. He has paid 21 shillings in the Treasury. And he owes 21 shillings.

For 74 shillings for the gift of Swinford. He has paid 37 shillings in the Treasury. And he owes 37 shillings.

For 24 shillings and 8 pence for the gift of Penkhull. He has paid in the Treasury. And he is quit.

For 43 shillings and 4 pence for the gift of Tamworth. He has paid 28 shillings and 4 pence in the Treasury. And he owes 15 shillings.

For 100 shillings for the gift of Wigginton. He has paid 60 shillings in the Treasury. And he owes 40 shillings.

For 4 pounds, 7 shillings and 4 pence for the gift of Aldridge. He has paid 44 shillings in the Treasury. And he owes 43 shillings and 4 pence.

For 20 shillings for the gift of "Lench." He has paid 10 shillings in the Treasury. And he owes 10 shillings.

The same sheriff owes 40 shillings for the gift of Arley.

Concerning the chattels of outlaws

The same sheriff accounts as follows:

For 6 shillings and 9 pence for the chattels of Richard of Great Barr for the same.

For 8 shillings and 2 pence for the chattels of Ordric of Great Barr for the same.

For 11 pence for the chattels of William Prutel for the same.

For 19 shillings and 3 pence for the chattels of William of Featherstone.

For 5 shillings for the chattels of Anschill of Madeley.

For 17 shillings and 8 pence for the chattels of Ralph of Himley.

For 14 pence for the chattels of William the clerk of Swinford.

For 12 shillings for the chattels of Aldred of Ketley.

For half a mark for the chattels of Adam and Robert of Pipe. The sum is 4 pounds, 12 shillings and 7 pence. He has paid this in the Treasury by means of 10 tallies. And he is quit. The same sheriff renders account for 43 shillings and 5 pence for the profit of the land of Simon "le Sage," which his of the fee of the bishop of Chester. He has paid this into the Treasury. And he is quit.

The same sheriff renders account for 28 shillings and 9 pence for the profit of Coton, which was in the possession of William, son of Alan, for a whole year and for a quarter of a year. He has paid this into the Treasury. And he is quit.

The same sheriff renders account for 8 shillings and 1 penny for the profit of the land of Ralph of Himley for three-quarters of a year. He has paid this into the Treasury. And he is quit.

Concerning the scutage[10] of the knights of Staffordshire who did not go with the king on the expedition to Galloway

The bishop of Chester renders account for 15 pounds of the scutage of his knights. He has paid 14 pounds in the Treasury. And he owes 20 shillings.

Bertram of Verdun renders account for 20 shillings of the scutage of 1 knight. He has paid this into the Treasury, and he is quit.

Robert "de Broc" and William of Stanton and Robert of "Haselea" render account for 6 pounds and 4 shillings and 2 pence in respect of the pannage of Herefordshire in Wales. And for 110 shillings and 9 pence of the pannage of Gloucestershire. And for 6 shillings for the pannage of Bushley in Worcestershire. And for 48 shillings and 2 pence for the pannage of Shropshire. The sum is 14 pounds and 9 shillings and 1 penny. They have made payment for this in the Treasury by means of 4 tallies. And they are quit.

---

10   Payment to the king in place of feudal service.

54. *MAGNA CARTA*

MAGNA CARTA, THE CONSERVATIVE baronial reaction to King John's policies and to his defeat at the hands of the French, took final form only over the course of several years. It is a unique document in which noble rights and royal responsibilities to the law are fully described, and eventually sets the groundwork for later English law. The following documents allow one to trace this evolution. The *Articles of the Barons* was the draft of terms demanded by the barons at Runnymede. The second is the form of *Magna Carta* issued by the royal chancery shortly after Runnymede. Within the year, John's nominal lord, Pope Innocent III declared the document, radical by ecclesiastical standards, null and void (third document). The final document is the altered version reissued by Henry III in 1216.

Source: Harry Rothwell (ed.), *English Historical Documents 1189–1327*, vol. III (London: Eyre & Spottiswoode, 1975), 311–32.

Further Reading: J.C. Holt, *Magna Carta*, 2nd ed. (Cambridge: Cambridge University Press, 1992).

The Articles of the Barons, June 15, 1215

These are the articles which the barons ask for and the lord king grants

1 After the death of their predecessors, heirs who are of full age shall have their inheritance on payment of the old relief, which is to be stated in the charter.

2 Heirs who are under age and are wards shall have their inheritance when they come of age without paying relief and without making fine.

3 The guardian of the land of an heir shall take reasonable revenues, customary dues and services without destruction and waste of his men and goods, and if the guardian of the land causes destruction and waste, he shall lose the wardship; and the guardian shall keep in repair the houses, parks, preserves, ponds, mills and other things pertaining to the land out of the revenue from it; and that heirs shall be so married that they are not disparaged and on the advice of those nearest in blood to them.

4 That a widow shall not pay anything to have her dower or marriage portion after the death of her husband, but shall remain in his house for forty days after his death, and within that term the dower shall be assigned to her; the marriage portion and her inheritance she shall have forthwith.

5 King or bailiff shall not seize any land for debt while the chattels of the debtor suffice; nor shall those who have gone surety for the debtor be distrained while the principal debtor is himself able to pay; if however the principal debtor fails to pay, the sureties shall, if they wish, have the lands of the debtor until that debt is fully paid, unless the principal debtor can show that he has discharged his obligation in the matter to the sureties.

6 The king shall not grant any baron the right to take an aid from his free men, except for ransoming his person, for making his eldest son a knight and for once marrying his eldest daughter, and this he shall do by a reasonable aid.

7 That no one shall do greater service for a knight's fee than is due from it.

8 That common pleas shall not follow the court of the lord king, but shall be assigned in some fixed place; and that recognitions be held in the counties to which they relate, in this manner—that the king shall send two justices four times a year, who with four knights of the same county chosen by

the county shall hold assizes of *novel disseisin, mort d'ancestor* and *darrein presentment*,[1] nor shall anyone be summoned on account of this save the jurors and the two parties.

9 That a free man shall be amerced for a trivial offense in accordance with the degree of the offense, and for a grave offense in accordance with its gravity, yet saving his way of living; a villein also shall be amerced in the same way, saving his means of livelihood; and a merchant in the same way, saving his stock-in-trade; by the oath of good men of the neighborhood.

10 That a clerk shall be amerced in respect of his lay fief after the manner of the others aforesaid and not according to his ecclesiastical benefice.

11 That no vill shall be amerced for the purpose of making bridges at river banks save where they used to be legally and of old.

12 That the measure for wine, corn and widths of cloths and other things be improved; and so with weights.

13 That assizes of *novel disseisin* and of *mort d'ancestor* be shortened; and similarly with other assizes.

14 That no sheriff shall concern himself with pleas pertaining to the crown without coroners; and that counties and hundreds be at the old rents without any additional payment, except the king's demesne manors.

15 If anyone holding of the king dies, it shall be lawful for the sheriff or other bailiff of the king to seize and make a list of his chattels under the supervision of lawworthy men, provided that none of the chattels shall be removed until it is more fully known whether he owes any manifest debt to the lord king and then the debt to the king is paid in full; the residue however shall be left to the executors for carrying out the will of the deceased. And if nothing is owing to the king, all the chattels shall accrue to the deceased.

16 If any free man dies without leaving a will, his goods shall be distributed by his nearest kinfolk and friends and under the supervision of the church.

17 That widows shall not be forced to marry, so long as they wish to live without a husband, provided that they give security not to marry without the consent of the king, if they hold of the king, or of the lords of whom they hold.

18 That no constable or other bailiff shall take corn or other chattels unless he pays on the spot in cash for them, unless he can delay payment by arrangement with the seller.

19 That no constable shall be able to compel any knight to give money instead of castle-guard if he is willing to do the guard himself or through another good man, if for some good reason he cannot do it himself; and if the king leads him on military service, let him be excused guard in proportion to the time.

20 That no sheriff or king's bailiff or anyone else shall take the horses or carts of any free man for transport work save with his agreement.

21 That neither the king nor his bailiff shall take another man's timber for castles or other works of his, except with the agreement of him whose timber it is.

22 That the king shall not hold for more than a year and a day the land of those convicted of felony, but then it shall be handed over to the lord of the fief.

23 That all fish-weirs be henceforth cleared completely from the Thames and Medway and throughout all England.

---

1 The "petty assizes" or actions by which a plantiff could obtain a royal writ ordering the sheriff to impanel a jury to determine not right but possession. *Novel disseisin* was an action claiming to have been recently dispossessed; *mort d'ancestor* was an action in which a plantiff claimed that the defendant had taken free property that should have gone to the plantiff following the death of one of his relatives; *darrein presentment* was an action that investigated who was the last person who exercised the right to appoint a cleric to an ecclesiastical benefice or church.

24 That the writ called *Praecipe* be not in future issued to anyone in respect of any holding whereby a free man may lose his court.

25 If any one has been disseised of or kept out of his lands, franchises and his right by the king without a judgment, let it be immediately restored to him; and if a dispute arises over this, then let it be decided by the judgment of the twenty-five barons; and that those who were disseised by the father or the brother of the king get justice without delay by the judgment of their peers in the king's court; and let the archbishop and bishops by a certain date give their decision, which shall be final, whether the king should have the respite allowed to other crusaders.

26 That nothing be given for the writ of inquisition of life or limbs, but that instead it be freely granted without charge and not refused.

27 If anyone holds of the king by fee-farm, by socage, or by burgage,[2] and of another by knight service, the lord king shall not, by reason of the burgage or socage, have the wardship of the knights of the fief of the other, nor ought he to have custody of the burgage, socage or fee-farm; and that a free man shall not lose his knight service by reason of petty serjeanties, such as those who hold any holding by rendering knives or arrows or the like for it.

28 That no bailiff be able to put anyone to trial [*lex*[3]] upon his own bare word without reliable witnesses.

29 That the body of a free man be not arrested or imprisoned or disseised or outlawed or exiled or in any way victimized, nor shall the king attack or send anyone to attack him with force, except by the judgment of his social equals or by the law of the land.

30 That right be not sold or delayed or forbidden to be done.

31 That merchants be able to go and come safely for buying or selling by the ancient and right customs, free from all evil tolls.

32 That no scutage or aid be imposed in the kingdom unless by common counsel of the kingdom, except for ransoming the king's person, for making his eldest son a knight, and for once marrying his eldest daughter; and for this a reasonable aid shall be levied. Be it done in like manner concerning tallages and aids from the city of London and from other cities which have liberties in respect thereof, and that the city of London have in full its ancient liberties and free customs as well by water as by land.

33 That it be lawful for any one, without prejudicing the allegiance due to the lord king, to leave the kingdom and return, save, in the public interest, for a short period in time of war.

34 If anyone who has borrowed from the Jews any sum, great or small, dies before it is repaid, the debt shall not bear interest as long as the heir is under age, of whomsoever he holds; and if the debt falls into the hand of the king, the king shall not take anything except the principal which is mentioned in the bond.

35 If anyone dies indebted to the Jews, his wife shall have her dower; and if children are left, they shall be provided with necessities befitting the holding; and the debt shall be paid out of the residue, reserving, however, service due to lords of the land; other debts shall be dealt with in like manner; and that the guardian of the land shall restore to the heir when he comes of full age his land stocked, according to what he can reasonably bear from the revenues of the land, with plows and the means of husbandry.

36 If anyone who holds of some escheat such as the honor of Wallingford, Nottingham, Boulogne, and Lancaster or of other escheats which are in the king's hands and are baronies, dies, his heir shall give no other relief or do no other service to

---

2   Sockage was a form of feudal land tenure in which the tenant either performed non-military service or paid a cash rent. Burgage was rental property in a town or borough owned by the king or by a lord.

3   Here a technical term for a trial, such as compurgation, ordeal or combat.

the king than he would have done to the baron; and that the king hold it in the same manner in which the baron held it.

37 That fines made for dowers, marriage portions, inheritances and amercements unjustly and against the law be entirely remitted, or else let them be settled by the judgment of the twenty-five barons, or by the judgment of the majority of the same, along with the archbishop and such others as he may wish to associate with himself, provided that if any one or more of the twenty-five are in a like suit they be removed and others put in their place by the rest of the twenty-five.

38 That hostages and charters given to the king as security be returned.

39 That those who were outside the forest need not come before justices of the forest upon a general summons, unless they are impleaded or are sureties; and that wicked customs connected with forests and with foresters and warrens and sheriffs and riverbanks be amended by twelve knights of every county who are to be chosen by good men of the same county.

40 That the king remove completely from office the relations and all the following of Gerard d'Athée so that they have no office in future, namely Engeland, Andrew, Peter and Guy de Chanceaux, Guy de Cigogné, Matthew de Martigny and his brothers and his nephew Geoffrey and Philip Marc.

41 And that the king remove foreign knights, mercenaries, cross-bowmen, routiers and serjeants, who come with horses and arms to the detriment of the kingdom.

42 That the king make justices, constables, sheriffs and bailiffs of such as know the law of the land and mean to observe it well.

43 That barons who have founded abbeys, for which they have royal charters or ancient tenure, have the custody of them during vacancies.

44 If the king has disseised or kept out Welshmen from lands or liberties or from other things in England or in Wales they shall be immediately restored to them without a lawsuit; and if they were disseised or kept out of their holdings in England by the king's father or brother without the judgment of their peers, the king shall without delay do justice to them in the way that he does justice to the English, for their holdings in England according to the law of England, and for holdings in Wales according to the law of Wales, and for holdings in the March according to the law of the March; Welshmen shall do the same to the king and his men.

45 That the king give back the son of Llywelyn and, besides, all the hostages from Wales and the charters that were handed over to him as security for peace (unless, in the judgment of the archbishop and of such others as he may wish to associate with himself, it ought to be otherwise by the charters which the king has).

46 That the king act towards the king of the Scots concerning the return of hostages and concerning his franchises and his right in the same manner in which he acts towards the barons of England (unless, in the judgment of the archbishop and of such others as he may wish to associate with himself, it ought to be otherwise by the charters which the king has).

47 And let all forests that have been made forest by the king in his time be dis-afforested, and so be it done with river-banks that have been made preserves[4] by the king himself.

48 All these customs and liberties which the king has granted to be observed in the kingdom as far as it pertains to him towards his men, all of the kingdom, clerks as well as laymen, shall observe as far as it pertains to them towards their men.

[A space in the manuscript between [48] and [49].]

49 This is the form of security for the observance of the peace and liberties between the king and

---

4   Literally, "are 'in defence.'"

the kingdom. The barons shall choose any twenty-five barons of the kingdom they wish, who must with all their might observe, hold and cause to be observed, the peace and liberties which the lord king has granted and confirmed to them by his charter; so that if the king or the justiciar or the king's bailiffs or any one of his servants offends in any way against any one or transgresses any of the articles of the peace or the security and the offence be notified to four of the aforesaid twenty-five barons, those four barons shall come to the lord king, or to his justiciar if the king is out of the kingdom, and, laying the transgression before him, shall petition him to have that transgression corrected without delay; and if the king or his justiciar does not correct it, if the king is out of the kingdom, within a reasonable time to be determined in the charter, the aforesaid four shall refer that case to the rest of the twenty-five barons and those twenty-five together with the community of the whole land shall distrain and distress the king in every way they can, namely, by seizing castles, lands, possessions, and in such other ways as they can, saving the person of the lord king and the persons of the queen and his children, until, in their opinion, amends have been made; and when amends have been made they shall obey the lord king as before. And anyone in the land who wishes shall take an oath to obey the orders of the said twenty-five barons for the execution of the aforesaid matters, and with them to distress the king as much as he can, and the king shall publicly and freely give anyone leave to take the oath who wishes to take it and he shall never prohibit anyone from taking it. Indeed, all those in the land who are unwilling of their own accord and of themselves to take an oath to the twenty-five barons to help them to distrain and distress the king, the king shall make them take the oath as aforesaid at his command. Also, if any of the said twenty-five barons dies or leaves the country or is in any other way prevented from carrying out the things aforesaid, the rest of the twenty-five shall choose as they think fit another one in his place, and he shall take the oath like the rest. In all matters the execution of which is committed to these twenty-five barons, if it should happen that these twenty-five are present yet disagree among themselves about anything, or if some of

those summoned will not or cannot be present, that shall be held, as fixed and established which the majority of them ordained or commanded, exactly as if all the twenty-five had consented to it; and the said twenty-five shall swear that they will faithfully observe all the things aforesaid and will do all they can to get them observed. Furthermore, the king shall give them security by charters of the archbishop and bishops and master Pandulf that he will procure nothing from the lord pope whereby any of the things here agreed might be revoked or diminished, and if he does procure any such thing, let it be reckoned void and null and let him never use it.

Magna Carta, 1215

John, by the grace of God, king of England, lord of Ireland, duke of Normandy and Aquitaine, and count of Anjou, to the archbishops, bishops, abbots, earls, barons, justiciars, foresters, sheriffs, stewards, servants, and to all his bailiffs and faithful subjects, greeting. Know that we, out of reverence for God and for the salvation of our soul and those of all our ancestors and heirs, for the honor of God and the exaltation of Holy Church, and for the reform of our realm, on the advice of our venerable fathers, Stephen, archbishop of Canterbury, primate of all England and cardinal of the Holy Roman Church, Henry archbishop of Dublin, William of London, Peter of Winchester, Jocelyn of Bath and Glastonbury, Hugh of Lincoln, Walter of Worcester, William of Coventry and Benedict of Rochester, bishops, of master Pandulf, sub-deacon and member of the household of the lord pope, of brother Aymeric, master of the order of Knights Templar in England, and of the noble men William Marshal earl of Pembroke, William earl of Salisbury, William earl of Warenne, William earl of Arundel, Alan of Galloway constable of Scotland, Warin fitz Gerold, Peter fitz Herbert, Hubert de Burgh seneschal of Poitou, Hugh de Neville, Matthew fitz Herbert, Thomas Basset, Alan Basset, Philip de Aubeney, Robert of Ropsley, John Marshal, John fitz Hugh, and others, our faithful subjects:

1 In the first place have granted to God, and by this our present charter confirmed for us and our

heirs for ever that the English church shall be free, and shall have its rights undiminished and its liberties unimpaired; and it is our will that it be thus observed; which is evident from the fact that, before the quarrel between us and our barons began, we willingly and spontaneously granted and by our charter confirmed the freedom of elections which is reckoned most important and very essential to the English church, and obtained confirmation of it from the lord pope Innocent III; the which we will observe and we wish our heirs to observe it in good faith for ever. We have also granted to all free men of our kingdom, for ourselves and our heirs for ever, all the liberties written below, to be had and held by them and their heirs of us and our heirs.

2 If any of our earls or barons or others holding of us in chief by knight service dies, and at his death his heir be of full age and owe relief he shall have his inheritance on payment of the old relief, namely the heir or heirs of an earl £100 for a whole earl's barony, the heir or heirs of a baron £100 for a whole barony, the heir or heirs of a knight 100s, at most, for a whole knight's fee; and he who owes less shall give less according to the ancient usage of fiefs.

3 If, however, the heir of any such be under age and a ward, he shall have his inheritance when he comes of age without paying relief and without making fine.

4 The guardian of the land of such an heir who is under age shall take from the land of the heir no more than reasonable revenues, reasonable customary dues and reasonable services, and that without destruction and waste of men or goods; and if we commit the wardship of the land of any such to a sheriff, or to any other who is answerable to us for its revenues, and he destroys or wastes what he has wardship of, we will take compensation from him and the land shall be committed to two lawful and discreet men of that fief, who shall be answerable for the revenues to us or to him to whom we have assigned them; and if we give or sell to anyone the wardship of any such land and he causes destruction or waste therein, he shall lose that wardship, and it shall be transferred to two lawful and discreet men of that fief, who shall similarly be answerable to us as is aforesaid.

5 Moreover, so long as he has the wardship of the land, the guardian shall keep in repair the houses, parks, preserves, ponds, mills and other things pertaining to the land out of the revenues from it; and he shall restore to the heir when he comes of age his land fully stocked with plows and the means of husbandry according to what the season of husbandry requires and the revenues of the land can reasonably bear.

6 Heirs shall be married without disparagement, yet so that before the marriage is contracted those nearest in blood to the heir shall have notice.

7 A widow shall have her marriage portion and inheritance forthwith and without difficulty after the death of her husband; nor shall she pay anything to have her dower or her marriage portion or the inheritance which she and her husband held on the day of her husband's death; and she may remain in her husband's house for forty days after his death, within which time her dower shall be assigned to her.

8 No widow shall be forced to marry so long as she wishes to live without a husband, provided that she gives security not to marry without our consent if she holds of us, or without the consent of her lord of whom she holds, if she holds of another.

9 Neither we nor our bailiffs will seize for any debt any land or rent, so long as the chattels of the debtor are sufficient to repay the debt; nor will those who have gone surety for the debtor be distrained so long as the principal debtor is himself able to pay the debt; and if the principal debtor fails to pay the debt, having nothing wherewith to pay it, then shall the sureties answer for the debt; and they shall, if they wish, have the lands and rents of the debtor until they are reimbursed for the debt which they have paid for him, unless the principal debtor can show that he has discharged his obligation in the matter to the said sureties.

10 If anyone who has borrowed from the Jews any sum, great or small, dies before it is repaid, the debt shall not bear interest as long as the heir is under age, of whomsoever he holds; and if the debt falls into our hands, we will not take anything except the principal mentioned in the bond.

11 And if anyone dies indebted to the Jews, his wife shall have her dower and pay nothing of that debt; and if the dead man leaves children who are under age, they shall be provided with necessaries befitting the holding of the deceased; and the debt shall be paid out of the residue, reserving, however, service due to lords of the land; debts owing to others than Jews shall be dealt with in like manner.

12 No scutage or aid shall be imposed in our kingdom unless by common counsel of our kingdom, except for ransoming our person, for making our eldest son a knight, and for once marrying our eldest daughter; and for these only a reasonable aid shall be levied. Be it done in like manner concerning aids from the city of London.

13 And the city of London shall have all its ancient liberties and free customs as well by land as by water. Furthermore, we will and grant that all other cities, boroughs, towns, and ports shall have all their liberties and free customs.

14 And to obtain the common counsel of the kingdom about the assessing of an aid (except in the three cases aforesaid) or of a scutage, we will cause to be summoned the archbishops, bishops, abbots, earls and greater barons, individually by our letters—and, in addition, we will cause to be summoned generally through our sheriffs and bailiffs all those holding of us in chief—for a fixed date, namely, after the expiry of at least forty days, and to a fixed place; and in all letters of such summons we will specify the reason for the summons. And when the summons has thus been made, the business shall proceed on the day appointed, according to the counsel of those present, though not all have come who were summoned.

15 We will not in future grant any one the right to take an aid from his free men, except for ransoming his person, for making his eldest son a knight and for once marrying his eldest daughter, and for these only a reasonable aid shall be levied.

16 No one shall be compelled to do greater service for a knight's fee or for any other free holding than is due from it.

17 Common pleas shall not follow our court, but shall be held in some fixed place.

18 Recognitions of *novel disseisin*, of *mort d'ancestor*, and of *darrein presentment*, shall not be held elsewhere than in the counties to which they relate, and in this manner—we, or, if we should be out of the realm, our chief justiciar, will send two justices through each county four times a year, who, with four knights of each county chosen by the county, shall hold the said assizes in the county and on the day and in the place of meeting of the county court.

19 And if the said assizes cannot all be held on the day of the county court, there shall stay behind as many of the knights and freeholders who were present at the county court on that day as are necessary for the sufficient making of judgments, according to the amount of business to be done.

20 A free man shall not be amerced for a trivial offense except in accordance with the degree of the offense, and for a grave offense he shall be amerced in accordance with its gravity, yet saving his way of living; and a merchant in the same way, saving his stock-in-trade; and a villein shall be amerced in the same way, saving his means of livelihood—if they have fallen into our mercy: and none of the aforesaid amercements shall be imposed except by the oath of good men of the neighborhood.

21 Earls and barons shall not be amerced except by their peers, and only in accordance with the degree of the offense.

22 No clerk shall be amerced in respect of his lay holding except after the manner of the others aforesaid and not according to the amount of his ecclesiastical benefice.

23 No vill or individual shall be compelled to make bridges at river banks, except those who from of old are legally bound to do so.

24 No sheriff, constable, coroners, or others of our bailiffs, shall hold pleas of our crown.

25 All counties, hundreds, wapentakes and trithings[5] shall be at the old rents without any additional payment, except our demesne manors.

26 If anyone holding a lay fief of us dies and our sheriff or bailiff shows our letters patent of summons for a debt that the deceased owed us, it shall be lawful for our sheriff or bailiff to attach and make a list of chattels of the deceased found upon the lay fief to the value of that debt under the supervision of law-worthy men, provided that none of the chattels shall be removed until the debt which is manifest has been paid to us in full; and the residue shall be left to the executors for carrying out the will of the deceased. And if nothing is owing to us from him, all the chattels shall accrue to the deceased, saving to his wife and children their reasonable shares.

27 If any free man dies without leaving a will, his chattels shall be distributed by his nearest kinfolk and friends under the supervision of the church, saving to every one the debts which the deceased owed him.

28 No constable or other bailiff of ours shall take anyone's corn or other chattels unless he pays on the spot in cash for them or can delay payment by arrangement with the seller.

29 No constable shall compel any knight to give money instead of castle-guard if he is willing to do the guard himself or through another good man, if for some good reason he cannot do it himself; and if we lead or send him on military service, he shall be excused guard in proportion to the time that because of us he has been on service.

30 No sheriff, or bailiff of ours, or anyone else shall take the horses or carts of any free man for transport work save with the agreement of that freeman.

31 Neither we nor our bailiffs will take, for castles or other works of ours, timber which is not ours, except with the agreement of him whose timber it is.

32 We will not hold for more than a year and a day the lands of those convicted of felony, and then the lands shall be handed over to the lords of the fiefs.

33 Henceforth all fish-weirs shall be cleared completely from the Thames and the Medway and throughout all England, except along the sea coast.

34 The writ called *Praecipe* shall not in future be issued to anyone in respect of any holding whereby a freeman may lose his court.

35 Let there be one measure for wine throughout our kingdom, and one measure for ale, and one measure for corn, namely "the London quarter"; and one width for cloths whether dyed, russet or halberget, namely two ells within the selvedges. Let it be the same with weights as with measures.

36 Nothing shall be given or taken in future for the writ of inquisition of life or limbs; instead it shall be granted free of charge and not refused.

37 If anyone holds of us by fee-farm, by socage, or by burgage, and holds land of another by knight service, we will not, by reason of that fee-farm, socage, or burgage, have the wardship of his heir or of land of his that is of the fief of the other; nor will we have custody of the fee-farm, socage, or burgage, unless such fee-farm owes knight service. We will not have custody of anyone's heir or land which he holds of another by knight service by reason of any petty serjeanty which he holds of us by the service of rendering to us knives or arrows or the like.

38 No bailiff shall in future put anyone to trial

---

5   I.e. ridings or districts.

[*lex*[6]] upon his own bare word, without reliable witnesses produced for this purpose.

39 No free man shall be arrested or imprisoned or disseised or outlawed or exiled or in any way victimized, neither will we attack him or send anyone to attack him, except by the lawful judgment of his peers or by the law of the land.

40 To no one will we sell, to no one will we refuse or delay right or justice.

41 All merchants shall be able to go out of and come into England safely and securely and stay and travel throughout England, as well by land as by water, for buying and selling by the ancient and right customs free from all evil tolls, except in time of war and if they are of the land that is at war with us. And if such are found in our land at the beginning of a war, they shall be attached, without injury to their persons or goods, until we, or our chief justiciar, know how merchants of our land are treated who were found in the land at war with us when war broke out; and if ours are safe there, the others shall be safe in our land.

42 It shall be lawful in future for anyone, without prejudicing the allegiance due to us, to leave our kingdom and return safely and securely by land and water, save, in the public interest, for a short period in time of war—except for those imprisoned or outlawed in accordance with the law of the kingdom and natives of a land that is at war with us and merchants (who shall be treated as aforesaid).

43 If anyone who holds of some escheat such as the honor of Wallingford, Nottingham, Boulogne, Lancaster, or of other escheats which are in our hands and are baronies dies, his heir shall give no other relief and do no other service to us than he would have done to the baron if that barony had been in the baron's hands; and we will hold it in the same manner in which the baron held it.

44 Men who live outside the forest need not henceforth come before our justices of the forest upon a general summons, unless they are impleaded or are sureties for any person or persons who are attached for forest offenses.

45 We will not make justices, constables, sheriffs or bailiffs save of such as know the law of the kingdom and mean to observe it well.

46 All barons who have founded abbeys for which they have charters of the kings of England or ancient tenure shall have the custody of them during vacancies, as they ought to have.

47 All forests that have been made forest in our time shall be immediately dis-afforested; and so be it done with river-banks that have been made preserves[7] by us in our time.

48 All evil customs connected with forests and warrens, foresters and warreners, sheriffs and their officials, river-banks and their wardens shall immediately be inquired into in each county by twelve sworn knights of the same county who are to be chosen by good men of the same county, and within forty days of the completion of the inquiry shall be utterly abolished by them so as never to be restored, provided that we, or our justiciar if we are not in England, know of it first.

49 We will immediately return all hostages and charters given to us by Englishmen, as security for peace or faithful service.

50 We will remove completely from office the relations of Gerard de Athée so that in future they shall have no office in England, namely Engelard de Cigogné, Peter and Guy and Andrew de Chanceaux, Guy de Cigogné, Geoffrey de Martigny and his brothers, Philip Mark and his brothers and his nephew Geoffrey, and all their following.

51 As soon as peace is restored, we will remove from the kingdom all foreign knights, crossbowmen, serjeants, and mercenaries, who have come with horses and arms to the detriment of the kingdom.

---

6   See n. 3 above.
7   Literally, "put 'in defence.'"

52 If anyone has been disseised of or kept out of his lands, castles, franchises or his right by us without the legal judgment of his peers, we will immediately restore them to him: and if a dispute arises over this, then let it be decided by the judgment of the twenty-five barons who are mentioned below in the clause for securing the peace: for all the things, however, which anyone has been disseised or kept out of without the lawful judgment of his peers by king Henry, our father, or by king Richard, our brother, which we have in our hand or are held by others, to whom we are bound to warrant them, we will have the usual period of respite of crusaders, excepting those things about which a plea was started or an inquest made by our command before we took the cross; when however we return from our pilgrimage, or if by any chance we do not go on it, we will at once do full justice therein.

53 We will have the same respite, and in the same manner, in the doing of justice in the matter of the disafforesting or retaining of the forests which Henry our father or Richard our brother afforested, and in the matter of the wardship of the lands which are of the fief of another, wardships of which sort we have hitherto had by reason of a fief which anyone held of us by knight service, and in the matter of abbeys founded on the fief of another, not on a fief of our own, in which the lord of the fief claims he has a right; and when we have returned, or if we do not set out on our pilgrimage, we will at once do full justice to those who complain of these things.

54 No one shall be arrested or imprisoned upon the appeal of a woman for the death of anyone except her husband.

55 All fines made with us unjustly and against the law of the land, and all amercements imposed unjustly and against the law of the land, shall be entirely remitted, or else let them be settled by the judgment of the twenty-five barons who are mentioned below in the clause for securing the peace, or by the judgment of the majority of the same, along with the aforesaid Stephen, archbishop of Canterbury, if he can be present, and such others as he may wish to associate with himself for this

purpose, and if he cannot be present the business shall nevertheless proceed without him, provided that if any one or more of the aforesaid twenty-five barons are in a like suit, they shall be removed from the judgment of the case in question, and others chosen, sworn and put in their place by the rest of the same twenty-five for this case only.

56 If we have disseised or kept out Welshmen from lands or liberties or other things without the legal judgment of their peers in England or in Wales, they shall be immediately restored to them; and if a dispute arises over this, then let it be decided in the March by the judgment of their peers— for holdings in England according to the law of England, for holdings in Wales according to the law of Wales, and for holdings in the March according to the law of the March. Welshmen shall do the same to us and ours.

57 For all the things, however, which any Welshman was disseised of or kept out of without the lawful judgment of his peers by king Henry, our father, or king Richard, our brother, which we have in our hand or which are held by others, to whom we are bound to warrant them, we will have the usual period of respite of crusaders, excepting those things about which a plea was started or an inquest made by our command before we took the cross; when however we return, or if by any chance we do not set out on our pilgrimage, we will at once do full justice to them in accordance with the laws of the Welsh and the fore-said regions.

58 We will give back at once the son of Llywelyn and all the hostages from Wales and the charters that were handed over to us as security for peace.

59 We will act toward Alexander, king of the Scots, concerning the return of his sisters and hostages and concerning his franchises and his right in the same manner in which we act towards our other barons of England, unless it ought to be otherwise by the charters which we have from William his father, formerly king of the Scots, and this shall be determined by the judgment of his peers in our court.

60 All these aforesaid customs and liberties which we have granted to be observed in our kingdom as far as it pertains to us towards our men, all of our kingdom, clerks as well as laymen, shall observe as far as it pertains to them towards their men.

61 Since, moreover, for God and the betterment of our kingdom and for the better allaying of the discord that has arisen between us and our barons we have granted all these things aforesaid, wishing them to enjoy the use of them unimpaired and unshaken for ever, we give and grant them the under-written security, namely, that the barons shall choose any twenty-five barons of the kingdom they wish, who must with all their might observe, hold and cause to be observed, the peace and liberties which we have granted and confirmed to them by this present charter of ours, so that if we, or our justiciar, or our bailiffs or any one of our servants offend in any way against anyone or transgress any of the articles of the peace or the security and the offence be notified to four of the aforesaid twenty-five barons, those four barons shall come to us, or to our justiciar if we are out of the kingdom, and, laying the transgression before us, shall petition us to have that transgression corrected without delay. And if we do not correct the transgression, or if we are out of the kingdom, if our justiciar does not correct it, within forty days, reckoning from the time it was brought to our notice or to that of our justiciar if we were out of the kingdom, the aforesaid four barons shall refer that case to the rest of the twenty-five barons and those twenty-five barons together with the community of the whole land shall distrain and distress us in every way they can, namely, by seizing castles, lands, possessions, and in such other ways as they can, saving our person and the persons of our queen and our children, until, in their opinion, amends have been made; and when amends have been made, they shall obey us as they did before. And let anyone in the land who wishes take an oath to obey the orders of the said twenty-five barons for the execution of all the aforesaid matters, and with them to distress us as much as he can, and we publicly and freely give anyone leave to take the oath who wishes to take it and we will never prohibit anyone from taking it. Indeed, all those in the land who are unwilling of themselves and of their own accord to take an oath to the twenty-five barons to help them to distrain and distress us, we will make them take the oath as aforesaid at our command. And if any of the twenty-five barons dies or leaves the country or is in any other way prevented from carrying out the things aforesaid, the rest of the aforesaid twenty-five barons shall choose as they think fit another one in his place, and he shall take the oath like the rest. In all matters the execution of which is committed to these twenty-five barons, if it should happen that these twenty-five are present yet disagree among themselves about anything, or if some of those summoned will not or cannot be present, that shall be held as fixed and established which the majority of those present ordained or commanded, exactly as if all the twenty-five had consented to it; and the said twenty-five shall swear that they will faithfully observe all the things aforesaid and will do all they can to get them observed. And we will procure nothing from anyone, either personally or through anyone else, whereby any of these concessions and liberties might be revoked or diminished; and if any such thing is procured, let it be void and null, and we will never use it either personally or through another.

62 And we have fully remitted and pardoned to everyone all the ill-will, indignation and rancor that have arisen between us and our men, clergy and laity, from the time of the quarrel. Furthermore, we have fully remitted to all, clergy and laity, and as far as pertains to us have completely forgiven, all trespasses occasioned by the same quarrel between Easter in the sixteenth year of our reign and the restoration of peace. And, besides, we have caused to be made for them letters testimonial patent of the lord Stephen archbishop of Canterbury, of the lord Henry archbishop of Dublin and of the aforementioned bishops and of master Pandulf about this security and the aforementioned concessions.

63 Wherefore we wish and firmly enjoin that the English church shall be free, and that the men in our kingdom shall have and hold all the aforesaid liberties, rights and concessions well and peacefully, freely and quietly, fully and completely, for

themselves and their heirs from us and our heirs, in all matters and in all places for ever, as is aforesaid. An oath, moreover, has been taken, as well on our part as on the part of the barons, that all these things aforesaid shall be observed in good faith and without evil disposition. Witness the above-mentioned and many others. Given by our hand in the meadow which is called Runnymede between Windsor and Staines on the fifteenth day of June, in the seventeenth year of our reign.

Pope Innocent III declares Magna Carta null and void, August 24, 1215

Innocent, bishop, servant of the servants of God, to all the faithful of Christ who will see this document, greeting and apostolic benediction.

Although our well-beloved son in Christ, John illustrious king of the English, grievously offended God and the church—in consequence of which we excommunicated him and put his kingdom under ecclesiastical interdict—yet, by the merciful inspiration of Him who desireth not the death of a sinner but rather that he should turn from his wickedness and live, the king at length returned to his senses, and humbly made to God and the church such complete amends that he not only paid compensation for losses and restored property wrongfully seized, but also conferred full liberty on the English church: and further, on the relaxation of the two sentences, he yielded his kingdom of England and of Ireland to St. Peter and the Roman church, and received it from us again as fief under an annual payment of one thousand marks, having sworn an oath of fealty to us, as is clearly stated in his privilege furnished with a golden seal; and desiring still further to please Almighty God, he reverently assumed the badge of the life-giving Cross, intending to go to the relief of the Holy Land—a project for which he was splendidly preparing. But the enemy of the human race, who always hates good impulses, by his cunning wiles stirred up against him the barons of England so that, with a wicked inconsistency, the men who supported him when injuring the church rebelled against him when he turned from his sin and made amends to the church. A matter of dispute had arisen between them: several days had been fixed for the parties to discuss

a settlement: meanwhile, formal envoys had been sent to us: with them we conferred diligently, and after full deliberation we sent letters by them to the archbishop and the English bishops, charging and commanding them to devote earnest attention and effective effort to restoring a genuine and full agreement between the two sides; by apostolic authority they were to denounce as void any leagues and conspiracies which might have been formed after the outbreak of trouble between the kingdom and the priesthood: they were to prohibit, under sentence of excommunication, any attempt to form such leagues in future: and they were prudently to admonish the magnates and nobles of England, and strongly to enjoin on them, to strive to conciliate the king by manifest proofs of loyalty and submission; and then, if they should decide to make a demand of him, to implore it respectfully and not arrogantly, maintaining his royal honor and rendering the customary services which they and their predecessors paid to him and his predecessors (since the king ought not to lose these services without a judicial decision), that in this way they might the more easily gain their object. For we in our letters, and equally through the archbishop and bishops, have asked and advised the king, enjoining it on him as he hopes to have his sins remitted, to treat these magnates and nobles kindly and to hear their just petitions graciously, so that they too might recognize with gladness how by divine grace he had had a change of heart, and that thereby they and their heirs should serve him and his heirs readily and loyally; and we also asked him to grant them full safe-conduct for the outward and homeward journey and the time between, so that if they could not arrive at agreement the dispute might be decided in his court by their peers according to the laws and customs of the kingdom. But before the envoys bearing this wise and just mandate had reached England, the barons threw over their oath of fealty; and though, even if the king had wrongfully oppressed them they should not have proceeded against him by constituting themselves both judges and executors of the judgment in their own suit, yet, openly conspiring as vassals against their lord and as knights against their own king, they leagued themselves with his acknowledged enemies as well as with others, and dared to make war on him, occupying and devastating his territory and even seizing the city of London, the capital of the kingdom, which had been treacherously surrendered to them. Meantime the aforesaid envoys returned to England and the king offered, in accordance with the terms of our mandate, to grant the barons full justice. This they altogether rejected and began to stretch forth their hands to deeds still worse. So the king, appealing to our tribunal, offered to grant them justice before us to whom the decision of this suit belonged by reason of our lordship: but this they utterly rejected. Then he offered that four discreet men chosen by him and four more chosen by themselves should, together with us, end the dispute, and he promised that, first in his reforms, he would repeal all abuses introduced into England in his reign: but this also they contemptuously refused. Finally, the king declared to them that, since the lordship of the kingdom belonged to the Roman church, he neither could nor should, without our special mandate, make any change in it to our prejudice: and so he again appealed to our tribunal, placing under apostolic protection both himself and his kingdom with all his honor and rights. But making no progress by any method, he asked the archbishop and the bishops to execute our mandate, to defend the rights of the Roman church, and to protect himself in accordance with the form of the privilege granted to crusaders. When the archbishop and bishops would not take any action, seeing himself bereft of almost all counsel and help, he did not dare to refuse what the barons had dared to demand. And so by such violence and fear as might affect the most courageous of men he was forced to accept an agreement which is not only shameful and demeaning but also illegal and unjust, thereby lessening unduly and impairing his royal rights and dignity.

But because the Lord has said to us by the prophet Jeremiah, "I have set thee over the nations and over the kingdoms, to root out, and to destroy, to build and to plant," and also by Isaiah, "Loose the bands of wickedness, undo the heavy burdens," we refuse to ignore such shameless presumption, for thereby the apostolic see would be dishonored, the king's rights injured, the English nation shamed, and the whole plan for a crusade seriously endangered; and as this danger would be imminent if concessions, thus extorted from a great prince who has taken the Cross, were not canceled by our authority, even though he himself should prefer them to be upheld, on behalf of Almighty God, Father, Son, and Holy Spirit, and by the authority of saints Peter and Paul His apostles, and by our own authority, acting on the general advice of our brethren, we utterly reject and condemn this settlement, and under threat of excommunication we order that the king should not dare to observe it and that the barons and their associates should not require it to be observed: the charter, with all undertakings and guarantees whether confirming it or resulting from it, we declare to be null, and void of all validity for ever. Wherefore, let no man deem it lawful to infringe this document of our annulment and prohibition, or presume to oppose it. If anyone should presume to do so, let him know that he will incur the anger of Almighty God and of saints Peter and Paul His apostles.

Anagni, the 24th of August, in the eighteenth year of our pontificate.

Magna Carta, 1216

Henry,[8] by the grace of God king of England, lord of Ireland, duke of Normandy and Aquitaine, and count of Anjou, to the archbishops, bishops, abbots, earls, barons, justiciars, foresters, sheriffs, stewards, servants, bailiffs and to all his faithful subjects, greeting. Know that we, out of reverence for God and for the salvation of our soul and those of all our ancestors and *successors,* for the honor of God and the exaltation of holy church, and for the reform of our realm, on the advice of our venerable fathers, *the lord Gualo, cardinal priest of St. Martin, legate of the apostolic see, Peter of Winchester, R. of St Asaph, J. of Bath and Glastonbury, S. of Exeter, R. of Chichester, W. of Coventry, B. of Rochester, H. of Llandaff,—of St David's,—of Bangor and S. of Worcester, bishops,* and of the noble men *William Marshal earl of Pembroke, Ranulf earl of Chester, William de Ferrers earl of Derby, William count of Aumale,*

---

8   Italicized text indicates new material in the revised charter.

Hubert de Burgh our justiciar, Savari de Mauléon, William Brewer the father, William Brewer the son, Robert de Courtenay, Fawkes de Breauté, Reynold de Vautort, Walter de Lacy, Hugh de Mortimer, John of Monmouth, Walter de Beauchamp, Walter de Clifford, Roger de Clifford, Robert de Mortimer, William de Cantilupe, Matthew fitz Herbert, John Marshal, Alan Basset, Philip de Aubeney, John Lestrange and others, our faithful subjects:

1 In the first place have granted to God, and by this our present charter confirmed for us and our heirs for ever, that the English church shall be free, and shall have its rights undiminished and its liberties unimpaired. We have also granted to all free men of our kingdom, for ourselves and our heirs for ever, all the liberties written below, to be had and held by them and their heirs of us and our heirs. [1215, c.1]

2 If any of our earls or barons or others holding of us in chief by knight service dies, and at his death his heir be of full age and owe relief he shall have his inheritance on payment of the old relief, namely the heir or heirs of an earl £100 for a whole earl's barony, the heir or heirs of a baron £100 for a whole barony, the heir or heirs of a knight 100*s*, at most, for a whole knight's fee; and he who owes less shall give less according to the ancient usage of fiefs. [1215, c.2]

3 If, however, the heir of any such be under age, *his lord shall not have wardship of him, nor of his land, before he has received his homage; and after being a ward such an heir* shall have his inheritance when he comes of age, *that is of twenty-one years*, without paying relief and without making fine, *so, however, that if he is made a knight while still under age, the land nevertheless shall remain in his lord's wardship for the full term.* [1215, c. 3]

4 The guardian of the land of such an heir who is under age shall take from the land of the heir no more than reasonable revenues, reasonable customary dues and reasonable services, and that without destruction and waste of men or goods; and if we commit the wardship of the land of any such to a sheriff, or to any other who is answerable to us for the revenues *of that land*, and he destroys or wastes what he has wardship of, we will

take compensation from him and the land shall be committed to two lawful and discreet men of that fief, who shall be answerable for the revenues to us or to him to whom we have assigned them; and if we give or sell to anyone the wardship of any such land and he causes destruction or waste therein, he shall lose that wardship and it shall be transferred to two lawful and discreet men of that fief, who shall similarly be answerable to us as is aforesaid. [1215, c. 4]

5 Moreover, so long as he has the wardship of the land, the guardian shall keep in repair the houses, parks, preserves, ponds, mills and other things pertaining to the land out of the revenues from it; and he shall restore to the heir when he comes of age his land fully stocked with plows and *all other things in at least the measure he has received. All these things shall be observed in the case of wardships of vacant archbishoprics, bishoprics, abbeys, priories, churches and dignities except that wardships of this kind may not be sold.* [1215, c. 5]

6 Heirs shall be married without disparagement. [1215, c.6]

7 A widow shall have her marriage portion and inheritance forthwith and without *any* difficulty after the death of her husband; nor shall she pay anything to have her dower or her marriage portion or the inheritance which she and her husband held on the day of her husband's death; and she may remain in her husband's house for forty days after his death, within which time her dower shall be assigned to her, *unless it has already been assigned to her or unless the house is a castle; and if she leaves the castle, a suitable house shall be immediately provided for her in which she can stay honorably until her dower is assigned to her in accordance with what is aforesaid.* [1215, c.7]

8 No widow shall be forced to marry so long as she wishes to live without a husband, provided that she gives security not to marry without our consent if she holds of us, or without the consent of her lord if she holds of another. [1215, c.8]

9 *We or our bailiffs will not* seize for any debt any land or rent, so long as the *available* chattels of the debtor are sufficient to repay the debt *and the*

debtor himself is prepared to have it paid therefrom; nor will those who have gone surety for the debtor be distrained so long as the principal debtor is himself able to pay the debt; and if the principal debtor fails to pay the debt, having nothing wherewith to pay it *or is able but unwilling to pay*, then shall the sureties answer for the debt; and they shall, if they wish, have the lands and rents of the debtor until they are reimbursed for the debt which they have paid for him, unless the principal debtor can show that he has discharged his obligation in the matter to the said sureties. [1215, c.9]

10 The city of London shall have all its ancient liberties and free customs. Furthermore, we will and grant that all other cities, boroughs, towns, *the barons of the Cinque Ports*, and *all* ports shall have all their liberties and free customs. [1215, c.13]

11 No one shall be compelled to do greater service for a knight's fee or for any other free holding than is due from it. [1215, c.16]

12 Common pleas shall not follow our court, but shall be held in some fixed place. [1215, c.17]

13 Recognitions of novel disseisin, of mort d'ancestor, and of darrein presentment, shall not be held elsewhere than in the counties to which they relate, and in this manner—we, or, if we should be out of the realm, our chief justiciar, will send two justices through each county four times a year, who, with four knights of each county chosen by the county, shall hold the said assizes in the county and on the day and in the place of meeting of the county court. [1215, c.18]

14 And if the said assizes cannot all be held on the day of the county court, there shall stay behind as many of the knights and freeholders who were present at the county court on that day as are necessary for the sufficient making of judgments, according to the amount of business to be done. [1215, c.19]

15 A free man shall not be amerced for a trivial offense except in accordance with the degree of the offense, and for a grave offense in accordance with its gravity, yet saving his way of living; and a merchant in the same way, saving his stock-in-trade;

and a villein shall be amerced in the same way, saving his means of livelihood; if *he has* fallen into our mercy: and none of the aforesaid amercements shall be imposed except by the oath of good *and law-worthy* men of the neighborhood. [1215, c.20]

16 Earls and barons shall not be amerced except by their peers, and only in accordance with the degree of the offense. [1215, c.21]

17 No clerk shall be amerced except after the fashion of the aforesaid and not according to the amount of his ecclesiastical benefice. [1215, c.22]

18 No vill or individual shall be compelled to make bridges at river banks, except *one* who from of old *is* legally bound to do so. [1215, c.23]

19 No sheriff, constable, coroners, or others of our bailiffs shall hold pleas of our crown. [1215, c.24]

20 If anyone holding a lay fief of us dies and our sheriff or bailiff shows our letters patent of summons for a debt that the deceased owed us, it shall be lawful for our sheriff or bailiff to attach and make a list of chattels of the deceased found upon the lay fief to the value of that debt under the supervision of law-worthy men, provided that none of the chattels shall be removed until the debt which is manifest has been paid to us in full; and the residue shall be left to the executors for carrying out the will of the deceased. And if nothing is owing to us from him, all the chattels shall accrue to the deceased, saving to his wife and *his* children their reasonable shares. [1215, c.26]

21 No constable *or his bailiff* shall take the corn or other chattels of anyone *who is not of the vill where the castle is situated* unless he pays on the spot in cash for them or can delay payment by arrangement with the seller; *if the seller is of the vill, he shall be bound to pay within three weeks.* [1215, c.28]

22 No constable shall compel any knight to give money instead of castle-guard if he is willing to do *it* himself or through another good man, if for some good reason he cannot do it himself; and if we lead or send him on military service, he shall

be excused guard in proportion to the time that because of us he has been on service. [1215, c.29]

23 No sheriff, or bailiff of ours, or *other person* shall take *anyone's* horses or carts for transport work unless *he pays for them at the old-established rates, namely at ten pence a day for a cart with two horses and fourteen pence a day for a cart with three horses.* [1215, c.30]

24 Neither we nor our bailiffs will take, for castles or other works of ours, timber which is not ours, except with the agreement of him whose timber it is. [1215, c.31]

25 We will not hold for more than a year and a day the lands of those convicted of felony, and then the lands shall be handed over to the lords of the fiefs. [1215, c.32]

26 Henceforth all fish-weirs shall be cleared completely from the Thames and the Medway and throughout all England, except along the sea coast. [1215, c.33]

27 The writ called Praecipe shall not in future be issued to anyone in respect of any holding whereby a free man may lose his court. [1215, c.34]

28 Let there be one measure for wine throughout our kingdom, and one measure for ale, and one measure for corn, namely "the London quarter"; and one width for cloths whether dyed, russet or halberget, namely two ells within the selvedges. Let it be the same with weights as with measures. [1215, c.35]

29 Nothing shall be given in future for the writ of inquisition of life or limbs: instead, it shall be granted free of charge and not refused. [1215, c.36]

30 If anyone holds of us by fee-farm, by socage, or by burgage, and holds land of another by knight service, we will not, by reason of that fee-farm, socage or burgage, have the wardship of his heir or of land of his that is of the fief of the other; nor will we have custody of the fee-farm, socage, or burgage, unless such fee-farm owes knight service. We will not have custody of anyone's heir or

land which he holds of another by knight service by reason of any petty serjeanty which he holds of us by the service of rendering to us knives or arrows or the like. [1215, c.37]

31 No bailiff shall in future put anyone to trial upon his own bare word without reliable witnesses produced for this purpose. [1215, c.38]

32 No free man shall be arrested or imprisoned or disseised or outlawed or exiled or victimised in any *other* way, neither will we attack him or send anyone to attack him, except by the lawful judgment of his peers or by the law of the land. [1215, c.39]

33 To no one will we sell, to no one will we refuse or delay right or justice. [1215, c.40]

34 All merchants, *unless they have been publicly prohibited beforehand*, shall be able to go out of and come into England safely and securely and stay and travel throughout England, as well by land as by water, for buying and selling by the ancient and right customs free from all evil tolls, except in time of war and if they are of the land that is at war with us. And if such are found in our land at the beginning of a war, they shall be attached, without injury to their persons or goods, until we, or our chief justiciar, know how merchants of our land are treated who were found in the land at war with us when war broke out; and if ours are safe there, the others shall be safe in our land. [1215, c.41]

35 If anyone who holds of some escheat such as the honor of Wallingford, Nottingham, Boulogne, Lancaster, or of other escheats which are in our hands and are baronies dies, his heir shall give no other relief and do no other service to us than he would have done to the baron if that *land* had been in the baron's hands; and we will hold it in the same manner in which the barons held it. [1215, c.43]

36 Men who live outside the forest need not henceforth come before our justices of the forest upon a general summons, unless they are impleaded or are sureties for any person or persons who are attached for forest offenses. [1215, c.44]

37 All barons who have founded abbeys for which they have charters of the kings of England or ancient tenure shall have the custody of them during vacancies, as they ought to have *and as it is made clear above.* [1215, c.46]

38 All forests that were made forest in the time *of King John, our father,* shall be immediately disafforested; and so be it done with river-banks that were made preserves by *the same J. in his* time. [1215, c.47]

39 No one shall be arrested or imprisoned upon the appeal of a woman for the death of anyone except her husband. [1215, c.54]

40 *And* if *King J. our father* disseised or kept out Welshmen from lands or liberties or other things without the legal judgment of their peers in England or in Wales, they shall be immediately restored to them; and if a dispute arises over this, then let it be decided in the March by the judgment of their peers—for holdings in England according to the law of England, for holdings in Wales according to the law of Wales, and for holdings in the March according to the law of the March. Welshmen shall do the same to us and ours. [1215, c.56]

41 All these aforesaid customs and liberties which we have granted to be observed in our kingdom as far as it pertains to us towards our men, all of our kingdoms, clerks as well as laymen, shall observe as far as it pertains to them towards their men. [1215, c.60]

42 *However, because there were certain articles contained in the former charter which seemed important yet doubtful, namely On the assessing of scutage and aids, On debts of Jews and others, On freedom to leave and return to our kingdom, On forests and foresters, warrens and warreners, On the customs of counties, and On river-banks and their wardens, the above-mentioned prelates and magnates have agreed to these being deferred until we have fuller counsel, when we will, most fully in these as well as other matters that have to be amended, do what is for the common good and the peace and estate of ourselves and our kingdom. Because we have not yet a seal, we have had the present charter sealed with the seals of our venerable father, the lord Gualo cardinal priest of St. Martin, legate of the apostolic see, and William Marshal earl of Pembroke, ruler of us and of our kingdom. Witness all the aforementioned and many others. Given by the hands of the aforesaid lord, the legate, and William Marshal earl of Pembroke at Bristol on the twelfth day of November in the first year of our reign.*

55. ROYAL COURTS OF ENGLAND

The Huntingdonshire Eyre of 1286

RECORDED IN LATIN, THE records of royal courts are a major source of information on the social, legal, and economic structures of England in the thirteenth century. The following excerpts from the Huntingdonshire Eyre of 1286 show typical types of actions brought before the royal justices.

Source: Anne Reiber DeWindt and Edwin Brezette DeWindt, *Royal Justice and the Medieval English Countryside*, vol. 2 (Toronto: Pontifical Institute of Medieval Studies, 1981).

Further Reading: See source volume above.

Action of Right

The Abbot of Crowland claims against Emma, who was the wife of Berenger le Moyne, one messuage and half of one virgate of land with appurtenances in Thurning as the right of his church of Crowland by *precipe in capite*,[1] whereupon he says that a certain Henry of Longchamp, former abbot of Crowland, his predecessor, was seised[2] of the aforesaid tenements with appurtenances in his demesne as of fee and right of his church of Saint Guthlac of Crowland in a time of peace, the time of the lord King Richard, kinsman of the present lord king, taking esplees [enjoyment] therein to the value of [unspecified]. And he offers to prove that such is the right of his church.

Emma comes, and on another occasion she said that the aforesaid tenements with appurtenance were given to Berenger, her late husband, and to her in free marriage, and of them were born Rose, wife of Geoffrey of Southorpe, Emma, wife of Richard of Carlby, and Margaret, wife of John Peche, whereupon she said that she could not answer therein without Geoffrey and Rose, Richard and Emma, [and] John and Margaret, so that the sheriff was ordered to summon them to be here on this day, namely on Monday, three weeks after Michaelmas, to answer together. They have not come, and they were summoned. Therefore, it is adjudged that the aforesaid Emma will answer without them.

Emma denies the right of the abbot and his church and the seisin of that Henry, predecessor of this abbot, of whose seisin, etc., as the right of his church of Saint Guthlac of Crowland, and everything, etc. And she puts herself on a jury of the country in place of the Grand Assize of the lord king and seeks that acknowledgment be made whether she has greater right in those tenements with appurtenances as her right and marriage gift, or the aforesaid abbot.

John Russel, John of Drayton, John Mowyn and Richard of Bevil, four knights summoned to elect both knights and other free and lawful men, came and elected these, namely: John of Drayton (sworn), John Mowyn (sworn), Richard of Bevil (sworn), Guy of Waterville (sworn), Robert of Beaumes (sworn), knights. Richard of Catworth (sworn), William Engayne (sworn), Richard of Hotot (sworn), Richard Marshall (sworn) of Stoneley, John of Cantelou (sworn), William of Hampton (sworn), (and) Geoffrey of Haddon (sworn), who say on their oath that the aforesaid abbot has greater right in the aforesaid tenements as the right of his church of Saint Guthlac of Crowland than the aforesaid Emma. Therefore, it is adjudged that the abbot recover his seisin of those tenements with appurtenances, to be held by him and his successors and his church, quit, from this Emma and her heirs in perpetuity. And Emma is in mercy.

---

1   A writ obtained to claim property when the property is held directly from the king.
2   Possessed.

Action of Dower

Agnes, who was the wife of John Gate of Offord Darcy, claims against the prior of Huntingdon the third part of one messuage and a half-virgate of land with appurtenances in Offord Darcy as her dower, *unde nichil habet*,[3] etc.

The prior comes and says that Agnes ought not to have dower from that, for he says that John, former husband of Agnes, neither on the day he married her nor afterward was ever seised of those tenements as of fee so that he could give her dower therein. For he says that those tenements were at one time a certain Reginald le Moyne's, of Offord, who gave those tenements, along with his body, to the church of Saint Mary of Huntingdon and to the canons serving there, in free, pure and perpetual alms, together with a certain Richard Gate, grandfather of this John, at that time a villein of this Reginald, with his entire family of that Richard [who were] at that time holding those tenements in villeinage, whereupon he says that the ancestors of this John always held those tenements in villeinage. And concerning this he puts himself on the country, and Agnes does the same. Therefore, let there be a jury.

Concerning this, a certain Geoffrey Gate, brother of the aforesaid John, comes and says that he is a villein on the prior and his church and holds those tenements from him in villeinage, and that his ancestors, from the time of the enfeoffment of that Reginald le Moyne, have been villeins of the predecessors of the prior and his church, and that they have held those tenements from him in villeinage. And the prior seeks that this jury consider the evidence mentioned above.

The jurors say on their oath that the aforesaid John, neither on the day that he married Agnes nor afterwards, was ever seised of those tenements as of fee so that he could give her dower therein. Therefore, it is adjudged that the prior go without a day and that Agnes take nothing by this jury but is in mercy for a false claim.

Action of Entry

Agnes, widow of Roger Knight, claims against Robert of Bedford and Juliana, his wife, two acres of land and three acres of meadow with appurtenances in Little Paxton; and against John, son of Roger Webster, one rod of meadow with appurtenances in the same vill; and against Roger of Daventry and Cecilia, his wife, one acre and one rod of land with appurtenances in that vill, as her right and inheritance, and in which Robert and Juliana, John, Roger and Cecilia do not have entry except after the surrender that Roger Knight, her late husband, whom she, in his lifetime, could not contradict, made to Hugh de la Mare.

Robert, Juliana, John, Roger and Cecilia come and deny Agnes' right. And Roger and Cecilia, concerning the judgment claimed against them, say that they are not obliged to answer her, for they say that they have nothing in the aforesaid tenements except only a tenancy at the will of a certain John of Offord, without whom they cannot bring those tenements into judgment. And Agnes cannot deny this. Therefore, Roger and Cecilia go without a day, and Agnes takes nothing against them by this writ but is in mercy for a false claim.

Robert and Juliana, concerning the tenements claimed against them, say that they cannot answer Agnes, for they say that they do not hold those tenements entirely, but that a certain Stephen of Dalham holds one rod of land therein and held it on the day Agnes sought her writ, namely: May 16, the fourteenth year of the present king. And concerning this they put themselves on the country, and Agnes does the same. Therefore, let there be a jury.

The jurors, elected by consent of the parties, say on their oath that Robert and Juliana do not hold those tenements entirely nor did they on the day she [Agnes] sought her writ, for a certain Stephen of Dalham holds one rod therein, as Robert and Juliana say. Therefore, it is adjudged that Robert and Juliana go without a day and that Agnes take nothing by this writ but is in mercy for a false claim.

---

3   If a widow had not been assigned a dower, she could obtain a writ requiring her to be given one.

John, son of Roger Webster, concerning the tenements claimed against him, says that Roger, late husband of this Agnes, was never in seisin of that rod of meadow so that he could have surrendered it to Hugh or to anyone else. And concerning this he puts himself on the country, and Agnes does the same. Therefore, let there be a jury.

The jurors, elected by consent of the parties, say on their oath that Roger, late husband of Agnes, was never in seisin of that rod of meadow so that he could have released it to anyone, as John says. Therefore, it is adjudged that John go without a day and that Agnes take nothing by this writ but is in mercy for a false claim.

Action of Novel Disseisin

An assize comes to declare whether William le Moyne Sr. of Raveley, John of Raveley and Alan le Kew unjustly disseised William, son of William le Moyne, and Eleanor of Lovetot of their free tenement in Sawtry le Moyne, whereupon they complain that they disseised them of one messuage and three carucates of land with appurtenances.

The same assize comes to declare whether William le Moyne Sr., John of Raveley and Alan le Kew unjustly disseised William, son of William le Moyne, of his free tenement in Gidding and Loddington, whereupon he complains that they disseised him of one messuage and one carucate of land with appurtenances in Gidding and of one messuage and two carucates of land with appurtenances in Loddington.

William le Moyne Sr. comes and answers for himself as tenant and for John and Alan as their bailiff, and he says nothing to stay the assize except only that William and Eleanor were never in seisin of the aforesaid tenements in Sawtry as of a free tenement so that they could be disseised therein. Nor was that William, son of William, in seisin of the aforesaid tenements in Gidding and Loddington as of his free tenement so that he could be disseised. And concerning this, he puts himself on the assize. Therefore, let the assize be taken.

The jurors say on their oath, regarding the tenements in Sawtry, that the aforesaid William Sr. and the others unjustly disseised William, son of William, and Eleanor, as they complain;

and regarding the tenements in Gidding and Loddington, they say on the same oath that William Sr. and the others unjustly disseised William, son of William, as he complains. Therefore, it is adjudged that William, son of William, and Eleanor recover their seisin of the aforesaid tenements in Sawtry by view of the recognitors, and that William, son of William, recover his seisin of the aforesaid tenements in Gidding and Loddington by view of the aforesaid recognitors. And William le Moyne Sr. and the others are in mercy.

Damages, regarding the first assize: 10s.; and regarding the second assize, concerning the tenements in Loddington: a half-mark; and concerning the tenements in Gidding: 40d., all to the clerks.

Later, the fine is excused at the request of John of Lovetot.

Damages to the clerks.

Action of Mort d'Ancestor

An assize comes to declare whether Ellen of Folksworth, the mother of Henry, son of Robert of Blymhill, was seised in her demesne as of fee of a half-virgate with appurtenances in Folksworth on the day that [she died], which Richard, son of Thomas of Wennington, holds.

Richard comes and vouches Geoffrey de la Hose to warrant. He is present and warrants him, and he says that Ellen did not die seised of the aforesaid tenements in her demesne as of fee. He says further that Ellen had nothing in this, except for the term of her life, from the surrender of Thomas de la Hose. And concerning this, he puts himself on the assize.

The jurors say on their oath that Ellen, concerning whose death [the assize is brought] died seised of the aforesaid tenement in her demesne as of fee and after the term, and that Henry is her closest heir. Therefore, it is adjudged that Henry recover his seisin of the tenements with appurtenances by view of the recognitors against Richard and that Richard have land from that of Geoffrey in a suitable place of the same value. And Geoffrey is in mercy.

Damages: 20s., to the clerks, etc.

Appeal of Felony

Unidentified malefactors, at night, encountered Simon Chyne in the fields of Hemingford and wounded him, so that three days later he died. Afterwards they fled, and it is not known who they were nor where they went.

Later it was determined by the coroners' rolls that Agnes, widow of the aforesaid Simon of Chyne, appealed in the county court Laurence, son of Robert Fenner of Saint Ives of the death of Simon, her husband. She also appealed Adam, son of Robert Fenner, brother of the aforesaid Laurence, as an accomplice. And it is determined by the coroners' rolls that Agnes brought suit against them up to the fourth county court, at which Laurence and Adam appeared and were arrested and delivered to Thomas of Belhus, the sheriff at that time.

Later, before William Musket, John Russel and his associates, justices assigned to jail delivery, they were delivered, having been accused by the county without a separate warrant. Therefore, the sheriff is ordered to make the aforesaid William and John, with their associates who were involved, come with the rolls and warrant. And the jurors attest that the aforesaid Laurence killed Simon. Therefore, the sheriff is ordered to arrest him if, etc., and saving, etc. And Geoffrey Fenner and John Aylmer, who were attached because they were present, come and are not suspected. Therefore, they are acquitted. Nothing is known of Laurence's chattels. He was not in tithing because he was a cleric.

Indictment of Felony

The jurors present that Margery Mouner of Keyston and William Mercer of Keyston were indicted by Robert Scochere of Oundle, and afterwards, because of that, they fled. William was later captured at Lincoln and hanged there. His chattels: 10s., for which the sheriff will answer. He had chattels in the county of Northampton at Islip worth 10s., for which William of Soule will answer. And because he took those chattels without warrant, he is in mercy. Margery's chattels, 2 s. 6 d., for which the sheriff will answer. And the twelve jurors concealed those chattels in their presentment. Therefore, they are in mercy. And because Margery is suspected, let her be exacted and waived. She was not in tithing because she is a woman.

Presentment of Felony by Jury

The jurors present that William, son of Thomas Beadle, put himself in the church of Warboys and acknowledged that he was a thief and abjured the realm before the coroner. He had no chattels. He was not in tithing because he is a free man, but he was of the household of the aforesaid Thomas, his father, who now does not have him to stand trial. Therefore, he is in mercy. And because the vill of Warboys did not capture him, it is in mercy. And the twelve jurors did not mention in their verdict before which coroner this abjuration was made. Therefore, they are in mercy.

Presentment of Death by Misadventure

Margery daughter of William Springolf was struck in the head by a kicking mare, so that three days later she died. The first-finder and four neighbors come and are not suspected, nor is anyone else. Judgment: misadventure. Price of the mare: 3s., for which the sheriff will answer. And the vills of Somersham and Earith falsely appraised that deodand.[4] Therefore, they are in mercy. And the twelve jurors concealed a part of that deodand. Therefore, they are in mercy.

---

4 An animal or inanimate object that has caused the death of a person.

56. A MEDIEVAL ENGLISH VILLAGE: PLANS OF WHARRAM PERCY

THE BEST PRESERVED AND studied abandoned village in England is Wharram Percy, Yorkshire East Riding. Excavations there have uncovered successive habitations from the Iron Age until its destruction in the early sixteenth century.

Throughout the medieval period, all houses were long houses except for a courtyard farm in the manorial enclosure. Prior to the thirteenth century, the houses were timber. After that time, they were constructed of chalk quarried on individual tofts. In the thirteenth century, houses were constructed at right angles with the gable to the street.

The site of the manor changed across time. The Anglo-Saxon manor was probably near the church. In the twelfth century, it was moved onto the hill at the north end of the village, and in the thirteenth century it was again moved several hundred yards farther north.

The village church shows the changes in the village. Its first period may be pre-Danish. Massive rebuilding took place in the Norman period. In the twelfth and thirteenth centuries, aisles and chapels were demolished and the chancel halved.

Source: Maurice Beresford and John G. Hurst (eds.), *Deserted Medieval Villages* (New York: St. Martin's Press, 1971).

Further Reading: Ann Clark, "Wharram Percy—Where are we Now?" *Current Archaeology* 200 (2005): 230–32.

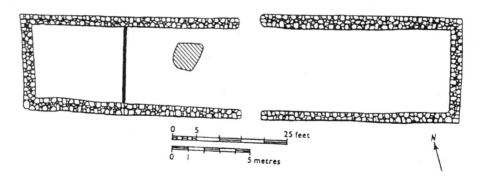

Plan, three-roomed long-house, Wharram Percy.

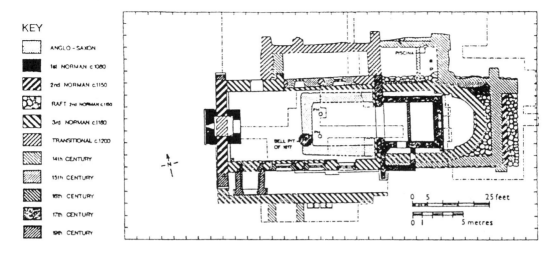

KEY

- ANGLO - SAXON
- 1st NORMAN c.1080
- 2nd NORMAN c.1150
- RAISED 2nd NORMAN c.1160
- 3rd NORMAN c.1180
- TRANSITIONAL c.1200
- 14th CENTURY
- 15th CENTURY
- 16th CENTURY
- 17th CENTURY
- 19th CENTURY

Plan of the parish church showing the expansion from the small Saxon church to the large medieval church with nave, chancel, north and south aisles, and chapels at the peak of the prosperity of the village in the fourteenth century. In the fifteenth and sixteenth centuries the aisles and chapels were pulled down, and in the seventeenth century the chancel was halved in size after the desertion of four of the five townships in the parish.

Plan of the village showing the early extent of the settlement (4–8) with the twelfth-century manor house and boundary bank; to the north the thirteenth-century planned extension of the village (12–18), with the new site for the manorial complex (A–N and 19–25).

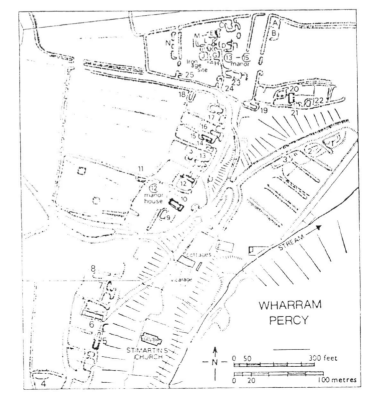

WHARRAM PERCY

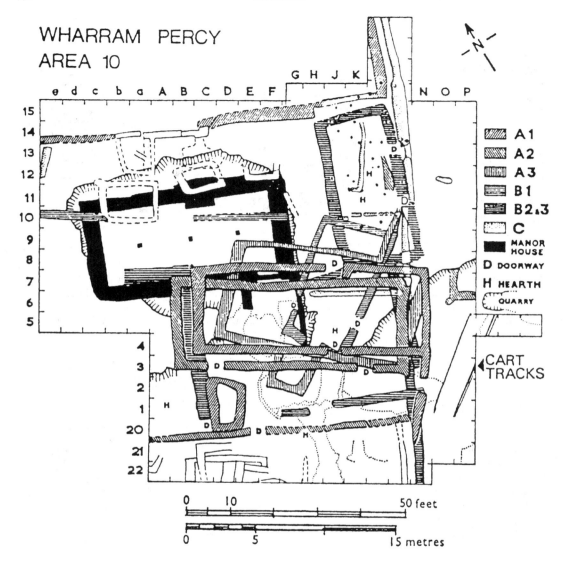

Plan of Area 10 showing the complex sequence of superimposed periods on different alignments. The late twelfth-century Percy Manor house and chalk quarries were replaced by two thirteenth-century houses oriented north-south (B2–3). In the fourteenth century these were replaced by a single house (B1) while in the fifteenth century the long-houses were built east-west on quite a different alignment (A1–3).

57. *FUERO DE CUENCA*

CUENCA IS A SMALL town captured by King Alfonso of Castile in 1189–90 during the Reconquista, the centuries-long conflict between the Christian kings of Spain and Portugal and the Muslim dynasties in southern Spain. Shortly after the conquest, King Alfonso issued a *Fuero* or code for the town, one of the earliest municipal codes in Europe. The *Fuero* was a distinctively Spanish phenomenon with roots in older Germanic traditions of the granting of royal privileges, and although it had close parallels in England and France, by the later part of the twelfth century *fueros* had become much more detailed and comprehensive legal charters. The following sections of the code deal with relations among Jews, Muslims, and Christians, all of whom were citizens of Cuenca.

Source: James F. Powers (ed. and trans.), *The Code of Cuenca: Municipal Law on the Twelfth-Century Castilian Frontier* (Philadelphia: University of Pennsylvania Press, 2000), 29, 31, 34, 40–41, 81, 85.

Further Reading: See the introduction to the translation above.

Chapter I. Concession of the Code and Outline of Its Privileges

First of all, I give and grant to all inhabitants of the city of Cuenca and to their successors, Cuenca itself with all its district; that is to say, with its mountains, springs, grass, rivers, salt-works, and mines of silver, iron, or any other metal....

10. *Privilege of the settlers*

I likewise grant to all settlers this prerogative: whoever may come to live in Cuenca, whatever condition he may be, whether Christian, Moor, or Jew, free or servile, should come in safety. He need not answer to anyone by reason of enmity, debt, bond, inheritance, *mayordomia*, *merindadico* [special taxes paid to royal officials] or any other thing that he may have done before the conquest of Cuenca [1177]. But if he had an enemy before the conquest of Cuenca, and he encounters his enemy while living here, both parties should designate bondsmen, according to the code of Cuenca, so that they remain in peace. He who does not want to designate a bondsman should leave the city and its district....

23. *Purchasing a Moor for exchange with a captive Christian*

Whoever purchases a Moor in Cuenca to be given in exchange for a captive Christian should pay the owner of the Moor the price the Moor cost him, plus ten *aurei* as profit, and the owner should surrender him; after the Moor is attested, regardless whether he is sold or undersold, after receiving the agreed-upon price, the owner of the Moor should release the Christian from captivity....

25. *Granting of fairs*

For the benefit and honor of the city, I also grant fairs that are to begin eight days before the celebration of Pentecost and last until eight days after this feast. Whoever comes to these fairs, whether Christian, Moor, or Jew, should come safely. Whoever impedes them or causes any damage should pay for the king's portion a fine of one thousand *aurei*, and to the plaintiff double the value of the damage done. If he is unable to pay the charges, let him be hanged. Whoever kills a man will be buried alive beneath the dead person. If he injures someone, he will have his hand cut off....

32. Concerning the bathhouse, and the testimony of women

Men may use the common bathhouses on Tuesdays, Thursdays, and Saturdays. Women may enter on Mondays, and Wednesdays. Jews should enter on Fridays and Sundays. No one, neither woman nor man, should pay more than an *obolus* entry fee. Servants and children of citizens should enter free of charge. If a man enters any part of the bathhouse premises on the women's day for bathing, he is liable for a fine of ten *aurei*. He should pay the same fine for spying on women in the bath on those days. However, if a woman enters a bathhouse on a day reserved for men, or is found there at night, and because of this the woman is publicly dishonored or harmed in some way, she should have no right to bring charges of a kind sufficient to exile the offending man. On the other hand, if a man commits these acts against a woman on the women's bathing days, or steals her clothing, let him be hurled from the city cliffs. Officials can gather testimony from women at the bathhouse, at the bakehouse, at the fountain and river, and also at the spinners' and weavers' workplaces. Female witnesses should be wives or daughters of citizens of the city.

If a Christian should intrude in a bathhouse on the Jewish bathing days, or if a Jew should intrude on the Christian bathing days, resulting in either person attacking or killing the other, no formal accusations should be accepted from either of the persons or their relatives.

The bathhouse manager should provide bathers with all bathing necessities, such as water and the like. Failing to provide these necessities will make the manager liable to a fine of ten *solidi*, five to be paid to the almutazaf [chief official of the city market] and five to the complainant. Anyone stealing bathhouse equipment should have his ears cut off; if bathers' belongings are worth up to ten *menkales* or more, then let the thief be hurled from the city cliffs.

Chapter XI.

...19. He who injures another's Moor.
If someone injures another's Moor, he should pay five *solidi* for doing it; he who kills him, fifteen *aurei*; but if he is a Moor set aside for prisoner exchange, and his senior already has bondsmen for the redemption and can confirm it, as is established in the code, he who killed the Moor should pay the promised redemption; for another Moor, whether or not a servant, he should not pay more than fifteen *aurei*, as has been said.

20. He who injures or kills a free Moor.
Anyone who injures or kills a free Moor should pay for him, as for a Christian.

21. The free Moor who injures or kills a Christian
If a free Moor injures or kills a Christian, for injuring him he should pay the pecuniary penalty according to the Code of Cuenca; for killing him, he [the Moor] should be put in the hands of the plaintiff, so that the plaintiff should take the money from the pecuniary penalties, and finally he should do with his [the Moor's] body what he wants.

22. He who violates another's Moorish woman.
Whoever violates another's Moorish woman should pay her dowry, as if she were a married woman of the city.

23. He who has a child with another's Moorish woman.
If someone has a child with another's Moorish woman, this child should be the servant of the senior of the Moorish woman, until his father redeems him. Also, we say that such a child should not divide with his siblings that which corresponds to the patrimony of their father, while he remains in servitude. Later should he become free, he should take a share of the goods of his father....

48. The woman who is surprised with an infidel
If a woman is surprised with a Moor or with a Jew, both should be burned alive.

58. *LAS SIETE PARTIDAS*

LAS SIETE PARTIDAS IS a seven-part law code prepared under the direction of King Alfonso X the Wise of Castille (1252–84) but only put into effect in 1348. This extraordinarily comprehensive legal code, written in Castilian, eventually spread to other Spanish kingdoms and then, following the unification of Spain, throughout the Spanish Empire. The following selection deals with three categories of people who were severely marginalized in medieval Spain: Jews, Muslims, and heretics. While the third group were severely persecuted, the first and second maintained some legal protections in their lives and their religion, although their rights were much more circumscribed than they had been in earlier Spanish legal traditions such as the *Fuero de Cuenca*.

Source: *Las Siete Partidas*, trans. Samuel Parsons Scott (Chicago: Published for the Comparative Law Bureau of the American Bar Association by Commerce Clearing House, Inc., 1931), 1431–44.

Further Reading: See the introduction to Robert I. Burns (ed.), *Las Siete Partidas*, trans. Samuel Parsons Scott (Philadelphia: University of Pennsylvania Press, 2001).

TITLE XXIV.

Concerning the Jews.

Jews are a people who, although they do not believe in the religion of Our Lord Jesus Christ, yet, the great Christian sovereigns have always permitted them to live among them. Wherefore, since in the preceding title we spoke of Diviners, and other men who allege that they know things that are to come, which is a kind of contempt of God, since they desire to make themselves equal to Him by learning his acts and his secrets; we intend to speak here of the Jews, who insult His name and deny the marvelous and holy acts which He performed when he sent His Son, Our Lord Jesus Christ, into the world to save sinners. We shall explain what the word Jew means; whence it derived this name; for what reasons the Church and the great Christian world permitted the Jews to live among them; in what way Jews should pass their lives among Christians; what things they should not use, or do, according to our religion; and what Jews those are who can be subjected to force on account of the wicked acts that they have performed, or the debt which they owe. Also why Jews who become Christians should not be subject to compulsion; what advantage a Jew, by becoming a Christian obtains over other Jews who do not; what penalty those deserve who cause him injury or dishonor; and to what punishment Christians, who become Jews, and also Jews who force their Moorish slaves to embrace their religion, are liable.

LAW I.
What the Word Jew Means, and Whence This Term Is Derived.

A party who believes in, and adheres to the law of Moses is called a Jew, according to the strict signification of the term, as well as one who is circumcised, and observes the other precepts commanded by his religion. This name derived from the tribe of Judah which was nobler and more powerful than the others, and, also possessed another advantage, because the king of the Jews had to be selected from that tribe, and its members always received the first wounds in battle. The reason that the church, emperors, kings and princes, permitted the Jews to dwell among them and with Christians, is because they always lived, as it were, in captivity, as it was constantly in the minds of men that they were descended from those who crucified Our Lord Jesus Christ.

LAW II.

What Way Jews Should Pass Their Lives among Christians; What Things They Should Not Make Use of or Practice According to Our Religion; and What Penalty Those Deserve Who Act Contrary to Its Ordinances.

Jews should pass their lives among Christians quietly and without disorder, practicing their own religious rites, and not speaking ill of the faith of Our Lord Jesus Christ, which Christians acknowledge. Moreover, a Jew should be very careful to avoid preaching to, or converting any Christian, to the end that he may become a Jew, by exalting his own belief and disparaging ours. Whoever violates this law shall be put to death and lose all his property. And because we have heard it said that in some places Jews celebrated, and still celebrate Good Friday, which commemorates the Passion Our Lord Jesus Christ, by way of contempt; stealing children and fastening them to crosses, and making images of wax and crucifying them, when they cannot obtain children; we order that, hereafter, if in any part of our dominions anything like this is done, and can be proved, all persons who were present when the act was committed shall be seized, arrested and brought before the king; and after the king ascertains that they are guilty, he shall cause them to be put to death in a disgraceful manner, no matter how many there may be.

We also forbid any Jew to dare to leave his house or his quarter on Good Friday, but they must all remain shut up until Saturday morning; and if they violate this regulation, we decree that they shall not be entitled to reparation for any injury or dishonor inflicted upon them by Christians.

LAW III.

No Jew Can Hold Any Office or Employment by Which He May Be Able to Oppress Christians.

Jews were formerly highly honored, and enjoyed privileges above all other races, for they alone were called the People of God. But for the reason that they disowned Him who had honored them and given them privileges; and instead of showing Him reverence humiliated Him, by shamefully putting Him to death on the cross; it was proper and just that, on account of the great crime and

wickedness which they committed, they should forfeit the honors and privileges which they enjoyed; and therefore from the day when they crucified Our Lord Jesus Christ they never had either king or priests among themselves, as they formerly did. The emperors, who in former times were lords of all the world, considered it fitting and right that, on account of the treason which they committed in killing their lord, they should lose all said honors and privileges, so that no Jew could ever afterwards hold an honorable position, or a public office by means of which he might, in any way, oppress a Christian.

LAW IV.

How Jews Can Have a Synagogue among Christians.

A synagogue is a place where the Jews pray, and a new building of this kind cannot be erected in any part of our dominions, except by our order. Where, however, those which formerly existed there are torn down, they can be built in the same spot where they originally stood; but they cannot be made any larger or raised to any greater height, or be painted. A synagogue constructed in any other manner shall be lost by the Jews, and shall belong to the principal church of the locality where it is built. And for the reason that a synagogue is a place where the name of God is praised, we forbid any Christian to deface it, or remove anything from it, or take anything out of it by force, except where some malefactor takes refuge there; for they have a right to remove him by force in order to bring him before the judge. Moreover, we forbid Christians to put any animal into a synagogue, or loiter in it, or place any hindrance in the way of the Jews while they are there performing their devotions according to their religion.

LAW V.

No Compulsion Shall Be Brought to Bear Upon the Jews on Saturday, and What Jews Can Be Subject to Compulsion.

Saturday is the day on which Jews perform their devotions, and remain quiet in their lodgings, and do not make contracts or transact any business; and for the reason that they are obliged by their religion, to keep it, no one should on that day summon them or bring them into court. Wherefore we order that no judge shall employ force or any constraint upon Jews on Saturday, in order to bring them into court on account of their debts; or arrest them; or cause them any other annoyance; for the remaining days of the week are sufficient for the purpose of employing compulsion against them, and for making demands for things which can be demanded of them, according to law. Jews are not bound to obey a summons served upon them on that day; and, moreover, we decree that any decision rendered against them on Saturday shall not be valid; but if a Jew should wound, kill, rob, steal, or commit any other offense like these for which he can be punished in person and property, then the judge can arrest him on Saturday.

We also decree that all claims that Christians have against Jews, and Jews against Christians shall be decided and determined by our judges in the district where they reside, and not by their old men. And as we forbid Christians to bring Jews into court or annoy them on Saturday; so we also decree that Jews, neither in person, nor by their attorneys, shall have the right to bring Christians into court, or annoy them on this day. And in addition we forbid any Christian, on his own responsibility, to arrest or wrong any Jew either in his person or property, but where he has any complaint against him he must bring it before our judges; and if anyone be so bold as to use violence against the Jews, or rob them of anything he shall return them double the value of the same.

LAW VI.
Jews Who Become Christians Shall Not Be Subject to Compulsion; What Advantage a Jew Has Who Becomes a Christian; and What Penalty Other Jews Deserve Who Do Him Harm.

No force or compulsion shall be employed in any way against a Jew to induce him to become a Christian; but Christians should convert him to the faith of Our Lord Jesus Christ by means of the texts of the Holy Scriptures and by kind words, for no one can love or appreciate a service which is done him by compulsion. We also decree that if any Jew or Jewess should voluntarily desire to become a Christian, the other Jews shall not interfere with this in any way, and if they stone, wound, or kill any such person, because they wish to become Christians, or after they have been baptized, and this can be proved; we order that all the murderers, or the abettors of said murder or attack shall be burned. But where the party was not killed, but wounded, or dishonored; we order that the judges of the neighborhood where this took place shall compel those guilty of the attack, or who caused the dishonor, to make amends to him for the same; and also that they be punished for the offense which they committed, as they think they deserve; and we also order that, after any Jews become Christians, all persons in our dominions shall honor them; and that no one shall dare to reproach them or their descendants, by way of insult, with having been Jews; and that they shall possess all their property, sharing the same with their brothers, and inheriting it from their fathers and mothers and other relatives, just as if they were Jews; and that they can hold all offices and dignities which other Christians can do.

LAW VII.
What Penalty a Christian Deserves Who Becomes a Jew.

Where a Christian is so unfortunate as to become a Jew, we order that he shall be put to death just as if he had become a heretic; and we decree that his property shall be disposed of in the same way that we stated should be done with that of heretics.

LAW VIII.
No Christian, Man or Woman Shall Live with a Jew.

We forbid any Jew to keep Christian men or women in his house, to be served by them; although he may have them to cultivate and take care of his lands, or protect him on the way when he is compelled to go to some dangerous place. Moreover, we forbid any Christian man or woman to invite a Jew or a Jewess, or to accept an invitation from them, to eat or drink together, or to drink any wine made by their hands. We also order that no Jews shall dare to bathe in company with Christians, and that no Christian shall take any medicine or cathartic made by a Jew; but he can take it by the advice of some intelligent person, only where it is made by a Christian, who knows and is familiar with its ingredients.

LAW IX.
What Penalty a Jew Deserves Who Has Intercourse with a Christian Woman.

Jews who live with Christian women are guilty of great insolence and boldness, for which reason we decree that all Jews who, hereafter, may be convicted of having done such a thing shall be put to death. For if Christians who commit adultery with married women deserve death on that account much more do Jews who have sexual intercourse with Christian women, who are spiritually the wives of Our Lord Jesus Christ because of the faith and the baptism which they receive in His name; nor do we consider it proper that a Christian woman who commits an offense of this kind shall escape without punishment. Wherefore we order that, whether she be a virgin, a married woman, a widow, or a common prostitute who gives herself to all men, she shall suffer the same penalty which we mentioned in the last law in the title concerning the Moors, to which a Christian woman is liable who has carnal intercourse with a Moor.

LAW X.
What Penalty Jews Deserve Who Hold Christians as Slaves.

A Jew shall not purchase, or keep as a slave a Christian man or woman and if anyone violates this law the Christian shall be restored to freedom and shall not pay any portion of the price given for him, although the Jew may not have been aware when he bought him, that he was a Christian; but if he knew that he was such when he purchased him, and makes use of him after wards as a slave, he shall be put to death for doing so. Moreover, we forbid any Jew to convert a captive to his religion, even though said captive may be Moor, or belong to some other barbarous race. If anyone violates this law we order that the said slave who has become a Jew shall be set at liberty, and removed from the control of the party to whom he

or she belonged. If any Moors who are the captives of Jews become Christians, they shall at once be freed, as is explained in the Fourth Partida of this book, in the title concerning liberty, in the laws which treat of this subject.

LAW XI.
Jews Shall Bear Certain Marks in Order That They May Be Known.

Many crimes and outrageous things occur between Christians and Jews because they live together in cities, and dress alike; and in order to avoid the offenses and evils which take place for this reason, we deem it proper, and we order that all Jews male and female living in our dominions shall bear some distinguishing mark upon their heads so that people may plainly recognize a Jew, or a Jewess; and any Jew who does not bear such a mark, shall pay for each time he is found without it ten *maravedis* of gold; and if he has not the means to do this he shall publicly receive ten lashes for his offense.

TITLE XXV.

Concerning the Moors.

The Moors are a people who believe that Mohammed was the prophet and messenger of God, and for the reason that the works which he performed do not indicate the extraordinary sanctity which belongs to such a sacred calling, his religion is, as it were, an insult to God. Wherefore, since in the preceding title we treated of the Jews and of the obstinacy which they display toward the true faith, we intend to speak here of the Moors, and of their foolish belief by which they think they will be saved. We shall show why they have this name; how many kinds of them there are; how they should live among Christians, and what things they are forbidden to do while they live there; how Christians should convert them to the faith by kind words, and not by violence or compulsion; and what punishment those deserve who prevent them from becoming Christians, or dishonor them by word or deed after they have been converted, and also to what penalty a Christian who becomes a Moor, is liable.

LAW I.
Whence the Name of Moor Is Derived, How Many Kinds of the Latter There Are, and in What Way They Should Live among Christians.

Surracenus, in Latin, means Moor, in Castilian, and this name is derived from Sarah, the free wife of Abraham, although the lineage of the Moors is not traced to her, but to Hagar, who was Abraham's servant. There are two kinds of Moors; some do not believe in either the New or the Old Testament; the others accept the five books of Moses, but reject the prophets and do not believe them. The latter are called Samaritans because they first appeared in the city called Samaria, and these are mentioned in the Gospel where it is stated that the Jews and the Samaritans should not associate with one another or live together.

We decree that Moors shall live among Christians in the same way that we mentioned in the preceding title that Jews shall do, by observing their own law and not insulting ours. Moors, however, shall not have mosques in Christian towns, or make their sacrifices publicly in the presence of men. The mosques which they formerly possessed shall belong to the king; and he can give them to whomsoever he wishes. Although the Moors do not acknowledge a good religion, so long as they live among Christians with their assurance of security, their property shall not be stolen from them or taken by force; and we order that whoever violates this law shall pay a sum equal to double the value of what he took.

LAW II.
Christians Should Convert the Moors by Kind Words, and Not by Compulsion.

Christians should endeavor to convert the Moors by causing them to believe in our religion, and bring them into it by kind words and suitable discourses, and not by violence or compulsion; for if it should be the will of Our Lord to bring them into it and to make them believe by force, He can use compulsion against them if He so desires, since He has full power to do so; but He is not pleased with the service which men perform through fear, but with that which they do voluntarily and without coercion, and as He does not

wish to restrain them or employ violence, we forbid anyone to do so for this purpose; and if the wish to become Christians should arise among them, we forbid anyone to refuse assent to it, or oppose it in any way whatsoever. Whoever violates this law shall receive the penalty we mentioned in the preceding title, which treats of how Jews who interfere with, or kill those belonging to their religion who afterwards become Christians, shall be punished.

LAW III.
What Punishment Those Deserve Who Insult Converts.

Many men live and die in strange beliefs, who would love to be Christians if it were not for the vilification and dishonor which they see others who become converted endure by being called turncoats, and calumniated and insulted in many evil ways; and we hold that those who do this wickedly offend, and that they should honor persons of this kind for many reasons, and not show them disrespect. One of these is because they renounce the religion in which they and their families were born; and another is because, after they have understanding, they acknowledge the superiority of our religion and accept it, separating from their parents and their relatives, and abandoning the life which they have been accustomed to live, and all other things from which they derive pleasure. There are some of them who, on account of the dishonor inflicted upon them after they have adopted our Faith, and become Christians, repent and desert it, closing their hearts against it on account of the insults and reproaches to which they are subjected; and for this reason we order all Christians, of both sexes, in our dominions to show honor and kindness, in every way they can, to persons of other or strange beliefs, who embrace our religion; just as they would do to any of their own parents or grandparents, who had embraced the faith or become Christians; and we forbid anyone to dishonor them by word or deed, or do them any wrong, injury, or harm in any way whatever. If anyone violates this law we order that he be punished for it, as seems best to the judges of the district; and that the punishment be more severe if the injury had been committed against another man or woman whose entire line of ancestors had been Christians.

LAW IV.
What Punishment a Christian Deserves Who Becomes a Moor.

Men sometimes become insane and lose their prudence and understanding, as, for instance, where unfortunate persons, and those who despair of everything, renounce the faith of Our Lord Jesus Christ, and become Moors; and there are some of them who are induced to do this through the desire to live according to their customs, or on account of the loss of relatives who have been killed or died or because they have lost their property and become poor; or awful acts which they commit, dreading the punishment which they deserve on account of them; and when they are induced to do a thing of this kind for any of the reasons aforesaid, or others similar to them, they are guilty of very great wickedness and treason, for on account of no loss or affliction which may come upon them, nor for any profit, riches, good fortune, or pleasure which they may expect to obtain in this world, should they renounce the faith of Our Lord Jesus Christ by which they will be saved and have everlasting life.

Wherefore we order that all those who are guilty of this wickedness shall lose all their possessions, and have no right to any portion of them, but that shall belong to their children (if they have any) who remain steadfast in our faith and do not renounce it; and if they have no children, their property shall belong to their nearest relatives within the tenth degree, who remain steadfast in the belief of the Christians; and if they have neither children nor relatives, all their possessions shall be forfeited to the royal treasury; and, in addition to this, we order that if any person who has committed such an offense shall be found in any part of our dominions he shall be put to death.

LAW V.
What Penalty a Christian Deserves Who Becomes a Moor, Even if He Subsequently Repents and Returns to Our Faith.

Apostata, in Latin, means, in Castilian, a Christian who becomes a Jew or a Moor, and afterwards repents and returns to the Christian religion; because a man of this kind is false, and manifests contempt for our faith, he should not remain unpunished, even though he repents; for which reason the learned men of the ancients declare that such a person must remain forever infamous, so that his testimony could never be taken, nor he hold office or any honorable position, nor make a will, nor be appointed an heir of others in any way whatsoever. And, in addition to this, we do not permit that any sale or donation which may be made to him or which he may make to another party shall be valid, after the day on which it entered into his heart to do this; and we hold that a penalty of this kind inflicted upon such a person is more severe than if he were put to death; for a dishonorable life will be worse to him than death itself, since he will not be able to make use of the honors and advantages which he sees others enjoy.

LAW VI.
What Penalty a Christian of Either Sex Who Becomes a Jew, a Moor, or a Heretic, Deserves.

Our Lord God desired that kings and princes should have dominion over the people, in order that through them justice might be maintained, and also because as often as disputes and controversies arise among men which cannot be decided by the ancient law, through their means new advice might be obtained by means of which said controversy could be equitably decided; and therefore we order that if, from this time forward, as it has formerly occurred, any married woman acknowledging our faith becomes a Jewess, a Moor, or a heretic, and marries again in accordance with the rites of her new religion, or commits adultery; her dowry, her marriage gifts, and all property which she held in common with her husband at the time when she committed this offense, shall belong to him; and we decree that her husband if he becomes a Jew, a Moor or a heretic, shall undergo the same penalty which we stated should be inflicted upon his wife. Where, however, the said woman has children, they, after the death of their father, shall inherit the property which the husband obtains on account of the offense committed by his wife, and although he may have children by another wife, the latter shall not be entitled to any of said property. We decree that the same disposition shall be made of his property if he committed an offense of this kind.

LAW VII.
Where Anyone Renounces the Faith of Our Lord Jesus Christ His Reputation Can Be Attacked Five Years after His Death.

Where anyone renounces the religion of Our Lord Jesus Christ and subsequently returns to it, as stated above, and he should not happen to be accused of said offense in his lifetime; we consider it proper, and we order, that any man can attack his reputation within five years after his death. If during said time anyone should accuse him and he should be convicted, his property shall be disposed of as we stated in the preceding law; but if he should not be accused while alive, or within five years after his death, then no one can accuse him afterwards.

LAW VIII.
What Reason a Christian Who Becomes a Jew or a Moor and Afterwards Repents, Returning to the Faith of the Christians, Can Escape the Penalty Aforesaid.

It may happen that some of those who renounce the Catholic faith and become Moors will attempt to render some great service to the Christians resulting in the substantial benefit of the country; and for the reason that they endeavor to perform such a service may not remain unrewarded, we consider it proper and we order that they be pardoned, and released from the penalty of death which we stated in the fourth law preceding this one shall be inflicted upon them on account of the offense of which they are guilty. For a party who commits an act of this kind makes it sufficiently understood that he is attached to the Christians,

and would return to the Catholic faith if he had not left it through shame, or on account of some reproach by his relatives or friends; therefore we order, and we desire that his life be granted him, even though he may remain a Moor. And if after he has rendered the service to the Christians, as aforesaid, he repents of his sin and returns to the Catholic faith, we order, and we consider it proper that he also be released from the penalty of being considered infamous, that he shall not lose his property; and that no one thereafter shall dare to reproach him or his conduct, or interfere with him in any way; and that he shall enjoy all the honors, and make use of all the things which Christians have and ordinarily use, just as if he had never renounced the Catholic faith.

LAW IX.
Moors Who Come on a Mission from Other Kingdoms to the Court of the King Should, with Their Property, Be Safe and Secure.

Envoys frequently come from the land of the Moors and other countries to the court of the king, and although they may come from the enemy's country and by his order, we consider it proper and we direct that every envoy who comes to our country, whether he be Christian, Moor, or Jew, shall come and go in safety and security through all our dominions, and we forbid anyone to do him violence, wrong, or harm, or to injure his property.

Moreover, we decree that although an envoy who visits our country may owe a debt to some man in our dominions, which was contracted before he came on the mission, he shall not be arrested or brought into court for it; but if he should not be willing to pay any debts which he contracted in our country after he came on the mission, suit can be brought against him for them, and he can be compelled to pay them by a judgment of court.

LAW X.
What Penalty a Moor and a Christian Woman Deserve Who Have Intercourse with One Another.

If a Moor has sexual intercourse with a Christian virgin, we order that he will be stoned, and that she, for the first offense, shall lose half of her property, that her father, mother, or grandfather shall have it, and if she has no such relatives, that it shall belong to the king. For the second offense, she shall lose all her property, and the heirs aforesaid, if she has any, shall obtain it, and if she has none, the king shall be entitled to it, and she shall be put to death. We decree and order that the same rule shall apply to a widow who commits this crime. If a Moor has sexual intercourse with a Christian married woman, he shall be put to death, and she shall be placed in the power of her husband who may burn her to death, or release her, or do what he pleases with her. If a Moor has intercourse with a common woman who abandons herself to everyone, for the first offense, they shall be scourged together through the town and for the second they shall be put to death.

TITLE XXVI.

Concerning Heretics.

Heretics are a species of insane people who endeavor to pervert the sayings of Our Lord Jesus Christ, and impart to them a different construction from that which the Holy Fathers gave them and which the Church of Rome believes, and orders to be observed. Wherefore, since in the preceding title we spoke of the Moors, we desire here to speak of heretics. We shall show why they have this name; how many kinds of them there are; what injury results to men from their society; who has the right to accuse them, and before whom this can be done; and what punishment they deserve after their heresy has been proved.

LAW I.
From What Source Heretics Derive Their Name; How Many Kinds of Them There Are; and What Injury Results to Men by Associating with Them.

Haeresis, in Latin, means, in Castilian, a separation, and a heretic derives his name from this source because he is separated from the Catholic faith of Christians; and although there are several sects and kinds of heretics there are only principal ones. The first includes every belief which a man has which does not agree with the true faith which the Church of Rome orders be acknowledged, and observed; the second includes the disbelief which some wicked and incredulous men entertain, who think that the soul dies with the body, and that a man will not be rewarded or punished in the next world for the good or evil which he does in this; and those who hold this opinion are worse than beasts. Great injury results to a country from heretics of every description, for they constantly endeavor to corrupt the minds of men and cause them to err.

LAW II.
Who Can Accuse Heretics, Before Whom This Can Be Done, What Penalty They Deserve after Their Heresy Has Been Proved, and Who Is Entitled to Inherit Their Property.

Heretics can be accused by anyone of the people before the bishops or the vicars who occupy their places, and they should examine them in the articles of faith and the sacraments, and if they find that they err with respect to them or any other matters which the Roman Church accepts and orders to be delivered and observed; they should then attempt to convert them, and withdraw them from said errors by means of good arguments and gentle words, and if they are willing to return to the faith and believe it, after they have been reconciled to the church they should be pardoned.

If they are not willing to abandon their obstinacy, they should be condemned as heretics, and afterwards delivered to the secular judge, and the latter shall punish them in the following way; that is, if the heretic is a preacher, or what is called a comforter, he should be put to death by fire; and the unbelievers whom we mentioned in the preceding law, who do not think that any reward or punishment exists in the other world, shall suffer the same penalty. If the heretic is not a preacher, but merely a believer who associates, or is present with those who perform sacrifices at the time when this is done, and listens daily, or whenever he can do so to their preaching; we order that he shall be put to death in the same manner, since he believes in, and is present at the sacrifices which are performed. Where he is not a believer in their doctrines, but practices them by attending their sacrifices, we order that he shall suffer perpetual banishment from our dominions, or be put in prison until he repents, or returns to the faith.

We also decree that the property of persons condemned as heretics, or who are known to die in heretical belief, shall belong to their children or to the descendants of the latter. If they have no children, we order that it shall belong to their next of kin who are Catholics; if they have no such relatives and are laymen, we decree that the king shall inherit all their property; and if they belong to the clergy, the church can claim and take possession of their estates within a year after their deaths; but the royal treasury shall be entitled to them after that time if the church was guilty of negligence in not claiming them within that period. If the heretic was a believer, and was not present at the sacrifices, as aforesaid, but went to hear the doctrines, we order he shall pay ten pounds of gold to the royal treasury, and if he should not have the means with which to do so, he shall receive fifty lashes in public.

LAW III.
Children, Who Are Not Catholics, Cannot, with the Others, Inherit the Property of Their Father, Who Was a Heretic.

When a man has been condemned as a heretic, and has some children who are heretics and some who adhere to the Catholic faith and observe it, we order that those who remain steadfast in our religion shall inherit the entire estate of their father, and shall not be bound to give the others any portion of the same. If, however, the others, acknowledging their error, subsequently become converted and return to the Catholic faith, their brothers will then be bound to give each one of them his share of the estate of their father; but the rents and profits of the property which the said Catholic brothers collected during the time that the others were heretics, they shall not be obliged to account for to the latter, or to give them any portion of the same, if they do not wish to.

LAW IV.
A Man Who Is Proclaimed a Heretic Cannot Hold Any Dignity or Public Office, but Shall Lose All Which He Formerly Held.

A man who has been condemned as a heretic shall not hold any dignity or public office, and therefore he cannot be a pope, a cardinal, a patriarch, an archbishop, or a bishop, nor can he enjoy any of the honors or dignities which belong to the Holy Church. We also decree that a person of this kind cannot be an emperor, a king, a duke, or a count, nor shall he hold any office or honorable position appertaining to secular sovereignty.

We also decree that if anyone is proved to be a heretic, he shall lose, for this reason, any dignity which he formerly held, and, in addition to this, he is forbidden by the ancient laws to make a will except where he desires to leave his property to his Catholic children; and no bequest can be left him by the will of anyone, nor can he be appointed the heir of another. We also decree that after the day on which he was condemned for heresy no will of his shall be valid, and that any sale or donation made to him shall be void, as well as any which he may make to another of his own property.

59. GIOVANNI SCRIBA

Notary Book

THE FOLLOWING CONTRACTS MAKE it possible to follow the business dealings of the Genoese merchant Oliverius Nivetelle in the 1160s. They were recorded in the Notary Book of Giovanni Scriba, the earliest extant notary book from Genoa. Most of the contracts are a form of bilateral commenda contract termed in Genoa *societas*. Traditionally, the investor who stays home contributed two thirds of the capital and the traveling partner one third plus his labor. The profits were divided by half according to the amount of the original investment, and losses were proportionally borne by both.

One text records a land transaction and can be compared with the text of the *Theodosian Code* above (doc. 1) to see the influence of Roman law in twelfth-century Italy.

Source: M. Chiaudano and M. Moresco (eds.), *Il cartolare di Giovanni Scriba II* (Turin: 1935).

Further Reading: Stephen Epstein, *Wills and Wealth in Medieval Genoa, 1150–1250* (Cambridge, MA: Harvard University Press, 1984).

---

654 Witnesses Oliverii Nivetele and Iohanis Cirbini Witnesses Ogerius Spion, Ioffredus the pelterer de Clavica and Iohannes de Doda. Oliverius Nivetella and Iohannes Cirbinus contracted a societas in which Oliverius brought 30 pounds and Iohannes Cirbinus 15 pounds. This same Iohannes must transact the business in Palermo and through Sicily and must come to Genoa and dissolve this societas into the hands of this Oliverus or his agent, the profits being equally divided. Done in the house of this same Oliverius, 1160, May 12, 7th indiction.

655 Oliverius Nivetelle and Oliverius de Reco.
Same witnesses, place and time and Iohannes Cirbinus and Ansaldinus Testa. Oliverius Nivetella and Oliverius de Reco contracted a societas in which Oliverius Nivetella invested 20 pounds 4-½ shillings and the above mentioned Oliverius invested 11 pounds. Oliverius must take the work of this societas to Palermo and through Sicily and then must settle accounts with Oliverius or his agent, and after the capital is returned the profits will be divided equally.

656 Oliverius Nivetelle and Oliverius Ferretus The same witnesses, day and place as above. Oliverius Nivetella and Oliverius Ferretus on the directive and authority of their lord Oto Dormacagar contracted a societas in which this Oliverius Nivetella states that he contributed 25 pounds and Oliverius Ferrerius and his lord and the same Oliverius contributed 17-½ pounds. Oliverius must take this societas to Palermo and then Sicily and from there this ship and its crew will return without exception and after the capital has been divided he will divide the profits of this venture equally with Oliverius or his agent....

878 Oliverius Nivetelle
Witnesses Bonus Vassallus Salsa, Bombellus the banker, Lanfrancus de Albario, Jordanus de Isa

and Nicolosus de domo. We Otobonus master and Druda his spouse have taken from you, Oliverius Nivetella, 60 pounds in Genovese pennies as full price for a house and a parcel of land of our hereditary right which is in Clavica. Its boundaries are on two sides the public road, and on two others your house.

We sell you the above-mentioned purchaser everything within these boundaries with its entrance and exit and all of its rights for you and your heirs or to whomever you may wish to give it to do whatever you wish as proprietor. We further promise not to hinder you and to defend you against everyone else under penalty of a double payment according to its present or future increased value, in order to make good our pledge that we have sold to you all that we have or should have and we promise that without your authority and advice we shall not make any evaluation or claims on it in for sale. We give you possession and lordship of this house. I Druda made this with the advice and authority of my kinsman Iordanus de Isa and Nicolosus de domo renouncing my rights in this case according to the senatusconsult of Velleianus[1] on the law of mortgages and the law of Julia on non-appraised values.[2] Done in the church of Saint Laurence, August 17, in the 8th indiction....

1125 Oliverius Nivetelle and Ferretus

Witnesses Bonus Vassallus Salsa, Aimericus, Master Bernardus, Oto Painardus and Enricus Nivetella. Oliverius Nivetella and Oliver Ferretus have contracted a societas in which they both state that Oliverius Nivetella invested 40 pounds and Oliverius Ferretus 20 pounds. Oliverius Ferretus must take this societas in the ship of Enrici Gagina and on his return must divide principal and interest with Oliverii Nivetelle. After the capital has been separated, the profits are to be divided equally. Oliverius Ferretus further swears that he has promised 20 pounds in this societas and that he will execute and will make every effort to advance this societas in good faith and legally according to the tenor of the contract of the societas and that he will return it as stipulated above and that as long as he is doing business with this Oliverius and had his property and this societas in his power he will keep faith and will restore to him or to his agent without fraud nor will he deprive him of more than 10 shillings per year which he expects in good faith unless he receives permission to do so by him or by his reliable agent. Done in the house of Iohannis the scribe, 1163, September 25, the 11th indiction.

1126 Oliverius Nivetella and Enricus Gagina

Witnesses Bonus Vassallus Salsa, Oto Rainardus, Donatus de Sancto Donato and Enricus Nivetella. Oliverius Nivetella and Enricus Gagina state that they have divided all of the societas which they had previously shared and that each has taken his share. Done before lord Bernardus the magistrate, in the same day as above.

1127 Oliverius Nivetella and Enricus Gagina

The above witnesses in the preceding document and on the same day and place. Oliverius Nivetella and Enricus Gagina have formed a societas in which Oliverius contributes 102 pounds and Enricus 51. Enricus undertakes this societas in a ship which is to depart and return and when the capital has been removed, the profits are to be divided in halves. In addition Enricus will carry 49 pounds of his own which he should spend and from which he should freely profit and which will be his own profit.

---

1   In Roman Law, the Senatusconsult Velleianum forbade surety by women.
2   The Julian law protected the alienation of a woman's dowry by her husband or guardian. See above, Theodosian Code 3,1,3 (doc. 1).

60. *DIALOGUES* OF CATHERINE OF SIENA

C ATHERINE OF SIENA (1347–80) was born Caterina Benincasa to a family of modest means in the city of Siena in central Italy. From childhood she had visions, and after entering the Third Order of St. Dominic at age sixteen she became famous for her austerity, contemplation, and work with the poor. She dictated letters and discussions of spiritual matters in a trance-like state to her confessor and spiritual director who, after 1374, was Raymond of Capua, future master-general of the Dominican order. Among the most significant of her writings were her Dialogues, a treatise in four books dedicated respectively to Divine Providence, Discretion, Prayer, and Obedience. The following passage from the second book deals with the nature of love. It is followed by an eye-witness account of her death by Barduccio di Piero Canigiani.

Source: *The Dialogue of the Seraphic Virgin Catherine of Siena (Dictated by her, while in a state of ecstasy, to her secretaries, and completed in the year of our lord 1370 together with an account of her death by an eye-witness)*, trans. Algar Thorold (Westminster, MD: The Newman Bookshop, 1944).

Further Reading: F. Thomas Luongo, *The Saintly Politics of Catherine of Siena* (Ithaca, NY: Cornell University Press, 2006).

Of the imperfection of those who love GOD for their own profit, delight, and consolation.

"Some there are who have become faithful servants, serving Me with fidelity without servile fear of punishment, but rather with love. This very love, however, if they serve Me with a view to their own profit, or the delight and pleasure which they find in Me, is imperfect. Dost thou know what proves the imperfection of this love? The withdrawal of the consolations which they found in Me, and the insufficiency and short duration of their love for their neighbor, which grows weak by degrees, and ofttimes disappears. Towards Me their love grows weak when, on occasion, in order to exercise them in virtue and raise them above their imperfection, I withdraw from their minds My consolation and allow them to fall into battles and perplexities. This I do so that, coming to perfect self-knowledge, they may know that of themselves they are nothing and have no grace, and accordingly in time of battle fly to Me, as their Benefactor, seeking Me alone, with true humility, for which purpose I treat them thus, without drawing from them consolation indeed, but not grace. At such a time these weak ones, of whom I speak, relax their energy, impatiently turning backwards, and sometimes abandon, under color of virtue, many of their exercises, saying to themselves, *This labor does not profit me.* All this they do, because they feel themselves deprived of mental consolation. Such a soul acts imperfectly, for she has not yet unwound the bandage of spiritual self-love, for, had she unwound it she would see that, in truth, everything proceeds from Me, that no leaf of a tree falls to the ground without My providence, and that what I give and promise to My creatures, I give and promise to them for their sanctification, which is the good and the end for which I created them. My creatures should see and know that I wish nothing but their good, through the blood of My only-begotten son, in which they are washed from their iniquities. By this blood they are enabled to know My truth, how, in order to give them eternal life, I created them in My image and likeness and re-created them to grace with the blood of My son, making them sons of adoption. But, since they are imperfect, they make use of Me only for their own profit, relaxing their love for their neighbor. Thus, those in the first state come to nought through the fear of enduring pain, and those in the second, because they slacken their pace, ceasing to render service to their neighbor, and withdrawing their charity if they see their own profit or consolation withdrawn from them: this happens because their love was originally impure, for they gave to their neighbor the same imperfect love which they gave to Me, that is to say, a love based only on desire of their own advantage. If, through a desire for perfection, they do not recognize this imperfection of theirs, it is impossible that they should not turn back. For those who desire Eternal Life, a pure love, prescinding from themselves, is necessary, for it is not enough for eternal life to fly sin from fear of punishment, or to embrace virtue from the motive of one's own advantage. Sin should be abandoned because it is displeasing to Me, and virtue should be loved for My sake. It is true that, generally speaking, every person is first called in this way, but this is because the soul herself is at first imperfect, from which imperfection she must advance to perfection, either while she lives, by a generous love to Me with a pure and virtuous heart that takes no thought for herself, or, at least, in the moment of death, recognizing her own imperfection, with the purpose, had she but time, of serving Me, irrespectively of herself. It was with this imperfect love that St. Peter loved the sweet and good Jesus, My only-begotten son, enjoying most pleasantly His sweet conversation, but, when the time of trouble came, he failed, and so disgraceful was his fall, that, not only could he not bear any pain himself, but his terror of the very approach of pain caused him to fall, and deny the Lord, with the words, '*I have never known Him.*' The soul who has climbed this step with servile fear and mercenary love alone, falls into many troubles. Such souls should arise and become sons, and serve Me, irrespective of themselves, for I, who am the rewarder of every labor, render to each man according to his state and his labor; wherefore, if these souls do not abandon the exercise of holy prayer and their other good works, but go on, with perseverance, to increase their virtues, they will arrive at the state of filial love, because I respond to them with the same love, with which they love Me, so that, if they love Me, as a servant does his master, I pay them their wages according to their deserts, but I do not reveal Myself to them, because secrets are revealed to a friend, who has become one thing with his friend, and not to a servant. Yet it is true, that a servant may so advance by the virtuous love, which he bears to his master, as to become a very

dear friend, and so do some of these of whom I have spoken, but while they remain in the state of mercenary love, I do not manifest Myself to them. If they, through displeasure at their imperfection, and love of virtue, dig up, with hatred, the root of spiritual self-love, and mount to the throne of conscience, reasoning with themselves, so as to quell the motions of servile fear in their heart, and to correct mercenary love by the light of the holy faith, they will be so pleasing to Me, that they will attain to the love of the friend. And I will manifest Myself to them, as My truth said in these words: '*He who loves Me shall be one thing with Me and I with him, and I will manifest Myself to him and we will dwell together.*' This is the state of two dear friends, for though they are two in body, yet they are one in soul through the affection of love, because love transforms the lover into the object loved, and where two friends have one soul, there can be no secret between them, wherefore My truth said: 'I will come and we will dwell together,' and this is the truth."

Of the way in which GOD manifests Himself to the soul who loves Him.

"Knowest thou how I manifest Myself to the soul who loves Me in truth, and follows the doctrine of My sweet and amorous word? In many is My virtue manifested in the soul in proportion to her desire, but I make three special manifestations. The first manifestation of My virtue, that is to say, of My love and charity in the soul, is made through the word of My son, and shown in the blood, which He spilled with such fire of love. Now this charity is manifested in two ways; first, in general, to ordinary people, that is to those who live in the ordinary grace of God. It is manifested to them by the many and diverse benefits which they receive from Me. The second mode of manifestation, which is developed from the first, is peculiar to those who have become My friends in the way mentioned above, and is known through a sentiment of the soul, by which they taste, know, prove, and feel it. This second manifestation, however, is in men themselves; they manifesting Me, through the affection of their love. For though I am no acceptor of creatures, I am an acceptor of holy desires, and Myself in the soul in that precise degree of perfection which she seeks in Me. Sometimes I manifest Myself (and this is also a part of the second manifestation) by endowing men with the spirit of prophecy, showing them the things of the future. This I do in many and diverse ways, according as I see need in the soul herself and in other creatures. At other times the third manifestation takes place. I then form in the mind the presence of the truth, My only-begotten son, in many ways, according to the will and the desire of the soul. Sometimes she seeks Me in prayer, wishing to know My power, and I satisfy her by causing her to taste and see My virtue. Sometimes she seeks Me in the wisdom of My son, and I satisfy her by placing His wisdom before the eye of her intellect, sometimes in the clemency of the Holy Spirit and then My goodness causes her to taste the fire of divine charity, and to conceive the true and royal virtues, which are founded on the pure love of her neighbor."

Why Christ did not say "I will manifest My father," but "I will manifest Myself."

"Thou seest now how truly My word spoke, when He said: '*He who loves Me shall be one thing with Me.*' Because, by following His doctrine with the affection of love, you are united with Him, and, being united with Him, you are united with Me, because We are one thing together. And so it is that I manifest Myself to you, because We are one and the same thing together. Wherefore if My truth said, '*I will manifest Myself to you,*' He said the truth, because, in manifesting Himself, He manifested Me, and, in manifesting Me, He manifested Himself. But why did He not say, '*I will manifest My father to you*'? For three reasons in particular. First, because He wished to show that He and I are not separate from each other, on which account He also made the following reply to St. Philip, when he said to Him, '*Show us the father, and it is enough for us.*' My word said, '*Who sees Me sees the father, and who sees the father sees Me.*' This He said because He was one thing with Me, and that which He had, He had from Me, I having nothing from Him; wherefore, again, He said to Judas, '*My doctrine is not Mine, but My father's who sent Me,*' because My son proceeds from Me, not I from Him, though

I with Him and He with Me are but one thing. For this reason He did not say '*I will manifest the father,*' but '*I will manifest Myself*' being one thing with the father. The second reason was because, in manifesting Himself to you, He did not present to you anything He had not received from Me, the Father. These words, then, mean the father has manifested Himself to Me, because I am one thing with Him, and I will manifest to you, by means of Myself, Me and Him. The third reason was, because I, being invisible, could not be seen by you, until you should be separated from your bodies. Then, indeed, will you see Me, your GOD, and My son, the word, face to face. From now until after the general Resurrection, when your humanity will be conformed with the humanity of the eternal word, according to what I told thee in the treatise of the Resurrection, you can see Me, with the eye of the intellect alone, for, as I am, you cannot see Me now. Wherefore I veiled the divine nature with your humanity, so that you might see Me through that medium. I, the invisible, made Myself, as it were, visible by sending you the word, My son, veiled in the flesh of your humanity. He manifested Me to you. Therefore it was that He did not say '*I will manifest the father to you,*' but rather, '*I will manifest Myself to you,*' as if He should say, '*According as My father manifests Himself to Me, will I manifest Myself to you, for, in this manifestation of Himself, He manifests Me.*' Now therefore thou understandest why He did not say '*I will manifest the father to you.*' Both, because such a vision is impossible for you, while yet in the mortal body, and because He is one thing with Me."

How the soul, after having mounted the first step of the bridge, should proceed to mount the second.

"Thou hast now seen how excellent is the state of him who has attained to the love of a friend; climbing with the foot of affection, he has reached the secret of the heart, which is the second of the three steps figured in the body of My son. I have told thee what was meant by the three powers of the soul, and now I will show thee how they signify the three states, through which the soul passes. Before treating of the third state, I wish to show thee how a man becomes a friend and how, from a friend, he grows into a son, attaining to filial love, and how a man may know if he has become a friend. And first of how a man arrives at being a friend. In the beginning, a man serves Me imperfectly through servile fear, but, by exercise and perseverance, he arrives at the love of delight, finding his own delight and profit in Me. This is a necessary stage, by which he must pass, who would attain to perfect love, to the love that is of friend and son. I call filial love perfect, because thereby, a man receives his inheritance from Me, the eternal father, and because a son's love includes that of a friend, which is why I told thee that a friend grows into a son. What means does he take to arrive thereat? I will tell thee. Every perfection and every virtue proceeds from charity, and charity is nourished by humility, which results from the knowledge and holy hatred of self, that is, sensuality. To arrive thereat, a man must persevere, and remain in the cellar of self-knowledge in which he will learn My mercy, in the blood of My only begotten son, drawing to Himself, with this love, My divine charity, exercising himself in the extirpation of his perverse self-will, both spiritual and temporal, hiding himself in his own house, as did Peter, who, after the sin of denying My Son, began to weep. Yet his lamentations were imperfect and remained so, until after the forty days, that is until after the Ascension. But when My truth returned to Me, in His humanity, Peter and the others concealed themselves in the house, awaiting the coming of the Holy Spirit, which My truth had promised them. They remained barred in from fear, because the soul always fears until she arrives at true love. But when they had persevered in fasting and in humble and continual prayer, until they had received the abundance of the Holy Spirit, they lost their fear, and followed and preached Christ crucified. So also the soul, who wishes to arrive at this perfection, after she has risen from the guilt of mortal sin, recognizing it for what it is, begins to weep from fear of the penalty, whence she rises to the consideration of My mercy, in which contemplation, she finds her own pleasure and profit. This is an imperfect state, and I, in order to develop perfection in the soul, after the forty days, that is after these two states, withdraw Myself from time to time, not in grace but in feeling. My Truth showed you this when He said

to the disciples, 'I will go and will return to you.'

"Everything that He said was said primarily, and in particular, to the disciples, but referred in general to the whole present and future, to those, that is to say, who should come after. He said '*I will go and will return to you*'; and so it was, for, when the Holy Spirit returned upon the disciples, He also returned, as I told you above, for the Holy Spirit did not return alone, but came with My power, and the wisdom of the son, who is one thing with Me, and with His own clemency, which proceeds from Me the father, and from the son. Now, as I told thee, in order to raise the soul from imperfection, I withdraw Myself from her sentiment, depriving her of former consolations. When she was in the guilt of mortal sin, she had separated herself from Me, and I deprived her of grace through her own guilt, because that guilt had barred the door of her desires. Wherefore the sun of grace did not shine, not through its own defect, but through the defect of the creature, who bars the door of desire. When she knows herself and her darkness, she opens the window and vomits her filth, by holy confession. Then I, having returned to the soul by grace, withdraw Myself from her by sentiment, which I do in order to humiliate her, and cause her to seek Me in truth, and to prove her in the light of faith, so that she come to prudence. Then, if she love Me without thought of self, and with lively faith and with hatred of her own sensuality, she rejoices in the time of trouble, deeming herself unworthy of peace and quietness of mind. Now comes the second of the three things of which I told thee, that is to say: how the soul arrives at perfection, and what she does when she is perfect. This is what she does. Though she perceives that I have withdrawn Myself, she does not, on that account, look back, but perseveres with humility in her exercises, remaining barred in the house of self-knowledge, and, continuing to dwell therein, awaits, with lively faith, the coming of the Holy Spirit, that is of Me, who am the fire of charity. How does she await me? Not in idleness, but in watching and continued prayer, and not only with physical, but also with intellectual watching, that is, with the eye of her mind alert, and, watching with the light of faith, she extirpates, with hatred, the wandering thoughts of her heart, looking for the affection of

My charity, and knowing that I desire nothing but her sanctification, which is certified to her in the blood of My son. As long as her eye thus watches, illumined by the knowledge of Me and of herself, she continues to pray with the prayer of holy desire, which is a continued prayer, and also with actual prayer, which she practices at the appointed times, according to the orders of Holy Church. This is what the soul does in order to rise from imperfection and arrive at perfection, and it is to this end, namely that she may arrive at perfection, that I withdraw from her, not by grace but by sentiment. Once more do I leave her, so that she may see and know her defects, so that, feeling herself deprived of consolation and afflicted by pain, she may recognize her own weakness, and learn how incapable she is of stability or perseverance, thus cutting down to the very root of spiritual self-love, for this should be the end and purpose of all her self-knowledge, to rise above herself, mounting the throne of conscience, and not permitting the sentiment of imperfect love to turn again in its death-struggle, but, with correction and reproof, digging up the root of self-love, with the knife of self-hatred and the love of virtue."

How an imperfect lover of GOD loves his neighbor also imperfectly, and of the signs of this imperfect love.

"And I would have thee know that just as every imperfection and perfection is acquired from Me, so is it manifested by means of the neighbor. And simple souls, who often love creatures with spiritual love, know this well, for, if they have received My love sincerely without any self-regarding considerations, they satisfy the thirst of their love for their neighbor equally sincerely. If a man carry away the vessel which he has filled at the fountain and then drink of it, the vessel becomes empty, but if he keep his vessel standing in the fountain, while he drinks, it always remains full. So the love of the neighbor, whether spiritual or temporal, should be drunk in Me, without any self-regarding considerations. I require that you should love Me with the same love with which I love you. This indeed you cannot do, because I loved you without being loved. All the love which you have for Me you owe to Me, so that it is not of

grace that you love Me, but because you ought to do so. While I love you of grace, and not because I owe you My love. Therefore to Me, in person, you cannot repay the love which I require of you, and I have placed you in the midst of your fellows, that you may do to them that which you cannot do to Me, that is to say, that you may love your neighbor of free grace, without expecting any return from him, and what you do to him, I count as done to Me, which My Truth showed forth when He said to Paul, My persecutor—'*Saul, Saul, why persecutest thou Me?*' This He said, judging that Paul persecuted Him in His faithful. This love must be sincere, because it is with the same love with which you love Me, that you must love your neighbor. Dost thou know how the imperfection of spiritual love for the creature is shown? It is shown when the lover feels pain if it appear to him that the object of his love does not satisfy or return his love, or when he sees the beloved one's conversation turned aside from him, or himself deprived of consolation, or another loved more than he. In these and in many other ways can it be seen that his neighborly love is still imperfect, and that, though his love was originally drawn from Me, the Fountain of all love, he took the vessel out of the water, in order to drink from it. It is because his love for Me is still imperfect, that his neighborly love is so weak, and because the root of self-love has not been properly dug out. Wherefore I often permit such a love to exist, so that the soul may in this way come to the knowledge of her own imperfection, and for the same reason do I withdraw myself from the soul by sentiment, that she may be thus led to enclose herself in the house of self-knowledge, where is acquired every perfection. After which I return into her with more light and with more knowledge of My truth in proportion to the degree in which she refers to grace the power of slaying her own will. And she never ceases to cultivate the vine of her soul, and to root out the thorns of evil thoughts, replacing them with the stones of virtues, cemented together in the blood of Christ crucified, which she has found on her journey across the bridge of Christ, My only-begotten Son. For I told thee, if thou remember, that upon the bridge, that is, upon the doctrine of My truth, were built up the stones, based upon the virtue of His blood, for it is in virtue of this blood that the virtues give life.

"Trinity, I have known in Thy light, which Thou hast given me with the light of holy faith, the many and wonderful things Thou hast declared to me, explaining to me the path of supreme perfection, so that I may no longer serve Thee in darkness, but with light, and that I may be the mirror of a good and holy life, and arise from my miserable sins, for through them I have hitherto served Thee in darkness. I have not known Thy truth and have not loved it. Why did I not know Thee? Because I did not see Thee with the glorious light of the holy faith; because the cloud of self-love darkened the eye of my intellect, and Thou, the Eternal Trinity, hast dissipated the darkness with Thy light. Who can attain to Thy greatness, and give Thee thanks for such immeasurable gifts and benefits as Thou hast given me in this doctrine of truth, which has been a special grace over and above the ordinary graces which Thou givest also to Thy other creatures? Thou hast been willing to condescend to my need and to that of Thy creatures—the need of introspection. Having first given the grace to ask the question, Thou repliest to it, and satisfiest Thy servant, penetrating me with a ray of grace, so that in that light I may give Thee thanks. Clothe me, clothe me with Thee, oh! Eternal Truth, that I may run my mortal course with true obedience and the light of holy faith, with which light I feel that my soul is about to become inebriated afresh."

A Letter of Ser Barduccio di Piero Canigiani, containing the Transit of the Seraphic Virgin, Saint Catherine of Siena, to Sister Catherine Petriboni in the Monastery of San Piero a Monticelli near Florence. In the Name of Jesus Christ.

Dearest Mother in Christ Jesus, and Sister in the holy memory of our blessed mother Catherine, I, Barduccio, a wretched and guilty sinner, recommend myself to your holy prayers as a feeble infant, orphaned by the death of so great a mother. I received your letter and read it with much pleasure, and communicated it to my afflicted mothers here, who, supremely grateful for your great charity and tender love towards them, recommend themselves greatly, for their part, to your prayers, and beg you to recommend them to the prioress and all the sisters that they may be ready to do all that may be pleasing to God concerning themselves and you. But since you, as a beloved and faithful daughter, desire to know the end of our common mother, I am constrained to satisfy your desire; and although I know myself to be but little fitted to give such a narration, I will write in any case what my feeble eyes have seen, and what the dull senses of my soul have been able to comprehend.

This blessed virgin and mother of thousands of souls, about the feast of the Circumcision, began to feel so great a change both in soul and body, that she was obliged to alter her mode of life, the action of taking food for her sustenance becoming so loathsome to her, that it was only with the greatest difficulty that she could force herself to take any, and, when she did so, she swallowed nothing of the substance of the food, but had the habit of rejecting it. Moreover, not one drop of water could she swallow for refreshment, whence came to her a most violent and tedious thirst, and so great an inflammation of her throat that her breath seemed to be fire, with all which, however, she remained in very good health, robust and fresh as usual. In these conditions we reached Sexagesima Sunday, when, about the hour of vespers, at the time of her prayer, she had so violent a stroke that from that day onwards she was no longer in health. Towards the night of the following Monday, just after I had written a letter, she had another stroke so terrific, that we all mourned her as dead, remaining under it for a long time without giving any sign of life. Then, rising, she stood for an equal space of time, and did not seem the same person as she who had fallen.

From that hour began new travail and bitter pains in her body, and, Lent having arrived, she began, in spite of her infirmity, to give herself with such application of mind to prayer that the frequency of the humble sighs and sorrowful plaints which she exhaled from the depth of her heart appeared to us a miracle. I think, too, that you know that her prayers were so fervent that one hour spent in prayer by her reduced that dear tender frame to greater weakness than would be suffered by one who should persist for two whole days in prayer. Meanwhile, every morning, after communion, she arose from the earth in such a state that any one who had seen her would have thought her dead, and was thus carried back to bed. Thence, after an hour or two, she would arise afresh, and we would go to St. Peter's, although a good mile distant, where she would place herself in prayer, so remaining until vespers, finally returning to the house so worn out that she seemed a corpse.

These were her exercises up till the third Sunday in Lent, when she finally succumbed, conquered by the innumerable sufferings, which daily increased, and consumed her body, and the infinite afflictions of the soul which she derived from the consideration of the sins which she saw being committed against God, and from the dangers ever more grave to which she knew the Holy Church to be exposed, on account of which she remained greatly overcome, and both internally and externally tormented. She lay in this state for eight weeks, unable to lift her head, and full of intolerable pains, from the soles of her feet to the crown of her head, to such an extent that she would often say: "These pains are truly physical, but not natural; for it seems that God has given permission to the devils to torment this body at their pleasure." And, in truth, it evidently was so; for, if I were to attempt to explain the patience which she practiced, under this terrible and unheard-of agony, I should fear to injure, by my explanations, facts which cannot be explained. This only will I say, that, every time that a new torment came upon her, she would joyously raise her eyes and her heart to God and say: "Thanks to Thee, oh eternal Spouse, for granting such graces afresh every day to me, Thy miserable and most unworthy handmaid!"

In this way her body continued to consume itself until the Sunday before the Ascension; but by that time it was reduced to such a state that it seemed like a corpse in a picture, though I speak not of the face, which remained ever angelical and breathed forth devotion, but of the bosom and limbs, in which nothing could be seen but the bones, covered by the thinnest skin, and so feeble was she from the waist downwards that she could not move herself, even a little, from one side to another. In the night preceding the aforesaid Sunday, about two hours or more before dawn, a great change was produced in her, and we thought that she was approaching the end.

The whole family was then called around her, and she, with singular humility and devotion, made signs to those who were standing near that she desired to receive Holy Absolution for her faults and the pains due to them, and so it was done. After which she became gradually reduced to such a state that we could observe no other movement than her breathing, continuous, sad, and feeble. On account of this it seemed right to give her extreme unction, which our abbot of Sant' Antimo did, while she lay as it were deprived of feeling.

After this unction she began altogether to change, and to make various signs with her head and her arms as if to show that she was suffering from grave assaults of demons, and remained in this calamitous state for an hour and a half, half of which time having been passed in silence, she began to say: "I have sinned! Oh Lord, have mercy on me!" And this, as I believe, she repeated more than sixty times, raising each time her right arm, and then letting it fall and strike the bed. Then, changing her words, she said as many times again, but without moving her arms, "Holy God, have mercy on me!" Finally she employed the remainder of the above-mentioned time with many other formulas of prayer both humble and devout, expressing various acts of virtue, after which her face suddenly changed from gloom to angelic light, and her tearful and clouded eyes became serene and joyous, in such a manner that I could not doubt that, like one saved from a deep sea, she was restored to herself, which circumstance greatly mitigated the grief of her sons and daughters who were standing around in the affliction you can imagine.

Catherine had been lying on the bosom of Mother Alessia and now succeeded in rising, and with a little help began to sit up, leaning against the same mother. In the meantime we had put before her eyes a pious picture, containing many relics and various pictures of the saints. She, however, fixed her eyes on the image of the cross set in it, and began to adore it, explaining, in words, certain of her most profound feelings of the goodness of God, and while she prayed, she accused herself in general of all her sins in the sight of God, and, in particular, said: "It is my fault, oh eternal Trinity, that I have offended Thee so miserably with my negligence, ignorance, ingratitude, and disobedience, and many other defects. Wretch that I am! for I have not observed Thy commandments, either those which are given in general to all, or those which Thy goodness laid upon me in particular! Oh mean creature that I am!" Saying which, she struck her breast, repeating her confession, and continued: "I have not observed Thy precept, with which Thou didst command me to seek always to give Thee honor, and to spend myself in labors for my neighbor, while I, on the contrary, have fled from labors, especially where they were necessary. Didst Thou not command me, oh, my God! to abandon all thought of myself and to consider solely the praise and glory of Thy Name in the salvation of souls, and with this food alone, taken from the table of the most holy Cross, to comfort myself? But I have sought my own consolation. Thou didst ever invite me to bind myself to Thee alone by sweet, loving, and fervent desires, by tears and humble and continuous prayers for the salvation of the whole world and for the reformation of the holy Church, promising me that, on account of them, Thou wouldst use mercy with the world, and give new beauty to Thy Spouse; but I, wretched one, have not corresponded with Thy desire, but have remained asleep in the bed of negligence.

"Oh, unhappy that I am! Thou hast placed me in charge of souls, assigning to me so many beloved sons, that I should love them with singular love and direct them to Thee by the way of Life, but I have been to them nothing but a mirror of human weakness; I have had no care of them; I have not helped them with continuous and humble prayer in Thy presence, nor have I given them sufficient examples of the good life or the warnings of salutary doctrine. Oh, mean creature that I am! with how little reverence have I received Thy innumerable gifts, the graces of such sweet torments and labours which it pleased Thee to accumulate on this fragile body, nor have I endured them with that burning desire and ardent love with which Thou didst send them to me. Alas! oh, my Love, through Thy excessive goodness Thou didst choose me for Thy spouse, from the beginning of my childhood, but I was not faithful enough; in fact, I was unfaithful to Thee, because I did not keep my memory faithful to Thee alone and to Thy most high benefits; nor have I fixed my intelligence on the thought of them only or disposed my will to love Thee immediately with all

its strength."

Of these and many other similar things did that pure dove accuse herself, rather, as I think, for our example than for her own need, and then, turning to the priest, said: "For the love of Christ crucified, absolve me of all these sins which I have confessed in the presence of God, and of all the others which I cannot remember." That done, she asked again for the plenary indulgence, saying that it had been granted her by Pope Gregory and Pope Urban, saying this as one an hungered for the blood of Christ. So I did what she asked, and she, keeping her eyes ever fixed on the crucifix, began afresh to adore it with the greatest devotion, and to say certain very profound things which I, for my sins, was not worthy to understand, and also on account of the grief with which I was laboring and the anguish with which her throat was oppressed, which was so great that she could hardly utter her words, while we, placing our ears to her mouth, were able to catch one or two now or again, passing them on from one to the other. After this she turned to certain of her sons, who had not been present at a memorable discourse which, many days previously, she had made to the whole family, showing us the way of salvation and perfection, and laying upon each of us the particular task which he was to perform after her death. She now did the same to these others, begging most humbly pardon of all for the slight care which she seemed to have had of our salvation. Then she said certain things to Lucio and to another, and finally to me, and then turned herself straightway to prayer.

Oh! had you seen with what humility and reverence she begged and received many times the blessing of her most sorrowful mother, all that I can say is that it was a bitter sweet to her. How full of tender affection was the spectacle of the mother, recommending herself to her blessed child, and begging her to obtain a particular grace from God—namely, that in these melancholy circumstances she might not offend Him. But all these things did not distract the holy virgin from the fervor of her prayer; and, approaching her end, she began to pray especially for the Catholic Church, for which she declared she was giving her life. She prayed again for Pope Urban VI, whom she resolutely confessed to be the true pontiff, and strengthened her sons never to hesitate to give their life for that truth. Then, with the greatest fervor, she besought all her beloved children whom the Lord had given her, to love Him alone, repeating many of the words which our Saviour used, when He recommended the disciples to the Father, praying with such affection, that, at hearing her, not only our hearts, but the very stones might have been broken. Finally, making the sign of the cross, she blessed us all, and thus continued in prayer to the end of her life for which she had so longed, saying: "Thou, oh Lord, callest me, and I come to Thee, not through my merits, but through Thy mercy alone, which I ask of Thee, in virtue of Thy blood!" and many times she called out: "Blood, Blood!" Finally, after the example of the Savior, she said: "Father, into Thy hands I commend my soul and my spirit," and thus sweetly, with a face all shining and angelical, she bent her head, and gave up the ghost.

Her transit occurred on the Sunday at the hour of sext, but we kept her unburied until the hour of compline on Tuesday, without any odour being perceptible, her body remaining so pure, intact, and fragrant, that her arms, her neck and her legs remained as flexible as if she were still alive. During those three days the body was visited by crowds of people, and lucky he thought himself who was able to touch it. Almighty God also worked many miracles in that time, which in my hurry I omit. Her tomb is visited devoutly by the faithful, like those of the other holy bodies which are in Rome, and Almighty God is granting many graces in the name of His blessed spouse, and I doubt not that there will be many more, and we are made great by hearing of them. I say no more. Recommend me to the prioress and all the sisters, for I have, at present, the greatest need of the help of prayer. May Almighty God preserve you and help you to grow in His grace.

61. FLORENCE: CATASTO OF 1427

THE CATASTO (A TYPE of tax survey) of 1427–30 is one of the earliest attempts to compile a precise record of a city's population and its wealth. This record is a unique source for exploring social and economic questions about types of households, the role of women, business ties, financial and kin networks, household composition, and social responsibilities. The particular examples below all describe members of the important Alberti family of Florence. Previously, the adult male members of the family had been exiled from the city, so the reports are all made by their wives, widows or minor children.

Source: Archivio di Stado di Firenze, Catasto 35, ff. 1337r–1341v and Cat. 72, f. 413r. Translated by Susannah Foster Baxendale for this volume.

Further Reading: David Herlihy and Christiane Klapisch-Zuber, *Tuscans and their Families: A Study of the Florentine Catasto of 1427* (New Haven, CT: Yale University Press, 1985).

Portata[1] for the "Heirs of Albertaccio"

In the Name of God

Before you, Sirs, officials of the Catasto of the people and Commune of Florence, this relates to the property and taxes that on this the 19th of January 1427 [1428] one finds of the estate of Albertaccio degli Alberti taxed in the quarter of Santa Croce, *gonfalone*[2] of Leon Nero and to report the holdings of Monna Ginevra wife of the late Albertaccio degli Alberti. And [the estate] has a *prestanzone*[3] rating of ƒ[lorins]18 which according to the testament of the said Monna Ginevra ¾ is to be paid by the said heirs and ½ by whoever gets the other estate. The said estate belongs to Piero di Bartolomeo degli Alberti during his life and after his life to his sons. And their property is this, that is:

A house with a courtyard, loggia, arcade, well and kitchen garden, situated in the parish of San Romeo of Florence, at the foot of the Rubaconte Bridge in the place called 'of the Alberti's house.' [It is bounded] on the first, second, third and fourth [sides], [by] the street. Monna Caterina wife of the late Piero di Messer Filippo Corsini lives in this house and Monna Sandra her aunt by hereditary privilege. Beneath this house are the following places, used as rented-out shops, as we will now state:

One shop for use as silk dyeing, under this house along the Arno, which is rented by Tommaso di Domenico, knifemaker, for his son and he owes a yearly rent of ƒ16.   ƒ16

One shop for use of a blacksmith, situated under the said house on the corner, which is rented by Aveduto Malischalcho and he owes a yearly rent of ƒ14.   ƒ14

One shop for use of a construction worker, situated under the said house. It is rented by Zanobi di Michele, construction worker, and he owes a yearly rent of L.48 fp.   ƒ12

One shop for use of a cooper, situated under the said house which is rented by Andrea di Niccolò, old clothes dealer, and he owes a yearly rent of ƒ14. [Added in a later hand: This shop belongs to Daniello de Piero himself.]   ƒ14

---

1   Report.
2   Neighborhood.
3   Tax.

Also facing the said house, seven little shops, one after the other, with arcades, [bounded] on the first [side], the street; the second, the Via Lungharno; third, Antonio degli Alberti; fourth, the *piazzuola*[4] of the said Alberti. The following renters are in the said shops:

In the shop on the corner facing Santa Maria delle Gratie and the blacksmith, is Andrea di Niccolò, flax-dresser, and he owes a yearly rent of ƒ13.   ƒ13

A shop next to the said one is rented by Lorenzo di Cristofano [son of] the late Naviolo and he owes a yearly rent of ƒ6.   ƒ6

A shop next to the said one is rented by Antonio di Piero, cooper, and he owes a yearly rent of ƒ6.   ƒ6

A shop next to the said one is rented by Filippo di Giovanni Gangaliardi, lasagna-maker, and he owes a yearly rent of ƒ6.   ƒ6

A shop next to the said one rented by Antonio di Loso, driver, and he owes a yearly rent of ƒ6.   ƒ6

A shop next to the said one rented by 'il Calamanza' and he owes a yearly rent of ƒ6.   ƒ6

A shop next to the said one rented by Lazaro di Zanobi, the 'barber' and he owes a yearly rent of ƒ8.   ƒ8

A house with stalls and land for use of silk dyeing, situated on the *piazzuola* in the place called 'of the Alberti's house,' [bounded] on the first, the said *piazzuola*; second, Antonio degli Alberti; third, the via Lungharno; fourth [left blank]. Of this, a half belongs to Daniello di Piero degli Alberti himself. Agniolo

di Ser Giovanni, dyer, rents it and owes a yearly rent of ƒ14.   ƒ14

The fourth part, indivisible, of the Palagietto, situated on the corner of Corso de'Tintori under which there is a shop for use of a barber, of which ¼ belongs to us and the other ¾ to Filippo degli Alberti and the Otto di Guardia. [Bounded] on the first, the street, that is, Corso de'-Tintori; on the second, the street which goes to the Ponte Rubaconte; third, Luigi degli Alberti; on the fourth, the Parte Guelfa. The said Palagietto is rented by Francesco di Betto Busini for ƒ6 a year for the ¼ and the barber shop is rented by Bartolo di Luigi, barber, and he owes ƒ1 for the ¼ a year. In all, ƒ7-¼.   ƒ7-¼

A half-house, situated on Corso de' Tintori over the entrance to the Fungha; the other half is held by the Otto di Guardia. [Bounded] on the first, the street of Corso de'Tintori; second, Fabiano d'Antonio Martini; on the third, the bake-house of the late Betto Busini; on the fourth, the Piazza of the Fungha. Benedetto di Michele, doublet-maker, rents this half-house and owes a yearly rent of L.9 fp.   ƒ2-¼

A house situated in the Fungha of Corso de'Tintori, [bounded] on the first, the piazza of the said Fungha; second, us ourselves; third, Bucello di Francesco; fourth, the cap-dyeing shop. There are 2 renters in this house, that is: Gualente di Tommaso, a dye worker, and he owes a yearly rent of L.6 fp. for the half.   ƒ1-½

Piero of Ravenna, dye worker, and he owes a yearly rent of L.6 fp. for half.   ƒ1-½

4   Small square.

A house situated in the Fungha of
Corso de'Tintori, next to the above-
mentioned [house, bounded] on the
first, the piazza of the said Fungha; on
the second, us ourselves; on the third,
the Otto di Guardia; on the fourth,
Bucello di Francesco. There are 2
renters in this house, that is: Giovanni
d'Orlanduccio, called Monteuchi,
and he owes a yearly rent of L.7 fp.   *f*1-¾

Giusto and Benedetto di Piero, por-
ters, and they owe a yearly rent of
L.6 fp.   *f*1-½

Also there are several houses in the Fungha held
by the Otto di Guardia which we claim to be ours
and of our ownership but [because of] the inability to re-enter the homeland, we have not been able
to demonstrate to the Otto that they [the houses]
are in our ownership. We are seeking [to recover]
our accounts and if we acquire anything, you will
be notified. And we are giving you this notice so
as to not prejudice our accounts.

[The "heirs" go on to list possessions outside the
city: an abandoned house and three attached
farms worth *f*69; a farm worth *f*33; a farm worth
*f*22; one worth *f*15; a house and three attached
farms worth *f*50; a farm worth *f*50; a farm worth
*f*40; and two farms with payments in kind.]

And further we find ourselves inscribed in the
Monte Comune of Florence in the quarter of
Santa Croce:

In the Monte Comune *f*898 *s*12 *d*9
with payments from 1423 til now,
inscribed in [the name of] Monna
Caterina wife of the late Piero di
Messer Filippo Corsini and previously in [the name of] Monna Ginevra the wife of the late Albertaccio
degli Alberti.   *f*898 *s*12 *d*9

In the Monte di Pisa *f*212 inscribed
in [the name of] the said Monna
Caterina and previously in the
said Monna Ginevra.   *f*212

In the Monte Comune *f* [left blank]
with all the payments from then on,
inscribed in Cherubino d'Albertaccio
degli Alberti and as of now it has not
been possible for us to claim them.
We mention it to you for the record
so as to not prejudice our accounts
and when they see we are right, you
will be notified.   *f* [blank]

*f*9 *s*3 *d*9 of payments received from
Monte Commune [credits] from 1415
to 1416 inscribed in Monna Caterina
wife of the late Piero di Messer Filippo
Corsini.   *f*9 *s*3 *d*9

*f*57 *s*10 of payments in the said
Monte inscribed in the same [Caterina]
from 1415 to 1419 at 20,000.   *f*57 *s*10

*f*62 *s*13 of said payments from
1419 to 1423 inscribed in the same
[Caterina] at 120,000.   *f*62 *s*13

*f*21 *s*4 of payments made from the
Monte of Pisa from 1415 to 1419,
at 126,000, inscribed in the said Monna
Caterina.   *f*21 *s*4

All the above-named monies were previously
in the name of Monna Ginevra d'Albertaccio.
Further we are owed the following by Carlo
Macinghi and others:

*f*275 of Monte di 5 complete, which
the said Carlo had inscribed in his
son Niccolò and which belong to us.   *f*275

*f*511 di Monte di 8, of which we retain ¼ and which begin to accrue
the first of January 1427 [1428] and
are inscribed in the said Niccolò.   *f*511

*f*37 of the said Monte which were invested in the Monte on 1 July
1427 and are inscribed in the said
Niccolò.   *f*37

*f*18-½ for one *prestanzone* paid by
Antonio di Bernardo di Luigi in his

name which were invested in the
Monte in July 1427.   *f*18-½

*f*93 *s*17 *d*4 of Monte Commune
inscribed in Francesco di Piero
degli Alberti, quarter of Santa
Croce.   *f*93 *s*17 *d*4

*f*9 *s*6 of payments received from the
said [credits].   *f*9 *s*6

Debtors

Zanobi di Michele, construction
worker, owes   *f*24

Andrea di Niccolò, flax-worker   *f*20

Tommaso di Domenico, knife-
maker   *f*15

Bartolo di Pagnio of Terina   *f*9

Monna Telda, wife of the late
Zanobi, barber   *f*3
Filippo di Giovanni, lasagna-
maker   *f*20

Aveduto Malischalco   *f*20

Agniolo di Ser Giovanni, dyer   *f*10

"Il Chalamanza"   *f*3

Antonio di Loso   *f*3

Antonio di Piero, cooper   *f*4

Lorenzo di Cristofano, rope-maker   *f*6

Niccolò and Domenico di Giovanni
del Calice   *f*49

Bernaba di Giovanni, called

Necha   *f*21

Berto di Monna Maddalena   *f*20

Pagholo di Masotto   *f*10

Andrea di Michele   *f*10

Piero di Ciecco, baker   *f*30

                                         *f*277
[Written to the side of the last of debtors]
    A total of 18 debtors who owe *f*277; these are
old monies and one could retrieve them only with
great effort and lots of time [at a rate of] *s*10 to the
lire or less. They [the debts] are all lost....

Creditors

We owe the following creditors, that is:

Carlo di Niccolò Macinghi is owed
*f*850, *f*500 of which are for a bequest which Cherubino made to
Mona Albiera his [Carlo's] wife, and
the remainder is for monies used by
the estate for *prestanze* and other
things.   *f*850

Monna Caterina wife of the late Piero
di Messer Filippo Corsini is owed   *f*150

Messer Iacopo di Totto of Modena
is owed 50 ducats for cloths received
from him for clothes for Piero and his
household [famiglia] a while ago.
They [the ducats] are   *f*55

Bartolomeo di Giovanni Chalora is
still owed for rent of the house we
rent from him in Modena and
other things received from him a
while ago. 30 ducats.   *f*33

Giovanni Charandini, druggist, in
Modena is owed for medicine receiv-
ed for Piero and for the funeral of
Iacopo's children. 15 ducats   *f*16 *s*10

Valets and other servants are still
owed 20 ducats by Piero.   *f*22

Bivigliano degli Alberti is owed 100
ducats which he paid for us on 6

August 1425 to Francesco di
Guidalotto of Bologna, which we
owed. They are   *f*110

Antonio di Ricciardo degli Alberti
is owed 300 ducats which Ricciardo
lent [us] on 12 October 1418 and
because of inability they have not
yet been repaid.   *f*330

Roberto Poggio of Lechlade [delle
Ceclade], English, is owed *l*123 *s*12 *d*6
sterling by Daniello himself. They
are, at 40 pounds sterling to the
florin,   *f*742

Ulichoccho, a draper of Cirencester
[Sirisestri] in England is owed *l*53 *s*15
sterling by Daniello himself. They
are, at 40 pounds sterling to the
florin,   *f*322 *s*10

Dominico Villani of London is still
owed for Daniello's living expenses
from a while ago. *l*sterling are, at 40
pounds sterling to the florin,   *f*144

Monna Ginevra wife of the late Albertaccio degli Alberti for the loss of 4
accatti sold at a bad loss, that is, *f*16
*s*19, and we list them here because
the said Monna Ginevra lists the
accatti   *f*16 *s*13

Obligations

It costs us for yearly rent of the house
we maintain in Modena 12 ducats
which are   *f*13

Daniello has yearly expenses in
England, 20 crowns, for his return
over his living [costs]   *f*21

It costs us a year to maintain the
houses and shops in Florence which
are 18 or so sites, *f*1-½ a year, site
for site, and more besides. In all,
*f*27

It costs us every year the loan of oxen
to work our possessions and maintain
the houses of the said possessions,
which are 16 or so houses. In all,
yearly   *f*30

It costs us a year for planting and
clearing of three farms in Monte
Chucchi al'Angella around *f*20 and
often more.   *f*20

And we cite to you the obligation of *f*13 for rent
in Modena and *f*21 for the return of Daniello to
England and, notwithstanding ours is one single
family, one can't do less since Daniello is exiled
and the limits of his exile are 100 miles and he
cannot, according to the limits, live in Modena.
And wanting to observe them [the limits], the
said Daniello has taken London in England for
his place of habitation such that one can do no
less than the obligation of the rent in Modena and
in London.

Mouths[5]

Piero di Bartolomeo degli Alberti, ill, stricken with gout.	
He is aged	73 years
Iacopo his son, aged	42 years
Daniello his son, aged	33 years
Benedetto, son of the said Iacopo, aged	2-½ years
Caterina, daughter of Daniello, aged	3 years
	5 mouths are *f*1000

property	*f*7198 *s*9
obligations	*f*3441 *s*13
remainder	*f*3756 *s*16

*f*27

---

5   That is, dependants who must be supported.

Portata for Caterina, wife of the late Piero Corsini

To you, the wise and prudent officials of the Catasto, empowered by the Commune of Florence, I, Caterina, daughter of the late Albertaccio degli Alberti and wife of the late Piero di Messer Filippo Corsini, reveal my property and my obligations:

Lorenzo di Messer Palla di Nofri degli Strozzi and partners have ƒ500 of mine at their discretion.

Antonio di Salvestro di Ser Ristoro and partners have ƒ300 of mine similarly.

Andrea Borghognoni and Ser Pagholo di Ser Lando and partners have ƒ200 similarly.

Antonio di Bernardo di Luigi has ƒ200 of mine in the above-said manner.

Francesco di Filippo di Messer Castellano and partners have ƒ100 of mine.

Bernardo di Messer Biagio Guasconi owes me around ƒ25 which are the remainder of ƒ300 which he had of mine when he defaulted and went bankrupt at less than 16 soldi to the lira. And for all that I do not think I will get this remainder.

The Commune of Florence owes me ƒ600 and they are in the Monte Commune account inscribed for the quarter of Santa Croce.

The abovementioned Commune owes me ƒ11 for 4 *accatti* inscribed for the quarter of Santa Croce.

The estate of Monna Ginevra wife of the late Albertaccio degli Alberti owes me ƒ150. Concerning these monies: when I recover them, it is agreed that I will use them to buy furnishings since the household furnishings I have been using until now will revert to the heirs of Albertaccio degli Alberti. And because of this, I entreat you [the officials] that it please you to not tax these 150 florins.

These are my obligations; and two servants with a salary enough to keep them; and I cannot manage with less.

And I am taxed in the *gonfalone* of Leon Nero and have as a *prestanze* rate ƒ2 s17 and I was not previously given any tax relief.

And I, the abovementioned Caterina, who lives in the house which was Albertaccio's, by right of inheritance as he left me the [privilege of] return to the house upon being widowed. The said house is in the parish of San Romeo [bounded] on the first and second and third [sides], the street; on the fourth, Daniello degli Alberti. To you, the abovementioned officials, I am sending this declaration which I have written in my own hand.

I Niccolò di Carlo Macinghi have carried this [to the officials] with the approval of the said Monna Caterina.

July 10, 1428

Portata for wife and heirs of Adovardo d'Alberto di Luigi degli Alberti

† In the name of God on the [blank] day of July 1427

Before you, Sirs, officials of the Catasto, Piero Cambini, as manager of the property which one finds belonging to the heirs of Adovardo d'Alberto di Luigi degli Alberti. There remain his wife whose name is Monna Caterina, aged 36, with four children, three feminine and one masculine, whom I will describe below. And they [the heirs] are not of age and are in exile and are staying in Bologna. And they live pretty meagerly because they have little; and they are taxed in Leon Nero, the quarter of Santa Croce, and have as a *prestanzone* rate ƒ [left blank]. And the goods they have are these. And I advise you that they have little income and wouldn't manage too well were it not that their mother stays with the children in the house of her brother who is Antonio di Lionardo [*sic*] degli Alberti. This is the utter truth.

A *palazzo* fronting on Via Mastia with a tower on the corner, and, on the Borgo Santa Croce [a part] like a house, all situated in the parish of San Iacopo tralle Fosse in the place called "of the Albertis' house" [bounded] first is the big street which goes to the Rubaconte Bridge; second, Borgo Santa Croce; third, Tommaso di Francesco Davizzi and partly the heirs of Bernardo d'Iacopo degli Alberti; fourth, Monna Catelana daughter of the late Alberto di Bernardo degli Alberti. The said *palazzo* facing [the street] with the tower is rented by Luca di Giovanni of Cortona for ƒ20 a year. The part on Borgo Santa Croce is rented by Asino di Bongianni for ƒ20-½ a year.

Five parts of nine parts, that is, ⁵⁄₉ of a farm situated in the contado of Florence in the place called "at the waters of Rinfusa" in the parish of

Sanminiato al Monte; and Monna Aura, wife of Tommaso Corsi, holds ⁴⁄₉ for life. It has workers' houses, hay-threshing floor and oven ... rent of ƒ28-¼ for all, of which ƒ15 *l*3 *s*8 *d*4 fp. belongs to the ⁵⁄₉th belonging to the heirs of Adovardo.

Five parts of nine parts, that is, ⁵⁄₉ of a casetta of which the other ⁴⁄₉ is held for life by the said Monna Aura, wife of Tommaso Corsi ... rent ƒ3-½ a year; our part is *l*7 *s*16 fp.

[He lists a farm, a *casetta*, a parcel of land, and 4 farms.]

You [the officials] need to take off for the loan of oxen ...

You need to take off for the maintenance of the houses in Florence and in the *contado*.

You need to take off for the factor who manages their affairs. Before he didn't want to be paid while in service; Piero Cambini, no price given.

The woman to account for, Monna Caterina aged 36, stays in Bologna in exile with her children for the sake of the male child who cannot stay here [in Florence]; she has three girl children and one boy child.

One named Costanza aged	12 or 13
Another named Margherita aged	9 or 10
Adovarda aged	4 or 5
Alberto the boy is aged	8 or 9

[The debtors are listed for a total worth of about ƒ150]

These people [the heirs] don't have cash because Alessio degli Alberti ruined his brother Adovardo, father of these children while he was in Barbery. And he lost his own and that of others in such a manner that they were left debtors for a goodly amount to their kin [*consorti*], an amount I don't see that they can ever pay any of it, but like good relatives [*parenti*], they help them [the heirs] with expenses.

They have these monies in the Monte, as we will write:

ƒ41 in the Monte Comune, inscribed in Monna Margherita wife of the late Alberto di Luigi degli Alberti ...

ƒ52 inscribed in the Monte Comune in the name of Adovardo d'Alberto di Luigi degli Alberti ...

property	ƒ1737 *s*9*d*4
obligations	ƒ1028
remainder	ƒ711 *s*9 *d*4

Portata of Antonia wife of Piero Dini

✝ In the name of God on the 31st day of July 1427

To you, the esteemed citizens elected to do the Catasto of the property of every citizen of the parishes of Florence. Monna Antonia, daughter of the late Alberto degli Alberti and wife of Piero di Giovanni Dini living in the city of Venice declares here following all of her moveable and immoveable property piece by piece and every obligation. First:

A half house [held] in common indivisibly with Monna Catalana, her sister and wife of the late Francesco Davizzi, situated in the gonfalone of Leon Nero in the street called Borgo Santa Croce, bounded on the first, the said street; second, the heirs of Adovardo degli Alberti; third, Tommaso Davizzi and Nerozzo degli Alberti; fourth, Francesco d'Altobianco degli Alberti. The said Monna Catelana lives in this [the house] by virtue of the testament of the said Alberto their father who bequeathed the return to and use of the said house should any of his daughters be left widowed. Documented by the hand of Ser Antonio di Ser chello. And for this reason, the said Monna Catelana has always held it and lived in it, because she is a widow, without paying anything; therefore this is not taxable [literally: is accounted valueless].

A half small farm [held] indivisibly in common with the said Monna Catelana ...

A half piece of land in the same place [held] indivisibly with the abovementioned [Catelana] ...

A piece [of land] in the same place, indivisible as above ...

All the above-mentioned lands are worked by Mane di Lapo Bugli and his son Meo. My part of the return, that is, the half is ...

12 *staia* of corn
3 *staia* of grain
9 or 10 barrels of wine
½ barrel of oil
30 pounds of pork

Further I find myself [owed] for the remainder of 200 florins of withheld costs for him, Tommaso di Frances-co Davizzi, from the heirs of Filippo Macinghi ƒ150

Further she is owed for 24 ordinary payments of Monte Comune on ƒ268 ƒ25

Further she is owed by Tomasso Davizzi and by Monna Catelana his mother, around ƒ55

Further she is owed the payments sustained from the said ƒ268 of Monte Comune from 1415 to 1419 and from 1419 to 1423. I believe she received [the payments] for 1411 to 1415 since she's not aware if there were any more. Her account is neither counted nor settled. ƒ [blank]

The said Monna Antonia lives in Venice, aged [blank] ƒ200

property	ƒ464 s10
obligations	ƒ200
remainder	ƒ264 s10

Portata of Tomasso di Francesco Davizzi and his mother

Tommaso di Francesco Davizzi and Monna Catelana his mother in the quarter of Santa Croce, *gonfalone* of Leon Nero; they have a *prestanzone* rate of ƒ7.

To you, revered citizens, elected officials to do the Catasto of the property of every citizen of the city of Florence. I Tommaso di Francesco Davizzi report to you all moveable and immoveable goods, debtors and creditors of mine and of Monna Catelana my mother here in every detail and, following, all our obligations. First:

A half-house, indivisible, where we presently live, situated in the *gonfalone* of Leon Nero in the parish of Sant'Iacopo tralle fosse in Borgo Santa Croce. [Bounded] first, the said street; second, the heirs of Adovardo degli Alberti; third, Tommaso Davizzi and Nerozzo degli Alberti;

fourth, Francesco d'Altobianco degli Alberti. Further, household furnishings for our use in the said house and in the summer house.

5 or 6 parts, indivisible, of a house situated in the said parish in the street called "of the Alberti's house." Bounded first, the street; second, the heirs of Adovardo degli Alberti; third, the above-named house of Monna Catelana and Monna Antonia d'Alberto degli Alberti; fourth, Francesco d'Altobianco degli Alberti. This [house] is rented by Tommaso Busini; he gives me ƒ20 yearly; I get, for my part, ƒ16 s13 d10 a year.

[He goes on to list ⅚ of a farm; ⅚ of a farm with one parcel of land; and a half farm.]

I find myself in the partnership which I have with Tommaso and Simone Corsi, a base capital of ƒ1500

We have not yet settled the accounts; we are overextended rather than settled; I will have to report to you what I have in the shop. I find myself, next, bankrupt in the new company, current account ƒ270 [He lists some small Monte credits.]

Here next I will write all the debtors I find, those whom I reckon to be good for payment ultimately.

The heirs of Cipriano and Ser Luigi di Simone Guiduccini ƒ60

Nastagio di Simone Guiduccini ƒ35

Niccolò di Sanminiato de'Ricci ƒ55

Antonio, priest, of Sant'Angelo ƒ65

The Commune of Assissi for 10 *accatti* ƒ28

Benedetto da Panzano ƒ8 s15

Pagolo Quaratesi ƒ9 s17

Rosso di Strozza ƒ6 s11

ƒ267 s20

Here next I will write all the credits to be recovered:

Cosimo and Lorenzo de'Medici and heirs	ƒ430
Monna Vaggia di Bindo Guasconi	ƒ150
Giovanni di Bartolo Morelli	ƒ500
Ilarione di Lipanno de'Bardi	ƒ42
Antonio di Salvestro and partners	ƒ20
Monna Antonia, wife of Piero Dini	ƒ50 +
The old company of Tommaso and Simone Corsi and with the remainder, I should have	ƒ450
	ƒ1542

Here below I will record the many debtors I find which are no-account, from whom I have not been able, in times past, to collect, nor do I expect to [ever]. These debtors are, that is:

Tommaso di Filippo di Michele	ƒ4-½
Lorenzo and Giovanni di Scholai degli Pini; I paid for them to their syndic	ƒ555
Santi Pisiro	ƒ1
The heirs and estate of Bernardo degli Alberti, for the remainder of a finding I got against them; and for money I paid to the gonfalone for them. They don't have their property, so one must let it [the debt] ride.	ƒ765
Bartolo di Maschio	ƒ765
Giovanni Manini	ƒ10

Monna Catelana is aged 44
Tommaso aged 26
Checca is a girl who Monna Catelana vowed to raise for the love of God since she has neither daddy nor mama to raise her aged 4 or 6

[He is not given credit for Checca]

property	ƒ3361 s4 d8
obligations	ƒ2042
remainder	ƒ1319 s4 d8

Portata of Messer Alberto di Giovanni degli Alberti

Jesus

Before you, the wise and prudent officials of the Catasto, reported for me, Messer Alberto di Giovanni degli Alberti, quarter of Santa Croce, *gonfalone* [left blank], parish of San Iacopo tralle Fosse, who has a *prestanzone* rate of [left blank] that in this [my *portata*] I will mention to you of my little houses, my furniture and obligations. And first:

A farm situated in the Valdarno di Sopra … the farm is worked by Bartolomeo di Mariotto and his brothers and they have rented it a long time. It yields 100 *staia* of grain a year, sequestered by the official; and it isn't run with oxen nor [has it] *prestanza*.

Another farm without a house … For many years rented by Ghezo di Giunta da Marrano. It yields 100 *staia* of grain a year.

With [the following] obligations, first:

I Messer Alberto, aged	48
Mariotto di Duccio my blood cousin, aged	30
Luigi and Antonio di Niccolo di Luigi, my second cousins,	45 and 35

[I am] omitting the other household members whom I know you won't accept.

I owe the Commune [blank], all that is posted in this last venture and even perhaps some old *prestanze*.

The present document done in the name of Messer Alberto was written by the hand of me, Valorino di Barna, at his behest and according to

how he directed that I set it out and record it by
me myself. I know that the abovesaid matters are
true, and because I am still weak from a long illness, I can't come to depose [the *portata*], but my
son Lapozzo will come or Piero Cambini.

Portata of Caterina wife of the late Messer Cipriano degli Alberti

Before you, Sirs, honorable and prudent officials of the Catasto of the city,
contado and territory of Florence, I am
producing my *portata* done by me,
Madonna Caterina, wife of the late
Messer Cipriano degli Alberti, of
moveable and immoveable property,
debts and credits and obligations
taxed in the *gonfalone* of Leon Nero in
the quarter of S. Croce in the parish of
San Iacopo tralle Fosse of Firenze.
And the said Madonna Caterina has a
prestaze rating of 1 florin 3 soldi, that is,   *f*1 *s*3

Property, that is:

[She then lists a farm with 10 parcels of land
worth *f*20; a farm with 16 parcels worth *f*25; a
farm with 7 parcels worth *f*20; a farm with 8 parcels worth *f*28; four small parcels rented for payment in kind.]
   A house in Empoli in which house I live myself and keep my crops, bounded [left blank]. I am
obliged to keep an animal to carry me and to ef-
ficiently carry my farm goods and I can manage
with no less.

Debts and obligations:

I spend 12 florins a year for the house
in Florence, used for my habitation,
which house I rent from Domenico
di Gherardino, on Borgo Santa Croce.
Bounded by first, the street; second,
Bartolino Bisarnesi and partly the
said Domenico; third, Antonio di Salvestro di Ser Ristoro; fourth, Fran-
cesdo d'Altobianco [degli Alberti;
it is] in the [area known as the] Fungha   *f*12

I owe Piero Cambini 18 florins, for
cloth for me from the warehouse of
the Alexandri   *f*18

Also I owe the said warehouse for
cloth I got for my servant who I keep
in the house   *f*7

And further I owe Messer Guiliano
Davanzati those monies still ow-
ing for my *prestanze*   *f*6

[The following entry was canceled:
And further I owe the heirs of Giovanni degli Peruzzi *f*30 which they
lent me to pay my debts and dues   *f*30]

I still must pay Lucia her dowry, when
she will be of age; she lives with me
in the house and I pay those expenses of hers which pertain to me   [blank]

I keep a servant for 12 florins a year
and pay his expenses   *f*12

Heads

Madonna Caterina, wife of the late
   Messer Cipriano degli Alberti, aged   60
Mariotto di Duccio, grandson of the
   said Madonna Caterina, aged   27
   The said Mariotto doesn't live in Florence. I am
obligated to support and pay his expenses in such
amounts that he is in my [household, as opposed
to anyone else's].
   [in the left margin of the official copy, next to
Mariotto's name, was written: Give him to Messer
Alberto for his "mouth," written on page 253 of
this (volume)].
   I Lodovico di Cheroso di Bartoli di Ser Segna
filled out this *portata* at the will of the said
Madonna Caterina abovesaid, and I have undersigned for me in my own hand.

property	*f*1808 *s*5 *do*
obligations	*f* 402 *s*8 *do*
remainder	*f*1405 *s*17

Portata of Maria wife of the late Ricciardo degli Alberti

(Source: ASF, Cat. 35, ff. 1048r-v and Cat. 72, f. 357v)

Before you, Sirs, officials of the Catasto, I Piero Cambini of Santa Felice in Piazza report to you as a factor of this property of Monna Maria wife of the late Ricciardo degli Alberti and daughter of Messer Mainardo Cavalcanti. And today she is a widow and lives in Bologna with her daughters of whom one is a widow. And she [Maria] is ill and has a lot of difficulty making ends meet, such that she is recommended to your consideration such as it can be. And this is the property that she holds between her dowry and bequests and monies.

[He lists two farms left to her by her mother]

This Monna Maria has not had *prestanze* nor do I find her taxed with *prestanze*. She is ill and somehow she must live as a woman of substance.

I Piero Cambini attest to these things I have written at the request of Monna Maria and I have never asked anything ever for my pains. However, I am here [in Florence] or in Venice, such that it will be necessary [to find] another factor to serve her. And I salute you.

Portata of Tommasa wife of Bivigliano degli Alberti

The property of Monna Tommasa, wife of Bivigliano degli Alberti, who [the Alberti] were consigned [to exile] and daughter of Noffo Ridolfi. And taxed in *prestanze* in the quarter of Santa Croce in the *gonfalone* of Leon Nero.   *f*1 *s*12 *d*5

A "noble house" with a kitchen garden in the place called "in the woods" in the parish of San Piero a Ema.

Below I will write her debtors:

Piero di Nofri dell'Antella   *f*33

Giovanni di [blank] who tends the vines [in the garden mentioned] holds a little farm which he rents from the commune. And because he

works the farm and the said vineyard,

I lent him *f*40   [blank]

Below I will write her creditors:

Schiatta Ridolfi and Giovanni Giugni   *f*20

I am here in his house [Schiatta's?] and I am about to take a rental [place]. Thus, use your discretion [as to how to tax me].

[In the official version, this portion is written: I am in the house of others and am about to take a house. Therefore take into account what is my (tax) responsibility.]

Monna Tommasa, aged	60
Bivigliano, her husband, aged	69
Francesco, her son, aged	42
Bertoldo, her son, aged	26
Monna Isabella, wife of Francesco her son, aged	24
Marco, son of the said Francesco, aged	6
Diamante, son of the said Francesco, aged	2-½
Bartolomea, daughter of the said Francesco, aged	3
Nera, daughter of the said Francesco, aged in months	18
Altobiancho, son of the said Francesco, aged in months	3

submitted July 12, 1427
[She is given only her 'mouth'.]

property	*f*841
obligations	*f*220
remainder	*f*621

Portata of Selvaggia wife of the late Filippo Magalotti

[From the outside of the *portata*]
July 12

Leon Nero. Monna Vaggia wife of the late Messer Filippo Magalotti *f*1 *s*12 *d*5

The said document for Monna Vaggia wife of the late Messer Filippo Magalotti. Fetched by me Folco Portinari with her consent.

[From the inside]

✝ In the name of God on the 10th day of July 1427

Before you, Sirs, officials of the Catasto, here following are written all the property and obligations of Monna Vaggia wife of the late Messer Filippo Magalotti of the quarter of Santa Croce, *gonfalone* of Leon Nero at the *prestanze* rate of ƒ1 *s*12 *d*5.

In the Monte Comune, inscribed in Monna Vaggia in the quarter of Santa Croce, ƒ2038 *s*10 *d*10 with payments from 1419 to 1423, ƒ100 at ⁶⁄₇

And for her lifetime, inscribed in the Hospital of Santa Maria Nuova in the same quarter, ƒ172 of Monte Comune [credit].

[She rents out two small houses and a shop, one right next to the other.]

All the said rents are mine for life.

A half farm, indivisible, [with nine parcels of land]. This farm is held in common with the heirs of Andrea di Messer Bindo de'Bardi. It is worked by Scuosino, called Tasso….

A farm …

Both farms are held for my lifetime.

Here following I will give the obligations of the abovementioned Monna Vaggia, aged 60 years.

Caterina, her granddaughter, daughter of the late Bernardo Magalotti.

Luca, her grandson, son of the late said Bernardo, aged 11; he is not legitimate.

And with a house rented from Piero Cambini which belongs to the grandsons of Messer Niccolaio degli Alberti. I pay yearly ƒ11.

And expenses to maintain my little houses which I rent out, ƒ2-½ a year. And to maintain the Valdarno property, ƒ2 a year.

Here following are the debts:

And to give to Piero Cambini for the rental of the house   ƒ11

And to him for wine I had [of him] for the year gone by   ƒ11

And to give for [the love of] God for the soul of Bernardo my son ƒ15 a day [sic] and I will give proof why it is as it is   ƒ15

And to give, in accordance with a vow I made, to a girl who married   ƒ10

And to give to Monna Dianora who stays with me, for her salary   ƒ8

And to give to a girl who stayed with me a while, *l*50 fp.   ƒ12-½

And to give to Tommaso di Lapo Corsi for velvet gotten from them [his company?] for one of my girls when I remarried her off   ƒ4

And to give Antonio di Piero   ƒ1 *l*3

And to give to Giovanni Charadori for furnishings   ƒ1

And to pay for 4 *prestanzoni*, ƒ2 *s*16 fp.   ƒ2 *s*16

Also to give for the farm of San Marcellino in Bisano, the *decima* to X, that is, 5 half barrels of wine and 5 half *staia* of grain.

To give to Maestro di Baldano who repairs the house of the farm for me, for my part,   ƒ2-½

property	ƒ1543 *s*10
obligations	ƒ 639
remainder	ƒ 904 *s*10

62. GREGORIO DATI

Diary

GREGORIO DATI WAS AN important businessman who was active primarily in the manufacture and sale of silk cloth. His private diary, kept to record his business dealings, provides a view into the private life of a successful Florentine merchant at the beginning of the fifteenth century. It is just one of many private "memory books" composed by men during this period in Italy, and it is typical in its lack of passion.

Source: Gene Brucker (ed.), *Two Memoirs of Renaissance Florence: The Diaries of Buonaccorso Pitti and Gregorio Dati*, trans. Julia Martinas (New York: Harper and Row, 1967).

Further Reading: Ionut Epurescu-Pascovici, "Gregorio Dati (1362–1435) and the Limits of Individual Agency," *The Medieval History Journal* 9 (2006): 297–325.

In the name of God, his mother and all the saints of Paradise, I shall begin this book wherein I shall set forth an account of our activities so as to have a record of them, and wherein having once more and always invoked the name of God, I shall record the secret affairs of our company and their progress from year to year. This ledger belongs to Goro [Gregorio], son of Stagio Dati, and I shall call it the secret ledger. In the name of God, Father, Son, and Holy Ghost, I shall here record some particular things known to myself. God grant they meet with the approval of whoever learns of them when I am gone.

I learn from old registers that Dato and Pero di Bencivenni were purse-vendors on the Ponte Vecchio next to the fishmongers, and that their shop was destroyed by the flood of 1333. It appears from there that Dato had a number of sons, the eldest of whom, Stagio, was born on March 9, 1317. His mother's name was Monna Filippa. According to Stagio's registers he married our mother, Monna Ghita, in the year …, giving her the ring on August 5 and celebrating the wedding on November 4.

I find that Stagio went into partnership with Vanni di Ser Lotto [Castellani]. The company was set up on January 1, 1353 with a capital of one thousand gold florins. This appears on page 3 of Register A.

I was born on April 15, 1362. This is recorded in a register marked with an asterisk on page 85 where the seventeen children he had by Monna Ghita are listed in order of age.

Our father Stagio left this world for a better one on September 11, 1374, when he was a consul of the Wool Guild and treasurer of the Commission on the Salt Tax and Forced Loans. He had been ill for several days before his death and, several days earlier, while still in health, had made a will. He received all the sacraments of the church as befits a devout Christian, and by the mercy of God passed on to eternal life in a state of grace.

On April 15, 1375, when I had learned enough arithmetic, I went to work in the silk merchant's shop belonging to Giovanni di Giano and his partners. I was thirteen years old and I won their esteem.

We gave Madalena [Goro's sister] in marriage in June 1380. This is recorded in register E, page 84.

I left Giovanni di Giano on October 2, 1380, spent fifteen months with the Wool Guild and returned to him on January 1, 1382.

Partnership Accounts—1384

In the name of God, the Virgin Mary and all the saints—may they grant me health in soul and body and prosperity in business—I shall record here all my dealings with our company.

On January 1, 1385, Giovanni di Giano and his partners made me a partner in their silk business for as long as it may please God. I am to invest 300 gold florins which I have not got, being actually in debt to the business. However, with God's help, I hope to have the money shortly and am to receive two out of every twenty-four shares, in other words, a twelfth of the total profit. We settled our accounts on June 8, 1387, on Giovanni di Giano's death. May he rest in peace. My share of the profits for the two years and five months I had been a partner came to 468 gold florins, 7 *soldi a fiorino*.[1] Thanks be to God. We formed a new partnership on the following terms: Buonaccorso Berardi is to invest 8,000 florins and have eleven shares; Michele di Ser Parente is to invest 3,500 florins and have eight shares; Goro, son of Stagio Dati, is to invest 500 florins and have three shares; Nardo di Lippo is to invest 500 and have two shares. Thus the capital of the company shall amount to 12,500 gold florins. And if any partner invests additional money in the company, that investment will earn one-half of the percentage of the profits earned by the regular shares.

On January 1, 1389, we settled our accounts, and my share of the profits for the nineteen months came to 552 gold florins, 6 *soldi a fiorino*. Praise and thanks be to God. On January 1, 1390, we reviewed our accounts for the year and my profit was 341 florins, 10 *soldi a fiorino*. Thanks be to God. I left for Valencia on the company's business on September 1, 1390 and got there on October 26. I was back in Florence on November 29, 1392. The accounts I kept regarding our business there is entered in the white ledger on page … in my name and Berardo's. The company did not pay any of our expenses for this trip. It is true that Giovanni left the business in a bad way and with a number of debts.

On January 1, 1393, we dissolved the company and Michele di Ser Parente withdrew all his investments. My profit was reckoned as 1,416 florins, 21 *soldi a fiorino*, and 60 florins were paid for Simone's salary. However this was assuming Giovanni Stefani's debt would be paid, which it has not been, and so it was decided instead that 954 florins, 25 *soldi a fiorino* cash should be deducted from my account corresponding to the debts outstanding, and that I should get back this

money when the debts were paid. This was done in order to enable us to set up a new company with real money. Anyway, between cash and expectations my profits came to 1,476 florins, 21 *soldi a fiorino*.

Recommending ourselves to God and good fortune, we set up a new company for a year, starting on January 1, 1393 on the following terms: Buonaccorso Berardi shall invest 4,000 florins and receive eleven shares; Goro di Stagio shall invest 1,000 florins and receive five shares; Nardo di Lippo shall invest 500 florins and receive three and one-half shares. The capital shall amount to 6,000 florins. May the Lord bless our enterprise.

In God's name I shall continue my review of the accounts written above on page two of our company's agreements, and of my shares, balance sheets and profits and shall record what followed and is yet to follow. As appears in these accounts, we renewed our partnership on January 1, 1393 when I undertook to invest 1,000 florins. I did not actually have the money but was about to get married—which I then did—and to receive the dowry which procured me a larger share and more consideration in our company. Yet we achieved little that year.

I set out for Valencia in September 1393 in order to wind up matters there but did not get beyond Genoa. When I reached the Riviera, I was set upon and robbed by a galley from Briganzone and returned to Florence on December 14, having lost 250 florins' worth of pearls, merchandise and clothes belonging to myself, and 300 gold florins' worth of the company's property.

On January 1, 1394, we drew up our balance sheet and my profit came to 162 florins, 2 *soldi a fiorino*. We renewed our partnership for another year and made a few changes. Whereas Buonaccorso Berardi had previously invested 4,000 florins and received eleven shares, under the new arrangement he was to invest 4,000 florins and receive twelve shares, and whereas I had previously invested 1,000 florins and received five shares, I was now to invest 500 florins and receive four shares. The reason for this was that I had not got the money and Antonio di Segna put it up. (In

---

1   The phrase *soldi a fiorino* refers to a money of account commonly used in Florentine monetary calculation. Twenty-nine *soldi a fiorino* were equivalent to one gold florin.

this agreement "this year" is to be read as "last year" and "Buonaccorso Berardi" is to be understood as including Antonio di Segna, who is to be paid what is due to him by Buonaccorso at the latter's discretion.)

I went to Valencia on April 20, 1394 and returned on January 24 of the next year. On 1 February 1395, our company expired and we settled our accounts. My profit was 295 florins, and Simone's salary for the outgoing year was 30 florins. May God be thanked. That December I left Simone in Valencia with Andrea Lopis who was to invest 500 florins in Simone's name on the understanding that all profits on cloth, silks, and other matters were to be divided equally between them and that any goods they might order from me for their own use were to be paid for within the usual time, six months. Moreover, I was to send them goods of my own and they were to sell them for me and take a commission.

On January 1, 1396, I found I had made 600 florins on my own, independently of any partnership, on goods sent to and received from Valencia and elsewhere. My expenditure, however, of which I have kept no account, came to about 250 florins, leaving a balance of 350. These sums, earned over three years in the three payments mentioned above, are entered like the others on page 2[2] above. Altogether I found myself in 1395 with little cash in hand, as a result of the great expenses to which I had gone in the hope that they would yield greater profits than they did. In addition, there were the expenses I was put to by our brother Don Jacopo,[3] my losses over Giovanni Stefani in Valencia, and the money which was stolen from me near Genoa. It is fitting to give praise to God for all things. Altogether, having reckoned my profits, the two dowries received and my outlay for the half-share in the farm in S. Andrea, bought from Monna Tita, I have about 200 florins in hand. God grant that henceforth we prosper in soul and body. This balance of 200 florins is entered on page 3 above under Receipt and Expenditure.

Memoranda, 1393

In God's name, I shall continue this record of my activities, which it is well to have in writing so as to recollect them, and which I began back on page 1. My beloved wife, Bandecca, went to Paradise after a nine-month illness started by a miscarriage in the fifth month of pregnancy. It was eleven o'clock at night on Friday, July 15, 1390, when she peacefully returned her soul to her Creator in Buonaccorso-Berardi's house. The next day I had her buried in S. Brancazio; she had received the last sacraments.

I went to Valencia on September 1, 1390, taking Bernardo with me. I came back on November 30, 1392, having suffered much hardship during my stay, both in mind and body. We were still owed 4,000 Barcelona pounds by Giovanni di Stefano, who acknowledged this debt in a notarized deed which I brought back with me to Florence. In Valencia I had an illegitimate male child by Margherita, a Tartar slave whom I had bought. He was born on December 21, 1391, in Valencia on St. Thomas's Day and I named him after that saint. I sent him to Florence in March on Felice del Pace's ship. God grant that he turn out well.

On the expiration of our partnership, on January 1, 1393, Michele di Ser Parente withdrew. Later, I made an agreement with him whereby he made over to me his share in Giovanni di Stefani's debt and a few other items which are entered on page 6.

I married my second wife, Isabetta, the daughter of Mari Vilanuzzi on Sunday, June 22, as is recorded on the other side of this page.

On September 10, 1393, I left Florence for Catalonia and, while we were at sea in a small galley a little beyond Portovenere, a galley from Briganzone came after us, held us up, and robbed us and took our goods to Baldo Spinoli at Briganzone. We got some of them back later, although with great difficulty and at great expense. I came back here on December 14. On April 20, I went to Valencia on Felice's ship. I visited Majorca and Barcelona where Simone joined me, after which we both went to Valencia where I left him. I returned home by land and reached Florence on January

---

2   These and other page references refer to pages in Dati's ledger.

3   Jacopo was a priest.

24, 1395. Thanks be to God. Our partnership expired on February 1, 1395, and that year I did business of my own and was very successful. Thanks be to God. I went into partnership once more with Michele di Ser Parente on January 1, 1396, and the terms and clauses are entered on page 6.

Our Simone, who had been in Valencia since December 1394, wanted to come to Florence. He arrived on December 12, 1396, and left to go back there on January 3, 1397. However, while he was at sea, a Neapolitan galley overtook him just outside Pisa and took him as a prisoner to Naples. On April 3, he was released for ransom at Gaeta, from whence he made his way back to Valencia.

A general remission and acquittance was granted to us, to Michele di Ridolfo's sons, and to the Commune of Florence with regard to the matter concerning Dato by Andrea da Bologna, an inhabitant of Montpellier, on February 14, 1398. The notary was Giovanni da Pino. This is entered in my long Ledger 'A, page 131. It cost us 100 gold francs and I have the deed in my strong-box.[4]

My Wife Betta's Personal Accounts—1393

In the name of God and the Virgin Mary, of Blessed Michael the Archangel, of saints John the Baptist and John the Evangelist, of saints Peter and Paul, of the holy scholars saints Gregory and Jerome, and of St. Mary Magdalene and St. Elisabeth and all the blessed saints in heaven—may they ever intercede for us—I shall record here how I married my second wife, Isabetta, known as Betta, the daughter of Mari di Lorenzo Vilanuzzi and of Monna Veronica, daughter of Pagolo d'Arrigo Guglielmi, and I shall also record the promises which were made to me. May God and his Saints grant by their grace that they be kept.

On March 31, 1393, I was betrothed to her and on Easter Monday, April 7, I gave her the ring. On June 22, a Sunday, I became her husband in the name of God and good fortune. Her first cousins, Giovanni and Lionardo di Domenico Arrighi, promised that she should have a dowry of 900 gold florins and that, apart from the dowry, she should have the income on a farm in S. Fiore a Elsa, which had been left her as a legacy by her mother, Monna Veronica. It was not stated at the time how much this amounted to, but it was understood that she would receive the amounts. We arranged our match very simply indeed and with scarcely any discussion. God grant that nothing but good may come of it. On the 26th of that same June, I received a payment of 800 gold florins from the bank of Giacomino and Company. This was the dowry. I invested it in the shop of Buonaccorso Berardi and his partners, and it is recorded here, on page 2 among the profits. At the same time I received the trousseau which my wife's cousins valued at 106 florins, in the light of which they deducted six florins from another account, leaving me the equivalent of 100 gold florins. But from what I heard from her and what I saw myself, they had overestimated it by 30 florins or more. However, from politeness, I said nothing about this.

I have not declared this dowry nor insured it on account of their negligence and in order to put off paying the tax. They dare not urge me to do so since they are obligated towards me. Yet I must do so, and if by God's will something were to happen before I do, I want her to be as assured as can be of having her dowry, just as though it had been declared and insured. For the fault is not hers. It turns out that the income she is to receive comes from a farm in S. Fiore on the Elsa on the way to Pisa. It is a nice piece of property which apparently belonged to Pagolo Guglielmi. Giovanni and Lionardo bought it from Betta's mother, Monna Veronica, or rather bought a half-share in it for 500 gold florins and paid a tax on this sale. Later they sold back their share to Monna Veronica, paying another tax, for 575 florins. These transactions are recorded in the register of taxes on contracts in register 500, 40; 500, 41 and 500, 42. When Monna Veronica died in April 1391, she left the income from this farm to Betta and to her children after her.

On September 26, 1402, as Simone was in Florence for a while before leaving for Catalonia, and as the penalties for evading tax on contracts were remitted by law for those who paid that day, I and Simone declared the dowry of 900 gold florins received from Leonardo and Domenico. The

---

4   This was apparently an old business dispute involving Gregorio Dati's grandfather, Dato.

notary was Ser Giunta Franceschi and on the 30th of the same September, I paid 30 gold florins, being 3-1/8 per cent, to the account of the taxes on contracts.

Our Lord God was pleased to call to himself the blessed soul of Isabetta, known as Betta, on Monday, October 2, between four and five o'clock in the afternoon. The next day, Tuesday, at three in the afternoon, she was buried in our grave at S. Spirito. May God receive her soul in His glory. Amen.

Children, 1393

In praise, glory, honor and benediction of Almighty God, I shall record the fruits that His grace will grant us, and may He in His mercy vouchsafe that they be such as to console our souls eternally, amen. On Sunday morning, May 17, 1394, Betta gave birth to a girl whom we called Bandecca in memory of my first wife. Goro d'Andrea, Niccolaio di Bartolommeo Niccoli, and Berardo di Buonaccorso were her sponsors.

On Friday evening, March 17, 1396, towards two o'clock in the morning, the Lord blessed our marriage with a male son whom we named Stagio and whom we had baptized in the love of God on Sunday morning by Fra Simone Bartoli of the Augustinian Hermits, my partner Nardo di Lippo, and Sandro di Jacopo, a pauper.

At two o'clock in the night of Monday, March 12, 1397, Betta gave birth to our third child, a girl. We called her after Betta's mother, giving her the names Veronica Gostanza, and Sandro di Jacopo baptized her in the love of God.

At midday on Saturday, April 27, 1398, Betta gave birth to our fourth child which was a boy. We called him Bernardo Agostino and he was baptized the same day in the love of God by Monna Agnola del Ciri and Monna Francesca Aldobrandino. God grant he turn out well.

At dawn on Tuesday, July 1, 1399, Betta had our fifth child and we baptized him in the love of God the same day, calling him Mari Piero. The sponsors were Master Lionardo[5] and Fra Zanobi.

On Tuesday evening, June 22, 1400, Betta gave birth for the sixth time. The child was a girl. We called her Filippa Giovanna and she was baptized on Friday morning in the love of God. Fra Simone Bartoli held her.

Our Lord God was pleased to take to Himself the fruits which He had lent us, and He took first our most beloved, Stagio, our darling and blessed first-born. He died of the plague on the morning of Friday, July 30, 1400, in Florence without my seeing him, for I was in the country. Master Lionardo and Monna Ghita were with him. May God bless him and grant that he pray for us.

On August 22 of the same year, the divine bounty was pleased to desire a companion for that beloved soul. God called our son Mari to Himself and he died at eleven o'clock on Sunday, of the plague. God grant us the grace to find favor with Him and to bless and thank Him for all things.

On Wednesday, July 13, 1401, after midnight, the Lord lent us a seventh child. Betta had a son who we called Stagio Benedetto. The sponsors were Nardo di Lippo and Domenico Benini. Divine providence was pleased to take him back and for this too may He be thanked and praised. The child suffered from a cough for a fortnight, and at midday on September 29, St. Michael's Day and the Eve of St. Jerome's Day, passed away to Paradise. God grant that we, when we leave this mortal life, may follow him there.

On July 5, 1402, before the hour of terce, Betta gave birth to our eighth child. We had him baptized straight after terce in the love of God. His godparents were Nardo and blind Margherita, and we called him Piero Antonio because of Betta's special devotion to St. Antonio. God bless him and grant that he become a good man.

After that my wife Isabetta passed on to Paradise as is recorded on the opposite page, and I shall have no more children by her to list here. God be praised.

Our Creator was pleased to call to Himself the soul of our gentle and good son Antonio. He left this life, I think, on August 2. For I was in great trouble and did not know it at the time. It was in Pisa where he is buried at S. Caterina's.

Betta and I had eight children, five boys and three girls.

---

5 Gregorio's brother, Lionardo Dati, was a Dominican friar, who later was elected General of the Order.

Memo, 1394

I record that on February 1 I withdrew from the partnership with Buonaccorso Berardi and did business on my own this year. I bought goods and sent them to Simone in Valencia, lent money to friends in Pisa and elsewhere, received goods from Valencia for sale here and continued like this for eight months until the beginning of October. I did very well during this period. I have not kept accounts but earned and spent on my own. Yet I can see that the transactions I carried out have been successful, and I hope those which are not yet concluded will be equally so. I may go through with them by myself or may go into partnership with someone.

And once more in God's name I have formed a partnership with Michele di Ser Parente from October 1, 1395. In our account books, it will be reckoned as beginning on January 1, 1396, when Mariotto di Lodovico is to withdraw. I am now beginning to do things for this new partnership. I shall record the terms and clauses of our agreements further on, on page 6, and may God bless our enterprise.

Going over my accounts, I find that when Michele di Ser Parente withdrew from our partnership on January 1, 1393, my total assets amounted to about 800 florins, which was all the actual money I would have possessed had I wished to withdraw in my turn. This meant I had made no profit. For I had to pay back about 950 florins which was the part of my profits corresponding to the debts owed us in Catalonia and elsewhere, which should not have been reckoned as recoverable for the moment. We realized this later when Antonio di Segna's guile made it seem advisable to check the various assets of the company. This was why I resolved to put up with anything for the next two years and to stay in their shop and suffer Antonio di Segna and everything else, as I was too short of money to try and do things my own way. I have been hoping that Matteo will help me to send Simone to Valencia where he will be very useful to me for my business here. I pray God that it may so turn out.

After that in 1393 I got the dowry which came to 800 florins, while my profits from our partnership were 162 florins, and for the year after were 325 florins which comes to a total of 1,287 florins. My expenditure, entered in folio 3 under "Expenditure," was in two amounts, totaling 1,425 florins. This includes my losses when I was robbed on the Riviera, about 275 florins paid for the farm and about 100 florins lent to Michele's heir. Whereas in 1392 I was owed 950 florins and owed about 150 florins, since then I find my debits exceeding my credits by about 140 florins, which makes a total debit of 290. I estimate that in the eight months I have been in business on my own, I have made good my losses and wiped out this debt, or will have done so when the ventures I embarked on then have been concluded. So now I can live within my capital. Would to God and the Virgin Mary that I were sure of continuing to do so from January 1, 1396, and were sure that my debits would not exceed my credits from the time I go into partnership with Michele. But God will grant us His grace as He has always done. I am not entering the 950 florins and 25 *soldi a fiorino* in my accounts since they cannot be put to any use.

After that year by God's grace I did better than I had expected, for the Valencia branch did well and paid up, and I have been able to transfer 200 florins from the credit side and deduct them from my debits as appears on Outgo, folio 3.

Account Book—1395

May God and His gentle Mother bestow their grace upon us. In their name I shall note here the terms and clauses of the new partnership which I and others formed with Michele di Ser Parente and the sums of money involved. Michele di Ser Parente shall invest 8,000 florins and receive thirteen and three-quarter shares; I, Goro di Stagio, am to invest 1,000 florins and have four and one-half shares; Nardo di Lippo Nardi is to invest 400 florins and have two shares. The total capital is to amount to 9,600 florins and be divided in twenty-four shares.[6]

I engage to contribute 1,000 florins to the capital of our partnership so as to enjoy a substantial share and consideration in the firm. I have not got the cash at present but expect that Matteo di Tommaso will lend me 400 florins belonging to his stepmother, Monna Lorenza, plus some money of his own. I shall try to raise the rest somewhere else if I can and will debit it to the Valencia account until I have made enough either in my business here or with Simone in Valencia to pay it back.

I have agreed with Michele to send his son Giovanni to Valencia, where he is to form a business partnership with Simone for as long as we shall decide. We will supply the goods they require and our firm will put 1,000 florins cash at their disposal. One half of whatever profits they make will be ours, and the other half is to be divided between them so that each will have one quarter of the total profits. Giovanni went to Valencia in May 1396, but only stayed there a short time as he did not get on with Simone. Simone came to Florence on December 12, 1396 and reached an agreement with myself and Michele whereby they were to keep whatever profits, good or bad, they might manage to make in Valencia, without giving our firm any share in them, and to pay us whatever they owed us on the usual terms.

Simone left here for Valencia on January 3 and, having set sail from Pisa on the 8th, was captured by one of King Louis's[7] admirals, Messer Giovanni Gonsalvo of Seville, who took him as a prisoner to Naples. When he had been held there for three months, he was taken to Gaeta and released for a ransom of 200 florins. This was paid for him by Doffo Spini, whom we reimbursed, and debited to the Valencia account with a number of other expenses. On April 3, he left for Majorca on the *nave dipungiata*.[8] May God grant he get there safely and that we recover our losses. Giovanni and Simone continued to wrangle and bicker even more than before, until finally Giovanni resolved to leave for Barcelona and settle there. They continued, however, to be partners. Then of their own accord they dissolved the partnership, agreeing that Simone should keep whatever profits he had made in Valencia and Giovanni should have what

he had made in Barcelona. God grant His grace to each of them.

Shop Accounts, 1403

When the partnership with Michele di Ser Parente expired, I set up shop on my own under the name of Goro Stagio and company. My partners are Piero and Jacopo di Tommaso Lana who contribute 3,000 [florins] while I contribute 2,000, and Nardo di Lippo who contributes his services. The partnership is to start on January 1, 1403 and to last three years. The clauses and articles of agreement and the amounts invested by each partner will be entered in a secret ledger covered with white leather belonging to our partnership.

On my account and with my own money, I paid 75 florins to the heirs of Simone Vespucci and their representative, Lapo Vespucci, for the goodwill and licence to exercise my profession in one of the shops of Por Santa Maria.[9] The brokers were Andrea di Bonaventura and Niccolaio Niccoli. On March 6, 1403, Isau d'Agnolo and Antonio Manni, a silk merchant who was in the shop, received 25 florins from me. The broker was Meo d'Andrea del Benino. The fixtures and repairs cost me about 100 florins, so altogether, between the goodwill and the fixtures I paid 200 florins out of my own pocket, in God's name, for myself and my heirs. The site of the shop belongs to the Carthusian monks, from whom I am to rent it on the usual terms for 35 gold florins a year. Ser Ludovico of the guild drew up the lease, which is to run for five years from the beginning of February 1403.

As already stated, I have undertaken to put up 2,000 florins. This is how I propose to raise them: 1,370 florins and 25 *soldi a fiorino* are still due to me from my old partnership with Michele di Ser Parente, as appears on page 118 of my ledger for stock and cash on hand. The rest I expect to obtain if I marry again this year, when I hope to find a woman with a dowry as large as God may be pleased to grant me. If I do not marry, I will find the money some other way.

The partnership with Piero was set up and formally notarized several months ago. Voluntarily

---

7 Louis of Anjou, claimant to the kingdom of Naples.
8 The phrase should perhaps be translated as "the ship owned [or captained] by Pungiata."
9 Por Santa Maria was the guild of the silk manufacturers.

and of his own accord, he asked me to see to the investments and the dividing into shares, leaving all this in my hands....

January 1, 1404

I know that in this wretched life our sins expose us to many tribulations of soul and passions of the body, that without God's grace and mercy which strengthens our weakness, enlightens our mind and supports our will, we would perish daily. I also see that since my birth forty years ago, I have given little heed to God's commandments. Distrusting my own power to reform, but hoping to advance by degrees along the path of virtue, I resolve from this day forward to refrain from going to the shop or conducting business on solemn church holidays, or from permitting others to work for me or seek temporal gain on such days. Whenever I make exceptions in cases of extreme necessity, I promise, on the following day, to distribute alms of one gold florin to God's poor. I have written this down so that I may remember my promise and be ashamed if I should chance to break it.

Also, in memory of the passion of Our Lord Jesus Christ who freed and saved us by His merits, that He may, by His grace and mercy preserve us from guilty passions, I resolve from this very day and in perpetuity to keep Friday as a day of total chastity—with Friday I include the following night—when I must abstain from the enjoyment of all carnal pleasures. God give me grace to keep my promise, yet if I should break it through forgetfulness, I engage to give 20 *soldi* to the poor for each time, and to say twenty Paternosters and Avemarias.

I resolve this day to do a third thing while I am in health and able to, remembering that each day we need Almighty God to provide for us. Each day I wish to honor God by some giving of alms or by the recitation of prayers or some other pious act. If, by inadvertence, I fail to do so, that day or the next day I must give alms to God's poor of at least 5 *soldi*. These however are not vows but intentions by which I shall do my best to abide.[10]

May 3, 1412. On April 28, my name was drawn as standard-bearer of the militia company.[11] Up until then I had not been sure whether my name was in the purses for that office, although I was eager that it should be both for my own honor and that of my heirs. I recalled that my father Stagio had held a number of appointments in the course of his life, being frequently a consul of the Guild of Por Santa Maria, a member of the Merchants' Court and one of the officials in charge of gabelles and the treasurers. Yet he was never drawn for any of the colleges during his lifetime, though shortly after his death he was drawn as a prior. I recalled that I had aroused a great deal of animosity eight years ago because of my business in Catalonia, and that last year I only just escaped being arrested for debt by the commune. On the very day my name was drawn for this office, only fifteen minutes before it was drawn, I had taken advantage of the reprieve granted by the new laws and finished paying off my debt to the commune. That was a veritable inspiration from God, may His name be praised and blessed! Now that I can obtain other offices, it seems to me that, having had a great benefit, I should be content to know that I have sat once in the colleges and should aspire no further. So, lest I should ungratefully give way to the insatiable appetites of those in whom success breeds renewed ambition, I have resolved and sworn to myself that I shall not henceforth invoke the aid of any or attempt to get myself elected to public offices or to have my name included in new purses. Rather, I shall let things take their course without interfering. I shall abide by God's will, accepting those offices of the guilds or commune for which my name shall be drawn, and not refusing the labor but serving and doing what good I may. In this way I shall restrain my own presumption and tendency towards ambition and shall live in freedom without demeaning myself by begging favors from any. And if I should depart from this resolve, I condemn myself each time to distribute two gold florins in alms within a month. I have taken this resolution in my fiftieth year.

Knowing my weakness in the face of sin, I make another resolve on the same day. In order to ensure the peace and good of my own conscience, I vowed that I would never accept any office, if

---

10   Dati meant that these obligations were not to be considered legally binding.

11   A member of one of the Signoria's advisory colleges. Dati's district (*gonfalone*) was Ferze, in the quarter of S. Spirito.

my name should be drawn, wherein I would have power to wield the death penalty. If I should depart from this resolution, I condemn myself to give 25 gold florins in alms to the poor within three months for each such office that I have agreed to accept. And I shall in no way attempt to influence those who make up the purses for such offices, either asking them to put or not put in my name, but shall let them do as they think fit. If I should do otherwise, I condemn myself to distribute a gold florin.

Children—1404

Glory, honor and praise be to Almighty God. Continuing from folio 5, I shall list the children which He shall in His grace bestow on me and my wife, Ginevra.

On Sunday morning at terce, April 27 of the same year, Ginevra gave birth to our first-born son. He was baptized at the hour of vespers on Monday the 28th in the church of S. Giovanni. We named him Manetto Domenico. His sponsors in God's love were Bartolo di Giovanni di Niccola, Giovanni di Michelozzo, a belt-maker, and Domenico di Deo, a goldsmith. God make him good.

At the third hour of Thursday, March 19, 1405, Ginevra gave birth to a female child of less than seven months. She had not realized she was pregnant, since for four months she had been ailing as though she were not, and in the end was unable to hold it. We baptized it at once in the church of S. Giovanni. The sponsors were Bartolo, Monna Buona, another lady, and the blind woman. Having thought at first that it was a boy, we named it Agnolo Giovanni. It died at dawn on Sunday morning, March 22, and was buried before the sermon.

At terce on Tuesday morning, June 8, 1406, Ginevra had her third child, a fine full-term baby girl whom we had baptized on Friday morning, June 9. We christened her Elisabetta Caterina and she will be called Lisabetta in memory of my dead wife, Betta. The sponsors were Fra Lorenzo, Bartolo, and the blind woman.

On June 4, 1407, a Saturday, Ginevra gave birth after a nine-month pregnancy to a little girl whom we had baptized on the evening of Tuesday the 7th. We named her Antonia Margherita and we shall call her Antonia. Her godfather was Nello di Ser Piero Nelli, a neighbor. God grant her good fortune.

At terce, Sunday, July 31, 1411, Ginevra gave birth to a very attractive baby boy whom we had baptized on August 4. The sponsors were my colleagues among the standard-bearers of the militia companies with the exception of two: Giorgio and Bartolomeo Fioravanti. We called the child Niccolò. God bless him. God was pleased to call the child very shortly to Himself. He died of dysentery on October 22 at terce. May he intercede with God for us.

At terce on Sunday, October 1, 1412, Ginevra had a son whom, from devotion to St. Jerome—since it was yesterday that her pains began—I called Girolamo Domenico. The sponsors were Master Bartolomeo del Carmine, Cristofano di Francesco di Ser Giovanni, and Lappuccio di Villa, and his son Bettino. God grant him and us health and make him a good man.

God willed that the blessed soul of our daughter Betta should return to Him after a long illness. She passed away during the night between Tuesday and the first Wednesday of Lent at four in the morning, February 21, 1414. She was seven years and seven months, and I was sorely grieved at her death. God grant she pray for us.

On May 1, 1415, at the hour of terce on a Wednesday, God granted us a fine little boy, and I had him baptized at four on Saturday morning. Jacopo di Francesco di Tura and Aringhieri di Jacopo, the wool merchant, were his godfathers. May God grant that he be healthy, wise, and good. We named him after the two holy apostles, Jacopo and Filippo, on whose feast day he was born and we shall call him Filippo.

At eleven o'clock on Friday, April 24, 1416, Ginevra gave birth to a baby girl after a painful and almost fatal labor. The child was baptized immediately on S. Marco's Day, the 25th. We called her Ghita in memory of our mother. Monna Mea di Franchino was her godmother.

Manetto died in Pisa in January 1418. He had been very sick and was buried in S. Martino. Pippo died on August 2, 1419 in Val di Pesa in a place called Polonia. This is recorded in notebook B.

At two o'clock on the night following Monday July 17, Lisa was born. She was baptized by Master Pagolo from Montepulciano, a preaching friar,[12] on Wednesday at seven o'clock. God console us, amen. She later died.

Altogether Ginevra and I had eleven children: four boys and seven girls.

Memorandum—1405

To take up my record of past years from folio 7, I served among the Ten on Liberty.[13] My term began on April 1 and ran four months. My colleagues were Arrigo Mazinghi, Niccoloso Cambi, Giraldo di Lorenzo, Piero Velluti, Nastagio di Benincasa, Uguccione Giandonati, Michele di Banco, two artisans, and myself. I pleased everyone and acted as rightly as I was able.

I was Guild Consul for the third time from May 1 of the same year. With me were Zanobi di Ser Gino, Agnolo di Ghezzo, Noze Manetti, and Agnolo di Filippo di Ser Giovanni [Pandolfini].

I began proceedings against Messer Giovanni Serristori and Company on the … of September before the Merchants' Court. I was reluctant to do this but had no choice. I had suffered grievous harm in spirit and pocket and was likely to be ruined if I did not defend myself. God bring me safely out of this! The partnership with Piero and Jacopo Lana and Nardo di Lippo expired on December 31, 1406. We did not renew it because of the risks we had run in connection with what had happened in Spain. It is advisable for us to lie low for a while and wait and pay our creditors and put our trust in God. I have reached an agreement with Piero establishing the time and manner in which I must pay him. I am to do so through Bernardo who has a copy of the agreement.

I was a guild consul for the fourth time from September 1, 1408, in company with Lapo Corsi, Chimento di Stefano, Filippo di Ghezo, Francesco di Messer Jacopo Marchi, and Matteo di Lorenzo, the goldsmith.

On November 11, 1408, I set out for Valencia and Murcia, and reached Murcia on December 30. I traveled overland in the company of Pagolo Mei and it was a difficult journey. I left Murcia in May 1410 and delayed in Valencia on account of the risks of both the sea and land route, due to the war between ourselves and the King[14] and the Genoese. In February I finally set out and took ship at Barcelona whence I sailed for Piombino which I reached on March 12 at terce on St. Gregory's Day and was in Florence on March 15, 1411.

In that year 1411, there was a plague, and Piero Lana died. That December I made an agreement with his brother and partner, Jacopo, who had been my partner too, and with Piero's sons through Dino di Messer Guccio and Bernardo and Pagolo di Vanni and Zanobi di Ser Benozzo, who acted as intermediaries.

Our Master Lionardo was elected father general of the Dominican Order by the chapter, with great harmony and festivities and honor on September 29, the Feast of the Angels, and the following day, the feast of S. Jerome, the holiday and procession were held. Praise be to God.

Mona Ghita, our beloved mother, departed this wretched life and returned her soul to her Creator before dawn on Monday morning, January 29, 1414. She received the last sacraments and passed away peacefully. May God receive her in his bosom. Amen.

Partnership with Pietro Lana, 1408

The accounts of the shop and company are written above on page 8. As a result of the adversity which overtook us in Barcelona, and of the lawsuit here which followed it, and of the suspicions concerning Simone's ventures and the calumnies that were spread about, we were very short of credit. So we were forced to withdraw from business and collect whatever we could to pay our creditors, borrowing from friends and using all our ingenuity, suffering losses, high interest and expense in order to avoid bankruptcy and shame. And although my partner was in favor of going bankrupt so as to avoid some losses and expenditure, I was resolved to face ruin rather than loss of honor. I held out so firmly and struggled to such

---

12 A member of the Dominican Order.
13 The Ten on Liberty (*Dieci di Libertà*) was a magistracy whose primary function was to settle quarrels between citizens.
14 Florence's antagonist was King Ladislaus of Naples. This war is described in Pitti's diary.

purpose that in the end we managed to pay all our debts, and I satisfied all claims except those of my partners. May God be praised and blessed. I am sure too that if I had managed to send Simone the silk and gold which he was to sell the King, he would have brought his business to a successful conclusion. But I could not send it, and indeed had to abandon all business activity until 1405. Then the lawsuit began and I had to sell whatever goods I had here so as to pay my debts, and I was obliged to renege on my promises to send him what he needed for the King. Consequently, his business began to collapse and stagnate. Indeed, it sank into such confusion that it has been impossible to set it back on its feet, and it has gone ever since from bad to worse.

As Simone was doing badly himself, he was unable to send us the consignments and remittances we needed. My partner, who had grown very impatient, kept complaining in public and behaving in a way unfavorable to our common interest. While I was in Spain, Antonio di Ser Bartolomeo and two other powerful companies took proceedings against him in connection with a transaction they had concluded with me. He defended our interest very badly, did not produce our accounts as evidence, and merely tried to show that he himself was not liable. The judgement went against him and he was forced to pay. Of the 500 florins we had received from them, I had already paid back 300 florins to their agent in Spain, so that we only owed them a residue of 200. Yet they were awarded 2,000 silver florins. I do not think such a thing ever happened before or since. And I hope it may bring them bad luck. Yet we have to stand to the loss of it and the fault lies with my partner and his crooked ways.

Hearing that Pagolo Mei was going to Spain, I decided to travel with him and see whether I could save something from the ruin of our branch there. We left Florence on November 12, 1408, traveled by land and, after a very wearisome journey in harsh wintry weather, reached Murcia[15] on December 30. Simone came to meet us there and for a while we had good hopes of his business but these were later deceived because of the falsity of the Spaniards, and because, through no error of

his, he was unfairly treated. I was back in Florence safe and sound on March 15, 1411, but all I brought with me was a great deal of sorrow and weariness.

My partner, Lana, kept tormenting me in every way he could and denounced me to the Merchant's Court as a bankrupt, asking them to have me publicly denounced by their herald. He did not succeed in getting them to pass sentence against me, for I had not gone bankrupt but had returned from abroad to settle my accounts with him and to do what I could towards satisfying him. In the middle of this dispute, he died of the plague in July 1411.

After that it was God's will to recall to Himself the blessed soul of my wife Ginevra. She died in childbirth after lengthy suffering, which she bore with remarkable strength and patience. She was perfectly lucid at the time of her death when she received all the sacraments: confession, communion, extreme unction, and a papal indulgence granting absolution for all her sins, which she received from Master Lionardo, who had been granted it by the pope. It comforted her greatly, and she returned her soul to her Creator on September 7, the Eve of the Feast of Our Lady, at nones: the hour when Our Blessed Lord Jesus Christ expired on the cross and yielded up his spirit to our Heavenly Father. On Friday the 8th she was honorably buried and on the 9th, masses were said for her soul. Her body lies in our plot at S. Spirito and her soul has gone to eternal life. God bless her and grant us fortitude. Her loss has sorely tried me. May He help me to bring up the unruly family which is left to me in the best way for their souls and bodies.

God who shows his wisdom in all things permitted the plague to strike our house. The first to succumb was our manservant Paccino at the end of June 1420. Three days later it was the turn of our slave-girl Marta, after her on July 1 my daughter Sandra and on July 5 my daughter Antonia. We left that house after that and went to live opposite, but a few days later Veronica died. Again we moved, this time to Via Chiara where Bandecca and Pippa fell ill and departed this life on August 1. All of them bore the marks

---

15 Murcia is an inland town in southeastern Castile, some 100 miles south of the port city of Valencia.

of the plague. It passed off after that and we returned to our own house. May God bless them all. Bandecca's will and her accounts appear on page … of my ledger A.

I then took another wife, Caterina, the daughter of Dardano Guicciardini. She was thirty years of age, and came to our house on March 30, 1421. Her personal accounts are written in detail further on in folio 13. God grant us a good life together, amen.

My name was drawn to serve among the Twelve Good Men, and I began my term of office on September 15, 1421. My colleagues were Antonio d'Ubaldo di Fetto, Buonaccorso Corsellini, Antonio di Piero di Fronte, Piero di Buonaccorso di Vanni, Lapo di Giovanni Bucelli, Dino di Messer Guccio, Tomaso di Giacomo di Goggio, Guarente the goldsmith, Michele di Nardo Pagnini, Bencivenni di Cristoforo, and Puccino di Ser Andrea. No greater unanimity could be found than that which reigned amongst us. Thanks be to God.

My name was drawn to be overseer for the Guild Hospital[16] for one year. I began to serve on May 1, 1422 with Bartolo Corsi, Giovanni di Deo, Salvi Lotti, Cione di Cecco Cioni, and Tommaso di Pazzino.

On September 9, 1422, the Signoria and Colleges elected me to serve among the Five Defenders of the County and District in lieu of Parigi Corbinelli who had been appointed Podestà. I took office on the 10th of the month and served during January with Giovanni di Messer Forese [Salviati], Salvestro Popoleschi, Giovanni Carradori, and Piero del Palagio. It is an onerous office, in which one may gain merit in the sight of God and acquire contempt for the world. We did a great deal to improve the lot of the unfortunate peasants.

My Fourth Wife's Personal Account

In the name of God and of the Virgin Mary, or SS. Gregory and Catherine, I shall note down here matters relating to my fourth wife.

Memo that on Tuesday, January 28, 1421, I made an agreement with Niccolò d'Andrea del Benino to take his niece, Caterina, for my lawful wife. She is the daughter of the late Dardano di Niccolò Guicciardini and of Monna Tita, Andrea del Benino's daughter. We were betrothed on the morning of Monday, February 3, the Eve of Carnival. I met Piero and Giovanni di Messer Luigi [Guicciardini] in the church of S. Maria sopra Porta, and Niccolò d'Andrea del Benino was our mediator. The dowry promised me was 600 florins, and the notary was Ser Niccolò di Ser Verdiano. I went to dine with her that evening in Piero's house and the Saturday after Easter— March 29, 1421—Ser Niccolò drew up a public instrument, whereby I attested to the receipt of a dowry amounting to 615 florins from Giovanni di Messer Luigi. I then received it from him and her as appears in my ledger B on page 128, including a trousseau worth fifteen florins. Madalena and Bernardo and Michele di Manetto went surety for me. That day I gave her the ring and then on Sunday evening, March 30, she came to live in our house simply and without ceremony. On May 7, 1421, I paid the tax on contracts. See Register A 72, page 56. It came to sixteen florins, four *soldi*, four *denari*. God be praised and thanked and may He grant us a peaceful and healthy life, amen.

Offspring—1422

The following is a list of the children begotten by me.

I was single when my first son, Maso,[17] was born on December 21, 1391—this appears on the back of page 4. Before his birth I had got Bandecca with child but she had a miscarriage in her sixth month in July 1390. After that, as I have indicated on page 5, I had eight children by my second wife, Betta; five boys and three girls. Then, as I show on page 10, I had eleven children by my third wife, Ginevra: four boys and seven girls. Altogether, not counting the one that did not live to be baptized, I have had twenty children: ten boys and ten girls. Of these, Maso, Bernardo, Girolamo, Ghita and Betta are still alive. Praise be to God for all things, amen.

---

16 The famous Spedale degli Innocenti, the foundling home in the Piazza SS. Annunziata. The construction of the building, for which Brunelleschi was architect, was begun two years earlier, in 1420.

17 Maso was the child born of the slave girl, Margherita, in Valencia.

Caterina, my fourth wife, miscarried after four months and the child did not live long enough to receive baptism. That was in August 1421.

On October 4, 1422, at one o'clock on a Sunday night, Caterina gave birth to a daughter. We had Fra Aducci and Fra Giovanni Masi baptize her on Monday the 5th and christen her Ginevra Francesca. May God bless her.

At three o'clock on Friday, January 7, 1424, Caterina gave birth to a fine healthy boy whom we had baptized on the morning of Saturday the 8th. The godparents were the Abbot Simone of S. Felice and Michele di Manetto. We christened the child Antonio Felice. God grant he turn out a good man.

Between eight and nine o'clock on the morning of Tuesday, March 20, 1425, Caterina had another healthy and attractive child who was baptized the following day—the 21st—which was the feast of St. Benedict. Fra Cristofano, Father Provincial of the monks of S. Maria Novella, the prior, Master Alessio, Master Girolamo, and Fra Benedetto were his sponsors. We christened him Lionardo Benedetto. God make him a good man.

At three in the morning of July 26, 1426, Caterina had a fine little girl whom we christened Anna Bandecca. The baptism was on the 27th and her sponsors were Antonina and Monna Lucia. God grant her His grace and that she be a comfort to us.

At two o'clock in the night of Monday, August 28, 1427, Caterina gave birth to a fine little girl. She was baptized on Wednesday morning the 22nd and christened Filippa Felice. The Abbot of S. Felice, Giovanni di Messer Forese Salviati, and Giuliano di Tommaso di Guccio, who had served in the same office with me, were her sponsors. God grant she be a source of consolation to us and fill her with His grace. Our Lord called her to Himself on October 19, 1430. This appears on page 30, notebook E. May God bless her.

At about eleven o'clock on Saturday, June 2, 1431, Caterina gave birth to a girl who was baptized on Monday the 4th in S. Giovanni's and christened Bartolomea Domenica. See notebook E, page 46.

Our Lord was pleased to call to Himself and to eternal life our two blessed children, Lionardo and Ginevra, on Saturday, October 6, 1431. This appears in notebook one, page 14. Lionardo had been in perfect health twenty-four hours before his death. God bless them and grant us the grace to bear their loss with fortitude.

Memoranda—1422

Some items worth bearing in mind are noted above on page 12. I shall follow them up with an account of events which happen during the course of the current year or of years to come.

We received news that our brother, Simone di Stagio, who had lived for about twenty-eight years in Spain and Valencia, had passed from this life of tribulation at the hour of nones on Saturday, May 23, after receiving the sacraments as befits a devout Christian. May Our Lord receive his soul in eternal life.

I bought the house next to my own house on the corner from Monna Mea through a third party to whom she had mortgaged it. The whole transaction is clearly described in my ledger B on page 132. It cost me 50 florins.

I was guild consul for the eighth time from the beginning of May 1423. With me served Francesco della Luna, Agnolo di Ghezo, Niccolò di Giovanni Carducci, Francesco Bartolelli, and Giovanni di Deo. Agnolo died during his term in office, and his place was taken by Lorenzo di Piero di Lenzo.

I agreed to serve as Podestà of Montale and Agliana in order to avoid the plague. My term of office was from April 12 to October 12, 1424. A great number of people accompanied me there and, by God's grace, none of us got sick. I was the first to stay in the residence at Montale and I saw to it that it was properly furnished and arranged. I acquired little wealth there but was highly esteemed by the inhabitants. Thanks be to God.

Our brother, Master Lionardo, general of the Preaching Friars, passed on from this life on Friday, March 16, 1425. He had been in very poor health. He received the sacraments and his funeral was honored by the Commune, the Parte Guelfa, the Merchant's Court, and the Guild Heads. His personal account is entered on page 116 of ledger B. I received a general acquittance from the friars and chapter covering all transactions I had ever conducted with him. The instrument was drawn up by Ser Cristofano da Laterina on the advice of

Messer Stefano Bonaccorsi on March 3, 1425 and I have it at home.

My name was drawn to serve among the Lord Priors of the city of Florence for a term of two months, starting on July 1 and finishing on the last day of August 1425. Serving with me were: Giovanni Grasso, Lapo Bucelli, Piero di Bonaccorso, Domenico di Tano, Giandonato di Cecco, Niccolò Valori, Cresci di Lorenzo, and Lorenzo di Piero di Lenzo, the Standard-bearer of Justice. The war[18] made our task extremely onerous but, by the grace of God, we left matters in a better way than we found them.

By the grace of God, I was standard-bearer of justice for two months from March 1, 1429. The priors serving with me were: Zanobi di Tommaso Bartoli, a feather-bed maker, Bianco d'Agnoli, a maker of wine glasses, as artisans of the quarter of S. Spirito; Riccardo di Niccolò Fagni and Berto di Lionardo Berti for S. Croce; Pierozzo di Francesco della Lana and Piero di Francesco Redditi for S. Maria Novella; Antonio di Ghezzo della Casa and Francesco di Piero Gherucci for S. Giovanni; and Ser Iacopo Salvestri, our notary. By God's grace we worked harmoniously together and accomplished a number of good things. I had a column placed in Piazza S. Felice; it was brought from the Mercato Vecchio, and the decision was taken by the priorate.

1428. Chronological notes concerning myself.

The first, which appears on page 12, records how I was born on April 15, 1362. Further on, mention is made of the death of Stagio in 1374 and of how I began to work in the silk business in 1375 and of how Madalena got married in 1380. It is true that we owed Manetto more than 200 florins at that time, and that we owned nothing but the house and some old furniture. On January 1, 1385, I was made a partner in the business and was supposed to invest 300 florins in it. However, as appears on page 3, I was already in debt for even more than that, largely on account of expenses to which I had been put by Don Jacopo. I did well for several years after that as can be seen on page 2. In 1388 I got married and received a dowry and was able to pay off the debt that year, as well as furnishing

the house decently and keeping almost within my capital. In 1390, my wife Bandecca died and I went to Valencia for the company. I returned in 1392. We had done well during this period, but due to the bad debt that Giovanni Stefani contracted with our company, I found myself rather short of money. In 1393 I married my second wife as is indicated on page 4. The dowry was substantial but I spent too much. In 1394 I was captured and robbed at sea and suffered considerable losses as is shown on page 4 of this diary. That year I bought a half share in the farm at Antella and neither made nor lost money. However, having left the company in 1395, I set up on my own and did well and made 300 or more florins. As appears on page 6, I bought Michele's share of Giovanni Stefani's debt from him for 600 florins with certain terms. I thought this to be a clever move, but it turned out not to be and I lost most of my investment. However I went into partnership with Michele in 1396, as is shown above on page 6. As I was short of money, I promised to put up 1,000 florins which, for as long as the company lasted, I was obliged to borrow on interest or raise in other ways, drawing money against Simone's account in Valencia by means of bills of exchange and other stratagems. And I did very well up to the year 1402, as appears on page 7. However, in 1400, I took refuge from the plague in Antella and spent more than 500 florins on the house and in planting vines. I had other expenses too, so that in 1402, when I parted company with Michele, I had about 1,000 florins. The entry indicates 1,370 [florins] but I owed the rest. That year, as is indicated earlier, I went into partnership with Piero Lana and engaged myself to invest 2,000 florins. I got married that same year for the third time and received over 600 florins cash as is shown on page 8. Thus I was able to invest that sum in the company, which meant that I still owed over 300 florins.

At this point, fortune turned against me. Simone had gone into business on his own account in Valencia and was involved in transactions with the king of Castile. I let him have great quantities of merchandise and bills of exchange for large sums of money. I had been against his engaging in this activity, but he was convinced that he was in trouble, litigation and losses so that

---

18 Florence was then at war with Filippo Maria Visconti, ruler of Milan.

we went deeply into debt and were on the point of going bankrupt. I had to join him in Spain in 1408, and spent almost three years there and in Valencia, recovering only a tiny portion of our losses. As ill fortune would have it, the king, with whom Simone had dealt, died in 1406 and as a result of this Simone was unjustly treated and ruined. Our company lost over 10,000 florins in this affair, which swallowed up all our capital. Over and above these losses, Piero Lana was forced to pay further sums, and so was I, for I paid over 1,000 florins from Matteo's legacy. Piero brought a lawsuit against me which might have harmed me greatly and, in 1412, I reached a settlement with his heirs as appears on page 72 of Ledger B. I agreed to pay them 2,400 florins and, as also appears from the ledger, I finished paying off this debt in 1422. The interest I had to pay in this period amounted to over 600 florins. So one may say that in 1412, according to a rough estimate that I made of my losses and the interest I had to pay on account of them, I was in debt for over 3,000 florins. That same year 1412, my name was drawn to be standard-bearer of justice, and I served in that office. This was the beginning of my recovery. After that, in 1414, I married off Bandecca and gave her a dowry of 550 florins. That same year our brother Lionardo was made father general of his order. So our trust in God aided and comforted us.

After reaching the settlement with Piero Lana's heirs in 1412, I found myself in debt for about 3,000 florins. God came to my aid then with the promotion of my brother who, as father general, was in a position to help me pay off the debt. The assistance he gave me from time to time and according to his means is recorded in ledger B, page 94. The sums he paid out to me and in my name up to the year 1420 amounted to 2,330 florins, and he made me a gift of them. There were still 700 florins to be paid off and, as my living expenses during that time amounted to more than that sum, my total debt was 1,500 florins. However, I had sold off various pieces of furniture, which

brought in 200 florins; the sale of the Campi farm brought in 250 gold florins; Ginevra's communal bonds brought in interest amounting to 200 florins. When Pope John [XXIII] came, I made 150 Bologna florins from cloths I made for him, and in 1418 I made 200 florins as *Proveditore*[19] in Pisa. All this amounted to 1,000 florins, so that I can say that in 1412 I only owed 500 florins.

I set up in business again, and in 1421 I remarried and my wife brought me 600 florins. In the course of 1421 and 1422, the father general lent me 1,000 florins. Michele joined my company and I did well so that when we drew up our third balance sheet on January 1, 1424, my own profit came to 1,100 florins. This profit, together with my wife's dowry and what the father general had lent me, came to 2,700. When I had subtracted the 500 florins for my debt and further sums for expenses, I had about 900 florins left in hand. In 1424 I got money from the father general in Cosimo's[20] name which he later turned into a gift, together with another sum which brought it to 500 florins, so that altogether I had 1,400 florins net. However, God called him to Himself that year and we did badly in the business. I don't know how this occurred, for I was at Montale and my losses amounted to 250 florins. Then the war started and we made very little while it lasted but had to bear heavy expenses. However, the greatest damage to me was the terrible tax burden imposed by the commune, which cost me 1,200 florins. I had to pay back a dowry, for which I had gone surety, to Nardo di Lippo's wife. This cost me 300 florins, and I have entered this debt against the heir on page 2 of register D. I don't know whether I will be able to recover the money. So, in 1427, I was almost able to keep within my capital. I set up a new company with Michele and Giovanni di Ser Guido and, in my red account book, the capital and merchandise assessed at the cash value amounted to 1,000 florins, allowing 300 florins to pay for the furnishings and goodwill. But in my old white purchases book B, I have a debt of about 700 florins, so I have practically no liquid capital at all.[21]

---

19 The *Proveditori*, a magistracy of five citizens with general responsibility for the government of Pisa and its contado.

20 The banker, Cosimo de' Medici.

21 Dati died on September 17, 1435; he did not keep his diary for the last eight years of his life.

GLOSSARY

Many specialized and technical terms appearing within only one document are defined in the notes to that document. The following terms appear more frequently.

Albigenses: adherents of the dualist Cathar heresy

allod: land fully owned and not held in fief

amerce: fine

anathema/to anathematize: a curse consigning one to damnation

assize: administrative and judicial meetings; also the decisions taken at these meetings

augur: *see* haruspices

bailiff: official charged with public administrative authority; executes writs and processes, distrains, and arrests

baillis: French royal officer responsible for justice and administration within a subdivision of the kingdom

breviary: from the latin *breviarium* (summary or abridged), a book containing the divine office recited by clergy each day

burgess: an elected member of the local urban council, or a freeman/citizen of a borough in general

catechumens: those receiving instruction in preparation for baptism

cellarers: member of a monastery responsible for supplies and provisions

centenarius (pl. centenarii): an agent of a count responsible for a jurisdiction termed a "hundred"

chatelain: possessor of a castle

compline: last of the monastic liturgical hours

consul ordinary: the consulship was the highest office in the Roman state; a consul ordinary distinguishes one who actually exercised this office from others given honorary consul status

contado: the immediate area surrounding an Italian city and which is under its control

dauphin: the title given to the heir to the French throne

demesne: portion of a manor worked by peasants for the direct profit of the lord

ealdorman: a high-ranking Anglo-Saxon royal official, roughly equivalent to a count

exegesis: the explanation and interpretation of a text, most frequently Christian scripture

fisc: originally the public treasury of Rome, but its meaning is extended to any imperial or royal treasury

Grey Friars: Franciscan monks

Guibiline/Guelf: During the thirteenth and fourteenth centuries in Northern Italy, the Guelphs supported the papacy while the Guibilines, also known as the Waiblinegens for their battle cry, supported the interests of the Holy Roman Empire. *See also* Waiblinegen

haruspices and augurs: Roman religious officials thought to predict future events, the haruspex through the examination of entrails, the augur through the flight of birds

hide: a measurement of land sufficient to support one peasant household

letter patent: legal document conferred by a monarch granting title or right

leudes (pl. of leud): the personal following of a Frankish king or magnate who had sworn a special oath of loyalty and from whom his personal bodyguard was formed.

lidus (pl. lidi): a semi-free person of low social status in the Frankish world

mancuse: a gold coin or a unit of accounting equal to thirty pennies

margrave: title, which became hereditary, given to rulers of principalities on the borders of the Holy Roman Empire (the marches).

master of the soldiers (magister militum): a top-level military commander in the late Roman empire

missal: liturgical book containing all the necessary liturgical texts for performing mass

missus: Carolingian court officer, normally a count or bishop, charged with delivering imperial judgments and acting as investigator in high-level disputes

modius: a unit of measure, often of grain

novel disseisin: in English law, an action to recover lands of which the plaintiff had been recently (hence novel) disseised, or dispossessed. The plantiff obtained a royal writ which ordered the sheriff to empanel a jury to determine not right to property but whether the plaintiff had been dispossessed of it.

pallium: a narrow cloth band, worn over the shoulders, presented by the pope to metropolitan archbishops

Paraclete: the Holy Spirit (from the Greek parakletos)

patrimony: any land, estate, or goods inherited after the death of the father

Peripatetics: members of the Aristotelian school of philosophy

podestà: in Italian cities, the title given to the head of local government, either appointed by the emperor or hired by the commune

postliminium: under Roman law, those who return from banishment or exile after a proscribed period of time are entitled to regain former privileges and rights under the right of postliminium

precentor: religious official responsible for choral services

preaching friar: Dominican monk

prebend: a clerical income from church estates

presbyter: originally an elder in the early Christian community; in time applied to priests, the ordained clergy subordinate to bishops

precarial holdings: land offered in exchange for service, but revocable by lender

prefect of the city: civic official responsible for the administration of a city, roughly equivalent to mayor

prevots: subordinate royal officials, with duties roughly equivalent to the viscounts, who were usually active in urban areas

prior: second-ranking member of monastery, below abbot

proconsul: Roman provincial governor

reeve: English chief royal magistrate of town or district (shire-reeve); more generally a local overseer (sometimes of large estates)

rescript: written command sent out by imperial authorities in answer to problem or question

sanctuary: in medieval law, a church or holy place designated as a place of refuge where fugitives could find immunity from their secular pursuers

Schöffe (pl. *Schöffen*): lay judge or juror

shriven: to be free of the guilt of sin after sacramental confession

scrofa: Latin for "boar"; movable shed which protected soldiers setting up sieges

scutage: payment to the king in place of feudal service

seneschal: in the Frankish period, a household officer; later a high royal official responsible for military and judicial administration; equivalent of bailiff

sextaria: a measure of land differing regionally

siccli: a unit of weight varying regionally

synod: meeting of clergy to discuss ecclesiastical affairs

Thing/Þing: Germanic legislative assembly or meeting, sometimes advisory in nature

usufruct: the legal right to the goods normally produced from the land, without actual ownership of it

venia: indulgence or favor

viscount: a royal official immediately subordinate to the count or *baillis* with important duties in supervising commerce and routine judicial work

vicedominus: administrator acting in the place of a count or bishop

Waiblinegen/Guibiline/Guelf: supporters of the Imperial party in Italy

wergeld: price to be paid to the family or the lord of a slain person; set by social standing or proximity to the king

White Friar: Carmelite monk

witan: an advisory council to the Saxon English king

SOURCES

Aquinas, St. Thomas, excerpts from *Summa Theologiae* (New York: McGraw-Hill, 1964). Reprinted by permission of Methuen Publishing Ltd., London.

Beech, George (trans.), "Hugh of Lusignan, Agreement Between Lord and Vassal." *English Historical Review* 84 (1969): 528–48, ed. Jane Martindale. Copyright © 1969 by George Beech. Reprinted by permission of Oxford University Press.

Brady, Ignatius (trans.), excerpts from *The Legend and Writing of Saint Clare of Assisi* (New York: St. Bonaventure, 1953). Reprinted by permission of Franciscan Institute Publications.

Butler-Bowdon, William (ed. and trans.), excerpts from *The Book of Margery Kempe* (New York: The Devin-Adair Company, 1944). Copyright © 1944 Devin-Adair, Publishers, Inc., Old Greenwich, Connecticut, 06870. All rights reserved. Reprinted by permission.

Deane, S.N. (ed. and trans.), excerpts from *Anselm: Basic Writings* (La Salle: Open Court Publishing, 1962). Copyright © 1962. Reprinted by permission of Open Court Publishing Company, a division of Carus Publishing Company, Peru, IL.

Dods, Marcus (trans.), excerpts from *A Select Library of the Nicene and Post-Nicene Fathers of the Christian Church*, ed. Philip Schaff (Buffalo: Christian Literature Co., 1987). Copyright © 1987. Reprinted by permission of The Continuum International Publishing Group.

Douglas, David C. and George W. Greenaway (eds.), "Domesday Book" and "Dialogue of the Exchequer," from *English Historical Documents 1042–1189, Volume II* (London: Eyre & Spottiswoode, 1953). Copyright © 2007

Taylor & Francis. Reprinted by permission of Taylor & Francis Books UK.

Eidelberg, Shlomo (ed. and trans.), "Solomon bar Simson," from *The Jews and the Crusaders: Hebrew Chronicles of the First and Second Crusades* (Madison: University of Wisconsin Press, 1977). Copyright © 1977 Shlomo Eidelberg. Reprinted by permission of Shlomo Eidelberg.

Knoll, Paul W. and Frank Shaer (ed. and trans.), excerpt from *Gesta Principum Polonorum: The Deeds of the Princes of the Poles, Central European Medieval Texts 3* (Budapest & New York: Central European Press, 2003). Reprinted by permission of Central European University Press.

Mierow, Charles Christopher (ed. and trans.), excerpt from *The Deeds of Fredrick Barbossa* (New York: Columbia University Press, 1953). Copyright © 1953 Columbia University Press. Reprinted by permission of Columbia University Press.

Musurillo, H.R. (trans.), excerpt from *The Acts of the Christian Martyrs* (Oxford: Clarendon Press, 1972). Copyright © 1972 by H.R. Musurillo. Reprinted by permission of Oxford University Press.

Neel, Carol (ed. and trans.), excerpts from *Handbook for William: A Carolingian Woman's Counsel for her Son by Dhuoda* (Lincoln & London: University of Nebraska Press, 1991). Copyright © 1991 University of Nebraska Press. Reprinted by permission of University of Nebraska Press.

Périn, Patrick and Laure-Charlotte Feffer, "The Tomb of Childeric" and "Father of Clovis," from *Les Francs* (Paris: Colin, 1987). Copyright © 1987 Armand Colin. Reprinted by permission.